INGENIX®
www.shopingenix.com

HCPCS Level II Professional

2012

Publisher's Notice

The OptumInsight *2012 HCPCS* is designed to be an accurate and authoritative source of information about this government coding system. Every effort has been made to verify the accuracy of the listings, and all information is believed reliable at the time of publication. Absolute accuracy cannot be guaranteed, however. This publication is made available with the understanding that the publisher is not engaged in rendering legal or other services that require a professional license.

Our Commitment to Accuracy

OptumInsight is committed to producing accurate and reliable materials. To report corrections, please visit www.shopingenix.com/accuracy or e-mail accuracy@ingenix.com. You can also reach customer service by calling 1.800.464.3649, option 1.

To view OptumInsight updates/correction notices, please visit http://www.shopingenix.com/Product/Announcements/

For Answers to Coding Questions Try Our New OptumInsight Coding Answers

Validate your coding accuracy and reduce denials. Find answers to those difficult coding questions in 48 to 72 hours.

Increase your productivity. Access the tool and submit your questions online 24 hours a day, seven days a week.

Save time and money associated with researching those hard to code procedures.

Use existing site content as a research tool. Quickly access previously submitted questions and answers by other users.

Always know where your questions stand during the Q&A process. Access real-time status of pending questions and receive email notifications when a question is answered.

No subscription necessary. Take advantage of the flexible pricing options based on the number of questions you purchase.

For information, please visit www.shopingenix.com or call customer service at 1.800.464.3649, option 1.

Copyright

Made in the USA

HP ISBN 978-1-60151-573-5

Acknowledgments

Julie Orton Van, CPC, CPC-P, *Product Manager*

Karen Schmidt, BSN, *Technical Director*

Stacy Perry, *Manager, Desktop Publishing*

Lisa Singley, *Project Manager*

Wendy Gabbert, CPC, CPC-H, PCS, FCS, *Clinical/Technical Editor*

Trudy Whitehead, CPC-H, CMAS, *Clinical/Technical Editor*

Tracy Betzler, *Desktop Publishing Specialist*

Hope M. Dunn, *Desktop Publishing Specialist*

Jean Parkinson, *Editor*

Technical Editors

Wendy Gabbert, CPC, CPC-H, PCS, FCS

Ms. Gabbert has more than 25 years of experience in the health care field. She has extensive background in CPT/HCPCS and ICD-9-CM coding. She served several years as a coding consultant. Her areas of expertise include physician and hospital CPT coding assessments, chargemaster reviews, and the outpatient prospective payment system (OPPS). She is a member of the American Academy of Professional Coders and American College of Medical Coding Specialists.

Trudy Whitehead, CPC-H, CMAS

Ms. Whitehead has more than 20 years of experience in hospital and physician coding and reimbursement. Recently she developed an APC review system for the postpayment review of Medicare FFS APC claims, including workflow, training, and development of an instruction manual as director of ambulatory review systems. She has conducted hospital and insurance bill auditing, managed facility claims processing and claims negotiations, developed outpatient repricer and rules engines, performed hospital chargemaster reviews, and worked on software development. Ms. Whitehead is a member of the American Academy of Professional Coders (AAPC) and the American Association of Medical Audit Specialists.

Introduction

ORGANIZATION OF HCPCS

The OptumInsight 2012 *HCPCS Level II* book contains mandated changes and new codes for use as of January 1, 2012. Deleted codes have also been indicated and cross-referenced to active codes when possible. New codes have been added to the appropriate sections, eliminating the time-consuming step of looking in two places for a code. However, keep in mind that the information in this book is a reproduction of the 2012 HCPCS; additional information on coverage issues may have been provided to Medicare contractors after publication. All contractors periodically update their systems and records throughout the year. If this book does not agree with your contractor, it is either because of a mid-year update or correction or a specific local or regional coverage policy.

Index

Because HCPCS is organized by code number rather than by service or supply name, the index enables the coder to locate any code without looking through individual ranges of codes. Just look up the medical or surgical supply, service, orthotic, prosthetic, or generic or brand name drug in question to find the appropriate codes. This index also refers to many of the brand names by which these items are known.

Table of Drugs and Biologicals

The brand names of drugs listed are examples only and may not include all products available for that type of drug. The table of drugs and biologicals lists HCPCS codes from any available sections including A codes, C codes, J codes, S codes, and Q codes under brand and generic drug names with amount, route of administration, and code numbers. While we try to make the table comprehensive, it is not all-inclusive.

Color-coded Coverage Instructions

The OptumInsight *HCPCS Level II* book provides colored symbols for each coverage and reimbursement instruction. A legend to these symbols is provided on the bottom of each two-page spread.

HOW TO USE OPTUMINSIGHT HCPCS LEVEL II BOOK

Blue Color Bar—Special Coverage Instructions

A blue bar for "special coverage instructions" over a code means that special coverage instructions apply to that code. These special instructions are also typically given in the form of Medicare Pub.100 reference numbers. The appendixes provide the full text of the cited Medicare Pub.100 references.

A4336 **Incontinence supply, urethral insert, any type, each**

Yellow Color Bar—Contractor Discretion

Issues that are left to "contractor discretion" are covered with a yellow bar. Contact the contractor for specific coverage information on those codes.

A9581 **Injection, gadoxetate disodium, 1 ml**

Red Color Bar—Not Covered by or Invalid for Medicare

Codes that are not covered by or are invalid for Medicare are covered by a red bar. The pertinent Medicare internet-only manuals (Pub. 100) reference numbers are also given explaining why a particular code is not covered. These numbers refer to the appendixes, where we have listed the Medicare references.

A4264 **Permanent implantable contraceptive intratubal occlusion device(s) and delivery system**

Codes in the OptumInsight *HCPCS Level II* follow the AMA CPT book conventions to indicate new, revised, and deleted codes.

- A black circle (●) precedes a new code.
- A black triangle (▲) precedes a code with revised terminology or rules.
- A circle (❍) precedes a reissued code.
- Codes deleted from the 2011 active codes appear with a strike-out.

● **J0490** **Injection, belimumab, 10 mg**

▲ **E0642** **Standing frame/table system, mobile (dynamic stander), any size including pediatric**

❍ **There are no reinstated codes for 2012.**

~~C9276~~ **~~Injection, cabazitaxel, 1 mg~~**

☑ Quantity Alert

Many codes in HCPCS report quantities that may not coincide with quantities available in the marketplace. For instance, a HCPCS code for an ostomy pouch with skin barrier reports each pouch, but the product is generally sold in a package of 10; "10" must be indicated in the quantity box on the CMS claim form to ensure proper reimbursement. This symbol indicates that care should be taken to verify quantities in this code. These quantity alerts do not represent Medicare Unlikely Edits (MUEs) and should not be used for MUEs. An appendix of the MUE's can be found in appendix 8 of the *HCPCS Level II Expert* editions.

☑ **J0120** **Injection, tetracycline, up to 250 mg**

♀ Female Only
This icon identifies procedures that some payers may consider female only.

A4280 **Adhesive skin support attachment for use with external breast prosthesis, each** ♀

♂ Male Only
This icon identifies procedures that some payers may consider male only.

A4326 **Male external catheter with integral collection chamber, anytype, each** ♂

A Age Edit
This icon denotes codes intended for use with a specific age group, such as neonate, newborn, pediatric, and adult. Carefully review the code description to ensure that the code you report most appropriately reflects the patient's age.

Q2037 **Influenza virus vaccine, split virus, when administered to individuals 3 years of age and older, for intramuscular use (FLUVIRIN)** A

M Maternity
This icon identifies procedures that by definition should only be used for maternity patients generally between 12 and 55 years of age.

H1001 **Prenatal care, at-risk enhanced service; antepartum management** M

A2-Z3 ASC Payment Indicators
Codes designated as being paid by ASC groupings that were effective at the time of printing are denoted by the group number.

G0105 **Colorectal cancer screening; colonoscopy on individual at high risk** A2

DMEPOS
Use this icon to identify when to consult the CMS durable medical equipment, prosthetics, orthotics, and supplies (DMEPOS) for payment of this durable medical item.

E0988 **Manual wheelchair accessory, lever-activated, wheel drive, pair**

⊘ Skilled Nursing Facility (SNF)
Use this icon to identify certain items and services excluded from SNF consolidated billing. These items may be billed directly to the Medicare contractor by the provider or supplier of the service or item.

A4653 **Peritoneal dialysis catheter anchoring device, belt, each** ⊘

Drugs commonly reported with a code are listed underneath by brand or generic name.

C9254 **Injection, lacosamide, 1 mg**
Use this code for VIMPAT.

PQ Physician Quality Reporting System (PQRS)
This icon identifies codes that are specific to a PQRS measure.

G8126 **Patient documented as being treated with antidepressant medication during the entire 12 week acute treatment phase** PQ

CMS does not use consistent terminology when a code for a specific procedure is not listed. The code description may include any of the following terms: unlisted, not otherwise classified (NOC), unspecified, unclassified, other, and miscellaneous. If you are sure there is no code for the service or supply provided or used, be sure to provide adequate documentation to the payer. Check with the payer for more information.

A0999 **Unlisted ambulance service**

The specific update of a new, revised, or deleted code is shown as a footnote, indicated to the right of the code and at the bottom of the page.

● **C9366** [Jan] **EpiFix, per sq cm**

OPPS Status Indicators

A-Y OPPS status indicators

Status indicators identify how individual HCPCS Level II codes are paid or not paid under the OPPS. The same status indicator is assigned to all the codes within an ambulatory payment classification (APC). Consult the payer or resource to learn which CPT codes fall within various APCs. Status indicators for HCPCS and their definitions follow:

A Services furnished to a hospital outpatient that are paid under a fee schedule or payment system other than OPPS, for example:

- Ambulance Services
- Clinical Diagnostic Laboratory Services
- Non-Implantable Prosthetic and Orthotic Devices
- EPO for ESRD Patients
- Physical, Occupational, and Speech Therapy
- Routine Dialysis Services for ESRD Patients Provided in a Certified Dialysis Unit of a Hospital
- Diagnostic Mammography
- Screening Mammography

B Codes that are not recognized by OPPS when submitted on an outpatient hospital Part B bill type (12x and 13x)

C Inpatient Procedures

E Items, Codes, and Services:

- That are not covered by any Medicare outpatient benefit based on statutory exclusion.
- That are not covered by any Medicare outpatient benefit for reasons other than statutory exclusion
- That are not recognized by Medicare for outpatient claims but for which an alternate code for the same item or service may be available
- For which separate payment is not provided on outpatient claims

F Corneal Tissue Acquisition; Certain CRNA Services and Hepatitis B Vaccines

G Pass-Through Drugs and Biologicals

H Pass-Through Device Categories

K Nonpass-Through Drugs and Nonimplantable Biologicals, Including Therapeutic Radiopharmaceuticals

L Influenza Vaccine; Pneumococcal Pneumonia Vaccine

M Items and Services Not Billable to the Fiscal Intermediary/MAC

N Items and Services Packaged into APC Rates

P Partial Hospitalization

Q1 STVX-Packaged Codes

Q2 T-Packaged Codes

Q3 Codes That May Be Paid Through a Composite APC

R Blood and Blood Products

S Significant Procedure, Not Discounted when Multiple

T Significant Procedure, Multiple Reduction Applies

U Brachytherapy Sources

V Clinic or Emergency Department Visit

X Ancillary Services

Y Nonimplantable Durable Medical Equipment

A	A4321	**Therapeutic agent for urinary catheter irrigation**
B	Q4005	**Cast supplies, long arm cast, adult (11 years +), plaster**
C	G0341	**Percutaneous islet cell transplant, includes portal vein catheterization and infusion**
E	A0021	**Ambulance service, outside state per mile, transport (Medicaid only)**
F	V2785	**Processing, preserving and transporting corneal tissue**
G	J0588	**Injection, incobotulinumtoxinA, 1 unit**
H	C1749	**Endoscope, retrograde imaging/illumination colonoscope device (implantable)**
K	J1750	**Injection, iron dextran, 50 mg**
L	Q2036	**Influenza virus vaccine, split virus, when administered to individuals 3 years of age and older, for intramuscular use (FLULAVAL)**
M	G0333	**Pharmacy dispensing fee for inhalation drug(s); initial 30-day supply as a beneficiary**
N	A4220	**Refill kit for implantable infusion pump**
P	G0129	**Occupational therapy services requiring the skills of a qualified occupational therapist, furnished as a component of a partial hospitalization treatment program, per session (45 minutes or more)**
Q3	G0379	**Direct admission of patient for hospital observation care**
R	P9010	**Blood (whole), for transfusion, per unit**
S	G0251	**Linear accelerator based stereotactic radiosurgery, delivery including collimator changes and custom plugging, fractionated treatment, all lesions, per session, maximum five sessions per course of treatment**
T	C9724	**Endoscopic full-thickness plication in the gastric cardia using endoscopic plication system (EPS); includes endoscopy**
U	A9527	**Iodine I-125, sodium iodide solution, therapeutic, per millicurie**
V	G0101	**Cervical or vaginal cancer screening; pelvic and clinical breast examination**
X	Q0035	**Cardiokymography**
Y	A4222	**Infusion supplies for external drug infusion pump, per cassette or bag (list drugs separately)**

ASC Payment Indicators

A2-Z3 **ASC Payment Indicators**
This icon identifies the new ASC status payment indicators, effective January 1, 2012. They indicate how the ASC payment rate was derived and/or how the procedure, item, or service is treated under the 2012 ASC payment system. For more information about these new indicators and how they affect billing, consult OptumInsight's *Outpatient Billing Editor.*

- **A2** Surgical procedure on ASC list in CY 2007; payment based on OPPS relative payment weight
- **C5** Inpatient procedure
- **F4** Corneal tissue acquisition, hepatitis B vaccine; paid at reasonable cost
- **G2** Nonoffice-based surgical procedure added in CY 2008 or later; payment based on OPPS relative payment weight
- **H2** Brachytherapy source paid separately when provided integral to a surgical procedure on ASC list; payment based on OPPS rate
- **J7** Device-intensive procedure; paid at adjusted rate
- **J8** Device-intensive procedure added to ASC list in CY 2008 or later; paid at adjusted rate
- **K2** Drugs and biologicals paid separately when provided integral to a surgical procedure on ASC list; payment based on OPPS rate
- **K7** Unclassified drugs and biologicals; payment contractor-priced
- **L1** Influenza vaccine; pneumococcal vaccine; packaged item/service; no separate payment made
- **L6** New Technology Intraocular Lens (NTIOL); special payment
- **M5** Quality measurement code used for reporting purposes only; no payment made
- **N1** Packaged service/item; no separate payment made
- **P2** Office-based surgical procedure added to ASC list in CY 2008 or later with MPFS nonfacility PE RVUs; payment based on OPPS relative payment weight
- **P3** Office-based surgical procedure added to ASC list in CY 2008 or later with MPFS nonfacility PE RVUs; payment based on MPFS nonfacility PE RVUs
- **R2** Office-based surgical procedure added to ASC list in CY 2008 or later without MPFS nonfacility PE RVUs; payment based on OPPS relative payment weight
- **Z2** Radiology service paid separately when provided integral to a surgical procedure on ASC list; payment based on OPPS relative payment weight
- **Z3** Radiology service paid separately when provided integral to a surgical procedure on ASC list; payment based on MPFS nonfacility PE RVUs

A2	G0105	**Coloerectal cancer screening; colonoscopy on individual at high risk**
C5	G0342	**Laparoscopy for islet cell transplant, includes portal vein catheterization and infusion**
F4	V2785	**Processing, preserving and transporting corneal tissue**
G2	C9716	**Creations of thermal anal lesions by radiofrequency energy**
H2	A9527	**Iodine I-125, sodium iodide solution, therapeutic per millicurie**
J7	C1749	**Endoscope, retrograde imaging/illumination colonoscope device (implantable)**
J8	G0448	**Insertion or replacement of a permanent pacing cardioverter-defibrillator system with transvenous lead(s), single or dual chamber with insertion of pacing electrode, cardiac venous system, for left ventricular pacing**
K2	C9121	**Injection, argatroban, per 5 mg**
K7	C9399	**Unclassified drugs or biologicals**
L1	Q2037	**Influenza virus vaccine, split virus, when administered to individuals 3 years of age and older, for intramuscular use (FLUVIRIN)**
N1	L8690	**Auditory osseointegrated device, includes all internal and external components**

MED: This notation precedes an instruction pertaining to this code in the CMS Publication 100 (Pub 100) electronic manual or in a National Coverage Determination (NCD). These CMS sources, formerly called the Medicare Carriers Manual (MCM) and Coverage Issues Manual (CIM), present the rules for submitting these services to the federal government or its contractors and are included in the appendix of this book.

A4300 **Implantable access catheter, (e.g., venous, arterial, epidural subarachnoid, or peritoneal, etc.) external access**
MED: 100-2, 15, 120

AHA: American Hospital Association Coding Clinic for HCPCS citations help you find expanded information about specific codes and their usage.

A4290 **Sacral nerve stimulation test lead, each**
AHA: 1Q, '02, 9

ABOUT HCPCS CODES

OptumInsight does not develop or maintain HCPCS Level II codes. The federal government does.

Any supplier or manufacturer can submit a request for coding modification to the HCPCS Level II national codes. A document explaining the HCPCS modification process, as well as a detailed format for submitting a recommendation for a modification to HCPCS Level II codes, is available on the HCPCS website at https://www.cms.gov/MedHCPCSGenInfo/01a_Application_Form_and_Instructions.asp#TopOfPage. Besides the information requested in this format, a requestor should also submit any additional descriptive material, including the manufacturer's product literature and information that is believed would be helpful in furthering CMS's understanding of the medical features of the item for which a coding modification is being recommended. The HCPCS coding review process is an ongoing, continuous process.

Requests for coding modifications should be sent to the following address:

Felicia Eggleston, CMS HCPCS Workgroup Coordinator
Centers for Medicare and Medicaid Services
C5-08-27
7500 Security Blvd
Baltimore, Maryland 21244-1850

The dental (D) codes are not included in the official 2012 HCPCS Level II code set. The American Dental Association (ADA) holds the copyright on those codes and instructed CMS to remove them. As a result, OptumInsight has removed them from this product; however, OptumInsight has additional resources available for customers requiring the dental codes. Please go to www.ShopIngenix.com or call 1.800.464.3649.

HOW TO USE HCPCS LEVEL II

Coders should keep in mind, however, that the insurance companies and government do not base payment solely on what was done for the patient. They need to know why the services were performed. In addition to using the HCPCS coding system for procedures and supplies, coders must also use the ICD-9-CM coding system to denote the diagnosis. This book will not discuss ICD-9-CM codes, which can be found in a current ICD-9-CM code book for diagnosis codes. To locate a HCPCS Level II code, follow these steps:

1. Identify the services or procedures that the patient received.

   Example:

   Patient administered PSA exam.

2. Look up the appropriate term in the index.

   Example:

   Screening

   prostate

   Coding Tip: Coders who are unable to find the procedure or service in the index can look in the table of contents for the type of procedure or device to narrow the code choices. Also, coders should remember to check the unlisted procedure guidelines for additional choices.

3. Assign a tentative code.

   Example:

   Code G0103

   Coding Tip: To the right of the terminology, there may be a single code or multiple codes, a cross-reference, or an indication that the code has been deleted. Tentatively assign all codes listed.

4. Locate the code or codes in the appropriate section. When multiple codes are listed in the index, be sure to read the narrative of all codes listed to find the appropriate code based on the service performed.

   Example:

   G0103 Prostate cancer screening; prostate specific antigen test (PSA)

5. Check for color bars, symbols, notes, and references.

   Example:

   A **G0103 Prostate cancer screening; prostate specific antigen test (PSA)** ♂

   MED: 100-3, 210.1; 100-4, 18, 50

6. Review the appendixes for the reference definitions and other guidelines for coverage issues that apply.

7. Determine whether any modifiers should be used.

8. Assign the code.

   Example:

   The code assigned is G0103.

CODING STANDARDS

Levels of Use

Coders may find that the same procedure is coded at two or even three levels. Which code is correct? There are certain rules to follow if this should occur.

When both a CPT and a HCPCS Level II code have virtually identical narratives for a procedure or service, the CPT code should be used. If, however, the narratives are not identical (e.g., the CPT code narrative is generic, whereas the HCPCS Level II code is specific), the Level II code should be used.

Be sure to check for a national code when a CPT code description contains an instruction to include additional information, such as describing a specific medication. For example, when billing Medicare or Medicaid for supplies, avoid using CPT code 99070 Supplies and materials (except spectacles), provided by the physician over and above those usually included with the office visit or other services rendered (list drugs, trays, supplies, or materials provided). There are many HCPCS Level II codes that specify supplies in more detail.

Special Reports

Submit a special report with the claim when a new, unusual, or variable procedure is provided or a modifier is used. Include the following information:

- A copy of the appropriate report (e.g., operative, x-ray), explaining the nature, extent, and need for the procedure
- Documentation of the medical necessity of the procedure
- Documentation of the time and effort necessary to perform the procedure

A

B

D

E

M

T

U

V

TRANSPORTATION SERVICES INCLUDING AMBULANCE A0021-A0999

This code range includes ground and air ambulance, nonemergency transportation (taxi, bus, automobile, wheelchair van), and ancillary transportation-related fees.

HCPCS Level II codes for ambulance services must be reported with modifiers that indicate pick-up origins and destinations. The modifier describing the arrangement (QM, QN) is listed first. The modifiers describing the origin and destination are listed second. Origin and destination modifiers are created by combining two alpha characters from the following list. Each alpha character, with the exception of X, represents either an origin or a destination. Each pair of alpha characters creates one modifier. The first position represents the origin and the second the destination. The modifiers most commonly used are:

D	Diagnostic or therapeutic site other than "P" or "H" when these are used as origin codes
E	Residential, domiciliary, custodial facility (other than 1819 facility)
G	Hospital-based ESRD facility
H	Hospital
I	Site of transfer (e.g., airport or helicopter pad) between modes of ambulance transport
J	Free standing ESRD facility
N	Skilled nursing facility (SNF)
P	Physician's office
R	Residence
S	Scene of accident or acute event
X	Intermediate stop at physician's office on way to hospital (destination code only)

Note: Modifier X can only be used as a destination code in the second position of a modifier.

See S0215. For Medicaid, see T codes and T modifiers.

AMBULANCE TRANSPORT AND SUPPLIES

E **A0021** **Ambulance service, outside state per mile, transport (Medicaid only)**

E **A0080** **Nonemergency transportation, per mile - vehicle provided by volunteer (individual or organization), with no vested interest**

E **A0090** **Nonemergency transportation, per mile - vehicle provided by individual (family member, self, neighbor) with vested interest**

E **A0100** **Nonemergency transportation; taxi**

E **A0110** **Nonemergency transportation and bus, intra- or interstate carrier**

E **A0120** **Nonemergency transportation: mini-bus, mountain area transports, or other transportation systems**

E **A0130** **Nonemergency transportation: wheelchair van**

E **A0140** **Nonemergency transportation and air travel (private or commercial) intra- or interstate**

E **A0160** **Nonemergency transportation: per mile - caseworker or social worker**

E **A0170** **Transportation ancillary: parking fees, tolls, other**

E **A0180** **Nonemergency transportation: ancillary: lodging-recipient**

E **A0190** **Nonemergency transportation: ancillary: meals, recipient**

E **A0200** **Nonemergency transportation: ancillary: lodging, escort**

E **A0210** **Nonemergency transportation: ancillary: meals, escort**

E **A0225** **Ambulance service, neonatal transport, base rate, emergency transport, one way**
MED: 100-4,1,10.1.4.1

E ☑ **A0380** **BLS mileage (per mile)**
See code(s): A0425
MED: 100-2,10,10.3.3; 100-4,1,10.1.4.1; 100-4,15,20.2; 100-4,15,30.2

A **A0382** **BLS routine disposable supplies**
MED: 100-2,10,30.1.1

A **A0384** **BLS specialized service disposable supplies; defibrillation (used by ALS ambulances and BLS ambulances in jurisdictions where defibrillation is permitted in BLS ambulances)**

E ☑ **A0390** **ALS mileage (per mile)**
See code(s): A0425
MED: 100-2,10,10.3.3; 100-4,1,10.1.4.1; 100-4,15,20.2; 100-4,15,30.2

A **A0392** **ALS specialized service disposable supplies; defibrillation (to be used only in jurisdictions where defibrillation cannot be performed in BLS ambulances)**
MED: 100-2,10,30.1.1

A **A0394** **ALS specialized service disposable supplies; IV drug therapy**

A **A0396** **ALS specialized service disposable supplies; esophageal intubation**

A **A0398** **ALS routine disposable supplies**

WAITING TIME

Units	Time
1	1/2 to 1 hr.
2	1 to 1-1/2 hrs.
3	1-1/2 to 2 hrs.
4	2 to 2-1/2 hrs.
5	2-1/2 to 3 hrs.
6	3 to 3-1/2 hrs.
7	3-1/2 to 4 hrs.
8	4 to 4-1/2 hrs.
9	4-1/2 to 5 hrs.
10	5 to 5-1/2 hrs.

A **A0420** **Ambulance waiting time (ALS or BLS), one-half (1/2) hour increments**

OTHER AMBULANCE SERVICES

A **A0422** **Ambulance (ALS or BLS) oxygen and oxygen supplies, life sustaining situation**

A **A0424** **Extra ambulance attendant, ground (ALS or BLS) or air (fixed or rotary winged); (requires medical review)**
Pertinent documentation to evaluate medical appropriateness should be included when this code is reported.
MED: 100-4,15,30.2.1

A **A0425** **Ground mileage, per statute mile**

A **A0426** **Ambulance service, advanced life support, nonemergency transport, level 1 (ALS 1)**
MED: 100-2,10,20; 100-4,1,10.1.4.1; 100-4,15,20.1.4; 100-4,15,30.2; 100-4,15,30.2.1

A **A0427** Ambulance service, advanced life support, emergency transport, level 1 (ALS 1 - emergency)
MED: 100-2,10,20; 100-4,1,10.1.4.1; 100-4,15,30.2.1

A **A0428** Ambulance service, basic life support, nonemergency transport, (BLS)
MED: 100-2,10,20; 100-4,1,10.1.4.1; 100-4,15,30.2.1

A **A0429** Ambulance service, basic life support, emergency transport (BLS, emergency)
MED: 100-2,10,20; 100-4,1,10.1.4.1; 100-4,15,30.2.1

A **A0430** Ambulance service, conventional air services, transport, one way (fixed wing)
MED: 100-2,10,20; 100-4,1,10.1.4.1; 100-4,15,20.3; 100-4,15,30.2.1

A **A0431** Ambulance service, conventional air services, transport, one way (rotary wing)
MED: 100-2,10,20; 100-4,1,10.1.4.1; 100-4,15,30.2.1

A **A0432** Paramedic intercept (PI), rural area, transport furnished by a volunteer ambulance company which is prohibited by state law from billing third-party payers
MED: 100-2,10,20; 100-2,10,30.1.1; 100-4,15,30.2.1

A **A0433** Advanced life support, level 2 (ALS 2)
MED: 100-2,10,20; 100-4,15,30.2.1

A **A0434** Specialty care transport (SCT)
MED: 100-2,10,20; 100-4,15,30.2.1

A **A0435** Fixed wing air mileage, per statute mile
MED: 100-2,10,20; 100-4,15,20.2; 100-4,15,20.3; 100-4,15,30.2; 100-4,15,30.2.1

A **A0436** Rotary wing air mileage, per statute mile
MED: 100-2,10,20; 100-4,15,20.2; 100-4,15,30.2.1

E **A0888** Noncovered ambulance mileage, per mile (e.g., for miles traveled beyond closest appropriate facility)
MED: 100-2,10,20; 100-4,15,20.2; 100-4,15,30.1.2; 100-4,15,30.2.4

E **A0998** Ambulance response and treatment, no transport

A **A0999** Unlisted ambulance service
MED: 100-2,10,20

MEDICAL AND SURGICAL SUPPLIES A4206-A9999

This section covers a wide variety of medical, surgical, and some durable medical equipment (DME) related supplies and accessories. DME-related supplies, accessories, maintenance, and repair required to ensure the proper functioning of this equipment is generally covered by Medicare under the prosthetic devices provision.

INJECTION SUPPLIES

E ☑ **A4206** Syringe with needle, sterile, 1 cc or less, each

E ☑ **A4207** Syringe with needle, sterile 2 cc, each

E ☑ **A4208** Syringe with needle, sterile 3 cc, each

E ☑ **A4209** Syringe with needle, sterile 5 cc or greater, each

E ☑ **A4210** Needle-free injection device, each
Sometimes covered by commercial payers with preauthorization and physician letter stating need (e.g., for insulin injection in young children).

E **A4211** Supplies for self-administered injections
When a drug that is usually injected by the patient (e.g., insulin or calcitonin) is injected by the physician, it is excluded from Medicare coverage unless administered in an emergency situation (e.g., diabetic coma).

B **A4212** Noncoring needle or stylet with or without catheter

E ☑ **A4213** Syringe, sterile, 20 cc or greater, each

E **A4215** Needle, sterile, any size, each

A ☑ **A4216** Sterile water, saline and/or dextrose, diluent/flush, 10 ml ♿

A ☑ **A4217** Sterile water/saline, 500 ml ♿

N ☑ **A4218** Sterile saline or water, metered dose dispenser, 10 ml NI

N **A4220** Refill kit for implantable infusion pump NI

Y **A4221** Supplies for maintenance of drug infusion catheter, per week (list drug separately) ♿

Y **A4222** Infusion supplies for external drug infusion pump, per cassette or bag (list drugs separately) ♿

E ☑ **A4223** Infusion supplies not used with external infusion pump, per cassette or bag (list drugs separately)

N ☑ **A4230** Infusion set for external insulin pump, nonneedle cannula type
Covered by some commercial payers as ongoing supply to preauthorized pump.

N ☑ **A4231** Infusion set for external insulin pump, needle type
Covered by some commercial payers as ongoing supply to preauthorized pump.

E ☑ **A4232** Syringe with needle for external insulin pump, sterile, 3 cc
Covered by some commercial payers as ongoing supply to preauthorized pump.

BATTERIES

Y ☑ **A4233** Replacement battery, alkaline (other than J cell), for use with medically necessary home blood glucose monitor owned by patient, each ♿
MED: 100-4,23,60.3

Y ☑ **A4234** Replacement battery, alkaline, J cell, for use with medically necessary home blood glucose monitor owned by patient, each ♿

Y ☑ **A4235** Replacement battery, lithium, for use with medically necessary home blood glucose monitor owned by patient, each ♿

Y ☑ **A4236** Replacement battery, silver oxide, for use with medically necessary home blood glucose monitor owned by patient, each ♿

OTHER SUPPLIES

E ☑ **A4244** Alcohol or peroxide, per pint

E ☑ **A4245** Alcohol wipes, per box

E ☑ **A4246** Betadine or pHisoHex solution, per pint

E ☑ **A4247** Betadine or iodine swabs/wipes, per box

N ☑ **A4248** Chlorhexidine containing antiseptic, 1 ml NI

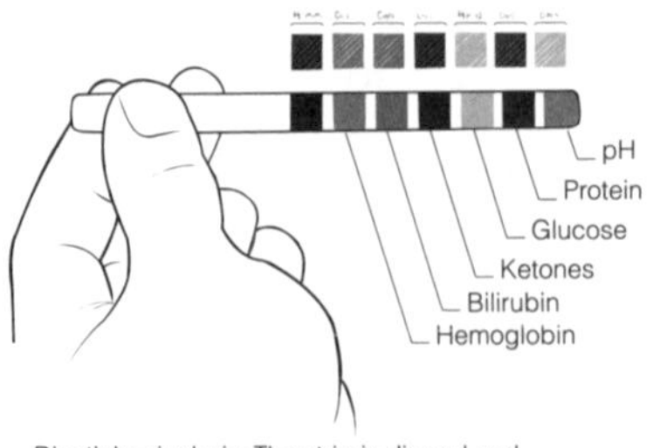

Dipstick urinalysis: The strip is dipped and color-coded squares are read at timed intervals (e.g., pH immediately; ketones at 15 sec., etc.). Results are compared against a reference chart

Tablet reagents turn specific colors when urine droplets are placed on them

E ☑ **A4250** Urine test or reagent strips or tablets (100 tablets or strips)
MED: 100-2,15,110

E ☑ **A4252** Blood ketone test or reagent strip, each

Y ☑ **A4253** Blood glucose test or reagent strips for home blood glucose monitor, per 50 strips ♿
Medicare covers glucose strips for diabetic patients using home glucose monitoring devices prescribed by their physicians.
MED: 100-4,23,60.3

Y ☑ **A4255** Platforms for home blood glucose monitor, 50 per box ♿
Some Medicare contractors cover monitor platforms for diabetic patients using home glucose monitoring devices prescribed by their physicians. Some commercial payers also provide this coverage to noninsulin dependent diabetics.

Y **A4256** Normal, low, and high calibrator solution/chips ♿
Some Medicare contractors cover calibration solutions or chips for diabetic patients using home glucose monitoring devices prescribed by their physicians. Some commercial payers also provide this coverage to noninsulin dependent diabetics.
MED: 100-4,23,60.3

Y ☑ **A4257** Replacement lens shield cartridge for use with laser skin piercing device, each ♿

Y ☑ **A4258** Spring-powered device for lancet, each ♿
Some Medicare contractors cover lancing devices for diabetic patients using home glucose monitoring devices prescribed by their physicians. Medicare jurisdiction: DME regional contractor. Some commercial payers also provide this coverage to noninsulin dependent diabetics.
MED: 100-4,23,60.3

Y ☑ **A4259** Lancets, per box of 100 ♿
Medicare covers lancets for diabetic patients using home glucose monitoring devices prescribed by their physicians. Medicare jurisdiction: DME regional contractor. Some commercial payers also provide this coverage to noninsulin dependent diabetics.

E **A4261** Cervical cap for contraceptive use ♀

N ☑ **A4262** Temporary, absorbable lacrimal duct implant, each N1
Always report concurrent to the implant procedure.

N ☑ **A4263** Permanent, long-term, nondissolvable lacrimal duct implant, each N1
Always report concurrent to the implant procedure.

E ☑ **A4264** Permanent implantable contraceptive intratubal occlusion device(s) and delivery system ♀

Y ☑ **A4265** Paraffin, per pound ♿

E **A4266** Diaphragm for contraceptive use ♀

E ☑ **A4267** Contraceptive supply, condom, male, each ♂

E ☑ **A4268** Contraceptive supply, condom, female, each ♀

E ☑ **A4269** Contraceptive supply, spermicide (e.g., foam, gel), each ♀

N ☑ **A4270** Disposable endoscope sheath, each N1

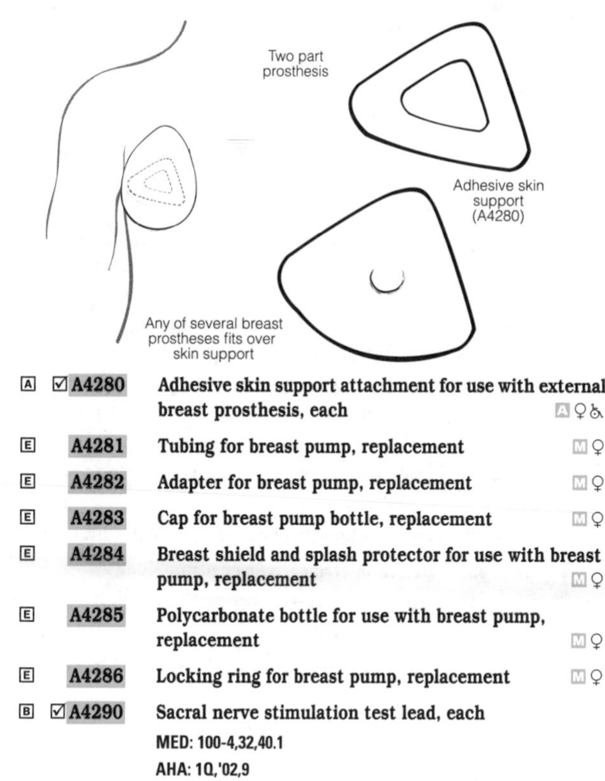

A ☑ **A4280** Adhesive skin support attachment for use with external breast prosthesis, each A ♀ ♿

E **A4281** Tubing for breast pump, replacement M ♀

E **A4282** Adapter for breast pump, replacement M ♀

E **A4283** Cap for breast pump bottle, replacement M ♀

E **A4284** Breast shield and splash protector for use with breast pump, replacement M ♀

E **A4285** Polycarbonate bottle for use with breast pump, replacement M ♀

E **A4286** Locking ring for breast pump, replacement M ♀

B ☑ **A4290** Sacral nerve stimulation test lead, each
MED: 100-4,32,40.1
AHA: 1Q,'02,9

VASCULAR CATHETERS AND DRUG DELIVERY SYSTEMS

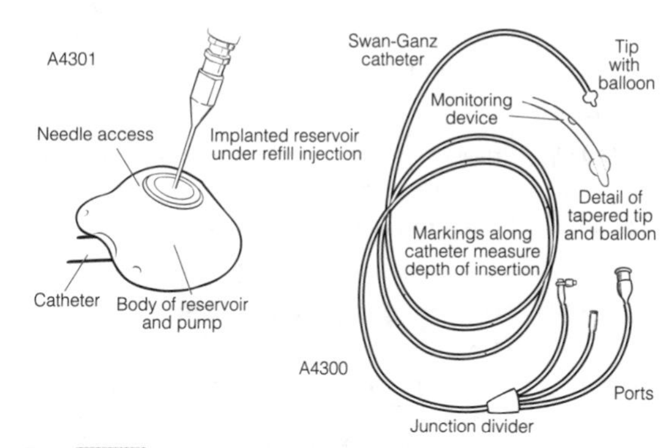

N **A4300** Implantable access catheter, (e.g., venous, arterial, epidural subarachnoid, or peritoneal, etc.) external access N1

N **A4301** Implantable access total catheter, port/reservoir (e.g., venous, arterial, epidural, subarachnoid, peritoneal, etc.) N1

N ☑ **A4305** Disposable drug delivery system, flow rate of 50 ml or greater per hour N1

N ☑ **A4306** Disposable drug delivery system, flow rate of less than 50 ml per hour N1

INCONTINENNCE APPLIANCES AND CARE SUPPLIES

Covered by Medicare when the medical record indicates incontinence is permanent, or of long and indefinite duration.

A **A4310** Insertion tray without drainage bag and without catheter (accessories only) ♿

A A4311 Insertion tray without drainage bag with indwelling catheter, Foley type, 2-way latex with coating (Teflon, silicone, silicone elastomer or hydrophilic, etc.)

A A4312 Insertion tray without drainage bag with indwelling catheter, Foley type, 2-way, all silicone

A A4313 Insertion tray without drainage bag with indwelling catheter, Foley type, 3-way, for continuous irrigation

A A4314 Insertion tray with drainage bag with indwelling catheter, Foley type, 2-way latex with coating (Teflon, silicone, silicone elastomer or hydrophilic, etc.)

A A4315 Insertion tray with drainage bag with indwelling catheter, Foley type, 2-way, all silicone

A A4316 Insertion tray with drainage bag with indwelling catheter, Foley type, 3-way, for continuous irrigation

A A4320 Irrigation tray with bulb or piston syringe, any purpose

A A4321 Therapeutic agent for urinary catheter irrigation

A ☑ A4322 Irrigation syringe, bulb or piston, each

A ☑ A4326 Male external catheter with integral collection chamber, any type, each ♂

A ☑ A4327 Female external urinary collection device; meatal cup, each ♀

A ☑ A4328 Female external urinary collection device; pouch, each ♀

A ☑ A4330 Perianal fecal collection pouch with adhesive, each

A ☑ A4331 Extension drainage tubing, any type, any length, with connector/adaptor, for use with urinary leg bag or urostomy pouch, each

A ☑ A4332 Lubricant, individual sterile packet, each

A ☑ A4333 Urinary catheter anchoring device, adhesive skin attachment, each

A ☑ A4334 Urinary catheter anchoring device, leg strap, each

A A4335 Incontinence supply; miscellaneous

A ☑ A4336 Incontinence supply, urethral insert, any type, each

A ☑ A4338 Indwelling catheter; Foley type, 2-way latex with coating (Teflon, silicone, silicone elastomer, or hydrophilic, etc.), each

A ☑ A4340 Indwelling catheter; specialty type, (e.g., Coude, mushroom, wing, etc.), each

A ☑ A4344 Indwelling catheter, Foley type, 2-way, all silicone, each

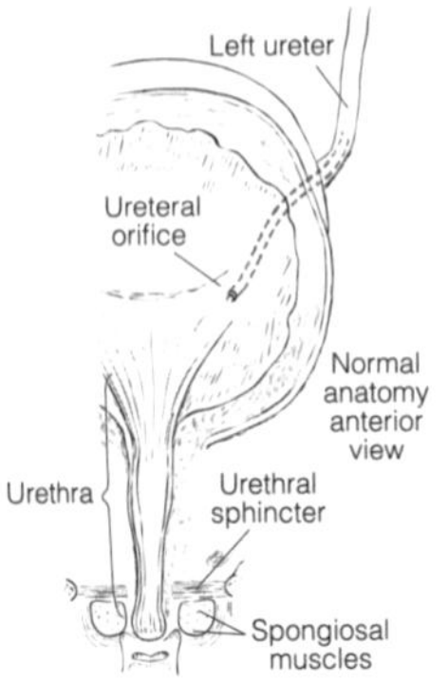

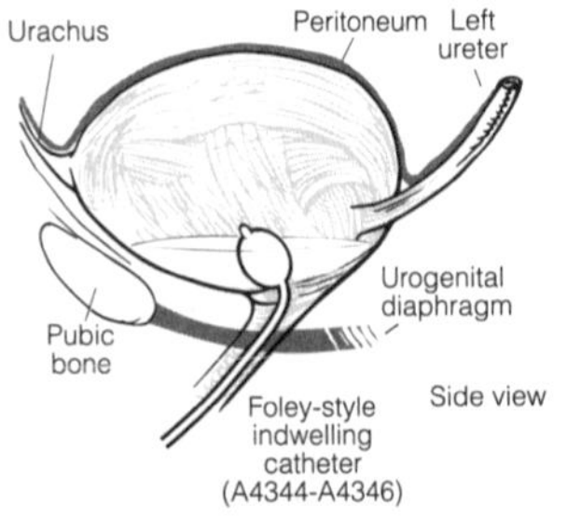

Multiple port indwelling catheters allow for irrigation and drainage

A ☑ A4346 Indwelling catheter; Foley type, 3-way for continuous irrigation, each

A ☑ A4349 Male external catheter, with or without adhesive, disposable, each ♂

A ☑ A4351 Intermittent urinary catheter; straight tip, with or without coating (Teflon, silicone, silicone elastomer, or hydrophilic, etc.), each

A ☑ A4352 Intermittent urinary catheter; Coude (curved) tip, with or without coating (Teflon, silicone, silicone elastomeric, or hydrophilic, etc.), each

A A4353 Intermittent urinary catheter, with insertion supplies

A A4354 Insertion tray with drainage bag but without catheter

A ☑ A4355 Irrigation tubing set for continuous bladder irrigation through a 3-way indwelling Foley catheter, each

A ☑ A4356 External urethral clamp or compression device (not to be used for catheter clamp), each

A ☑ A4357 Bedside drainage bag, day or night, with or without antireflux device, with or without tube, each

A ☑ A4358 Urinary drainage bag, leg or abdomen, vinyl, with or without tube, with straps, each

A ☑ A4360 Disposable external urethral clamp or compression device, with pad and/or pouch, each

OSTOMY SUPPLIES

A ☑ A4361 Ostomy faceplate, each

A ☑ A4362 Skin barrier; solid, 4 x 4 or equivalent; each
See code(s) A4461 or A4463

A A4363 Ostomy clamp, any type, replacement only, each

A ☑ A4364 Adhesive, liquid or equal, any type, per oz

A ☑ A4366 Ostomy vent, any type, each

A ☑ A4367 Ostomy belt, each

A ☑ A4368 Ostomy filter, any type, each

A ☑ A4369 Ostomy skin barrier, liquid (spray, brush, etc.), per oz

A ☑ A4371 Ostomy skin barrier, powder, per oz

A ☑ A4372 Ostomy skin barrier, solid 4 x 4 or equivalent, standard wear, with built-in convexity, each

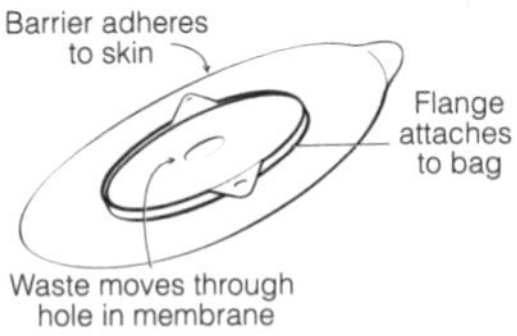

Faceplate flange and skin barrier combination (A4373)

A ☑ A4373 Ostomy skin barrier, with flange (solid, flexible or accordian), with built-in convexity, any size, each

A ☑ A4375 Ostomy pouch, drainable, with faceplate attached, plastic, each

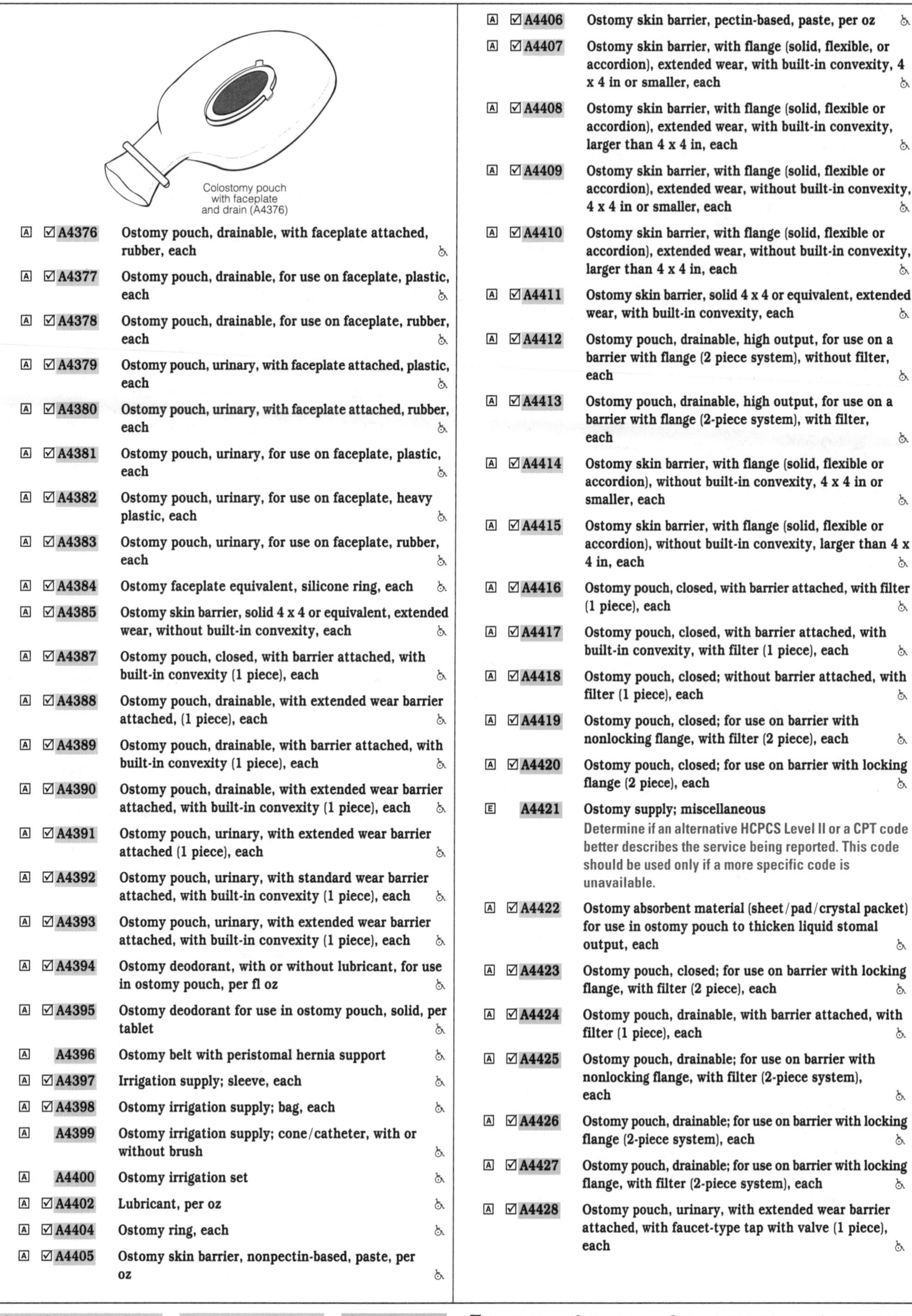

Colostomy pouch with faceplate and drain (A4376)

[A] ☑ **A4376** Ostomy pouch, drainable, with faceplate attached, rubber, each ♿

[A] ☑ **A4377** Ostomy pouch, drainable, for use on faceplate, plastic, each ♿

[A] ☑ **A4378** Ostomy pouch, drainable, for use on faceplate, rubber, each ♿

[A] ☑ **A4379** Ostomy pouch, urinary, with faceplate attached, plastic, each ♿

[A] ☑ **A4380** Ostomy pouch, urinary, with faceplate attached, rubber, each ♿

[A] ☑ **A4381** Ostomy pouch, urinary, for use on faceplate, plastic, each ♿

[A] ☑ **A4382** Ostomy pouch, urinary, for use on faceplate, heavy plastic, each ♿

[A] ☑ **A4383** Ostomy pouch, urinary, for use on faceplate, rubber, each ♿

[A] ☑ **A4384** Ostomy faceplate equivalent, silicone ring, each ♿

[A] ☑ **A4385** Ostomy skin barrier, solid 4 x 4 or equivalent, extended wear, without built-in convexity, each ♿

[A] ☑ **A4387** Ostomy pouch, closed, with barrier attached, with built-in convexity (1 piece), each ♿

[A] ☑ **A4388** Ostomy pouch, drainable, with extended wear barrier attached, (1 piece), each ♿

[A] ☑ **A4389** Ostomy pouch, drainable, with barrier attached, with built-in convexity (1 piece), each ♿

[A] ☑ **A4390** Ostomy pouch, drainable, with extended wear barrier attached, with built-in convexity (1 piece), each ♿

[A] ☑ **A4391** Ostomy pouch, urinary, with extended wear barrier attached (1 piece), each ♿

[A] ☑ **A4392** Ostomy pouch, urinary, with standard wear barrier attached, with built-in convexity (1 piece), each ♿

[A] ☑ **A4393** Ostomy pouch, urinary, with extended wear barrier attached, with built-in convexity (1 piece), each ♿

[A] ☑ **A4394** Ostomy deodorant, with or without lubricant, for use in ostomy pouch, per fl oz ♿

[A] ☑ **A4395** Ostomy deodorant for use in ostomy pouch, solid, per tablet ♿

[A] **A4396** Ostomy belt with peristomal hernia support ♿

[A] ☑ **A4397** Irrigation supply; sleeve, each ♿

[A] ☑ **A4398** Ostomy irrigation supply; bag, each ♿

[A] **A4399** Ostomy irrigation supply; cone/catheter, with or without brush ♿

[A] **A4400** Ostomy irrigation set ♿

[A] ☑ **A4402** Lubricant, per oz ♿

[A] ☑ **A4404** Ostomy ring, each ♿

[A] ☑ **A4405** Ostomy skin barrier, nonpectin-based, paste, per oz ♿

[A] ☑ **A4406** Ostomy skin barrier, pectin-based, paste, per oz ♿

[A] ☑ **A4407** Ostomy skin barrier, with flange (solid, flexible, or accordion), extended wear, with built-in convexity, 4 x 4 in or smaller, each ♿

[A] ☑ **A4408** Ostomy skin barrier, with flange (solid, flexible or accordion), extended wear, with built-in convexity, larger than 4 x 4 in, each ♿

[A] ☑ **A4409** Ostomy skin barrier, with flange (solid, flexible or accordion), extended wear, without built-in convexity, 4 x 4 in or smaller, each ♿

[A] ☑ **A4410** Ostomy skin barrier, with flange (solid, flexible or accordion), extended wear, without built-in convexity, larger than 4 x 4 in, each ♿

[A] ☑ **A4411** Ostomy skin barrier, solid 4 x 4 or equivalent, extended wear, with built-in convexity, each ♿

[A] ☑ **A4412** Ostomy pouch, drainable, high output, for use on a barrier with flange (2 piece system), without filter, each ♿

[A] ☑ **A4413** Ostomy pouch, drainable, high output, for use on a barrier with flange (2-piece system), with filter, each ♿

[A] ☑ **A4414** Ostomy skin barrier, with flange (solid, flexible or accordion), without built-in convexity, 4 x 4 in or smaller, each ♿

[A] ☑ **A4415** Ostomy skin barrier, with flange (solid, flexible or accordion), without built-in convexity, larger than 4 x 4 in, each ♿

[A] ☑ **A4416** Ostomy pouch, closed, with barrier attached, with filter (1 piece), each ♿

[A] ☑ **A4417** Ostomy pouch, closed, with barrier attached, with built-in convexity, with filter (1 piece), each ♿

[A] ☑ **A4418** Ostomy pouch, closed; without barrier attached, with filter (1 piece), each ♿

[A] ☑ **A4419** Ostomy pouch, closed; for use on barrier with nonlocking flange, with filter (2 piece), each ♿

[A] ☑ **A4420** Ostomy pouch, closed; for use on barrier with locking flange (2 piece), each ♿

[E] **A4421** Ostomy supply; miscellaneous

Determine if an alternative HCPCS Level II or a CPT code better describes the service being reported. This code should be used only if a more specific code is unavailable.

[A] ☑ **A4422** Ostomy absorbent material (sheet/pad/crystal packet) for use in ostomy pouch to thicken liquid stomal output, each ♿

[A] ☑ **A4423** Ostomy pouch, closed; for use on barrier with locking flange, with filter (2 piece), each ♿

[A] ☑ **A4424** Ostomy pouch, drainable, with barrier attached, with filter (1 piece), each ♿

[A] ☑ **A4425** Ostomy pouch, drainable; for use on barrier with nonlocking flange, with filter (2-piece system), each ♿

[A] ☑ **A4426** Ostomy pouch, drainable; for use on barrier with locking flange (2-piece system), each ♿

[A] ☑ **A4427** Ostomy pouch, drainable; for use on barrier with locking flange, with filter (2-piece system), each ♿

[A] ☑ **A4428** Ostomy pouch, urinary, with extended wear barrier attached, with faucet-type tap with valve (1 piece), each ♿

A ☑ A4429 Ostomy pouch, urinary, with barrier attached, with built-in convexity, with faucet-type tap with valve (1 piece), each ♿

A ☑ A4430 Ostomy pouch, urinary, with extended wear barrier attached, with built-in convexity, with faucet-type tap with valve (1 piece), each ♿

A ☑ A4431 Ostomy pouch, urinary; with barrier attached, with faucet-type tap with valve (1 piece), each ♿

A ☑ A4432 Ostomy pouch, urinary; for use on barrier with nonlocking flange, with faucet-type tap with valve (2 piece), each ♿

A ☑ A4433 Ostomy pouch, urinary; for use on barrier with locking flange (2 piece), each ♿

A ☑ A4434 Ostomy pouch, urinary; for use on barrier with locking flange, with faucet-type tap with valve (2 piece), each ♿

MISCELLANEOUS SUPPLIES

A ☑ A4450 Tape, nonwaterproof, per 18 sq in ♿
See also code A4452.

A ☑ A4452 Tape, waterproof, per 18 sq in ♿
See also code A4450.

A ☑ A4455 Adhesive remover or solvent (for tape, cement or other adhesive), per oz ♿

A ☑ A4456 Adhesive remover, wipes, any type, each ♿

E A4458 Enema bag with tubing, reusable

A ☑ A4461 Surgical dressing holder, nonreusable, each ♿

A ☑ A4463 Surgical dressing holder, reusable, each ♿

N A4465 Nonelastic binder for extremity

E ☑ A4466 Garment, belt, sleeve or other covering, elastic or similar stretchable material, any type, each

N A4470 Gravlee jet washer

N A4480 VABRA aspirator ♀

A ☑ A4481 Tracheostoma filter, any type, any size, each ♿

A A4483 Moisture exchanger, disposable, for use with invasive mechanical ventilation ♿

E ☑ A4490 Surgical stockings above knee length, each
MED: 100-2,15,110

E ☑ A4495 Surgical stockings thigh length, each
MED: 100-2,15,110

E ☑ A4500 Surgical stockings below knee length, each
MED: 100-2,15,110

E ☑ A4510 Surgical stockings full-length, each
MED: 100-2,15,110

E ☑ A4520 Incontinence garment, any type, (e.g., brief, diaper), each

B A4550 Surgical trays

E ☑ A4554 Disposable underpads, all sizes

Y ☑ A4556 Electrodes (e.g., apnea monitor), per pair ♿

Y ☑ A4557 Lead wires (e.g., apnea monitor), per pair ♿

Y ☑ A4558 Conductive gel or paste, for use with electrical device (e.g., TENS, NMES), per oz ♿

Y ☑ A4559 Coupling gel or paste, for use with ultrasound device, per oz ♿

N A4561 Pessary, rubber, any type A ♀ ♿

N A4562 Pessary, nonrubber, any type A ♀ ♿
Medicare jurisdiction: DME regional contractor.

N A4565 Slings

E A4566 Shoulder sling or vest design, abduction restrainer, with or without swathe control, prefabricated, includes fitting and adjustment

E A4570 Splint
Dressings applied by a physician are included as part of the professional service.

E A4575 Topical hyperbaric oxygen chamber, disposable

E A4580 Cast supplies (e.g., plaster)
See Q4001-Q4048.

E A4590 Special casting material (e.g., fiberglass)
See Q4001-Q4048.

Y A4595 Electrical stimulator supplies, 2 lead, per month, (e.g., TENS, NMES) ♿
MED: 100-3,160.13

Y ☑ A4600 Sleeve for intermittent limb compression device, replacement only, each

Y A4601 Lithium ion battery for nonprosthetic use, replacement

Y A4604 Tubing with integrated heating element for use with positive airway pressure device ♿
MED: 100-4,23,60.3; 100-4,36,50.14

Y ☑ A4605 Tracheal suction catheter, closed system, each ♿

A A4606 Oxygen probe for use with oximeter device, replacement

Y ☑ A4608 Transtracheal oxygen catheter, each ♿
MED: 100-4,23,60.3

SUPPLIES FOR OXYGEN AND RELATED RESPIRATORY EQUIPMENT

Y A4611 Battery, heavy-duty; replacement for patient-owned ventilator ♿

Y A4612 Battery cables; replacement for patient-owned ventilator ♿

Y ☑ A4613 Battery charger; replacement for patient-owned ventilator ♿

Y A4614 Peak expiratory flow rate meter, hand held ♿

Y A4615 Cannula, nasal ♿
MED: 100-4,20,100.2; 100-4,23,60.3

Y ☑ A4616 Tubing (oxygen), per foot ♿
MED: 100-4,20,100.2

Y A4617 Mouthpiece ♿
MED: 100-4,20,100.2

Y A4618 Breathing circuits ♿
MED: 100-4,20,100.2

Y A4619 Face tent ♿
MED: 100-4,20,100.2

Y A4620 Variable concentration mask ♿
MED: 100-4,20,100.2; 100-4,23,60.3

A A4623 Tracheostomy, inner cannula ♿

Y ☑ A4624 Tracheal suction catheter, any type other than closed system, each ♿

A A4625 Tracheostomy care kit for new tracheostomy ♿

A ☑ A4626 Tracheostomy cleaning brush, each ♿

E A4627 Spacer, bag or reservoir, with or without mask, for use with metered dose inhaler
MED: 100-2,15,110

Y ☑ **A4628** Oropharyngeal suction catheter, each ♿

A **A4629** Tracheostomy care kit for established tracheostomy ♿

REPLACEMENT SUPPLIES FOR DME

Y ☑ **A4630** Replacement batteries, medically necessary, transcutaneous electrical stimulator, owned by patient ♿

Y ☑ **A4633** Replacement bulb/lamp for ultraviolet light therapy system, each ♿

A **A4634** Replacement bulb for therapeutic light box, tabletop model

Y ☑ **A4635** Underarm pad, crutch, replacement, each ♿

Y ☑ **A4636** Replacement, handgrip, cane, crutch, or walker, each ♿
MED: 100-4,23,60.3; 100-4,36,50,15

Y ☑ **A4637** Replacement, tip, cane, crutch, walker, each ♿

Y ☑ **A4638** Replacement battery for patient-owned ear pulse generator, each ♿

Y ☑ **A4639** Replacement pad for infrared heating pad system, each ♿

Y **A4640** Replacement pad for use with medically necessary alternating pressure pad owned by patient ♿

RADIOPHARMACEUTICALS

N **A4641** Radiopharmaceutical, diagnostic, not otherwise classified N1
MED: 100-4,13,60.3; 100-4,13,60.3.1; 100-4,13,60.3.2

N ☑ **A4642** Indium In-111 satumomab pendetide, diagnostic, per study dose, up to 6 millicuries N1
Use this code for Oncoscint.

MISCELLANEOUS SUPPLIES

N ☑ **A4648** Tissue marker, implantable, any type, each N1

N **A4649** Surgical supply; miscellaneous
Determine if an alternative HCPCS Level II or a CPT code better describes the service being reported. This code should be used only if a more specific code is unavailable.

N ☑ **A4650** Implantable radiation dosimeter, each N1

A ☑ **A4651** Calibrated microcapillary tube, each ⃠

A **A4652** Microcapillary tube sealant ⃠

DIALYSIS SUPPLIES

A ☑ **A4653** Peritoneal dialysis catheter anchoring device, belt, each ⃠

N ☑ **A4657** Syringe, with or without needle, each ⃠
MED: 100-4,8,60.4; 100-4,8,60.7; 100-4,8,60.7.3; 100-4,13,60.7.1

N **A4660** Sphygmomanometer/blood pressure apparatus with cuff and stethoscope ⃠

N **A4663** Blood pressure cuff only ⃠

E **A4670** Automatic blood pressure monitor

B ☑ **A4671** Disposable cycler set used with cycler dialysis machine, each ⃠

B ☑ **A4672** Drainage extension line, sterile, for dialysis, each ⃠

B **A4673** Extension line with easy lock connectors, used with dialysis ⃠

B ☑ **A4674** Chemicals/antiseptics solution used to clean/sterilize dialysis equipment, per 8 oz ⃠

N ☑ **A4680** Activated carbon filter for hemodialysis, each ⃠

N ☑ **A4690** Dialyzer (artificial kidneys), all types, all sizes, for hemodialysis, each ⃠

N ☑ **A4706** Bicarbonate concentrate, solution, for hemodialysis, per gallon ⃠

N ☑ **A4707** Bicarbonate concentrate, powder, for hemodialysis, per packet ⃠

N ☑ **A4708** Acetate concentrate solution, for hemodialysis, per gallon ⃠

N ☑ **A4709** Acid concentrate, solution, for hemodialysis, per gallon ⃠

N ☑ **A4714** Treated water (deionized, distilled, or reverse osmosis) for peritoneal dialysis, per gallon ⃠

N **A4719** "Y set" tubing for peritoneal dialysis ⃠

N ☑ **A4720** Dialysate solution, any concentration of dextrose, fluid volume greater than 249 cc, but less than or equal to 999 cc, for peritoneal dialysis ⃠

N ☑ **A4721** Dialysate solution, any concentration of dextrose, fluid volume greater than 999 cc but less than or equal to 1999 cc, for peritoneal dialysis ⃠

N ☑ **A4722** Dialysate solution, any concentration of dextrose, fluid volume greater than 1999 cc but less than or equal to 2999 cc, for peritoneal dialysis ⃠

N ☑ **A4723** Dialysate solution, any concentration of dextrose, fluid volume greater than 2999 cc but less than or equal to 3999 cc, for peritoneal dialysis ⃠

N ☑ **A4724** Dialysate solution, any concentration of dextrose, fluid volume greater than 3999 cc but less than or equal to 4999 cc, for peritoneal dialysis ⃠

N ☑ **A4725** Dialysate solution, any concentration of dextrose, fluid volume greater than 4999 cc but less than or equal to 5999 cc, for peritoneal dialysis ⃠

N ☑ **A4726** Dialysate solution, any concentration of dextrose, fluid volume greater than 5999 cc, for peritoneal dialysis ⃠

B ☑ **A4728** Dialysate solution, nondextrose containing, 500 ml ⃠

N ☑ **A4730** Fistula cannulation set for hemodialysis, each ⃠

N ☑ **A4736** Topical anesthetic, for dialysis, per g ⃠

N ☑ **A4737** Injectable anesthetic, for dialysis, per 10 ml ⃠

N **A4740** Shunt accessory, for hemodialysis, any type, each ⃠

N ☑ **A4750** Blood tubing, arterial or venous, for hemodialysis, each ⃠

N ☑ **A4755** Blood tubing, arterial and venous combined, for hemodialysis, each ⃠

N ☑ **A4760** Dialysate solution test kit, for peritoneal dialysis, any type, each ⃠

N ☑ **A4765** Dialysate concentrate, powder, additive for peritoneal dialysis, per packet ⃠

N ☑ **A4766** Dialysate concentrate, solution, additive for peritoneal dialysis, per 10 ml ⃠

N ☑ **A4770** Blood collection tube, vacuum, for dialysis, per 50 ⃠

N ☑ **A4771** Serum clotting time tube, for dialysis, per 50 ⃠

N ☑ **A4772** Blood glucose test strips, for dialysis, per 50 ⃠

N ☑ **A4773** Occult blood test strips, for dialysis, per 50 ⃠

N ☑ A4774 Ammonia test strips, for dialysis, per 50

N ☑ A4802 Protamine sulfate, for hemodialysis, per 50 mg

N ☑ A4860 Disposable catheter tips for peritoneal dialysis, per 10

N A4870 Plumbing and/or electrical work for home hemodialysis equipment

N A4890 Contracts, repair and maintenance, for hemodialysis equipment

N ☑ A4911 Drain bag/bottle, for dialysis, each

N A4913 Miscellaneous dialysis supplies, not otherwise specified

Pertinent documentation to evaluate medical appropriateness should be included when this code is reported. Determine if an alternative HCPCS Level II or a CPT code better describes the service being reported. This code should be used only if a more specific code is unavailable.

N ☑ A4918 Venous pressure clamp, for hemodialysis, each

N ☑ A4927 Gloves, nonsterile, per 100

N ☑ A4928 Surgical mask, per 20

N ☑ A4929 Tourniquet for dialysis, each

N ☑ A4930 Gloves, sterile, per pair

N ☑ A4931 Oral thermometer, reusable, any type, each

E ☑ A4932 Rectal thermometer, reusable, any type, each

OSTOMY POUCHES AND SUPPLIES

A ☑ A5051 Ostomy pouch, closed; with barrier attached (1 piece), each

A ☑ A5052 Ostomy pouch, closed; without barrier attached (1 piece), each

A ☑ A5053 Ostomy pouch, closed; for use on faceplate, each

A ☑ A5054 Ostomy pouch, closed; for use on barrier with flange (2 piece), each

A A5055 Stoma cap

● A ☑ A5056 Jan Ostomy pouch, drainable, with extended wear barrier attached, with filter, (1 piece), each

● A ☑ A5057 Jan Ostomy pouch, drainable, with extended wear barrier attached, with built in convexity, with filter, (1 piece), each

A ☑ A5061 Ostomy pouch, drainable; with barrier attached, (1 piece), each

A ☑ A5062 Ostomy pouch, drainable; without barrier attached (1 piece), each

A ☑ A5063 Ostomy pouch, drainable; for use on barrier with flange (2-piece system), each

A ☑ A5071 Ostomy pouch, urinary; with barrier attached (1 piece), each

A ☑ A5072 Ostomy pouch, urinary; without barrier attached (1 piece), each

A ☑ A5073 Ostomy pouch, urinary; for use on barrier with flange (2 piece), each

A A5081 Continent device; plug for continent stoma

A A5082 Continent device; catheter for continent stoma

A A5083 Continent device, stoma absorptive cover for continent stoma

A A5093 Ostomy accessory; convex insert

INCONTINENCE SUPPLIES

A ☑ A5102 Bedside drainage bottle with or without tubing, rigid or expandable, each

A ☑ A5105 Urinary suspensory with leg bag, with or without tube, each

A ☑ A5112 Urinary drainage bag, leg or abdomen, latex, with or without tube, with straps, each

A ☑ A5113 Leg strap; latex, replacement only, per set

A ☑ A5114 Leg strap; foam or fabric, replacement only, per set

A ☑ A5120 Skin barrier, wipes or swabs, each

A ☑ A5121 Skin barrier; solid, 6 x 6 or equivalent, each

A ☑ A5122 Skin barrier; solid, 8 x 8 or equivalent, each

A A5126 Adhesive or nonadhesive; disk or foam pad

A ☑ A5131 Appliance cleaner, incontinence and ostomy appliances, per 16 oz

A A5200 Percutaneous catheter/tube anchoring device, adhesive skin attachment

DIABETIC SHOES, FITTING, AND MODIFICATIONS

According to Medicare, documentation from the prescribing physician must certify the diabetic patient has one of the following conditions: peripheral neuropathy with evidence of callus formation; history of preulcerative calluses; history of ulceration; foot deformity; previous amputation; or poor circulation. The footwear must be fitted and furnished by a podiatrist, pedorthist, orthotist, or prosthetist.

Y ☑ A5500 For diabetics only, fitting (including follow-up), custom preparation and supply of off-the-shelf depth-inlay shoe manufactured to accommodate multidensity insert(s), per shoe

MED: 100-2,15,140

Y ☑ A5501 For diabetics only, fitting (including follow-up), custom preparation and supply of shoe molded from cast(s) of patient's foot (custom molded shoe), per shoe

MED: 100-2,15,140

Y ☑ A5503 For diabetics only, modification (including fitting) of off-the-shelf depth-inlay shoe or custom molded shoe with roller or rigid rocker bottom, per shoe

MED: 100-2,15,140

Y ☑ A5504 For diabetics only, modification (including fitting) of off-the-shelf depth-inlay shoe or custom molded shoe with wedge(s), per shoe

MED: 100-2,15,140

Y ☑ A5505 For diabetics only, modification (including fitting) of off-the-shelf depth-inlay shoe or custom molded shoe with metatarsal bar, per shoe

MED: 100-2,15,140

Y ☑ A5506 For diabetics only, modification (including fitting) of off-the-shelf depth-inlay shoe or custom molded shoe with off-set heel(s), per shoe

MED: 100-2,15,140

Y ☑ A5507 For diabetics only, not otherwise specified modification (including fitting) of off-the-shelf depth-inlay shoe or custom molded shoe, per shoe

MED: 100-2,15,140

Y ☑ A5508 For diabetics only, deluxe feature of off-the-shelf depth-inlay shoe or custom molded shoe, per shoe

MED: 100-2,15,140

Jan January Update

Special Coverage Instructions | Noncovered by Medicare | Carrier Discretion | ☑ Quantity Alert | ● New Code | ○ Recycled/Reinstated | ▲ Revised Code

 A Age Edit | M Maternity Edit | ♀ Female Only | ♂ Male Only | A-Y OPPS Status Indicators

E ☑ A5510 For diabetics only, direct formed, compression molded to patient's foot without external heat source, multiple-density insert(s) prefabricated, per shoe
MED: 100-2,15,140

Y ☑ A5512 For diabetics only, multiple density insert, direct formed, molded to foot after external heat source of 230 degrees Fahrenheit or higher, total contact with patient's foot, including arch, base layer minimum of 1/4 inch material of shore a 35 durometer or 3/16 inch material of shore a 40 durometer (or higher), prefabricated, each ♿

Y ☑ A5513 For diabetics only, multiple density insert, custom molded from model of patient's foot, total contact with patient's foot, including arch, base layer minimum of 3/16 inch material of shore a 35 durometer or higher), includes arch filler and other shaping material, custom fabricated, each ♿

DRESSINGS

E A6000 Noncontact wound-warming wound cover for use with the noncontact wound-warming device and warming card

A ☑ A6010 Collagen based wound filler, dry form, sterile, per g of collagen ♿

A ☑ A6011 Collagen based wound filler, gel/paste, per g of collagen ♿

A ☑ A6021 Collagen dressing, sterile, pad size 16 sq in or less, each ♿

A ☑ A6022 Collagen dressing, sterile, pad size more than 16 sq in but less than or equal to 48 sq in, each ♿

A ☑ A6023 Collagen dressing, sterile, pad size more than 48 sq in, each ♿

A ☑ A6024 Collagen dressing wound filler, sterile, per 6 in ♿

E ☑ A6025 Gel sheet for dermal or epidermal application, (e.g., silicone, hydrogel, other), each

A ☑ A6154 Wound pouch, each ♿

A ☑ A6196 Alginate or other fiber gelling dressing, wound cover, sterile, pad size 16 sq in or less, each dressing ♿

A ☑ A6197 Alginate or other fiber gelling dressing, wound cover, sterile, pad size more than 16 sq in but less than or equal to 48 sq in, each dressing ♿

A ☑ A6198 Alginate or other fiber gelling dressing, wound cover, sterile, pad size more than 48 sq in, each dressing

A ☑ A6199 Alginate or other fiber gelling dressing, wound filler, sterile, per 6 in ♿

A ☑ A6203 Composite dressing, sterile, pad size 16 sq in or less, with any size adhesive border, each dressing ♿

A ☑ A6204 Composite dressing, sterile, pad size more than 16 sq in, but less than or equal to 48 sq in, with any size adhesive border, each dressing ♿

A ☑ A6205 Composite dressing, sterile, pad size more than 48 sq in, with any size adhesive border, each dressing

A ☑ A6206 Contact layer, sterile, 16 sq in or less, each dressing

A ☑ A6207 Contact layer, sterile, more than 16 sq in but less than or equal to 48 sq in, each dressing ♿

A ☑ A6208 Contact layer, sterile, more than 48 sq in, each dressing

A ☑ A6209 Foam dressing, wound cover, sterile, pad size 16 sq in or less, without adhesive border, each dressing ♿

A ☑ A6210 Foam dressing, wound cover, sterile, pad size more than 16 sq in but less than or equal to 48 sq in, without adhesive border, each dressing ♿

A ☑ A6211 Foam dressing, wound cover, sterile, pad size more than 48 sq in, without adhesive border, each dressing ♿

A ☑ A6212 Foam dressing, wound cover, sterile, pad size 16 sq in or less, with any size adhesive border, each dressing ♿

A ☑ A6213 Foam dressing, wound cover, sterile, pad size more than 16 sq in but less than or equal to 48 sq in, with any size adhesive border, each dressing

A ☑ A6214 Foam dressing, wound cover, sterile, pad size more than 48 sq in, with any size adhesive border, each dressing ♿

A ☑ A6215 Foam dressing, wound filler, sterile, per g

A ☑ A6216 Gauze, nonimpregnated, nonsterile, pad size 16 sq in or less, without adhesive border, each dressing ♿

A ☑ A6217 Gauze, nonimpregnated, nonsterile, pad size more than 16 sq in but less than or equal to 48 sq in, without adhesive border, each dressing ♿

A ☑ A6218 Gauze, nonimpregnated, nonsterile, pad size more than 48 sq in, without adhesive border, each dressing

A ☑ A6219 Gauze, nonimpregnated, sterile, pad size 16 sq in or less, with any size adhesive border, each dressing ♿

A ☑ A6220 Gauze, nonimpregnated, sterile, pad size more than 16 sq in but less than or equal to 48 sq in, with any size adhesive border, each dressing ♿

A ☑ A6221 Gauze, nonimpregnated, sterile, pad size more than 48 sq in, with any size adhesive border, each dressing

A ☑ A6222 Gauze, impregnated with other than water, normal saline, or hydrogel, sterile, pad size 16 sq in or less, without adhesive border, each dressing ♿

A ☑ A6223 Gauze, impregnated with other than water, normal saline, or hydrogel, sterile, pad size more than 16 sq in, but less than or equal to 48 sq in, without adhesive border, each dressing ♿

A ☑ A6224 Gauze, impregnated with other than water, normal saline, or hydrogel, sterile, pad size more than 48 sq in, without adhesive border, each dressing ♿

A ☑ A6228 Gauze, impregnated, water or normal saline, sterile, pad size 16 sq in or less, without adhesive border, each dressing

A ☑ A6229 Gauze, impregnated, water or normal saline, sterile, pad size more than 16 sq in but less than or equal to 48 sq in, without adhesive border, each dressing ♿

A ☑ A6230 Gauze, impregnated, water or normal saline, sterile, pad size more than 48 sq in, without adhesive border, each dressing

A ☑ A6231 Gauze, impregnated, hydrogel, for direct wound contact, sterile, pad size 16 sq in or less, each dressing ♿

A ☑ A6232 Gauze, impregnated, hydrogel, for direct wound contact, sterile, pad size greater than 16 sq in, but less than or equal to 48 sq in, each dressing ♿

A ☑ A6233 Gauze, impregnated, hydrogel, for direct wound contact, sterile, pad size more than 48 sq in, each dressing ♿

A ☑ A6234 Hydrocolloid dressing, wound cover, sterile, pad size 16 sq in or less, without adhesive border, each dressing ♿

A ☑ **A6235** Hydrocolloid dressing, wound cover, sterile, pad size more than 16 sq in but less than or equal to 48 sq in, without adhesive border, each dressing ♿

A ☑ **A6236** Hydrocolloid dressing, wound cover, sterile, pad size more than 48 sq in, without adhesive border, each dressing ♿

A ☑ **A6237** Hydrocolloid dressing, wound cover, sterile, pad size 16 sq in or less, with any size adhesive border, each dressing ♿

A ☑ **A6238** Hydrocolloid dressing, wound cover, sterile, pad size more than 16 sq in but less than or equal to 48 sq in, with any size adhesive border, each dressing ♿

A ☑ **A6239** Hydrocolloid dressing, wound cover, sterile, pad size more than 48 sq in, with any size adhesive border, each dressing

A ☑ **A6240** Hydrocolloid dressing, wound filler, paste, sterile, per oz ♿

A ☑ **A6241** Hydrocolloid dressing, wound filler, dry form, sterile, per g ♿

A ☑ **A6242** Hydrogel dressing, wound cover, sterile, pad size 16 sq in or less, without adhesive border, each dressing ♿

A ☑ **A6243** Hydrogel dressing, wound cover, sterile, pad size more than 16 sq in but less than or equal to 48 sq in, without adhesive border, each dressing ♿

A ☑ **A6244** Hydrogel dressing, wound cover, sterile, pad size more than 48 sq in, without adhesive border, each dressing ♿

A ☑ **A6245** Hydrogel dressing, wound cover, sterile, pad size 16 sq in or less, with any size adhesive border, each dressing ♿

A ☑ **A6246** Hydrogel dressing, wound cover, sterile, pad size more than 16 sq in but less than or equal to 48 sq in, with any size adhesive border, each dressing ♿

A ☑ **A6247** Hydrogel dressing, wound cover, sterile, pad size more than 48 sq in, with any size adhesive border, each dressing ♿

A ☑ **A6248** Hydrogel dressing, wound filler, gel, per fl oz ♿

A **A6250** Skin sealants, protectants, moisturizers, ointments, any type, any size
Surgical dressings applied by a physician are included as part of the professional service. Surgical dressings obtained by the patient to perform homecare as prescribed by the physician are covered.

A ☑ **A6251** Specialty absorptive dressing, wound cover, sterile, pad size 16 sq in or less, without adhesive border, each dressing ♿

A ☑ **A6252** Specialty absorptive dressing, wound cover, sterile, pad size more than 16 sq in but less than or equal to 48 sq in, without adhesive border, each dressing ♿

A ☑ **A6253** Specialty absorptive dressing, wound cover, sterile, pad size more than 48 sq in, without adhesive border, each dressing ♿

A ☑ **A6254** Specialty absorptive dressing, wound cover, sterile, pad size 16 sq in or less, with any size adhesive border, each dressing ♿

A ☑ **A6255** Specialty absorptive dressing, wound cover, sterile, pad size more than 16 sq in but less than or equal to 48 sq in, with any size adhesive border, each dressing ♿

A ☑ **A6256** Specialty absorptive dressing, wound cover, sterile, pad size more than 48 sq in, with any size adhesive border, each dressing

A ☑ **A6257** Transparent film, sterile, 16 sq in or less, each dressing ♿
Surgical dressings applied by a physician are included as part of the professional service. Surgical dressings obtained by the patient to perform homecare as prescribed by the physician are covered. Use this code for Polyskin, Tegaderm, and Tegaderm HP.

A ☑ **A6258** Transparent film, sterile, more than 16 sq in but less than or equal to 48 sq in, each dressing ♿
Surgical dressings applied by a physician are included as part of the professional service. Surgical dressings obtained by the patient to perform homecare as prescribed by the physician are covered.

A ☑ **A6259** Transparent film, sterile, more than 48 sq in, each dressing ♿
Surgical dressings applied by a physician are included as part of the professional service. Surgical dressings obtained by the patient to perform homecare as prescribed by the physician are covered.

A **A6260** Wound cleansers, any type, any size
Surgical dressings applied by a physician are included as part of the professional service. Surgical dressings obtained by the patient to perform homecare as prescribed by the physician are covered.

A ☑ **A6261** Wound filler, gel/paste, per fl oz, not otherwise specified
Surgical dressings applied by a physician are included as part of the professional service. Surgical dressings obtained by the patient to perform homecare as prescribed by the physician are covered.

A ☑ **A6262** Wound filler, dry form, per g, not otherwise specified

A ☑ **A6266** Gauze, impregnated, other than water, normal saline, or zinc paste, sterile, any width, per linear yd ♿
Surgical dressings applied by a physician are included as part of the professional service. Surgical dressings obtained by the patient to perform homecare as prescribed by the physician are covered.

A ☑ **A6402** Gauze, nonimpregnated, sterile, pad size 16 sq in or less, without adhesive border, each dressing ♿
Surgical dressings applied by a physician are included as part of the professional service. Surgical dressings obtained by the patient to perform homecare as prescribed by the physician are covered.

A ☑ **A6403** Gauze, nonimpregnated, sterile, pad size more than 16 sq in, less than or equal to 48 sq in, without adhesive border, each dressing ♿
Surgical dressings applied by a physician are included as part of the professional service. Surgical dressings obtained by the patient to perform homecare as prescribed by the physician are covered.

A ☑ **A6404** Gauze, nonimpregnated, sterile, pad size more than 48 sq in, without adhesive border, each dressing

A ☑ **A6407** Packing strips, nonimpregnated, sterile, up to 2 in in width, per linear yd ♿

A ☑ **A6410** Eye pad, sterile, each ♿

A ☑ **A6411** Eye pad, nonsterile, each ♿

A ☑ **A6412** Eye patch, occlusive, each

E ☑ **A6413** Adhesive bandage, first aid type, any size, each

A ☑ **A6441** Padding bandage, nonelastic, nonwoven/nonknitted, width greater than or equal to 3 in and less than 5 in, per yd ♿

A ☑ **A6442** Conforming bandage, nonelastic, knitted/woven, nonsterile, width less than 3 in, per yd ♿

A ☑ A6443 Conforming bandage, nonelastic, knitted/woven, nonsterile, width greater than or equal to 3 in and less than 5 in, per yd ♿

A ☑ A6444 Conforming bandage, nonelastic, knitted/woven, nonsterile, width greater than or equal to 5 in, per yd ♿

A ☑ A6445 Conforming bandage, nonelastic, knitted/woven, sterile, width less than 3 in, per yd ♿

A ☑ A6446 Conforming bandage, nonelastic, knitted/woven, sterile, width greater than or equal to 3 in and less than 5 in, per yd ♿

A ☑ A6447 Conforming bandage, nonelastic, knitted/woven, sterile, width greater than or equal to 5 in, per yd ♿

A ☑ A6448 Light compression bandage, elastic, knitted/woven, width less than 3 in, per yd ♿

A ☑ A6449 Light compression bandage, elastic, knitted/woven, width greater than or equal to 3 in and less than 5 in, per yd ♿

A ☑ A6450 Light compression bandage, elastic, knitted/woven, width greater than or equal to 5 in, per yd ♿

A ☑ A6451 Moderate compression bandage, elastic, knitted/woven, load resistance of 1.25 to 1.34 ft lbs at 50% maximum stretch, width greater than or equal to 3 in and less than 5 in, per yd ♿

A ☑ A6452 High compression bandage, elastic, knitted/woven, load resistance greater than or equal to 1.35 ft lbs at 50% maximum stretch, width greater than or equal to 3 in and less than 5 in, per yd ♿

A ☑ A6453 Self-adherent bandage, elastic, nonknitted/nonwoven, width less than 3 in, per yd ♿

A ☑ A6454 Self-adherent bandage, elastic, nonknitted/nonwoven, width greater than or equal to 3 in and less than 5 in, per yd ♿

A ☑ A6455 Self-adherent bandage, elastic, nonknitted/nonwoven, width greater than or equal to 5 in, per yd ♿

A ☑ A6456 Zinc paste impregnated bandage, nonelastic, knitted/woven, width greater than or equal to 3 in and less than 5 in, per yd ♿

A A6457 Tubular dressing with or without elastic, any width, per linear yd ♿

COMPRESSION GARMENTS

A A6501 Compression burn garment, bodysuit (head to foot), custom fabricated ♿

A A6502 Compression burn garment, chin strap, custom fabricated ♿

A A6503 Compression burn garment, facial hood, custom fabricated ♿

A A6504 Compression burn garment, glove to wrist, custom fabricated ♿

A A6505 Compression burn garment, glove to elbow, custom fabricated ♿

A A6506 Compression burn garment, glove to axilla, custom fabricated ♿

A A6507 Compression burn garment, foot to knee length, custom fabricated ♿

A A6508 Compression burn garment, foot to thigh length, custom fabricated ♿

A A6509 Compression burn garment, upper trunk to waist including arm openings (vest), custom fabricated ♿

A A6510 Compression burn garment, trunk, including arms down to leg openings (leotard), custom fabricated ♿

A A6511 Compression burn garment, lower trunk including leg openings (panty), custom fabricated ♿

A A6512 Compression burn garment, not otherwise classified

B A6513 Compression burn mask, face and/or neck, plastic or equal, custom fabricated ♿

E ☑ A6530 Gradient compression stocking, below knee, 18-30 mm Hg, each

A ☑ A6531 Gradient compression stocking, below knee, 30-40 mm Hg, each ♿

A ☑ A6532 Gradient compression stocking, below knee, 40-50 mm Hg, each ♿

E ☑ A6533 Gradient compression stocking, thigh length, 18-30 mm Hg, each

E ☑ A6534 Gradient compression stocking, thigh length, 30-40 mm Hg, each

E ☑ A6535 Gradient compression stocking, thigh length, 40-50 mm Hg, each

E ☑ A6536 Gradient compression stocking, full-length/chap style, 18-30 mm Hg, each

E ☑ A6537 Gradient compression stocking, full-length/chap style, 30-40 mm Hg, each

E ☑ A6538 Gradient compression stocking, full-length/chap style, 40-50 mm Hg, each

E ☑ A6539 Gradient compression stocking, waist length, 18-30 mm Hg, each

E ☑ A6540 Gradient compression stocking, waist length, 30-40 mm Hg, each

E ☑ A6541 Gradient compression stocking, waist length, 40-50 mm Hg, each

E A6544 Gradient compression stocking, garter belt

A ☑ A6545 Gradient compression wrap, nonelastic, below knee, 30-50 mm Hg, each ♿

E A6549 Gradient compression stocking/sleeve, not otherwise specified

Y ☑ A6550 Wound care set, for negative pressure wound therapy electrical pump, includes all supplies and accessories ♿

MED: 100-4,23,60.3

RESPIRATORY SUPPLIES

Y ☑ A7000 Canister, disposable, used with suction pump, each ♿

MED: 100-4,23,60.3

Y ☑ A7001 Canister, nondisposable, used with suction pump, each ♿

Y ☑ A7002 Tubing, used with suction pump, each ♿

Y A7003 Administration set, with small volume nonfiltered pneumatic nebulizer, disposable ♿

Y A7004 Small volume nonfiltered pneumatic nebulizer, disposable ♿

Y A7005 Administration set, with small volume nonfiltered pneumatic nebulizer, nondisposable ♿

Y A7006 Administration set, with small volume filtered pneumatic nebulizer ♿

Y A7007 Large volume nebulizer, disposable, unfilled, used with aerosol compressor ♿

Y A7008 Large volume nebulizer, disposable, prefilled, used with aerosol compressor ♿

Y A7009 Reservoir bottle, nondisposable, used with large volume ultrasonic nebulizer ♿

Y ☑A7010 Corrugated tubing, disposable, used with large volume nebulizer, 100 ft ♿

Y ☑A7011 Corrugated tubing, nondisposable, used with large volume nebulizer, 10 ft

Y A7012 Water collection device, used with large volume nebulizer ♿

Y A7013 Filter, disposable, used with aerosol compressor or ultrasonic generator ♿

Y A7014 Filter, nondisposable, used with aerosol compressor or ultrasonic generator ♿

Y A7015 Aerosol mask, used with DME nebulizer ♿

Y A7016 Dome and mouthpiece, used with small volume ultrasonic nebulizer ♿

Y A7017 Nebulizer, durable, glass or autoclavable plastic, bottle type, not used with oxygen ♿

Y ☑A7018 Water, distilled, used with large volume nebulizer, 1000 ml ♿

Y A7020 Interface for cough stimulating device, includes all components, replacement only ♿

Y ☑A7025 High frequency chest wall oscillation system vest, replacement for use with patient-owned equipment, each ♿

Y ☑A7026 High frequency chest wall oscillation system hose, replacement for use with patient-owned equipment, each ♿

Y ☑A7027 Combination oral/nasal mask, used with continuous positive airway pressure device, each ♿

Y ☑A7028 Oral cushion for combination oral/nasal mask, replacement only, each ♿

Y ☑A7029 Nasal pillows for combination oral/nasal mask, replacement only, pair ♿

Y ☑A7030 Full face mask used with positive airway pressure device, each ♿

MED: 100-4,23,60.3; 100-4,36,50.14

Y ☑A7031 Face mask interface, replacement for full face mask, each ♿

Y ☑A7032 Cushion for use on nasal mask interface, replacement only, each ♿

MED: 100-3,240.4

Y ☑A7033 Pillow for use on nasal cannula type interface, replacement only, pair ♿

Y A7034 Nasal interface (mask or cannula type) used with positive airway pressure device, with or without head strap ♿

Y A7035 Headgear used with positive airway pressure device ♿

Y A7036 Chinstrap used with positive airway pressure device ♿

Y A7037 Tubing used with positive airway pressure device ♿

Y A7038 Filter, disposable, used with positive airway pressure device ♿

Y A7039 Filter, nondisposable, used with positive airway pressure device ♿

A A7040 One way chest drain valve ♿

A A7041 Water seal drainage container and tubing for use with implanted chest tube ♿

N ☑A7042 Implanted pleural catheter, each ♿

A A7043 Vacuum drainage bottle and tubing for use with implanted catheter ♿

Y ☑A7044 Oral interface used with positive airway pressure device, each ♿

MED: 100-3,240.4; 100-4,23,60.3; 100-4,36,50.14

Y A7045 Exhalation port with or without swivel used with accessories for positive airway devices, replacement only ♿

Y ☑A7046 Water chamber for humidifier, used with positive airway pressure device, replacement, each ♿

TRACHEOSTOMY SUPPLIES

A ☑A7501 Tracheostoma valve, including diaphragm, each ♿

A ☑A7502 Replacement diaphragm/faceplate for tracheostoma valve, each ♿

A ☑A7503 Filter holder or filter cap, reusable, for use in a tracheostoma heat and moisture exchange system, each ♿

A ☑A7504 Filter for use in a tracheostoma heat and moisture exchange system, each ♿

A ☑A7505 Housing, reusable without adhesive, for use in a heat and moisture exchange system and/or with a tracheostoma valve, each ♿

A ☑A7506 Adhesive disc for use in a heat and moisture exchange system and/or with tracheostoma valve, any type each ♿

A ☑A7507 Filter holder and integrated filter without adhesive, for use in a tracheostoma heat and moisture exchange system, each ♿

A ☑A7508 Housing and integrated adhesive, for use in a tracheostoma heat and moisture exchange system and/or with a tracheostoma valve, each ♿

A ☑A7509 Filter holder and integrated filter housing, and adhesive, for use as a tracheostoma heat and moisture exchange system, each ♿

A ☑A7520 Tracheostomy/laryngectomy tube, noncuffed, polyvinylchloride (PVC), silicone or equal, each ♿

MED: 100-2,1,40

A ☑A7521 Tracheostomy/laryngectomy tube, cuffed, polyvinylchloride (PVC), silicone or equal, each ♿

MED: 100-2,1,40

A ☑A7522 Tracheostomy/laryngectomy tube, stainless steel or equal (sterilizable and reusable), each ♿

MED: 100-2,1,40

A ☑A7523 Tracheostomy shower protector, each

A ☑A7524 Tracheostoma stent/stud/button, each ♿

A ☑A7525 Tracheostomy mask, each ♿

A ☑A7526 Tracheostomy tube collar/holder, each ♿

A ☑A7527 Tracheostomy/laryngectomy tube plug/stop, each ♿

PROTECTIVE HELMET

Y A8000 Helmet, protective, soft, prefabricated, includes all components and accessories ♿

Y A8001 Helmet, protective, hard, prefabricated, includes all components and accessories ♿

Y A8002 Helmet, protective, soft, custom fabricated, includes all components and accessories ♿

Y A8003 Helmet, protective, hard, custom fabricated, includes all components and accessories ♿

Y A8004 Soft interface for helmet, replacement only ♿

OTHER SUPPLIES AND DEVICES

B A9150 Nonprescription drugs

E ☑ A9152 Single vitamin/mineral/trace element, oral, per dose, not otherwise specified

E ☑ A9153 Multiple vitamins, with or without minerals and trace elements, oral, per dose, not otherwise specified

B ☑ A9155 Artificial saliva, 30 ml

E A9180 Pediculosis (lice infestation) treatment, topical, for administration by patient/caretaker

E A9270 Noncovered item or service

● E ☑ A9272 Jan Mechanical wound suction, disposable, includes dressing, all accessories and components, each

Y A9273 Hot water bottle, ice cap or collar, heat and/or cold wrap, any type

E ☑ A9274 External ambulatory insulin delivery system, disposable, each, includes all supplies and accessories

E A9275 Home glucose disposable monitor, includes test strips

E ☑ A9276 Sensor; invasive (e.g., subcutaneous), disposable, for use with interstitial continuous glucose monitoring system, 1 unit = 1 day supply

E A9277 Transmitter; external, for use with interstitial continuous glucose monitoring system

E A9278 Receiver (monitor); external, for use with interstitial continuous glucose monitoring system

E A9279 Monitoring feature/device, stand-alone or integrated, any type, includes all accessories, components and electronics, not otherwise classified

E A9280 Alert or alarm device, not otherwise classified

E ☑ A9281 Reaching/grabbing device, any type, any length, each

E ☑ A9282 Wig, any type, each

E ☑ A9283 Foot pressure off loading/supportive device, any type, each

N A9284 Spirometer, nonelectronic, includes all accessories

E A9300 Exercise equipment

RADIOPHARMACEUTICALS

N ☑ A9500 Technetium tc-99m sestamibi, diagnostic, per study dose N1 ⊘
Use this code for Cardiolite.

N ☑ A9501 Technetium Tc-99m teboroxime, diagnostic, per study dose N1 ⊘

N ☑ A9502 Technetium Tc-99m tetrofosmin, diagnostic, per study dose N1 ⊘
Use this code for Myoview.

N ☑ A9503 Technetium Tc-99m medronate, diagnostic, per study dose, up to 30 millicuries N1 ⊘
Use this code for CIS-MDP, Draximage MDP-10, Draximage MDP-25, MDP-Bracco, Technetium Tc-99m MPI-MDP
AHA: 2Q,'02,9

N ☑ A9504 Technetium Tc-99m apcitide, diagnostic, per study dose, up to 20 millicuries N1 ⊘
Use this code for Acutect
AHA: 2Q,'02,9; 4Q,'01,5

N ☑ A9505 Thallium Tl-201 thallous chloride, diagnostic, per millicurie N1 ⊘
Use this code for MIBG, Thallous Chloride USP.
AHA: 2Q,'02,9

N ☑ A9507 Indium In-111 capromab pendetide, diagnostic, per study dose, up to 10 millicuries N1 ⊘
Use this code for Prostascint.

N ☑ A9508 Iodine I-131 iobenguane sulfate, diagnostic, per 0.5 millicurie N1 ⊘
Use this code for MIBG.
AHA: 2Q,'02,9

N ☑ A9509 Iodine I-123 sodium iodide, diagnostic, per millicurie N1 ⊘

N ☑ A9510 Technetium Tc-99m disofenin, diagnostic, per study dose, up to 15 millicuries N1 ⊘
Use this code for Hepatolite.

N ☑ A9512 Technetium Tc-99m pertechnetate, diagnostic, per millicurie N1 ⊘
Use this code for Technelite, Ultra-Technelow.

N ☑ A9516 Iodine I-123 sodium iodide, diagnostic, per 100 microcuries, up to 999 microcuries N1 ⊘

K ☑ A9517 Iodine I-131 sodium iodide capsule(s), therapeutic, per millicurie ⊘

N ☑ A9521 Technetium Tc-99m exametazime, diagnostic, per study dose, up to 25 millicuries N1 ⊘
Use this code for Ceretec.

N ☑ A9524 Iodine I-131 iodinated serum albumin, diagnostic, per 5 microcuries N1 ⊘

N ☑ A9526 Nitrogen N-13 ammonia, diagnostic, per study dose, up to 40 millicuries N1 ⊘
MED: 100-4,13,60.3; 100-4,13,60.3.1; 100-4,13,60.3.2

U ☑ A9527 Iodine I-125, sodium iodide solution, therapeutic, per millicurie H2 ⊘

N ☑ A9528 Iodine I-131 sodium iodide capsule(s), diagnostic, per millicurie N1 ⊘

N ☑ A9529 Iodine I-131 sodium iodide solution, diagnostic, per millicurie N1 ⊘

K ☑ A9530 Iodine I-131 sodium iodide solution, therapeutic, per millicurie ⊘

N ☑ A9531 Iodine I-131 sodium iodide, diagnostic, per microcurie (up to 100 microcuries) N1 ⊘

N ☑ A9532 Iodine I-125 serum albumin, diagnostic, per 5 microcuries N1 ⊘

N ☑ A9536 Technetium Tc-99m depreotide, diagnostic, per study dose, up to 35 millicuries N1 ⊘

N ☑ A9537 Technetium Tc-99m mebrofenin, diagnostic, per study dose, up to 15 millicuries N1 ⊘

N ☑ A9538 Technetium Tc-99m pyrophosphate, diagnostic, per study dose, up to 25 millicuries N1 ⊘
Use this code for CIS-PYRO, Phosphostec, Technescan Pyp Kit

N ☑ A9539 Technetium Tc-99m pentetate, diagnostic, per study dose, up to 25 millicuries N1 ⊘
Use this code for AN-DTPA, DTPA, MPI-DTPA Kit-Chelate, MPI Indium DTPA IN-111, Pentate Calcium Trisodium, Pentate Zinc Trisodium

N ☑ **A9540** Technetium Tc-99m macroaggregated albumin, diagnostic, per study dose, up to 10 millicuries N1 ⊘

N ☑ **A9541** Technetium Tc-99m sulfur colloid, diagnostic, per study dose, up to 20 millicuries N1 ⊘

N ☑ **A9542** Indium In-111 ibritumomab tiuxetan, diagnostic, per study dose, up to 5 millicuries N1 ⊘
Use this code for Zevalin

K ☑ **A9543** Yttrium Y-90 ibritumomab tiuxetan, therapeutic, per treatment dose, up to 40 millicuries ⊘

N ☑ **A9544** Iodine I-131 tositumomab, diagnostic, per study dose N1 ⊘

K ☑ **A9545** Iodine I-131 tositumomab, therapeutic, per treatment dose ⊘
Use this code for Bexxar.

N ☑ **A9546** Cobalt Co-57/58, cyanocobalamin, diagnostic, per study dose, up to 1 microcurie N1 ⊘

N ☑ **A9547** Indium In-111 oxyquinoline, diagnostic, per 0.5 millicurie N1 ⊘

N ☑ **A9548** Indium In-111 pentetate, diagnostic, per 0.5 millicurie N1 ⊘

N ☑ **A9550** Technetium Tc-99m sodium gluceptate, diagnostic, per study dose, up to 25 millicurie N1 ⊘

N ☑ **A9551** Technetium Tc-99m succimer, diagnostic, per study dose, up to 10 millicuries N1 ⊘
Use this code for MPI-DMSA Kidney Reagent.

N ☑ **A9552** Fluorodeoxyglucose F-18 FDG, diagnostic, per study dose, up to 45 millicuries N1 ⊘
MED: 100-3,220.6.13; 100-3,220.6.14; 100-3,220.6.17; 100-4,13,60.3.2

N ☑ **A9553** Chromium Cr-51 sodium chromate, diagnostic, per study dose, up to 250 microcuries N1 ⊘
Use this code for Chromitope Sodium.

N ☑ **A9554** Iodine I-125 sodium iothalamate, diagnostic, per study dose, up to 10 microcuries N1 ⊘
Use this code for Glofil-125.

N ☑ **A9555** Rubidium Rb-82, diagnostic, per study dose, up to 60 millicuries N1 ⊘
Use this code for Cardiogen 82.
MED: 100-3,220.6.1; 100-4,13,60.3.2

N ☑ **A9556** Gallium Ga-67 citrate, diagnostic, per millicurie N1 ⊘

N ☑ **A9557** Technetium Tc-99m bicisate, diagnostic, per study dose, up to 25 millicuries N1 ⊘
Use this code for Neurolite.

N ☑ **A9558** Xenon Xe-133 gas, diagnostic, per 10 millicuries N1 ⊘

N ☑ **A9559** Cobalt Co-57 cyanocobalamin, oral, diagnostic, per study dose, up to 1 microcurie N1 ⊘

N ☑ **A9560** Technetium Tc-99m labeled red blood cells, diagnostic, per study dose, up to 30 millicuries N1 ⊘

N ☑ **A9561** Technetium Tc-99m oxidronate, diagnostic, per study dose, up to 30 millicuries N1 ⊘
Use this code for TechneScan.

N ☑ **A9562** Technetium Tc-99m mertiatide, diagnostic, per study dose, up to 15 millicuries N1 ⊘
Use this code for TechneScan MAG-3.

K ☑ **A9563** Sodium phosphate P-32, therapeutic, per millicurie ⊘

K ☑ **A9564** Chromic phosphate P-32 suspension, therapeutic, per millicurie ⊘
Use this code for Phosphocol (P32).

N ☑ **A9566** Technetium Tc-99m fanolesomab, diagnostic, per study dose, up to 25 millicuries N1 ⊘

N ☑ **A9567** Technetium Tc-99m pentetate, diagnostic, aerosol, per study dose, up to 75 millicuries N1 ⊘
Use this code for AN-DTPA, DTPA, MPI-DTPA Kit-Chelate, MPI Indium DTPA IN-111, Pentate Calcium Trisodium, Pentate Zinc Trisodium.

N ☑ **A9568** Technetium Tc-99m arcitumomab, diagnostic, per study dose, up to 45 millicuries N1 ⊘
Use this code for CEA Scan.

N ☑ **A9569** Technetium Tc-99m exametazime labeled autologous white blood cells, diagnostic, per study dose N1 ⊘
Use this code for Ceretec.

N ☑ **A9570** Indium In-111 labeled autologous white blood cells, diagnostic, per study dose N1 ⊘

N ☑ **A9571** Indium In-111 labeled autologous platelets, diagnostic, per study dose N1 ⊘

N ☑ **A9572** Indium In-111 pentetreotide, diagnostic, per study dose, up to 6 millicuries N1 ⊘
Use this code for Ostreoscan.

N ☑ **A9576** Injection, gadoteridol, (ProHance multipack), per ml N1

N ☑ **A9577** Injection, gadobenate dimeglumine (MultiHance), per ml N1

N ☑ **A9578** Injection, gadobenate dimeglumine (MultiHance multipack), per ml N1

N ☑ **A9579** Injection, gadolinium-based magnetic resonance contrast agent, not otherwise specified (NOS), per ml N1
Use this code for Omniscan, Magnevist.

N ☑ **A9580** Sodium fluoride F-18, diagnostic, per study dose, up to 30 millicuries N1 ⊘
MED: 100-3,220.6.19; 100-4,13,60.3.2; 100-4,13,60.18

N ☑ **A9581** Injection, gadoxetate disodium, 1 ml N1
Use this code for Eovist.

N ☑ **A9582** Iodine I-123 iobenguane, diagnostic, per study dose, up to 15 millicuries N1

N ☑ **A9583** Injection, gadofosveset trisodium, 1 ml N1
Use this code for Ablavar, Vasovist.

● G ☑ **A9584** Jan Iodine I-123 ioflupane, diagnostic, per study dose, up to 5 millicuries K2
Use this code for DaTscan.

● N ☑ **A9585** Jan Injection, gadobutrol, 0.1 ml N1
Use this code for Gadavist.

K ☑ **A9600** Strontium Sr-89 chloride, therapeutic, per millicurie ⊘
Use this code for Metastron.
AHA: 2Q,'02,9

K ☑ **A9604** Samarium sm-153 lexidronam, therapeutic, per treatment dose, up to 150 millicuries
Use this code for Quadramet.

N **A9698** Nonradioactive contrast imaging material, not otherwise classified, per study N1 ⊘

N **A9699** Radiopharmaceutical, therapeutic, not otherwise classified ⊘

B **A9700** Supply of injectable contrast material for use in echocardiography, per study
AHA: 4Q,'01,5

Jan January Update

Special Coverage Instructions | Noncovered by Medicare | Carrier Discretion | ☑ Quantity Alert | ● New Code | ○ Recycled/Reinstated | ▲ Revised Code

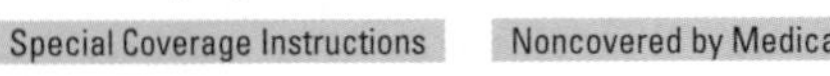

A Age Edit | M Maternity Edit | ♀ Female Only | ♂ Male Only | A-Y OPPS Status Indicators

MISCELLANEOUS

Y **A9900** Miscellaneous DME supply, accessory, and/or service component of another HCPCS code

A **A9901** DME delivery, set up, and/or dispensing service component of another HCPCS code

Y **A9999** Miscellaneous DME supply or accessory, not otherwise specified

ENTERAL AND PARENTERAL THERAPY B4000-B9999

This section includes codes for supplies, formulae, nutritional solutions, and infusion pumps.

ENTERAL FORMULAE AND ENTERAL MEDICAL SUPPLIES

Y ☑ **B4034** **Enteral feeding supply kit; syringe fed, per day, includes but not limited to feeding/flushing syringe, administration set tubing, dressings, tape**
MED: 100-4,23,60.3

Y ☑ **B4035** **Enteral feeding supply kit; pump fed, per day, includes but not limited to feeding/flushing syringe, administration set tubing, dressings, tape**

Y ☑ **B4036** **Enteral feeding supply kit; gravity fed, per day, includes but not limited to feeding/flushing syringe, administration set tubing, dressings, tape**

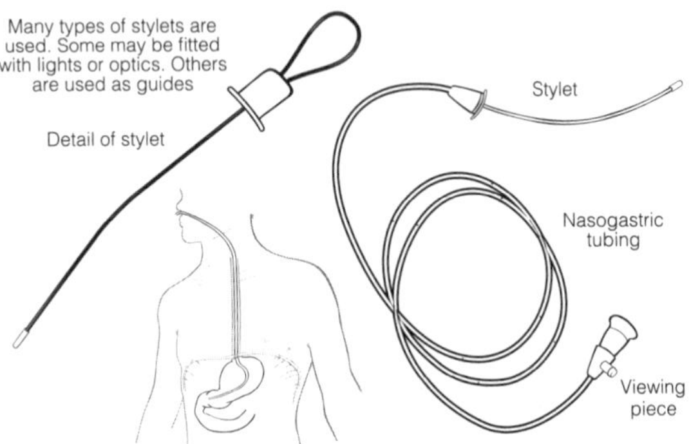
Many types of stylets are used. Some may be fitted with lights or optics. Others are used as guides
Detail of stylet
Stylet
Nasogastric tubing
Viewing piece

Y **B4081** **Nasogastric tubing with stylet**
MED: 100-4,23,60.3

Y **B4082** **Nasogastric tubing without stylet**

Y **B4083** **Stomach tube - Levine type**

A ☑ **B4087** **Gastrostomy/jejunostomy tube, standard, any material, any type, each**

A ☑ **B4088** **Gastrostomy/jejunostomy tube, low-profile, any material, any type, each**

E ☑ **B4100** **Food thickener, administered orally, per oz**

Y ☑ **B4102** **Enteral formula, for adults, used to replace fluids and electrolytes (e.g., clear liquids), 500 ml = 1 unit**

Y ☑ **B4103** **Enteral formula, for pediatrics, used to replace fluids and electrolytes (e.g., clear liquids), 500 ml = 1 unit**

E **B4104** **Additive for enteral formula (e.g., fiber)**

Y ☑ **B4149** **Enteral formula, manufactured blenderized natural foods with intact nutrients, includes proteins, fats, carbohydrates, vitamins and minerals, may include fiber, administered through an enteral feeding tube, 100 calories = 1 unit**
MED: 100-4,23,60.3

Y ☑ **B4150** **Enteral formula, nutritionally complete with intact nutrients, includes proteins, fats, carbohydrates, vitamins and minerals, may include fiber, administered through an enteral feeding tube, 100 calories = 1 unit**
Use this code for Enrich, Ensure, Ensure HN, Ensure Powder, Isocal, Lonalac Powder, Meritene, Meritene Powder, Osmolite, Osmolite HN, Portagen Powder, Sustacal, Renu, Sustagen Powder, Travasorb.

Y ☑ **B4152** **Enteral formula, nutritionally complete, calorically dense (equal to or greater than 1.5 kcal/ml) with intact nutrients, includes proteins, fats, carbohydrates, vitamins and minerals, may include fiber, administered through an enteral feeding tube, 100 calories = 1 unit**
Use this code for Magnacal, Isocal HCN, Sustacal HC, Ensure Plus, Ensure Plus HN.

Y ☑ **B4153** **Enteral formula, nutritionally complete, hydrolyzed proteins (amino acids and peptide chain), includes fats, carbohydrates, vitamins and minerals, may include fiber, administered through an enteral feeding tube, 100 calories = 1 unit**
Use this code for Criticare HN, Vivonex t.e.n. (Total Enteral Nutrition), Vivonex HN, Vital (Vital HN), Travasorb HN, Isotein HN, Precision HN, Precision Isotonic.

Y ☑ **B4154** **Enteral formula, nutritionally complete, for special metabolic needs, excludes inherited disease of metabolism, includes altered composition of proteins, fats, carbohydrates, vitamins and/or minerals, may include fiber, administered through an enteral feeding tube, 100 calories = 1 unit**
Use this code for Hepatic-aid, Travasorb Hepatic, Travasorb MCT, Travasorb Renal, Traum-aid, Tramacal, Aminaid.

Y ☑ **B4155** **Enteral formula, nutritionally incomplete/modular nutrients, includes specific nutrients, carbohydrates (e.g., glucose polymers), proteins/amino acids (e.g., glutamine, arginine), fat (e.g., medium chain triglycerides) or combination, administered through an enteral feeding tube, 100 calories = 1 unit**
Use this code for Propac, Gerval Protein, Promix, Casec, Moducal, Controlyte, Polycose Liquid or Powder, Sumacal, Microlipids, MCT Oil, Nutri-source.

Y ☑ **B4157** **Enteral formula, nutritionally complete, for special metabolic needs for inherited disease of metabolism, includes proteins, fats, carbohydrates, vitamins and minerals, may include fiber, administered through an enteral feeding tube, 100 calories = 1 unit**

Y ☑ **B4158** **Enteral formula, for pediatrics, nutritionally complete with intact nutrients, includes proteins, fats, carbohydrates, vitamins and minerals, may include fiber and/or iron, administered through an enteral feeding tube, 100 calories = 1 unit**

Y ☑ **B4159** **Enteral formula, for pediatrics, nutritionally complete soy based with intact nutrients, includes proteins, fats, carbohydrates, vitamins and minerals, may include fiber and/or iron, administered through an enteral feeding tube, 100 calories = 1 unit**

Y ☑ **B4160** **Enteral formula, for pediatrics, nutritionally complete calorically dense (equal to or greater than 0.7 kcal/ml) with intact nutrients, includes proteins, fats, carbohydrates, vitamins and minerals, may include fiber, administered through an enteral feeding tube, 100 calories = 1 unit**

Y ☑ **B4161** **Enteral formula, for pediatrics, hydrolyzed/amino acids and peptide chain proteins, includes fats, carbohydrates, vitamins and minerals, may include fiber, administered through an enteral feeding tube, 100 calories = 1 unit**

Y ☑ **B4162** **Enteral formula, for pediatrics, special metabolic needs for inherited disease of metabolism, includes proteins, fats, carbohydrates, vitamins and minerals, may include fiber, administered through an enteral feeding tube, 100 calories = 1 unit**

PARENTERAL NUTRITION SOLUTIONS AND SUPPLIES

Y ☑ **B4164** Parenteral nutrition solution: carbohydrates (dextrose), 50% or less (500 ml = 1 unit), home mix

Y ☑ **B4168** Parenteral nutrition solution; amino acid, 3.5%, (500 ml = 1 unit) - home mix

Y ☑ **B4172** Parenteral nutrition solution; amino acid, 5.5% through 7%, (500 ml = 1 unit) - home mix

Y ☑ **B4176** Parenteral nutrition solution; amino acid, 7% through 8.5%, (500 ml = 1 unit) - home mix

Y ☑ **B4178** Parenteral nutrition solution: amino acid, greater than 8.5% (500 ml = 1 unit), home mix

Y ☑ **B4180** Parenteral nutrition solution: carbohydrates (dextrose), greater than 50% (500 ml = 1 unit), home mix

B ☑ **B4185** Parenteral nutrition solution, per 10 grams lipids

Y ☑ **B4189** Parenteral nutrition solution: compounded amino acid and carbohydrates with electrolytes, trace elements, and vitamins, including preparation, any strength, 10 to 51 g of protein, premix

Y ☑ **B4193** Parenteral nutrition solution: compounded amino acid and carbohydrates with electrolytes, trace elements, and vitamins, including preparation, any strength, 52 to 73 g of protein, premix

Y ☑ **B4197** Parenteral nutrition solution; compounded amino acid and carbohydrates with electrolytes, trace elements and vitamins, including preparation, any strength, 74 to 100 grams of protein - premix

Y ☑ **B4199** Parenteral nutrition solution; compounded amino acid and carbohydrates with electrolytes, trace elements and vitamins, including preparation, any strength, over 100 grams of protein - premix

Y **B4216** Parenteral nutrition; additives (vitamins, trace elements, Heparin, electrolytes), home mix, per day

Y **B4220** Parenteral nutrition supply kit; premix, per day

Y **B4222** Parenteral nutrition supply kit; home mix, per day

Y **B4224** Parenteral nutrition administration kit, per day

Y **B5000** Parenteral nutrition solution: compounded amino acid and carbohydrates with electrolytes, trace elements, and vitamins, including preparation, any strength, renal - Amirosyn RF, NephrAmine, RenAmine - premix
Use this code for Amirosyn-RF, NephrAmine, RenAmin.

Y **B5100** Parenteral nutrition solution: compounded amino acid and carbohydrates with electrolytes, trace elements, and vitamins, including preparation, any strength, hepatic - FreAmine HBC, HepatAmine - premix
Use this code for FreAmine HBC, HepatAmine.

Y **B5200** Parenteral nutrition solution: compounded amino acid and carbohydrates with electrolytes, trace elements, and vitamins, including preparation, any strength, stress - branch chain amino acids - premix

ENTERAL AND PARENTERAL PUMPS

Y **B9000** Enteral nutrition infusion pump - without alarm
MED: 100-4,23,60.3

Y **B9002** Enteral nutrition infusion pump - with alarm

Y **B9004** Parenteral nutrition infusion pump, portable

Y **B9006** Parenteral nutrition infusion pump, stationary

Y **B9998** NOC for enteral supplies

Y **B9999** NOC for parenteral supplies
Determine if an alternative HCPCS Level II or a CPT code better describes the service being reported. This code should be used only if a more specific code is unavailable.

OUTPATIENT PPS C1300 - C9899

This section reports drugs, biologicals, and devices codes that must be used by OPPS hospitals. Non-OPPS hospitals, Critical Access Hospitals (CAHs), Indian Health Service Hospitals (HIS), hospitals located in American Samoa, Guam, Saipan, or the Virgin Islands, and Maryland waiver hospitals may report these codes at their discretion. The codes can only be reported for facility (technical) services.

The C series of HCPCS may include device catagories, new technology procedures, and drugs, biologicals and radiopharmaceuticals that do not have other HCPCS codes assigned. Some of these items and services are eligible for transitional pass-through payments for OPPS hospitals, have separate APC payments, or are items that are packaged. Hospitals are encouraged to report all appropriate C codes regardless of payment status.

S ☑ **C1300** Hyperbaric oxygen under pressure, full body chamber, per 30 minute interval
MED: 100-4,32,30.1

N **C1713** Anchor/screw for opposing bone-to-bone or soft tissue-to-bone (implantable) N1
AHA: 3Q,'02,5; 1Q,'01,5

N **C1714** Catheter, transluminal atherectomy, directional N1
AHA: 4Q,'03,8; 3Q,'02,5; 1Q,'01,5

N **C1715** Brachytherapy needle N1
AHA: 3Q,'02,5; 1Q,'01,5

U ☑ **C1716** Brachytherapy source, nonstranded, gold-198, per source H2
AHA: 3Q,'02,5; 1Q,'01,5

U ☑ **C1717** Brachytherapy source, nonstranded, high dose rate iridium-192, per source H2
AHA: 3Q,'02,5; 1Q,'01,5

U ☑ **C1719** Brachytherapy source, nonstranded, nonhigh dose rate iridium-192, per source H2
AHA: 3Q,'02,5; 1Q,'01,5

N **C1721** Cardioverter-defibrillator, dual chamber (implantable) N1
MED: 100-4,14,40.8
AHA: 3Q,'02,5; 1Q,'01,5

N **C1722** Cardioverter-defibrillator, single chamber (implantable) N1
AHA: 3Q,'02,5; 1Q,'01,5

N **C1724** Catheter, transluminal atherectomy, rotational N1
AHA: 4Q,'03,8; 3Q,'02,5; 1Q,'01,5

N **C1725** Catheter, transluminal angioplasty, nonlaser (may include guidance, infusion/perfusion capability) N1
AHA: 4Q,'03,8; 3Q,'02,5; 1Q,'01,5

N **C1726** Catheter, balloon dilatation, nonvascular N1
AHA: 3Q,'02,5; 1Q,'01,5

N **C1727** Catheter, balloon tissue dissector, nonvascular (insertable) N1
AHA: 3Q,'02,5; 1Q,'01,5

N **C1728** Catheter, brachytherapy seed administration N1
AHA: 3Q,'02,5; 1Q,'01,5

N **C1729** Catheter, drainage N1
AHA: 3Q,'02,5; 1Q,'01,5

N **C1730** Catheter, electrophysiology, diagnostic, other than 3D mapping (19 or fewer electrodes) N1
AHA: 3Q,'02,5; 1Q,'01,5

N **C1731** Catheter, electrophysiology, diagnostic, other than 3D mapping (20 or more electrodes) N1
AHA: 3Q,'02,5; 1Q,'01,5

N **C1732** Catheter, electrophysiology, diagnostic/ablation, 3D or vector mapping N1
AHA: 1Q,'01,5

N **C1733** Catheter, electrophysiology, diagnostic/ablation, other than 3D or vector mapping, other than cool-tip N1
AHA: 3Q,'02,5; 1Q,'01,5

H **C1749** Endoscope, retrograde imaging/illumination colonoscope device (implantable) J7

N **C1750** Catheter, hemodialysis/peritoneal, long-term N1
AHA: 4Q,'03,8; 3Q,'02,5; 1Q,'01,5

N **C1751** Catheter, infusion, inserted peripherally, centrally or midline (other than hemodialysis) N1
AHA: 4Q,'03,8; 3Q,'02,5; 3Q,'01,5

N **C1752** Catheter, hemodialysis/peritoneal, short-term N1
AHA: 4Q,'03,8; 3Q,'02,5; 1Q,'01,5

N **C1753** Catheter, intravascular ultrasound N1
AHA: 4Q,'03,8; 3Q,'02,5; 1Q,'01,5

N **C1754** Catheter, intradiscal N1
AHA: 4Q,'03,8; 3Q,'02,5; 1Q,'01,5

N **C1755** Catheter, intraspinal N1
AHA: 4Q,'03,8; 3Q,'02,5; 1Q,'01,5

N **C1756** Catheter, pacing, transesophageal N1
AHA: 4Q,'03,8; 3Q,'02,5; 1Q,'01,5

N **C1757** Catheter, thrombectomy/embolectomy N1
AHA: 4Q,'03,8; 3Q,'02,5; 1Q,'01,5

N **C1758** Catheter, ureteral N1
AHA: 4Q,'03,8; 3Q,'02,5; 1Q,'01,6

N **C1759** Catheter, intracardiac echocardiography N1
AHA: 4Q,'03,8; 3Q,'02,5; 1Q,'01,5; 3Q,'01,4

N **C1760** Closure device, vascular (implantable/insertable) N1
AHA: 4Q,'03,8; 3Q,'02,5; 1Q,'01,6

N **C1762** Connective tissue, human (includes fascia lata) N1
AHA: 3Q,'03,12; 4Q,'03,8; 3Q,'02,5; 1Q,'01,6

N **C1763** Connective tissue, nonhuman (includes synthetic) N1
AHA: 3Q,'03,12; 4Q,'03,8; 3Q,'02,5; 1Q,'01,6

N **C1764** Event recorder, cardiac (implantable) N1
MED: 100-4,14,40.8
AHA: 4Q,'03,8; 3Q,'02,5; 1Q,'01,6

N **C1765** Adhesion barrier N1

N **C1766** Introducer/sheath, guiding, intracardiac electrophysiological, steerable, other than peel-away N1
AHA: 3Q,'02,5; 3Q,'01,5

N **C1767** Generator, neurostimulator (implantable), nonrechargeable N1
MED: 100-4,14,40.8; 100-4,32,40.1
AHA: 4Q,'03,8; 1Q,'02,9; 3Q,'02,5

N **C1768** Graft, vascular N1
AHA: 4Q,'03,8; 3Q,'02,5; 1Q,'01,6

N **C1769** Guide wire N1
AHA: 4Q,'03,8; 3Q,'02,5; 1Q,'01,6; 3Q,'01,4

N **C1770** Imaging coil, magnetic resonance (insertable) N1
AHA: 4Q,'03,8; 3Q,'02,5; 1Q,'01,6

N **C1771** Repair device, urinary, incontinence, with sling graft N1
MED: 100-4,14,40.8
AHA: 4Q,'03,8; 3Q,'02,5; 1Q,'01,6

N **C1772** Infusion pump, programmable (implantable) N1
AHA: 3Q,'02,5; 1Q,'01,6

N **C1773** Retrieval device, insertable (used to retrieve fractured medical devices) N1
AHA: 4Q,'03,8; 3Q,'02,5; 1Q,'01,6

N **C1776** Joint device (implantable) N1
MED: 100-4,14,40.8
AHA: 3Q,'02,5; 1Q,'01,6; 3Q,'01,5

N **C1777** Lead, cardioverter-defibrillator, endocardial single coil (implantable) N1
AHA: 3Q,'02,5; 1Q,'01,6

N **C1778** Lead, neurostimulator (implantable) N1
MED: 100-4,14,40.8; 100-4,32,40.1
AHA: 3Q,'02,5; 1Q,'02,9

N **C1779** Lead, pacemaker, transvenous VDD single pass N1
AHA: 3Q,'02,5; 1Q,'01,6

N **C1780** Lens, intraocular (new technology) N1
AHA: 3Q,'02,5; 1Q,'01,6

N **C1781** Mesh (implantable) N1
Use this code for OrthADAPT Bioimplant.
AHA: 3Q,'02,5; 1Q,'01,6

N **C1782** Morcellator N1
AHA: 3Q,'02,5; 1Q,'01,6

N **C1783** Ocular implant, aqueous drainage assist device N1

N **C1784** Ocular device, intraoperative, detached retina N1
AHA: 3Q,'02,5; 1Q,'01,6

N **C1785** Pacemaker, dual chamber, rate-responsive (implantable) N1
MED: 100-4,14,40.8
AHA: 4Q,'03,8; 3Q,'02,5; 1Q,'01,6

N **C1786** Pacemaker, single chamber, rate-responsive (implantable) N1
MED: 100-2,1,40
AHA: 4Q,'03,8; 3Q,'02,5; 1Q,'01,6

N **C1787** Patient programmer, neurostimulator N1
AHA: 4Q,'03,8; 3Q,'02,5; 1Q,'01,6

N **C1788** Port, indwelling (implantable) N1
AHA: 4Q,'03,8; 3Q,'02,5; 1Q,'01,6; 3Q,'01,4

N **C1789** Prosthesis, breast (implantable) N1
AHA: 4Q,'03,8; 3Q,'02,5; 1Q,'01,6

N **C1813** Prosthesis, penile, inflatable N1
MED: 100-4,14,40.8
AHA: 4Q,'03,8; 3Q,'02,5; 1Q,'01,6

N **C1814** Retinal tamponade device, silicone oil N1

N **C1815** Prosthesis, urinary sphincter (implantable) N1
MED: 100-4,14,40.8
AHA: 4Q,'03,8; 3Q,'02,5; 1Q,'01,6

N **C1816** Receiver and/or transmitter, neurostimulator (implantable) N1
AHA: 4Q,'03,8; 3Q,'02,5; 1Q,'01,6

N **C1817** Septal defect implant system, intracardiac N1
AHA: 4Q,'03,8; 3Q,'02,5; 1Q,'01,6

N **C1818** Integrated keratoprosthesis N1
AHA: 4Q,'03,4

N **C1819** Surgical tissue localization and excision device (implantable) N1

N **C1820** Generator, neurostimulator (implantable), with rechargeable battery and charging system N1
MED: 100-4,4,10.12; 100-4,14,40.8

N **C1821** Interspinous process distraction device (implantable) N1

● H C1830 Jan Powered bone marrow biopsy needle J7

● H C1840 Jan Lens, intraocular (telescopic) J7

N **C1874** Stent, coated/covered, with delivery system N1
AHA: 4Q,'03,8; 1Q,'01,6

N **C1875** Stent, coated/covered, without delivery system N1
AHA: 4Q,'03,8; 1Q,'01,6

N **C1876** Stent, noncoated/noncovered, with delivery system N1
AHA: 4Q,'03,8; 3Q,'02,5; 1Q,'01,6; 3Q,'01,4

N **C1877** Stent, noncoated/noncovered, without delivery system N1
AHA: 4Q,'03,8; 3Q,'02,5; 1Q,'01,6; 3Q,'01,4

N **C1878** Material for vocal cord medialization, synthetic (implantable) N1
AHA: 3Q,'02,5; 1Q,'01,6

N **C1879** Tissue marker (implantable) N1
AHA: 4Q,'03,8; 3Q,'02,5; 1Q,'01,6

N **C1880** Vena cava filter N1
AHA: 4Q,'03,8; 3Q,'02,5; 1Q,'01,6

N **C1881** Dialysis access system (implantable) N1
MED: 100-4,14,40.8
AHA: 4Q,'03,8; 3Q,'02,5; 1Q,'01,6

N **C1882** Cardioverter-defibrillator, other than single or dual chamber (implantable) N1
AHA: 3Q,'02,5; 1Q,'01,5

N **C1883** Adaptor/extension, pacing lead or neurostimulator lead (implantable) N1
MED: 100-4,32,40.1
AHA: 1Q,'02,9; 3Q,'02,5; 1Q,'01,5

N **C1884** Embolization protective system N1

N **C1885** Catheter, transluminal angioplasty, laser N1
AHA: 4Q,'03,8; 3Q,'02,5; 1Q,'01,5

● H **C1886** Jan Catheter, extravascular tissue ablation, any modality (insertable)

N **C1887** Catheter, guiding (may include infusion/perfusion capability) N1
AHA: 3Q,'02,5; 1Q,'01,5

N **C1888** Catheter, ablation, noncardiac, endovascular (implantable) N1

N **C1891** Infusion pump, nonprogrammable, permanent (implantable) N1
MED: 100-4,14,40.8
AHA: 4Q,'03,8; 3Q,'02,5; 1Q,'01,6

N **C1892** Introducer/sheath, guiding, intracardiac electrophysiological, fixed-curve, peel-away N1
AHA: 3Q,'02,5; 1Q,'01,6

N **C1893** Introducer/sheath, guiding, intracardiac electrophysiological, fixed-curve, other than peel-away N1
AHA: 3Q,'02,5; 1Q,'01,6; 3Q,'01,4

N **C1894** Introducer/sheath, other than guiding, other than intracardiac electrophysiological, nonlaser N1
AHA: 3Q,'02,5

N **C1895** Lead, cardioverter-defibrillator, endocardial dual coil (implantable) N1
AHA: 3Q,'02,5; 1Q,'01,6

N **C1896** Lead, cardioverter-defibrillator, other than endocardial single or dual coil (implantable) N1
AHA: 3Q,'02,5; 1Q,'01,6

N **C1897** Lead, neurostimulator test kit (implantable) N1
MED: 100-4,14,40.8; 100-4,32,40.1
AHA: 1Q,'02,9; 3Q,'02,5; 1Q,'01,6

N **C1898** Lead, pacemaker, other than transvenous VDD single pass N1
AHA: 1Q,'01,6; 3Q,'01,4

N **C1899** Lead, pacemaker/cardioverter-defibrillator combination (implantable) N1
AHA: 3Q,'02,5; 1Q,'01,6

Status	Code	Description	APC
N	C1900	Lead, left ventricular coronary venous system MED: 100-4,14,40.8	N1
N	C2614	Probe, percutaneous lumbar discectomy	N1
N	C2615	Sealant, pulmonary, liquid AHA: 3Q,'02,5; 1Q,'01,6	N1
U	☑ C2616	Brachytherapy source, nonstranded, yttrium-90, per source AHA: 3Q,'03,11; 3Q,'02,5	H2
N	C2617	Stent, noncoronary, temporary, without delivery system AHA: 4Q,'03,8; 3Q,'02,5; 1Q,'01,6	N1
N	C2618	Probe, cryoablation AHA: 4Q,'03,8; 3Q,'02,5; 1Q,'01,6	N1
N	C2619	Pacemaker, dual chamber, nonrate-responsive (implantable) MED: 100-4,14,40.8 AHA: 3Q,'02,5; 1Q,'01,6; 3Q,'01,4	N1
N	C2620	Pacemaker, single chamber, nonrate-responsive (implantable) AHA: 4Q,'03,8; 3Q,'02,5; 1Q,'01,6	N1
N	C2621	Pacemaker, other than single or dual chamber (implantable) AHA: 4Q,'03,8; 1Q,'01,6	N1
N	C2622	Prosthesis, penile, noninflatable AHA: 4Q,'03,8; 3Q,'02,5; 1Q,'01,6	N1
N	C2625	Stent, noncoronary, temporary, with delivery system AHA: 4Q,'03,8; 3Q,'02,5; 1Q,'01,6	N1
N	C2626	Infusion pump, nonprogrammable, temporary (implantable) MED: 100-4,14,40.8 AHA: 3Q,'02,5; 1Q,'01,6	N1
N	C2627	Catheter, suprapubic/cystoscopic AHA: 4Q,'03,8; 3Q,'02,5; 1Q,'01,5	N1
N	C2628	Catheter, occlusion AHA: 4Q,'03,8; 3Q,'02,5; 1Q,'01,5	N1
N	C2629	Introducer/sheath, other than guiding, intracardiac electrophysiological, laser AHA: 3Q,'02,5; 1Q,'01,6	N1
N	C2630	Catheter, electrophysiology, diagnostic/ablation, other than 3D or vector mapping, cool-tip AHA: 3Q,'02,5; 1Q,'01,5	N1
N	C2631	Repair device, urinary, incontinence, without sling graft MED: 100-4,14,40.8 AHA: 4Q,'03,8; 3Q,'02,5; 1Q,'01,6	N1
U	☑ C2634	Brachytherapy source, nonstranded, high activity, iodine-125, greater than 1.01 mCi (NIST), per source AHA: 2Q,'05,8	H2
U	☑ C2635	Brachytherapy source, nonstranded, high activity, palladium-103, greater than 2.2 mCi (NIST), per source AHA: 2Q,'05,8	H2
U	☑ C2636	Brachytherapy linear source, nonstranded, palladium-103, per 1 mm	H2
B	☑ C2637	Brachytherapy source, nonstranded, ytterbium-169, per source AHA: 3Q,'05,7	
U	☑ C2638	Brachytherapy source, stranded, iodine-125, per source	H2
U	☑ C2639	Brachytherapy source, nonstranded, iodine-125, per source	H2
U	☑ C2640	Brachytherapy source, stranded, palladium-103, per source	H2
U	☑ C2641	Brachytherapy source, nonstranded, palladium-103, per source	H2
U	☑ C2642	Brachytherapy source, stranded, cesium-131, per source	H2
U	☑ C2643	Brachytherapy source, nonstranded, cesium-131, per source	H2
U	☑ C2698	Brachytherapy source, stranded, not otherwise specified, per source	H2
U	☑ C2699	Brachytherapy source, nonstranded, not otherwise specified, per source	H2
Q3	C8900	Magnetic resonance angiography with contrast, abdomen MED: 100-4,13,40.1.2	Z2
Q3	C8901	Magnetic resonance angiography without contrast, abdomen MED: 100-4,13,40.1.2	Z2
Q3	C8902	Magnetic resonance angiography without contrast followed by with contrast, abdomen MED: 100-4,13,40.1.2	Z2
Q3	C8903	Magnetic resonance imaging with contrast, breast; unilateral	Z2
Q3	C8904	Magnetic resonance imaging without contrast, breast; unilateral	Z2
Q3	C8905	Magnetic resonance imaging without contrast followed by with contrast, breast; unilateral	Z2
Q3	C8906	Magnetic resonance imaging with contrast, breast; bilateral	Z2
Q3	C8907	Magnetic resonance imaging without contrast, breast; bilateral	Z2
Q3	C8908	Magnetic resonance imaging without contrast followed by with contrast, breast; bilateral	Z2
Q3	C8909	Magnetic resonance angiography with contrast, chest (excluding myocardium) MED: 100-4,13,40.1.2	Z2
Q3	C8910	Magnetic resonance angiography without contrast, chest (excluding myocardium) MED: 100-4,13,40.1.2	Z2
Q3	C8911	Magnetic resonance angiography without contrast followed by with contrast, chest (excluding myocardium) MED: 100-4,13,40.1.2	Z2
Q3	C8912	Magnetic resonance angiography with contrast, lower extremity MED: 100-4,13,40.1.2	Z2
Q3	C8913	Magnetic resonance angiography without contrast, lower extremity MED: 100-4,13,40.1.2	Z2
Q3	C8914	Magnetic resonance angiography without contrast followed by with contrast, lower extremity MED: 100-4,13,40.1.2	Z2
Q3	C8918	Magnetic resonance angiography with contrast, pelvis MED: 100-4,13,40.1.2 AHA: 4Q,'03,4	Z2
Q3	C8919	Magnetic resonance angiography without contrast, pelvis MED: 100-4,13,40.1.2 AHA: 4Q,'03,4	Z2

Q3 C8920 Magnetic resonance angiography without contrast followed by with contrast, pelvis Z2
MED: 100-4,13,40.1.2
AHA: 4Q,'03,4

S C8921 Transthoracic echocardiography with contrast, or without contrast followed by with contrast, for congenital cardiac anomalies; complete
MED: 100-4,4,200.7.2

S C8922 Transthoracic echocardiography with contrast, or without contrast followed by with contrast, for congenital cardiac anomalies; follow-up or limited study

S C8923 Transthoracic echocardiography with contrast, or without contrast followed by with contrast, real-time with image documentation (2D), includes M-mode recording, when performed, complete, without spectral or color doppler echocardiography

S C8924 Transthoracic echocardiography with contrast, or without contrast followed by with contrast, real-time with image documentation (2D), includes M-mode recording when performed, follow-up or limited study

S C8925 Transesophageal echocardiography (TEE) with contrast, or without contrast followed by with contrast, real time with image documentation (2D) (with or without M-mode recording); including probe placement, image acquisition, interpretation and report

S C8926 Transesophageal echocardiography (TEE) with contrast, or without contrast followed by with contrast, for congenital cardiac anomalies; including probe placement, image acquisition, interpretation and report

S C8927 Transesophageal echocardiography (TEE) with contrast, or without contrast followed by with contrast, for monitoring purposes, including probe placement, real time 2-dimensional image acquisition and interpretation leading to ongoing (continuous) assessment of (dynamically changing) cardiac pumping function and to therapeutic measures on an immediate time basis

S C8928 Transthoracic echocardiography with contrast, or without contrast followed by with contrast, real-time with image documentation (2D), includes M-mode recording, when performed, during rest and cardiovascular stress test using treadmill, bicycle exercise and/or pharmacologically induced stress, with interpretation and report

S C8929 Transthoracic echocardiography with contrast, or without contrast followed by with contrast, real-time with image documentation (2D), includes M-mode recording, when performed, complete, with spectral doppler echocardiography, and with color flow doppler echocardiography

S C8930 Transthoracic echocardiography, with contrast, or without contrast followed by with contrast, real-time with image documentation (2D), includes M-mode recording, when performed, during rest and cardiovascular stress test using treadmill, bicycle exercise and/or pharmacologically induced stress, with interpretation and report; including performance of continuous electrocardiographic monitoring, with physician supervision

▲ Q3 C8931 Jan Magnetic resonance angiography with contrast, spinal canal and contents Z2

Q3 C8932 Magnetic resonance angiography without contrast, spinal canal and contents Z2

Q3 C8933 Magnetic resonance angiography without contrast followed by with contrast, spinal canal and contents Z2

Q3 C8934 Magnetic resonance angiography with contrast, upper extremity Z2

Q3 C8935 Magnetic resonance angiography without contrast, upper extremity Z2

Q3 C8936 Magnetic resonance angiography without contrast followed by with contrast, upper extremity Z2

S C8957 Intravenous infusion for therapy/diagnosis; initiation of prolonged infusion (more than 8 hours), requiring use of portable or implantable pump
MED: 100-4,4,230.2; 100-4,4,230.2.1

N C9113 Injection, pantoprazole sodium, per vial N1
Use this code for Protonix.

K ☑ C9121 Injection, argatroban, per 5 mg K2

K ☑ C9248 Injection, clevidipine butyrate, 1 mg K2
Use this code for Cleviprex.

K ☑ C9250 Human plasma fibrin sealant, vapor-heated, solvent-detergent (Artiss), 2 ml K2

K ☑ C9254 Injection, lacosamide, 1 mg K2
Use this code for VIMPAT.

K ☑ C9257 Injection, bevacizumab, 0.25 mg K2
Use this code for Avastin.

~~C9270~~ Jan ~~Injection, immune globulin (Gammaplex), intravenous, nonlyophilized (e.g., liquid), 500 mg~~
To report, see J1557

~~C9272~~ Jan ~~Injection, denosumab, 1 mg~~
To report, see J0897

~~C9273~~ Jan ~~Sipuleucel-T, minimum of 50 million autologous CD54+ cells activated with PAP-GM-CSF, including leukapheresis and all other preparatory procedures, per infusion~~
To report, see Q2043

~~C9274~~ Jan ~~Crotalidae polyvalent immune fab (Ovine), 1 vial~~
To report, see J0840

G ☑ C9275 Injection, hexaminolevulinate HCl, 100 mg, per study dose K2
Use this code for Cysview.

~~C9276~~ Jan ~~Injection, cabazitaxel, 1 mg~~
To report, see J9043

~~C9277~~ Jan ~~Injection, alglucosidase alfa (Lumizyme), 1 mg~~
To report, see J0221

~~C9278~~ Jan ~~Injection, incobotulinumtoxina, 1 unit~~
To report, see J0588

G ☑ C9279 Injection, ibuprofen, 100 mg K2

~~C9280~~ Jan ~~Injection, eribulin mesylate, 1 mg~~

~~C9281~~ Jan ~~Injection, pegloticase, 1 mg~~
To report, see J2507

~~C9282~~ Jan ~~Injection, ceftaroline fosamil, 10 mg~~
To report, see J0712

~~C9283~~ Jan ~~Injection, acetaminophen, 10 mg~~
To report, see J0131

~~C9284~~ Jan ~~Injection, ipilimumab, 1 mg~~
To report, see J9228

● G ☑ C9285 Jan Lidocaine 70 mg/tetracaine 70 mg, per patch K2
Use this code for SYNERA.

● G ☑ **C9286** Jan **Injection, belatacept, 1 mg** K2
Use this code for NULOJIX.

● G ☑ **C9287** Jan **Injection, brentuximab vedotin, 1 mg** K2
Use this code for ADCETRIS.

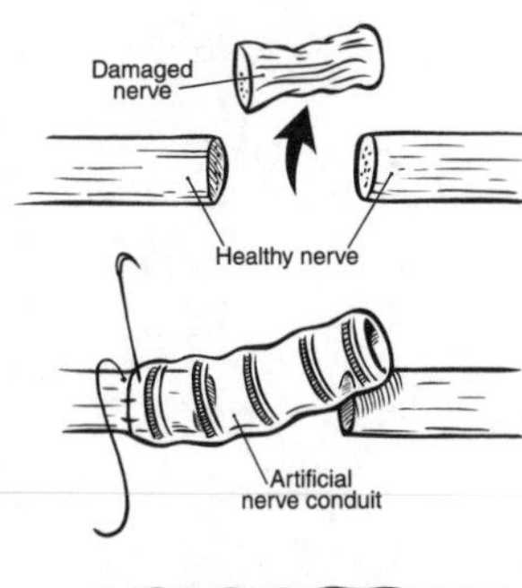

A synthetic "bridge" is affixed to each end of a severed nerve with sutures
This procedure is performed using an operating microscope

N ☑ **C9352** **Microporous collagen implantable tube (NeuraGen Nerve Guide), per cm length** N1

N ☑ **C9353** **Microporous collagen implantable slit tube (NeuraWrap Nerve Protector), per cm length** N1

N ☑ **C9354** **Acellular pericardial tissue matrix of nonhuman origin (Veritas), per sq cm** N1

N ☑ **C9355** **Collagen nerve cuff (NeuroMatrix), per 0.5 cm length** N1

N ☑ **C9356** **Tendon, porous matrix of cross-linked collagen and glycosaminoglycan matrix (TenoGlide Tendon Protector Sheet), per sq cm** N1

K ☑ **C9358** **Dermal substitute, native, nondenatured collagen, fetal bovine origin (SurgiMend Collagen Matrix), per 0.5 sq cm** K2

N ☑ **C9359** **Porous purified collagen matrix bone void filler (Integra Mozaik Osteoconductive Scaffold Putty, Integra OS Osteoconductive Scaffold Putty), per 0.5 cc** N1

K ☑ **C9360** **Dermal substitute, native, nondenatured collagen, neonatal bovine origin (SurgiMend Collagen Matrix), per 0.5 sq cm** K2

N ☑ **C9361** **Collagen matrix nerve wrap (NeuroMend Collagen Nerve Wrap), per 0.5 cm length** N1

N ☑ **C9362** **Porous purified collagen matrix bone void filler (Integra Mozaik Osteoconductive Scaffold Strip), per 0.5 cc** N1

K ☑ **C9363** **Skin substitute (Integra Meshed Bilayer Wound Matrix), per square cm** K2

N ☑ **C9364** **Porcine implant, Permacol, per sq cm** N1

~~C9365~~ Jan ~~**Oasis Ultra Tri-Layer Matrix, per square centimeter**~~
To report, see Q4102-Q4103

● G ☑ **C9366** Jan **EpiFix, per sq cm** K2

G ☑ **C9367** **Skin substitute, Endoform Dermal Template, per sq cm** K2

A **C9399** **Unclassified drugs or biologicals** K7
MED: 100-4,17,90.3

~~C9406~~ Jan ~~**Iodine I-123 ioflupane, diagnostic, per study dose, up to 5 millicuries**~~
To report, see A9584

T **C9716** **Creations of thermal anal lesions by radiofrequency energy** G2

T **C9724** **Endoscopic full-thickness plication in the gastric cardia using endoscopic plication system (EPS); includes endoscopy** G2

T **C9725** **Placement of endorectal intracavitary applicator for high intensity brachytherapy** G2
AHA: 3Q,'05,7

T **C9726** **Placement and removal (if performed) of applicator into breast for radiation therapy** G2

T ☑ **C9727** **Insertion of implants into the soft palate; minimum of 3 implants** G2

X **C9728** **Placement of interstitial device(s) for radiation therapy/surgery guidance (e.g., fiducial markers, dosimeter), for other than the following sites (any approach): abdomen, pelvis, prostate, retroperitoneum, thorax, single or multiple**

~~C9729~~ Jan ~~**Percutaneous laminotomy/laminectomy (intralaminar approach) for decompression of neural elements, (with ligamentous resection, discectomy, facetectomy and/or foraminotomy, when performed) any method under indirect image guidance, with the use of an endoscope when performed, single or multiple levels, unilateral or bilateral; lumbar**~~

~~C9730~~ Jan ~~**Bronchoscopic bronchial thermoplasty with imaging guidance (if performed), radiofrequency ablation of airway smooth muscle, 1 lobe**~~

~~C9731~~ Jan ~~**Bronchoscopic bronchial thermoplasty with imaging guidance (if performed), radiofrequency ablation of airway smooth muscle, 2 or more lobes**~~

● T **C9732** Jan **Insertion of ocular telescope prosthetic including removal of crystalline lens**

T **C9800** **Dermal injection procedure(s) for facial lipodystrophy syndrome (LDS) and provision of Radiesse or Sculptra dermal filler, including all items and supplies** R2
MED: 100-3,250.5; 100-4,32,260.1; 100-4,32,260.2.1

N **C9898** **Radiolabeled product provided during a hospital inpatient stay**

A **C9899** **Implanted prosthetic device, payable only for inpatients who do not have inpatient coverage**

DURABLE MEDICAL EQUIPMENT E0100-E9999

E codes include durable medical equipment such as canes, crutches, walkers, commodes, decubitus care, bath and toilet aids, hospital beds, oxygen and related respiratory equipment, monitoring equipment, pacemakers, patient lifts, safety equipment, restraints, traction equipment, fracture frames, wheelchairs, and artificial kidney machines.

CANES

Y **E0100** **Cane, includes canes of all materials, adjustable or fixed, with tip** ♿
White canes for the blind are not covered under Medicare.

Y **E0105** **Cane, quad or 3-prong, includes canes of all materials, adjustable or fixed, with tips** ♿

CRUTCHES

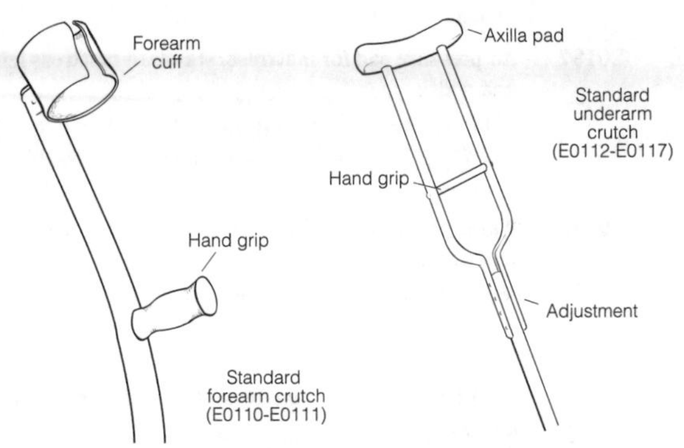

Y ☑ **E0110** **Crutches, forearm, includes crutches of various materials, adjustable or fixed, pair, complete with tips and handgrips** ♿

Y ☑ **E0111** **Crutch, forearm, includes crutches of various materials, adjustable or fixed, each, with tip and handgrips** ♿

Y ☑ **E0112** **Crutches, underarm, wood, adjustable or fixed, pair, with pads, tips, and handgrips** ♿

Y ☑ **E0113** **Crutch, underarm, wood, adjustable or fixed, each, with pad, tip, and handgrip** ♿

Y ☑ **E0114** **Crutches, underarm, other than wood, adjustable or fixed, pair, with pads, tips, and handgrips** ♿

Y ☑ **E0116** **Crutch, underarm, other than wood, adjustable or fixed, with pad, tip, handgrip, with or without shock absorber, each** ♿

Y ☑ **E0117** **Crutch, underarm, articulating, spring assisted, each** ♿

E ☑ **E0118** **Crutch substitute, lower leg platform, with or without wheels, each**
Medicare covers walkers if patient's ambulation is impaired.

WALKERS

Y **E0130** **Walker, rigid (pickup), adjustable or fixed height** ♿
MED: 100-4,23,60.3; 100-4,36,50,15

Y **E0135** **Walker, folding (pickup), adjustable or fixed height** ♿
Medicare covers walkers if patient's ambulation is impaired.
MED: 100-4,36,50,15

Y **E0140** **Walker, with trunk support, adjustable or fixed height, any type** ♿
MED: 100-4,36,50,15

Y **E0141** **Walker, rigid, wheeled, adjustable or fixed height** ♿
Medicare covers walkers if patient's ambulation is impaired.

Y **E0143** **Walker, folding, wheeled, adjustable or fixed height** ♿
Medicare covers walkers if patient's ambulation is impaired.
MED: 100-4,36,50,15

Y **E0144** **Walker, enclosed, 4 sided framed, rigid or folding, wheeled with posterior seat** ♿

Y **E0147** **Walker, heavy-duty, multiple braking system, variable wheel resistance** ♿
Medicare covers safety roller walkers only in patients with severe neurological disorders or restricted use of one hand. In some cases, coverage will be extended to patients with a weight exceeding the limits of a standard wheeled walker.
MED: 100-4,36,50,15

Y ☑ **E0148** **Walker, heavy-duty, without wheels, rigid or folding, any type, each** ♿

Y **E0149** **Walker, heavy-duty, wheeled, rigid or folding, any type** ♿

ATTACHMENTS

Y ☑ **E0153** **Platform attachment, forearm crutch, each** ♿

Y ☑ **E0154** **Platform attachment, walker, each** ♿
MED: 100-4,23,60.3; 100-4,36,50.14; 100-4,36,50,15

Y ☑ **E0155** **Wheel attachment, rigid pick-up walker, per pair** ♿

Y **E0156** **Seat attachment, walker** ♿
MED: 100-4,36,50.14

Y ☑ **E0157** **Crutch attachment, walker, each** ♿

Y ☑ **E0158** **Leg extensions for walker, per set of 4** ♿

Y ☑ **E0159** **Brake attachment for wheeled walker, replacement, each** ♿

COMMODES

Y **E0160** **Sitz type bath or equipment, portable, used with or without commode** ♿
Medicare covers sitz baths if medical record indicates that the patient has an infection or injury of the perineal area and the sitz bath is prescribed by the physician.

Y **E0161** **Sitz type bath or equipment, portable, used with or without commode, with faucet attachment(s)** ♿
Medicare covers sitz baths if medical record indicates that the patient has an infection or injury of the perineal area and the sitz bath is prescribed by the physician.

Y **E0162** **Sitz bath chair** ♿
Medicare covers sitz baths if medical record indicates that the patient has an infection or injury of the perineal area and the sitz bath is prescribed by the physician.

Y **E0163** **Commode chair, mobile or stationary, with fixed arms** ♿
Medicare covers commodes for patients confined to their beds or rooms, for patients without indoor bathroom facilities, and to patients who cannot climb or descend the stairs necessary to reach the bathrooms in their homes.

Y **E0165** Commode chair, mobile or stationary, with detachable arms ♿
Medicare covers commodes for patients confined to their beds or rooms, for patients without indoor bathroom facilities, and to patients who cannot climb or descend the stairs necessary to reach the bathrooms in their homes.

Y **E0167** Pail or pan for use with commode chair, replacement only ♿
Medicare covers commodes for patients confined to their beds or rooms, for patients without indoor bathroom facilities, and to patients who cannot climb or descend the stairs necessary to reach the bathrooms in their homes.

Y ☑ **E0168** Commode chair, extra wide and/or heavy-duty, stationary or mobile, with or without arms, any type, each ♿

Y **E0170** Commode chair with integrated seat lift mechanism, electric, any type ♿

Y **E0171** Commode chair with integrated seat lift mechanism, nonelectric, any type ♿

E **E0172** Seat lift mechanism placed over or on top of toilet, any type

Y ☑ **E0175** Footrest, for use with commode chair, each ♿

DECUBITUS CARE EQUIPMENT

Y **E0181** Powered pressure reducing mattress overlay/pad, alternating, with pump, includes heavy-duty ♿
Medicare covers pads if physicians supervise their use in patients who have decubitus ulcers or susceptibility to them. Prior authorization is required by Medicare for this item.

Y **E0182** Pump for alternating pressure pad, for replacement only ♿
Medicare covers pads if physicians supervise their use in patients who have decubitus ulcers or susceptibility to them. Prior authorization is required by Medicare for this item.

Y **E0184** Dry pressure mattress ♿
Medicare covers pads if physicians supervise their use in patients who have decubitus ulcers or susceptibility to them. Prior authorization is required by Medicare for this item.

Y **E0185** Gel or gel-like pressure pad for mattress, standard mattress length and width ♿
Medicare covers pads if physicians supervise their use in patients who have decubitus ulcers or susceptibility to them. Prior authorization is required by Medicare for this item.

Y **E0186** Air pressure mattress ♿
Medicare covers pads if physicians supervise their use in patients who have decubitus ulcers or susceptibility to them.

Y **E0187** Water pressure mattress ♿
Medicare covers pads if physicians supervise their use in patients who have decubitus ulcers or susceptibility to them.

Y **E0188** Synthetic sheepskin pad ♿
Medicare covers pads if physicians supervise their use in patients who have decubitus ulcers or susceptibility to them. Prior authorization is required by Medicare for this item.

Y **E0189** Lambswool sheepskin pad, any size ♿
Medicare covers pads if physicians supervise their use in patients who have decubitus ulcers or susceptibility to them. Prior authorization is required by Medicare for this item.

E **E0190** Positioning cushion/pillow/wedge, any shape or size, includes all components and accessories

Y ☑ **E0191** Heel or elbow protector, each ♿

Y **E0193** Powered air flotation bed (low air loss therapy) ♿
MED: 100-4,23,60.3

Y **E0194** Air fluidized bed ♿
An air fluidized bed is covered by Medicare if the patient has a stage 3 or stage 4 pressure sore and, without the bed, would require institutionalization. A physician's prescription is required.

Y **E0196** Gel pressure mattress ♿
Medicare covers pads if physicians supervise their use in patients who have decubitus ulcers or susceptibility to them.

Y **E0197** Air pressure pad for mattress, standard mattress length and width ♿
Medicare covers pads if physicians supervise their use in patients who have decubitus ulcers or susceptibility to them.

Y **E0198** Water pressure pad for mattress, standard mattress length and width ♿
Medicare covers pads if physicians supervise their use in patients who have decubitus ulcers or susceptibility to them.

Y **E0199** Dry pressure pad for mattress, standard mattress length and width ♿
Medicare covers pads if physicians supervise their use in patients who have decubitus ulcers or susceptibility to them.

HEAT/COLD APPLICATION

Y **E0200** Heat lamp, without stand (table model), includes bulb, or infrared element ♿

Y **E0202** Phototherapy (bilirubin) light with photometer ♿

E **E0203** Therapeutic lightbox, minimum 10,000 lux, table top model

Y **E0205** Heat lamp, with stand, includes bulb, or infrared element ♿

Y **E0210** Electric heat pad, standard ♿

Y **E0215** Electric heat pad, moist ♿

Y **E0217** Water circulating heat pad with pump ♿

Y **E0218** Water circulating cold pad with pump

Y **E0221** Infrared heating pad system

Y **E0225** Hydrocollator unit, includes pads ♿
MED: 100-2,15,230

E **E0231** Noncontact wound-warming device (temperature control unit, AC adapter and power cord) for use with warming card and wound cover

E **E0232** Warming card for use with the noncontact wound-warming device and noncontact wound-warming wound cover

Y **E0235** Paraffin bath unit, portable (see medical supply code A4265 for paraffin) ♿
MED: 100-2,15,230

Y **E0236** Pump for water circulating pad ♿

Y E0239 Hydrocollator unit, portable ♿
MED: 100-2,15,230

BATH AND TOILET AIDS

E E0240 Bath/shower chair, with or without wheels, any size

E ☑ E0241 Bathtub wall rail, each

E E0242 Bathtub rail, floor base

E ☑ E0243 Toilet rail, each

E E0244 Raised toilet seat

E E0245 Tub stool or bench

E E0246 Transfer tub rail attachment

E E0247 Transfer bench for tub or toilet with or without commode opening

E E0248 Transfer bench, heavy-duty, for tub or toilet with or without commode opening

Y E0249 Pad for water circulating heat unit, for replacement only ♿

HOSPITAL BEDS AND ACCESSORIES

Y E0250 Hospital bed, fixed height, with any type side rails, with mattress ♿
MED: 100-4,23,60.3

Y E0251 Hospital bed, fixed height, with any type side rails, without mattress ♿

Y E0255 Hospital bed, variable height, hi-lo, with any type side rails, with mattress ♿

Y E0256 Hospital bed, variable height, hi-lo, with any type side rails, without mattress ♿

Y E0260 Hospital bed, semi-electric (head and foot adjustment), with any type side rails, with mattress ♿

Y E0261 Hospital bed, semi-electric (head and foot adjustment), with any type side rails, without mattress ♿

Y E0265 Hospital bed, total electric (head, foot, and height adjustments), with any type side rails, with mattress ♿

Y E0266 Hospital bed, total electric (head, foot, and height adjustments), with any type side rails, without mattress ♿

E E0270 Hospital bed, institutional type includes: oscillating, circulating and Stryker frame, with mattress

Y E0271 Mattress, innerspring ♿
MED: 100-4,23,60.3; 100-4,36,50.14

Y E0272 Mattress, foam rubber ♿

E E0273 Bed board

E E0274 Over-bed table

Y E0275 Bed pan, standard, metal or plastic ♿
Reusable, autoclavable bedpans are covered by Medicare for bed-confined patients.

Y E0276 Bed pan, fracture, metal or plastic ♿
Reusable, autoclavable bedpans are covered by Medicare for bed-confined patients.

Y E0277 Powered pressure-reducing air mattress ♿
MED: 100-4,23,60.3

Y E0280 Bed cradle, any type ♿
MED: 100-4,36,50.14

Y E0290 Hospital bed, fixed height, without side rails, with mattress ♿

Y E0291 Hospital bed, fixed height, without side rails, without mattress ♿

Y E0292 Hospital bed, variable height, hi-lo, without side rails, with mattress ♿

Y E0293 Hospital bed, variable height, hi-lo, without side rails, without mattress ♿

Y E0294 Hospital bed, semi-electric (head and foot adjustment), without side rails, with mattress ♿

Y E0295 Hospital bed, semi-electric (head and foot adjustment), without side rails, without mattress ♿

Y E0296 Hospital bed, total electric (head, foot, and height adjustments), without side rails, with mattress ♿

Y E0297 Hospital bed, total electric (head, foot, and height adjustments), without side rails, without mattress ♿

Y E0300 Pediatric crib, hospital grade, fully enclosed ♿

Y E0301 Hospital bed, heavy-duty, extra wide, with weight capacity greater than 350 pounds, but less than or equal to 600 pounds, with any type side rails, without mattress ♿

Y E0302 Hospital bed, extra heavy-duty, extra wide, with weight capacity greater than 600 pounds, with any type side rails, without mattress ♿

Y E0303 Hospital bed, heavy-duty, extra wide, with weight capacity greater than 350 pounds, but less than or equal to 600 pounds, with any type side rails, with mattress ♿

Y E0304 Hospital bed, extra heavy-duty, extra wide, with weight capacity greater than 600 pounds, with any type side rails, with mattress ♿

Y E0305 Bedside rails, half-length ♿

Y E0310 Bedside rails, full-length ♿
MED: 100-4,36,50.14

E E0315 Bed accessory: board, table, or support device, any type

Y E0316 Safety enclosure frame/canopy for use with hospital bed, any type ♿
MED: 100-4,23,60.3

Y E0325 Urinal; male, jug-type, any material ♂♿

Y E0326 Urinal; female, jug-type, any material ♀♿

Y E0328 Hospital bed, pediatric, manual, 360 degree side enclosures, top of headboard, footboard and side rails up to 24 in above the spring, includes mattress

Y E0329 Hospital bed, pediatric, electric or semi-electric, 360 degree side enclosures, top of headboard, footboard and side rails up to 24 in above the spring, includes mattress

E E0350 Control unit for electronic bowel irrigation/evacuation system

E E0352 Disposable pack (water reservoir bag, speculum, valving mechanism, and collection bag/box) for use with the electronic bowel irrigation/evacuation system

E E0370 Air pressure elevator for heel

Y E0371 Nonpowered advanced pressure reducing overlay for mattress, standard mattress length and width ♿
MED: 100-4,23,60.3

Y E0372 Powered air overlay for mattress, standard mattress length and width ♿

Y E0373 Nonpowered advanced pressure reducing mattress ♿

OXYGEN AND RELATED RESPIRATORY EQUIPMENT

Y **E0424** Stationary compressed gaseous oxygen system, rental; includes container, contents, regulator, flowmeter, humidifier, nebulizer, cannula or mask, and tubing ♿

For the first claim filed for home oxygen equipment or therapy, submit a certificate of medical necessity that includes the oxygen flow rate, anticipated frequency and duration of oxygen therapy, and physician signature. Medicare accepts oxygen therapy as medically necessary in cases documenting any of the following: erythocythemia with a hematocrit greater than 56 percent; a P pulmonale on EKG; or dependent edema consistent with congestive heart failure.

E **E0425** Stationary compressed gas system, purchase; includes regulator, flowmeter, humidifier, nebulizer, cannula or mask, and tubing

E **E0430** Portable gaseous oxygen system, purchase; includes regulator, flowmeter, humidifier, cannula or mask, and tubing

Y **E0431** Portable gaseous oxygen system, rental; includes portable container, regulator, flowmeter, humidifier, cannula or mask, and tubing ♿

Y **E0433** Portable liquid oxygen system, rental; home liquefier used to fill portable liquid oxygen containers, includes portable containers, regulator, flowmeter, humidifier, cannula or mask and tubing, with or without supply reservoir and contents gauge ♿

Y **E0434** Portable liquid oxygen system, rental; includes portable container, supply reservoir, humidifier, flowmeter, refill adaptor, contents gauge, cannula or mask, and tubing ♿

E **E0435** Portable liquid oxygen system, purchase; includes portable container, supply reservoir, flowmeter, humidifier, contents gauge, cannula or mask, tubing and refill adaptor

Y **E0439** Stationary liquid oxygen system, rental; includes container, contents, regulator, flowmeter, humidifier, nebulizer, cannula or mask, & tubing ♿

E **E0440** Stationary liquid oxygen system, purchase; includes use of reservoir, contents indicator, regulator, flowmeter, humidifier, nebulizer, cannula or mask, and tubing

Y ☑ **E0441** Stationary oxygen contents, gaseous, 1 month's supply = 1 unit ♿

Y ☑ **E0442** Stationary oxygen contents, liquid, 1 month's supply = 1 unit ♿

Y ☑ **E0443** Portable oxygen contents, gaseous, 1 month's supply = 1 unit ♿

Y ☑ **E0444** Portable oxygen contents, liquid, 1 month's supply = 1 unit ♿

N **E0445** Oximeter device for measuring blood oxygen levels noninvasively

E **E0446** Topical oxygen delivery system, not otherwise specified, includes all supplies and accessories

Y **E0450** Volume control ventilator, without pressure support mode, may include pressure control mode, used with invasive interface (e.g., tracheostomy tube) ♿

Y **E0455** Oxygen tent, excluding croup or pediatric tents

Y **E0457** Chest shell (cuirass) ♿

Y **E0459** Chest wrap ♿

Y **E0460** Negative pressure ventilator; portable or stationary ♿

Y **E0461** Volume control ventilator, without pressure support mode, may include pressure control mode, used with noninvasive interface (e.g., mask) ♿

Y **E0462** Rocking bed, with or without side rails ♿

Y **E0463** Pressure support ventilator with volume control mode, may include pressure control mode, used with invasive interface (e.g., tracheostomy tube) ♿

Y **E0464** Pressure support ventilator with volume control mode, may include pressure control mode, used with noninvasive interface (e.g., mask) ♿

Y **E0470** Respiratory assist device, bi-level pressure capability, without backup rate feature, used with noninvasive interface, e.g., nasal or facial mask (intermittent assist device with continuous positive airway pressure device) ♿

MED: 100-3,240.4; 100-4,23,60.3

Y **E0471** Respiratory assist device, bi-level pressure capability, with back-up rate feature, used with noninvasive interface, e.g., nasal or facial mask (intermittent assist device with continuous positive airway pressure device) ♿

Y **E0472** Respiratory assist device, bi-level pressure capability, with backup rate feature, used with invasive interface, e.g., tracheostomy tube (intermittent assist device with continuous positive airway pressure device) ♿

Y **E0480** Percussor, electric or pneumatic, home model ♿

E **E0481** Intrapulmonary percussive ventilation system and related accessories

Y **E0482** Cough stimulating device, alternating positive and negative airway pressure ♿

Y ☑ **E0483** High frequency chest wall oscillation air-pulse generator system, (includes hoses and vest), each ♿

Y ☑ **E0484** Oscillatory positive expiratory pressure device, nonelectric, any type, each ♿

Y **E0485** Oral device/appliance used to reduce upper airway collapsibility, adjustable or nonadjustable, prefabricated, includes fitting and adjustment ♿

Y **E0486** Oral device/appliance used to reduce upper airway collapsibility, adjustable or nonadjustable, custom fabricated, includes fitting and adjustment ♿

N **E0487** Spirometer, electronic, includes all accessories

IPPB MACHINES

IPPB unit in use

Battery pack and controls

Nebulizer

Nebulizer reservoir

Oxygen supply tube

Intermittent Positive Pressure Breathing (IPPB) devices

Y **E0500** IPPB machine, all types, with built-in nebulization; manual or automatic valves; internal or external power source ♿

HUMIDIFIERS/COMPRESSORS/NEBULIZERS

Y **E0550** Humidifier, durable for extensive supplemental humidification during IPPB treatments or oxygen delivery ♿

Y **E0555** Humidifier, durable, glass or autoclavable plastic bottle type, for use with regulator or flowmeter

Y **E0560** Humidifier, durable for supplemental humidification during IPPB treatment or oxygen delivery ♿
MED: 100-4,23,60.3

Y **E0561** Humidifier, nonheated, used with positive airway pressure device ♿
MED: 100-3,240.4; 100-4,36,50.14

Y **E0562** Humidifier, heated, used with positive airway pressure device ♿

Y **E0565** Compressor, air power source for equipment which is not self-contained or cylinder driven ♿

Y **E0570** Nebulizer, with compressor ♿

~~**E0571**~~ [Jan] ~~Aerosol compressor, battery powered, for use with small volume nebulizer~~

Y **E0572** Aerosol compressor, adjustable pressure, light duty for intermittent use ♿

Y **E0574** Ultrasonic/electronic aerosol generator with small volume nebulizer ♿

Y **E0575** Nebulizer, ultrasonic, large volume ♿

Y **E0580** Nebulizer, durable, glass or autoclavable plastic, bottle type, for use with regulator or flowmeter ♿
MED: 100-4,23,60.3

Y **E0585** Nebulizer, with compressor and heater ♿

PUMPS AND VAPORIZERS

Y **E0600** Respiratory suction pump, home model, portable or stationary, electric ♿

Y **E0601** Continuous airway pressure (CPAP) device ♿
MED: 100-3,240.4; 100-4,23,60.3

Y **E0602** Breast pump, manual, any type M ♀ ♿

N **E0603** Breast pump, electric (AC and/or DC), any type M ♀

A **E0604** Breast pump, hospital grade, electric (AC and/or DC), any type M ♀

Y **E0605** Vaporizer, room type ♿

Y **E0606** Postural drainage board ♿

MONITORING DEVICES

Y **E0607** Home blood glucose monitor ♿
Medicare covers home blood testing devices for diabetic patients when the devices are prescribed by the patients' physicians. Many commercial payers provide this coverage to non-insulin dependent diabetics as well.

Y **E0610** Pacemaker monitor, self-contained, (checks battery depletion, includes audible and visible check systems) ♿

Y **E0615** Pacemaker monitor, self-contained, checks battery depletion and other pacemaker components, includes digital/visible check systems ♿

N **E0616** Implantable cardiac event recorder with memory, activator, and programmer N1

Y **E0617** External defibrillator with integrated electrocardiogram analysis ♿

Y **E0618** Apnea monitor, without recording feature ♿

Y **E0619** Apnea monitor, with recording feature ♿

Y **E0620** Skin piercing device for collection of capillary blood, laser, each ♿

PATIENT LIFTS

Y **E0621** Sling or seat, patient lift, canvas or nylon ♿

E **E0625** Patient lift, bathroom or toilet, not otherwise classified

Y **E0627** Seat lift mechanism incorporated into a combination lift-chair mechanism ♿
MED: 100-4,20,100; 100-4,20,130.2; 100-4,20,130.3; 100-4,20,130.4; 100-4,20,130.5

Y **E0628** Separate seat lift mechanism for use with patient-owned furniture, electric ♿
MED: 100-4,20,100; 100-4,20,130.2; 100-4,20,130.3; 100-4,20,130.4; 100-4,20,130.5

Y **E0629** Separate seat lift mechanism for use with patient-owned furniture, nonelectric ♿
MED: 100-4,20,100; 100-4,20,130.2; 100-4,20,130.3; 100-4,20,130.4; 100-4,20,130.5

Y **E0630** Patient lift, hydraulic or mechanical, includes any seat, sling, strap(s), or pad(s) ♿

Y **E0635** Patient lift, electric, with seat or sling ♿

Y **E0636** Multipositional patient support system, with integrated lift, patient accessible controls ♿

▲ E **E0637** [Jan] Combination sit-to-stand frame/table system, any size including pediatric, with seat lift feature, with or without wheels

▲ E **E0638** [Jan] Standing frame/table system, one position (e.g., upright, supine or prone stander), any size including pediatric, with or without wheels

E **E0639** Patient lift, moveable from room to room with disassembly and reassembly, includes all components/accessories

E **E0640** Patient lift, fixed system, includes all components/accessories

▲ E **E0641** [Jan] Standing frame/table system, multi-position (e.g., 3-way stander), any size including pediatric, with or without wheels

▲ E **E0642** [Jan] Standing frame/table system, mobile (dynamic stander), any size including pediatric

COMPRESSION DEVICES

Y **E0650** Pneumatic compressor, nonsegmental home model ♿

Y **E0651** Pneumatic compressor, segmental home model without calibrated gradient pressure ♿

Y **E0652** Pneumatic compressor, segmental home model with calibrated gradient pressure ♿

Y **E0655** Nonsegmental pneumatic appliance for use with pneumatic compressor, half arm ♿

Y **E0656** Segmental pneumatic appliance for use with pneumatic compressor, trunk ♿

Y **E0657** Segmental pneumatic appliance for use with pneumatic compressor, chest ♿

Y **E0660** Nonsegmental pneumatic appliance for use with pneumatic compressor, full leg ♿

Y **E0665** Nonsegmental pneumatic appliance for use with pneumatic compressor, full arm ♿

[Jan] January Update

Special Coverage Instructions | Noncovered by Medicare | Carrier Discretion | ☑ Quantity Alert | ● New Code | ○ Recycled/Reinstated | ▲ Revised Code

Y **E0666** Nonsegmental pneumatic appliance for use with pneumatic compressor, half leg

Y **E0667** Segmental pneumatic appliance for use with pneumatic compressor, full leg

Y **E0668** Segmental pneumatic appliance for use with pneumatic compressor, full arm

Y **E0669** Segmental pneumatic appliance for use with pneumatic compressor, half leg

Y **E0671** Segmental gradient pressure pneumatic appliance, full leg

Y **E0672** Segmental gradient pressure pneumatic appliance, full arm

Y **E0673** Segmental gradient pressure pneumatic appliance, half leg

Y **E0675** Pneumatic compression device, high pressure, rapid inflation/deflation cycle, for arterial insufficiency (unilateral or bilateral system)

Y **E0676** Intermittent limb compression device (includes all accessories), not otherwise specified

ULTRAVIOLET LIGHT

▲ Y **E0691** Jan Ultraviolet light therapy system, includes bulbs/lamps, timer and eye protection; treatment area 2 sq ft or less

Y **E0692** Ultraviolet light therapy system panel, includes bulbs/lamps, timer and eye protection, 4 ft panel

Y **E0693** Ultraviolet light therapy system panel, includes bulbs/lamps, timer and eye protection, 6 ft panel

Y **E0694** Ultraviolet multidirectional light therapy system in 6 ft cabinet, includes bulbs/lamps, timer, and eye protection

SAFETY EQUIPMENT

Fabric wrist restraint

Padded leather restraints may feature a locking device

Restraints (E0710)

Fabric gait belt for assistance in walking (E0700)

Body restraint

E **E0700** Safety equipment, device or accessory, any type

B ☑ **E0705** Transfer device, any type, each

E **E0710** Restraints, any type (body, chest, wrist, or ankle)

NERVE STIMULATORS AND DEVICES

Y **E0720** Transcutaneous electrical nerve stimulation (TENS) device, 2 lead, localized stimulation

While TENS is covered when employed to control chronic pain, it is not covered for experimental treatment, as in motor function disorders like MS. Prior authorization is required by Medicare for this item.

MED: 100-3,160.13

Y **E0730** Transcutaneous electrical nerve stimulation (TENS) device, 4 or more leads, for multiple nerve stimulation

While TENS is covered when employed to control chronic pain, it is not covered for experimental treatment, as in motor function disorders like MS. Prior authorization is required by Medicare for this item.

MED: 100-3,160.13

Y **E0731** Form-fitting conductive garment for delivery of TENS or NMES (with conductive fibers separated from the patient's skin by layers of fabric)

MED: 100-3,160.13

Y **E0740** Incontinence treatment system, pelvic floor stimulator, monitor, sensor, and/or trainer

Y **E0744** Neuromuscular stimulator for scoliosis

Y **E0745** Neuromuscular stimulator, electronic shock unit

N **E0746** Electromyography (EMG), biofeedback device

Biofeedback therapy is covered by Medicare only for re-education of specific muscles or for treatment of incapacitating muscle spasm or weakness.

Y **E0747** Osteogenesis stimulator, electrical, noninvasive, other than spinal applications

Medicare covers noninvasive osteogenic stimulation for nonunion of long bone fractures, failed fusion, or congenital pseudoarthroses.

Y **E0748** Osteogenesis stimulator, electrical, noninvasive, spinal applications

Medicare covers noninvasive osteogenic stimulation as an adjunct to spinal fusion surgery for patients at high risk of pseudoarthroses due to previously failed spinal fusion, or for those undergoing fusion of three or more vertebrae.

N **E0749** Osteogenesis stimulator, electrical, surgically implanted

Medicare covers invasive osteogenic stimulation for nonunion of long bone fractures or as an adjunct to spinal fusion surgery for patients at high risk of pseudoarthroses due to previously failed spinal fusion, or for those undergoing fusion of three or more vertebrae.

MED: 100-4,4,190

E **E0755** Electronic salivary reflex stimulator (intraoral/noninvasive)

Y **E0760** Osteogenesis stimulator, low intensity ultrasound, noninvasive

MED: 100-4,32,110.5

E **E0761** Nonthermal pulsed high frequency radiowaves, high peak power electromagnetic energy treatment device

B **E0762** Transcutaneous electrical joint stimulation device system, includes all accessories

Y **E0764** Functional neuromuscular stimulation, transcutaneous stimulation of sequential muscle groups of ambulation with computer control, used for walking by spinal cord injured, entire system, after completion of training program

Y **E0765** FDA approved nerve stimulator, with replaceable batteries, for treatment of nausea and vomiting

B **E0769** Electrical stimulation or electromagnetic wound treatment device, not otherwise classified

MED: 100-4,32,11.1

Y **E0770** Functional electrical stimulator, transcutaneous stimulation of nerve and/or muscle groups, any type, complete system, not otherwise specified

Jan January Update

INFUSION SUPPLIES

Y E0776 IV pole ♿
MED: 100-4,23,60.3

Y E0779 Ambulatory infusion pump, mechanical, reusable, for infusion 8 hours or greater ♿

Y E0780 Ambulatory infusion pump, mechanical, reusable, for infusion less than 8 hours ♿

Y E0781 Ambulatory infusion pump, single or multiple channels, electric or battery operated, with administrative equipment, worn by patient ♿

N E0782 Infusion pump, implantable, nonprogrammable (includes all components, e.g., pump, catheter, connectors, etc.) N1
MED: 100-4,4,190

N E0783 Infusion pump system, implantable, programmable (includes all components, e.g., pump, catheter, connectors, etc.) N1
MED: 100-4,4,190

Y E0784 External ambulatory infusion pump, insulin ♿
Covered by some commercial payers with preauthorization.

N E0785 Implantable intraspinal (epidural/intrathecal) catheter used with implantable infusion pump, replacement N1 ♿
MED: 100-4,4,190

N E0786 Implantable programmable infusion pump, replacement (excludes implantable intraspinal catheter) N1

Y E0791 Parenteral infusion pump, stationary, single, or multichannel ♿

TRACTION EQUIPMENT

N E0830 Ambulatory traction device, all types, each

Y E0840 Traction frame, attached to headboard, cervical traction ♿

Y E0849 Traction equipment, cervical, free-standing stand/frame, pneumatic, applying traction force to other than mandible ♿

Y E0850 Traction stand, freestanding, cervical traction ♿

Y E0855 Cervical traction equipment not requiring additional stand or frame ♿

Y E0856 Cervical traction device, cervical collar with inflatable air bladder ♿

Y E0860 Traction equipment, overdoor, cervical ♿

Y E0870 Traction frame, attached to footboard, extremity traction (e.g., Buck's) ♿

Y E0880 Traction stand, freestanding, extremity traction (e.g., Buck's) ♿

Y E0890 Traction frame, attached to footboard, pelvic traction ♿

Y E0900 Traction stand, freestanding, pelvic traction (e.g., Buck's) ♿

ORTHOPEDIC DEVICES

Y E0910 Trapeze bars, also known as Patient Helper, attached to bed, with grab bar ♿
MED: 100-4,23,60.3

Y E0911 Trapeze bar, heavy-duty, for patient weight capacity greater than 250 pounds, attached to bed, with grab bar ♿

Y E0912 Trapeze bar, heavy-duty, for patient weight capacity greater than 250 pounds, freestanding, complete with grab bar ♿

Y E0920 Fracture frame, attached to bed, includes weights ♿

Y E0930 Fracture frame, freestanding, includes weights ♿

Y E0935 Continuous passive motion exercise device for use on knee only ♿

E E0936 Continuous passive motion exercise device for use other than knee

Y E0940 Trapeze bar, freestanding, complete with grab bar ♿
MED: 100-4,23,60.3

Y E0941 Gravity assisted traction device, any type ♿

Y E0942 Cervical head harness/halter ♿

Y E0944 Pelvic belt/harness/boot ♿

Y E0945 Extremity belt/harness ♿

Y E0946 Fracture, frame, dual with cross bars, attached to bed, (e.g., Balken, 4 Poster) ♿

Y E0947 Fracture frame, attachments for complex pelvic traction ♿

Y E0948 Fracture frame, attachments for complex cervical traction ♿

WHEELCHAIR ACCESSORIES

Y ☑ E0950 Wheelchair accessory, tray, each ♿
MED: 100-4,23,60.3

Y ☑ E0951 Heel loop/holder, any type, with or without ankle strap, each ♿

Y ☑ E0952 Toe loop/holder, any type, each ♿

Y ☑ E0955 Wheelchair accessory, headrest, cushioned, any type, including fixed mounting hardware, each ♿

Y ☑ E0956 Wheelchair accessory, lateral trunk or hip support, any type, including fixed mounting hardware, each ♿

Y ☑ E0957 Wheelchair accessory, medial thigh support, any type, including fixed mounting hardware, each ♿

Y ☑ E0958 Manual wheelchair accessory, one-arm drive attachment, each ♿

B ☑ E0959 Manual wheelchair accessory, adapter for amputee, each ♿

Y E0960 Wheelchair accessory, shoulder harness/straps or chest strap, including any type mounting hardware ♿
MED: 100-4,23,60.3

B ☑ E0961 Manual wheelchair accessory, wheel lock brake extension (handle), each ♿

B ☑ E0966 Manual wheelchair accessory, headrest extension, each ♿

Y ☑ E0967 Manual wheelchair accessory, hand rim with projections, any type, each ♿

Y E0968 Commode seat, wheelchair ♿

Y E0969 Narrowing device, wheelchair ♿

E E0970 No. 2 footplates, except for elevating legrest
See code(s): K0037, K0042

B ☑ E0971 Manual wheelchair accessory, antitipping device, each ♿

B ☑ E0973 Wheelchair accessory, adjustable height, detachable armrest, complete assembly, each
MED: 100-4,23,60.3

B ☑ E0974 Manual wheelchair accessory, antirollback device, each

B ☑ E0978 Wheelchair accessory, positioning belt/safety belt/pelvic strap, each
MED: 100-4,23,60.3

Y E0980 Safety vest, wheelchair

Y ☑ E0981 Wheelchair accessory, seat upholstery, replacement only, each
MED: 100-4,23,60.3

Y ☑ E0982 Wheelchair accessory, back upholstery, replacement only, each

Y E0983 Manual wheelchair accessory, power add-on to convert manual wheelchair to motorized wheelchair, joystick control

Y E0984 Manual wheelchair accessory, power add-on to convert manual wheelchair to motorized wheelchair, tiller control

Y E0985 Wheelchair accessory, seat lift mechanism

Y ☑ E0986 Manual wheelchair accessory, push activated power assist, each

● Y ☑ E0988 Jan Manual wheelchair accessory, lever-activated, wheel drive, pair

B ☑ E0990 Wheelchair accessory, elevating legrest, complete assembly, each
MED: 100-4,23,60.3

B E0992 Manual wheelchair accessory, solid seat insert

Y ☑ E0994 Armrest, each

B ☑ E0995 Wheelchair accessory, calf rest/pad, each
MED: 100-4,23,60.3

Y E1002 Wheelchair accessory, power seating system, tilt only
MED: 100-4,23,60.3

Y E1003 Wheelchair accessory, power seating system, recline only, without shear reduction

Y E1004 Wheelchair accessory, power seating system, recline only, with mechanical shear reduction

Y E1005 Wheelchair accessory, power seating system, recline only, with power shear reduction

Y E1006 Wheelchair accessory, power seating system, combination tilt and recline, without shear reduction

Y E1007 Wheelchair accessory, power seating system, combination tilt and recline, with mechanical shear reduction

Y E1008 Wheelchair accessory, power seating system, combination tilt and recline, with power shear reduction

Y ☑ E1009 Wheelchair accessory, addition to power seating system, mechanically linked leg elevation system, including pushrod and legrest, each

Y ☑ E1010 Wheelchair accessory, addition to power seating system, power leg elevation system, including legrest, pair

Y E1011 Modification to pediatric size wheelchair, width adjustment package (not to be dispensed with initial chair)

Y E1014 Reclining back, addition to pediatric size wheelchair

Y ☑ E1015 Shock absorber for manual wheelchair, each

Y ☑ E1016 Shock absorber for power wheelchair, each
MED: 100-4,23,60.3

Y ☑ E1017 Heavy-duty shock absorber for heavy-duty or extra heavy-duty manual wheelchair, each

Y ☑ E1018 Heavy-duty shock absorber for heavy-duty or extra heavy-duty power wheelchair, each

Y E1020 Residual limb support system for wheelchair
MED: 100-4,23,60.3

Y E1028 Wheelchair accessory, manual swingaway, retractable or removable mounting hardware for joystick, other control interface or positioning accessory
MED: 100-4,23,60.3; 100-4,23,60.3

Y E1029 Wheelchair accessory, ventilator tray, fixed

Y E1030 Wheelchair accessory, ventilator tray, gimbaled

Y E1031 Rollabout chair, any and all types with castors 5 in or greater

Y E1035 Multi-positional patient transfer system, with integrated seat, operated by care giver, patient weight capacity up to and including 300 lbs
MED: 100-2,15,110

Y E1036 Multi-positional patient transfer system, extra-wide, with integrated seat, operated by caregiver, patient weight capacity greater than 300 lbs

Y E1037 Transport chair, pediatric size

Y E1038 Transport chair, adult size, patient weight capacity up to and including 300 pounds

Y E1039 Transport chair, adult size, heavy-duty, patient weight capacity greater than 300 pounds

WHEELCHAIRS

Y E1050 Fully-reclining wheelchair, fixed full-length arms, swing-away detachable elevating legrests

Y E1060 Fully-reclining wheelchair, detachable arms, desk or full-length, swing-away detachable elevating legrests

Y E1070 Fully-reclining wheelchair, detachable arms (desk or full-length) swing-away detachable footrest

Y E1083 Hemi-wheelchair, fixed full-length arms, swing-away detachable elevating legrest

Y E1084 Hemi-wheelchair, detachable arms desk or full-length arms, swing-away detachable elevating legrests

E E1085 Hemi-wheelchair, fixed full-length arms, swing-away detachable footrests
See code(s): K0002

E E1086 Hemi-wheelchair, detachable arms, desk or full-length, swing-away detachable footrests
See code(s): K0002

Y E1087 High strength lightweight wheelchair, fixed full-length arms, swing-away detachable elevating legrests

Y E1088 High strength lightweight wheelchair, detachable arms desk or full-length, swing-away detachable elevating legrests

E E1089 High-strength lightweight wheelchair, fixed-length arms, swing-away detachable footrest
See code(s): K0004

Jan January Update

Special Coverage Instructions | Noncovered by Medicare | Carrier Discretion | ☑ Quantity Alert | ● New Code | ○ Recycled/Reinstated | ▲ Revised Code

 A Age Edit | M Maternity Edit | ♀ Female Only | ♂ Male Only | A-Y OPPS Status Indicators

E E1090 High-strength lightweight wheelchair, detachable arms, desk or full-length, swing-away detachable footrests
See code(s): K0004

Y E1092 Wide heavy-duty wheel chair, detachable arms (desk or full-length), swing-away detachable elevating legrests

Y E1093 Wide heavy-duty wheelchair, detachable arms, desk or full-length arms, swing-away detachable footrests

Y E1100 Semi-reclining wheelchair, fixed full-length arms, swing-away detachable elevating legrests

Y E1110 Semi-reclining wheelchair, detachable arms (desk or full-length) elevating legrest

E E1130 Standard wheelchair, fixed full-length arms, fixed or swing-away detachable footrests
See code(s): K0001

E E1140 Wheelchair, detachable arms, desk or full-length, swing-away detachable footrests
See code(s): K0001

Y E1150 Wheelchair, detachable arms, desk or full-length swing-away detachable elevating legrests

Y E1160 Wheelchair, fixed full-length arms, swing-away detachable elevating legrests

Y E1161 Manual adult size wheelchair, includes tilt in space

Y E1170 Amputee wheelchair, fixed full-length arms, swing-away detachable elevating legrests

Y E1171 Amputee wheelchair, fixed full-length arms, without footrests or legrest

Y E1172 Amputee wheelchair, detachable arms (desk or full-length) without footrests or legrest

Y E1180 Amputee wheelchair, detachable arms (desk or full-length) swing-away detachable footrests

Y E1190 Amputee wheelchair, detachable arms (desk or full-length) swing-away detachable elevating legrests

Y E1195 Heavy-duty wheelchair, fixed full-length arms, swing-away detachable elevating legrests

Y E1200 Amputee wheelchair, fixed full-length arms, swing-away detachable footrest

Y E1220 Wheelchair; specially sized or constructed, (indicate brand name, model number, if any) and justification

Y E1221 Wheelchair with fixed arm, footrests

Y E1222 Wheelchair with fixed arm, elevating legrests

Y E1223 Wheelchair with detachable arms, footrests

Y E1224 Wheelchair with detachable arms, elevating legrests

Y ☑E1225 Wheelchair accessory, manual semi-reclining back, (recline greater than 15 degrees, but less than 80 degrees), each

B ☑E1226 Wheelchair accessory, manual fully reclining back, (recline greater than 80 degrees), each
See also K0028

Y E1227 Special height arms for wheelchair

Y E1228 Special back height for wheelchair

Y E1229 Wheelchair, pediatric size, not otherwise specified

Y E1230 Power operated vehicle (3- or 4-wheel nonhighway), specify brand name and model number
Prior authorization is required by Medicare for this item.

Y E1231 Wheelchair, pediatric size, tilt-in-space, rigid, adjustable, with seating system

Y E1232 Wheelchair, pediatric size, tilt-in-space, folding, adjustable, with seating system

Y E1233 Wheelchair, pediatric size, tilt-in-space, rigid, adjustable, without seating system

Y E1234 Wheelchair, pediatric size, tilt-in-space, folding, adjustable, without seating system

Y E1235 Wheelchair, pediatric size, rigid, adjustable, with seating system

Y E1236 Wheelchair, pediatric size, folding, adjustable, with seating system

Y E1237 Wheelchair, pediatric size, rigid, adjustable, without seating system

Y E1238 Wheelchair, pediatric size, folding, adjustable, without seating system

Y E1239 Power wheelchair, pediatric size, not otherwise specified

Y E1240 Lightweight wheelchair, detachable arms, (desk or full-length) swing-away detachable, elevating legrest

E E1250 Lightweight wheelchair, fixed full-length arms, swing-away detachable footrest
See code(s): K0003

E E1260 Lightweight wheelchair, detachable arms (desk or full-length) swing-away detachable footrest
See code(s): K0003

Y E1270 Lightweight wheelchair, fixed full-length arms, swing-away detachable elevating legrests

Y E1280 Heavy-duty wheelchair, detachable arms (desk or full-length) elevating legrests

E E1285 Heavy-duty wheelchair, fixed full-length arms, swing-away detachable footrest
See code(s): K0006

E E1290 Heavy-duty wheelchair, detachable arms (desk or full-length) swing-away detachable footrest
See code(s): K0006

Y E1295 Heavy-duty wheelchair, fixed full-length arms, elevating legrest

Y E1296 Special wheelchair seat height from floor

Y E1297 Special wheelchair seat depth, by upholstery

Y E1298 Special wheelchair seat depth and/or width, by construction

WHIRLPOOL - EQUIPMENT

E E1300 Whirlpool, portable (overtub type)

Y E1310 Whirlpool, nonportable (built-in type)

ADDITIONAL OXYGEN RELATED EQUIPMENT

Y E1353 Regulator
MED: 100-4,23,60.3

Y ☑E1354 Oxygen accessory, wheeled cart for portable cylinder or portable concentrator, any type, replacement only, each

Y E1355 Stand/rack
MED: 100-4,23,60.3

Y ☑E1356 Oxygen accessory, battery pack/cartridge for portable concentrator, any type, replacement only, each

Y ☑E1357 Oxygen accessory, battery charger for portable concentrator, any type, replacement only, each

Y ☑E1358 Oxygen accessory, DC power adapter for portable concentrator, any type, replacement only, each

Y E1372 Immersion external heater for nebulizer

Y E1390 Oxygen concentrator, single delivery port, capable of delivering 85 percent or greater oxygen concentration at the prescribed flow rate

Y ☑E1391 Oxygen concentrator, dual delivery port, capable of delivering 85 percent or greater oxygen concentration at the prescribed flow rate, each

Y E1392 Portable oxygen concentrator, rental

Y E1399 Durable medical equipment, miscellaneous
MED: 100-4,32,110.5

Y E1405 Oxygen and water vapor enriching system with heated delivery
MED: 100-4,20,20; 100-4,20,20.4

Y E1406 Oxygen and water vapor enriching system without heated delivery
MED: 100-4,20,20; 100-4,20,20.4

ARTIFICIAL KIDNEY MACHINES AND ACCESSORIES

A E1500 Centrifuge, for dialysis

A E1510 Kidney, dialysate delivery system kidney machine, pump recirculating, air removal system, flowrate meter, power off, heater and temperature control with alarm, IV poles, pressure gauge, concentrate container

A E1520 Heparin infusion pump for hemodialysis

A ☑E1530 Air bubble detector for hemodialysis, each, replacement

A ☑E1540 Pressure alarm for hemodialysis, each, replacement

A ☑E1550 Bath conductivity meter for hemodialysis, each

A ☑E1560 Blood leak detector for hemodialysis, each, replacement

A E1570 Adjustable chair, for ESRD patients

A ☑E1575 Transducer protectors/fluid barriers, for hemodialysis, any size, per 10

A E1580 Unipuncture control system for hemodialysis

A E1590 Hemodialysis machine

A E1592 Automatic intermittent peritoneal dialysis system

A E1594 Cycler dialysis machine for peritoneal dialysis

A E1600 Delivery and/or installation charges for hemodialysis equipment

A E1610 Reverse osmosis water purification system, for hemodialysis

A E1615 Deionizer water purification system, for hemodialysis

A E1620 Blood pump for hemodialysis, replacement

A E1625 Water softening system, for hemodialysis

A E1630 Reciprocating peritoneal dialysis system

A ☑E1632 Wearable artificial kidney, each

B ☑E1634 Peritoneal dialysis clamps, each

A E1635 Compact (portable) travel hemodialyzer system

A ☑E1636 Sorbent cartridges, for hemodialysis, per 10

A ☑E1637 Hemostats, each

A ☑E1639 Scale, each

A E1699 Dialysis equipment, not otherwise specified

JAW MOTION REHABILITATION SYSTEM AND ACCESSORIES

Y E1700 Jaw motion rehabilitation system
Medicare jurisdiction: local contractor.

Y ☑E1701 Replacement cushions for jaw motion rehabilitation system, package of 6
Medicare jurisdiction: local contractor.

Y ☑E1702 Replacement measuring scales for jaw motion rehabilitation system, package of 200
Medicare jurisdiction: local contractor.

FEXION/EXTENSION DEVICE

Y E1800 Dynamic adjustable elbow extension/flexion device, includes soft interface material

Y E1801 Static progressive stretch elbow device, extension and/or flexion, with or without range of motion adjustment, includes all components and accessories

Y E1802 Dynamic adjustable forearm pronation/supination device, includes soft interface material

Y E1805 Dynamic adjustable wrist extension/flexion device, includes soft interface material

Y E1806 Static progressive stretch wrist device, flexion and/or extension, with or without range of motion adjustment, includes all components and accessories

Y E1810 Dynamic adjustable knee extension/flexion device, includes soft interface material

Y E1811 Static progressive stretch knee device, extension and/or flexion, with or without range of motion adjustment, includes all components and accessories

Y E1812 Dynamic knee, extension/flexion device with active resistance control

Y E1815 Dynamic adjustable ankle extension/flexion device, includes soft interface material

Y E1816 Static progressive stretch ankle device, flexion and/or extension, with or without range of motion adjustment, includes all components and accessories

Y E1818 Static progressive stretch forearm pronation/supination device, with or without range of motion adjustment, includes all components and accessories

Y E1820 Replacement soft interface material, dynamic adjustable extension/flexion device

Y E1821 Replacement soft interface material/cuffs for bi-directional static progressive stretch device

Y E1825 Dynamic adjustable finger extension/flexion device, includes soft interface material

Y E1830 Dynamic adjustable toe extension/flexion device, includes soft interface material

Y E1831 Static progressive stretch toe device, extension and/or flexion, with or without range of motion adjustment, includes all components and accessories

Y E1840 Dynamic adjustable shoulder flexion/abduction/rotation device, includes soft interface material

Y E1841 Static progressive stretch shoulder device, with or without range of motion adjustment, includes all components and accessories

OTHER DEVICES

Y	E1902	Communication board, nonelectronic augmentative or alternative communication device
Y	E2000	Gastric suction pump, home model, portable or stationary, electric ♿
Y	E2100	Blood glucose monitor with integrated voice synthesizer ♿
Y	E2101	Blood glucose monitor with integrated lancing/blood sample ♿
Y	E2120	Pulse generator system for tympanic treatment of inner ear endolymphatic fluid ♿

DME WHEELCHAIR ACCESSORY

Y	☑ E2201	Manual wheelchair accessory, nonstandard seat frame, width greater than or equal to 20 in and less than 24 in ♿
Y	☑ E2202	Manual wheelchair accessory, nonstandard seat frame width, 24-27 in ♿
Y	☑ E2203	Manual wheelchair accessory, nonstandard seat frame depth, 20 to less than 22 in ♿
Y	☑ E2204	Manual wheelchair accessory, nonstandard seat frame depth, 22 to 25 in ♿
Y	☑ E2205	Manual wheelchair accessory, handrim without projections (includes ergonomic or contoured), any type, replacement only, each ♿
Y	☑ E2206	Manual wheelchair accessory, wheel Lock assembly, complete, each ♿
Y	☑ E2207	Wheelchair accessory, crutch and cane holder, each ♿
Y	☑ E2208	Wheelchair accessory, cylinder tank carrier, each ♿ MED: 100-4,23,60.3
Y	☑ E2209	Accessory, arm trough, with or without hand support, each ♿
Y	☑ E2210	Wheelchair accessory, bearings, any type, replacement only, each ♿
Y	☑ E2211	Manual wheelchair accessory, pneumatic propulsion tire, any size, each ♿
Y	☑ E2212	Manual wheelchair accessory, tube for pneumatic propulsion tire, any size, each ♿
Y	☑ E2213	Manual wheelchair accessory, insert for pneumatic propulsion tire (removable), any type, any size, each ♿
Y	☑ E2214	Manual wheelchair accessory, pneumatic caster tire, any size, each ♿
Y	☑ E2215	Manual wheelchair accessory, tube for pneumatic caster tire, any size, each ♿
Y	☑ E2216	Manual wheelchair accessory, foam filled propulsion tire, any size, each ♿
Y	☑ E2217	Manual wheelchair accessory, foam filled caster tire, any size, each ♿
Y	☑ E2218	Manual wheelchair accessory, foam propulsion tire, any size, each ♿
Y	☑ E2219	Manual wheelchair accessory, foam caster tire, any size, each ♿
Y	☑ E2220	Manual wheelchair accessory, solid (rubber/plastic) propulsion tire, any size, each ♿
Y	☑ E2221	Manual wheelchair accessory, solid (rubber/plastic) caster tire (removable), any size, each ♿
Y	☑ E2222	Manual wheelchair accessory, solid (rubber/plastic) caster tire with integrated wheel, any size, each ♿
Y	☑ E2224	Manual wheelchair accessory, propulsion wheel excludes tire, any size, each ♿
Y	☑ E2225	Manual wheelchair accessory, caster wheel excludes tire, any size, replacement only, each ♿
Y	☑ E2226	Manual wheelchair accessory, caster fork, any size, replacement only, each ♿
Y	☑ E2227	Manual wheelchair accessory, gear reduction drive wheel, each ♿
Y	☑ E2228	Manual wheelchair accessory, wheel braking system and lock, complete, each ♿
E	E2230	Manual wheelchair accessory, manual standing system
Y	E2231	Manual wheelchair accessory, solid seat support base (replaces sling seat), includes any type mounting hardware ♿
Y	E2291	Back, planar, for pediatric size wheelchair including fixed attaching hardware
Y	E2292	Seat, planar, for pediatric size wheelchair including fixed attaching hardware
Y	E2293	Back, contoured, for pediatric size wheelchair including fixed attaching hardware
Y	E2294	Seat, contoured, for pediatric size wheelchair including fixed attaching hardware
Y	E2295	Manual wheelchair accessory, for pediatric size wheelchair, dynamic seating frame, allows coordinated movement of multiple positioning features
Y	E2300	Power wheelchair accessory, power seat elevation system
Y	E2301	Power wheelchair accessory, power standing system
Y	E2310	Power wheelchair accessory, electronic connection between wheelchair controller and one power seating system motor, including all related electronics, indicator feature, mechanical function selection switch, and fixed mounting hardware ♿ MED: 100-4,23,60.3
Y	E2311	Power wheelchair accessory, electronic connection between wheelchair controller and 2 or more power seating system motors, including all related electronics, indicator feature, mechanical function selection switch, and fixed mounting hardware ♿
Y	E2312	Power wheelchair accessory, hand or chin control interface, mini-proportional remote joystick, proportional, including fixed mounting hardware ♿
Y	☑ E2313	Power wheelchair accessory, harness for upgrade to expandable controller, including all fasteners, connectors and mounting hardware, each ♿
Y	E2321	Power wheelchair accessory, hand control interface, remote joystick, nonproportional, including all related electronics, mechanical stop switch, and fixed mounting hardware ♿ MED: 100-4,23,60.3
Y	E2322	Power wheelchair accessory, hand control interface, multiple mechanical switches, nonproportional, including all related electronics, mechanical stop switch, and fixed mounting hardware ♿
Y	E2323	Power wheelchair accessory, specialty joystick handle for hand control interface, prefabricated ♿
Y	E2324	Power wheelchair accessory, chin cup for chin control interface ♿

Y **E2325** Power wheelchair accessory, sip and puff interface, nonproportional, including all related electronics, mechanical stop switch, and manual swingaway mounting hardware

Y **E2326** Power wheelchair accessory, breath tube kit for sip and puff interface

Y **E2327** Power wheelchair accessory, head control interface, mechanical, proportional, including all related electronics, mechanical direction change switch, and fixed mounting hardware

Y **E2328** Power wheelchair accessory, head control or extremity control interface, electronic, proportional, including all related electronics and fixed mounting hardware

Y **E2329** Power wheelchair accessory, head control interface, contact switch mechanism, nonproportional, including all related electronics, mechanical stop switch, mechanical direction change switch, head array, and fixed mounting hardware

Y **E2330** Power wheelchair accessory, head control interface, proximity switch mechanism, nonproportional, including all related electronics, mechanical stop switch, mechanical direction change switch, head array, and fixed mounting hardware

Y **E2331** Power wheelchair accessory, attendant control, proportional, including all related electronics and fixed mounting hardware

Y ☑ **E2340** Power wheelchair accessory, nonstandard seat frame width, 20-23 in

Y ☑ **E2341** Power wheelchair accessory, nonstandard seat frame width, 24-27 in

Y ☑ **E2342** Power wheelchair accessory, nonstandard seat frame depth, 20 or 21 in

Y ☑ **E2343** Power wheelchair accessory, nonstandard seat frame depth, 22-25 in

Y **E2351** Power wheelchair accessory, electronic interface to operate speech generating device using power wheelchair control interface

MED: 100-4,23,60.3

● Y ☑ **E2358** Jan Power wheelchair accessory, group 34 nonsealed lead acid battery, each

● Y **E2359** Jan Power wheelchair accessory, group 34 sealed lead acid battery, each (e.g., gel cell, absorbed glass mat)

Y ☑ **E2360** Power wheelchair accessory, 22 NF nonsealed lead acid battery, each

Y ☑ **E2361** Power wheelchair accessory, 22 NF sealed lead acid battery, each (e.g., gel cell, absorbed glassmat)

MED: 100-4,23,60.3

Y ☑ **E2362** Power wheelchair accessory, group 24 nonsealed lead acid battery, each

Y ☑ **E2363** Power wheelchair accessory, group 24 sealed lead acid battery, each (e.g., gel cell, absorbed glassmat)

MED: 100-4,23,60.3

Y ☑ **E2364** Power wheelchair accessory, U-1 nonsealed lead acid battery, each

Y ☑ **E2365** Power wheelchair accessory, U-1 sealed lead acid battery, each (e.g., gel cell, absorbed glassmat)

MED: 100-4,23,60.3

Y ☑ **E2366** Power wheelchair accessory, battery charger, single mode, for use with only one battery type, sealed or nonsealed, each

Y ☑ **E2367** Power wheelchair accessory, battery charger, dual mode, for use with either battery type, sealed or nonsealed, each

Y **E2368** Power wheelchair component, motor, replacement only

Y **E2369** Power wheelchair component, gear box, replacement only

Y **E2370** Power wheelchair component, motor and gear box combination, replacement only

Y ☑ **E2371** Power wheelchair accessory, group 27 sealed lead acid battery, (e.g., gel cell, absorbed glassmat), each

Y ☑ **E2372** Power wheelchair accessory, group 27 nonsealed lead acid battery, each

Y **E2373** Power wheelchair accessory, hand or chin control interface, compact remote joystick, proportional, including fixed mounting hardware

MED: 100-4,23,60.3

Y **E2374** Power wheelchair accessory, hand or chin control interface, standard remote joystick (not including controller), proportional, including all related electronics and fixed mounting hardware, replacement only

Y **E2375** Power wheelchair accessory, nonexpandable controller, including all related electronics and mounting hardware, replacement only

Y **E2376** Power wheelchair accessory, expandable controller, including all related electronics and mounting hardware, replacement only

Y **E2377** Power wheelchair accessory, expandable controller, including all related electronics and mounting hardware, upgrade provided at initial issue

Y ☑ **E2381** Power wheelchair accessory, pneumatic drive wheel tire, any size, replacement only, each

Y ☑ **E2382** Power wheelchair accessory, tube for pneumatic drive wheel tire, any size, replacement only, each

Y ☑ **E2383** Power wheelchair accessory, insert for pneumatic drive wheel tire (removable), any type, any size, replacement only, each

Y ☑ **E2384** Power wheelchair accessory, pneumatic caster tire, any size, replacement only, each

Y ☑ **E2385** Power wheelchair accessory, tube for pneumatic caster tire, any size, replacement only, each

Y ☑ **E2386** Power wheelchair accessory, foam filled drive wheel tire, any size, replacement only, each

Y ☑ **E2387** Power wheelchair accessory, foam filled caster tire, any size, replacement only, each

Y ☑ **E2388** Power wheelchair accessory, foam drive wheel tire, any size, replacement only, each

Y ☑ **E2389** Power wheelchair accessory, foam caster tire, any size, replacement only, each

Y ☑ **E2390** Power wheelchair accessory, solid (rubber/plastic) drive wheel tire, any size, replacement only, each

Y ☑ **E2391** Power wheelchair accessory, solid (rubber/plastic) caster tire (removable), any size, replacement only, each

Y ☑ **E2392** Power wheelchair accessory, solid (rubber/plastic) caster tire with integrated wheel, any size, replacement only, each

Y ☑ **E2394** Power wheelchair accessory, drive wheel excludes tire, any size, replacement only, each

[Y] ☑ **E2395** Power wheelchair accessory, caster wheel excludes tire, any size, replacement only, each ♿

[Y] ☑ **E2396** Power wheelchair accessory, caster fork, any size, replacement only, each ♿

[Y] ☑ **E2397** Power wheelchair accessory, lithium-based battery, each ♿

WOUND THERAPY

[Y] **E2402** Negative pressure wound therapy electrical pump, stationary or portable ♿
MED: 100-4,23,60.3

SPEECH GENERATING DEVICE

[Y] ☑ **E2500** Speech generating device, digitized speech, using prerecorded messages, less than or equal to 8 minutes recording time ♿

[Y] ☑ **E2502** Speech generating device, digitized speech, using prerecorded messages, greater than 8 minutes but less than or equal to 20 minutes recording time ♿

[Y] ☑ **E2504** Speech generating device, digitized speech, using prerecorded messages, greater than 20 minutes but less than or equal to 40 minutes recording time ♿

[Y] ☑ **E2506** Speech generating device, digitized speech, using prerecorded messages, greater than 40 minutes recording time ♿

[Y] **E2508** Speech generating device, synthesized speech, requiring message formulation by spelling and access by physical contact with the device ♿

[Y] **E2510** Speech generating device, synthesized speech, permitting multiple methods of message formulation and multiple methods of device access ♿

[Y] **E2511** Speech generating software program, for personal computer or personal digital assistant ♿

[Y] **E2512** Accessory for speech generating device, mounting system ♿

[Y] **E2599** Accessory for speech generating device, not otherwise classified

WHEELCHAIR CUSHION

[Y] **E2601** General use wheelchair seat cushion, width less than 22 in, any depth ♿
MED: 100-4,23,60.3

[Y] **E2602** General use wheelchair seat cushion, width 22 in or greater, any depth ♿

[Y] **E2603** Skin protection wheelchair seat cushion, width less than 22 in, any depth ♿

[Y] **E2604** Skin protection wheelchair seat cushion, width 22 in or greater, any depth ♿

[Y] **E2605** Positioning wheelchair seat cushion, width less than 22 in, any depth ♿

[Y] **E2606** Positioning wheelchair seat cushion, width 22 in or greater, any depth ♿

[Y] **E2607** Skin protection and positioning wheelchair seat cushion, width less than 22 in, any depth ♿

[Y] **E2608** Skin protection and positioning wheelchair seat cushion, width 22 in or greater, any depth ♿

[Y] **E2609** Custom fabricated wheelchair seat cushion, any size

[B] **E2610** Wheelchair seat cushion, powered

[Y] **E2611** General use wheelchair back cushion, width less than 22 in, any height, including any type mounting hardware ♿
MED: 100-4,23,60.3

[Y] **E2612** General use wheelchair back cushion, width 22 in or greater, any height, including any type mounting hardware ♿

[Y] **E2613** Positioning wheelchair back cushion, posterior, width less than 22 in, any height, including any type mounting hardware ♿

[Y] **E2614** Positioning wheelchair back cushion, posterior, width 22 in or greater, any height, including any type mounting hardware ♿

[Y] **E2615** Positioning wheelchair back cushion, posterior-lateral, width less than 22 in, any height, including any type mounting hardware ♿

[Y] **E2616** Positioning wheelchair back cushion, posterior-lateral, width 22 in or greater, any height, including any type mounting hardware ♿

[Y] **E2617** Custom fabricated wheelchair back cushion, any size, including any type mounting hardware

[Y] ☑ **E2619** Replacement cover for wheelchair seat cushion or back cushion, each ♿
MED: 100-4,23,60.3

[Y] **E2620** Positioning wheelchair back cushion, planar back with lateral supports, width less than 22 in, any height, including any type mounting hardware ♿

[Y] **E2621** Positioning wheelchair back cushion, planar back with lateral supports, width 22 in or greater, any height, including any type mounting hardware ♿

[Y] **E2622** Skin protection wheelchair seat cushion, adjustable, width less than 22 in, any depth ♿

[Y] **E2623** Skin protection wheelchair seat cushion, adjustable, width 22 in or greater, any depth ♿

[Y] **E2624** Skin protection and positioning wheelchair seat cushion, adjustable, width less than 22 in, any depth ♿

[Y] **E2625** Skin protection and positioning wheelchair seat cushion, adjustable, width 22 in or greater, any depth ♿

WHEELCHAIR ARM SUPPORT

● [Y] **E2626** Jan Wheelchair accessory, shoulder elbow, mobile arm support attached to wheelchair, balanced, adjustable ♿

● [Y] **E2627** Jan Wheelchair accessory, shoulder elbow, mobile arm support attached to wheelchair, balanced, adjustable Rancho type ♿

● [Y] **E2628** Jan Wheelchair accessory, shoulder elbow, mobile arm support attached to wheelchair, balanced, reclining ♿

● [Y] **E2629** Jan Wheelchair accessory, shoulder elbow, mobile arm support attached to wheelchair, balanced, friction arm support (friction dampening to proximal and distal joints) ♿

● [Y] **E2630** Jan Wheelchair accessory, shoulder elbow, mobile arm support, monosuspension arm and hand support, overhead elbow forearm hand sling support, yoke type suspension support ♿

● [Y] **E2631** Jan Wheelchair accessory, addition to mobile arm support, elevating proximal arm ♿

● [Y] **E2632**[Jan] Wheelchair accessory, addition to mobile arm support, offset or lateral rocker arm with elastic balance control ♿

● [Y] **E2633**[Jan] Wheelchair accessory, addition to mobile arm support, supinator ♿

GAIT TRAINER

[E] **E8000** Gait trainer, pediatric size, posterior support, includes all accessories and components

[E] **E8001** Gait trainer, pediatric size, upright support, includes all accessories and components

[E] **E8002** Gait trainer, pediatric size, anterior support, includes all accessories and components

Jan January Update

PROCEDURES/PROFESSIONAL SERVICES (TEMPORARY) G0008-G9156

The G codes are used to identify professional health care procedures and services that would otherwise be coded in CPT but for which there are no CPT codes.

Please refer to your CPT book for possible alternate code(s).

IMMUNIZATION ADMINISTRATION

S **G0008** **Administration of influenza virus vaccine**

MED: 100-2,12,40.11; 100-2,12,40.11; 100-4,18,10.2.1; 100-4,18,10.2.2.1; 100-4,18,10.2.2.1; 100-4,18,10.2.5.2; 100-4,18,10.3.1.1; 100-4,18,10.4.1; 100-4,18,10.4.2; 100-4,18,10.4.3

S **G0009** **Administration of pneumococcal vaccine**

MED: 100-2,12,40.11; 100-4,18,10.2.2.1

S **G0010** **Administration of hepatitis B vaccine**

MED: 100-2,12,40.11; 100-4,18,10.2.2.1

SEMEN ANALYSIS

A **G0027** **Semen analysis; presence and/or motility of sperm excluding Huhner** ♂

SCREENING SERVICES

V **G0101** **Cervical or vaginal cancer screening; pelvic and clinical breast examination** ♀ ⃠ PQ

G0101 can be reported with an E/M code when a separately identifiable E/M service was provided.

AHA: 4Q,'02,8; 3Q,'01,6

N **G0102** **Prostate cancer screening; digital rectal examination** ♂ ⃠

A **G0103** **Prostate cancer screening; prostate specific antigen test (PSA)** ♂

S **G0104** **Colorectal cancer screening; flexible sigmoidoscopy** P3 ⃠

Medicare covers colorectal screening for cancer via flexible sigmoidoscopy once every four years for patients 50 years or older.

MED: 100-4,18,60.1; 100-4,18,60.2; 100-4,18,60.6

T **G0105** **Colorectal cancer screening; colonoscopy on individual at high risk** A2 ⃠ PQ

An individual with ulcerative enteritis or a history of a malignant neoplasm of the lower gastrointestinal tract is considered at high-risk for colorectal cancer, as defined by CMS.

MED: 100-4,18,60.1; 100-4,18,60.2; 100-4,18,60.6

AHA: 3Q,'01,6

S **G0106** **Colorectal cancer screening; alternative to G0104, screening sigmoidoscopy, barium enema** PQ

MED: 100-4,18,60.1; 100-4,18,60.2; 100-4,18,60.6

A ☑ **G0108** **Diabetes outpatient self-management training services, individual, per 30 minutes** ⃠ PQ

MED: 100-2,13,30; 100-2,15,270.2; 100-2,15,270.4.3; 100-2,15,300; 100-2,15,300.2; 100-2,15,300.3; 100-2,15,300.4; 100-4,4,300.6; 100-4,9,181; 100-4,12,190.3; 100-4,18,120.1

A ☑ **G0109** **Diabetes outpatient self-management training services, group session (2 or more), per 30 minutes** ⃠ PQ

MED: 100-2,13,30; 100-2,15,300.2; 100-4,4,300.6; 100-4,9,181

S **G0117** **Glaucoma screening for high risk patients furnished by an optometrist or ophthalmologist** ⃠

MED: 100-2,15,280.1

AHA: 1Q,'02,4; 3Q,'01,12

S **G0118** **Glaucoma screening for high risk patient furnished under the direct supervision of an optometrist or ophthalmologist** ⃠

MED: 100-2,15,280.1

AHA: 1Q,'02,4; 3Q,'01,12

S **G0120** **Colorectal cancer screening; alternative to G0105, screening colonoscopy, barium enema** PQ

MED: 100-4,18,60.1; 100-4,18,60.2; 100-4,18,60.6

T **G0121** **Colorectal cancer screening; colonoscopy on individual not meeting criteria for high risk** A2 ⃠

MED: 100-4,18,60.1; 100-4,18,60.2; 100-4,18,60.6

AHA: 1Q,'02,4; 3Q,'01,12

E **G0122** **Colorectal cancer screening; barium enema**

MED: 100-4,18,60.2; 100-4,18,60.6

A **G0123** **Screening cytopathology, cervical or vaginal (any reporting system), collected in preservative fluid, automated thin layer preparation, screening by cytotechnologist under physician supervision** ♀

See also P3000-P3001.

B **G0124** **Screening cytopathology, cervical or vaginal (any reporting system), collected in preservative fluid, automated thin layer preparation, requiring interpretation by physician** ♀ ⃠

See also P3000-P3001.

MISCELLANEOUS SERVICES

T **G0127** **Trimming of dystrophic nails, any number** P3 ⃠

MED: 100-2,15,290; 100-2,15,290

B ☑ **G0128** **Direct (face-to-face with patient) skilled nursing services of a registered nurse provided in a comprehensive outpatient rehabilitation facility, each 10 minutes beyond the first 5 minutes** ⃠

MED: 100-2,12,30.1; 100-2,12,40.8; 100-4,5,20.4; 100-4,5,100.3

P ☑ **G0129** **Occupational therapy services requiring the skills of a qualified occupational therapist, furnished as a component of a partial hospitalization treatment program, per session (45 minutes or more)**

X **G0130** **Single energy x-ray absorptiometry (SEXA) bone density study, one or more sites; appendicular skeleton (peripheral) (e.g., radius, wrist, heel)** Z3

B **G0141** **Screening cytopathology smears, cervical or vaginal, performed by automated system, with manual rescreening, requiring interpretation by physician** ♀ ⃠

A **G0143** **Screening cytopathology, cervical or vaginal (any reporting system), collected in preservative fluid, automated thin layer preparation, with manual screening and rescreening by cytotechnologist under physician supervision** ♀

A **G0144** **Screening cytopathology, cervical or vaginal (any reporting system), collected in preservative fluid, automated thin layer preparation, with screening by automated system, under physician supervision** ♀

A **G0145** **Screening cytopathology, cervical or vaginal (any reporting system), collected in preservative fluid, automated thin layer preparation, with screening by automated system and manual rescreening under physician supervision** ♀

A **G0147** **Screening cytopathology smears, cervical or vaginal, performed by automated system under physician supervision** ♀

A **G0148** Screening cytopathology smears, cervical or vaginal, performed by automated system with manual rescreening ♀

B ☑ **G0151** Services performed by a qualified physical therapist in the home health or hospice setting, each 15 minutes
MED: 100-4,11,30.3; 100-4,11,30.3

B ☑ **G0152** Services performed by a qualified occupational therapist in the home health or hospice setting, each 15 minutes

B ☑ **G0153** Services performed by a qualified speech-language pathologist in the home health or hospice setting, each 15 minutes

B ☑ **G0154** Direct skilled nursing services of a licensed nurse (LPN or RN) in the home health or hospice setting, each 15 minutes

B ☑ **G0155** Services of clinical social worker in home health or hospice settings, each 15 minutes

B ☑ **G0156** Services of home health/hospice aide in home health or hospice settings, each 15 minutes

B ☑ **G0157** Services performed by a qualified physical therapist assistant in the home health or hospice setting, each 15 minutes

B ☑ **G0158** Services performed by a qualified occupational therapist assistant in the home health or hospice setting, each 15 minutes

▲ B ☑ **G0159** Jan Services performed by a qualified physical therapist, in the home health setting, in the establishment or delivery of a safe and effective physical therapy maintenance program, each 15 minutes

▲ B ☑ **G0160** Jan Services performed by a qualified occupational therapist, in the home health setting, in the establishment or delivery of a safe and effective occupational therapy maintenance program, each 15 minutes

▲ B ☑ **G0161** Jan Services performed by a qualified speech-language pathologist, in the home health setting, in the establishment or delivery of a safe and effective speech-language pathology maintenance program, each 15 minutes

B ☑ **G0162** Skilled services by a registered nurse (RN) for management and evaluation of the plan of care; each 15 minutes (the patient's underlying condition or complication requires an RN to ensure that essential nonskilled care achieves its purpose in the home health or hospice setting)

B ☑ **G0163** Skilled services of a licensed nurse (LPN or RN) for the observation and assessment of the patient's condition, each 15 minutes (the change in the patient's condition requires skilled nursing personnel to identify and evaluate the patient's need for possible modification of treatment in the home health or hospice setting)

▲ B ☑ **G0164** Jan Skilled services of a licensed nurse (LPN or RN), in the training and/or education of a patient or family member, in the home health or hospice setting, each 15 minutes

T ☑ **G0166** External counterpulsation, per treatment session ⊘
MED: 100-4,32,130; 100-4,32,130.1

B **G0168** Wound closure utilizing tissue adhesive(s) only ⊘
AHA: 3Q,'01,13; 4Q,'01,12

S **G0173** Linear accelerator based stereotactic radiosurgery, complete course of therapy in one session Z2
MED: 100-4,4,200.3.4; 100-4,4,200.3.4

V **G0175** Scheduled interdisciplinary team conference (minimum of 3 exclusive of patient care nursing staff) with patient present

P **G0176** Activity therapy, such as music, dance, art or play therapies not for recreation, related to the care and treatment of patient's disabling mental health problems, per session (45 minutes or more)

N **G0177** Training and educational services related to the care and treatment of patient's disabling mental health problems per session (45 minutes or more)

M **G0179** Physician re-certification for Medicare-covered home health services under a home health plan of care (patient not present), including contacts with home health agency and review of reports of patient status required by physicians to affirm the initial implementation of the plan of care that meets patient's needs, per re-certification period ⊘
MED: 100-4,11,40.1.3.1; 100-4,12,180; 100-4,12,180.1

M **G0180** Physician certification for Medicare-covered home health services under a home health plan of care (patient not present), including contacts with home health agency and review of reports of patient status required by physicians to affirm the initial implementation of the plan of care that meets patient's needs, per certification period ⊘
MED: 100-4,11,40.1.3.1; 100-4,12,180; 100-4,12,180.1

M **G0181** Physician supervision of a patient receiving Medicare-covered services provided by a participating home health agency (patient not present) requiring complex and multidisciplinary care modalities involving regular physician development and/or revision of care plans, review of subsequent reports of patient status, review of laboratory and other studies, communication (including telephone calls) with other health care professionals involved in the patient's care, integration of new information into the medical treatment plan and/or adjustment of medical therapy, within a calendar month, 30 minutes or more ⊘
MED: 100-4,11,40.1.3.1; 100-4,12,180; 100-4,12,180.1

M **G0182** Physician supervision of a patient under a Medicare-approved hospice (patient not present) requiring complex and multidisciplinary care modalities involving regular physician development and/or revision of care plans, review of subsequent reports of patient status, review of laboratory and other studies, communication (including telephone calls) with other health care professionals involved in the patient's care, integration of new information into the medical treatment plan and/or adjustment of medical therapy, within a calendar month, 30 minutes or more ⊘
MED: 100-4,11,40.1.3.1; 100-4,12,180; 100-4,12,180.1

T **G0186** Destruction of localized lesion of choroid (for example, choroidal neovascularization); photocoagulation, feeder vessel technique (one or more sessions) R2 ⊘

A **G0202** Screening mammography, producing direct digital image, bilateral, all views ♀ P0
AHA: 1Q,'02,3

A **G0204** Diagnostic mammography, producing direct digital image, bilateral, all views
MED: 100-4,18,20.4
AHA: 1Q,'03,7

A **G0206** Diagnostic mammography, producing direct digital image, unilateral, all views
MED: 100-4,18,20.4
AHA: 1Q,'03,7

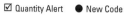

Jan January Update

E **G0219** PET imaging whole body; melanoma for noncovered indications

MED: 100-3,220.6.3; 100-3,220.6.4; 100-3,220.6.6; 100-3,220.6.7; 100-3,220.6.10; 100-3,220.6.11; 100-3,220.6.12; 100-3,220.6.17; 100-4,13,60; 100-4,13,60.15; 100-4,13,60.16

AHA: 1Q,'02,10

E **G0235** PET imaging, any site, not otherwise specified

MED: 100-3,220.6.2; 100-3,220.6.3; 100-3,220.6.4; 100-3,220.6.5; 100-3,220.6.6; 100-3,220.6.7; 100-3,220.6.9; 100-3,220.6.10; 100-3,220.6.11; 100-3,220.6.12; 100-3,220.6.13; 100-3,220.6.17; 100-4,13,60; 100-4,13,60.13; 100-4,13,60.14; 100-4,13,60.15; 100-4,13,60.16; 100-4,13,60.17

S ☑ **G0237** Therapeutic procedures to increase strength or endurance of respiratory muscles, face-to-face, one-on-one, each 15 minutes (includes monitoring) ⃠

MED: 100-2,12,30.1; 100-2,12,40.5

S ☑ **G0238** Therapeutic procedures to improve respiratory function, other than described by G0237, one-on-one, face-to-face, per 15 minutes (includes monitoring)

MED: 100-2,12,40.5

S **G0239** Therapeutic procedures to improve respiratory function or increase strength or endurance of respiratory muscles, 2 or more individuals (includes monitoring)

MED: 100-2,12,40.5

V **G0245** Initial physician evaluation and management of a diabetic patient with diabetic sensory neuropathy resulting in a loss of protective sensation (LOPS) which must include: (1) the diagnosis of LOPS, (2) a patient history, (3) a physical examination that consists of at least the following elements: (a) visual inspection of the forefoot, hindfoot, and toe web spaces, (b) evaluation of a protective sensation, (c) evaluation of foot structure and biomechanics, (d) evaluation of vascular status and skin integrity, and (e) evaluation and recommendation of footwear, and (4) patient education ⃠

MED: 100-4,32,80.2; 100-4,32,80.8

AHA: 4Q,'02,9

V **G0246** Follow-up physician evaluation and management of a diabetic patient with diabetic sensory neuropathy resulting in a loss of protective sensation (LOPS) to include at least the following: (1) a patient history, (2) a physical examination that includes: (a) visual inspection of the forefoot, hindfoot, and toe web spaces, (b) evaluation of protective sensation, (c) evaluation of foot structure and biomechanics, (d) evaluation of vascular status and skin integrity, and (e) evaluation and recommendation of footwear, and (3) patient education ⃠

MED: 100-4,32,80; 100-4,32,80.8

AHA: 4Q,'02,9

T **G0247** Routine foot care by a physician of a diabetic patient with diabetic sensory neuropathy resulting in a loss of protective sensation (LOPS) to include the local care of superficial wounds (i.e., superficial to muscle and fascia) and at least the following, if present: (1) local care of superficial wounds, (2) debridement of corns and calluses, and (3) trimming and debridement of nails P3 ⃠

MED: 100-4,32,80.8

AHA: 4Q,'02,9

V **G0248** Demonstration, prior to initiation of home INR monitoring, for patient with either mechanical heart valve(s), chronic atrial fibrillation, or venous thromboembolism who meets Medicare coverage criteria, under the direction of a physician; includes: face-to-face demonstration of use and care of the INR monitor, obtaining at least one blood sample, provision of instructions for reporting home INR test results, and documentation of patient's ability to perform testing and report results

MED: 100-3,190.11; 100-4,32,60.4.1; 100-4,32,60.5.2

AHA: 4Q,'02,9

V ☑ **G0249** Provision of test materials and equipment for home INR monitoring of patient with either mechanical heart valve(s), chronic atrial fibrillation, or venous thromboembolism who meets Medicare coverage criteria; includes: provision of materials for use in the home and reporting of test results to physician; testing not occurring more frequently than once a week; testing materials, billing units of service include 4 tests

AHA: 4Q,'02,9

M ☑ **G0250** Physician review, interpretation, and patient management of home INR testing for patient with either mechanical heart valve(s), chronic atrial fibrillation, or venous thromboembolism who meets Medicare coverage criteria; testing not occurring more frequently than once a week; billing units of service include 4 tests ⃠

AHA: 4Q,'02,9

S ☑ **G0251** Linear accelerator based stereotactic radiosurgery, delivery including collimator changes and custom plugging, fractionated treatment, all lesions, per session, maximum 5 sessions per course of treatment Z2

MED: 100-4,4,200.3.4; 100-4,4,200.3.4

E **G0252** PET imaging, full and partial-ring PET scanners only, for initial diagnosis of breast cancer and/or surgical planning for breast cancer (e.g., initial staging of axillary lymph nodes)

MED: 100-3,220.6.3; 100-3,220.6.10; 100-4,13,60; 100-4,13,60.15; 100-4,13,60.16

E **G0255** Current perception threshold/sensory nerve conduction test, (SNCT) per limb, any nerve

AHA: 4Q,'02,9

S **G0257** Unscheduled or emergency dialysis treatment for an ESRD patient in a hospital outpatient department that is not certified as an ESRD facility

AHA: 1Q,'03,9; 4Q,'02,9

N **G0259** Injection procedure for sacroiliac joint; arthrography N1

AHA: 4Q,'02,9

T **G0260** Injection procedure for sacroiliac joint; provision of anesthetic, steroid and/or other therapeutic agent, with or without arthrography A2

AHA: 4Q,'02,9

N **G0268** Removal of impacted cerumen (one or both ears) by physician on same date of service as audiologic function testing N1 ⃠

AHA: 1Q,'03,12

N **G0269** Placement of occlusive device into either a venous or arterial access site, postsurgical or interventional procedure (e.g., angioseal plug, vascular plug) N1

A ☑ **G0270** Medical nutrition therapy; reassessment and subsequent intervention(s) following second referral in same year for change in diagnosis, medical condition or treatment regimen (including additional hours needed for renal disease), individual, face-to-face with the patient, each 15 minutes

MED: 100-2,15,270; 100-2,15,270.2; 100-4,9,182; 100-4,12,190.3; 100-4,12,190.3; 100-4,12,190.7

A ☑ **G0271** Medical nutrition therapy, reassessment and subsequent intervention(s) following second referral in same year for change in diagnosis, medical condition, or treatment regimen (including additional hours needed for renal disease), group (2 or more individuals), each 30 minutes

MED: 100-4,9,182

N **G0275** Renal angiography, nonselective, one or both kidneys, performed at the same time as cardiac catheterization and/or coronary angiography, includes positioning or placement of any catheter in the abdominal aorta at or near the origins (ostia) of the renal arteries, injection of dye, flush aortogram, production of permanent images, and radiologic supervision and interpretation (List separately in addition to primary procedure)

N **G0278** Iliac and/or femoral artery angiography, nonselective, bilateral or ipsilateral to catheter insertion, performed at the same time as cardiac catheterization and/or coronary angiography, includes positioning or placement of the catheter in the distal aorta or ipsilateral femoral or iliac artery, injection of dye, production of permanent images, and radiologic supervision and interpretation (List separately in addition to primary procedure)

A **G0281** Electrical stimulation, (unattended), to one or more areas, for chronic Stage III and Stage IV pressure ulcers, arterial ulcers, diabetic ulcers, and venous stasis ulcers not demonstrating measurable signs of healing after 30 days of conventional care, as part of a therapy plan of care

MED: 100-4,32,11.1

AHA: 1Q,'03,7; 2Q,'03,7

E **G0282** Electrical stimulation, (unattended), to one or more areas, for wound care other than described in G0281

MED: 100-4,32,11.1

AHA: 1Q,'03,7; 2Q,'03,7

A **G0283** Electrical stimulation (unattended), to one or more areas for indication(s) other than wound care, as part of a therapy plan of care

AHA: 1Q,'03,7; 2Q,'03,7

N **G0288** Reconstruction, computed tomographic angiography of aorta for surgical planning for vascular surgery

N **G0289** Arthroscopy, knee, surgical, for removal of loose body, foreign body, debridement/shaving of articular cartilage (chondroplasty) at the time of other surgical knee arthroscopy in a different compartment of the same knee

T **G0290** Transcatheter placement of a drug eluting intracoronary stent(s), percutaneous, with or without other therapeutic intervention, any method; single vessel

AHA: 3Q,'03,11; 4Q,'03,7; 4Q,'02,9

T **G0291** Transcatheter placement of a drug eluting intracoronary stent(s), percutaneous, with or without other therapeutic intervention, any method; each additional vessel

AHA: 3Q,'03,11; 4Q,'03,7; 4Q,'02,9

X ☑ **G0293** Noncovered surgical procedure(s) using conscious sedation, regional, general, or spinal anesthesia in a Medicare qualifying clinical trial, per day

AHA: 4Q,'02,9

X ☑ **G0294** Noncovered procedure(s) using either no anesthesia or local anesthesia only, in a Medicare qualifying clinical trial, per day

AHA: 4Q,'02,9

E **G0295** Electromagnetic therapy, to one or more areas, for wound care other than described in G0329 or for other uses

AHA: 1Q,'03,7

S ☑ **G0302** Preoperative pulmonary surgery services for preparation for LVRS, complete course of services, to include a minimum of 16 days of services

S ☑ **G0303** Preoperative pulmonary surgery services for preparation for LVRS, 10 to 15 days of services

S ☑ **G0304** Preoperative pulmonary surgery services for preparation for LVRS, 1 to 9 days of services

S ☑ **G0305** Postdischarge pulmonary surgery services after LVRS, minimum of 6 days of services

A **G0306** Complete CBC, automated (HgB, HCT, RBC, WBC, without platelet count) and automated WBC differential count

A **G0307** Complete (CBC), automated (HgB, Hct, RBC, WBC; without platelet count)

A **G0328** Colorectal cancer screening; fecal occult blood test, immunoassay, 1-3 simultaneous determinations

MED: 100-4,16,70.8; 100-4,18,60.1; 100-4,18,60.2; 100-4,18,60.6

A **G0329** Electromagnetic therapy, to one or more areas for chronic Stage III and Stage IV pressure ulcers, arterial ulcers, diabetic ulcers and venous stasis ulcers not demonstrating measurable signs of healing after 30 days of conventional care as part of a therapy plan of care

MED: 100-4,32,11.2

M **G0333** Pharmacy dispensing fee for inhalation drug(s); initial 30-day supply as a beneficiary

B **G0337** Hospice evaluation and counseling services, preelection

MED: 100-4,11,10.1

S **G0339** Image guided robotic linear accelerator-based stereotactic radiosurgery, complete course of therapy in one session or first session of fractionated treatment

MED: 100-4,4,200.3.4; 100-4,4,200.3.4

S **G0340** Image guided robotic linear accelerator-based stereotactic radiosurgery, delivery including collimator changes and custom plugging, fractionated treatment, all lesions, per session, second through fifth sessions, maximum 5 sessions per course of treatment

MED: 100-4,4,200.3.4; 100-4,4,200.3.4

C **G0341** Percutaneous islet cell transplant, includes portal vein catheterization and infusion

MED: 100-4,32,70

C **G0342** Laparoscopy for islet cell transplant, includes portal vein catheterization and infusion

MED: 100-4,32,70

C **G0343** Laparotomy for islet cell transplant, includes portal vein catheterization and infusion

MED: 100-4,32,70

X **G0364** Bone marrow aspiration performed with bone marrow biopsy through the same incision on the same date of service P3 ⊘

S **G0365** Vessel mapping of vessels for hemodialysis access (services for preoperative vessel mapping prior to creation of hemodialysis access using an autogenous hemodialysis conduit, including arterial inflow and venous outflow) G2

M **G0372** Physician service required to establish and document the need for a power mobility device ⊘

OBSERVATION/EMERGENCY DEPARTMENT SERVICES

N **G0378** Hospital observation service, per hour

MED: 100-2,6,20.6; 100-4,4,290.1; 100-4,4,290.2.2; 100-4,4,290.4.1; 100-4,4,290.4.2; 100-4,4,290.4.3; 100-4,4,290.5.1; 100-4,4,290.5.2

Q3 **G0379** Direct admission of patient for hospital observation care

MED: 100-2,6,20.6; 100-4,4,290.4.1; 100-4,4,290.4.2; 100-4,4,290.4.3; 100-4,4,290.5.1; 100-4,4,290.5.2

V **G0380** Level 1 hospital emergency department visit provided in a type B emergency department; (the ED must meet at least one of the following requirements: (1) it is licensed by the state in which it is located under applicable state law as an emergency room or emergency department; (2) it is held out to the public (by name, posted signs, advertising, or other means) as a place that provides care for emergency medical conditions on an urgent basis without requiring a previously scheduled appointment; or (3) during the calendar year immediately preceding the calendar year in which a determination under 42 CFR 489.24 is being made, based on a representative sample of patient visits that occurred during that calendar year, it provides at least one-third of all of its outpatient visits for the treatment of emergency medical conditions on an urgent basis without requiring a previously scheduled appointment)

MED: 100-4,4,160

V **G0381** Level 2 hospital emergency department visit provided in a type B emergency department; (the ED must meet at least one of the following requirements: (1) it is licensed by the state in which it is located under applicable state law as an emergency room or emergency department; (2) it is held out to the public (by name, posted signs, advertising, or other means) as a place that provides care for emergency medical conditions on an urgent basis without requiring a previously scheduled appointment; or (3) during the calendar year immediately preceding the calendar year in which a determination under 42 CFR 489.24 is being made, based on a representative sample of patient visits that occurred during that calendar year, it provides at least one-third of all of its outpatient visits for the treatment of emergency medical conditions on an urgent basis without requiring a previously scheduled appointment)

MED: 100-4,4,160

V **G0382** Level 3 hospital emergency department visit provided in a type B emergency department; (the ED must meet at least one of the following requirements: (1) it is licensed by the state in which it is located under applicable state law as an emergency room or emergency department; (2) it is held out to the public (by name, posted signs, advertising, or other means) as a place that provides care for emergency medical conditions on an urgent basis without requiring a previously scheduled appointment; or (3) during the calendar year immediately preceding the calendar year in which a determination under 42 CFR 489.24 is being made, based on a representative sample of patient visits that occurred during that calendar year, it provides at least one-third of all of its outpatient visits for the treatment of emergency medical conditions on an urgent basis without requiring a previously scheduled appointment)

MED: 100-4,4,160

V **G0383** Level 4 hospital emergency department visit provided in a type B emergency department; (the ED must meet at least one of the following requirements: (1) it is licensed by the state in which it is located under applicable state law as an emergency room or emergency department; (2) it is held out to the public (by name, posted signs, advertising, or other means) as a place that provides care for emergency medical conditions on an urgent basis without requiring a previously scheduled appointment; or (3) during the calendar year immediately preceding the calendar year in which a determination under 42 CFR 489.24 is being made, based on a representative sample of patient visits that occurred during that calendar year, it provides at least one-third of all of its outpatient visits for the treatment of emergency medical conditions on an urgent basis without requiring a previously scheduled appointment)

MED: 100-4,4,160

Q3 **G0384** Level 5 hospital emergency department visit provided in a type B emergency department; (the ED must meet at least one of the following requirements: (1) it is licensed by the state in which it is located under applicable state law as an emergency room or emergency department; (2) it is held out to the public (by name, posted signs, advertising, or other means) as a place that provides care for emergency medical conditions on an urgent basis without requiring a previously scheduled appointment; or (3) during the calendar year immediately preceding the calendar year in which a determination under 42 CFR 489.24 is being made, based on a representative sample of patient visits that occurred during that calendar year, it provides at least one-third of all of its outpatient visits for the treatment of emergency medical conditions on an urgent basis without requiring a previously scheduled appointment)

MED: 100-4,4,160; 100-4,4,290.5.1

OTHER SERVICES

S **G0389** Ultrasound B-scan and/or real time with image documentation; for abdominal aortic aneurysm (AAA) screening

MED: 100-4,9,160

S **G0390** Trauma response team associated with hospital critical care service

MED: 100-4,4,160.1

ALCOHOL OR SUBSTANCE ABUSE

S ☑ **G0396** Alcohol and/or substance (other than tobacco) abuse structured assessment (e.g., AUDIT, DAST), and brief intervention 15 to 30 minutes ⊘

MED: 100-4,4,200.6

S ☑ **G0397** Alcohol and/or substance (other than tobacco) abuse structured assessment (e.g., AUDIT, DAST), and intervention, greater than 30 minutes ⊘

MED: 100-4,4,200.6

HOME SLEEP STUDY

S **G0398** Home sleep study test (HST) with type II portable monitor, unattended; minimum of 7 channels: EEG, EOG, EMG, ECG/heart rate, airflow, respiratory effort and oxygen saturation

MED: 100-3,240.4

S **G0399** Home sleep test (HST) with type III portable monitor, unattended; minimum of 4 channels: 2 respiratory movement/airflow, 1 ECG/heart rate and 1 oxygen saturation

S **G0400** Home sleep test (HST) with type IV portable monitor, unattended; minimum of 3 channels

INITIAL PHYSICAL EXAM

V **G0402** Initial preventive physical examination; face-to-face visit, services limited to new beneficiary during the first 12 months of Medicare enrollment ⊘

MED: 100-4,9,150; 100-4,12,80.1; 100-4,12,100.1.1; 100-4,18,80; 100-4,18,80.1; 100-4,18,80.2; 100-4,18,80.3.3; 100-4,18,80.3.3; 100-4,18,80.4

M **G0403** Electrocardiogram, routine ECG with 12 leads; performed as a screening for the initial preventive physical examination with interpretation and report

S **G0404** Electrocardiogram, routine ECG with 12 leads; tracing only, without interpretation and report, performed as a screening for the initial preventive physical examination

MED: 100-4,18,80.3.3

B **G0405** Electrocardiogram, routine ECG with 12 leads; interpretation and report only, performed as a screening for the initial preventive physical examination ⊘

FOLLOW-UP TELEHEALTH

▲ B **G0406** Jan Follow-up inpatient consultation, limited, physicians typically spend 15 minutes communicating with the patient via telehealth ⊘

MED: 100-2,15,270; 100-2,15,270.2; 100-4,12,190.3; 100-4,12,190.3; 100-4,12,190.3.1; 100-4,12,190.3.3

▲ B **G0407** Jan Follow-up inpatient consultation, intermediate, physicians typically spend 25 minutes communicating with the patient via telehealth ⊘

▲ B **G0408** Jan Follow-up inpatient consultation, complex, physicians typically spend 35 minutes communicating with the patient via telehealth ⊘

PSYCHOLOGICAL SERVICES

M ☑ **G0409** Social work and psychological services, directly relating to and/or furthering the patient's rehabilitation goals, each 15 minutes, face-to-face; individual (services provided by a CORF qualified social worker or psychologist in a CORF)

MED: 100-2,12,30.1

P **G0410** Group psychotherapy other than of a multiple-family group, in a partial hospitalization setting, approximately 45 to 50 minutes

P **G0411** Interactive group psychotherapy, in a partial hospitalization setting, approximately 45 to 50 minutes

FRACTURE CARE

C **G0412** Open treatment of iliac spine(s), tuberosity avulsion, or iliac wing fracture(s), unilateral or bilateral for pelvic bone fracture patterns which do not disrupt the pelvic ring, includes internal fixation, when performed CS ⊘

T **G0413** Percutaneous skeletal fixation of posterior pelvic bone fracture and/or dislocation, for fracture patterns which disrupt the pelvic ring, unilateral or bilateral, (includes ilium, sacroiliac joint and/or sacrum) ⊘

C **G0414** Open treatment of anterior pelvic bone fracture and/or dislocation for fracture patterns which disrupt the pelvic ring, unilateral or bilateral, includes internal fixation when performed (includes pubic symphysis and/or superior/inferior rami) CS ⊘

C **G0415** Open treatment of posterior pelvic bone fracture and/or dislocation, for fracture patterns which disrupt the pelvic ring, unilateral or bilateral, includes internal fixation, when performed (includes ilium, sacroiliac joint and/or sacrum) CS ⊘

SURGICAL PATHOLOGY

X **G0416** Surgical pathology, gross and microscopic examination for prostate needle saturation biopsy sampling, 1-20 specimens ♂

S **G0417** Surgical pathology, gross and microscopic examination for prostate needle saturation biopsy sampling, 21-40 specimens ♂

S **G0418** Surgical pathology, gross and microscopic examination for prostate needle saturation biopsy sampling, 41-60 specimens ♂

S **G0419** Surgical pathology, gross and microscopic examination for prostate needle saturation biopsy sampling, greater than 60 specimens ♂

EDUCATIONAL SERVICES

A ☑ **G0420** Face-to-face educational services related to the care of chronic kidney disease; individual, per session, per one hour ⊘

MED: 100-2,15,270.2; 100-2,15,310; 100-2,15,310.1; 100-2,15,310.2; 100-2,15,310.3; 100-2,15,310.4; 100-2,15,310.5; 100-2,32,20.2; 100-4,12,190.3

A ☑ **G0421** Face-to-face educational services related to the care of chronic kidney disease; group, per session, per one hour ⊘

CARDIAC AND PULMONARY REHABILITATION

S ☑ **G0422** Intensive cardiac rehabilitation; with or without continuous ECG monitoring with exercise, per session ⊘

MED: 100-2,15,232; 100-4,32,140.2.2.1; 100-4,32,140.3.1; 100-8,10,2.2.8

S ☑ **G0423** Intensive cardiac rehabilitation; with or without continuous ECG monitoring; without exercise, per session ⊘

MED: 100-4,32,140.3.1

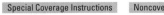

S ☑ **G0424** Pulmonary rehabilitation, including exercise (includes monitoring), one hour, per session, up to 2 sessions per day ⊘

MED: 100-2,15,231; 100-4,32,140.4; 100-4,32,140.4; 100-4,32,140.4.1; 100-4,32,140.4.1

INPATIENT TELEHEALTH

▲ B ☑ **G0425** Jan Telehealth consultation, emergency department or initial inpatient, typically 30 minutes communicating with the patient via telehealth ⊘

MED: 100-2,15,270; 100-2,15,270.2; 100-4,12,190.3; 100-4,12,190.3.1; 100-4,12,190.3.2

▲ B ☑ **G0426** Jan Telehealth consultation, emergency department or initial inpatient, typically 50 minutes communicating with the patient via telehealth ⊘

▲ B ☑ **G0427** Jan Telehealth consultation, emergency department or initial inpatient, typically 70 minutes or more communicating with the patient via telehealth ⊘

DEFECT FILLERS

E **G0428** Collagen meniscus implant procedure for filling meniscal defects (e.g., CMI, collagen scaffold, Menaflex)

MED: 100-3,150.12

B **G0429** Dermal filler injection(s) for the treatment of facial lipodystrophy syndrome (LDS) (e.g., as a result of highly active antiretroviral therapy)

MED: 100-3,250.5; 100-4,32,260.1; 100-4,32,260.2.1; 100-4,32,260.2.2; 100-4,32,260.2.2

LABORATORY SERVICES

A ☑ **G0431** Drug screen, qualitative; multiple drug classes by high complexity test method (e.g., immunoassay, enzyme assay), per patient encounter

A **G0432** Infectious agent antibody detection by enzyme immunoassay (EIA) technique, HIV-1 and/or HIV-2, screening

MED: 100-3,190.14; 100-3,210.7; 100-4,18,130; 100-4,18,130.1; 100-4,18,130.4

A **G0433** Infectious agent antibody detection by enzyme-linked immunosorbent assay (ELISA) technique, HIV-1 and/or HIV-2, screening

MED: 100-3,210.7; 100-4,18,130; 100-4,18,130.1; 100-4,18,130.4

A **G0434** Drug screen, other than chromatographic; any number of drug classes, by CLIA waived test or moderate complexity test, per patient encounter

▲ A **G0435** Jan Infectious agent antigen detection by rapid antibody test of oral mucosa transudate, HIV-1 or HIV-2, screening

MED: 100-3,210.7; 100-4,18,130; 100-4,18,130.1; 100-4,18,130.4

OTHER SERVICES

X ☑ **G0436** Smoking and tobacco cessation counseling visit for the asymptomatic patient; intermediate, greater than 3 minutes, up to 10 minutes

MED: 100-4,18,150.2; 100-4,18,150.4

▲ X ☑ **G0437** Jan Smoking and tobacco cessation counseling visit for the asymptomatic patient; intermediate, greater than 10 minutes

A **G0438** Annual wellness visit; includes a personalized prevention plan of service (pps), initial visit

MED: 100-2,15,280.5; 100-4,12,100.1.1; 100-4,18,140; 100-4,18,140.1; 100-4,18,140.5

A **G0439** Annual wellness visit, includes a personalized prevention plan of service (pps), subsequent visit

MED: 100-2,15,280.5; 100-4,18,140; 100-4,18,140.1; 100-4,18,140.5

~~G0440~~ Jan ~~Application of tissue cultured allogeneic skin substitute or dermal substitute; for use on lower limb, includes the site preparation and debridement if performed; first 25 sq cm or less~~

~~G0441~~ Jan ~~Application of tissue cultured allogeneic skin substitute or dermal substitute; for use on lower limb, includes the site preparation and debridement if performed; each additional 25 sq cm~~

● ☑ **G0442** Jan Annual alcohol misuse screening, 15 minutes

● ☑ **G0443** Jan Brief face-to-face behavioral counseling for alcohol misuse, 15 minutes

● ☑ **G0444** Jan Annual depression screening, 15 minutes

● ☑ **G0445** Jan High intensity behavioral counseling to prevent sexually transmitted infection; face-to-face, individual, includes: education, skills training and guidance on how to change sexual behavior; performed semi-annually, 30 minutes

● ☑ **G0446** Jan Intensive behavioral therapy to reduce cardiovascular disease risk, individual, face-to-face, bi-annual, 15 minutes

● ☑ **G0447** Jan Face-to-face behavioral counseling for obesity, 15 minutes

● B **G0448** Jan Insertion or replacement of a permanent pacing cardioverter-defibrillator system with transvenous lead(s), single or dual chamber with insertion of pacing electrode, cardiac venous system, for left ventricular pacing J8

● ☑ **G0449** Jan Annual face-to-face obesity screening, 15 minutes

● **G0450** Jan Screening for sexually transmitted infections, includes laboratory tests for chlamydia, gonorrhea, syphilis and hepatitis B

● S **G0451** Jan Development testing, with interpretation and report, per standardized instrument form

QUALITY MEASURES

● M **G0908** Jan Most recent hemoglobin (HgB) level > 12.0 g/dl

● M **G0909** Jan Hemoglobin level measurement not documented, reason not otherwise specified

● M **G0910** Jan Most recent hemoglobin level ≤ 12.0 g/dl

● M **G0911** Jan Assessed level of activity and symptoms

● M **G0912** Jan Level of activity and symptoms not assessed

● M **G0913** Jan Improvement in visual function achieved within 90 days following cataract surgery

● M **G0914** Jan Patient care survey was not completed by patient

● M **G0915** Jan Improvement in visual function not achieved within 90 days following cataract surgery

● M **G0916** Jan Satisfaction with care achieved within 90 days following cataract surgery

● M **G0917** Jan Patient satisfaction survey was not completed by patient

● M **G0918** Jan Satisfaction with care not achieved within 90 days following cataract surgery

● M **G0919** Jan Influenza immunization ordered or recommended (to be given at alternate location or alternate provider); vaccine not available at time of visit

● M **G0920** Jan Type, anatomic location, and activity all documented

Jan January Update

Special Coverage Instructions | Noncovered by Medicare | Carrier Discretion | ☑ Quantity Alert | ● New Code | ○ Recycled/Reinstated | ▲ Revised Code

● M **G0921** Jan Documentation of patient reason(s) for not being able to assess

● M **G0922** Jan No documentation of disease type, anatomic location, and activity, reason not otherwise specified

MEDICATION

S ☑ **G3001** Administration and supply of tositumomab, 450 mg ⊘

QUALITY MEASURES

M **G8126** Patient documented as being treated with antidepressant medication during the entire 12 week acute treatment phase A PQ

M **G8127** Patient not documented as being treated with antidepressant medication during the entire 12 weeks acute treatment phase A PQ

M **G8128** Clinician documented that patient was not an eligible candidate for antidepressant medication during the entire 12 week acute treatment phase measure A PQ

M **G8395** Left ventricular ejection fraction (LVEF) >= 40% or documentation as normal or mildly depressed left ventricular systolic function PQ

M **G8396** Left ventricular ejection fraction (LVEF) not performed or documented PQ

M **G8397** Dilated macular or fundus exam performed, including documentation of the presence or absence of macular edema and level of severity of retinopathy PQ

M **G8398** Dilated macular or fundus exam not performed PQ

M **G8399** Patient with central dual-energy x-ray absorptiometry (DXA) results documented or ordered or pharmacologic therapy (other than minerals/vitamins) for osteoporosis prescribed PQ

M **G8400** Patient with central dual-energy x-ray absorptiometry (DXA) results not documented or not ordered or pharmacologic therapy (other than minerals/vitamins) for osteoporosis not prescribed PQ

M **G8401** Clinician documented that patient was not an eligible candidate for screening or therapy for osteoporosis for women measure ♀ PQ

M **G8404** Lower extremity neurological exam performed and documented PQ

M **G8405** Lower extremity neurological exam not performed PQ

M **G8406** Clinician documented that patient was not an eligible candidate for lower extremity neurological exam measure PQ

M **G8410** Footwear evaluation performed and documented PQ

M **G8415** Footwear evaluation was not performed PQ

M **G8416** Clinician documented that patient was not an eligible candidate for footwear evaluation measure PQ

M **G8417** Calculated BMI above the upper parameter and a follow-up plan was documented in the medical record PQ

M **G8418** Calculated BMI below the lower parameter and a follow-up plan was documented in the medical record PQ

M **G8419** Calculated BMI outside normal parameters, no follow-up plan was documented in the medical record PQ

M **G8420** Calculated BMI within normal parameters and documented PQ

M **G8421** BMI not calculated PQ

M **G8422** Patient not eligible for BMI calculation PQ

M **G8427** List of current medications (includes prescription, over-the-counter, herbals, vitamin/mineral/dietary [nutritional] supplements) documented by the provider, including drug name, dosage, frequency and route PQ

M **G8428** Current medications (includes prescription, over-the-counter, herbals, vitamin/mineral/dietary [nutritional] supplements) with drug name, dosage, frequency and route not documented by the provider, reason not specified PQ

M **G8430** Provider documentation that patient is not eligible for medication assessment PQ

▲ M **G8431** Jan Positive screen for clinical depression using an age appropriate standardized tool and a follow-up plan documented PQ

▲ M **G8432** Jan No documentation of clinical depression screening using an age appropriate standardized tool PQ

▲ M **G8433** Jan Screening for clinical depression using an age appropriate standardized tool not documented, patient not eligible/appropriate PQ

~~G8440~~ Jan ~~Documentation of pain assessment (including location, intensity and description) prior to initiation of therapy or documentation of the absence of pain as a result of assessment through discussion with the patient including the use of a standardized tool and a follow-up plan is documented~~

To report, see G8493, G8502, G8509, G8730-G8732

~~G8441~~ Jan ~~No documentation of pain assessment (including location, intensity and description) prior to initiation of therapy~~

To report, see G8493, G8502, G8509, G8730-G8732

M **G8442** Documentation that patient is not eligible for pain assessment PQ

M **G8447** Patient encounter was documented using an EHR system that has been certified by an authorized testing and certification body (ATCB) PQ

M **G8448** Patient encounter was documented using a PQRI qualified EHR or other acceptable systems PQ

M **G8450** Beta-blocker therapy prescribed for patients with left ventricular ejection fraction (LVEF) < 40% or documentation as moderately or severely depressed left ventricular systolic function PQ

M **G8451** Clinician documented patient with left ventricular ejection fraction (LVEF) < 40% or documentation as moderately or severely depressed left ventricular systolic function was not eligible candidate for beta-blocker therapy PQ

M **G8452** Beta-blocker therapy not prescribed for patients with left ventricular ejection fraction (LVEF) < 40% or documentation as moderately or severely depressed left ventricular systolic function PQ

M **G8458** Clinician documented that patient is not an eligible candidate for genotype testing; patient not receiving antiviral treatment for hepatitis C PQ

M **G8459** Clinician documented that patient is receiving antiviral treatment for hepatitis C PQ

M **G8460** Clinician documented that patient is not an eligible candidate for quantitative RNA testing at week 12; patient not receiving antiviral treatment for hepatitis C PQ

M **G8461** Patient receiving antiviral treatment for hepatitis C PQ

M G8462 Clinician documented that patient is not an eligible candidate for counseling regarding contraception prior to antiviral treatment; patient not receiving antiviral treatment for hepatitis C PQ

M G8463 Patient receiving antiviral treatment for hepatitis C documented PQ

M G8464 Clinician documented that prostate cancer patient is not an eligible candidate for adjuvant hormonal therapy; low or intermediate risk of recurrence or risk of recurrence not determined PQ

M G8465 High risk of recurrence of prostate cancer PQ

M G8468 Angiotensin converting enzyme (ACE) inhibitor or angiotensin receptor blocker (ARB) therapy prescribed for patients with a left ventricular ejection fraction (LVEF) < 40% or documentation of moderately or severely depressed left ventricular systolic function PQ

M G8469 Clinician documented that patient with a left ventricular ejection fraction (LVEF) < 40% or documentation of moderately or severely depressed left ventricular systolic function was not an eligible candidate for angiotensin converting enzyme (ACE) inhibitor or angiotensin receptor blocker (ARB) therapy PQ

M G8470 Patient with left ventricular ejection fraction (LVEF) ≥ 40% or documentation as normal or mildly depressed left ventricular systolic function PQ

M G8471 Left ventricular ejection fraction (LVEF) was not performed or documented PQ

M G8472 Angiotensin converting enzyme (ACE) inhibitor or angiotensin receptor blocker (ARB) therapy not prescribed for patients with a left ventricular ejection fraction (LVEF) < 40% or documentation of moderately or severely depressed left ventricular systolic function, reason not specified PQ

M G8473 Angiotensin converting enzyme (ACE) inhibitor or angiotensin receptor blocker (ARB) therapy prescribed PQ

M G8474 Angiotensin converting enzyme (ACE) inhibitor or angiotensin receptor blocker (ARB) therapy not prescribed for reasons documented by the clinician PQ

M G8475 Angiotensin converting enzyme (ACE) inhibitor or angiotensin receptor blocker (ARB) therapy not prescribed, reason not specified PQ

M G8476 Most recent blood pressure has a systolic measurement of < 130 mm Hg and a diastolic measurement of < 80 mm Hg PQ

M G8477 Most recent blood pressure has a systolic measurement of >= 130 mm Hg and/or a diastolic measurement of >= 80 mm Hg PQ

M G8478 Blood pressure measurement not performed or documented, reason not specified PQ

▲ M G8482 Jan Influenza immunization administered or previously received PQ

M G8483 Influenza immunization was not ordered or administered for reasons documented by clinician PQ

M G8484 Influenza immunization was not ordered or administered, reason not specified PQ

M G8485 I intend to report the diabetes mellitus measures group

M G8486 I intend to report the preventive care measures group

M G8487 I intend to report the chronic kidney disease (CKD) measures group

M G8489 I intend to report the coronary artery disease (CAD) measures group

M G8490 I intend to report the rheumatoid arthritis measures group

M G8491 I intend to report the HIV/AIDS measures group

M G8492 I intend to report the perioperative care measures group

M G8493 I intend to report the back pain measures group

M G8494 All quality actions for the applicable measures in the diabetes mellitus measures group have been performed for this patient

M G8495 All quality actions for the applicable measures in the CKD measures group have been performed for this patient

M G8496 All quality actions for the applicable measures in the preventive care measures group have been performed for this patient

M G8497 All quality actions for the applicable measures in the coronary artery bypass graft (CABG) measures group have been performed for this patient

M G8498 All quality actions for the applicable measures in the coronary artery disease (CAD) measures group have been performed for this patient

M G8499 All quality actions for the applicable measures in the rheumatoid arthritis measures group have been performed for this patient

M G8500 All quality actions for the applicable measures in the HIV/AIDS measures group have been performed for this patient

M G8501 All quality actions for the applicable measures in the perioperative care measures group have been performed for this patient

M G8502 All quality actions for the applicable measures in the back pain measures group have been performed for this patient

M G8506 Patient receiving angiotensin converting enzyme (ACE) inhibitor or angiotensin receptor blocker (ARB) therapy PQ

~~G8508~~ Jan ~~Documentation of pain assessment (including location, intensity and description) prior to initiation of therapy or documentation of the absence of pain as a result of assessment through discussion with the patient including the use of a standardized tool; no documentation of a follow-up plan, patient not eligible~~

To report, see G8493, G8502, G8509, G8730-G8732

▲ M G8509 Jan Documentation of positive pain assessment; no documentation of a follow-up plan, reason not specified PQ

▲ M G8510 Jan Negative screen for clinical depression using an age appropriate standardized tool, follow-up not required PQ

▲ M G8511 Jan Positive screen for clinical depression using an age appropriate standardized tool documented, follow up plan not documented, reason not specified PQ

M G8524 Patch closure used for patient undergoing conventional CEA PQ

Jan January Update

M G8525 Clinician documented that patient did not receive conventional CEA PQ

M G8526 Patch closure not used for patient undergoing conventional CEA, reason not specified PQ

M G8530 Autogenous AV fistula received PQ

M G8531 Clinician documented that patient was not an eligible candidate for autogenous AV fistula PQ

M G8532 Clinician documented that patient received vascular access other than autogenous AV fistula, reason not specified PQ

~~G8534~~ Jan ~~Documentation of an elder maltreatment screen and follow-up plan~~
To report, see G8535-G8536, G8733-G8735

M G8535 No documentation of an elder maltreatment screen, patient not eligible PQ

M G8536 No documentation of an elder maltreatment screen, reason not specified PQ

~~G8537~~ Jan ~~Elder maltreatment screen documented, follow-up plan not documented, patient not eligible~~
To report, see G8535, G8733-G8735

~~G8538~~ Jan ~~Elder maltreatment screen documented, follow-up plan not documented, reason not specified~~
To report, see G8535, G8733-G8735

▲ M G8539 Jan Documentation of a current functional outcome assessment using a standardized tool and documentation of a care plan based on identified deficiencies PQ

M G8540 Documentation that the patient is not eligible for a functional outcome assessment using a standardized tool PQ

M G8541 No documentation of a current functional outcome assessment using a standardized tool, reason not specified PQ

▲ M G8542 Jan Documentation of a current functional outcome assessment using a standardized tool; no functional deficiencies identified, care plan not required PQ

M G8543 Documentation of a current functional outcome assessment using a standardized tool; no documentation of a care plan, reason not specified PQ

M G8544 I intend to report the coronary artery bypass graft (CABG) measures group

M G8545 I intend to report the hepatitis C measures group

M G8546 I intend to report the community-acquired pneumonia (CAP) measures group

M G8547 I intend to report the ischemic vascular disease (IVD) measures group

M G8548 I intend to report the heart failure (HF) measures group

M G8549 All quality actions for the applicable measures in the hepatitis C measures group have been performed for this patient

M G8550 All quality actions for the applicable measures in the community-acquired pneumonia (CAP) measures group have been performed for this patient

M G8551 All quality actions for the applicable measures in the heart failure (HF) measures group have been performed for this patient

M G8552 All quality actions for the applicable measures in the ischemic vascular disease (IVD) measures group have been performed for this patient

▲ M G8553 Jan Prescription(s) generated and transmitted via a qualified ERX system or a certified EHR system

M G8556 Referred to a physician (preferably a physician with training in disorders of the ear) for an otologic evaluation PQ

M G8557 Patient is not eligible for the referral for otologic evaluation measure PQ

M G8558 Not referred to a physician (preferably a physician with training in disorders of the ear) for an otologic evaluation, reason not specified PQ

M G8559 Patient referred to a physician (preferably a physician with training in disorders of the ear) for an otologic evaluation PQ

M G8560 Patient has a history of active drainage from the ear within the previous 90 days PQ

M G8561 Patient is not eligible for the referral for otologic evaluation for patients with a history of active drainage measure PQ

M G8562 Patient does not have a history of active drainage from the ear within the previous 90 days PQ

M G8563 Patient not referred to a physician (preferably a physician with training in disorders of the ear) for an otologic evaluation, reason not specified PQ

M G8564 Patient was referred to a physician (preferably a physician with training in disorders of the ear) for an otologic evaluation, reason not specified) PQ

M G8565 Verification and documentation of sudden or rapidly progressive hearing loss PQ

M G8566 Patient is not eligible for the "referral for otologic evaluation for sudden or rapidly progressive hearing loss" measure PQ

M G8567 Patient does not have verification and documentation of sudden or rapidly progressive hearing loss PQ

M G8568 Patient was not referred to a physician (preferably a physician with training in disorders of the ear) for an otologic evaluation, reason not specified) PQ

M G8569 Prolonged intubation (> 24 hrs) required PQ

M G8570 Prolonged intubation (> 24 hrs) not required PQ

M G8571 Development of deep sternal wound infection within 30 days postoperatively PQ

M G8572 No deep sternal wound infection PQ

▲ M G8573 Jan Stroke following isolated CABG surgery PQ

▲ M G8574 Jan No stroke following isolated CABG surgery PQ

▲ M G8575 Jan Developed postoperative renal failure or required dialysis PQ

▲ M G8576 Jan No postoperative renal failure/dialysis not required PQ

▲ M G8577 Jan Reexploration required due to mediastinal bleeding with or without tamponade, graft occlusion, valve dysfunction or other cardiac reason PQ

▲ M G8578 Jan Reexploration not required due to mediastinal bleeding with or without tamponade, graft occlusion, valve dysfunction or other cardiac reason PQ

M G8579 Antiplatelet medication at discharge PQ

▲ M G8580 Jan Antiplatelet medication contraindicated PQ

M G8581 No antiplatelet medication at discharge PQ

M G8582 Beta-blocker at discharge PQ

▲ M G8583[Jan] Beta blocker contraindicated PQ

M G8584 No beta-blocker at discharge PQ

M G8585 Antilipid treatment at discharge PQ

▲ M G8586[Jan] Antilipid treatment contraindicated PQ

M G8587 No antilipid treatment at discharge PQ

M G8588 Most recent systolic blood pressure < 140 mm Hg PQ

M G8589 Most recent systolic blood pressure ≥ 140 mm Hg PQ

M G8590 Most recent diastolic blood pressure < 90 mm Hg PQ

M G8591 Most recent diastolic blood pressure ≥ 90 mm Hg PQ

M G8592 No documentation of blood pressure measurement PQ

M G8593 Lipid profile results documented and reviewed (must include total cholesterol, HDL-C, triglycerides and calculated LDL-C) PQ

M G8594 Lipid profile not performed, reason not otherwise specified PQ

M G8595 Most recent LDL-C < 100 mg/dL PQ

M G8596 LDL-C was not performed PQ

M G8597 Most recent LDL-C ≥ 100 mg/dL PQ

M G8598 Aspirin or another antithrombotic therapy used PQ

M G8599 Aspirin or another antithrombotic therapy not used, reason not otherwise specified PQ

M G8600 IV tPA initiated within 3 hours (≤ 180 minutes) of time last known well PQ

M G8601 IV tPA not initiated within 3 hours (≤ 180 minutes) of time last known well for reasons documented by clinician PQ

M G8602 IV tPA not initiated within 3 hours (≤ 180 minutes) of time last known well, reason not specified PQ

M G8603 Score on the spoken language comprehension functional communication measure at discharge was higher than at admission PQ

M G8604 Score on the spoken language comprehension functional communication measure at discharge was not higher than at admission, reason not specified PQ

▲ M G8605[Jan] Patient treated for spoken language comprehension but not scored on the spoken language comprehension functional communication measure either at admission or at discharge PQ

M G8606 Score on the attention functional communication measure at discharge was higher than at admission PQ

M G8607 Score on the attention functional communication measure at discharge was not higher than at admission, reason not specified PQ

▲ M G8608[Jan] Patient treated for attention but not scored on the attention functional communication measure either at admission or at discharge PQ

M G8609 Score on the memory functional communication measure at discharge was higher than at admission PQ

M G8610 Score on the memory functional communication measure at discharge was not higher than at admission, reason not specified PQ

▲ M G8611[Jan] Patient treated for memory but not scored on the memory functional communication measure either at admission or at discharge PQ

M G8612 Score on the motor speech functional communication measure at discharge was higher than at admission PQ

M G8613 Score on the motor speech functional communication measure at discharge was not higher than at admission, reason not specified PQ

▲ M G8614[Jan] Patient treated for motor speech but not scored on the motor speech comprehension functional communication measure either at admission or at discharge PQ

M G8615 Score on the reading functional communication measure at discharge was higher than at admission PQ

M G8616 Score on the reading functional communication measure at discharge was not higher than at admission, reason not specified PQ

▲ M G8617[Jan] Patient treated for reading but not scored on the reading functional communication measure either at admission or at discharge PQ

M G8618 Score on the spoken language expression functional communication measure at discharge was higher than at admission PQ

M G8619 Score on the spoken language expression functional communication measure at discharge was not higher than at admission, reason not specified PQ

▲ M G8620[Jan] Patient treated for spoken language expression but not scored on the spoken language expression functional communication measure either at admission or at discharge PQ

M G8621 Score on the writing functional communication measure at discharge was higher than at admission PQ

M G8622 Score on the writing functional communication measure at discharge was not higher than at admission, reason not specified PQ

▲ M G8623[Jan] Patient treated for writing but not scored on the writing functional communication measure either at admission or at discharge PQ

M G8624 Score on the swallowing functional communication measure at discharge was higher than at admission PQ

M G8625 Score on the swallowing functional communication measure at discharge was not higher than at admission, reason not specified PQ

▲ M G8626[Jan] Patient treated for swallowing but not scored on the swallowing functional communication measure at admission or at discharge PQ

M G8627 Surgical procedure performed within 30 days following cataract surgery for major complications (e.g., retained nuclear fragments, endophthalmitis, dislocated or wrong power iol, retinal detachment, or wound dehiscence) PQ

M G8628 Surgical procedure not performed within 30 days following cataract surgery for major complications (e.g., retained nuclear fragments, endophthalmitis, dislocated or wrong power iol, retinal detachment, or wound dehiscence) PQ

M ☑ G8629 Documentation of order for prophylactic parenteral antibiotic to be given within one hour (if fluoroquinolone or vancomycin, 2 hours) prior to surgical incision (or start of procedure when no incision is required)

[Jan] January Update

M ☑ **G8630** Documentation that administration of prophylactic parenteral antibiotics was initiated within one hour (if fluoroquinolone or vancomycin, 2 hours) prior to surgical incision (or start of procedure when no incision is required), as ordered

M ☑ **G8631** Clinician documented that patient was not an eligible candidate for ordering prophylactic parenteral antibiotics to be given within one hour (if fluoroquinolone or vancomycin, 2 hours) prior to surgical incision (or start of procedure when no incision is required)

M ☑ **G8632** Prophylactic parenteral antibiotics were not ordered to be given or given within one hour (if fluoroquinolone or vancomycin, 2 hours) prior to the surgical incision (or start of procedure when no incision is required), reason not otherwise specified)

M **G8633** Pharmacologic therapy (other than minerals/vitamins) for osteoporosis prescribed

M **G8634** Clinician documented patient not an eligible candidate to receive pharmacologic therapy for osteoporosis

M **G8635** Pharmacologic therapy for osteoporosis was not prescribed, reason not otherwise specified

~~G8636~~ Jan ~~Influenza immunization administered or previously received~~
To report, see G8482

~~G8637~~ Jan ~~Clinician documented that patient is not eligible to receive the influenza immunization~~
To report, see G8483-G8484

~~G8638~~ Jan ~~Influenza immunization not administered or previously received, reason not otherwise specified~~
To report, see G8484

~~G8639~~ Jan ~~Influenza immunization was administered or previously received~~
To report, see G8482

~~G8640~~ Jan ~~Clinician has documented that patient is not eligible to receive the influenza immunization~~
To report, see G8483-G8484

~~G8641~~ Jan ~~Influenza immunization was not administered or previously received, reason not otherwise specified~~
To report, see G8484

M **G8642** The eligible professional practices in a rural area without sufficient high speed internet access and requests a hardship exemption from the application of the payment adjustment under section 1848(a)(5) (a) of the Social Security Act

M **G8643** The eligible professional practices in an area without sufficient available pharmacies for electronic prescribing and requests a hardship exemption for the application of the payment adjustment under section 1848(a)(5) (a) of the Social Security Act

M **G8644** Eligible professional does not have prescribing privileges

M **G8645** I intend to report the asthma measures group

M **G8646** All quality actions for the applicable measures in the asthma measures group have been performed for this patient

M ☑ **G8647** Risk-adjusted functional status change residual score for the knee successfully calculated and the score was equal to zero (0) or greater than zero (> 0)

M ☑ **G8648** Risk-adjusted functional status change residual score for the knee successfully calculated and the score was less than zero (< 0)

M **G8649** Risk-adjusted functional status change residual scores for the knee not measured because the patient did not complete foto's functional intake on admission and/or follow up status survey near discharge, patient not eligible/not appropriate

M **G8650** Risk-adjusted functional status change residual scores for the knee not measured because the patient did not complete FOTO's functional intake on admission and/or follow up status survey near discharge, reason not specified

M ☑ **G8651** Risk-adjusted functional status change residual score for the hip successfully calculated and the score was equal to zero (0) or greater than zero (> 0)

M ☑ **G8652** Risk-adjusted functional status change residual score for the hip successfully calculated and the score was less than zero (< 0)

M **G8653** Risk-adjusted functional status change residual scores for the hip not measured because the patient did not complete foto's functional intake on admission and/or follow up status survey near discharge, patient not eligible/not appropriate

M **G8654** Risk-adjusted functional status change residual scores for the hip not measured because the patient did not complete foto's functional intake on admission and/or follow up status survey near discharge, reason not specified

M ☑ **G8655** Risk-adjusted functional status change residual score for the lower leg, foot or ankle successfully calculated and the score was equal to zero (0) or greater than zero(> 0)

M ☑ **G8656** Risk-adjusted functional status change residual score for the lower leg, foot or ankle successfully calculated and the score was less than zero (< 0)

M **G8657** Risk-adjusted functional status change residual scores for the lower leg, foot or ankle not measured because the patient did not complete foto's functional intake on admission and/or follow up status survey near discharge, patient not eligible/not appropriate

M **G8658** Risk-adjusted functional status change residual scores for the lower leg, foot or ankle not measured because the patient did not complete foto's functional intake on admission and/or follow up status survey near discharge, reason not specified

M ☑ **G8659** Risk-adjusted functional status change residual score for the lumbar spine successfully calculated and the score was equal to zero (0) or greater than zero (> 0)

M ☑ **G8660** Risk-adjusted functional status change residual score for the lumbar spine successfully calculated and the score was less than zero (< 0)

M **G8661** Risk-adjusted functional status change residual scores for the lumbar spine not measured because the patient did not complete foto's functional intake on admission and/or follow up status survey near discharge, patient not eligible/not appropriate

M **G8662** Risk-adjusted functional status change residual scores for the lumbar spine not measured because the patient did not complete foto's functional intake on admission and/or follow up status survey near discharge, reason not specified

M ☑ **G8663** Risk-adjusted functional status change residual score for the shoulder successfully calculated and the score was equal to zero (0) or greater than zero (> 0)

M ☑ **G8664** Risk-adjusted functional status change residual score for the shoulder successfully calculated and the score was less than zero (< 0)

Jan January Update

M **G8665** Risk-adjusted functional status change residual scores for the shoulder not measured because the patient did not complete FOTO's functional intake on admission and/or follow up status survey near discharge, patient not eligible/not appropriate

M **G8666** Risk-adjusted functional status change residual scores for the shoulder not measured because the patient did not complete foto's functional intake on admission and/or follow up status survey near discharge, reason not specified

M ☑ **G8667** Risk-adjusted functional status change residual score for the elbow, wrist or hand successfully calculated and the score was equal to zero (0) or greater than zero (> 0)

M ☑ **G8668** Risk-adjusted functional status change residual score for the elbow, wrist or hand successfully calculated and the score was less than zero (< 0)

M **G8669** Risk-adjusted functional status change residual scores for the elbow, wrist or hand not measured because the patient did not complete foto's functional intake on admission and/or follow up status survey near discharge, patient not eligible/not appropriate

M **G8670** Risk-adjusted functional status change residual scores for the elbow, wrist or hand not measured because the patient did not complete foto's functional intake on admission and/or follow up status survey near discharge, reason not specified

M ☑ **G8671** Risk-adjusted functional status change residual score for the neck, cranium, mandible, thoracic spine, ribs, or other general orthopedic impairment successfully calculated and the score was equal to zero (0) or greater than zero (> 0)

M ☑ **G8672** Risk-adjusted functional status change residual score for the neck, cranium, mandible, thoracic spine, ribs, or other general orthopedic impairment successfully calculated and the score was less than zero (< 0)

M **G8673** Risk-adjusted functional status change residual scores for the neck, cranium, mandible, thoracic spine, ribs, or other general orthopedic impairment not measured because the patient did not complete foto's functional intake on admission and/or follow up status survey near discharge, patient not eligible/not appropriate

M **G8674** Risk-adjusted functional status change residual scores for the neck, cranium, mandible, thoracic spine, ribs, or other general orthopedic impairment not measured because the patient did not complete foto's functional intake on admission and/or follow up status survey near discharge, reason not specified

~~G8675~~ Jan ~~Most recent systolic blood pressure >= 140 mm hg~~
To report, see G8589

~~G8676~~ Jan ~~Most recent diastolic blood pressure >= 90 mm hg~~
To report, see G8591

~~G8677~~ Jan ~~Most recent systolic blood pressure < 130 mm hg~~
To report, see G8790

~~G8678~~ Jan ~~Most recent systolic blood pressure 130 to 139 mm hg~~
To report, see G8791

~~G8679~~ Jan ~~Most recent diastolic blood pressure < 80 mm hg~~
To report, see G8793

~~G8680~~ Jan ~~Most recent diastolic blood pressure 80 - 89 mm hg~~
To report, see G8794

~~G8681~~ Jan ~~Patient hospitalized with principal diagnosis of heart failure during the measurement period~~

M **G8682** Left ventricular function testing performed during the measurement period

M **G8683** Clinician documented that patient is not an eligible candidate for left ventricular function testing during the measurement period

~~G8684~~ Jan ~~Patient not hospitalized with principal diagnosis of heart failure during the measurement period~~

M **G8685** Left ventricular function testing not performed during the measurement period, reason not specified

~~G8686~~ Jan ~~Currently a tobacco smoker or current exposure to secondhand smoke~~

~~G8687~~ Jan ~~Currently a tobacco nonuser and no exposure to secondhand smoke~~

~~G8688~~ Jan ~~Currently a smokeless tobacco user (e.g., chew, snuff) and no exposure to secondhand smoke~~

~~G8689~~ Jan ~~Tobacco use not assessed, reason not otherwise specified~~
To report, see G8751

~~G8690~~ Jan ~~Current tobacco smoker or current exposure to secondhand smoke~~

~~G8691~~ Jan ~~Current tobacco nonuser and no exposure to secondhand smoke~~

~~G8692~~ Jan ~~Current smokeless tobacco user (e.g., chew, snuff) and no exposure to secondhand smoke~~

~~G8693~~ Jan ~~Tobacco use not assessed, reason not specified~~
To report, see G8751

● M ☑ **G8694** Jan Left ventriucular ejection fraction (LVEF) < 40%

● M ☑ **G8695** Jan Left ventricular ejection fraction (LVEF) ≥ 40% or documentation as mildly depressed left ventricular systolic function or normal

● M **G8696** Jan Antithrombotic therapy prescribed at discharge

● M **G8697** Jan Antithrombotic therapy not prescribed for documented reasons

● M **G8698** Jan Antithrombotic therapy was not prescribed at discharge, reason not otherwise specified

● M **G8699** Jan Rehabilitation services (occupational, physical or speech) ordered at or prior to discharge

● M **G8700** Jan Rehabilitation services (occupational, physical or speech) not indicated at or prior to discharge

● M **G8701** Jan Rehabilitation services were not ordered, reason not otherwise specified

● M **G8702** Jan Documentation that prophylactic antibiotics were given within 4 hours prior to surgical incision or intraoperatively

● M **G8703** Jan Documentation that prophylactic antibiotics were neither given within 4 hours prior to surgical incision nor intraoperatively

● M **G8704** Jan 12-lead electrocardiogram (ECG) performed

● M **G8705** Jan Documentation of medical reason(s) for not performing a 12-lead electrocardiogram (ECG)

● M **G8706** Jan Documentation of patient reason(s) for not performing a 12-lead electrocardiogram (ECG)

● M **G8707** Jan 12-lead electrocardiogram (ECG) not performed, reason not otherwise specified

● M **G8708** Jan Patient not prescribed or dispensed antibiotic

● M **G8709** Jan Patient prescribed or dispensed antibiotic for documented medical reason(s)

● M **G8710** Jan Patient prescribed or dispensed antibiotic

● M **G8711** Jan Prescribed or dispensed antibiotic

● M G8712 Jan Antibiotic not prescribed or dispensed

● M G8713 Jan SpKt/V greater than or equal to 1.2 (single-pool clearance of urea [Kt] / volume V])

● M ☑ G8714 Jan Hemodialysis treatment performed exactly 3 times per week

● M ☑ G8715 Jan Hemodialysis treatment performed less than 3 times per week or greater than 3 times per week

● M G8716 Jan Documentation of reason(s) for patient not having greater than or equal to 1.2 (single-pool clearance of urea [Kt] / volume [V])

● M G8717 Jan SpKt/V less than 1.2 (single-pool clearance of urea [Kt] / volume V]), reason not specified

● M G8718 Jan Total Kt/V greater than or equal to 1.7 per week (total clearance of urea [Kt] / volume V])

● M G8720 Jan Total Kt/V less than 1.7 per week (total clearance of urea [Kt] / volume V]), reason not specified

● M G8721 Jan PT category (primary tumor), pN category (regional lymph nodes), and histologic grade were documented in pathology report

● M G8722 Jan Medical reason(s) documented for not including pT category, pN category and histologic grade in the pathology report

● M G8723 Jan Specimen site is other than anatomic location of primary tumor

● M G8724 Jan PT category, pN category and histologic grade were not documented in the pathology report, reason not otherwise specified

● M G8725 Jan Fasting lipid profile performed (triglycerides, LDL-C, HDL-C and total cholesterol)

● M G8726 Jan Clinician has documented reason for not performing fasting lipid profile

● M G8727 Jan Patient receiving hemodialysis, peritoneal dialysis or kidney transplantation

● M G8728 Jan Fasting lipid profile not performed, reason not otherwise specified

● M G8730 Jan Pain assessment documented as positive utilizing a standardized tool and a follow-up plan is documented

● M G8731 Jan Pain assessment documented as negative, no follow-up plan is required

● M G8732 Jan No documentation of pain assessment

● M G8733 Jan Documentation of a positive elder maltreatment screen and documented follow-up plan A

● M G8734 Jan Elder maltreatment screen documented as negative, no follow-up required A

● M G8735 Jan Elder maltreatment screen documented as positive, follow-up plan not documented, reason not specified A

● M ☑ G8736 Jan Most current LDL-C < 100 mg/dL

● M ☑ G8737 Jan Most current LDL-C ≥ 100 mg/dL

● M ☑ G8738 Jan Left ventricular ejection fraction (LVEF) < 40% or documentation of severely or moderately depressed left ventricular systolic function

● M ☑ G8739 Jan Left ventricular ejection fraction (LVEF) ≥ 40% or documentation as normal or mildly depressed left ventricular systolic function

● M G8740 Jan Left ventricular ejection fraction (LVEF) not performed or assessed, reason not specified

● M G8741 Jan Patient not treated for spoken language comprehension disorder

● M G8742 Jan Patient not treated for attention disorder

● M G8743 Jan Patient not treated for memory disorder

● M G8744 Jan Patient not treated for motor speech disorder

● M G8745 Jan Patient not treated for reading disorder

● M G8746 Jan Patient not treated for spoken language expression disorder

● M G8747 Jan Patient not treated for writing disorder

● M G8748 Jan Patient not treated for swallowing disorder

● M G8749 Jan Absence of signs of melanoma (cough, dyspnea, tenderness, localized neurologic signs such as weakness, jaundice or any other sign suggesting systemic spread) or absence of symptoms of melanoma (pain, paresthesia, or any other symptom suggesting the possibility of systemic spread of melanoma)

● M G8750 Jan Presence of signs of melanoma (cough, dyspnea, tenderness, localized neurologic signs such as weakness, jaundice or any other sign suggesting systemic spread) or presence of symptoms of melanoma (pain, paresthesia, or any other symptom suggesting the possibility of systemic spread of melanoma)

● M G8751 Jan Smoking status and exposure to secondhand smoke in the home not assessed, reason not specified

● M ☑ G8752 Jan Most recent systolic blood pressure < 140 mm Hg

● M ☑ G8753 Jan Most recent systolic blood pressure ≥ 140 mm Hg

● M ☑ G8754 Jan Most recent diastolic blood pressure < 90 mm Hg

● M ☑ G8755 Jan Most recent diastolic blood pressure ≥ 90 mmHg

● M G8756 Jan No documentation of blood pressure measurement, reason not otherwise specified

● M G8757 Jan All quality actions for the applicable measures in the chronic obstructive pulmonary disease measures group have been performed for this patient

● M G8758 Jan All quality actions for the applicable measures in the inflammatory bowel disease measures group have been performed for this patient

● M G8759 Jan All quality actions for the applicable measures in the obstructive sleep apnea measures group have been performed for this patient

● M G8760 Jan All quality actions for the applicable measures in the epilepsy measures group have been performed for this patient

● M G8761 Jan All quality actions for the applicable measures in the dementia measures group have been performed for this patient

● M G8762 Jan All quality actions for the applicable measures in the Parkinson's disease measures group have been performed for this patient

● M G8763 Jan All quality actions for the applicable measures in the hypertension measures group have been performed for this patient

● M G8764 Jan All quality actions for the applicable measures in the cardiovascular prevention measures group have been performed for this patient

● M G8765 Jan All quality actions for the applicable measures in the cataract measures group have been performed for this patient

● M G8767 Jan Lipid panel results documented and reviewed (must include total cholesterol, HDL-C, triglycerides and calculated LDL-C)

Jan January Update

Special Coverage Instructions | Noncovered by Medicare | Carrier Discretion | ☑ Quantity Alert | ● New Code | ○ Recycled/Reinstated | ▲ Revised Code

 A Age Edit | M Maternity Edit | ♀ Female Only | ♂ Male Only | A-Y OPPS Status Indicators

● M G8768 Jan Documentation of medical reason(s) for not performing lipid profile (e.g., patients who have a terminal illness or for whom treatment of hypertension with standard treatment goals is not clinically appropriate)

● M G8769 Jan Lipid profile not performed, reason not otherwise specified

● M G8770 Jan Urine protein test result documented and reviewed

● M G8771 Jan Documentation of diagnosis of chronic kidney disease

● M G8772 Jan Documentation of medical reason(s) for not performing urine protein test (e.g., patients who have a terminal illness or for whom treatment of hypertension with standard treatment goals is not cllinically appropriate)

● M G8773 Jan Urine protein test was not performed, reason not otherwise specified

● M G8774 Jan Serum creatinine test result documented and reviewed

● M G8775 Jan Documentation of medical reason(s) for not performing serum creatinine test (e.g., patients who have a terminal illness or for whom treatment of hypertension with standard treatment goals is not clinically appropriate)

● M G8776 Jan Serum creatinine test not performed, reason not otherwise specified

● M G8777 Jan Diabetes screening test performed

● M G8778 Jan Documentation of medical reason(s) for not performing diabetes screening test (e.g., patients who have a terminal illness or for whom treatment of hypertension with standard treatment goals is not clinically appropriate, or patients with a diagnosis of diabetes)

● M G8779 Jan Diabetes screening test not performed, reason not otherwise specified

● M G8780 Jan Counseling for diet and physical activity performed

● M G8781 Jan Documentation of medical reason(s) for patient not receiving counseling for diet and physical activity (e.g., patients who have a terminal illness or for whom treatment of hypertension with standard treatment goals is not clinically appropriate)

● M G8782 Jan Counseling for diet and physical activity not performed, reason not otherwise specified

● M G8783 Jan Blood pressure screening performed as recommended by the defined screening interval

● M G8784 Jan Blood pressure not assessed, patient not eligible

● M G8785 Jan Blood pressure screening not performed as recommended by screening interval, reason not otherwise specified

● M G8786 Jan Severity of angina assessed according to level of activity

● M G8787 Jan Angina assessed as present

● M G8788 Jan Angina assessed as absent

● M G8789 Jan Severity of angina not assessed according to level of activity

● M ☑ G8790 Jan Most recent office visit systolic blood pressure < 130 mm hg

● M ☑ G8791 Jan Most recent office visit systolic blood pressure, 130-139 mm hg

● M ☑ G8792 Jan Most recent office visit systolic blood pressure ≥ 140 mm Hg

● M ☑ G8793 Jan Most recent office visit diastolic blood pressure, < 80 mm hg

● M ☑ G8794 Jan Most recent office visit diastolic blood pressure, 80-89 mm hg

● M ☑ G8795 Jan Most recent office visit diastolic blood pressure >= 90 mm Hg

● M G8796 Jan Blood pressure measurement not documented, reason not otherwise specified

● M G8797 Jan Specimen site other than anatomic location of esophagus

● M G8798 Jan Specimen site other than anatomic location of prostate

● M G8799 Jan Anticoagulation ordered

● M G8800 Jan Anticoagulation not ordered for reasons documented by clinician

● M G8801 Jan Anticoagulation was not ordered, reason not specified

● M G8802 Jan Pregnancy test (urine or serum) ordered ♀

● M G8803 Jan Pregnancy test (urine or serum) not ordered for reasons documented by clinician ♀

● M G8805 Jan Pregnancy test (urine or serum) was not ordered, reason not specified ♀

● M G8806 Jan Performance of transabdominal or transvaginal ultrasound ♀

● M G8807 Jan Transabdominal or transvaginal ultrasound not performed for reasons documented by clinician ♀

● M G8808 Jan Performance of transabdominal or transvaginal ultrasound not ordered, reason not specified ♀

● M G8809 Jan Rh immune globulin (RhoGam) ordered

● M G8810 Jan R immune globulin (RhoGam) not ordered for reasons documented by clinician

● M G8811 Jan Documentation Rh immune globulin (RhoGam) was not ordered, reason not specified

● M G8812 Jan Patient is not eligible for follow-up CTA, duplex, or MRA

● M G8813 Jan Follow-up CTA, duplex, or MRA of the abdomen and pelvis performed

● M G8814 Jan Follow-up CTA, duplex, or MRA of the abdomen and pelvis not performed

● M G8815 Jan Statin therapy not prescribed for documented reasons

● M G8816 Jan Statin medication prescribed at discharge

● M G8817 Jan Statin therapy not prescribed at discharge, reason not specified

● M G8818 Jan Patient discharge to home no later than postoperative day #7

● M G8819 Jan Aneurysm minor diameter ≤ 5.5 cm

● M ☑ G8820 Jan Aneurysm minor diameter 5.6-6.0 cm

● M G8821 Jan Abdominal aortic aneurysm is not infrarenal

● M ☑ G8822 Jan Male patients with aneurysms minor diameter > 6 cm ♂

● M ☑ G8823 Jan Female patients with aneurysm minor diameter > 6 cm ♀

● M ☑ G8824 Jan Female patients with aneurysm minor diameter 5.6-6.0 cm ♀

● M G8825 Jan Patient not discharged to home by postoperative day #7

Jan January Update

● M G8826 Jan Patient discharged to home no later than postoperative day #2 following EVAR

● M ☑G8827 Jan Aneurysm minor diameter ≤ 5.5 cm for women ♀

● M ☑G8828 Jan Aneurysm minor diameter ≤ 5.5 cm for men ♂

● M ☑G8829 Jan Aneurysm minor diameter 5.6-6.0 cm for men ♂

● M ☑G8830 Jan Aneurysm minor diameter > 6 cm for men ♂

● M ☑G8831 Jan Aneurysm minor diameter > 6 cm for women ♀

● M ☑G8832 Jan Aneurysm minor diameter 5.6-6.0 cm for women ♀

● M G8833 Jan Patient not discharged to home by postoperative day #2 following EVAR

● M G8834 Jan Patient discharged to home no later than postoperative day #2 following CEA

● M G8835 Jan Asymptomatic patient with no history of any transient ischemic attack or stroke in any carotid or vertebrobasilar territory

● M G8836 Jan Symptomatic patient with ipsilateral stroke or TIA within 120 days prior to CEA

● M ☑G8837 Jan Other symptomatic patient with ipsilateral carotid territory TIA or stroke > 120 days prior to CEA, or contralateral carotid territory TIA or stroke or vertebrobasilar TIA or stroke

● M G8838 Jan Patient not discharged to home by postoperative day #2

● M G8839 Jan Sleep apnea symptoms assessed, including presence or absence of snoring and daytime sleepiness

● M G8840 Jan Documentation of reason(s) for not performing an assessment of sleep symptoms (e.g., patient didn't have initial daytime sleepiness, patient visits between initial testing and initiation of therapy)

● M G8841 Jan Sleep apnea symptoms not assessed, reason not otherwise specified

● M G8842 Jan Apnea hypopnea index (AHI) or respiratory disturbance index (RDI) measured at the time of initial diagnosis

● M G8843 Jan Documentation of reason(s) for not measuring an apnea hypopnea index (AHI) or a respiratory disturbance index (RDI) at the time of initial diagnosis

● M G8844 Jan Apnea hypopna index (AHI) or respiratory disturbance index (RDI) not measured at the time of initial diagnosis, reason not specified

● M G8845 Jan Positive airway pressure therapy prescribed

● M ☑G8846 Jan Moderate or severe obstructive sleep apnea (apnea hypopnea index (AHI) or respiratory disturbance index (RDI) of 15 or greater)

● M G8847 Jan Positive airway pressure therapy not prescribed

● M G8848 Jan Mild obstructive sleep apnea (apnea hypopnea index (AHI) or respiratory disturbance index (RDI) of less than 15)

● M G8849 Jan Documentation of reason(s) for not prescribing positive airway pressure therapy

● M G8850 Jan Positive airway pressure therapy not prescribed, reason not otherwise specified

● M G8851 Jan Objective measurement of adherence to positive airway pressure therapy, documented

● M G8852 Jan Positive airway pressure therapy prescribed

● M G8853 Jan Positive airway pressure therapy not prescribed

● M G8854 Jan Documentation of reason(s) for not objectively measuring adherence to positive airway pressure therapy

● M G8855 Jan Objective measurement of adherence to positive airway pressure therapy not performed, reason not otherwise specified

● M G8856 Jan Referral to a physician for an otologic evaluation performed

● M G8857 Jan Patient is not eligible for the referral for otologic evaluation measure (e.g., patients who are already under the care of a physician for acute or chronic dizziness)

● M G8858 Jan Referral to a physician for an otologic evaluation not performed, reason not specified

● M ☑G8859 Jan Patient receiving corticosteroids greater than or equal to 10 mg/day for 60 or greater consecutive days

● M ☑G8860 Jan Patients who have received dose of corticosteroids greater than or equal to 10 mg/day for 60 or greater consecutive days

● M G8861 Jan Central dual-energy x-ray absorptiometry (DXA) ordered or documented, review of systems and medication history or pharmacologic therapy (other than minerals/vitamins) for osteoporosis prescribed

● M ☑G8862 Jan Patients not receiving corticosteroids greater than or equal to 10 mg/day for 60 or greater consecutive days

● M G8863 Jan Patients not assessed for risk of bone loss, reason not otherwise specified

● M G8864 Jan Pneumococcal vaccine administered or previously received

● M G8865 Jan Documentation of medical reason(s) for not administering or previously receiving pneumococcal vaccine (e.g., patient allergic reaction, potential adverse drug reaction)

● M G8866 Jan Documentation of patient reason(s) for not administering or previously receiving pneumococcal vaccine (e.g., patient refusal)

● M G8867 Jan Pneumococcal vaccine not administered or previously received, reason not otherwise specified

● M G8868 Jan Patients receiving a first course of anti-TNF therapy

● M G8869 Jan Patient has documented immunity to hepatitis B and is receiving a first course of anti-TNF therapy

● M G8870 Jan Hepatitis B vaccine injection administered or previously received and is receiving a first course of anti-TNF therapy

● M G8871 Jan Patient not receiving a first course of anti-TNF therapy

● M G8872 Jan Excised tissue evaluated by imaging intraoperatively to confirm successful inclusion of targeted lesion

● M G8873 Jan Patients with needle localization specimens which are not amenable to intraoperative imaging such as MRI needle wire localization, or targets which are tentatively identified on mammogram or ultrasound which do not contain a biopsy marker but which can be verified on intraoperative inspection or pathology

● M G8874 Jan Excised tissue not evaluated by imaging intraoperatively to confirm successful inclusion of targeted lesion

● M G8875 Jan Clinician diagnosed breast cancer preoperatively by a minimally invasive biopsy method

● M G8876 Jan Documentation of reason(s) for not performing minimally invasive biopsy to diagnose breast cancer preoperatively

● M G8877 Jan Clinician did not attempt to achieve the diagnosis of breast cancer preoperatively by a minimally invasive biopsy method, reason not otherwise specified

● M G8878 Jan Sentinel lymph node biopsy procedure performed

● M G8879 Jan Clinically node negative (T1N0M0 or T2N0M0) invasive breast cancer

● M G8880 Jan Documentation of reason(s) sentinel lymph node biopsy not performed

● M G8881 Jan Stage of breast cancer is greater than T1N0M0 or T2N0M0

● M G8882 Jan Sentinel lymph node biopsy procedure not performed

● M G8883 Jan Biopsy results reviewed, communicated, tracked and documented

● M G8884 Jan Clinician documented reason that patient's biopsy results were not reviewed

● M G8885 Jan Biopsy results not reviewed, communicated, tracked or documented

● M G8886 Jan Most recent blood pressure under control

● M G8887 Jan Documentation of medical reason(s) for most recent blood pressure not being under control (e.g., patients with comorbid conditions that cause an increase in blood pressure or require treatment with medications that cause an increase in blood pressure, or patients who had a terminal illness or for whom treatment of hypertension with standard treatment goals is not clinically appropriate)

● M G8888 Jan Most recent blood pressure not under control, results documented and reviewed

● M G8889 Jan No documentation of blood pressure measurement, reason not otherwise specified

● M G8890 Jan Most recent LDL-C under control, results documented and reviewed

● M G8891 Jan Documentation of medical reason(s) for most recent LDL-C not under control (e.g., patients who had a terminal illness or for whom treatment of hypertension with standard treatment goals is not clinically appropriate)

● M G8892 Jan Documentation of medical reason(s) for not performing LDL-C test (e.g., patients who had a terminal illness or for whom treatment of hypertension with standard treatment goals is not clinically appropriate)

● M G8893 Jan Most recent LDL-C not under control, results documented and reviewed

● M G8894 Jan LDL-C not performed, reason not specified

● M G8895 Jan Oral aspirin or other anticoagulant/antiplatelet therapy prescribed

● M G8896 Jan Documentation of medical reason(s) for not prescribing oral aspirin or other anticoagulant/antiplatelet therapy (e.g., under age 30, patient documented to be low risk, patient with terminal illness or treatment of hypertension with standard treatment goals is not clinically appropriate)

● M G8897 Jan Oral aspirin or other anticoagulant/antiplatelet therapy was not prescribed, reason not otherwise specified

● M G8898 Jan I intend to report the chronic obstructive pulmonary disease measures group

● M G8899 Jan I intend to report the inflammatory bowel disease measures group

● M G8900 Jan I intend to report the obstructive sleep apnea measures group

● M G8901 Jan I intend to report the epilepsy measures group

● M G8902 Jan I intend to report the dementia measures group

● M G8903 Jan I intend to report the Parkinson's disease measures group

● M G8904 Jan I intend to report the hypertension measures group

● M G8905 Jan I intend to report the cardiovascular prevention measures group

● M G8906 Jan I intend to report the cataract measures group

COORDINATED CARE

B G9001 Coordinated care fee, initial rate

B G9002 Coordinated care fee, maintenance rate

B G9003 Coordinated care fee, risk adjusted high, initial

B G9004 Coordinated care fee, risk adjusted low, initial

B G9005 Coordinated care fee, risk adjusted maintenance

B G9006 Coordinated care fee, home monitoring

B G9007 Coordinated care fee, scheduled team conference

B G9008 Coordinated care fee, physician coordinated care oversight services

B G9009 Coordinated care fee, risk adjusted maintenance, Level 3

B G9010 Coordinated care fee, risk adjusted maintenance, Level 4

B G9011 Coordinated care fee, risk adjusted maintenance, Level 5

B G9012 Other specified case management service not elsewhere classified

DEMONSTRATION PROJECT

E G9013 ESRD demo basic bundle Level I

E G9014 ESRD demo expanded bundle including venous access and related services

E ☑ G9016 Smoking cessation counseling, individual, in the absence of or in addition to any other evaluation and management service, per session (6-10 minutes) [demo project code only]

A ☑ G9017 Amantadine HCl, oral, per 100 mg (for use in a Medicare-approved demonstration project)

A ☑ G9018 Zanamivir, inhalation powder, administered through inhaler, per 10 mg (for use in a Medicare-approved demonstration project)

A ☑ G9019 Oseltamivir phosphate, oral, per 75 mg (for use in a Medicare-approved demonstration project)

A ☑ G9020 Rimantadine HCl, oral, per 100 mg (for use in a Medicare-approved demonstration project)

A ☑ G9033 Amantadine HCl, oral brand, per 100 mg (for use in a Medicare-approved demonstration project)

A ☑ G9034 Zanamivir, inhalation powder, administered through inhaler, brand, per 10 mg (for use in a Medicare-approved demonstration project)

A ☑ G9035 Oseltamivir phosphate, oral, brand, per 75 mg (for use in a Medicare-approved demonstration project)

A ☑ G9036 Rimantadine HCl, oral, brand, per 100 mg (for use in a Medicare-approved demonstration project)

~~G9041~~ Jan ~~Rehabilitation services for low vision by qualified occupational therapist, direct one-on-one contact, each 15 minutes~~

~~G9042~~ Jan ~~Rehabilitation services for low vision by certified orientation and mobility specialists, direct one-on-one contact, each 15 minutes~~

~~G9043~~ Jan ~~Rehabilitation services for low vision by certified low vision rehabilitation therapist, direct one-on-one contact, each 15 minutes~~

~~G9044~~ Jan ~~Rehabilitation services for low vision by certified low vision rehabilitation teacher, direct one-on-one contact, each 15 minutes~~

E **G9050** Oncology; primary focus of visit; work-up, evaluation, or staging at the time of cancer diagnosis or recurrence (for use in a Medicare-approved demonstration project)

E **G9051** Oncology; primary focus of visit; treatment decision-making after disease is staged or restaged, discussion of treatment options, supervising/coordinating active cancer-directed therapy or managing consequences of cancer-directed therapy (for use in a Medicare-approved demonstration project)

E **G9052** Oncology; primary focus of visit; surveillance for disease recurrence for patient who has completed definitive cancer-directed therapy and currently lacks evidence of recurrent disease; cancer-directed therapy might be considered in the future (for use in a Medicare-approved demonstration project)

E **G9053** Oncology; primary focus of visit; expectant management of patient with evidence of cancer for whom no cancer-directed therapy is being administered or arranged at present; cancer-directed therapy might be considered in the future (for use in a Medicare-approved demonstration project)

E **G9054** Oncology; primary focus of visit; supervising, coordinating or managing care of patient with terminal cancer or for whom other medical illness prevents further cancer treatment; includes symptom management, end-of-life care planning, management of palliative therapies (for use in a Medicare-approved demonstration project)

E **G9055** Oncology; primary focus of visit; other, unspecified service not otherwise listed (for use in a Medicare-approved demonstration project)

E **G9056** Oncology; practice guidelines; management adheres to guidelines (for use in a Medicare-approved demonstration project)

E **G9057** Oncology; practice guidelines; management differs from guidelines as a result of patient enrollment in an institutional review board-approved clinical trial (for use in a Medicare-approved demonstration project)

E **G9058** Oncology; practice guidelines; management differs from guidelines because the treating physician disagrees with guideline recommendations (for use in a Medicare-approved demonstration project)

E **G9059** Oncology; practice guidelines; management differs from guidelines because the patient, after being offered treatment consistent with guidelines, has opted for alternative treatment or management, including no treatment (for use in a Medicare-approved demonstration project)

E **G9060** Oncology; practice guidelines; management differs from guidelines for reason(s) associated with patient comorbid illness or performance status not factored into guidelines (for use in a Medicare-approved demonstration project)

E **G9061** Oncology; practice guidelines; patient's condition not addressed by available guidelines (for use in a Medicare-approved demonstration project)

E **G9062** Oncology; practice guidelines; management differs from guidelines for other reason(s) not listed (for use in a Medicare-approved demonstration project)

M **G9063** Oncology; disease status; limited to nonsmall cell lung cancer; extent of disease initially established as Stage I (prior to neoadjuvant therapy, if any) with no evidence of disease progression, recurrence, or metastases (for use in a Medicare-approved demonstration project)

M **G9064** Oncology; disease status; limited to nonsmall cell lung cancer; extent of disease initially established as Stage II (prior to neoadjuvant therapy, if any) with no evidence of disease progression, recurrence, or metastases (for use in a Medicare-approved demonstration project)

M **G9065** Oncology; disease status; limited to nonsmall cell lung cancer; extent of disease initially established as Stage III a (prior to neoadjuvant therapy, if any) with no evidence of disease progression, recurrence, or metastases (for use in a Medicare-approved demonstration project)

M **G9066** Oncology; disease status; limited to nonsmall cell lung cancer; Stage III B-IV at diagnosis, metastatic, locally recurrent, or progressive (for use in a Medicare-approved demonstration project)

M **G9067** Oncology; disease status; limited to nonsmall cell lung cancer; extent of disease unknown, staging in progress, or not listed (for use in a Medicare-approved demonstration project)

M **G9068** Oncology; disease status; limited to small cell and combined small cell/nonsmall cell; extent of disease initially established as limited with no evidence of disease progression, recurrence, or metastases (for use in a Medicare-approved demonstration project)

M **G9069** Oncology; disease status; small cell lung cancer, limited to small cell and combined small cell/nonsmall cell; extensive Stage at diagnosis, metastatic, locally recurrent, or progressive (for use in a Medicare-approved demonstration project)

M **G9070** Oncology; disease status; small cell lung cancer, limited to small cell and combined small cell/nonsmall; extent of disease unknown, staging in progress, or not listed (for use in a Medicare-approved demonstration project)

M **G9071** Oncology; disease status; invasive female breast cancer (does not include ductal carcinoma in situ); adenocarcinoma as predominant cell type; stage I or stage IIA-IIB; or T3, N1, M0; and ER and/or PR positive; with no evidence of disease progression, recurrence, or metastases (for use in a Medicare-approved demonstration project) ♀

M **G9072** Oncology; disease status; invasive female breast cancer (does not include ductal carcinoma in situ); adenocarcinoma as predominant cell type; stage I, or stage IIA-IIB; or T3, N1, M0; and ER and PR negative; with no evidence of disease progression, recurrence, or metastases (for use in a Medicare-approved demonstration project) ♀

M **G9073** Oncology; disease status; invasive female breast cancer (does not include ductal carcinoma in situ); adenocarcinoma as predominant cell type; stage IIIA-IIIB; and not T3, N1, M0; and ER and/or PR positive; with no evidence of disease progression, recurrence, or metastases (for use in a Medicare-approved demonstration project) ♀

M **G9074** Oncology; disease status; invasive female breast cancer (does not include ductal carcinoma in situ); adenocarcinoma as predominant cell type; stage IIIA-IIIB; and not T3, N1, M0; and ER and PR negative; with no evidence of disease progression, recurrence, or metastases (for use in a Medicare-approved demonstration project) ♀

M **G9075** Oncology; disease status; invasive female breast cancer (does not include ductal carcinoma in situ); adenocarcinoma as predominant cell type; M1 at diagnosis, metastatic, locally recurrent, or progressive (for use in a Medicare-approved demonstration project) ♀

M **G9077** Oncology; disease status; prostate cancer, limited to adenocarcinoma as predominant cell type; T1-T2C and Gleason 2-7 and PSA < or equal to 20 at diagnosis with no evidence of disease progression, recurrence, or metastases (for use in a Medicare-approved demonstration project) ♂

M **G9078** Oncology; disease status; prostate cancer, limited to adenocarcinoma as predominant cell type; T2 or T3a Gleason 8-10 or PSA > 20 at diagnosis with no evidence of disease progression, recurrence, or metastases (for use in a Medicare-approved demonstration project) ♂

M **G9079** Oncology; disease status; prostate cancer, limited to adenocarcinoma as predominant cell type; T3B-T4, any N; any T, N1 at diagnosis with no evidence of disease progression, recurrence, or metastases (for use in a Medicare-approved demonstration project) ♂

M **G9080** Oncology; disease status; prostate cancer, limited to adenocarcinoma; after initial treatment with rising PSA or failure of PSA decline (for use in a Medicare-approved demonstration project) ♂

M **G9083** Oncology; disease status; prostate cancer, limited to adenocarcinoma; extent of disease unknown, staging in progress, or not listed (for use in a Medicare-approved demonstration project) ♂

M **G9084** Oncology; disease status; colon cancer, limited to invasive cancer, adenocarcinoma as predominant cell type; extent of disease initially established as T1-3, N0, M0 with no evidence of disease progression, recurrence or metastases (for use in a Medicare-approved demonstration project)

M **G9085** Oncology; disease status; colon cancer, limited to invasive cancer, adenocarcinoma as predominant cell type; extent of disease initially established as T4, N0, M0 with no evidence of disease progression, recurrence, or metastases (for use in a Medicare-approved demonstration project)

M **G9086** Oncology; disease status; colon cancer, limited to invasive cancer, adenocarcinoma as predominant cell type; extent of disease initially established as T1-4, N1-2, M0 with no evidence of disease progression, recurrence, or metastases (for use in a Medicare-approved demonstration project)

M **G9087** Oncology; disease status; colon cancer, limited to invasive cancer, adenocarcinoma as predominant cell type; M1 at diagnosis, metastatic, locally recurrent, or progressive with current clinical, radiologic, or biochemical evidence of disease (for use in a Medicare-approved demonstration project)

M **G9088** Oncology; disease status; colon cancer, limited to invasive cancer, adenocarcinoma as predominant cell type; M1 at diagnosis, metastatic, locally recurrent, or progressive without current clinical, radiologic, or biochemical evidence of disease (for use in a Medicare-approved demonstration project)

M **G9089** Oncology; disease status; colon cancer, limited to invasive cancer, adenocarcinoma as predominant cell type; extent of disease unknown, staging in progress or not listed (for use in a Medicare-approved demonstration project)

M **G9090** Oncology; disease status; rectal cancer, limited to invasive cancer, adenocarcinoma as predominant cell type; extent of disease initially established as T1-2, N0, M0 (prior to neoadjuvant therapy, if any) with no evidence of disease progression, recurrence, or metastases (for use in a Medicare-approved demonstration project)

M **G9091** Oncology; disease status; rectal cancer, limited to invasive cancer, adenocarcinoma as predominant cell type; extent of disease initially established as T3, N0, M0 (prior to neoadjuvant therapy, if any) with no evidence of disease progression, recurrence, or metastases (for use in a Medicare-approved demonstration project)

M **G9092** Oncology; disease status; rectal cancer, limited to invasive cancer, adenocarcinoma as predominant cell type; extent of disease initially established as T1-3, N1-2, M0 (prior to neoadjuvant therapy, if any) with no evidence of disease progression, recurrence or metastases (for use in a Medicare-approved demonstration project)

M **G9093** Oncology; disease status; rectal cancer, limited to invasive cancer, adenocarcinoma as predominant cell type; extent of disease initially established as T4, any N, M0 (prior to neoadjuvant therapy, if any) with no evidence of disease progression, recurrence, or metastases (for use in a Medicare-approved demonstration project)

M **G9094** Oncology; disease status; rectal cancer, limited to invasive cancer, adenocarcinoma as predominant cell type; M1 at diagnosis, metastatic, locally recurrent, or progressive (for use in a Medicare-approved demonstration project)

M **G9095** Oncology; disease status; rectal cancer, limited to invasive cancer, adenocarcinoma as predominant cell type; extent of disease unknown, staging in progress or not listed (for use in a Medicare-approved demonstration project)

M **G9096** Oncology; disease status; esophageal cancer, limited to adenocarcinoma or squamous cell carcinoma as predominant cell type; extent of disease initially established as T1-T3, N0-N1 or NX (prior to neoadjuvant therapy, if any) with no evidence of disease progression, recurrence, or metastases (for use in a Medicare-approved demonstration project)

M **G9097** Oncology; disease status; esophageal cancer, limited to adenocarcinoma or squamous cell carcinoma as predominant cell type; extent of disease initially established as T4, any N, M0 (prior to neoadjuvant therapy, if any) with no evidence of disease progression, recurrence, or metastases (for use in a Medicare-approved demonstration project)

M **G9098** Oncology; disease status; esophageal cancer, limited to adenocarcinoma or squamous cell carcinoma as predominant cell type; M1 at diagnosis, metastatic, locally recurrent, or progressive (for use in a Medicare-approved demonstration project)

M **G9099** Oncology; disease status; esophageal cancer, limited to adenocarcinoma or squamous cell carcinoma as predominant cell type; extent of disease unknown, staging in progress, or not listed (for use in a Medicare-approved demonstration project)

M **G9100** Oncology; disease status; gastric cancer, limited to adenocarcinoma as predominant cell type; post R0 resection (with or without neoadjuvant therapy) with no evidence of disease recurrence, progression, or metastases (for use in a Medicare-approved demonstration project)

M **G9101** Oncology; disease status; gastric cancer, limited to adenocarcinoma as predominant cell type; post R1 or R2 resection (with or without neoadjuvant therapy) with no evidence of disease progression, or metastases (for use in a Medicare-approved demonstration project)

M **G9102** Oncology; disease status; gastric cancer, limited to adenocarcinoma as predominant cell type; clinical or pathologic M0, unresectable with no evidence of disease progression, or metastases (for use in a Medicare-approved demonstration project)

M **G9103** Oncology; disease status; gastric cancer, limited to adenocarcinoma as predominant cell type; clinical or pathologic M1 at diagnosis, metastatic, locally recurrent, or progressive (for use in a Medicare-approved demonstration project)

M **G9104** Oncology; disease status; gastric cancer, limited to adenocarcinoma as predominant cell type; extent of disease unknown, staging in progress, or not listed (for use in a Medicare-approved demonstration project)

M **G9105** Oncology; disease status; pancreatic cancer, limited to adenocarcinoma as predominant cell type; post R0 resection without evidence of disease progression, recurrence, or metastases (for use in a Medicare-approved demonstration project)

M **G9106** Oncology; disease status; pancreatic cancer, limited to adenocarcinoma; post R1 or R2 resection with no evidence of disease progression, or metastases (for use in a Medicare-approved demonstration project)

M **G9107** Oncology; disease status; pancreatic cancer, limited to adenocarcinoma; unresectable at diagnosis, M1 at diagnosis, metastatic, locally recurrent, or progressive (for use in a Medicare-approved demonstration project)

M **G9108** Oncology; disease status; pancreatic cancer, limited to adenocarcinoma; extent of disease unknown, staging in progress, or not listed (for use in a Medicare-approved demonstration project)

M **G9109** Oncology; disease status; head and neck cancer, limited to cancers of oral cavity, pharynx and larynx with squamous cell as predominant cell type; extent of disease initially established as T1-T2 and N0, M0 (prior to neoadjuvant therapy, if any) with no evidence of disease progression, recurrence, or metastases (for use in a Medicare-approved demonstration project)

M **G9110** Oncology; disease status; head and neck cancer, limited to cancers of oral cavity, pharynx and larynx with squamous cell as predominant cell type; extent of disease initially established as T3-4 and/or N1-3, M0 (prior to neoadjuvant therapy, if any) with no evidence of disease progression, recurrence, or metastases (for use in a Medicare-approved demonstration project)

M **G9111** Oncology; disease status; head and neck cancer, limited to cancers of oral cavity, pharynx and larynx with squamous cell as predominant cell type; M1 at diagnosis, metastatic, locally recurrent, or progressive (for use in a Medicare-approved demonstration project)

M **G9112** Oncology; disease status; head and neck cancer, limited to cancers of oral cavity, pharynx and larynx with squamous cell as predominant cell type; extent of disease unknown, staging in progress, or not listed (for use in a Medicare-approved demonstration project)

M **G9113** Oncology; disease status; ovarian cancer, limited to epithelial cancer; pathologic stage 1A-B (Grade 1) without evidence of disease progression, recurrence, or metastases (for use in a Medicare-approved demonstration project) ♀

M **G9114** Oncology; disease status; ovarian cancer, limited to epithelial cancer; pathologic stage IA-B (grade 2-3); or stage IC (all grades); or stage II; without evidence of disease progression, recurrence, or metastases (for use in a Medicare-approved demonstration project) ♀

M **G9115** Oncology; disease status; ovarian cancer, limited to epithelial cancer; pathologic stage III-IV; without evidence of progression, recurrence, or metastases (for use in a Medicare-approved demonstration project) ♀

M **G9116** Oncology; disease status; ovarian cancer, limited to epithelial cancer; evidence of disease progression, or recurrence, and/or platinum resistance (for use in a Medicare-approved demonstration project) ♀

M **G9117** Oncology; disease status; ovarian cancer, limited to epithelial cancer; extent of disease unknown, staging in progress, or not listed (for use in a Medicare-approved demonstration project) ♀

M **G9123** Oncology; disease status; chronic myelogenous leukemia, limited to Philadelphia chromosome positive and/or BCR-ABL positive; chronic phase not in hematologic, cytogenetic, or molecular remission (for use in a Medicare-approved demonstration project)

M **G9124** Oncology; disease status; chronic myelogenous leukemia, limited to Philadelphia chromosome positive and /or BCR-ABL positive; accelerated phase not in hematologic cytogenetic, or molecular remission (for use in a Medicare-approved demonstration project)

M **G9125** Oncology; disease status; chronic myelogenous leukemia, limited to Philadelphia chromosome positive and/or BCR-ABL positive; blast phase not in hematologic, cytogenetic, or molecular remission (for use in a Medicare-approved demonstration project)

M **G9126** Oncology; disease status; chronic myelogenous leukemia, limited to Philadelphia chromosome positive and/or BCR-ABL positive; in hematologic, cytogenetic, or molecular remission (for use in a Medicare-approved demonstration project)

M **G9128** Oncology; disease status; limited to multiple myeloma, systemic disease; smoldering, stage I (for use in a Medicare-approved demonstration project)

M **G9129** Oncology; disease status; limited to multiple myeloma, systemic disease; stage II or higher (for use in a Medicare-approved demonstration project)

M **G9130** Oncology; disease status; limited to multiple myeloma, systemic disease; extent of disease unknown, staging in progress, or not listed (for use in a Medicare-approved demonstration project)

M **G9131** Oncology; disease status; invasive female breast cancer (does not include ductal carcinoma in situ); adenocarcinoma as predominant cell type; extent of disease unknown, staging in progress, or not listed (for use in a Medicare-approved demonstration project) ♀

M **G9132** Oncology; disease status; prostate cancer, limited to adenocarcinoma; hormone-refractory/androgen-independent (e.g., rising PSA on antiandrogen therapy or postorchiectomy); clinical metastases (for use in a Medicare-approved demonstration project) ♂

M **G9133** Oncology; disease status; prostate cancer, limited to adenocarcinoma; hormone-responsive; clinical metastases or M1 at diagnosis (for use in a Medicare-approved demonstration project) ♂

M **G9134** Oncology; disease status; non-Hodgkin's lymphoma, any cellular classification; Stage I, II at diagnosis, not relapsed, not refractory (for use in a Medicare-approved demonstration project)

M **G9135** Oncology; disease status; non-Hodgkin's lymphoma, any cellular classification; Stage III, IV, not relapsed, not refractory (for use in a Medicare-approved demonstration project)

M **G9136** Oncology; disease status; non-Hodgkin's lymphoma, transformed from original cellular diagnosis to a second cellular classification (for use in a medicare-approved demonstration project)

M **G9137** Oncology; disease status; non-Hodgkin's lymphoma, any cellular classification; relapsed/refractory (for use in a medicare-approved demonstration project)

M **G9138** Oncology; disease status; non-Hodgkin's lymphoma, any cellular classification; diagnostic evaluation, stage not determined, evaluation of possible relapse or nonresponse to therapy, or not listed (for use in a Medicare-approved demonstration project)

M **G9139** Oncology; disease status; chronic myelogenous leukemia, limited to Philadelphia chromosome positive and/or BCR-ABL positive; extent of disease unknown, staging in progress, not listed (for use in a Medicare-approved demonstration project)

A ☑ **G9140** Frontier extended stay clinic demonstration; for a patient stay in a clinic approved for the CMS demonstration project; the following measures should be present: the stay must be equal to or greater than 4 hours; weather or other conditions must prevent transfer or the case falls into a category of monitoring and observation cases that are permitted by the rules of the demonstration; there is a maximum frontier extended stay clinic (FESC) visit of 48 hours, except in the case when weather or other conditions prevent transfer; payment is made on each period up to 4 hours, after the first 4 hours

H1N1 ADMINISTRATION AND VACCINE

S **G9141** Influenza A (H1N1) immunization administration (includes the physician counseling the patient/family)

E **G9142** Influenza A (H1N1) vaccine, any route of administration

WARFARIN TESTING

A **G9143** Warfarin responsiveness testing by genetic technique using any method, any number of specimen(s)

MED: 100-3,90.1; 100-4,32,250.1; 100-4,32,250.2

OUTPATIENT IV INSULIN TX

E **G9147** Outpatient Intravenous Insulin Treatment (OIVIT) either pulsatile or continuous, by any means, guided by the results of measurements for: respiratory quotient; and/or, urine urea nitrogen (UUN); and/or, arterial, venous or capillary glucose; and/or potassium concentration

MED: 100-3,40.7; 100-4,4,320.1; 100-4,4,320.2

WHEELCHAIR EVALUATION

● M **G9156** [Jan] Evaluation for wheelchair requiring face-to-face visit with physician

ALCOHOL AND DRUG ABUSE TREATMENT SERVICES H0001-H2037

The H codes are used by those state Medicaid agencies that are mandated by state law to establish separate codes for identifying mental health services that include alcohol and drug treatment services.

H0001 Alcohol and/or drug assessment

H0002 Behavioral health screening to determine eligibility for admission to treatment program

H0003 Alcohol and/or drug screening; laboratory analysis of specimens for presence of alcohol and/or drugs

☑ H0004 Behavioral health counseling and therapy, per 15 minutes

H0005 Alcohol and/or drug services; group counseling by a clinician

H0006 Alcohol and/or drug services; case management

H0007 Alcohol and/or drug services; crisis intervention (outpatient)

H0008 Alcohol and/or drug services; subacute detoxification (hospital inpatient)

H0009 Alcohol and/or drug services; acute detoxification (hospital inpatient)

H0010 Alcohol and/or drug services; subacute detoxification (residential addiction program inpatient)

H0011 Alcohol and/or drug services; acute detoxification (residential addiction program inpatient)

H0012 Alcohol and/or drug services; subacute detoxification (residential addiction program outpatient)

H0013 Alcohol and/or drug services; acute detoxification (residential addiction program outpatient)

H0014 Alcohol and/or drug services; ambulatory detoxification

H0015 Alcohol and/or drug services; intensive outpatient (treatment program that operates at least 3 hours/day and at least 3 days/week and is based on an individualized treatment plan), including assessment, counseling; crisis intervention, and activity therapies or education

H0016 Alcohol and/or drug services; medical/somatic (medical intervention in ambulatory setting)

☑ H0017 Behavioral health; residential (hospital residential treatment program), without room and board, per diem

☑ H0018 Behavioral health; short-term residential (nonhospital residential treatment program), without room and board, per diem

☑ H0019 Behavioral health; long-term residential (nonmedical, nonacute care in a residential treatment program where stay is typically longer than 30 days), without room and board, per diem

H0020 Alcohol and/or drug services; methadone administration and/or service (provision of the drug by a licensed program)

H0021 Alcohol and/or drug training service (for staff and personnel not employed by providers)

H0022 Alcohol and/or drug intervention service (planned facilitation)

H0023 Behavioral health outreach service (planned approach to reach a targeted population)

H0024 Behavioral health prevention information dissemination service (one-way direct or nondirect contact with service audiences to affect knowledge and attitude)

H0025 Behavioral health prevention education service (delivery of services with target population to affect knowledge, attitude and/or behavior)

H0026 Alcohol and/or drug prevention process service, community-based (delivery of services to develop skills of impactors)

H0027 Alcohol and/or drug prevention environmental service (broad range of external activities geared toward modifying systems in order to mainstream prevention through policy and law)

H0028 Alcohol and/or drug prevention problem identification and referral service (e.g., student assistance and employee assistance programs), does not include assessment

H0029 Alcohol and/or drug prevention alternatives service (services for populations that exclude alcohol and other drug use e.g., alcohol free social events)

H0030 Behavioral health hotline service

H0031 Mental health assessment, by nonphysician

H0032 Mental health service plan development by nonphysician

H0033 Oral medication administration, direct observation

☑ H0034 Medication training and support, per 15 minutes

☑ H0035 Mental health partial hospitalization, treatment, less than 24 hours

☑ H0036 Community psychiatric supportive treatment, face-to-face, per 15 minutes

☑ H0037 Community psychiatric supportive treatment program, per diem

☑ H0038 Self-help/peer services, per 15 minutes

☑ H0039 Assertive community treatment, face-to-face, per 15 minutes

☑ H0040 Assertive community treatment program, per diem

☑ H0041 Foster care, child, nontherapeutic, per diem A

☑ H0042 Foster care, child, nontherapeutic, per month A

☑ H0043 Supported housing, per diem

☑ H0044 Supported housing, per month

☑ H0045 Respite care services, not in the home, per diem

H0046 Mental health services, not otherwise specified

H0047 Alcohol and/or other drug abuse services, not otherwise specified

H0048 Alcohol and/or other drug testing: collection and handling only, specimens other than blood

H0049 Alcohol and/or drug screening

☑ H0050 Alcohol and/or drug services, brief intervention, per 15 minutes

H1000 Prenatal care, at-risk assessment M ♀

H1001 Prenatal care, at-risk enhanced service; antepartum management M ♀

H1002 Prenatal care, at risk enhanced service; care coordination M ♀

H1003 Prenatal care, at-risk enhanced service; education M ♀

H1004 Prenatal care, at-risk enhanced service; follow-up home visit M ♀

H1005 Prenatal care, at-risk enhanced service package (includes H1001-H1004) M ♀

☑ H1010 Nonmedical family planning education, per session

H1011 Family assessment by licensed behavioral health professional for state defined purposes

H2000 Comprehensive multidisciplinary evaluation

☑ H2001 Rehabilitation program, per 1/2 day

☑ H2010 Comprehensive medication services, per 15 minutes

☑ H2011 Crisis intervention service, per 15 minutes

☑ H2012 Behavioral health day treatment, per hour

☑ H2013 Psychiatric health facility service, per diem

☑ H2014 Skills training and development, per 15 minutes

☑ H2015 Comprehensive community support services, per 15 minutes

☑ H2016 Comprehensive community support services, per diem

☑ H2017 Psychosocial rehabilitation services, per 15 minutes

☑ H2018 Psychosocial rehabilitation services, per diem

☑ H2019 Therapeutic behavioral services, per 15 minutes

☑ H2020 Therapeutic behavioral services, per diem

☑ H2021 Community-based wrap-around services, per 15 minutes

☑ H2022 Community-based wrap-around services, per diem

☑ H2023 Supported employment, per 15 minutes

☑ H2024 Supported employment, per diem

☑ H2025 Ongoing support to maintain employment, per 15 minutes

☑ H2026 Ongoing support to maintain employment, per diem

☑ H2027 Psychoeducational service, per 15 minutes

☑ H2028 Sexual offender treatment service, per 15 minutes

☑ H2029 Sexual offender treatment service, per diem

☑ H2030 Mental health clubhouse services, per 15 minutes

☑ H2031 Mental health clubhouse services, per diem

☑ H2032 Activity therapy, per 15 minutes

☑ H2033 Multisystemic therapy for juveniles, per 15 minutes

☑ H2034 Alcohol and/or drug abuse halfway house services, per diem

☑ H2035 Alcohol and/or other drug treatment program, per hour

☑ H2036 Alcohol and/or other drug treatment program, per diem

☑ H2037 Developmental delay prevention activities, dependent child of client, per 15 minutes A

J CODES DRUGS J0120-J8499

J codes include drugs that ordinarily cannot be self-administered, chemotherapy drugs, immunosuppressive drugs, inhalation solutions, and other miscellaneous drugs and solutions

N ☑ J0120 Injection, tetracycline, up to 250 mg N1

▲ K ☑ J0129 Jan Injection, abatacept, 10 mg (code may be used for Medicare when drug administered under the direct supervision of a physician, not for use when drug is self-administered) K2
Use this code for Orencia

K ☑ J0130 Injection abciximab, 10 mg K2
Use this code for ReoPro.

● G ☑ J0131 Jan Injection, acetaminophen, 10 mg K2
Use this code for OFIRMEV.

K ☑ J0132 Injection, acetylcysteine, 100 mg K2
Use this code for Acetadote.

N ☑ J0133 Injection, acyclovir, 5 mg N1
Use this code for Zovirax

K ☑ J0135 Injection, adalimumab, 20 mg K2
Use this code for Humira.

N ☑ J0150 Injection, adenosine for therapeutic use, 6 mg (not to be used to report any adenosine phosphate compounds, instead use A9270) N1
Use this code for Adenocard.
AHA: 2Q,'02,10

K ☑ J0152 Injection, adenosine for diagnostic use, 30 mg (not to be used to report any adenosine phosphate compounds; instead use A9270) K2
Use this code for Adenoscan.

N ☑ J0171 Injection, Adrenalin, epinephrine, 0.1 mg N1

K ☑ J0180 Injection, agalsidase beta, 1 mg K2
Use this code for Fabrazyme.

E ☑ J0190 Injection, biperiden lactate, per 5 mg

N ☑ J0200 Injection, alatrofloxacin mesylate, 100 mg N1
MED: 100-2,15,50.5

K ☑ J0205 Injection, alglucerase, per 10 units K2
Use this code for Ceredase.

K ☑ J0207 Injection, amifostine, 500 mg K2
Use this code for Ethyol.

K ☑ J0210 Injection, methyldopate HCl, up to 250 mg K2
Use this code for Aldomet.

K ☑ J0215 Injection, alefacept, 0.5 mg K2
Use this for Amevive.

▲ K ☑ J0220 Jan Injection, alglucosidase alfa, 10 mg, not otherwise specified K2
Use this code for Myozyme.

● G ☑ J0221 Jan Injection, alglucosidase alfa, (Lumizyme), 10 mg K2

▲ K ☑ J0256 Jan Injection, alpha 1-proteinase inhibitor (human), not otherwise specified, 10 mg K2
Use this code for Aralast, Aralast NP, Prolastin C, Zemira.

● K ☑ J0257 Jan Injection, alpha 1 proteinase inhibitor (human), (GLASSIA), 10 mg K2

B J0270 Injection, alprostadil, 1.25 mcg (code may be used for Medicare when drug administered under the direct supervision of a physician, not for use when drug is self-administered)
Use this code for Alprostadil, Caverject, Edex, Prostin VR Pediatric.

B J0275 Alprostadil urethral suppository (code may be used for Medicare when drug administered under the direct supervision of a physician, not for use when drug is self-administered)
Use this code for Muse.

N ☑ J0278 Injection, amikacin sulfate, 100 mg N1
Use this code for Amikin.

N ☑ J0280 Injection, aminophyllin, up to 250 mg N1

N ☑ J0282 Injection, amiodarone HCl, 30 mg N1
Use this code for Cordarone IV.

N ☑ J0285 Injection, amphotericin B, 50 mg N1
Use this for Amphocin, Fungizone

K ☑ J0287 Injection, amphotericin B lipid complex, 10 mg K2
Use this code for Abelcet

K ☑ J0288 Injection, amphotericin B cholesteryl sulfate complex, 10 mg K2
Use this code for Amphotec.

K ☑ J0289 Injection, amphotericin B liposome, 10 mg K2
Use this code for Ambisome.

N ☑ J0290 Injection, ampicillin sodium, 500 mg N1

N ☑ J0295 Injection, ampicillin sodium/sulbactam sodium, per 1.5 g N1
Use this code for Unasyn.

K ☑ J0300 Injection, amobarbital, up to 125 mg K2
Use this code for Amytal.

N ☑ J0330 Injection, succinylcholine chloride, up to 20 mg N1
Use this code for Anectine, Quelicin.

K ☑ J0348 Injection, anidulafungin, 1 mg K2
Use this code for Eraxis.

E ☑ J0350 Injection, anistreplase, per 30 units
Use this code for Eminase.

N ☑ J0360 Injection, hydralazine HCl, up to 20 mg N1

K ☑ J0364 Injection, apomorphine HCl, 1 mg K2
Use this code for Apokyn.

N ☑ J0365 Injection, aprotinin, 10,000 kiu N1
Use this code for Trasylol.

N ☑ J0380 Injection, metaraminol bitartrate, per 10 mg N1
Use this code for Aramine.

N ☑ J0390 Injection, chloroquine HCl, up to 250 mg N1
Use this code for Aralen.

E ☑ J0395 Injection, arbutamine HCl, 1 mg

N ☑ J0400 Injection, aripiprazole, intramuscular, 0.25 mg N1
Use this code for Abilify.

N ☑ J0456 Injection, azithromycin, 500 mg N1
Use this code for Zithromax.
MED: 100-2,15,50.5

N ☑ J0461 Injection, atropine sulfate, 0.01 mg N1
Use this code for AtroPen.

N ☑ J0470 Injection, dimercaprol, per 100 mg N1
Use this code for BAL

K ☑ J0475 Injection, baclofen, 10 mg K2
Use this code for Lioresal, Gablofen.

K ☑ J0476 Injection, baclofen, 50 mcg for intrathecal trial K2
Use this code for Lioresal, Gablofen.

K J0480 Injection, basiliximab, 20 mg K2
Use this code for Simulect.

● G ☑ J0490 Jan Injection, belimumab, 10 mg K2
Use this code for BENLYSTA.

N ☑ J0500 Injection, dicyclomine HCl, up to 20 mg N1
Use this code for Bentyl.

N ☑ J0515 Injection, benztropine mesylate, per 1 mg N1
Use this code for Cogentin.

N ☑ J0520 Injection, bethanechol chloride, Myotonachol or Urecholine, up to 5 mg N1

N ☑ J0558 Injection, penicillin G benzathine and penicillin G procaine, 100,000 units N1
Use this code for Bicillin CR, Bicillin CR 900/300, Bicillin CR Tubex.

N ☑ J0561 Injection, penicillin G benzathine, 100,000 units N1

K ☑ J0583 Injection, bivalirudin, 1 mg K2
Use this code for Angiomax.

K ☑ J0585 Injection, onabotulinumtoxinA, 1 unit K2
Use this code for Botox, Botox Cosmetic.

K ☑ J0586 Injection, abobotulinumtoxinA, 5 units K2
Use this code for Dysport.

K ☑ J0587 Injection, rimabotulinumtoxinB, 100 units K2
Use this code for Myobloc.
AHA: 2Q,'02,8

● G ☑ J0588 Jan Injection, incobotulinumtoxinA, 1 unit K2
Use this code for XEOMIN.

N ☑ J0592 Injection, buprenorphine HCl, 0.1 mg N1
Use this code for Buprenex.

K ☑ J0594 Injection, busulfan, 1 mg K2
Use this code for Busulfex.

N ☑ J0595 Injection, butorphanol tartrate, 1 mg N1
Use this code for Stadol.

G ☑ J0597 Injection, C-1 esterase inhibitor (human), Berinert, 10 units K2

K ☑ J0598 Injection, C-1 esterase inhibitor (human), Cinryze, 10 units K2

K ☑ J0600 Injection, edetate calcium disodium, up to 1,000 mg K2
Use this code for Calcium Disodium Versenate, Calcium EDTA.

N ☑ J0610 Injection, calcium gluconate, per 10 ml N1

N ☑ J0620 Injection, calcium glycerophosphate and calcium lactate, per 10 ml N1

N ☑ J0630 Injection, calcitonin salmon, up to 400 units N1
Use this code for Calcimar, Miacalcin.
MED: 100-4,10,90.1

N ☑ J0636 Injection, calcitriol, 0.1 mcg N1
Use this code for Calcijex.

K J0637 Injection, caspofungin acetate, 5 mg K2
Use this code for Cancidas.

G J0638 Injection, canakinumab, 1 mg K2
Use this code for ILARIS.

N ☑ J0640 Injection, leucovorin calcium, per 50 mg N1

K ☑ J0641 Injection, levoleucovorin calcium, 0.5 mg K2
Use this code for Fusilev.

N ☑ J0670 Injection, mepivacaine HCl, per 10 ml N1
Use this code for Carbocaine, Polocaine, Isocaine HCl, Scandonest

N ☑ J0690 Injection, cefazolin sodium, 500 mg N1
Use this code for Ancef, Kefzol

N ☑ J0692 Injection, cefepime HCl, 500 mg N1
Use this code for Maxipime.

N ☑ J0694 Injection, cefoxitin sodium, 1 g N1

N ☑ J0696 Injection, ceftriaxone sodium, per 250 mg N1
Use this code for Rocephin.

N ☑ J0697 Injection, sterile cefuroxime sodium, per 750 mg N1
Use this code for Zinacef.

N ☑ J0698 Injection, cefotaxime sodium, per g N1
Use this code for Claforan.

N ☑ J0702 Injection, betamethasone acetate 3 mg and betamethasone sodium phosphate 3 mg N1
Use this code for Celestone Soluspan.

N ☑ J0706 Injection, caffeine citrate, 5 mg N1
Use this code for Cafcit.
AHA: 2Q,'02,8

N ☑ J0710 Injection, cephapirin sodium, up to 1 g N1

● G ☑ J0712 Jan Injection, ceftaroline fosamil, 10 mg K2
Use this code for Teflaro.

N ☑ J0713 Injection, ceftazidime, per 500 mg N1
Use this code for Ceptax, Fortaz, Tazicef

N ☑ J0715 Injection, ceftizoxime sodium, per 500 mg N1
Use this code for Cefizox.

K ☑ J0718 Injection, certolizumab pegol, 1 mg K2
Use this code for Cimzia.

N ☑ J0720 Injection, chloramphenicol sodium succinate, up to 1 g N1
Use this code for Chlormycetin.

N ☑ J0725 Injection, chorionic gonadotropin, per 1,000 USP units N1

N ☑ J0735 Injection, clonidine HCl, 1 mg N1
Use this code for Clorpres, Duraclon, Iopidine

K ☑ J0740 Injection, cidofovir, 375 mg K2
Use this code for Vistide.

N ☑ J0743 Injection, cilastatin sodium; imipenem, per 250 mg N1
Use this code for Primaxin I.M., Primaxin I.V.

N ☑ J0744 Injection, ciprofloxacin for intravenous infusion, 200 mg N1
Use this code for Cipro.

N ☑ J0745 Injection, codeine phosphate, per 30 mg N1

N ☑ J0760 Injection, colchicine, per 1 mg N1

N ☑ J0770 Injection, colistimethate sodium, up to 150 mg N1
Use this code for Coly-Mycin M.

G ☑ J0775 Injection, collagenase, clostridium histolyticum, 0.01 mg K2
Use this code for XIAFLEX.

N ☑ J0780 Injection, prochlorperazine, up to 10 mg N1
Use this code for Compazine, Ultrazine-10.

K ☑ J0795 Injection, corticorelin ovine triflutate, 1 mcg K2
Use this code for Acthrel.

K ☑ J0800 Injection, corticotropin, up to 40 units K2
Use this code for H.P. Acthar gel

K ☑ **J0833** **Injection, cosyntropin, not otherwise specified, 0.25 mg** K2
Use this code for Cortrosyn.

N ☑ **J0834** **Injection, cosyntropin (Cortrosyn), 0.25 mg** N1

● G ☑ **J0840**Jan **Injection, crotalidae polyvalent immune fab (ovine), up to 1 g** K2
Use this code for CroFab, FabAV.

K ☑ **J0850** **Injection, cytomegalovirus immune globulin intravenous (human), per vial** K2
Use this code for Cytogam.

K ☑ **J0878** **Injection, daptomycin, 1 mg** K2
Use this code for Cubicin.

K ☑ **J0881** **Injection, darbepoetin alfa, 1 mcg (non-ESRD use)** K2
Use this code for Aranesp.
MED: 100-4,8,60.7.4

A ☑ **J0882** **Injection, darbepoetin alfa, 1 mcg (for ESRD on dialysis)** ⊘
Use this code for Aranesp.
MED: 100-4,8,60.4; 100-4,8,60.7; 100-4,8,60.7.4; 100-4,13,60.7.1

K ☑ **J0885** **Injection, epoetin alfa, (for non-ESRD use), 1000 units** K2
Use this code for Epogen/Procrit.

A ☑ **J0886** **Injection, epoetin alfa, 1000 units (for ESRD on dialysis)** ⊘
Use this code for Epogen/Procrit.
MED: 100-4,8,60.4

K ☑ **J0894** **Injection, decitabine, 1 mg** K2 ⊘ ⊘
Use this code for Dacogen.

N ☑ **J0895** **Injection, deferoxamine mesylate, 500 mg** N1
Use this code for Desferal.

● G ☑ **J0897**Jan **Injection, denosumab, 1 mg** K2
Use this code for XGEVA, Prolia.

N ☑ **J0900** **Injection, testosterone enanthate and estradiol valerate, up to 1 cc** N1

N ☑ **J0945** **Injection, brompheniramine maleate, per 10 mg** N1

N ☑ **J1000** **Injection, depo-estradiol cypionate, up to 5 mg** N1
Use this code for depGynogen, Depogen, Estradiol Cypionate

N ☑ **J1020** **Injection, methylprednisolone acetate, 20 mg** N1
Use this code for Depo-Medrol.

N ☑ **J1030** **Injection, methylprednisolone acetate, 40 mg** N1
Use this code for DepoMedalone40, Depo-Medrol, Sano-Drol

N ☑ **J1040** **Injection, methylprednisolone acetate, 80 mg** N1
Use this code for Cortimed, DepMedalone, DepoMedalone 80, Depo-Medrol, Duro Cort, Methylcotolone, Pri-Methylate, Sano-Drol

N ☑ **J1051** **Injection, medroxyprogesterone acetate, 50 mg** N1
Use this code for Depo-Provera.

E **J1055** **Injection, medroxyprogesterone acetate for contraceptive use, 150 mg** ♀
Use this code for Depo-Provera.

E **J1056** **Injection, medroxyprogesterone acetate/estradiol cypionate, 5 mg/25 mg** ♀
Use this code for Lunelle monthly contraceptive.

N ☑ **J1060** **Injection, testosterone cypionate and estradiol cypionate, up to 1 ml** N1
Use this code for Depo-Testadiol, Duo-Span, Duo-Span II.

N ☑ **J1070** **Injection, testosterone cypionate, up to 100 mg** N1
Use this code for Depo Testosterone Cypionate

N ☑ **J1080** **Injection, testosterone cypionate, 1 cc, 200 mg** N1
Use this code for Depandrante, Depo-Testosterone, Virilon

N **J1094** **Injection, dexamethasone acetate, 1 mg** N1
Use this code for Cortastat LA, Dalalone L.A., Dexamethasone Acetate Anhydrous, Dexone LA.

N ☑ **J1100** **Injection, dexamethasone sodium phosphate, 1 mg** N1
Use this code for Cortastat, Dalalone, Decaject, Dexone, Solurex, Adrenocort, Primethasone, Dexasone, Dexim, Medidex, Spectro-Dex.

N ☑ **J1110** **Injection, dihydroergotamine mesylate, per 1 mg** N1
Use this code for D.H.E. 45.

N ☑ **J1120** **Injection, acetazolamide sodium, up to 500 mg** N1
Use this code for Diamox.

N ☑ **J1160** **Injection, digoxin, up to 0.5 mg** N1
Use this code for Lanoxin.

K ☑ **J1162** **Injection, digoxin immune fab (ovine), per vial** K2
Use this code for Digibind, Digifab.

N ☑ **J1165** **Injection, phenytoin sodium, per 50 mg** N1
Use this code for Dilantin.

N ☑ **J1170** **Injection, hydromorphone, up to 4 mg** N1
Use this code for Dilaudid, Dilaudid-HP.

N ☑ **J1180** **Injection, dyphylline, up to 500 mg** N1

K ☑ **J1190** **Injection, dexrazoxane HCl, per 250 mg** K2
Use this code for Zinecard.

N ☑ **J1200** **Injection, diphenhydramine HCl, up to 50 mg** N1
Use this code for Benadryl, Benahist 10, Benahist 50, Benoject-10, Benoject-50, Bena-D 10, Bena-D 50, Nordryl, Dihydrex, Dimine, Diphenacen-50, Hyrexin-50, Truxadryl, Wehdryl.
AHA: 1Q,'02,2

K ☑ **J1205** **Injection, chlorothiazide sodium, per 500 mg** K2
Use this code for Diuril Sodium.

K ☑ **J1212** **Injection, DMSO, dimethyl sulfoxide, 50%, 50 ml** K2
Use this code for Rimso 50. DMSO is covered only as a treatment of interstitial cystitis.

N ☑ **J1230** **Injection, methadone HCl, up to 10 mg** N1
Use this code for Dolophine HCl.

N ☑ **J1240** **Injection, dimenhydrinate, up to 50 mg** N1
Use this code for Dramamine, Dinate, Dommanate, Dramanate, Dramilin, Dramocen, Dramoject, Dymenate, Hydrate, Marmine, Wehamine.

N ☑ **J1245** **Injection, dipyridamole, per 10 mg** N1
Use this code for Persantine IV.

N ☑ **J1250** **Injection, Dobutamine HCl, per 250 mg** N1

N ☑ **J1260** **Injection, dolasetron mesylate, 10 mg** N1
Use this code for Anzemet.

N ☑ **J1265** **Injection, dopamine HCl, 40 mg** N1

N **J1267** **Injection, doripenem, 10 mg** N1
Use this code for Doribax

N ☑ **J1270** **Injection, doxercalciferol, 1 mcg** N1
Use this code for Hectorol.

G ☑ **J1290** **Injection, ecallantide, 1 mg** K2
Use this code for KALBITOR.

K ☑ **J1300** **Injection, eculizumab, 10 mg** K2
Use this code for Soliris.

Jan **January Update**

N ☑ **J1320** **Injection, amitriptyline HCl, up to 20 mg** N1
Use this code for Elavil

K ☑ **J1324** **Injection, enfuvirtide, 1 mg** K2
Use this code for Fuzeon.

N ☑ **J1325** **Injection, epoprostenol, 0.5 mg** N1
Use this code for Flolan. See K0455 for infusion pump for epoprosterol.

K ☑ **J1327** **Injection, eptifibatide, 5 mg** K2
Use this code for Integrilin.

N ☑ **J1330** **Injection, ergonovine maleate, up to 0.2 mg** N1
Medicare jurisdiction: local contractor. Use this code for Ergotrate Maleate.

N ☑ **J1335** **Injection, ertapenem sodium, 500 mg** N1
Use this code for Invanz.

N ☑ **J1364** **Injection, erythromycin lactobionate, per 500 mg** N1

N ☑ **J1380** **Injection, estradiol valerate, up to 10 mg** N1
Use this code for Delestrogen, Dioval, Dioval XX, Dioval 40, Duragen-10, Duragen-20, Duragen-40, Estradiol L.A., Estradiol L.A. 20, Estradiol L.A. 40, Gynogen L.A. 10, Gynogen L.A. 20, Gynogen L.A. 40, Valergen 10, Valergen 20, Valergen 40, Estra-L 20, Estra-L 40, L.A.E. 20.

K ☑ **J1410** **Injection, estrogen conjugated, per 25 mg** K2
Use this code for Natural Estrogenic Substance, Premarin Intravenous, Primestrin Aqueous.

K **J1430** **Injection, ethanolamine oleate, 100 mg** K2
Use this code for Ethamiolin.

E ☑ **J1435** **Injection, estrone, per 1 mg**
Use this code for Estone Aqueous, Estragyn, Estro-A, Estrone, Estronol, Theelin Aqueous, Estone 5, Kestrone 5.

N ☑ **J1436** **Injection, etidronate disodium, per 300 mg** N1
Use this code for Didronel.

K ☑ **J1438** **Injection, etanercept, 25 mg (code may be used for Medicare when drug administered under the direct supervision of a physician, not for use when drug is self-administered)** K2
Use this code for Enbrel.

K ☑ **J1440** **Injection, filgrastim (G-CSF), 300 mcg** K2
Use this code for Neupogen.

K ☑ **J1441** **Injection, filgrastim (G-CSF), 480 mcg** K2
Use this code for Neupogen.

N ☑ **J1450** **Injection, fluconazole, 200 mg** N1
Use this code for Diflucan.
MED: 100-2,15,50.5

K ☑ **J1451** **Injection, fomepizole, 15 mg** K2
Use this code for Antizol.

E ☑ **J1452** **Injection, fomivirsen sodium, intraocular, 1.65 mg**
Use this code for Vitavene.
MED: 100-2,15,50.4.2

K **J1453** **Injection, fosaprepitant, 1 mg** K2
Use this code for Emend.

K ☑ **J1455** **Injection, foscarnet sodium, per 1,000 mg** K2
Use this code for Foscavir.

N ☑ **J1457** **Injection, gallium nitrate, 1 mg** N1
Use this code for Ganite.

K ☑ **J1458** **Injection, galsulfase, 1 mg** K2
Use this code for Naglazyme.

K **J1459** **Injection, immune globulin (Privigen), intravenous, nonlyophilized (e.g., liquid), 500 mg** K2

K ☑ **J1460** **Injection, gamma globulin, intramuscular, 1 cc** K2
Use this code for GamaSTAN SD.

● G ☑ **J1557** Jan **Injection, immune globulin, (Gammaplex), intravenous, nonlyophilized (e.g., liquid), 500 mg** K2

K ☑ **J1559** **Injection, immune globulin (Hizentra), 100 mg** K2

K ☑ **J1560** **Injection, gamma globulin, intramuscular, over 10 cc** K2
Use this code for GamaSTAN SD.

▲ K ☑ **J1561** Jan **Injection, immune globulin, (Gamunex/Gamunex-C/Gammaked), nonlyophilized (e.g., liquid), 500 mg** K2

K ☑ **J1562** **Injection, immune globulin (Vivaglobin), 100 mg** K2

K ☑ **J1566** **Injection, immune globulin, intravenous, lyophilized (e.g., powder), not otherwise specified, 500 mg** K2
Use this code for Carimune.

K ☑ **J1568** **Injection, immune globulin, (Octagam), intravenous, nonlyophilized (e.g., liquid), 500 mg** K2

K ☑ **J1569** **Injection, immune globulin, (Gammagard liquid), intravenous, nonlyophilized, (e.g., liquid), 500 mg** K2

K ☑ **J1570** **Injection, ganciclovir sodium, 500 mg** K2
Use this code for Cytovene.

K ☑ **J1571** **Injection, hepatitis B immune globulin (Hepagam B), intramuscular, 0.5 ml** K2

G ☑ **J1572** **Injection, immune globulin, (Flebogamma/Flebogamma Dif), intravenous, nonlyophilized (e.g., liquid), 500 mg** K2

K ☑ **J1573** **Injection, hepatitis B immune globulin (Hepagam B), intravenous, 0.5 ml** K2

N ☑ **J1580** **Injection, garamycin, gentamicin, up to 80 mg** N1
Use this code for Gentamicin Sulfate, Jenamicin.

N ☑ **J1590** **Injection, gatifloxacin, 10 mg** N1
MED: 100-4,4,10.4

K ☑ **J1595** **Injection, glatiramer acetate, 20 mg** K2
Use this code for Copaxone.

N ☑ **J1599** **Injection, immune globulin, intravenous, nonlyophilized (e.g., liquid), not otherwise specified, 500 mg** N1

N ☑ **J1600** **Injection, gold sodium thiomalate, up to 50 mg** N1
Use this code for Myochrysine.
MED: 100-4,4,10.4

K ☑ **J1610** **Injection, glucagon HCl, per 1 mg** K2
Use this code for Glucagen.

K ☑ **J1620** **Injection, gonadorelin HCl, per 100 mcg** K2
Use this code for Factrel, Lutrepulse.

N ☑ **J1626** **Injection, granisetron HCl, 100 mcg** N1
Use this code for Kytril.
MED: 100-4,4,10.4

N ☑ **J1630** **Injection, haloperidol, up to 5 mg** N1
Use this code for Haldol.
MED: 100-4,4,10.4

N ☑ **J1631** **Injection, haloperidol decanoate, per 50 mg** N1
Use this code for Haldol Decanoate-50.

K ☑ **J1640** **Injection, hemin, 1 mg** K2
Use this code for Panhematin.

K ☑ J1642 Injection, heparin sodium, (heparin lock flush), per 10 units K2
Use this code for Hep-Lock, Hep-Lock U/P, Hep-Pak, Lok-Pak.
MED: 100-4,4,10.4

K ☑ J1644 Injection, Heparin sodium, per 1000 units K2
Use this code for Heparin Sodium, Liquaemin Sodium.
MED: 100-4,4,10.4

N ☑ J1645 Injection, dalteparin sodium, per 2500 IU N1
Use this code for Fragmin.

N ☑ J1650 Injection, enoxaparin sodium, 10 mg N1
Use this code for Lovenox.
MED: 100-4,4,10.4

N ☑ J1652 Injection, fondaparinux sodium, 0.5 mg N1
Use this code for Atrixtra.

N ☑ J1655 Injection, tinzaparin sodium, 1000 IU N1
Use this code for Innohep.
MED: 100-4,4,10.4

K ☑ J1670 Injection, tetanus immune globulin, human, up to 250 units K2
Use this code for HyperTET SD.

B J1675 Injection, histrelin acetate, 10 mcg
Use this code for Supprelin LA.

K ☑ J1680 Injection, human fibrinogen concentrate, 100 mg K2
Use this code for RiaSTAP.

N ☑ J1700 Injection, hydrocortisone acetate, up to 25 mg N1
Use this code for Hydrocortone Acetate.
MED: 100-4,4,10.4

N ☑ J1710 Injection, hydrocortisone sodium phosphate, up to 50 mg N1
Use this code for Hydrocortone Phosphate.
MED: 100-4,4,10.4

N ☑ J1720 Injection, hydrocortisone sodium succinate, up to 100 mg N1
Use this code for Solu-Cortef, A-Hydrocort.
MED: 100-4,4,10.4

● K J1725 Jan Injection, hydroxyprogesterone caproate, 1 mg M ♀ K2
Use this code for Makena.

N ☑ J1730 Injection, diazoxide, up to 300 mg N1

K ☑ J1740 Injection, ibandronate sodium, 1 mg K2
Use this code for Boniva.

K ☑ J1742 Injection, ibutilide fumarate, 1 mg K2
Use this code for Corvert.

K J1743 Injection, idursulfase, 1 mg K2
Use this code for Elaprase.

K ☑ J1745 Injection infliximab, 10 mg K2
Use this code for Remicade.

K J1750 Injection, iron dextran, 50 mg K2
Use this code for INFeD.

K ☑ J1756 Injection, iron sucrose, 1 mg K2
Use this code for Venofer.

K ☑ J1786 Injection, imiglucerase, 10 units K2
Use this code for Cerezyme.

N ☑ J1790 Injection, droperidol, up to 5 mg N1
Use this code for Inapsine.
MED: 100-4,4,10.4

N ☑ J1800 Injection, propranolol HCl, up to 1 mg N1
Use this code for Inderal.
MED: 100-4,4,10.4

E ☑ J1810 Injection, droperidol and fentanyl citrate, up to 2 ml ampule
AHA: 2Q,'02,8

N ☑ J1815 Injection, insulin, per 5 units N1
Use this code for Humalog, Humulin, Iletin, Insulin Lispo, Lantus, Levemir, NPH, Pork insulin, Regular insulin, Ultralente, Velosulin, Humulin R, Iletin II Regular Pork, Insulin Purified Pork, Relion, Lente Iletin I, Novolin R, Humulin R U-500.
MED: 100-4,4,10.4

N ☑ J1817 Insulin for administration through DME (i.e., insulin pump) per 50 units N1
Use this code for Humalog, Humulin, Vesolin BR, Iletin II NPH Pork, Lispro-PFC, Novolin, Novolog, Novolog Flexpen, Novolog Mix, Relion Novolin.

E ☑ J1826 Injection, interferon beta-1a, 30 mcg
Use this code for AVONEX, Rebif.

K ☑ J1830 Injection interferon beta-1b, 0.25 mg (code may be used for Medicare when drug administered under the direct supervision of a physician, not for use when drug is self-administered) K2
Use this code for Betaseron.

K ☑ J1835 Injection, itraconazole, 50 mg K2
Use this code for Sporonox IV.
MED: 100-4,4,10.4

N ☑ J1840 Injection, kanamycin sulfate, up to 500 mg N1
Use this code for Kantrex
MED: 100-4,4,10.4

N ☑ J1850 Injection, kanamycin sulfate, up to 75 mg N1
Use this code for Kantrex
MED: 100-4,4,10.4

N ☑ J1885 Injection, ketorolac tromethamine, per 15 mg N1
Use this code for Toradol.
MED: 100-4,4,10.4

N ☑ J1890 Injection, cephalothin sodium, up to 1 g N1
MED: 100-4,4,10.4

K ☑ J1930 Injection, lanreotide, 1 mg K2
Use this code for Somatuline.

K ☑ J1931 Injection, laronidase, 0.1 mg K2
Use this code for Aldurazyme.

N ☑ J1940 Injection, furosemide, up to 20 mg N1
Use this code for Lasix
MED: 100-4,4,10.4

K ☑ J1945 Injection, lepirudin, 50 mg K2
Use this code for Refludan.
This drug is used for patients with heparin induced thrombocytopenia.

K ☑ J1950 Injection, leuprolide acetate (for depot suspension), per 3.75 mg K2
Use this code for Eliguard, Lupron, Lupron-3, Lupron-4, Lupron Depot.

N ☑ J1953 Injection, levetiracetam, 10 mg N1
Use this code for Keppra.

B ☑ J1955 Injection, levocarnitine, per 1 g
Use this code for Carnitor

N ☑ J1956 Injection, levofloxacin, 250 mg N1
Use this code for Levaquin.
MED: 100-4,4,10.4

N ☑ J1960 Injection, levorphanol tartrate, up to 2 mg N1
Use this code for Levo-Dromoran.
MED: 100-4,4,10.4

N ☑ J1980 Injection, hyoscyamine sulfate, up to 0.25 mg N1
Use this code for Levsin.
MED: 100-4,4,10.4

N ☑ J1990 Injection, chlordiazepoxide HCl, up to 100 mg N1
Use this code for Librium.
MED: 100-4,4,10.4

N ☑ J2001 Injection, lidocaine HCl for intravenous infusion, 10 mg N1
Use this code for Xylocaine.
MED: 100-4,4,10.4

N ☑ J2010 Injection, lincomycin HCl, up to 300 mg N1
Use this code for Lincocin
MED: 100-4,4,10.4

K ☑ J2020 Injection, linezolid, 200 mg K2
Use this code for Zyvok.
AHA: 2Q,'02,8

N ☑ J2060 Injection, lorazepam, 2 mg N1
Use this code for Ativan.
MED: 100-4,4,10.4

N ☑ J2150 Injection, mannitol, 25% in 50 ml N1
Use this code for Osmitrol.
MED: 100-4,4,10.4

K ☑ J2170 Injection, mecasermin, 1 mg K2
Use this code for Iplex, Increlex.
MED: 100-4,4,10.4

N ☑ J2175 Injection, meperidine HCl, per 100 mg N1
Use this code for Demerol.
MED: 100-4,4,10.4

N ☑ J2180 Injection, meperidine and promethazine HCl, up to 50 mg N1
Use this code for Mepergan Injection.
MED: 100-4,4,10.4

N ☑ J2185 Injection, meropenem, 100 mg N1
Use this code for Merrem
MED: 100-4,4,10.4

N ☑ J2210 Injection, methylergonovine maleate, up to 0.2 mg N1
Use this code for Methergine.
MED: 100-4,4,10.4

K ☑ J2248 Injection, micafungin sodium, 1 mg K2
Use this code for Mycamine.

N ☑ J2250 Injection, midazolam HCl, per 1 mg N1
Use this code for Versed.
MED: 100-4,4,10.4

N ☑ J2260 Injection, milrinone lactate, 5 mg N1
Use this code for Primacor.
MED: 100-4,4,10.4

● E ☑ J2265 Jan Injection, minocycline HCl, 1 mg
Use this code for MINOCIN.

N ☑ J2270 Injection, morphine sulfate, up to 10 mg N1
Use this code for Depodur, Infumorph
MED: 100-4,4,10.4

N ☑ J2271 Injection, morphine sulfate, 100 mg N1
Use this code for Depodur, Infumorph
MED: 100-4,4,10.4

N ☑ J2275 Injection, morphine sulfate (preservative-free sterile solution), per 10 mg N1
Use this code for Astramorph PF, Duramorph, Infumorph.
MED: 100-4,4,10.4

K ☑ J2278 Injection, ziconotide, 1 mcg K2
Use this code for Prialt

N ☑ J2280 Injection, moxifloxacin, 100 mg N1
Use this code for Avelox.
MED: 100-4,4,10.4

N ☑ J2300 Injection, nalbuphine HCl, per 10 mg N1
Use this code for Nubain.
MED: 100-4,4,10.4

N ☑ J2310 Injection, naloxone HCl, per 1 mg N1
Use this code for Narcan.

K ☑ J2315 Injection, naltrexone, depot form, 1 mg K2
Use this code for Vivitrol.

N ☑ J2320 Injection, nandrolone decanoate, up to 50 mg N1

K J2323 Injection, natalizumab, 1 mg K2
Use this code for Tysabri.

K ☑ J2325 Injection, nesiritide, 0.1 mg K2
Use this code for Natrecor.

K ☑ J2353 Injection, octreotide, depot form for intramuscular injection, 1 mg K2
Use this code for Sandostatin LAR.

N ☑ J2354 Injection, octreotide, nondepot form for subcutaneous or intravenous injection, 25 mcg N1
Use this code for Sandostatin.

K ☑ J2355 Injection, oprelvekin, 5 mg K2
Use this code for Neumega.

K ☑ J2357 Injection, omalizumab, 5 mg K2
Use this code for Xolair.

K ☑ J2358 Injection, olanzapine, long-acting, 1 mg K2
Use this code for ZYPREXA RELPREVV.

N ☑ J2360 Injection, orphenadrine citrate, up to 60 mg N1
Use this code for Norflex

N ☑ J2370 Injection, phenylephrine HCl, up to 1 ml N1

N ☑ J2400 Injection, chloroprocaine HCl, per 30 ml N1
Use this code for Nesacaine, Nesacaine-MPF.

N ☑ J2405 Injection, ondansetron HCl, per 1 mg N1
Use this code for Zofran.

N ☑ J2410 Injection, oxymorphone HCl, up to 1 mg N1
Use this code for Numorphan, Oxymorphone HCl.

K ☑ J2425 Injection, palifermin, 50 mcg K2
Use this code for Kepivance.

K J2426 Injection, paliperidone palmitate extended release, 1 mg K2
Use this code for INVEGA SUSTENNA.

N ☑ J2430 Injection, pamidronate disodium, per 30 mg N1
Use this code for Aredia

N ☑ J2440 Injection, papaverine HCl, up to 60 mg N1

E ☑ J2460 Injection, oxytetracycline HCl, up to 50 mg
Use this code for Terramycin IM.

K ☑ J2469 Injection, palonosetron HCl, 25 mcg K2
Use this code for Aloxi.

Jan January Update

Special Coverage Instructions | Noncovered by Medicare | Carrier Discretion | ☑ Quantity Alert | ● New Code | ○ Recycled/Reinstated | ▲ Revised Code

 A Age Edit | M Maternity Edit | ♀ Female Only | ♂ Male Only | A-Y OPPS Status Indicators

N ☑ J2501 Injection, paricalcitol, 1 mcg N1
Use this code For Zemplar.

K J2503 Injection, pegaptanib sodium, 0.3 mg K2
Use this code for Mucagen.

K ☑ J2504 Injection, pegademase bovine, 25 IU K2
Use this code for Adagen.

K ☑ J2505 Injection, pegfilgrastim, 6 mg K2
Use this code for Neulasta.

● G ☑ J2507 Jan Injection, pegloticase, 1 mg K2
Use this code for KRYSTEXXA.

N ☑ J2510 Injection, penicillin G procaine, aqueous, up to 600,000 units N1
Use this code for Wycillin, Duracillin A.S., Pfizerpen A.S., Crysticillin 300 A.S., Crysticillin 600 A.S.

K J2513 Injection, pentastarch, 10% solution, 100 ml K2

N ☑ J2515 Injection, pentobarbital sodium, per 50 mg N1
Use this code for Nembutal Sodium Solution.

N ☑ J2540 Injection, penicillin G potassium, up to 600,000 units N1
Use this code for Pfizerpen.

N ☑ J2543 Injection, piperacillin sodium/tazobactam sodium, 1 g/0.125 g (1.125 g) N1
Use this code for Zosyn.

B ☑ J2545 Pentamidine isethionate, inhalation solution, FDA-approved final product, noncompounded, administered through DME, unit dose form, per 300 mg
Use this code for Nebupent, Pentam 300

N ☑ J2550 Injection, promethazine HCl, up to 50 mg N1
Use this code for Phenergan

N ☑ J2560 Injection, phenobarbital sodium, up to 120 mg N1

K ☑ J2562 Injection, plerixafor, 1 mg K2
Use this code for Mozobil.

N ☑ J2590 Injection, oxytocin, up to 10 units N1
Use this code for Pitocin, Syntocinon.

N ☑ J2597 Injection, desmopressin acetate, per 1 mcg N1
Use this code for DDAVP.

N ☑ J2650 Injection, prednisolone acetate, up to 1 ml N1

N ☑ J2670 Injection, tolazoline HCl, up to 25 mg N1

N J2675 Injection, progesterone, per 50 mg N1
Use this code for Gesterone, Gestrin.

N ☑ J2680 Injection, fluphenazine decanoate, up to 25 mg N1

N ☑ J2690 Injection, procainamide HCl, up to 1 g N1
Use this code for Pronestyl.

K ☑ J2700 Injection, oxacillin sodium, up to 250 mg K2
Use this code for Bactocill

N ☑ J2710 Injection, neostigmine methylsulfate, up to 0.5 mg N1
Use this code for Prostigmin.

N ☑ J2720 Injection, protamine sulfate, per 10 mg N1

K J2724 Injection, protein C concentrate, intravenous, human, 10 IU K2

K ☑ J2725 Injection, protirelin, per 250 mcg K2
Use this code for Thyrel TRH

K ☑ J2730 Injection, pralidoxime chloride, up to 1 g K2
Use this code for Protopam Chloride.

K ☑ J2760 Injection, phentolamine mesylate, up to 5 mg K2
Use this code for Regitine.

N ☑ J2765 Injection, metoclopramide HCl, up to 10 mg N1
Use this code for Reglan

K ☑ J2770 Injection, quinupristin/dalfopristin, 500 mg (150/350) K2
Use this code for Synercid.

K ☑ J2778 Injection, ranibizumab, 0.1 mg K2
Use this code for Lucentis.

N ☑ J2780 Injection, ranitidine HCl, 25 mg N1
Use this code for Zantac.

K ☑ J2783 Injection, rasburicase, 0.5 mg K2
Use this code for Elitek.

K ☑ J2785 Injection, regadenoson, 0.1 mg K2
Use this code for Lexiscan.

K ☑ J2788 Injection, Rho D immune globulin, human, minidose, 50 mcg (250 i.u.) K2
Use this code for RhoGam, MiCRhoGAM.

K ☑ J2790 Injection, Rho D immune globulin, human, full dose, 300 mcg (1500 i.u.) K2
Use this code for RhoGam, HypRho SD.

K J2791 Injection, Rho(D) immune globulin (human), (Rhophylac), intramuscular or intravenous, 100 IU K2
Use this for Rhophylac .

K ☑ J2792 Injection, Rho D immune globulin, intravenous, human, solvent detergent, 100 IU K2
Use this code for WINRho SDF

K ☑ J2793 Injection, rilonacept, 1 mg K2
Use this code for Arcalyst.

K ☑ J2794 Injection, risperidone, long acting, 0.5 mg K2
Use this code for Risperidal Consta Long Acting.

N ☑ J2795 Injection, ropivacaine HCl, 1 mg N1
Use this code for Naropin.

K ☑ J2796 Injection, romiplostim, 10 mcg K2
Use this code for Nplate.

N ☑ J2800 Injection, methocarbamol, up to 10 ml N1
Use this code for Robaxin

N J2805 Injection, sincalide, 5 mcg N1
Use this code for Kinevac.

N ☑ J2810 Injection, theophylline, per 40 mg N1

K ☑ J2820 Injection, sargramostim (GM-CSF), 50 mcg K2
Use this code for Leukine

K ☑ J2850 Injection, secretin, synthetic, human, 1 mcg K2

N ☑ J2910 Injection, aurothioglucose, up to 50 mg N1
Use this code for Solganal.

N ☑ J2916 Injection, sodium ferric gluconate complex in sucrose injection, 12.5 mg N1
MED: 100-2,15,50.2; 100-3,110.10

N ☑ J2920 Injection, methylprednisolone sodium succinate, up to 40 mg N1
Use this code for Solu-Medrol, A-methaPred.

N ☑ J2930 Injection, methylprednisolone sodium succinate, up to 125 mg N1
Use this code for Solu-Medrol, A-methaPred.

E ☑ J2940 Injection, somatrem, 1 mg
Use this code for Protropin.
AHA: 2Q,'02,8

K ☑J2941 **Injection, somatropin, 1 mg** K2
Use this code for Humatrope, Genotropin Nutropin, Biotropin, Genotropin, Genotropin Miniquick, Norditropin, Nutropin, Nutropin AQ, Saizen, Saizen Somatropin RDNA Origin, Serostim, Serostim RDNA Origin, Zorbtive.
AHA: 2Q,'02,8

N ☑J2950 **Injection, promazine HCl, up to 25 mg** N1
Use this code for Sparine, Prozine-50.

K ☑J2993 **Injection, reteplase, 18.1 mg** K2
Use this code for Retavase

K ☑J2995 **Injection, streptokinase, per 250,000 IU** K2
Use this code for Streptase

K ☑J2997 **Injection, alteplase recombinant, 1 mg** K2
Use this code for Activase, Cathflo.

N ☑J3000 **Injection, streptomycin, up to 1 g** N1
Use this code for Streptomycin Sulfate.

N ☑J3010 **Injection, fentanyl citrate, 0.1 mg** N1
Use this code for Sublimaze.

K ☑J3030 **Injection, sumatriptan succinate, 6 mg (code may be used for Medicare when drug administered under the direct supervision of a physician, not for use when drug is self-administered)** K2
Use this code for Imitrex.

N ☑J3070 **Injection, pentazocine, 30 mg** N1
Use this code for Talwin.

G ☑J3095 **Injection, telavancin, 10 mg** K2
Use this code for VIBATIV.

K ☑J3101 **Injection, tenecteplase, 1 mg** K2
Use this code for TNKase.

N ☑J3105 **Injection, terbutaline sulfate, up to 1 mg** N1
For terbutaline in inhalation solution, see K0525 and K0526.

B ☑J3110 **Injection, teriparatide, 10 mcg**
Use this code for Forteo.
MED: 100-4,10,90.1

N ☑J3120 **Injection, testosterone enanthate, up to 100 mg** N1
Use this code for Delatestryl.

N ☑J3130 **Injection, testosterone enanthate, up to 200 mg** N1
Use this code for Delatestryl.

N ☑J3140 **Injection, testosterone suspension, up to 50 mg** N1

N ☑J3150 **Injection, testosterone propionate, up to 100 mg** N1

N ☑J3230 **Injection, chlorpromazine HCl, up to 50 mg** N1
Use this code for Thorazine.

K ☑J3240 **Injection, thyrotropin alpha, 0.9 mg, provided in 1.1 mg vial** K2
Use this code for Thyrogen.

K ☑J3243 **Injection, tigecycline, 1 mg** K2
Use this code for Tygacil.

K ☑J3246 **Injection, tirofiban HCl, 0.25 mg** K2
Use this code for Aggrastat.

N ☑J3250 **Injection, trimethobenzamide HCl, up to 200 mg** N1
Use this code for Tigan, Tiject-20, Arrestin.

N ☑J3260 **Injection, tobramycin sulfate, up to 80 mg** N1
Use this code for Nebcin.

G ☑J3262 **Injection, tocilizumab, 1 mg** K2
Use this code for ACTEMRA.

N ☑J3265 **Injection, torsemide, 10 mg/ml** N1
Use this code for Demadex, Torsemide.

N ☑J3280 **Injection, thiethylperazine maleate, up to 10 mg** N1

K ☑J3285 **Injection, treprostinil, 1 mg** K2
Use this code for Remodulin.

K J3300 **Injection, triamcinolone acetonide, preservative free, 1 mg** K2
Use this code for TRIVARIS, TRIESENCE

N ☑J3301 **Injection, triamcinolone acetonide, not otherwise specified, 10 mg** N1
Use this code for Kenalog-10, Kenalog-40, Tri-Kort, Kenaject-40, Cenacort A-40, Triam-A, Trilog.

N ☑J3302 **Injection, triamcinolone diacetate, per 5 mg** N1
Use this code for Aristocort, Aristocort Intralesional, Aristocort Forte, Amcort, Trilone, Cenacort Forte.

N ☑J3303 **Injection, triamcinolone hexacetonide, per 5 mg** N1
Use this code for Aristospan Intralesional, Aristospan Intra-articular.

E ☑J3305 **Injection, trimetrexate glucuronate, per 25 mg**
Use this code for Neutrexin.

K ☑J3310 **Injection, perphenazine, up to 5 mg** K2
Use this code for Trilafon.

K ☑J3315 **Injection, triptorelin pamoate, 3.75 mg** ♂ K2
Use this code for Trelstar Depot, Trelstar Depot Plus Debioclip Kit, Trelstar LA.

E ☑J3320 **Injection, spectinomycin dihydrochloride, up to 2 g**
Use this code for Trobicin.

K ☑J3350 **Injection, urea, up to 40 g** K2

K J3355 **Injection, urofollitropin, 75 IU** K2
Use this code for Metrodin, Bravelle, Fertinex.

G ☑J3357 **Injection, ustekinumab, 1 mg** K2
Use this code for STELARA.

N ☑J3360 **Injection, diazepam, up to 5 mg** N1
Use this code for Diastat, Dizac, Valium.

N ☑J3364 **Injection, urokinase, 5,000 IU vial** N1
Use this code for Kinlytic

K ☑J3365 **Injection, IV, urokinase, 250,000 IU vial** K2
Use this code for Kinlytic

N ☑J3370 **Injection, vancomycin HCl, 500 mg** N1
Use this code for Vancocin.

G ☑J3385 **Injection, velaglucerase alfa, 100 units** K2
Use this code for VPRIV.

K ☑J3396 **Injection, verteporfin, 0.1 mg** K2
Use this code for Visudyne.

E ☑J3400 **Injection, triflupromazine HCl, up to 20 mg**

N ☑J3410 **Injection, hydroxyzine HCl, up to 25 mg** N1
Use this code for Vistaril, Vistaject-25, Hyzine, Hyzine-50.

N ☑J3411 **Injection, thiamine HCl, 100 mg** N1

N ☑J3415 **Injection, pyridoxine HCl, 100 mg** N1

N ☑J3420 **Injection, vitamin B-12 cyanocobalamin, up to 1,000 mcg** N1
Use this code for Sytobex, Redisol, Rubramin PC, Betalin 12, Berubigen, Cobex, Cobal, Crystal B12, Cyano, Cyanocobalamin, Hydroxocobalamin, Hydroxycobal, Nutri-Twelve.

N ☑J3430 **Injection, phytonadione (vitamin K), per 1 mg** N1
Use this code for AquaMephyton, Konakion, Menadione, Phytonadione.

K ☑J3465 **Injection, voriconazole, 10 mg** K2

N ☑ J3470 Injection, hyaluronidase, up to 150 units N1

N ☑ J3471 Injection, hyaluronidase, ovine, preservative free, per 1 USP unit (up to 999 USP units) N1

N ☑ J3472 Injection, hyaluronidase, ovine, preservative free, per 1,000 USP units N1

N ☑ J3473 Injection, hyaluronidase, recombinant, 1 USP unit N1

N ☑ J3475 Injection, magnesium sulfate, per 500 mg N1
Use this code for Mag Sul, Sulfa Mag.

N ☑ J3480 Injection, potassium chloride, per 2 mEq N1

N ☑ J3485 Injection, zidovudine, 10 mg N1
Use this code for Retrovir, Zidovudine.

N ☑ J3486 Injection, ziprasidone mesylate, 10 mg N1
Use this code for Geodon.

K ☑ J3487 Injection, zoledronic acid (Zometa), 1 mg K2

K ☑ J3488 Injection, zoledronic acid (Reclast), 1 mg K2

N J3490 Unclassified drugs N1

E ☑ J3520 Edetate disodium, per 150 mg
Use this code for Endrate, Disotate, Meritate, Chealamide, E.D.T.A. This drug is used in chelation therapy, a treatment for atherosclerosis that is not covered by Medicare.

N J3530 Nasal vaccine inhalation N1

E J3535 Drug administered through a metered dose inhaler

E J3570 Laetrile, amygdalin, vitamin B-17
The FDA has found Laetrile to have no safe or effective therapeutic purpose.

N J3590 Unclassified biologics N1

N ☑ J7030 Infusion, normal saline solution, 1,000 cc N1

N ☑ J7040 Infusion, normal saline solution, sterile (500 ml=1 unit) N1

N ☑ J7042 5% dextrose/normal saline (500 ml = 1 unit) N1

N ☑ J7050 Infusion, normal saline solution, 250 cc N1

N ☑ J7060 5% dextrose/water (500 ml = 1 unit) N1

N ☑ J7070 Infusion, D-5-W, 1,000 cc N1

N ☑ J7100 Infusion, dextran 40, 500 ml N1
Use this code for Gentran, 10% LMD, Rheomacrodex.

N ☑ J7110 Infusion, dextran 75, 500 ml N1
Use this code for Gentran 75.

N ☑ J7120 Ringers lactate infusion, up to 1,000 cc N1

~~J7130~~ Jan ~~Hypertonic saline solution, 50 or 100 mEq, 20 cc vial~~
To report, see J7131

● N ☑ J7131 Jan Hypertonic saline solution, 1 ml N1

● G ☑ J7180 Jan Injection, factor XIII (antihemophilic factor, human), 1 IU K2
Use this code for Corifact.

● G ☑ J7183 Jan Injection, von Willebrand factor complex (human), Wilate, 1 IU vWF:RCo K2

~~J7184~~ Jan ~~Injection, von Willebrand factor complex (human), Wilate, per 100 IU VWF:RCo~~
To report, see J7183

K ☑ J7185 Injection, factor VIII (antihemophilic factor, recombinant) (XYNTHA), per IU K2
Use this code for Xyntha.

K J7186 Injection, antihemophilic factor VIII/von Willebrand factor complex (human), per factor VIII i.u. K2
Use this code for Alphanate.
MED: 100-4,17,80.4.1

K J7187 Injection, von Willebrand factor complex (Humate-P), per IU VWF:RCO K2
MED: 100-4,17,80.4.1

K ☑ J7189 Factor VIIa (antihemophilic factor, recombinant), per 1 mcg K2
MED: 100-4,17,80.4.1

K ☑ J7190 Factor VIII (antihemophilic factor, human) per IU K2
Use this code for Koate-DVI, Monarc-M, Monoclate-P.
FACTOR VIII
Antihemophilic factor that is part of the intrinsic coagulation cascade used to treat Hemophilia A. The most common and oldest form of this is human derived factor concentrated from human plasma (HCPCS Level II code J7190). The Porcine variety (J7191) is supplied as lyophilized Factor VIII from concentrated pig's blood. Recombinant, purified factor VIII (J7192) without the albumin is produced by recombinant genes. May be sold under the brand names Hexilate, Kogenate.
MED: 100-4,17,80.4; 100-4,17,80.4.1

K ☑ J7191 Factor VIII (antihemophilic factor (porcine)), per IU K2
FACTOR VIII
Antihemophilic factor that is part of the intrinsic coagulation cascade used to treat Hemophilia A. The most common and oldest form of this is human derived factor concentrated from human plasma (HCPCS Level II code J7190). The Porcine variety (J7191) is supplied as lyophilized Factor VIII from concentrated pig's blood. Recombinant, purified factor VIII (J7192) without the albumin is produced by recombinant genes. May be sold under the brand names Hexilate, Kogenate.
MED: 100-4,17,80.4; 100-4,17,80.4.1

K ☑ J7192 Factor VIII (antihemophilic factor, recombinant) per IU, not otherwise specified K2
Use this code for Recombinate, Kogenate FS, Helixate FX, Advate rAHF-PFM, Antihemophilic Factor Human Method M Monoclonal Purified, Refacto.
FACTOR VIII
Antihemophilic factor that is part of the intrinsic coagulation cascade used to treat Hemophilia A. The most common and oldest form of this is human derived factor concentrated from human plasma (HCPCS Level II code J7190). The Porcine variety (J7191) is supplied as lyophilized Factor VIII from concentrated pig's blood. Recombinant, purified factor VIII (J7192) without the albumin is produced by recombinant genes. May be sold under the brand names Hexilate, Kogenate.
MED: 100-4,17,80.4; 100-4,17,80.4.1

K ☑ J7193 Factor IX (antihemophilic factor, purified, nonrecombinant) per IU K2
Use this code for AlphaNine SD, Mononine.
MED: 100-4,17,80.4; 100-4,17,80.4.1
AHA: 2Q,'02,8

K ☑ J7194 Factor IX complex, per IU K2
Use this code for Konyne-80, Profilnine SD, Proplex T, Proplex T, Bebulin VH, factor IX+ complex, Profilnine SD.
MED: 100-4,17,80.4; 100-4,17,80.4.1

K ☑ **J7195** **Factor IX (antihemophilic factor, recombinant) per IU** K2
Use this code for Benefix.
MED: 100-4,17,80.4; 100-4,17,80.4.1
AHA: 2Q,'02,8

K ☑ **J7196** **Injection, antithrombin recombinant, 50 i.u.** K2
Use this code for ATryn.

K ☑ **J7197** **Antithrombin III (human), per IU** K2
Use this code for Thrombate III, ATnativ.
MED: 100-4,17,80.4.1

K ☑ **J7198** **Antiinhibitor, per IU** K2
Medicare jurisdiction: local contractor. Use this code for Autoplex T, Feiba VH AICC.
MED: 100-3,110.3; 100-4,17,80.4; 100-4,17,80.4.1

B **J7199** **Hemophilia clotting factor, not otherwise classified**
Medicare jurisdiction: local contractor.
MED: 100-4,17,80.4; 100-4,17,80.4.1

E **J7300** **Intrauterine copper contraceptive**
Use this code for Paragard T380A.

E ☑ **J7302** **Levonorgestrel-releasing intrauterine contraceptive system, 52 mg** ♀
Use this code for Mirena.

E ☑ **J7303** **Contraceptive supply, hormone containing vaginal ring, each** ♀
Use this code for Nuvaring Vaginal Ring.

E ☑ **J7304** **Contraceptive supply, hormone containing patch, each**

E **J7306** **Levonorgestrel (contraceptive) implant system, including implants and supplies**
Use this code for Norplant II.

E **J7307** **Etonogestrel (contraceptive) implant system, including implant and supplies**
Use this code for Implanon.

K ☑ **J7308** **Aminolevulinic acid HCl for topical administration, 20%, single unit dosage form (354 mg)** K2

K ☑ **J7309** **Methyl aminolevulinate (MAL) for topical administration, 16.8%, 1 g** K2
Use this code for Metvixia.

K ☑ **J7310** **Ganciclovir, 4.5 mg, long-acting implant** K2
Use this code for Vitrasert.

K **J7311** **Fluocinolone acetonide, intravitreal implant** K2
Use this code for Retisert.

K ☑ **J7312** **Injection, dexamethasone, intravitreal implant, 0.1 mg** K2
Use this code for OZURDEX.

K ☑ **J7321** **Hyaluronan or derivative, Hyalgan or Supartz, for intra-articular injection, per dose** K2

K ☑ **J7323** **Hyaluronan or derivative, Euflexxa, for intra-articular injection, per dose** K2

K ☑ **J7324** **Hyaluronan or derivative, Orthovisc, for intra-articular injection, per dose** K2

K ☑ **J7325** **Hyaluronan or derivative, Synvisc or Synvisc-One, for intra-articular injection, 1 mg** K2

● K **J7326** Jan **Hyaluronan or derivative, Gel-One, for intra-articular injection, per dose** K2

B ☑ **J7330** **Autologous cultured chondrocytes, implant**
Medicare jurisdiction: local contractor. Use this code for Carticel.

G **J7335** **Capsaicin 8% patch, per 10 sq cm** K2
Use this code for Qutenza.

N ☑ **J7500** **Azathioprine, oral, 50 mg** N1
Use this code for Azasan, Imuran.
MED: 100-2,15,50.5; 100-4,17,80.3

K ☑ **J7501** **Azathioprine, parenteral, 100 mg** K2
MED: 100-4,17,80.3

N ☑ **J7502** **Cyclosporine, oral, 100 mg** N1
Use this code for Neoral, Sandimmune, Gengraf, Sangcya
MED: 100-2,15,50.5; 100-4,17,80.3

K ☑ **J7504** **Lymphocyte immune globulin, antithymocyte globulin, equine, parenteral, 250 mg** K2
Use this code for Atgam.
MED: 100-4,17,80.3

K ☑ **J7505** **Muromonab-CD3, parenteral, 5 mg** K2
Use this code for Orthoclone OKT3.
MED: 100-4,17,80.3

N ☑ **J7506** **Prednisone, oral, per 5 mg** N1
MED: 100-2,15,50.5; 100-4,17,80.3

N ☑ **J7507** **Tacrolimus, oral, per 1 mg** N1
Use this code for Prograf.
MED: 100-2,15,50.5; 100-4,17,80.3

N ☑ **J7509** **Methylprednisolone, oral, per 4 mg** N1
Use this code for Medrol, Methylpred.
MED: 100-2,15,50.5; 100-4,17,80.3

N ☑ **J7510** **Prednisolone, oral, per 5 mg** N1
Use this code for Delta-Cortef, Cotolone, Pediapred, Prednoral, Prelone.
MED: 100-2,15,50.5; 100-4,17,80.3

K ☑ **J7511** **Lymphocyte immune globulin, antithymocyte globulin, rabbit, parenteral, 25 mg** K2
Use this code for Thymoglobulin.
MED: 100-4,17,80.3
AHA: 2Q,'02,8

K ☑ **J7513** **Daclizumab, parenteral, 25 mg** K2
Use this code for Zenapax.
MED: 100-2,15,50.5; 100-4,17,80.3

N ☑ **J7515** **Cyclosporine, oral, 25 mg** N1
Use this code for Neoral, Sandimmune, Gengraf, Sangcya.
MED: 100-4,17,80.3

N ☑ **J7516** **Cyclosporine, parenteral, 250 mg** N1
Use this code for Neoral, Sandimmune, Gengraf, Sangcya.
MED: 100-4,17,80.3

N ☑ **J7517** **Mycophenolate mofetil, oral, 250 mg** N1
Use this code for CellCept.
MED: 100-4,17,80.3

N ☑ **J7518** **Mycophenolic acid, oral, 180 mg** N1
Use this code for Myfortic Delayed Release.
MED: 100-4,17,80.3.1

N ☑ **J7520** **Sirolimus, oral, 1 mg** N1
Use this code for Rapamune.
MED: 100-2,15,50.5; 100-4,17,80.3

K ☑ **J7525** **Tacrolimus, parenteral, 5 mg** K2
Use this code for Prograf.
MED: 100-2,15,50.5; 100-4,17,80.3

N **J7599** **Immunosuppressive drug, not otherwise classified** N1
Determine if an alternative HCPCS Level II or a CPT code better describes the service being reported. This code should be used only if a more specific code is unavailable.
MED: 100-2,15,50.5; 100-4,17,80.3

INHALATION DRUGS

M ☑ J7604 Acetylcysteine, inhalation solution, compounded product, administered through DME, unit dose form, per g

M ☑ J7605 Arformoterol, inhalation solution, FDA approved final product, noncompounded, administered through DME, unit dose form, 15 mcg

M J7606 Formoterol fumarate, inhalation solution, FDA approved final product, noncompounded, administered through DME, unit dose form, 20 mcg
Use this code for PERFOROMIST.

M ☑ J7607 Levalbuterol, inhalation solution, compounded product, administered through DME, concentrated form, 0.5 mg

M ☑ J7608 Acetylcysteine, inhalation solution, FDA-approved final product, noncompounded, administered through DME, unit dose form, per g
Use this code for Acetadote, Mucomyst, Mucosil.

M ☑ J7609 Albuterol, inhalation solution, compounded product, administered through DME, unit dose, 1 mg

M ☑ J7610 Albuterol, inhalation solution, compounded product, administered through DME, concentrated form, 1 mg

M ☑ J7611 Albuterol, inhalation solution, FDA-approved final product, noncompounded, administered through DME, concentrated form, 1 mg
Use this code for Accuneb, Proventil, Respirol, Ventolin.

M ☑ J7612 Levalbuterol, inhalation solution, FDA-approved final product, noncompounded, administered through DME, concentrated form, 0.5 mg
Use this code for Xopenex HFA.

M ☑ J7613 Albuterol, inhalation solution, FDA-approved final product, noncompounded, administered through DME, unit dose, 1 mg
Use this code for Accuneb, Proventil, Respirol, Ventolin.

M ☑ J7614 Levalbuterol, inhalation solution, FDA-approved final product, noncompounded, administered through DME, unit dose, 0.5 mg
Use this code for Xopenex.

M ☑ J7615 Levalbuterol, inhalation solution, compounded product, administered through DME, unit dose, 0.5 mg

M ☑ J7620 Albuterol, up to 2.5 mg and ipratropium bromide, up to 0.5 mg, FDA-approved final product, noncompounded, administered through DME

M ☑ J7622 Beclomethasone, inhalation solution, compounded product, administered through DME, unit dose form, per mg
Use this code for Beclovent, Beconase.

M ☑ J7624 Betamethasone, inhalation solution, compounded product, administered through DME, unit dose form, per mg

M ☑ J7626 Budesonide, inhalation solution, FDA-approved final product, noncompounded, administered through DME, unit dose form, up to 0.5 mg
Use this code for Pulmicort, Pulmicort Flexhaler, Pulmicort Respules, Vanceril.

M ☑ J7627 Budesonide, inhalation solution, compounded product, administered through DME, unit dose form, up to 0.5 mg

M ☑ J7628 Bitolterol mesylate, inhalation solution, compounded product, administered through DME, concentrated form, per mg

M ☑ J7629 Bitolterol mesylate, inhalation solution, compounded product, administered through DME, unit dose form, per mg

M ☑ J7631 Cromolyn sodium, inhalation solution, FDA-approved final product, noncompounded, administered through DME, unit dose form, per 10 mg
Use this code for Intal, Nasalcrom

M ☑ J7632 Cromolyn sodium, inhalation solution, compounded product, administered through DME, unit dose form, per 10 mg

M ☑ J7633 Budesonide, inhalation solution, FDA-approved final product, noncompounded, administered through DME, concentrated form, per 0.25 mg
Use this code for Pulmicort, Pulmicort Flexhaler, Pulmicort Respules, Vanceril

M ☑ J7634 Budesonide, inhalation solution, compounded product, administered through DME, concentrated form, per 0.25 mg

M ☑ J7635 Atropine, inhalation solution, compounded product, administered through DME, concentrated form, per mg

M ☑ J7636 Atropine, inhalation solution, compounded product, administered through DME, unit dose form, per mg

M ☑ J7637 Dexamethasone, inhalation solution, compounded product, administered through DME, concentrated form, per mg

M ☑ J7638 Dexamethasone, inhalation solution, compounded product, administered through DME, unit dose form, per mg

M ☑ J7639 Dornase alfa, inhalation solution, FDA-approved final product, noncompounded, administered through DME, unit dose form, per mg
Use this code for Pulmozyme.

E ☑ J7640 Formoterol, inhalation solution, compounded product, administered through DME, unit dose form, 12 mcg

M ☑ J7641 Flunisolide, inhalation solution, compounded product, administered through DME, unit dose, per mg
Use this code for Aerobid, Flunisolide.

M ☑ J7642 Glycopyrrolate, inhalation solution, compounded product, administered through DME, concentrated form, per mg

M ☑ J7643 Glycopyrrolate, inhalation solution, compounded product, administered through DME, unit dose form, per mg

M ☑ J7644 Ipratropium bromide, inhalation solution, FDA-approved final product, noncompounded, administered through DME, unit dose form, per mg
Use this code for Atrovent.

M ☑ J7645 Ipratropium bromide, inhalation solution, compounded product, administered through DME, unit dose form, per mg

M ☑ J7647 Isoetharine HCl, inhalation solution, compounded product, administered through DME, concentrated form, per mg

M ☑ J7648 Isoetharine HCl, inhalation solution, FDA-approved final product, noncompounded, administered through DME, concentrated form, per mg
Use this code for Beta-2.

M ☑ J7649 Isoetharine HCl, inhalation solution, FDA-approved final product, noncompounded, administered through DME, unit dose form, per mg

M ☑ J7650 Isoetharine HCl, inhalation solution, compounded product, administered through DME, unit dose form, per mg

M ☑ J7657 Isoproterenol HCl, inhalation solution, compounded product, administered through DME, concentrated form, per mg

M ☑ J7658 Isoproterenol HCl, inhalation solution, FDA-approved final product, noncompounded, administered through DME, concentrated form, per mg
Use this code for Isuprel HCl.

M ☑ J7659 Isoproterenol HCl, inhalation solution, FDA-approved final product, noncompounded, administered through DME, unit dose form, per mg
Use this code for Isuprel HCl

M ☑ J7660 Isoproterenol HCl, inhalation solution, compounded product, administered through DME, unit dose form, per mg

● M ☑ J7665 Jan Mannitol, administered through an inhaler, 5 mg
Use this code for ARIDOL.

M ☑ J7667 Metaproterenol sulfate, inhalation solution, compounded product, concentrated form, per 10 mg

M ☑ J7668 Metaproterenol sulfate, inhalation solution, FDA-approved final product, noncompounded, administered through DME, concentrated form, per 10 mg
Use this code for Alupent

M ☑ J7669 Metaproterenol sulfate, inhalation solution, FDA-approved final product, noncompounded, administered through DME, unit dose form, per 10 mg
Use this code for Alupent.

M ☑ J7670 Metaproterenol sulfate, inhalation solution, compounded product, administered through DME, unit dose form, per 10 mg

N ☑ J7674 Methacholine chloride administered as inhalation solution through a nebulizer, per 1 mg N1

M ☑ J7676 Pentamidine isethionate, inhalation solution, compounded product, administered through DME, unit dose form, per 300 mg

M ☑ J7680 Terbutaline sulfate, inhalation solution, compounded product, administered through DME, concentrated form, per mg
Use this code for Brethine.

M ☑ J7681 Terbutaline sulfate, inhalation solution, compounded product, administered through DME, unit dose form, per mg
Use this code for Brethine.

M ☑ J7682 Tobramycin, inhalation solution, FDA-approved final product, noncompounded, unit dose form, administered through DME, per 300 mg
Use this code for Tobi.

M ☑ J7683 Triamcinolone, inhalation solution, compounded product, administered through DME, concentrated form, per mg
Use this code for Azmacort.

M ☑ J7684 Triamcinolone, inhalation solution, compounded product, administered through DME, unit dose form, per mg
Use this code for Azmacort.

M ☑ J7685 Tobramycin, inhalation solution, compounded product, administered through DME, unit dose form, per 300 mg

M ☑ J7686 Treprostinil, inhalation solution, FDA-approved final product, noncompounded, administered through DME, unit dose form, 1.74 mg
Use this code for Tyvaso.

M J7699 NOC drugs, inhalation solution administered through DME

N J7799 NOC drugs, other than inhalation drugs, administered through DME N1

B J8498 Antiemetic drug, rectal/suppository, not otherwise specified

E J8499 Prescription drug, oral, nonchemotherapeutic, NOS

J CODES CHEMOTHERAPY DRUGS J8501-J9999

ORAL CHEMOTHERAPY DRUGS

K ☑ J8501 Aprepitant, oral, 5 mg K2
Use this code for Emend.
MED: 100-4,17,80.2.1; 100-4,17,80.2.4

K ☑ J8510 Busulfan; oral, 2 mg K2
Use this code for Busulfex, Myleran.
MED: 100-2,15,50.5; 100-4,17,80.1.1

E ☑ J8515 Cabergoline, oral, 0.25 mg
Use this code for Dostinex.
MED: 100-2,15,50.5

K ☑ J8520 Capecitabine, oral, 150 mg K2
Use this code for Xeloda.
MED: 100-2,15,50.5; 100-4,17,80.1.1

K ☑ J8521 Capecitabine, oral, 500 mg K2
Use this code for Xeloda.
MED: 100-2,15,50.5; 100-4,17,80.1.1

N ☑ J8530 Cyclophosphamide; oral, 25 mg N1
Use this code for Cytoxan.
MED: 100-2,15,50.5; 100-4,17,80.1.1

N ☑ J8540 Dexamethasone, oral, 0.25 mg N1
Use this code for Decadron.

K ☑ J8560 Etoposide; oral, 50 mg K2
Use this code for VePesid.
MED: 100-2,15,50.5; 100-4,17,80.1.1

● K ☑ J8561 Jan Everolimus, oral, 0.25 mg K2
Use this code for Zortress, AFINITOR.

G ☑ J8562 Fludarabine phosphate, oral, 10 mg K2
Use this code for Oforta.

E ☑ J8565 Gefitinib, oral, 250 mg
Use this code for Iressa.
MED: 100-4,17,80.1.1

N J8597 Antiemetic drug, oral, not otherwise specified N1

N ☑ J8600 Melphalan; oral, 2 mg N1
Use this code for Alkeran.
MED: 100-2,15,50.5; 100-4,17,80.1.1

N ☑ J8610 Methotrexate; oral, 2.5 mg N1
Use this code for Trexall, RHEUMATREX.
MED: 100-2,15,50.5; 100-4,17,80.1.1

E ☑ J8650 Nabilone, oral, 1 mg
Use this code for Cesamet

K ☑ J8700 Temozolomide, oral, 5 mg K2
Use this code for Temodar.
MED: 100-2,15,50.5

K ☑ J8705 Topotecan, oral, 0.25 mg K2
Use this code for Hycamtin.

B J8999 Prescription drug, oral, chemotherapeutic, NOS
Determine if an alternative HCPCS Level II or a CPT code better describes the service being reported. This code should be used only if a more specific code is unavailable.
MED: 100-2,15,50.5; 100-4,17,80.1.1; 100-4,17,80.1.2

INJECTABLE CHEMOTHERAPY DRUGS

These codes cover the cost of the chemotherapy drug only, not the administration.

N ☑ J9000 Injection, doxorubicin HCl, 10 mg N1 ⊘
Use this code for Adriamycin PFS, Adriamycin RDF, Rubex.

K ☑ J9001 Injection, doxorubicin HCl, all lipid formulations, 10 mg K2 ⊘
Use this code for Doxil.

K ☑ J9010 Injection, alemtuzumab, 10 mg K2 ⊘
Use this code for Campath.

K ☑ J9015 Injection, aldesleukin, per single use vial K2 ⊘
Use this code for Proleukin, IL-2, Interleukin.

K ☑ J9017 Injection, arsenic trioxide, 1 mg K2 ⊘
Use this code for Trisenox.
AHA: 2Q,'02,8

K ☑ J9020 Injection, asparaginase, 10,000 units K2 ⊘
Use this code for Elspar.

K ☑ J9025 Injection, azacitidine, 1 mg K2 ⊘
Use this code for Vidaza.

K ☑ J9027 Injection, clofarabine, 1 mg K2 ⊘
Use this code for Clolar.

K ☑ J9031 BCG (intravesical) per instillation K2
Use this code for Tice BCG, PACIS BCG, TheraCys.

K ☑ J9033 Injection, bendamustine HCl, 1 mg K2 ⊘
Use this code for TREANDA.

K ☑ J9035 Injection, bevacizumab, 10 mg K2 ⊘
Use this code for Avastin.

N ☑ J9040 Injection, bleomycin sulfate, 15 units N1 ⊘
Use this code for Blenoxane.

K ☑ J9041 Injection, bortezomib, 0.1 mg K2 ⊘
Use this code for Velcade.

● G ☑ J9043 Jan Injection, cabazitaxel, 1 mg K2
Use this code for Jevtana.

N ☑ J9045 Injection, carboplatin, 50 mg N1 ⊘
Use this code for Paraplatin.

K ☑ J9050 Injection, carmustine, 100 mg K2 ⊘
Use this code for BiCNU.

K ☑ J9055 Injection, cetuximab, 10 mg K2 ⊘
Use this code for Erbitux.

N ☑ J9060 Injection, cisplatin, powder or solution, 10 mg N1 ⊘
Use this code for Plantinol AQ.

K ☑ J9065 Injection, cladribine, per 1 mg K2 ⊘
Use this code for Leustatin.

K ☑ J9070 Cyclophosphamide, 100 mg K2 ⊘
Use this code for Endoxan-Asta.

K ☑ J9098 Injection, cytarabine liposome, 10 mg K2 ⊘
Use this code for Depocyt.

N ☑ J9100 Injection, cytarabine, 100 mg N1 ⊘
Use this code for Cytosar-U, Ara-C, Tarabin CFS.

K ☑ J9120 Injection, dactinomycin, 0.5 mg K2 ⊘
Use this code for Cosmegen.

N ☑ J9130 Dacarbazine, 100 mg N1 ⊘
Use this code for DTIC-Dome.

K ☑ J9150 Injection, daunorubicin, 10 mg K2 ⊘
Use this code for Cerubidine.

K ☑ J9151 Injection, daunorubicin citrate, liposomal formulation, 10 mg K2 ⊘
Use this code for Daunoxome.

K ☑ J9155 Injection, degarelix, 1 mg K2

K ☑ J9160 Injection, denileukin diftitox, 300 mcg K2 ⊘
Use this code for Ontak.

E ☑ J9165 Injection, diethylstilbestrol diphosphate, 250 mg

K ☑ J9171 Injection, docetaxel, 1 mg K2 ⊘
Use this code for Taxotere.

N ☑ J9175 Injection, Elliotts' B solution, 1 ml N1

K ☑ J9178 Injection, epirubicin HCl, 2 mg K2 ⊘
Use this code for Ellence.

● G ☑ J9179 Jan Injection, eribulin mesylate, 0.1 mg K2
Use this code for HALAVEN.

N ☑ J9181 Injection, etoposide, 10 mg N1 ⊘
Use this code for VePesid, Toposar.

K ☑ J9185 Injection, fludarabine phosphate, 50 mg K2 ⊘
Use this code for Fludara.

N ☑ J9190 Injection, fluorouracil, 500 mg N1
Use this code for Adrucil.

K ☑ J9200 Injection, floxuridine, 500 mg K2 ⊘
Use this code for FUDR.

K ☑ J9201 Injection, gemcitabine HCl, 200 mg K2 ⊘
Use this code for Gemzar.

K ☑ J9202 Goserelin acetate implant, per 3.6 mg K2
Use this code for Zoladex.

K ☑ J9206 Injection, irinotecan, 20 mg K2 ⊘
Use this code for Camptosar.

K ☑ J9207 Injection, ixabepilone, 1 mg K2 ⊘
Use this code for IXEMPRA.

K ☑ J9208 Injection, ifosfamide, 1 g K2 ⊘
Use this code for IFEX, Mitoxana.

N ☑ J9209 Injection, mesna, 200 mg N1
Use this code for Mesnex.

K ☑ J9211 Injection, idarubicin HCl, 5 mg K2 ⊘
Use this code for Idamycin.

N ☑ J9212 Injection, interferon alfacon-1, recombinant, 1 mcg N1
Use this code for Infergen.

N ☑ J9213 Injection, interferon, alfa-2a, recombinant, 3 million units N1
Use this code for Roferon-A.

K ☑ J9214 Injection, interferon, alfa-2b, recombinant, 1 million units K2
Use this code for Intron A, Rebetron Kit.

K ☑ J9215 **Injection, interferon, alfa-N3, (human leukocyte derived), 250,000 IU** K2
Use this code for Alferon N.

K ☑ J9216 **Injection, interferon, gamma 1-b, 3 million units** K2
Use this code for Actimmune.

K ☑ J9217 **Leuprolide acetate (for depot suspension), 7.5 mg** K2
Use this code for Lupron Depot, Eligard.

K ☑ J9218 **Leuprolide acetate, per 1 mg** K2
Use this code for Lupron.

K ☑ J9219 **Leuprolide acetate implant, 65 mg** K2
Use this code for Lupron Implant.
AHA: 4Q,'01,5

K ☑ J9225 **Histrelin implant (Vantas), 50 mg** K2 ⊘

K ☑ J9226 **Histrelin implant (Supprelin LA), 50 mg** K2

● G ☑ J9228 Jan **Injection, ipilimumab, 1 mg** K2
Use this code for YERVOY.

K ☑ J9230 **Injection, mechlorethamine HCl, (nitrogen mustard), 10 mg** K2 ⊘
Use this code for Mustargen.

K ☑ J9245 **Injection, melphalan HCl, 50 mg** K2 ⊘
Use this code for Alkeran, L-phenylalanine mustard.

N ☑ J9250 **Methotrexate sodium, 5 mg** N1
Use this code for Folex, Folex PFS, Methotrexate LPF.

N ☑ J9260 **Methotrexate sodium, 50 mg** N1
Use this code for Folex, Folex PFS, Methotrexate LPF.

K ☑ J9261 **Injection, nelarabine, 50 mg** K2 ⊘
Use this code for Arranon

K ☑ J9263 **Injection, oxaliplatin, 0.5 mg** K2 ⊘
Use this code for Eloxatin.

K ☑ J9264 **Injection, paclitaxel protein-bound particles, 1 mg** K2 ⊘
Use this code for Abraxane.

N ☑ J9265 **Injection, paclitaxel, 30 mg** N1 ⊘
Use this code for Taxol, Nov-Onxol.

K ☑ J9266 **Injection, pegaspargase, per single dose vial** K2 ⊘
Use this code for Oncaspar.
AHA: 2Q,'02,8

K ☑ J9268 **Injection, pentostatin, 10 mg** K2 ⊘
Use this code for Nipent.

N ☑ J9270 **Injection, plicamycin, 2.5 mg** N1 ⊘
Use this code for Mithacin.

K ☑ J9280 **Mitomycin, 5 mg** K2 ⊘
Use this code for Mutamycin.

K ☑ J9293 **Injection, mitoxantrone HCl, per 5 mg** K2 ⊘
Use this code for Navantrone.

K ☑ J9300 **Injection, gemtuzumab ozogamicin, 5 mg** K2 ⊘
AHA: 2Q,'02,8

G ☑ J9302 **Injection, ofatumumab, 10 mg** K2
Use this code for ARZERRA.

K ☑ J9303 **Injection, panitumumab, 10 mg** K2 ⊘
Use this code for Vectibix.

K ☑ J9305 **Injection, pemetrexed, 10 mg** K2 ⊘
Use this code for Alimta.

G ☑ J9307 **Injection, pralatrexate, 1 mg** K2
Use this code for FOLOTYN.

K ☑ J9310 **Injection, rituximab, 100 mg** K2 ⊘
Use this code for RituXan.

G ☑ J9315 **Injection, romidepsin, 1 mg** K2
Use this code for ISTODAX.

K ☑ J9320 **Injection, streptozocin, 1 g** K2 ⊘
Use this code for Zanosar.

K ☑ J9328 **Injection, temozolomide, 1 mg** K2 ⊘
Use this code for Temodar.

K ☑ J9330 **Injection, temsirolimus, 1 mg** K2 ⊘
Use this code for TORISEL.

K ☑ J9340 **Injection, thiotepa, 15 mg** K2 ⊘
Use this code for Thioplex.

K ☑ J9351 **Injection, topotecan, 0.1 mg** K2
Use this code for HYCAMTIN.

K ☑ J9355 **Injection, trastuzumab, 10 mg** K2 ⊘
Use this code for Herceptin.

K ☑ J9357 **Injection, valrubicin, intravesical, 200 mg** K2 ⊘
Use this code for Valstar.

N ☑ J9360 **Injection, vinblastine sulfate, 1 mg** N1 ⊘
Use this code for Velban.

N ☑ J9370 **Vincristine sulfate, 1 mg** N1 ⊘
Use this code for Oncovin, Vincasar PFS.

K ☑ J9390 **Injection, vinorelbine tartrate, 10 mg** K2 ⊘
Use this code for Navelbine.

K ☑ J9395 **Injection, fulvestrant, 25 mg** K2 ⊘
Use this code for Fastodex.

K ☑ J9600 **Injection, porfimer sodium, 75 mg** K2 ⊘
Use this code for Photofrin.

N J9999 **Not otherwise classified, antineoplastic drugs** N1
Determine if an alternative HCPCS Level II or a CPT code better describes the service being reported. This code should be used only if a more specific code is unavailable.

TEMPORARY CODES K0000-K9999

The K codes were established for use by the DME Medicare Administrative Contractors (DME MACs). The K codes are developed when the currently existing permanent national codes for supplies and certain product categories do not include the codes needed to implement a DME MAC medical review policy.

WHEELCHAIR AND WHEELCHAIR ACCESSORIES

Y K0001 Standard wheelchair

Y K0002 Standard hemi (low seat) wheelchair

Y K0003 Lightweight wheelchair

Y K0004 High strength, lightweight wheelchair

Y K0005 Ultralightweight wheelchair

Y K0006 Heavy-duty wheelchair

Y K0007 Extra heavy-duty wheelchair

Y K0009 Other manual wheelchair/base

Y K0010 Standard-weight frame motorized/power wheelchair

Y K0011 Standard-weight frame motorized/power wheelchair with programmable control parameters for speed adjustment, tremor dampening, acceleration control and braking

Y K0012 Lightweight portable motorized/power wheelchair

Y K0014 Other motorized/power wheelchair base

Y ☑ K0015 Detachable, nonadjustable height armrest, each
MED: 100-4,23,60.3

Y ☑ K0017 Detachable, adjustable height armrest, base, each

Y ☑ K0018 Detachable, adjustable height armrest, upper portion, each

Y ☑ K0019 Arm pad, each

Y ☑ K0020 Fixed, adjustable height armrest, pair

Y ☑ K0037 High mount flip-up footrest, each

Y ☑ K0038 Leg strap, each

Y ☑ K0039 Leg strap, H style, each

Y ☑ K0040 Adjustable angle footplate, each

Y ☑ K0041 Large size footplate, each

Y ☑ K0042 Standard size footplate, each

Y ☑ K0043 Footrest, lower extension tube, each

Y ☑ K0044 Footrest, upper hanger bracket, each

Y K0045 Footrest, complete assembly

Y ☑ K0046 Elevating legrest, lower extension tube, each

Y ☑ K0047 Elevating legrest, upper hanger bracket, each

Y K0050 Ratchet assembly

Y ☑ K0051 Cam release assembly, footrest or legrest, each

Y ☑ K0052 Swingaway, detachable footrests, each

Y ☑ K0053 Elevating footrests, articulating (telescoping), each

Y ☑ K0056 Seat height less than 17 in or equal to or greater than 21 in for a high-strength, lightweight, or ultralightweight wheelchair

Y ☑ K0065 Spoke protectors, each

Y ☑ K0069 Rear wheel assembly, complete, with solid tire, spokes or molded, each

Y ☑ K0070 Rear wheel assembly, complete, with pneumatic tire, spokes or molded, each

Y ☑ K0071 Front caster assembly, complete, with pneumatic tire, each

Y ☑ K0072 Front caster assembly, complete, with semipneumatic tire, each

Y ☑ K0073 Caster pin lock, each

Y ☑ K0077 Front caster assembly, complete, with solid tire, each

Y K0098 Drive belt for power wheelchair
MED: 100-4,23,60.3

Y ☑ K0105 IV hanger, each

Y K0108 Wheelchair component or accessory, not otherwise specified

Y K0195 Elevating legrests, pair (for use with capped rental wheelchair base)
MED: 100-4,23,60.3

EQUIPMENT, REPLACEMENT, REPAIR, RENTAL

Y K0455 Infusion pump used for uninterrupted parenteral administration of medication, (e.g., epoprostenol or treprostinol)

Y K0462 Temporary replacement for patient-owned equipment being repaired, any type
MED: 100-4,20,40.1

Y ☑ K0552 Supplies for external drug infusion pump, syringe type cartridge, sterile, each

Y ☑ K0601 Replacement battery for external infusion pump owned by patient, silver oxide, 1.5 volt, each
AHA: 2Q,'03,7

Y ☑ K0602 Replacement battery for external infusion pump owned by patient, silver oxide, 3 volt, each
AHA: 2Q,'03,7

Y ☑ K0603 Replacement battery for external infusion pump owned by patient, alkaline, 1.5 volt, each
AHA: 2Q,'03,7

Y ☑ K0604 Replacement battery for external infusion pump owned by patient, lithium, 3.6 volt, each
AHA: 2Q,'03,7

Y ☑ K0605 Replacement battery for external infusion pump owned by patient, lithium, 4.5 volt, each
AHA: 2Q,'03,7

Y K0606 Automatic external defibrillator, with integrated electrocardiogram analysis, garment type
AHA: 4Q,'03,4

Y ☑ K0607 Replacement battery for automated external defibrillator, garment type only, each
AHA: 4Q,'03,4

Y ☑ K0608 Replacement garment for use with automated external defibrillator, each
AHA: 4Q,'03,4

Y ☑ K0609 Replacement electrodes for use with automated external defibrillator, garment type only, each
AHA: 4Q,'03,4

Y K0669 Wheelchair accessory, wheelchair seat or back cushion, does not meet specific code criteria or no written coding verification from DME PDAC

A ☑ K0672 Addition to lower extremity orthotic, removable soft interface, all components, replacement only, each

Y K0730 Controlled dose inhalation drug delivery system

Y K0733 Power wheelchair accessory, 12 to 24 amp hour sealed lead acid battery, each (e.g., gel cell, absorbed glassmat)
MED: 100-4,23,60.3

Y K0738 Portable gaseous oxygen system, rental; home compressor used to fill portable oxygen cylinders; includes portable containers, regulator, flowmeter, humidifier, cannula or mask, and tubing

Y ☑ K0739 Repair or nonroutine service for durable medical equipment other than oxygen equipment requiring the skill of a technician, labor component, per 15 minutes

E ☑ K0740 Repair or nonroutine service for oxygen equipment requiring the skill of a technician, labor component, per 15 minutes

● Y K0741 Jan Portable gaseous oxygen system, rental, includes portable container, regulator, flowmeter, humidifier, cannula or mask, and tubing, for cluster headaches

● Y K0742 Jan Portable oxygen contents, gaseous, 1 month's supply = 1 unit, for cluster headaches, for initial months supply or to replace used contents

● Y K0743 Jan Suction pump, home model, portable, for use on wounds

● A ☑ K0744 Jan Absorptive wound dressing for use with suction pump, home model, portable, pad size 16 sq in or less

● A ☑ K0745 Jan Absorptive wound dressing for use with suction pump, home model, portable, pad size more than 16 sq in but less than or equal to 48 sq in

● A K0746 Jan Absorptive wound dressing for use with suction pump, home model, portable, pad size greater than 48 sq in

POWER OPERATED VEHICLE AND ACCESSORIES

Y K0800 Power operated vehicle, group 1 standard, patient weight capacity up to and including 300 pounds
MED: 100-4,23,60.3

Y K0801 Power operated vehicle, group 1 heavy-duty, patient weight capacity 301 to 450 pounds

Y K0802 Power operated vehicle, group 1 very heavy-duty, patient weight capacity 451 to 600 pounds

Y K0806 Power operated vehicle, group 2 standard, patient weight capacity up to and including 300 pounds

Y K0807 Power operated vehicle, group 2 heavy-duty, patient weight capacity 301 to 450 pounds

Y K0808 Power operated vehicle, group 2 very heavy-duty, patient weight capacity 451 to 600 pounds

Y K0812 Power operated vehicle, not otherwise classified

POWER WHEELCHAIRS

Y K0813 Power wheelchair, group 1 standard, portable, sling/solid seat and back, patient weight capacity up to and including 300 pounds
MED: 100-4,23,60.3

Y K0814 Power wheelchair, group 1 standard, portable, captain's chair, patient weight capacity up to and including 300 pounds

Y K0815 Power wheelchair, group 1 standard, sling/solid seat and back, patient weight capacity up to and including 300 pounds

Y K0816 Power wheelchair, group 1 standard, captain's chair, patient weight capacity up to and including 300 pounds

Y K0820 Power wheelchair, group 2 standard, portable, sling/solid seat/back, patient weight capacity up to and including 300 pounds

Y K0821 Power wheelchair, group 2 standard, portable, captain's chair, patient weight capacity up to and including 300 pounds

Y K0822 Power wheelchair, group 2 standard, sling/solid seat/back, patient weight capacity up to and including 300 pounds

Y K0823 Power wheelchair, group 2 standard, captain's chair, patient weight capacity up to and including 300 pounds

Y K0824 Power wheelchair, group 2 heavy-duty, sling/solid seat/back, patient weight capacity 301 to 450 pounds

Y K0825 Power wheelchair, group 2 heavy-duty, captain's chair, patient weight capacity 301 to 450 pounds

Y K0826 Power wheelchair, group 2 very heavy-duty, sling/solid seat/back, patient weight capacity 451 to 600 pounds

Y K0827 Power wheelchair, group 2 very heavy-duty, captain's chair, patient weight capacity 451 to 600 pounds

Y K0828 Power wheelchair, group 2 extra heavy-duty, sling/solid seat/back, patient weight capacity 601 pounds or more

Y K0829 Power wheelchair, group 2 extra heavy-duty, captain's chair, patient weight 601 pounds or more

Y K0830 Power wheelchair, group 2 standard, seat elevator, sling/solid seat/back, patient weight capacity up to and including 300 pounds

Y K0831 Power wheelchair, group 2 standard, seat elevator, captain's chair, patient weight capacity up to and including 300 pounds

Y K0835 Power wheelchair, group 2 standard, single power option, sling/solid seat/back, patient weight capacity up to and including 300 pounds
MED: 100-4,23,60.3

Y K0836 Power wheelchair, group 2 standard, single power option, captain's chair, patient weight capacity up to and including 300 pounds

Y K0837 Power wheelchair, group 2 heavy-duty, single power option, sling/solid seat/back, patient weight capacity 301 to 450 pounds

Y K0838 Power wheelchair, group 2 heavy-duty, single power option, captain's chair, patient weight capacity 301 to 450 pounds

Y K0839 Power wheelchair, group 2 very heavy-duty, single power option sling/solid seat/back, patient weight capacity 451 to 600 pounds

Y K0840 Power wheelchair, group 2 extra heavy-duty, single power option, sling/solid seat/back, patient weight capacity 601 pounds or more

Y K0841 Power wheelchair, group 2 standard, multiple power option, sling/solid seat/back, patient weight capacity up to and including 300 pounds

Y K0842 Power wheelchair, group 2 standard, multiple power option, captain's chair, patient weight capacity up to and including 300 pounds

Y K0843 Power wheelchair, group 2 heavy-duty, multiple power option, sling/solid seat/back, patient weight capacity 301 to 450 pounds

Y **K0848** Power wheelchair, group 3 standard, sling/solid seat/back, patient weight capacity up to and including 300 pounds ♿

Y **K0849** Power wheelchair, group 3 standard, captain's chair, patient weight capacity up to and including 300 pounds ♿

Y **K0850** Power wheelchair, group 3 heavy-duty, sling/solid seat/back, patient weight capacity 301 to 450 pounds ♿

Y **K0851** Power wheelchair, group 3 heavy-duty, captain's chair, patient weight capacity 301 to 450 pounds ♿

Y **K0852** Power wheelchair, group 3 very heavy-duty, sling/solid seat/back, patient weight capacity 451 to 600 pounds ♿

Y **K0853** Power wheelchair, group 3 very heavy-duty, captain's chair, patient weight capacity 451 to 600 pounds ♿

Y **K0854** Power wheelchair, group 3 extra heavy-duty, sling/solid seat/back, patient weight capacity 601 pounds or more ♿

Y **K0855** Power wheelchair, group 3 extra heavy-duty, captain's chair, patient weight capacity 601 pounds or more ♿

Y **K0856** Power wheelchair, group 3 standard, single power option, sling/solid seat/back, patient weight capacity up to and including 300 pounds ♿

Y **K0857** Power wheelchair, group 3 standard, single power option, captain's chair, patient weight capacity up to and including 300 pounds ♿

Y **K0858** Power wheelchair, group 3 heavy-duty, single power option, sling/solid seat/back, patient weight 301 to 450 pounds ♿

Y **K0859** Power wheelchair, group 3 heavy-duty, single power option, captain's chair, patient weight capacity 301 to 450 pounds ♿

Y **K0860** Power wheelchair, group 3 very heavy-duty, single power option, sling/solid seat/back, patient weight capacity 451 to 600 pounds ♿

Y **K0861** Power wheelchair, group 3 standard, multiple power option, sling/solid seat/back, patient weight capacity up to and including 300 pounds ♿

Y **K0862** Power wheelchair, group 3 heavy-duty, multiple power option, sling/solid seat/back, patient weight capacity 301 to 450 pounds ♿

Y **K0863** Power wheelchair, group 3 very heavy-duty, multiple power option, sling/solid seat/back, patient weight capacity 451 to 600 pounds ♿

Y **K0864** Power wheelchair, group 3 extra heavy-duty, multiple power option, sling/solid seat/back, patient weight capacity 601 pounds or more ♿

Y **K0868** Power wheelchair, group 4 standard, sling/solid seat/back, patient weight capacity up to and including 300 pounds

Y **K0869** Power wheelchair, group 4 standard, captain's chair, patient weight capacity up to and including 300 pounds

Y **K0870** Power wheelchair, group 4 heavy-duty, sling/solid seat/back, patient weight capacity 301 to 450 pounds

Y **K0871** Power wheelchair, group 4 very heavy-duty, sling/solid seat/back, patient weight capacity 451 to 600 pounds

Y **K0877** Power wheelchair, group 4 standard, single power option, sling/solid seat/back, patient weight capacity up to and including 300 pounds

Y **K0878** Power wheelchair, group 4 standard, single power option, captain's chair, patient weight capacity up to and including 300 pounds

Y **K0879** Power wheelchair, group 4 heavy-duty, single power option, sling/solid seat/back, patient weight capacity 301 to 450 pounds

Y **K0880** Power wheelchair, group 4 very heavy-duty, single power option, sling/solid seat/back, patient weight 451 to 600 pounds

Y **K0884** Power wheelchair, group 4 standard, multiple power option, sling/solid seat/back, patient weight capacity up to and including 300 pounds

Y **K0885** Power wheelchair, group 4 standard, multiple power option, captain's chair, patient weight capacity up to and including 300 pounds

Y **K0886** Power wheelchair, group 4 heavy-duty, multiple power option, sling/solid seat/back, patient weight capacity 301 to 450 pounds

Y **K0890** Power wheelchair, group 5 pediatric, single power option, sling/solid seat/back, patient weight capacity up to and including 125 pounds

Y **K0891** Power wheelchair, group 5 pediatric, multiple power option, sling/solid seat/back, patient weight capacity up to and including 125 pounds

Y **K0898** Power wheelchair, not otherwise classified

Y **K0899** Power mobility device, not coded by DME PDAC or does not meet criteria

ORTHOTIC PROCEDURES AND DEVICES L0000-L4999

L codes include orthotic and prosthetic procedures and devices, as well as scoliosis equipment, orthopedic shoes, and prosthetic implants.

CERVICAL

- A **L0112** Cranial cervical orthotic, congenital torticollis type, with or without soft interface material, adjustable range of motion joint, custom fabricated ♿
- A **L0113** Cranial cervical orthotic, torticollis type, with or without joint, with or without soft interface material, prefabricated, includes fitting and adjustment ♿
- A **L0120** Cervical, flexible, nonadjustable (foam collar) ♿
- A **L0130** Cervical, flexible, thermoplastic collar, molded to patient ♿
- A **L0140** Cervical, semi-rigid, adjustable (plastic collar) ♿
- A **L0150** Cervical, semi-rigid, adjustable molded chin cup (plastic collar with mandibular/occipital piece) ♿
- A **L0160** Cervical, semi-rigid, wire frame occipital/mandibular support ♿
- A **L0170** Cervical, collar, molded to patient model ♿
- A **L0172** Cervical, collar, semi-rigid thermoplastic foam, 2 piece ♿
- A **L0174** Cervical, collar, semi-rigid, thermoplastic foam, 2 piece with thoracic extension ♿

MULTIPLE POST COLLAR

- A **L0180** Cervical, multiple post collar, occipital/mandibular supports, adjustable ♿
- A **L0190** Cervical, multiple post collar, occipital/mandibular supports, adjustable cervical bars (SOMI, Guilford, Taylor types) ♿
- A **L0200** Cervical, multiple post collar, occipital/mandibular supports, adjustable cervical bars, and thoracic extension ♿

THORACIC

- A **L0220** Thoracic, rib belt, custom fabricated ♿
- A **L0430** Spinal orthotic, anterior-posterior-lateral control, with interface material, custom fitted (DeWall Posture Protector only) ♿

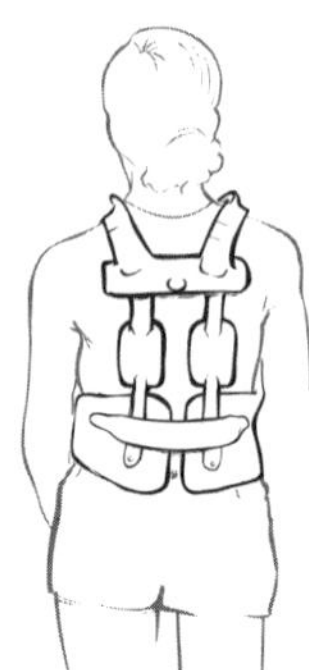

TLSO brace with adjustable straps and pads (L0450). The model at right and similar devices such as the Boston brace are molded polymer over foam and may be bivalve (front and back components)

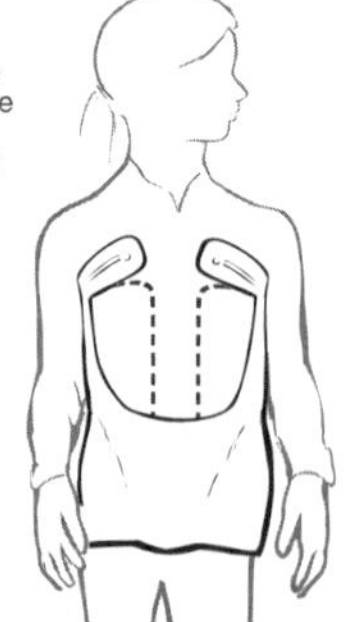

Thoracic lumbar sacral orthosis (TLSO)

- A **L0450** Thoracic-lumbar-sacral orthotic (TLSO), flexible, provides trunk support, upper thoracic region, produces intracavitary pressure to reduce load on the intervertebral disks with rigid stays or panel(s), includes shoulder straps and closures, prefabricated, includes fitting and adjustment ♿
- A **L0452** Thoracic-lumbar-sacral orthotic (TLSO), flexible, provides trunk support, upper thoracic region, produces intracavitary pressure to reduce load on the intervertebral disks with rigid stays or panel(s), includes shoulder straps and closures, custom fabricated ♿
- A **L0454** Thoracic-lumbar-sacral orthotic (TLSO) flexible, provides trunk support, extends from sacrococcygeal junction to above T-9 vertebra, restricts gross trunk motion in the sagittal plane, produces intracavitary pressure to reduce load on the intervertebral disks with rigid stays or panel(s), includes shoulder straps and closures, prefabricated, includes fitting and adjustment ♿
- A **L0456** Thoracic-lumbar-sacral orthotic (TLSO), flexible, provides trunk support, thoracic region, rigid posterior panel and soft anterior apron, extends from the sacrococcygeal junction and terminates just inferior to the scapular spine, restricts gross trunk motion in the sagittal plane, produces intracavitary pressure to reduce load on the intervertebral disks, includes straps and closures, prefabricated, includes fitting and adjustment ♿
- A **L0458** Thoracic-lumbar-sacral orthotic (TLSO), triplanar control, modular segmented spinal system, 2 rigid plastic shells, posterior extends from the sacrococcygeal junction and terminates just inferior to the scapular spine, anterior extends from the symphysis pubis to the xiphoid, soft liner, restricts gross trunk motion in the sagittal, coronal, and transverse planes, lateral strength is provided by overlapping plastic and stabilizing closures, includes straps and closures, prefabricated, includes fitting and adjustment ♿
- A **L0460** Thoracic-lumbar-sacral orthotic (TLSO), triplanar control, modular segmented spinal system, 2 rigid plastic shells, posterior extends from the sacrococcygeal junction and terminates just inferior to the scapular spine, anterior extends from the symphysis pubis to the sternal notch, soft liner, restricts gross trunk motion in the sagittal, coronal, and transverse planes, lateral strength is provided by overlapping plastic and stabilizing closures, includes straps and closures, prefabricated, includes fitting and adjustment ♿
- A **L0462** Thoracic-lumbar-sacral orthotic (TLSO), triplanar control, modular segmented spinal system, 3 rigid plastic shells, posterior extends from the sacrococcygeal junction and terminates just inferior to the scapular spine, anterior extends from the symphysis pubis to the sternal notch, soft liner, restricts gross trunk motion in the sagittal, coronal, and transverse planes, lateral strength is provided by overlapping plastic and stabilizing closures, includes straps and closures, prefabricated, includes fitting and adjustment ♿

A **L0464** Thoracic-lumbar-sacral orthotic (TLSO), triplanar control, modular segmented spinal system, 4 rigid plastic shells, posterior extends from sacrococcygeal junction and terminates just inferior to scapular spine, anterior extends from symphysis pubis to the sternal notch, soft liner, restricts gross trunk motion in sagittal, coronal, and transverse planes, lateral strength is provided by overlapping plastic and stabilizing closures, includes straps and closures, prefabricated, includes fitting and adjustment ♿

A **L0466** Thoracic-lumbar-sacral orthotic (TLSO), sagittal control, rigid posterior frame and flexible soft anterior apron with straps, closures and padding, restricts gross trunk motion in sagittal plane, produces intracavitary pressure to reduce load on intervertebral disks, includes fitting and shaping the frame, prefabricated, includes fitting and adjustment ♿

A **L0468** Thoracic-lumbar-sacral orthotic (TLSO), sagittal-coronal control, rigid posterior frame and flexible soft anterior apron with straps, closures and padding, extends from sacrococcygeal junction over scapulae, lateral strength provided by pelvic, thoracic, and lateral frame pieces, restricts gross trunk motion in sagittal, and coronal planes, produces intracavitary pressure to reduce load on intervertebral disks, includes fitting and shaping the frame, prefabricated, includes fitting and adjustment ♿

▲ A **L0470** [Jan] TLSO, triplanar control, rigid posterior frame and flexible soft anterior apron with straps, closures and padding extends from sacrococcygeal junction to scapula, lateral strength provided by pelvic, thoracic, and lateral frame pieces, rotational strength provided by subclavicular extensions, restricts gross trunk motion in sagittal, coronal, and transverse planes, provides intracavitary pressure to reduce load on the intervertebral disks, includes fitting and shaping the frame, prefabricated, includes fitting and adjustment ♿

A **L0472** Thoracic-lumbar-sacral orthotic (TLSO), triplanar control, hyperextension, rigid anterior and lateral frame extends from symphysis pubis to sternal notch with 2 anterior components (one pubic and one sternal), posterior and lateral pads with straps and closures, limits spinal flexion, restricts gross trunk motion in sagittal, coronal, and transverse planes, includes fitting and shaping the frame, prefabricated, includes fitting and adjustment ♿

A **L0480** Thoracic-lumbar-sacral orthotic (TLSO), triplanar control, 1 piece rigid plastic shell without interface liner, with multiple straps and closures, posterior extends from sacrococcygeal junction and terminates just inferior to scapular spine, anterior extends from symphysis pubis to sternal notch, anterior or posterior opening, restricts gross trunk motion in sagittal, coronal, and transverse planes, includes a carved plaster or CAD-CAM model, custom fabricated ♿

A **L0482** Thoracic-lumbar-sacral orthotic (TLSO), triplanar control, 1 piece rigid plastic shell with interface liner, multiple straps and closures, posterior extends from sacrococcygeal junction and terminates just inferior to scapular spine, anterior extends from symphysis pubis to sternal notch, anterior or posterior opening, restricts gross trunk motion in sagittal, coronal, and transverse planes, includes a carved plaster or CAD-CAM model, custom fabricated ♿

A **L0484** Thoracic-lumbar-sacral orthotic TLSO, triplanar control, 2 piece rigid plastic shell without interface liner, with multiple straps and closures, posterior extends from sacrococcygeal junction and terminates just inferior to scapular spine, anterior extends from symphysis pubis to sternal notch, lateral strength is enhanced by overlapping plastic, restricts gross trunk motion in the sagittal, coronal, and transverse planes, includes a carved plaster or CAD-CAM model, custom fabricated ♿

A **L0486** Thoracic-lumbar-sacral orthotic (TLSO), triplanar control, 2 piece rigid plastic shell with interface liner, multiple straps and closures, posterior extends from sacrococcygeal junction and terminates just inferior to scapular spine, anterior extends from symphysis pubis to sternal notch, lateral strength is enhanced by overlapping plastic, restricts gross trunk motion in the sagittal, coronal, and transverse planes, includes a carved plaster or CAD-CAM model, custom fabricated ♿

A **L0488** Thoracic-lumbar-sacral orthotic (TLSO), triplanar control, 1 piece rigid plastic shell with interface liner, multiple straps and closures, posterior extends from sacrococcygeal junction and terminates just inferior to scapular spine, anterior extends from symphysis pubis to sternal notch, anterior or posterior opening, restricts gross trunk motion in sagittal, coronal, and transverse planes, prefabricated, includes fitting and adjustment ♿

A **L0490** Thoracic-lumbar-sacral orthotic (TLSO), sagittal-coronal control, 1 piece rigid plastic shell, with overlapping reinforced anterior, with multiple straps and closures, posterior extends from sacrococcygeal junction and terminates at or before the T-9 vertebra, anterior extends from symphysis pubis to xiphoid, anterior opening, restricts gross trunk motion in sagittal and coronal planes, prefabricated, includes fitting and adjustment ♿

A **L0491** Thoracic-lumbar-sacral orthotic (TLSO), sagittal-coronal control, modular segmented spinal system, 2 rigid plastic shells, posterior extends from the sacrococcygeal junction and terminates just inferior to the scapular spine, anterior extends from the symphysis pubis to the xiphoid, soft liner, restricts gross trunk motion in the sagittal and coronal planes, lateral strength is provided by overlapping plastic and stabilizing closures, includes straps and closures, prefabricated, includes fitting and adjustment ♿

A **L0492** Thoracic-lumbar-sacral orthotic (TLSO), sagittal-coronal control, modular segmented spinal system, 3 rigid plastic shells, posterior extends from the sacrococcygeal junction and terminates just inferior to the scapular spine, anterior extends from the symphysis pubis to the xiphoid, soft liner, restricts gross trunk motion in the sagittal and coronal planes, lateral strength is provided by overlapping plastic and stabilizing closures, includes straps and closures, prefabricated, includes fitting and adjustment ♿

CERVICAL-THORACIC-LUMBAR-SACRAL ORTHOTIC

A **L0621** Sacroiliac orthotic, flexible, provides pelvic-sacral support, reduces motion about the sacroiliac joint, includes straps, closures, may include pendulous abdomen design, prefabricated, includes fitting and adjustment ♿

[Jan] January Update

A **L0622** Sacroiliac orthotic, flexible, provides pelvic-sacral support, reduces motion about the sacroiliac joint, includes straps, closures, may include pendulous abdomen design, custom fabricated ♿

A **L0623** Sacroiliac orthotic, provides pelvic-sacral support, with rigid or semi-rigid panels over the sacrum and abdomen, reduces motion about the sacroiliac joint, includes straps, closures, may include pendulous abdomen design, prefabricated, includes fitting and adjustment ♿

A **L0624** Sacroiliac orthotic, provides pelvic-sacral support, with rigid or semi-rigid panels placed over the sacrum and abdomen, reduces motion about the sacroiliac joint, includes straps, closures, may include pendulous abdomen design, custom fabricated ♿

A **L0625** Lumbar orthotic, flexible, provides lumbar support, posterior extends from L-1 to below L-5 vertebra, produces intracavitary pressure to reduce load on the intervertebral discs, includes straps, closures, may include pendulous abdomen design, shoulder straps, stays, prefabricated, includes fitting and adjustment ♿

A **L0626** Lumbar orthotic, sagittal control, with rigid posterior panel(s), posterior extends from L-1 to below L-5 vertebra, produces intracavitary pressure to reduce load on the intervertebral discs, includes straps, closures, may include padding, stays, shoulder straps, pendulous abdomen design, prefabricated, includes fitting and adjustment ♿

A **L0627** Lumbar orthotic, sagittal control, with rigid anterior and posterior panels, posterior extends from L-1 to below L-5 vertebra, produces intracavitary pressure to reduce load on the intervertebral discs, includes straps, closures, may include padding, shoulder straps, pendulous abdomen design, prefabricated, includes fitting and adjustment ♿

A **L0628** Lumbar-sacral orthotic, flexible, provides lumbo-sacral support, posterior extends from sacrococcygeal junction to T-9 vertebra, produces intracavitary pressure to reduce load on the intervertebral discs, includes straps, closures, may include stays, shoulder straps, pendulous abdomen design, prefabricated, includes fitting and adjustment ♿

A **L0629** Lumbar-sacral orthotic, flexible, provides lumbo-sacral support, posterior extends from sacrococcygeal junction to T-9 vertebra, produces intracavitary pressure to reduce load on the intervertebral discs, includes straps, closures, may include stays, shoulder straps, pendulous abdomen design, custom fabricated ♿

A **L0630** Lumbar-sacral orthotic, sagittal control, with rigid posterior panel(s), posterior extends from sacrococcygeal junction to T-9 vertebra, produces intracavitary pressure to reduce load on the intervertebral discs, includes straps, closures, may include padding, stays, shoulder straps, pendulous abdomen design, prefabricated, includes fitting and adjustment ♿

A **L0631** Lumbar-sacral orthotic (LSO), sagittal control, with rigid anterior and posterior panels, posterior extends from sacrococcygeal junction to T-9 vertebra, produces intracavitary pressure to reduce load on the intervertebral discs, includes straps, closures, may include padding, shoulder straps, pendulous abdomen design, prefabricated, includes fitting and adjustment ♿

A **L0632** Lumbar-sacral orthotic (LSO), sagittal control, with rigid anterior and posterior panels, posterior extends from sacrococcygeal junction to T-9 vertebra, produces intracavitary pressure to reduce load on the intervertebral discs, includes straps, closures, may include padding, shoulder straps, pendulous abdomen design, custom fabricated ♿

A **L0633** Lumbar-sacral orthotic (LSO), sagittal-coronal control, with rigid posterior frame/panel(s), posterior extends from sacrococcygeal junction to T-9 vertebra, lateral strength provided by rigid lateral frame/panels, produces intracavitary pressure to reduce load on intervertebral discs, includes straps, closures, may include padding, stays, shoulder straps, pendulous abdomen design, prefabricated, includes fitting and adjustment ♿

A **L0634** Lumbar-sacral orthotic (LSO), sagittal-coronal control, with rigid posterior frame/panel(s), posterior extends from sacrococcygeal junction to T-9 vertebra, lateral strength provided by rigid lateral frame/panel(s), produces intracavitary pressure to reduce load on intervertebral discs, includes straps, closures, may include padding, stays, shoulder straps, pendulous abdomen design, custom fabricated ♿

A **L0635** Lumbar-sacral orthotic (LSO), sagittal-coronal control, lumbar flexion, rigid posterior frame/panel(s), lateral articulating design to flex the lumbar spine, posterior extends from sacrococcygeal junction to T-9 vertebra, lateral strength provided by rigid lateral frame/panel(s), produces intracavitary pressure to reduce load on intervertebral discs, includes straps, closures, may include padding, anterior panel, pendulous abdomen design, prefabricated, includes fitting and adjustment ♿

A **L0636** Lumbar-sacral orthotic (LSO), sagittal-coronal control, lumbar flexion, rigid posterior frame/panels, lateral articulating design to flex the lumbar spine, posterior extends from sacrococcygeal junction to T-9 vertebra, lateral strength provided by rigid lateral frame/panels, produces intracavitary pressure to reduce load on intervertebral discs, includes straps, closures, may include padding, anterior panel, pendulous abdomen design, custom fabricated ♿

A **L0637** Lumbar-sacral orthotic (LSO), sagittal-coronal control, with rigid anterior and posterior frame/panels, posterior extends from sacrococcygeal junction to T-9 vertebra, lateral strength provided by rigid lateral frame/panels, produces intracavitary pressure to reduce load on intervertebral discs, includes straps, closures, may include padding, shoulder straps, pendulous abdomen design, prefabricated, includes fitting and adjustment ♿

A **L0638** Lumbar-sacral orthotic (LSO), sagittal-coronal control, with rigid anterior and posterior frame/panels, posterior extends from sacrococcygeal junction to T-9 vertebra, lateral strength provided by rigid lateral frame/panels, produces intracavitary pressure to reduce load on intervertebral discs, includes straps, closures, may include padding, shoulder straps, pendulous abdomen design, custom fabricated ♿

A **L0639** **Lumbar-sacral orthotic (LSO), sagittal-coronal control, rigid shell(s)/panel(s), posterior extends from sacrococcygeal junction to T-9 vertebra, anterior extends from symphysis pubis to xyphoid, produces intracavitary pressure to reduce load on the intervertebral discs, overall strength is provided by overlapping rigid material and stabilizing closures, includes straps, closures, may include soft interface, pendulous abdomen design, prefabricated, includes fitting and adjustment** ♿

A **L0640** **Lumbar-sacral orthotic (LSO), sagittal-coronal control, rigid shell(s)/panel(s), posterior extends from sacrococcygeal junction to T-9 vertebra, anterior extends from symphysis pubis to xyphoid, produces intracavitary pressure to reduce load on the intervertebral discs, overall strength is provided by overlapping rigid material and stabilizing closures, includes straps, closures, may include soft interface, pendulous abdomen design, custom fabricated** ♿

A **L0700** **Cervical-thoracic-lumbar-sacral orthosis (CTLSO), anterior-posterior-lateral control, molded to patient model, (Minerva type)** ♿

A **L0710** **Cervical-thoracic-lumbar-sacral orthotic (CTLSO), anterior-posterior-lateral-control, molded to patient model, with interface material, (Minerva type)** ♿

HALO PROCEDURE

A **L0810** **Halo procedure, cervical halo incorporated into jacket vest** ♿

A **L0820** **Halo procedure, cervical halo incorporated into plaster body jacket** ♿

A **L0830** **Halo procedure, cervical halo incorporated into Milwaukee type orthotic** ♿

A **L0859** **Addition to halo procedure, magnetic resonance image compatible systems, rings and pins, any material** ♿

A **L0861** **Addition to halo procedure, replacement liner/interface material** ♿

ADDITIONS TO SPINAL ORTHOTIC

A **L0970** **Thoracic-lumbar-sacral orthotic (TLSO), corset front** ♿

A **L0972** **Lumbar-sacral orthotic (LSO), corset front** ♿

A **L0974** **Thoracic-lumbar-sacral orthotic (TLSO), full corset** ♿

A **L0976** **Lumbar-sacral orthotic (LSO), full corset** ♿

A **L0978** **Axillary crutch extension** ♿

A ☑ **L0980** **Peroneal straps, pair** ♿

A ☑ **L0982** **Stocking supporter grips, set of 4** ♿

A ☑ **L0984** **Protective body sock, each** ♿

A **L0999** **Addition to spinal orthotic, not otherwise specified**
Determine if an alternative HCPCS Level II or a CPT code better describes the service being reported. This code should be used only if a more specific code is unavailable.

ORTHOTIC DEVICES - SCOLIOSIS PROCEDURES

The orthotic care of scoliosis differs from other orthotic care in that the treatment is more dynamic in nature and uses continual modification of the orthosis to the patient's changing condition. This coding structure uses the proper names - or eponyms - of the procedures because they have historic and universal acceptance in the profession. It should be recognized that variations to the basic procedures described by the founders/developers are accepted in various medical and orthotic practices throughout the country. All procedures include model of patient when indicated.

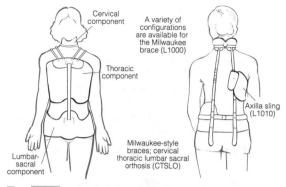

A **L1000** **Cervical-thoracic-lumbar-sacral orthotic (CTLSO) (Milwaukee), inclusive of furnishing initial orthotic, including model** ♿

A **L1001** **Cervical-thoracic-lumbar-sacral orthotic (CTLSO), immobilizer, infant size, prefabricated, includes fitting and adjustment** A ♿

A **L1005** **Tension based scoliosis orthotic and accessory pads, includes fitting and adjustment** ♿

A **L1010** **Addition to cervical-thoracic-lumbar-sacral orthotic (CTLSO) or scoliosis orthotic, axilla sling** ♿

A **L1020** **Addition to cervical-thoracic-lumbar-sacral orthotic (CTLSO) or scoliosis orthotic, kyphosis pad** ♿

A **L1025** **Addition to cervical-thoracic-lumbar-sacral orthotic (CTLSO) or scoliosis orthotic, kyphosis pad, floating** ♿

A **L1030** **Addition to cervical-thoracic-lumbar-sacral orthotic (CTLSO) or scoliosis orthotic, lumbar bolster pad** ♿

A **L1040** **Addition to cervical-thoracic-lumbar-sacral orthotic (CTLSO) or scoliosis orthotic, lumbar or lumbar rib pad** ♿

A **L1050** **Addition to cervical-thoracic-lumbar-sacral orthotic (CTLSO) or scoliosis orthotic, sternal pad** ♿

A **L1060** **Addition to cervical-thoracic-lumbar-sacral orthotic (CTLSO) or scoliosis orthotic, thoracic pad** ♿

A **L1070** **Addition to cervical-thoracic-lumbar-sacral orthotic (CTLSO) or scoliosis orthotic, trapezius sling** ♿

A **L1080** **Addition to cervical-thoracic-lumbar-sacral orthotic (CTLSO) or scoliosis orthotic, outrigger** ♿

A **L1085** **Addition to cervical-thoracic-lumbar-sacral orthotic (CTLSO) or scoliosis orthotic, outrigger, bilateral with vertical extensions** ♿

A **L1090** **Addition to cervical-thoracic-lumbar-sacral orthotic (CTLSO) or scoliosis orthotic, lumbar sling** ♿

A **L1100** **Addition to cervical-thoracic-lumbar-sacral orthotic (CTLSO) or scoliosis orthotic, ring flange, plastic or leather** ♿

A **L1110** **Addition to cervical-thoracic-lumbar-sacral orthotic (CTLSO) or scoliosis orthotic, ring flange, plastic or leather, molded to patient model** ♿

A ☑ **L1120** **Addition to cervical-thoracic-lumbar-sacral orthotic (CTLSO), scoliosis orthotic, cover for upright, each** ♿

THORACIC-LUMBAR-SACRAL ORTHOSIS (TLSO) (LOW PROFILE)

A **L1200** **Thoracic-lumbar-sacral orthotic (TLSO), inclusive of furnishing initial orthotic only** ♿

A L1210 Addition to thoracic-lumbar-sacral orthotic (TLSO), (low profile), lateral thoracic extension ♿

A L1220 Addition to thoracic-lumbar-sacral orthotic (TLSO), (low profile), anterior thoracic extension ♿

A L1230 Addition to thoracic-lumbar-sacral orthotic (TLSO), (low profile), Milwaukee type superstructure ♿

A L1240 Addition to thoracic-lumbar-sacral orthotic (TLSO), (low profile), lumbar derotation pad ♿

A L1250 Addition to thoracic-lumbar-sacral orthotic (TLSO), (low profile), anterior ASIS pad ♿

A L1260 Addition to thoracic-lumbar-sacral orthotic (TLSO), (low profile), anterior thoracic derotation pad ♿

A L1270 Addition to thoracic-lumbar-sacral orthotic (TLSO), (low profile), abdominal pad ♿

A ☑ L1280 Addition to thoracic-lumbar-sacral orthotic (TLSO), (low profile), rib gusset (elastic), each ♿

A L1290 Addition to thoracic-lumbar-sacral orthotic (TLSO), (low profile), lateral trochanteric pad ♿

OTHER SCOLIOSIS PROCEDURES

A L1300 Other scoliosis procedure, body jacket molded to patient model ♿

A L1310 Other scoliosis procedure, postoperative body jacket ♿

A L1499 Spinal orthotic, not otherwise specified

Determine if an alternative HCPCS Level II or a CPT code better describes the service being reported. This code should be used only if a more specific code is unavailable.

THORACIC-HIP-KNEE-ANKLE ORTHOTIC (THKAO)

~~L1500~~ Jan ~~Thoracic-hip-knee-ankle orthosis (thoracic-hip-knee-ankle orthosis), mobility frame (Newington, Parapodium types)~~

~~L1510~~ Jan ~~Thoracic-hip-knee-ankle orthosis, standing frame, with or without tray and accessories~~

~~L1520~~ Jan ~~Thoracic-hip-knee-ankle orthotic (THKAO), swivel walker~~

HIP ORTHOTIC (HO) - FLEXIBLE

A L1600 Hip orthotic (HO), abduction control of hip joints, flexible, Frejka type with cover, prefabricated, includes fitting and adjustment ♿

A L1610 Hip orthotic (HO), abduction control of hip joints, flexible, (Frejka cover only), prefabricated, includes fitting and adjustment ♿

A L1620 Hip orthosis (HO), abduction control of hip joints, flexible, (Pavlik harness), prefabricated, includes fitting and adjustment ♿

A L1630 Hip orthotic (HO), abduction control of hip joints, semi-flexible (Von Rosen type), custom fabricated ♿

A L1640 Hip orthotic (HO), abduction control of hip joints, static, pelvic band or spreader bar, thigh cuffs, custom fabricated ♿

A L1650 Hip orthotic (HO), abduction control of hip joints, static, adjustable, (Ilfled type), prefabricated, includes fitting and adjustment ♿

A L1652 Hip orthotic, bilateral thigh cuffs with adjustable abductor spreader bar, adult size, prefabricated, includes fitting and adjustment, any type ♿

A L1660 Hip orthotic (HO), abduction control of hip joints, static, plastic, prefabricated, includes fitting and adjustment ♿

A L1680 Hip orthotic (HO), abduction control of hip joints, dynamic, pelvic control, adjustable hip motion control, thigh cuffs (Rancho hip action type), custom fabricated ♿

A L1685 Hip orthosis (HO), abduction control of hip joint, postoperative hip abduction type, custom fabricated ♿

A L1686 Hip orthotic (HO), abduction control of hip joint, postoperative hip abduction type, prefabricated, includes fitting and adjustment ♿

A L1690 Combination, bilateral, lumbo-sacral, hip, femur orthotic providing adduction and internal rotation control, prefabricated, includes fitting and adjustment ♿

LEGG PERTHES

A L1700 Legg Perthes orthotic, (Toronto type), custom fabricated ♿

A L1710 Legg Perthes orthotic, (Newington type), custom fabricated ♿

A L1720 Legg Perthes orthotic, trilateral, (Tachdijan type), custom fabricated ♿

A L1730 Legg Perthes orthotic, (Scottish Rite type), custom fabricated ♿

A L1755 Legg Perthes orthotic, (Patten bottom type), custom fabricated ♿

KNEE ORTHOTIC

A L1810 Knee orthotic (KO), elastic with joints, prefabricated, includes fitting and adjustment ♿

A L1820 Knee orthotic, elastic with condylar pads and joints, with or without patellar control, prefabricated, includes fitting and adjustment ♿

A L1830 Knee orthotic (KO), immobilizer, canvas longitudinal, prefabricated, includes fitting and adjustment ♿

A L1831 Knee orthotic, locking knee joint(s), positional orthotic, prefabricated, includes fitting and adjustment ♿

A L1832 Knee orthotic, adjustable knee joints (unicentric or polycentric), positional orthotic, rigid support, prefabricated, includes fitting and adjustment ♿

A L1834 Knee orthotic (KO), without knee joint, rigid, custom fabricated ♿

A L1836 Knee orthotic, rigid, without joint(s), includes soft interface material, prefabricated, includes fitting and adjustment ♿

A L1840 Knee orthotic (KO), derotation, medial-lateral, anterior cruciate ligament, custom fabricated ♿

A L1843 Knee orthotic (KO), single upright, thigh and calf, with adjustable flexion and extension joint (unicentric or polycentric), medial-lateral and rotation control, with or without varus/valgus adjustment, prefabricated, includes fitting and adjustment ♿

A L1844 Knee orthotic (KO), single upright, thigh and calf, with adjustable flexion and extension joint (unicentric or polycentric), medial-lateral and rotation control, with or without varus/valgus adjustment, custom fabricated ♿

A **L1845** Knee orthotic, double upright, thigh and calf, with adjustable flexion and extension joint (unicentric or polycentric), medial-lateral and rotation control, with or without varus/valgus adjustment, prefabricated, includes fitting and adjustment ♿

A **L1846** Knee orthotic, double upright, thigh and calf, with adjustable flexion and extension joint (unicentric or polycentric), medial-lateral and rotation control, with or without varus/valgus adjustment, custom fabricated ♿

A **L1847** Knee orthotic (KO), double upright with adjustable joint, with inflatable air support chamber(s), prefabricated, includes fitting and adjustment ♿

A **L1850** Knee orthotic (KO), Swedish type, prefabricated, includes fitting and adjustment ♿

A **L1860** Knee orthotic (KO), modification of supracondylar prosthetic socket, custom fabricated (SK) ♿

ANKLE-FOOT ORTHOTIC (AFO)

A **L1900** Ankle-foot orthotic (AFO), spring wire, dorsiflexion assist calf band, custom fabricated ♿

A **L1902** Ankle-foot orthotic (AFO), ankle gauntlet, prefabricated, includes fitting and adjustment ♿

A **L1904** Ankle-foot orthotic (AFO), molded ankle gauntlet, custom fabricated ♿

A **L1906** Ankle-foot orthosis (AFO), multiligamentus ankle support, prefabricated, includes fitting and adjustment ♿

A **L1907** AFO, supramalleolar with straps, with or without interface/pads, custom fabricated ♿

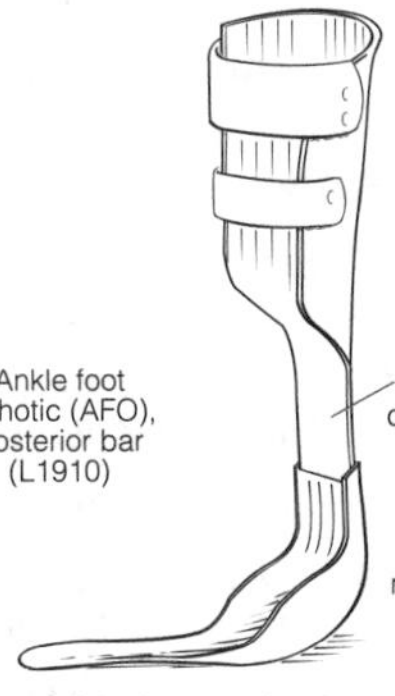

Ankle foot orthotic (AFO), posterior bar (L1910)

Flexible carbon component

Foot component may fit inside shoe

A **L1910** Ankle-foot orthotic (AFO), posterior, single bar, clasp attachment to shoe counter, prefabricated, includes fitting and adjustment ♿

A **L1920** Ankle-foot orthotic (AFO), single upright with static or adjustable stop (Phelps or Perlstein type), custom fabricated ♿

A **L1930** Ankle-foot orthotic (AFO), plastic or other material, prefabricated, includes fitting and adjustment ♿

A **L1932** AFO, rigid anterior tibial section, total carbon fiber or equal material, prefabricated, includes fitting and adjustment ♿

A **L1940** Ankle-foot orthotic (AFO), plastic or other material, custom fabricated ♿

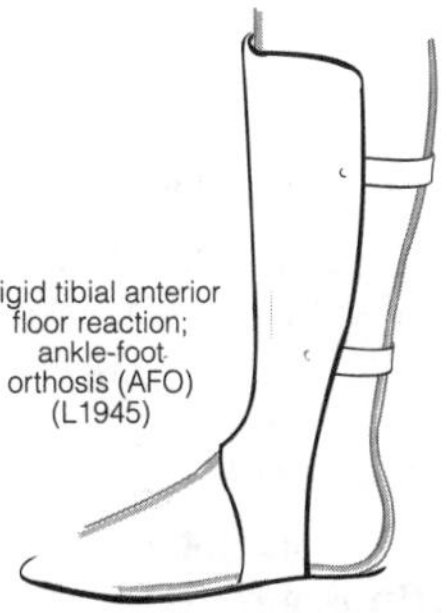

Rigid tibial anterior floor reaction; ankle-foot orthosis (AFO) (L1945)

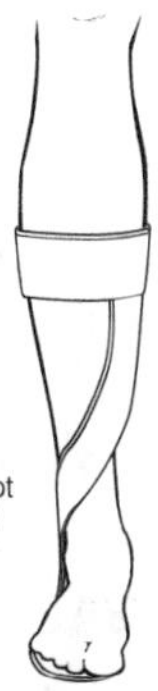

Spiral; ankle-foot orthosis (AFO) (L1950)

A **L1945** Ankle-foot orthotic (AFO), plastic, rigid anterior tibial section (floor reaction), custom fabricated ♿

A **L1950** Ankle-foot orthotic (AFO), spiral, (Institute of Rehabilitative Medicine type), plastic, custom fabricated ♿

A **L1951** Ankle-foot orthotic (AFO), spiral, (Institute of rehabilitative Medicine type), plastic or other material, prefabricated, includes fitting and adjustment ♿

A **L1960** Ankle-foot orthotic (AFO), posterior solid ankle, plastic, custom fabricated ♿

A **L1970** Ankle-foot orthotic (AFO), plastic with ankle joint, custom fabricated ♿

A **L1971** Ankle-foot orthotic (AFO), plastic or other material with ankle joint, prefabricated, includes fitting and adjustment ♿

A **L1980** Ankle-foot orthotic (AFO), single upright free plantar dorsiflexion, solid stirrup, calf band/cuff (single bar 'BK' orthotic), custom fabricated ♿

A **L1990** Ankle-foot orthotic (AFO), double upright free plantar dorsiflexion, solid stirrup, calf band/cuff (double bar 'BK' orthotic), custom fabricated ♿

KNEE-ANKLE-FOOT ORTHOTIC (KAFO) - OR ANY COMBINATION

A **L2000** Knee-ankle-foot orthotic (KAFO), single upright, free knee, free ankle, solid stirrup, thigh and calf bands/cuffs (single bar 'AK' orthotic), custom fabricated ♿

A **L2005** Knee-ankle-foot orthosis, any material, single or double upright, stance control, automatic lock and swing phase release, any type activation, includes ankle joint, any type, custom fabricated ♿

A **L2010** Knee-ankle-foot orthotic (KAFO), single upright, free ankle, solid stirrup, thigh and calf bands/cuffs (single bar 'AK' orthotic), without knee joint, custom fabricated ♿

A **L2020** Knee-ankle-foot orthotic (KAFO), double upright, free ankle, solid stirrup, thigh and calf bands/cuffs (double bar 'AK' orthotic), custom fabricated ♿

A **L2030** Knee-ankle-foot orthotic (KAFO), double upright, free ankle, solid stirrup, thigh and calf bands/cuffs, (double bar 'AK' orthotic), without knee joint, custom fabricated ♿

A **L2034** Knee-ankle-foot orthotic (KAFO), full plastic, single upright, with or without free motion knee, medial-lateral rotation control, with or without free motion ankle, custom fabricated ♿

A **L2035** Knee-ankle-foot orthotic (KAFO), full plastic, static (pediatric size), without free motion ankle, prefabricated, includes fitting and adjustment ♿

A **L2036** Knee-ankle-foot orthotic (KAFO), full plastic, double upright, with or without free motion knee, with or without free motion ankle, custom fabricated ♿

A **L2037** Knee-ankle-foot orthotic (KAFO), full plastic, single upright, with or without free motion knee, with or without free motion ankle, custom fabricated ♿

A **L2038** Knee-ankle-foot orthotic (KAFO), full plastic, with or without free motion knee, multi-axis ankle, custom fabricated ♿

TORSION CONTROL: HIP-KNEE-ANKLE-FOOT ORTHOTIC (HKAFO)

A **L2040** Hip-knee-ankle-foot orthotic (HKAFO), torsion control, bilateral rotation straps, pelvic band/belt, custom fabricated ♿

A **L2050** Hip-knee-ankle-foot orthotic (HKAFO), torsion control, bilateral torsion cables, hip joint, pelvic band/belt, custom fabricated ♿

A **L2060** Hip-knee-ankle-foot orthotic (HKAFO), torsion control, bilateral torsion cables, ball bearing hip joint, pelvic band/ belt, custom fabricated ♿

A **L2070** Hip-knee-ankle-foot orthotic (HKAFO), torsion control, unilateral rotation straps, pelvic band/belt, custom fabricated ♿

A **L2080** Hip-knee-ankle-foot orthotic (HKAFO), torsion control, unilateral torsion cable, hip joint, pelvic band/belt, custom fabricated ♿

A **L2090** Hip-knee-ankle-foot orthotic (HKAFO), torsion control, unilateral torsion cable, ball bearing hip joint, pelvic band/ belt, custom fabricated ♿

A **L2106** Ankle-foot orthotic (AFO), fracture orthotic, tibial fracture cast orthotic, thermoplastic type casting material, custom fabricated ♿

A **L2108** Ankle-foot orthotic (AFO), fracture orthotic, tibial fracture cast orthotic, custom fabricated ♿

A **L2112** Ankle-foot orthotic (AFO), fracture orthotic, tibial fracture orthotic, soft, prefabricated, includes fitting and adjustment ♿

A **L2114** Ankle-foot orthosis (AFO), fracture orthosis, tibial fracture orthosis, semi-rigid, prefabricated, includes fitting and adjustment ♿

A **L2116** Ankle-foot orthotic (AFO), fracture orthotic, tibial fracture orthotic, rigid, prefabricated, includes fitting and adjustment ♿

A **L2126** Knee-ankle-foot orthotic (KAFO), fracture orthotic, femoral fracture cast orthotic, thermoplastic type casting material, custom fabricated ♿

A **L2128** Knee-ankle-foot orthotic (KAFO), fracture orthotic, femoral fracture cast orthotic, custom fabricated ♿

A **L2132** Knee-ankle-foot orthotic (KAFO), fracture orthotic, femoral fracture cast orthotic, soft, prefabricated, includes fitting and adjustment ♿

A **L2134** Knee-ankle-foot orthotic (KAFO), fracture orthotic, femoral fracture cast orthotic, semi-rigid, prefabricated, includes fitting and adjustment ♿

A **L2136** KAFO, fracture orthotic, femoral fracture cast orthotic, rigid, prefabricated, includes fitting and adjustment ♿

ADDITIONS TO FRACTURE ORTHOTIC

A **L2180** Addition to lower extremity fracture orthotic, plastic shoe insert with ankle joints ♿

A **L2182** Addition to lower extremity fracture orthotic, drop lock knee joint ♿

A **L2184** Addition to lower extremity fracture orthotic, limited motion knee joint ♿

A **L2186** Addition to lower extremity fracture orthotic, adjustable motion knee joint, Lerman type ♿

A **L2188** Addition to lower extremity fracture orthotic, quadrilateral brim ♿

A **L2190** Addition to lower extremity fracture orthotic, waist belt ♿

A **L2192** Addition to lower extremity fracture orthotic, hip joint, pelvic band, thigh flange, and pelvic belt ♿

ADDITIONS TO LOWER EXTREMITY ORTHOTIC: SHOE-ANKLE-SHIN-KNEE

A ☑ **L2200** Addition to lower extremity, limited ankle motion, each joint ♿

A ☑ **L2210** Addition to lower extremity, dorsiflexion assist (plantar flexion resist), each joint ♿

A ☑ **L2220** Addition to lower extremity, dorsiflexion and plantar flexion assist/resist, each joint ♿

A **L2230** Addition to lower extremity, split flat caliper stirrups and plate attachment ♿

A **L2232** Addition to lower extremity orthotic, rocker bottom for total contact ankle-foot orthotic (AFO), for custom fabricated orthotic only ♿

A **L2240** Addition to lower extremity, round caliper and plate attachment ♿

A **L2250** Addition to lower extremity, foot plate, molded to patient model, stirrup attachment ♿

A **L2260** Addition to lower extremity, reinforced solid stirrup (Scott-Craig type) ♿

A **L2265** Addition to lower extremity, long tongue stirrup ♿

A **L2270** Addition to lower extremity, varus/valgus correction (T) strap, padded/lined or malleolus pad ♿

A **L2275** Addition to lower extremity, varus/valgus correction, plastic modification, padded/lined ♿

A **L2280** Addition to lower extremity, molded inner boot ♿

A **L2300** Addition to lower extremity, abduction bar (bilateral hip involvement), jointed, adjustable ♿

A **L2310** Addition to lower extremity, abduction bar, straight ♿

A **L2320** Addition to lower extremity, nonmolded lacer, for custom fabricated orthotic only ♿

A **L2330** Addition to lower extremity, lacer molded to patient model, for custom fabricated orthotic only ♿

A **L2335** Addition to lower extremity, anterior swing band ♿

A **L2340** Addition to lower extremity, pretibial shell, molded to patient model ♿

A **L2350** Addition to lower extremity, prosthetic type, (BK) socket, molded to patient model, (used for PTB, AFO orthoses) ♿

A **L2360** Addition to lower extremity, extended steel shank ♿

A **L2370** Addition to lower extremity, Patten bottom ♿

A **L2375** Addition to lower extremity, torsion control, ankle joint and half solid stirrup ♿

A ☑ L2380 Addition to lower extremity, torsion control, straight knee joint, each joint ♿

A ☑ L2385 Addition to lower extremity, straight knee joint, heavy-duty, each joint ♿

A ☑ L2387 Addition to lower extremity, polycentric knee joint, for custom fabricated knee-ankle-foot orthotic(KAFO), each joint ♿

A ☑ L2390 Addition to lower extremity, offset knee joint, each joint ♿

A ☑ L2395 Addition to lower extremity, offset knee joint, heavy-duty, each joint ♿

A L2397 Addition to lower extremity orthotic, suspension sleeve ♿

ADDITIONS TO STRAIGHT KNEE OR OFFSET KNEE JOINTS

A ☑ L2405 Addition to knee joint, drop lock, each ♿

A ☑ L2415 Addition to knee lock with integrated release mechanism (bail, cable, or equal), any material, each joint ♿

A ☑ L2425 Addition to knee joint, disc or dial lock for adjustable knee flexion, each joint ♿

A ☑ L2430 Addition to knee joint, ratchet lock for active and progressive knee extension, each joint ♿

A L2492 Addition to knee joint, lift loop for drop lock ring ♿

ADDITIONS: THIGH/WEIGHT BEARING - GLUTEAL/ISCHIAL WEIGHT BEARING

A L2500 Addition to lower extremity, thigh/weight bearing, gluteal/ischial weight bearing, ring ♿

A L2510 Addition to lower extremity, thigh/weight bearing, quadri-lateral brim, molded to patient model ♿

A L2520 Addition to lower extremity, thigh/weight bearing, quadri-lateral brim, custom fitted ♿

A L2525 Addition to lower extremity, thigh/weight bearing, ischial containment/narrow M-L brim molded to patient model ♿

A L2526 Addition to lower extremity, thigh/weight bearing, ischial containment/narrow M-L brim, custom fitted ♿

A L2530 Addition to lower extremity, thigh/weight bearing, lacer, nonmolded ♿

A L2540 Addition to lower extremity, thigh/weight bearing, lacer, molded to patient model ♿

A L2550 Addition to lower extremity, thigh/weight bearing, high roll cuff ♿

ADDITIONS: PELVIC AND THORACIC CONTROL

A ☑ L2570 Addition to lower extremity, pelvic control, hip joint, Clevis type 2 position joint, each ♿

A L2580 Addition to lower extremity, pelvic control, pelvic sling ♿

A ☑ L2600 Addition to lower extremity, pelvic control, hip joint, Clevis type, or thrust bearing, free, each ♿

A ☑ L2610 Addition to lower extremity, pelvic control, hip joint, Clevis or thrust bearing, lock, each ♿

A ☑ L2620 Addition to lower extremity, pelvic control, hip joint, heavy-duty, each ♿

A ☑ L2622 Addition to lower extremity, pelvic control, hip joint, adjustable flexion, each ♿

A ☑ L2624 Addition to lower extremity, pelvic control, hip joint, adjustable flexion, extension, abduction control, each ♿

A L2627 Addition to lower extremity, pelvic control, plastic, molded to patient model, reciprocating hip joint and cables ♿

A L2628 Addition to lower extremity, pelvic control, metal frame, reciprocating hip joint and cables ♿

A L2630 Addition to lower extremity, pelvic control, band and belt, unilateral ♿

A L2640 Addition to lower extremity, pelvic control, band and belt, bilateral ♿

A ☑ L2650 Addition to lower extremity, pelvic and thoracic control, gluteal pad, each ♿

A L2660 Addition to lower extremity, thoracic control, thoracic band ♿

A L2670 Addition to lower extremity, thoracic control, paraspinal uprights ♿

A L2680 Addition to lower extremity, thoracic control, lateral support uprights ♿

ADDITIONS: GENERAL

A ☑ L2750 Addition to lower extremity orthotic, plating chrome or nickel, per bar ♿

A L2755 Addition to lower extremity orthotic, high strength, lightweight material, all hybrid lamination/prepreg composite, per segment, for custom fabricated orthotic only ♿

A ☑ L2760 Addition to lower extremity orthotic, extension, per extension, per bar (for lineal adjustment for growth) ♿

A ☑ L2768 Orthotic side bar disconnect device, per bar ♿

A ☑ L2780 Addition to lower extremity orthotic, noncorrosive finish, per bar ♿

A ☑ L2785 Addition to lower extremity orthotic, drop lock retainer, each ♿

A L2795 Addition to lower extremity orthotic, knee control, full kneecap ♿

A L2800 Addition to lower extremity orthotic, knee control, knee cap, medial or lateral pull, for use with custom fabricated orthotic only ♿

A L2810 Addition to lower extremity orthotic, knee control, condylar pad ♿

A L2820 Addition to lower extremity orthotic, soft interface for molded plastic, below knee section ♿

A L2830 Addition to lower extremity orthotic, soft interface for molded plastic, above knee section ♿

A ☑ L2840 Addition to lower extremity orthotic, tibial length sock, fracture or equal, each ♿

A ☑ L2850 Addition to lower extremity orthotic, femoral length sock, fracture or equal, each ♿

E ☑ L2861 Addition to lower extremity joint, knee or ankle, concentric adjustable torsion style mechanism for custom fabricated orthotics only, each

A L2999 Lower extremity orthoses, not otherwise specified

Determine if an alternative HCPCS Level II or a CPT code better describes the service being reported. This code should be used only if a more specific code is unavailable.

ORTHOPEDIC FOOTWEAR

INSERTS

A ☑L3000 Foot insert, removable, molded to patient model, UCB type, Berkeley shell, each
MED: 100-2,15,290

A ☑L3001 Foot, insert, removable, molded to patient model, Spenco, each
MED: 100-2,15,290

A ☑L3002 Foot insert, removable, molded to patient model, Plastazote or equal, each
MED: 100-2,15,290

A ☑L3003 Foot insert, removable, molded to patient model, silicone gel, each
MED: 100-2,15,290

A ☑L3010 Foot insert, removable, molded to patient model, longitudinal arch support, each
MED: 100-2,15,290

A ☑L3020 Foot insert, removable, molded to patient model, longitudinal/metatarsal support, each
MED: 100-2,15,290

A ☑L3030 Foot insert, removable, formed to patient foot, each
MED: 100-2,15,290

A ☑L3031 Foot, insert/plate, removable, addition to lower extremity orthotic, high strength, lightweight material, all hybrid lamination/prepreg composite, each

ARCH SUPPORT, REMOVABLE, PREMOLDED

A ☑L3040 Foot, arch support, removable, premolded, longitudinal, each
MED: 100-2,15,290

A ☑L3050 Foot, arch support, removable, premolded, metatarsal, each
MED: 100-2,15,290

A ☑L3060 Foot, arch support, removable, premolded, longitudinal/metatarsal, each
MED: 100-2,15,290

ARCH SUPPORT, NONREMOVABLE, ATTACHED TO SHOE

A ☑L3070 Foot, arch support, nonremovable, attached to shoe, longitudinal, each
MED: 100-2,15,290

A ☑L3080 Foot, arch support, nonremovable, attached to shoe, metatarsal, each
MED: 100-2,15,290

A ☑L3090 Foot, arch support, nonremovable, attached to shoe, longitudinal/metatarsal, each
MED: 100-2,15,290

A L3100 Hallus-valgus night dynamic splint
MED: 100-2,15,290

ABDUCTION AND ROTATION BARS

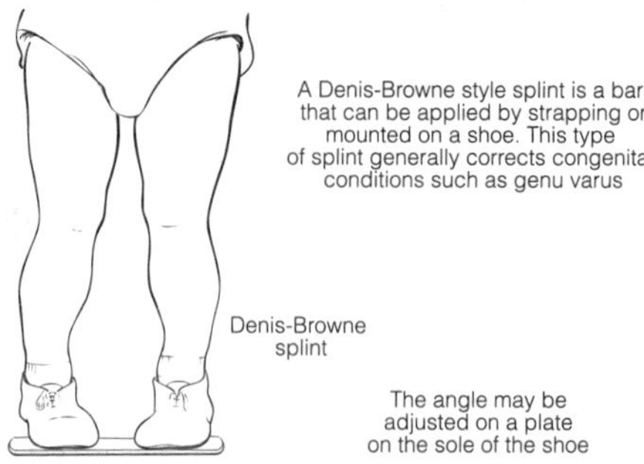

A Denis-Browne style splint is a bar that can be applied by strapping or mounted on a shoe. This type of splint generally corrects congenital conditions such as genu varus
Denis-Browne splint
The angle may be adjusted on a plate on the sole of the shoe

A L3140 Foot, abduction rotation bar, including shoes
MED: 100-2,15,290

A L3150 Foot, abduction rotation bar, without shoes
MED: 100-2,15,290

A L3160 Foot, adjustable shoe-styled positioning device

A ☑L3170 Foot, plastic, silicone or equal, heel stabilizer, each
MED: 100-2,15,290

ORTHOPEDIC SHOES AND BOOTS

A L3201 Orthopedic shoe, Oxford with supinator or pronator, infant A
MED: 100-2,15,290

A L3202 Orthopedic shoe, Oxford with supinator or pronator, child A
MED: 100-2,15,290

A L3203 Orthopedic shoe, Oxford with supinator or pronator, junior A
MED: 100-2,15,290

A L3204 Orthopedic shoe, hightop with supinator or pronator, infant A
MED: 100-2,15,290

A L3206 Orthopedic shoe, hightop with supinator or pronator, child A
MED: 100-2,15,290

A L3207 Orthopedic shoe, hightop with supinator or pronator, junior A
MED: 100-2,15,290

A ☑L3208 Surgical boot, each, infant A

A ☑L3209 Surgical boot, each, child A

A ☑L3211 Surgical boot, each, junior A

A ☑L3212 Benesch boot, pair, infant A

A ☑L3213 Benesch boot, pair, child A

A ☑L3214 Benesch boot, pair, junior A

E ☑L3215 Orthopedic footwear, ladies shoe, oxford, each A ♀

E ☑L3216 Orthopedic footwear, ladies shoe, depth inlay, each A ♀

E ☑L3217 Orthopedic footwear, ladies shoe, hightop, depth inlay, each A ♀

E ☑L3219 Orthopedic footwear, mens shoe, oxford, each A ♂

E ☑L3221 Orthopedic footwear, mens shoe, depth inlay, each A ♂

E ☑L3222 Orthopedic footwear, mens shoe, hightop, depth inlay, each A ♂

A L3224 Orthopedic footwear, woman's shoe, oxford, used as an integral part of a brace (orthotic) ♀ ♿
MED: 100-2,15,290

A L3225 Orthopedic footwear, man's shoe, oxford, used as an integral part of a brace (orthotic) ♂ ♿
MED: 100-2,15,290

A ☑ L3230 Orthopedic footwear, custom shoe, depth inlay, each
MED: 100-2,15,290

A ☑ L3250 Orthopedic footwear, custom molded shoe, removable inner mold, prosthetic shoe, each
MED: 100-2,15,290

A ☑ L3251 Foot, shoe molded to patient model, silicone shoe, each
MED: 100-2,15,290

A ☑ L3252 Foot, shoe molded to patient model, Plastazote (or similar), custom fabricated, each
MED: 100-2,15,290

A ☑ L3253 Foot, molded shoe, Plastazote (or similar), custom fitted, each
MED: 100-2,15,290

A L3254 Nonstandard size or width
MED: 100-2,15,290

A L3255 Nonstandard size or length
MED: 100-2,15,290

A L3257 Orthopedic footwear, additional charge for split size
MED: 100-2,15,290

E ☑ L3260 Surgical boot/shoe, each

A ☑ L3265 Plastazote sandal, each

SHOE MODIFICATION - LIFTS

A ☑ L3300 Lift, elevation, heel, tapered to metatarsals, per in ♿
MED: 100-2,15,290

A ☑ L3310 Lift, elevation, heel and sole, neoprene, per in ♿
MED: 100-2,15,290

A ☑ L3320 Lift, elevation, heel and sole, cork, per in
MED: 100-2,15,290

A L3330 Lift, elevation, metal extension (skate) ♿
MED: 100-2,15,290

A ☑ L3332 Lift, elevation, inside shoe, tapered, up to one-half in ♿
MED: 100-2,15,290

A ☑ L3334 Lift, elevation, heel, per in ♿
MED: 100-2,15,290

SHOE MODIFICATION - WEDGES

A L3340 Heel wedge, SACH ♿
MED: 100-2,15,290

A L3350 Heel wedge ♿
MED: 100-2,15,290

A L3360 Sole wedge, outside sole ♿
MED: 100-2,15,290

A L3370 Sole wedge, between sole ♿
MED: 100-2,15,290

A L3380 Clubfoot wedge ♿
MED: 100-2,15,290

A L3390 Outflare wedge ♿
MED: 100-2,15,290

A L3400 Metatarsal bar wedge, rocker ♿
MED: 100-2,15,290

A L3410 Metatarsal bar wedge, between sole ♿
MED: 100-2,15,290

A L3420 Full sole and heel wedge, between sole ♿
MED: 100-2,15,290

SHOE MODIFICATIONS - HEELS

A L3430 Heel, counter, plastic reinforced ♿
MED: 100-2,15,290

A L3440 Heel, counter, leather reinforced ♿
MED: 100-2,15,290

A L3450 Heel, SACH cushion type ♿
MED: 100-2,15,290

A L3455 Heel, new leather, standard ♿
MED: 100-2,15,290

A L3460 Heel, new rubber, standard ♿
MED: 100-2,15,290

A L3465 Heel, Thomas with wedge ♿
MED: 100-2,15,290

A L3470 Heel, Thomas extended to ball ♿
MED: 100-2,15,290

A L3480 Heel, pad and depression for spur ♿
MED: 100-2,15,290

A L3485 Heel, pad, removable for spur
MED: 100-2,15,290

MISCELLANEOUS SHOE ADDITIONS

A L3500 Orthopedic shoe addition, insole, leather ♿
MED: 100-2,15,290

A L3510 Orthopedic shoe addition, insole, rubber ♿
MED: 100-2,15,290

A L3520 Orthopedic shoe addition, insole, felt covered with leather ♿
MED: 100-2,15,290

A L3530 Orthopedic shoe addition, sole, half ♿
MED: 100-2,15,290

A L3540 Orthopedic shoe addition, sole, full ♿
MED: 100-2,15,290

A L3550 Orthopedic shoe addition, toe tap, standard ♿
MED: 100-2,15,290

A L3560 Orthopedic shoe addition, toe tap, horseshoe ♿
MED: 100-2,15,290

A L3570 Orthopedic shoe addition, special extension to instep (leather with eyelets) ♿
MED: 100-2,15,290

A L3580 Orthopedic shoe addition, convert instep to Velcro closure ♿
MED: 100-2,15,290

A L3590 Orthopedic shoe addition, convert firm shoe counter to soft counter ♿
MED: 100-2,15,290

A L3595 Orthopedic shoe addition, March bar ♿
MED: 100-2,15,290

TRANSFER OR REPLACEMENT

A **L3600** Transfer of an orthotic from one shoe to another, caliper plate, existing ♿
MED: 100-2,15,290

A **L3610** Transfer of an orthotic from one shoe to another, caliper plate, new ♿
MED: 100-2,15,290

A **L3620** Transfer of an orthotic from one shoe to another, solid stirrup, existing ♿
MED: 100-2,15,290

A **L3630** Transfer of an orthotic from one shoe to another, solid stirrup, new ♿
MED: 100-2,15,290

A **L3640** Transfer of an orthotic from one shoe to another, Dennis Browne splint (Riveton), both shoes ♿
MED: 100-2,15,290

A **L3649** Orthopedic shoe, modification, addition or transfer, not otherwise specified
Determine if an alternative HCPCS Level II or a CPT code better describes the service being reported. This code should be used only if a more specific code is unavailable.
MED: 100-2,15,290

SHOULDER ORTHOTIC (SO)

A **L3650** Shoulder orthotic (SO), figure of eight design abduction restrainer, prefabricated, includes fitting and adjustment ♿

A **L3660** Jan Shoulder orthotic (SO), figure of eight design abduction restrainer, canvas and webbing, prefabricated, includes fitting and adjustment

A **L3670** Jan Shoulder orthotic (SO), acromio/clavicular (canvas and webbing type), prefabricated, includes fitting and adjustment

A **L3671** Shoulder orthotic (SO), shoulder joint design, without joints, may include soft interface, straps, custom fabricated, includes fitting and adjustment ♿

A **L3674** Shoulder orthotic, abduction positioning (airplane design), thoracic component and support bar, with or without nontorsion joint/turnbuckle, may include soft interface, straps, custom fabricated, includes fitting and adjustment ♿

A **L3675** Jan Shoulder orthotic (SO), vest type abduction restrainer, canvas webbing type or equal, prefabricated, includes fitting and adjustment

A **L3677** Shoulder orthotic, shoulder joint design, without joints, may include soft interface, straps, prefabricated, includes fitting and adjustment

ELBOW ORTHOTIC (EO)

A **L3702** Elbow orthotic (EO), without joints, may include soft interface, straps, custom fabricated, includes fitting and adjustment ♿

A **L3710** Elbow orthotic (EO), elastic with metal joints, prefabricated, includes fitting and adjustment ♿

A **L3720** Elbow orthotic (EO), double upright with forearm/arm cuffs, free motion, custom fabricated ♿

A **L3730** Elbow orthotic (EO), double upright with forearm/arm cuffs, extension/ flexion assist, custom fabricated ♿

A **L3740** Elbow orthotic (EO), double upright with forearm/arm cuffs, adjustable position lock with active control, custom fabricated ♿

A **L3760** Elbow orthotic (EO), with adjustable position locking joint(s), prefabricated, includes fitting and adjustments, any type ♿

A **L3762** Elbow orthotic (EO), rigid, without joints, includes soft interface material, prefabricated, includes fitting and adjustment ♿

A **L3763** Elbow-wrist-hand orthotic (EWHO), rigid, without joints, may include soft interface, straps, custom fabricated, includes fitting and adjustment ♿

A **L3764** Elbow-wrist-hand orthotic (EWHO), includes one or more nontorsion joints, elastic bands, turnbuckles, may include soft interface, straps, custom fabricated, includes fitting and adjustment ♿

A **L3765** Elbow-wrist-hand-finger orthotic (EWHFO), rigid, without joints, may include soft interface, straps, custom fabricated, includes fitting and adjustment ♿

A **L3766** Elbow-wrist-hand-finger orthotic (EWHFO), includes one or more nontorsion joints, elastic bands, turnbuckles, may include soft interface, straps, custom fabricated, includes fitting and adjustment ♿

WRIST-HAND-FINGER ORTHOTIC (WHFO)

A **L3806** Wrist-hand-finger orthotic (WHFO), includes one or more nontorsion joint(s), turnbuckles, elastic bands/springs, may include soft interface material, straps, custom fabricated, includes fitting and adjustment ♿

A **L3807** Wrist-hand-finger orthotic (WHFO), without joint(s), prefabricated, includes fitting and adjustments, any type ♿

A **L3808** Wrist-hand-finger orthotic (WHFO), rigid without joints, may include soft interface material; straps, custom fabricated, includes fitting and adjustment ♿

ADDITIONS TO UPPER EXTREMITY ORTHOTIC

E ☑ **L3891** Addition to upper extremity joint, wrist or elbow, concentric adjustable torsion style mechanism for custom fabricated orthotics only, each

DYNAMIC FLEXOR HINGE, RECIPROCAL WRIST EXTENSION/FLEXION, FINGER FLEXION/EXTENSION

A **L3900** Wrist-hand-finger orthotic (WHFO), dynamic flexor hinge, reciprocal wrist extension/ flexion, finger flexion/extension, wrist or finger driven, custom fabricated ♿

A **L3901** Wrist-hand-finger orthotic (WHFO), dynamic flexor hinge, reciprocal wrist extension/ flexion, finger flexion/extension, cable driven, custom fabricated ♿

EXTERNAL POWER

A **L3904** Wrist-hand-finger orthotic (WHFO), external powered, electric, custom fabricated ♿

OTHER UPPER EXTREMITY ORTHOTICS

A **L3905** Wrist-hand orthotic (WHO), includes one or more nontorsion joints, elastic bands, turnbuckles, may include soft interface, straps, custom fabricated, includes fitting and adjustment ♿

A **L3906** Wrist-hand orthosis (WHO), without joints, may include soft interface, straps, custom fabricated, includes fitting and adjustment ♿

A **L3908** Wrist-hand orthotic (WHO), wrist extension control cock-up, nonmolded, prefabricated, includes fitting and adjustment ♿

A **L3912** Hand-finger orthotic (HFO), flexion glove with elastic finger control, prefabricated, includes fitting and adjustment ♿

A **L3913** Hand finger orthotic (HFO), without joints, may include soft interface, straps, custom fabricated, includes fitting and adjustment ♿

A **L3915** Wrist hand orthotic (WHO), includes one or more nontorsion joint(s), elastic bands, turnbuckles, may include soft interface, straps, prefabricated, includes fitting and adjustment ♿

A **L3917** Hand orthotic (HO), metacarpal fracture orthotic, prefabricated, includes fitting and adjustment ♿

A **L3919** Hand orthotic (HO), without joints, may include soft interface, straps, custom fabricated, includes fitting and adjustment ♿

A **L3921** Hand finger orthotic (HFO), includes one or more nontorsion joints, elastic bands, turnbuckles, may include soft interface, straps, custom fabricated, includes fitting and adjustment ♿

A **L3923** Hand finger orthotic (HFO), without joints, may include soft interface, straps, prefabricated, includes fitting and adjustment ♿

A **L3925** Finger orthotic (FO), proximal interphalangeal (PIP)/distal interphalangeal (DIP), nontorsion joint/spring, extension/flexion, may include soft interface material, prefabricated, includes fitting and adjustment ♿

A **L3927** Finger orthotic (FO), proximal interphalangeal (PIP)/distal interphalangeal (DIP), without joint/spring, extension/flexion (e.g., static or ring type), may include soft interface material, prefabricated, includes fitting and adjustment ♿

A **L3929** Hand-finger orthotic (HFO), includes one or more nontorsion joint(s), turnbuckles, elastic bands/springs, may include soft interface material, straps, prefabricated, includes fitting and adjustment ♿

A **L3931** Wrist-hand-finger orthotic (WHFO), includes one or more nontorsion joint(s), turnbuckles, elastic bands/springs, may include soft interface material, straps, prefabricated, includes fitting and adjustment ♿

A **L3933** Finger orthotic (FO), without joints, may include soft interface, custom fabricated, includes fitting and adjustment ♿

A **L3935** Finger orthotic, nontorsion joint, may include soft interface, custom fabricated, includes fitting and adjustment ♿

A ☑ **L3956** Addition of joint to upper extremity orthotic, any material; per joint ♿

SHOULDER, ELBOW, WRIST, HAND ORTHOTIC

A **L3960** Shoulder-elbow-wrist-hand orthotic (SEWHO), abduction positioning, airplane design, prefabricated, includes fitting and adjustment ♿

A **L3961** Shoulder elbow wrist hand orthotic (SEWHO), shoulder cap design, without joints, may include soft interface, straps, custom fabricated, includes fitting and adjustment ♿

A **L3962** Shoulder-elbow-wrist-hand orthotic (SEWHO), abduction positioning, Erb's palsy design, prefabricated, includes fitting and adjustment ♿

~~**L3964**~~ Jan ~~Shoulder-elbow orthotic (SEO), mobile arm support attached to wheelchair, balanced, adjustable, prefabricated, includes fitting and adjustment~~
To report, see E2626

~~**L3965**~~ Jan ~~Shoulder-elbow orthotic (SEO), mobile arm support attached to wheelchair, balanced, adjustable Rancho type, prefabricated, includes fitting and adjustment~~
To report, see E2627

~~**L3966**~~ Jan ~~Shoulder-elbow orthotic (SEO), mobile arm support attached to wheelchair, balanced, reclining, prefabricated, includes fitting and adjustment~~
To report, see E2628

A **L3967** Shoulder-elbow-wrist-hand orthotic (SEWHO), abduction positioning (airplane design), thoracic component and support bar, without joints, may include soft interface, straps, custom fabricated, includes fitting and adjustment ♿

~~**L3968**~~ Jan ~~Shoulder-elbow orthotic (SEO), mobile arm support attached to wheelchair, balanced, friction arm support (friction dampening to proximal and distal joints), prefabricated, includes fitting and adjustment~~
To report, see E2629

~~**L3969**~~ Jan ~~Shoulder-elbow orthotic (SEO), mobile arm support, monosuspension arm and hand support, overhead elbow forearm hand sling support, yoke type suspension support, prefabricated, includes fitting and adjustment~~
To report, see E2630

ADDITIONS TO MOBILE ARM SUPPORTS

~~**L3970**~~ Jan ~~Shoulder-elbow orthotic (SEO), addition to mobile arm support, elevating proximal arm~~
To report, see E2631

A **L3971** Shoulder-elbow-wrist-hand orthotic (SEWHO), shoulder cap design, includes one or more nontorsion joints, elastic bands, turnbuckles, may include soft interface, straps, custom fabricated, includes fitting and adjustment ♿

~~**L3972**~~ Jan ~~Shoulder-elbow orthotic (SEO), addition to mobile arm support, offset or lateral rocker arm with elastic balance control~~
To report, see E2632

A **L3973** Shoulder-elbow-wrist-hand orthotic (SEWHO), abduction positioning (airplane design), thoracic component and support bar, includes one or more nontorsion joints, elastic bands, turnbuckles, may include soft interface, straps, custom fabricated, includes fitting and adjustment ♿

~~**L3974**~~ Jan ~~Shoulder-elbow orthotic (SEO), addition to mobile arm support, supinator~~

A **L3975** Shoulder-elbow-wrist-hand-finger orthotic (SEWHO), shoulder cap design, without joints, may include soft interface, straps, custom fabricated, includes fitting and adjustment ♿

A L3976 Shoulder-elbow-wrist-hand-finger orthotic (SEWHO), abduction positioning (airplane design), thoracic component and support bar, without joints, may include soft interface, straps, custom fabricated, includes fitting and adjustment

A L3977 Shoulder-elbow-wrist-hand-finger orthotic (SEWHO), shoulder cap design, includes one or more nontorsion joints, elastic bands, turnbuckles, may include soft interface, straps, custom fabricated, includes fitting and adjustment

A L3978 Shoulder-elbow-wrist-hand-finger orthotic (SEWHO), abduction positioning (airplane design), thoracic component and support bar, includes one or more nontorsion joints, elastic bands, turnbuckles, may include soft interface, straps, custom fabricated, includes fitting and adjustment

FRACTURE ORTHOTIC

A L3980 Upper extremity fracture orthotic, humeral, prefabricated, includes fitting and adjustment

A L3982 Upper extremity fracture orthotic, radius/ulnar, prefabricated, includes fitting and adjustment

A L3984 Upper extremity fracture orthotic, wrist, prefabricated, includes fitting and adjustment

A ☑ L3995 Addition to upper extremity orthotic, sock, fracture or equal, each

A L3999 Upper limb orthosis, not otherwise specified

REPAIRS

A L4000 Replace girdle for spinal orthotic (cervical-thoracic-lumbar-sacral orthotic (CTLSO) or spinal orthotic SO)

A L4002 Replacement strap, any orthotic, includes all components, any length, any type

A L4010 Replace trilateral socket brim

A L4020 Replace quadrilateral socket brim, molded to patient model

A L4030 Replace quadrilateral socket brim, custom fitted

A L4040 Replace molded thigh lacer, for custom fabricated orthotic only

A L4045 Replace nonmolded thigh lacer, for custom fabricated orthotic only

A L4050 Replace molded calf lacer, for custom fabricated orthotic only

A L4055 Replace nonmolded calf lacer, for custom fabricated orthotic only

A L4060 Replace high roll cuff

A L4070 Replace proximal and distal upright for KAFO

A L4080 Replace metal bands KAFO, proximal thigh

A L4090 Replace metal bands KAFO-AFO, calf or distal thigh

A L4100 Replace leather cuff KAFO, proximal thigh

A L4110 Replace leather cuff KAFO-AFO, calf or distal thigh

A L4130 Replace pretibial shell

A ☑ L4205 Repair of orthotic device, labor component, per 15 minutes

A L4210 Repair of orthotic device, repair or replace minor parts

MISCELLANEOUS LOWER LIMB SUPPORTS

A L4350 Ankle control orthotic, stirrup style, rigid, includes any type interface (e.g., pneumatic, gel), prefabricated, includes fitting and adjustment

A L4360 Walking boot, pneumatic and/or vacuum, with or without joints, with or without interface material, prefabricated, includes fitting and adjustment

A L4370 Pneumatic full leg splint, prefabricated, includes fitting and adjustment

~~L4380~~ Jan ~~Pneumatic knee splint, prefabricated, includes fitting and adjustment~~

To report, see L4370-L3470

A L4386 Walking boot, nonpneumatic, with or without joints, with or without interface material, prefabricated, includes fitting and adjustment

A L4392 Replacement, soft interface material, static AFO

A L4394 Replace soft interface material, foot drop splint

A L4396 Static or dynamic ankle-foot orthotic (AFO), including soft interface material, adjustable for fit, for positioning, may be used for minimal ambulation, prefabricated, includes fitting and adjustment

A L4398 Foot drop splint, recumbent positioning device, prefabricated, includes fitting and adjustment

A L4631 Ankle-foot orthotic, walking boot type, varus/valgus correction, rocker bottom, anterior tibial shell, soft interface, custom arch support, plastic or other material, includes straps and closures, custom fabricated

PROSTHETIC PROCEDURES L5000-L9999

The procedures in this section are considered as "base" or "basic procedures" and may be modified by listing items/procedures or special materials from the "additions" sections and adding them to the base procedure.

PARTIAL FOOT

A L5000 Partial foot, shoe insert with longitudinal arch, toe filler

MED: 100-2,15,290

A L5010 Partial foot, molded socket, ankle height, with toe filler

MED: 100-2,15,290

A L5020 Partial foot, molded socket, tibial tubercle height, with toe filler

MED: 100-2,15,290

ANKLE

A L5050 Ankle, Symes, molded socket, SACH foot

A L5060 Ankle, Symes, metal frame, molded leather socket, articulated ankle/foot

BELOW KNEE

A L5100 Below knee, molded socket, shin, SACH foot

A L5105 Below knee, plastic socket, joints and thigh lacer, SACH foot

KNEE DISARTICULATION

A L5150 Knee disarticulation (or through knee), molded socket, external knee joints, shin, SACH foot

A L5160 Knee disarticulation (or through knee), molded socket, bent knee configuration, external knee joints, shin, SACH foot

ABOVE KNEE

A L5200 Above knee, molded socket, single axis constant friction knee, shin, SACH foot

A ☑L5210 Above knee, short prosthesis, no knee joint (stubbies), with foot blocks, no ankle joints, each

A ☑L5220 Above knee, short prosthesis, no knee joint (stubbies), with articulated ankle/foot, dynamically aligned, each

A L5230 Above knee, for proximal femoral focal deficiency, constant friction knee, shin, SACH foot

HIP DISARTICULATION

A L5250 Hip disarticulation, Canadian type; molded socket, hip joint, single axis constant friction knee, shin, SACH foot

A L5270 Hip disarticulation, tilt table type; molded socket, locking hip joint, single axis constant friction knee, shin, SACH foot

HEMIPELVECTOMY

A L5280 Hemipelvectomy, Canadian type; molded socket, hip joint, single axis constant friction knee, shin, SACH foot

A L5301 Below knee, molded socket, shin, SACH foot, endoskeletal system

~~L5311~~ Jan ~~Knee disarticulation (or through knee), molded socket, external knee joints, shin, SACH foot, endoskeletal system~~

To report, see L5150, L5160

● A L5312 Jan Knee disarticulation (or through knee), molded socket, single axis knee, pylon, SACH foot, endoskeletal system

A L5321 Above knee, molded socket, open end, SACH foot, endoskeletal system, single axis knee

A L5331 Hip disarticulation, Canadian type, molded socket, endoskeletal system, hip joint, single axis knee, SACH foot

A L5341 Hemipelvectomy, Canadian type, molded socket, endoskeletal system, hip joint, single axis knee, SACH foot

IMMEDIATE POSTSURGICAL OR EARLY FITTING PROCEDURES

Above-the-knee test socket

Test sockets are often made of clear plastic so the prosthetist can visualize the fit against the residual limb

Below-the-knee early fitting rigid dressing (L5400)

A ☑L5400 Immediate postsurgical or early fitting, application of initial rigid dressing, including fitting, alignment, suspension, and one cast change, below knee

A ☑L5410 Immediate postsurgical or early fitting, application of initial rigid dressing, including fitting, alignment and suspension, below knee, each additional cast change and realignment

A ☑L5420 Immediate postsurgical or early fitting, application of initial rigid dressing, including fitting, alignment and suspension and one cast change AK or knee disarticulation

A ☑L5430 Immediate postsurgical or early fitting, application of initial rigid dressing, including fitting, alignment and suspension, AK or knee disarticulation, each additional cast change and realignment

A L5450 Immediate postsurgical or early fitting, application of nonweight bearing rigid dressing, below knee

A L5460 Immediate postsurgical or early fitting, application of nonweight bearing rigid dressing, above knee

INITIAL PROSTHESIS

A L5500 Initial, below knee PTB type socket, nonalignable system, pylon, no cover, SACH foot, plaster socket, direct formed

MED: 100-2,1,40

A L5505 Initial, above knee, knee disarticulation, ischial level socket, nonalignable system, pylon, no cover, SACH foot, plaster socket, direct formed

MED: 100-2,1,40

PREPARATORY PROSTHESIS

A L5510 Preparatory, below knee PTB type socket, nonalignable system, pylon, no cover, SACH foot, plaster socket, molded to model

A L5520 Preparatory, below knee PTB type socket, nonalignable system, pylon, no cover, SACH foot, thermoplastic or equal, direct formed

A L5530 Preparatory, below knee PTB type socket, nonalignable system, pylon, no cover, SACH foot, thermoplastic or equal, molded to model

A L5535 Preparatory, below knee PTB type socket, nonalignable system, no cover, SACH foot, prefabricated, adjustable open end socket

A L5540 Preparatory, below knee PTB type socket, nonalignable system, pylon, no cover, SACH foot, laminated socket, molded to model

A L5560 Preparatory, above knee, knee disarticulation, ischial level socket, nonalignable system, pylon, no cover, SACH foot, plaster socket, molded to model

A L5570 Preparatory, above knee - knee disarticulation, ischial level socket, nonalignable system, pylon, no cover, SACH foot, thermoplastic or equal, direct formed

A L5580 Preparatory, above knee, knee disarticulation, ischial level socket, nonalignable system, pylon, no cover, SACH foot, thermoplastic or equal, molded to model

A L5585 Preparatory, above knee - knee disarticulation, ischial level socket, nonalignable system, pylon, no cover, SACH foot, prefabricated adjustable open end socket

A L5590 Preparatory, above knee, knee disarticulation, ischial level socket, nonalignable system, pylon, no cover, SACH foot, laminated socket, molded to model

A L5595 Preparatory, hip disarticulation/hemipelvectomy, pylon, no cover, SACH foot, thermoplastic or equal, molded to patient model

A L5600 Preparatory, hip disarticulation/hemipelvectomy, pylon, no cover, SACH foot, laminated socket, molded to patient model

ADDITIONS

ADDITIONS: LOWER EXTREMITY

A L5610 Addition to lower extremity, endoskeletal system, above knee, hydracadence system

A L5611 Addition to lower extremity, endoskeletal system, above knee, knee disarticulation, 4-bar linkage, with friction swing phase control

A L5613 Addition to lower extremity, endoskeletal system, above knee, knee disarticulation, 4-bar linkage, with hydraulic swing phase control

A L5614 Addition to lower extremity, exoskeletal system, above knee-knee disarticulation, 4 bar linkage, with pneumatic swing phase control

A L5616 Addition to lower extremity, endoskeletal system, above knee, universal multiplex system, friction swing phase control

A ☑ L5617 Addition to lower extremity, quick change self-aligning unit, above knee or below knee, each

ADDITIONS: TEST SOCKETS

A L5618 Addition to lower extremity, test socket, Symes

A L5620 Addition to lower extremity, test socket, below knee

A L5622 Addition to lower extremity, test socket, knee disarticulation

A L5624 Addition to lower extremity, test socket, above knee

A L5626 Addition to lower extremity, test socket, hip disarticulation

A L5628 Addition to lower extremity, test socket, hemipelvectomy

A L5629 Addition to lower extremity, below knee, acrylic socket

ADDITIONS: SOCKET VARIATIONS

A L5630 Addition to lower extremity, Symes type, expandable wall socket

A L5631 Addition to lower extremity, above knee or knee disarticulation, acrylic socket

A L5632 Addition to lower extremity, Symes type, PTB brim design socket

A L5634 Addition to lower extremity, Symes type, posterior opening (Canadian) socket

A L5636 Addition to lower extremity, Symes type, medial opening socket

A L5637 Addition to lower extremity, below knee, total contact

A L5638 Addition to lower extremity, below knee, leather socket

A L5639 Addition to lower extremity, below knee, wood socket

A L5640 Addition to lower extremity, knee disarticulation, leather socket

A L5642 Addition to lower extremity, above knee, leather socket

A L5643 Addition to lower extremity, hip disarticulation, flexible inner socket, external frame

A L5644 Addition to lower extremity, above knee, wood socket

A L5645 Addition to lower extremity, below knee, flexible inner socket, external frame

A L5646 Addition to lower extremity, below knee, air, fluid, gel or equal, cushion socket

A L5647 Addition to lower extremity, below knee, suction socket

A L5648 Addition to lower extremity, above knee, air, fluid, gel or equal, cushion socket

A L5649 Addition to lower extremity, ischial containment/narrow M-L socket

A L5650 Additions to lower extremity, total contact, above knee or knee disarticulation socket

A L5651 Addition to lower extremity, above knee, flexible inner socket, external frame

A L5652 Addition to lower extremity, suction suspension, above knee or knee disarticulation socket

A L5653 Addition to lower extremity, knee disarticulation, expandable wall socket

ADDITIONS: SOCKET INSERT AND SUSPENSION

A L5654 Addition to lower extremity, socket insert, Symes, (Kemblo, Pelite, Aliplast, Plastazote or equal)

A L5655 Addition to lower extremity, socket insert, below knee (Kemblo, Pelite, Aliplast, Plastazote or equal)

A L5656 Addition to lower extremity, socket insert, knee disarticulation (Kemblo, Pelite, Aliplast, Plastazote or equal)

A L5658 Addition to lower extremity, socket insert, above knee (Kemblo, Pelite, Aliplast, Plastazote or equal)

A L5661 Addition to lower extremity, socket insert, multidurometer Symes

A L5665 Addition to lower extremity, socket insert, multidurometer, below knee

A L5666 Addition to lower extremity, below knee, cuff suspension

A L5668 Addition to lower extremity, below knee, molded distal cushion

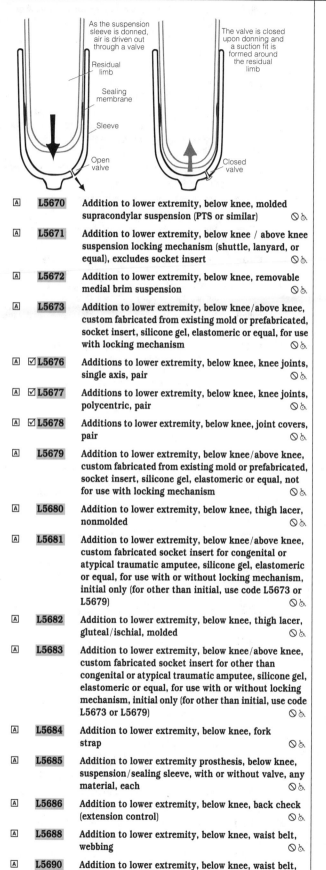

As the suspension sleeve is donned, air is driven out through a valve

Residual limb

Sealing membrane

Sleeve

Open valve

The valve is closed upon donning and a suction fit is formed around the residual limb

Closed valve

- A **L5670** Addition to lower extremity, below knee, molded supracondylar suspension (PTS or similar) ⊘ ♿
- A **L5671** Addition to lower extremity, below knee / above knee suspension locking mechanism (shuttle, lanyard, or equal), excludes socket insert ⊘ ♿
- A **L5672** Addition to lower extremity, below knee, removable medial brim suspension ⊘ ♿
- A **L5673** Addition to lower extremity, below knee/above knee, custom fabricated from existing mold or prefabricated, socket insert, silicone gel, elastomeric or equal, for use with locking mechanism ⊘ ♿
- A ☑ **L5676** Additions to lower extremity, below knee, knee joints, single axis, pair ⊘ ♿
- A ☑ **L5677** Additions to lower extremity, below knee, knee joints, polycentric, pair ⊘ ♿
- A ☑ **L5678** Additions to lower extremity, below knee, joint covers, pair ⊘ ♿
- A **L5679** Addition to lower extremity, below knee/above knee, custom fabricated from existing mold or prefabricated, socket insert, silicone gel, elastomeric or equal, not for use with locking mechanism ⊘ ♿
- A **L5680** Addition to lower extremity, below knee, thigh lacer, nonmolded ⊘ ♿
- A **L5681** Addition to lower extremity, below knee/above knee, custom fabricated socket insert for congenital or atypical traumatic amputee, silicone gel, elastomeric or equal, for use with or without locking mechanism, initial only (for other than initial, use code L5673 or L5679) ⊘ ♿
- A **L5682** Addition to lower extremity, below knee, thigh lacer, gluteal/ischial, molded ⊘ ♿
- A **L5683** Addition to lower extremity, below knee/above knee, custom fabricated socket insert for other than congenital or atypical traumatic amputee, silicone gel, elastomeric or equal, for use with or without locking mechanism, initial only (for other than initial, use code L5673 or L5679) ⊘ ♿
- A **L5684** Addition to lower extremity, below knee, fork strap ⊘ ♿
- A **L5685** Addition to lower extremity prosthesis, below knee, suspension/sealing sleeve, with or without valve, any material, each ⊘ ♿
- A **L5686** Addition to lower extremity, below knee, back check (extension control) ⊘ ♿
- A **L5688** Addition to lower extremity, below knee, waist belt, webbing ⊘ ♿
- A **L5690** Addition to lower extremity, below knee, waist belt, padded and lined ⊘ ♿
- A **L5692** Addition to lower extremity, above knee, pelvic control belt, light ⊘ ♿
- A **L5694** Addition to lower extremity, above knee, pelvic control belt, padded and lined ⊘ ♿
- A ☑ **L5695** Addition to lower extremity, above knee, pelvic control, sleeve suspension, neoprene or equal, each ⊘ ♿
- A **L5696** Addition to lower extremity, above knee or knee disarticulation, pelvic joint ⊘ ♿
- A **L5697** Addition to lower extremity, above knee or knee disarticulation, pelvic band ⊘ ♿
- A **L5698** Addition to lower extremity, above knee or knee disarticulation, Silesian bandage ⊘ ♿
- A **L5699** All lower extremity prostheses, shoulder harness ⊘ ♿
- A **L5610** Addition to lower extremity, endoskeletal system, above knee, hydracadence system ⊘ ♿
- A **L5611** Addition to lower extremity, endoskeletal system, above knee, knee disarticulation, 4-bar linkage, with friction swing phase control ⊘ ♿
- A **L5613** Addition to lower extremity, endoskeletal system, above knee, knee disarticulation, 4-bar linkage, with hydraulic swing phase control ⊘ ♿
- A **L5614** Addition to lower extremity, exoskeletal system, above knee-knee disarticulation, 4 bar linkage, with pneumatic swing phase control ⊘ ♿
- A **L5616** Addition to lower extremity, endoskeletal system, above knee, universal multiplex system, friction swing phase control ⊘ ♿
- A ☑ **L5617** Addition to lower extremity, quick change self-aligning unit, above knee or below knee, each ⊘ ♿
- A **L5618** Addition to lower extremity, test socket, Symes ⊘ ♿
- A **L5620** Addition to lower extremity, test socket, below knee ⊘ ♿
- A **L5622** Addition to lower extremity, test socket, knee disarticulation ⊘ ♿
- A **L5624** Addition to lower extremity, test socket, above knee ⊘ ♿
- A **L5626** Addition to lower extremity, test socket, hip disarticulation ⊘ ♿
- A **L5628** Addition to lower extremity, test socket, hemipelvectomy ⊘ ♿
- A **L5629** Addition to lower extremity, below knee, acrylic socket ⊘ ♿
- A **L5630** Addition to lower extremity, Symes type, expandable wall socket ⊘ ♿
- A **L5631** Addition to lower extremity, above knee or knee disarticulation, acrylic socket ⊘ ♿
- A **L5632** Addition to lower extremity, Symes type, PTB brim design socket ⊘ ♿
- A **L5634** Addition to lower extremity, Symes type, posterior opening (Canadian) socket ⊘ ♿
- A **L5636** Addition to lower extremity, Symes type, medial opening socket ⊘ ♿
- A **L5637** Addition to lower extremity, below knee, total contact ⊘ ♿
- A **L5638** Addition to lower extremity, below knee, leather socket ⊘ ♿

A L5639 Addition to lower extremity, below knee, wood socket

A L5640 Addition to lower extremity, knee disarticulation, leather socket

A L5642 Addition to lower extremity, above knee, leather socket

A L5643 Addition to lower extremity, hip disarticulation, flexible inner socket, external frame

A L5644 Addition to lower extremity, above knee, wood socket

A L5645 Addition to lower extremity, below knee, flexible inner socket, external frame

A L5646 Addition to lower extremity, below knee, air, fluid, gel or equal, cushion socket

A L5647 Addition to lower extremity, below knee, suction socket

A L5648 Addition to lower extremity, above knee, air, fluid, gel or equal, cushion socket

A L5649 Addition to lower extremity, ischial containment/narrow M-L socket

A L5650 Additions to lower extremity, total contact, above knee or knee disarticulation socket

A L5651 Addition to lower extremity, above knee, flexible inner socket, external frame

A L5652 Addition to lower extremity, suction suspension, above knee or knee disarticulation socket

A L5653 Addition to lower extremity, knee disarticulation, expandable wall socket

A L5654 Addition to lower extremity, socket insert, Symes, (Kemblo, Pelite, Aliplast, Plastazote or equal)

A L5655 Addition to lower extremity, socket insert, below knee (Kemblo, Pelite, Aliplast, Plastazote or equal)

A L5656 Addition to lower extremity, socket insert, knee disarticulation (Kemblo, Pelite, Aliplast, Plastazote or equal)

A L5658 Addition to lower extremity, socket insert, above knee (Kemblo, Pelite, Aliplast, Plastazote or equal)

A L5661 Addition to lower extremity, socket insert, multidurometer Symes

A L5665 Addition to lower extremity, socket insert, multidurometer, below knee

A L5666 Addition to lower extremity, below knee, cuff suspension

A L5668 Addition to lower extremity, below knee, molded distal cushion

As the suspension sleeve is donned, air is driven out through a valve
Residual limb
Sealing membrane
Sleeve
Open valve
The valve is closed upon donning and a suction fit is formed around the residual limb
Closed valve

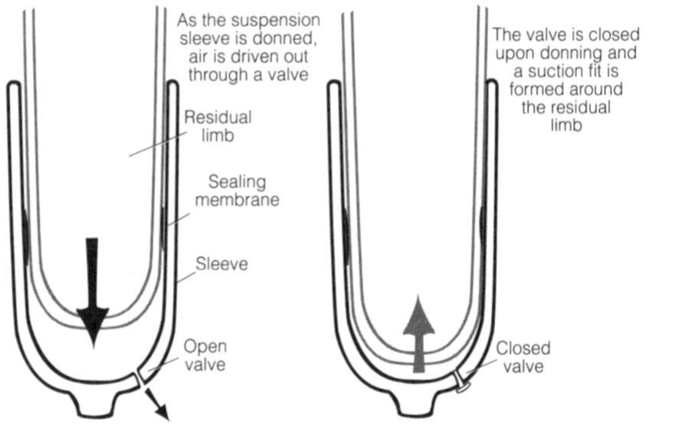

A L5670 Addition to lower extremity, below knee, molded supracondylar suspension (PTS or similar)

A L5671 Addition to lower extremity, below knee / above knee suspension locking mechanism (shuttle, lanyard, or equal), excludes socket insert

A L5672 Addition to lower extremity, below knee, removable medial brim suspension

A L5673 Addition to lower extremity, below knee/above knee, custom fabricated from existing mold or prefabricated, socket insert, silicone gel, elastomeric or equal, for use with locking mechanism

A ☑ L5676 Additions to lower extremity, below knee, knee joints, single axis, pair

A ☑ L5677 Additions to lower extremity, below knee, knee joints, polycentric, pair

A ☑ L5678 Additions to lower extremity, below knee, joint covers, pair

A L5679 Addition to lower extremity, below knee/above knee, custom fabricated from existing mold or prefabricated, socket insert, silicone gel, elastomeric or equal, not for use with locking mechanism

A L5680 Addition to lower extremity, below knee, thigh lacer, nonmolded

A L5681 Addition to lower extremity, below knee/above knee, custom fabricated socket insert for congenital or atypical traumatic amputee, silicone gel, elastomeric or equal, for use with or without locking mechanism, initial only (for other than initial, use code L5673 or L5679)

A L5682 Addition to lower extremity, below knee, thigh lacer, gluteal/ischial, molded

A L5683 Addition to lower extremity, below knee/above knee, custom fabricated socket insert for other than congenital or atypical traumatic amputee, silicone gel, elastomeric or equal, for use with or without locking mechanism, initial only (for other than initial, use code L5673 or L5679)

A L5684 Addition to lower extremity, below knee, fork strap

A L5685 Addition to lower extremity prosthesis, below knee, suspension/sealing sleeve, with or without valve, any material, each

A L5686 Addition to lower extremity, below knee, back check (extension control)

A L5688 Addition to lower extremity, below knee, waist belt, webbing

A L5690 Addition to lower extremity, below knee, waist belt, padded and lined

A L5692 Addition to lower extremity, above knee, pelvic control belt, light

A L5694 Addition to lower extremity, above knee, pelvic control belt, padded and lined

A ☑ L5695 Addition to lower extremity, above knee, pelvic control, sleeve suspension, neoprene or equal, each

A L5696 Addition to lower extremity, above knee or knee disarticulation, pelvic joint

A L5697 Addition to lower extremity, above knee or knee disarticulation, pelvic band

A L5698 Addition to lower extremity, above knee or knee disarticulation, Silesian bandage

A L5699 All lower extremity prostheses, shoulder harness ⊘ ♿

REPLACEMENTS

A L5700 Replacement, socket, below knee, molded to patient model ⊘ ♿

A L5701 Replacement, socket, above knee/knee disarticulation, including attachment plate, molded to patient model ⊘ ♿

A L5702 Replacement, socket, hip disarticulation, including hip joint, molded to patient model ⊘ ♿

A L5703 Ankle, Symes, molded to patient model, socket without solid ankle cushion heel (SACH) foot, replacement only ⊘ ♿

A L5704 Custom shaped protective cover, below knee ⊘ ♿

A L5705 Custom shaped protective cover, above knee ⊘ ♿

A L5706 Custom shaped protective cover, knee disarticulation ⊘ ♿

A L5707 Custom shaped protective cover, hip disarticulation ⊘ ♿

ADDITIONS: EXOSKELETAL KNEE-SHIN SYSTEM

A L5710 Addition, exoskeletal knee-shin system, single axis, manual lock ⊘ ♿

A L5711 Additions exoskeletal knee-shin system, single axis, manual lock, ultra-light material ⊘ ♿

A L5712 Addition, exoskeletal knee-shin system, single axis, friction swing and stance phase control (safety knee) ⊘ ♿

A L5714 Addition, exoskeletal knee-shin system, single axis, variable friction swing phase control ⊘ ♿

A L5716 Addition, exoskeletal knee-shin system, polycentric, mechanical stance phase lock ⊘ ♿

A L5718 Addition, exoskeletal knee-shin system, polycentric, friction swing and stance phase control ⊘ ♿

A L5722 Addition, exoskeletal knee-shin system, single axis, pneumatic swing, friction stance phase control ⊘ ♿

A L5724 Addition, exoskeletal knee-shin system, single axis, fluid swing phase control ⊘ ♿

A L5726 Addition, exoskeletal knee/shin system, single axis, external joints, fluid swing phase control ⊘ ♿

A L5728 Addition, exoskeletal knee-shin system, single axis, fluid swing and stance phase control ⊘ ♿

A L5780 Addition, exoskeletal knee-shin system, single axis, pneumatic/hydra pneumatic swing phase control ⊘ ♿

A L5781 Addition to lower limb prosthesis, vacuum pump, residual limb volume management and moisture evacuation system ⊘ ♿

A L5782 Addition to lower limb prosthesis, vacuum pump, residual limb volume management and moisture evacuation system, heavy-duty ⊘ ♿

COMPONENT MODIFICATION

A L5785 Addition, exoskeletal system, below knee, ultra-light material (titanium, carbon fiber or equal) ⊘ ♿

A L5790 Addition, exoskeletal system, above knee, ultra-light material (titanium, carbon fiber or equal) ⊘ ♿

A L5795 Addition, exoskeletal system, hip disarticulation, ultra-light material (titanium, carbon fiber or equal) ⊘ ♿

ADDITIONS: ENDOSKELETAL KNEE-SHIN SYSTEM

A L5810 Addition, endoskeletal knee-shin system, single axis, manual lock ⊘ ♿

A L5811 Addition, endoskeletal knee-shin system, single axis, manual lock, ultra-light material ⊘ ♿

A L5812 Addition, endoskeletal knee-shin system, single axis, friction swing and stance phase control (safety knee) ⊘ ♿

A L5814 Addition, endoskeletal knee-shin system, polycentric, hydraulic swing phase control, mechanical stance phase lock ⊘ ♿

A L5816 Addition, endoskeletal knee-shin system, polycentric, mechanical stance phase lock ⊘ ♿

A L5818 Addition, endoskeletal knee/shin system, polycentric, friction swing and stance phase control ⊘ ♿

A L5822 Addition, endoskeletal knee-shin system, single axis, pneumatic swing, friction stance phase control ⊘ ♿

A L5824 Addition, endoskeletal knee-shin system, single axis, fluid swing phase control ⊘ ♿

A L5826 Addition, endoskeletal knee-shin system, single axis, hydraulic swing phase control, with miniature high activity frame ⊘ ♿

A L5828 Addition, endoskeletal knee-shin system, single axis, fluid swing and stance phase control ⊘ ♿

A L5830 Addition, endoskeletal knee/shin system, single axis, pneumatic/swing phase control ⊘ ♿

A L5840 Addition, endoskeletal knee/shin system, 4-bar linkage or multiaxial, pneumatic swing phase control ⊘ ♿

A L5845 Addition, endoskeletal knee/shin system, stance flexion feature, adjustable ⊘ ♿

A L5848 Addition to endoskeletal knee-shin system, fluid stance extension, dampening feature, with or without adjustability ⊘ ♿

A L5850 Addition, endoskeletal system, above knee or hip disarticulation, knee extension assist ⊘ ♿

A L5855 Addition, endoskeletal system, hip disarticulation, mechanical hip extension assist ⊘ ♿

A L5856 Addition to lower extremity prosthesis, endoskeletal knee-shin system, microprocessor control feature, swing and stance phase, includes electronic sensor(s), any type ⊘ ♿

A L5857 Addition to lower extremity prosthesis, endoskeletal knee-shin system, microprocessor control feature, swing phase only, includes electronic sensor(s), any type ⊘ ♿

A L5858 Addition to lower extremity prosthesis, endoskeletal knee shin system, microprocessor control feature, stance phase only, includes electronic sensor(s), any type ⊘ ♿

A L5910 Addition, endoskeletal system, below knee, alignable system ⊘ ♿

A L5920 Addition, endoskeletal system, above knee or hip disarticulation, alignable system ⊘ ♿

A L5925 Addition, endoskeletal system, above knee, knee disarticulation or hip disarticulation, manual lock ⊘ ♿

A	L5930	Addition, endoskeletal system, high activity knee control frame
A	L5940	Addition, endoskeletal system, below knee, ultra-light material (titanium, carbon fiber or equal)
A	L5950	Addition, endoskeletal system, above knee, ultra-light material (titanium, carbon fiber or equal)
A	L5960	Addition, endoskeletal system, hip disarticulation, ultra-light material (titanium, carbon fiber or equal)
A	L5961	Addition, endoskeletal system, polycentric hip joint, pneumatic or hydraulic control, rotation control, with or without flexion and/or extension control
A	L5962	Addition, endoskeletal system, below knee, flexible protective outer surface covering system
A	L5964	Addition, endoskeletal system, above knee, flexible protective outer surface covering system
A	L5966	Addition, endoskeletal system, hip disarticulation, flexible protective outer surface covering system
A	L5968	Addition to lower limb prosthesis, multiaxial ankle with swing phase active dorsiflexion feature
A	L5970	All lower extremity prostheses, foot, external keel, SACH foot
A	L5971	All lower extremity prosthesis, solid ankle cushion heel (SACH) foot, replacement only
A	L5972	All lower extremity prostheses, flexible keel foot (SAFE, STEN, Bock Dynamic or equal)
A	L5973	Endoskeletal ankle foot system, microprocessor controlled feature, dorsiflexion and/or plantar flexion control, includes power source

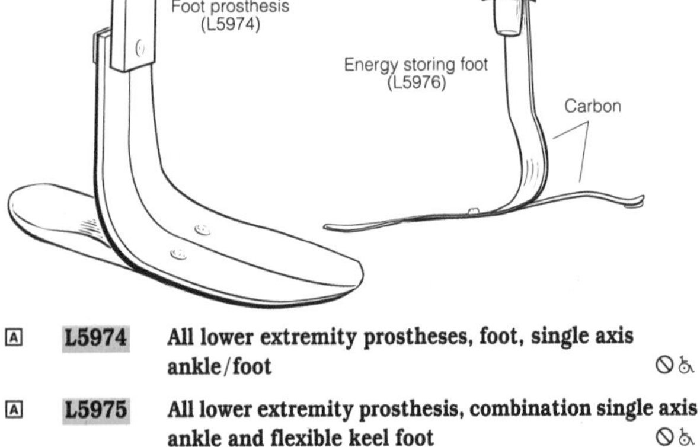

A	L5974	All lower extremity prostheses, foot, single axis ankle/foot
A	L5975	All lower extremity prosthesis, combination single axis ankle and flexible keel foot
A	L5976	All lower extremity prostheses, energy storing foot (Seattle Carbon Copy II or equal)

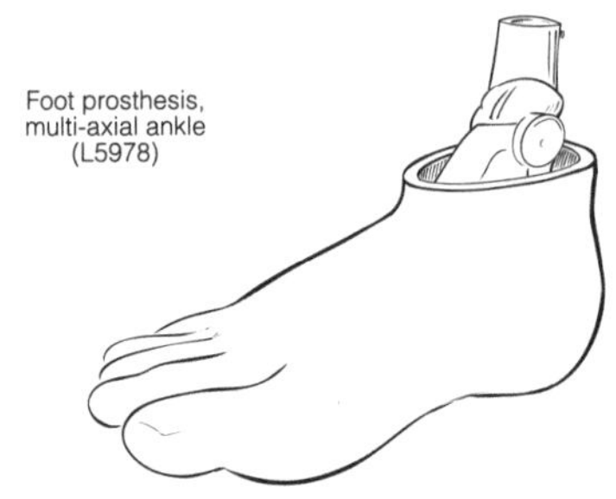

A	L5978	All lower extremity prostheses, foot, multiaxial ankle/foot
A	L5979	All lower extremity prostheses, multiaxial ankle, dynamic response foot, one piece system
A	L5980	All lower extremity prostheses, flex-foot system
A	L5981	All lower extremity prostheses, flex-walk system or equal
A	L5982	All exoskeletal lower extremity prostheses, axial rotation unit
A	L5984	All endoskeletal lower extremity prosthesis, axial rotation unit, with or without adjustability
A	L5985	All endoskeletal lower extremity prostheses, dynamic prosthetic pylon
A	L5986	All lower extremity prostheses, multiaxial rotation unit (MCP or equal)
A	L5987	All lower extremity prosthesis, shank foot system with vertical loading pylon
A	L5988	Addition to lower limb prosthesis, vertical shock reducing pylon feature
A	L5990	Addition to lower extremity prosthesis, user adjustable heel height
A	L5999	Lower extremity prosthesis, not otherwise specified Determine if an alternative HCPCS Level II or a CPT code better describes the service being reported. This code should be used only if a more specific code is unavailable.

PARTIAL HAND

▲	A	L6000 Jan	Partial hand, thumb remaining
▲	A	L6010 Jan	Partial hand, little and/or ring finger remaining
▲	A	L6020 Jan	Partial hand, no finger remaining
	A	L6025	Transcarpal/metacarpal or partial hand disarticulation prosthesis, external power, self-suspended, inner socket with removable forearm section, electrodes and cables, 2 batteries, charger, myoelectric control of terminal device

WRIST DISARTICULATION

A	L6050	Wrist disarticulation, molded socket, flexible elbow hinges, triceps pad
A	L6055	Wrist disarticulation, molded socket with expandable interface, flexible elbow hinges, triceps pad

BELOW ELBOW

A	L6100	Below elbow, molded socket, flexible elbow hinge, triceps pad
A	L6110	Below elbow, molded socket (Muenster or Northwestern suspension types)
A	L6120	Below elbow, molded double wall split socket, step-up hinges, half cuff
A	L6130	Below elbow, molded double wall split socket, stump activated locking hinge, half cuff

ELBOW DISARTICULATION

A	L6200	Elbow disarticulation, molded socket, outside locking hinge, forearm
A	L6205	Elbow disarticulation, molded socket with expandable interface, outside locking hinges, forearm

ABOVE ELBOW

A L6250 Above elbow, molded double wall socket, internal locking elbow, forearm

SHOULDER DISARTICULATION

A L6300 Shoulder disarticulation, molded socket, shoulder bulkhead, humeral section, internal locking elbow, forearm

A L6310 Shoulder disarticulation, passive restoration (complete prosthesis)

A L6320 Shoulder disarticulation, passive restoration (shoulder cap only)

INTERSCAPULAR THORACIC

A L6350 Interscapular thoracic, molded socket, shoulder bulkhead, humeral section, internal locking elbow, forearm

A L6360 Interscapular thoracic, passive restoration (complete prosthesis)

A L6370 Interscapular thoracic, passive restoration (shoulder cap only)

IMMEDIATE AND EARLY POSTSURGICAL PROCEDURES

A L6380 Immediate postsurgical or early fitting, application of initial rigid dressing, including fitting alignment and suspension of components, and one cast change, wrist disarticulation or below elbow

A ☑L6382 Immediate postsurgical or early fitting, application of initial rigid dressing including fitting alignment and suspension of components, and one cast change, elbow disarticulation or above elbow

A ☑L6384 Immediate postsurgical or early fitting, application of initial rigid dressing including fitting alignment and suspension of components, and one cast change, shoulder disarticulation or interscapular thoracic

A ☑L6386 Immediate postsurgical or early fitting, each additional cast change and realignment

A L6388 Immediate postsurgical or early fitting, application of rigid dressing only

MOLDED SOCKET

A L6400 Below elbow, molded socket, endoskeletal system, including soft prosthetic tissue shaping

A L6450 Elbow disarticulation, molded socket, endoskeletal system, including soft prosthetic tissue shaping

A L6500 Above elbow, molded socket, endoskeletal system, including soft prosthetic tissue shaping

A L6550 Shoulder disarticulation, molded socket, endoskeletal system, including soft prosthetic tissue shaping

A L6570 Interscapular thoracic, molded socket, endoskeletal system, including soft prosthetic tissue shaping

PREPARATORY SOCKET

A L6580 Preparatory, wrist disarticulation or below elbow, single wall plastic socket, friction wrist, flexible elbow hinges, figure of eight harness, humeral cuff, Bowden cable control, USMC or equal pylon, no cover, molded to patient model

A L6582 Preparatory, wrist disarticulation or below elbow, single wall socket, friction wrist, flexible elbow hinges, figure of eight harness, humeral cuff, Bowden cable control, USMC or equal pylon, no cover, direct formed

A L6584 Preparatory, elbow disarticulation or above elbow, single wall plastic socket, friction wrist, locking elbow, figure of eight harness, fair lead cable control, USMC or equal pylon, no cover, molded to patient model

A L6586 Preparatory, elbow disarticulation or above elbow, single wall socket, friction wrist, locking elbow, figure of eight harness, fair lead cable control, USMC or equal pylon, no cover, direct formed

A L6588 Preparatory, shoulder disarticulation or interscapular thoracic, single wall plastic socket, shoulder joint, locking elbow, friction wrist, chest strap, fair lead cable control, USMC or equal pylon, no cover, molded to patient model

A L6590 Preparatory, shoulder disarticulation or interscapular thoracic, single wall socket, shoulder joint, locking elbow, friction wrist, chest strap, fair lead cable control, USMC or equal pylon, no cover, direct formed

ADDITIONS: UPPER LIMB

The following procedures/modifications/components may be added to other base procedures. The items in this section should reflect the additional complexity of each modification procedure, in addition to the base procedure, at the time of the original order.

A ☑L6600 Upper extremity additions, polycentric hinge, pair

A ☑L6605 Upper extremity additions, single pivot hinge, pair

A ☑L6610 Upper extremity additions, flexible metal hinge, pair

A L6611 Addition to upper extremity prosthesis, external powered, additional switch, any type

A L6615 Upper extremity addition, disconnect locking wrist unit

A ☑L6616 Upper extremity addition, additional disconnect insert for locking wrist unit, each

A L6620 Upper extremity addition, flexion/extension wrist unit, with or without friction

A L6621 Upper extremity prosthesis addition, flexion/extension wrist with or without friction, for use with external powered terminal device

A L6623 Upper extremity addition, spring assisted rotational wrist unit with latch release

A L6624 Upper extremity addition, flexion/extension and rotation wrist unit

A L6625 Upper extremity addition, rotation wrist unit with cable lock

A L6628 Upper extremity addition, quick disconnect hook adapter, Otto Bock or equal

A L6629 Upper extremity addition, quick disconnect lamination collar with coupling piece, Otto Bock or equal

A L6630 Upper extremity addition, stainless steel, any wrist

A ☑L6632 Upper extremity addition, latex suspension sleeve, each

A L6635 Upper extremity addition, lift assist for elbow

A L6637 Upper extremity addition, nudge control elbow lock

A L6638 Upper extremity addition to prosthesis, electric locking feature, only for use with manually powered elbow

A ☑ L6640 Upper extremity additions, shoulder abduction joint, pair

A L6641 Upper extremity addition, excursion amplifier, pulley type

A L6642 Upper extremity addition, excursion amplifier, lever type

A ☑ L6645 Upper extremity addition, shoulder flexion-abduction joint, each

A L6646 Upper extremity addition, shoulder joint, multipositional locking, flexion, adjustable abduction friction control, for use with body powered or external powered system

A L6647 Upper extremity addition, shoulder lock mechanism, body powered actuator

A L6648 Upper extremity addition, shoulder lock mechanism, external powered actuator

A ☑ L6650 Upper extremity addition, shoulder universal joint, each

A L6655 Upper extremity addition, standard control cable, extra

A L6660 Upper extremity addition, heavy-duty control cable

A L6665 Upper extremity addition, Teflon, or equal, cable lining

A L6670 Upper extremity addition, hook to hand, cable adapter

A L6672 Upper extremity addition, harness, chest or shoulder, saddle type

A L6675 Upper extremity addition, harness, (e.g., figure of eight type), single cable design

A L6676 Upper extremity addition, harness, (e.g., figure of eight type), dual cable design

A L6677 Upper extremity addition, harness, triple control, simultaneous operation of terminal device and elbow

A L6680 Upper extremity addition, test socket, wrist disarticulation or below elbow

A L6682 Upper extremity addition, test socket, elbow disarticulation or above elbow

A L6684 Upper extremity addition, test socket, shoulder disarticulation or interscapular thoracic

A L6686 Upper extremity addition, suction socket

A L6687 Upper extremity addition, frame type socket, below elbow or wrist disarticulation

A L6688 Upper extremity addition, frame type socket, above elbow or elbow disarticulation

A L6689 Upper extremity addition, frame type socket, shoulder disarticulation

A L6690 Upper extremity addition, frame type socket, interscapular-thoracic

A ☑ L6691 Upper extremity addition, removable insert, each

A ☑ L6692 Upper extremity addition, silicone gel insert or equal, each

A L6693 Upper extremity addition, locking elbow, forearm counterbalance

A L6694 Addition to upper extremity prosthesis, below elbow/above elbow, custom fabricated from existing mold or prefabricated, socket insert, silicone gel, elastomeric or equal, for use with locking mechanism

A L6695 Addition to upper extremity prosthesis, below elbow/above elbow, custom fabricated from existing mold or prefabricated, socket insert, silicone gel, elastomeric or equal, not for use with locking mechanism

A L6696 Addition to upper extremity prosthesis, below elbow/above elbow, custom fabricated socket insert for congenital or atypical traumatic amputee, silicone gel, elastomeric or equal, for use with or without locking mechanism, initial only (for other than initial, use code L6694 or L6695)

A L6697 Addition to upper extremity prosthesis, below elbow/above elbow, custom fabricated socket insert for other than congenital or atypical traumatic amputee, silicone gel, elastomeric or equal, for use with or without locking mechanism, initial only (for other than initial, use code L6694 or L6695)

A L6698 Addition to upper extremity prosthesis, below elbow/above elbow, lock mechanism, excludes socket insert

TERMINAL DEVICE

A L6703 Terminal device, passive hand/mitt, any material, any size

A L6704 Terminal device, sport/recreational/work attachment, any material, any size

A L6706 Terminal device, hook, mechanical, voluntary opening, any material, any size, lined or unlined

A L6707 Terminal device, hook, mechanical, voluntary closing, any material, any size, lined or unlined

A L6708 Terminal device, hand, mechanical, voluntary opening, any material, any size

A L6709 Terminal device, hand, mechanical, voluntary closing, any material, any size

A L6711 Terminal device, hook, mechanical, voluntary opening, any material, any size, lined or unlined, pediatric

A L6712 Terminal device, hook, mechanical, voluntary closing, any material, any size, lined or unlined, pediatric

A L6713 Terminal device, hand, mechanical, voluntary opening, any material, any size, pediatric

A L6714 Terminal device, hand, mechanical, voluntary closing, any material, any size, pediatric

● A L6715 Jan Terminal device, multiple articulating digit, includes motor(s), initial issue or replacement

A L6721 Terminal device, hook or hand, heavy-duty, mechanical, voluntary opening, any material, any size, lined or unlined

A L6722 Terminal device, hook or hand, heavy-duty, mechanical, voluntary closing, any material, any size, lined or unlined

ADDITION TO TERMINAL DEVICE

- A **L6805** Addition to terminal device, modifier wrist unit
- A **L6810** Addition to terminal device, precision pinch device
- ● A **L6880** Jan Electric hand, switch or myolelectric controlled, independently articulating digits, any grasp pattern or combination of grasp patterns, includes motor(s)
- A **L6881** Automatic grasp feature, addition to upper limb electric prosthetic terminal device
- A **L6882** Microprocessor control feature, addition to upper limb prosthetic terminal device

REPLACEMENT SOCKET

- A **L6883** Replacement socket, below elbow/wrist disarticulation, molded to patient model, for use with or without external power
- A **L6884** Replacement socket, above elbow/elbow disarticulation, molded to patient model, for use with or without external power
- A **L6885** Replacement socket, shoulder disarticulation/interscapular thoracic, molded to patient model, for use with or without external power

HAND RESTORATION

- A **L6890** Addition to upper extremity prosthesis, glove for terminal device, any material, prefabricated, includes fitting and adjustment
- A **L6895** Addition to upper extremity prosthesis, glove for terminal device, any material, custom fabricated
- A **L6900** Hand restoration (casts, shading and measurements included), partial hand, with glove, thumb or one finger remaining
- A **L6905** Hand restoration (casts, shading and measurements included), partial hand, with glove, multiple fingers remaining
- A **L6910** Hand restoration (casts, shading and measurements included), partial hand, with glove, no fingers remaining
- A **L6915** Hand restoration (shading and measurements included), replacement glove for above

EXTERNAL POWER

- A **L6920** Wrist disarticulation, external power, self-suspended inner socket, removable forearm shell, Otto Bock or equal switch, cables, 2 batteries and 1 charger, switch control of terminal device
- A **L6925** Wrist disarticulation, external power, self-suspended inner socket, removable forearm shell, Otto Bock or equal electrodes, cables, 2 batteries and one charger, myoelectronic control of terminal device
- A **L6930** Below elbow, external power, self-suspended inner socket, removable forearm shell, Otto Bock or equal switch, cables, 2 batteries and one charger, switch control of terminal device
- A **L6935** Below elbow, external power, self-suspended inner socket, removable forearm shell, Otto Bock or equal electrodes, cables, 2 batteries and one charger, myoelectronic control of terminal device
- A **L6940** Elbow disarticulation, external power, molded inner socket, removable humeral shell, outside locking hinges, forearm, Otto Bock or equal switch, cables, 2 batteries and one charger, switch control of terminal device
- A **L6945** Elbow disarticulation, external power, molded inner socket, removable humeral shell, outside locking hinges, forearm, Otto Bock or equal electrodes, cables, 2 batteries and one charger, myoelectronic control of terminal device
- A **L6950** Above elbow, external power, molded inner socket, removable humeral shell, internal locking elbow, forearm, Otto Bock or equal switch, cables, 2 batteries and one charger, switch control of terminal device
- A **L6955** Above elbow, external power, molded inner socket, removable humeral shell, internal locking elbow, forearm, Otto Bock or equal electrodes, cables, 2 batteries and one charger, myoelectronic control of terminal device
- A **L6960** Shoulder disarticulation, external power, molded inner socket, removable shoulder shell, shoulder bulkhead, humeral section, mechanical elbow, forearm, Otto Bock or equal switch, cables, 2 batteries and one charger, switch control of terminal device
- A **L6965** Shoulder disarticulation, external power, molded inner socket, removable shoulder shell, shoulder bulkhead, humeral section, mechanical elbow, forearm, Otto Bock or equal electrodes, cables, 2 batteries and one charger, myoelectronic control of terminal device
- A **L6970** Interscapular-thoracic, external power, molded inner socket, removable shoulder shell, shoulder bulkhead, humeral section, mechanical elbow, forearm, Otto Bock or equal switch, cables, 2 batteries and one charger, switch control of terminal device
- A **L6975** Interscapular-thoracic, external power, molded inner socket, removable shoulder shell, shoulder bulkhead, humeral section, mechanical elbow, forearm, Otto Bock or equal electrodes, cables, 2 batteries and one charger, myoelectronic control of terminal device

ELECTRIC HAND AND ACCESSORIES

- A **L7007** Electric hand, switch or myoelectric controlled, adult
- A **L7008** Electric hand, switch or myoelectric, controlled, pediatric
- A **L7009** Electric hook, switch or myoelectric controlled, adult
- A **L7040** Prehensile actuator, switch controlled
- A **L7045** Electric hook, switch or myoelectric controlled, pediatric

ELECTRONIC ELBOW AND ACCESSORIES

- A **L7170** Electronic elbow, Hosmer or equal, switch controlled
- A **L7180** Electronic elbow, microprocessor sequential control of elbow and terminal device
- A **L7181** Electronic elbow, microprocessor simultaneous control of elbow and terminal device
- A **L7185** Electronic elbow, adolescent, Variety Village or equal, switch controlled

Jan January Update

- A **L7186** Electronic elbow, child, Variety Village or equal, switch controlled ⊘ ♿
- A **L7190** Electronic elbow, adolescent, Variety Village or equal, myoelectronically controlled ⊘ ♿
- A **L7191** Electronic elbow, child, Variety Village or equal, myoelectronically controlled ⊘ ♿
- A **L7260** Electronic wrist rotator, Otto Bock or equal ⊘ ♿
- A **L7261** Electronic wrist rotator, for Utah arm ⊘ ♿
- ~~L7266~~ Jan ~~Servo control, Steeper or equal~~
- ~~L7272~~ Jan ~~Analogue control, UNB or equal~~
- ~~L7274~~ Jan ~~Proportional control, 6-12 volt, Liberty, Utah or equal~~

BATTERY COMPONENTS

- A ☑ **L7360** Six volt battery, each ♿
- A ☑ **L7362** Battery charger, 6 volt, each ⊘ ♿
- A ☑ **L7364** Twelve volt battery, each ⊘ ♿
- A ☑ **L7366** Battery charger, twelve volt, each ⊘ ♿
- A **L7367** Lithium ion battery, replacement ⊘ ♿
- ▲ A **L7368** Jan Lithium ion battery charger, replacement only ⊘ ♿

ADDITIONS TO UPPER EXTREMITY PROSTHESIS

- A **L7400** Addition to upper extremity prosthesis, below elbow/wrist disarticulation, ultralight material (titanium, carbon fiber or equal) ⊘ ♿
- A **L7401** Addition to upper extremity prosthesis, above elbow disarticulation, ultralight material (titanium, carbon fiber or equal) ⊘ ♿
- A **L7402** Addition to upper extremity prosthesis, shoulder disarticulation/interscapular thoracic, ultralight material (titanium, carbon fiber or equal) ⊘ ♿
- A **L7403** Addition to upper extremity prosthesis, below elbow/wrist disarticulation, acrylic material ⊘ ♿
- A **L7404** Addition to upper extremity prosthesis, above elbow disarticulation, acrylic material ⊘ ♿
- A **L7405** Addition to upper extremity prosthesis, shoulder disarticulation/interscapular thoracic, acrylic material ⊘ ♿
- A **L7499** Upper extremity prosthesis, not otherwise specified

REPAIRS

- ~~L7500~~ Jan ~~Repair of prosthetic device, hourly rate (excludes V5335 repair of oral or laryngeal prosthesis or artificial larynx)~~
  To report, see L7520
- A **L7510** Repair of prosthetic device, repair or replace minor parts
  Medicare jurisdiction: local contractor if repair of implanted prosthetic device.
- A ☑ **L7520** Repair prosthetic device, labor component, per 15 minutes ♿
  Medicare jurisdiction: local contractor if repair of implanted prosthetic device.

MALE PROSTHETIC

- E ☑ **L7600** Prosthetic donning sleeve, any material, each
- A **L7900** Male vacuum erection system A ♂ ♿

BREAST PROSTHETICS

- A **L8000** Breast prosthesis, mastectomy bra A ♀ ♿
- A **L8001** Breast prosthesis, mastectomy bra, with integrated breast prosthesis form, unilateral A ♀ ♿
- A **L8002** Breast prosthesis, mastectomy bra, with integrated breast prosthesis form, bilateral A ♀ ♿
- A **L8010** Breast prosthesis, mastectomy sleeve A ♀
- A **L8015** External breast prosthesis garment, with mastectomy form, post mastectomy A ♀ ♿
- A **L8020** Breast prosthesis, mastectomy form A ♀ ♿
- A **L8030** Breast prosthesis, silicone or equal, without integral adhesive A ♀ ♿
- A **L8031** Breast prosthesis, silicone or equal, with integral adhesive ♿
- A ☑ **L8032** Nipple prosthesis, reusable, any type, each ♿
- A **L8035** Custom breast prosthesis, post mastectomy, molded to patient model A ♀ ♿
- A **L8039** Breast prosthesis, not otherwise specified A ♀

FACE AND EAR PROSTHETICS

Orbital and midfacial prosthesis (L8041-L8042)

Nasal prosthesis (L8040)

Frontal bone

Nasal bone

Maxilla

Zygoma

(L8043-L8044)

Facial prosthetics are typically custom manufactured from polymers and carefully matched to the original features. The maxilla, zygoma, frontal, and nasal bones are often involved, either singly or in combination (L8040-L8044)

- A **L8040** Nasal prosthesis, provided by a nonphysician ♿
- A **L8041** Midfacial prosthesis, provided by a nonphysician ♿
- A **L8042** Orbital prosthesis, provided by a nonphysician ♿
- A **L8043** Upper facial prosthesis, provided by a nonphysician ♿
- A **L8044** Hemi-facial prosthesis, provided by a nonphysician ♿
- A **L8045** Auricular prosthesis, provided by a nonphysician ♿
- A **L8046** Partial facial prosthesis, provided by a nonphysician ♿
- A **L8047** Nasal septal prosthesis, provided by a nonphysician ♿
- A **L8048** Unspecified maxillofacial prosthesis, by report, provided by a nonphysician
- A **L8049** Repair or modification of maxillofacial prosthesis, labor component, 15 minute increments, provided by a nonphysician

TRUSSES

- A **L8300** Truss, single with standard pad ♿
- A **L8310** Truss, double with standard pads ♿
- A **L8320** Truss, addition to standard pad, water pad ♿
- A **L8330** Truss, addition to standard pad, scrotal pad ♂ ♿

PROSTHETIC SOCKS

A ☑L8400 Prosthetic sheath, below knee, each

A ☑L8410 Prosthetic sheath, above knee, each

A ☑L8415 Prosthetic sheath, upper limb, each

A ☑L8417 Prosthetic sheath/sock, including a gel cushion layer, below knee or above knee, each

A ☑L8420 Prosthetic sock, multiple ply, below knee, each

A ☑L8430 Prosthetic sock, multiple ply, above knee, each

A ☑L8435 Prosthetic sock, multiple ply, upper limb, each

A ☑L8440 Prosthetic shrinker, below knee, each

A ☑L8460 Prosthetic shrinker, above knee, each

A ☑L8465 Prosthetic shrinker, upper limb, each

A ☑L8470 Prosthetic sock, single ply, fitting, below knee, each

A ☑L8480 Prosthetic sock, single ply, fitting, above knee, each

A ☑L8485 Prosthetic sock, single ply, fitting, upper limb, each

A L8499 Unlisted procedure for miscellaneous prosthetic services

Determine if an alternative HCPCS Level II or a CPT code better describes the service being reported. This code should be used only if a more specific code is unavailable.

LARYNX AND TRACHEA PROTHETICS AND ACCESSORIES

A L8500 Artificial larynx, any type

A L8501 Tracheostomy speaking valve

A L8505 Artificial larynx replacement battery/accessory, any type

A ☑L8507 Tracheo-esophageal voice prosthesis, patient inserted, any type, each

A L8509 Tracheo-esophageal voice prosthesis, inserted by a licensed health care provider, any type

A L8510 Voice amplifier

A ☑L8511 Insert for indwelling tracheoesophageal prosthesis, with or without valve, replacement only, each

A ☑L8512 Gelatin capsules or equivalent, for use with tracheoesophageal voice prosthesis, replacement only, per 10

A ☑L8513 Cleaning device used with tracheoesophageal voice prosthesis, pipet, brush, or equal, replacement only, each

A ☑L8514 Tracheoesophageal puncture dilator, replacement only, each

A ☑L8515 Gelatin capsule, application device for use with tracheoesophageal voice prosthesis, each

BREAST IMPLANT

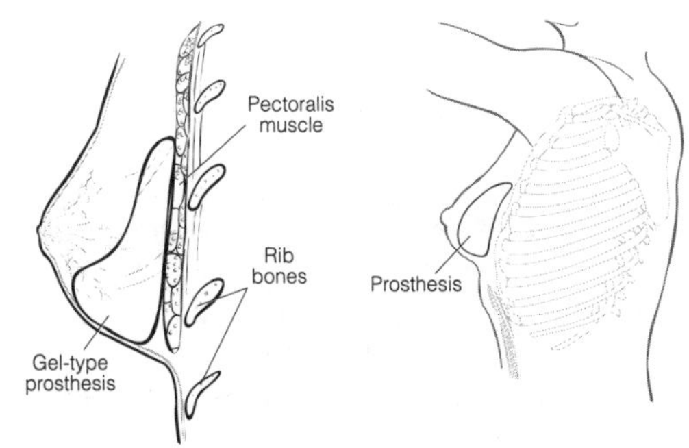

N L8600 Implantable breast prosthesis, silicone or equal

Medicare covers implants inserted in post-mastectomy reconstruction in a breast cancer patient. Always report concurrent to the implant procedure.

MED: 100-4,4,190

URINARY BULKING AGENTS

N ☑L8603 Injectable bulking agent, collagen implant, urinary tract, 2.5 ml syringe, includes shipping and necessary supplies

Medicare covers up to five separate collagen implant treatments in patients with intrinsic sphincter deficiency. Who have passed a collagen sensitivity test.

MED: 100-4,4,190

N ☑L8604 Injectable bulking agent, dextranomer/hyaluronic acid copolymer implant, urinary tract, 1 ml, includes shipping and necessary supplies

N ☑L8606 Injectable bulking agent, synthetic implant, urinary tract, 1 ml syringe, includes shipping and necessary supplies

EYE AND EAR IMPLANTS AND ACCESSORIES

N L8609 Artificial cornea

N L8610 Ocular implant

MED: 100-4,4,190

N L8612 Aqueous shunt

MED: 100-4,4,190

N L8613 Ossicula implant

MED: 100-4,4,190

N L8614 Cochlear device, includes all internal and external components

A cochlear implant is covered by Medicare when the patient has bilateral sensorineural deafness.

MED: 100-4,4,190; 100-4,14,40.8

AHA: 4Q,'03,8; 3Q,'02,5

A L8615 Headset/headpiece for use with cochlear implant device, replacement

A L8616 Microphone for use with cochlear implant device, replacement

A L8617 Transmitting coil for use with cochlear implant device, replacement

A L8618 Transmitter cable for use with cochlear implant device, replacement

A L8619 Cochlear implant, external speech processor and controller, integrated system, replacement

Medicare jurisdiction: local contractor.

A ☑ L8621 Zinc air battery for use with cochlear implant device, replacement, each

A ☑ L8622 Alkaline battery for use with cochlear implant device, any size, replacement, each

A ☑ L8623 Lithium ion battery for use with cochlear implant device speech processor, other than ear level, replacement, each

A ☑ L8624 Lithium ion battery for use with cochlear implant device speech processor, ear level, replacement, each

A L8627 Cochlear implant, external speech processor, component, replacement

A L8628 Cochlear implant, external controller component, replacement

A L8629 Transmitting coil and cable, integrated, for use with cochlear implant device, replacement

UPPER EXTREMITY IMPLANTS

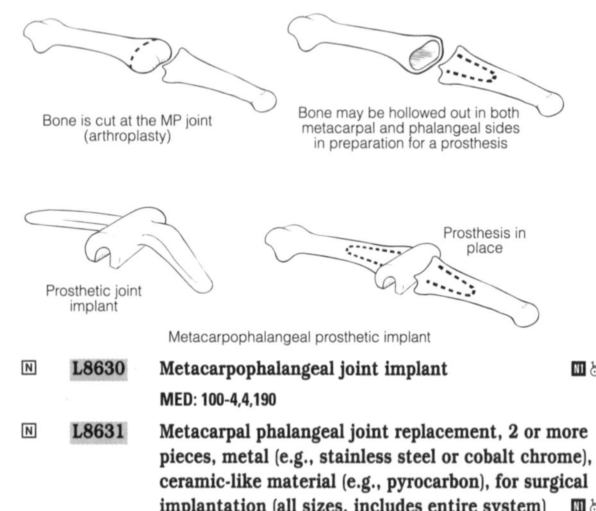
Bone is cut at the MP joint (arthroplasty)
Bone may be hollowed out in both metacarpal and phalangeal sides in preparation for a prosthesis
Prosthetic joint implant
Prosthesis in place
Metacarpophalangeal prosthetic implant

N L8630 Metacarpophalangeal joint implant
MED: 100-4,4,190

N L8631 Metacarpal phalangeal joint replacement, 2 or more pieces, metal (e.g., stainless steel or cobalt chrome), ceramic-like material (e.g., pyrocarbon), for surgical implantation (all sizes, includes entire system)

LOWER EXTREMITY IMPLANT

N L8641 Metatarsal joint implant
MED: 100-4,4,190

N L8642 Hallux implant
MED: 100-4,4,190

INTERPHALANGEAL IMPLANTS

N ☑ L8658 Interphalangeal joint spacer, silicone or equal, each
MED: 100-4,4,190

N L8659 Interphalangeal finger joint replacement, 2 or more pieces, metal (e.g., stainless steel or cobalt chrome), ceramic-like material (e.g., pyrocarbon) for surgical implantation, any size

CARDIOVASCULAR IMPLANT

N L8670 Vascular graft material, synthetic, implant
MED: 100-4,4,190

NEUROSTIMULATOR AND ACCESSORIES

N ☑ L8680 Implantable neurostimulator electrode, each

A L8681 Patient programmer (external) for use with implantable programmable neurostimulator pulse generator, replacement only

N L8682 Implantable neurostimulator radiofrequency receiver

A L8683 Radiofrequency transmitter (external) for use with implantable neurostimulator radiofrequency receiver

A L8684 Radiofrequency transmitter (external) for use with implantable sacral root neurostimulator receiver for bowel and bladder management, replacement

N L8685 Implantable neurostimulator pulse generator, single array, rechargeable, includes extension

N L8686 Implantable neurostimulator pulse generator, single array, nonrechargeable, includes extension

N L8687 Implantable neurostimulator pulse generator, dual array, rechargeable, includes extension

N L8688 Implantable neurostimulator pulse generator, dual array, nonrechargeable, includes extension

A L8689 External recharging system for battery (internal) for use with implantable neurostimulator, replacement only

MISCELLANEOUS PROSTHETICS AND ACCESSORIES

N L8690 Auditory osseointegrated device, includes all internal and external components
MED: 100-4,14,40.8

A L8691 Auditory osseointegrated device, external sound processor, replacement

E L8692 Auditory osseointegrated device, external sound processor, used without osseointegration, body worn, includes headband or other means of external attachment

A L8693 Auditory osseointegrated device abutment, any length, replacement only

A L8695 External recharging system for battery (external) for use with implantable neurostimulator, replacement only

N L8699 Prosthetic implant, not otherwise specified
Determine if an alternative HCPCS Level II or a CPT code better describes the service being reported. This code should be used only if a more specific code is unavailable.
MED: 100-4,4,190

N L9900 Orthotic and prosthetic supply, accessory, and/or service component of another HCPCS L code

MEDICAL SERVICES M0000-M0301

OTHER MEDICAL SERVICES

M codes include office services, cellular therapy, prolotherapy, intragastric hypothermia, IV chelation therapy, and fabric wrapping of an abdominal aneurysm.

Q3 **M0064** **Brief office visit for the sole purpose of monitoring or changing drug prescriptions used in the treatment of mental psychoneurotic and personality disorders** ⊘

MED: 100-4,12,210.1

E **M0075** **Cellular therapy**

The therapeutic efficacy of injecting foreign proteins has not been established.

E **M0076** **Prolotherapy**

The therapeutic efficacy of prolotherapy and joint sclerotherapy has not been established.

E **M0100** **Intragastric hypothermia using gastric freezing**

Code with caution: This procedure is considered obsolete.

CARDIOVASCULAR SERVICES

E **M0300** **IV chelation therapy (chemical endarterectomy)**

Chelation therapy is considered experimental in the United States.

MED: 100-3,20.21; 100-3,20.22

E **M0301** **Fabric wrapping of abdominal aneurysm**

Code with caution: This procedure has largely been replaced with more effective treatment modalities. Submit documentation.

PATHOLOGY AND LABORATORY SERVICES P0000-P9999

P codes include chemistry, toxicology, and microbiology tests, screening Papanicolaou procedures, and various blood products.

CHEMISTRY AND TOXICOLOGY TESTS

A **P2028** Cephalin floculation, blood
Code with caution: This test is considered obsolete. Submit documentation.

A **P2029** Congo red, blood
Code with caution: This test is considered obsolete. Submit documentation.

E **P2031** Hair analysis (excluding arsenic)

A **P2033** Thymol turbidity, blood
Code with caution: This test is considered obsolete. Submit documentation.

A **P2038** Mucoprotein, blood (seromucoid) (medical necessity procedure)
Code with caution: This test is considered obsolete. Submit documentation.

PATHOLOGY SCREENING TESTS

A **P3000** Screening Papanicolaou smear, cervical or vaginal, up to 3 smears, by technician under physician supervision A ♀
One Pap test is covered by Medicare every two years, unless the physician suspects cervical abnormalities and shortens the interval. See also G0123-G0124.

B **P3001** Screening Papanicolaou smear, cervical or vaginal, up to 3 smears, requiring interpretation by physician A ♀ ⊘
One Pap test is covered by Medicare every two years, unless the physician suspects cervical abnormalities and shortens the interval. See also G0123-G0124.

MICROBIOLOGY TESTS

E **P7001** Culture, bacterial, urine; quantitative, sensitivity study

MISCELLANEOUS

R ☑ **P9010** Blood (whole), for transfusion, per unit
MED: 100-1,3,20.5; 100-2,1,10; 100-4,3,40.2.2

R ☑ **P9011** Blood, split unit
MED: 100-1,3,20.5; 100-2,1,10; 100-4,3,40.2.2; 100-4,4,231.4

R ☑ **P9012** Cryoprecipitate, each unit
MED: 100-1,3,20.5; 100-2,1,10; 100-4,3,40.2.2

R ☑ **P9016** Red blood cells, leukocytes reduced, each unit
MED: 100-1,3,20.5; 100-2,1,10; 100-4,3,40.2.2

R ☑ **P9017** Fresh frozen plasma (single donor), frozen within 8 hours of collection, each unit
MED: 100-1,3,20.5; 100-2,1,10; 100-4,3,40.2.2

R ☑ **P9019** Platelets, each unit
MED: 100-1,3,20.5; 100-2,1,10; 100-4,3,40.2.2

R ☑ **P9020** Platelet rich plasma, each unit
MED: 100-1,3,20.5; 100-4,3,40.2.2

R ☑ **P9021** Red blood cells, each unit
MED: 100-1,3,20.5; 100-2,1,10; 100-4,3,40.2.2

R ☑ **P9022** Red blood cells, washed, each unit
MED: 100-1,3,20.5; 100-2,1,10; 100-4,3,40.2.2

R ☑ **P9023** Plasma, pooled multiple donor, solvent/detergent treated, frozen, each unit
MED: 100-1,3,20.5; 100-2,1,10; 100-4,3,40.2.2

R ☑ **P9031** Platelets, leukocytes reduced, each unit
MED: 100-1,3,20.5; 100-1,3,20.5.2; 100-1,3,20.5.3; 100-2,1,10; 100-4,3,40.2.2

R ☑ **P9032** Platelets, irradiated, each unit
MED: 100-1,3,20.5; 100-1,3,20.5.2; 100-1,3,20.5.3; 100-2,1,10; 100-4,3,40.2.2

R ☑ **P9033** Platelets, leukocytes reduced, irradiated, each unit
MED: 100-1,3,20.5; 100-1,3,20.5.2; 100-1,3,20.5.3; 100-2,1,10; 100-4,3,40.2.2

R ☑ **P9034** Platelets, pheresis, each unit
MED: 100-1,3,20.5; 100-1,3,20.5.2; 100-1,3,20.5.3; 100-2,1,10; 100-4,3,40.2.2

R ☑ **P9035** Platelets, pheresis, leukocytes reduced, each unit
MED: 100-1,3,20.5; 100-1,3,20.5.2; 100-1,3,20.5.3; 100-2,1,10; 100-4,3,40.2.2

R ☑ **P9036** Platelets, pheresis, irradiated, each unit
MED: 100-1,3,20.5; 100-1,3,20.5.2; 100-1,3,20.5.3; 100-2,1,10; 100-4,3,40.2.2

R ☑ **P9037** Platelets, pheresis, leukocytes reduced, irradiated, each unit
MED: 100-1,3,20.5; 100-1,3,20.5.2; 100-1,3,20.5.3; 100-2,1,10; 100-4,3,40.2.2

R ☑ **P9038** Red blood cells, irradiated, each unit
MED: 100-1,3,20.5; 100-1,3,20.5.2; 100-1,3,20.5.3; 100-2,1,10; 100-4,3,40.2.2

R ☑ **P9039** Red blood cells, deglycerolized, each unit
MED: 100-1,3,20.5; 100-1,3,20.5.2; 100-1,3,20.5.3; 100-2,1,10; 100-4,3,40.2.2

R ☑ **P9040** Red blood cells, leukocytes reduced, irradiated, each unit
MED: 100-1,3,20.5; 100-1,3,20.5.2; 100-1,3,20.5.3; 100-2,1,10; 100-4,3,40.2.2

K ☑ **P9041** Infusion, albumin (human), 5%, 50 ml K2
MED: 100-2,1,10; 100-4,3,40.2.2

R ☑ **P9043** Infusion, plasma protein fraction (human), 5%, 50 ml
MED: 100-1,3,20.5; 100-2,1,10; 100-4,3,40.2.2

R ☑ **P9044** Plasma, cryoprecipitate reduced, each unit
MED: 100-1,3,20.5; 100-2,1,10; 100-4,3,40.2.2

K ☑ **P9045** Infusion, albumin (human), 5%, 250 ml K2
MED: 100-2,1,10; 100-4,3,40.2.2

K ☑ **P9046** Infusion, albumin (human), 25%, 20 ml K2
MED: 100-2,1,10; 100-4,3,40.2.2

K ☑ **P9047** Infusion, albumin (human), 25%, 50 ml K2
MED: 100-2,1,10; 100-4,3,40.2.2

R ☑ **P9048** Infusion, plasma protein fraction (human), 5%, 250 ml
MED: 100-2,1,10; 100-4,3,40.2.2

R ☑ **P9050** Granulocytes, pheresis, each unit
MED: 100-2,1,10; 100-4,3,40.2.2

R ☑ **P9051** Whole blood or red blood cells, leukocytes reduced, CMV-negative, each unit
MED: 100-2,1,10; 100-4,3,40.2.2

R ☑ **P9052** Platelets, HLA-matched leukocytes reduced, apheresis/pheresis, each unit
MED: 100-2,1,10; 100-4,3,40.2.2

R ☑ **P9053** Platelets, pheresis, leukocytes reduced, CMV-negative, irradiated, each unit

MED: 100-2,1,10; 100-4,3,40.2.2

R ☑ **P9054** Whole blood or red blood cells, leukocytes reduced, frozen, deglycerol, washed, each unit

MED: 100-2,1,10; 100-4,3,40.2.2

R ☑ **P9055** Platelets, leukocytes reduced, CMV-negative, apheresis/pheresis, each unit

MED: 100-2,1,10; 100-4,3,40.2.2

R ☑ **P9056** Whole blood, leukocytes reduced, irradiated, each unit

MED: 100-2,1,10; 100-4,3,40.2.2

R ☑ **P9057** Red blood cells, frozen/deglycerolized/washed, leukocytes reduced, irradiated, each unit

MED: 100-2,1,10; 100-4,3,40.2.2

R ☑ **P9058** Red blood cells, leukocytes reduced, CMV-negative, irradiated, each unit

MED: 100-2,1,10; 100-4,3,40.2.2

R ☑ **P9059** Fresh frozen plasma between 8-24 hours of collection, each unit

MED: 100-2,1,10; 100-4,3,40.2.2

R ☑ **P9060** Fresh frozen plasma, donor retested, each unit

MED: 100-2,1,10; 100-4,3,40.2.2

A ☑ **P9603** Travel allowance, one way in connection with medically necessary laboratory specimen collection drawn from homebound or nursing homebound patient; prorated miles actually travelled.

MED: 100-4,16,60; 100-4,16,60.2

A ☑ **P9604** Travel allowance, one way in connection with medically necessary laboratory specimen collection drawn from homebound or nursing homebound patient; prorated trip charge

MED: 100-4,16,60; 100-4,16,60.2

A **P9612** Catheterization for collection of specimen, single patient, all places of service

MED: 100-4,16,60

N **P9615** Catheterization for collection of specimen(s) (multiple patients)

MED: 100-4,16,60

Q CODES (TEMPORARY) Q0035 - Q9968

Temporary Q codes are used to pay health care providers for supplies, drugs, and biologicals to which no permanent code has been assigned.

X **Q0035** **Cardiokymography**
Covered only in conjunction with electrocardiographic stress testing in male patients with atypical angina or nonischemic chest pain, or female patients with angina.

B ☑ **Q0081** **Infusion therapy, using other than chemotherapeutic drugs, per visit**
AHA: 1Q,'02,7; 4Q,'02,7

B ☑ **Q0083** **Chemotherapy administration by other than infusion technique only (e.g., subcutaneous, intramuscular, push), per visit**

B ☑ **Q0084** **Chemotherapy administration by infusion technique only, per visit**

B ☑ **Q0085** **Chemotherapy administration by both infusion technique and other technique(s) (e.g. subcutaneous, intramuscular, push), per visit**

T **Q0091** **Screening Papanicolaou smear; obtaining, preparing and conveyance of cervical or vaginal smear to laboratory** A ♀ ⊘
One pap test is covered by Medicare every two years for low risk patients and every one year for high risk patients. Q0091 can be reported with an E/M code when a separately identifiable E/M service is provided.
MED: 100-3, 190.2
AHA: 4Q,'02,8

N **Q0092** **Set-up portable x-ray equipment**
MED: 100-4,13,90.4

A **Q0111** **Wet mounts, including preparations of vaginal, cervical or skin specimens**

A **Q0112** **All potassium hydroxide (KOH) preparations**

A **Q0113** **Pinworm examinations**

A **Q0114** **Fern test** ♀

A **Q0115** **Postcoital direct, qualitative examinations of vaginal or cervical mucous** A ♀

K ☑ **Q0138** **Injection, ferumoxytol, for treatment of iron deficiency anemia, 1 mg (non-ESRD use)** K2
Use this code for Feraheme.

A ☑ **Q0139** **Injection, ferumoxytol, for treatment of iron deficiency anemia, 1 mg (for ESRD on dialysis)**
Use this code for Feraheme.

E ☑ **Q0144** **Azithromycin dihydrate, oral, capsules/powder, 1 g**
Use this code for Zithromax, Zithromax Z-PAK.

● N ☑ **Q0162** Jan **Ondansetron 1 mg, oral, FDA approved prescription antiemetic, for use as a complete therapeutic substitute for an IV antiemetic at the time of chemotherapy treatment, not to exceed a 48 hour dosage regimen** N1
Use this code for Zofran, Zuplenz.

N ☑ **Q0163** **Diphenhydramine HCl, 50 mg, oral, FDA approved prescription antiemetic, for use as a complete therapeutic substitute for an IV antiemetic at time of chemotherapy treatment not to exceed a 48-hour dosage regimen** N1
See also J1200. Medicare covers at the time of chemotherapy if regimen doesn't exceed 48 hours. Submit on the same claim as the chemotherapy. Use this code for Truxadryl.
AHA: 1Q,'02,2

N ☑ **Q0164** **Prochlorperazine maleate, 5 mg, oral, FDA approved prescription antiemetic, for use as a complete therapeutic substitute for an IV antiemetic at the time of chemotherapy treatment, not to exceed a 48-hour dosage regimen** N1
Medicare covers at the time of chemotherapy if regimen doesn't exceed 48 hours. Submit on the same claim as the chemotherapy. Use this code for Compazine.

N ☑ **Q0165** **Prochlorperazine maleate, 10 mg, oral, FDA approved prescription antiemetic, for use as a complete therapeutic substitute for an IV antiemetic at the time of chemotherapy treatment, not to exceed a 48-hour dosage regimen**
Medicare covers at the time of chemotherapy if regimen doesn't exceed 48 hours. Submit on the same claim as the chemotherapy. Use this code for Compazine.

N ☑ **Q0166** **Granisetron HCl, 1 mg, oral, FDA approved prescription antiemetic, for use as a complete therapeutic substitute for an IV antiemetic at the time of chemotherapy treatment, not to exceed a 24-hour dosage regimen** N1
Medicare covers at the time of chemotherapy if regimen doesn't exceed 48 hours. Submit on the same claim as the chemotherapy. Use this code for Kytril.

N ☑ **Q0167** **Dronabinol, 2.5 mg, oral, FDA approved prescription antiemetic, for use as a complete therapeutic substitute for an IV antiemetic at the time of chemotherapy treatment, not to exceed a 48-hour dosage regimen** N1
Medicare covers at the time of chemotherapy if regimen doesn't exceed 48 hours. Submit on the same claim as the chemotherapy. Use this code for Marinol.

N ☑ **Q0168** **Dronabinol, 5 mg, oral, FDA approved prescription antiemetic, for use as a complete therapeutic substitute for an IV antiemetic at the time of chemotherapy treatment, not to exceed a 48-hour dosage regimen**
Use this code for Marinol.

N ☑ **Q0169** **Promethazine HCl, 12.5 mg, oral, FDA approved prescription antiemetic, for use as a complete therapeutic substitute for an IV antiemetic at the time of chemotherapy treatment, not to exceed a 48-hour dosage regimen** N1
Medicare covers at the time of chemotherapy if regimen doesn't exceed 48 hours. Submit on the same claim as the chemotherapy. Use this code for Phenergan, Amergan.

N ☑ **Q0170** **Promethazine HCl, 25 mg, oral, FDA approved prescription antiemetic, for use as a complete therapeutic substitute for an IV antiemetic at the time of chemotherapy treatment, not to exceed a 48-hour dosage regimen**
Medicare covers at the time of chemotherapy if regimen doesn't exceed 48 hours. Submit on the same claim as the chemotherapy. Use this code for Phenergan, Amergan.

N ☑ **Q0171** **Chlorpromazine HCl, 10 mg, oral, FDA approved prescription antiemetic, for use as a complete therapeutic substitute for an IV antiemetic at the time of chemotherapy treatment, not to exceed a 48-hour dosage regimen** N1
Medicare covers at the time of chemotherapy if regimen doesn't exceed 48 hours. Submit on the same claim as the chemotherapy. Use this code for Thorazine.

Jan January Update

Special Coverage Instructions | Noncovered by Medicare | Carrier Discretion | ☑ Quantity Alert | ● New Code | ○ Recycled/Reinstated | ▲ Revised Code

 A Age Edit | M Maternity Edit | ♀ Female Only | ♂ Male Only | A-Y OPPS Status Indicators

N ☑ Q0172 **Chlorpromazine HCl, 25 mg, oral, FDA approved prescription antiemetic, for use as a complete therapeutic substitute for an IV antiemetic at the time of chemotherapy treatment, not to exceed a 48-hour dosage regimen**
Medicare covers at the time of chemotherapy if regimen doesn't exceed 48 hours. Submit on the same claim as the chemotherapy. Use this code for Thorazine.

N ☑ Q0173 **Trimethobenzamide HCl, 250 mg, oral, FDA approved prescription antiemetic, for use as a complete therapeutic substitute for an IV antiemetic at the time of chemotherapy treatment, not to exceed a 48-hour dosage regimen** N1
Medicare covers at the time of chemotherapy if regimen doesn't exceed 48 hours. Submit on the same claim as the chemotherapy. Use this code for Tebamide, T-Gen, Ticon, Tigan, Triban, Thimazide.

E ☑ Q0174 **Thiethylperazine maleate, 10 mg, oral, FDA approved prescription antiemetic, for use as a complete therapeutic substitute for an IV antiemetic at the time of chemotherapy treatment, not to exceed a 48-hour dosage regimen**
Medicare covers at the time of chemotherapy if regimen doesn't exceed 48 hours. Submit on the same claim as the chemotherapy.

N ☑ Q0175 **Perphenazine, 4 mg, oral, FDA approved prescription antiemetic, for use as a complete therapeutic substitute for an IV antiemetic at the time of chemotherapy treatment, not to exceed a 48 hour dosage regimen** N1
Medicare covers at the time of chemotherapy if regimen doesn't exceed 48 hours. Submit on the same claim as the chemotherapy. Use this code for Trilifon.

N ☑ Q0176 **Perphenazine, 8 mg, oral, FDA approved prescription antiemetic, for use as a complete therapeutic substitute for an IV antiemetic at the time of chemotherapy treatment, not to exceed a 48 hour dosage regimen**
Medicare covers at the time of chemotherapy if regimen doesn't exceed 48 hours. Submit on the same claim as the chemotherapy. Use this code for Trilifon.

N ☑ Q0177 **Hydroxyzine pamoate, 25 mg, oral, FDA approved prescription antiemetic, for use as a complete therapeutic substitute for an IV antiemetic at the time of chemotherapy treatment, not to exceed a 48-hour dosage regimen** N1
Medicare covers at the time of chemotherapy if regimen doesn't exceed 48 hours. Submit on the same claim as the chemotherapy. Use this code for Vistaril.

N ☑ Q0178 **Hydroxyzine pamoate, 50 mg, oral, FDA approved prescription antiemetic, for use as a complete therapeutic substitute for an IV antiemetic at the time of chemotherapy treatment, not to exceed a 48-hour dosage regimen**
Medicare covers at the time of chemotherapy if regimen doesn't exceed 48 hours. Submit on the same claim as the chemotherapy.

~~Q0179~~ Jan ~~Ondansetron HCl 8 mg, oral, FDA approved prescription antiemetic, for use as a complete therapeutic substitute for an IV antiemetic at the time of chemotherapy treatment, not to exceed a 48-hour dosage regimen~~
To report, see Q0162

N ☑ Q0180 **Dolasetron mesylate, 100 mg, oral, FDA approved prescription antiemetic, for use as a complete therapeutic substitute for an IV antiemetic at the time of chemotherapy treatment, not to exceed a 24-hour dosage regimen** N1
Medicare covers at the time of chemotherapy if regimen doesn't exceed 24 hours. Submit on the same claim as the chemotherapy. Use this code for Anzemet.

E Q0181 **Unspecified oral dosage form, FDA approved prescription antiemetic, for use as a complete therapeutic substitute for an IV antiemetic at the time of chemotherapy treatment, not to exceed a 48-hour dosage regimen**
Medicare covers at the time of chemotherapy if regimen doesn't exceed 48-hours. Submit on the same claim as the chemotherapy.

A Q0478 **Power adapter for use with electric or electric/pneumatic ventricular assist device, vehicle type** ♿

A Q0479 **Power module for use with electric or electric/pneumatic ventricular assist device, replacement only** ♿

A Q0480 **Driver for use with pneumatic ventricular assist device, replacement only** ♿
AHA: 3Q,'05,2

A Q0481 **Microprocessor control unit for use with electric ventricular assist device, replacement only** ♿
AHA: 3Q,'05,2

A Q0482 **Microprocessor control unit for use with electric/pneumatic combination ventricular assist device, replacement only** ♿
AHA: 3Q,'05,2

A Q0483 **Monitor/display module for use with electric ventricular assist device, replacement only** ♿
AHA: 3Q,'05,2

A Q0484 **Monitor/display module for use with electric or electric/pneumatic ventricular assist device, replacement only** ♿
AHA: 3Q,'05,2

A Q0485 **Monitor control cable for use with electric ventricular assist device, replacement only** ♿
AHA: 3Q,'05,2

A Q0486 **Monitor control cable for use with electric/pneumatic ventricular assist device, replacement only** ♿
AHA: 3Q,'05,2

A Q0487 **Leads (pneumatic/electrical) for use with any type electric/pneumatic ventricular assist device, replacement only** ♿
AHA: 3Q,'05,2

A Q0488 **Power pack base for use with electric ventricular assist device, replacement only**
AHA: 3Q,'05,2

A Q0489 **Power pack base for use with electric/pneumatic ventricular assist device, replacement only** ♿
AHA: 3Q,'05,2

A Q0490 **Emergency power source for use with electric ventricular assist device, replacement only** ♿
AHA: 3Q,'05,2

A Q0491 **Emergency power source for use with electric/pneumatic ventricular assist device, replacement only** ♿
AHA: 3Q,'05,2

A Q0492 **Emergency power supply cable for use with electric ventricular assist device, replacement only** ♿
AHA: 3Q,'05,2

A **Q0493** Emergency power supply cable for use with electric/pneumatic ventricular assist device, replacement only
AHA: 3Q,'05,2

A **Q0494** Emergency hand pump for use with electric or electric/pneumatic ventricular assist device, replacement only
AHA: 3Q,'05,2

A **Q0495** Battery/power pack charger for use with electric or electric/pneumatic ventricular assist device, replacement only
AHA: 3Q,'05,2

A **Q0496** Battery, other than lithium-ion, for use with electric or electric/pneumatic ventricular assist device, replacement only
AHA: 3Q,'05,2

A **Q0497** Battery clips for use with electric or electric/pneumatic ventricular assist device, replacement only
AHA: 3Q,'05,2

A **Q0498** Holster for use with electric or electric/pneumatic ventricular assist device, replacement only
AHA: 3Q,'05,2

A **Q0499** Belt/vest/bag for use to carry external peripheral components of any type ventricular assist device, replacement only
AHA: 3Q,'05,2

A ☑ **Q0500** Filters for use with electric or electric/pneumatic ventricular assist device, replacement only
The base unit for this code is for each filter.
AHA: 3Q,'05,2

A **Q0501** Shower cover for use with electric or electric/pneumatic ventricular assist device, replacement only
AHA: 3Q,'05,2

A **Q0502** Mobility cart for pneumatic ventricular assist device, replacement only
AHA: 3Q,'05,2

A ☑ **Q0503** Battery for pneumatic ventricular assist device, replacement only, each
AHA: 3Q,'05,2

A **Q0504** Power adapter for pneumatic ventricular assist device, replacement only, vehicle type
AHA: 3Q,'05,2

A **Q0505** Miscellaneous supply or accessory for use with ventricular assist device
AHA: 3Q,'05,2

A **Q0506** Battery, lithium-ion, for use with electric or electric/pneumatic ventricular assist device, replacement only

B **Q0510** Pharmacy supply fee for initial immunosuppressive drug(s), first month following transplant

B **Q0511** Pharmacy supply fee for oral anticancer, oral antiemetic, or immunosuppressive drug(s); for the first prescription in a 30-day period

B **Q0512** Pharmacy supply fee for oral anticancer, oral antiemetic, or immunosuppressive drug(s); for a subsequent prescription in a 30-day period

B **Q0513** Pharmacy dispensing fee for inhalation drug(s); per 30 days

B **Q0514** Pharmacy dispensing fee for inhalation drug(s); per 90 days

K ☑ **Q0515** Injection, sermorelin acetate, 1 mcg K2

~~Q1003~~ Jan ~~New technology, intraocular lens, category 3 (reduced spherical aberration)~~
To report, see C1780-C1300

▲ E **Q1004** Jan New technology, intraocular lens, category 4 as defined in Federal Register notice

▲ E **Q1005** Jan New technology, intraocular lens, category 5 as defined in Federal Register notice

N ☑ **Q2004** Irrigation solution for treatment of bladder calculi, for example renacidin, per 500 ml N1

N ☑ **Q2009** Injection, fosphenytoin, 50 mg phenytoin equivalent N1
Use this code for Cerebyx.

K ☑ **Q2017** Injection, teniposide, 50 mg K2
Use this code for Vumon.

B ☑ **Q2026** Injection, Radiesse, 0.1 ml
MED: 100-3,250.5; 100-4,32,260.1; 100-4,32,260.2.1; 100-4,32,260.2.2; 100-4,32,260.2.2

B ☑ **Q2027** Injection, Sculptra, 0.1 ml
MED: 100-3,250.5; 100-4,32,260.1; 100-4,32,260.2.2

L **Q2035** Influenza virus vaccine, split virus, when administered to individuals 3 years of age and older, for intramuscular use (AFLURIA) A L1
MED: 100-2,15,50.4.4.2

L **Q2036** Influenza virus vaccine, split virus, when administered to individuals 3 years of age and older, for intramuscular use (FLULAVAL) A L1

L **Q2037** Influenza virus vaccine, split virus, when administered to individuals 3 years of age and older, for intramuscular use (FLUVIRIN) A L1

L **Q2038** Influenza virus vaccine, split virus, when administered to individuals 3 years of age and older, for intramuscular use (Fluzone) A L1

L **Q2039** Influenza virus vaccine, split virus, when administered to individuals 3 years of age and older, for intramuscular use (not otherwise specified) A L1

~~Q2040~~ Jan ~~Injection, incobotulinumtoxinA, 1 unit~~
To report, see J0588

~~Q2041~~ Jan ~~Injection, von Willebrand factor complex (human), Wilate, 1 IU VWF:RCo~~
To report, see J7183

~~Q2042~~ Jan ~~Injection, hydroxyprogesterone caproate, 1 mg~~
To report, see J1725

● G ☑ **Q2043** Jan Sipuleucel-T, minimum of 50 million autologous cd54+ cells activated with PAP-GM-CSF, including leukapheresis and all other preparatory procedures, per infusion ♂ K2
Use this code for PROVENGE.

~~Q2044~~ Jan ~~Injection, belimumab, 10 mg~~
To report, see J0490

B ☑ **Q3001** Radioelements for brachytherapy, any type, each ⊘

A **Q3014** Telehealth originating site facility fee ⊘

K ☑ **Q3025** Injection, interferon beta-1a, 11 mcg for intramuscular use K2
Use this code for Avonex, Rebif. See also J1825.

E ☑ **Q3026** Injection, interferon beta-1a, 11 mcg for subcutaneous use
Use this code for Avonex, Rebif. See also J1825.

N **Q3031** Collagen skin test

Jan January Update

Special Coverage Instructions | Noncovered by Medicare | Carrier Discretion | ☑ Quantity Alert | ● New Code | ○ Recycled/Reinstated | ▲ Revised Code

 A Age Edit | M Maternity Edit | ♀ Female Only | ♂ Male Only | A-Y OPPS Status Indicators

B **Q4001** Casting supplies, body cast adult, with or without head, plaster A
MED: 100-4,20,170

B **Q4002** Cast supplies, body cast adult, with or without head, fiberglass A
MED: 100-4,20,170

B **Q4003** Cast supplies, shoulder cast, adult (11 years +), plaster A
MED: 100-4,20,170

B **Q4004** Cast supplies, shoulder cast, adult (11 years +), fiberglass A
MED: 100-4,20,170

B **Q4005** Cast supplies, long arm cast, adult (11 years +), plaster A
MED: 100-4,20,170

B **Q4006** Cast supplies, long arm cast, adult (11 years +), fiberglass A
MED: 100-4,20,170

B **Q4007** Cast supplies, long arm cast, pediatric (0-10 years), plaster A
MED: 100-4,20,170

B **Q4008** Cast supplies, long arm cast, pediatric (0-10 years), fiberglass A
MED: 100-4,20,170

B **Q4009** Cast supplies, short arm cast, adult (11 years +), plaster A
MED: 100-4,20,170

B **Q4010** Cast supplies, short arm cast, adult (11 years +), fiberglass A
MED: 100-4,20,170

B **Q4011** Cast supplies, short arm cast, pediatric (0-10 years), plaster A
MED: 100-4,20,170

B **Q4012** Cast supplies, short arm cast, pediatric (0-10 years), fiberglass A
MED: 100-4,20,170

B **Q4013** Cast supplies, gauntlet cast (includes lower forearm and hand), adult (11 years +), plaster A
MED: 100-4,20,170

B **Q4014** Cast supplies, gauntlet cast (includes lower forearm and hand), adult (11 years +), fiberglass A
MED: 100-4,20,170

B **Q4015** Cast supplies, gauntlet cast (includes lower forearm and hand), pediatric (0-10 years), plaster A
MED: 100-4,20,170

B **Q4016** Cast supplies, gauntlet cast (includes lower forearm and hand), pediatric (0-10 years), fiberglass A
MED: 100-4,20,170

B **Q4017** Cast supplies, long arm splint, adult (11 years +), plaster A
MED: 100-4,20,170

B **Q4018** Cast supplies, long arm splint, adult (11 years +), fiberglass A
MED: 100-4,20,170

B **Q4019** Cast supplies, long arm splint, pediatric (0-10 years), plaster A
MED: 100-4,20,170

B **Q4020** Cast supplies, long arm splint, pediatric (0-10 years), fiberglass A
MED: 100-4,20,170

B **Q4021** Cast supplies, short arm splint, adult (11 years +), plaster A
MED: 100-4,20,170

B **Q4022** Cast supplies, short arm splint, adult (11 years +), fiberglass A
MED: 100-4,20,170

B **Q4023** Cast supplies, short arm splint, pediatric (0-10 years), plaster A
MED: 100-4,20,170

B **Q4024** Cast supplies, short arm splint, pediatric (0-10 years), fiberglass A
MED: 100-4,20,170

B **Q4025** Cast supplies, hip spica (one or both legs), adult (11 years +), plaster A
MED: 100-4,20,170

B **Q4026** Cast supplies, hip spica (one or both legs), adult (11 years +), fiberglass A
MED: 100-4,20,170

B **Q4027** Cast supplies, hip spica (one or both legs), pediatric (0-10 years), plaster A
MED: 100-4,20,170

B **Q4028** Cast supplies, hip spica (one or both legs), pediatric (0-10 years), fiberglass A
MED: 100-4,20,170

B **Q4029** Cast supplies, long leg cast, adult (11 years +), plaster A
MED: 100-4,20,170

B **Q4030** Cast supplies, long leg cast, adult (11 years +), fiberglass A
MED: 100-4,20,170

B **Q4031** Cast supplies, long leg cast, pediatric (0-10 years), plaster A
MED: 100-4,20,170

B **Q4032** Cast supplies, long leg cast, pediatric (0-10 years), fiberglass A
MED: 100-4,20,170

B **Q4033** Cast supplies, long leg cylinder cast, adult (11 years +), plaster A
MED: 100-4,20,170

B **Q4034** Cast supplies, long leg cylinder cast, adult (11 years +), fiberglass A
MED: 100-4,20,170

B **Q4035** Cast supplies, long leg cylinder cast, pediatric (0-10 years), plaster A
MED: 100-4,20,170

B **Q4036** Cast supplies, long leg cylinder cast, pediatric (0-10 years), fiberglass A
MED: 100-4,20,170

B **Q4037** Cast supplies, short leg cast, adult (11 years +), plaster A
MED: 100-4,20,170

B **Q4038** Cast supplies, short leg cast, adult (11 years +), fiberglass A
MED: 100-4,20,170

B **Q4039** Cast supplies, short leg cast, pediatric (0-10 years), plaster A
MED: 100-4,20,170

B **Q4040** Cast supplies, short leg cast, pediatric (0-10 years), fiberglass A
MED: 100-4,20,170

B Q4041 Cast supplies, long leg splint, adult (11 years +), plaster A
MED: 100-4,20,170

B Q4042 Cast supplies, long leg splint, adult (11 years +), fiberglass A
MED: 100-4,20,170

B Q4043 Cast supplies, long leg splint, pediatric (0-10 years), plaster A
MED: 100-4,20,170

B Q4044 Cast supplies, long leg splint, pediatric (0-10 years), fiberglass A
MED: 100-4,20,170

B Q4045 Cast supplies, short leg splint, adult (11 years +), plaster A
MED: 100-4,20,170

B Q4046 Cast supplies, short leg splint, adult (11 years +), fiberglass A
MED: 100-4,20,170

B Q4047 Cast supplies, short leg splint, pediatric (0-10 years), plaster A
MED: 100-4,20,170

B Q4048 Cast supplies, short leg splint, pediatric (0-10 years), fiberglass A
MED: 100-4,20,170

B Q4049 Finger splint, static
MED: 100-4,20,170

B Q4050 Cast supplies, for unlisted types and materials of casts
MED: 100-4,20,170

B Q4051 Splint supplies, miscellaneous (includes thermoplastics, strapping, fasteners, padding and other supplies)
MED: 100-4,20,170

Y ☑ Q4074 Iloprost, inhalation solution, FDA-approved final product, noncompounded, administered through DME, unit dose form, up to 20 mcg

A ☑ Q4081 Injection, epoetin alfa, 100 units (for ESRD on dialysis)
MED: 100-4,8,60.4; 100-4,8,60.4.1

B Q4082 Drug or biological, not otherwise classified, Part B drug competitive acquisition program (CAP)

N ☑ Q4100 Skin substitute, not otherwise specified N1

K ☑ Q4101 Apligraf, per sq cm K2

K ☑ Q4102 Oasis wound matrix, per sq cm K2

K ☑ Q4103 Oasis burn matrix, per sq cm K2

K ☑ Q4104 Integra bilayer matrix wound dressing (BMWD), per sq cm K2

K ☑ Q4105 Integra dermal regeneration template (DRT), per sq cm K2

K ☑ Q4106 Dermagraft, per sq cm K2

K ☑ Q4107 GRAFTJACKET, per sq cm K2

K ☑ Q4108 Integra matrix, per sq cm K2

K ☑ Q4110 PriMatrix, per sq cm K2

K ☑ Q4111 GammaGraft, per sq cm K2

K ☑ Q4112 Cymetra, injectable, 1 cc K2

▲ K ☑ Q4113 Jan GRAFTJACKET XPRESS, injectable, 1cc K2

K ☑ Q4114 Integra flowable wound matrix, injectable, 1 cc K2

K ☑ Q4115 AlloSkin, per sq cm K2

K ☑ Q4116 AlloDerm, per sq cm K2

E ☑ Q4117 HYALOMATRIX, per sq cm

K ☑ Q4118 MatriStem micromatrix, 1 mg K2

K Q4119 MatriStem wound matrix, per sq cm K2

E ☑ Q4120 MatriStem burn matrix, per sq cm

K ☑ Q4121 TheraSkin, per sq cm K2

● K ☑ Q4122 Jan DermACELL, per sq cm K2

● E ☑ Q4123 Jan AlloSkin RT, per sq cm

● G ☑ Q4124 Jan OASIS ultra tri-layer wound matrix, per sq cm K2

● E ☑ Q4125 Jan Arthroflex, per sq cm

● E ☑ Q4126 Jan MemoDerm, per sq cm

● E ☑ Q4127 Jan Talymed, per sq cm

● E ☑ Q4128 Jan FlexHD or AllopatchHD, per sq cm

● E ☑ Q4129 Jan Unite biomatrix, per sq cm

● N ☑ Q4130 Jan Strattice TM, per sq cm N1

B Q5001 Hospice care provided in patient's home/residence
MED: 100-4,11,30.3

B Q5002 Hospice care provided in assisted living facility

B Q5003 Hospice care provided in nursing long-term care facility (LTC) or nonskilled nursing facility (NF)
MED: 100-4,11,30.3

B Q5004 Hospice care provided in skilled nursing facility (SNF)

B Q5005 Hospice care provided in inpatient hospital

B Q5006 Hospice care provided in inpatient hospice facility

B Q5007 Hospice care provided in long-term care facility

B Q5008 Hospice care provided in inpatient psychiatric facility

B Q5009 Hospice care provided in place not otherwise specified (NOS)

B Q5010 Hospice home care provided in a hospice facility

N ☑ Q9951 Low osmolar contrast material, 400 or greater mg/ml iodine concentration, per ml N1
Use this code for ULTRAVIST 240, 300, 370.
MED: 100-4,13,40

N ☑ Q9953 Injection, iron-based magnetic resonance contrast agent, per ml N1

N ☑ Q9954 Oral magnetic resonance contrast agent, per 100 ml N1

N ☑ Q9955 Injection, perflexane lipid microspheres, per ml N1

N ☑ Q9956 Injection, octafluoropropane microspheres, per ml N1

N ☑ Q9957 Injection, perflutren lipid microspheres, per ml N1

N ☑ Q9958 High osmolar contrast material, up to 149 mg/ml iodine concentration, per ml N1
MED: 100-4,13,40
AHA: 3Q,'05,7

N ☑ Q9959 High osmolar contrast material, 150-199 mg/ml iodine concentration, per ml N1
AHA: 3Q,'05,7

N ☑ Q9960 High osmolar contrast material, 200-249 mg/ml iodine concentration, per ml N1
AHA: 3Q,'05,7

N ☑ Q9961 High osmolar contrast material, 250-299 mg/ml iodine concentration, per ml N1
AHA: 3Q,'05,7

N ☑ **Q9962** **High osmolar contrast material, 300-349 mg/ml iodine concentration, per ml** N1

AHA: 3Q,'05,7

N ☑ **Q9963** **High osmolar contrast material, 350-399 mg/ml iodine concentration, per ml** N1

AHA: 3Q,'05,7

N ☑ **Q9964** **High osmolar contrast material, 400 or greater mg/ml iodine concentration, per ml** N1

AHA: 3Q,'05,7

N ☑ **Q9965** **Low osmolar contrast material, 100-199 mg/ml iodine concentration, per ml** N1

Use this code for Omnipaque 140, Omnipaque 180, Optiray 160, Optiray 140.

N ☑ **Q9966** **Low osmolar contrast material, 200-299 mg/ml iodine concentration, per ml** N1

Use this code for Omnipaque 240, Optiray 240.

N ☑ **Q9967** **Low osmolar contrast material, 300-399 mg/ml iodine concentration, per ml** N1

Use this code for Omnipaque 300, Omnipaque 350, Optiray, Optiray 300, Optiray 320, Oxilan 300, Oxilan 350, ULTRAVIST 150.

N ☑ **Q9968** **Injection, nonradioactive, noncontrast, visualization adjunct (e.g., methylene blue, isosulfan blue), 1 mg** N1

DIAGNOSTIC RADIOLOGY SERVICES R0000-R5999

R codes are used for the transportation of portable x-ray and/or EKG equipment.

B ☑ **R0070** **Transportation of portable x-ray equipment and personnel to home or nursing home, per trip to facility or location, one patient seen**

Only a single, reasonable transportation charge is allowed for each trip the portable x-ray supplier makes to a location. When more than one patient is x-rayed at the same location, prorate the single allowable transport charge among all patients.

MED: 100-4,13,90.3

B ☑ **R0075** **Transportation of portable x-ray equipment and personnel to home or nursing home, per trip to facility or location, more than one patient seen**

Only a single, reasonable transportation charge is allowed for each trip the portable x-ray supplier makes to a location. When more than one patient is x-rayed at the same location, prorate the single allowable transport charge among all patients.

MED: 100-4,13,90.3

B ☑ **R0076** **Transportation of portable EKG to facility or location, per patient**

Only a single, reasonable transportation charge is allowed for each trip the portable EKG supplier makes to a location. When more than one patient is tested at the same location, prorate the single allowable transport charge among all patients.

MED: 100-4,13,90.3

TEMPORARY NATIONAL CODES (NON-MEDICARE) S0000-S9999

The S codes are used by the Blue Cross/Blue Shield Association (BCBSA) and the Health Insurance Association of America (HIAA) to report drugs, services, and supplies for which there are no national codes but for which codes are needed by the private sector to implement policies, programs, or claims processing. They are for the purpose of meeting the particular needs of the private sector. These codes are also used by the Medicaid program, but they are not payable by Medicare.

☑ **S0012** **Butorphanol tartrate, nasal spray, 25 mg**
Use this code for Stadol NS.

☑ **S0014** **Tacrine HCl, 10 mg**
Use this code for Cognex.

☑ **S0017** **Injection, aminocaproic acid, 5 g**
Use this code for Amicar.

☑ **S0020** **Injection, bupivicaine HCl, 30 ml**
Use this code for Marcaine, Sensorcaine.

☑ **S0021** **Injection, cefoperazone sodium, 1 g**
Use this code for Cefobid.

☑ **S0023** **Injection, cimetidine HCl, 300 mg**
Use this code for Tagamet HCl.

☑ **S0028** **Injection, famotidine, 20 mg**
Use this code for Pepcid.

☑ **S0030** **Injection, metronidazole, 500 mg**
Use this code for Flagyl IV RTU.

☑ **S0032** **Injection, nafcillin sodium, 2 g**
Use this code for Nallpen, Unipen.

☑ **S0034** **Injection, ofloxacin, 400 mg**
Use this code for Floxin IV.

☑ **S0039** **Injection, sulfamethoxazole and trimethoprim, 10 ml**
Use this code for Bactrim IV, Septra IV, SMZ-TMP, Sulfutrim.

☑ **S0040** **Injection, ticarcillin disodium and clavulanate potassium, 3.1 g**
Use this code for Timentin.

☑ **S0073** **Injection, aztreonam, 500 mg**
Use this code for Azactam.

☑ **S0074** **Injection, cefotetan disodium, 500 mg**
Use this code for Cefotan.

☑ **S0077** **Injection, clindamycin phosphate, 300 mg**
Use this code for Cleocin Phosphate.

☑ **S0078** **Injection, fosphenytoin sodium, 750 mg**
Use this code for Cerebryx.

☑ **S0080** **Injection, pentamidine isethionate, 300 mg**
Use this code for NebuPent, Pentam 300, Pentacarinat. See also code J2545.

☑ **S0081** **Injection, piperacillin sodium, 500 mg**
Use this code for Pipracil.

☑ **S0088** **Imatinib, 100 mg**
Use this code for Gleevec.

☑ **S0090** **Sildenafil citrate, 25 mg** A
Use this code for Viagra.

☑ **S0091** **Granisetron HCl, 1 mg (for circumstances falling under the Medicare statute, use Q0166)**
Use this code for Kytril.

☑ **S0092** **Injection, hydromorphone HCl, 250 mg (loading dose for infusion pump)**
Use this code for Dilaudid, Hydromophone. See also J1170.

☑ **S0093** **Injection, morphine sulfate, 500 mg (loading dose for infusion pump)**
Use this code for Duramorph, MS Contin, Morphine Sulfate. See also J2270, J2271, J2275.

S0104 **Zidovudine, oral, 100 mg**
See also J3485 for Retrovir.

☑ **S0106** **Bupropion HCl sustained release tablet, 150 mg, per bottle of 60 tablets**
Use this code for Wellbutrin SR tablets.

☑ **S0108** **Mercaptopurine, oral, 50 mg**
Use this code for Purinethol oral.

☑ **S0109** **Methadone, oral, 5 mg**
Use this code for Dolophine.

☑ **S0117** **Tretinoin, topical, 5 g**

● ☑ **S0119** Jan **Ondansetron, oral, 4 mg (for circumstances falling under the Medicare statute, use HCPCS Q code)**
Use this code for Zofran, Zuplenz.

☑ **S0122** **Injection, menotropins, 75 IU**
Use this code for Humegon, Pergonal, Repronex.

☑ **S0126** **Injection, follitropin alfa, 75 IU**
Use this code for Gonal-F.

☑ **S0128** **Injection, follitropin beta, 75 IU** ♀
Use this code for Follistim.

S0132 **Injection, ganirelix acetate, 250 mcg** ♀
Use this code for Antagon.

☑ **S0136** **Clozapine, 25 mg**
Use this code for Clozaril.

☑ **S0137** **Didanosine (ddI), 25 mg**
Use this code for Videx.

☑ **S0138** **Finasteride, 5 mg** ♂
Use this code for Propecia (oral), Proscar (oral).

☑ **S0139** **Minoxidil, 10 mg**

☑ **S0140** **Saquinavir, 200 mg**
Use this code for Fortovase (oral), Invirase (oral).

☑ **S0142** **Colistimethate sodium, inhalation solution administered through DME, concentrated form, per mg**

S0145 **Injection, pegylated interferon alfa-2a, 180 mcg per ml**
Use this code for Pegasys.

☑ **S0148** **Injection, pegylated interferon alfa-2B, 10 mcg**

☑ **S0155** **Sterile dilutant for epoprostenol, 50 ml**
Use this code for Flolan.

☑ **S0156** **Exemestane, 25 mg**
Use this code for Aromasin.

☑ **S0157** **Becaplermin gel 0.01%, 0.5 gm**
Use this code for Regraex Gel.

☑ **S0160** **Dextroamphetamine sulfate, 5 mg**

☑ **S0164** **Injection, pantoprazole sodium, 40 mg**
Use this code for Protonix IV.

☑ **S0166** **Injection, olanzapine, 2.5 mg**
Use this code for Zyprexa.

☑ **S0169** **Calcitrol, 0.25 mcg**
Use this code for Calcijex.

Jan January Update

☑ **S0170** Anastrozole, oral, 1 mg
Use this code for Arimidex.

☑ **S0171** Injection, bumetanide, 0.5 mg
Use this code for Bumex.

☑ **S0172** Chlorambucil, oral, 2 mg
Use this code for Leukeran.

☑ **S0174** Dolasetron mesylate, oral 50 mg (for circumstances falling under the Medicare statute, use Q0180)
Use this code for Anzemet.

☑ **S0175** Flutamide, oral, 125 mg
Use this code for Eulexin.

☑ **S0176** Hydroxyurea, oral, 500 mg
Use this code for Droxia, Hydrea, Mylocel.

☑ **S0177** Levamisole HCl, oral, 50 mg
Use this code for Ergamisol.

☑ **S0178** Lomustine, oral, 10 mg
Use this code for Ceenu.

☑ **S0179** Megestrol acetate, oral, 20 mg
Use this code for Megace.

~~S0181~~ Jan ~~Ondansetron HCl, oral, 4 mg (for circumstances falling under the Medicare statute, use Q0179)~~
To report, see S0119

☑ **S0182** Procarbazine HCl, oral, 50 mg
Use this code for Matulane.

☑ **S0183** Prochlorperazine maleate, oral, 5 mg (for circumstances falling under the Medicare statute, use Q0164-Q0165)
Use this code for Compazine.

☑ **S0187** Tamoxifen citrate, oral, 10 mg
Use this code for Nolvadex.

☑ **S0189** Testosterone pellet, 75 mg

☑ **S0190** Mifepristone, oral, 200 mg ♀
Use this code for Mifoprex 200 mg oral.

☑ **S0191** Misoprostol, oral, 200 mcg

☑ **S0194** Dialysis/stress vitamin supplement, oral, 100 capsules

S0195 Pneumococcal conjugate vaccine, polyvalent, intramuscular, for children from 5 years to 9 years of age who have not previously received the vaccine A
Use this code for Pneumovax II.

☑ **S0197** Prenatal vitamins, 30-day supply M ♀

S0199 Medically induced abortion by oral ingestion of medication including all associated services and supplies (e.g., patient counseling, office visits, confirmation of pregnancy by HCG, ultrasound to confirm duration of pregnancy, ultrasound to confirm completion of abortion) except drugs ♀

S0201 Partial hospitalization services, less than 24 hours, per diem

S0207 Paramedic intercept, nonhospital-based ALS service (nonvoluntary), nontransport

S0208 Paramedic intercept, hospital-based ALS service (nonvoluntary), nontransport

☑ **S0209** Wheelchair van, mileage, per mile

☑ **S0215** Nonemergency transportation; mileage, per mile
See also codes A0021-A0999 for transportation.

☑ **S0220** Medical conference by a physician with interdisciplinary team of health professionals or representatives of community agencies to coordinate activities of patient care (patient is present); approximately 30 minutes

☑ **S0221** Medical conference by a physician with interdisciplinary team of health professionals or representatives of community agencies to coordinate activities of patient care (patient is present); approximately 60 minutes

S0250 Comprehensive geriatric assessment and treatment planning performed by assessment team A

S0255 Hospice referral visit (advising patient and family of care options) performed by nurse, social worker, or other designated staff

S0257 Counseling and discussion regarding advance directives or end of life care planning and decisions, with patient and/or surrogate (list separately in addition to code for appropriate evaluation and management service)

S0260 History and physical (outpatient or office) related to surgical procedure (list separately in addition to code for appropriate evaluation and management service)

☑ **S0265** Genetic counseling, under physician supervision, each 15 minutes

☑ **S0270** Physician management of patient home care, standard monthly case rate (per 30 days)

☑ **S0271** Physician management of patient home care, hospice monthly case rate (per 30 days)

☑ **S0272** Physician management of patient home care, episodic care monthly case rate (per 30 days)

S0273 Physician visit at member's home, outside of a capitation arrangement

S0274 Nurse practitioner visit at member's home, outside of a capitation arrangement

S0280 Medical home program, comprehensive care coordination and planning, initial plan

S0281 Medical home program, comprehensive care coordination and planning, maintenance of plan

S0302 Completed early periodic screening diagnosis and treatment (EPSDT) service (list in addition to code for appropriate evaluation and management service)

S0310 Hospitalist services (list separately in addition to code for appropriate evaluation and management service)

S0315 Disease management program; initial assessment and initiation of the program

S0316 Disease management program, follow-up/reassessment

☑ **S0317** Disease management program; per diem

S0320 Telephone calls by a registered nurse to a disease management program member for monitoring purposes; per month

S0340 Lifestyle modification program for management of coronary artery disease, including all supportive services; first quarter/stage

S0341 Lifestyle modification program for management of coronary artery disease, including all supportive services; second or third quarter/stage

S0342 Lifestyle modification program for management of coronary artery disease, including all supportive services; 4th quarter / stage

Jan January Update

Special Coverage Instructions | Noncovered by Medicare | Carrier Discretion | ☑ Quantity Alert | ● New Code | ○ Recycled/Reinstated | ▲ Revised Code

 A Age Edit | M Maternity Edit | ♀ Female Only | ♂ Male Only | A-Y OPPS Status Indicators

S0390 Routine foot care; removal and/or trimming of corns, calluses and/or nails and preventive maintenance in specific medical conditions (e.g., diabetes), per visit

S0395 Impression casting of a foot performed by a practitioner other than the manufacturer of the orthotic

S0400 Global fee for extracorporeal shock wave lithotripsy treatment of kidney stone(s)

☑ S0500 Disposable contact lens, per lens

☑ S0504 Single vision prescription lens (safety, athletic, or sunglass), per lens

☑ S0506 Bifocal vision prescription lens (safety, athletic, or sunglass), per lens

☑ S0508 Trifocal vision prescription lens (safety, athletic, or sunglass), per lens

☑ S0510 Nonprescription lens (safety, athletic, or sunglass), per lens

☑ S0512 Daily wear specialty contact lens, per lens

☑ S0514 Color contact lens, per lens

S0515 Scleral lens, liquid bandage device, per lens

S0516 Safety eyeglass frames

S0518 Sunglasses frames

S0580 Polycarbonate lens (list this code in addition to the basic code for the lens)

S0581 Nonstandard lens (list this code in addition to the basic code for the lens)

S0590 Integral lens service, miscellaneous services reported separately

S0592 Comprehensive contact lens evaluation

S0595 Dispensing new spectacle lenses for patient supplied frame

S0601 Screening proctoscopy ♂

S0610 Annual gynecological examination, new patient ♀

S0612 Annual gynecological examination, established patient ♀

S0613 Annual gynecological examination; clinical breast examination without pelvic evaluation ♀

S0618 Audiometry for hearing aid evaluation to determine the level and degree of hearing loss

S0620 Routine ophthalmological examination including refraction; new patient

S0621 Routine ophthalmological examination including refraction; established patient

S0622 Physical exam for college, new or established patient (list separately in addition to appropriate evaluation and management code) A

~~S0625~~ Jan ~~Retinal telescreening by digital imaging of multiple different fundus areas to screen for vision-threatening conditions, including imaging, interpretation and report~~

S0630 Removal of sutures; by a physician other than the physician who originally closed the wound

S0800 Laser in situ keratomileusis (LASIK)

S0810 Photorefractive keratectomy (PRK)

S0812 Phototherapeutic keratectomy (PTK)

S1001 Deluxe item, patient aware (list in addition to code for basic item)
MED: 100-2,1,10.1.4

S1002 Customized item (list in addition to code for basic item)

S1015 IV tubing extension set

S1016 Non-PVC (polyvinyl chloride) intravenous administration set, for use with drugs that are not stable in PVC e.g., Paclitaxel

S1030 Continuous noninvasive glucose monitoring device, purchase (for physician interpretation of data, use CPT code)

S1031 Continuous noninvasive glucose monitoring device, rental, including sensor, sensor replacement, and download to monitor (for physician interpretation of data, use CPT code)

S1040 Cranial remolding orthotic, pediatric, rigid, with soft interface material, custom fabricated, includes fitting and adjustment(s)

S2053 Transplantation of small intestine and liver allografts

S2054 Transplantation of multivisceral organs

S2055 Harvesting of donor multivisceral organs, with preparation and maintenance of allografts; from cadaver donor

S2060 Lobar lung transplantation

S2061 Donor lobectomy (lung) for transplantation, living donor

S2065 Simultaneous pancreas kidney transplantation

S2066 Breast reconstruction with gluteal artery perforator (GAP) flap, including harvesting of the flap, microvascular transfer, closure of donor site and shaping the flap into a breast, unilateral ♀

S2067 Breast reconstruction of a single breast with "stacked" deep inferior epigastric perforator (DIEP) flap(s) and/or gluteal artery perforator (GAP) flap(s), including harvesting of the flap(s), microvascular transfer, closure of donor site(s) and shaping the flap into a breast, unilateral ♀

S2068 Breast reconstruction with deep inferior epigastric perforator (DIEP) flap or superficial inferior epigastric artery (SIEA) flap, including harvesting of the flap, microvascular transfer, closure of donor site and shaping the flap into a breast, unilateral ♀

S2070 Cystourethroscopy, with ureteroscopy and/or pyeloscopy; with endoscopic laser treatment of ureteral calculi (includes ureteral catheterization)

S2079 Laparoscopic esophagomyotomy (Heller type)

S2080 Laser-assisted uvulopalatoplasty (LAUP)

S2083 Adjustment of gastric band diameter via subcutaneous port by injection or aspiration of saline

S2095 Transcatheter occlusion or embolization for tumor destruction, percutaneous, any method, using yttrium-90 microspheres

S2102 Islet cell tissue transplant from pancreas; allogeneic

S2103 Adrenal tissue transplant to brain

S2107 Adoptive immunotherapy i.e. development of specific antitumor reactivity (e.g., tumor-infiltrating lymphocyte therapy) per course of treatment

S2112 Arthroscopy, knee, surgical for harvesting of cartilage (chondrocyte cells)

S2115 Osteotomy, periacetabular, with internal fixation

S2117 Arthroereisis, subtalar

Jan January Update

Special Coverage Instructions | Noncovered by Medicare | Carrier Discretion | ☑ Quantity Alert | ● New Code | ○ Recycled/Reinstated | ▲ Revised Code

S2118 Metal-on-metal total hip resurfacing, including acetabular and femoral components

S2120 Low density lipoprotein (LDL) apheresis using heparin-induced extracorporeal LDL precipitation

S2140 Cord blood harvesting for transplantation, allogeneic

S2142 Cord blood-derived stem-cell transplantation, allogeneic

S2150 Bone marrow or blood-derived stem cells (peripheral or umbilical), allogeneic or autologous, harvesting, transplantation, and related complications; including: pheresis and cell preparation/storage; marrow ablative therapy; drugs, supplies, hospitalization with outpatient follow-up; medical/surgical, diagnostic, emergency, and rehabilitative services; and the number of days of pre and post transplant care in the global definition

S2152 Solid organ(s), complete or segmental, single organ or combination of organs; deceased or living donor (s), procurement, transplantation, and related complications; including: drugs; supplies; hospitalization with outpatient follow-up; medical/surgical, diagnostic, emergency, and rehabilitative services, and the number of days of pre and posttransplant care in the global definition

S2202 Echosclerotherapy

S2205 Minimally invasive direct coronary artery bypass surgery involving mini-thoracotomy or mini-sternotomy surgery, performed under direct vision; using arterial graft(s), single coronary arterial graft

S2206 Minimally invasive direct coronary artery bypass surgery involving mini-thoracotomy or mini-sternotomy surgery, performed under direct vision; using arterial graft(s), 2 coronary arterial grafts

S2207 Minimally invasive direct coronary artery bypass surgery involving mini-thoracotomy or mini-sternotomy surgery, performed under direct vision; using venous graft only, single coronary venous graft

S2208 Minimally invasive direct coronary artery bypass surgery involving mini-thoracotomy or mini-sternotomy surgery, performed under direct vision; using single arterial and venous graft(s), single venous graft

S2209 Minimally invasive direct coronary artery bypass surgery involving mini-thoracotomy or mini-sternotomy surgery, performed under direct vision; using 2 arterial grafts and single venous graft

S2225 Myringotomy, laser-assisted

S2230 Implantation of magnetic component of semi-implantable hearing device on ossicles in middle ear

S2235 Implantation of auditory brain stem implant

S2260 Induced abortion, 17 to 24 weeks M ♀

S2265 Induced abortion, 25 to 28 weeks M ♀

S2266 Induced abortion, 29 to 31 weeks M ♀

S2267 Induced abortion, 32 weeks or greater M ♀

~~**S2270**~~ Jan ~~Insertion of vaginal cylinder for application of radiation source or clinical brachytherapy (report separately in addition to radiation source delivery)~~

S2300 Arthroscopy, shoulder, surgical; with thermally-induced capsulorrhaphy

S2325 Hip core decompression

S2340 Chemodenervation of abductor muscle(s) of vocal cord

S2341 Chemodenervation of adductor muscle(s) of vocal cord

S2342 Nasal endoscopy for postoperative debridement following functional endoscopic sinus surgery, nasal and/or sinus cavity(s), unilateral or bilateral

~~**S2344**~~ Jan ~~Nasal/sinus endoscopy, surgical; with enlargement of sinus ostium opening using inflatable device (i.e., balloon sinuplasty)~~

S2348 Decompression procedure, percutaneous, of nucleus pulposus of intervertebral disc, using radiofrequency energy, single or multiple levels, lumbar

S2350 Diskectomy, anterior, with decompression of spinal cord and/or nerve root(s), including osteophytectomy; lumbar, single interspace

S2351 Diskectomy, anterior, with decompression of spinal cord and/or nerve root(s), including osteophytectomy; lumbar, each additional interspace (list separately in addition to code for primary procedure)

S2360 Percutaneous vertebroplasty, one vertebral body, unilateral or bilateral injection; cervical

S2361 Each additional cervical vertebral body (list separately in addition to code for primary procedure)

S2400 Repair, congenital diaphragmatic hernia in the fetus using temporary tracheal occlusion, procedure performed in utero M ♀

S2401 Repair, urinary tract obstruction in the fetus, procedure performed in utero M ♀

S2402 Repair, congenital cystic adenomatoid malformation in the fetus, procedure performed in utero M ♀

S2403 Repair, extralobar pulmonary sequestration in the fetus, procedure performed in utero M ♀

S2404 Repair, myelomeningocele in the fetus, procedure performed in utero M ♀

S2405 Repair of sacrococcygeal teratoma in the fetus, procedure performed in utero M ♀

S2409 Repair, congenital malformation of fetus, procedure performed in utero, not otherwise classified M ♀

S2411 Fetoscopic laser therapy for treatment of twin-to-twin transfusion syndrome M ♀

S2900 Surgical techniques requiring use of robotic surgical system (list separately in addition to code for primary procedure)

S3000 Diabetic indicator; retinal eye exam, dilated, bilateral

S3005 Performance measurement, evaluation of patient self assessment, depression

S3600 STAT laboratory request (situations other than S3601)

S3601 Emergency STAT laboratory charge for patient who is homebound or residing in a nursing facility

S3620 Newborn metabolic screening panel, includes test kit, postage and the laboratory tests specified by the state for inclusion in this panel (e.g., galactose; hemoglobin, electrophoresis; hydroxyprogesterone, 17-d; phenylanine (PKU); and thyroxine, total) A

S3625 Maternal serum triple marker screen including alpha-fetoprotein (AFP), estriol, and human chorionic gonadotropin (HCG) M ♀

S3626 Maternal serum quadruple marker screen including alpha-fetoprotein (AFP), estriol, human chorionic gonadotropin hCG) and inhibin A

~~S3628~~ Jan ~~Placental alpha microglobulin-1 rapid immunoassay for detection of rupture of fetal membranes~~

S3630 Eosinophil count, blood, direct

S3645 HIV-1 antibody testing of oral mucosal transudate

S3650 Saliva test, hormone level; during menopause A ♀

S3652 Saliva test, hormone level; to assess preterm labor risk M ♀

S3655 Antisperm antibodies test (immunobead) A ♀

S3708 Gastrointestinal fat absorption study

S3711 Circulating tumor cell test

S3713 Kras mutation analysis testing

● S3722 Jan Dose optimization by area under the curve (AUC) analysis, for infusional 5-fluorouracil

S3800 Genetic testing for amyotrophic lateral sclerosis (ALS)

S3818 Complete gene sequence analysis; BRCA1 gene

S3819 Complete gene sequence analysis; BRCA2 gene

S3820 Complete BRCA1 and BRCA2 gene sequence analysis for susceptibility to breast and ovarian cancer ♀

S3822 Single mutation analysis (in individual with a known BRCA1 or BRCA2 mutation in the family) for susceptibility to breast and ovarian cancer ♀

S3823 Three-mutation BRCA1 and BRCA2 analysis for susceptibility to breast and ovarian cancer in Ashkenazi individuals ♀

S3828 Complete gene sequence analysis; MLH1 gene

S3829 Complete gene sequence analysis; MSH2 gene

S3830 Complete MLH1 and MSH2 gene sequence analysis for hereditary nonpolyposis colorectal cancer (HNPCC) genetic testing

S3831 Single-mutation analysis (in individual with a known MLH1 and MSH2 mutation in the family) for hereditary nonpolyposis colorectal cancer (HNPCC) genetic testing

S3833 Complete APC gene sequence analysis for susceptibility to familial adenomatous polyposis (FAP) and attenuated fap

S3834 Single-mutation analysis (in individual with a known APC mutation in the family) for susceptibility to familial adenomatous polyposis (FAP) and attenuated FAP

S3835 Complete gene sequence analysis for cystic fibrosis genetic testing

S3837 Complete gene sequence analysis for hemochromatosis genetic testing

S3840 DNA analysis for germline mutations of the RET proto-oncogene for susceptibility to multiple endocrine neoplasia type 2

S3841 Genetic testing for retinoblastoma

S3842 Genetic testing for Von Hippel-Lindau disease

S3843 DNA analysis of the F5 gene for susceptibility to factor V Leiden thrombophilia

S3844 DNA analysis of the connexin 26 gene (GJB2) for susceptibility to congenital, profound deafness

S3845 Genetic testing for alpha-thalassemia

S3846 Genetic testing for hemoglobin E beta-thalassemia

S3847 Genetic testing for Tay-Sachs disease

S3848 Genetic testing for Gaucher disease

S3849 Genetic testing for Niemann-Pick disease

S3850 Genetic testing for sickle cell anemia

S3851 Genetic testing for Canavan disease

S3852 DNA analysis for APOE epsilon 4 allele for susceptibility to Alzheimer's disease

S3853 Genetic testing for myotonic muscular dystrophy

S3854 Gene expression profiling panel for use in the management of breast cancer treatment

S3855 Genetic testing for detection of mutations in the presenilin - 1 gene

S3860 Genetic testing, comprehensive cardiac ion channel analysis, for variants in 5 major cardiac ion channel genes for individuals with high index of suspicion for familial long QT syndrome (LQTS) or related syndromes

S3861 Genetic testing, sodium channel, voltage-gated, type V, alpha subunit (SCN5A) and variants for suspected Brugada Syndrome

S3862 Genetic testing, family-specific ion channel analysis, for blood-relatives of individuals (index case) who have previously tested positive for a genetic variant of a cardiac ion channel syndrome using either one of the above test configurations or confirmed results from another laboratory

S3865 Comprehensive gene sequence analysis for hypertrophic cardiomyopathy

S3866 Genetic analysis for a specific gene mutation for hypertrophic cardiomyopathy (HCM) in an individual with a known HCM mutation in the family

S3870 Comparative genomic hybrization (CGH) microarray testing for developmental delay, autism spectrum disorder and/or mental retardation

S3890 DNA analysis, fecal, for colorectal cancer screening

S3900 Surface electromyography (EMG)

S3902 Ballistocardiogram

S3904 Masters 2 step

~~S3905~~ Jan ~~Noninvasive electrodiagnostic testing with automatic computerized hand-held device to stimulate and measure neuromuscular signals in diagnosing and evaluating systemic and entrapment neuropathies~~

S4005 Interim labor facility global (labor occurring but not resulting in delivery) M ♀

S4011 In vitro fertilization; including but not limited to identification and incubation of mature oocytes, fertilization with sperm, incubation of embryo(s), and subsequent visualization for determination of development M ♀

S4013 Complete cycle, gamete intrafallopian transfer (GIFT), case rate M ♀

S4014 Complete cycle, zygote intrafallopian transfer (ZIFT), case rate M ♀

S4015 Complete in vitro fertilization cycle, not otherwise specified, case rate M ♀

S4016 Frozen in vitro fertilization cycle, case rate ♀

S4017 Incomplete cycle, treatment cancelled prior to stimulation, case rate ♀

S4018 Frozen embryo transfer procedure cancelled before transfer, case rate ♀

S4020 In vitro fertilization procedure cancelled before aspiration, case rate ♀

Jan January Update

Special Coverage Instructions | Noncovered by Medicare | Carrier Discretion | ☑ Quantity Alert | ● New Code | ○ Recycled/Reinstated | ▲ Revised Code

Code	Description	Edits
S4021	In vitro fertilization procedure cancelled after aspiration, case rate	♀
S4022	Assisted oocyte fertilization, case rate	♀
S4023	Donor egg cycle, incomplete, case rate	♀
S4025	Donor services for in vitro fertilization (sperm or embryo), case rate	A
S4026	Procurement of donor sperm from sperm bank	♂
S4027	Storage of previously frozen embryos	♀
S4028	Microsurgical epididymal sperm aspiration (MESA)	A ♂
S4030	Sperm procurement and cryopreservation services; initial visit	A ♂
S4031	Sperm procurement and cryopreservation services; subsequent visit	A ♂
S4035	Stimulated intrauterine insemination (IUI), case rate	♀
S4037	Cryopreserved embryo transfer, case rate	♀
S4040	Monitoring and storage of cryopreserved embryos, per 30 days	♀
S4042	Management of ovulation induction (interpretation of diagnostic tests and studies, nonface-to-face medical management of the patient), per cycle	
S4981	Insertion of levonorgestrel-releasing intrauterine system	♀
S4989	Contraceptive intrauterine device (e.g., Progestacert IUD), including implants and supplies	♀
☑ S4990	Nicotine patches, legend	
☑ S4991	Nicotine patches, nonlegend	
S4993	Contraceptive pills for birth control	♀
S4995	Smoking cessation gum	
☑ S5000	Prescription drug, generic	
☑ S5001	Prescription drug, brand name	
☑ S5010	5% dextrose and 0.45% normal saline, 1000 ml	
☑ S5011	5% dextrose in lactated ringer's, 1000 ml	
☑ S5012	5% dextrose with potassium chloride, 1000 ml	
☑ S5013	5% dextrose/0.45% normal saline with potassium chloride and magnesium sulfate, 1000 ml	
☑ S5014	5% dextrose/0.45% normal saline with potassium chloride and magnesium sulfate, 1500 ml	
S5035	Home infusion therapy, routine service of infusion device (e.g., pump maintenance)	
S5036	Home infusion therapy, repair of infusion device (e.g., pump repair)	
☑ S5100	Day care services, adult; per 15 minutes	A
☑ S5101	Day care services, adult; per half day	A
☑ S5102	Day care services, adult; per diem	A
☑ S5105	Day care services, center-based; services not included in program fee, per diem	
☑ S5108	Home care training to home care client, per 15 minutes	
☑ S5109	Home care training to home care client, per session	
☑ S5110	Home care training, family; per 15 minutes	
S5111	Home care training, family; per session	
☑ S5115	Home care training, nonfamily; per 15 minutes	
☑ S5116	Home care training, nonfamily; per session	
☑ S5120	Chore services; per 15 minutes	
☑ S5121	Chore services; per diem	
☑ S5125	Attendant care services; per 15 minutes	
☑ S5126	Attendant care services; per diem	
☑ S5130	Homemaker service, NOS; per 15 minutes	
☑ S5131	Homemaker service, NOS; per diem	
☑ S5135	Companion care, adult (e.g., IADL/ADL); per 15 minutes	A
☑ S5136	Companion care, adult (e.g., IADL/ADL); per diem	A
☑ S5140	Foster care, adult; per diem	A
☑ S5141	Foster care, adult; per month	A
☑ S5145	Foster care, therapeutic, child; per diem	A
☑ S5146	Foster care, therapeutic, child; per month	A
☑ S5150	Unskilled respite care, not hospice; per 15 minutes	
☑ S5151	Unskilled respite care, not hospice; per diem	
S5160	Emergency response system; installation and testing	
☑ S5161	Emergency response system; service fee, per month (excludes installation and testing)	
S5162	Emergency response system; purchase only	
S5165	Home modifications; per service	
S5170	Home delivered meals, including preparation; per meal	
S5175	Laundry service, external, professional; per order	
S5180	Home health respiratory therapy, initial evaluation	
S5181	Home health respiratory therapy, NOS, per diem	
☑ S5185	Medication reminder service, nonface-to-face; per month	
S5190	Wellness assessment, performed by nonphysician	
S5199	Personal care item, NOS, each	
☑ S5497	Home infusion therapy, catheter care/maintenance, not otherwise classified; includes administrative services, professional pharmacy services, care coordination, and all necessary supplies and equipment (drugs and nursing visits coded separately), per diem	
☑ S5498	Home infusion therapy, catheter care/maintenance, simple (single lumen), includes administrative services, professional pharmacy services, care coordination and all necessary supplies and equipment, (drugs and nursing visits coded separately), per diem	
☑ S5501	Home infusion therapy, catheter care/maintenance, complex (more than one lumen), includes administrative services, professional pharmacy services, care coordination, and all necessary supplies and equipment (drugs and nursing visits coded separately), per diem	
☑ S5502	Home infusion therapy, catheter care/maintenance, implanted access device, includes administrative services, professional pharmacy services, care coordination and all necessary supplies and equipment (drugs and nursing visits coded separately), per diem (use this code for interim maintenance of vascular access not currently in use)	
S5517	Home infusion therapy, all supplies necessary for restoration of catheter patency or declotting	
S5518	Home infusion therapy, all supplies necessary for catheter repair	

S5520 Home infusion therapy, all supplies (including catheter) necessary for a peripherally inserted central venous catheter (PICC) line insertion

S5521 Home infusion therapy, all supplies (including catheter) necessary for a midline catheter insertion

S5522 Home infusion therapy, insertion of peripherally inserted central venous catheter (PICC), nursing services only (no supplies or catheter included)

S5523 Home infusion therapy, insertion of midline venous catheter, nursing services only (no supplies or catheter included)

☑ S5550 Insulin, rapid onset, 5 units

☑ S5551 Insulin, most rapid onset (Lispro or Aspart); 5 units

☑ S5552 Insulin, intermediate acting (NPH or LENTE); 5 units

☑ S5553 Insulin, long acting; 5 units

☑ S5560 Insulin delivery device, reusable pen; 1.5 ml size

☑ S5561 Insulin delivery device, reusable pen; 3 ml size

☑ S5565 Insulin cartridge for use in insulin delivery device other than pump; 150 units

☑ S5566 Insulin cartridge for use in insulin delivery device other than pump; 300 units

☑ S5570 Insulin delivery device, disposable pen (including insulin); 1.5 ml size

☑ S5571 Insulin delivery device, disposable pen (including insulin); 3 ml size

S8030 Scleral application of tantalum ring(s) for localization of lesions for proton beam therapy

S8035 Magnetic source imaging

S8037 Magnetic resonance cholangiopancreatography (MRCP)

S8040 Topographic brain mapping

S8042 Magnetic resonance imaging (MRI), low-field

S8049 Intraoperative radiation therapy (single administration)

S8055 Ultrasound guidance for multifetal pregnancy reduction(s), technical component (only to be used when the physician doing the reduction procedure does not perform the ultrasound, guidance is included in the CPT code for multifetal pregnancy reduction (59866) M ♀

S8080 Scintimammography (radioimmunoscintigraphy of the breast), unilateral, including supply of radiopharmaceutical

S8085 Fluorine-18 fluorodeoxyglucose (F-18 FDG) imaging using dual-head coincidence detection system (nondedicated PET scan)

S8092 Electron beam computed tomography (also known as ultrafast CT, cine CT)

S8096 Portable peak flow meter

☑ S8097 Asthma kit (including but not limited to portable peak expiratory flow meter, instructional video, brochure, and/or spacer)

S8100 Holding chamber or spacer for use with an inhaler or nebulizer; without mask

S8101 Holding chamber or spacer for use with an inhaler or nebulizer; with mask

S8110 Peak expiratory flow rate (physician services)

☑ S8120 Oxygen contents, gaseous, 1 unit equals 1 cubic foot

☑ S8121 Oxygen contents, liquid, 1 unit equals 1 pound

● S8130 Jan Interferential current stimulator, 2 channel

● S8131 Jan Interferential current stimulator, 4 channel

S8185 Flutter device

S8186 Swivel adaptor

S8189 Tracheostomy supply, not otherwise classified

S8210 Mucus trap

S8262 Mandibular orthopedic repositioning device, each

S8265 Haberman feeder for cleft lip/palate

S8270 Enuresis alarm, using auditory buzzer and/or vibration device

S8301 Infection control supplies, not otherwise specified

S8415 Supplies for home delivery of infant M ♀

S8420 Gradient pressure aid (sleeve and glove combination), custom made

S8421 Gradient pressure aid (sleeve and glove combination), ready made

S8422 Gradient pressure aid (sleeve), custom made, medium weight

S8423 Gradient pressure aid (sleeve), custom made, heavy weight

S8424 Gradient pressure aid (sleeve), ready made

S8425 Gradient pressure aid (glove), custom made, medium weight

S8426 Gradient pressure aid (glove), custom made, heavy weight

S8427 Gradient pressure aid (glove), ready made

S8428 Gradient pressure aid (gauntlet), ready made

S8429 Gradient pressure exterior wrap

☑ S8430 Padding for compression bandage, roll

☑ S8431 Compression bandage, roll

Various types of digit splints (S8450)

☑ S8450 Splint, prefabricated, digit (specify digit by use of modifier)

☑ S8451 Splint, prefabricated, wrist or ankle

☑ S8452 Splint, prefabricated, elbow

S8460 Camisole, postmastectomy

☑ S8490 Insulin syringes (100 syringes, any size)

S8940 Equestrian/hippotherapy, per session

☑ S8948 Application of a modality (requiring constant provider attendance) to one or more areas; low-level laser; each 15 minutes

☑ S8950 Complex lymphedema therapy, each 15 minutes

S8990 Physical or manipulative therapy performed for maintenance rather than restoration

S8999 Resuscitation bag (for use by patient on artificial respiration during power failure or other catastrophic event)

S9001 Home uterine monitor with or without associated nursing services M ♀

S9007 Ultrafiltration monitor

S9015 Automated EEG monitoring

S9024 Paranasal sinus ultrasound

S9025 Omnicardiogram/cardiointegram

S9034 Extracorporeal shockwave lithotripsy for gall stones (if performed with ERCP, use 43265)

S9055 Procuren or other growth factor preparation to promote wound healing

☑ S9056 Coma stimulation per diem

☑ S9061 Home administration of aerosolized drug therapy (e.g., Pentamidine); administrative services, professional pharmacy services, care coordination, all necessary supplies and equipment (drugs and nursing visits coded separately), per diem

~~S9075~~ Jan ~~Smoking cessation treatment~~
To report, see G0436-G0437

S9083 Global fee urgent care centers

S9088 Services provided in an urgent care center (list in addition to code for service)

☑ S9090 Vertebral axial decompression, per session

S9097 Home visit for wound care

☑ S9098 Home visit, phototherapy services (e.g., Bili-lite), including equipment rental, nursing services, blood draw, supplies, and other services, per diem

☑ S9109 Congestive heart failure telemonitoring, equipment rental, including telescale, computer system and software, telephone connections, and maintenance, per month

☑ S9117 Back school, per visit

☑ S9122 Home health aide or certified nurse assistant, providing care in the home; per hour

☑ S9123 Nursing care, in the home; by registered nurse, per hour (use for general nursing care only, not to be used when CPT codes 99500-99602 can be used)

☑ S9124 Nursing care, in the home; by licensed practical nurse, per hour

☑ S9125 Respite care, in the home, per diem

☑ S9126 Hospice care, in the home, per diem

☑ S9127 Social work visit, in the home, per diem

☑ S9128 Speech therapy, in the home, per diem

☑ S9129 Occupational therapy, in the home, per diem

☑ S9131 Physical therapy; in the home, per diem

☑ S9140 Diabetic management program, follow-up visit to non-MD provider

☑ S9141 Diabetic management program, follow-up visit to MD provider

S9145 Insulin pump initiation, instruction in initial use of pump (pump not included)

S9150 Evaluation by ocularist

S9152 Speech therapy, re-evaluation

☑ S9208 Home management of preterm labor, including administrative services, professional pharmacy services, care coordination, and all necessary supplies or equipment (drugs and nursing visits coded separately), per diem (do not use this code with any home infusion per diem code) M ♀

☑ S9209 Home management of preterm premature rupture of membranes (PPROM), including administrative services, professional pharmacy services, care coordination, and all necessary supplies or equipment (drugs and nursing visits coded separately), per diem (do not use this code with any home infusion per diem code) M ♀

☑ S9211 Home management of gestational hypertension, includes administrative services, professional pharmacy services, care coordination and all necessary supplies and equipment (drugs and nursing visits coded separately); per diem (do not use this code with any home infusion per diem code) M ♀

☑ S9212 Home management of postpartum hypertension, includes administrative services, professional pharmacy services, care coordination, and all necessary supplies and equipment (drugs and nursing visits coded separately), per diem (do not use this code with any home infusion per diem code) ♀

☑ S9213 Home management of preeclampsia, includes administrative services, professional pharmacy services, care coordination, and all necessary supplies and equipment (drugs and nursing services coded separately); per diem (do not use this code with any home infusion per diem code) M ♀

☑ S9214 Home management of gestational diabetes, includes administrative services, professional pharmacy services, care coordination, and all necessary supplies and equipment (drugs and nursing visits coded separately); per diem (do not use this code with any home infusion per diem code) M ♀

☑ S9325 Home infusion therapy, pain management infusion; administrative services, professional pharmacy services, care coordination, and all necessary supplies and equipment, (drugs and nursing visits coded separately), per diem (do not use this code with S9326, S9327 or S9328)

☑ S9326 Home infusion therapy, continuous (24 hours or more) pain management infusion; administrative services, professional pharmacy services, care coordination and all necessary supplies and equipment (drugs and nursing visits coded separately), per diem

☑ S9327 Home infusion therapy, intermittent (less than 24 hours) pain management infusion; administrative services, professional pharmacy services, care coordination, and all necessary supplies and equipment (drugs and nursing visits coded separately), per diem

☑ S9328 Home infusion therapy, implanted pump pain management infusion; administrative services, professional pharmacy services, care coordination, and all necessary supplies and equipment (drugs and nursing visits coded separately), per diem

☑ S9329 Home infusion therapy, chemotherapy infusion; administrative services, professional pharmacy services, care coordination, and all necessary supplies and equipment (drugs and nursing visits coded separately), per diem (do not use this code with S9330 or S9331)

Jan January Update

☑ S9330 Home infusion therapy, continuous (24 hours or more) chemotherapy infusion; administrative services, professional pharmacy services, care coordination, and all necessary supplies and equipment (drugs and nursing visits coded separately), per diem

☑ S9331 Home infusion therapy, intermittent (less than 24 hours) chemotherapy infusion; administrative services, professional pharmacy services, care coordination, and all necessary supplies and equipment (drugs and nursing visits coded separately), per diem

☑ S9335 Home therapy, hemodialysis; administrative services, professional pharmacy services, care coordination, and all necessary supplies and equipment (drugs and nursing services coded separately), per diem

☑ S9336 Home infusion therapy, continuous anticoagulant infusion therapy (e.g., Heparin), administrative services, professional pharmacy services, care coordination and all necessary supplies and equipment (drugs and nursing visits coded separately), per diem

☑ S9338 Home infusion therapy, immunotherapy, administrative services, professional pharmacy services, care coordination, and all necessary supplies and equipment (drugs and nursing visits coded separately), per diem

☑ S9339 Home therapy; peritoneal dialysis, administrative services, professional pharmacy services, care coordination and all necessary supplies and equipment (drugs and nursing visits coded separately), per diem

☑ S9340 Home therapy; enteral nutrition; administrative services, professional pharmacy services, care coordination, and all necessary supplies and equipment (enteral formula and nursing visits coded separately), per diem

☑ S9341 Home therapy; enteral nutrition via gravity; administrative services, professional pharmacy services, care coordination, and all necessary supplies and equipment (enteral formula and nursing visits coded separately), per diem

☑ S9342 Home therapy; enteral nutrition via pump; administrative services, professional pharmacy services, care coordination, and all necessary supplies and equipment (enteral formula and nursing visits coded separately), per diem

☑ S9343 Home therapy; enteral nutrition via bolus; administrative services, professional pharmacy services, care coordination, and all necessary supplies and equipment (enteral formula and nursing visits coded separately), per diem

☑ S9345 Home infusion therapy, antihemophilic agent infusion therapy (e.g., factor VIII); administrative services, professional pharmacy services, care coordination, and all necessary supplies and equipment (drugs and nursing visits coded separately), per diem

☑ S9346 Home infusion therapy, alpha-1-proteinase inhibitor (e.g., Prolastin); administrative services, professional pharmacy services, care coordination, and all necessary supplies and equipment (drugs and nursing visits coded separately), per diem

☑ S9347 Home infusion therapy, uninterrupted, long-term, controlled rate intravenous or subcutaneous infusion therapy (e.g., epoprostenol); administrative services, professional pharmacy services, care coordination, and all necessary supplies and equipment (drugs and nursing visits coded separately), per diem

☑ S9348 Home infusion therapy, sympathomimetic/inotropic agent infusion therapy (e.g., Dobutamine); administrative services, professional pharmacy services, care coordination, all necessary supplies and equipment (drugs and nursing visits coded separately), per diem

☑ S9349 Home infusion therapy, tocolytic infusion therapy; administrative services, professional pharmacy services, care coordination, and all necessary supplies and equipment (drugs and nursing visits coded separately), per diem M ♀

☑ S9351 Home infusion therapy, continuous or intermittent antiemetic infusion therapy; administrative services, professional pharmacy services, care coordination, and all necessary supplies and equipment (drugs and visits coded separately), per diem

☑ S9353 Home infusion therapy, continuous insulin infusion therapy; administrative services, professional pharmacy services, care coordination, and all necessary supplies and equipment (drugs and nursing visits coded separately), per diem

☑ S9355 Home infusion therapy, chelation therapy; administrative services, professional pharmacy services, care coordination, and all necessary supplies and equipment (drugs and nursing visits coded separately), per diem

☑ S9357 Home infusion therapy, enzyme replacement intravenous therapy; (e.g., Imiglucerase); administrative services, professional pharmacy services, care coordination, and all necessary supplies and equipment (drugs and nursing visits coded separately), per diem

☑ S9359 Home infusion therapy, antitumor necrosis factor intravenous therapy; (e.g., Infliximab); administrative services, professional pharmacy services, care coordination, and all necessary supplies and equipment (drugs and nursing visits coded separately), per diem

☑ S9361 Home infusion therapy, diuretic intravenous therapy; administrative services, professional pharmacy services, care coordination, and all necessary supplies and equipment (drugs and nursing visits coded separately), per diem

☑ S9363 Home infusion therapy, antispasmotic therapy; administrative services, professional pharmacy services, care coordination, and all necessary supplies and equipment (drugs and nursing visits coded separately), per diem

☑ S9364 Home infusion therapy, total parenteral nutrition (TPN); administrative services, professional pharmacy services, care coordination, and all necessary supplies and equipment including standard TPN formula (lipids, specialty amino acid formulas, drugs other than in standard formula and nursing visits coded separately), per diem (do not use with home infusion codes S9365-S9368 using daily volume scales)

☑ S9365 Home infusion therapy, total parenteral nutrition (TPN); 1 liter per day, administrative services, professional pharmacy services, care coordination, and all necessary supplies and equipment including standard TPN formula (lipids, specialty amino acid formulas, drugs other than in standard formula and nursing visits coded separately), per diem

☑ S9366 Home infusion therapy, total parenteral nutrition (TPN); more than 1 liter but no more than 2 liters per day, administrative services, professional pharmacy services, care coordination, and all necessary supplies and equipment including standard TPN formula (lipids, specialty amino acid formulas, drugs other than in standard formula and nursing visits coded separately), per diem

☑ S9367 Home infusion therapy, total parenteral nutrition (TPN); more than 2 liters but no more than 3 liters per day, administrative services, professional pharmacy services, care coordination, and all necessary supplies and equipment including standard TPN formula (lipids, specialty amino acid formulas, drugs other than in standard formula and nursing visits coded separately), per diem

☑ S9368 Home infusion therapy, total parenteral nutrition (TPN); more than 3 liters per day, administrative services, professional pharmacy services, care coordination, and all necessary supplies and equipment including standard TPN formula (lipids, specialty amino acid formulas, drugs other than in standard formula and nursing visits coded separately), per diem

S9370 Home therapy, intermittent antiemetic injection therapy; administrative services, professional pharmacy services, care coordination, and all necessary supplies and equipment (drugs and nursing visits coded separately), per diem

S9372 Home therapy; intermittent anticoagulant injection therapy (e.g., Heparin); administrative services, professional pharmacy services, care coordination, and all necessary supplies and equipment (drugs and nursing visits coded separately), per diem (do not use this code for flushing of infusion devices with Heparin to maintain patency)

S9373 Home infusion therapy, hydration therapy; administrative services, professional pharmacy services, care coordination, and all necessary supplies and equipment (drugs and nursing visits coded separately), per diem (do not use with hydration therapy codes S9374-S9377 using daily volume scales)

S9374 Home infusion therapy, hydration therapy; 1 liter per day, administrative services, professional pharmacy services, care coordination, and all necessary supplies and equipment (drugs and nursing visits coded separately), per diem

S9375 Home infusion therapy, hydration therapy; more than 1 liter but no more than 2 liters per day, administrative services, professional pharmacy services, care coordination, and all necessary supplies and equipment (drugs and nursing visits coded separately), per diem

S9376 Home infusion therapy, hydration therapy; more than 2 liters but no more than 3 liters per day, administrative services, professional pharmacy services, care coordination, and all necessary supplies and equipment (drugs and nursing visits coded separately), per diem

S9377 Home infusion therapy, hydration therapy; more than 3 liters per day, administrative services, professional pharmacy services, care coordination, and all necessary supplies (drugs and nursing visits coded separately), per diem

S9379 Home infusion therapy, infusion therapy, not otherwise classified; administrative services, professional pharmacy services, care coordination, and all necessary supplies and equipment (drugs and nursing visits coded separately), per diem

S9381 Delivery or service to high risk areas requiring escort or extra protection, per visit

S9401 Anticoagulation clinic, inclusive of all services except laboratory tests, per session

S9430 Pharmacy compounding and dispensing services

S9433 Medical food nutritionally complete, administered orally, providing 100% of nutritional intake

S9434 Modified solid food supplements for inborn errors of metabolism

S9435 Medical foods for inborn errors of metabolism

☑ S9436 Childbirth preparation/Lamaze classes, nonphysician provider, per session M ♀

S9437 Childbirth refresher classes, nonphysician provider, per session M ♀

☑ S9438 Cesarean birth classes, nonphysician provider, per session M ♀

☑ S9439 VBAC (vaginal birth after cesarean) classes, nonphysician provider, per session M ♀

☑ S9441 Asthma education, nonphysician provider, per session

☑ S9442 Birthing classes, nonphysician provider, per session M ♀

☑ S9443 Lactation classes, nonphysician provider, per session M ♀

☑ S9444 Parenting classes, nonphysician provider, per session

☑ S9445 Patient education, not otherwise classified, nonphysician provider, individual, per session

☑ S9446 Patient education, not otherwise classified, nonphysician provider, group, per session

☑ S9447 Infant safety (including CPR) classes, nonphysician provider, per session

☑ S9449 Weight management classes, nonphysician provider, per session

S9451 Exercise classes, nonphysician provider, per session

S9452 Nutrition classes, nonphysician provider, per session

S9453 Smoking cessation classes, nonphysician provider, per session

S9454 Stress management classes, nonphysician provider, per session

S9455 Diabetic management program, group session

S9460 Diabetic management program, nurse visit

S9465 Diabetic management program, dietitian visit

S9470 Nutritional counseling, dietitian visit

S9472 Cardiac rehabilitation program, nonphysician provider, per diem

S9473 Pulmonary rehabilitation program, nonphysician provider, per diem

S9474 Enterostomal therapy by a registered nurse certified in enterostomal therapy, per diem

S9475 Ambulatory setting substance abuse treatment or detoxification services, per diem

S9476 Vestibular rehabilitation program, nonphysician provider, per diem

S9480 Intensive outpatient psychiatric services, per diem

☑ S9482 Family stabilization services, per 15 minutes

☑ S9484 Crisis intervention mental health services, per hour

S9485 Crisis intervention mental health services, per diem

S9490 Home infusion therapy, corticosteroid infusion; administrative services, professional pharmacy services, care coordination, and all necessary supplies and equipment (drugs and nursing visits coded separately), per diem

S9494 Home infusion therapy, antibiotic, antiviral, or antifungal therapy; administrative services, professional pharmacy services, care coordination, and all necessary supplies and equipment (drugs and nursing visits coded separately), per diem (do not use this code with home infusion codes for hourly dosing schedules S9497-S9504)

S9497 Home infusion therapy, antibiotic, antiviral, or antifungal therapy; once every 3 hours; administrative services, professional pharmacy services, care coordination, and all necessary supplies and equipment (drugs and nursing visits coded separately), per diem

S9500 Home infusion therapy, antibiotic, antiviral, or antifungal therapy; once every 24 hours; administrative services, professional pharmacy services, care coordination, and all necessary supplies and equipment (drugs and nursing visits coded separately), per diem

S9501 Home infusion therapy, antibiotic, antiviral, or antifungal therapy; once every 12 hours; administrative services, professional pharmacy services, care coordination, and all necessary supplies and equipment (drugs and nursing visits coded separately), per diem

S9502 Home infusion therapy, antibiotic, antiviral, or antifungal therapy; once every 8 hours, administrative services, professional pharmacy services, care coordination, and all necessary supplies and equipment (drugs and nursing visits coded separately), per diem

S9503 Home infusion therapy, antibiotic, antiviral, or antifungal; once every 6 hours; administrative services, professional pharmacy services, care coordination, and all necessary supplies and equipment (drugs and nursing visits coded separately), per diem

S9504 Home infusion therapy, antibiotic, antiviral, or antifungal; once every 4 hours; administrative services, professional pharmacy services, care coordination, and all necessary supplies and equipment (drugs and nursing visits coded separately), per diem

S9529 Routine venipuncture for collection of specimen(s), single homebound, nursing home, or skilled nursing facility patient

S9537 Home therapy; hematopoietic hormone injection therapy (e.g., erythropoietin, G-CSF, GM-CSF); administrative services, professional pharmacy services, care coordination, and all necessary supplies and equipment (drugs and nursing visits coded separately), per diem

S9538 Home transfusion of blood product(s); administrative services, professional pharmacy services, care coordination and all necessary supplies and equipment (blood products, drugs, and nursing visits coded separately), per diem

S9542 Home injectable therapy, not otherwise classified, including administrative services, professional pharmacy services, care coordination, and all necessary supplies and equipment (drugs and nursing visits coded separately), per diem

S9558 Home injectable therapy; growth hormone, including administrative services, professional pharmacy services, care coordination, and all necessary supplies and equipment (drugs and nursing visits coded separately), per diem

S9559 Home injectable therapy, interferon, including administrative services, professional pharmacy services, care coordination, and all necessary supplies and equipment (drugs and nursing visits coded separately), per diem

S9560 Home injectable therapy; hormonal therapy (e.g., leuprolide, goserelin), including administrative services, professional pharmacy services, care coordination, and all necessary supplies and equipment (drugs and nursing visits coded separately), per diem

S9562 Home injectable therapy, palivizumab, including administrative services, professional pharmacy services, care coordination, and all necessary supplies and equipment (drugs and nursing visits coded separately), per diem

S9590 Home therapy, irrigation therapy (e.g., sterile irrigation of an organ or anatomical cavity); including administrative services, professional pharmacy services, care coordination, and all necessary supplies and equipment (drugs and nursing visits coded separately), per diem

S9810 Home therapy; professional pharmacy services for provision of infusion, specialty drug administration, and/or disease state management, not otherwise classified, per hour (do not use this code with any per diem code)

▲ S9900 Jan Services by a Journal-listed Christian Science practitioner for the purpose of healing, per diem

S9970 Health club membership, annual

S9975 Transplant related lodging, meals and transportation, per diem

S9976 Lodging, per diem, not otherwise classified

S9977 Meals, per diem, not otherwise specified

S9981 Medical records copying fee, administrative

☑ S9982 Medical records copying fee, per page

S9986 Not medically necessary service (patient is aware that service not medically necessary)

S9988 Services provided as part of a Phase I clinical trial

S9989 Services provided outside of the United States of America (list in addition to code(s) for services(s))

S9990 Services provided as part of a Phase II clinical trial

S9991 Services provided as part of a Phase III clinical trial

S9992 Transportation costs to and from trial location and local transportation costs (e.g., fares for taxicab or bus) for clinical trial participant and one caregiver/companion

S9994 Lodging costs (e.g., hotel charges) for clinical trial participant and one caregiver/companion

S9996 Meals for clinical trial participant and one caregiver/companion

S9999 Sales tax

NATIONAL T CODES ESTABLISHED FOR STATE MEDICAID AGENCIES T1000-T9999

The T codes are designed for use by Medicaid state agencies to establish codes for items for which there are no permanent national codes but for which codes are necessary to administer the Medicaid program (T codes are not accepted by Medicare but can be used by private insurers). This range of codes describes nursing and home health-related services, substance abuse treatment, and certain training-related procedures.

☑ **T1000** Private duty/independent nursing service(s), licensed, up to 15 minutes

T1001 Nursing assessment/evaluation

☑ **T1002** RN services, up to 15 minutes

☑ **T1003** LPN/LVN services, up to 15 minutes

☑ **T1004** Services of a qualified nursing aide, up to 15 minutes

☑ **T1005** Respite care services, up to 15 minutes

T1006 Alcohol and/or substance abuse services, family/couple counseling

T1007 Alcohol and/or substance abuse services, treatment plan development and/or modification

T1009 Child sitting services for children of the individual receiving alcohol and/or substance abuse services

T1010 Meals for individuals receiving alcohol and/or substance abuse services (when meals not included in the program)

T1012 Alcohol and/or substance abuse services, skills development

☑ **T1013** Sign language or oral interpretive services, per 15 minutes

T1014 Telehealth transmission, per minute, professional services bill separately

T1015 Clinic visit/encounter, all-inclusive

☑ **T1016** Case management, each 15 minutes

☑ **T1017** Targeted case management, each 15 minutes

T1018 School-based individualized education program (IEP) services, bundled

☑ **T1019** Personal care services, per 15 minutes, not for an inpatient or resident of a hospital, nursing facility, ICF/MR or IMD, part of the individualized plan of treatment (code may not be used to identify services provided by home health aide or certified nurse assistant)

T1020 Personal care services, per diem, not for an inpatient or resident of a hospital, nursing facility, ICF/MR or IMD, part of the individualized plan of treatment (code may not be used to identify services provided by home health aide or certified nurse assistant)

T1021 Home health aide or certified nurse assistant, per visit

T1022 Contracted home health agency services, all services provided under contract, per day

T1023 Screening to determine the appropriateness of consideration of an individual for participation in a specified program, project or treatment protocol, per encounter

T1024 Evaluation and treatment by an integrated, specialty team contracted to provide coordinated care to multiple or severely handicapped children, per encounter A

T1025 Intensive, extended multidisciplinary services provided in a clinic setting to children with complex medical, physical, mental and psychosocial impairments, per diem A

T1026 Intensive, extended multidisciplinary services provided in a clinic setting to children with complex medical, physical, medical and psychosocial impairments, per hour A

☑ **T1027** Family training and counseling for child development, per 15 minutes

T1028 Assessment of home, physical and family environment, to determine suitability to meet patient's medical needs

T1029 Comprehensive environmental lead investigation, not including laboratory analysis, per dwelling

☑ **T1030** Nursing care, in the home, by registered nurse, per diem

☑ **T1031** Nursing care, in the home, by licensed practical nurse, per diem

☑ **T1502** Administration of oral, intramuscular and/or subcutaneous medication by health care agency/professional, per visit

☑ **T1503** Administration of medication, other than oral and/or injectable, by a health care agency/professional, per visit

T1505 Electronic medication compliance management device, includes all components and accessories, not otherwise classified

T1999 Miscellaneous therapeutic items and supplies, retail purchases, not otherwise classified; identify product in "remarks"

T2001 Nonemergency transportation; patient attendant/escort

☑ **T2002** Nonemergency transportation; per diem

T2003 Nonemergency transportation; encounter/trip

T2004 Nonemergency transport; commercial carrier, multipass

T2005 Nonemergency transportation; stretcher van

☑ **T2007** Transportation waiting time, air ambulance and nonemergency vehicle, one-half (1/2) hour increments

☑ **T2010** Preadmission screening and resident review (PASRR) level I identification screening, per screen

T2011 Preadmission screening and resident review (PASRR) level II evaluation, per evaluation

☑ **T2012** Habilitation, educational; waiver, per diem

☑ **T2013** Habilitation, educational, waiver; per hour

☑ **T2014** Habilitation, prevocational, waiver; per diem

☑ **T2015** Habilitation, prevocational, waiver; per hour

☑ **T2016** Habilitation, residential, waiver; per diem

☑ **T2017** Habilitation, residential, waiver; 15 minutes

☑ **T2018** Habilitation, supported employment, waiver; per diem

☑ **T2019** Habilitation, supported employment, waiver; per 15 minutes

☑ **T2020** Day habilitation, waiver; per diem

☑ **T2021** Day habilitation, waiver; per 15 minutes

☑ **T2022** Case management, per month

☑ T2023 Targeted case management; per month

T2024 Service assessment/plan of care development, waiver

T2025 Waiver services; not otherwise specified (NOS)

☑ T2026 Specialized childcare, waiver; per diem

☑ T2027 Specialized childcare, waiver; per 15 minutes

T2028 Specialized supply, not otherwise specified, waiver

T2029 Specialized medical equipment, not otherwise specified, waiver

☑ T2030 Assisted living, waiver; per month

☑ T2031 Assisted living; waiver, per diem

☑ T2032 Residential care, not otherwise specified (NOS), waiver; per month

☑ T2033 Residential care, not otherwise specified (NOS), waiver; per diem

☑ T2034 Crisis intervention, waiver; per diem

T2035 Utility services to support medical equipment and assistive technology/devices, waiver

☑ T2036 Therapeutic camping, overnight, waiver; each session

☑ T2037 Therapeutic camping, day, waiver; each session

☑ T2038 Community transition, waiver; per service

☑ T2039 Vehicle modifications, waiver; per service

☑ T2040 Financial management, self-directed, waiver; per 15 minutes

☑ T2041 Supports brokerage, self-directed, waiver; per 15 minutes

☑ T2042 Hospice routine home care; per diem

☑ T2043 Hospice continuous home care; per hour

☑ T2044 Hospice inpatient respite care; per diem

☑ T2045 Hospice general inpatient care; per diem

☑ T2046 Hospice long-term care, room and board only; per diem

☑ T2048 Behavioral health; long-term care residential (nonacute care in a residential treatment program where stay is typically longer than 30 days), with room and board, per diem

☑ T2049 Nonemergency transportation; stretcher van, mileage; per mile

T2101 Human breast milk processing, storage and distribution only ♀

☑ T4521 Adult sized disposable incontinence product, brief/diaper, small, each

☑ T4522 Adult sized disposable incontinence product, brief/diaper, medium, each

☑ T4523 Adult sized disposable incontinence product, brief/diaper, large, each

☑ T4524 Adult sized disposable incontinence product, brief/diaper, extra large, each

☑ T4525 Adult sized disposable incontinence product, protective underwear/pull-on, small size, each

☑ T4526 Adult sized disposable incontinence product, protective underwear/pull-on, medium size, each

☑ T4527 Adult sized disposable incontinence product, protective underwear/pull-on, large size, each

☑ T4528 Adult sized disposable incontinence product, protective underwear/pull-on, extra large size, each

☑ T4529 Pediatric sized disposable incontinence product, brief/diaper, small/medium size, each

☑ T4530 Pediatric sized disposable incontinence product, brief/diaper, large size, each

☑ T4531 Pediatric sized disposable incontinence product, protective underwear/pull-on, small/medium size, each

☑ T4532 Pediatric sized disposable incontinence product, protective underwear/pull-on, large size, each

☑ T4533 Youth sized disposable incontinence product, brief/diaper, each

☑ T4534 Youth sized disposable incontinence product, protective underwear/pull-on, each

☑ T4535 Disposable liner/shield/guard/pad/undergarment, for incontinence, each

☑ T4536 Incontinence product, protective underwear/pull-on, reusable, any size, each

☑ T4537 Incontinence product, protective underpad, reusable, bed size, each

☑ T4538 Diaper service, reusable diaper, each diaper

☑ T4539 Incontinence product, diaper/brief, reusable, any size, each

☑ T4540 Incontinence product, protective underpad, reusable, chair size, each

☑ T4541 Incontinence product, disposable underpad, large, each

☑ T4542 Incontinence product, disposable underpad, small size, each

☑ T4543 Disposable incontinence product, brief/diaper, bariatric, each

T5001 Positioning seat for persons with special orthopedic needs

T5999 Supply, not otherwise specified

VISION SERVICES V0000-V2999

These V codes include vision-related supplies, including spectacles, lenses, contact lenses, prostheses, intraocular lenses, and miscellaneous lenses.

FRAMES

- A **V2020** Frames, purchases ♿
- E **V2025** Deluxe frame
  MED: 100-4,1,30.3.5

SINGLE VISION, GLASS, OR PLASTIC

Monofocal spectacles (V2100-V2114)

Trifocal spectacles (V2300-V2314)

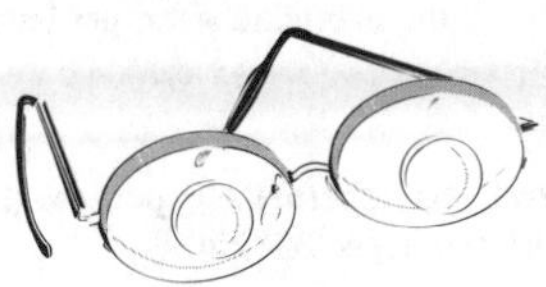

Low vision aids mounted to spectacles (V2610)

Telescopic or other compound lens fitted on spectacles as a low vision aid (V2615)

- A ☑ **V2100** Sphere, single vision, plano to plus or minus 4.00, per lens ♿
- A ☑ **V2101** Sphere, single vision, plus or minus 4.12 to plus or minus 7.00d, per lens ♿
- A ☑ **V2102** Sphere, single vision, plus or minus 7.12 to plus or minus 20.00d, per lens ♿
- A ☑ **V2103** Spherocylinder, single vision, plano to plus or minus 4.00d sphere, 0.12 to 2.00d cylinder, per lens ♿
- A ☑ **V2104** Spherocylinder, single vision, plano to plus or minus 4.00d sphere, 2.12 to 4.00d cylinder, per lens ♿
- A ☑ **V2105** Spherocylinder, single vision, plano to plus or minus 4.00d sphere, 4.25 to 6.00d cylinder, per lens ♿
- A ☑ **V2106** Spherocylinder, single vision, plano to plus or minus 4.00d sphere, over 6.00d cylinder, per lens ♿
- A ☑ **V2107** Spherocylinder, single vision, plus or minus 4.25 to plus or minus 7.00 sphere, 0.12 to 2.00d cylinder, per lens ♿
- A ☑ **V2108** Spherocylinder, single vision, plus or minus 4.25d to plus or minus 7.00d sphere, 2.12 to 4.00d cylinder, per lens ♿
- A ☑ **V2109** Spherocylinder, single vision, plus or minus 4.25 to plus or minus 7.00d sphere, 4.25 to 6.00d cylinder, per lens ♿
- A ☑ **V2110** Spherocylinder, single vision, plus or minus 4.25 to 7.00d sphere, over 6.00d cylinder, per lens ♿
- A ☑ **V2111** Spherocylinder, single vision, plus or minus 7.25 to plus or minus 12.00d sphere, 0.25 to 2.25d cylinder, per lens ♿
- A ☑ **V2112** Spherocylinder, single vision, plus or minus 7.25 to plus or minus 12.00d sphere, 2.25d to 4.00d cylinder, per lens ♿
- A ☑ **V2113** Spherocylinder, single vision, plus or minus 7.25 to plus or minus 12.00d sphere, 4.25 to 6.00d cylinder, per lens ♿
- A ☑ **V2114** Spherocylinder, single vision, sphere over plus or minus 12.00d, per lens ♿
- A ☑ **V2115** Lenticular (myodisc), per lens, single vision ♿
- A **V2118** Aniseikonic lens, single vision ♿
- A ☑ **V2121** Lenticular lens, per lens, single ♿
- A **V2199** Not otherwise classified, single vision lens

BIFOCAL, GLASS, OR PLASTIC

- A ☑ **V2200** Sphere, bifocal, plano to plus or minus 4.00d, per lens ♿
- A ☑ **V2201** Sphere, bifocal, plus or minus 4.12 to plus or minus 7.00d, per lens ♿
- A ☑ **V2202** Sphere, bifocal, plus or minus 7.12 to plus or minus 20.00d, per lens ♿
- A ☑ **V2203** Spherocylinder, bifocal, plano to plus or minus 4.00d sphere, 0.12 to 2.00d cylinder, per lens ♿
- A ☑ **V2204** Spherocylinder, bifocal, plano to plus or minus 4.00d sphere, 2.12 to 4.00d cylinder, per lens ♿
- A ☑ **V2205** Spherocylinder, bifocal, plano to plus or minus 4.00d sphere, 4.25 to 6.00d cylinder, per lens ♿
- A ☑ **V2206** Spherocylinder, bifocal, plano to plus or minus 4.00d sphere, over 6.00d cylinder, per lens ♿
- A ☑ **V2207** Spherocylinder, bifocal, plus or minus 4.25 to plus or minus 7.00d sphere, 0.12 to 2.00d cylinder, per lens ♿
- A ☑ **V2208** Spherocylinder, bifocal, plus or minus 4.25 to plus or minus 7.00d sphere, 2.12 to 4.00d cylinder, per lens ♿
- A ☑ **V2209** Spherocylinder, bifocal, plus or minus 4.25 to plus or minus 7.00d sphere, 4.25 to 6.00d cylinder, per lens ♿
- A ☑ **V2210** Spherocylinder, bifocal, plus or minus 4.25 to plus or minus 7.00d sphere, over 6.00d cylinder, per lens ♿
- A ☑ **V2211** Spherocylinder, bifocal, plus or minus 7.25 to plus or minus 12.00d sphere, 0.25 to 2.25d cylinder, per lens ♿
- A ☑ **V2212** Spherocylinder, bifocal, plus or minus 7.25 to plus or minus 12.00d sphere, 2.25 to 4.00d cylinder, per lens ♿
- A ☑ **V2213** Spherocylinder, bifocal, plus or minus 7.25 to plus or minus 12.00d sphere, 4.25 to 6.00d cylinder, per lens ♿
- A ☑ **V2214** Spherocylinder, bifocal, sphere over plus or minus 12.00d, per lens ♿
- A ☑ **V2215** Lenticular (myodisc), per lens, bifocal ♿
- A ☑ **V2218** Aniseikonic, per lens, bifocal ♿
- A ☑ **V2219** Bifocal seg width over 28mm ♿
- A ☑ **V2220** Bifocal add over 3.25d ♿
- A **V2221** Lenticular lens, per lens, bifocal ♿
- A **V2299** Specialty bifocal (by report)
  Pertinent documentation to evaluate medical appropriateness should be included when this code is reported.

TRIFOCAL, GLASS, OR PLASTIC

- A ☑ **V2300** Sphere, trifocal, plano to plus or minus 4.00d, per lens ♿
- A ☑ **V2301** Sphere, trifocal, plus or minus 4.12 to plus or minus 7.00d per lens ♿

A ☑ **V2302** Sphere, trifocal, plus or minus 7.12 to plus or minus 20.00, per lens

A ☑ **V2303** Spherocylinder, trifocal, plano to plus or minus 4.00d sphere, 0.12 to 2.00d cylinder, per lens

A ☑ **V2304** Spherocylinder, trifocal, plano to plus or minus 4.00d sphere, 2.25 to 4.00d cylinder, per lens

A ☑ **V2305** Spherocylinder, trifocal, plano to plus or minus 4.00d sphere, 4.25 to 6.00 cylinder, per lens

A ☑ **V2306** Spherocylinder, trifocal, plano to plus or minus 4.00d sphere, over 6.00d cylinder, per lens

A ☑ **V2307** Spherocylinder, trifocal, plus or minus 4.25 to plus or minus 7.00d sphere, 0.12 to 2.00d cylinder, per lens

A ☑ **V2308** Spherocylinder, trifocal, plus or minus 4.25 to plus or minus 7.00d sphere, 2.12 to 4.00d cylinder, per lens

A ☑ **V2309** Spherocylinder, trifocal, plus or minus 4.25 to plus or minus 7.00d sphere, 4.25 to 6.00d cylinder, per lens

A ☑ **V2310** Spherocylinder, trifocal, plus or minus 4.25 to plus or minus 7.00d sphere, over 6.00d cylinder, per lens

A ☑ **V2311** Spherocylinder, trifocal, plus or minus 7.25 to plus or minus 12.00d sphere, 0.25 to 2.25d cylinder, per lens

A ☑ **V2312** Spherocylinder, trifocal, plus or minus 7.25 to plus or minus 12.00d sphere, 2.25 to 4.00d cylinder, per lens

A ☑ **V2313** Spherocylinder, trifocal, plus or minus 7.25 to plus or minus 12.00d sphere, 4.25 to 6.00d cylinder, per lens

A ☑ **V2314** Spherocylinder, trifocal, sphere over plus or minus 12.00d, per lens

A ☑ **V2315** Lenticular, (myodisc), per lens, trifocal

A **V2318** Aniseikonic lens, trifocal

A ☑ **V2319** Trifocal seg width over 28 mm

A ☑ **V2320** Trifocal add over 3.25d

A **V2321** Lenticular lens, per lens, trifocal

A **V2399** Specialty trifocal (by report)
Pertinent documentation to evaluate medical appropriateness should be included when this code is reported.

VARIABLE ASPHERICITY LENS, GLASS, OR PLASTIC

A ☑ **V2410** Variable asphericity lens, single vision, full field, glass or plastic, per lens

A ☑ **V2430** Variable asphericity lens, bifocal, full field, glass or plastic, per lens

A **V2499** Variable sphericity lens, other type

CONTACT LENS

A ☑ **V2500** Contact lens, PMMA, spherical, per lens

A ☑ **V2501** Contact lens, PMMA, toric or prism ballast, per lens

A ☑ **V2502** Contact lens PMMA, bifocal, per lens

A ☑ **V2503** Contact lens, PMMA, color vision deficiency, per lens

A ☑ **V2510** Contact lens, gas permeable, spherical, per lens

A ☑ **V2511** Contact lens, gas permeable, toric, prism ballast, per lens

A ☑ **V2512** Contact lens, gas permeable, bifocal, per lens

A ☑ **V2513** Contact lens, gas permeable, extended wear, per lens

A ☑ **V2520** Contact lens, hydrophilic, spherical, per lens
Hydrophilic contact lenses are covered by Medicare only for aphakic patients. Local contractor if incident to physician services.

A ☑ **V2521** Contact lens, hydrophilic, toric, or prism ballast, per lens
Hydrophilic contact lenses are covered by Medicare only for aphakic patients. Local contractor if incident to physician services.

A ☑ **V2522** Contact lens, hydrophilic, bifocal, per lens
Hydrophilic contact lenses are covered by Medicare only for aphakic patients. Local contractor if incident to physician services.

A ☑ **V2523** Contact lens, hydrophilic, extended wear, per lens
Hydrophilic contact lenses are covered by Medicare only for aphakic patients.

A ☑ **V2530** Contact lens, scleral, gas impermeable, per lens (for contact lens modification, see 92325)

A ☑ **V2531** Contact lens, scleral, gas permeable, per lens (for contact lens modification, see 92325)

A **V2599** Contact lens, other type
Local contractor if incident to physician services.

VISION AIDS

A **V2600** Hand held low vision aids and other nonspectacle mounted aids

A **V2610** Single lens spectacle mounted low vision aids

A **V2615** Telescopic and other compound lens system, including distance vision telescopic, near vision telescopes and compound microscopic lens system

PROSTHETIC EYE

Implant
Peg
One type of eye implant
Reverse angle
Previously placed prosthetic receptacle
Implant
Peg hole drilled into prosthetic
Side view
Peg

A **V2623** Prosthetic eye, plastic, custom

A **V2624** Polishing/resurfacing of ocular prosthesis

A **V2625** Enlargement of ocular prosthesis

A **V2626** Reduction of ocular prosthesis

A **V2627** Scleral cover shell
A scleral shell covers the cornea and the anterior sclera. Medicare covers a scleral shell when it is prescribed as an artificial support to a shrunken and sightless eye or as a barrier in the treatment of severe dry eye.

A **V2628** Fabrication and fitting of ocular conformer

A	V2629	Prosthetic eye, other type

INTRAOCULAR LENSES

N	V2630	Anterior chamber intraocular lens N1 The IOL must be FDA-approved for reimbursement. Medicare payment for an IOL is included in the payment for ASC facility services. Medicare jurisdiction: local contractor.
N	V2631	Iris supported intraocular lens N1 The IOL must be FDA-approved for reimbursement. Medicare payment for an IOL is included in the payment for ASC facility services. Medicare jurisdiction: local contractor.
N	V2632	Posterior chamber intraocular lens N1 The IOL must be FDA-approved for reimbursement. Medicare payment for an IOL is included in the payment for ASC facility services. Medicare jurisdiction: local contractor. MED: 100-4,32,120.2

MISCELLANEOUS

A	☑ V2700	Balance lens, per lens ♿
E	V2702	Deluxe lens feature
A	☑ V2710	Slab off prism, glass or plastic, per lens ♿
A	☑ V2715	Prism, per lens ♿
A	☑ V2718	Press-on lens, Fresnel prism, per lens ♿
A	☑ V2730	Special base curve, glass or plastic, per lens ♿
A	☑ V2744	Tint, photochromatic, per lens ♿
A	☑ V2745	Addition to lens; tint, any color, solid, gradient or equal, excludes photochromatic, any lens material, per lens ♿
A	☑ V2750	Antireflective coating, per lens ♿
A	☑ V2755	U-V lens, per lens ♿
E	V2756	Eye glass case
A	☑ V2760	Scratch resistant coating, per lens ♿
B	☑ V2761	Mirror coating, any type, solid, gradient or equal, any lens material, per lens
A	☑ V2762	Polarization, any lens material, per lens ♿
A	☑ V2770	Occluder lens, per lens ♿
A	☑ V2780	Oversize lens, per lens ♿
B	☑ V2781	Progressive lens, per lens
A	☑ V2782	Lens, index 1.54 to 1.65 plastic or 1.60 to 1.79 glass, excludes polycarbonate, per lens ♿
A	☑ V2783	Lens, index greater than or equal to 1.66 plastic or greater than or equal to 1.80 glass, excludes polycarbonate, per lens ♿
A	☑ V2784	Lens, polycarbonate or equal, any index, per lens ♿
F	V2785	Processing, preserving and transporting corneal tissue F4 Medicare jurisdiction: local contractor. MED: 100-4,4,200.1
A	☑ V2786	Specialty occupational multifocal lens, per lens ♿
E	V2787	Astigmatism correcting function of intraocular lens MED: 100-4,32,120.1; 100-4,32,120.2
E	V2788	Presbyopia correcting function of intraocular lens MED: 100-4,32,120.1; 100-4,32,120.2
N	V2790	Amniotic membrane for surgical reconstruction, per procedure N1 Medicare jurisdiction: local contractor. MED: 100-4,4,200.4
A	V2797	Vision supply, accessory and/or service component of another HCPCS vision code
A	V2799	Vision service, miscellaneous Determine if an alternative HCPCS Level II or a CPT code better describes the service being reported. This code should be used only if a more specific code is unavailable.

HEARING SERVICES V5000-V5999

This range of codes describes hearing tests and related supplies and equipment, speech-language pathology screenings, and repair of augmentative communicative system.

HEARING SERVICES

E	V5008	Hearing screening
E	V5010	Assessment for hearing aid
E	V5011	Fitting/orientation/checking of hearing aid
E	V5014	Repair/modification of a hearing aid
E	V5020	Conformity evaluation

MONAURAL HEARING AID

E	V5030	Hearing aid, monaural, body worn, air conduction
E	V5040	Hearing aid, monaural, body worn, bone conduction
E	V5050	Hearing aid, monaural, in the ear
E	V5060	Hearing aid, monaural, behind the ear

OTHER HEARING SERVICES

E	V5070	Glasses, air conduction
E	V5080	Glasses, bone conduction
E	V5090	Dispensing fee, unspecified hearing aid
E	V5095	Semi-implantable middle ear hearing prosthesis
E	V5100	Hearing aid, bilateral, body worn
E	V5110	Dispensing fee, bilateral

HEARING AIDS, SERVICES, AND ACCESSORIES

E	V5120	Binaural, body
E	V5130	Binaural, in the ear
E	V5140	Binaural, behind the ear
E	V5150	Binaural, glasses
E	V5160	Dispensing fee, binaural
E	V5170	Hearing aid, CROS, in the ear
E	V5180	Hearing aid, CROS, behind the ear
E	V5190	Hearing aid, CROS, glasses
E	V5200	Dispensing fee, CROS
E	V5210	Hearing aid, BICROS, in the ear
E	V5220	Hearing aid, BICROS, behind the ear
E	V5230	Hearing aid, BICROS, glasses
E	V5240	Dispensing fee, BICROS
E	V5241	Dispensing fee, monaural hearing aid, any type
E	V5242	Hearing aid, analog, monaural, CIC (completely in the ear canal)

E V5243 Hearing aid, analog, monaural, ITC (in the canal)

E V5244 Hearing aid, digitally programmable analog, monaural, CIC

E V5245 Hearing aid, digitally programmable, analog, monaural, ITC

E V5246 Hearing aid, digitally programmable analog, monaural, ITE (in the ear)

E V5247 Hearing aid, digitally programmable analog, monaural, BTE (behind the ear)

E V5248 Hearing aid, analog, binaural, CIC

E V5249 Hearing aid, analog, binaural, ITC

E V5250 Hearing aid, digitally programmable analog, binaural, CIC

E V5251 Hearing aid, digitally programmable analog, binaural, ITC

E V5252 Hearing aid, digitally programmable, binaural, ITE

E V5253 Hearing aid, digitally programmable, binaural, BTE

E V5254 Hearing aid, digital, monaural, CIC

E V5255 Hearing aid, digital, monaural, ITC

E V5256 Hearing aid, digital, monaural, ITE

E V5257 Hearing aid, digital, monaural, BTE

E V5258 Hearing aid, digital, binaural, CIC

E V5259 Hearing aid, digital, binaural, ITC

E V5260 Hearing aid, digital, binaural, ITE

E V5261 Hearing aid, digital, binaural, BTE

E V5262 Hearing aid, disposable, any type, monaural

E V5263 Hearing aid, disposable, any type, binaural

E V5264 Ear mold/insert, not disposable, any type

E V5265 Ear mold/insert, disposable, any type

E V5266 Battery for use in hearing device

E V5267 Hearing aid supplies/accessories

ASSISTIVE LISTENING DEVICE

E V5268 Assistive listening device, telephone amplifier, any type

E V5269 Assistive listening device, alerting, any type

E V5270 Assistive listening device, television amplifier, any type

E V5271 Assistive listening device, television caption decoder

E V5272 Assistive listening device, TDD

E V5273 Assistive listening device, for use with cochlear implant

E V5274 Assistive listening device, not otherwise specified

MISCELLANEOUS HEARING SERVICES

E ☑ V5275 Ear impression, each

E V5298 Hearing aid, not otherwise classified

B V5299 Hearing service, miscellaneous ⊘

Determine if an alternative HCPCS Level II or a CPT code better describes the service being reported. This code should be used only if a more specific code is unavailable.

SPEECH-LANGUAGE PATHOLOGY SERVICES

E V5336 Repair/modification of augmentative communicative system or device (excludes adaptive hearing aid)

Medicare jurisdiction: DME regional contractor.

E V5362 Speech screening

E V5363 Language screening

E V5364 Dysphagia screening

APPENDIX 1 — TABLE OF DRUGS AND BIOLOGICALS

Introduction and Directions

The HCPCS 2012 Table of Drugs and Biologicals is designed to quickly and easily direct the user to drug names and their corresponding codes. Both generic and brand or trade names are alphabetically listed in the "Drug Name" column of the table. The associated A, C, J, K, Q, or S code is given only for the generic name of the drug. While we try to make the table comprehensive, it is not all-inclusive.

The "Unit Per" column lists the stated amount for the referenced generic drug as provided by CMS. "Up to" listings are inclusive of all quantities up to and including the listed amount. All other listings are for the amount of the drug as listed. The editors recognize that the availability of some drugs in the quantities listed is dependent on many variables beyond the control of the clinical ordering clerk. The availability in your area of regularly used drugs in the most cost-effective quantities should be relayed to your third-party payers.

The "Route of Administration" column addresses the most common methods of delivering the referenced generic drug as described in current pharmaceutical literature. The official definitions for Level II drug codes generally describe administration other than by oral method. Therefore, with a handful of exceptions, oral-delivered options for most drugs are omitted from the Route of Administration column.

Intravenous administration includes all methods, such as gravity infusion, injections, and timed pushes. When several routes of administration are listed, the first listing is simply the first, or most common, method as described in current reference literature. The "VAR" posting denotes various routes of administration and is used for drugs that are commonly administered into joints, cavities, tissues, or topical applications, in addition to other parenteral administrations. Listings posted with "OTH" alert the user to other administration methods, such as suppositories or catheter injections.

Please be reminded that the Table of Drugs, as well as all HCPCS Level II national definitions and listings, constitutes a post-treatment medical reference for billing purposes only. Although the editors have exercised all normal precautions to ensure the accuracy of the table and related material, the use of any of this information to select medical treatment is entirely inappropriate. Do not code directly from the table of drugs. Refer to the tabular section for complete information.

See Appendix 3 for abbreviations.

Drug Name	Unit Per	Route	Code
10% LMD	500 ML	IV	J7100
5% DEXTROSE AND .45% NORMAL SALINE	1000 ML	IV	S5010
5% DEXTROSE IN LACTATED RINGER'S	1000 ML	IV	S5011
5% DEXTROSE WITH POSTASSIUM CHLORIDE	1000 ML	IV	S5012
5% DEXTROSE/.45% NS WITH KCL AND MAG SULFATE	1000ML	IV	S5013
5% DEXTROSE/.45% NS WITH KCL AND MAG SULFATE	1500 ML	IV	S5014
5% DEXTROSE/NORMAL SALINE	5%	VAR	J7042
5% DEXTROSE/WATER	500 ML	IV	J7060
ABATACEPT	10 MG	IV	J0129
ABCIXIMAB	10 MG	IV	J0130
ABELCET	10 MG	IV	J0287
ABILIFY	0.25 MG	IM	J0400
ABLAVAR	1 ML	IV	A9583
ABOBOTULINUMTOXINA	5 UNITS	IM	J0586
ABRAXANE	1 MG	IV	J9264
ACCELULAR PERICARDIAL TISSUE MATRIX NONHUMAN	SQ CM	OTH	C9354
ACCUNEB NONCOMPOUNDED, CONCENTRATED	1 MG	INH	J7611
ACCUNEB NONCOMPOUNDED, UNIT DOSE	1 MG	INH	J7613
ACETADOTE	1 G	INH	J7608
ACETADOTE	100 MG	IV	J0132
ACETAMINOPHEN	10 MG	IV	J0131
ACETAZOLAMIDE SODIUM	500 MG	IM, IV	J1120

Drug Name	Unit Per	Route	Code
ACETYLCYSTEINE COMPOUNDED	PER G	INH	J7604
ACETYLCYSTEINE NONCOMPOUNDED	1 G	INH	J7608
ACTEMRA	1 MG	IV	J3262
ACTHREL	1 MCG	IV	J0795
ACTIMMUNE	3 MU	SC	J9216
ACTIVASE	1 MG	IV	J2997
ACUTECT	STUDY DOSE UP TO 20 MCI	IV	A9504
ACYCLOVIR	5 MG	[illegible]	[illegible]
ADAGEN	25 IU	[illegible]	[illegible]
ADALIMUMAB	20 MG	[illegible]	[illegible]
ADCETRIS	1 MG	[illegible]	[illegible]
ADENOCARD	6 MG	[illegible]	[illegible]
ADENOSCAN	30 MG	[illegible]	[illegible]
ADENOSINE	30 MG	[illegible]	[illegible]
ADENOSINE	6 MG	[illegible]	[illegible]
ADRENALIN	0.1 MG	[illegible]	[illegible]
ADRENOCORT	1 MG	[illegible]	[illegible]
ADRIAMYCIN	10 MG	[illegible]	[illegible]
ADRUCIL	500 MG	IV	J9190
AEROBID	1 MG	INH	J7641
AFINITOR	0.25 MG	ORAL	J8561
AFLURIA	EA	IM	Q2035
AGALSIDASE BETA	1 MG	IV	J0180
AGGRASTAT	12.5 MG	IM, IV	J3246
A-HYDROCORT	100 MG	IV, IM, SC	J1720
ALATROFLOXACIN MESYLATE	100 MG	IV	J0200
ALBUTEROL AND IPRATROPIUM BROMIDE NONCOMPOUNDED	2.5MG/0.5 MG	INH	J7620
ALBUTEROL COMPOUNDED, CONCENTRATED	1 MG	INH	J7610
ALBUTEROL COMPOUNDED, UNIT DOSE	1 MG	INH	J7609
ALBUTEROL NONCOMPOUNDED, UNIT DOSE	1 MG	INH	J7613
ALBUTEROL, NONCOMPOUNDED, CONCENTRATED FORM	1 MG	INH	J7611
ALDESLEUKIN	1 VIAL	IV	J9015
ALDURAZYME	0.1 MG	IV	J1931
ALEFACEPT	0.5 MG	IV, IM	J0215
ALEMTUZUMAB	10 MG	IV	J9010
ALFERON N	250,000 IU	IM	J9215
ALGLUCERASE	10 U	IV	J0205
~~ALGLUCOSIDASE ALFA (LUMIZYME)~~	~~1 MG~~	~~IV~~	~~C9277~~
ALGLUCOSIDASE ALFA (LUMIZYME)	10 MG	IV	J0221
ALGLUCOSIDASE ALFA NOS	10 MG	IV	J0220
ALIMTA	10 MG	IV	J9305
ALKERAN	2 MG	ORAL	J8600
ALKERAN	50 MG	IV	J9245
ALLODERM	SQ CM	OTH	Q4116
ALLOGRAFT, CYMETRA	1 CC	INJ	Q4112
ALLOGRAFT, GRAFTJACKET EXPRESS	1 CC	INJ	Q4113
ALLOPATCHHD	SQ CM	OTH	Q4128
ALLOSKIN	SQ CM	OTH	Q4115
ALLOSKIN RT	SQ CM	OTH	Q4123
ALOXI	25 MCG	IV	J2469
ALPHA 1 - PROTEINASE INHIBITOR (HUMAN) NOS	10 MG	IV	J0256

Drug Name	Unit Per	Route	Code
ALPHA 1-PROTENIASE INHIBITOR (HUMAN) (GLASSIA)	10 MG	IV	J0257
ALPHANATE	PER FACTOR VIII IU	IV	J7186
ALPHANINE SD	1 IU	IV	J7193
ALPROSTADIL	1.25 MCG	IV	J0270
ALPROSTADIL	EA	OTH	J0275
ALTEPLASE RECOMBINANT	1 MG	IV	J2997
ALUPENT, NONCOMPOUNDED, CONCENTRATED	10 MG	INH	J7668
ALUPENT, NONCOMPOUNDED, UNIT DOSE	10 MG	INH	J7669
AMANTADINE HCL (DEMONSTRATION PROJECT)	100 MG	ORAL	G9017
AMANTADINE HYDROCHLORIDE (BRAND NAME) (DEMONSTRTION PROJECT)	100 MG	ORAL	G9033
AMANTADINE HYDROCHLORIDE (GENERIC)	100 MG	ORAL	G9017
AMBISOME	10 MG	IV	J0289
AMCORT	5 MG	IM	J3302
AMERGAN	12.5 MG	ORAL	Q0169
A-METHAPRED	125 MG	IM, IV	J2930
A-METHAPRED	40 MG	IM, IV	J2920
AMEVIVE	0.5 MG	IV, IM	J0215
AMICAR	5 G	IV	S0017
AMIFOSTINE	500 MG	IV	J0207
AMIKACIN SULFATE	100 MG	IM, IV	J0278
AMINOCAPRIOC ACID	5 G	IV	S0017
AMINOPHYLLINE	250 MG	IV	J0280
AMIODARONE HCL	30 MG	IV	J0282
AMITRIPTYLINE HCL	20 MG	IM	J1320
AMMONIA N-13	STUDY DOSE UP TO 40 MCI	IV	A9526
AMOBARBITAL	125 MG	IM, IV	J0300
AMPHOCIN	50 MG	IV	J0285
AMPHOTEC	10 MG	IV	J0287
AMPHOTERICIN B	50 MG	IV	J0285
AMPHOTERICIN B CHOLESTERYL SULFATE COMPLEX	10 MG	IV	J0288
AMPHOTERICIN B LIPID COMPLEX	10 MG	IV	J0287
AMPHOTERICIN B LIPOSOME	10 MG	IV	J0289
AMPICILLIN SODIUM	500 MG	IM, IV	J0290
AMPICILLIN SODIUM/SULBACTAM SODIUM	1.5 G	IM, IV	J0295
AMYTAL	125 MG	IM, IV	J0300
ANASTROZOLE	1 MG	ORAL	S0170
ANCEF	500 MG	IM, IV	J0690
AN-DTPA DIAGNOSTIC	STUDY DOSE UP TO 25 MCI	IV	A9539
AN-DTPA THERAPEUTIC	STUDY DOSE UP TO 25 MCI	INH	A9567
ANECTINE	20 MG	IM, IV	J0330
ANGIOMAX	1 MG	IV	J0583
ANIDULAFUNGIN	1 MG	IV	J0348
ANISTREPLASE	30 U	IV	J0350
ANTAGON	250 MCG	SC	S0132
ANTIEMETIC NOC	VAR	ORAL	Q0181
ANTIEMETIC DRUG NOC	VAR	OTH	J8498
ANTIEMETIC DRUG NOS	VAR	ORAL	J8597
ANTIHEMOPHILIC FACTOR HUMAN METHOD M MONOCLONAL PURIFIED	1 IU	IV	J7192
ANTIHEMOPHILIC FACTOR PORCINE	1 IU	IV	J7191
ANTIHEMOPHILIC FACTOR VIII, XYNTHA, RECOMBINANT	1 IU	IV	J7185
ANTIHEMOPHILIC FACTOR VIII/VON WILLEBRAND FACTOR COMPLEX, HUMAN	PER FACTOR VIII IU	IV	J7186
ANTI-INHIBITOR	1 IU	IV	J7198
ANTITHROMBIN III	1 IU	IV	J7195
ANTITHROMBIN RECOMBINANT	50 IU	IV	J7196
ANTI-THYMOCYTE GLOBULIN,EQUINE	250 MG	OTH	J7504
ANTIZOL	15 MG	IV	J1451
ANZEMET	10 MG	IV	J1260
ANZEMET	100 MG	ORAL	Q0180
ANZEMET	50 MG	ORAL	S0174
APLIGRAF	SQ CM	OTH	Q4101
APOKYN	1 MG	SC	J0364
APOMORPHINE HYDROCHLORIDE	1 MG	SC	J0364
APREPITANT	5 MG	ORAL	J8501
APROTININ	10,000 KIU	IV	J0365
AQUAMEPHYTON	1 MG	IM, SC, IV	J3430
ARA-C	100 MG	SC, IV	J9100
ARALEN	UP TO 250 MG	IM, IV	J0390
ARAMINE	10 MG	IV, IM, SC	J0380
ARANESP, ESRD USE	1 MCG	SC, IV	J0882
ARANESP, NON-ESRD USE	1 MCG	SC, IV	J0881
ARBUTAMINE HCL	1 MG	IV	J0395
ARCALYST	1 MG	SC	J2793
AREDIA	30 MG	IV	J2430
ARFORMOTEROL	15 MCG	INH	J7605
ARIDOL	5 MG	INH	J7665
ARIMIDEX	1 MG	ORAL	S0170
ARIPIPRAZOLE	0.25 MG	IM	J0400
ARISTOCORT	5 MG	IM	J3302
ARISTOCORTE FORTE	5 MG	IM	J3302
ARISTOCORTE INTRALESIONAL	5 MG	OTH	J3302
ARISTOSPAN	5 MG	VAR	J3303
ARIXTRA	0.5 MG	SC	J1652
AROMASIN	25 MG	ORAL	S0156
ARRANON	50 MG	IV	J9261
ARRESTIN	200 MG	IM	J3250
ARSENIC TRIOXIDE	1 MG	IV	J9017
ARTHROFLEX	SQ CM	OTH	Q4125
ARTISS FIBRIN SEALANT	2 ML	OTH	C9250
ARZERRA	10 MG	IV	J9302
ASPARAGINASE	10,000 U	VAR	J9020
ASTRAMORPH PF	10 MG	IM, IV, SC	J2275
ATGAM	250 MG	OTH	J7504
ATIVAN	2 MG	IM, IV	J2060
ATOPICLAIR	ANY SIZE	OTH	A6250
ATROPEN	0.01 MG	IM	J0461
ATROPINE SULFATE	0.01 MG	IM, IV, SC	J0461
ATROPINE, COMPOUNDED, CONCENTRATED	I MG	INH	J7635
ATROPINE, COMPOUNDED, UNIT DOSE	1 MG	INH	J7636
ATROVENT, NONCOMPOUNDED, UNIT DOSE	1 MG	INH	J7644

Drug Name	Unit Per	Route	Code
ATRYN	50 IU	IV	J7196
AUROTHIOGLUCOSE	50 MG	IM	J2910
AUTOPLEX T	1 IU	IV	J7198
AVASTIN	10 MG	IV	J9035
AVASTIN	0.25 MG	IV	C9257
AVELOX	100 MG	IV	J2280
AVONEX	11 MCG	IM	Q3025
AVONEX	30 MCG	IM	J1826
AZACITIDINE	1 MG	SC	J9025
AZACTAM	500 MG	IV	S0073
AZASAN	50 MG	ORAL	J7500
AZATHIOPRINE	100 MG	OTH	J7501
AZATHIOPRINE	50 MG	ORAL	J7500
AZITHROMYCIN	500 MG	IV	J0456
AZMACORT	PER MG	INH	J7684
AZMACORT CONCENTRATED	PER MG	INH	J7683
AZTREONAM	500 MG	IV	S0073
BACLOFEN	10 MG	IT	J0475
BACLOFEN	50 MCG	IT	J0476
BACTOCILL	250 MG	IM, IV	J2700
BACTRIM IV	10 ML	IV	S0039
BAL	100 MG	IM	J0470
BASILIXIMAB	20 MG	IV	J0480
BCG INTRAVESICLE	VIAL	OTH	J9031
BEBULIN VH	1 IU	IV	J7194
BECAPLERMIN GEL 0.01%	0.5 G	OTH	S0157
BECLOMETHASONE COMPOUNDED	1 MG	INH	J7622
BECLOVENT COMPOUNDED	1 MG	INH	J7622
BECONASE COMPOUNDED	1 MG	INH	J7622
BELATACEPT	1 MG	IV	C9286
~~BELIMUMAB~~	~~10 MG~~	~~IV~~	~~Q2044~~
BELIMUMAB	10 MG	IV	J0490
BENA-D 10	50 MG	IV, IM	J1200
BENA-D 50	50 MG	IV, IM	J1200
BENADRYL	50 MG	IV, IM	J1200
BENAHIST 10	50 MG	IV, IM	J1200
BENAHIST 50	50 MG	IV, IM	J1200
BENDAMUSTINE HCL	1 MG	IV	J9033
BENEFIX	1 IU	IV	J7195
~~BENLYSTA~~	~~10 MG~~	~~IV~~	~~Q2044~~
BENLYSTA	10 MG	IV	J0490
BENOJECT-10	50 MG	IV, IM	J1200
BENOJECT-50	50 MG	IV, IM	J1200
BENTYL	20 MG	IM	J0500
BENZTROPINE MESYLATE	1 MG	IM, IV	J0515
BERINERT	10 U	IV	J0597
BERUBIGEN	1,000 MCG	SC, IM	J3420
BETA-2	1 MG	INH	J7648
BETALIN 12	1,000 MCG	SC, IM	J3420
BETAMETHASONE ACETATE AND BETAMETHASONE SODIUM PHOSPHATE	3 MG, OF EACH	IM	J0702
BETAMETHASONE COMPOUNDED, UNIT DOSE	1 MG	INH	J7624
BETASERON	0.25 MG	SC	J1830
BETHANECHOL CHLORIDE, MYOTONACHOL OR URECHOLINE	5 MG	SC	J0520
BEVACIZUMAB	10 MG	IV	J9035

Drug Name	Unit Per	Route	Code
BEVACIZUMAB	0.25 MG	IV	C9257
BEXXAR THERAPEUTIC	TX DOSE	IV	A9545
BICILLIN CR	100,000 UNITS	IM	J0558
BICILLIN CR 900/300	100,000 UNITS	IM	J0558
BICILLIN CR TUBEX	100,000 UNITS	IM	J0558
BICILLIN LA	100,000 U	IM	J0561
BICNU	100 MG	IV	J9050
BIOCLATE	1 IU	IV	J7192
BIOTROPIN	1 MG	SC	J2941
BIPERIDEN LACTATE	5 MG	IM, IV	J0190
BITOLTEROL MESYLATE, COMPOUNDED CONCENTRATED	PER MG	INH	J7628
BITOLTEROL MESYLATE, COMPOUNDED UNIT DOSE	PER MG	INH	J7629
BIVALIRUDIN	1 MG	IV	J0583
BLENOXANE	15 U	IM, IV, SC	J9040
BLEOMYCIN LYOPHILLIZED	15 U	IM, IV, SC	J9040
BLEOMYCIN SULFATE	15 U	IM, IV, SC	J9040
BONIVA	1 MG	IV	J1740
BORTEZOMIB	0.1 MG	IV	J9041
BOTOX	1 UNIT	IM, OTH	J0585
BOTOX COSMETIC	1 UNIT	IM, OTH	J0585
BOTULINUM TOXIN TYPE A	1 UNIT	IM, OTH	J0585
BOTULINUM TOXIN TYPE B	100 U	OTH	J0587
BRAVELLE	75 IU	SC, IM	J3355
BRENTUXIMAB VENDOTIN	1 MG	IV	C9287
BRETHINE	PER MG	INH	J7681
BRETHINE CONCENTRATED	PER MG	INH	J7680
BRICANYL	PER MG	INH	J7681
BRICANYL CONCENTRATED	PER MG	INH	J7680
BROM-A-COT	10 MG	IM, SC, IV	J0945
BROMPHENIRAMINE MALEATE	10 MG	IM, SC, IV	J0945
BUDESONIDE COMPOUNDED, CONCETRATED	0.25 MG	INH	J7634
BUDESONIDE, COMPOUNDED, UNIT DOSE	0.5 MG	INH	J7627
BUDESONIDE, NONCOMPOUNDED, CONCENTRATED	0.25 MG	INH	J7633
BUDESONIDE, NONCOMPOUNDED, UNIT DOSE	0.5 MG	INH	J7626
BUMETANIDE	0.5 MG	IM, IV	S0171
BUPIVACAINE HCL	30 ML	OTH	S0020
BUPRENEX	0.1 MG	IM, IV	J0592
BUPRENORPHINE HCL	0.1 MG	IM, IV	J0592
BUPROPION HCL	150 MG	ORAL	S0106
BUSULFAN	1 MG	IV	J0594
BUSULFAN	2 MG	ORAL	J8510
BUSULFEX	2 MG	ORAL	J8510
BUTORPHANOL TARTRATE	2 MG	IM, IV	J0595
BUTORPHANOL TARTRATE	25 MG	OTH	S0012
C 1 ESTERASE INHIBITOR (HUMAN) (BERINERT)	10 UNITS	IV	J0597
C1 ESTERASE INHIBITOR (HUMAN) (CINRYZE)	10 UNITS	IV	J0598
CABAZITAXEL	1 MG	IV	J9043
~~CABAZITAXEL~~	~~1 MG~~	~~IV~~	~~C9276~~
CABERGOLINE	0.25 MG	ORAL	J8515

Drug Name	Unit Per	Route	Code
CAFCIT	5 MG	IV	J0706
CAFFEINE CITRATE	5 MG	IV	J0706
CALCIJEX	0.1 MCG	IM	J0636
CALCIJEX	0.25 MCG	INJ	S0169
CALCIMAR	UP TO 400 U	SC, IM	J0630
CALCITONIN SALMON	400 U	SC, IM	J0630
CALCITRIOL	0.1 MCG	IM	J0636
CALCITROL	0.25 MCG	IM	S0169
CALCIUM DISODIUM VERSENATE	1,000 MG	IV, SC, IM	J0600
CALCIUM GLUCONATE	10 ML	IV	J0610
CALCIUM GLYCEROPHOSPHATE AND CALCIUM LACTATE	10 ML	IM, SC	J0620
CALDOLOR	100 MG	IV	C9279
CAMPATH	10 MG	IV	J9010
CAMPTOSAR	20 MG	IV	J9206
CANAKINUMAB	1 MG	SC	J0638
CANCIDAS	5 MG	IV	J0637
CAPECITABINE	150 MG	ORAL	J8520
CAPROMAB PENDETIDE	STUDY DOSE UP TO 10 MCI	IV	A9507
CAPSAICIN 8% PATCH	10 SQ CM	OTH	J7335
CARBOCAINE	10 ML	VAR	J0670
CARBOPLATIN	50 MG	IV	J9045
CARDIOGEN 82	STUDY DOSE UP TO 60 MCI	IV	A9555
CARDIOLITE	STUDY DOSE	IV	A9500
CARIMUNE	500 MG	IV	J1566
CARMUSTINE	100 MG	IV	J9050
CARNITOR	1 G	IV	J1955
CARTICEL		OTH	J7330
CASPOFUNGIN ACETATE	5 MG	IV	J0637
CATAPRES	1 MG	OTH	J0735
CATHFLO	1 MG	IV	J2997
CAVERJECT	1.25 MCG	VAR	J0270
CEA SCAN	STUDY DOSE UP TO 45 MCI	IV	A9568
CEENU	10 MG	ORAL	S0178
CEFAZOLIN SODIUM	500 MG	IM, IV	J0690
CEFEPIME HCL	500 MG	IV	J0692
CEFIZOX	500 MG	IV, IM	J0715
CEFOBID	1 G	IV	S0021
CEFOPERAZONE SODIUM	1 G	IV	S0021
CEFOTAN	500 MG	IM, IV	S0074
CEFOTAXIME SODIUM	1 GM	IV, IM	J0698
CEFOTETAN DISODIUM	500 MG	IM. IV	S0074
CEFOXITIN SODIUM	1 GM	IV, IM	J0694
~~CEFTAROLINE FOSAMIL~~	~~10 MG~~	~~IV~~	~~C9282~~
CEFTAROLINE FOSAMIL	10 MG	IV	J0712
CEFTAZIDIME	500 MG	IM, IV	J0713
CEFTIZOXIME SODIUM	500 MG	IV, IM	J0715
CEFTRIAXONE SODIUM	250 MG	IV, IM	J0696
CEFUROXIME	750 MG	IM, IV	J0697
CEFUROXIME SODIUM STERILE	750 MG	IM, IV	J0697
CELESTONE SOLUSPAN	3 MG	IM	J0702
CELLCEPT	250 MG	ORAL	J7517
CENACORT A-40	10 MG	IM	J3301
CENACORT FORTE	5 MG	IM	J3302
CEPHALOTHIN SODIUM	UP TO 1 G	INJ	J1890
CEPHAPIRIN SODIUM	1 G	IV	J0710
CEPTAZ	500 MG	IM, IV	J0713
CEREBRYX	50 MG	IM, IV	Q2009
CEREBRYX	750 MG	IM, IV	S0078
CEREDASE	10 U	IV	J0205
CERETEC	STUDY DOSE UP TO 25 MCI	IV	A9521
CERETEC	STUDY DOSE	IV	A9569
CEREZYME	10 U	IV	J1786
CERTOLIZUMAB PEGOL	1 MG	SC	J0718
CERUBIDINE	10 MG	IV	J9150
CESAMET	1 MG	ORAL	J8650
CETUXIMAB	10 MG	IV	J9055
CHEALAMIDE	150 MG	IV	J3520
CHLORAMBUCIL	2 MG	ORAL	S0172
CHLORAMPHENICOL SODIUM SUCCINATE	1 G	IV	J0720
CHLORDIAZEPOXIDE HCL	100 MG	IM, IV	J1990
CHLOROMYCETIN	1 G	IV	J0720
CHLOROPROCAINE HCL	30 ML	VAR	J2400
CHLOROQUINE HCL	UP TO 250 MG	IM, IV	J0390
CHLOROTHIAZIDE SODIUM	500 MG	IV	J1205
CHLORPROMAZINE HCL	10 MG	ORAL	Q0171
CHLORPROMAZINE HCL	25 MG	ORAL	Q0172
CHLORPROMAZINE HCL	50 MG	IM, IV	J3230
CHOLETEC	STUDY DOSE UP TO 15 MCI	IV	A9537
CHOREX	1000 USP	IM	J0725
CHORIONIC GONADOTROPIN	1,000 USP U	IM	J0725
CHROMIC PHOSPHATE P32 (THERAPEUTIC)	1 MCI	IV	A9564
CHROMITOPE SODIUM	STUDY DOSE UP TO 250 UCI	IV	A9553
CHROMIUM CR-51 SODIUM IOTHALAMATE, DIAGNOSTIC	STUDY DOSE UP TO 250 UCI	IV	A9553
CIDOFOVIR	375 MG	IV	J0740
CILASTATIN SODIUM	250 MG	IV, IM	J0743
CIMETIDINE HCL	300 MG	IM, IV	S0023
CIMZIA	1 MG	SC	J0718
CINRZYE	10 UNITS	IV	J0598
CIPRO	200 MG	IV	J0744
CIPROFLOXACIN FOR INTRAVENOUS INFUSION	200 MG	IV	J0744
CIS-MDP	STUDY DOSE UP TO 30 MCI	IV	A9503
CISPLATIN	10 MG	IV	J9060
CIS-PYRO	STUDY DOSE UP TO 25 MCI	IV	A9538
CLADRIBINE	1 MG	IV	J9065
CLAFORAN	1 GM	IV, IM	J0698
CLEOCIN PHOSPHATE	300 MG	IV	S0077
CLEVIDIPINE BUTYRATE	1 MG	IV	C9248
CLEVIPREX	1 MG	IV	C9248
CLINDAMYCIN PHOSPHATE	300 MG	IV	S0077
CLOFARABINE	1 MG	IV	J9027
CLOLAR	1 MG	IV	J9027
CLONIDINE HCL	1 MG	OTH	J0735
CLOZAPINE	25 MG	ORAL	S0136

Drug Name	Unit Per	Route	Code
CLOZARIL	25 MG	ORAL	S0136
COBAL	1,000 MCG	IM, SC	J3420
COBALT CO-57 CYNOCOBALAMIN, DIAGNOSTIC	STUDY DOSE UP TO 1 UCI	ORAL	A9559
COBATOPE 57	STUDY DOSE UP TO 1 UCI	ORAL	A9559
COBEX	1,000 MCG	SC, IM	J3420
CODEINE PHOSPHATE	30 MG	IM, IV, SC	J0745
COGENTIN	1 MG	IM, IV	J0515
COGNEX	10 MG	ORAL	S0014
COLCHICINE	1 MG	IV	J0760
COLHIST	10 MG	IM, SC, IV	J0945
COLISTIMETHATE SODIUM	150 MG	IM, IV	J0770
COLISTIMETHATE SODIUM	1 MG	INH	S0142
COLLAGEN BASED WOUND FILLER DRY FOAM	1 GM	OTH	A6010
COLLAGEN BASED WOUND FILLER, GEL/PASTE	1 GM	OTH	A6011
COLLAGEN MATRIX NERVE WRAP	0.5 CM	OTH	C9361
COLLAGEN NERVE CUFF	0.5 CM LENGTH	OTH	C9355
COLLAGENASE, CLOSTRIDIUM HISTOLYTICUM	0.01 MG	OTH	J0775
COLY-MYCIN M	150 MG	IM, IV	J0770
COMPAZINE	10 MG	IM, IV	J0780
COMPAZINE	5 MG	ORAL	S0183
COMPAZINE	10 MG	ORAL	Q0165
COMPAZINE	5 MG	ORAL	Q0164
CONTRACEPTIVE SUPPLY, HORMONE CONTAINING PATCH	EACH	OTH	J7304
CONTRAST FOR ECHOCARDIOGRAM	STUDY	IV	A9700
COPAXONE	20 MG	SC	J1595
COPPER T MODEL TCU380A IUD COPPER WIRE/COPPER COLLAR	EA	OTH	J7300
CORDARONE	30 MG	IV	J0282
CORIFACT	1 IU	IV	J7180
CORTASTAT	1 MG	IM, IV, OTH	J1100
CORTASTAT LA	1 MG	IM	J1094
CORTICORELIN OVINE TRIFLUTATE	1 MCG	IV	J0795
CORTICOTROPIN	40 U	IV, IM, SC	J0800
CORTIMED	80 MG	IM	J1040
CORTROSYN	0.25 MG	IM, IV	J0834
CORVERT	1 MG	IV	J1742
COSMEGEN	0.5 MG	IV	J9120
COSYNTROPIN	0.25 MG	IM, IV	J0833
COTOLONE	5 MG	ORAL	J7510
CROFAB	UP TO 1 GM	IV	J0840
CROMOLYN SODIUM COMPOUNDED	PER 10 MG	INH	J7632
CROMOLYN SODIUM NONCOMPOUNDED	10 MG	INH	J7631
~~CROTALIDAE POLYVALENT IMMUNE FAB~~	~~1 VIAL~~	~~IV~~	~~C9274~~
CROTALIDAE POLYVALENT IMMUNE FAB (OVINE)	UP TO 1 GM	IV	J0840
CRYSTAL B12	1,000 MCG	IM, SC	J3420
CRYSTICILLIN 300 A.S.	600,000 UNITS	IM, IV	J2510
CRYSTICILLIN 600 A.S.	600,000 UNITS	IM, IV	J2510
CUBICIN	1 MG	IV	J0878
CYANO	1,000 MCG	IM, SC	J3420
CYANOCOBALAMIN	1,000 MCG	IM, SC	J3420
CYANOCOBALAMIN COBALT 57/58	STUDY DOSE UP TO 1 UCI	IV	A9546
CYANOCOBALAMIN COBALT CO-57	STUDY DOSE UP TO 1 UCI	ORAL	A9559
CYCLOPHOSPHAMIDE	100 MG	IV	J9070
CYCLOPHOSPHAMIDE	25 MG	ORAL	J8530
CYCLOSPORINE	100 MG	ORAL	J7502
CYCLOSPORINE	250 MG	IV	J7516
CYCLOSPORINE	25 MG	ORAL	J7515
CYMETRA	1 CC	INJ	Q4112
CYSVIEW	STUDY DOSE	OTH	C9275
CYTARABINE	100 MG	SC, IV	J9100
CYTARABINE LIPOSOME	10 MG	IT	J9098
CYTOGAM	VIAL	IV	J0850
CYTOMEGALOVIRUS IMMUNE GLOB	VIAL	IV	J0850
CYTOSAR-U	100 MG	SC, IV	J9100
CYTOTEC	200 MCG	ORAL	S0191
CYTOVENE	500 MG	IV	J1570
CYTOXAN	100 MG	IV	J9070
CYTOXAN	25 MG	ORAL	J8530
D.H.E. 45	1 MG	IM, IV	J1110
DACARBAZINE	100 MG	IV	J9130
DACLIZUMAB	25 MG	OTH	J7513
DACOGEN	1 MG	IV	J0894
DACTINOMYCIN	0.5 MG	IV	J9120
DALALONE	1 MG	IM, IV, OTH	J1100
DALALONE LA	1 MG	IM	J1094
DALTEPARIN SODIUM	2,500 IU	SC	J1645
DAPTOMYCIN	1 MG	IV	J0878
DARBEPOETIN ALFA, ESRD USE	1 MCG	SC, IV	J0882
DARBEPOETIN ALFA, NON-ESRD USE	1 MCG	SC, IV	J0881
DATSCAN	STUDY DOSE	IV	A9584
DAUNORUBICIN	10 MG	IV	J9150
DAUNORUBICIN CITRATE, LIPOOSOMAL FORMULATION	10 MG	IV	J9151
DAUNOXOME	10 MG	IV	J9151
DDAVP	1 MCG	IV, SC	J2597
DECADRON	0.25 MG	ORAL	J8540
DECAJECT	1 MG	IM, IV, OTH	J1100
DECITABINE	1 MG	IV	J0894
DECOLONE-50	50 MG	IM	J2320
DEFEROXAMINE MESYLATE	500 MG	IM, SC, IV	J0895
DEGARELIX	1 MG	SC	J9155
DELATESTRYL	100 MG	IM	J3120
DELATESTRYL	200 MG	IM	J3130
DELESTROGEN	10 MG	IM	J1380
DELTA-CORTEF	5 MG	ORAL	J7510
DEMADEX	10 MG	IV	J3265
DEMEROL	100 MG	IM, IV, SC	J2175
DENILEUKIN DIFTITOX	300 MCG	IV	J9160
~~DENOSUMAB~~	~~1 MG~~	~~SC~~	~~C9272~~
DENOSUMAB	1 MG	SC	J0897
DEPANDRATE	1 CC, 200 MG	IM	J1080
DEPANDROGYN	1 ML	IM	J1060
DEPGYNOGEN	UP TO 5 MG	IM	J1000
DEPHENACEN-50	50 MG	IM, IV	J1200
DEPMEDALONE	40 MG	IM	J1030

Drug Name	Unit Per	Route	Code
DEPMEDALONE	80 MG	IM	J1040
DEPOCYT	10 MG	IT	J9098
DEPODUR	UP TO 10 MG	IV	J2270
DEPODUR	100 MG	IV	J2271
DEPO-ESTRADIOL CYPIONATE	UP TO 5 MG	IM	J1000
DEPOGEN	UP TO 5 MG	IM	J1000
DEPO-MEDROL	20 MG	IM, OTH	J1020
DEPO-MEDROL	80 MG	IM, OTH	J1040
DEPO-MEDROL	40 MG	IM, OTH	J1030
DEPO-PROVERA	150 MG	IM	J1055
DEPO-PROVERA	50 MG	IM	J1051
DEPO-TESTADIOL	1 ML	IM	J1060
DEPO-TESTOSTERONE	200 MG	IM	J1080
DEPO-TESTOSTERONE	UP TO 100 MG	IM	J1070
DEPO-TESTOSTERONE CYPIONATE	UP TO 100 MG	IM	J1070
DEPTESTROGEN	UP TO 100 MG	IM	J1070
DERMACELL	SQ CM	OTH	Q4122
DERMAGRAFT	SQ CM	OTH	Q4106
DERMAL SUBSTITUTE, NATIVE, NONDENATURED COLLAGEN, FETAL	0.5 SQ CM	OTH	C9358
DERMAL SUBSTITUTE, NATIVE, NONDENATURED COLLAGEN, NEONATAL	0.5 SQ CM	OTH	C9360
DESFERAL	500 MG	IM, SC, IV	J0895
DESMOPRESSIN ACETATE	1 MCG	IV, SC	J2597
DEXAMETHASONE	0.25 MG	ORAL	J8540
DEXAMETHASONE ACETATE	1 MG	IM	J1094
DEXAMETHASONE ACETATE ANHYDROUS	1 MG	IM	J1094
DEXAMETHASONE INTRAVITREAL IMPLANT	0.1 MG	OTH	J7312
DEXAMETHASONE SODIUM PHOSPHATE	1 MG	IM, IV, OTH	J1100
DEXAMETHASONE, COMPOUNDED, CONCENTRATED	1 MG	INH	J7637
DEXAMETHASONE, COMPOUNDED, UNIT DOSE	1 MG	INH	J7638
DEXASONE	1 MG	IM, IV, OTH	J1100
DEXEDRINE	5 MG	ORAL	S0160
DEXIM	1 MG	IM, IV, OTH	J1100
DEXONE	0.25 MG	ORAL	J8540
DEXONE	1 MG	IM, IV, OTH	J1100
DEXONE LA	1 MG	IM	J1094
DEXRAZOXANE HCL	250 MG	IV	J1190
DEXTRAN 40	500 ML	IV	J7100
DEXTROAMPHETAMINE SULFATE	5 MG	ORAL	S0160
DEXTROSE	500 ML	IV	J7060
DEXTROSE, STERILE WATER, AND/OR DEXTROSE DILUENT/FLUSH	10 ML	VAR	A4216
DEXTROSE/SODIUM CHLORIDE	5%	VAR	J7042
DEXTROSE/THEOPHYLLINE	40 MG	IV	J2810
DEXTROSTAT	5 MG	ORAL	S0160
DIALYSIS/STRESS VITAMINS	100 CAPS	ORAL	S0194
DIAMOX	500 MG	IM, IV	J1120
DIASTAT	5 MG	IV, IM	J3360
DIAZEPAM	5 MG	IV, IM	J3360
DIAZOXIDE	300 MG	IV	J1730
DIBENT	UP TO 20 MG	IM	J0500
DICYCLOMINE HCL	20 MG	IM	J0500
DIDANOSINE (DDI)	25 MG	ORAL	S0137
DIDRONEL	300 MG	IV	J1436
DIETHYLSTILBESTROL DIPHOSPHATE	250 MG	INJ	J9165
DIFLUCAN	200 MG	IV	J1450
DIGIBIND	VIAL	IV	J1162
DIGIFAB	VIAL	IV	J1162
DIGOXIN	0.5 MG	IM, IV	J1160
DIGOXIN IMMUNE FAB	VIAL	IV	J1162
DIHYDROERGOTAMINE MESYLATE	1 MG	IM, IV	J1110
DILANTIN	50 MG	IM, IV	J1165
DILAUDID	250 MG	OTH	S0092
DILAUDID	4 MG	SC, IM, IV	J1170
DIMENHYDRINATE	50 MG	IM, IV	J1240
DIMERCAPROL	100 MG	IM	J0470
DIMINE	50 MG	IV, IM	J1200
DINATE	50 MG	IM, IV	J1240
DIOVAL	10 MG	IM	J1380
DIOVAL 40	10 MG	IM	J1380
DIOVAL XX	10 MG	IM	J1380
DIPHENHYDRAMINE HCL	50 MG	IV, IM	J1200
DIPHENHYDRAMINE HCL	50 MG	ORAL	Q0163
DIPYRIDAMOLE	10 MG	IV	J1245
DISOTATE	150 MG	IV	J3520
DI-SPAZ	UP TO 20 MG	IM	J0500
DIURIL	500 MG	IV	J1205
DIURIL SODIUM	500 MG	IV	J1205
DIZAC	5 MG	IV, IM	J3360
DMSO, DIMETHYL SULFOXIDE	50%, 50 ML	OTH	J1212
DOBUTAMINE HCL	250 MG	IV	J1250
DOBUTREX	250 MG	IV	J1250
DOCETAXEL	1 MG	IV	J9171
DOLASETRON MESYLATE	10 MG	IV	J1260
DOLASETRON MESYLATE	50 MG	ORAL	S0174
DOLASETRON MESYLATE	100 MG	ORAL	Q0180
DOLOPHINE	5 MG	ORAL	S0109
DOLOPHINE HCL	10 MG	IM, SC	J1230
DOMMANATE	50 MG	IM, IV	J1240
DOPAMINE HCL	40 MG	IV	J1265
DORIBAX	10 MG	IV	J1267
DORIPENEM	10 MG	IV	J1267
DORNASE ALPHA, NONCOMPOUNDED, UNIT DOSE	1 MG	INH	J7639
DOSTINEX	0.25 MG	ORAL	J8515
DOXERCALCIFEROL	1 MG	IV	J1270
DOXIL	10 MG	IV	J9001
DOXORUBICIN HCL	10 MG	IV	J9000
DOXORUBICIN HCL, ALL LIPID FORMULATIONS	10 MG	IV	J9001
DRAMAMINE	50 MG	IM, IV	J1240
DRAMANATE	50 MG	IM, IV	J1240
DRAMILIN	50 MG	IM, IV	J1240
DRAMOCEN	50 MG	IM, IV	J1240
DRAMOJECT	50 MG	IM, IV	J1240
DRAXIMAGE MDP-10	STUDY DOSE UP TO 30 MCI	IV	A9503
DRAXIMAGE MDP-25	STUDY DOSE UP TO 30 MCI	IV	A9503

Drug Name	Unit Per	Route	Code
DRONABINAL	2.5 MG	ORAL	Q0167
DRONABINAL	5 MG	ORAL	Q0168
DROPERIDOL	5 MG	IM, IV	J1790
DROPERIDOL AND FENTANYL CITRATE	2 ML	IM, IV	J1810
DROXIA	500 MG	ORAL	S0176
DTIC-DOME	100 MG	IV	J9130
DTPA	STUDY DOSE UP TO 25 MCI	IV	A9539
DTPA	STUDY DOSE UP TO 25 MCI	INH	A9567
DUO-SPAN	1 ML	IM	J1060
DUO-SPAN II	1 ML	IM	J1060
DURACILLIN A.S.	600,000 UNITS	IM, IV	J2510
DURACLON	1 MG	OTH	J0735
DURAGEN-10	10 MG	IM	J1380
DURAGEN-20	10 MG	IM	J1380
DURAGEN-40	10 MG	IM	J1380
DURAMORPH	10 MG	IM, IV, SC	J2275
DURAMORPH	500 MG	OTH	S0093
DURO CORT	80 MG	IM	J1040
DYMENATE	50 MG	IM, IV	J1240
DYPHYLLINE	500 MG	IM	J1180
DYSPORT	5 UNITS	IM	J0586
E.D.T.A	150 MG	IV	J3520
ECALLANTIDE	1 MG	SC	J1290
ECHOCARDIOGRAM IMAGE ENHANCER	1 ML	INJ	Q9956
ECHOCARDIOGRAM IMAGE ENHANCER	1 ML	IV	Q9955
ECULIZUMAB	10 MG	IV	J1300
EDETATE CALCIUM DISODIUM	1,000 MG	IV, SC, IM	J0600
EDETATE DISODIUM	150 MG	IV	J3520
EDEX	1.25 MCG	VAR	J0270
ELAPRASE	1 MG	IV	J1743
ELAVIL	20 MG	IM	J1320
ELIGARD	7.5 MG	IM	J9217
ELIGARD	PER 3.75 MG	SC	J1950
ELITEK	50 MCG	IM	J2783
ELLENCE	2 MG	IV	J9178
ELLIOTTS B SOLUTION	1 ML	IV, IT	J9175
ELOXATIN	0.5 MG	IV	J9263
ELSPAR	10,000 U	VAR	J9020
EMEND	5 MG	ORAL	J8501
EMEND	1 MG	IV	J1453
EMINASE	30 U	IV	J0350
ENBREL	25 MG	IM, IV	J1438
ENDOFORM DERMAL TEMPLATE	1 SQ CM	OTH	C9367
ENDOXAN-ASTA	100 MG	IV	J9070
ENDRATE	150 MG	IV	J3520
ENFUVIRTIDE	1 MG	SC	J1324
ENOXAPARIN SODIUM	10 MG	SC	J1650
EOVIST	1 ML	IV	A9581
EPIFIX	PER SQ IN	OTH	C9366
EPINEPHRINE	0.1 MG	VAR	J0171
EPIRUBICIN HCL	2 MG	IV	J9178
EPOETIN ALFA FOR ESRD DIALYSIS	100 U	INJ	Q4081
EPOETIN ALFA, ESRD USE	1,000 U	SC, IV	J0886
EPOETIN ALFA, NON-ESRD USE	1,000 U	SC, IV	J0885
EPOGEN/ESRD	1,000 U	SC, IV	J0886
EPOGEN/NON-ESRD	1,000 U	SC, IV	J0885
EPOPROSTENOL	0.5 MG	IV	J1325
EPOPROSTENOL STERILE DILUTANT	50 ML	IV	S0155
EPTIFIBATIDE	5 MG	IM, IV	J1327
ERAXIS	1 MG	IV	J0348
ERBITUX	10 MG	IV	J9055
ERGAMISOL	50 MG	ORAL	S0177
ERGONOVINE MALEATE	0.2 MG	IM, IV	J1330
~~ERIBULIN MESYLATE~~	~~1 MG~~	~~IV~~	~~C9280~~
ERIBULIN MESYLATE	0.1 MG	IV	J9179
ERTAPENEM SODIUM	500 MG	IM, IV	J1335
ERYTHROCIN LACTOBIONATE	500 MG	IV	J1364
ESTONE AQUEOUS	1 MG	IM, IV	J1435
ESTRADIOL CYPIONATE	UP TO 5 MG	IM	J1000
ESTRADIOL L.A.	10 MG	IM	J1380
ESTRADIOL L.A. 20	10 MG	IM	J1380
ESTRADIOL L.A. 40	10 MG	IM	J1380
ESTRADIOL VALERATE	10 MG	IM	J1380
ESTRAGYN	1 MG	IV, IM	J1435
ESTRA-L 20	10 MG	IM	J1380
ESTRA-L 40	10 MG	IM	J1380
ESTRO-A	1 MG	IV, IM	J1435
ESTROGEN CONJUGATED	25 MG	IV, IM	J1410
ESTRONE	1 MG	IV, IM	J1435
ESTRONOL	1 MG	IM, IV	J1435
ETANERCEPT	25 MG	IM, IV	J1438
ETHAMOLIN	100 MG	IV	J1430
ETHANOLAMINE OLEATE	100 MG	IV	J1430
ETHYOL	500 MG	IV	J0207
ETIDRONATE DISODIUM	300 MG	IV	J1436
ETONOGESTREL	IMPLANT	OTH	J7307
ETOPOSIDE	10 MG	IV	J9181
ETOPOSIDE	50 MG	ORAL	J8560
EUFLEXXA	DOSE	OTH	J7323
EULEXIN	125 MG	ORAL	S0175
EVEROLIMUS	0.25 MG	ORAL	J8561
EXAMETAZIME LABELED AUTOLOGOUS WHITE BLOOD CELLS, TECHNETIUM TC-99M	STUDY DOSE	IV	A9569
EXMESTANE	25 MG	ORAL	S0156
FABRAZYME	1 MG	IV	J0180
FACTOR IX NON-RECOMBINANT	1 IU	IV	J7193
FACTOR IX RECOMBINANT	1 IU	IV	J7195
FACTOR IX+ COMPLEX	1 IU	IV	J7194
FACTOR VIIA RECOMBINANT	1 MCG	IV	J7189
FACTOR VIII PORCINE	1 IU	IV	J7191
FACTOR VIII RECOMBINANT	1 IU	IV	J7192
FACTOR VIII, HUMAN	1 IU	IV	J7190
FACTOR XIII (ANTIHEMOPHILIC FACTOR, HUMAN)	1 IU	IV	J7180
FACTREL	100 MCG	SC, IV	J1620
FAMOTIDINE	20 MG	IV	S0028
FASLODEX	25 MG	IM	J9395
FDG	STUDY DOSE UP TO 45 MCI	IV	A9552
FEIBA-VH AICC	1 IU	IV	J7198
FENTANYL CITRATE	0.1 MG	IM, IV	J3010
FERAHEME (FOR ESRD)	1 MG	IV	Q0139

Drug Name	Unit Per	Route	Code
FERAHEME (NON-ESRD)	1 MG	IV	Q0138
FERIDEX IV	1 ML	IV	Q9953
FERRLECIT	12.5 MG	IV	J2916
FERTINEX	75 IU	SC	J3355
FERUMOXYTOL (FOR ESRD)	1 MG	IV	Q0139
FERUMOXYTOL (NON-ESRD)	1 MG	IV	Q0138
FIBRIN SEALANT (HUMAN)	2ML	OTH	C9250
FIBRINOGEN CONCENTRATE (HUMAN)	100 MG	IV	J1680
FILGRASTIM	300 MCG	SC, IV	J1440
FILGRASTIM	480 MCG	SC, IV	J1441
FINASTERIDE	5 MG	ORAL	S0138
FLAGYL	500 MG	IV	S0030
FLEBOGAMMA	500 MG	IV	J1572
FLEXHD	SQ CM	OTH	Q4128
FLEXON	60 MG	IV, IM	J2360
FLOLAN	0.5 MG	IV	J1325
FLOXIN IV	400 MG	IV	S0034
FLOXURIDINE	500 MG	IV	J9200
FLUCONAZOLE	200 MG	IV	J1450
FLUDARA	50 MG	IV	J9185
FLUDARABINE PHOSPHATE	50 MG	IV	J9185
FLUDARABINE PHOSPHATE	10 MG	ORAL	J8562
FLUDEOXYGLUCOSE F18	STUDY DOSE UP TO 45 MCI	IV	A9552
FLULAVAL	EA	IM	Q2036
FLUMADINE (DEMONSTATION PROJECT)	100 MG	ORAL	G9036
FLUNISOLIDE, COMPOUNDED, UNIT DOSE	1 MG	INH	J7641
FLUOCINOLONE ACETONIDE INTRAVITREAL	IMPLANT	OTH	J7311
FLUORODEOXYGLUCOSE F-18 FDG, DIAGNOSTIC	STUDY DOSE UP TO 45 MCI	IV	A9552
FLUOROURACIL	500 MG	IV	J9190
FLUPHENAZINE DECANOATE	25 MG	SC, IM	J2680
FLUTAMIDE	125 MG	ORAL	S0175
FLUVIRIN	EA	IM	Q2037
FLUZONE	EA	IM	Q2038
FOLEX	5 MG	IV, IM, IT, IA	J9250
FOLEX	50 MG	IV, IM, IT, IA	J9260
FOLEX PFS	5 MG	IV, IM, IT, IA	J9250
FOLEX PFS	50 MG	IV, IM, IT, IA	J9260
FOLLISTIM	75 IU	SC, IM	S0128
FOLLITROPIN ALFA	75 IU	SC	S0126
FOLLITROPIN BETA	75 IU	SC, IM	S0128
FOLOTYN	1 MG	IV	J9307
FOMEPIZOLE	15 MG	IV	J1451
FOMIVIRSEN SODIUM	1.65 MG	OTH	J1452
FONDAPARINUX SODIUM	0.5 MG	SC	J1652
FORMOTEROL FUMERATE NONCOMPOUNDED UNIT DOSE FORM	20 MCG	INH	J7606
FORMOTEROL, COMPOUNDED, UNIT DOSE	12 MCG	INH	J7640
FORTAZ	500 MG	IM, IV	J0713
FORTEO	10 MCG	SC	J3110
FORTOVASE	200 MG	ORAL	S0140
FOSAPREPITANT	1 MG	IV	J1453
FOSCARNET SODIUM	1,000 MG	IV	J1455
FOSCAVIR	1,000 MG	IV	J1455
FOSPHENYTOIN	50 MG	IM, IV	Q2009
FOSPHENYTOIN SODIUM	750 MG	IM, IV	S0078
FRAGMIN	2,500 IU	SC	J1645
FUDR	500 MG	IV	J9200
FULVESTRANT	25 MG	IM	J9395
FUNGIZONE	50 MG	IV	J0285
FUROSEMIDE	20 MG	IM, IV	J1940
FUSILEV	0.5 MG	IV	J0641
FUZEON	1 MG	SC	J1324
GABLOFEN	10 MG	IT	J0475
GABLOFEN	50 MCG	IT	J0476
GADAVIST	0.1 ML	IV	A9585
GADOBENATE DIMEGLUMINE (MULTIHANCE MULTIPACK)	1 ML	IV	A9577
GADOBUTROL	0.1 ML	IV	A9585
GADOFOSVESET TRISODIUM	1 ML	IV	A9583
GADOLINIUM -BASED CONTRAST NOS	1 ML	IV	A9579
GADOTERIDOL (PROHANCE MULTIPACK)	1 ML	IV	A9576
GADOXETATE DISODIUM	1 ML	IV	A9581
GALLIUM GA-67	1 MCI	IV	A9556
GALLIUM NITRATE	1 MG	IV	J1457
GALSULFASE	1 MG	IV	J1458
GAMASTAN	1 CC	IM	J1460
GAMASTAN	OVER 10 CC	IM	J1560
GAMASTAN SD	1 CC	IM	J1460
GAMASTAN SD	OVER 10 CC	IM	J1560
GAMMA GLOBULIN	1 CC	IM	J1460
GAMMA GLOBULIN	OVER 10 CC	IM	J1560
GAMMAGARD	500 MG	IV	J1569
GAMMAGRAFT	SQ CM	OTH	Q4111
GAMMAKED	500 MG	IV, SC	J1561
~~GAMMAPLEX~~	~~500 MG~~	~~IV~~	~~C9270~~
GAMMAPLEX	500 MG	IV	J1557
GAMUNEX	500 MG	IV, SQ	J1561
GAMUNEX-C	500 MG	IV, SC	J1561
GANCICLOVIR	4.5 MG	OTH	J7310
GANCICLOVIR SODIUM	500 MG	IV	J1570
GANIRELIX ACETATE	250 MCG	SC	S0132
GANITE	1 MG	IV	J1457
GARAMYCIN	80 MG	IM, IV	J1580
GASTROCROM	10 MG	INH	J7631
GASTROMARK	1 ML	ORAL	Q9954
GATIFLOXACIN	10 MG	IV	J1590
GEFITINIB	250 MG	ORAL	J8565
GEL-ONE	DOSE	OTH	J7326
GEMCITABINE HCL	200 MG	IV	J9201
GEMTUZUMAB OZOGAMICIN	5 MG	IV	J9300
GEMZAR	200 MG	IV	J9201
GENGRAF	100 MG	ORAL	J7502
GENGRAF	25 MG	ORAL	J7515
GENOTROPIN	1 MG	SC	J2941
GENOTROPIN MINIQUICK	1 MG	SC	J2941
GENOTROPIN NUTROPIN	1 MG	SC	J2941
GENTAMICIN	80 MG	IM, IV	J1580
GENTRAN	500 ML	IV	J7100
GENTRAN 75	500 ML	IV	J7110

Drug Name	Unit Per	Route	Code
GEODON	10 MG	IM	J3486
GEREF	1MCG	SC	Q0515
GLASSIA	10 MG	IV	J0257
GLATIRAMER ACETATE	20 MG	SC	J1595
GLEEVEC	100 MG	ORAL	S0088
GLOFIL-125	STUDY DOSE UP TO 10 UCI	IV	A9554
GLUCAGEN	1 MG	SC, IM, IV	J1610
GLUCAGON	1 MG	SC, IM, IV	J1610
GLUCOTOPE	STUDY DOSE UP TO 45 MCI	IV	A9552
GLYCOPYRROLATE, COMPOUNDED CONCENTRATED	PER MG	INH	J7642
GLYCOPYRROLATE, COMPOUNDED, UNIT DOSE	1 MG	INH	J7643
GOLD SODIUM THIOMALATE	50 MG	IM	J1600
GONADORELIN HCL	100 MCG	SC, IV	J1620
GONAL-F	75 IU	SC	S0126
GOSERELIN ACETATE	3.6 MG	SC	J9202
GRAFTJACKET	SQ CM	OTH	Q4107
GRAFTJACKET EXPRESS	1 CC	INJ	Q4113
GRANISETRON HCL	1 MG	ORAL	Q0166
GRANISETRON HCL	100 MCG	IV	J1626
GRANISETRON HCL	1 MG	IV	S0091
GYNOGEN L.A. 10	10 MG	IM	J1380
GYNOGEN L.A. 20	10 MG	IM	J1380
GYNOGEN L.A. 40	10 MG	IM	J1380
H.P. ACTHAR GEL	UP TO 40 UNITS	OTH	J0800
HALAVEN	0.1 MG	IV	J9179
HALDOL	5 MG	IM, IV	J1630
HALDOL DECANOATE	50 MG	IM	J1631
HALOPERIDOL	5 MG	IM, IV	J1630
HECTOROL	1 MG	IV	J1270
HELIXATE FS	1 IU	IV	J7192
HEMIN	1 MG	IV	J1640
HEMOFIL-M	1 IU	IV	J7190
HEP LOCK	10 U	IV	J1642
HEPAGAM B	0.5 ML	IM	J1571
HEPAGAM B	0.5 ML	IV	J1573
HEPARIN SODIUM	1,000 U	IV, SC	J1644
HEPARIN SODIUM	10 U	IV	J1642
HEPATITIS B IMMUNE GLOBULIN	0.5 ML	IV	J1573
HEPATOLITE	STUDY DOSE UP TO 15 MCI	IV	A9510
HEP-PAK	10 UNITS	IV	J1642
HERCEPTIN	10 MG	IV	J9355
HEXADROL	0.25 MG	ORAL	J8540
HEXAMINOLEVULINATE	STUDY DOSE	OTH	C9275
HIGH OSMOLAR CONTRAST MATERIAL, UP TO 149 MG/ML IODINE CONCENTRATION	1 ML	IV	Q9958
HIGH OSMOLAR CONTRAST MATERIAL, UP TO 150-199 MG/ML IODINE CONCENTRATION	1 ML	IV	Q9959
HIGH OSMOLAR CONTRAST MATERIAL, UP TO 200-249 MG/ML IODINE CONCENTRATION	1 ML	IV	Q9960
HIGH OSMOLAR CONTRAST MATERIAL, UP TO 250-299 MG/ML IODINE CONCENTRATION	1 ML	IV	Q9961
HIGH OSMOLAR CONTRAST MATERIAL, UP TO 300-349 MG/ML IODINE CONCENTRATION	1 ML	IV	Q9962
HIGH OSMOLAR CONTRAST MATERIAL, UP TO 350-399 MG/ML IODINE CONCENTRATION	1 ML	IV	Q9963
HIGH OSMOLAR CONTRAST MATERIAL, UP TO 400 OR GREATER MG/ML IODINE CONCENTRATION	1 ML	IV	Q9964
HISTERLIN IMPLANT (VANTAS)	50 MG	OTH	J9225
HISTRELIN ACETATE	10 MG	INJ	J1675
HISTRELIN IMPLANT (SUPPRELIN LA)	50 MG	OTH	J9226
HIZENTRA	100 MG	IV	J1559
HUMALOG	5 U	SC	J1815
HUMALOG	50 U	SC	J1817
HUMATE-P	1 IU	IV	J7187
HUMATROPE	1 MG	SC	J2941
HUMIRA	20 MG	SC	J0135
HUMULIN	5 U	SC	J1815
HUMULIN	50 U	SC	J1817
HUMULIN R	5 U	SC	J1815
HUMULIN R U-500	5 U	SC	J1815
HYALGAN	DOSE	OTH	J7321
HYALOMATRIX	SQ CM	OTH	Q4117
HYALURONAN OR DERITIVE, GEL-ONE	DOSE	OTH	J7326
HYALURONAN, EUFLEXXA	DOSE	OTH	J7323
HYALURONAN, HYALGAN OR SUPARTZ	DOSE	OTH	J7321
HYALURONAN, ORTHOVISC	DOSE	OTH	J7324
HYALURONAN, SYNVISC/SYNVISC-ONE	1 MG	OTH	J7325
HYALURONIDASE	150 UNITS	VAR	J3470
HYALURONIDASE RECOMBINANT	1 USP UNIT	SC	J3473
HYALURONIDASE, OVINE, PRESERVATIVE FREE	1000 USP	OTH	J3472
HYALURONIDASE, OVINE, PRESERVATIVE FREE	1 USP	OTH	J3471
HYCAMTIN	0.25 MG	ORAL	J8705
HYCAMTIN	0.1 MG	IV	J9351
HYDRALAZINE HCL	20 MG	IV, IM	J0360
HYDRATE	50 MG	IM, IV	J1240
HYDREA	500 MG	ORAL	S0176
HYDROCORTISONE ACETATE	25 MG	IV, IM, SC	J1700
HYDROCORTISONE SODIUM PHOSPHATE	50 MG	IV, IM, SC	J1710
HYDROCORTISONE SODIUM SUCCINATE	100 MG	IV, IM, SC	J1720
HYDROCORTONE PHOSPHATE	50 MG	SC, IM, IV	J1710
HYDROMORPHONE HCL	4 MG	SC, IM, IV	J1170
HYDROMORPHONE HCL	250 MG	OTH	S0092
HYDROXOCOBALAMIN	1,000 MCG	IM, SC	J3420
HYDROXYCOBAL	1,000 MCG	IM, SC	J3420
HYDROXYPROGESTERONE CAPROATE	1 MG	IM	J1725
HYDROXYUREA	500 MG	ORAL	S0176
HYDROXYZINE HCL	25 MG	IM	J3410
HYDROXYZINE PAMOATE	25 MG	ORAL	Q0177
HYDROXYZINE PAMOATE	50 MG	ORAL	Q0178
HYOSCYAMINE SULFATE	0.25 MG	SC, IM, IV	J1980
HYPERRHO S/D	300 MCG	IV	J2790
HYPERTET SD	UP TO 250 MG	IM	J1670
HYPERTONIC SALINE SOLUTION	1 ML	VAR	J7131

Drug Name	Unit Per	Route	Code
HYREXIN	50 MG	IV, IM	J1200
HYZINE	25 MG	IM	J3410
HYZINE-50	25 MG	IM	J3410
I-131 TOSITUMOMAB DIAGNOSTIC	STUDY DOSE	IV	A9544
I-131 TOSITUMOMAB THERAPEUTIC	TX DOSE	IV	A9545
IBANDRONATE SODIUM	1 MG	IV	J1740
IBRITUMOMAB TUXETAN	STUDY DOSE UP TO 5 MCI	IV	A9542
IBUPROFEN	100 MG	IV	C9279
IBUTILIDE FUMARATE	1 MG	IV	J1742
IDAMYCIN	5 MG	IV	J9211
IDAMYCIN PFS	5 MG	IV	J9211
IDARUBICIN HCL	5 MG	IV	J9211
IDURSULFASE	1 MG	IV	J1743
IFEX	1 G	IV	J9208
IFOSFAMIDE	1 G	IV	J9208
IL-2	1 VIAL	IV	J9015
ILARIS	1 MG	SC	J0638
ILETIN	5 UNITS	SC	J1815
ILETIN II NPH PORK	50 U	SC	J1817
ILETIN II REGULAR PORK	5 U	SC	J1815
ILOPROST INHALATION SOLUTION	PER DOSE UP TO 20 MCG	INH	Q4074
IMAGENT	1 ML	IV	Q9955
IMATINIB	100 MG	ORAL	S0088
IMIGLUCERASE	10 U	IV	J1786
IMITREX	6 MG	SC	J3030
IMMUNE GLOBULIN (FLEBOGAMMA, FLEBOGAMMA DIF	500 MG	IV	J1572
IMMUNE GLOBULIN (GAMMAGARD LIQUID)	500 MG	IV	J1569
IMMUNE GLOBULIN (GAMMAPLEX)	500 MG	IV	J1557
~~IMMUNE GLOBULIN (GAMMAPLEX)~~	~~500 MG~~	~~IV~~	~~C9270~~
IMMUNE GLOBULIN (GAMUNEX)	500 MG	IV	J1561
IMMUNE GLOBULIN (HIZENTRA)	100 MG	IV	J1559
IMMUNE GLOBULIN (OCTAGAM)	500 MG	IV	J1568
IMMUNE GLOBULIN (PRIVIGEN) NONLYOPHILIZED	500 MG	IV	J1459
IMMUNE GLOBULIN (RHOPHYLAC)	100 IU	IM, IV	J2791
IMMUNE GLOBULIN LYOPHILIZED	500 MG	IV	J1566
IMMUNE GLOBULIN SUBCUTANEOUS	100 MG	SC	J1562
IMMUNE GLOBULIN, NONLYOPHILIZED (NOS)	500 MG	IV	J1599
IMPLANON	IMPLANT	OTH	J7307
IMURAN	50 MG	ORAL	J7500
IN-111 SATUMOMAB PENDETIDE	STUDY DOSE UP TO MCI	IV	A4642
INAPSINE	5 MG	IM, IV	J1790
~~INCOBOTULINUMTOXINA~~	~~1 UNIT~~	~~IM~~	~~C9278~~
~~INCOBOTULINUMTOXINA~~	~~1 UNIT~~	~~IM~~	~~Q2040~~
INCOBUTULINUMTOXINA	1 UNIT	IM	J0588
INDERAL	1 MG	IV	J1800
INDIUM IN-111 IBRITUMOMAB TIUXETAN, DIAGNOSTIC	STUDY DOSE UP TO 5 MCI	IV	A9542
INDIUM IN-111 LABELED AUTOLOGOUS PLATELETS	STUDY DOSAGE	IV	A9571
INDIUM IN-111 LABELED AUTOLOGOUS WHITE BLOOD CELLS	STUDY DOSE	IV	A9570
INDIUM IN-111 OXYQUINOLINE	0.5 MCI	IV	A9547
INDIUM IN-111 PENTETREOTIDE	STUDY DOSE UP TO 6 MCI	IV	A9572
INDURSALFASE	1 MG	IV	J1743
INFED	50 MG	IM, IV	J1750
INFERGEN	1 MCG	SC	J9212
INFLIXIMAB	10 MG	IV	J1745
INFLUENZA A (H1N1) VACCINE	EA	VAR	G9142
INFLUENZA VIRUS VACCINE (AFLURIA)	EA	IM	Q2035
INFLUENZA VIRUS VACCINE (FLULAVAL)	EA	IM	Q2036
INFLUENZA VIRUS VACCINE (FLUVIRIN)	EA	IM	Q2037
INFLUENZA VIRUS VACCINE (FLUZONE)	EA	IM	Q2038
INFLUENZA VIRUS VACCINE, NOT OTHERWISE SPECIFIED	EA	IM	Q2039
INFUMORPH	10 MG	IM, IV, SC	J2270
INFUMORPH	10 MG	OTH	J2275
INFUMORPH PRESERVATIVE FREE	100 MG	IM, IV, SC	J2271
INNOHEP	1,000 IU	SC	J1655
INSULIN	5 U	SC	J1815
INSULIN	50 U	SC	J1817
INSULIN LISPRO	5 U	SC	S5551
INSULIN LISPRO	5 U	SC	J1815
INSULIN PURIFIED REGULAR PORK	5 U	SC	J1815
INTAL	10 MG	INH	J7631
INTEGRA BILAYER MATRIX DRESSING	SQ CM	OTH	Q4104
INTEGRA DERMAL REGENERATION TEMPLATE	SQ CM	OTH	Q4105
INTEGRA FLOWABLE WOUND MATRIX	1 CC	INJ	Q4114
INTEGRA MATRIX	SQ CM	OTH	Q4108
INTEGRA MESHED BILAYER WOUND MATRIX	SQ CM	OTH	C9363
INTEGRA MOZAIK OSTEOCONDUCTIVE SCAFFOLD PUTTY	0.5 CC	OTH	C9359
INTEGRA MOZAIK OSTEOCONDUCTIVE SCAFFOLD STRIP	0.5 CC	OTH	C9362
INTEGRA OS OSTEOCONDUCTIVE SCAFFOLD PUTTY	0.5 CC	OTH	C9359
INTEGRILIN	5 MG	IM, IV	J1327
INTERFERON ALFA-2A	3,000,000 U	SC, IM	J9213
INTERFERON ALFA-2B	1,000,000 U	SC, IM	J9214
INTERFERON ALFACON-1	1 MCG	SC	J9212
INTERFERON ALFA-N3	250,000 IU	IM	J9215
INTERFERON BETA-1A	11 MCG	IM	Q3025
INTERFERON BETA-1A	30 MCG	IM, SC	J1826
INTERFERON BETA-1A	11 MCG	SC	Q3026
INTERFERON BETA-1B	0.25 MG	SC	J1830
INTERFERON, ALFA-2A, RECOMBINANT	3,000,000 U	SC, IM	J9213
INTERFERON, ALFA-2B, RECOMBINANT	1,000,000 U	SC, IM	J9214
INTERFERON, ALFA-N3, (HUMAN LEUKOCYTE DERIVED)	250,000 IU	IM	J9215
INTERFERON, GAMMA 1-B	3,000,000 U	SC	J9216
INTERLUEKIN	1 VIAL	IV	J9015
INTRON A	1,000,000 U	SC, IM	J9214
INVANZ	500 MG	IM, IV	J1335
INVEGA SUSTENNA	1 MG	IM	J2426
INVIRASE	200 MG	ORAL	S0140
IOBENGUANE SULFATE I-131	0.5 MCI	IV	A9508

Drug Name	Unit Per	Route	Code
IOBENGUANE, I-123, DIAGNOSTIC	PER STUDY DOSE UP TO 15 MCI	IV	A9582
IODINE I-123 IOBENGUANE, DIAGNOSTIC	15 MCI	IV	A9582
IODINE I-123 IOFLUPANE	STUDY DOSE UP TO 5 MCI	IV	A9584
IODINE I-123 SODIUM IODIDE CAPSULE(S), DIAGNOSTIC	100-9999 UCI	ORAL	A9516
IODINE I-123 SODIUM IODIDE, DIAGNOSTIC	1 MCI	IV	A9509
IODINE I-125 SERUM ALBUMIN, DIAGNOSTIC	5 UCI	IV	A9532
IODINE I-125 SODIUM IOTHALAMATE, DIAGNOSTIC	STUDY DOSE UP TO 10 UCI	IV	A9554
IODINE I-125, SODIUM IODIDE SOLUTION, THERAPEUTIC	1 MCI	ORAL	A9527
IODINE I-131 IOBENGUANE SULFATE, DIAGNOSTIC	0.5 MCI	IV	A9508
IODINE I-131 IODINATED SERUM ALBUMIN, DIAGNOSTIC	PER 5 UCI	IV	A9524
IODINE I-131 SODIUM IODIDE CAPSULE(S), DIAGNOSTIC	1 MCI	ORAL	A9528
IODINE I-131 SODIUM IODIDE CAPSULE(S), THERAPEUTIC	1 MCI	ORAL	A9517
IODINE I-131 SODIUM IODIDE SOLUTION, DIAGNOSTIC	1 MCI	ORAL	A9529
IODINE I-131 SODIUM IODIDE SOLUTION, THERAPEUTIC	1 MCI	ORAL	A9530
IODINE I-131 SODIUM IODIDE, DIAGNOSTIC	PER UCI UP TO 100 UCI	IV	A9531
IODINE I-131 TOSITUMOMAB, DIAGNOSTIC	STUDY DOSE	IV	A9544
IODINE I-131 TOSITUMOMAB, THERAPEUTIC	TX DOSE	IV	A9545
IODOTOPE THERAPEUTIC CAPSULE(S)	1 MCI	ORAL	A9517
IODOTOPE THERAPEUTIC SOLUTION	1 MCI	ORAL	A9530
IOFLUPANE	STUDY DOSE UP TO 5 MCI	IV	A9584
ION-BASED MAGNETIC RESONANCE CONTRAST AGENT	1 ML	IV	Q9953
IOTHALAMATE SODIUM I-125	STUDY DOSE UP TO 10 UCI	IV	A9554
IPILIMUMAB	1 MG	IV	J9228
IPLEX	1 MG	SC	J2170
IPRATROPIUM BROMIDE, NONCOMPOUNDED, UNIT DOSE	1 MG	INH	J7644
IPTRATROPIUM BROMIDE COMPOUNDED, UNIT DOSE	1 MG	INH	J7645
IRESSA	250 MG	ORAL	J8565
IRINOTECAN	20 MG	IV	J9206
IRON DEXTRAN, 50 MG	50 MG	IM, IV	J1750
IRON SUCROSE	1 MG	IV	J1756
ISOCAINE	10 ML	VAR	J0670
ISOETHARINE HCL COMPOUNDED, CONCENTRATED	1 MG	INH	J7647
ISOETHARINE HCL COMPOUNDED, UNIT DOSE	1 MG	INH	J7650
ISOETHARINE HCL, NONCOMPOUNDED CONCENTRATED	PER MG	INH	J7648
ISOETHARINE HCL, NONCOMPOUNDED, UNIT DOSE	1 MG	INH	J7649
ISOJEX	5 UCI	IV	A9532
ISOPROTERENOL HCL COMPOUNDED, CONCENTRATED	1 MG	INH	J7657
ISOPROTERENOL HCL COMPOUNDED, UNIT DOSE	1 MG	INH	J7660
ISOPROTERENOL HCL, NONCOMPOUNDED CONCENTRATED	1 MG	INH	J7658
ISOPROTERNOL HCL, NONCOMPOUNDED, UNIT DOSE	1MG	INH	J7659
ISOSULFAN BLUE	1 MG	SC	Q9968
ISTODAX	1 MG	IV	J9315
ISUPREL	1 MG	INH	J7658
ISUPREL	I MG	INH	J7659
ITRACONAZOLE	50 MG	IV	J1835
IVEEGAM	500 MG	IV	J1566
IXABEPILONE	1 MG	IV	J9207
IXEMPRA	1 MG	IV	J9207
JEVTANA	1 MG	IV	J9043
~~JEVTANA~~	~~1 MG~~	~~IV~~	~~C9276~~
KALBITOR	1 MG	SC	J1290
KANAMYCIN	500 MG	IM, IV	J1840
KANAMYCIN	75 MG	IM, IV	J1850
KANTREX	500 MG	IM, IV	J1840
KANTREX	75 MG	IM, IV	J1850
KEFZOL	500 MG	IM, IV	J0690
KENAJECT-40	10 MG	IM	J3301
KENALOG-10	10 MG	IM	J3301
KEPIVANCE	50 MCG	IV	J2425
KEPPRA	10 MG	IV	J1953
KESTRONE	1 MG	IV, IM	J1435
KETOROLAC TROMETHAMINE	15 MG	IM, IV	J1885
KINEVAC	5 MCG	IV	J2805
KOATE-DVI	1 IU	IV	J7190
KOGENATE FS	1 IU	IV	J7192
KONAKION	1 MG	SC, IM, IV	J3430
KONYNE 80	1 IU	IV	J7194
KRYSTEXXA	1 MG	IV	J2507
KYTRIL	1 MG	ORAL	Q0166
KYTRIL	1 MG	IV	S0091
KYTRIL	100 MCG	IV	J1626
L.A.E. 20	10 MG	IM	J1380
LACOSAMIDE	1 MG	IV	C9254
LANOXIN	0.5 MG	IM, IV	J1160
LANREOTIDE	1 MG	SC	J1930
LANTUS	50 U	SC	J1815
LARONIDASE	0.1 MG	IV	J1931
LASIX	20 MG	IM, IV	J1940
LENTE ILETIN I	5 U	SC	J1815
LEPIRUDIN	50 MG	IV	J1945
LEUCOVORIN CALCIUM	50 MG	IM, IV	J0640
LEUKERAN	2 MG	ORAL	S0172
LEUKINE	50 MCG	IV	J2820
LEUPROLIDE ACETATE	1 MG	IM	J9218
LEUPROLIDE ACETATE	7.5 MG	IM	J9217
LEUPROLIDE ACETATE (FOR DEPOT SUSPENSION)	3.75 MG	IM	J1950
LEUPROLIDE ACETATE DEPOT	7.5 MG	IM	J9217
LEUPROLIDE ACETATE IMPLANT	65 MG	OTH	J9219
LEUSTATIN	1 MG	IV	J9065
LEVABUTEROL COMPOUNDED, UNIT DOSE	1 MG	INH	J7615

Drug Name	Unit Per	Route	Code
LEVABUTEROL, COMPOUNDED, CONCENTRATED	0.5 MG	INH	J7607
LEVALBUTEROL NONCOMPOUNDED, CONCENTRATED FORM	0.5 MG	INH	J7612
LEVALBUTEROL, NONCOMPOUNDED, UNIT DOSE	0.5 MG	INH	J7614
LEVAMISOLE HCL	50 MG	ORAL	S0177
LEVAQUIN	250 MG	IV	J1956
LEVEMIR	5 U	SC	J1815
LEVETIRACETAM	10 MG	IV	J1953
LEVOCARNITINE	1 G	IV	J1955
LEVO-DROMORAN	UP TO 2 MG	IV, IM	J1960
LEVOFLOXACIN	250 MG	IV	J1956
LEVOLEUCOVORIN CALCIUM	0.5 MG	IV	J0641
LEVONORGESTREL	52 MG	OTH	J7302
LEVORPHANOL TARTRATE	2 MG	SC, IV, IM	J1960
LEVSIN	0.25 MG	SC, IM, IV	J1980
LEVULAN KERASTICK	354 MG	OTH	J7308
LEXISCAN	0.1 MG	IV	J2785
LIBRIUM	100 MG	IM, IV	J1990
LIDOCAINE 70 MG/TETRACAINE 70 MG	PATCH	OTH	C9285
LIDOCAINE HCL	10 MG	IV	J2001
LINCOCIN HCL	300 MG	IV	J2010
LINCOMYCIN HCL	300 MG	IM, IV	J2010
LINEZOLID	200 MG	IV	J2020
LIORESAL	10 MG	IT	J0475
LIORESAL INTRATHECAL REFILL	50 MCG	IT	J0476
LIQUAEMIN SODIUM	1,000 UNITS	SC, IV	J1644
LISPRO-PFC	50 U	SC	J1817
LOK-PAK	10 UNITS	IV	J1642
LOMUSTINE	10 MG	ORAL	S0178
LORAZEPAM	2 MG	IM, IV	J2060
LOVENOX	10 MG	SC	J1650
LOW OSMOLAR CONTRAST MATERIAL, 100-199 MG/ML IODINE CONCENTRATIONS	1 ML	IV	Q9965
LOW OSMOLAR CONTRAST MATERIAL, 200-299 MG/ML IODINE CONCENTRATION	1 ML	IV	Q9966
LOW OSMOLAR CONTRAST MATERIAL, 300-399 MG/ML IODINE CONCENTRATION	1 ML	IV	Q9967
LOW OSMOLAR CONTRAST MATERIAL, 400 OR GREATER MG/ML IODINE CONCENTRATION	1 ML	IV	Q9951
L-PHENYLALANINE MUSTARD	50 MG	IV	J9245
LUCENTIS	0.1 MG	IV	J2778
~~LUMIZYME~~	~~1 MG~~	~~IV~~	~~C9277~~
LUMIZYME	10 MG	IV	J0221
LUNELLE	5 MG/25 MG	IM	J1056
LUPRON	1 MG	SC	J9218
LUPRON DEPOT	PER 3.75 MG	IM	J1950
LUPRON DEPOT	7.5 MG	IM	J9217
LUPRON IMPLANT	65 MG	OTH	J9219
LUTREPULSE	100 MCG	SC, IV	J1620
LYMPHAZURIN	1 MG	SC	Q9968
LYMPHOCYTE IMMUNE GLOBULIN, ANTITHYMOCYTE GLOBULIN, EQUINE	250 MG	OTH	J7504
LYMPHOCYTE IMMUNE GLOBULIN, ANTITHYMOCYTE GLOBULIN, RABBIT	25 MG	OTH	J7511
MACUGEN	0.3 MG	OTH	J2503
MAGNESIUM SULFATE	500 MG	IV	J3475
MAGNETIC RESONANCE CONTRAST AGENT	1 ML	ORAL	Q9954
MAGNEVIST	1 ML	IV	A9579
MAGROTEC	STUDY DOSE UP TO 10 MCI	IV	A9540
MAKENA	1 MG	IM	J1725
MANNITOL	25% IN 50 ML	IV	J2150
MANNITOL	5 MG	INH	J7665
MARCAINE HCL	30 ML	VAR	S0020
MARINOL	2.5 MG	ORAL	Q0167
MARINOL	5 MG	ORAL	Q0168
MARMINE	50 MG	IM, IV	J1240
MATRISTEM BURN MATRIX	SQ CM	OTH	Q4120
MATRISTEM MICROMATRIX	1 MG	OTH	Q4118
MATRISTEM WOUND MATRIX	SQ CM	OTH	Q4119
MATULANE	50 MG	ORAL	S0182
MAXIPIME	500 MG	IV	J0692
MDP-BRACCO	STUDY DOSE UP TO 30 MCI	IV	A9503
MECASERMIN	1 MG	SC	J2170
MECHLORETHAMINE HCL (NITROGEN MUSTARD)	10 MG	IV	J9230
MEDIDEX	1 MG	IM, IV, OTH	J1100
MEDROL	4 MG	ORAL	J7509
MEDROXYPROGESTERONE ACETATE	50 MG	IM	J1051
MEDROXYPROGESTERONE ACETATE (CONTRACEPTIVE)	150 MG	IM	J1055
MEDROXYPROGESTERONE ACETATE/ESTRADIOL CYPIONATE	5 MG/25 MG	IM	J1056
MEFOXIN	1 G	IV	J0694
MEGACE	20 MG	ORAL	S0179
MEGESTROL ACETATE	20 MG	ORAL	S0179
MELPHALAN HCL	2 MG	ORAL	J8600
MELPHALAN HCL	50 MG	IV	J9245
MEMODERM	SQ CM	OTH	Q4126
MENADIONE	1 MG	IM, SC, IV	J3430
MENOTROPINS	75 IU	SC, IM, IV	S0122
MEPERGAN	50 MG	IM, IV	J2180
MEPERIDINE AND PROMETHAZINE HCL	50 MG	IM, IV	J2180
MEPERIDINE HCL	100 MG	IM, IV, SC	J2175
MEPIVACAINE HCL	10 ML	VAR	J0670
MERCAPTOPURINE	50 MG	ORAL	S0108
MERITATE	150 MG	IV	J3520
MEROPENEM	100 MG	IV	J2185
MERREM	100 MG	IV	J2185
MESNA	200 MG	IV	J9209
MESNEX	200 MG	IV	J9209
METAPROTERENOL SULFATE COMPOUNDED, UNIT DOSE	10 MG	INH	J7670
METAPROTERENOL SULFATE, NONCOMPOUNDED, CONCENTRATED	10 MG	INH	J7668
METAPROTERENOL SULFATE, NONCOMPOUNDED, UNIT DOSE	10 MG	INH	J7669
METARAMINOL BITARTRATE	10 MG	IV, IM, SC	J0380
METASTRON STRONTIUM 89 CHLORIDE	1 MCI	IV	A9600
METATRACE	STUDY DOSE UP TO 45 MCI	IV	A9552
METHACHOLINE CHLORIDE	1 MG	INH	J7674

Drug Name	Unit Per	Route	Code
METHADONE	5 MG	ORAL	S0109
METHADONE HCL	10 MG	IM, SC	J1230
METHAPREL, COMPOUNDED, UNIT DOSE	10 MG	INH	J7670
METHAPREL, NONCOMPOUNDED, CONCENTRATED	10 MG	INH	J7668
METHAPREL, NONCOMPOUNDED, UNIT DOSE	10 MG	INH	J7669
METHERGINE	0.2 MG	IM, IV	J2210
METHOTREXATE	5 MG	IV, IM, IT, IA	J9250
METHOTREXATE	2.5 MG	ORAL	J8610
METHOTREXATE	50 MG	IV, IM, IT, IA	J9260
METHOTREXATE LPF	5 MG	IV, IM, IT, IA	J9250
METHOTREXATE LPF	50 MG	IV, IM, IT, IA	J9260
METHYL AMINOLEVULINATE 16.8%	1 G	OTH	J7309
METHYLCOTOLONE	80 MG	IM	J1040
METHYLDOPA HCL	UP TO 250 MG	IV	J0210
METHYLDOPATE HCL	UP TO 250 MG	IV	J0210
METHYLENE BLUE	1 MG	SC	Q9968
METHYLERGONOVINE MALEATE	0.2 MG	IM, IV	J2210
METHYLPRED	4 MG	ORAL	J7509
METHYLPREDNISOLONE	4 MG	ORAL	J7509
METHYLPREDNISOLONE	125 MG	IM, IV	J2930
METHYLPREDNISOLONE	UP TO 40 MG	IM, IV	J2920
METHYLPREDNISOLONE ACETATE	20 MG	IM	J1020
METHYLPREDNISOLONE ACETATE	40 MG	IM	J1030
METHYLPREDNISOLONE ACETATE	80 MG	IM	J1040
METOCLOPRAMIDE	10 MG	IV	J2765
METRONIDAZOLE	500 MG	IV	S0030
METVIXIA 16.8%	1 G	OTH	J7309
MIACALCIN	400 U	SC, IM	J0630
MIBG	0.5 MCI	IV	A9508
MICAFUNGIN SODIUM	1 MG	IV	J2248
MICRHOGAM	50 MCG	IV	J2788
MICROPOROUS COLLAGEN IMPLANTABLE SLIT TUBE	1 CM LENGTH	OTH	C9353
MICROPOROUS COLLAGGEN IMPLANTABLE TUBE	1 CM LENGTH	OTH	C9352
MIDAZOLAM HCI	1 MG	IM, IV	J2250
MIFEPRISTONE	200 MG	ORAL	S0190
MILRINONE LACTATE	5 MG	IV	J2260
MINOCIN	1 MG	IV	J2265
MINOCYCLINE HCL	1 MG	IV	J2265
MINOXIDIL	10 MG	ORAL	S0139
MIRENA	52 MG	OTH	J7302
MISOPROSTOL	200 MG	ORAL	S0191
MITHRACIN	2.5 MG	IV	J9270
MITOMYCIN	5 MG	IV	J9280
MITOXANA	1 G	IV	J9208
MITOXANTRONE HCL	5 MG	IV	J9293
MONARC-M	1 IU	IV	J7190
MONOCLATE-P	1 IU	IV	J7190
MONONINE	1 IU	IV	J7193
MONOPUR	75 IU	SC, IM	S0122
MORPHINE SULFATE	10 MG	IM, IV, SC	J2270
MORPHINE SULFATE	500 MG	OTH	S0093
MORPHINE SULFATE	100 MG	IM, IV, SC	J2271
MORPHINE SULFATE, PRESERVATIVE FREE, STERILE SOLUTION	10 MG	VAR	J2275
MOXIFLOXACIN	100 MG	IV	J2280
MOZOBIL	1 MG	SC	J2562
MPI INDIUM DTPA	0.5 MCI	IV	A9548
MS CONTIN	500 MG	OTH	S0093
MUCOMYST	1 G	INH	J7608
MUCOSIL	1 G	INH	J7608
MULTIHANCE	1 ML	IV	A9577
MULTIHANCE MULTIPACK	1 ML	IV	A9578
MUROMONAB-CD3	5 MG	OTH	J7505
MUSE	EA	OTH	J0275
MUSTARGEN	10 MG	IV	J9230
MUTAMYCIN	5 MG	IV	J9280
MYCAMINE	1 MG	IV	J2248
MYCOPHENOLATE MOFETIL	250 MG	ORAL	J7517
MYCOPHENOLIC ACID	180 MG	ORAL	J7518
MYFORTIC DELAYED RELEASE	180 MG	ORAL	J7518
MYLERAN	2 MG	ORAL	J8510
MYLOCEL	500 MG	ORAL	S0176
MYOBLOC	100 U	IM	J0587
MYOCHRYSINE	50 MG	IM	J1600
MYOZYME	10 MG	IV	J0220
NABILONE	1 MG	ORAL	J8650
NAFCILLIN SODIUM	2 GM	IM, IV	S0032
NAGLAZYME	1 MG	IV	J1458
NALBUPHINE HCL	10 MG	IM, IV, SC	J2300
NALLPEN	2 GM	IM, IV	S0032
NALOXONE HCL	1 MG	IM, IV, SC	J2310
NALTREXONE, DEPOT FORM	1 MG	IM	J2315
NANDROLONE DECANOATE	50 MG	IM	J2320
NARCAN	1 MG	IM, IV, SC	J2310
NAROPIN	1 MG	VAR	J2795
NASALCROM	10 MG	INH	J7631
NATALIZUMAB	1 MG	IV	J2323
NATRECOR	0.1 MG	IV	J2325
NATURAL ESTROGENIC SUBSTANCE	1 MG	IM, IV	J1410
NAVELBINE	10 MG	IV	J9390
ND-STAT	10 MG	IM, SC, IV	J0945
NEBCIN	80 MG	IM, IV	J3260
NEBUPENT	300 MG	INH	J2545
NEBUPENT	300 MG	IM, IV	S0080
NELARABINE	50 MG	IV	J9261
NEMBUTAL SODIUM	50 MG	IM, IV, OTH	J2515
NEORAL	25 MG	ORAL	J7515
NEORAL	250 MG	ORAL	J7516
NEOSAR	100 MG	IV	J9070
NEOSCAN	1 MCI	IV	A9556
NEOSTIGMINE METHYLSULFATE	250 MG	IM, IV	J2710
NEOTECT	STUDY DOSE UP TO 35 MCI	IV	A9536
NESACAINE	30 ML	VAR	J2400
NESACAINE-MPF	30 ML	VAR	J2400
NESIRITIDE	0.1 MG	IV	J2325
NEULASTA	6 MG	SC, SQ	J2505
NEUMEGA	5 MG	SC	J2355
NEUPOGEN	300 MCG	SC, IV	J1440

Drug Name	Unit Per	Route	Code
NEUPOGEN	480 MCG	SC, IV	J1441
NEURAGEN NERVE GUIDE	1 CM LENGTH	OTH	C9352
NEUROLITE	STUDY DOSE UP TO 25 MCI	IV	A9557
NEUROMATRIX	0.5 CM LENGTH	OTH	C9355
NEUROMEND NERVE WRAP	0.5 CM	OTH	C9361
NEUROWRAP NERVE PROTECTOR	1 CM LENGTH	OTH	C9353
NEUTREXIN	25 MG	IV	J3305
NEUTROSPEC	STUDY DOSE UP TO 25 MCI	IV	A9566
NIPENT	10 MG	IV	J9268
NITROGEN MUSTARD	10 MG	IV	J9230
NITROGEN N-13 AMMONIA, DIAGNOSTIC	STUDY DOSE UP TO 40 MCI	INJ	A9526
NOC DRUGS, INHALATION SOLUTION ADMINISTERED THROUGH DME	1 EA		J7699
NOLVADEX	10 MG	ORAL	S0187
NORDITROPIN	1 MG	SC	J2941
NORDYL	50 MG	IV, IM	J1200
NORFLEX	60 MG	IV, IM	J2360
NORMAL SALINE SOLUTION	250 CC	IV	J7050
NORMAL SALINE SOLUTION	1000 CC	IV	J7030
NORMAL SALINE SOLUTION	500 ML	IV	J7040
NORPLANT II	IMPLANT	OTH	J7306
NOT OTHERWISE CLASSIFIED, ANTINEOPLASTIC DRUGS			J9999
NOVANTRONE	5 MG	IV	J9293
NOVAREL	1,000 USP U	IM	J0725
NOVASTAN	5 MG	IV	C9121
NOVOLIN	50 U	SC	J1817
NOVOLIN R	5 U	SC	J1815
NOVOLOG	50 U	SC	J1817
NOV-ONXOL	30 MG	IV	J9265
NOVOSEVEN	1 MCG	IV	J7189
NPH	5 UNITS	SC	J1815
NPLATE	10 MCG	SC	J2796
NUBAIN	10 MG	IM, IV, SC	J2300
NULOJIX	1 MG	IV	C9286
NUMORPHAN	1 MG	IV, SC, IM	J2410
NUTRI-TWELVE	1,000 MCG	IM, SC	J3420
NUTROPIN	1 MG	SC	J2941
NUTROPIN A.Q.	1 MG	SC	J2941
NUVARING VAGINAL RING	EACH	OTH	J7303
OASIS BURN MATRIX	SQ CM	OTH	Q4103
OASIS ULTRA TRI-LAYER WOUND MATRIX	SQ CM	OTH	Q4124
OASIS WOUND MATRIX	SQ CM	OTH	Q4102
OCTAFLUOROPROPANE UCISPHERES	1 ML	IV	Q9956
OCTAGAM	500 MG	IV	J1568
OCTREOSCAN	STUDY DOSE UP TO 6 MCI	IV	A9572
OCTREOTIDE ACETATE DEPOT	1 MG	IM	J2353
OCTREOTIDE, NON-DEPOT FORM	25 MCG	SC, IV	J2354
OFATUMUMAB	10 MG	IV	J9302
OFIRMEV	10 MG	IV	J0131
OFLOXACIN	400 MG	IV	S0034
OFORTA	10 MG	ORAL	J8562
OLANZAPINE	2.5 MG	IM	S0166
OLANZAPINE LONG ACTING	1 MG	IM	J2358
OMALIZUMAB	5 MG	SC	J2357
OMNIPAQUE 140	PER ML	IV	Q9965
OMNIPAQUE 180	PER ML	IV	Q9965
OMNIPAQUE 240	PER ML	IV	Q9966
OMNIPAQUE 300	PER ML	IV	Q9966
OMNIPAQUE 350	PER ML	IV	Q9967
OMNISCAN	1 ML	IV	A9579
ONABOTULINUMTOXINA	1 UNIT	IM, OTH	J0585
ONCASPAR	VIAL	IM, IV	J9266
ONCOSCINT	STUDY DOSE, UP TO 6 MCI	IV	A4642
ONDANSETRON	1 MG	ORAL	Q0162
ONDANSETRON	4 MG	ORAL	S0119
~~ONDANSETRON HCL~~	~~4 MG~~	~~ORAL~~	~~S0181~~
~~ONDANSETRON HCL~~	~~8 MG~~	~~ORAL~~	~~Q0179~~
ONDANSETRON HYDROCHLORIDE	1 MG	IV	J2405
ONTAK	300 MCG	IV	J9160
ONXOL	30 MG	IV	J9265
OPRELVEKIN	5 MG	SC	J2355
OPTIRAY	PER ML	IV	Q9967
OPTIRAY 160	PER ML	IV	Q9965
OPTIRAY 240	PER ML	IV	Q9966
OPTIRAY 300	PER ML	IV	Q9967
OPTIRAY 320	PER ML	IV	Q9967
OPTISON	1 ML	IV	Q9957
ORAL MAGNETIC RESONANCE CONTRAST AGENT, PER 100 ML	100 ML	ORAL	Q9954
ORENCIA	10 MG	IV	J0129
ORPHENADRINE CITRATE	60 MG	IV, IM	J2360
ORTHADAPT BIOIMPLANT	SQ CM	OTH	C1781
ORTHOCLONE OKT3	5 MG	OTH	J7505
ORTHOVISC	DOSE	OTH	J7324
OSELTAMIVIR PHOSPHATE (BRAND NAME) (DEMONSTRATION PROJECT)	75 MG	ORAL	G9035
OSELTAMIVIR PHOSPHATE (GENERIC) (DEMONSTRATION PROJECT)	75 MG	ORAL	G9019
OSMITROL	25% IN 50 ML	IV	J2150
OXACILLIN SODIUM	250 MG	IM, IV	J2700
OXALIPLATIN	0.5 MG	IV	J9263
OXILAN 300	PER ML	IV	Q9967
OXILAN 350	PER ML	IV	Q9967
OXYMORPHONE HCL	1 MG	IV, SC, IM	J2410
OXYTETRACYCLINE HCL	50 MG	IM	J2460
OXYTOCIN	10 U	IV, IM	J2590
OZURDEX	0.1 MG	OTH	J7312
PACIS BCG	VIAL	OTH	J9031
PACLITAXEL	30 MG	IV	J9265
PACLITAXEL PROTEIN-BOUND PARTICLES	1 MG	IV	J9264
PALIFERMIN	50 MCG	IV	J2425
PALIPERIDONE PALMITATE EXTENDED RELEASED	1 MG	IM	J2426
PALONOSETRON HCL	25 MCG	IV	J2469
PAMIDRONATE DISODIUM	30 MG	IV	J2430
PANHEMATIN	1 MG	IV	J1640
PANITUMUMAB	10 MG	IV	J9303
PANTOPRAZOLE SODIUM	40 MG	IV	S0164
PANTOPRAZOLE SODIUM	VIAL	IV	C9113

Drug Name	Unit Per	Route	Code
PAPAVERINE HCL	60 MG	IV, IM	J2440
PARAGARD T380A	EA	OTH	J7300
PARAPLANTIN	50 MG	IV	J9045
PARICALCITOL	1 MCG	IV, IM	J2501
PEDIAPRED	5 MG	ORAL	J7510
PEGADEMASE BOVINE	25 IU	IM	J2504
PEGAPTANIB SODIUM	0.3 MG	OTH	J2503
PEGASPARGASE	VIAL	IM, IV	J9266
PEGFILGRASTIM	6 MG	SC	J2505
PEGINTERFERON ALFA-2A	180 MCG	SC	S0145
PEG-INTRON	180 MCG	SC	S0145
~~PEGLOTICASE~~	~~1 MG~~	~~IV~~	~~C9281~~
PEGLOTICASE	1 MG	IV	J2507
PEGYLATED INTERFERON ALFA-2A	180 MCG	SC	S0145
PEGYLATED INTERFERON ALFA-2B	10 MCG	SC	S0148
PEMETREXED	10 MG	IV	J9305
PENICILLIN G BENZATHINE	100,000 U	IM	J0561
PENICILLIN G BENZATHINE AND PENICILLIN G PROCAINE	100,000 UNITS	IM	J0558
PENICILLIN G POTASSIUM	600,000 U	IM, IV	J2540
PENICILLIN G PROCAINE	600,000 U	IM, IV	J2510
PENTACARINAT	300 MG	INH	S0080
PENTAM	300 MG	IM, IV	J2545
PENTAM 300	300 MG	IM, IV	S0080
PENTAMIDINE ISETHIONATE	300 MG	IM, IV	S0080
PENTAMIDINE ISETHIONATE COMPOUNDED	PER 300 MG	INH	J7676
PENTAMIDINE ISETHIONATE NONCOMPOUNDED	300 MG	INH	J2545
PENTASPAN	100 ML	IV	J2513
PENTASTARCH 10% SOLUTION	100 ML	IV	J2513
PENTATE CALCIUM TRISODIUM	STUDY DOSE UP TO 25 MCI	IV	A9539
PENTATE CALCIUM TRISODIUM	STUDY DOSE UP TO 75 MCI	INH	A9567
PENTATE ZINC TRISODIUM	STUDY DOSE UP TO 25 MCI	IV	A9539
PENTATE ZINC TRISODIUM	STUDY DOSE UP TO 75 MCI	INH	A9567
PENTAZOCINE	30 MG	IM, SC, IV	J3070
PENTOBARBITAL SODIUM	50 MG	IM, IV, OTH	J2515
PENTOSTATIN	10 MG	IV	J9268
PEPCID	20 MG	IV	S0028
PERFLEXANE LIPID MICROSPHERE	1 ML	IV	Q9955
PERFLUTREN LIPID MICROSPHERE	1 ML	IV	Q9957
PERFOROMIST	20 MCG	INH	J7606
PERMACOL	SQ CM	OTH	C9364
PERPHENAZINE	4 MG	ORAL	Q0175
PERPHENAZINE	5 MG	IM, IV	J3310
PERPHENAZINE	8 MG	ORAL	Q0176
PERSANTINE	10 MG	IV	J1245
PFIZERPEN A.S.	600,000 U	IM, IV	J2510
PHENERGAN	12.5 MG	ORAL	Q0169
PHENERGAN	50 MG	IM, IV	J2550
PHENOBARBITAL SODIUM	120 MG	IM, IV	J2560
PHENTOLAMINE MESYLATE	5 MG	IM, IV	J2760
PHENYLEPHRINE HCL	1 ML	SC, IM, IV	J2370
PHENYTOIN SODIUM	50 MG	IM, IV	J1165
PHOSPHOCOL	1 MCI	IV	A9563

Drug Name	Unit Per	Route	Code
PHOSPHOTEC	STUDY DOSE UP TO 25 MCI	IV	A9538
PHOTOFRIN	75 MG	IV	J9600
PHYTONADIONE	1 MG	IM, SC, IV	J3430
PIPERACILLIN SODIUM	500 MG	IM, IV	S0081
PIPERACILLIN SODIUM/TAZOBACTAM SODIUM	1 G/1.125 GM	IV	J2543
PITOCIN	10 U	IV, IM	J2590
PLATINOL AQ	10 MG	IV	J9060
PLERIXAFOR	1 MG	SC	J2562
PLICAMYCIN	2.5 MG	IV	J9270
PNEUMOCOCCAL CONJUGATE	EA	IM	S0195
PNEUMOVAX II	EA	IM	S0195
POLOCAINE	10 ML	VAR	J0670
POLYGAM	500 MG	IV	J1566
POLYGAM S/D	500 MG	IV	J1566
PORCINE IMPLANT, PERMACOL	SQ CM	OTH	C9364
PORFIMER SODIUM	75 MG	IV	J9600
PORK INSULIN	5 U	SC	J1815
POROUS PURIFIED COLLAGEN MATRIX BONE VOID FILLER	0.5 CC	OTH	C9362
POROUS PURIFIED COLLAGEN MATRIX BONE VOID FILLER, PUTTY	0.5 CC	OTH	C9359
POTASSIUM CHLORIDE	2 MEQ	IV	J3480
PRALATREXATE	1 MG	IV	J9307
PRALIDOXIME CHLORIDE	1 MG	IV, IM, SC	J2730
PREDNISOLONE	5 MG	ORAL	J7510
PREDNISOLONE ACETATE	1 ML	IM	J2650
PREDNISONE	5 MG	ORAL	J7506
PREDNORAL	5 MG	ORAL	J7510
PREGNYL	1,000 USP U	IM	J0725
PRELONE	5 MG	ORAL	J7510
PREMARIN	25 MG	IV, IM	J1410
PRENATAL VITAMINS	30 TABS	ORAL	S0197
PRIALT	1 MCG	OTH	J2278
PRIMACOR	5 MG	IV	J2260
PRIMATRIX	SQ CM	OTH	Q4110
PRIMAXIN	250 MG	IV, IM	J0743
PRIMESTRIN AQUEOUS	1 MG	IM, IV	J1410
PRIMETHASONE	1 MG	IM, IV, OTH	J1100
PRI-METHYLATE	80 MG	IM	J1040
PRIVIGEN	500 MG	IV	J1459
PROCAINAMIDE HCL	1 G	IM, IV	J2690
PROCARBAZINE HCL	50 MG	ORAL	S0182
PROCHLOPERAZINE MALEATE	5 MG	ORAL	S0183
PROCHLORPERAZINE	10 MG	IM, IV	J0780
PROCHLORPERAZINE MALEATE	10 MG	ORAL	Q0165
PROCHLORPERAZINE MALEATE	5 MG	ORAL	Q0164
PROCRIT, ESRD USE	1,000 U	SC, IV	J0886
PROCRIT, NON-ESRD USE	1,000 U	SC, IV	J0885
PROFILNINE HEAT-TREATED	1 IU	IV	J7194
PROFILNINE SD	1 IU	IV	J7194
PROFONIX	VIAL	INJ	C9113
PROGESTERONE	50 MG	IM	J2675
PROGRAF	1 MG	ORAL	J7507
PROGRAF	5 MG	OTH	J7525
PROLASTIN	10 MG	IV	J0256
PROLEUKIN	1 VIAL	VAR	J9015

Drug Name	Unit Per	Route	Code
PROLIA	1 MG	SC	J0897
PROLIXIN DECANOATE	25 MG	SC, IM	J2680
PROMAZINE HCL	25 MG	IM	J2950
PROMETHAZINE HCL	12.5 MG	ORAL	Q0169
PROMETHAZINE HCL	50 MG	IM, IV	J2550
PROMETHAZINE HCL	25 MG	ORAL	Q0170
PRONESTYL	1 G	IM, IV	J2690
PROPECIA	5 MG	ORAL	S0138
PROPLEX SX-T	1 IU	IV	J7194
PROPLEX T	1 IU	IV	J7194
PROPRANOLOL HCL	1 MG	IV	J1800
PROREX	50 MG	IM, IV	J2550
PROSCAR	5 MG	ORAL	S0138
PROSTASCINT	STUDY DOSE UP TO 10 MCI	IV	A9507
PROSTIGMIN	0.5 MG	IM, IV	J2710
PROSTIN VR	1.25 MCG	INJ	J0270
PROTAMINE SULFATE	10 MG	IV	J2720
PROTEIN C CONCENTRATE	10 IU	IV	J2724
PROTEINASE INHIBITOR (HUMAN)	10 MG	IV	J0256
PROTIRELIN	250 MCG	IV	J2725
PROTONIX IV	40 MG	IV	S0164
PROTONIX IV	VIAL	IV	C9113
PROTOPAM CHLORIDE	1 G	SC, IM, IV	J2730
PROTROPIN	1 MG	SC, IM	J2940
~~PROVENGE~~	~~INFUSION~~	~~IV~~	~~C9273~~
PROVENGE	INFUSION	IV	Q2043
PROVENTIL NONCOMPOUNDED, CONCENTRATED	1 MG	INH	J7611
PROVENTIL NONCOMPOUNDED, UNIT DOSE	1 MG	INH	J7613
PROVOCHOLINE POWDER	1 MG	INH	J7674
PROZINE-50	25 MG	IM	J2950
PULMICORT	0.25 MG	INH	J7633
PULMICORT RESPULES	0.5 MG	INH	J7627
PULMICORT RESPULES NONCOMPOUNDED, CONCETRATED	0.25 MG	INH	J7626
PULMOZYME	1 MG	INH	J7639
PURINETHOL	50 MG	ORAL	S0108
PYRIDOXINE HCL	100 MG	IM, IV	J3415
QUADRAMET	PER DOSE UP TO 150 MCI	IV	A9604
QUELICIN	20 MG	IM, IV	J0330
QUINUPRISTIN/DALFOPRISTIN	500 MG	IV	J2770
QUTENZA	10 SQ CM	OTH	J7335
RADIESSE	0.1 ML	OTH	Q2026
RANIBIZUMAB	0.5 MG	OTH	J2778
RANITIDINE HCL	25 MG	INJ	J2780
RAPAMUNE	1 MG	ORAL	J7520
RASBURICASE	50 MCG	IM	J2783
REBETRON KIT	1,000,000 U	SC, IM	J9214
REBIF	11 MCG	SC	Q3026
REBIF	30 MCG	SC	J1826
RECLAST	1 MG	IV	J3488
RECOMBINATE	1 IU	IV	J7192
REDISOL	1,000 MCG	SC. IM	J3420
REFACTO	1 IU	IV	J7192
REFLUDAN	50 MG	IM, IV	J1945
REGADENOSON	0.1 MG	IV	J2785
REGITINE	5 MG	IM, IV	J2760
REGLAN	10 MG	IV	J2765
REGRANEX GEL	0.5 G	OTH	S0157
REGULAR INSULIN	5 UNITS	SC	J1815
RELAXIN	10 ML	IV, IM	J2800
RELENZA (DEMONSTRATION PROJECT)	10 MG	INH	G9034
RELION	5 U	SC	J1815
RELION NOVOLIN	50 U	SC	J1817
REMICADE	10 MG	IV	J1745
REMODULIN	1 MG	SC	J3285
REODULIN	1 MG	SC	J3285
REOPRO	10 MG	IV	J0130
REPRONEX	75 IU	SC, IM, IV	S0122
RESPIROL NONCOMPOUNDED, CONCENTRATED	1 MG	INH	J7611
RESPIROL NONCOMPOUNDED, UNIT DOSE	1 MG	INH	J7613
RETAVASE	18.1 MG	IV	J2993
RETEPLASE	18.1 MG	IV	J2993
RETISERT	IMPLANT	OTH	J7311
RETROVIR	10 MG	IV	J3485
RETROVIR	100 MG	ORAL	S0104
RHEOMACRODEX	500 ML	IV	J7100
RHEUMATREX	2.5 MG	ORAL	J8610
RHEUMATREX DOSE PACK	2.5 MG	ORAL	J8610
RHO D IMMUNE GLOBULIN	300 MCG	IV	J2790
RHO D IMMUNE GLOBULIN (RHOPHYLAC)	100 IU	IM, IV	J2791
RHO D IMMUNE GLOBULIN MINIDOSE	50 MCG	IM	J2788
RHO D IMMUNE GLOBULIN SOLVENT DETERGENT	100 IU	IV	J2792
RHOGAM	300 MCG	IM	J2790
RHOGAM	50 MCG	IM	J2788
RHOPHYLAC	100 IU	IM, IV	J2791
RIASTAP	100 MG	IV	J1680
RILONACEPT	1 MG	SC	J2793
RIMANTADINE HCL (DEMONSTRATION PROJECT)	100 MG	ORAL	G9036
RIMANTADINE HCL (DEMONSTRATION PROJECT)	100 MG	ORAL	G9020
RIMSO 50	50 ML	IV	J1212
RINGERS LACTATE INFUSION	UP TO 1000 CC	IV	J7120
RISPERDAL COSTA LONG ACTING	0.5 MG	IM	J2794
RISPERIDONE, LONG ACTING	0.5 MG	IM	J2794
RITUXAN	100 MG	IV	J9310
RITUXIMAB	100 MG	IV	J9310
ROBAXIN	10 ML	IV, IM	J2800
ROCEPHIN	250 MG	IV, IM	J0696
ROFERON-A	3,000,000 U	SC, IM	J9213
ROMIDEPSIN	1 MG	IV	J9315
ROMIPLOSTIM	10 MCG	SC	J2796
ROPIVACAINE HYDROCHLORIDE	1 MG	VAR	J2795
RUBEX	10 MG	IV	J9000
RUBIDIUM RB-82	STUDY DOSE UP TO 60 MCI	IV	A9555
RUBRAMIN PC	1,000 MCG	SC, IM	J3420

Drug Name	Unit Per	Route	Code
RUBRATOPE 57	STUDY DOSE UP TO 1 UCI	ORAL	A9559
SAIZEN	1 MG	SC	J2941
SAIZEN SOMATROPIN RDNA ORIGIN	1 MG	SC	J2941
SALINE OR STERILE WATER, METERED DOSE DISPENSER	10 ML	INH	A4218
SALINE, STERILE WATER, AND/OR DEXTROSE DILUENT/FLUSH	10 ML	VAR	A4216
SALINE/STERILE WATER	500 ML	VAR	A4217
SAMARIUM LEXIDRONAM	PER DOSE UP TO 150 MCI	IV	A9604
SANDIMMUNE	100 MG	ORAL	J7502
SANDIMMUNE	250 MG	IV	J7516
SANDIMMUNE	25 MG	ORAL	J7515
SANDOSTATIN	25 MCG	SC, IV	J2354
SANDOSTATIN LAR	1 MG	IM	J2353
SANGCYA	100 MG	ORAL	J7502
SANO-DROL	40 MG	IM	J1030
SANO-DROL	80 MG	IM	J1040
SAQUINAVIR	200 MG	ORAL	S0140
SARGRAMOSTIM (GM-CSF)	50 MCG	IV	J2820
SCANDONEST	PER 10 ML	IV	J0670
SCULPTRA	0.1 ML	OTH	Q2027
SECREFLO	1 MCG	IV	J2850
SECRETIN, SYNTHETIC, HUMAN	1 MCG	IV	J2850
SENSORCAINE	30 ML	VAR	S0020
SEPTRA IV	10 ML	IV	S0039
SERMORELIN ACETATE	1 MCG	IV	Q0515
SEROSTIM	1 MG	SC	J2941
SEROSTIM RDNA ORIGIN	1 MG	SC	J2941
SILDENAFIL CITRATE	25 MG	ORAL	S0090
SIMULECT	20 MG	IV	J0480
SINCALIDE	5 MCG	IV	J2805
~~SIPULEUCEL-T~~	~~INFUSION~~	~~IV~~	~~C9273~~
SIPULEUCEL-T	INFUSION	IV	Q2043
SIROLIMUS	1 MG	ORAL	J7520
SKIN SUBSTITUTE (ENDOFORM DERMAL TEMPLATE)	SQ CM	OTH	C9367
SKIN SUBSTITUTE, ALLODERM	SQ CM	OTH	Q4116
SKIN SUBSTITUTE, ALLOSKIN	SQ CM	OTH	Q4115
SKIN SUBSTITUTE, APLIGRAF	SQ CM	OTH	Q4101
SKIN SUBSTITUTE, DERMAGRAFT	SQ CM	OTH	Q4106
SKIN SUBSTITUTE, GAMMAGRAFT	SQ CM	OTH	Q4111
SKIN SUBSTITUTE, GRAFTJACKET	SQ CM	OTH	Q4107
SKIN SUBSTITUTE, INTEGRA BILAYER MATRIX WOUND DRESSING	SQ CM	OTH	Q4104
SKIN SUBSTITUTE, INTEGRA DERMAL REGENERATION TEMPLATE	SQ CM	OTH	Q4105
SKIN SUBSTITUTE, INTEGRA MATRIX	SQ CM	OTH	Q4108
SKIN SUBSTITUTE, INTEGRA MESHED BILAYER WOUND MATRIX	SQ CM	OTH	C9363
SKIN SUBSTITUTE, OASIS BURN MATRIX	SQ CM	OTH	Q4103
SKIN SUBSTITUTE, OASIS WOUND MATRIX	SQ CM	OTH	Q4102
SKIN SUBSTITUTE, PRIMATRIX	SQ CM	OTH	Q4110
SMZ-TMP	10 ML	IV	S0039
SODIUM FERRIC GLUCONATE COMPLEX IN SUCROSE	12.5 MG	IV	J2916
SODIUM FLUORIDE F-18, DIAGNOSTIC	STUDY DOSE UP TO 30 MCI	IV	A9580
SODIUM IODIDE I-131 CAPSULE DIAGNOSTIC	1 MCI	ORAL	A9528
SODIUM IODIDE I-131 CAPSULE THERAPEUTIC	1 MCI	ORAL	A9517
SODIUM IODIDE I-131 SOLUTION THERAPEUTIC	1 MCI	ORAL	A9530
SODIUM PHOSPHATE P32	1 MCI	IV	A9563
SOLGANAL	50 MG	IM	J2910
SOLIRIS	10 MG	IV	J1300
SOLTAMOX	10 MG	ORAL	S0187
SOLU-CORTEF	100 MG	IV, IM, SC	J1720
SOLU-MEDROL	125 MG	IM, IV	J2930
SOLU-MEDROL	40 MG	IM, IV	J2920
SOLUREX	1 MG	IM, IV, OTH	J1100
SOMATREM	1 MG	SC, IM	J2940
SOMATROPIN	1 MG	SC	J2941
SOMATULINE	1 MG	SC	J1930
SPECTINOMYCIN DIHYDROCHLORIDE	2 G	IM	J3320
SPECTRO-DEX	1 MG	IM, IV, OTH	J1100
SPORANOX	50 MG	IV	J1835
STADOL	1 MG	IM, IV	J0595
STADOL NS	25 MG	OTH	S0012
STELARA	1 MG	SC	J3357
STERILE WATER OR SALINE, METERED DOSE DISPENSER	10 ML	INH	A4218
STERILE WATER, SALINE, AND/OR DEXTROSE DILUENT/FLUSH	10 ML	VAR	A4216
STERILE WATER/SALINE	500 ML	VAR	A4217
STRATTICE TM	SQ CM	OTH	Q4130
STREPTASE	250,000 IU	IV	J2995
STREPTOKINASE	250,000 IU	IV	J2995
STREPTOMYCIN	1 G	IM	J3000
STREPTOZOCIN	1 G	IV	J9320
STRONTIUM 89 CHLORIDE	1 MCI	IV	A9600
SUBLIMAZE	0.1 MG	IM, IV	J3010
SUCCINYLCHOLINE CHLORIDE	20 MG	IM, IV	J0330
SULFAMETHOXAZOLE AND TRIMETHOPRIM	10 ML	IV	S0039
SULFUTRIM	10 ML	IV	S0039
SUMATRIPTAN SUCCINATE	6 MG	SC	J3030
SUPARTZ	DOSE	OTH	J7321
SUPPRELIN LA	10 MCG	OTH	J1675
SURGIMEND COLLAGEN MATRIX, FETAL	0.5 SQ CM	OTH	C9358
SURGIMEND COLLAGEN MATRIX, NEONATAL	0.5 SQ CM	OTH	C9360
SYMMETREL (DEMONSTRATION PROJECT)	100 MG	ORAL	G9033
SYNERA	70 MG/70 MG	OTH	C9285
SYNERCID	500 MG	IV	J2770
SYNTOCINON	10 UNITS	IV	J2590
SYNVISC/SYNVISC-ONE	1 MG	OTH	J7325
SYTOBEX	1,000 MCG	SC, IM	J3420
TACRINE HCL	10 MG	ORAL	S0014
TACROLIMUS	1 MG	ORAL	J7507
TACROLIMUS	5 MG	OTH	J7525
TAGAMET HCL	300 MG	IM, IV	S0023
TALWIN	30 MG	IM, SC, IV	J3070
TALYMED	SQ CM	OTH	Q4127
TAMIFLU (DEMONSTRATION PROJECT)	75 MG	ORAL	G9019

Drug Name	Unit Per	Route	Code
TAMIFLU (DEMONSTRATION PROJECT)	75 MG	ORAL	G9035
TAMOXIFEN CITRATE	10 MG	ORAL	S0187
TAXOL	30 MG	IV	J9265
TAXOTERE	1 MG	IV	J9171
TAZICEF	500 MG	IM, IV	J0713
TEBAMIDE	250 MG	ORAL	Q0173
TEBOROXIME TECHNETIUM TC 99	STUDY DOSE	IV	A9501
TEBOROXIME, TECHNETIUM	STUDY DOSE	IV	A9501
TECHNEPLEX	STUDY DOSE UP TO 25 MCI	IV	A9539
TECHNESCAN	STUDY DOSE UP TO 30 MCI	IV	A9561
TECHNESCAN FANOLESOMAB	STUDY DOSE UP TO 25 MCI	IV	A9566
TECHNESCAN MAA	STUDY DOSE UP TO 10 MCI	IV	A9540
TECHNESCAN MAG3	STUDY DOSE UP TO 15 MCI	IV	A9562
TECHNESCAN PYP	STUDY DOSE UP TO 25 MCI	IV	A9538
TECHNESCAN PYP KIT	STUDY DOSE UP TO 25 MCI	IV	A9538
TECHNETIUM SESTAMBI	STUDY DOSE	IV	A9500
TECHNETIUM TC 99M APCITIDE	STUDY DOES UP TO 20 MCI	IV	A9504
TECHNETIUM TC 99M ARCITUMOMAB, DIAGNOSTIC	STUDY DOSE UP TO 45 MCI	IV	A9568
TECHNETIUM TC 99M BICISATE	STUDY DOSE UP TO 25 MCI	IV	A9557
TECHNETIUM TC 99M DEPREOTIDE	STUDY DOSE UP TO 35 MCI	IV	A9536
TECHNETIUM TC 99M EXAMETAZIME	STUDY DOSE UP TO 25 MCI	IV	A9521
TECHNETIUM TC 99M FANOLESOMAB	STUDY DOSE UP TO 25 MCI	IV	A9566
TECHNETIUM TC 99M LABELED RED BLOOD CELLS	STUDY DOSE UP TO 30 MCI	IV	A9560
TECHNETIUM TC 99M MACROAGGREGATED ALBUMIN	STUDY DOSE UP TO 10 MCI	IV	A9540
TECHNETIUM TC 99M MDI-MDP	STUDY DOSE UP TO 30 MCI	IV	A9503
TECHNETIUM TC 99M MEBROFENIN	STUDY DOSE UP TO 15 MCI	IV	A9537
TECHNETIUM TC 99M MEDRONATE	STUDY DOSE UP TO 30 MCI	IV	A9503
TECHNETIUM TC 99M MERTIATIDE	STUDY DOSE UP TO 15 MCI	IV	A9562
TECHNETIUM TC 99M OXIDRONATE	STUDY DOSE UP TO 30 MCI	IV	A9561
TECHNETIUM TC 99M PENTETATE	STUDY DOSE UP TO 25 MCI	IV	A9539
TECHNETIUM TC 99M PYROPHOSPHATE	STUDY DOSE UP TO 25 MCI	IV	A9538
TECHNETIUM TC 99M SODIUM GLUCEPATATE	STUDY DOSE UP TO 25 MCI	IV	A9550
TECHNETIUM TC 99M SUCCIMER	STUDY DOSE UP TO 10 MCI	IV	A9551
TECHNETIUM TC 99M SULFUR COLLOID	STUDY DOSE UP TO 20 MCI	IV	A9541
TECHNETIUM TC 99M TETROFOSMIN, DIAGNOSTIC	STUDY DOSE	IV	A9502
TECHNETIUM TC-99M EXAMETAZIME LABELED AUTOLOGOUS WHITE BLOOD CELLS	STUDY DOSE	IV	A9569
TECHNETIUM TC-99M TEBOROXIME	STUDY DOSE	IV	A9501
TECHNILITE	1 MCI	IV	A9512
TEFLARO	10 MG	IV	J0712
TELAVANCIN	10 MG	IV	J3095
TEMODAR	5 MG	ORAL	J8700
TEMODAR	1 MG	IV	J9328
TEMOZOLOMIDE	5 MG	ORAL	J8700
TEMOZOLOMIDE	1 MG	IV	J9328
TEMSIROLIMUS	1 MG	IV	J9330
TENDON, POROUS MATRIX	SQ CM	OTH	C9356
TENDON, POROUS MATRIX CROSS-LINKED AND GLYCOSAMINOGLYCAN MATRIX	SQ CM	OTH	C9356
TENECTEPLASE	1 MG	IV	J3101
TENIPOSIDE	50 MG	IV	Q2017
TENOGLIDE TENDON PROTECTOR	SQ CM	OTH	C9356
TENOGLIDE TENDON PROTECTOR SHEET	SQ CM	OTH	C9356
TEQUIN	10 MG	IV	J1590
TERBUTALINE SULFATE	1 MG	SC, IV	J3105
TERBUTALINE SULFATE, COMPOUNDED, CONCENTRATED	1 MG	INH	J7680
TERBUTALINE SULFATE, COMPOUNDED, UNIT DOSE	1 MG	INH	J7681
TERIPARATIDE	10 MCG	SC	J3110
TERRAMYCIN	50 MG	IM	J2460
TESTERONE	50 MG	IM	J3140
TESTOSTERONE CYPIONATE	1 CC, 200 MG	IM	J1080
TESTOSTERONE CYPIONATE	UP TO 100 MG	IM	J1070
TESTOSTERONE CYPIONATE & ESTRADIOL CYPIONATE	1 ML	IM	J1060
TESTOSTERONE ENANTHATE	100 MG	IM	J3120
TESTOSTERONE ENANTHATE	200 MG	IM	J3130
TESTOSTERONE ENANTHATE & ESTRADIOL VALERATE	1 CC	IM	J0900
TESTOSTERONE PELLET	75 MG	OTH	S0189
TESTOSTERONE PROPIONATE	100 MG	IM	J3150
TESTOSTERONE SUSPENSION	50 MG	IM	J3140
TESTRO AQ	50 MG	IM	J3140
TETANUS IMMUNE GLOBULIN	250 U	IM	J1670
TETRACYCLINE HCL	250 MG	IV	J0120
T-GEN	250 MG	ORAL	Q0173
THALLOUS CHLORIDE	1 MCI	IV	A9505
THALLOUS CHLORIDE TL-201	1 MCI	IV	A9505
THALLOUS CHLORIDE USP	1 MCI	IV	A9505
THEELIN AQUEOUS	1 MG	IM, IV	J1435
THEOPHYLLINE	40 MG	IV	J2810
THERACYS	VIAL	OTH	J9031
THERASKIN	SQ CM	OTH	Q4121
THIAMINE HCL	100 MG	INJ	J3411
THIETHYLPERAZINE MALEATE	10 MG	ORAL	Q0174
THIETHYLPERAZINE MALEATE	10 MG	IM	J3280
THIMAZIDE	250 MG	ORAL	Q0173
THIOTEPA	15 MG	IV	J9340
THORAZINE	10 MG	ORAL	Q0171
THORAZINE	50 MG	IM, IV	J3230
THORAZINE	25 MG	ORAL	Q0172
THROMBATE III	1 IU	IV	J7197
THYMOGLOBULIN	25 MG	OTH	J7511
THYROGEN	0.9 MG	IM, SC	J3240

Drug Name	Unit Per	Route	Code
THYROTROPIN ALPHA	0.9 MG	IM, SC	J3240
TICARCILLIN DISODIUM AND CLAVULANATE	3.1 G	IV	S0040
TICE BCG	VIAL	OTH	J9031
TICON	250 MG	IM	Q0173
TIGAN	200 MG	IM	J3250
TIGECYCLINE	1 MG	IV	J3243
TIJECT-20	200 MG	IM	J3250
TIMENTIN	3.1 G	IV	S0040
TINZAPARIN	1,000 IU	SC	J1655
TIROFIBAN HCL	0.25 MG	IM, IV	J3246
TNKASE	1 MG	IV	J3101
TOBI	300 MG	INH	J7682
TOBRAMYCIN COMPOUNDED, UNIT DOSE	300 MG	INH	J7685
TOBRAMYCIN SULFATE	80 MG	IM, IV	J3260
TOBRAMYCIN, NONCOMPOUNDED, UNIT DOSE	300 MG	INH	J7682
TOCILIZUMAB	1 MG	IV	J3262
TOLAZOLINE HCL	25 MG	IV	J2670
TOPOSAR	10 MG	IV	J9181
TOPOTECAN	0.25 MG	ORAL	J8705
TOPOTECAN	0.1 MG	IV	J9351
TORADOL	15 MG	IV	J1885
TORISEL	1 MG	IV	J9330
TORNALATE	PER MG	INH	J7629
TORNALATE CONCENTRATE	PER MG	INH	J7628
TORSEMIDE	10 MG	IV	J3265
TOSITUMOMAB	450 MG	IV	G3001
TOSITUMOMAB I-131 DIAGNOSTIC	STUDY DOSE	IV	A9544
TOSITUMOMAB I-131 THERAPEUTIC	TX DOSE	IV	A9545
TOTECT	PER 250 MG	IV	J1190
TRASTUZUMAB	10 MG	IV	J9355
TRASYLOL	10,000 KIU	IV	J0365
TREANDA	1 MG	IV	J9033
TRELSTAR DEPOT	3.75 MG	IM	J3315
TRELSTAR DEPOT PLUS DEBIOCLIP KIT	3.75 MG	IM	J3315
TRELSTAR LA	3.75 MG	IM	J3315
TREPROSTINIL	1 MG	SC	J3285
TREPROSTINIL, INHALATION SOLUTION	1.74 MG	INH	J7686
TRETINOIN	5 G	OTH	S0117
TRIAM-A	10 MG	IM	J3301
TRIAMCINOLONE ACETONIDE	10 MG	IM	J3301
TRIAMCINOLONE ACETONIDE, PRESERVATIVE FREE	1 MG	INJ	J3300
TRIAMCINOLONE DIACETATE	5 MG	IM	J3302
TRIAMCINOLONE HEXACETONIDE	5 MG	VAR	J3303
TRIAMCINOLONE, COMPOUNDED, CONCENTRATED	1 MG	INH	J7683
TRIAMCINOLONE, COMPOUNDED, UNIT DOSE	1 MG	INH	J7684
TRIBAN	250 MG	ORAL	Q0173
TRIESENCE	1 MG	OTH	J3300
TRIFLUPROMAZINE HCL	UP TO 20 MG	INJ	J3400
TRI-KORT	10 MG	IM	J3301
TRILIFON	4 MG	ORAL	Q0175
TRILOG	10 MG	IM	J3301
TRILONE	5 MG	IM	J3302
TRIMETHOBENZAMIDE HCL	200 MG	IM	J3250
TRIMETHOBENZAMIDE HCL	250 MG	ORAL	Q0173
TRIMETREXATE GLUCURONATE	25 MG	IV	J3305
TRIPTORELIN PAMOATE	3.75 MG	IM	J3315
TRISENOX	1 MG	IV	J9017
TRIVARIS	1 MG	VAR	J3300
TROBICIN	2 G	IM	J3320
TRUXADRYL	50 MG	IV, IM	J1200
TYGACIL	1 MG	IV	J3243
TYPE A BOTOX	1 UNIT	IM, OTH	J0585
TYSABRI	1 MG	IV	J2323
TYVASO	1.74 MG	INH	J7686
ULTRALENTE	5 U	SC	J1815
ULTRATAG	STUDY DOSE UP TO 30 MCI	IV	A9560
ULTRA-TECHNEKOW	1 MCI	IV	A9512
ULTRAVIST 150	1 ML	IV	Q9967
ULTRAVIST 240	1 ML	IV	Q9951
ULTRAVIST 300	1 ML	IV	Q9951
ULTRAVIST 370	1 ML	IV	Q9951
UNASYN	1.5 G	IM, IV	J0295
UNCLASSIFIED BIOLOGICS			J3590
UNCLASSIFIED DRUGS OR BIOLOGICALS	VAR	VAR	C9399
UNITE BIOMATRIX	SQ CM	OTH	Q4129
UREA	40 G	IV	J3350
URECHOLINE	UP TO 5 MG	SC	J0520
UROFOLLITROPIN	75 IU	SC, IM	J3355
UROKINASE	250,000 IU	IV	J3365
UROKINASE	5,000 IU	IV	J3364
USTEKINUMAB	1 MG	SC	J3357
VALERGEN	10 MG	IM	J1380
VALIUM	5 MG	IV, IM	J3360
VALRUBICIN INTRAVESICAL	200 MG	OTH	J9357
VALSTAR	200 MG	OTH	J9357
VANCOCIN	500 MG	IM, IV	J3370
VANCOMYCIN HCL	500 MG	IV, IM	J3370
VANTAS	50 MG	OTH	J9225
VECTIBIX	10 MG	IV	J9303
VELAGLUCERASE ALFA	100 U	IV	J3385
VELBAN	I MG	IV	J9370
VELCADE	0.1 MG	IV	J9041
VELOSULIN	5 U	SC	J1815
VELOSULIN BR	5 U	SC	J1815
VENOFER	1 MG	IV	J1756
VENTOLIN NONCOMPOUNDED, CONCENTRATED	1 MG	INH	J7611
VENTOLIN NONCOMPOUNDED, UNIT DOSE	1 MG	INH	J7613
VEPESID	10 MG	IV	J9181
VEPESID	50 MG	ORAL	J8560
VERITAS	SQ CM	OTH	C9354
VERSED	1 MG	IM, IV	J2250
VERTEPORFIN	0.1 MG	IV	J3396
VFEND	200 MG	IV	J3465
VIAGRA	25 MG	ORAL	S0090
VIBATIV	10 MG	IV	J3095

Drug Name	*Unit Per*	*Route*	*Code*
VIDAZA	1 MG	SC	J9025
VIDEX	25 MG	ORAL	S0137
VIMPAT	1 MG	IV, ORAL	C9254
VINBLASTINE SULFATE	1 MG	IV	J9360
VINCASCAR	1 MG	IV	J9370
VINCRISTINE SULFATE	1 MG	IV	J9370
VINORELBINE TARTRATE	10 MG	IV	J9390
VIRILON	1 CC, 200 MG	IM	J1080
VISTAJECT-25	25 MG	IM	J3410
VISTARIL	25 MG	IM	J3410
VISTARIL	25 MG	ORAL	Q0177
VISTIDE	375 MG	IV	J0740
VISUDYNE	0.1 MG	IV	J3396
VITAMIN B-12 CYANOCOBALAMIN	1,000 MCG	IM, SC	J3420
VITRASE	1 USP	OTH	J3471
VITRASE	1,000 USP	OTH	J3472
VITRASERT	4.5 MG	OTH	J7310
VITRAVENE	1.65 MG	OTH	J1452
VIVITROL	1 MG	IM	J2315
VON WILLEBRAND FACTOR COMPLEX (HUMAN) (WILATE)	1 IU	IV	J7183
~~VON WILLEBRAND FACTOR COMPLEX, HUMAN (WILATE)~~	~~100 IU~~	~~IV~~	~~J7184~~
~~VON WILLEBRAND FACTOR COMPLEX, HUMAN (WILATEO~~	~~1 I.U.~~	~~IV~~	~~Q2041~~
VON WILLEBRAND FACTOR COMPLEX, HUMATE-P	1 IU	IV	J7187
VON WILLEBRAND FACTOR VIII COMPLEX, HUMAN	PER FACTOR VIII IU	IV	J7186
VORICONAZOLE	200 MG	IV	J3465
VPRIV	100 U	IV	J3385
VUMON	50 MG	IV	Q2017
WEHAMINE	50 MG	IM, IV	J1240
WEHDRYL	50 MG	IM, IV	J1200
WELBUTRIN SR	150 MG	ORAL	S0106
WILATE	1 IU	IV	J7183
~~WILATE~~	~~100 IU~~	~~IV~~	~~J7184~~
~~WILATE~~	~~1 I.U.~~	~~IV~~	~~Q2041~~
WINRHO SDF	100 IU	IV	J2792
WYCILLIN	600,000 U	IM, IV	J2510
XELODA	150 MG	ORAL	J8520
XELODA	500 MG	ORAL	J8521
XENON XE-133	10 MCI	INH	A9558
XEOMIN	1 UNIT	IM	J0588
XGEVA	1 MG	SC	J0897
XIAFLEX	0.01 MG	OTH	J0775
XOLAIR	5 MG	SC	J2357
XYLOCAINE	10 MG	IV	J2001
XYNTHA	1 IU	IV	J7185
YERVOY	1 MG	IV	J9228
YTTRIUM 90 IBRITUMOMAB TIUXETAN	TX DOSE UP TO 40 MCI	IV	A9543
ZANAMIVIR (BRAND) (DEMONSTRATION PROJECT)	10 MG	INH	G9034
ZANAMIVIR (GENERIC) (DEMONSTRATION PROJECT)	10 MG	INH	G9018
ZANOSAR	1 GM	IV	J9320
ZANTAC	25 MG	INJ	J2780
ZEMAIRA	10 MG	IV	J0256
ZEMPLAR	1 MCG	IV, IM	J2501
ZENAPAX	25 MG	OTH	J7513
ZEVALIN	STUDY DOSE UP TO 5 MCI	IV	A9542
ZEVALIN DIAGNOSTIC	STUDY DOSE UP TO 5 MCI	IV	A9542
ZEVALIN THERAPEUTIC	TX DOSE UP TO 40 MCI	IV	A9543
ZICONOTIDE	1 MCG	IT	J2278
ZIDOVUDINE	10 MG	IV	J3485
ZIDOVUDINE	100 MG	ORAL	S0104
ZINACEFT	PER 750 MG	IM, IV	J0697
ZINECARD	250 MG	IV	J1190
ZIPRASIDONE MESYLATE	10 MG	IM	J3486
ZITHROMAX	1 G	ORAL	Q0144
ZITHROMAX	500 MG	IV	J0456
ZOFRAN	4 MG	ORAL	S0119
~~ZOFRAN~~	~~8 MG~~	~~ORAL~~	~~Q0179~~
ZOFRAN	1 MG	IV	J2405
ZOFRAN	1 MG	ORAL	Q0162
ZOLADEX	3.6 MG	SC	J9202
ZOLEDRONIC ACID (RECLAST)	1 MG	IV	J3488
ZOLEDRONIC ACID (ZOMETA)	1 MG	IV	J3487
ZOMETA	1 MG	IV	J3487
ZORBTIVE	1 MG	SC	J2941
ZORTRESS	0.25 MG	ORAL	J8561
ZOSYN	1 G/1.125 GM	IV	J2543
ZOVIRAX	5 MG	IV	J0133
ZUPLENZ	1 MG	ORAL	Q0162
ZUPLENZ	4 MG	ORAL	S0119
ZYPREXA	2.5 MG	IM	S0166
ZYPREXA RELPREVV	1 MG	IM	J2358
ZYVOX	200 MG	IV	J2020

NOT OTHERWISE CLASSIFIED DRUGS

Drug Name	*Unit Per*	*Route*	*Code*
ALFENTANIL	500 MCG	IV	J3490
ALLOPURINOL SODIUM	500 MG	IV	J3490
AMINOCAPROIC ACID	250 MG	IV	J3490
~~ARGININE HYDROCHLORIDE~~	~~300 ML~~	~~IV~~	~~J3490~~
~~ASCORBIC ACID~~	~~250 MG~~	~~IV~~	~~J3490~~
~~ATROPINE SULFATE/EDROPHONIUM CHLORIDE~~	~~10 MG~~	~~IV~~	~~J3490~~
AZTREONAM	25 MG	INH	J3490
AZTREONAM	500 MG	IV	J3490
BUMETANIDE	0.25 MG	IM, IV	J3490
BUPIVACAINE, 0.25%	1 ML	OTH	J3490
BUPIVACAINE, 0.50%	1 ML	OTH	J3490
BUPIVACAINE, 0.75%	1 ML	OTH	J3490
~~CABAZITAXEL~~	~~1 MG~~	~~IV~~	~~J3490~~
CALCIUM CHLORIDE	100 MG	IV	J3490
~~CIMETIDINE HCL~~	~~150 MG~~	~~IM, IV~~	~~J3490~~
CLAVULANTE POTASSIUM/TICARCILLIN DISODIUM	0.1-3 GM	IV	J3490
CLEVIDIPINE BUTYRATE	1 MG	IV	J3490
CLINDAMYCIN PHOSPHATE	150 MG	IV	J3490
COPPER SULFATE	0.4 MG	INJ	J3490

Drug Name	*Unit Per*	*Route*	*Code*
~~DENOSUMAB~~	~~1MG~~	~~SC~~	~~J3490~~
DILTIAZEM HCL	5 MG	IV	J3490
DOXAPRAM HCL	20 MG	IV	J3490
DOXYCYCLINE HYCLATE	100 MG	INJ	J3490
~~EDROPHONIUM CHLORIDE~~	~~10 MG~~	~~IM, IV~~	~~J3490~~
~~ENALAPRILAT~~	~~1.25 MG~~	~~IV~~	~~J3490~~
ESMOLOL HYDROCHLORIDE	10 MG	IV	J3490
ESOMEPRAZOLE SODIUM	20 MG	IV	J3490
ETOMIDATE	2 MG	IV	J3490
FAMOTIDINE	10 MG	IV	J3490
FLUMAZENIL	0.1 MG	IV	J3490
FOLIC ACID	5 MG	SC, IM, IV	J3490
FOSPROPOFOL DISODIUM	35 MG	IV	J3490
GLYCOPYRROLATE	0.2 MG	IM, IV	J3490
HEXAMINOLEVULINATE HCL	100 MG PER STUDY DOSE	IV	J3490
~~HUMAN IMMUNE GLOBULIN INTRAVENOUS (GAMMAPLEX)~~	~~500 MG~~	~~IV~~	~~J3490~~
~~KETAMINE HCL~~	~~10 MG~~	~~IM, IV~~	~~J3490~~
LABETALOL HCL	5 MG	INJ	J3490
LIDOCAINE	1 ML	VAR	J3490
LUMIZYME	1 MG	IV	J3590
METOPROLOL TARTRATE	1 MG	IV	J3490
METRONIDAZOLE INJ	500 MG	IV	J3490
MORRHUATE SODIUM	50 MG	OTH	J3490
~~NAFCILLIN SODIUM~~	~~1 GM~~	~~IM, IV~~	~~J3490~~
NITROGLYCERIN	5 MG	IV	J3490
~~OFIRMEV~~	~~10 MG~~	~~IV~~	~~J3490~~
OLANZAPINE SHORT ACTING	0.5 MG	IM	J3490
~~POTASSIUM ACETATE~~	~~2 MEQ~~	~~IV~~	~~J3490~~
~~POTASSIUM PHOSPHATE~~	~~3 MMOL~~	~~IV~~	~~J3490~~
PROPOFOL	10 MG	IV	J3490
~~PROTONIX~~	~~40 MG~~	~~IV~~	~~J3490~~
RIFAMPIN	600 MG	IV	J3490
~~SARRACENIA PURPURA~~	~~1 ML~~	~~INJ~~	~~J3490~~
~~SIPULEUCEL-T~~	~~50 MILLION CD54 CELLS~~	~~IV~~	~~J3490~~
SODIUM ACETATE	2 MEQ	IV	J3490
~~SODIUM BICARBONATE, 8.4%~~	~~50 ML~~	~~IV~~	~~J3490~~
SODIUM CHLORIDE, HYPERTONIC	250 CC	IV	J3490
~~SODIUM THIOSULFATE~~	~~100 MG~~	~~IV~~	~~J3490~~
~~SULFAMETHOXAZOLE-TRIMETHOPRIM~~	~~400-80 MG~~	~~ORAL~~	~~J8499~~
SURGIMEND	0.5 SQ CM	OTH	J3490
~~SYNERA~~	~~70 MG/70 MG~~	~~TOP~~	~~J3490~~
~~VALPROATE SODIUM~~	~~100 MG~~	~~IV~~	~~J3490~~
VASOPRESSIN	20 UNITS	SC, IM	J3490
VECURONIUM BROMIDE	1 MG	IV	J3490
~~VERAPAMIL HCL~~	~~2.5 MG~~	~~IV~~	~~J3490~~
~~VON WILLEBRAND FACTOR COMPLEX (HUMAN), WILATE~~	~~100 IU~~	~~IV~~	~~J3490~~

APPENDIX 2 — MODIFIERS

A modifier is a two-position alpha or numeric code that is added to the end of a CPT code to clarify the services being billed. Modifiers provide a means by which a service can be altered without changing the procedure code. They add more information, such as the anatomical site, to the code. In addition, they help to eliminate the appearance of duplicate billing and unbundling. Modifiers are used to increase accuracy in reimbursement, coding consistency, editing, and to capture payment data.

A1 Dressing for one wound

A2 Dressing for 2 wounds

A3 Dressing for 3 wounds

A4 Dressing for 4 wounds

A5 Dressing for 5 wounds

A6 Dressing for 6 wounds

A7 Dressing for 7 wounds

A8 Dressing for 8 wounds

A9 Dressing for 9 or more wounds

AA Anesthesia services performed personally by anesthesiologist

AD Medical supervision by a physician: more than 4 concurrent anesthesia procedures

AE Registered dietician

AF Specialty physician

AG Primary physician

AH Clinical psychologist

AI Principal physician of record

AJ Clinical social worker

AK Nonparticipating physician

AM Physician, team member service

AP Determination of refractive state was not performed in the course of diagnostic ophthalmological examination

AQ Physician providing a service in an unlisted health professional shortage area (HPSA)

AR Physician provider services in a physician scarcity area

AS Physician assistant, nurse practitioner, or clinical nurse specialist services for assistant at surgery

AT Acute treatment (this modifier should be used when reporting service 98940, 98941, 98942)

AU Item furnished in conjunction with a urological, ostomy, or tracheostomy supply

AV Item furnished in conjunction with a prosthetic device, prosthetic or orthotic

AW Item furnished in conjunction with a surgical dressing

AX Item furnished in conjunction with dialysis services

AY Item or service furnished to an ESRD patient that is not for the treatment of ESRD

AZ Physician providing a service in a dental health professional shortage area for the purpose of an electronic health record incentive payment

BA Item furnished in conjunction with parenteral enteral nutrition (PEN) services

BL Special acquisition of blood and blood products

BO Orally administered nutrition, not by feeding tube

BP The beneficiary has been informed of the purchase and rental options and has elected to purchase the item

BR The beneficiary has been informed of the purchase and rental options and has elected to rent the item

BU The beneficiary has been informed of the purchase and rental options and after 30 days has not informed the supplier of his/her decision

CA Procedure payable only in the inpatient setting when performed emergently on an outpatient who expires prior to admission

CB Service ordered by a renal dialysis facility (RDF) phy[illegible] the ESRD beneficiary's dialysis benefit, is not part [illegible] rate, and is separately reimbursable

CC Procedure code change (use CC when the procedur[illegible] was changed either for administrative reasons or [illegible] incorrect code was filed)

CD AMCC test has been ordered by an ESRD facility [illegible] that is part of the composite rate and is not separ[illegible]

CE AMCC test has been ordered by an ESRD facility [illegible] that is a composite rate test but is beyond the no[illegible] covered under the rate and is separately reimbursable based on medical necessity

CF AMCC test has been ordered by an ESRD facility or MCP physician that is not part of the composite rate and is separately billable

CG Policy criteria applied

CR Catastrophe/Disaster related

CS Item or service related, in whole or in part, to an illness, injury, or condition that was caused by or exacerbated by the effects, direct or indirect, of the 2010 oil spill in the gulf of Mexico, including but not limited to subsequent clean up activities

DA Oral health assessment by a licensed health professional other than a dentist

E1 Upper left, eyelid

E2 Lower left, eyelid

E3 Upper right, eyelid

E4 Lower right, eyelid

EA Erythropoetic stimulating agent (ESA) administered to treat anemia due to anticancer chemotherapy

EB Erythropoetic stimulating agent (ESA) administered to treat anemia due to anticancer radiotherapy

EC Erythropoetic stimulating agent (ESA) administered to treat anemia not due to anticancer radiotherapy or anticancer chemotherapy

ED Hematocrit level has exceeded 39% (or hemoglobin level has exceeded 13.0 G/dl) for 3 or more consecutive billing cycles immediately prior to and including the current cycle

EE Hematocrit level has not exceeded 39% (or hemoglobin level has not exceeded 13.0 G/dl) for 3 or more consecutive billing cycles immediately prior to and including the current cycle

EJ Subsequent claims for a defined course of therapy, e.g., EPO, sodium hyaluronate, infliximab

EM Emergency reserve supply (for ESRD benefit only)

EP Service provided as part of Medicaid early periodic screening diagnosis and treatment (EPSDT) program

ET Emergency services

EY No physician or other licensed health care provider order for this item or service

F1 Left hand, 2nd digit

F2 Left hand, third digit

F3 Left hand, 4th digit

F4 Left hand, fifth digit

F5 Right hand, thumb

F6 Right hand, 2nd digit

F7 Right hand, third digit

F8 Right hand, 4th digit

F9 Right hand, 5th digit

FA Left hand, thumb

FB Item provided without cost to provider, supplier or practitioner, or full credit received for replaced device (examples, but not limited to, covered under warranty, replaced due to defect, free samples)

FC Partial credit received for replaced device

FP Service provided as part of family planning program

G1 Most recent URR reading of less than 60

G2 Most recent URR reading of 60 to 64.9

G3 Most recent URR reading of 65 to 69.9

G4 Most recent URR reading of 70 to 74.9

G5 Most recent URR reading of 75 or greater

G6 ESRD patient for whom less than 6 dialysis sessions have been provided in a month

G7 Pregnancy resulted from rape or incest or pregnancy certified by physician as life threatening

G8 Monitored anesthesia care (MAC) for deep complex, complicated, or markedly invasive surgical procedure

G9 Monitored anesthesia care for patient who has history of severe cardiopulmonary condition

GA Waiver of liability statement issued as required by payer policy, individual case

GB Claim being resubmitted for payment because it is no longer covered under a global payment demonstration

GC This service has been performed in part by a resident under the direction of a teaching physician

GD Units of service exceeds medically unlikely edit value and represents reasonable and necessary services

GE This service has been performed by a resident without the presence of a teaching physician under the primary care exception

GF Nonphysician (e.g., nurse practitioner (NP), certified registered nurse anesthetist (CRNA), certified registered nurse (CRN), clinical nurse specialist (CNS), physician assistant (PA)) services in a critical access hospital

GG Performance and payment of a screening mammogram and diagnostic mammogram on the same patient, same day

GH Diagnostic mammogram converted from screening mammogram on same day

GJ "Opt out" physician or practitioner emergency or urgent service

GK Reasonable and necessary item/service associated with GA or GZ modifier

GL Medically unnecessary upgrade provided instead of nonupgraded item, no charge, no advance beneficiary notice (ABN)

GM Multiple patients on one ambulance trip

GN Services delivered under an outpatient speech language pathology plan of care

GO Services delivered under an outpatient occupational therapy plan of care

GP Services delivered under an outpatient physical therapy plan of care

GQ Via asynchronous telecommunications system

GR This service was performed in whole or in part by a resident in a department of veterans affairs medical center or clinic, supervised in accordance with VA policy

GS Dosage of EPO or darbepoetin alfa has been reduced and maintained in response to hematocrit or hemoglobin level

GT Via interactive audio and video telecommunication systems

GU Waiver of liability statement issued as required by payer policy, routine notice

GV Attending physician not employed or paid under arrangement by the patient's hospice provider

GW Service not related to the hospice patient's terminal condition

GX Notice of liability issued, voluntary under payer policy

GY Item or service statutorily excluded, does not meet the definition of any Medicare benefit or for non-Medicare insurers, is not a contract benefit

GZ Item or service expected to be denied as not reasonable and necessary

H9 Court-ordered

HA Child/adolescent program

HB Adult program, nongeriatric

HC Adult program, geriatric

HD Pregnant/parenting women's program

HE Mental health program

HF Substance abuse program

HG Opioid addiction treatment program

HH Integrated mental health/substance abuse program

HI Integrated mental health and mental retardation/developmental disabilities program

HJ Employee assistance program

HK Specialized mental health programs for high-risk populations

HL Intern

HM Less than bachelor degree level

HN Bachelors degree level

HO Masters degree level

HP Doctoral level

HQ Group setting

HR Family/couple with client present

HS Family/couple without client present

HT Multi-disciplinary team

HU Funded by child welfare agency

HV Funded state addictions agency

HW Funded by state mental health agency

HX Funded by county/local agency

HY Funded by juvenile justice agency

HZ Funded by criminal justice agency

J1 Competitive acquisition program no-pay submission for a prescription number

J2 Competitive acquisition program, restocking of emergency drugs after emergency administration

J3 Competitive acquisition program (CAP), drug not available through CAP as written, reimbursed under average sales price methodology

J4 DMEPOS item subject to DMEPOS competitive bidding program that is furnished by a hospital upon discharge

JA Administered intravenously

JB Administered subcutaneously

JC Skin substitute used as a graft

JD Skin substitute not used as a graft

JW Drug amount discarded/not administered to any patient

K0 Lower extremity prosthesis functional level 0-does not have the ability or potential to ambulate or transfer safely with or without assistance and a prosthesis does not enhance their quality of life or mobility

K1 Lower extremity prosthesis functional level 1 - has the ability or potential to use a prosthesis for transfers or ambulation on level surfaces at fixed cadence, typical of the limited and unlimited household ambulator.

K2 Lower extremity prosthesis functional level 2 - has the ability or potential for ambulation with the ability to traverse low level environmental barriers such as curbs, stairs or uneven surfaces, typical of the limited community ambulator.

K3 Lower extremity prosthesis functional level 3-has the ability or potential for ambulation with variable cadence, typical of the community ambulator who has the ability to traverse most environmental barriers and may have vocational, therapeutic, or exercise activity that demands prosthetic utilization beyond simple locomotion

K4 Lower extremity prosthesis functional level 4 - has the ability or potential for prosthetic ambulation that exceeds the basic ambulation skills, exhibiting high impact, stress, or energy levels, typical of the prosthetic demands of the child, active adult, or athlete.

KA Add on option/accessory for wheelchair

KB Beneficiary requested upgrade for ABN, more than 4 modifiers identified on claim

KC	Replacement of special power wheelchair interface
KD	Drug or biological infused through DME
KE	Bid under round one of the DMEPOS competitive bidding program for use with noncompetitive bid base equipment
KF	Item designated by FDA as class III device
KG	DMEPOS item subject to DMEPOS competitive bidding program number 1
KH	DMEPOS item, initial claim, purchase or first month rental
KI	DMEPOS item, 2nd or 3rd month rental
KJ	DMEPOS item, parenteral enteral nutrition (PEN) pump or capped rental, months 4 to 15
KK	DMEPOS item subject to DMEPOS competitive bidding program number 2
KL	DMEPOS item delivered via mail
KM	Replacement of facial prosthesis including new impression/moulage
KN	Replacement of facial prosthesis using previous master model
KO	Single drug unit dose formulation
KP	First drug of a multiple drug unit dose formulation
KQ	Second or subsequent drug of a multiple drug unit dose formulation
KR	Rental item, billing for partial month
KS	Glucose monitor supply for diabetic beneficiary not treated with insulin
KT	Beneficiary resides in a competitive bidding area and travels outside that competitive bidding area and receives a competitive bid item.
KU	DMEPOS item subject to DMEPOS competitive bidding program number 3
KV	DMEPOS item subject to DMEPOS competitive bidding program that is furnished as part of a professional service
KW	DMEPOS item subject to DMEPOS competitive bidding program number 4
KX	Requirements specified in the medical policy have been met
KY	DMEPOS item subject to DMEPOS competitive bidding program number 5
KZ	New coverage not implemented by managed care
LC	Left circumflex coronary artery
LD	Left anterior descending coronary artery
LL	Lease/rental (use the LL modifier when DME equipment rental is to be applied against the purchase price)
LR	Laboratory round trip
LS	FDA-monitored intraocular lens implant
LT	Left side (used to identify procedures performed on the left side of the body)
M2	Medicare secondary payer (MSP)
MS	Six month maintenance and servicing fee for reasonable and necessary parts and labor which are not covered under any manufacturer or supplier warranty
NB	Nebulizer system, any type, FDA-cleared for use with specific drug
NR	New when rented (use the NR modifier when DME which was new at the time of rental is subsequently purchased)
NU	New equipment
P1	A normal healthy patient
P2	A patient with mild systemic disease
P3	A patient with severe systemic disease
P4	A patient with severe systemic disease that is a constant threat to life
P5	A moribund patient who is not expected to survive without the operation
P6	A declared brain-dead patient whose organs are being removed for donor purposes
PA	Surgical or other invasive procedure on wrong body part
PB	Surgical or other invasive procedure on wrong patient
PC	Wrong surgery or other invasive procedure on patient
PD	Diagnostic or related non diagnostic item or service provided in a wholly owned or operated entity to a patient who is admitted as an inpatient within 3 days
PI	Positron emission tomography (PET) or PET/computed tomography (CT) to inform the initial treatment strategy of tumors that are biopsy proven or strongly suspected of being cancerous based on other diagnostic testing
PL	Progressive addition lenses
PS	Positron emission tomography (PET) or PET/computed tomography (CT) to inform the subsequent treatment strategy of cancerous tumors when the beneficiary's treating physician determines that the PET study is needed to inform subsequent anti-tumor strategy
PT	Colorectal cancer screening test; converted to diagnostic test or other procedure
Q0	Investigational clinical service provided in a clinical research study that is in an approved clinical research study
Q1	Routine clinical service provided in a clinical research study that is in an approved clinical research study
Q2	HCFA/ORD demonstration project procedure/service
Q3	Live kidney donor surgery and related services
Q4	Service for ordering/referring physician qualifies as a service exemption
Q5	Service furnished by a substitute physician under a reciprocal billing arrangement
Q6	Service furnished by a locum tenens physician
Q7	One Class A finding
Q8	Two Class B findings
Q9	One class B and 2 class C findings
QC	Single channel monitoring
QD	Recording and storage in solid state memory by a digital recorder
QE	Prescribed amount of oxygen is less than 1 liter per minute (LPM)
QF	Prescribed amount of oxygen exceeds 4 liters per minute (LPM) and portable oxygen is prescribed
QG	Prescribed amount of oxygen is greater than 4 liters per minute (LPM)
QH	Oxygen conserving device is being used with an oxygen delivery system
QJ	Services/items provided to a prisoner or patient in state or local custody, however the state or local government, as applicable, meets the requirements in 42 CFR 411.4(B)
QK	Medical direction of 2, 3, or 4 concurrent anesthesia procedures involving qualified individuals
QL	Patient pronounced dead after ambulance called
QM	Ambulance service provided under arrangement by a provider of services
QN	Ambulance service furnished directly by a provider of services
QP	Documentation is on file showing that the laboratory test(s) was ordered individually or ordered as a CPT-recognized panel other than automated profile codes 80002-80019, G0058, G0059, and G0060
QS	Monitored anesthesia care service
QT	Recording and storage on tape by an analog tape recorder
QW	CLIA waived test
QX	CRNA service: with medical direction by a physician
QY	Medical direction of one certified registered nurse anesthetist (CRNA) by an anesthesiologist
QZ	CRNA service: without medical direction by a physician
RA	Replacement of a DME, orthotic or prosthetic item
RB	Replacement of a part of a DME, orthotic or prosthetic item furnished as part of a repair
RC	Right coronary artery

RD Drug provided to beneficiary, but not administered "incident-to"

RE Furnished in full compliance with FDA-mandated risk evaluation and mitigation strategy (REMS)

RR Rental (use the RR modifier when DME is to be rented)

RT Right side (used to identify procedures performed on the right side of the body)

SA Nurse practitioner rendering service in collaboration with a physician

SB Nurse midwife

SC Medically necessary service or supply

SD Services provided by registered nurse with specialized, highly technical home infusion training

SE State and/or federally-funded programs/services

SF Second opinion ordered by a professional review organization (PRO) per section 9401, p.l. 99-272 (100% reimbursement - no Medicare deductible or coinsurance)

SG Ambulatory surgical center (ASC) facility service

SH Second concurrently administered infusion therapy

SJ Third or more concurrently administered infusion therapy

SK Member of high risk population (use only with codes for immunization)

SL State supplied vaccine

SM Second surgical opinion

SN Third surgical opinion

SQ Item ordered by home health

SS Home infusion services provided in the infusion suite of the IV therapy provider

ST Related to trauma or injury

SU Procedure performed in physician's office (to denote use of facility and equipment)

SV Pharmaceuticals delivered to patient's home but not utilized

SW Services provided by a certified diabetic educator

SY Persons who are in close contact with member of high-risk population (use only with codes for immunization)

T1 Left foot, 2nd digit

T2 Left foot, 3rd digit

T3 Left foot, 4th digit

T4 Left foot, 5th digit

T5 Right foot, great toe

T6 Right foot, 2nd digit

T7 Right foot, 3rd digit

T8 Right foot, 4th digit

T9 Right foot, 5th digit

TA Left foot, great toe

TC Technical component. Under certain circumstances, a charge may be made for the technical component alone. Under those circumstances the technical component charge is identified by adding modifier 'TC' to the usual procedure number. Technical component charges are institutional charges and not billed separately by physicians. However, portable x-ray suppliers only bill for technical component and should utilize modifier TC. The charge data from portable x-ray suppliers will then be used to build customary and prevailing profiles.

TD RN

TE LPN/LVN

TF Intermediate level of care

TG Complex/high tech level of care

TH Obstetrical treatment/services, prenatal or postpartum

TJ Program group, child and/or adolescent

TK Extra patient or passenger, nonambulance

TL Early intervention/individualized family service plan (IFSP)

TM Individualized education program (IEP)

TN Rural/outside providers' customary service area

TP Medical transport, unloaded vehicle

TQ Basic life support transport by a volunteer ambulance provider

TR School-based individualized education program (IEP) services provided outside the public school district responsible for the student

TS Follow-up service

TT Individualized service provided to more than one patient in same setting

TU Special payment rate, overtime

TV Special payment rates, holidays/weekends

TW Back-up equipment

U1 Medicaid level of care 1, as defined by each state

U2 Medicaid level of care 2, as defined by each state

U3 Medicaid level of care 3, as defined by each state

U4 Medicaid level of care 4, as defined by each state

U5 Medicaid level of care 5, as defined by each state

U6 Medicaid level of care 6, as defined by each state

U7 Medicaid level of care 7, as defined by each state

U8 Medicaid level of care 8, as defined by each state

U9 Medicaid level of care 9, as defined by each state

UA Medicaid level of care 10, as defined by each state

UB Medicaid level of care 11, as defined by each state

UC Medicaid level of care 12, as defined by each state

UD Medicaid level of care 13, as defined by each state

UE Used durable medical equipment

UF Services provided in the morning

UG Services provided in the afternoon

UH Services provided in the evening

UJ Services provided at night

UK Services provided on behalf of the client to someone other than the client (collateral relationship)

UN 2 patients served

UP 3 patients served

UQ 4 patients served

UR 5 patients served

US 6 or more patients served

V5 Vascular catheter (alone or with any other vascular access)

V6 Arteriovenous graft (or other vascular access not including a vascular catheter)

V7 Arteriovenous fistula only (in use with 2 needles)

V8 Infection present

V9 No infection present

VP Aphakic patient

APPENDIX 3 — ABBREVIATIONS AND ACRONYMS

HCPCS Abbreviations and Acronyms

The following abbreviations and acronyms are used in the HCPCS descriptions:

/	or
<	less than
<=	less than equal to
>	greater than
>=	greater than equal to
AC	alternating current
AFO	ankle-foot orthosis
AICC	anti-inhibitor coagulant complex
AK	above the knee
AKA	above knee amputation
ALS	advanced life support
AMP	ampule
ART	artery
ART	Arterial
ASC	ambulatory surgery center
ATT	attached
A-V	Arteriovenous
AVF	arteriovenous fistula
BICROS	bilateral routing of signals
BK	below the knee
BLS	basic life support
BMI	body mass index
BP	blood pressure
BTE	behind the ear (hearing aid)
CAPD	continuous ambulatory peritoneal dialysis
Carb	carbohydrate
CBC	complete blood count
cc	cubic centimeter
CCPD	continuous cycling peritoneal analysis
CHF	congestive heart failure
CIC	completely in the canal (hearing aid)
CIM	Coverage Issue Manual
Clsd	closed
cm	centimeter
CMN	certificate of medical necessity
CMS	Centers for Medicare and Medicaid Services
CMV	Cytomegalovirus
Conc	concentrate
Conc	concentrated
Cont	continuous
CP	clinical psychologist
CPAP	continuous positive airway pressure
CPT	Current Procedural Terminology
CRF	chronic renal failure
CRNA	certified registered nurse anesthetist
CROS	contralateral routing of signals
CSW	clinical social worker
CT	computed tomography
CTLSO	cervical-thoracic-lumbar-sacral orthosis
cu	cubic
DC	direct current
DI	diurnal rhythm
Dx	diagnosis
DLI	donor leukocyte infusion
DME	durable medical equipment
DME MAC	durable medical equipment Medicare administrative contractor
DMEPOS	Durable Medical Equipment, Prosthestics, Orthotics and Other Supplies
DMERC	durable medical equipment regional carrier
DR	diagnostic radiology
DX	diagnostic
e.g.	for example
Ea	each
ECF	extended care facility
EEG	electroencephalogram
EKG	electrocardiogram
EMG	electromyography
EO	elbow orthosis
EP	electrophysiologic
EPO	epoetin alfa
EPSDT	early periodic screening, diagnosis and treatment
ESRD	end-stage renal disease
Ex	extended
Exper	experimental
Ext	external
F	french
FDA	Food and Drug Administration
FDG-PET	Positron emission with tomography with 18 fluorodeoxyglucose
Fem	female
FO	finger orthosis
FPD	fixed partial denture
Fr	french
ft	foot
G-CSF	filgrastim (granulocyte colony-stimulating factor)
gm	gram (g)
H20	water
HCl	hydrochloric acid, hydrochloride
HCPCS	Healthcare Common Procedural Coding System
HCT	hematocrit
HFO	hand-finger orthosis
HHA	home health agency
HI	high
HI-LO	high-low
HIT	home infusion therapy
HKAFO	hip-knee-ankle foot orthosis
HLA	human leukocyte antigen
HMES	heat and moisture exchange system
HNPCC	hereditary non-polyposis colorectal cancer
HO	hip orthosis
HPSA	health professional shortage area
HST	home sleep test
IA	intra-arterial administration
ip	interphalangeal
I-131	Iodine 131
ICF	intermediate care facility
ICU	intensive care facility
IM	intramuscular
in	inch
INF	infusion
INH	inhalation solution
INJ	injection
IOL	intraocular lens
IPD	intermittent peritoneal dialysis
IPPB	intermittent positive pressure breathing
IT	intrathecal administration
ITC	in the canal (hearing aid)
ITE	in the ear (hearing aid)

IU	international units
IV	intravenous
IVF	in vitro fertilization
KAFO	knee-ankle-foot orthosis
KO	knee orthosis
KOH	potassium hydroxide
L	left
LASIK	laser in situ keratomileusis
LAUP	laser assisted uvulopalatoplasty
lbs	pounds
LDL	low density lipoprotein
LDS	lipodystrophy syndrome
Lo	low
LPM	liters per minute
LPN/LVN	Licensed Practical Nurse/Licensed Vocational Nurse
LSO	lumbar-sacral orthosis
MAC	Medicare administrative contractor
mp	metacarpophalangeal
mcg	microgram
mCi	millicurie
MCM	Medicare Carriers Manual
MCP	metacarparpophalangeal joint
MCP	monthly capitation payment
mEq	milliequivalent
MESA	microsurgical epididymal sperm aspiration
mg	milligram
mgs	milligrams
MHT	megahertz
ml	milliliter
mm	millimeter
mmHg	millimeters of Mercury
MRA	magnetic resonance angiography
MRI	magnetic resonance imaging
NA	sodium
NCI	National Cancer Institute
NEC	not elsewhere classified
NG	nasogastric
NH	nursing home
NMES	neuromuscular electrical stimulation
NOC	not otherwise classified
NOS	not otherwise specified
O2	oxygen
OBRA	Omnibus Budget Reconciliation Act
OMT	osteopathic manipulation therapy
OPPS	outpatient prospective payment system
ORAL	oral administration
OSA	obstructive sleep apnea
Ost	ostomy
OTH	other routes of administration
oz	ounce
PA	physician's assistant
PAR	parenteral
PCA	patient controlled analgesia
PCH	pouch
PEN	parenteral and enteral nutrition
PENS	percutaneous electrical nerve stimulation
PET	positron emission tomography
PHP	pre-paid health plan
PHP	physician hospital plan
PI	paramedic intercept
PICC	peripherally inserted central venous catheter
PKR	photorefractive keratotomy
Pow	powder
PQRS	Physician Quality Reporting System
PRK	photoreactive keratectomy
PRO	peer review organization
PSA	prostate specific antigen
PTB	patellar tendon bearing
PTK	phototherapeutic keratectomy
PVC	polyvinyl chloride
R	right
Repl	replace
RN	registered nurse
RP	retrograde pyelogram
Rx	prescription
SACH	solid ankle, cushion heel
SC	subcutaneous
SCT	specialty care transport
SEO	shoulder-elbow orthosis
SEWHO	shoulder-elbow-wrist-hand orthosis
SEXA	single energy x-ray absorptiometry
SGD	speech generating device
SGD	sinus rhythm
SM	samarium
SNCT	sensory nerve conduction test
SNF	skilled nursing facility
SO	sacroilliac othrosis
SO	shoulder orthosis
Sol	solution
SQ	square
SR	screen
ST	standard
ST	sustained release
Syr	syrup
TABS	tablets
Tc	Technetium
Tc 99m	technetium isotope
TENS	transcutaneous electrical nerve stimulator
THKAO	thoracic-hip-knee-ankle orthosis
TLSO	thoracic-lumbar-sacral-orthosis
TM	temporomandibular
TMJ	temporomandibular joint
TPN	total parenteral nutrition
U	unit
uCi	microcurie
VAR	various routes of administration
w	with
w/	with
w/o	with or without
WAK	wearable artificial kidney
wc	wheelchair
WHFO	wrist-hand-finger orthotic
Wk	week
w/o	without
Xe	xenon (isotope mass of xenon 133)

APPENDIX 4 — PUB 100 REFERENCES

The Centers for Medicare and Medicaid Services restructured its paper-based manual system as a web-based system on October 1, 2003. Called the online CMS manual system, it combines all of the various program instructions into internet-only manuals (IOMs), which are used by all CMS programs and contractors. In many instances, the references from the online manuals in appendix E contain a mention of the old paper manuals from which the current information was obtained when the manuals were converted. This information is shown in the header of the text, in the following format, when applicable, as A3-3101, HO-210, and B3-2049. Complete versions of all of the manuals can be found at http://www.cms.gov/manuals.

Effective with implementation of the IOMs, the former method of publishing program memoranda (PMs) to communicate program instructions was replaced by the following four templates:

- One-time notification
- Manual revisions
- Business requirements
- Confidential requirements

The web-based system has been organized by functional area (e.g., eligibility, entitlement, claims processing, benefit policy, program integrity) in an effort to eliminate redundancy within the manuals, simplify updating, and make CMS program instructions available more quickly. The web-based system contains the functional areas included below:

Pub. 100	Introduction
Pub. 100-1	Medicare General Information, Eligibility, and Entitlement Manual
Pub. 100-2	Medicare Benefit Policy Manual
Pub. 100-3	Medicare National Coverage Determinations (NCD) Manual
Pub. 100-4	Medicare Claims Processing Manual
Pub. 100-5	Medicare Secondary Payer Manual
Pub. 100-6	Medicare Financial Management Manual
Pub. 100-7	State Operations Manual
Pub. 100-8	Medicare Program Integrity Manual
Pub. 100-9	Medicare Contractor Beneficiary and Provider Communications Manual
Pub. 100-10	Quality Improvement Organization Manual
Pub. 100-11	Programs of All-Inclusive Care for the Elderly (PACE) Manual
Pub. 100-12	State Medicaid Manual (under development)
Pub. 100-13	Medicaid State Children's Health Insurance Program (under development)
Pub. 100-14	Medicare ESRD Network Organizations Manual
Pub. 100-15	Medicaid Integrity Program (MIP)
Pub. 100-16	Medicare Managed Care Manual
Pub. 100-17	CMS/Business Partners Systems Security Manual
Pub. 100-18	Medicare Prescription Drug Benefit Manual
Pub. 100-19	Demonstrations
Pub. 100-20	One-Time Notification
Pub. 100-21	Recurring Update Notification
Pub. 100-22	Medicare Quality Reporting Incentive Programs Manual
Pub. 100-24	State Buy-In Manual
Pub. 100-25	Information Security Acceptable Risk Safeguards Manual

A brief description of the Medicare manuals primarily used for *CPC Expert* follows:

The ***National Coverage Determinations Manual*** (NCD), is organized according to categories such as diagnostic services, supplies, and medical procedures. The table of contents lists each category and subject within that category. Revision transmittals identify any new or background material, recap the changes, and provide an effective date for the change.

When complete, the manual will contain two chapters. Chapter 1 currently includes a description of CMS's national coverage determinations. When available, chapter 2 will contain a list of HCPCS codes related to each coverage determination. The manual is organized in accordance with CPT category sequences.

The ***Medicare Benefit Policy Manual*** contains Medicare general coverage instructions that are not national coverage determinations. As a general rule, in the past these instructions have been found in chapter II of the ***Medicare Carriers Manual***, the ***Medicare Intermediary Manual***, other provider manuals, and program memoranda.

The ***Medicare Claims Processing Manual*** contains instructions for processing claims for contractors and providers.

The ***Medicare Program Integrity Manual*** communicates the priorities and standards for the Medicare integrity programs.

100-1, 1, 10.1

Hospital Insurance (Part A) for Inpatient Hospital, Hospice, Home Health and Skilled Nursing Facility (SNF) Services - A Brief Description

Hospital insurance is designed to help patients defray the expenses incurred by hospitalization and related care. In addition to inpatient hospital benefits, hospital insurance covers post hospital extended care in SNFs and post hospital care furnished by a home health agency in the patient's home. Blood clotting factors, for hemophilia patients competent to use such factors to control bleeding without medical or other supervision, and items related to the administration of such factors, are also a Part A benefit for beneficiaries in a covered Part A stay. The purpose of these additional benefits is to provide continued treatment after hospitalization and to encourage the appropriate use of more economical alternatives to inpatient hospital care. Program payments for services rendered to beneficiaries by providers (i.e., hospitals, SNFs, and home health agencies) are generally made to the provider. In each benefit period, payment may be made for up to 90 inpatient hospital days, and 100 days of post hospital extended care services .Hospices also provide Part A hospital insurance services such as short-term inpatient care. In order to be eligible to elect hospice care under Medicare, an individual must be entitled to Part A of Medicare and be certified as being terminally ill. An individual is considered to be terminally ill if the individual has a medical prognosis that his or her life expectancy is 6 months or less if the illness runs its normal course.

100-1, 3, 20.5

Blood Deductibles (Part A and Part B)

Program payment may not be made for the first 3 pints of whole blood or equivalent units of packed red cells received under Part A and Part B combined in a calendar year. However, blood processing (e.g., administration, storage) is not subject to the deductible.

The blood deductibles are in addition to any other applicable deductible and coinsurance amounts for which the patient is responsible.

The deductible applies only to the first 3 pints of blood furnished in a calendar year, even if more than one provider furnished blood.

100-1, 3, 20.5.2

Part B Blood Deductible

Blood is furnished on an outpatient basis or is subject to the Part B blood deductible and is counted toward the combined limit. It should be noted that payment for blood may be made to the hospital under Part B only for blood furnished in an outpatient setting. Blood is not covered for inpatient Part B services.

100-1,3,20.5.3

Items Subject to Blood Deductibles

The blood deductibles apply only to whole blood and packed red cells. The term whole blood means human blood from which none of the liquid or cellular components have been removed. Where packed red cells are furnished, a unit of packed red cells is considered equivalent to a pint of whole blood. Other components of blood such as platelets, fibrinogen, plasma, gamma globulin, and serum albumin are not subject to the blood deductible. However, these components of blood are covered as biologicals.

Refer to Pub. 100-04, Medicare Claims Processing Manual, chapter 4, Sec.231 regarding billing for blood and blood products under the Hospital Outpatient Prospective Payment System (OPPS).

100-1, 5, 90.2

Laboratory Defined

Laboratory means a facility for the biological, microbiological, serological, chemical, immuno-hematological, hematological, biophysical, cytological, pathological, or other examination of materials derived from the human body for the purpose of providing information for the diagnosis, prevention, or treatment of any disease or impairment of, or the assessment of the health of, human beings. These examinations also include procedures to determine, measure, or otherwise describe the presence or absence of various substances or organisms in the body. Facilities only collecting or preparing specimens (or both) or only serving as a mailing service and not performing testing are not considered laboratories.

100-2, 1, 10

Covered Inpatient Hospital Services Covered Under Part A

A3-3101, HO-210

Patients covered under hospital insurance are entitled to have payment made on their behalf for inpatient hospital services. (Inpatient hospital services do not include extended care services provided by hospitals pursuant to swing bed approvals. See Pub. 100-1, Chapter 8, Sec.10.1, "Hospital Providers of Extended Care Services."). However, both inpatient hospital and inpatient SNF benefits are provided under Part A - Hospital Insurance Benefits for the Aged and Disabled, of Title XVIII).

Additional information concerning the following topics can be found in the following manual chapters:

- Benefit periods is found in Chapter 3, "Duration of Covered Inpatient Services";
- Copayment days is found in Chapter 2, "Duration of Covered Inpatient Services";
- Lifetime reserve days is found in Chapter 5, "Lifetime Reserve Days";
- Related payment information is housed in the Provider Reimbursement Manual.

Blood must be furnished on a day which counts as a day of inpatient hospital services to be covered as a Part A service and to count toward the blood deductible. Thus, blood is not covered under Part A and does not count toward the Part A blood deductible when furnished to an inpatient after the inpatient has exhausted all benefit days in a benefit period, or where the individual has elected not to use lifetime reserve days. However, where the patient is discharged on their first day of entitlement or on the hospital's first day of participation, the hospital is permitted to submit a billing form with no accommodation charge, but with ancillary charges including blood.

The records for all Medicare hospital inpatient discharges are maintained in CMS for statistical analysis and use in determining future PPS DRG classifications and rates.

Non-PPS hospitals do not pay for noncovered services generally excluded from coverage in the Medicare Program. This may result in denial of a part of the billed charges or in denial of the entire admission, depending upon circumstance. In PPS hospitals, the following are also possible:

1. In appropriately admitted cases where a noncovered procedure was performed, denied services may result in payment of a different DRG (i.e., one which excludes payment for the noncovered procedure); or
2. In appropriately admitted cases that become cost outlier cases, denied services may lead to denial of some or all of an outlier payment.

The following examples illustrate this principle. If care is noncovered because a patient does not need to be hospitalized, the intermediary denies the admission and makes no Part A (i.e., PPS) payment unless paid under limitation on liability. Under limitation on liability, Medicare payment may be made when the provider and the beneficiary were not aware the services were not necessary and could not reasonably be expected to know that he services were not necessary. For detailed instructions, see the Medicare Claims Processing Manual, Chapter 30,"Limitation on Liability." If a patient is appropriately hospitalized but receives (beyond routine services) only noncovered care, the admission is denied.

NOTE: The intermediary does not deny an admission that includes covered care, even if noncovered care was also rendered. Under PPS, Medicare assumes that it is paying for only the covered care rendered whenever covered services needed to treat and/or diagnose the illness were in fact provided.

If a noncovered procedure is provided along with covered nonroutine care, a DRG change rather than an admission denial might occur. If noncovered procedures are elevating costs into the cost outlier category, outlier payment is denied in whole or in part.

When the hospital is included in PPS, most of the subsequent discussion regarding coverage of inpatient hospital services is relevant only in the context of determining the appropriateness of admissions, which DRG, if any, to pay, and the appropriateness of payment for any outlier cases.

If a patient receives items or services in excess of, or more expensive than, those for which payment can be made, payment is made only for the covered items or services or for only the appropriate prospective payment amount. This provision applies not only to inpatient services, but also to all hospital services under Parts A and B of the program. If the items or services were requested by the patient, the hospital may charge him the difference between the amount customarily charged for the services requested and the amount customarily charged for covered services.

An inpatient is a person who has been admitted to a hospital for bed occupancy for purposes of receiving inpatient hospital services. Generally, a patient is considered an inpatient if formally admitted as inpatient with the expectation that he or she will remain at least overnight and occupy a bed even though it later develops that the patient can be discharged or transferred to another hospital and not actually use a hospital bed overnight.

The physician or other practitioner responsible for a patient's care at the hospital is also responsible for deciding whether the patient should be admitted as an inpatient. Physicians should use a 24-hour period as a benchmark, i.e., they should order admission for patients who are expected to need hospital care for 24 hours or more, and treat other patients on an outpatient basis. However, the decision to admit a patient is a complex medical judgment which can be made only after the physician has considered a number of factors, including the patient's medical history and current medical needs, the types of facilities available to inpatients and to outpatients, the hospital's by-laws and admissions policies, and the relative appropriateness of treatment in each setting. Factors to be considered when making the decision to admit include such things as:

The severity of the signs and symptoms exhibited by the patient;

The medical predictability of something adverse happening to the patient;

The need for diagnostic studies that appropriately are outpatient services (i.e., their performance does not ordinarily require the patient to remain at the hospital for 24 hours or more) to assist in assessing whether the patient should be admitted; and

The availability of diagnostic procedures at the time when and at the location where the patient presents.

Admissions of particular patients are not covered or noncovered solely on the basis of the length of time the patient actually spends in the hospital. In certain specific situations coverage of services on an inpatient or outpatient basis is determined by the following rules:

Minor Surgery or Other Treatment - When patients with known diagnoses enter a hospital for a specific minor surgical procedure or other treatment that is expected to keep them in the hospital for only a few hours (less than 24), they are considered outpatients for coverage purposes regardless of: the hour they came to the hospital, whether they used a bed, and whether they remained in the hospital past midnight.

Renal Dialysis - Renal dialysis treatments are usually covered only as outpatient services but may under certain circumstances be covered as inpatient services depending on the patient's condition. Patients staying at home, who are ambulatory, whose conditions are stable and who come to the hospital for routine chronic dialysis treatments, and not for a diagnostic workup or a change in therapy, are considered outpatients. On the other hand, patients undergoing short-term dialysis until their kidneys recover from an acute illness (acute dialysis), or persons with borderline renal failure who develop acute renal failure every time they have an illness and require dialysis (episodic dialysis) are usually inpatients. A patient may begin dialysis as an inpatient and then progress to an outpatient status.

Under original Medicare, the Quality Improvement Organization (QIO), for each hospital is responsible for deciding, during review of inpatient admissions on a case-by-case basis, whether the admission was medically necessary. Medicare law authorizes the QIO to make these judgments, and the judgments are binding for purposes of Medicare coverage. In making these judgments, however, QIOs consider only the medical evidence which was available to the physician at the time an admission decision had to be made. They do not take into account other information (e.g., test results) which became available only after admission, except in cases where considering the post-admission information would support a finding that an admission was medically necessary.

Refer to Parts 4 and 7 of the QIO Manual with regard to initial determinations for these services. The QIO will review the swing bed services in these PPS hospitals as well.

NOTE: When patients requiring extended care services are admitted to beds in a hospital, they are considered inpatients of the hospital. In such cases, the services furnished in the hospital will not be considered extended care services, and payment may not be made under the program for such services unless the services are extended care services furnished pursuant to a swing bed agreement granted to the hospital by the Secretary of Health and Human Services.

100-2, 1, 10.1.4

Charges for Deluxe Private Room

A3-3101.1.D, HO-210.1.D

Beneficiaries found to need a private room (either because they need isolation for medical reasons or because they need immediate admission when no other accommodations are available) may be assigned to any of the provider's private rooms. They do not have the right to insist on the private room of their choice, but their preferences should be given the same consideration as if they were paying all provider charges themselves. The program does not, under any circumstances, pay for personal comfort items. Thus, the program does not pay for deluxe accommodations and/or services. These would include a suite, or a room substantially more spacious than is required for treatment, or specially equipped or decorated, or serviced for the comfort and convenience of persons willing to pay a differential for such amenities. If the beneficiary (or representative) requests such deluxe accommodations, the provider should advise that there will be a charge, not covered by Medicare, of a specified amount per day (not exceeding the differential defined in the next sentence); and may charge the beneficiary that amount for each day he/she occupies the deluxe accommodations. The maximum amount the provider may charge the beneficiary for such accommodations is the differential between the most prevalent private room rate at the time of admission and the customary charge for the room occupied. Beneficiaries may not be charged this differential if they (or their representative) do not request the deluxe accommodations.

The beneficiary may not be charged such a differential in private room rates if that differential is based on factors other than personal comfort items. Such factors might include differences between older and newer wings, proximity to lounge, elevators or nursing stations, desirable view, etc. Such rooms are standard 1-bed units and not deluxe rooms for purposes of these instructions, even though the provider may call them deluxe and have a higher customary charge for them. No additional charge may be imposed upon the beneficiary who is assigned to a room that may be somewhat more desirable because of these factors.

100-2, 1, 40

Supplies, Appliances, and Equipment

Supplies, appliances, and equipment, which are ordinarily furnished by the hospital for the care and treatment of the beneficiary solely during the inpatient hospital stay, are covered inpatient hospital services.

Under certain circumstances, supplies, appliances, and equipment used during the beneficiary's inpatient stay are covered under Part A even though the supplies, appliances and equipment leave the hospital with the patient upon discharge. These are circumstances in which it would be unreasonable or impossible from a medical standpoint to limit the patient's use of the item to the periods during which the individual is an inpatient. Examples of items covered under this rule are:

- Items permanently installed in or attached to the patient's body while an inpatient, such as cardiac valves, cardiac pacemakers, and artificial limbs; and
- Items which are temporarily installed in or attached to the patient's body while an inpatient, and which are also necessary to permit or facilitate the patient's release from the hospital, such as tracheotomy or drainage tubes.

Hospital "admission packs" containing primarily toilet articles, such as soap, toothbrushes, toothpaste, and combs, are covered under Part A if routinely furnished by the hospital to all its inpatients. If not routinely furnished to all patients, the packs are not covered. In that situation, the hospital may charge beneficiaries for the pack, but only if they request it with knowledge of what they are requesting and what the charge to them will be.

Supplies, appliances, and equipment furnished to an inpatient for use only outside the hospital are not, in general, covered as inpatient hospital services. However, a temporary or disposable item, which is medically necessary to permit or facilitate the patient's departure from the hospital and is required until the patient can obtain a continuing supply, is covered as an inpatient hospital service.

Oxygen furnished to hospital inpatients is covered under Part A as an inpatient supply.

100-2, 6, 10

Medical and Other Health Services Furnished to Inpatients of Participating Hospitals

Payment may be made under Part B for physician services and for the nonphysician medical and other health services listed below when furnished by a participating hospital (either directly or under arrangements) to an inpatient of the hospital, but only if payment for these services cannot be made under Part A.

In PPS hospitals, this means that Part B payment could be made for these services if:

- No Part A prospective payment is made at all for the hospital stay because of patient exhaustion of benefit days before admission;
- The admission was disapproved as not reasonable and necessary (and waiver of liability payment was not made);
- The day or days of the otherwise covered stay during which the services were provided were not reasonable and necessary (and no payment was made under waiver of liability);
- The patient was not otherwise eligible for or entitled to coverage under Part A (See the Medicare Benefit Policy Manual, Chapter 1, Sec.150, for services received as a result of noncovered services); or
- No Part A day outlier payment is made (for discharges before October 1997) for one or more outlier days due to patient exhaustion of benefit days after admission but before the case's arrival at outlier status, or because outlier days are otherwise not covered and waiver of liability payment is not made.

However, if only day outlier payment is denied under Part A (discharges before October 1997), Part B payment may be made for only the services covered under Part B and furnished on the denied outlier days.

In non-PPS hospitals, Part B payment may be made for services on any day for which Part A payment is denied (i.e., benefit days are exhausted; services are not at the hospital level of care; or patient is not otherwise eligible or entitled to payment under Part A).

Services payable are:

- Diagnostic x-ray tests, diagnostic laboratory tests, and other diagnostic tests;
- X-ray, radium, and radioactive isotope therapy, including materials and services of technicians;
- Surgical dressings, and splints, casts, and other devices used for reduction of fractures and dislocations;
- Prosthetic devices (other than dental) which replace all or part of an internal body organ (including contiguous tissue), or all or part of the function of a permanently inoperative or malfunctioning internal body organ, including replacement or repairs of such devices;
- Leg, arm, back, and neck braces, trusses, and artificial legs, arms, and eyes including adjustments, repairs, and replacements required because of breakage, wear, loss, or a change in the patient's physical condition;
- Outpatient physical therapy, outpatient speech-language pathology services, and outpatient occupational therapy (see the Medicare Benefit Policy Manual, Chapter 15, "Covered Medical and Other Health Services," Sec.Sec.220 and 230);
- Screening mammography services;
- Screening pap smears;
- Influenza, pneumococcal pneumonia, and hepatitis B vaccines;
- Colorectal screening;
- Bone mass measurements;
- Diabetes self-management;
- Prostate screening;
- Ambulance services;
- Hemophilia clotting factors for hemophilia patients competent to use these factors without supervision);
- Immunosuppressive drugs;
- Oral anti-cancer drugs;
- Oral drug prescribed for use as an acute anti-emetic used as part of an anti-cancer chemotherapeutic regimen; and
- Epoetin Alfa (EPO).

Coverage rules for these services are described in the Medicare Benefit Policy Manual, Chapters: 11, "End Stage Renal Disease (ESRD);" 14, "Medical Devices;" or 15, "Medical and Other Health Services."

For services to be covered under Part A or Part B, a hospital must furnish nonphysician services to its inpatients directly or under arrangements. A nonphysician service is one which does not meet the criteria defining physicians' services specifically provided for in regulation at 42 CFR 415.102. Services "incident to" physicians' services (except for the services of nurse anesthetists employed by anesthesiologists) are nonphysician services for purposes of this provision. This provision is applicable to all hospitals participating in Medicare, including those paid under alternative arrangements such as State cost control systems, and to emergency hospital services furnished by nonparticipating hospitals.

In all hospitals, every service provided to a hospital inpatient other than those listed in the next paragraph must be treated as an inpatient hospital service to be paid for under Part A, if Part A coverage is available and the beneficiary is entitled to Part A. This is because every hospital must provide directly or arrange for any nonphysician service rendered to its inpatients, and a hospital can be paid under Part B for a service provided in this manner only if Part A coverage does not exist.

These services, when provided to a hospital inpatient, may be covered under Part B, even though the patient has Part A coverage for the hospital stay. This is because these services are covered under Part B and not covered under Part A. They are:

- Physicians' services (including the services of residents and interns in unapproved teaching programs);
- Influenza vaccine;
- Pneumococcal vaccine and its administration;

- Hepatitis B vaccine and its administration;
- Screening mammography services;
- Screening pap smears and pelvic exams;
- Colorectal screening;
- Bone mass measurements;
- Diabetes self management training services; and
- Prostate screening.

However, note that in order to have any Medicare coverage at all (Part A or Part B), any nonphysician service rendered to a hospital inpatient must be provided directly or arranged for by the hospital.

100-2, 6, 20.6

Outpatient Observation Services

A. Outpatient Observation Services Defined

Observation care is a well-defined set of specific, clinically appropriate services, which include ongoing short term treatment, assessment, and reassessment before a decision can be made regarding whether patients will require further treatment as hospital inpatients or if they are able to be discharged from the hospital. Observation services are commonly ordered for patients who present to the emergency department and who then require a significant period of treatment or monitoring in order to make a decision concerning their admission or discharge.

Observation services are covered only when provided by the order of a physician or another individual authorized by State licensure law and hospital staff bylaws to admit patients to the hospital or to order outpatient tests. In the majority of cases, the decision whether to discharge a patient from the hospital following resolution of the reason for the observation care or to admit the patient as an inpatient can be made in less than 48 hours, usually in less than 24 hours. In only rare and exceptional cases do reasonable and necessary outpatient observation services span more than 48 hours.

Hospitals may bill for patients who are directly referred to the hospital for outpatient observation services. A direct referral occurs when a physician in the community refers a patient to the hospital for outpatient observation, bypassing the clinic or emergency department (ED) visit. Effective for services furnished on or after January 1, 2003, hospitals may bill for patients directly referred for observation services.

See Pub. 100-04,*Medicare Claims Processing Manual*,chapter 4, section 290, at http://www.cms.hhs.gov/manuals/downloads/clm104c04.pdf for billing and payment instructions for outpatient observation services.

Future updates will be issued in a Recurring Update Notification.

B. Coverage of Outpatient Observation Services

When a physician orders that a patient receive observation care, the patient's status is that of an outpatient. The purpose of observation is to determine the need for further treatment or for inpatient admission. Thus, a patient receiving observation services may improve and be released, or be admitted as an inpatient (see Pub. 100-02,*Medicare Benefit Policy Manual*, Chapter 1, Section 10 "Covered Inpatient Hospital Services Covered Under Part A" at http://www.cms.hhs.gov/manuals/Downloads/bp102c01.pdf). For more information on correct reporting of observation services, see Pub. 100-04,*Medicare Claims Processing Manual*, chapter 4, section 290.2.2.)

All hospital observation services, regardless of the duration of the observation care, that are medically reasonable and necessary are covered by Medicare.

Observation services are reported using HCPCS code G0378 (Hospital observation service, per hour). Beginning January 1, 2008, HCPCS code G0378 for hourly observation services is assigned status indicator N, signifying that its payment is always packaged. No separate payment is made for observation services reported with HCPCS code G0378. In most circumstances, observation services are supportive and ancillary to the other separately payable services provided to a patient. In certain circumstances when observation care is billed in conjunction with a high level clinic visit (Level 5), high level Type A emergency department visit (Level 4 or 5), high level Type B emergency department visit (Level 5), critical care services, or direct referral for observation services as an integral part of a patient's extended encounter of care, payment may be made for the entire extended care encounter through one of two composite APCs when certain criteria are met. For information about billing and payment methodology for observation services in years prior to CY 2008, see Pub. 100-04,*Medicare Claims Processing Manual*, Chapter 4, Sec.Sec.290.3-290.4. For information about payment for extended assessment and management under composite APCs, see Sec.290.5.

Payment for all reasonable and necessary observation services is packaged into the payments for other separately payable services provided to the patient in the same encounter. Observation services packaged through assignment of status indicator N are covered OPPS services. Since the payment for these services is included in the APC payment for other separately payable services on the claim, hospitals must not bill Medicare beneficiaries directly for the packaged services.

C. Services Not Covered by Medicare and Notification to the Beneficiary

In making the determination whether an ABN can be used to shift liability to a beneficiary for the cost of non-covered items or services related to an encounter that includes observation care, the provider should follow a two step process. First, the provider must decide whether the item or service meets either the definition of observation care or would be otherwise covered. If the item or service does not meet the definitional requirements of any Medicare-covered benefit under Part B, then the item or service is not covered by Medicare and an ABN is not required to shift the liability to the beneficiary. However, the provider may choose to provide voluntary notification for these items or services.

Second, if the item or service meets the definition of observation services or would be otherwise covered, then the provider must decide whether the item or service is "reasonable and necessary" for the beneficiary on the occasion in question, or if the item or service exceeds any frequency limitation for the particular benefit or falls outside of a timeframe for receipt of a particular benefit. In these cases, the ABN would be used to shift the liability to the beneficiary (see Pub. 100-04,*Medicare Claims Processing Manual*; Chapter 30, "Financial Liability Protections," Section 20, at http://www.cms.hhs.gov/manuals/downloads/clm104c30.pdf for information regarding Limitation On Liability (LOL) Under Sec.1879 Where Medicare Claims Are Disallowed).

If an ABN is not issued to the beneficiary, the provider may be held liable for the cost of the item or service unless the provider/supplier is able to demonstrate that they did not know and could not have reasonably been expected to know that Medicare would not pay for the item or service.

100-2, 10, 10.2.2

Reasonableness of the Ambulance Trip

Under the FS payment is made according to the level of medically necessary services actually furnished. That is, payment is based on the level of service furnished (provided they were medically necessary), not simply on the vehicle used. Even if a local government requires an ALS response for all calls, payment under the FS is made only for the level of service furnished, and then only when the service is medically necessary.

100-2, 10, 10.3.3

Separately Payable Ambulance Transport Under Part B versus Patient Transportation that is Covered Under a Packaged Hospital Service

Transportation of a beneficiary from his or her home, an accident scene, or any other point of origin is covered under Part B as an ambulance service only to the nearest hospital, critical access hospital (CAH), or skilled nursing facility (SNF) that is capable of furnishing the required level and type of care for the beneficiary's illness or injury and only if medical necessity and other program coverage criteria are met.

Medicare-covered ambulance services are paid either as separately billed services, in which case the entity furnishing the ambulance service bills Part B of the program, or as a packaged service, in which case the entity furnishing the ambulance service must seek payment from the provider who is responsible for the beneficiary's care. If either the origin or the destination of the ambulance transport is the beneficiary's home, then the ambulance transport is paid separately by Medicare Part B, and the entity that furnishes the ambulance transport may bill its Medicare carrier or intermediary directly. If both the origin and destination of the ambulance transport are providers, e.g., a hospital, critical access hospital (CAH), skilled nursing facility (SNF), then responsibility for payment for the ambulance transport is determined in accordance with the following sequential criteria.

NOTE: These criteria must be applied in sequence as a flow chart and not independently of one another.

1. Provider Numbers:

   If the Medicare-assigned provider numbers of the two providers are different, then the ambulance service is separately billable to the program. If the provider number of both providers is the same, then consider criterion 2, "campus".

2. Campus:

   Following criterion 1, if the campuses of the two providers (sharing the same provider numbers) are the same, then the transport is not separately billable to the program. In this case the provider is responsible for payment. If the campuses of the two providers are different, then consider criterion 3, "patient status." "Campus" means the physical area immediately adjacent to the provider's main buildings, other areas and structures that are not strictly contiguous to the main buildings, but are located within 250 yards of the main buildings, and any of the other areas determined on an individual case basis by the CMS regional office to be part of the provider's campus.

3. Patient Status: Inpatient vs. Outpatient

   Following criteria 1 and 2, if the patient is an inpatient at both providers (i.e., inpatient status both at the origin and at the destination, providers sharing the same provider number but located on different campuses), then the transport is not separately billable. In this case the provider is responsible for payment. All other combinations (i.e., outpatient-to-inpatient, inpatient-to-outpatient, outpatient-to-outpatient) are separately billable to the program.

In the case where the point of origin is not a provider, Part A coverage is not available because, at the time the beneficiary is being transported, the beneficiary is not an inpatient of any provider paid under Part A of the program and ambulance services are excluded from the 3-day preadmission payment window.

The transfer, i.e., the discharge of a beneficiary from one provider with a subsequent admission to another provider, is also payable as a Part B ambulance transport, provided all program coverage criteria are met, because, at the time that the beneficiary is in transit, the beneficiary is not a patient of either provider and not subject to either the inpatient preadmission payment window or outpatient payment packaging requirements. This includes an outpatient transfer from a remote, off-campus emergency department (ER) to becoming an inpatient or outpatient at the main campus hospital, even if the ER is owned and operated by the hospital.

Once a beneficiary is admitted to a hospital, CAH, or SNF, it may be necessary to transport the beneficiary to another hospital or other site temporarily for specialized care while the beneficiary maintains inpatient status with the original provider. This movement of the patient is considered "patient transportation" and is covered as an inpatient hospital or CAH service and as a SNF service when the SNF is furnishing it as a covered SNF service and payment is made under Part A for that service. (If the beneficiary is a resident of a SNF and must be transported by ambulance to receive dialysis or certain other high-end outpatient hospital services, the ambulance transport may be separately payable under Part B.) Because the service is covered and payable as a beneficiary transportation service under Part A, the service cannot be classified and paid for as an ambulance service under Part B. This includes intra-campus transfers between different departments of the same hospital, even where the departments are located in separate buildings. Such intra-campus transfers are not separately payable under the Part B ambulance benefit. Such costs are accounted for in the same manner as the costs of such a transfer within a single building.

100-2, 10, 20

Coverage Guidelines for Ambulance Service Claims

Payment may be made for expenses incurred by a patient for ambulance service provided conditions l, 2, and 3 in the left-hand column have been met. The right-hand column indicates the documentation needed to establish that the condition has been met.

Conditions	Review Action
1. Patient was transported by an approved supplier of ambulance services.	1. Ambulance suppliers are explained in greater detail in Sec.10.1.3
2. The patient was suffering from an illness or injury, which contraindicated transportation by other means. (Sec.10.2)	2. (a) The contractor presumes the requirement was met if the submitted documentation indicates that the patient: • Was transported in an emergency situation, e.g., as a result of an accident, injury or acute illness, or • Needed to be restrained to prevent injury to the beneficiary or others; or • Was unconscious or in shock; or • Required oxygen or other emergency treatment during transport to the nearest appropriate facility; or • Exhibits signs and symptoms of acute respiratory distress or cardiac distress such as shortness of breath or chest pain; or • Exhibits signs and symptoms that indicate the possibility of acute stroke; or • Had to remain immobile because of a fracture that had not been set or the possibility of a fracture; or • Was experiencing severe hemorrhage; or • Could be moved only by stretcher; or • Was bed-confined before and after the ambulance trip. (b) In the absence of any of the conditions listed in
2. Continued	(a) above additional documentation should be obtained to establish medical need where the evidence indicates the existence of the circumstances listed below: i Patient's condition would not ordinarily require movement by stretcher, or ii The individual was not admitted as a hospital inpatient (except in accident cases), or iii The ambulance was used solely because other means of transportation were unavailable, or
3. The patient was transported from and to points listed below. (a) From patient's residence (or other place where need arose) to hospital or skilled nursing facility.	3. Claims should show the ZIP Code of the point of pickup. (a) i. Condition met if trip began within the institution's service area as shown in the carrier's locality guide. ii. Condition met where the trip began outside the institution's service area if the institution was the nearest one with appropriate facilities.

NOTE: A patient's residence is the place where he or she makes his/her home and dwells permanently, or for an extended period of time. A skilled nursing facility is one, which is listed in the Directory of Medical Facilities as a participating SNF or as an institution which meets §1861(j)(1) of the Act.

NOTE: A claim for ambulance service to a participating hospital or skilled nursing facility should not be denied on the grounds that there is a nearer nonparticipating institution having appropriate facilities.

(b) Skilled nursing facility to a hospital or hospital to a skilled nursing facility.	(b) i Condition met if the ZIP Code of the pickup point is within the service area of the destination as shown in the carrier's locality guide. ii Condition met where the ZIP Code of the pickup point is outside the service area of the destination if the destination institution was the nearest appropriate facility.
(c) Hospital to hospital or skilled nursing facility to skilled nursing facility.	(c) Condition met if the discharging institution was not an appropriate facility and the admitting institution was the nearest appropriate facility.
(c) Hospital to hospital or skilled nursing facility to skilled nursing facility.	(c) Condition met if the discharging institution was not an appropriate facility and the admitting institution was the nearest appropriate facility.
(d) From a hospital or skilled nursing facility to patient's residence.	(d) i Condition met if patient's residence is within the institution's service area as shown in the carrier's locality guide. ii Condition met where the patient's residence is outside the institution's service area if the institution was the nearest appropriate facility.
(e) Round trip for hospital or participating skilled nursing facility inpatients to the nearest hospital or nonhospital treatment facility	(e) Condition met if the reasonable and necessary diagnostic or therapeutic service required by patient's condition is not available at the institution where the beneficiary is an inpatient.

NOTE: Ambulance service to a physician's office or a physician-directed clinic is not covered. See §10.3.8 above, where a stop is made at a physician's office en route to a hospital and §10.3.3 for additional exceptions.)

Conditions	Review Action
4. Ambulance services involving hospital admissions in Canada or Mexico are covered (Medicare Claims Processing Manual, Chapter 1, "General Billing Requirements, "§10.1.3.) if the following conditions are met:	4. (a) The foreign hospitalization has been determined to be covered; and (b) The ambulance service meets the coverage requirements set forth in §§10-10.3. If the foreign hospitalization has been determined to be covered on the basis of emergency services (See the Medicare Claims Processing Manual, Chapter 1, "General Billing Requirements," §10.1.3), the necessity requirement (§10.2) and the destination requirement (§10.3) are considered met.
5. The carrier will make partial payment for otherwise covered ambulance service, which exceeded limits defined in item 6. The carrier will base the payment on the amount payable had the patient been transported:	5 & 6 (a) From the pickup point to the nearest appropriate facility, or 5 & 6 (b) From the nearest appropriate facility to the beneficiary's residence where he or she is being returned home from a distant institution.

100-2, 12, 30.1

Rules for Payment of CORF Services

The payment basis for CORF services is 80 percent of the lesser of: (1) the actual charge for the service or (2) the physician fee schedule amount for the service when the physician fee schedule establishes a payment amount for such service. Payment for CORF services under the physician fee schedule is made for physical therapy, occupational therapy, speech-language pathology and respiratory therapy services, as well as the nursing and social and/or psychological services, which are a part of, or directly relate to, the rehabilitation plan of treatment.

Payment for covered durable medical equipment, orthotic and prosthetic (DMEPOS) devices and supplies provided by a CORF is based upon: the lesser of 80 percent of actual charges or the payment amount established under the DMEPOS fee schedule; or, the single payment amount established under the DMEPOS competitive bidding program, provided that payment for such an item is not included in the payment amount for other CORF services.

If there is no fee schedule amount for a covered CORF item or service, payment should be based on the lesser of 80 percent of the actual charge for the service provided or an amount determined by the local Medicare contractor.

Payment for CORF social and/or psychological services is made under the physician fee schedule only for HCPCS code G0409, as appropriate, and only when billed using revenue codes 0560, 0569, 0910, 0911, 0914 and 0919.

Payment for CORF respiratory therapy services is made under the physician fee schedule when provided by a respiratory therapist as defined at 42CFR485.70(j) and, only to the extent that these services support or are an adjunct to the rehabilitation plan of treatment, when billed using revenue codes 0410, 0412 and 0419. Separate payment is not made for diagnostic tests or for services related to physiologic monitoring services which are bundled into other respiratory therapy services appropriately performed by a respiratory therapist, such as Healthcare Common Procedure Coding System (HCPCS) codes G0237, G0238 and G0239.

Payment for CORF nursing services is made under the physician fee schedule only when provided by a registered nurse as defined at 42CFR485.70(h) for nursing services only to the extent that these services support or are an adjunct to the rehabilitation plan of treatment. In addition, payment for CORF nursing services is made only when provided by a registered nurse. HCPCS code G0128 is used to bill for these services and only with revenue codes 0550 and 0559.

For specific payment requirements for CORF, items and services see Pub. 100-04, Medicare Claims Processing Manual, Chapter 5, Part B Outpatient Rehabilitation and CORF/OPT Services.

100-2,10,30.1.1

Ground Ambulance Services:

Basic Life Support (BLS)

Definition: Basic life support (BLS) is transportation by ground ambulance vehicle and the provision of medically necessary supplies and services, including BLS ambulance services as defined by the State. The ambulance must be staffed by an individual who is qualified in accordance with State and local laws as an emergency medical technician-basic (EMT-Basic). These laws may vary from State to State or within a State. For example, only in some jurisdictions is an EMT-Basic permitted to operate limited equipment onboard the vehicle, assist more qualified personnel in performing assessments and interventions, and establish a peripheral intravenous (IV) line.

Basic Life Support (BLS) - Emergency

Definition: When medically necessary, the provision of BLS services, as specified above, in the context of an emergency response. An emergency response is one that, at the time the ambulance provider or supplier is called, it responds immediately. An immediate response is one in which the ambulance provider/supplier begins as quickly as possible to take the steps necessary to respond to the call.

Application: The determination to respond emergently with a BLS ambulance must be in accord with the local 911 or equivalent service dispatch protocol. If the call came in directly to the ambulance provider/supplier, then the provider's/supplier's dispatch protocol must meet, at a minimum, the standards of the dispatch protocol of the local 911 or equivalent service. In areas that do not have a local 911 or equivalent service, then the protocol must meet, at a minimum, the standards of a dispatch protocol in another similar jurisdiction within the State or, if there is no similar jurisdiction within the State, then the standards of any other dispatch protocol within the State. Where the dispatch was inconsistent with this standard of protocol, including where no protocol was used, the beneficiary's condition (for example, symptoms) at the scene determines the appropriate level of payment.

Advanced Life Support, Level 1 (ALS1)

Definition: Advanced life support, level 1 (ALS1) is the transportation by ground ambulance vehicle and the provision of medically necessary supplies and services including the provision of an ALS assessment or at least one ALS intervention.

Advanced Life Support Assessment

Definition: An advanced life support (ALS) assessment is an assessment performed by an ALS crew as part of an emergency response that was necessary because the patient's reported condition at the time of dispatch was such that only an ALS crew was qualified to perform the assessment. An ALS assessment does not necessarily result in a determination that the patient requires an ALS level of service.

Application: The determination to respond emergently with an ALS ambulance must be in accord with the local 911 or equivalent service dispatch protocol. If the call came in directly to the ambulance provider/supplier, then the provider's/supplier's dispatch protocol must meet, at a minimum, the standards of the dispatch protocol of the local 911 or equivalent service. In areas that do not have a local 911 or equivalent service, then the protocol must meet, at a minimum, the standards of a dispatch protocol in another similar jurisdiction within the State or, if there is no similar jurisdiction within the State, then the standards of any other dispatch protocol within the State. Where the dispatch was inconsistent with this standard of protocol, including where no protocol was used, the beneficiary's condition (for example, symptoms) at the scene determines the appropriate level of payment.

Advanced Life Support Intervention

Definition: An advanced life support (ALS) intervention is a procedure that is in accordance with State and local laws, required to be done by an emergency medical technician-intermediate (EMT-Intermediate) or EMT-Paramedic.

Application: An ALS intervention must be medically necessary to qualify as an intervention for payment for an ALS level of service. An ALS intervention applies only to ground transports.

Advanced Life Support, Level 1 (ALS1) - Emergency

Definition: When medically necessary, the provision of ALS1 services, as specified above, in the context of an emergency response. An emergency response is one that, at the time the ambulance provider or supplier is called, it responds immediately. An immediate response is one in which the ambulance provider/supplier begins as quickly as possible to take the steps necessary to respond to the call.

Application: The determination to respond emergently with an ALS ambulance must be in accord with the local 911 or equivalent service dispatch protocol. If the call came in directly to the ambulance provider/supplier, then the provider's/supplier's dispatch protocol must meet, at a minimum, the standards of the dispatch protocol of the local 911 or equivalent service. In areas that do not have a local 911 or equivalent service, then the protocol must meet, at a minimum, the standards of a dispatch protocol in another similar jurisdiction within the State or, if there is no similar jurisdiction within the State, then the standards of any other dispatch protocol within the State. Where the dispatch was inconsistent with this standard of protocol, including where no protocol was used, the beneficiary's condition (for example, symptoms) at the scene determines the appropriate level of payment.

Advanced Life Support, Level 2 (ALS2)

Definition: Advanced life support, level 2 (ALS2) is the transportation by ground ambulance vehicle and the provision of medically necessary supplies and services including (1) at least three separate administrations of one or more medications by intravenous push/bolus or by continuous infusion (excluding crystalloid fluids) or (2) ground ambulance transport, medically necessary supplies and services, and the provision of at least one of the ALS2 procedures listed below:

a. Manual defibrillation/cardioversion;

b. Endotracheal intubation;

c. Central venous line;

d. Cardiac pacing;

e. Chest decompression;

f. Surgical airway; or

g. Intraosseous line.

Application: Crystalloid fluids include fluids such as 5 percent Dextrose in water, Saline and Lactated Ringer's. Medications that are administered by other means, for example: intramuscular/subcutaneous injection, oral, sublingually or nebulized, do not qualify to determine whether the ALS2 level rate is payable. However, this is not an all-inclusive list. Likewise, a single dose of medication administered fractionally (i.e., one-third of a single dose quantity) on three separate occasions does not qualify for the ALS2 payment rate. The criterion of multiple administrations of the same drug requires a suitable quantity and amount of time between administrations that is in accordance with standard medical practice guidelines. The fractional administration of a single dose (for this purpose meaning a standard or protocol dose) on three separate occasions does not qualify for ALS2 payment.

In other words, the administration of 1/3 of a qualifying dose 3 times does not equate to three qualifying doses for purposes of indicating ALS2 care. One-third of X given 3 times might = X (where X is a standard/protocol drug amount), but the same sequence does not equal 3 times X. Thus, if 3 administrations of the same drug are required to show that ALS2 care was given, each of those administrations must be in accord with local protocols. The run will not qualify on the basis of drug administration if that administration was not according to protocol.

An example of a single dose of medication administered fractionally on three separate occasions that would not qualify for the ALS2 payment rate would be the use of Intravenous (IV) Epinephrine in the treatment of pulseless Ventricular Tachycardia/Ventricular Fibrillation (VF/VT) in the adult patient. Administering this medication in increments of 0.25 mg, 0.25 mg, and 0.50 mg would not qualify for the ALS2 level of payment. This medication, according to the American Heart Association (AHA), Advanced Cardiac Life Support (ACLS) protocol, calls for Epinephrine to be administered in 1 mg increments every 3 to 5 minutes. Therefore, in order to receive payment for an ALS2 level of service, based in part on the administration of Epinephrine, three separate administrations of Epinephrine in 1 mg increments must be administered for the treatment of pulseless VF/VT.

A second example that would not qualify for the ALS2 payment level is the use of Adenosine in increments of 2 mg, 2 mg, and 2 mg for a total of 6 mg in the treatment of an adult patient with Paroxysmal Supraventricular Tachycardia (PSVT). According to ACLS guidelines, 6 mg of Adenosine should be given by rapid intravenous push (IVP) over 1 to 2 seconds. If the first dose does not result in the elimination of the supraventricular tachycardia within 1 to 2 minutes, 12 mg of Adenosine should be administered IVP. If the supraventricular tachycardia persists, a second 12 mg dose of Adenosine can be administered for a total of 30 mg of Adenosine. Three separate administrations of the drug Adenosine in the dosage amounts outlined in the later case would qualify for ALS2 payment.

Endotracheal intubation is one of the services that qualifies for the ALS2 level of payment; therefore, it is not necessary to consider medications administered by endotracheal intubation for the purpose of determining whether the ALS2 rate is payable. The monitoring and maintenance of an endotracheal tube that was previously inserted prior to transport also qualifies as an ALS2 procedure.

Advanced Life Support (ALS) Personnel

Definition: ALS personnel are individuals trained to the level of the emergency medical technician-intermediate (EMT-Intermediate) or paramedic.

Specialty Care Transport (SCT)

Definition: Specialty care transport (SCT) is the interfacility transportation of a critically injured or ill beneficiary by a ground ambulance vehicle, including the provision of medically necessary supplies and services, at a level of service beyond the scope of the EMT-Paramedic. SCT is necessary when a beneficiary's condition requires ongoing care that must be furnished by one or more health professionals in an appropriate specialty area, for example, emergency or critical care nursing, emergency medicine, respiratory care, cardiovascular care, or a paramedic with additional training.

Application: The EMT-Paramedic level of care is set by each State. SCT is necessary when a beneficiary's condition requires ongoing care that must be furnished by one or more health professionals in an appropriate specialty area. Care above that level that is medically necessary and that is furnished at a level of service above the EMT-Paramedic level of care is considered SCT. That is to say, if EMT-Paramedics - without specialty care certification or qualification - are permitted to furnish a given service in a State, then that service does not qualify for SCT. The phrase "EMT-Paramedic with additional training" recognizes that a State may permit a person who is not only certified as an EMT-Paramedic, but who also has successfully completed additional education as determined by the State in furnishing higher level medical services required by critically ill or critically injured patients, to furnish a level of service that otherwise would require a health professional in an appropriate specialty care area (for example, a nurse) to provide. "Additional training" means the specific additional training that a State requires a paramedic to complete in order to qualify to furnish specialty care to a critically ill or injured patient during an SCT.

Paramedic Intercept (PI)

Definition: Paramedic Intercept services are ALS services provided by an entity that does not provide the ambulance transport. This type of service is most often provided for an emergency ambulance transport in which a local volunteer ambulance that can provide only basic life support (BLS) level of service is dispatched to transport a patient. If the patient needs ALS services such as EKG monitoring, chest decompression, or I.V. therapy, another entity dispatches a paramedic to meet the BLS ambulance at the scene or once the ambulance is on the way to the hospital. The ALS paramedics then provide services to the patient.

This tiered approach to life saving is cost effective in many areas because most volunteer ambulances do not charge for their services and one paramedic service can cover many communities. Prior to March 1, 1999, Medicare payment could be made for these services, but only when the claim was submitted by the entity that actually furnished the ambulance transport. Payment could not be made directly to the intercept service provider. In those areas where State laws prohibit volunteer ambulances from billing Medicare and other health insurance, the intercept service could not receive payment for treating a Medicare beneficiary and was forced to bill the beneficiary for the entire service.

Paramedic intercept services furnished on or after March 1, 1999, may be payable separate from the ambulance transport, subject to the requirements specified below.

The intercept service(s) is:

- Furnished in a rural area;
- Furnished under a contract with one or more volunteer ambulance services; and,
- Medically necessary based on the condition of the beneficiary receiving the ambulance service.
- In addition, the volunteer ambulance service involved must:
- Meet the program's certification requirements for furnishing ambulance services;
- Furnish services only at the BLS level at the time of the intercept; and,
- Be prohibited by State law from billing anyone for any service.
- Finally, the entity furnishing the ALS paramedic intercept service must:
- Meet the program's certification requirements for furnishing ALS services, and,
- Bill all recipients who receive ALS paramedic intercept services from the entity, regardless of whether or not those recipients are Medicare beneficiaries.

For purposes of the paramedic intercept benefit, a rural area is an area that is designated as rural by a State law or regulation or any area outside of a Metropolitan Statistical Area or in New England, outside a New England County Metropolitan Area as defined by the Office of Management and Budget. The current list of these areas is periodically published in the Federal Register.

See the Medicare Claims Processing Manual, Chapter 15, "Ambulance," Sec.20.1.4 for payment of paramedic intercept services.

Services in a Rural Area

Definition: Services in a rural area are services that are furnished (1) in an area outside a Metropolitan Statistical Area (MSA); or, (2) in New England, outside a New England County Metropolitan Area (NECMA); or, (3) an area identified as rural using the Goldsmith modification even though the area is within an MSA.

Emergency Response

Definition: Emergency response is a BLS or ALS1 level of service that has been provided in immediate response to a 911 call or the equivalent. An immediate response is one in which the ambulance provider/supplier begins as quickly as possible to take the steps necessary to respond to the call.

Application: The phrase "911 call or equivalent" is intended to establish the standard that the nature of the call at the time of dispatch is the determining factor. Regardless of the medium by which the call is made (e.g., a radio call could be appropriate) the call is of an emergent nature when, based on the information available to the dispatcher at the time of the call, it is reasonable for the dispatcher to issue an emergency dispatch in light of accepted, standard dispatch protocol. An emergency call need not come through 911 even in areas where a 911 call system exists. However, the determination to respond emergently must be in accord with the local 911 or equivalent service dispatch protocol. If the call came in directly to the ambulance provider/supplier, then the provider's/supplier's dispatch protocol and the dispatcher's actions must meet, at a minimum, the standards of the dispatch protocol of the local 911 or equivalent service. In areas that do not have a local 911 or equivalent service, then both the protocol and the dispatcher's actions must meet, at a minimum, the standards of the dispatch protocol in another similar jurisdiction within the State, or if there is no similar jurisdiction, then the standards of any other dispatch protocol within the State. Where the dispatch was inconsistent with this standard of protocol, including where no protocol was used, the beneficiary's condition (for example, symptoms) at the scene determines the appropriate level of payment.

EMT-Intermediate
Definition: EMT-Intermediate is an individual who is qualified, in accordance with State and local laws, as an EMT-Basic and who is also certified in accordance with State and local laws to perform essential advanced techniques and to administer a limited number of medications.

EMT-Paramedic
Definition: EMT-Paramedic possesses the qualifications of the EMT-Intermediate and, in accordance with State and local laws, has enhanced skills that include being able to administer additional interventions and medications.

Relative Value Units
Definition: Relative value units (RVUs) measure the value of ambulance services relative to the value of a base level ambulance service.

Application: The RVUs for the ambulance fee schedule are as follows:

Service Level RVUs

- BLS 1.00
- BLS - Emergency 1.60
- ALS1 1.20
- ALS1 - Emergency 1.90
- ALS2 2.75
- SCT 3.25
- PI 1.75
- RVUs are not applicable to FW and RW services

100-2, 12, 40.5

Respiratory Therapy Services

A respiratory therapy plan of treatment is wholly established and signed by the referring physician before the respiratory therapist initiates the actual treatment.

A. Definition
Respiratory therapy services include only those services that can be appropriately provided to CORF patients by a qualified respiratory therapist, as defined at 42CFR485.70(j), under a physician-established respiratory therapy plan of treatment. The facility physician must be present in the facility for a sufficient time to provide, in accordance with accepted principles of medical practice, medical direction, medical care services and consultation. Respiratory therapy services include the physiological monitoring necessary to furnish these services. Payment for these services is bundled into the payment for respiratory therapy services and is not payable separately. Diagnostic and other medical services provided in the CORF setting are not considered CORF services, and therefore may not be included in a respiratory therapy plan of treatment because these are covered under separate benefit categories.

The respiratory therapist assesses the patient to determine the appropriateness of pursed lip breathing activity and may check the patient's oxygen saturation level (via pulse oximetry). If appropriate, the respiratory therapist then provides the initial training in order to ensure that the patient can accurately perform the activity. The respiratory therapist may again check the patient's oxygen saturation level, or perform peak respiratory flow, or check other respiratory parameters. These types of services are considered "physiological monitoring" and are bundled into the payment for HCPCS codes G0237, G0238 and G0239. Physiological monitoring also includes the provision of a 6-minute walk test that is typically conducted before the start of the patient's respiratory therapy activities. The time to provide this walk "test" assessment is included as part of the HCPCS code G0238. When provided as part of a CORF respiratory therapy plan of treatment, payment for these monitoring activities is bundled into the payment for other services provided by the respiratory therapist, such as the three respiratory therapy specific G-codes.

B. Guidelines for Applying Coverage Criteria
There are some conditions for which respiratory therapy services may be indicated. However, respiratory therapy performed as part of a standard protocol without regard to the individual patient's actual condition, capacity for improving, and the need for such services as established, is not reasonable and medically necessary. All respiratory therapy services must meet the test of being "reasonable and medically necessary" pursuant to Sec.1862(a)(1)(A) of the Act. Determinations of medical necessity are made based on local contractor decisions on a claim-by-claim basis.

The three HCPCS codes G0237, G0238, and G0239 are specific to services provided under the respiratory therapy plan of treatment and, as such, are not designated as subject to the therapy caps.

C. Patient Education Programs
Instructing a patient in the use of equipment, breathing exercises, etc. may be considered reasonable and necessary to the patient's respiratory therapy plan of treatment and can usually be given to a patient during the course of treatment by the respiratory therapist. These educational instructions are bundled into the covered service and separate payment is not made.

100-2, 12, 40.8

Nursing Services

CORF nursing services may only be provided by an individual meeting the qualifications of a registered nurse, as defined at 42CFR485.70(h). They must relate to, or be a part of, the rehabilitation plan of treatment.

CORF nursing services must be reasonable and medically necessary and are provided as an adjunct to the rehabilitation plan of treatment. For example, a registered nurse may perform or instruct a patient, as appropriate, in the proper procedure of "in and out" urethral catheterization, tracheostomy tube suctioning, or the cleaning for ileostomy or colostomy bags.

Nursing services may not substitute for or supplant the services of physical therapists, occupational therapists, speech-language pathologists and respiratory therapists, but instead must support or further the services and goals provided in the rehabilitation plan of treatment.

CORF nursing services must be provided by a registered nurse and may only be coded as HCPCS code G0128 indicating that CORF "nursing services" were provided.

100-2, 12, 40.11

Vaccines

A CORF may provide pneumococcal pneumonia, influenza virus, and hepatitis B vaccines to its patients. While not included as a service under the CORF benefit, Medicare will make payment to the CORF for certain vaccines and their administration provided to CORF patients (CY 2008 PFS Rule 72 FR 66293).

The following three vaccinations are covered in a CORF if a physician who is a doctor of medicine or osteopathy orders it for a CORF patient:

Pneumococcal pneumonia vaccine and its administration;

Hepatitis B vaccine and its administration furnished to a beneficiary who is at high or intermediate risk of contracting hepatitis B; and

Influenza virus vaccine and its administration

Payment for covered pneumococcal pneumonia, influenza virus, and hepatitis B vaccines provided in the CORF setting is based on 95 percent of the average wholesale price. The CORF registered nurse provides administration of any of these vaccines using HCPCS codes G0008, G0009 or G0010 with payment based on CPT code 90471.

100-2, 13, 30

Rural Health Clinic and Federally Qualified Health Center Service Defined

Payments for covered RHC/FQHC services furnished to Medicare beneficiaries are made on the basis of an all-inclusive rate per covered visit (except for pneumococcal and influenza vaccines and their administration, which is paid at 100 percent of reasonable cost). The term "visit" is defined as a face-to-face encounter between the patient and a physician, physician assistant, nurse practitioner, certified nurse midwife, visiting nurse, clinical psychologist, or clinical social worker during which an RHC/FQHC service is rendered. As a result of section 5114 of the Deficit Reduction Act of 2005 (DRA), the FQHC definition of a face-to-face encounter is expanded to include encounters with qualified practitioners of Outpatient Diabetes Self-Management Training Services (DSMT) and medical nutrition therapy (MNT) services when the FQHC meets all relevant program requirements for the provision of such services.

Encounters with (1) more than one health professional; and (2) multiple encounters with the same health professional which take place on the same day and at a single location, constitute a single visit. An exception occurs in cases in which the patient, subsequent to the first encounter, suffers an illness or injury requiring additional diagnosis or treatment.

100-2, 15, 50

Drugs and Biologicals

B3-2049, A3-3112.4.B, HO-230.4.B

The Medicare program provides limited benefits for outpatient drugs. The program covers drugs that are furnished "incident to" a physician's service provided that the drugs are not usually self-administered by the patients who take them.

Generally, drugs and biologicals are covered only if all of the following requirements are met:

- They meet the definition of drugs or biologicals (see Sec.50.1);
- They are of the type that are not usually self-administered. (see Sec.50.2);
- They meet all the general requirements for coverage of items as incident to a physician's services (see Sec.Sec.50.1 and 50.3);
- They are reasonable and necessary for the diagnosis or treatment of the illness or injury for which they are administered according to accepted standards of medical practice (see Sec.50.4);
- They are not excluded as noncovered immunizations (see Sec.50.4.4.2); and
- They have not been determined by the FDA to be less than effective. (See Sec.Sec.50.4.4).

Medicare Part B does generally not cover drugs that can be self-administered, such as those in pill form, or are used for self-injection. However, the statute provides for the coverage of some self-administered drugs. Examples of self-administered drugs that are covered include blood-clotting factors, drugs used in immunosuppressive therapy, erythropoietin for dialysis patients, osteoporosis drugs for certain homebound patients, and certain oral cancer drugs. (See Sec.110.3 for coverage of drugs, which are necessary to the effective use of Durable Medical Equipment (DME) or prosthetic devices.)

100-2, 15, 50.2

Determining Self-Administration of Drug or Biological

AB-02-072, AB-02-139, B3-2049.2

The Medicare program provides limited benefits for outpatient prescription drugs. The program covers drugs that are furnished "incident to" a physician's service provided that the drugs are not usually self-administered by the patients who take them. Section 112 of the Benefits, Improvements & Protection Act of 2000 (BIPA) amended sections 1861(s)(2)(A) and 1861(s)(2)(B) of the Act to redefine this exclusion. The prior statutory language referred to those drugs "which cannot be self-administered." Implementation of the BIPA provision requires interpretation of the phrase "not usually self-administered by the patient".

A. Policy

Fiscal intermediaries and carriers are instructed to follow the instructions below when applying the exclusion for drugs that are usually self-administered by the patient. Each individual contractor must make its own individual determination on each drug. Contractors must continue to apply the policy that not only the drug is medically reasonable and necessary for any individual claim, but also that the route of administration is medically reasonable and necessary. That is, if a drug is available in both oral and injectable forms, the injectable form of the drug must be medically reasonable and necessary as compared to using the oral form.

For certain injectable drugs, it will be apparent due to the nature of the condition(s) for which they are administered or the usual course of treatment for those conditions, they are, or are not, usually self-administered. For example, an injectable drug used to treat migraine headaches is usually self-administered. On the other hand, an injectable drug, administered at the same time as chemotherapy, used to treat anemia secondary to chemotherapy is not usually self-administered.

B. Administered

The term "administered" refers only to the physical process by which the drug enters the patient's body. It does not refer to whether the process is supervised by a medical professional (for example, to observe proper technique or side-effects of the drug). Only injectable (including intravenous) drugs are eligible for inclusion under the "incident to" benefit. Other routes of administration including, but not limited to, oral drugs, suppositories, topical medications are all considered to be usually self-administered by the patient.

C. Usually

For the purposes of applying this exclusion, the term "usually" means more than 50 percent of the time for all Medicare beneficiaries who use the drug. Therefore, if a drug is self-administered by more than 50 percent of Medicare beneficiaries, the drug is excluded from coverage and the contractor may not make any Medicare payment for it. In arriving at a single determination as to whether a drug is usually self-administered, contractors should make a separate determination for each indication for a drug as to whether that drug is usually self-administered.

After determining whether a drug is usually self-administered for each indication, contractors should determine the relative contribution of each indication to total use of the drug (i.e., weighted average) in order to make an overall determination as to whether the drug is usually self-administered. For example, if a drug has three indications, is not self-administered for the first indication, but is self administered for the second and third indications, and the first indication makes up 40 percent of total usage, the second indication makes up 30 percent of total usage, and the third indication makes up 30 percent of total usage, then the drug would be considered usually self-administered.

Reliable statistical information on the extent of self-administration by the patient may not always be available. Consequently, CMS offers the following guidance for each contractor's consideration in making this determination in the absence of such data:

1. Absent evidence to the contrary, presume that drugs delivered intravenously are not usually self-administered by the patient.
2. Absent evidence to the contrary, presume that drugs delivered by intramuscular injection are not usually self-administered by the patient. (Avonex, for example, is delivered by intramuscular injection, not usually self-administered by the patient.) The contractor may consider the depth and nature of the particular intramuscular injection in applying this presumption. In applying this presumption, contractors should examine the use of the particular drug and consider the following factors:
3. Absent evidence to the contrary, presume that drugs delivered by subcutaneous injection are self-administered by the patient. However, contractors should examine the use of the particular drug and consider the following factors:
   - A. Acute Condition - Is the condition for which the drug is used an acute condition? If so, it is less likely that a patient would self-administer the drug. If the condition were longer term, it would be more likely that the patient would self-administer the drug.
   - B. Frequency of Administration - How often is the injection given? For example, if the drug is administered once per month, it is less likely to be self-administered by the patient. However, if it is administered once or more per week, it is likely that the drug is self-administered by the patient. In some instances, carriers may have provided payment for one or perhaps several doses of a drug that would otherwise not be paid for because the drug is usually self-administered. Carriers may have exercised this discretion for limited coverage, for example, during a brief time when the patient is being trained under the supervision of a physician in the proper technique for self-administration. Medicare will no longer pay for such doses. In addition, contractors may no longer pay for any drug when it is administered on an outpatient emergency basis, if the drug is excluded because it is usually self-administered by the patient.

D. Definition of Acute Condition

For the purposes of determining whether a drug is usually self-administered, an acute condition means a condition that begins over a short time period, is likely to be of short duration and/or the expected course of treatment is for a short, finite interval. A course of treatment consisting of scheduled injections lasting less than two weeks, regardless of frequency or route of administration, is considered acute. Evidence to support this may include Food and Drug administration (FDA) approval language, package inserts, drug compendia, and other information.

E. By the Patient

The term "by the patient" means Medicare beneficiaries as a collective whole. The carrier includes only the patients themselves and not other individuals (that is, spouses, friends, or other care-givers are not considered the patient). The determination is based on whether the drug is self-administered by the patient a majority of the time that the drug is used on an outpatient basis by Medicare beneficiaries for medically necessary indications.

The carrier ignores all instances when the drug is administered on an inpatient basis. The carrier makes this determination on a drug-by-drug basis, not on a beneficiary-by-beneficiary basis. In evaluating whether beneficiaries as a collective whole self-administer, individual beneficiaries who do not have the capacity to self-administer any drug due to a condition other than the condition for which they are taking the drug in question are not considered. For example, an individual afflicted with paraplegia or advanced dementia would not have the capacity to self-administer any injectable drug, so such individuals would not be included in the population upon which the determination for self-administration by the patient was based. Note that some individuals afflicted with a less severe stage of an otherwise debilitating condition would be included in the population upon which the determination for "self-administered by the patient" was based; for example, an early onset of dementia.

F. Evidentiary Criteria

Contractors are only required to consider the following types of evidence: peer reviewed medical literature, standards of medical practice, evidence-based practice guidelines, FDA approved label, and package inserts. Contractors may also consider other evidence submitted by interested individuals or groups subject to their judgment.

Contractors should also use these evidentiary criteria when reviewing requests for making a determination as to whether a drug is usually self-administered, and requests for reconsideration of a pending or published determination.

Please note that prior to the August 1, 2002, one of the principal factors used to determine whether a drug was subject to the self-administered exclusion was whether the FDA label contained instructions for self-administration. However, CMS notes that under the new standard, the fact that the FDA label includes instructions for self-administration is not, by itself, a determining factor that a drug is subject to this exclusion.

G. Provider Notice of Noncovered Drugs
Contractors must describe on their Web site the process they will use to determine whether a drug is usually self-administered and thus does not meet the "incident to" benefit category. Contractors must publish a list of the injectable drugs that are subject to the self-administered exclusion on their Web site, including the data and rationale that led to the determination. Contractors will report the workload associated with developing new coverage statements in CAFM 21208.

Contractors must provide notice 45 days prior to the date that these drugs will not be covered. During the 45-day time period, contractors will maintain existing medical review and payment procedures. After the 45-day notice, contractors may deny payment for the drugs subject to the notice.

Contractors must not develop local medical review policies (LMRPs) for this purpose because further elaboration to describe drugs that do not meet the ‚Äòincident to' and the ‚Äònot usually self-administered' provisions of the statute are unnecessary. Current LMRPs based solely on these provisions must be withdrawn. LMRPs that address the self-administered exclusion and other information may be reissued absent the self-administered drug exclusion material. Contractors will report this workload in CAFM 21206. However, contractors may continue to use and write LMRPs to describe reasonable and necessary uses of drugs that are not usually self-administered. H. Conferences Between Contractors Contractors' Medical Directors may meet and discuss whether a drug is usually self-administered without reaching a formal consensus. Each contractor uses its discretion as to whether or not it will participate in such discussions. Each contractor must make its own individual determinations, except that fiscal intermediaries may, at their discretion, follow the determinations of the local carrier with respect to the self-administered exclusion.

I. Beneficiary Appeals
If a beneficiary's claim for a particular drug is denied because the drug is subject to the "self-administered drug" exclusion, the beneficiary may appeal the denial. Because it is a "benefit category" denial and not a denial based on medical necessity, an Advance Beneficiary Notice (ABN) is not required. A "benefit category" denial (i.e., a denial based on the fact that there is no benefit category under which the drug may be covered) does not trigger the financial liability protection provisions of Limitation On Liability (under Sec.1879 of the Act). Therefore, physicians or providers may charge the beneficiary for an excluded drug.

J. Provider and Physician Appeals
A physician accepting assignment may appeal a denial under the provisions found in Chapter 29 of the Medicare Claims Processing Manual.

K. Reasonable and Necessary
Carriers and fiscal intermediaries will make the determination of reasonable and necessary with respect to the medical appropriateness of a drug to treat the patient's condition. Contractors will continue to make the determination of whether the intravenous or injection form of a drug is appropriate as opposed to the oral form. Contractors will also continue to make the determination as to whether a physician's office visit was reasonable and necessary. However, contractors should not make a determination of whether it was reasonable and necessary for the patient to choose to have his or her drug administered in the physician's office or outpatient hospital setting. That is, while a physician's office visit may not be reasonable and necessary in a specific situation, in such a case an injection service would be payable.

L. Reporting Requirements
Each carrier and intermediary must report to CMS, every September 1 and March 1, its complete list of injectable drugs that the contractor has determined are excluded when furnished incident to a physician's service on the basis that the drug is usually self-administered. The CMS anticipates that contractors will review injectable drugs on a rolling basis and publish their list of excluded drugs as it is developed. For example, contractors should not wait to publish this list until every drug has been reviewed.

Contractors must send their exclusion list to the following e-mail address: drugdata@cms.hhs.gov a template that CMS will provide separately, consisting of the following data elements in order:

1. Carrier Name
2. State
3. Carrier ID#
4. HCPCS
5. Descriptor
6. Effective Date of Exclusion
7. End Date of Exclusion
8. Comments

Any exclusion list not provided in the CMS mandated format will be returned for correction. To view the presently mandated CMS format for this report, open the file located at: http://cms.hhs.gov/manuals/pm_trans/AB02_139a

100-2, 15, 50.4.2

Unlabeled Use of Drug

B3-2049.3

An unlabeled use of a drug is a use that is not included as an indication on the drug's label as approved by the FDA. FDA approved drugs used for indications other than what is indicated on the official label may be covered under Medicare if the carrier determines the use to be medically accepted, taking into consideration the major drug compendia, authoritative medical literature and/or accepted standards of medical practice. In the case of drugs used in an anti-cancer chemotherapeutic regimen, unlabeled uses are covered for a medically accepted indication as defined in Sec.50.5. These decisions are made by the contractor on a case-by-case basis.

100-2, 15, 50.4.4.2

Immunizations

Vaccinations or inoculations are excluded as immunizations unless they are directly related to the treatment of an injury or direct exposure to a disease or condition, such as anti-rabies treatment, tetanus antitoxin or booster vaccine, botulin antitoxin, antivenin sera, or immune globulin. In the absence of injury or direct exposure, preventive immunization (vaccination or inoculation) against such diseases as smallpox, polio, diphtheria, etc., is not covered. However, pneumococcal, hepatitis B, and influenza virus vaccines are exceptions to this rule. (See items A, B, and C below.) In cases where a vaccination or inoculation is excluded from coverage, related charges are also not covered.

A. Pneumococcal Pneumonia Vaccinations
Effective for services furnished on or after May 1, 1981, the Medicare Part B program covers pneumococcal pneumonia vaccine and its administration when furnished in compliance with any applicable State law by any provider of services or any entity or individual with a supplier number. This includes revaccination of patients at highest risk of pneumococcal infection. Typically, these vaccines are administered once in a lifetime except for persons at highest risk. Effective July 1, 2000, Medicare does not require for coverage purposes that a doctor of medicine or osteopathy order the vaccine. Therefore, the beneficiary may receive the vaccine upon request without a physician's order and without physician supervision.

An initial vaccine may be administered only to persons at high risk (see below) of pneumococcal disease. Revaccination may be administered only to persons at highest risk of serious pneumococcal infection and those likely to have a rapid decline in pneumococcal antibody levels, provided that at least 5 years have [passed since the previous dose of pneumococcal vaccine.

Persons at high risk for whom an initial vaccine may be administered include all people age 65 and older; immunocompetent adults who are at increased risk of pneumococcal disease or its complications because of chronic illness (e.g., cardiovascular disease, pulmonary disease, diabetes mellitus, alcoholism, cirrhosis, or cerebrospinal fluid leaks); and individuals with compromised immune

(e.g., splenic dysfunction or anatomic asplenia, Hodgkin's disease, lymphoma, multiple myeloma, chronic renal failure, HIV infection, nephrotic syndrome, sickle cell disease, or organ transplantation).

Persons at highest risk and those most likely to have rapid declines in antibody levels are those for whom revaccination may be appropriate. This group includes persons with functional or anatomic asplenia (e.g., sickle cell disease, splenectomy), HIV infection, leukemia, lymphoma, Hodgkin's disease, multiple myeloma, generalized malignancy, chronic renal failure, nephrotic syndrome, or other conditions associated with immunosuppression such as organ or bone marrow transplantation, and those receiving immunosuppressive chemotherapy. It is not appropriate for routine revaccination of people age 65 or older that are not at highest risk.

Those administering the vaccine should not require the patient to present an immunization record prior to administering the pneumococcal vaccine, nor should they feel compelled to review the patient's complete medical record if it is not available. Instead, provided that the patient is competent, it is acceptable to rely on the patient's verbal history to determine prior vaccination status. If the patient is uncertain about his or her vaccination history in the past 5 years, the vaccine should be given. However, if the patient is certain he/she was were vaccinated in the last

5 years, the vaccine should not be given. If the patient is certain that the vaccine was given more than 5 years ago, revaccination is covered only if the patient is at high risk.

B. Hepatitis B Vaccine

Effective for services furnished on or after September 1, 1984, P.L. 98-369 provides coverage under Part B for hepatitis B vaccine and its administration, furnished to a Medicare beneficiary who is at high or intermediate risk of contracting hepatitis B. This coverage is effective for services furnished on or after September 1, 1984. High-risk groups currently identified include (see exception below):

- ESRD patients;
- Hemophiliacs who receive Factor VIII or IX concentrates;
- Clients of institutions for the mentally retarded;
- Persons who live in the same household as a Hepatitis B Virus (HBV) carrier;
- Homosexual men; and
- Illicit injectable drug abusers.

Intermediate risk groups currently identified include:

- Staff in institutions for the mentally retarded; and
- Workers in health care professions who have frequent contact with blood or blood-derived body fluids during routine work.

EXCEPTION: Persons in both of the above-listed groups in paragraph B, would not be considered at high or intermediate risk of contracting hepatitis B, however, if there were laboratory evidence positive for antibodies to hepatitis B. (ESRD patients are routinely tested for hepatitis B antibodies as part of their continuing monitoring and therapy.)

For Medicare program purposes, the vaccine may be administered upon the order of a doctor of medicine or osteopathy, by a doctor of medicine or osteopathy, or by home health agencies, skilled nursing facilities, ESRD facilities, hospital outpatient departments, and persons recognized under the incident to physicians' services provision of law.

A charge separate from the ESRD composite rate will be recognized and paid for administration of the vaccine to ESRD patients.

C. Influenza Virus Vaccine

Effective for services furnished on or after May 1, 1993, the Medicare Part B program covers influenza virus vaccine and its administration when furnished in compliance with any applicable State law by any provider of services or any entity or individual with a supplier number. Typically, these vaccines are administered once a flu season. Medicare does not require, for coverage purposes, that a doctor of medicine or osteopathy order the vaccine. Therefore, the beneficiary may receive the vaccine upon request without a physician's order and without physician supervision

100-2, 15, 50.5

Self-Administered Drugs and Biologicals

B3-2049.5

Medicare Part B does not cover drugs that are usually self-administered by the patient unless the statute provides for such coverage. The statute explicitly provides coverage, for blood clotting factors, drugs used in immunosuppressive therapy, erythropoietin for dialysis patients, certain oral anti-cancer drugs and anti-emetics used in certain situations.

100-2, 15, 100

Surgical Dressings, Splints, Casts, and Other Devices Used for Reductions of Fractures and Dislocations

B3-2079, A3-3110.3, HO-228.3

Surgical dressings are limited to primary and secondary dressings required for the treatment of a wound caused by, or treated by, a surgical procedure that has been performed by a physician or other health care professional to the extent permissible under State law. In addition, surgical dressings required after debridement of a wound are also covered, irrespective of the type of debridement, as long as the debridement was reasonable and necessary and was performed by a health care professional acting within the scope of his/her legal authority when performing this function. Surgical dressings are covered for as long as they are medically necessary. Primary dressings are therapeutic or protective coverings applied directly to wounds or lesions either on the skin or caused by an opening to the skin. Secondary dressing materials that serve a therapeutic or protective function and that are needed to secure a primary dressing are also covered. Items such as adhesive tape, roll gauze, bandages, and disposable compression material are examples of secondary dressings. Elastic stockings, support hose, foot coverings, leotards, knee supports, surgical leggings, gauntlets, and pressure garments for the arms and hands are examples of items that are not ordinarily covered as surgical dressings. Some items, such as transparent film, may be used as a primary or secondary dressing. If a physician, certified nurse midwife, physician assistant, nurse practitioner, or clinical nurse specialist applies surgical dressings as part of a professional service that is billed to Medicare, the surgical dressings are considered incident to the professional services of the health care practitioner. (See Sec. 60.1, 180, 190, 200, and 210.) When surgical dressings are not covered incident to the services of a health care practitioner and are obtained by the patient from a supplier (e.g., a drugstore, physician, or other health care practitioner that qualifies as a supplier) on an order from a physician or other health care professional authorized under State law or regulation to make such an order, the surgical dressings are covered separately under Part B. Splints and casts, and other devices used for reductions of fractures and dislocations are covered under Part B of Medicare. This includes dental splints.

100-2, 15, 110

Durable Medical Equipment - General

B3-2100, A3-3113, HO-235, HHA-220

Expenses incurred by a beneficiary for the rental or purchases of durable medical equipment (DME) are reimbursable if the following three requirements are met:

- The equipment meets the definition of DME (Sec.110.1);
- The equipment is necessary and reasonable for the treatment of the patient's illness or injury or to improve the functioning of his or her malformed body member (Sec.110.1); and
- The equipment is used in the patient's home. The decision whether to rent or purchase an item of equipment generally resides with the beneficiary, but the decision on how to pay rests with CMS. For some DME, program payment policy calls for lump sum payments and in others for periodic payment. Where covered DME is furnished to a beneficiary by a supplier of services other than a provider of services, the DMERC makes the reimbursement. If a provider of services furnishes the equipment, the intermediary makes the reimbursement. The payment method is identified in the annual fee schedule update furnished by CMS. The CMS issues quarterly updates to a fee schedule file that contains rates by HCPCS code and also identifies the classification of the HCPCS code within the following categories. Category Code Definition IN Inexpensive and Other Routinely Purchased Items FS Frequently Serviced Items CR Capped Rental Items OX Oxygen and Oxygen Equipment OS Ostomy, Tracheostomy & Urological Items SD Surgical Dressings PO Prosthetics & Orthotics SU Supplies TE Transcutaneous Electrical Nerve Stimulators The DMERCs, carriers, and intermediaries, where appropriate, use the CMS files to determine payment rules. See the Medicare Claims Processing Manual, Chapter 20, "Durable Medical Equipment, Surgical Dressings and Casts, Orthotics and Artificial Limbs, and Prosthetic Devices," for a detailed description of payment rules for each classification. Payment may also be made for repairs, maintenance, and delivery of equipment and for expendable and nonreusable items essential to the effective use of the equipment subject to the conditions in Sec.110.2. See the Medicare Benefit Policy Manual, Chapter 11, "End Stage Renal Disease," for hemodialysis equipment and supplies.

100-2, 15, 110.1

Definition of Durable Medical Equipment

B3-2100.1, A3-3113.1, HO-235.1, HHA-220.1, B3-2100.2, A3-3113.2, HO-235.2, HHA-220.2

- Durable medical equipment is equipment which:
- Can withstand repeated use;
- Is primarily and customarily used to serve a medical purpose;
- Generally is not useful to a person in the absence of an illness or injury; and
- Is appropriate for use in the home.

All requirements of the definition must be met before an item can be considered to be durable medical equipment. The following describes the underlying policies for determining whether an item meets the definition of DME and may be covered.

A. Durability

An item is considered durable if it can withstand repeated use, i.e., the type of item that could normally be rented. Medical supplies of an expendable nature, such as incontinent pads, lambs wool pads, catheters, ace bandages, elastic stockings, surgical facemasks, irrigating kits, sheets, and bags are not considered "durable" within the meaning of the definition. There are other items that, although durable in nature, may fall into other coverage categories such as supplies, braces, prosthetic devices, artificial arms, legs, and eyes.

B. Medical Equipment

Medical equipment is equipment primarily and customarily used for medical purposes and is not generally useful in the absence of illness or injury. In most instances, no development will be needed to determine whether a specific item of equipment is medical in nature. However, some cases will require development to determine whether the item constitutes medical equipment. This development would include the advice of local medical organizations (hospitals, medical schools, medical societies) and specialists in the field of physical medicine and rehabilitation. If the equipment is new on the market, it may be necessary, prior to seeking professional advice, to obtain information from the supplier or manufacturer explaining the design, purpose, effectiveness and method of using the equipment in the home as well as the results of any tests or clinical studies that have been conducted.

1. Equipment Presumptively
   MedicalItems such as hospital beds, wheelchairs, hemodialysis equipment, iron lungs, respirators, intermittent positive pressure breathing machines, medical regulators, oxygen tents, crutches, canes, trapeze bars, walkers, inhalators, nebulizers, commodes, suction machines, and traction equipment presumptively constitute medical equipment. (Although hemodialysis equipment is covered as a prosthetic device (Sec.120), it also meets the definition of DME, and reimbursement for the rental or purchase of such equipment for use in the beneficiary's home will be made only under the provisions for payment applicable to DME. See the Medicare Benefit Policy Manual, Chapter 11, "End Stage Renal Disease," Sec.30.1, for coverage of home use of hemodialysis.) NOTE: There is a wide variety in types of respirators and suction machines. The DMERC's medical staff should determine whether the apparatus specified in the claim is appropriate for home use.

2. Equipment Presumptively Nonmedical
   Equipment which is primarily and customarily used for a nonmedical purpose may not be considered "medical" equipment for which payment can be made under the medical insurance program. This is true even though the item has some remote medically related use. For example, in the case of a cardiac patient, an air conditioner might possibly be used to lower room temperature to reduce fluid loss in the patient and to restore an environment conducive to maintenance of the proper fluid balance. Nevertheless, because the primary and customary use of an air conditioner is a nonmedical one, the air conditioner cannot be deemed to be medical equipment for which payment can be made. Other devices and equipment used for environmental control or to enhance the environmental setting in which the beneficiary is placed are not considered covered DME. These include, for example, room heaters, humidifiers, dehumidifiers, and electric air cleaners. Equipment which basically serves comfort or convenience functions or is primarily for the convenience of a person caring for the patient, such as elevators, stairway elevators, and posture chairs, do not constitute medical equipment. Similarly, physical fitness equipment (such as an exercycle), first-aid or precautionary-type equipment (such as preset portable oxygen units), self-help devices (such as safety grab bars), and training equipment (such as Braille training texts) are considered nonmedical in nature.

3. Special Exception Items
   Specified items of equipment may be covered under certain conditions even though they do not meet the definition of DME because they are not primarily and customarily used to serve a medical purpose and/or are generally useful in the absence of illness or injury. These items would be covered when it is clearly established that they serve a therapeutic purpose in an individual case and would include:

   a. Gel pads and pressure and water mattresses (which generally serve a preventive purpose) when prescribed for a patient who had bed sores or there is medical evidence indicating that they are highly susceptible to such ulceration; and

   b. Heat lamps for a medical rather than a soothing or cosmetic purpose, e.g., where the need for heat therapy has been established.

In establishing medical necessity for the above items, the evidence must show that the item is included in the physician's course of treatment and a physician is supervising its use.

NOTE: The above items represent special exceptions and no extension of coverage to other items should be inferred

C. Necessary and Reasonable

Although an item may be classified as DME, it may not be covered in every instance. Coverage in a particular case is subject to the requirement that the equipment be necessary and reasonable for treatment of an illness or injury, or to improve the functioning of a malformed body member. These considerations will bar payment for equipment which cannot reasonably be expected to perform a therapeutic function in an individual case or will permit only partial therapeutic function in an individual case or will permit only partial payment when the type of equipment furnished substantially exceeds that required for the treatment of the illness or injury involved. See the Medicare Claims Processing Manual, Chapter 1, "General Billing Requirements;" Sec.60, regarding the rules for providing advance beneficiary notices (ABNs) that advise beneficiaries, before items or services actually are furnished, when Medicare is likely to deny payment for them. ABNs allow beneficiaries to make an informed consumer decision about receiving items or services for which they may have to pay out-of-pocket and to be more active participants in their own health care treatment decisions.

1. Necessity for the Equipment
   Equipment is necessary when it can be expected to make a meaningful contribution to the treatment of the patient's illness or injury or to the improvement of his or her malformed body member. In most cases the physician's prescription for the equipment and other medical information available to the DMERC will be sufficient to establish that the equipment serves this purpose.

2. Reasonableness of the Equipment
   Even though an item of DME may serve a useful medical purpose, the DMERC or intermediary must also consider to what extent, if any, it would be reasonable for the Medicare program to pay for the item prescribed. The following considerations should enter into the determination of reasonableness:

   1. Would the expense of the item to the program be clearly disproportionate to the therapeutic benefits which could ordinarily be derived from use of the equipment?

   2. Is the item substantially more costly than a medically appropriate and realistically feasible alternative pattern of care?

   3. Does the item serve essentially the same purpose as equipment already available to the beneficiary?

3. Payment Consistent With What is Necessary and Reasonable
   Where a claim is filed for equipment containing features of an aesthetic nature or features of a medical nature which are not required by the patient's condition or where there exists a reasonably feasible and medically appropriate alternative pattern of care which is less costly than the equipment furnished, the amount payable is based on the rate for the equipment or alternative treatment which meets the patient's medical needs. The acceptance of an assignment binds the supplier-assignee to accept the payment for the medically required equipment or service as the full charge and the supplier-assignee cannot charge the beneficiary the differential attributable to the equipment actually furnished.

4. Establishing the Period of Medical Necessity
   Generally, the period of time an item of durable medical equipment will be considered to be medically necessary is based on the physician's estimate of the time that his or her patient will need the equipment. See the Medicare Program Integrity Manual, Chapters 5 and 6, for medical review guideline

D. Definition of a Beneficiary's Home

For purposes of rental and purchase of DME a beneficiary's home may be his/her own dwelling, an apartment, a relative's home, a home for the aged, or some other type of institution. However, an institution may not be considered a beneficiary's home if it:

- Meets at least the basic requirement in the definition of a hospital, i.e., it is primarily engaged in providing by or under the supervision of physicians, to inpatients, diagnostic and therapeutic services for medical diagnosis, treatment, and care of injured, disabled, and sick persons, or rehabilitation services for the rehabilitation of injured, disabled, or sick persons; or

- Meets at least the basic requirement in the definition of a skilled nursing facility, i.e., it is primarily engaged in providing to inpatients skilled nursing care and related services for patients who require medical or nursing care, or rehabilitation services for the rehabilitation of injured, disabled, or sick persons.

Thus, if an individual is a patient in an institution or distinct part of an institution which provides the services described in the bullets above, the individual is not entitled to have separate Part B payment made for rental or purchase of DME. This is because such an institution may not be considered the individual's home. The same concept applies even if the patient resides in a bed or portion of the institution not certified for Medicare.

If the patient is at home for part of a month and, for part of the same month is in an institution that cannot qualify as his or her home, or is outside the U.S., monthly payments may be made for the entire month. Similarly, if DME is returned to the provider before the end of a payment month because the beneficiary died in that month or because the equipment became unnecessary in that month, payment may be made for the entire month.

100-2, 15, 110.2

Repairs, Maintenance, Replacement, and Delivery

Under the circumstances specified below, payment may be made for repair, maintenance, and replacement of medically required DME, including equipment which had been in use before the user enrolled in Part B of the program. However, do not pay for repair, maintenance, or replacement of equipment in the frequent and substantial servicing or oxygen equipment payment categories. In addition, payments for repair and maintenance may not include payment for parts and labor covered under a manufacturer's or supplier's warranty.

A. Repairs

To repair means to fix or mend and to put the equipment back in good condition after damage or wear. Repairs to equipment which a beneficiary owns are covered when necessary to make the equipment serviceable. However, do not pay for repair of previously denied equipment or equipment in the frequent and substantial servicing or oxygen equipment payment categories. If the expense for repairs exceeds the estimated expense of purchasing or renting another item of equipment for the remaining period of medical need, no payment can be made for the amount of the excess. (See subsection C where claims for repairs suggest malicious damage or culpable neglect.) Since renters of equipment recover from the rental charge the expenses they incur in maintaining in working order the equipment they rent out, separately itemized charges for repair of rented equipment are not covered. This includes items in the frequent and substantial servicing, oxygen equipment, capped rental, and inexpensive or routinely purchased payment categories which are being rented. A new Certificate of Medical Necessity (CMN) and/or physician's order is not needed for repairs. For replacement items, see Subsection C below.

B. Maintenance

Routine periodic servicing, such as testing, cleaning, regulating, and checking of the beneficiary's equipment, is not covered. The owner is expected to perform such routine maintenance rather than a retailer or some other person who charges the beneficiary. Normally, purchasers of DME are given operating manuals which describe the type of servicing an owner may perform to properly maintain the equipment. It is reasonable to expect that beneficiaries will perform this maintenance. Thus, hiring a third party to do such work is for the convenience of the beneficiary and is not covered. However, more extensive maintenance which, based on the manufacturers' recommendations, is to be performed by authorized technicians, is covered as repairs for medically necessary equipment which a beneficiary owns. This might include, for example, breaking down sealed components and performing tests which require specialized testing equipment not available to the beneficiary. Do not pay for maintenance of purchased items that require frequent and substantial servicing or oxygen equipment. Since renters of equipment recover from the rental charge the expenses they incur in maintaining in working order the equipment they rent out, separately itemized charges for maintenance of rented equipment are generally not covered. Payment may not be made for maintenance of rented equipment other than the maintenance and servicing fee established for capped rental items. For capped rental items which have reached the 15-month rental cap, contractors pay claims for maintenance and servicing fees after 6 months have passed from the end of the final paid rental month or from the end of the period the item is no longer covered under the supplier's or manufacturer's warranty, whichever is later. See the Medicare Claims Processing Manual, Chapter 20, "Durable Medical Equipment, Prosthetics and Orthotics, and Supplies (DMEPOS)," for additional instruction and an example. A new CMN and/or physician's order is not needed for covered maintenance.

C. Replacement

Replacement refers to the provision of an identical or nearly identical item. Situations involving the provision of a different item because of a change in medical condition are not addressed in this section.

Equipment which the beneficiary owns or is a capped rental item may be replaced in cases of loss or irreparable damage. Irreparable damage refers to a specific accident or to a natural disaster (e.g., fire, flood). A physician's order and/or new Certificate of Medical Necessity (CMN), when required, is needed to reaffirm the medical necessity of the item.

Irreparable wear refers to deterioration sustained from day-to-day usage over time and a specific event cannot be identified. Replacement of equipment due to irreparable wear takes into consideration the reasonable useful lifetime of the equipment. If the item of equipment has been in continuous use by the patient on either a rental or purchase basis for the equipment's useful lifetime, the beneficiary may elect to obtain a new piece of equipment. Replacement may be reimbursed when a new physician order and/or new CMN, when required, is needed to reaffirm the medical necessity of the item.

The reasonable useful lifetime of durable medical equipment is determined through program instructions. In the absence of program instructions, carriers may determine the reasonable useful lifetime of equipment, but in no case can it be less than 5 years. Computation of the useful lifetime is based on when the equipment is delivered to the beneficiary, not the age of the equipment. Replacement due to wear is not covered during the reasonable useful lifetime of the equipment. During the reasonable useful lifetime, Medicare does cover repair up to the cost of replacement (but not actual replacement) for medically necessary equipment owned by the beneficiary. (See subsection A.)

Charges for the replacement of oxygen equipment, items that require frequent and substantial servicing or inexpensive or routinely purchased items which are being rented are not covered. Cases suggesting malicious damage, culpable neglect, or wrongful disposition of equipment should be investigated and denied where the DMERC determines that it is unreasonable to make program payment under the circumstances. DMERCs refer such cases to the program integrity specialist in the RO.

D. Delivery

Payment for delivery of DME whether rented or purchased is generally included in the fee schedule allowance for the item. See Pub. 100-04, Medicare Claims Processing Manual, Chapter 20, "Durable Medical Equipment, Prosthetics and Orthotics, and Supplies (DMEPOS)," for the rules that apply to making reimbursement for exceptional cases.

100-2, 15, 110.3

Coverage of Supplies and Accessories

B3-2100.5, A3-3113.4, HO-235.4, HHA-220.5 B3-2100.5, A3-3113.4, HO-235.4, HHA-220.5

Payment may be made for supplies, e.g., oxygen, that are necessary for the effective use of durable medical equipment. Such supplies include those drugs and biologicals which must be put directly into the equipment in order to achieve the therapeutic benefit of the durable medical equipment or to assure the proper functioning of the equipment, e.g., tumor chemotherapy agents used with an infusion pump or heparin used with a home dialysis system. However, the coverage of such drugs or biologicals does not preclude the need for a determination that the drug or biological itself is reasonable and necessary for treatment of the illness or injury or to improve the functioning of a malformed body member. In the case of prescription drugs, other than oxygen, used in conjunction with durable medical equipment, prosthetic, orthotics, and supplies (DMEPOS) or prosthetic devices, the entity that dispenses the drug must furnish it directly to the patient for whom a prescription is written. The entity that dispenses the drugs must have a Medicare supplier number, must possess a current license to dispense prescription drugs in the State in which the drug is dispensed, and must bill and receive payment in its own name. A supplier that is not the entity that dispenses the drugs cannot purchase the drugs used in conjunction with DME for resale to the beneficiary. Reimbursement may be made for replacement of essential accessories such as hoses, tubes, mouthpieces, etc., for necessary DME, only if the beneficiary owns or is purchasing the equipment.Payment may be made for supplies, e.g., oxygen, that are necessary for the effective use of durable medical equipment. Such supplies include those drugs and biologicals which must be put directly into the equipment in order to achieve the therapeutic benefit of the durable medical equipment or to assure the proper functioning of the equipment, e.g., tumor chemotherapy agents used with an infusion pump or heparin used with a home dialysis system. However, the coverage of such drugs or biologicals does not preclude the need for a determination that the drug or biological itself is reasonable and necessary for treatment of the illness or injury or to improve the functioning of a malformed body member. In the case of prescription drugs, other than oxygen, used in conjunction with durable medical equipment, prosthetic, orthotics, and supplies (DMEPOS) or prosthetic devices, the entity that dispenses the drug must furnish it directly to the patient for whom a prescription is written. The entity that dispenses the drugs must have a Medicare supplier number, must possess a current license to dispense prescription drugs in the State in which the drug is dispensed, and must bill and receive payment in its own name. A supplier that is not the entity that dispenses the drugs cannot purchase the drugs used in conjunction with DME for resale to the beneficiary. Reimbursement may be made for replacement of essential accessories such as hoses, tubes, mouthpieces, etc., for necessary DME, only if the beneficiary owns or is purchasing the equipment.

100-2, 15, 120

Prosthetic Devices

B3-2130, A3-3110.4, HO-228.4, A3-3111, HO-229

A. General

Prosthetic devices (other than dental) which replace all or part of an internal body organ (including contiguous tissue), or replace all or part of the function of a permanently inoperative or malfunctioning internal body organ are covered when furnished on a physician's order. This does not require a determination that there is no possibility that the patient's condition may improve sometime in the future. If the medical record, including the judgment of the attending physician, indicates the condition is of long and indefinite duration, the test of permanence is considered met. (Such a device may also be covered under Sec.60.l as a supply when furnished incident to a physician's service.)

Examples of prosthetic devices include artificial limbs, parenteral and enteral (PEN) nutrition, cardiac pacemakers, prosthetic lenses (see subsection B), breast prostheses (including a surgical brassiere) for postmastectomy patients, maxillofacial devices, and devices which replace all or part of the ear or nose. A urinary collection and retention system with or without a tube is a prosthetic device replacing bladder function in case of permanent urinary incontinence. The foley catheter is also considered a prosthetic device when ordered for a patient with permanent urinary incontinence. However, chucks, diapers, rubber sheets, etc., are supplies that are not covered under this provision. Although hemodialysis equipment is a prosthetic device, payment for the rental or purchase of such equipment in the home is made only for use under the provisions for payment applicable to durable medical equipment.

An exception is that if payment cannot be made on an inpatient's behalf under Part A, hemodialysis equipment, supplies, and services required by such patient could be covered under Part B as a prosthetic device, which replaces the function of a kidney. See the Medicare Benefit Policy Manual, Chapter 11, "End Stage Renal Disease," for payment for hemodialysis equipment used in the home. See the Medicare Benefit Policy Manual, Chapter 1, "Inpatient Hospital Services," Sec.10, for additional instructions on hospitalization for renal dialysis.

NOTE: Medicare does not cover a prosthetic device dispensed to a patient prior to the time at which the patient undergoes the procedure that makes necessary the use of the device. For example, the carrier does not make a separate Part B payment for an intraocular lens (IOL) or pacemaker that a physician, during an office visit prior to the actual surgery, dispenses to the patient for his or her use. Dispensing a prosthetic device in this manner raises health and safety issues. Moreover, the need for the device cannot be clearly established until the procedure that makes its use possible is successfully performed. Therefore, dispensing a prosthetic device in this manner is not considered reasonable and necessary for the treatment of the patient's condition.

Colostomy (and other ostomy) bags and necessary accouterments required for attachment are covered as prosthetic devices. This coverage also includes irrigation and flushing equipment and other items and supplies directly related to ostomy care, whether the attachment of a bag is required.

Accessories and/or supplies which are used directly with an enteral or parenteral device to achieve the therapeutic benefit of the prosthesis or to assure the proper functioning of the device may also be covered under the prosthetic device benefit subject to the additional guidelines in the Medicare National Coverage Determinations Manual.

Covered items include catheters, filters, extension tubing, infusion bottles, pumps (either food or infusion), intravenous (I.V.) pole, needles, syringes, dressings, tape, Heparin Sodium (parenteral only), volumetric monitors (parenteral only), and parenteral and enteral nutrient solutions. Baby food and other regular grocery products that can be blenderized and used with the enteral system are not covered. Note that some of these items, e.g., a food pump and an I.V. pole, qualify as DME. Although coverage of the enteral and parenteral nutritional therapy systems is provided on the basis of the prosthetic device benefit, the payment rules relating to lump sum or monthly payment for DME apply to such items.

The coverage of prosthetic devices includes replacement of and repairs to such devices as explained in subsection D.

Finally, the Benefits Improvement and Protection Act of 2000 amended Sec.1834(h)(1) of the Act by adding a provision (1834 (h)(1)(G)(i)) that requires Medicare payment to be made for the replacement of prosthetic devices which are artificial limbs, or for the replacement of any part of such devices, without regard to continuous use or useful lifetime restrictions if an ordering physician determines that the replacement device, or replacement part of such a device, is necessary.

Payment may be made for the replacement of a prosthetic device that is an artificial limb, or replacement part of a device if the ordering physician determines that the replacement device or part is necessary because of any of the following:

1. A change in the physiological condition of the patient;
2. An irreparable change in the condition of the device, or in a part of the device; or
3. The condition of the device, or the part of the device, requires repairs and the cost of such repairs would be more than 60 percent of the cost of a replacement device, or, as the case may be, of the part being replaced.

This provision is effective for items replaced on or after April 1, 2001. It supersedes any rule that that provided a 5-year or other replacement rule with regard to prosthetic devices.

B. Prosthetic Lenses

The term "internal body organ" includes the lens of an eye. Prostheses replacing the lens of an eye include post-surgical lenses customarily used during convalescence from eye surgery in which the lens of the eye was removed. In addition, permanent lenses are also covered when required by an individual lacking the organic lens of the eye because of surgical removal or congenital absence. Prosthetic lenses obtained on or after the beneficiary's date of entitlement to supplementary medical insurance benefits may be covered even though the surgical removal of the crystalline lens occurred before entitlement.

1. Prosthetic Cataract Lenses
   One of the following prosthetic lenses or combinations of prosthetic lenses furnished by a physician (see Sec.30.4 for coverage of prosthetic lenses prescribed by a doctor of optometry) may be covered when determined to be reasonable and necessary to restore essentially the vision provided by the crystalline lens of the eye:
   - Prosthetic bifocal lenses in frames;
   - Prosthetic lenses in frames for far vision, and prosthetic lenses in frames for near vision; or
   - When a prosthetic contact lens(es) for far vision is prescribed (including cases of binocular and monocular aphakia), make payment for the contact lens(es) and prosthetic lenses in frames for near vision to be worn at the same time as the contact lens(es), and prosthetic lenses in frames to be worn when the contacts have been removed.

   Lenses which have ultraviolet absorbing or reflecting properties may be covered, in lieu of payment for regular (untinted) lenses, if it has been determined that such lenses are medically reasonable and necessary for the individual patient. Medicare does not cover cataract sunglasses obtained in addition to the regular (untinted) prosthetic lenses since the sunglasses duplicate the restoration of vision function performed by the regular prosthetic lenses.
2. Payment for Intraocular Lenses (IOLs) Furnished in Ambulatory Surgical Centers (ASCs)
   Effective for services furnished on or after March 12, 1990, payment for intraocular lenses (IOLs) inserted during or subsequent to cataract surgery in a Medicare certified ASC is included with the payment for facility services that are furnished in connection with the covered surgery. Refer to the Medicare Claims Processing Manual, Chapter 14, "Ambulatory Surgical Centers," for more information.
3. Limitation on Coverage of Conventional Lenses One pair of conventional eyeglasses or conventional contact lenses furnished after each cataract surgery with insertion of an IOL is covered.

C. Dentures

Dentures are excluded from coverage. However, when a denture or a portion of the denture is an integral part (built-in) of a covered prosthesis (e.g., an obturator to fill an opening in the palate), it is covered as part of that prosthesis.

D. Supplies, Repairs, Adjustments, and Replacement

Supplies are covered that are necessary for the effective use of a prosthetic device (e.g., the batteries needed to operate an artificial larynx). Adjustment of prosthetic devices required by wear or by a change in the patient's condition is covered when ordered by a physician. General provisions relating to the repair and replacement of durable medical equipment in Sec.110.2 for the repair and replacement of prosthetic devices are applicable. (See the Medicare Benefit Policy Manual, Chapter 16, "General Exclusions from Coverage," Sec.40.4, for payment for devices replaced under a warranty.) Replacement of conventional eyeglasses or contact lenses furnished in accordance with Sec.120.B.3 is not covered. Necessary supplies, adjustments, repairs, and replacements are covered even when the device had been in use before the user enrolled in Part B of the program, so long as the device continues to be medically required.

100-2, 15, 130

Leg, Arm, Back, and Neck Braces, Trusses, and Artificial Legs, Arms, and Eyes

B3-2133, A3-3110.5, HO-228.5, AB-01-06 dated 1/18/01

These appliances are covered under Part B when furnished incident to physicians' services or on a physician's order. A brace includes rigid and semi-rigid devices which are used for the purpose of supporting a weak or deformed body member or restricting or eliminating motion in a diseased or injured part of the body. Elastic stockings, garter belts, and similar devices do not come within the scope of the definition of a brace. Back braces include, but are not limited to, special corsets, e.g., sacroiliac, sacrolumbar, dorsolumbar corsets, and belts. A terminal device (e.g., hand or hook) is covered under this provision whether an artificial limb is required by the patient. Stump stockings and harnesses (including replacements) are also covered when these appliances are essential to the effective use of the artificial limb.

Adjustments to an artificial limb or other appliance required by wear or by a change in the patient's condition are covered when ordered by a physician.

Adjustments, repairs and replacements are covered even when the item had been in use before the user enrolled in Part B of the program so long as the device continues to be medically required.

100-2, 15, 140

Therapeutic Shoes for Individuals with Diabetes

B3-2134

Coverage of therapeutic shoes (depth or custom-molded) along with inserts for individuals with diabetes is available as of May 1, 1993. These diabetic shoes are covered if the requirements as specified in this section concerning certification and prescription are fulfilled. In addition, this benefit provides for a pair of diabetic shoes even if only one foot suffers from diabetic foot disease. Each shoe is equally equipped so that the affected limb, as well as the remaining limb, is protected. Claims for therapeutic shoes for diabetics are processed by the Durable Medical Equipment Regional Carriers (DMERCs). Therapeutic shoes for diabetics are not DME and are not considered DME nor orthotics, but a separate category of coverage under Medicare Part B. (See Sec.1861(s)(12) and Sec.1833(o) of the Act.)

A. Definitions

The following items may be covered under the diabetic shoe benefit:

1. Custom-Molded ShoesCustom-molded shoes are shoes that:
   - Are constructed over a positive model of the patient's foot;
   - Are made from leather or other suitable material of equal quality;

- Have removable inserts that can be altered or replaced as the patient's condition warrants; and
- Have some form of shoe closure.

2. Depth Shoes
   Depth shoes are shoes that:
   - Have a full length, heel-to-toe filler that, when removed, provides a minimum of 3/16 inch of additional depth used to accommodate custom-molded or customized inserts;
   - Are made from leather or other suitable material of equal quality;
   - Have some form of shoe closure; and
   - Are available in full and half sizes with a minimum of three widths so that the sole is graded to the size and width of the upper portions of the shoes according to the American standard last sizing schedule or its equivalent. (The American standard last sizing schedule is the numerical shoe sizing system used for shoes sold in the United States.)

3. Inserts
   Inserts are total contact, multiple density, removable inlays that are directly molded to the patient's foot or a model of the patient's foot and that are made of a suitable material with regard to the patient's condition.

B. Coverage

1. Limitations
   For each individual, coverage of the footwear and inserts is limited to one of the following within one calendar year:
   - No more than one pair of custom-molded shoes (including inserts provided with such shoes) and two additional pairs of inserts; or
   - No more than one pair of depth shoes and three pairs of inserts (not including the noncustomized removable inserts provided with such shoes).

2. Coverage of Diabetic Shoes and Brace
   Orthopedic shoes, as stated in the Medicare Claims Processing Manual, Chapter 20, "Durable Medical Equipment, Surgical Dressings and Casts, Orthotics and Artificial Limbs, and Prosthetic Devices," generally are not covered. This exclusion does not apply to orthopedic shoes that are an integral part of a leg brace. In situations in which an individual qualifies for both diabetic shoes and a leg brace, these items are covered separately. Thus, the diabetic shoes may be covered if the requirements for this section are met, while the brace may be covered if the requirements of Sec.130 are met.

3. Substitution of Modifications for Inserts
   An individual may substitute modification(s) of custom-molded or depth shoes instead of obtaining a pair(s) of inserts in any combination. Payment for the modification(s) may not exceed the limit set for the inserts for which the individual is entitled. The following is a list of the most common shoe modifications available, but it is not meant as an exhaustive list of the modifications available for diabetic shoes:

   Rigid Rocker Bottoms - These are exterior elevations with apex positions for 51 percent to 75 percent distance measured from the back end of the heel. The apex is a narrowed or pointed end of an anatomical structure. The apex must be positioned behind the metatarsal heads and tapered off sharply to the front tip of the sole. Apex height helps to eliminate pressure at the metatarsal heads. Rigidity is ensured by the steel in the shoe. The heel of the shoe tapers off in the back in order to cause the heel to strike in the middle of the heel;
   - Roller Bottoms (Sole or Bar) - These are the same as rocker bottoms, but the heel is tapered from the apex to the front tip of the sole;
   - Metatarsal Bars- An exterior bar is placed behind the metatarsal heads in order to remove pressure from the metatarsal heads. The bars are of various shapes, heights, and construction depending on the exact purpose;
   - Wedges (Posting) - Wedges are either of hind foot, fore foot, or both and may be in the middle or to the side. The function is to shift or transfer weight bearing upon standing or during ambulation to the opposite side for added support, stabilization, equalized weight distribution, or balance; and
   - Offset Heels- This is a heel flanged at its base either in the middle, to the side, or a combination, that is then extended upward to the shoe in order to stabilize extreme positions of the hind foot. Other modifications to diabetic shoes include, but are not limited to flared heels, Velcro closures, and inserts for missing toes.

4. Separate Inserts Inserts may be covered and dispensed independently of diabetic shoes if the supplier of the shoes verifies in writing that the patient has appropriate footwear into which the insert can be placed. This footwear must meet the definitions found above for depth shoes and custom-molded shoes.

C. Certification

The need for diabetic shoes must be certified by a physician who is a doctor of medicine or a doctor of osteopathy and who is responsible for diagnosing and treating the patient's diabetic systemic condition through a comprehensive plan of care. This managing physician must:

- Document in the patient's medical record that the patient has diabetes;
- Certify that the patient is being treated under a comprehensive plan of care for diabetes, and that the patient needs diabetic shoes; and
- Document in the patient's record that the patient has one or more of the following conditions:
- Peripheral neuropathy with evidence of callus formation;
  - History of pre-ulcerative calluses;
  - History of previous ulceration;
  - Foot deformity;
  - Previous amputation of the foot or part of the foot; or
  - Poor circulation.

D. Prescription

Following certification by the physician managing the patient's systemic diabetic condition, a podiatrist or other qualified physician who is knowledgeable in the fitting of diabetic shoes and inserts may prescribe the particular type of footwear necessary.

E. Furnishing

Footwear The footwear must be fitted and furnished by a podiatrist or other qualified individual such as a pedorthist, an orthotist, or a prosthetist. The certifying physician may not furnish the diabetic shoes unless the certifying physician is the only qualified individual in the area. It is left to the discretion of each carrier to determine the meaning of "in the area."

100-2, 15, 150

Dental Services

B3-2136

As indicated under the general exclusions from coverage, items and services in connection with the care, treatment, filling, removal, or replacement of teeth or structures directly supporting the teeth are not covered. "Structures directly supporting the teeth" means the periodontium, which includes the gingivae, dentogingival junction, periodontal membrane, cementum of the teeth, and alveolar process.

In addition to the following, see Pub 100-01, the Medicare General Information, Eligibility, and Entitlement Manual, Chapter 5, Definitions and Pub 3, the Medicare National Coverage Determinations Manual for specific services which may be covered when furnished by a dentist. If an otherwise noncovered procedure or service is performed by a dentist as incident to and as an integral part of a covered procedure or service performed by the dentist, the total service performed by the dentist on such an occasion is covered.

EXAMPLE 1: The reconstruction of a ridge performed primarily to prepare the mouth for dentures is a noncovered procedure. However, when the reconstruction of a ridge is performed as a result of and at the same time as the surgical removal of a tumor (for other than dental purposes), the totality of surgical procedures is a covered service.

EXAMPLE 2: Medicare makes payment for the wiring of teeth when this is done in connection with the reduction of a jaw fracture.

The extraction of teeth to prepare the jaw for radiation treatment of neoplastic disease is also covered. This is an exception to the requirement that to be covered, a noncovered procedure or service performed by a dentist must be an incident to and an integral part of a covered procedure or service performed by the dentist. Ordinarily, the dentist extracts the patient's teeth, but another physician, e.g., a radiologist, administers the radiation treatments.

When an excluded service is the primary procedure involved, it is not covered, regardless of its complexity or difficulty. For example, the extraction of an impacted tooth is not covered. Similarly, an alveoplasty (the surgical improvement of the shape and condition of the alveolar process) and a frenectomy are excluded from coverage when either of these procedures is performed in connection with an excluded service, e.g., the preparation of the mouth for dentures. In a like manner, the removal of a torus palatinus (a bony protuberance of the hard palate) may be a covered service. However, with rare exception, this surgery is performed in connection with an excluded service, i.e., the preparation of the mouth for dentures. Under such circumstances, Medicare does not pay for this procedure.

Dental splints used to treat a dental condition are excluded from coverage under 1862(a)(12) of the Act. On the other hand, if the treatment is determined to be a covered medical condition (i.e., dislocated upper/lower jaw joints), then the splint can be covered.

Whether such services as the administration of anesthesia, diagnostic x-rays, and other related procedures are covered depends upon whether the primary procedure being performed by the dentist is itself covered. Thus, an x-ray taken in connection with the reduction of a fracture of the jaw or facial bone is covered. However, a single x-ray or x-ray survey taken in connection with the care or treatment of teeth or the periodontium is not covered.

Medicare makes payment for a covered dental procedure no matter where the service is performed. The hospitalization or nonhospitalization of a patient has no direct bearing on the coverage or exclusion of a given dental procedure.

Payment may also be made for services and supplies furnished incident to covered dental services. For example, the services of a dental technician or nurse who is under the direct supervision of the dentist or physician are covered if the services are included in the dentist's or physician's bill.

100-2, 15, 230

Practice of Physical Therapy, Occupational Therapy, and Speech-Language Pathology

A. Group Therapy Services.
Contractors pay for outpatient physical therapy services (which includes outpatient speech-language pathology services) and outpatient occupational therapy services provided simultaneously to two or more individuals by a practitioner as group therapy services (97150). The individuals can be, but need not be performing the same activity. The physician or therapist involved in group therapy services must be in constant attendance, but one-on-one patient contact is not required.

B. Therapy Students

1. General
   Only the services of the therapist can be billed and paid under Medicare Part B. The services performed by a student are not reimbursed even if provided under "line of sight" supervision of the therapist; however, the presence of the student "in the room" does not make the service unbillable. Pay for the direct (one-to-one) patient contact services of the physician or therapist provided to Medicare Part B patients. Group therapy services performed by a therapist or physician may be billed when a student is also present "in the room".

   EXAMPLES:

   Therapists may bill and be paid for the provision of services in the following scenarios:

   - The qualified practitioner is present and in the room for the entire session. The student participates in the delivery of services when the qualified practitioner is directing the service, making the skilled judgment, and is responsible for the assessment and treatment.
   - The qualified practitioner is present in the room guiding the student in service delivery when the therapy student and the therapy assistant student are participating in the provision of services, and the practitioner is not engaged in treating another patient or doing other tasks at the same time
   - The qualified practitioner is responsible for the services and as such, signs all documentation. (A student may, of course, also sign but it is not necessary since the Part B payment is for the clinician's service, not for the student's services).
2. Therapy Assistants as Clinical Instructors
   Physical therapist assistants and occupational therapy assistants are not precluded from serving as clinical instructors for therapy students, while providing services within their scope of work and performed under the direction and supervision of a licensed physical or occupational therapist to a Medicare beneficiary.
3. Services Provided Under Part A and Part B
   The payment methodologies for Part A and B therapy services rendered by a student are different. Under the MPFS (Medicare Part B), Medicare pays for services provided by physicians and practitioners that are specifically authorized by statute. Students do not meet the definition of practitioners under Medicare Part B. Under SNF PPS, payments are based upon the case mix or Resource Utilization Group (RUG) category that describes the patient. In the rehabilitation groups, the number of therapy minutes delivered to the patient determines the RUG category. Payment levels for each category are based upon the costs of caring for patients in each group rather than providing pecific payment for each therapy service as is done in Medicare Part B.

100-2, 15, 231

Pulmonary Rehabilitation (PR) Program Services Furnished On or After January 1, 2010

A pulmonary rehabilitation (PR) program is typically a physician-supervised, multidisciplinary program individually tailored and designed to optimize physical and social performance and autonomy of care for patients with chronic respiratory impairment. The main goal is to empower the individuals' ability to exercise independently. Exercise is combined with other training and support mechanisms to encourage long-term adherence to the treatment plan. Effective January 1, 2010, Medicare Part B pays for PR programs and related items and services if specific criteria is met by the Medicare beneficiary, the PR program itself, the setting in which it is administered, and the physician administering the program, as outlined below:

PR Program Beneficiary Requirements:

- As specified in 42 CFR 410.47, Medicare covers PR items and services for patients with moderate to very severe chronic obstructive pulmonary disease (COPD) (defined as GOLD classification II, III, and IV), when referred by the physician treating the chronic respiratory disease. Additional medical indications for coverage for PR program services may be established through the national coverage determination process.

PR Program Component Requirements:

- Physician-prescribed exercise. This physical activity includes techniques such as exercise conditioning, breathing retraining, and step and strengthening exercises. Some aerobic exercise must be included in each PR session. Both low- and high- intensity exercise is recommended to produce clinical benefits and a combination of endurance and strength training should be conducted at least twice per week.
- Education or training. This should be closely and clearly related to the individual's care and treatment and tailored to the individual's needs, including information on respiratory problem management and, if appropriate, brief smoking cessation counseling. Any education or training must assist in achievement of individual goals towards independence in activities of daily living, adaptation to limitations, and improved quality of life (QoL).
- Psychosocial assessment. This assessment means a written evaluation of an individual's mental and emotional functioning as it relates to the individual's rehabilitation or respiratory condition. It should include: (1) an assessment of those aspects of the individual's family and home situation that affects the individual's rehabilitation treatment, and, (2) a psychological evaluation of the individual's response to, and rate of progress under, the treatment plan. Periodic re-evaluations are necessary to ensure the individual's psychosocial needs are being met.
- Outcomes assessment. These should include: (1) beginning and end evaluations based on patient-centered outcomes, which are conducted by the physician at the start and end of the program, and, (2) objective clinical measures of the effectiveness of the PR program for the individual patient, including exercise performance and self-reported measures of shortness of breath, and behavior. The assessments should include clinical measures such as the 6-minute walk, weight, exercise performance, self-reported dyspnea, behavioral measures (supplemental oxygen use, smoking status,) and a QoL assessment.
- An individualized treatment plan describing the individual's diagnosis and detailing how components are utilized for each patient. The plan must be established, reviewed, and signed by a physician every 30 days. The plan may initially be developed by the referring physician or the PR physician. If the plan is developed by the referring physician who is not the PR physician, the PR physician must also review and sign the plan prior to imitation of the PR program. It is expected that the supervising physician would have initial, direct contact with the individual prior to subsequent treatment by ancillary personnel, and also have at least one direct contact in each 30-day period. The plan must have written specificity with regards to the type, amount, frequency, and duration of PR items and services furnished to the individual, and specify the appropriate mix of services for the patient's needs. It must include measurable and expected outcomes and estimated timetables to achieve these outcomes.

As specified at 42 CFR 410.47(f), PR program sessions are limited to a maximum of 2 1-hour sessions per day for up to 36 sessions, with the option for an additional 36 sessions if medically necessary.

PR Program Setting Requirements:
PR items and services must be furnished in a physician's office or a hospital outpatient setting. The setting must have the necessary cardio-pulmonary, emergency, diagnostic, and therapeutic life-saving equipment accepted by the medical community as medically necessary (for example, oxygen , cardiopulmonary resuscitation equipment, and a defibrillator) to treat chronic respiratory disease. All settings must have a physician immediately available and accessible for medical consultations and emergencies at all times that the PR items and services are being furnished under the program. This provision is satisfied if the physician meets the requirements for direct supervision of physician office services as specified at 42 CFR 410.26, and for hospital outpatient therapeutic services as specified at 42 CFR 410.27.

PR Program Physician Requirements:
Medicare Part B pays for PR services supervised by a physician only if the physician meets all of the following requirements: (1) expertise in the management of individuals with respiratory pathophysiology, (2) licensed to practice medicine in the state in which the PR program is

offered, (3) responsible and accountable for the PR program, and, (4) involved substantially, in consultation with staff, in directing the progress of the individual in the PR program.

(See Publication 100-04, Claims Processing Manual, chapter 32, section 140.4, for specific claims processing, coding, and billing requirements for PR program services.)

100-2, 15, 232

Cardiac Rehabilitation (CR) and Intensive Cardiac Rehabilitation (ICR) Services Furnished On or After January 1, 2010

Cardiac rehabilitation (CR) services mean a physician-supervised program that furnishes physician prescribed exercise, cardiac risk factor modification, including education, counseling, and behavioral intervention; psychosocial assessment, outcomes assessment, and other items/services as determined by the Secretary under certain conditions. Intensive cardiac rehabilitation (ICR) services mean a physician-supervised program that furnishes the same items/services under the same conditions as a CR program but must also demonstrate, as shown in peer-reviewed published research, that it improves patients' cardiovascular disease through specific outcome measurements described in 42 CFR 410.49(c). Effective January 1, 2010, Medicare Part B pays for CR/ICR programs and related items/services if specific criteria is met by the Medicare beneficiary, the CR/ICR program itself, the setting in which is it administered, and the physician administering the program, as outlined below:

CR/ICR Program Beneficiary Requirements:

- Medicare covers CR/ICR program services for beneficiaries who have experienced one or more of the following:
- Acute myocardial infarction within the preceding 12 months;
- Coronary artery bypass surgery;
- Current stable angina pectoris;
- Heart valve repair or replacement;
- Percutaneous transluminal coronary angioplasty (PTCA) or coronary stenting;
- Heart or heart-lung transplant.

For CR only, other cardiac conditions as specified through a national coverage determination (NCD).

CR/ICR Program Component Requirements:

Physician-prescribed exercise. This physical activity includes aerobic exercise combined with other types of exercise (i.e., strengthening, stretching) as determined to be appropriate for individual patients by a physician each day CR/ICR items/services are furnished.

Cardiac risk factor modification. This includes education, counseling, and behavioral intervention, tailored to the patients' individual needs.

Psychosocial assessment. This assessment means an evaluation of an individual's mental and emotional functioning as it relates to the individual's rehabilitation. It should include: (1) an assessment of those aspects of the individual's family and home situation that affects the individual's rehabilitation treatment, and, (2) a psychosocial evaluation of the individual's response to, and rate of progress under, the treatment plan.

Outcomes assessment. These should include: (i) minimally, assessments from the commencement and conclusion of CR/ICR, based on patient-centered outcomes which must be measured by the physician immediately at the beginning and end of the program, and, (ii) objective clinical measures of the effectiveness of the CR/ICR program for the individual patient, including exercise performance and self-reported measures of exertion and behavior.

Individualized treatment plan. This plan should be written and tailored to each individual patient and include (i) a description of the individual's diagnosis; (ii) the type, amount, frequency, and duration of the CR/ICR items/services furnished; and (iii) the goals set for the individual under the plan. The individualized treatment plan must be established, reviewed, and signed by a physician every 30 days.

As specified at 42 CFR 410.49(f)(1), CR sessions are limited to a maximum of 2 1-hour sessions per day for up to 36 sessions over up to 36 weeks with the option for an additional 36 sessions over an extended period of time if approved by the contractor under section 1862(a)(1)(A) of the Act. ICR sessions are limited to 72 1-hour sessions (as defined in section 1848(b)(5) of the Act), up to 6 sessions per day, over a period of up to 18 weeks.

CR/ICR Program Setting Requirements:

CR/ICR services must be furnished in a physician's office or a hospital outpatient setting (for ICR, the hospital outpatient setting must provide ICR using an approved ICR program). All settings must have a physician immediately available and accessible for medical consultations and emergencies at all times when items/services are being furnished under the program. This provision is satisfied if the physician meets the requirements for direct supervision of physician office services as specified at 42 CFR 410.26, and for hospital outpatient services as specified at 42 CFR 410.27.

ICR Program Approval Requirements:

All prospective ICR programs must be approved through the national coverage determination (NCD) process. To be approved as an ICR program, it must demonstrate through peer-reviewed, published research that it has accomplished one or more of the following for its patients: (i) positively affected the progression of coronary heart disease, (ii) reduced the need for coronary bypass surgery, or, (iii) reduced the need for percutaneous coronary interventions.

An ICR program must also demonstrate through peer-reviewed, published research that it accomplished a statistically significant reduction in five or more of the following measures for patients from their levels before CR services to after CR services: (i) low density lipoprotein, (ii) triglycerides, (iii) body mass index, (iv) systolic blood pressure, (v) diastolic blood pressure, and (vi) the need for cholesterol, blood pressure, and diabetes medications.

A list of approved ICR programs, identified through the NCD process, will be posted to the CMS Web site and listed in the Federal Register.

Once an ICR program is approved through the NCD process, all prospective ICR sites wishing to furnish ICR items/services via an approved ICR program may enroll with their local contractor to become an ICR program supplier using the designated forms as specified at 42 CFR 424.510, and report specialty code 31 to be identified as an enrolled ICR supplier. For purposes of appealing an adverse determination concerning site approval, an ICR site is considered a supplier (or prospective supplier) as defined in 42 CFR 498.2.

CR/ICR Program Physician Requirements:

Physicians responsible for CR/ICR programs are identified as medical directors who oversee or supervise the CR/ICR program at a particular site. The medical director, in consultation with staff, is involved in directing the progress of individuals in the program. The medical director, as well as physicians acting as the supervising physician, must possess all of the following: (1) expertise in the management of individuals with cardiac pathophysiology, (2) cardiopulmonary training in basic life support or advanced cardiac life support, and (3) licensed to practice medicine in the state in which the CR/ICR program is offered. Direct physician supervision may be provided by a supervising physician or the medical director.

(See Pub. 100-04, Medicare Claims Processing Manual, chapter 32, section 140.2, for specific claims processing, coding, and billing requirements for CR/ICR program services.)

100-2, 15, 270

Telehealth Services

Background

Section 223 of the Medicare, Medicaid and SCHIP Benefits Improvement and Protection Act of 2000 (BIPA) - Revision of Medicare Reimbursement for Telehealth Services amended §1834 of the Act to provide for an expansion of Medicare payment for telehealth services.

Effective October 1, 2001, coverage and payment for Medicare telehealth includes consultation, office visits, individual psychotherapy, and pharmacologic management delivered via a telecommunications system. Eligible geographic areas include rural health professional shortage areas (HPSA) and counties not classified as a metropolitan statistical area (MSA). Additionally, Federal telemedicine demonstration projects as of December 31, 2000, may serve as the originating site regardless of geographic location.

An interactive telecommunications system is required as a condition of payment; however, BIPA does allow the use of asynchronous "store and forward" technology in delivering these services when the originating site is a Federal telemedicine demonstration program in Alaska or Hawaii. BIPA does not require that a practitioner present the patient for interactive telehealth services.

With regard to payment amount, BIPA specified that payment for the professional service performed by the distant site practitioner (i.e., where the expert physician or practitioner is physically located at time of telemedicine encounter) is equal to what would have been paid without the use of telemedicine. Distant site practitioners include only a physician as described in §1861(r) of the Act and a medical practitioner as described in §1842(b)(18)(C) of the Act. BIPA also expanded payment under Medicare to include a $20 originating site facility fee (location of beneficiary).

Previously, the Balanced Budget Act of 1997 (BBA) limited the scope of Medicare telehealth coverage to consultation services and the implementing regulation prohibited the use of an asynchronous 'store and forward' telecommunications system. The BBA of 1997 also required the professional fee to be shared between the referring and consulting practitioners, and prohibited Medicare payment for facility fees and line charges associated with the telemedicine encounter.

The BIPA required that Medicare Part B (Supplementary Medical Insurance) pay for this expansion of telehealth services beginning with services furnished on October 1, 2001.

Section 149 of the Medicare Improvements for Patients and Providers Act of 2008 (MIPPA) amended §1834(m) of the Act to add certain entities as originating sites for payment of telehealth services. Effective for services furnished on or after January 1, 2009, eligible originating sites include a hospital-based or critical access hospital-based renal dialysis center (including satellites); a skilled nursing facility (as defined in §1819(a) of the Act); and a community mental health center (as defined in §1861(ff)(3)(B) of the Act). MIPPA also amended§1888(e)(2)(A)(ii) of the Act to exclude telehealth services furnished under §1834(m)(4)(C)(ii)(VII) from the consolidated billing provisions of the skilled nursing facility prospective payment system (SNF PPS).

NOTE: MIPPA did not add independent renal dialysis facilities as originating sites for payment of telehealth services.

The telehealth provisions authorized by §1834(m) of the Act are implemented in 42 CFR 410.78 and 414.65.

100-2, 15, 270.2

List of Medicare Telehealth Services

The use of a telecommunications system may substitute for an in-person encounter for professional consultations, office visits, office psychiatry services, and a limited number of other physician fee schedule (PFS) services. These services are listed below.

- Consultations (Effective October 1, 2001- December 31, 2009)
- Initial inpatient telehealth consultations (Effective January 1, 2010)
- Follow-up inpatient telehealth consultations (Effective January 1, 2009)
- Office or other outpatient visits
- Subsequent hospital care services (with the limitation of one telehealth visit every 3 days) (Effective January 1, 2011)
- Subsequent nursing facility care services (with the limitation of one telehealth visit every 30 days) (Effective January 1, 2011)
- Individual psychotherapy
- Pharmacologic management
- Psychiatric diagnostic interview examination (Effective March 1, 2003)
- End stage renal disease related services (Effective January 1, 2005)
- Individual and group medical nutrition therapy (Individual effective January 1, 2006; group effective January 1, 2011)
- Neurobehavioral status exam (Effective January 1, 2008)
- Individual and group health and behavior assessment and intervention (Individual effective January 1, 2010; group effective January 1, 2011)
- Individual and group kidney disease education (KDE) services (Effective January 1, 2011)
- Individual and group diabetes self-management training (DSMT) services (with a minimum of 1 hour of in-person instruction to be furnished in the initial year training period to ensure effective injection training) (Effective January 1, 2011)

NOTE: Beginning January 1, 2010, CMS eliminated the use of all consultation codes, except for inpatient telehealth consultation G-codes. CMS no longer recognizes office/outpatient or inpatient consultation CPT codes for payment of office/outpatient or inpatient visits. Instead, physicians and practitioners are instructed to bill a new or established patient office/outpatient visit CPT code or appropriate hospital or nursing facility care code, as appropriate to the particular patient, for all office/outpatient or inpatient visits. For detailed instructions regarding reporting these and other telehealth services, see Pub. 100-04, Medicare Claims Processing Manual, chapter 12, section 190.3.

The conditions of payment for Medicare telehealth services, including qualifying originating sites and the types of telecommunications systems recognized by Medicare, are subject to the provisions of 42 CFR 410.78. Payment for these services is subject to the provisions of 42 CFR 414.65.

100-2, 15, 270.4.3

Payment for Diabetes Self-Management Training (DSMT) as a Telehealth Service

Payment for Diabetes Self-Management Training (DSMT) as a Telehealth Service

Individual and group DSMT services may be paid as a Medicare telehealth service; however, at least 1 hour of the 10 hour benefit in the year following the initial DSMT service must be furnished in-person to allow for effective injection training. The injection training may be furnished through either individual or group DSMT services. By reporting the –GT or –GQ modifier with HCPCS code G0108 (Diabetes outpatient self-management training services, individual, per 30 minutes) or G0109 Diabetes outpatient self-management training services, group session (2 or more), per 30 minutes), the distant site practitioner certifies that the beneficiary has received or will receive 1 hour of in-person DSMT services for purposes of injection training during the year following the initial DSMT service.

As specified in 42 CFR 410.141(e) and stated in section 300.2 of this chapter, individual DSMT services may be furnished by a physician, individual, or entity that furnishes other services for which direct Medicare payment may be made and that submits necessary documentation to, and is accredited by, an accreditation organization approved by CMS. However, consistent with the statutory requirements of section 1834(m)(1) of the Act, as provided in 42 CFR 410.78(b)(1) and (b)(2) and stated in section 270.4 of this chapter, Medicare telehealth services, including individual DSMT services furnished as a telehealth service, could only be furnished by a licensed physician assistant (PA), nurse practitioner (NP), clinical nurse specialist (CNS), certified nurse-midwife (CNM), clinical psychologist, clinical social worker, or registered dietitian or nutrition professional.

100-2, 15, 280.1

Glaucoma Screening

A. Conditions of Coverage

The regulations implementing the Benefits Improvements and Protection Act of 2000, Sec.102, provide for annual coverage for glaucoma screening for beneficiaries in the following high risk categories:

- Individuals with diabetes mellitus;
- Individuals with a family history of glaucoma; or
- African-Americans age 50 and over. In addition, beginning with dates of service on or after January 1, 2006, 42 CFR 410.23(a)(2), revised, the definition of an eligible beneficiary in a high-risk category is expanded to include:
- Hispanic-Americans age 65 and over.

Medicare will pay for glaucoma screening examinations where they are furnished by or under the direct supervision in the office setting of an ophthalmologist or optometrist, who is legally authorized to perform the services under State law. Screening for glaucoma is defined to include:

- A dilated eye examination with an intraocular pressure measurement; and
- A direct ophthalmoscopy examination, or a slit-lamp biomicroscopic examination.

Payment may be made for a glaucoma screening examination that is performed on an eligible beneficiary after at least 11 months have passed following the month in which the last covered glaucoma screening examination was performed.

The following HCPCS codes apply for glaucoma screening:

G0117 Glaucoma screening for high-risk patients furnished by an optometrist or ophthalmologist; and

G0118 Glaucoma screening for high-risk patients furnished under the direct supervision of an optometrist or ophthalmologist.

The type of service for the above G codes is: TOS Q.

For providers who bill intermediaries, applicable types of bill for screening glaucoma services are 13X, 22X, 23X, 71X, 73X, 75X, and 85X. The following revenue codes should be reported when billing for screening glaucoma services:

- Comprehensive outpatient rehabilitation facilities (CORFs), critical access hospitals (CAHs), skilled nursing facilities (SNFs), independent and provider-based RHCs and free standing and provider-based FQHCs bill for this service under revenue code 770. CAHs electing the optional method of payment for outpatient services report this service under revenue codes 96X, 97X, or 98X.
- Hospital outpatient departments bill for this service under any valid/appropriate revenue code. They are not required to report revenue code 770.

B. Calculating the Frequency

Once a beneficiary has received a covered glaucoma screening procedure, the beneficiary may receive another procedure after 11 full months have passed. To determine the 11-month period, start the count beginning with the month after the month in which the previous covered screening procedure was performed.

C. Diagnosis Coding Requirements

Providers bill glaucoma screening using screening ("V") code V80.1 (Special Screening for Neurological, Eye, and Ear Diseases, Glaucoma). Claims submitted without a screening diagnosis code may be returned to the provider as unprocessable.

D. Payment Methodology

1. Carriers

   Contractors pay for glaucoma screening based on the Medicare physician fee schedule. Deductible and coinsurance apply. Claims from physicians or other providers where assignment was not taken are subject to the Medicare limiting charge (refer to the Medicare Claims Processing Manual, Chapter 12, "Physician/Non-physician Practitioners," for more information about the Medicare limiting charge).

2. Intermediaries

   Payment is made for the facility expense as follows:

   - Independent and provider-based RHC/free standing and provider-based FQHC - payment is made under the all inclusive rate for the screening glaucoma service based on the visit furnished to the RHC/FQHC patient;
   - CAH - payment is made on a reasonable cost basis unless the CAH has elected the optional method of payment for outpatient services in which case, procedures outlined in the Medicare Claims Processing Manual, Chapter 3, Sec.30.1.1, should be followed;
   - CORF - payment is made under the Medicare physician fee schedule;
   - Hospital outpatient department - payment is made under outpatient prospective payment system (OPPS);
   - Hospital inpatient Part B - payment is made under OPPS;
   - SNF outpatient - payment is made under the Medicare physician fee schedule (MPFS); and
   - SNF inpatient Part B - payment is made under MPFS. Deductible and coinsurance apply.

E. Special Billing Instructions for RHCs and FQHCs

Screening glaucoma services are considered RHC/FQHC services. RHCs and FQHCs bill the contractor under bill type 71X or 73X along with revenue code 770 and HCPCS codes G0117 or G0118 and RHC/FQHC revenue code 520 or 521 to report the related visit. Reporting of revenue code 770 and HCPCS codes G0117 and G0118 in addition to revenue code 520 or 521 is required for this service in order for CWF to perform frequency editing.

Payment should not be made for a screening glaucoma service unless the claim also contains a visit code for the service. Therefore, the contractor installs an edit in its system to assure payment is not made for revenue code 770 unless the claim also contains a visit revenue code (520 or 521).

100-2, 15, 280.5

Annual Wellness Visit (AWV) Including Personalized Prevention Plan Services (PPPS)

A. General

Pursuant to section 4103 of the Affordable Care Act of 2010 (the ACA), the Centers for Medicare & Medicaid Services (CMS) amended section 411.15(a)(1) and 411.15(k)(15) of the Code of Federal Regulations (CFR)(list of examples of routine physical examinations excluded from coverage), effective for services furnished on or after January 1, 2011. This expanded coverage, as established at 42 CFR 410.15, is subject to certain eligibility and other limitations that allow payment for an annual wellness visit (AWV), including personalized prevention plan services (PPPS), when performed by qualified health professionals, for an individual who is no longer within 12 months after the effective date of his/her first Medicare Part B coverage period, and has not received either an initial preventive physical examination (IPPE) or an AWV within the past 12 months. Medicare coinsurance and Part B deductibles do not apply.

The AWV will include the establishment of, or update to, the individual's medical/family history, measurement of his/her height, weight, body-mass index (BMI) or waist circumference, and blood pressure (BP), with the goal of health promotion and disease detection and encouraging patients to obtain the screening and preventive services that may already be covered and paid for under Medicare Part B. Definitions relative to the AWV are included below.

Coverage is available for an AWV that meets the following requirements:

1. It is performed by a health professional; and,
2. It is furnished to an eligible beneficiary who is no longer within 12 months after the effective date of his/her first Medicare Part B coverage period, and he/she has not received either an IPPE or an AWV providing PPPS within the past 12 months.

Sections 4103 and 4104 of the ACA also provide for a waiver of the Medicare coinsurance and Part B deductible requirements for an AWV effective for services furnished on or after January 1, 2011.

B. Definitions Relative to the AWV:

Detection of any cognitive impairment: The assessment of an individual's cognitive function by direct observation, with due consideration of information obtained by way of patient reports, concerns raised by family members, friends, caretakers, or others.

Eligible beneficiary: An individual who is no longer within 12 months after the effective date of his/her first Medicare Part B coverage period and who has not received either an IPPE or an AWV providing PPPS within the past 12 months.

Establishment of, or an update to, the individual's medical/family history: At a minimum, the collection and documentation of the following:

a. Past medical and surgical history, including experiences with illnesses, hospital stays, operations, allergies, injuries, and treatments.

b. Use or exposure to medications and supplements, including calcium and vitamins.

c. Medical events in the beneficiary's parents and any siblings and children, including diseases that may be hereditary or place the individual at increased risk.

First AWV providing PPPS: The provision of the following services to an eligible beneficiary by a health professional as those terms are defined in this section:

a. Establishment of an individual's medical/family history.

b. Establishment of a list of current providers and suppliers that are regularly involved in providing medical care to the individual.

c. Measurement of an individual's height, weight, BMI (or waist circumference, if appropriate), BP, and other routine measurements as deemed appropriate, based on the beneficiary's medical/family history.

d. Detection of any cognitive impairment that the individual may have as defined in this section.

e. Review of the individual's potential (risk factors) for depression, including current or past experiences with depression or other mood disorders, based on the use of an appropriate screening instrument for persons without a current diagnosis of depression, which the health professional may select from various available standardized screening tests designed for this purpose and recognized by national medical professional organizations.

f. Review of the individual's functional ability and level of safety based on direct observation, or the use of appropriate screening questions or a screening questionnaire, which the health professional may select from various available screening questions or standardized questionnaires designed for this purpose and recognized by national professional medical organizations.

g. Establishment of the following:

   (1) A written screening schedule for the individual, such as a checklist for the next 5 to 10 years, as appropriate, based on recommendations of the United States Preventive Services Task Force (USPSTF) and the Advisory Committee on Immunization Practices (ACIP), as well as the individual's health status, screening history, and age-appropriate preventive services covered by Medicare.

   (2) A list of risk factors and conditions for which primary, secondary, or tertiary interventions are recommended or are underway for the individual, including any mental health conditions or any such risk factors or conditions that have been identified through an IPPE, and a list of treatment options and their associated risks and benefits.

h. Furnishing of personalized health advice to the individual and a referral, as appropriate, to health education or preventive counseling services or programs aimed at reducing identified risk factors and improving self-management, or community-based lifestyle interventions to reduce health risks and promote self-management and wellness, including weight loss, physical activity, smoking cessation, fall prevention, and nutrition.

i. Any other element determined appropriate through the National Coverage Determination (NCD) process.

Health professional:

a. A physician who is a doctor of medicine or osteopathy (as defined in section 1861(r)(1) of the Social Security Act (the Act); or,

b. A physician assistant, nurse practitioner, or clinical nurse specialist (as defined in section 1861(aa)(5) of the Act); or,

c. A medical professional (including a health educator, registered dietitian, or nutrition professional or other licensed practitioner) or a team of such medical professionals, working under the direct supervision (as defined in 42CFR 410.32(b)(3)(ii)) of a physician as defined in this section.

Review of the individual's functional ability and level of safety: At a minimum, includes assessment of the following topics:

a. Hearing impairment,

b. Ability to successfully perform activities of daily living,

c. Fall risk, and, d. Home safety.

Subsequent AWV providing PPPS: The provision of the following services to an eligible beneficiary by a health professional as those terms are defined in this section:

a. An update of the individual's medical/family history.

b. An update of the list of current providers and suppliers that are regularly involved in providing medical care to the individual, as that list was developed for the first AWV providing PPPS.

c. Measurement of an individual's weight (or waist circumference), BP, and other routine measurements as deemed appropriate, based on the individual's medical/family history.

d. Detection of any cognitive impairment that the individual may have as defined in this section.

e. An update to the following:

(1) The written screening schedule for the individual as that schedule is defined in this section, that was developed at the first AWV providing PPPS, and,

(2) The list of risk factors and conditions for which primary, secondary, or tertiary interventions are recommended or are under way for the individual, as that list was developed at the first AWV providing PPPS.

f. Furnishing of personalized health advice to the individual and a referral, as appropriate, to health education or preventive counseling services or programs as that advice and related services are defined for the first AWV providing PPPS.

g. Any other element determined appropriate by the Secretary through the NCD process.

See Pub. 100-04, Medicare Claims Processing Manual, chapter 18, section 140, for detailed claims processing and billing instructions.

100-2, 15, 290

Foot Care

A. Treatment of Subluxation of Foot

Subluxations of the foot are defined as partial dislocations or displacements of joint surfaces, tendons ligaments, or muscles of the foot. Surgical or nonsurgical treatments undertaken for the sole purpose of correcting a subluxated structure in the foot as an isolated entity are not covered.

However, medical or surgical treatment of subluxation of the ankle joint (talo-crural joint) is covered. In addition, reasonable and necessary medical or surgical services, diagnosis, or treatment for medical conditions that have resulted from or are associated with partial displacement of structures is covered. For example, if a patient has osteoarthritis that has resulted in a partial displacement of joints in the foot, and the primary treatment is for the osteoarthritis, coverage is provided.

B. Exclusions from Coverage

The following foot care services are generally excluded from coverage under both Part A and Part B. (See Sec.290.F and Sec.290.G for instructions on applying foot care exclusions.)

1. Treatment of Flat Foot
   The term "flat foot" is defined as a condition in which one or more arches of the foot have flattened out. Services or devices directed toward the care or correction of such conditions, including the prescription of supportive devices, are not covered.

2. Routine Foot Care
   Except as provided above, routine foot care is excluded from coverage. Services that normally are considered routine and not covered by Medicare include the following:
   - The cutting or removal of corns and calluses;
   - The trimming, cutting, clipping, or debriding of nails; and
   - Other hygienic and preventive maintenance care, such as cleaning and soaking the feet, the use of skin creams to maintain skin tone of either ambulatory or bedfast patients, and any other service performed in the absence of localized illness, injury, or symptoms involving the foot.

3. Supportive Devices for Feet
   Orthopedic shoes and other supportive devices for the feet generally are not covered. However, this exclusion does not apply to such a shoe if it is an integral part of a leg brace, and its expense is included as part of the cost of the brace. Also, this exclusion does not apply to therapeutic shoes furnished to diabetics.

C. Exceptions to Routine Foot Care Exclusion

1. Necessary and Integral Part of Otherwise Covered Services
   In certain circumstances, services ordinarily considered to be routine may be covered if they are performed as a necessary and integral part of otherwise covered services, such as diagnosis and treatment of ulcers, wounds, or infections.

2. Treatment of Warts on Foot
   The treatment of warts (including plantar warts) on the foot is covered to the same extent as services provided for the treatment of warts located elsewhere on the body.

3. Presence of Systemic Condition
   The presence of a systemic condition such as metabolic, neurologic, or peripheral vascular disease may require scrupulous foot care by a professional that in the absence of such condition(s) would be considered routine (and, therefore, excluded from coverage). Accordingly, foot care that would otherwise be considered routine may be covered when systemic condition(s) result in severe circulatory embarrassment or areas of diminished sensation in the individual's legs or feet. (See subsection A.)

   In these instances, certain foot care procedures that otherwise are considered routine (e.g., cutting or removing corns and calluses, or trimming, cutting, clipping, or debriding nails) may pose a hazard when performed by a nonprofessional person on patients with such systemic conditions. (See Sec.290.G for procedural instructions.)

4. Mycotic Nails
   In the absence of a systemic condition, treatment of mycotic nails may be covered.
   The treatment of mycotic nails for an ambulatory patient is covered only when the physician attending the patient's mycotic condition documents that (1) there is clinical evidence of mycosis of the toenail, and (2) the patient has marked limitation of ambulation, pain, or secondary infection resulting from the thickening and dystrophy of the infected toenail plate.

   The treatment of mycotic nails for a nonambulatory patient is covered only when the physician attending the patient's mycotic condition documents that (1) there is clinical evidence of mycosis of the toenail, and (2) the patient suffers from pain or secondary infection resulting from the thickening and dystrophy of the infected toenail plate.

   For the purpose of these requirements, documentation means any written information that is required by the carrier in order for services to be covered. Thus, the information submitted with claims must be substantiated by information found in the patient's medical record. Any information, including that contained in a form letter, used for documentation purposes is subject to carrier verification in order to ensure that the information adequately justifies coverage of the treatment of mycotic nails.

D. Systemic Conditions That Might Justify Coverage

Although not intended as a comprehensive list, the following metabolic, neurologic, and peripheral vascular diseases (with synonyms in parentheses) most commonly represent the underlying conditions that might justify coverage for routine foot care.

- Diabetes mellitus *
- Arteriosclerosis obliterans (A.S.O., arteriosclerosis of the extremities, occlusive peripheral arteriosclerosis)
- Buerger's disease (thromboangiitis obliterans)
- Chronic thrombophlebitis *
- Peripheral neuropathies involving the feet -
- Associated with malnutrition and vitamin deficiency *
  - Malnutrition (general, pellagra)
  - Alcoholism
  - Malabsorption (celiac disease, tropical sprue)
  - Pernicious anemia
- Associated with carcinoma *
- Associated with diabetes mellitus *
- Associated with drugs and toxins *
- Associated with multiple sclerosis *
- Associated with uremia (chronic renal disease) *
- Associated with traumatic injury
- Associated with leprosy or neurosyphilis
- Associated with hereditary disorders
- Hereditary sensory radicular neuropathy
- Angiokeratoma corporis diffusum (Fabry's)
- Amyloid neuropathy

When the patient's condition is one of those designated by an asterisk (*), routine procedures are covered only if the patient is under the active care of a doctor of medicine or osteopathy who documents the condition.

E. Supportive Devices for Feet

Orthopedic shoes and other supportive devices for the feet generally are not covered. However, this exclusion does not apply to such a shoe if it is an integral part of a leg brace, and its expense is included as part of the cost of the brace. Also, this exclusion does not apply to therapeutic shoes furnished to diabetics.

F. Presumption of Coverage

In evaluating whether the routine services can be reimbursed, a presumption of coverage may be made where the evidence available discloses certain physical and/or clinical findings consistent with the diagnosis and indicative of severe peripheral involvement. For purposes of applying this presumption the following findings are pertinent:

Class A Findings

Nontraumatic amputation of foot or integral skeletal portion thereof.

Class B Findings

Absent posterior tibial pulse;

Advanced trophic changes as: hair growth (decrease or absence) nail changes (thickening) pigmentary changes (discoloration) skin texture (thin, shiny) skin color (rubor or redness) (Three required); and

Absent dorsalis pedis pulse.

Class C Findings

Claudication;

Temperature changes (e.g., cold feet);

Edema;

Paresthesias (abnormal spontaneous sensations in the feet); and

Burning.

The presumption of coverage may be applied when the physician rendering the routine foot care has identified:

1. A Class A finding;
2. Two of the Class B findings; or
3. One Class B and two Class C findings.

Cases evidencing findings falling short of these alternatives may involve podiatric treatment that may constitute covered care and should be reviewed by the intermediary's medical staff and developed as necessary.

For purposes of applying the coverage presumption where the routine services have been rendered by a podiatrist, the contractor may deem the active care requirement met if the claim or other evidence available discloses that the patient has seen an M.D. or D.O. for treatment and/or evaluation of the complicating disease process during the 6-month period prior to the rendition of the routine-type services. The intermediary may also accept the podiatrist's statement that the diagnosing and treating M.D. or D.O. also concurs with the podiatrist's findings as to the severity of the peripheral involvement indicated.

Services ordinarily considered routine might also be covered if they are performed as a necessary and integral part of otherwise covered services, such as diagnosis and treatment of diabetic ulcers, wounds, and infections.

G. Application of Foot Care Exclusions to Physician's Services

The exclusion of foot care is determined by the nature of the service. Thus, payment for an excluded service should be denied whether performed by a podiatrist, osteopath, or a doctor of medicine, and without regard to the difficulty or complexity of the procedure.

When an itemized bill shows both covered services and noncovered services not integrally related to the covered service, the portion of charges attributable to the noncovered services should be denied. (For example, if an itemized bill shows surgery for an ingrown toenail and also removal of calluses not necessary for the performance of toe surgery, any additional charge attributable to removal of the calluses should be denied.)

In reviewing claims involving foot care, the carrier should be alert to the following exceptional situations:

1. Payment may be made for incidental noncovered services performed as a necessary and integral part of, and secondary to, a covered procedure. For example, if trimming of toenails is required for application of a cast to a fractured foot, the carrier need not allocate and deny a portion of the charge for the trimming of the nails. However, a separately itemized charge for such excluded service should be disallowed. When the primary procedure is covered the administration of anesthesia necessary for the performance of such procedure is also covered.
2. Payment may be made for initial diagnostic services performed in connection with a specific symptom or complaint if it seems likely that its treatment would be covered even though the resulting diagnosis may be one requiring only noncovered care.

The name of the M.D. or D.O. who diagnosed the complicating condition must be submitted with the claim. In those cases, where active care is required, the approximate date the beneficiary was last seen by such physician must also be indicated.

NOTE: Section 939 of P.L. 96-499 removed "warts" from the routine foot care exclusion effective July 1, 1981.

Relatively few claims for routine-type care are anticipated considering the severity of conditions contemplated as the basis for this exception. Claims for this type of foot care should not be paid in the absence of convincing evidence that nonprofessional performance of the service would have been hazardous for the beneficiary because of an underlying systemic disease. The mere statement of a diagnosis such as those mentioned in Sec.D above does not of itself indicate the severity of the condition. Where development is indicated to verify diagnosis and/or severity the carrier should follow existing claims processing practices which may include review of carrier's history and medical consultation as well as physician contacts.

The rules in Sec.290.F concerning presumption of coverage also apply.

Codes and policies for routine foot care and supportive devices for the feet are not exclusively for the use of podiatrists. These codes must be used to report foot care services regardless of the specialty of the physician who furnishes the services. Carriers must instruct physicians to use the most appropriate code available when billing for routine foot care.

100-2, 15, 300

Diabetes Self-Management Training Services

Section 4105 of the Balanced Budget Act of 1997 permits Medicare coverage of diabetes self-management training (DSMT) services when these services are furnished by a certified provider who meets certain quality standards. This program is intended to educate beneficiaries in the successful self-management of diabetes. The program includes instructions in self-monitoring of blood glucose; education about diet and exercise; an insulin treatment plan developed specifically for the patient who is insulin-dependent; and motivation for patients to use the skills for self-management.

Diabetes self-management training services may be covered by Medicare only if the treating physician or treating qualified non-physician practitioner who is managing the beneficiary's diabetic condition certifies that such services are needed. The referring physician or qualified non-physician practitioner must maintain the plan of care in the beneficiary's medical record and documentation substantiating the need for training on an individual basis when group training is typically covered, if so ordered. The order must also include a statement signed by the physician that the service is needed as well as the following:

- The number of initial or follow-up hours ordered (the physician can order less than 10 hours of training);
- The topics to be covered in training (initial training hours can be used for the full initial training program or specific areas such as nutrition or insulin training); and
- A determination that the beneficiary should receive individual or group training.

The provider of the service must maintain documentation in a file that includes the original order from the physician and any special conditions noted by the physician.

When the training under the order is changed, the training order/referral must be signed by the physician or qualified non-physician practitioner treating the beneficiary and maintained in the beneficiary's file in the DSMT's program records.

NOTE: All entities billing for DSMT under the fee-for-service payment system or other payment systems must meet all national coverage requirements.

100-2, 15, 300.2

Certified Providers

A designated certified provider bills for DSMT provided by an accredited DSMT program. Certified providers must submit a copy of their accreditation certificate to the contractor. The statute states that a "certified provider" is a physician or other individual or entity designated by the Secretary that, in addition to providing outpatient self-management training services, provides other items and services for which payment may be made under title XVIII, and meets certain quality standards. The CMS is designating all providers and suppliers that bill Medicare for other individual services such as hospital outpatient departments, renal dialysis facilities, physicians and durable medical equipment suppliers as certified. All suppliers/providers who may bill for other Medicare services or items and who represent a DSMT program that is accredited as meeting quality standards can bill and receive payment for the entire DSMT program. Registered dietitians are eligible to bill on behalf of an entire DSMT program on or after January 1, 2002, as long as the provider has obtained a Medicare provider number. A dietitian may not be the sole provider of the DSMT service. There is an exception for rural areas. In a rural area, an individual who is qualified as a registered dietitian and as a certified diabetic educator who is currently certified by an organization approved by CMS may furnish training and is deemed to meet the multidisciplinary team requirement.

The CMS will not reimburse services on a fee-for-service basis rendered to a beneficiary under Part A.

NOTE: While separate payment is not made for this service to Rural Health Clinics (RHCs), the service is covered but is considered included in the all-inclusive encounter rate. Effective January 1, 2006, payment for DSMT provided in a Federally Qualified Health Clinic (FQHC) that meets all of the requirements identified in Pub. 100-04, chapter 18, section 120 may be made in addition to one other visit the beneficiary had during the same day.

All DSMT programs must be accredited as meeting quality standards by a CMS approved national accreditation organization. Currently, CMS recognizes the American Diabetes Association, American Association of Diabetes Educators and the Indian Health Service as approved national accreditation organizations. Programs without accreditation by a CMS-approved national accreditation organization are not covered. Certified providers may be asked to submit updated accreditation documents at any time or to submit outcome data to an organization designated by CMS.

Enrollment of DMEPOS Suppliers
The DMEPOS suppliers are reimbursed for diabetes training through local carriers. In order to file claims for DSMT, a DMEPOS supplier must be enrolled in the Medicare program with the National Supplier Clearinghouse (NSC). The supplier must also meet the quality standards of a CMS-approved national accreditation organization as stated above. DMEPOS suppliers must obtain a provider number from the local carrier in order to bill for DSMT.

The carrier requires a completed Form CMS-855, along with an accreditation certificate as part of the provider application process. After it has been determined that the quality standards are met, a billing number is assigned to the supplier. Once a supplier has received a provider identification (PIN) number, the supplier can begin receiving reimbursement for this service.

Carriers should contact the National Supplier Clearinghouse (NSC) according to the instruction in Pub 100-08, the Medicare Program Integrity Manual, Chapter 10, "Healthcare Provider/Supplier Enrollment," to verify an applicant is currently enrolled and eligible to receive direct payment from the Medicare program.

The applicant is assigned specialty 87.

Any DMEPOS supplier that has its billing privileges deactivated or revoked by the NSC will also have the billing number deactivated by the carrier.

100-2, 15, 300.3

Frequency of Training

A - Initial Training
The initial year for DSMT is the 12 month period following the initial date.

Medicare will cover initial training that meets the following conditions:

- Is furnished to a beneficiary who has not previously received initial or follow-up training under HCPCS codes G0108 or G0109;
- Is furnished within a continuous 12-month period;
- Does not exceed a total of 10 hours* (the 10 hours of training can be done in any combination of 1/2 hour increments);
- With the exception of 1 hour of individual training, training is usually furnished in a group setting, which can contain other patients besides Medicare beneficiaries, and;
- One hour of individual training may be used for any part of the training including insulin training.

* When a claim contains a DSMT HCPCS code and the associated units cause the total time for the DSMT initial year to exceed '10' hours, a CWF error will set.

B - Follow-Up Training
Medicare covers follow-up training under the following conditions:

- No more than 2 hours individual or group training per beneficiary per year;
- Group training consists of 2 to 20 individuals who need not all be Medicare beneficiaries;
- Follow-up training for subsequent years is based on a 12 month calendar after completion of the full 10 hours of initial training;
- Follow-up training is furnished in increments of no less than one-half hour*; and
- The physician (or qualified non-physician practitioner) treating the beneficiary must document in the beneficiary's medical record that the beneficiary is a diabetic.

*When a claim contains a DSMT HCPCS code and the associated units cause the total time for any follow-up year to exceed 2 hours, a CWF error will set.

100-2, 15, 300.4

Coverage Requirements for Individual Training

Medicare covers training on an individual basis for a Medicare beneficiary under any of the following conditions:

- No group session is available within 2 months of the date the training is ordered;
- The beneficiary's physician (or qualified non-physician practitioner) documents in the beneficiary's medical record that the beneficiary has special needs resulting from conditions, such as severe vision, hearing or language limitations or other such special conditions as identified by the treating physician or non-physician practitioner, that will hinder effective participation in a group training session; or
- The physician orders additional insulin training.

The need for individual training must be identified by the physician or non-physician practitioner in the referral.

NOTE: If individual training has been provided to a Medicare beneficiary and subsequently the carrier or intermediary determines that training should have been provided in a group, carriers and intermediaries down-code the reimbursement from individual to the group level and provider education would be the appropriate actions instead of denying the service as billed.

100-2, 15, 310

Kidney Disease Patient Education Services

By definition, chronic kidney disease (CKD) is kidney damage for 3 months or longer, regardless of the cause of kidney damage. CKD typically evolves over a long period of time and patients may not have symptoms until significant, possibly irreversible, damage has been done. Complications can develop from kidneys that do not function properly, such as high blood pressure, anemia, and weak bones. When CKD progresses, it may lead to kidney failure, which requires artificial means to perform kidney functions (dialysis) or a kidney transplant to maintain life.

Patients can be classified into 5 stages based on their glomerular filtration rate (GFR, how quickly blood is filtered through the kidneys), with stage I having kidney damage with normal or increased GFR to stage V with kidney failure, also called end-stage renal disease (ESRD). Once patients with CKD are identified, treatment is available to help prevent complications of decreased kidney function, slow the progression of kidney disease, and reduce the risk of other diseases such as heart disease.

Beneficiaries with CKD may benefit from kidney disease education (KDE) interventions due to the large amount of medical information that could affect patient outcomes, including the increasing emphasis on self-care and patients' desire for informed, autonomous decision-making. Pre-dialysis education can help patients achieve better understanding of their illness, dialysis modality options, and may help delay the need for dialysis. Education interventions should be patient-centered, encourage collaboration, offer support to the patient, and be delivered consistently.

Effective for claims with dates of service on and after January 1, 2010, Section 152(b) of the Medicare Improvements for Patients and Providers Act of 2008 (MIPPA) covers KDE services under Medicare Part B. KDE services are designed to provide beneficiaries with Stage IV CKD comprehensive information regarding: the management of comorbidities, including delaying the need for dialysis; prevention of uremic complications; all therapeutic options (each option for renal replacement therapy, dialysis access options, and transplantation); ensuring that the beneficiary has opportunities to actively participate in his/her choice of therapy; and that the services be tailored to meet the beneficiary's needs.

Regulations for KDE services were established at 42 CFR 410.48. Claims processing instructions and billing requirements can be found in Pub. 100-04, Medicare Claims Processing Manual, Chapter 32 - Billing Requirements for Special Services, Section 20.

100-2, 15, 310.1

Beneficiaries Eligible for Coverage

Medicare Part B covers outpatient, face-to-face KDE services for a beneficiary that:

- is diagnosed with Stage IV CKD, using the Modification of Diet in Renal Disease (MDRD) Study formula (severe decrease in GFR, GFR value of 15-29 mL/min/1.73 m2), and
- obtains a referral from the physician managing the beneficiary's kidney condition. The referral should be documented in the beneficiary's medical records.

100-2, 15, 310.2

Qualified Person

Medicare Part B covers KDE services provided by a ‚Äòqualified person,' meaning a: physician (as defined in section 30 of this chapter), physician assistant, nurse practitioner, or clinical nurse specialist (as defined in sections 190, 200, and 210 of this chapter), hospital, critical access hospital (CAH), skilled nursing facility (SNF), comprehensive outpatient rehabilitation facility (CORF), home health agency (HHA), or hospice, if the KDE services are provided in a rural area (using the actual geographic location core based statistical area (CBSA) to identify facilities located in rural areas), or hospital or CAH that is treated as being rural (was reclassified from urban to rural status per 42 CFR 412.103).

NOTE: The "incident to" requirements at section 1861(s)(2)(A) of the Social Security Act (the Act) do not apply to KDE services.

The following providers are not ‚Äòqualified persons' and are excluded from furnishing KDE services:

- A hospital, CAH, SNF, CORF, HHA, or hospice located outside of a rural area (using the actual geographic location CBSA to identify facilities located outside of a rural area), unless the services are furnished by a hospital or CAH that is treated as being in a rural area; and
- Renal dialysis facilities.

100-2, 15, 310.3

Limitations for Coverage

Medicare Part B covers KDE services: Up to six (6) sessions as a beneficiary lifetime maximum. A session is 1 hour. In order to bill for a session, a session must be at least 31 minutes in duration. A session that lasts at least 31 minutes, but less than 1 hour still constitutes 1 session.

On an individual basis or in group settings; if the services are provided in a group setting, a group consists of 2 to 20 individuals who need not all be Medicare beneficiaries.

NOTE: Two HCPCS codes were created for this benefit and one or the other must be present, along with ICD-9-CM code 585.4 (chronic kidney disease, Stage IV (severe)), in order for a claim to be processed and paid correctly. They are: G0420: Face-to-face educational services related to the care of chronic kidney disease; individual, per session, per one hour G0421: Face-to-face educational services related to the care of chronic kidney disease; group, per session, per one hour

100-2, 15, 310.4

Standards for Content

Medicare Part B covers KDE services, provided by a qualified person, which provide comprehensive information regarding:

A. The management of comorbidities, including delaying the need for dialysis, which includes, but is not limited to, the following topics:

- Prevention and treatment of cardiovascular disease,
- Prevention and treatment of diabetes,
- Hypertension management,
- Anemia management,
- Bone disease and disorders of calcium and phosphorus metabolism management,
- Symptomatic neuropathy management, and
- Impairments in functioning and well-being.

B. Prevention of uremic complications, which includes, but is not limited to, the following topics:

- Information on how the kidneys work and what happens when the kidneys fail,
- Understanding if remaining kidney function can be protected, preventing disease progression, and realistic chances of survival,
- Diet and fluid restrictions, and
- Medication review, including how each medication works, possible side effects and minimization of side effects, the importance of compliance, and informed decision making if the patient decides not to take a specific drug.

C. Therapeutic options, treatment modalities and settings, advantages and disadvantages of each treatment option, and how the treatments replace the kidney, including, but not limited to, the following topics: Hemodialysis, both at home and in-facility;

- Peritoneal dialysis (PD), including intermittent PD, continuous ambulatory PD, and continuous cycling PD, both at home and in-facility;
- All dialysis access options for hemodialysis and peritoneal dialysis; and
- Transplantation.

D. Opportunities for beneficiaries to actively participate in the choice of therapy and be tailored to meet the needs of the individual beneficiary involved, which includes, but is not limited to, the following topics: Physical symptoms,

- Impact on family and social life,
- Exercise,
- The right to refuse treatment,
- Impact on work and finances,
- The meaning of test results, and
- Psychological impact.

100-2, 15, 310.5

Outcomes Assessment

Qualified persons that provide KDE services must develop outcomes assessments that are designed to measure beneficiary knowledge about CKD and its treatment. The assessment must be administered to the beneficiary during a KDE session, and be made available to the Centers for Medicare & Medicaid Services (CMS) upon request. The outcomes assessments serve to assist KDE educators and CMS in improving subsequent KDE programs, patient understanding, and assess program effectiveness of:

Preparing the beneficiary to make informed decisions about their healthcare options related to CKD, and

Meeting the communication needs of underserved populations, including persons with disabilities, persons with limited English proficiency, and persons with health literacy needs.

100-2, 16, 10

General Exclusions From Coverage

A3-3150, HO-260, HHA-232, B3-2300

No payment can be made under either the hospital insurance or supplementary medical insurance program for certain items and services, when the following conditions exist:

- Not reasonable and necessary (Sec.20);
- No legal obligation to pay for or provide (Sec.40);
- Paid for by a governmental entity (Sec.50);
- Not provided within United States (Sec.60);
- Resulting from war (Sec.70);
- Personal comfort (Sec.80);
- Routine services and appliances (Sec.90);
- Custodial care (Sec.110);
- Cosmetic surgery (Sec.120);
- Charges by immediate relatives or members of household (Sec.130);
- Dental services (Sec.140);
- Paid or expected to be paid under workers' compensation (Sec.150);
- Nonphysician services provided to a hospital inpatient that were not provided directly or arranged for by the hospital (Sec.170);
- Services Related to and Required as a Result of Services Which are not Covered Under Medicare (Sec.180);
- Excluded foot care services and supportive devices for feet (Sec.30); or
- Excluded investigational devices (See Chapter 14, Sec.30).

100-2, 16, 20

Services Not Reasonable and Necessary

A3-3151, HO-260.1, B3-2303, AB-00-52 - 6/00

Items and services which are not reasonable and necessary for the diagnosis or treatment of illness or injury or to improve the functioning of a malformed body member are not covered, e.g., payment cannot be made for the rental of a special hospital bed to be used by the patient in their home unless it was a reasonable and necessary part of the patient's treatment. See also Sec.80.

A health care item or service for the purpose of causing, or assisting to cause, the death of any individual (assisted suicide) is not covered. This prohibition does not apply to the provision of an item or service for the purpose of alleviating pain or discomfort, even if such use may increase the risk of death, so long as the item or service is not furnished for the specific purpose of causing death.

100-2, 16, 90

Routine Services and Appliances

A3-3157, HO-260.7, B3-2320, R-1797A3 - 5/00

Routine physical checkups; eyeglasses, contact lenses, and eye examinations for the purpose of prescribing, fitting, or changing eyeglasses; eye refractions by whatever practitioner and for whatever purpose performed; hearing aids and examinations for hearing aids; and immunizations are not covered.

The routine physical checkup exclusion applies to (a) examinations performed without relationship to treatment or diagnosis for a specific illness, symptom, complaint, or injury; and

(b) examinations required by third parties such as insurance companies business establishments, or Government agencies.

If the claim is for a diagnostic test or examination performed solely for the purpose of establishing a claim under title IV of Public Law 91-173, "Black Lung Benefits," the service is not covered under Medicare and the claimant should be advised to contact their Social Security office regarding the filing of a claim for reimbursement under the "Black Lung" program.

The exclusions apply to eyeglasses or contact lenses, and eye examinations for the purpose of prescribing, fitting, or changing eyeglasses or contact lenses for refractive errors. The exclusions do not apply to physicians' services (and services incident to a physicians' service) performed in conjunction with an eye disease, as for example, glaucoma or cataracts, or to post-surgical prosthetic lenses which are customarily used during convalescence from eye surgery in which the lens of the eye was removed, or to permanent prosthetic lenses required by an individual lacking the organic lens of the eye whether by surgical removal or congenital disease. Such prosthetic lens is a replacement for an internal body organ - the lens of the eye. (See the Medicare Benefit Policy Manual, Chapter 15, "Covered Medical and Other Health Services," Sec.120). Expenses for all refractive procedures, whether performed by an ophthalmologist (or any other physician) or an optometrist and without regard to the reason for performance of the refraction, are excluded from coverage.

A. Immunizations
Vaccinations or inoculations are excluded as immunizations unless they are either

Directly related to the treatment of an injury or direct exposure to a disease or condition, such as antirabies treatment, tetanus antitoxin or booster vaccine, botulin antitoxin, antivenin sera, or immune globulin. (In the absence of injury or direct exposure, preventive immunization (vaccination or inoculation) against such diseases as smallpox, polio, diphtheria, etc., is not covered.); or

Specifically covered by statute, as described in the Medicare Benefit Policy Manual, Chapter 15, "Covered Medical and Other Health Services," Sec.50.

B. Antigens
Prior to the Omnibus Reconciliation Act of 1980, a physician who prepared an antigen for a patient could not be reimbursed for that service unless the physician also administered the antigen to the patient. Effective January 1, 1981, payment may be made for a reasonable supply of antigens that have been prepared for a particular patient even though they have not been administered to the patient by the same physician who prepared them if:

The antigens are prepared by a physician who is a doctor of medicine or osteopathy, and "The physician who prepared the antigens has examined the patient and has determined a plan of treatment and a dosage regimen.

A reasonable supply of antigens is considered to be not more than a 12-week supply of antigens that has been prepared for a particular patient at any one time. The purpose of the reasonable supply limitation is to assure that the antigens retain their potency and effectiveness over the period in which they are to be administered to the patient. (See the Medicare Benefit Policy Manual, Chapter 15, "Covered Medical and Other Health Services," Sec.50.4.4.2)

100-2, 16, 140

Dental Services Exclusion

A3-3162, HO-260.13, B3-2336

Items and services in connection with the care, treatment, filling, removal, or replacement of teeth, or structures directly supporting the teeth are not covered. Structures directly supporting the teeth mean the periodontium, which includes the gingivae, dentogingival junction, periodontal membrane, cementum, and alveolar process. However, payment may be made for certain other services of a dentist. (See the Medicare Benefit Policy Manual, Chapter 15, "Covered Medical and Other Health Services," Sec.150.)

The hospitalization or nonhospitalization of a patient has no direct bearing on the coverage or exclusion of a given dental procedure.

When an excluded service is the primary procedure involved, it is not covered regardless of its complexity or difficulty. For example, the extraction of an impacted tooth is not covered. Similarly, an alveoplasty (the surgical improvement of the shape and condition of the alveolar process) and a frenectomy are excluded from coverage when either of these procedures is performed in connection with an excluded service, e.g., the preparation of the mouth for dentures. In like manner, the removal of the torus palatinus (a bony protuberance of the hard palate) could be a covered service. However, with rare exception, this surgery is performed in connection with an excluded service, i.e., the preparation of the mouth for dentures. Under such circumstances, reimbursement is not made for this purpose.

The extraction of teeth to prepare the jaw for radiation treatments of neoplastic disease is also covered. This is an exception to the requirement that to be covered, a noncovered procedure or service performed by a dentist must be an incident to and an integral part of a covered procedure or service performed by the dentist. Ordinarily, the dentist extracts the patient's teeth, but another physician, e.g., a radiologist, administers the radiation treatments.

Whether such services as the administration of anesthesia, diagnostic x-rays, and other related procedures are covered depends upon whether the primary procedure being performed by the dentist is covered. Thus, an x-ray taken in connection with the reduction of a fracture of the jaw or facial bone is covered. However, a single x-ray or xray survey taken in connection with the care or treatment of teeth or the periodontium is not covered.

See also the Medicare Benefit Policy Manual, Chapter 1, "Inpatient Hospital Services, Sec.70, and Chapter 15, "Covered Medical and Other Health Services," Sec.150 for additional information on dental services.

100-2, 32, 20.2

Healthcare Common Procedure Coding System (HCPCS) Procedure Codes and Applicable Diagnosis Codes

Effective for services performed on and after January 1, 2010, the following new HCPCS codes have been created for KDE services when provided to patients with stage IV CKD.

G0420: Face-to-face educational services related to the care of chronic kidney disease; individual, per session, per one hour

G0421: Face-to-face educational services related to the care of chronic kidney disease; group, per session, per one hour

The following diagnosis code should be reported when billing for KDE services:

585.4 (chronic kidney disease, Stage IV (severe)).

NOTE: Claims with HCPCS codes G0420 or G0421 and ICD-9 code 585.4 that are billed for KDE services are not allowed on a professional and institutional claim on the same service date.

100-3, 20.21

NCD for Chelation Therapy for Treatment of Atherosclerosis (20.21)

The application of chelation therapy using ethylenediamine-tetra-acetic acid (EDTA) for the treatment and prevention of atherosclerosis is controversial. There is no widely accepted rationale to explain the beneficial effects attributed to this therapy. Its safety is questioned and its clinical effectiveness has never been established by well designed, controlled clinical trials. It is not widely accepted and practiced by American physicians. EDTA chelation therapy for atherosclerosis is considered experimental. For these reasons, EDTA chelation therapy for the treatment or prevention of atherosclerosis is not covered.

Some practitioners refer to this therapy as chemoendarterectomy and may also show a diagnosis other than atherosclerosis, such as arteriosclerosis or calcinosis. Claims employing such variant terms should also be denied under this section.

100-3, 20.22

NCD for Ethylenediamine-Tetra-Acetic (EDTA) Chelation Therapy for Treatment of Atherosclerosis (20.22)

The use of EDTA as a chelating agent to treat atherosclerosis, arteriosclerosis, calcinosis, or similar generalized condition not listed by the FDA as an approved use is not covered. Any such use of EDTA is considered experimental.

100-3, 40.7

NCD for Outpatient Intravenous Insulin Treatment (40.7) (Effective December 23, 2009)

Indications and Limitations of Coverage

B. Nationally Covered Indications
N/A

C. Nationally Non-Covered Indications
Effective for claims with dates of service on and after December 23, 2009, the Centers for Medicare and Medicaid Services (CMS) determines that the evidence is adequate to conclude that OIVIT does not improve health outcomes in Medicare beneficiaries. Therefore, CMS determines that OIVIT is not reasonable and necessary for any indication under section 1862(a)(1)(A) of the Social Security Act. Services comprising an Outpatient Intravenous Insulin Therapy regimen are nationally non-covered under Medicare when furnished pursuant to an OIVIT regimen (see subsection A. above).

D. Other
Individual components of OIVIT may have medical uses in conventional treatment regimens for diabetes and other conditions. Coverage for such other uses may be determined by other local or national Medicare determinations, and do not pertain to OIVIT. For example, see Pub. 100-03, NCD Manual, Section 40.2, Home Blood Glucose Monitors, Section 40.3, Closed-loop Blood Glucose Control Devices (CBGCD), Section 190.20, Blood Glucose Testing, and Section 280.14,

Infusion Pumps, as well as Pub. 100-04, Claims Processing Manual, Chapter 18, Section 90, Diabetics Screening.

(This NCD last reviewed December 2009.)

100-3, 90.1

Pharmacogenomic Testing to Predict Warfarin Responsiveness (Effective August 3, 2009)

A. General

Warfarin sodium is an orally administered anticoagulant drug that is marketed most commonly as Coumadin(R). (The Food and Drug Administration (FDA) approved labeling for Coumadin(R) includes a Black Box Warning dating back to 2007.) Anticoagulant drugs are sometimes referred to as blood thinners by the lay public. Warfarin affects the vitamin K-dependent clotting factors II, VII, IX, and X. Warfarin is thought to interfere with clotting factor synthesis by inhibition of the C1 subunit of the vitamin K epoxide reductase (VKORC1) enzyme complex, thereby reducing the regeneration of vitamin K1 epoxide. The elimination of warfarin is almost entirely by metabolic conversion to inactive metabolites by cytochrome P450 (CYP) enzymes in liver cells. CYP2C9 is the principal cytochrome P450 enzyme that modulates the anticoagulant activity of warfarin. From results of clinical studies, genetic variation in the CYP2C9 and/or VKORC1 genes can, in concert with clinical factors, predict how each individual responds to warfarin

Pharmacogenomics denotes the study of how an individual's genetic makeup, or genotype, affects the body's response to drugs. Pharmacogenomics as a science examines associations among variations in genes with individual responses to a drug or medication. In application, pharmacogenomic results (i.e., information on the patient's genetic variations) can contribute to predicting a patient's response to a given drug: good, bad, or none at all. Pharmacogenomic testing of CYP2C9 or VKORC1 alleles to predict a patient's response to warfarin occurs ideally prior to initiation of the drug. This would be an once-in-a-lifetime test, absent any reason to believe that the patient's personal genetic characteristics would change over time. Although such pharmacogenomic testing would be used to attempt to better approximate the best starting dose of warfarin, it would not eliminate the need for periodic PT/INR testing, a standard diagnostic test for coagulation activity and for assessing how a patient is reacting to a warfarin dose.

Nationally Covered Indications

Effective August 3, 2009, the Centers for Medicare & Medicaid Services (CMS) believes that the available evidence supports that coverage with evidence development (CED) under Sec.1862(a)(1)(E) of the Social Security Act (the Act) is appropriate for pharmacogenomic testing of CYP2C9 or VKORC1 alleles to predict warfarin responsiveness by any method, and is therefore covered only when provided to Medicare beneficiaries who are candidates for anticoagulation therapy with warfarin who:

1. Have not been previously tested for CYP2C9 or VKORC1 alleles; and
2. Have received fewer than five days of warfarin in the anticoagulation regimen for which the testing is ordered; and
3. Are enrolled in a prospective, randomized, controlled clinical study when that study meets the following standards. A clinical study seeking Medicare payment for pharmacogenomic testing of CYP2C9 or VKORC1 alleles to predict warfarin responsiveness provided to the Medicare beneficiary who is a candidate for anticoagulation therapy with warfarin pursuant to CED must address one or more aspects of the following question:

   Prospectively, in Medicare-aged subjects whose warfarin therapy management includes pharmacogenomic testing of CYP2C9 or VKORC1 alleles to predict warfarin response, what is the frequency and severity of the following outcomes, compared to subjects whose warfarin therapy management does not include pharmacogenomic testing?

   Major hemorrhage

   Minor hemorrhage

   Thromboembolism related to the primary indication for anticoagulation

   Other thromboembolic event

   Mortality

   The study must adhere to the following standards of scientific integrity and relevance to the Medicare population:

   a. The principal purpose of the research study is to test whether a particular intervention potentially improves the participants' health outcomes.
   b. The research study is well-supported by available scientific and medical information or it is intended to clarify or establish the health outcomes of interventions already in common clinical use.
   c. The research study does not unjustifiably duplicate existing studies.
   d. The research study design is appropriate to answer the research question being asked in the study.
   e. The research study is sponsored by an organization or individual capable of executing the proposed study successfully.
   f. The research study is in compliance with all applicable Federal regulations concerning the protection of human subjects found in the Code of Federal Regulations (CFR) at 45 CFR Part 46. If a study is regulated by the FDA, it also must be in compliance with 21 CFR Parts 50 and 56.
   g. All aspects of the research study are conducted according to the appropriate standards of scientific integrity.
   h. The research study has a written protocol that clearly addresses, or incorporates by reference, the Medicare standards.
   i. The clinical research study is not designed to exclusively test toxicity or disease pathophysiology in healthy individuals. Trials of all medical technologies measuring therapeutic outcomes as one of the objectives meet this standard only if the disease or condition being studied is life-threatening as defined in 21 CFR Sec. 312.81(a) and the patient has no other viable treatment options.
   j. The clinical research study is registered on the www.ClinicalTrials.gov website by the principal sponsor/investigator prior to the enrollment of the first study subject.
   k. The research study protocol specifies the method and timing of public release of all pre-specified outcomes to be measured including release of outcomes if outcomes are negative or study is terminated early. The results must be made public within 24 months of the end of data collection. If a report is planned to be published in a peer-reviewed journal, then that initial release may be an abstract that meets the requirements of the International Committee of Medical Journal Editors. However, a full report of the outcomes must be made public no later than 3 years after the end of data collection.
   l. The research study protocol must explicitly discuss subpopulations affected by the treatment under investigation, particularly traditionally underrepresented groups in clinical studies, how the inclusion and exclusion criteria affect enrollment of these populations, and a plan for the retention and reporting of said populations on the trial. If the inclusion and exclusion criteria are expected to have a negative effect on the recruitment or retention of underrepresented populations, the protocol must discuss why these criteria are necessary.
   m. The research study protocol explicitly discusses how the results are or are not expected to be generalizable to the Medicare population to infer whether Medicare patients may benefit from the intervention. Separate discussions in the protocol may be necessary for populations eligible for Medicare due to age, disability or Medicaid eligibility. Consistent with section 1142 of the Act, the Agency for Healthcare Research and Quality (AHRQ) supports clinical research studies that CMS determines meet the above-listed standards and address the above-listed research questions.

B. Nationally Non-Covered Indications

The CMS believes that the available evidence does not demonstrate that pharmacogenomic testing of CYP2C9 or VKORC1 alleles to predict warfarin responsiveness improves health outcomes in Medicare beneficiaries outside the context of CED, and is therefore not reasonable and necessary under Sec.1862(a)(1)(A) of the Act.

C. Other

This NCD does not determine coverage to identify CYP2C9 or VKORC1 alleles for other purposes, nor does it determine national coverage to identify other alleles to predict warfarin responsiveness.

(This NCD last reviewed August 2009.)

100-3, 1, 110.22

Autologous Cellular Immunotherapy Treatment (Effective June 30, 2011)

A. General

Prostate cancer is the most common non-cutaneous cancer in men in the United States. In 2009, an estimated 192, 280 new cases of prostate cancer were diagnosed and an estimated 27,360 deaths were reported. The National Cancer Institute states that prostate cancer is predominantly a cancer of older men; the median age at diagnosis is 72 years. Once the patient has castration-resistant, metastatic prostate cancer the median survival is generally less than two years.

In 2010 the Food and Drug Administration (FDA) approved sipuleucel-T (PROVENGE®; APC8015), for patients with castration-resistant, metastatic prostate cancer. The posited mechanism of action, immunotherapy, is different from that of anti-cancer chemotherapy such as docetaxel. This is the first immunotherapy for prostate cancer to receive FDA approval.

The goal of immunotherapy is to stimulate the body's natural defenses (such as the white blood cells called dendritic cells, T-lymphocytes and mononuclear cells) in a specific manner so that they attack and destroy, or at least prevent, the proliferation of cancer cells. Specificity is attained by intentionally exposing a patient's white blood cells to a particular protein (called an antigen) associated with the prostate cancer. This exposure "trains" the white blood cells to target and attack the prostate cancer cells. Clinically, this is expected to result in a decrease in the size and/or number of cancer sites, an increase in the time to cancer progression, and/or an increase in survival of the patient.

Sipuleucel-T differs from other infused anti-cancer therapies. Most such anti-cancer therapies are manufactured and sold by a biopharmaceutical company and then purchased by and dispensed from a pharmacy. In contrast, once the decision is made to treat with sipuleucel-T, a multi-step process is used to produce sipuleucel-T. Sipuleucel-T is made individually for each patient with his own white blood cells. The patient's white blood cells are removed via a procedure called leukapheresis. In a laboratory the white blood cells are exposed to PA2024, which is a molecule created by linking prostatic acid phosphatase (PAP) with granulocyte/macrophage-colony stimulating factor (GM-CSF). PAP is an antigen specifically associated with prostate cancer cells; GM-CSF is a protein that targets a receptor on the surface of white blood cells. Hence, PAP serves to externally manipulate the immunological functioning of the patient's white blood cells while GM-CSF serves to stimulate the white blood cells into action. As noted in the FDA's clinical review, each dose of sipuleucel-T contains a minimum of 40 million treated white blood cells, however there is "high inherent variability" in the yield of sipuleucel-T from leukapheresis to leukapheresis in the same patient as well as from patient to patient. The treated white blood cells are then infused back into the same patient. The FDA-approved dosing regimen is three doses with each dose administered two weeks apart. The total treatment period is four weeks.

Indications and Limitations of Coverage

B. Nationally Covered Indications
Effective for services performed on or after June 30, 2011, The Centers for Medicare and Medicaid Services (CMS) proposes that the evidence is adequate to conclude that the use of autologous cellular immunotherapy treatment - sipuleucel-T; PROVENGE® improves health outcomes for Medicare beneficiaries with asymptomatic or minimally symptomatic metastatic castrate-resistant (hormone refractory) prostate cancer, and thus is reasonable and necessary for this on-label indication under 1862(a)(1)(A) of the Social Security Act.

C. Nationally Non-Covered Indications
N/A

D. Other
Effective for services performed on or after June 30, 2011, coverage of all off-label uses of autologous cellular immunotherapy treatment – sipuleucel-T; PROVENGE® for the treatment of prostate cancer is left to the discretion of the local Medicare Administrative Contractors.

(NCD last reviewed June 2011.)

100-3, 150.11

Thermal Intradiscal Procedures (TIPs)

A. General
Percutaneous thermal intradiscal procedures (TIPs) involve the insertion of a catheter(s)/probe(s) in the spinal disc under fluoroscopic guidance for the purpose of producing or applying heat and/or disruption within the disc to relieve low back pain.

The scope of this national coverage determination on TIPs includes percutaneous intradiscal techniques that employ the use of a radiofrequency energy source or electrothermal energy to apply or create heat and/or disruption within the disc for coagulation and/or decompression of disc material to treat symptomatic patients with annular disruption of a contained herniated disc, to seal annular tears or fissures, or destroy nociceptors for the purpose of relieving pain.

This includes techniques that use single or multiple probe(s)/catheter(s), which utilize a resistance coil or other delivery system technology, are flexible or rigid, and are placed within the nucleus, the nuclear-annular junction, or the annulus. Although not intended to be an all inclusive list, TIPs are commonly identified as intradiscal electrothermal therapy (IDET), intradiscal thermal annuloplasty (IDTA), percutaneous intradiscal radiofrequency thermocoagulation (PIRFT), radiofrequency annuloplasty (RA), intradiscal biacuplasty (IDB), percutaneous (or plasma) disc decompression (PDD) or coblation, or targeted disc decompression (TDD). At times, TIPs are identified or labeled based on the name of the catheter/probe that is used (e.g., SpineCath, discTRODE, SpineWand, Accutherm, or TransDiscal electrodes). Each technique or device has it own protocol for application of the therapy. Percutaneous disc decompression or nucleoplasty procedures that do not utilize a radiofrequency energy source or electrothermal energy (such as the disc decompressor procedure or laser procedure) are not within the scope of this NCD.

B. Nationally Covered Indications
N/A

C. Nationally Non-Covered Indications
Effective for services performed on or after September 29, 2008, the Centers for Medicare and Medicaid Services has determined that TIPs are not reasonable and necessary for the treatment of low back pain. Therefore, TIPs, which include procedures that employ the use of a radiofrequency energy source or electrothermal energy to apply or create heat and/or disruption within the disc for the treatment of low back pain, are noncovered.

D. Other
N/A

(This NCD last reviewed September 2008.)

100-3, 150.12

Collagen Meniscus Implant (Effective May 25, 2010)

A. General
The knee menisci are wedge-shaped, semi-lunar discs of fibrous tissue located in the knee joint between the ends of the femur and the tibia and fibula. There is a lateral and medial meniscus in each knee. It is known now that the menisci provide mechanical support, localized pressure distribution, and lubrication of the knee joint. Initially, meniscal tears were treated with total meniscectomy; however, as knowledge of the function of the menisci and the potential long term effects of total meniscectomy on the knee joint evolved, treatment of symptomatic meniscal tears gravitated to repair of the tear, when possible, or partial meniscectomy.

The collagen meniscus implant (also referred to as collagen scaffold (CS), CMI or MenaflexTM meniscus implant throughout the published literature) is used to fill meniscal defects that result from partial meniscectomy. The collagen meniscus implant is not intended to replace the entire meniscus at it requires a meniscal rim for attachment. The literature describes the placement of the collagen meniscus implant through an arthroscopic procedure with an additional incision for capture of the repair needles and tying of the sutures. After debridement of the damaged meniscus, the implant is trimmed to the size of meniscal defect and sutured into place. The collagen meniscus implant is described as a tissue engineered scaffold to support the generation of new meniscus-like tissue. The collagen meniscus implant is manufactured from bovine collagen and should not be confused with the meniscus transplant which involves the replacement of the meniscus with a transplant meniscus from a cadaver donor. The meniscus transplant is not addressed under this national coverage determination.

B. Nationally Covered Indications
N/A

C. Nationally Non-Covered Indications
Effective for claims with dates of service performed on or after May 25, 2010, the Centers for Medicare & Medicaid Services has determined that the evidence is adequate to conclude that the collagen meniscus implant does not improve health outcomes and, therefore, is not reasonable and necessary for the treatment of meniscal injury/tear under section 1862(a)(1)(A) of the Social Security Act. Thus, the collagen meniscus implant is non-covered by Medicare.

D. Other
N/A

(This NCD last reviewed May 2010.)

100-3, 190.11

NCD for Home Prothrombin Time International Normalized Ratio (INR) Monitoring for Anticoagulation Management (190.11)

A. General
Use of the International Normalized Ratio (INR) or prothrombin time (PT) - standard measurement for reporting the blood's clotting time) - allows physicians to determine the level of anticoagulation in a patient independent of the laboratory reagents used. The INR is the ratio of the patient's PT (extrinsic or tissue-factor dependent coagulation pathway) compared to the mean PT for a group of normal individuals. Maintaining patients within his/her prescribed therapeutic range minimizes adverse events associated with inadequate or excessive anticoagulation such as serious bleeding or thromboembolic events. Patient self-testing and self-management through the use of a home INR monitor may be used to improve the time in therapeutic rate (TTR) for select groups of patients. Increased TTR leads to improved clinical outcomes and reductions in thromboembolic and hemorrhagic events.

Warfarin (also prescribed under other trade names, e.g., Coumadin(R)) is a self-administered, oral anticoagulant (blood thinner) medication that affects the vitamin K- dependent clotting factors II, VII, IX and X. It is widely used for various medical conditions, and has a narrow therapeutic index, meaning it is a drug with less than a 2-fold difference between median lethal dose and median effective dose. For this reason, since October 4, 2006, it falls under the category of a Food and Drug administration (FDA) "black-box" drug whose dosage must be closely monitored to avoid serious complications. A PT/INR monitoring system is a portable testing device that includes a finger-stick and an FDA-cleared meter that measures the time it takes for a person's blood plasma to clot.

B. Nationally Covered Indications

For services furnished on or after March 19, 2008, Medicare will cover the use of home PT/INR monitoring for chronic, oral anticoagulation management for patients with mechanical heart valves, chronic atrial fibrillation, or venous thromboembolism (inclusive of deep venous thrombosis and pulmonary embolism) on warfarin. The monitor and the home testing must be prescribed by a treating physician as provided at 42 CFR 410.32(a), and all of the following requirements must be met:

1. The patient must have been anticoagulated for at least 3 months prior to use of the home INR device; and,
2. The patient must undergo a face-to-face educational program on anticoagulation management and must have demonstrated the correct use of the device prior to its use in the home; and,
3. The patient continues to correctly use the device in the context of the management of the anticoagulation therapy following the initiation of home monitoring; and,
4. Self-testing with the device should not occur more frequently than once a week.

C. Nationally Non-Covered Indications

N/A

D. Other

1. All other indications for home PT/INR monitoring not indicated as nationally covered above remain at local Medicare contractor discretion.
2. This national coverage determination (NCD) is distinct from, and makes no changes to, the PT clinical laboratory NCD at section 190.17 of Publication 100-03 of the NCD Manual.

100-3,190.14

NCD for Human Immunodeficiency Virus (HIV) Testing (Diagnosis) (190.14)

Indications and Limitations of Coverage

Indications

Diagnostic testing to establish HIV infection may be indicated when there is a strong clinical suspicion supported by one or more of the following clinical findings:

The patient has a documented, otherwise unexplained, AIDS-defining or AIDS-associated opportunistic infection.

The patient has another documented sexually transmitted disease which identifies significant risk of exposure to HIV and the potential for an early or subclinical infection.

The patient has documented acute or chronic hepatitis B or C infection that identifies a significant risk of exposure to HIV and the potential for an early or subclinical infection.

The patient has a documented AIDS-defining or AIDS-associated neoplasm.

The patient has a documented AIDS-associated neurologic disorder or otherwise unexplained dementia.

The patient has another documented AIDS-defining clinical condition, or a history of other severe, recurrent, or persistent conditions which suggest an underlying immune deficiency (for example, cutaneous or mucosal disorders).

The patient has otherwise unexplained generalized signs and symptoms suggestive of a chronic process with an underlying immune deficiency (for example, fever, weight loss, malaise, fatigue, chronic diarrhea, failure to thrive, chronic cough, hemoptysis, shortness of breath, or lymphadenopathy).

The patient has otherwise unexplained laboratory evidence of a chronic disease process with an underlying immune deficiency (for example, anemia, leukopenia, pancytopenia, lymphopenia, or low CD4+ lymphocyte count).

The patient has signs and symptoms of acute retroviral syndrome with fever, malaise, lymphadenopathy, and skin rash.

The patient has documented exposure to blood or body fluids known to be capable of transmitting HIV (for example, needlesticks and other significant blood exposures) and antiviral therapy is initiated or anticipated to be initiated.

The patient is undergoing treatment for rape. (HIV testing is a part of the rape treatment protocol.)

Limitations

HIV antibody testing in the United States is usually performed using HIV-1 or HIV-¬¾ combination tests. HIV-2 testing is indicated if clinical circumstances suggest HIV-2 is likely (that is, compatible clinical findings and HIV-1 test negative). HIV-2 testing may also be indicated in areas of the country where there is greater prevalence of HIV-2 infections.

The Western Blot test should be performed only after documentation that the initial EIA tests are repeatedly positive or equivocal on a single sample.

The HIV antigen tests currently have no defined diagnostic usage.

Direct viral RNA detection may be performed in those situations where serologic

testing does not establish a diagnosis but strong clinical suspicion persists (for example, acute retroviral syndrome, nonspecific serologic evidence of HIV, or perinatal HIV infection).

If initial serologic tests confirm an HIV infection, repeat testing is not indicated.

If initial serologic tests are HIV EIA negative and there is no indication for confirmation of infection by viral RNA detection, the interval prior to retesting is 3-6 months.

Testing for evidence of HIV infection using serologic methods may be medically appropriate in situations where there is a risk of exposure to HIV. However, in the absence of a documented AIDS defining or HIV- associated disease, an HIV associated sign or symptom, or documented exposure to a known HIV-infected source, the testing is considered by Medicare to be screening and thus is not covered by Medicare (for example, history of multiple blood component transfusions, exposure to blood or body fluids not resulting in consideration of therapy, history of transplant, history of illicit drug use, multiple sexual partners, same-sex encounters, prostitution, or contact with prostitutes).

The CPT Editorial Panel has issued a number of codes for infectious agent detection by direct antigen or nucleic acid probe techniques that have not yet been developed or are only being used on an investigational basis. Laboratory providers are advised to remain current on FDA-approval status for these tests.

100-3, 210.3

Colorectal Cancer Screening Tests

A. General

Section 4104 of the Balanced Budget Act of 1997 provides for coverage of screening colorectal cancer procedures under Medicare Part B. Medicare currently covers: (1) annual fecal occult blood tests (FOBTs); (2) flexible sigmoidoscopy over 4 years; (3) screening colonoscopy for persons at average risk for colorectal cancer every 10 years, or for persons at high risk for colorectal cancer every 2 years; (4) barium enema every 4 years as an alternative to flexible sigmoidoscopy, or every 2 years as an alternative to colonoscopy for persons at high risk for colorectal cancer; and, (5) other procedures the Secretary finds appropriate based on consultation with appropriate experts and organizations.

Coverage of the above screening examinations was implemented in regulations through a final rule that was published on October 31, 1997 (62 FR 59079), and was effective January 1, 1998. At that time, based on consultation with appropriate experts and organizations, the definition of the term "FOBT" was defined in 42 CFR Sec.410.37(a)(2) of the regulation to mean a "guaiac-based test for peroxidase activity, testing two samples from each of three consecutive stools."

In the 2003 Physician Fee Schedule Final Rule (67 FR 79966) effective March 1, 2003, the Centers for Medicare & Medicaid Services (CMS) amended the FOBT screening test regulation definition to provide that it could include either: (1) a guaiac-based FOBT, or, (2) other tests determined by the Secretary through a national coverage determination.

B. Nationally Covered Indications

Fecal Occult Blood Tests (FOBT) (effective for services performed on or after January 1, 2004)

1. History

   The FOBTs are generally divided into two types: immunoassay and guaiac types. Immunoassay (or immunochemical) fecal occult blood tests (iFOBT) use "antibodies directed against human globin epitopes. While most iFOBTs use spatulas to collect stool samples, some use a brush to collect toilet water surrounding the stool. Most iFOBTs require laboratory processing.

   Guaiac fecal occult blood tests (gFOBT) use a peroxidase reaction to indicate presence of the heme portion of hemoglobin. Guaiac turns blue after oxidation by oxidants or peroxidases in the presence of an oxygen donor such as hydrogen peroxide. Most FOBTs use sticks to collect stool samples and may be developed in a physician's office or a laboratory. In 1998, Medicare began reimbursement for guaiac FOBTs, but not immunoassay type tests for colorectal cancer screening. Since the fundamental process is similar for other iFOBTs, CMS evaluated colorectal cancer screening using immunoassay FOBTs in general.

2. Expanded Coverage

Medicare covers one screening FOBT per annum for the early detection of colorectal cancer. This means that Medicare will cover one guaiac-based (gFOBT) or one immunoassay-based (iFOBT) at a frequency of every 12 months; i.e., at least 11 months have passed following the month in which the last covered screening FOBT was performed, for beneficiaries aged 50 years and older. The beneficiary completes the existing gFOBT by taking samples from two different sites of three consecutive stools; the beneficiary completes the iFOBT by taking the appropriate number of stool samples according to the specific manufacturer's instructions. This screening requires a written order from the beneficiary's attending physician. ("Attending physician means a doctor of medicine or osteopathy (as defined in Sec.1861(r)(1) of the Social Security Act) who is fully knowledgeable about the beneficiary's medical condition, and who would be responsible for using the results of any examination performed in the overall management of the beneficiary's specific medical problem.)

C. Nationally Non-Covered Indications

All other indications for colorectal cancer screening not otherwise specified above remain non-covered. Non-coverage specifically includes:

1. Screening DNA (Deoxyribonucleic acid) stool tests, effective April 28, 2008, and,
2 Screening computed tomographic colonography (CTC), effective May 12, 2009.

D. Other

N/A

(This NCD last reviewed May 2009.)

100-3, 210.7

NCD for Screening for the Human Immunodeficiency Virus (HIV) Infection (210.7)

A. General

Infection with the human immunodeficiency virus (HIV) is a continuing, worldwide pandemic described by the World Health Organization as "the most serious infectious disease challenge to global public health". Acquired immunodeficiency syndrome (AIDS) is diagnosed when a HIV-infected person's immune system becomes severely compromised and/or a person becomes ill with a HIV-related opportunistic infection. Without treatment, AIDS usually develops within 8-10 years after a person's initial HIV infection. While there is presently no cure for HIV, an infected individual can be recognized by screening, and subsequent access to skilled care plus vigilant monitoring and adherence to continuous antiretroviral therapy may delay the onset of AIDS and increase quality of life for many years.

Significantly, more than half of new HIV infections are estimated to be sexually transmitted from infected individuals who are unaware of their HIV status. Consequently, improved secondary disease prevention and wider availability of screening linked to HIV care and treatment would not only delay disease progression and complications in untested or unaware older individuals, but could also decrease the spread of disease to those living with or partnered with HIV-infected individuals.

HIV antibody testing first became available in 1985. These commonly used, Food and Drug Administration (FDA)-approved HIV antibody screening tests – using serum or plasma from a venipuncture or blood draw – are known as EIA (enzyme immunoassay) or ELISA (enzyme-linked immunosorbent assay) tests.

Developed for point-of-care testing using alternative samples, six rapid HIV-1 and/or HIV-2 antibody tests – using fluid obtained from the oral cavity or using whole blood, serum, or plasma from a blood draw or fingerstick – were approved by the FDA from 2002-2006.

Effective January 1, 2009, the Centers for Medicare & Medicaid Services (CMS) is allowed to add coverage of "additional preventive services" through the national coverage determination (NCD) process if certain statutory requirements are met, as provided under section 101(a) of the Medicare Improvements for Patients and Providers Act. One of those requirements is that the service(s) be categorized as a grade A (strongly recommends) or grade B (recommends) rating by the US Preventive Services Task Force (USPSTF). The USPSTF strongly recommends screening for all adolescents and adults at risk for HIV infection, as well as all pregnant women.

B. Nationally Covered Indications

Effective for claims with dates of service on and after December 8, 2009, CMS determines that the evidence is adequate to conclude that screening for HIV infection is reasonable and necessary for early detection of HIV and is appropriate for individuals entitled to benefits under

Part A or enrolled under Part B. Therefore, CMS proposes to cover both standard and FDA-approved HIV rapid screening tests for:

1. A maximum of one, annual voluntary HIV screening of Medicare beneficiaries at increased risk for HIV infection per USPSTF guidelines as follows:
   - Men who have had sex with men after 1975
   - Men and women having unprotected sex with multiple [more than one] partners
   - Past or present injection drug users
   - Men and women who exchange sex for money or drugs, or have sex partners who do
   - Individuals whose past or present sex partners were HIV-infected, bisexual or injection drug users
   - Persons being treated for sexually transmitted diseases
   - Persons with a history of blood transfusion between 1978 and 1985
   - Persons who request an HIV test despite reporting no individual risk factors, since this group is likely to include individuals not willing to disclose high-risk behaviors; and,
2. A maximum of three, voluntary HIV screenings of pregnant Medicare beneficiaries: (1) when the diagnosis of pregnancy is known, (2) during the third trimester, and (3) at labor, if ordered by the woman's clinician.

C. Nationally Non-Covered Indications

Effective for claims with dates of service on and after December 8, 2009, Medicare beneficiaries with any known diagnosis of a HIV-related illness are not eligible for this screening test.

Medicare beneficiaries (other than those who are pregnant) who have had a prior HIV screening test within one year are not eligible (11 full months must have elapsed following the month in which the previous test was performed in order for the subsequent test to be covered).

Pregnant Medicare beneficiaries who have had three screening tests within their respective term of pregnancy are not eligible (beginning with the date of the first test).

D. Other

N/A

(This NCD last reviewed November 2009.)

100-3, 220.6

NCD for Positron Emission Tomography (PET) Scans (220.6)

Item/Service Description

Positron Emission Tomography (PET) is a minimally invasive diagnostic imaging procedure used to evaluate metabolism in normal tissue as well as in diseased tissues in conditions such as cancer, ischemic heart disease, and some neurologic disorders. A radiopharmaceutical is injected into the patient that gives off sub-atomic particles, known as positrons, as it decays. PET uses a positron camera (tomograph) to measure the decay of the radiopharmaceutical. The rate of decay provides biochemical information on the metabolism of the tissue being studied.

(This NCD last reviewed March 2009.)

100-3, 220.6.1

NCD for PET for Perfusion of the Heart (220.6.1)

Indications and Limitations of Coverage

1. Rubidium 82 (Effective March 14, 1995)

   Effective for services performed on or after March 14, 1995, PET scans performed at rest or with pharmacological stress used for noninvasive imaging of the perfusion of the heart for the diagnosis and management of patients with known or suspected coronary artery disease using the FDA-approved radiopharmaceutical Rubidium 82 (Rb 82) are covered, provided the requirements below are met:

   The PET scan, whether at rest alone, or rest with stress, is performed in place of, but not in addition to, a single photon emission computed tomography (SPECT); or

   The PET scan, whether at rest alone or rest with stress, is used following a SPECT that was found to be inconclusive. In these cases, the PET scan must have been considered necessary in order to determine what medical or surgical intervention is required to treat the patient. (For purposes of this requirement, an inconclusive test is a test(s) whose results are equivocal, technically uninterpretable, or discordant with a patient's other clinical data and must be documented in the beneficiary's file.)

   For any PET scan for which Medicare payment is claimed for dates of services prior to July 1, 2001, the claimant must submit additional specified information on the claim form (including proper codes and/or modifiers), to indicate the results of the PET scan. The claimant must also include information on whether the PET scan was performed after an inconclusive noninvasive cardiac test. The information submitted with respect to the previous noninvasive cardiac test must specify the type of test performed prior to the PET scan and whether it was inconclusive or unsatisfactory. These explanations are in the form of special G codes used for billing PET scans using Rb 82. Beginning July 1, 2001, claims should be submitted with the appropriate codes.
2. Ammonia N-13 (Effective October 1, 2003)

   Effective for services performed on or after October 1, 2003, PET scans performed at rest or with pharmacological stress used for noninvasive imaging of the perfusion of the heart for the diagnosis and management of patients with known or suspected coronary artery disease using the FDA-approved radiopharmaceutical ammonia N-13 are covered, provided the requirements below are met:

The PET scan, whether at rest alone, or rest with stress, is performed in place of, but not in addition to, a SPECT; or

The PET scan, whether at rest alone or rest with stress, is used following a SPECT that was found to be inconclusive. In these cases, the PET scan must have been considered necessary in order to determine what medical or surgical intervention is required to treat the patient. (For purposes of this requirement, an inconclusive test is a test whose results are equivocal, technically uninterpretable, or discordant with a patient's other clinical data and must be documented in the beneficiary's file.)

(This NCD last reviewed March 2005.)

100-3, 220.6.2

NCD for PET (FDG) for Lung Cancer (220.6.2)

220.6.2 - FDG PET for Lung Cancer (Replaced with Section 220.6.17)

100-3, 220.6.3

NCD for PET (FDG) for Esophageal Cancer (220.6.3)

220.6.3 - FDG PET for Esophageal Cancer (Replaced with Section 220.6.17)

100-3, 220.6.4

NCD for PET (FDG) for Colorectal Cancer (220.6.4)

220.6.4 - FDG PET for Colorectal Cancer (Replaced with Section 220.6.17

100-3, 220.6.5

NCD for PET (FDG) for Lymphoma (220.6.5)

220.6.5 - FDG PET for Lymphoma (Replaced with Section 220.6.17)

100-3, 220.6.6

NCD for PET (FDG) for Melanoma (220.6.6)

220.6.6 - FDG PET for Melanoma (Replaced with Section 220.6.17)

100-3, 220.6.7

NCD for PET (FDG) for Head and Neck Cancers (220.6.7)

220.6.7 - FDG PET for Head and Neck Cancers (Replaced with Section 220.6.17)

100-3, 220.6.9

NCD for PET (FDG) for Refractory Seizures (220.6.9)

Beginning July 1, 2001, Medicare covers FDG PET for pre-surgical evaluation for the purpose of localization of a focus of refractory seizure activity.

Limitations: Covered only for pre-surgical evaluation.

Documentation that these conditions are met should be maintained by the referring physician in the beneficiary's medical record, as is normal business practice.

(This NCD last reviewed June 2001.)

100-3, 220.6.10

NCD for PET (FDG) for Breast Cancer (220.6.10)

220.6.10 - FDG PET for Breast Cancer (Effective October 1, 2002) (Replaced with Section 220.6.17)

100-3, 220.6.11

NCD for PET (FDG) for Thyroid Cancer (220.6.11)

220.6.11 - FDG PET for Thyroid Cancer (Various Effective Dates Below) (Replaced with Section 220.6.17)

100-3, 220.6.12

NCD for PET (FDG) for Soft Tissue Sarcoma (220.6.12)

220.6.12 - FDG PET for Soft Tissue Sarcoma (Various Effective Dates Below) (Replaced with Section 220.6.17)

100-3, 220.6.13

NCD for PET (FDG) for Dementia and Neurodegenerative Diseases (220.6.13)

A. General

Medicare covers FDG PET scans for either the differential diagnosis of fronto-temporal dementia (FTD) and Alzheimer's disease (AD) under specific requirements; OR, its use in a Centers for Medicare & Medicaid Services (CMS)-approved practical clinical trial focused on the utility of FDG PET in the diagnosis or treatment of dementing neurodegenerative diseases. Specific requirements for each indication are clarified below:

B. Nationally Covered Indications

1. FDG PET Requirements for Coverage in the Differential Diagnosis of AD and FTD

   An FDG PET scan is considered reasonable and necessary in patients with a recent diagnosis of dementia and documented cognitive decline of at least 6 months, who meet diagnostic criteria for both AD and FTD. These patients have been evaluated for specific alternate neurodegenerative diseases or other causative factors, but the cause of the clinical symptoms remains uncertain.

   The following additional conditions must be met before an FDG PET scan will be covered:

   a. The patient's onset, clinical presentation, or course of cognitive impairment is such that FTD is suspected as an alternative neurodegenerative cause of the cognitive decline. Specifically, symptoms such as social disinhibition, awkwardness, difficulties with language, or loss of executive function are more prominent early in the course of FTD than the memory loss typical of AD;

   b. The patient has had a comprehensive clinical evaluation (as defined by the American Academy of Neurology (AAN)) encompassing a medical history from the patient and a well-acquainted informant (including assessment of activities of daily living), physical and mental status examination (including formal documentation of cognitive decline occurring over at least 6 months) aided by cognitive scales or neuropsychological testing, laboratory tests, and structural imaging such as magnetic resonance imaging (MRI) or computed tomography (CT);

   c. The evaluation of the patient has been conducted by a physician experienced in the diagnosis and assessment of dementia;

   d. The evaluation of the patient did not clearly determine a specific neurodegenerative disease or other cause for the clinical symptoms, and information available through FDG PET is reasonably expected to help clarify the diagnosis between FTD and AD and help guide future treatment;

   e. The FDG PET scan is performed in a facility that has all the accreditation necessary to operate nuclear medicine equipment. The reading of the scan should be done by an expert in nuclear medicine, radiology, neurology, or psychiatry, with experience interpreting such scans in the presence of dementia;

   f. A brain single photon emission computed tomography (SPECT) or FDG PET scan has not been obtained for the same indication. (The indication can be considered to be different in patients who exhibit important changes in scope or severity of cognitive decline, and meet all other qualifying criteria listed above and below (including the judgment that the likely diagnosis remains uncertain). The results of a prior SPECT or

   FDG PET scan must have been inconclusive or, in the case of SPECT, difficult to interpret due to immature or inadequate technology. In these instances, an FDG PET scan may be covered after 1 year has passed from the time the first SPECT or FDG PET scan was performed.)

   g. The referring and billing provider(s) have documented the appropriate evaluation of the Medicare beneficiary. Providers should establish the medical necessity of an FDG PET scan by ensuring that the following information has been collected and is maintained in the beneficiary medical record:

      - Date of onset of symptoms;
      - Diagnosis of clinical syndrome (normal aging; mild cognitive impairment (MCI); mild, moderate or severe dementia);
      - Mini mental status exam (MMSE) or similar test score;
      - Presumptive cause (possible, probable, uncertain AD);
      - Any neuropsychological testing performed;
      - Results of any structural imaging (MRI or CT) performed;
      - Relevant laboratory tests (B12, thyroid hormone); and,
      - Number and name of prescribed medications.

   The billing provider must furnish a copy of the FDG PET scan result for use by CMS and its contractors upon request. These verification requirements are consistent with federal requirements set forth in 42 Code of Federal Regulations section 410.32 generally for diagnostic x-ray tests, diagnostic laboratory tests, and other tests. In summary, section 410.32 requires the billing physician and the referring physician to maintain information in the medical record of each patient to demonstrate medical necessity [410.32(d) (2)] and submit the information demonstrating medical necessity to CMS and/or its agents upon request [410.32(d)(3)(I)] (OMB number 0938-0685).

2. FDG PET Requirements for Coverage in the Context of a CMS-approved Practical Clinical Trial Utilizing a Specific Protocol to Demonstrate the Utility of FDG PET in the Diagnosis, and

Treatment of Neurodegenerative Dementing Diseases An FDG PET scan is considered reasonable and necessary in patients with MCI or early dementia (in clinical circumstances other than those specified in subparagraph 1) only in the context of an approved clinical trial that contains patient safeguards and protections to ensure proper administration, use and evaluation of the FDG PET scan.

The clinical trial must compare patients who do and do not receive an FDG PET scan and have as its goal to monitor, evaluate, and improve clinical outcomes. In addition, it must meet the following basic criteria:

a. Written protocol on file;

b. Institutional Review Board review and approval;

c. Scientific review and approval by two or more qualified individuals who are not part of the research team; and,

d. Certification that investigators have not been disqualified.

C. Nationally Non-Covered Indications
All other uses of FDG PET for patients with a presumptive diagnosis of dementia-causing neurodegenerative disease (e.g., possible or probable AD, clinically typical FTD, dementia of Lewy bodies, or Creutzfeld-Jacob disease) for which CMS has not specifically indicated coverage continue to be non-covered.

D. Other
Not applicable.

(This NCD last reviewed September 2004.)

100-3, 220.6.14

NCD for PET (FDG) for Brain, Cervical, Ovarian, Pancreatic, Small Cell Lung, and Testicular Cancers (220.6.14)

See section 220.6.17

100-3, 220.6.17

Positron Emission Tomography (PET) (FDG) for Oncologic Conditions - (Various Effective Dates)

General
The Centers for Medicare and Medicaid Services (CMS) was asked to reconsider section 220.6, of the National Coverage Determinations (NCD) Manual, to end the prospective data collection requirements across all oncologic indications of FDG PET except for monitoring response to treatment. Section 220.6 of the NCD Manual, establishes the requirement for prospective data collection for FDG PET used in the diagnosis, staging, restaging, and monitoring response to treatment for brain, cervical, ovarian, pancreatic, small cell lung and testicular cancers, as well as for cancer indications not previously specified in section 220.6 in its entirety.

The CMS received public input indicating that the current coverage framework, which required cancer-by-cancer consideration of diagnosis, staging, restaging, and monitoring response to treatment should be replaced by a more omnibus consideration. Thus, CMS broadened the scope of this review through an announcement on the Web site and solicited additional public comment on the use of FDG PET imaging for solid tumors so that it could transparently consider this possibility.

1. Framework

   Effective for claims with dates of service on and after April 3, 2009, CMS is adopting a coverage framework that replaces the four-part diagnosis, staging, restaging and monitoring response to treatment categories with a two-part framework that differentiates FDG PET imaging used to inform the initial antitumor treatment strategy from other uses related to guiding subsequent antitumor treatment strategies after the completion of initial treatment. CMS is making this change for all NCDs that address coverage of FDG PET for the specific oncologic conditions addressed in this decision.

2. Initial Anti-tumor Treatment Strategy

   Effective for claims with dates of service on and after April 3, 2009, CMS has determined that the evidence is adequate to determine that the results of FDG PET imaging are useful in determining the appropriate initial treatment strategy for beneficiaries with suspected solid tumors and myeloma and improve health outcomes and thus are reasonable and necessary under Sec.1862(a)(1)(A) of the Social Security Act (the Act).

   Therefore, CMS will cover only one FDG PET study for beneficiaries who have solid tumors that are biopsy proven or strongly suspected based on other diagnostic testing when the beneficiary's treating physician determines that the FDG PET study is needed to determine the location and/or extent of the tumor for the following therapeutic purposes related to the initial treatment strategy:

   - To determine whether or not the beneficiary is an appropriate candidate for an invasive diagnostic or therapeutic procedure; or
   - To determine the optimal anatomic location for an invasive procedure; or
   - To determine the anatomic extent of tumor when the recommended anti-tumor treatment reasonably depends on the extent of the tumor.

   As exceptions to the April 3, 2009, initial treatment strategy section above:

   a. The CMS has reviewed evidence on the use of FDG PET imaging to determine initial anti-tumor treatment in patients with adenocarcinoma of the prostate. CMS has determined that the available evidence does not demonstrate that FDG PET imaging improves physician decision making in the determination of initial anti-tumor treatment strategy in Medicare beneficiaries who have adenocarcinoma of the prostate, does not improve health outcomes and is thus not reasonable and necessary under Sec.1862(a)(1)(A) of the Act. Therefore, FDG PET is nationally non-covered for this indication of this tumor type.

   b. The CMS received no new evidence demonstrating a change was warranted with respect to the use of FDG PET imaging to determine initial anti-tumor treatment in breast cancer; thus CMS is not making any change to the current coverage policy for FDG PET in breast cancer. CMS is continuing to cover FDG PET imaging for the initial treatment strategy for male and female breast cancer only when used in staging distant metastasis. FDG PET imaging for diagnosis and initial staging of axillary nodes will remain non-covered.

   c. The CMS received no new evidence demonstrating a change was warranted with respect to use of FDG PET imaging of regional lymph nodes in melanoma; thus CMS is not changing the current NCD for FDG PET in melanoma. CMS will continue non-coverage of FDG PET for the evaluation of regional lymph nodes in melanoma. Other uses to determine initial treatment strategy remain covered.

   d. The CMS received no new evidence demonstrating a change was warranted with respect to use of FDG PET imaging in the initial treatment strategy for cervical cancer. CMS is continuing to cover FDG PET imaging as an adjunct test for the detection of pre-treatment metastasis (i.e., staging) in newly diagnosed cervical cancers following conventional imaging that is negative for extra-pelvic metastasis. All other uses of FDG PET for the initial treatment strategy for beneficiaries diagnosed with cervical cancer will continue to only be covered as research under Sec.1862(a)(1)(E) of the Act through Coverage with Evidence Development (CED). Therefore, CMS will cover one initial FDG PET study for newly diagnosed cervical cancer when not used as an adjunct test for the detection of pre-treatment metastases following conventional imaging that is negative for extra-pelvic metastasis only when the beneficiary's treating physician determines that the FDG PET study is needed to inform the initial anti-tumor treatment strategy and the beneficiary is enrolled in, and the FDG PET provider is participating in, the specific type of prospective clinical study outlined under subsequent treatment strategy below.

   e. Effective November 10, 2009, as a result of a reconsideration request, CMS ended the prospective data collection requirements, or coverage with evidence development, for the use of FDG PET imaging in the initial staging of cervical cancer related to initial treatment strategy.

   CMS is continuing to cover FDG PET imaging as an adjunct test for the detection of pre-treatment metastasis (i.e., staging) in newly diagnosed cervical cancers following conventional imaging that is negative for extra-pelvic metastasis.

   Therefore, CMS will cover one initial FDG PET study for staging in beneficiaries who have biopsy-proven cervical cancer when the beneficiary's treating physician determines that the FDG PET study is needed to determine the location and/or extent of the tumor for the following therapeutic purposes related to initial treatment strategy:

   - To determine whether or not the beneficiary is an appropriate candidate for an invasive diagnostic or therapeutic procedure; or
   - To determine the optimal anatomic location for an invasive procedure; or
   - To determine the anatomic extent of the tumor when the recommended anti-tumor treatment reasonably depends on the extent of the tumor.

   Additionally, effective November 10, 2009, following a reconsideration request, CMS determines that there is no credible evidence that the results of FDG PET imaging are useful to make the initial diagnoses of cervical cancer, does not improve health outcomes, and is not reasonable and necessary under section 1862(a)(1)(A) of the Social Security Act. Therefore, CMS will non-cover FDG PET imaging for initial diagnosis of cervical cancer related to initial treatment strategy.

3. Subsequent Anti-tumor Treatment Strategy

   As part of its April 3, 2009, NCD, the CMS reviewed evidence on the use of FDG PET in the subsequent treatment strategy for patients with tumor types other than those seven indications currently covered without exception (breast, colorectal, esophagus, head and neck (non-CNS/thyroid), lymphoma, melanoma, and non-small cell lung).

As a result, CMS determined that the available evidence is adequate to determine that FDG PET imaging also improves physician decision making in the determination of subsequent treatment strategy in Medicare beneficiaries who have ovarian cancer, cervical cancer, and myeloma, improves health outcomes, and is thus reasonable and necessary under Sec.1862(a)(1)(A) of the Act.

Therefore, effective for claims with dates of service on and after April 3, 2009, for tumor types other than breast, colorectal, esophagus, head and neck (non-CNS/thyroid), lymphoma, melanoma, non-small cell lung, ovarian, cervical, and myeloma, CMS has determined that the available evidence is not adequate to determine that FDG PET imaging improves physician decision making in the determination of subsequent anti-tumor treatment strategy or improves health outcomes in Medicare beneficiaries and thus is not reasonable and necessary under Sec.1862(a)(1)(A) of the Act.

However, CMS has determined that the available evidence is sufficient to determine that FDG PET imaging for subsequent anti-tumor treatment strategy for all other tumor types other than the 10 indications noted above may be covered as research under Sec.1862(a)(1)(E) of the Act through CED. Therefore, CMS will cover a subsequent FDG PET study for all other tumor types other than the 10 indications noted above, when the beneficiary's treating physician determines that the FDG PET study is needed to inform the subsequent anti-tumor treatment strategy and the beneficiary is enrolled in, and the FDG PET provider is participating in, the following type of prospective clinical study:

An FDG PET clinical study that is designed to collect additional information at the time of the scan to assist in patient management. Qualifying clinical studies must ensure that specific hypotheses are addressed; appropriate data elements are collected; hospitals and providers are qualified to provide the FDG PET scan and interpret the results; participating hospitals and providers accurately report data on all enrolled patients not included in other qualifying trials through adequate auditing mechanisms; and all patient confidentiality, privacy, and other Federal laws must be followed.

The clinical studies for which CMS will provide coverage must answer one or more of the following three questions:

Prospectively, in Medicare beneficiaries whose treating physician determines that the FDG PET study is needed to inform the subsequent anti-tumor treatment strategy, does the addition of FDG PET imaging lead to:

- A change in the likelihood of appropriate referrals for palliative care;
- Improved quality of life; or,
- Improved survival?

The study must adhere to the following standards of scientific integrity and relevance to the Medicare population:

a. The principal purpose of the research study is to test whether a particular intervention potentially improves the participants' health outcomes.

b. The research study is well-supported by available scientific and medical information or it is intended to clarify or establish the health outcomes of interventions already in common clinical use.

c. The research study does not unjustifiably duplicate existing studies.

d. The research study design is appropriate to answer the research question being asked in the study.

e. The research study is sponsored by an organization or individual capable of executing the proposed study successfully.

f. The research study is in compliance with all applicable Federal regulations concerning the protection of human subjects found in the Code of Federal Regulations (CFR) at 45 CFR Part 46.

If a study is regulated by the Food and Drug Administration (FDA), it also must be in compliance with 21 CFR Parts 50 and 56.

g. All aspects of the research study are conducted according to the appropriate standards of scientific integrity.

h. The research study has a written protocol that clearly addresses, or incorporates by reference, the Medicare standards.

i. The clinical research study is not designed to exclusively test toxicity or disease pathophysiology in healthy individuals. Trials of all medical technologies measuring therapeutic outcomes as one of the objectives meet this standard only if the disease or condition being studied is life-threatening as defined in 21 CFR 312.81(a) and the patient has no other viable treatment options.

j. The clinical research study is registered on the www.ClinicalTrials.gov Web site by the principal sponsor/investigator prior to the enrollment of the first study subject.

k. The research study protocol specifies the method and timing of public release of all pre-specified outcomes to be measured including release of outcomes if outcomes are negative or study is terminated early. The results must be made public within 24 months of the end of data collection. If a report is planned to be published in a peer-reviewed journal, then that initial release may be an abstract that meets the requirements of the International Committee of Medical Journal Editors. However, a full report of the outcomes must be made public no later than 3 years after the end of data collection.

l. The research study protocol must explicitly discuss subpopulations affected by the treatment under investigation, particularly traditionally underrepresented groups in clinical studies, how the inclusion and exclusion criteria affect enrollment of these populations, and a plan for the retention and reporting of said populations on the trial. If the inclusion and exclusion criteria are expected to have a negative effect on the recruitment or retention of underrepresented populations, the protocol must discuss why these criteria are necessary.

m. The research study protocol explicitly discusses how the results are or are not expected to be generalizable to the Medicare population to infer whether Medicare patients may benefit from the intervention. Separate discussions in the protocol may be necessary for populations eligible for Medicare due to age, disability or Medicaid eligibility.

Consistent with section 1142 of the Act, the Agency for Healthcare Research and Quality (AHRQ) supports clinical research studies that CMS determines meet the above-listed standards and address the above-listed research questions.

4. Synopsis of New Framework

Effective for claims with dates of service on and after April 3, 2009, the CMS transitioned the prior framework-diagnosis, staging, restaging, and monitoring response to treatment-into the initial treatment strategy and subsequent treatment strategy framework. The chart below summarizes FDG PET coverage as of November 10, 2009:

FDG PET Coverage for Solid Tumors and Myeloma

Tumor Type	Initial Treatment Strategy (formerly "diagnosis" & "staging")	Subsequent Treatment Strategy (formerly "restaging" & "monitoring response to treatment")
Colorectal	Cover	Cover
Esophagus	Cover	Cover
Head & Neck (not Thyroid, CNS)	Cover	Cover
Lymphoma	Cover	Cover
Non-Small Cell Lung	Cover	Cover
Ovary	Cover	Cover
Brain	Cover	CED
Cervix	Cover w/exception*	Cover
Small Cell Lung	Cover	CED
Soft Tissue Sarcoma	Cover	CED
Pancreas	Cover	CED
Testes	Cover	CED
Breast (female and male)	Cover w/exception*	Cover
Melanoma	Cover w/exception*	Cover
Prostate	Non-Cover	CED
Thyroid	Cover	Cover w/exception or CED*
All Other Solid Tumors	Cover	CED
Myeloma	Cover	Cover
All other cancers not listed	CED	CED

* Cervix: Non-covered for the initial diagnosis of cervical cancer related to initial treatment strategy. All other indications for initial treatment strategy are covered.

* Breast: Non-covered for initial diagnosis and/or staging of axillary lymph nodes. Covered for initial staging of metastatic disease. All other indications for initial treatment strategy are covered.

* Melanoma: Non-covered for initial staging of regional lymph nodes. All other indications for initial treatment strategy are covered.

* Thyroid: Covered for subsequent treatment strategy of recurrent or residual thyroid cancer of follicular cell origin previously treated by thyroidectomy and radioiodine ablation and have a serum thyroglobulin >10ng/ml and have a negative I-131 whole body scan. All other indications for subsequent treatment strategy are CED.

(This NCD last reviewed November 2009.)

100-3, 220.6.19

Positron Emission Tomography NaF-18 (NaF-18 PET) to Identify Bone Metastasis of Cancer (Effective February 26, 2010)

A. General

Positron Emission Tomography (PET) is a non-invasive, diagnostic imaging procedure that assesses the level of metabolic activity and perfusion in various organ systems of the body. A positron camera (tomograph) is used to produce cross-sectional tomographic images, which are obtained from positron-emitting radioactive tracer substances (radiopharmaceuticals) such as

F-18 sodium fluoride. NaF-18 PET has been recognized as an excellent technique for imaging areas of altered osteogenic activity in bone. The clinical value of detecting and assessing the initial extent of metastatic cancer in bone is attested by a number of professional guidelines for oncology. Imaging to detect bone metastases is also recommended when a patient, following completion of initial treatment, is symptomatic with bone pain suspicious for metastases from a known primary tumor.

B. Nationally Covered Indications

Effective February 26, 2010, the Centers for Medicare & Medicaid Services (CMS) will cover NaF-18 PET imaging when the beneficiary's treating physician determines that the NaF-18 PET study is needed to inform to inform the initial antitumor treatment strategy or to guide subsequent antitumor treatment strategy after the completion of initial treatment, and when the beneficiary is enrolled in, and the NaF-18 PET provider is participating in, the following type of prospective clinical study:

A NaF-18 PET clinical study that is designed to collect additional information at the time of the scan to assist in initial antitumor treatment planning or to guide subsequent treatment strategy by the identification, location and quantification of bone metastases in beneficiaries in whom bone metastases are strongly suspected based on clinical symptoms or the results of other diagnostic studies. Qualifying clinical studies must ensure that specific hypotheses are addressed; appropriate data elements are collected; hospitals and providers are qualified to provide the PET scan and interpret the results; participating hospitals and providers accurately report data on all enrolled patients not included in other qualifying trials through adequate auditing mechanisms; and all patient confidentiality, privacy, and other Federal laws must be followed.

The clinical studies for which Medicare will provide coverage must answer one or more of the following questions:

Prospectively, in Medicare beneficiaries whose treating physician determines that the NaF-18 PET study results are needed to inform the initial antitumor treatment strategy or to guide subsequent antitumor treatment strategy after the completion of initial treatment, does the addition of NaF-18 PET imaging lead to:

A change in patient management to more appropriate palliative care; or A change in patient management to more appropriate curative care; or Improved quality of life; or Improved survival?

The study must adhere to the following standards of scientific integrity and relevance to the Medicare population:

a. The principal purpose of the research study is to test whether a particular intervention potentially improves the participants' health outcomes.

b. The research study is well-supported by available scientific and medical information or it is intended to clarify or establish the health outcomes of interventions already in common clinical use.

c. The research study does not unjustifiably duplicate existing studies.

d. The research study design is appropriate to answer the research question being asked in the study.

e. The research study is sponsored by an organization or individual capable of executing the proposed study successfully.

f. The research study is in compliance with all applicable Federal regulations concerning the protection of human subjects found in the Code of Federal Regulations (CFR) at 45 CFR Part 46. If a study is regulated by the Food and Drug Administration (FDA), it also must be in compliance with 21 CFR Parts 50 and 56.

g. All aspects of the research study are conducted according to the appropriate standards of scientific integrity.

h. The research study has a written protocol that clearly addresses, or incorporates by reference, the Medicare standards.

i. The clinical research study is not designed to exclusively test toxicity or disease pathophysiology in healthy individuals. Trials of all medical technologies measuring therapeutic outcomes as one of the objectives meet this standard only if the disease or condition being studied is life-threatening as defined in 21 CFR Sec.312.81(a) and the patient has no other viable treatment options.

j. The clinical research study is registered on the www.ClinicalTrials.gov Web site by the principal sponsor/investigator prior to the enrollment of the first study subject.

k. The research study protocol specifies the method and timing of public release of all pre-specified outcomes to be measured including release of outcomes if outcomes are negative or study is terminated early. The results must be made public within 24 months of the end of data collection. If a report is planned to be published in a peer-reviewed journal, then that initial release may be an abstract that meets the requirements of the International Committee of Medical Journal Editors. However, a full report of the outcomes must be made public no later than three (3) years after the end of data collection.

l. The research study protocol must explicitly discuss subpopulations affected by the treatment under investigation, particularly traditionally underrepresented groups in clinical studies, how the inclusion and exclusion criteria affect enrollment of these populations, and a plan for the retention and reporting of said populations on the trial. If the inclusion and exclusion criteria are expected to have a negative effect on the recruitment or retention of underrepresented populations, the protocol must discuss why these criteria are necessary.

m. The research study protocol explicitly discusses how the results are or are not expected to be generalizable to the Medicare population to infer whether Medicare patients may benefit from the intervention. Separate discussions in the protocol may be necessary for populations eligible for Medicare due to age, disability or Medicaid eligibility.

Consistent with section 1142 of the Social Security Act (the Act), the Agency for Healthcare Research and Quality (AHRQ) supports clinical research studies that the Centers for Medicare and Medicaid Services (CMS) determines meet the above-listed standards and address the above-listed research questions.

C. Nationally Non-Covered Indications

Effective February 26, 2010, CMS determines that the evidence is not sufficient to determine that the results of NaF-18 PET imaging to identify bone metastases improve health outcomes of beneficiaries with cancer and is not reasonable and necessary under Sec.1862(a)(1)(A) of the Act unless it is to inform initial antitumor treatment strategy or to guide subsequent antitumor treatment strategy after completion of initial treatment, and then only under CED. All other uses and clinical indications of NaF-18 PET are nationally non-covered.

D. Other

The only radiopharmaceutical diagnostic imaging agents covered by Medicare for PET cancer imaging are 2-[F-18] Fluoro-D-Glucose (FDG) and NaF-18 (sodium fluoride-18). All other PET radiopharmaceutical diagnostic imaging agents are non-covered for this indication.

(This NCD was last reviewed in February 2010.)

100-3, 220.6.2

NCD for PET (FDG) for Lung Cancer (220.6.2)

220.6.2 - FDG PET for Lung Cancer (Replaced with Section 220.6.17)

100-3, 220.6.3

NCD for PET (FDG) for Esophageal Cancer (220.6.3)

220.6.3 - FDG PET for Esophageal Cancer (Replaced with Section 220.6.17)

100-3, 220.6.4

NCD for PET (FDG) for Colorectal Cancer (220.6.4)

220.6.4 - FDG PET for Colorectal Cancer (Replaced with Section 220.6.17

100-3, 220.6.5

NCD for PET (FDG) for Lymphoma (220.6.5)

220.6.5 - FDG PET for Lymphoma (Replaced with Section 220.6.17)

100-3, 220.6.6

NCD for PET (FDG) for Melanoma (220.6.6)

220.6.6 - FDG PET for Melanoma (Replaced with Section 220.6.17)

100-3, 220.6.7

NCD for PET (FDG) for Head and Neck Cancers (220.6.7)

220.6.7 - FDG PET for Head and Neck Cancers (Replaced with Section 220.6.17)

100-3, 220.6.9

FDG PET for Refractory Seizures (Effective July 1, 2001)

Beginning July 1, 2001, Medicare covers FDG PET for pre-surgical evaluation for the purpose of localization of a focus of refractory seizure activity.

Limitations: Covered only for pre-surgical evaluation.

Documentation that these conditions are met should be maintained by the referring physician in the beneficiary's medical record, as is normal business practice.

(This NCD last reviewed June 2001.)

100-3, 240.4

NCD for Continuous Positive Airway Pressure (CPAP) Therapy For Obstructive Sleep Apnea (OSA) (240.4)

B. Nationally Covered Indications

Effective for claims with dates of service on and after March 13, 2008, the Centers for Medicare & Medicaid Services (CMS) determines that CPAP therapy when used in adult patients with OSA is considered reasonable and necessary under the following situations:

1. The use of CPAP is covered under Medicare when used in adult patients with OSA. Coverage of CPAP is initially limited to a 12-week period to identify beneficiaries diagnosed with OSA as subsequently described who benefit from CPAP. CPAP is subsequently covered only for those beneficiaries diagnosed with OSA who benefit from CPAP during this 12-week period.
2. The provider of CPAP must conduct education of the beneficiary prior to the use of the CPAP device to ensure that the beneficiary has been educated in the proper use of the device. A caregiver, for example a family member, may be compensatory, if consistently available in the beneficiary's home and willing and able to safely operate the CPAP device.
3. A positive diagnosis of OSA for the coverage of CPAP must include a clinical evaluation and a positive:
   a. attended PSG performed in a sleep laboratory; or
   b. unattended HST with a Type II home sleep monitoring device; or
   c. unattended HST with a Type III home sleep monitoring device; or
   d. unattended HST with a Type IV home sleep monitoring device that measures at least 3 channels.
4. The sleep test must have been previously ordered by the beneficiaryÔø¾s treating physician and furnished under appropriate physician supervision.
5. An initial 12-week period of CPAP is covered in adult patients with OSA if either of the following criterion using the AHI or RDI are met:
   a. AHI or RDI greater than or equal to 15 events per hour, or
   b. AHI or RDI greater than or equal to 5 events and less than or equal to 14 events per hour with documented symptoms of excessive daytime sleepiness, impaired cognition, mood disorders or insomnia, or documented hypertension, ischemic heart disease, or history of stroke.
6. The AHI or RDI is calculated on the average number of events of per hour. If the AHI or RDI is calculated based on less than 2 hours of continuous recorded sleep, the total number of recorded events to calculate the AHI or RDI during sleep testing must be at a minimum the number of events that would have been required in a 2-hour period.
7. Apnea is defined as a cessation of airflow for at least 10 seconds. Hypopnea is defined as an abnormal respiratory event lasting at least 10 seconds with at least a 30% reduction in thoracoabdominal movement or airflow as compared to baseline, and with at least a 4% oxygen desaturation.
8. Coverage with Evidence Development (CED): Medicare provides the following limited coverage for CPAP in adult beneficiaries who do not qualify for CPAP coverage based on criteria 1-7 above. A clinical study seeking Medicare payment for CPAP provided to a beneficiary who is an enrolled subject in that study must address one or more of the following questions
   a. In Medicare-aged subjects with clinically identified risk factors for OSA, how does the diagnostic accuracy of a clinical trial of CPAP compare with PSG and Type II, III & IV HST in identifying subjects with OSA who will respond to CPAP?
   b. In Medicare-aged subjects with clinically identified risk factors for OSA who have not undergone confirmatory testing with PSG or Type II, III & IV HST, does CPAP cause clinically meaningful harm?

   The study must meet the following additional standards:

   c. The principal purpose of the research study is to test whether a particular intervention potentially improves the participantsÔø¾ health outcomes.
   d. The research study is well-supported by available scientific and medical information or it is intended to clarify or establish the health outcomes of interventions already in common clinical use.
   e. The research study does not unjustifiably duplicate existing studies.
   f. The research study design is appropriate to answer the research question being asked in the study.
   g. The research study is sponsored by an organization or individual capable of executing the proposed study successfully.
   h. The research study is in compliance with all applicable Federal regulations concerning the protection of human subjects found at 45 CFR Part 46. If a study is Food and Drug Administration-regulated, it also must be in compliance with 21 CFR Parts 50 and 56.
   i. All aspects of the research study are conducted according to the appropriate standards of scientific integrity.
   j. The research study has a written protocol that clearly addresses, or incorporates by reference, the Medicare standards.
   k. The clinical research study is not designed to exclusively test toxicity or disease pathophysiology in healthy individuals. Trials of all medical technologies measuring therapeutic outcomes as one of the objectives meet this standard only if the disease or condition being studied is life-threatening as defined in 21 CFR Ôø¾ 312.81(a) and the patient has no other viable treatment options.
   l. The clinical research study is registered on the ClinicalTrials.gov Web site by the principal sponsor/investigator prior to the enrollment of the first study subject.
   m. The research study protocol specifies the method and timing of public release of all pre-specified outcomes to be measured, including release of outcomes if outcomes are negative or study is terminated early. The results must be made public within 24 months of the end of data collection. If a report is planned for publication in a peer-reviewed journal, then that initial release may be an abstract that meets the requirements of the International Committee of Medical Journal Editors. However, a full report of the outcomes must be made public no later than 3 years after the end of data collection.
   n. The research study protocol must explicitly discuss subpopulations affected by the treatment under investigation, particularly traditionally underrepresented groups in clinical studies, how the inclusion and exclusion criteria affect enrollment of these populations, and a plan for the retention and reporting of said populations in the trial. If the inclusion and exclusion criteria are expected to have a negative effect on the recruitment or retention of underrepresented populations, the protocol must discuss why these criteria are necessary.
   o. The research study protocol explicitly discusses how the results are or are not expected to be generalizable to the Medicare population to infer whether Medicare patients may benefit from the intervention. Separate discussions in the protocol may be necessary for populations eligible for Medicare due to age, disability, or Medicaid eligibility.

C. Nationally Non-covered Indications

Effective for claims with dates of services on and after March 13, 2008, other diagnostic tests for the diagnosis of OSA, other than those noted above for prescribing CPAP, are not sufficient for the coverage of CPAP.

D. Other

N/A

(This NCD last reviewed March

100-3, 240.4.1

Sleep Testing for Obstructive Sleep Apnea (OSA) (Effective March 3, 2009)

A. General

Obstructive sleep apnea (OSA) is the collapse of the oropharyngeal walls and the obstruction of airflow occurring during sleep. Diagnostic tests for OSA have historically been classified into four types. The most comprehensive is designated Type I attended facility based polysomnography (PSG), which is considered the reference standard for diagnosing OSA. Attended facility based polysomnogram is a comprehensive diagnostic sleep test including at least electroencephalography (EEG), electro-oculography (EOG), electromyography (EMG), heart rate or electrocardiography (ECG), airflow, breathing/respiratory effort, and arterial oxygen saturation (SaO2) furnished in a sleep laboratory facility in which a technologist supervises the recording during sleep time and has the ability to intervene if needed. Overnight PSG is the conventional diagnostic test for OSA. The American Thoracic Society and the American Academy of Sleep Medicine have recommended supervised PSG in the sleep laboratory over 2 nights for the diagnosis of OSA and the initiation of continuous positive airway pressure (CPAP).

Three categories of portable monitors (used both in attended and unattended settings) have been developed for the diagnosis of OSA. Type II monitors have a minimum of 7 channels (e.g., EEG, EOG, EMG, ECG-heart rate, airflow, breathing/respiratory effort, SaO2)-this type of device monitors sleep staging, so AHI can be calculated). Type III monitors have a minimum of 4 monitored channels including ventilation or airflow (at least two channels of respiratory movement or respiratory movement and airflow), heart rate or ECG, and oxygen saturation. Type IV devices may measure one, two, three or more parameters but do not meet all the criteria of a higher category device. Some monitors use an actigraphy algorithm to identify periods of sleep and wakefulness.

B. Nationally Covered Indications
Effective for claims with dates of service on and after March 3, 2009, the Centers for Medicare & Medicaid Services finds that the evidence is sufficient to determine that the results of the sleep tests identified below can be used by a beneficiary's treating physician to diagnose OSA, that the use of such sleep testing technologies demonstrates improved health outcomes in Medicare beneficiaries who have OSA and receive the appropriate treatment, and that these tests are thus reasonable and necessary under section 1862(a)(1)(A) of the Social Security Act.

1. Type I PSG is covered when used to aid the diagnosis of OSA in beneficiaries who have clinical signs and symptoms indicative of OSA if performed attended in a sleep lab facility.
2. Type II or Type III sleep testing devices are covered when used to aid the diagnosis of OSA in beneficiaries who have clinical signs and symptoms indicative of OSA if performed unattended in or out of a sleep lab facility or attended in a sleep lab facility.
3. Type IV sleep testing devices measuring three or more channels, one of which is airflow, are covered when used to aid the diagnosis of OSA in beneficiaries who have signs and symptoms indicative of OSA if performed unattended in or out of a sleep lab facility or attended in a sleep lab facility.
4. Sleep testing devices measuring three or more channels that include actigraphy, oximetry, and peripheral arterial tone, are covered when used to aid the diagnosis of OSA in beneficiaries who have signs and symptoms indicative of OSA if performed unattended in or out of a sleep lab facility or attended in a sleep lab facility.

C. Nationally Non-Covered Indications
Effective for claims with dates of services on and after March 3, 2009, other diagnostic sleep tests for the diagnosis of OSA, other than those noted above for prescribing CPAP, are not sufficient for the coverage of CPAP and are not covered.

D. Other
N/A

(This NCD last reviewed March 2009.)

100-3, 250.5

Dermal Injections for the Treatment of Facial Lipodystrophy Syndrome (LDS) - Effective March 23, 2010

A. General
Treatment of persons infected with the human immunodeficiency virus (HIV) or persons who have Acquired Immune Deficiency Syndrome (AIDS) may include highly active antiretroviral therapy (HAART). Drug reactions commonly associated with long-term use of HAART include metabolic complications such as, lipid abnormalities, e.g., hyperlipidemia, hyperglycemia, diabetes, lipodystrophy, and heart disease. Lipodystrophy is characterized by abnormal fat distribution in the body.

The LDS is often characterized by a loss of fat that results in a facial abnormality such as severely sunken cheeks. The patient's physical appearance may contribute to psychological conditions (e.g., depression) or adversely impact a patient's adherence to antiretroviral regimens (therefore jeopardizing their health) and both of these are important health-related outcomes of interest in this population. Therefore, improving a patient's physical appearance through the use of dermal injections could improve these health-related outcomes.

B. Nationally Covered Indications
Effective for claims with dates of service on and after March 23, 2010, dermal injections for LDS are only reasonable and necessary using dermal fillers approved by the Food and Drug Administration (FDA) for this purpose, and then only in HIV-infected beneficiaries when LDS caused by antiretroviral HIV treatment is a significant contributor to their depression.

C. Nationally Non-Covered Indications
1. Dermal fillers that are not approved by the FDA for the treatment of LDS.
2. Dermal fillers that are used for any indication other than LDS in HIV-infected individuals who manifest depression as a result of their antiretroviral HIV treatments.

D. Other
N/A

(This NCD last reviewed March 2010.)

100-4, 1, 10.1.4.1

Physician and Ambulance Services Furnished in Connection With Covered Foreign Inpatient Hospital Services

Payment is made for necessary physician and ambulance services that meet the other coverage requirements of the Medicare program, and are furnished in connection with and during a period of covered foreign hospitalization.

A. Coverage of Physician and Ambulance Services Furnished Outside the U.S.
Where inpatient services in a foreign hospital are covered, payment may also be made for

- Physicians' services furnished to the beneficiary while he/she is an inpatient,
- Physicians' services furnished to the beneficiary outside the hospital on the day of his/her admission as an inpatient, provided the services were for the same condition for which the beneficiary was hospitalized (including the services of a Canadian ship's physician who furnishes emergency services in Canadian waters on the day the patient is admitted to a Canadian hospital for a covered emergency stay and,
- Ambulance services, where necessary, for the trip to the hospital in conjunction with the beneficiary's admission as an inpatient. Return trips from a foreign hospital are not covered.

In cases involving foreign ambulance services, the general requirements in Chapter 15 are also applicable, subject to the following special rules:

- If the foreign hospitalization was determined to be covered on the basis of emergency services, the medical necessity requirements outlined in Chapter 15 are considered met.
- The definition of:
  - physician
  - for purposes of coverage of services furnished outside the U.S., is expanded to include a foreign practitioner, provided the practitioner is legally licensed to practice in the country in which the services are furnished.
- Only the enrollee can file for Part B benefits; the assignment method may not be used.
- Where the enrollee is deceased, the rules for settling Part B underpayments are applicable. Payment is made to the foreign physician or foreign ambulance company on an unpaid bill provided the physician or ambulance company accepts the payment as the full charge for the service, or payment an be made to a person who has agreed to assume legal liability to pay the physician or supplier. Where the bill is paid, payment may be made in accordance with Medicare regulations. The regular deductible and coinsurance requirements apply to physicians' and ambulance service

100-4, 1, 30.3.5

Effect of Assignment Upon Purchase of Cataract Glasses FromParticipating Physician or Supplier on Claims Submitted to Carriers

B3-3045.4

A pair of cataract glasses is comprised of two distinct products: a professional product (the prescribed lenses) and a retail commercial product (the frames). The frames serve not only as a holder of lenses but also as an article of personal apparel. As such, they are usually selected on the basis of personal taste and style. Although Medicare will pay only for standard frames, most patients want deluxe frames. Participating physicians and suppliers cannot profitably furnish such deluxe frames unless they can make an extra (noncovered) charge for the frames even though they accept assignment.

Therefore, a participating physician or supplier (whether an ophthalmologist, optometrist, or optician) who accepts assignment on cataract glasses with deluxe frames may charge the Medicare patient the difference between his/her usual charge to private pay patients for glasses with standard frames and his/her usual charge to such patients for glasses with deluxe frames, in addition to the applicable deductible and coinsurance on glasses with standard frames, if all of the following requirements are met:

A. The participating physician or supplier has standard frames available, offers them for saleto the patient, and issues and ABN to the patient that explains the price and other differences between standard and deluxe frames. Refer to Chapter 30.

B. The participating physician or supplier obtains from the patient (or his/her representative) and keeps on file the following signed and dated statement:

Name of Patient — Medicare Claim Number

Having been informed that an extra charge is being made by the physician or supplier for deluxe frames, that this extra charge is not covered by Medicare, and that standard frames are available for purchase from the physician or supplier at no extra charge, I have chosen to purchase deluxe frames.

Signature — Date

C. The participating physician or supplier itemizes on his/her claim his/her actual charge for the lenses, his/her actual charge for the standard frames, and his/her actual extra charge for the deluxe frames (charge differential). Once the assigned claim for deluxe frames has been processed, the carrier will follow the ABN instructions as described in Sec.60.

100-4, 3, 10.4

Payment of Nonphysician Services for Inpatients

All items and nonphysician services furnished to inpatients must be furnished directly by the hospital or billed through the hospital under arrangements. This provision applies to all hospitals, regardless of whether they are subject to PPS.

Other Medical Items, Supplies, and Services the following medical items, supplies, and services furnished to inpatients are covered under Part A. Consequently, they are covered by the prospective payment rate or reimbursed as reasonable costs under Part A to hospitals excluded from PPS.

- Laboratory services (excluding anatomic pathology services and certain clinical pathology services);
- Pacemakers and other prosthetic devices including lenses, and artificial limbs, knees, and hips;
- Radiology services including computed tomography (CT) scans furnished to inpatients by a physician's office, other hospital, or radiology clinic;
- Total parenteral nutrition (TPN) services; and
- Transportation, including transportation by ambulance, to and from another hospital or freestanding facility to receive specialized diagnostic or therapeutic services not available at the facility where the patient is an inpatient.

The hospital must include the cost of these services in the appropriate ancillary service cost center, i.e., in the cost of the diagnostic or therapeutic service. It must not show them separately under revenue code 0540.

EXCEPTIONS

Pneumococcal Vaccine -is payable under Part B only and is billed by the hospital on the Form CMS-1450.

Ambulance Service For purposes of this section "hospital inpatient" means beneficiary who has been formally admitted it does not include a beneficiary who is in the process of being transferred from one hospital to another. Where the patient is transferred from one hospital to another, and is admitted as an inpatient to the second, the ambulance service is payable under only Part B. If transportation is by a hospital owned and operated ambulance, the hospital bills separately on Form CMS-1450 as appropriate. Similarly, if the hospital arranges for the ambulance transportation with an ambulance operator, including paying the ambulance operator, it bills separately. However, if the hospital does not assume any financial responsibility, the billing is to the carrier by the ambulance operator or beneficiary, as appropriate, if an ambulance is used for the transportation of a hospital inpatient to another facility for diagnostic tests or special treatment the ambulance trip is considered part of the DRG, and not separately billable, if the resident hospital is under PPS.

Part B Inpatient Services Where Part A benefits are not payable, payment maybe made to the hospital under Part B for certain medical and other health services. See Chapter 4 for a description of Part B inpatient services.

Anesthetist Services "Incident to" Physician Services

If a physician's practice was to employ anesthetists and to bill on a reasonable charge basis for these services and that practice was in effect as of the last day of the hospital's most recent 12-month cost reporting period ending before September 30, 1983, the physician may continue that practice through cost reporting periods beginning October 1, 1984. However, if the physician chooses to continue this practice, the hospital may not add costs of the anesthetist's service to its base period costs for purposes of its transition payment rates. If it is the existing or new practice of the physician to employ certified registered nurse anesthetists (CRNAs) and other qualified anesthetists and include charges for their services in the physician bills for anesthesiology services for the hospital's cost report periods beginning on or after October 1, 1984, and before October 1, 1987, the physician may continue to do so.

B. Exceptions/Waivers

These provisions were waived before cost reporting periods beginning on or after October1, 1986, under certain circumstances. The basic criteria for waiver was that services furnished by outside suppliers are so extensive that a sudden change in billing practices would threaten the stability of patient care. Specific criteria for waiver and processing procedures are in Sec.2804 of the Provider Reimbursement Manual (CMS Pub. 15-1).

100-4, 3, 20.7.3

Payment for Blood Clotting Factor Administered to Hemophilia Patients

Section 6011 of Public Law (P.L.) 101-239 amended Sec.1886(a)(4) of the Social Security Act (the Act) to provide that prospective payment system (PPS) hospitals receive anadditional payment for the costs of administering blood clotting factor to Medicare hemophiliacs who are hospital inpatients. Section 6011(b) of P.L. 101.239 specified that the payment be based on a predetermined price per unit of clotting factor multiplied by the number of units provided. This add-on payment originally was effective for blood clotting factors furnished on or after June 19, 1990, and before December 19, 1991. Section 13505 of P. L. 103-66 amended Sec.6011 (d) of P.L. 101-239 to extend the period covered by the add-on payment for blood clotting factors administered to Medicare inpatients with hemophilia through September 30, 1994. Section 4452 of P.L. 105-33 amended Sec.6011(d) of P.L. 101-239 to reinstate the add-on payment for the costs of administering blood clotting factor to Medicare beneficiaries who have hemophilia and who are hospital inpatients for discharges occurring on or after October 1, 1998.

Local carriers shall process non-institutional blood clotting factor claims.

The FIs shall process institutional blood clotting factor claims payable under either Part A or Part B.

A. Inpatient Bills

Under the Inpatient Prospective Payment System (PPS), hospitals receive a special add-on payment for the costs of furnishing blood clotting factors to Medicare beneficiaries with hemophilia, admitted as inpatients of PPS hospitals. The clotting factor add-on payment is calculated using the number of units (as defined in the HCPCS code long descriptor) billed by the provider under special instructions for units of service.

The PPS Pricer software does not calculate the payment amount. The Fiscal Intermediary Standard System (FISS) calculates the payment amount and subtracts the charges from those submitted to Pricer so that the clotting factor charges are not included in cost outlier computations.

Blood clotting factors not paid on a cost or PPS basis are priced as a drug/biological under the Medicare Part B Drug Pricing File effective for the specific date of service. As of January 1, 2005, the average sales price (ASP) plus 6 percent shall be used.

If a beneficiary is in a covered Part A stay in a PPS hospital, the clotting factors are paid in addition to the DRG/HIPPS payment (For FY 2004, this payment is based on 95 percent of average wholesale price.) For a SNF subject to SNF/PPS, the payment is bundled into the SNF/PPS rate.

For SNF inpatient Part A, there is no add-on payment for blood clotting factors.

The codes for blood-clotting factors are found on the Medicare Part B Drug Pricing File. This file is distributed on a quarterly basis.

For discharges occurring on or after October 1, 2000, and before December 31, 2005, report HCPCS Q0187 based on 1 billing unit per 1.2 mg. Effective January 1, 2006, HCPCS code J7189 replaces Q0187 and is defined as 1 billing unit per 1 microgram (mcg).

The examples below include the HCPCS code and indicate the dosage amount specified in the descriptor of that code. Facilities use the units field as a multiplier to arrive at the dosage amount.

EXAMPLE 1

HCPCS	Drug	Dosage
J7189	Factor VIIa	1 mcg

Actual dosage: 13, 365 mcg

On the bill, the facility shows J7189 and 13, 365 in the units field (13, 365 mcg divided by 1 mcg = 13, 365 units).

NOTE:The process for dealing with one international unit (IU) is the same as the process of dealing with one microgram.

EXAMPLE 21

HCPCS	Drug	Dosage
J9355	Trastuzumab	10 mg

Actual dosage: 140 mg

On the bill, the facility shows J9355 and 14 in the units field (140 mg divided by 10mg = 14 units). When the dosage amount is greater than the amount indicated for the HCPCS code, the facility rounds up to determine units. When the dosage amount is less than the amount indicated for the HCPCS code, use 1 as the unit of measure.

EXAMPLE 3

HCPCS	Drug	Dosage
J3100	Tenecteplase	50 mg

Actual Dosage: 40 mg

The provider would bill for 1 unit, even though less than 1 full unit was furnished.

At times, the facility provides less than the amount provided in a single use vial and there is waste, i.e.; some drugs may be available only in packaged amounts that exceed the needs of an individual patient. Once the drug is reconstituted in the hospital's pharmacy, it may have a limited shelf life. Since an individual patient may receive less than the fully reconstituted amount, we encourage hospitals to schedule patients in such a way that the hospital can use the drug most efficiently. However, if the hospital must discard the remainder of a vial after administering part of it to a Medicare patient, the provider may bill for the amount of drug discarded plus the amount administered.

Example 1:
Drug X is available only in a 100-unit size. A hospital schedules three Medicare patients to receive drug X on the same day within the designated shelf life of the product. An appropriate hospital staff member administers 30 units to each patient. The remaining 10 units are billed to Medicare on the account of the last patient. Therefore, 30 units are billed on behalf of the first patient seen and 30 units are billed on behalf of the second patient seen. Forty units are billed on behalf of the last patient seen because the hospital had to discard 10 units at that point.

Example 2:
An appropriate hospital staff member must administer 30 units of drug X to a Medicare patient, and it is not practical to schedule another patient who requires the same drug. For example, the hospital has only one patient who requires drug X, or the hospital sees the patient for the first time and did not know the patient's condition. The hospital bills for 100 units on behalf of the patient, and Medicare pays for 100 units.

When the number of units of blood clotting factor administered to hemophiliac inpatients exceeds 99, 999, the hospital reports the excess as a second line for revenue code 0636 and repeats the HCPCS code. One hundred thousand fifty (100,050) units are reported on one line as 99, 999, and another line shows 1,051.

Revenue Code 0636 is used. It requires HCPCS. Some other inpatient drugs continue to be billed without HCPCS codes under pharmacy.

No changes in beneficiary notices are required. Coverage is applicable to hospital Part A claims only. Coverage is also applicable to inpatient Part B services in SNFs and all types of hospitals, including CAHs. Separate payment is not made to SNFs for beneficiaries in an inpatient Part A stay.

B. FI Action
The FI is responsible for the following:

- It accepts HCPCS codes for inpatient services;
- It edits to require HCPCS codes with Revenue Code 0636. Multiple iterations of the revenue code are possible with the same or different HCPCS codes. It does not edit units except to ensure a numeric value;
- It reduces charges forwarded to Pricer by the charges for hemophilia clotting factors in revenue code 0636. It retains the charges and revenue and HCPCS codes for CWF; and
- It modifies data entry screens to accept HCPCS codes for hospital (including CAH) swing bed, and SNF inpatient claims (bill types 11X, 12X, 18x, 21x and, 22x).

The September 1, 1993, IPPS final rule (58 FR 46304) states that payment will be made for the blood clotting factor only if an ICD-9-CM diagnosis code for hemophilia is included on the bill.

Since inpatient blood-clotting factors are covered only for beneficiaries with hemophilia, the FI must ensure that one of the following hemophilia diagnosis codes is listed on the bill before payment is made:

- 286.0 Congenital factor VIII disorder
- 286.1 Congenital factor IX disorder
- 286.2 Congenital factor IX disorder
- 286.3 Congenital deficiency of other clotting factor
- 286.4 von Willebrands' disease

Effective for discharges on or after August 1, 2001, payment may also be made if one of the following diagnosis codes is reported:

- 286.5 Hemorrhagic disorder due to circulating anticoagulants
- 286.7 Acquired coagulation factor deficiency

C. Part A Remittance Advice

1. X12.835 Ver. 003030M

   For remittance reporting PIP and/or non-PIP payments, the Hemophilia Add on will be reported in a claims level 2-090-CAS segment (CAS is the element identifier) exhibiting an "OA" Group Code and adjustment reason code "97" (payment is included in the allowance for the basic service/ procedure) followed by the associated dollar amount (POSITIVE) and units of service. For this version of the 835, "OA" group coded line level CAS segments are informational and are not included in the balancing routine. The Hemophilia Add On amount will always be included in the 2-010-CLP04 Claim Payment Amount.

   For remittance reporting PIP payments, the Hemophilia Add On will also be reported in the provider level adjustment (element identifier PLB) segment with the provider level adjustment reason code "CA" (Manual claims adjustment) followed by the associated dollar amount (NEGATIVE).

   NOTE: A data maintenance request will be submitted to ANSI ASC X12 for a new PLB adjustment reason code specifically for PIP payment Hemophilia Add On situations for future use. However, continue to use adjustment reason code "CA" until further notice.

   The FIs enter MA103 (Hemophilia Add On) in an open MIA (element identifier) remark code data element. This will alert the provider that the reason code 97 and PLB code "CA" adjustments are related to the Hemophilia Add On.

2. X12.835 Ver. 003051

   For remittances reporting PIP and/or non-PIP payments, Hemophilia Add On information will be reported in the claim level 2-062-AMT and 2-064-QTY segments. The 2-062-AMT01 element will carry a "ZK" (Federal Medicare claim MANDATE - Category 1) qualifier code followed by the total claim level Hemophilia Add On amount (POSITIVE). The 2-064QTY01 element will carry a "FL" (Units) qualifier code followed by the number of units approved for the Hemophilia Add On for the claim. The Hemophilia Add On amount will always be included in the 2-010-CLP04 Claim Payment Amount.

   NOTE: A data maintenance request will be submitted to ANSI ASC X12 for a new AMT qualifier code specifically for the Hemophilia Add On for future use. However, continue to use adjustment reason code "ZK" until further notice.

   For remittances reporting PIP payments, the Hemophilia Add On will be reported in the provider level adjustment PLB segment with the provider level adjustment reason "ZZ" followed by the associated dollar amount (NEGATIVE).

   NOTE: A data maintenance request will be submitted to ANSI ASC X12 for a new PLB, adjustment reason code specifically for the Hemophilia Add On for future use. However, continue to use PLB adjustment reason code "ZZ" until further notice. The FIs enter MA103 (Hemophilia Add On) in an open MIA remark code data element. This will alert the provider that the ZK, FL and ZZ entries are related to the Hemophilia Add On. (Effective with version 4010 of the 835, report ZK in lieu of FL in the QTY segment.)

3. Standard Hard Copy Remittance Advice

   For paper remittances reporting non-PIP payments involving Hemophilia Add On, add a "Hemophilia Add On" category to the end of the "Pass Thru Amounts" listings in the "Summary" section of the paper remittance. Enter the total of the Hemophilia Add On amounts due for the claims covered by this remittance next to the Hemophilia Add On heading.

   The FIs add the Remark Code "MA103" (Hemophilia Add On) to the remittance advice under the REM column for those claims that qualify for Hemophilia Add On payments.

   This will be the full extent of Hemophilia Add On reporting on paper remittance notices; providers wishing more detailed information must subscribe to the Medicare Part A specifications for the ANSI ASC X12N 835, where additional information is available.

   See chapter 22, for detailed instructions and definitions.

100-4, 3, 40.2.2

Charges to Beneficiaries for Part A Services
The hospital submits a bill even where the patient is responsible for a deductible which covers the entire amount of the charges for non-PPS hospitals, or in PPS hospitals, where the DRG payment amount will be less than the deductible.

A hospital receiving payment for a covered hospital stay (or PPS hospital that includes at least one covered day, or one treated as covered under guarantee of payment or limitation on liability) may charge the beneficiary, or other person, for items and services furnished during the stay only as described in subsections A through H. If limitation of liability applies, a beneficiary's liability for payment is governed by the limitation on liability notification rules in Chapter 30 of this manual. For related notices for inpatient hospitals, see CMS Transmittal 594, Change Request3903, dated June 24, 2005.

A. Deductible and Coinsurance
The hospital may charge the beneficiary or other person for applicable deductible and coinsurance amounts. The deductible is satisfied only by charges for covered services. The FI deducts the deductible and coinsurance first from the PPS payment. Where the deductible exceeds the PPS amount, the excess will be applied to a subsequent payment to the hospital. (See Chapter 3 of the Medicare General Information, Eligibility, and Entitlement Manual for specific policies.)

B. Blood Deductible
The Part A blood deductible provision applies to whole blood and red blood cells, and reporting of the number of pints is applicable to both PPS and non-PPS hospitals. (See Chapter 3 of the Medicare General Information, Eligibility, and Entitlement Manual for specific policies.) Hospitals shall report charges for red blood cells using revenue code 381, and charges for whole blood using revenue code 382.

C. Inpatient Care No Longer Required
The hospital may charge for services that are not reasonable and necessary or that constitute custodial care. Notification may be required under limitation of liability. See CMS Transmittal 594, Change Request3903, dated June 24, 2005, section V. of the attachment, for specific notification requirements. Note this transmittal will be placed in Chapter 30 of this manual at a future point. Chapter 1, section 150 of this manual also contains related billing information in addition to that provided below.

In general, after proper notification has occurred, and assuming an expedited decision is received from a Quality Improvement Organization (QIO), the following entries are required on the bill the hospital prepares:

- Occurrence code 3l (and date) to indicate the date the hospital notified the patient in accordance with the first bullet above;
- Occurrence span code 76 (and dates) to indicate the period of noncovered care for which it is charging the beneficiary;
- Occurrence span code 77 (and dates) to indicate the period of noncovered care for which the provider is liable, when it is aware of this prior to billing; and
- Value code 3l (and amount) to indicate the amount of charges it may bill the beneficiary for days for which inpatient care was no longer required. They are included as noncovered charges on the bill.

D. Change in the Beneficiary's Condition
If the beneficiary remains in the hospital after receiving notice as described in subsection C, and the hospital, the physician who concurred in the hospital's determination, or the QIO, subsequently determines that the beneficiary again requires inpatient hospital care, the hospital may not charge the beneficiary or other person for services furnished after the beneficiary again required inpatient hospital care until proper notification occurs (see subsection C).

If a patient who needs only a SNF level of care remains in the hospital after the SNF bed becomes available, and the bed ceases to be available, the hospital may continue to charge the beneficiary. It need not provide the beneficiary with another notice when the patient chose not to be discharged to the SNF bed.

E. Admission Denied
If the entire hospital admission is determined to be not reasonable or necessary, limitation of liability may apply. See 2005 CMS transmittal 594, section V. of the attachment, for specific notification requirements.

NOTE: This transmittal will be placed in Chapter 30 of this manual at a future point.

In such cases the following entries are required on the bill:

- Occurrence code 3l (and date) to indicate the date the hospital notified the beneficiary.
- Occurrence span code 76 (and dates) to indicate the period of noncovered care for which the hospital is charging the beneficiary.
- Occurrence span code 77 (and dates) to indicate any period of noncovered care for which the provider is liable (e.g., the period between issuing the notice and the time it may charge the beneficiary) when the provider is aware of this prior to billing.
- Value code 3l (and amount) to indicate the amount of charges the hospital may bill the beneficiary for hospitalization that was not necessary or reasonable. They are included as noncovered charges on the bill.

F. Procedures, Studies and Courses of Treatment That Are Not Reasonable or Necessary
If diagnostic procedures, studies, therapeutic studies and courses of treatment are excluded from coverage as not reasonable and necessary (even though the beneficiary requires inpatient hospital care) the hospital may charge the beneficiary or other person for the services or care according the procedures given in CMS Transmittal 594, Change Request3903, dated June 24, 2005.

The following bill entries apply to these circumstances:

- Occurrence code 32 (and date) to indicate the date the hospital provided the notice to the beneficiary.
- Value code 3l (and amount) to indicate the amount of such charges to be billed to the beneficiary. They are included as noncovered charges on the bill.

G. Nonentitlement Days and Days after Benefits Exhausted
If a hospital stay exceeds the day outlier threshold, the hospital may charge for some, or all, of the days on which the patient is not entitled to Medicare Part A, or after the Part A benefits are exhausted (i.e., the hospital may charge its customary charges for services furnished on those days). It may charge the beneficiary for the lesser of:

- The number of days on which the patient was not entitled to benefits or after the benefits were exhausted; or
- The number of outlier days. (Day outliers were discontinued at the end of FY 1997.)

If the number of outlier days exceeds the number of days on which the patient was not entitled to benefits, or after benefits were exhausted, the hospital may charge for all days on which the patient was not entitled to benefits or after benefits were exhausted. If the number of days on which the beneficiary was not entitled to benefits, or after benefits were exhausted, exceeds the number of outlier days, the hospital determines the days for which it may charge by starting with the last day of the stay (i.e., the day before the day of discharge) and identifying and counting off in reverse order, days on which the patient was not entitled to benefits or after the benefits were exhausted, until the number of days counted off equals the number of outlier days. The days counted off are the days for which the hospital may charge.

H. Contractual Exclusions
In addition to receiving the basic prospective payment, the hospital may charge the beneficiary for any services that are excluded from coverage for reasons other than, or in addition to, absence of medical necessity, provision of custodial care, non-entitlement to Part A, or exhaustion of benefits. For example, it may charge for most cosmetic and dental surgery.

I. Private Room Care
Payment for medically necessary private room care is included in the prospective payment. Where the beneficiary requests private room accommodations, the hospital must inform the beneficiary of the additional charge. (See the Medicare Benefit Policy Manual, Chapter 1.) When the beneficiary accepts the liability, the hospital will supply the service, and bill the beneficiary directly. If the beneficiary believes the private room was medically necessary, the beneficiary has a right to a determination and may initiate a Part A appeal.

J. Deluxe Item or Service
Where a beneficiary requests a deluxe item or service, i.e., an item or service which is more expensive than is medically required for the beneficiary's condition, the hospital may collect the additional charge if it informs the beneficiary of the additional charge. That charge is the difference between the customary charge for the item or service most commonly furnished by the hospital to private pay patients with the beneficiary's condition, and the charge for the more expensive item or service requested. If the beneficiary believes that the more expensive item or service was medically necessary, the beneficiary has a right to a determination and may initiate a Part A appeal.

K - Inpatient Acute Care Hospital Admission Followed By a Death or Discharge Prior To Room Assignment
A patient of an acute care hospital is considered an inpatient upon issuance of written doctor's orders to that effect. If a patient either dies or is discharged prior to being assigned and/or occupying a room, a hospital may enter an appropriate room and board charge on the claim. If a patient leaves of their own volition prior to being assigned and/or occupying a room, a hospital may enter an appropriate room and board charge on the claim as well as a patient status code 07 which indicates they left against medical advice. A hospital is not required to enter a room and board charge, but failure to do so may have a minimal impact on future DRG weight calculations.

100-4, 3, 40.3

Outpatient Services Treated as Inpatient Services

A3-3610.3, HO-415.6, HO-400D, A-03-008, A-03-013, A-03-054

A. Outpatient Services Followed by Admission Before Midnight of the Following Day (Effective For Services Furnished Before October 1, 1991)

When a beneficiary receives outpatient hospital services during the day immediately preceding the hospital admission, the outpatient hospital services are treated as inpatient services if the beneficiary has Part A coverage. Hospitals and FIs apply this provision only when the beneficiary is admitted to the hospital before midnight of the day following receipt of outpatient services. The day on which the patient is formally admitted as an inpatient is counted as the first inpatient day.

When this provision applies, services are included in the applicable PPS payment and not billed separately. When this provision applies to hospitals and units excluded from the hospital PPS, services are shown on the bill and included in the Part A payment. See Chapter 1 for FI requirements for detecting duplicate claims in such cases.

B. Preadmission Diagnostic Services (Effective for Services Furnished On or After January 1, 1991)

Diagnostic services (including clinical diagnostic laboratory tests) provided to a beneficiary by the admitting hospital, or by an entity wholly owned or wholly operated by the admitting hospital (or by another entity under arrangements with the admitting hospital), within 3 days prior to and including the date of the beneficiary's admission are deemed to be inpatient services and included in the inpatient payment, unless there is no Part A coverage. For example, if a patient is admitted on a Wednesday, outpatient services provided by the hospital on Sunday, Monday, Tuesday, or Wednesday are included in the inpatient Part A payment.

This provision does not apply to ambulance services and maintenance renal dialysis services (see the Medicare Benefit Policy Manual, Chapters 10 and 11, respectively). Additionally, Part A services furnished by skilled nursing facilities, home health agencies, and hospices are excluded from the payment window provisions.

For services provided before October 31, 1994, this provision applies to both hospitals subject to the hospital inpatient prospective payment system (IPPS) as well as those hospitals and units excluded from IPPS.

For services provided on or after October 31, 1994, for hospitals and units excluded from IPPS, this provision applies only to services furnished within one day prior to and including the date of the beneficiary's admission. The hospitals and units that are excluded from IPPS are: psychiatric hospitals and units; inpatient rehabilitation facilities (IRF) and units; long-term care hospitals (LTCH); children's hospitals; and cancer hospitals.

Critical access hospitals (CAHs) are not subject to the 3-day (nor 1-day) DRG payment window.

An entity is considered to be "wholly owned or operated" by the hospital if the hospital is the sole owner or operator. A hospital need not exercise administrative control over a facility in order to operate it. A hospital is considered the sole operator of the facility if the hospital has exclusive responsibility for implementing facility policies (i.e., conducting or overseeing the facility's routine operations), regardless of whether it also has the authority to make the policies.

For this provision, diagnostic services are defined by the presence on the bill of the following revenue and/or CPT codes:

- 0254 - Drugs incident to other diagnostic services
- 0255 - Drugs incident to radiology
- 030X - Laboratory
- 031X - Laboratory pathological
- 032X - Radiology diagnostic
- 0341, 0343 - Nuclear medicine, diagnostic/Diagnostic Radiopharmaceuticals
- 035X - CT scan
- 0371 - Anesthesia incident to Radiology
- 0372 - Anesthesia incident to other diagnostic services
- 040X - Other imaging services
- 046X - Pulmonary function
- 0471 - Audiology diagnostic
- 0481, 0489- Cardiology, Cardiac Catheter Lab/Other Cardiology with CPT codes 93501, 93503, 93505, 93508, 93510, 93526, 93541, 93542, 93543, 93544, 93556, 93561, or 93562 diagnostic
- 0482- Cardiology, Stress Test
- 0483- Cardiology, Echocardiology
- 053X - Osteopathic services
- 061X - MRT
- 062X - Medical/surgical supplies, incident to radiology or other diagnostic services
- 073X - EKG/ECG
- 074X - EEG
- 0918- Testing- Behavioral Health
- 092X - Other diagnostic services

The CWF rejects services furnished January 1, 1991, or later when outpatient bills for diagnostic services with through dates or last date of service (occurrence span code 72) fall on the day of admission or any of the 3 days immediately prior to admission to an IPPS or IPPS-excluded hospital. This reject applies to the bill in process, regardless of whether the outpatient or inpatient bill is processed first. Hospitals must analyze the two bills and report appropriate corrections. For services on or after October 31, 1994, for hospitals and units excluded from IPPS, CWF will reject outpatient diagnostic bills that occur on the day of or one day before admission. For IPPS hospitals, CWF will continue to reject outpatient diagnostic bills for services that occur on the day of or any of the 3 days prior to admission. Effective for dates of service on or after July 1, 2008, CWF will reject diagnostic services when the line item date of service (LIDOS) falls on the day of admission or any of the 3 days immediately prior to an admission to an IPPS hospital or on the day of admission or one day prior to admission for hospitals excluded from IPPS.

Hospitals in Maryland that are under the jurisdiction of the Health Services Cost Review Commission are subject to the 3-day payment window.

C. Other Preadmission Services (Effective for Services Furnished On or After October 1, 1991)

Nondiagnostic outpatient services that are related to a patient's hospital admission and that are provided by the hospital, or by an entity wholly owned or wholly operated by the admitting hospital (or by another entity under arrangements with the admitting hospital), to the patient during the 3 days immediately preceding and including the date of the patient's admission are deemed to be inpatient services and are included in the inpatient payment. Effective March 13, 1998, we defined nondiagnostic preadmission services as being related to the admission only when there is an exact match (for all digits) between the ICD-9-CM principal diagnosis code assigned for both the preadmission services and the inpatient stay. Thus, whenever Part A covers an admission, the hospital may bill nondiagnostic preadmission services to Part B as outpatient services only if they are not related to the admission. The FI shall assume, in the absence of evidence to the contrary, that such bills are not admission related and, therefore, are not deemed to be inpatient (Part A) services. If there are both diagnostic and nondiagnostic preadmission services and the nondiagnostic services are unrelated to the admission, the hospital may separately bill the nondiagnostic preadmission services to Part B. This provision applies only when the patient has Part A coverage. This provision does not apply to ambulance services and maintenance renal dialysis. Additionally, Part A services furnished by skilled nursing facilities, home health agencies, and hospices are excluded from the payment window provisions.

For services provided before October 31, 1994, this provision applies to both hospitals subject to IPPS as well as those hospitals and units excluded from IPPS (see section B above).

For services provided on or after October 31, 1994, for hospitals and units excluded from IPPS, this provision applies only to services furnished within one day prior to and including the date of the beneficiary's admission.

Critical access hospitals (CAHs) are not subject to the 3-day (nor 1-day) DRG payment window.

Hospitals in Maryland that are under the jurisdiction of the Health Services Cost Review Commission are subject to the 3-day payment window.

Effective for dates of service on or after July 1, 2008, CWF will reject therapeutic services when the line item date of service (LIDOS) falls on the day of admission or any of the 3 days immediately prior to an admission to an IPPS hospital or on the day of admission or one day prior to admission for hospitals excluded from IPPS.

100-4, 4, 10.4

Packaging

Under the OPPS, packaged services are items and services that are considered to be an integral part of another service that is paid under the OPPS. No separate payment is made for packaged services, because the cost of these items and services is included in the APC payment for the service of which they are an integral part. For example, routine supplies, anesthesia, recovery room use, and most drugs are considered to be an integral part of a surgical procedure so payment for these items is packaged into the APC payment for the surgical procedure.

A. Packaging for Claims Resulting in APC Payments

If a claim contains services that result in an APC payment but also contains packaged services, separate payment for the packaged services is not made since payment is included in the APC. However, charges related to the packaged services are used for outlier and Transitional Corridor Payments (TOPs) as well as for future rate setting.

Therefore, it is extremely important that hospitals report all HCPCS codes and all charges for all services they furnish, whether payment for the services is made separately paid or is packaged.

B. Packaging for Claims Resulting in No APC Payments

If the claim contains only services payable under cost reimbursement, such as corneal tissue, and services that would be packaged services if an APC were payable, then the packaged services are not separately payable. In addition, these charges for the packaged services are not used to calculate TOPs.

If the claim contains only services payable under a fee schedule, such as clinical diagnostic laboratory tests, and also contains services that would be packaged services if an APC were payable, the packaged services are not separately payable. In addition, the charges are not used to calculate TOPs.

If a claim contains services payable under cost reimbursement, services payable under a fee schedule, and services that would be packaged services if an APC were payable, the packaged services are not separately payable. In addition, the charges are not used to calculate TOPs payments.

C. Packaging Types Under the OPPS

1. Unconditionally packaged services are services for which separate payment is never made because the payment for the service is always packaged into the payment for other services. Unconditionally packaged services are identified in the OPPS Addendum B with status indictor of N. See the OPPS Web site at http://www.cms.hhs.gov/HospitalOutpatientPPS/ for the most recent Addendum B (HCPCS codes with status indicators). In general, the charges for unconditionally packaged services are used to calculate outlier and TOPS payments when they appear on a claim with a service that is separately paid under the OPPS because the packaged service is considered to be part of the package of services for which payment is being made through the APC payment for the separately paid service.

2. STVX-packaged services are services for which separate payment is made only if there is no service with status indicator S, T, V or X reported with the same date of service on the same claim. If a claim includes a service that is assigned status indicator S, T, V, or X reported on the same date of service as the STVXpackaged service, the payment for the STVX-packaged service is packaged into the payment for the service(s) with status indicator S, T, V or X and no separate payment is made for the STVX-packaged service. STVX-packaged services are assigned status indicator Q. See the OPPS Webpage at http://www.cms.hhs.gov/HospitalOutpatientPPS/ for identification of STVXpackaged codes.

3. T-packaged services are services for which separate payment is made only if there is no service with status indicator T reported with the same date of service on the same claim. When there is a claim that includes a service that is assigned status indicator T reported on the same date of service as the T-packaged service, the payment for the T-packaged service is packaged into the payment for the service(s) with status indicator T and no separate payment is made for the T-packaged service. T-packaged services are assigned status indicator Q. See the OPPS Web site at http://www.cms.hhs.gov/HospitalOutpatientPPS/ for identification of T-packaged codes.

4. A service that is assigned to a composite APC is a major component of a single episode of care. The hospital receives one payment through a composite APC for multiple major separately identifiable services. Services mapped to composite APCs are assigned status indicator Q. See the discussion of composite APCs in section 10.2.1.

100-4, 4, 160

Clinic and Emergency Visits

CMS has acknowledged from the beginning of the OPPS that CMS believes that CPT Evaluation and Management (E/M) codes were designed to reflect the activities of physicians and do not describe well the range and mix of services provided by hospitals during visits of clinic and emergency department patients. While awaiting the development of a national set of facility-specific codes and guidelines, providers should continue to apply their current internal guidelines to the existing CPT codes. Each hospital's internal guidelines should follow the intent of the CPT code descriptors, in that the guidelines should be designed to reasonably relate the intensity of hospital resources to the different levels of effort represented by the codes. Hospitals should ensure that their guidelines accurately reflect resource distinctions between the five levels of codes.

Effective January 1, 2007, CMS is distinguishing between two types of emergency departments: Type A emergency departments and Type B emergency departments.

A Type A emergency department is defined as an emergency department that is available 24 hours a day, 7 days a week and is either licensed by the State in which it is located under applicable State law as an emergency room or emergency department or it is held out to the public (by name, posted signs, advertising, or other means) as a place that provides care for emergency medical conditions on an urgent basis without requiring a previously scheduled appointment.

A Type B emergency department is defined as an emergency department that meets the definition of a "dedicated emergency department" as defined in 42 CFR 489.24 under the EMTALA regulations. It must meet at least one of the following requirements: (1) It is licensed by the State in which it is located under applicable State law as an emergency room or emergency department; (2) It is held out to the public (by name, posted signs, advertising, or other means) as a place that provides care for emergency medical conditions on an urgent basis without requiring a previously scheduled appointment; or (3) During the calendar year immediately preceding the calendar year in which a determination under 42 CFR 489.24 is being made, based on a representative sample of patient visits that occurred during that calendar year, it provides at least one-third of all of its outpatient visits for the treatment of emergency medical conditions on an urgent basis without requiring a previously scheduled appointment.

Hospitals must bill for visits provided in Type A emergency departments using CPT emergency department E/M codes. Hospitals must bill for visits provided in Type B emergency departments using the G-codes that describe visits provided in Type B emergency departments.

Hospitals that will be billing the new Type B ED visit codes may need to update their internal guidelines to report these codes.

Emergency department and clinic visits are paid in some cases separately and in other cases as part of a composite APC payment. See section 10.2.1 of this chapter for further details.

100-4, 4, 160.1

Critical Care Services

Beginning January 1, 2007, critical care services will be paid at two levels, depending on the presence or absence of trauma activation. Providers will receive one payment rate for critical care without trauma activation and will receive additional payment when critical care is associated with trauma activation.

To determine whether trauma activation occurs, follow the National Uniform Billing Committee (NUBC) guidelines in the Claims Processing Manual, Pub 100-04, Chapter 25, Sec.75.4 related to the reporting of the trauma revenue codes in the 68x series. The revenue code series 68x can be used only by trauma centers/hospitals as licensed or designated by the state or local government authority authorized to do so, or as verified by the American College of Surgeons. Different subcategory revenue codes are reported by designated Level 1-4 hospital trauma centers. Only patients for whom there has been prehospital notification based on triage information from prehospital caregivers, who meet either local, state or American College of Surgeons field triage criteria, or are delivered by inter-hospital transfers, and are given the appropriate team response can be billed a trauma activation charge.

When critical care services are provided without trauma activation, the hospital may bill CPT code 99291, Critical care, evaluation and management of the critically ill or critically injured patient; first 30-74 minutes (and 99292, if appropriate). If trauma activation occurs under the circumstances described by the NUBC guidelines that would permit reporting a charge under 68x, the hospital may also bill one unit of code G0390, which describes trauma activation associated with hospital critical care services. Revenue code 68x must be reported on the same date of service. The OCE will edit to ensure that G0390 appears with revenue code 68x on the same date of service and that only one unit of G0390 is billed. CMS believes that trauma activation is a one-time occurrence in association with critical care services, and therefore, CMS will only pay for one unit of G0390 per day.

The CPT code 99291 is defined by CPT as the first 30-74 minutes of critical care. This 30 minute minimum has always applied under the OPPS. The CPT code 99292, Critical care, evaluation and management of the critically ill or critically injured patient; each additional 30 minutes, remains a packaged service under the OPPS, so that hospitals do not have the ongoing administrative burden of reporting precisely the time for each critical service provided. As the CPT guidelines indicate, hospitals that provide less than 30 minutes of critical care should bill for a visit, typically an emergency department visit, at a level consistent with their own internal guidelines.

Under the OPPS, the time that can be reported as critical care is the time spent by a physician and/or hospital staff engaged in active face-to-face critical care of a critically ill or critically injured patient. If the physician and hospital staff or multiple hospital staff members are simultaneously engaged in this active face-to-face care, the time involved can only be counted once.

In CY 2007 hospitals may continue to report a charge with RC 68x without any HCPCS code when trauma team activation occurs. In order to receive additional payment when critical care services are associated with trauma activation, the hospital must report G0390 on the same date of service as RC 68x, in addition to CPT code 99291 (or 99292, if appropriate.)

In CY 2007 hospitals should continue to report 99291 (and 99292 as appropriate) for critical care services furnished without trauma team activation. CPT 99291 maps to APC 0617 (Critical Care). (CPT 99292 is packaged and not paid separately, but should be reported if provided.)

Critical care services are paid in some cases separately and in other cases as part of a composite APC payment. See Section 10.2.1 of this chapter for further details.

100-4, 4, 200.1

Billing for Corneal Tissue

Corneal tissue will be paid on a cost basis, not under OPPS. To receive cost based reimbursement hospitals must bill charges for corneal tissue using HCPCS code V2785.

100-4, 4, 200.3.4

Billing for Linear Accelerator (Robotic Image-Guided and Non-Robotic Image-Guided) SRS Planning and Delivery

Effective for services furnished on or after January 1, 2006, hospitals must bill using existing CPT codes that most accurately describe the service furnished for both robotic and non-robotic image-guided SRS planning. For robotic image-guided SRS delivery, hospitals must bill using HCPCS code G0339 for the first session and HCPCS code G0340 for the second through the fifth sessions. For non-robotic image-guided SRS delivery, hospitals must bill G0173 for delivery if the delivery occurs in one session, and G0251 for delivery per session (not to exceed five sessions) if delivery occurs during multiple sessions.

Linear Accelerator-Based Robotic Image-Guided SRS	
Planning	Use existing CPT codes
Delivery	G0339 (complete, 1st session)
	G0340 (2nd – 5th session)

Linear Accelerator-Based Non-Robotic Image-Guided SRS	
Planning	Use existing CPT codes
Delivery	G0173 (single session)
	G0251 (multiple)

HCPCS Code	Long Descriptors
G0173	Linear accelerator based stereotactic radiosurgery, delivery including collimator changes and custom plugging, complete course of treatment in one session, all lesions.
G0251	Linear accelerator based stereotactic radiosurgery, delivery including collimator changes and custom plugging, fractionated treatment, all lesions, per session, maximum 5 sessions per course of treatment.
G0339	Image-guided robotic linear accelerator-based stereotactic radiosurgery, complete course of therapy in one session or first session of fractionated treatment.
G0340	Image-guided robotic linear accelerator-based stereotactic radiosurgery, delivery including collimator changes and custom plugging, fractionated treatment, all lesions, per session, second through fifth sessions, maximum five sessions per course of treatment

100-4, 4, 200.4

Billing for Amniotic Membrane

Hospitals should report HCPCS code V2790 (Amniotic membrane for surgical reconstruction, per procedure) to report amniotic membrane tissue when the tissue is used. A specific procedure code associated with use of amniotic membrane tissue is CPT code 65780 (Ocular surface reconstruction; amniotic membrane transplantation).

Payment for the amniotic membrane tissue is packaged into payment for CPT code 65780 or other procedures with which the amniotic membrane is used.

100-4, 4, 200.6

Billing and Payment for Alcohol and/or Substance Abuse Assessment and Intervention Services

For CY 2008, the CPT Editorial Panel has created two new Category I CPT codes for reporting alcohol and/or substance abuse screening and intervention services. They are CPT code 99408 (Alcohol and/or substance (other than tobacco) abuse structured screening (e.g., AUDIT, DAST), and brief intervention (SBI) services; 15 to 30 minutes); and CPT code 99409 (Alcohol and/or substance (other than tobacco) abuse structured screening (e.g., AUDIT, DAST), and brief intervention (SBI) services; greater than 30 minutes). However, screening services are not covered by Medicare without specific statutory authority, such as has been provided for mammography, diabetes, and colorectal cancer screening. Therefore, beginning January 1, 2008, the OPPS recognizes two parallel G-codes (HCPCS codes G0396 and G0397) to allow for appropriate reporting and payment of alcohol and substance abuse structured assessment and intervention services that are not provided as screening services, but that are performed in the context of the diagnosis or treatment of illness or injury.

Contractors shall make payment under the OPPS for HCPCS code G0396 (Alcohol and/or substance (other than tobacco) abuse structured assessment (e.g., AUDIT, DAST) and brief intervention, 15 to 30 minutes) and HCPCS code G0397, (Alcohol and/or substance(other than tobacco) abuse structured assessment (e.g., AUDIT, DAST) and intervention greater than 30 minutes), only when reasonable and necessary (i.e., when the service is provided to evaluate patients with signs/symptoms of illness or injury) as per section 1862(a)(1)(A) of the Act.

HCPCS codes G0396 and G0397 are to be used for structured alcohol and/or substance (other than tobacco) abuse assessment and intervention services that are distinct from other clinic and emergency department visit services performed during the same encounter. Hospital resources expended performing services described by HCPCS codes G0396 and G0397 may not be counted as resources for determining the level of a visit service and vice versa (i.e., hospitals may not double count the same facility resources in order to reach a higher level clinic or emergency department visit). However, alcohol and/or substance structured assessment or intervention services lasting less than 15 minutes should not be reported using these HCPCS codes, but the hospital resources expended should be included in determining the level of the visit service reported.

100-4, 4, 200.7.2

Cardiac Echocardiography With Contrast

Hospitals are instructed to bill for echocardiograms with contrast using the applicable HCPCS code(s) included in Table 200.7.2 below. Hospitals should also report the appropriate units of the HCPCS codes for the contrast agents used in the performance of the echocardiograms.

Table 200.7.2 - HCPCS Codes For Echocardiograms With Contrast HCPCS Long Descriptor C8921 Transthoracic echocardiography with contrast for congenital cardiac anomalies; complete C8922 Transthoracic echocardiography with contrast for congenital cardiac anomalies; follow-up or limited study C8923 Transthoracic echocardiography with contrast, realtime with image documentation (2D) with or without HCPCS Long Descriptor M-mode recording; complete C8924 Transthoracic echocardiography with contrast, realtime with image documentation (2D) with or without M-mode recording; follow-up or limited study C8925 Transesophageal echocardiography (TEE) with contrast, real time with image documentation (2D) (with or without M-mode recording); including probe placement, image acquisition, interpretation and report C8926 Transesophageal echocardiography (TEE) with contrast for congenital cardiac anomalies; including probe placement, image acquisition, interpretation and report C8927 Transesophageal echocardiography (TEE) with contrast for monitoring purposes, including probe placement, real time 2-dimensional image acquisition and interpretation leading to ongoing (continuous) assessment of (dynamically changing) cardiac pumping function and to therapeutic measures on an immediate time basis C8928 Transthoracic echocardiography with contrast, realtime with image documentation (2D), with or without M-mode recording, during rest and cardiovascular stress test using treadmill, bicycle exercise and/or pharmacologically induced stress, with interpretation and report

100-4, 4, 230.2

Coding and Payment for Drug Administration

Coding and Payment for Drug Administration

A. Overview

Drug administration services furnished under the Hospital Outpatient Prospective Payment System (OPPS) during CY 2005 were reported using CPT codes 90780, 90781, and 96400-96459.

Effective January 1, 2006, some of these CPT codes were replaced with more detailed CPT codes incorporating specific procedural concepts, as defined and described by the CPT manual, such as initial, concurrent, and sequential.

Hospitals are instructed to use the full set of CPT codes, including those codes referencing concepts of initial, concurrent, and sequential, to bill for drug administration services furnished in the hospital outpatient department beginning January 1, 2007. In addition, hospitals are instructed to continue billing the HCPCS codes that most accurately describe the service(s) provided.

Hospitals are reminded to bill a separate Evaluation and Management code (with modifier 25) only if a significant, separately identifiable E/M service is performed in the same encounter with OPPS drug administration services.

B. Billing for Infusions and Injections

Beginning in CY 2007, hospitals were instructed to use the full set of drug administration CPT codes (90760-90779; 96401-96549), (96413-96523 beginning in CY 2008) (96360-96549 beginning in CY 2009) when billing for drug administration services provided in the hospital outpatient department. In addition, hospitals are to continue to bill HCPCS code C8957 (Intravenous infusion for therapy/diagnosis; initiation of prolonged infusion (more than 8 hours), requiring use of portable or implantable pump) when appropriate. Hospitals are expected to report all drug administration CPT codes in a manner consistent with their descriptors, CPT instructions, and correct coding principles. Hospitals should note the conceptual changes between CY 2006 drug administration codes effective under the OPPS and the CPT codes in effect beginning January 1, 2007, in order to ensure accurate billing under the OPPS. Hospitals should report all HCPCS codes that describe the drug administration services provided, regardless of whether or not those services are separately paid or their payment is packaged.

Medicare's general policy regarding physician supervision within hospital outpatient departments meets the physician supervision requirements for use of CPT codes 90760-90779, 96401-96549, (96413-96523 beginning in CY 2008). (Reference: Pub.100-02, Medicare Benefit Policy Manual, Chapter 6, §20.4.)

Drug administration services are to be reported with a line item date of service on the day they are provided. In addition, only one initial drug administration service is to be reported per vascular access site per encounter, including during an encounter where observation services span more than 1 calendar day.

C. Payments For Drug Administration Services

For CY 2007, OPPS drug administration APCs were restructured, resulting in a six-level hierarchy where active HCPCS codes have been assigned according to their clinical coherence and resource use. Contrary to the CY 2006 payment structure that bundled payment for several instances of a type of service (non-chemotherapy, chemotherapy by infusion, non-infusion chemotherapy) into a per-encounter APC payment, structure introduced in CY 2007 provides a separate APC payment for each reported unit of a separately payable HCPCS code.

Hospitals should note that the transition to the full set of CPT drug administration codes provides for conceptual differences when reporting, such as those noted below.

- In CY 2006, hospitals were instructed to bill for the first hour (and any additional hours) by each type of infusion service (non-chemotherapy, chemotherapy by infusion, non-infusion chemotherapy). Beginning in CY 2007, the first hour concept no longer exists. CPT codes in CY 2007 and beyond allow for only one initial service per encounter, for each vascular access site, no matter how many types of infusion services are provided; however, hospitals will receive an APC payment for the initial service and separate APC payment(s) for additional hours of infusion or other drug administration services provided that are separately payable.
- In CY 2006, hospitals providing infusion services of different types (non-chemotherapy, chemotherapy by infusion, non-infusion chemotherapy) received payment for the associated per-encounter infusion APC even if these infusions occurred during the same time period. Beginning in CY 2007, hospitals should report only one initial drug administration service, including infusion services, per encounter for each distinct vascular access site, with other services through the same vascular access site being reported via the sequential, concurrent or additional hour codes. Although new CPT guidance has been issued for reporting initial drug administration services, Medicare contractors shall continue to follow the guidance given in this manual.

(NOTE: This list above provides a brief overview of a limited number of the conceptual changes between CY 2006 OPPS drug administration codes and CY 2007 OPPS drug administration codes - this list is not comprehensive and does not include all items hospitals will need to consider during this transition)

For APC payment rates, refer to the most current quarterly version of Addendum B on the CMS Web site at http://www.cms.hhs.gov/HospitalOutpatientPPS/.

D. Infusions Started Outside the Hospital

Hospitals may receive Medicare beneficiaries for outpatient services who are in the process of receiving an infusion at their time of arrival at the hospital (e.g., a patient who arrives via ambulance with an ongoing intravenous infusion initiated by paramedics during transport). Hospitals are reminded to bill for all services provided using the HCPCS code(s) that most accurately describe the service(s) they provided. This includes hospitals reporting an initial hour of infusion, even if the hospital did not initiate the infusion, and additional HCPCS codes for additional or sequential infusion services if needed.

100-4, 4, 230.2.1

Administration of Drugs Via Implantable or Portable Pumps

for Implantable or Portable Pumps 2005 CPT Final CY 2006 OPPS 2005 CPT 2005 Description Code Description SI APC n/a n/a C8957 Intravenous infusion for therapy/diagnosis; initiation of prolonged infusion (more than 8 hours), requiring use of portable or implantable pump S 0120 96414 Chemotherapy administration, intravenous; infusion technique, initiation of prolonged infusion (more than 8 hours), requiring the use of a portable or implantable pump 96416 Chemotherapy administration, intravenous infusion technique; initiation of prolonged chemotherapy infusion (more than 8 hours), requiring use of portable or implantable pump S 0117 96425 Chemotherapy administration, infusion technique, initiation of prolonged infusion (more than 8 hours), requiring the use of a portable or implantable pump) 96425 Chemotherapy administration, intra-arterial; infusion technique, initiation of prolonged infusion (more than 8 hours), requiring the use of a portable or implantable pump S 0117 96520 Refilling and maintenance of portable pump 96521 Refilling and maintenance of portable pump T 0125 2005 CPT Final CY 2006 OPPS 2005 CPT 2005 Description Code Description SI APC 96530 Refilling and maintenance of implantable pump or reservoir for drug delivery, systemic [e.g. Intravenous, intra-arterial] 96522 Refilling and maintenance of implantable pump or reservoir for drug delivery, systemic (e.g., intravenous, intra-arterial) T 0125 n/a n/a 96523 Irrigation of implanted venous access device for drug delivery systems N - Hospitals are to report HCPCS code C8957 and CPT codes 96416 and 96425 to indicate the initiation of a prolonged infusion that requires the use of an implantable or portable pump. CPT codes 96521, 92522, and 96523 should be used by hospitals to indicate refilling and maintenance of drug delivery systems or irrigation of implanted venous access devices for such systems, and may be reported for the servicing of devices used for therapeutic drugs other than chemotherapy.

100-4, 4, 230.2.3

Non-Chemotherapy Drug Administration

Table 5: CY 2006 OPPS Non-Chemotherapy Drug Administration -Intravenous Infusion Technique

2005 CPT	Final CY 2006 OPPS	2005 CPT	2005 Description	Code	Desc	SI	APC
90780	Intravenous infusion for therapy/diagnosis, administered by physician or under direct supervision of physician; up to one hour	C8950	Intravenous infusion for therapy/diagnosis; up to 1 hour	S	0120		
90781	Intravenous infusion for therapy/diagnosis, administered by physician or under direct supervision of physician; each additional hour, up to eight (8) hours (List separately in addition to code for primary procedure)	C8951	Intravenous infusion for therapy/diagnosis; each additional hour (List separately in addition to C8950)	N	-	n/a	n/a
		C8957	Intravenous infusion for therapy/diagnosis; initiation of prolonged infusion (more than 8 hours), requiring use of portable or implantable pump	S	120		

Hospitals are to report HCPCS code C8950 to indicate an infusion of drugs other than anti-neoplastic drugs furnished on or after January 1, 2006 (except as noted at 230.2.2(A) above). HCPCS code C8951 should be used to report all additional infusion hours, with no limit on the number of hours billed per line. Medically necessary separate therapeutic or diagnostic hydration services should be reported with C8950 and C8951, as these are considered intravenous infusions for therapy/diagnosis.

HCPCS codes C8950 and C8951 should not be reported when the infusion is a necessary and integral part of a separately payable OPPS procedure.

When more than one nonchemotherapy drug is infused, hospitals are to code HCPCS codes C8950 and C8951 (if necessary) to report the total duration of an infusion, regardless of the number of substances or drugs infused. Hospitals are reminded to bill separately for each drug infused, in addition to the drug administration services.

The OCE pays one APC for each encounter reported by HCPCS code C8950, and only pays one APC for C8950 per day (unless Modifier 59 is used). Payment for additional hours of infusion reported by HCPCS code C8951 is packaged into the payment for the initial infusion. While no separate payment will be made for units of HCPCS code C8951, hospitals are instructed to report all codes that appropriately describe the services provided and the corresponding charges so that CMS may capture specific historical hospital cost data for future payment rate setting activities.

OCE logic assumes that all services for non-chemotherapy infusions billed on the same date of service were provided during the same encounter. Where a beneficiary makes two separate visits to the hospital for non-chemotherapy infusions in the same day, hospitals are to report modifier 59 for non-chemotherapy infusion codes during the second encounter that were also furnished in the first encounter. The OCE identifies modifier 59 and pays up to a maximum number of units per day, as listed in Table 1.

EXAMPLE 1

A beneficiary receives infused drugs that are not anti-neoplastic drugs (including hydrating solutions) for 2 hours. The hospital reports one unit of HCPCS code C8950 and one unit of HCPCS code C8951. The OCE will pay one unit of APC 0120. Payment for the unit of HCPCS code C8951 is packaged into the payment for one unit of APC 0120. (NOTE: See 230.1 for drug billing instructions.)

EXAMPLE 2

A beneficiary receives infused drugs that are not anti-neoplastic drugs (including hydrating solutions) for 12 hours. The hospital reports one unit of HCPCS code C8950 and eleven units of HCPCS code C8951. The OCE will pay one unit of APC 0120. Payment for the 11 units of HCPCS code C8951 is packaged into the payment for one unit of APC 0120. (NOTE: See 230.1 for drug billing instructions.)

EXAMPLE 3

A beneficiary experiences multiple attempts to initiate an intravenous infusion before a successful infusion is started 20 minutes after the first attempt. Once started, the infusion lasts one hour. The hospital reports one unit of HCPCS code C8950 to identify the 1 hour of infusion time. The 20 minutes spent prior to the infusion attempting to establish an IV line are not separately billable in the OPPS. The OCE pays one unit of APC 0120. (NOTE: See 230.1 for drug billing instructions.)

B. Administration of Non-Chemotherapy Drugs by a Route Other Than Intravenous Infusion

Table 6: CY 2006 OPPS Non-Chemotherapy Drug Administration -Route Other Than Intravenous Infusion

2005 CPT	Final CY 2006 OPPS	2005 CPT	2005 Description	Code	Description	SI	APC
90784	Therapeutic, prophylactic or diagnostic injection (specify material injected); intravenous	C8952	Therapeutic, prophylactic or diagnostic injection; intravenous push	X	0359		
90782	Therapeutic, prophylactic or diagnostic injection (specify material injected); subcutaneous or intramuscular	90772	Therapeutic, prophylactic or diagnostic injection (specify substance or drug); subcutaneous or intramuscular	X	0353		
90783	Therapeutic, prophylactic or diagnostic injection (specify material injected); intra-arterial	90773	Therapeutic, prophylactic or diagnostic injection (specify substance or drug); intra-arterial	X	0359		
90779	Unlisted therapeutic, prophylactic or diagnostic intravenous or intra-arterial, injection or infusion	90779	Unlisted therapeutic, prophylactic or diagnostic intravenous or intra-arterial injection or infusion	X	0352		

100-4, 4, 231.4

Billing for Split Unit of Blood

HCPCS code P9011 was created to identify situations where one unit of blood or a blood product is split and some portion of the unit is transfused to one patient and the other portions are transfused to other patients or to the same patient at other times. When a patient receives a transfusion of a split unit of blood or blood product, OPPS providers should bill P9011 for the blood product transfused, as well as CPT 86985 (Splitting, blood products) for each splitting procedure performed to prepare the blood product for a specific patient.

Providers should bill split units of packed red cells and whole blood using Revenue Code 389 (Other blood), and should not use Revenue Codes 381 (Packed red cells) or 382 (Whole blood). Providers should bill split units of other blood products using the applicable revenue codes for the blood product type, such as 383 (Plasma) or 384 (Platelets), rather than 389. Reporting revenue codes according to these specifications will ensure the Medicare beneficiary's blood deductible is applied correctly.

EXAMPLE: OPPS provider splits off a 100cc aliquot from a 250 cc unit of leukocytereduced red blood cells for a transfusion to Patient X. The hospital then splits off an 80cc aliquot of the remaining unit for a transfusion to Patient Y. At a later time, the remaining 70cc from the unit is transfused to Patient Z.

In billing for the services for Patient X and Patient Y, the OPPS provider should report the charges by billing P9011 and 86985 in addition to the CPT code for the transfusion service, because a specific splitting service was required to prepare a split unit for transfusion to each of those patients. However, the OPPS provider should report only P9011 and the CPT code for the transfusion service for Patient Z because no additional splitting was necessary to prepare the split unit for transfusion to Patient Z. The OPPS provider should bill Revenue Code 0389 for each split unit of the leukocyte-reduced red blood cells that was transfused.

100-4, 4, 240

Inpatient Part B Hospital Services

Inpatient Part B services which are paid under OPPS include:

- Diagnostic x-ray tests, and other diagnostic tests (excluding clinical diagnostic laboratory tests); X-ray, radium, and radioactive isotope therapy, including materials and services of technicians;
- Surgical dressings applied during an encounter at the hospital and splints, casts, and other devices used for reduction of fractures and dislocations (splints and casts, etc., include dental splints);
- Implantable prosthetic devices;
- Hepatitis B vaccine and its administration, and certain preventive screening services (pelvic exams, screening sigmoidoscopies, screening colonoscopies, bone mass measurements, and prostate screening.)
- Bone Mass measurements;
- Prostate screening;
- Immunosuppressive drugs;
- Oral anti-cancer drugs;
- Oral drug prescribed for use as an acute anti-emetic used as part of an anti-cancer chemotherapeutic regimen; and
- Epoetin Alfa (EPO)

When a hospital that is not paid under the OPPS furnishes an implantable prosthetic device that meets the criteria for coverage in Medicare Benefits Policy Manual, Pub.100-02, Chapter 6, Sec.10 to an inpatient who has coverage under Part B, payment for the implantable prosthetic device is made under the payment mechanism that applies to other hospital outpatient services (e.g. reasonable cost, all inclusive rate, waiver).

When a hospital that is paid under the OPPS furnishes an implantable prosthetic device to an inpatient who has coverage under Part B, but who does not have coverage of inpatient services on the date that the implanted prosthetic device is furnished, the hospital should report new HCPCS code, C9899, Implanted Prosthetic Device, Payable Only for Inpatients who do not Have Inpatient Coverage, that will be effective for services furnished on or after January 1, 2009. This code may be reported only on claims with TOB 12X when the prosthetic device is implanted on a day on which the beneficiary does not have coverage of the hospital inpatient services he or she is receiving. The line containing this new code will be rejected if it is reported on a claim that is not a TOB 12X or if it is reported with a line item date of service on which the beneficiary has coverage of inpatient hospital services. By reporting C9899, the hospital is reporting that all of the criteria for payment under Part B are met as specified in the

Medicare Benefits Policy Manual, Pub.100-02, Chapter 6, Sec.10, and that the item meets all Medicare criteria for coverage as an implantable prosthetic device as defined in that section.

Medicare contractors shall first determine that the item furnished meets the Medicare criteria for coverage as an implantable prosthetic device as specified in the *Medicare Benefits Policy Manual*, Pub. 100-02, Chapter 6, Sec.10. If the item does not meet the criteria for coverage as an implantable prosthetic device, the contractor shall deny payment on the basis that the item is outside the scope of the benefits for which there is coverage for Part B inpatients. The beneficiary is liable for the charges for the noncovered item when the item does not meet the criteria for coverage as an implanted prosthetic device as specified in the *Medicare Benefits Policy Manual*, Pub.100-02, Chapter 6, Sec.10.

If the contractor determines that the device is covered, the contractor shall determine if the device has pass through status under the OPPS. If so, the contractor shall establish the payment amount for the device at the product of the charge for the device and the hospital specific cost to charge ratio. Where the device does not have pass through status under the OPPS, the contractor shall establish the payment amount for the device at the amount for a comparable device in the DMEPOS fee schedule where there is such an amount. Payment under the DMEPOS fee schedule is made at the lesser of charges or the fee schedule amount and therefore if there is a fee for the specific item on the DMEPOS fee schedule, the payment amount for the item will be set at the lesser of the actual charges or the DMEPOS fee schedule amount. Where the item does not have pass through payment status and where there is no amount for a comparable device in the DMEPOS fee schedule, the contractor shall establish a payment amount that is specific to the particular implanted prosthetic device for the applicable calendar year. This amount (less applicable unpaid deductible and coinsurance) will be paid for that specific device for services furnished in the applicable calendar year unless the actual charge for the item is less than the established amount). Where the actual charge is less than the established amount, the contractor will pay the actual charge for the item (less applicable unpaid deductible and coinsurance).

In setting a contractor established payment rate for the specific device, the contractor takes into account the cost information available at the time the payment rate is established. This information may include, but is not limited to, the amount of device cost that would be removed from an applicable APC payment for implantation of the device if the provider received a device without cost or a full credit for the cost of the device.

If the contractor chooses to use this amount, see www.cms.hhs.gov/HospitalOutpatientPPS/ for the amount of reduction to the APC payment that would apply in these cases. From the OPPS webpage, select "Device, Radiolabeled Product, and Procedure Edits" from the list on the left side of the page. Open the file "Procedure to Device edits" to determine the HCPCS code that best describes the procedure in which the device would be used. Then identify the APC to which that procedure code maps from the most recent Addenda B on the OPPS webpage and open the file "FB/FC Modifier Procedures and Devices". Select the applicable year's file of APCs subject to full and partial credit reductions (for example: CY 2008 APCs Subject to Full and Partial Credit Reduction Policy"). Select the "Full offset reduction amount" that pertains to the APC that is most applicable to the device described by C9899. It would be reasonable to set this amount as a payment for a device furnished to a Part B inpatient.

For example, if C9899 is reporting insertion of a single chamber pacemaker (C1786 or equivalent narrative description on the claim in "remarks") the file of procedure to device edits shows that a single chamber pacemaker is the dominant device for APC 0090 (APC 0089 is for insertion of both pacemaker and electrodes and therefore would not apply if electrodes are not also billed). The table of offset reduction amounts for CY 2008 shows that the estimated cost of a single chamber pacemaker for APC 0090 is $4881.77. It would therefore be reasonable for the contractor/MAC to set the payment rate for a single chamber pacemaker furnished to a Part B inpatient to $4881.77. In this case the coinsurance would be $936.75 (20 percent of $4881.77, which is less than the inpatient deductible).

The beneficiary coinsurance is 20 percent of the payment amount for the device (i.e. the pass through payment amount, the DMEPOS fee schedule amount, the contractor established amount, or the actual charge if less than the DMEPOS fee schedule amount or the contractor established amount for the specific device), not to exceed the Medicare inpatient deductible that is applicable to the year in which the implanted prosthetic device is furnished.

Inpatient Part B services paid under other payment methods include:

- Clinical diagnostic laboratory tests, prosthetic devices other than implantable ones and other than dental which replace all or part of an internal body organ (including contiguous tissue), or all or part of the function of a permanently inoperative or malfunctioning internal body organ, including replacement or repairs of such devices;
- Leg, arm, back and neck braces; trusses and artificial legs; arms and eyes including adjustments, repairs, and replacements required because of breakage, wear, loss, or a change in the patient's physical condition; take home surgical dressings; outpatient physical therapy; outpatient occupational therapy; and outpatient speech-language pathology services;
- Ambulance services;
- Screening pap smears, screening colorectal tests, and screening mammography;
- Influenza virus vaccine and its administration, pneumococcal vaccine and its administration;
- Diabetes self-management training;
- Hemophilia clotting factors for hemophilia patients competent to use these factors without supervision).

See Chapter 6 of the Medicare Benefit Policy Manual for a discussion of the circumstances under which the above services may be covered as Part B Inpatient services.

100-4, 4, 290.1

Observation Services Overview

Observation care is a well-defined set of specific, clinically appropriate services, which include ongoing short term treatment, assessment, and reassessment, that are furnished while a decision is being made regarding whether patients will require further treatment as hospital inpatients or if they are able to be discharged from the hospital. Observation status is commonly assigned to patients who present to the emergency department and who then require a significant period of treatment or monitoring in order to make a decision concerning their admission or discharge. Observation services are covered only when provided by the order of a physician or another individual authorized by State licensure law and hospital staff bylaws to admit patients to the hospital or to order outpatient services.

Observation services must also be reasonable and necessary to be covered by Medicare. In only rare and exceptional cases do reasonable and necessary outpatient observation services span more than 48 hours. In the majority of cases, the decision whether to discharge a patient from the hospital following resolution of the reason for the observation care or to admit the patient as an inpatient can be made in less than 48 hours, usually in less than 24 hours.

100-4, 4, 290.2.2

Reporting Hours of Observation

Observation time begins at the clock time documented in the patient's medical record, which coincides with the time the patient is placed in a bed for the purpose of initiating observation care in accordance with a physician's order. Hospitals should round to the nearest hour. For example, a patient who was placed in an observation bed at 3:03 p.m. according to the nurses' notes and discharged to home at 9:45 p.m. should have a "7" placed in the units field of the reported observation HCPCS code.

General standing orders for observation services following all outpatient surgery are not recognized. Hospitals should not report as observation care, services that are part of another Part B service, such as postoperative monitoring during a standard recovery period (e.g., 4-6 hours), which should be billed as recovery room services. Similarly, in the case of patients who undergo diagnostic testing in a hospital outpatient department, routine preparation services furnished prior to the testing and recovery afterwards are included in the payments for those diagnostic services. Observation services should not be billed concurrently with diagnostic or therapeutic services for which active monitoring is a part of the procedure (e.g., colonoscopy, chemotherapy). In situations where such a procedure interrupts observation services, hospitals would record for each period of observation services the beginning and ending times during the hospital outpatient encounter and add the length of time for the periods of observation services together to reach the total number of units reported on the claim for the hourly observation services HCPCS code G0378 (Hospital observation service, per hour).

Observation time ends when all medically necessary services related to observation care are completed. For example, this could be before discharge when the need for observation has ended, but other medically necessary services not meeting the definition of observation care are provided (in which case, the additional medically necessary services would be billed separately or included as part of the emergency department or clinic visit). Alternatively, the end time of observation services may coincide with the time the patient is actually discharged from the hospital or admitted as an inpatient.

Observation time may include medically necessary services and follow-up care provided after the time that the physician writes the discharge order, but before the patient is discharged. However, reported observation time would not include the time patients remain in the observation area after treatment is finished for reasons such as waiting for transportation home.

If a period of observation spans more than 1 calendar day, all of the hours for the entire period of observation must be included on a single line and the date of service for that line is the date that observation care begins.

100-4, 4, 290.4.1

Billing and Payment for All Hospital Observation Services Furnished Between January 1, 2006 and December 31, 2007

Since January 1, 2006, two G-codes have been used to report observation services and direct referral for observation care. For claims for dates of service January 1, 2006 through December 31, 2007, the Integrated Outpatient Code Editor (I/OCE) determines whether the observation care or direct referral services are packaged or separately payable. Thus, hospitals provide consistent coding and billing under all circumstances in which they deliver observation care.

Beginning January 1, 2006, hospitals should not report CPT codes 99217-99220 or 99234-99236 for observation services. In addition, the following HCPCS codes were discontinued as of January 1, 2006: G0244 (Observation care by facility to patient), G0263 (Direct Admission with congestive heart failure, chest pain or asthma), and G0264 (Assessment other than congestive heart failure, chest pain, or asthma).

The three discontinued G-codes and the CPT codes that were no longer recognized were replaced by two new G-codes to be used by hospitals to report all observation services, whether separately payable or packaged, and direct referral for observation care, whether separately payable or packaged:

G0378- Hospital observation service, per hour; and

G0379- Direct admission of patient for hospital observation care.

The I/OCE determines whether observation services billed as units of G0378 are separately payable under APC 0339 (Observation) or whether payment for observation services will be packaged into the payment for other services provided by the hospital in the same encounter. Therefore, hospitals should bill HCPCS code G0378 when observation services are ordered and provided to any patient regardless of the patient's condition. The units of service should equal the number of hours the patient receives observation services.

Hospitals should report G0379 when observation services are the result of a direct referral for observation care without an associated emergency room visit, hospital outpatient clinic visit, critical care service, or hospital outpatient surgical procedure (status indicator T procedure) on the day of initiation of observation services. Hospitals should only report HCPCS code G0379 when a patient is referred directly for observation care after being seen by a physician in the community (see Sec.290.4.2 below)

Some non-repetitive OPPS services provided on the same day by a hospital may be billed on different claims, provided that all charges associated with each procedure or service being reported are billed on the same claim with the HCPCS code which describes that service. See chapter 1, section 50.2.2 of this manual. It is vitally important that all of the charges that pertain to a non-repetitive, separately paid procedure or service be reported on the same claim with that procedure or service. It should also be emphasized that this relaxation of same day billing requirements for some non-repetitive services does not apply to non-repetitive services provided on the same day as either direct referral to observation care or observation services because the OCE claim-by-claim logic cannot function properly unless all services related to the episode of observation care, including diagnostic tests, lab services, hospital clinic visits, emergency department visits, critical care services, and status indicator T procedures, are reported on the same claim. Additional guidance can be found in chapter 1, section 50.2.2 of this manual.

100-4, 4, 290.4.2

Separate and Packaged Payment for Direct Admission to Observation

In order to receive separate payment for a direct referral for observation care (APC 0604), the claim must show:

1. Both HCPCS codes G0378 (Hourly Observation) and G0379 (Direct Admit to Observation) with the same date of service;
2. That no services with a status indicator T or V or Critical care (APC 0617) were provided on the same day of service as HCPCS code G0379; and
3. The observation care does not qualify for separate payment under APC 0339.

Only a direct referral for observation services billed on a 13X bill type may be considered for a separate APC payment.

Separate payment is not allowed for HCPCS code G0379, direct admission to observation care, when billed with the same date of service as a hospital clinic visit, emergency room visit, critical care service, or "T" status procedure.

If a bill for the direct referral for observation services does not meet the three requirements listed above, then payment for the direct referral service will be packaged into payments for other separately payable services provided to the beneficiary in the same encounter.

100-4, 4, 290.4.3

Separate and Packaged Payment for Observation Services Furnished Between January 1, 2006 and December 31, 2007

Separate payment may be made for observation services provided to a patient with congestive heart failure, chest pain, or asthma. The list of ICD-9-CM diagnosis codes eligible for separate payment is reviewed annually. Any changes in applicable ICD-9-CM diagnosis codes are included in the October quarterly update of the OPPS and also published in the annual OPPS Final Rule. The list of qualifying ICD-9-CM diagnosis codes is also published on the OPPS Web page.

All of the following requirements must be met in order for a hospital to receive a separate APC payment for observation services through APC 0339:

1. Diagnosis Requirements
   a. The beneficiary must have one of three medical conditions: congestive heart failure, chest pain, or asthma.
   b. Qualifying ICD-9-CM diagnosis codes must be reported in Form Locator (FL) 76, Patient Reason for Visit, or FL 67, principal diagnosis, or both in order for the hospital to receive separate payment for APC 0339. If a qualifying ICD-9-CM diagnosis code(s) is reported in the secondary diagnosis field, but is not reported in either the Patient Reason for Visit field (FL 76) or in the principal diagnosis field (FL 67), separate payment for APC 0339 is not allowed.
2. Observation Time
   a. Observation time must be documented in the medical record.
   b. Hospital billing for observation services begins at the clock time documented in the patient's medical record, which coincides with the time that observation services are initiated in accordance with a physician's order for observation services.
   c. A beneficiary's time receiving observation services (and hospital billing) ends when all clinical or medical interventions have been completed, including follow-up care furnished by hospital staff and physicians that may take place after a physician has ordered the patient be released or admitted as an inpatient.
   d. The number of units reported with HCPCS code G0378 must equal or exceed 8 hours.
3. Additional Hospital Services
   a. The claim for observation services must include one of the following services in addition to the reported observation services. The additional services listed below must have a line item date of service on the same day or the day before the date reported for observation:

      An emergency department visit (APC 0609, 0613, 0614, 0615, 0616) or

      A clinic visit (APC 0604, 0605, 0606, 0607, 0608); or

      Critical care (APC 0617); or

      Direct referral for observation care reported with HCPCS code G0379 (APC 0604); must be reported on the same date of service as the date reported for observation services.
   b. No procedure with a T status indicator can be reported on the same day or day before observation care is provided.
4. Physician Evaluation
   a. The beneficiary must be in the care of a physician during the period of observation, as documented in the medical record by outpatient registration, discharge, and other appropriate progress notes that are timed, written, and signed by the physician.
   b. The medical record must include documentation that the physician explicitly assessed patient risk to determine that the beneficiary would benefit from observation care.

   Only observation services that are billed on a 13X bill type may be considered for a separate APC payment.

   Hospitals should bill all of the other services associated with the observation care, including direct referral for observation, hospital clinic visits, emergency room visits, critical care services, and T status procedures, on the same claim so that the claims processing logic may appropriately determine the payment status (either packaged or separately payable) of HCPCS codes G0378 and G0379.

   If a bill for observation care does not meet all of the requirements listed above, then payment for the observation care will be packaged into payments for other separately payable services provided to the beneficiary in the same encounter.

100-4, 4, 290.5.1

Billing and Payment for Observation Services Beginning January 1, 2008

Observation services are reported using HCPCS code G0378 (Hospital observation service, per hour). Beginning January 1, 2008, HCPCS code G0378 for hourly observation services is assigned status indicator N, signifying that its payment is always packaged. No separate payment is made for observation services reported with HCPCS code G0378, and APC 0339 is deleted as of January 1, 2008. In most circumstances, observation services are supportive and ancillary to the other services provided to a patient. In certain circumstances when observation care is billed in conjunction with a high level clinic visit (Level 5), high level Type A emergency department visit (Level 4 or 5), high level Type B emergency department visit (Level 5), critical care services, or a direct referral as an integral part of a patient's extended encounter of care, payment may be made for the entire extended care encounter through one of two composite APCs when certain criteria are met. For information about payment for extended assessment and management composite APCs, see Sec.10.2.1 (Composite APCs) of this chapter.

APC 8002 (Level I Extended Assessment and Management Composite) describes an encounter for care provided to a patient that includes a high level (Level 5) clinic visit or direct referral for observation in conjunction with observation services of substantial duration (8 or more hours). APC 8003 (Level II Extended Assessment and Management Composite) describes an encounter for care provided to a patient that includes a high level (Level 4 or 5) emergency department visit or critical care services in conjunction with observation services of substantial duration. Beginning January 1, 2009, APC 8003 also includes high level (Level 5) Type B emergency department visits. There is no limitation on diagnosis for payment of these composite APCs; however, composite APC payment will not be made when observation services are reported in association with a surgical procedure (T status procedure) or the hours of observation care reported are less than 8. The I/OCE evaluates every claim received to determine if payment through a composite APC is appropriate. If payment through a composite APC is inappropriate, the I/OCE, in conjunction with the Pricer, determines the appropriate status indicator, APC, and payment for every code on a claim.

All of the following requirements must be met in order for a hospital to receive an APC payment for an extended assessment and management composite APC:

1. Observation Time
   a. Observation time must be documented in the medical record.
   b. Hospital billing for observation services begins at the clock time documented in the patient's medical record, which coincides with the time that observation services are initiated in accordance with a physician's order for observation services.
   c. A beneficiary's time receiving observation services (and hospital billing) ends when all clinical or medical interventions have been completed, including follow-up care furnished by hospital staff and physicians that may take place after a physician has ordered the patient be released or admitted as an inpatient.
   d. The number of units reported with HCPCS code G0378 must equal or exceed 8 hours.
2. Additional Hospital Services
   a. The claim for observation services must include one of the following services in addition to the reported observation services. The additional services listed below must have a line item date of service on the same day or the day before the date reported for observation:

      A Type A or B emergency department visit (CPT codes 99284 or 99285 or HCPCS code G0384); or

      A clinic visit (CPT code 99205 or 99215); or

      Critical care (CPT code 99291); or

      Direct referral for observation care reported with HCPCS code G0379 (APC 0604) must be reported on the same date of service as the date reported for observation services.
   b. No procedure with a T status indicator can be reported on the same day or day before observation care is provided.
3. Physician Evaluation
   a. The beneficiary must be in the care of a physician during the period of observation, as documented in the medical record by outpatient registration, discharge, and other appropriate progress notes that are timed, written, and signed by the physician.
   b. The medical record must include documentation that the physician explicitly assessed patient risk to determine that the beneficiary would benefit from observation care.

Criteria 1 and 3 related to observation care beginning and ending time and physician evaluation apply regardless of whether the hospital believes that the criteria will be met for payment of the extended encounter through extended assessment and management composite payment.

Only visits, critical care and observation services that are billed on a 13X bill type may be considered for a composite APC payment.

Non-repetitive services provided on the same day as either direct referral for observation care or observation services must be reported on the same claim because the OCE claim-by-claim logic cannot function properly unless all services related to the episode of observation care, including hospital clinic visits, emergency department visits, critical care services, and T status procedures, are reported on the same claim. Additional guidance can be found in chapter 1, section 50.2.2 of this manual.

If a claim for services provided during an extended assessment and management encounter including observation care does not meet all of the requirements listed above, then the usual APC logic will apply to separately payable items and services on the claim; the special logic for direct admission will apply, and payment for the observation care will be packaged into payments for other separately payable services provided to the beneficiary in the same encounter.

100-4, 4, 290.5.2

Billing and Payment for Direct Referral for Observation Care Furnished Beginning January 1, 2008

Direct referral for observation care continues to be reported using HCPCS code G0379 (Direct admission of patient for hospital observation care). Hospitals should report G0379 when observation services are the result of a direct referral for observation care without an associated emergency room visit, hospital outpatient clinic visit, or critical care service on the day of initiation of observation services. Hospitals should only report HCPCS code G0379 when a patient is referred directly to observation care after being seen by a physician in the community.

Payment for direct referral for observation care will be made either separately as a low level hospital clinic visit under APC 0604 or packaged into payment for composite APC 8002 (Level I Prolonged Assessment and Management Composite) or packaged into the payment for other separately payable services provided in the same encounter. For information about payment for extended assessment and management composite APCs, see, Sec.10.2.1 (Composite APCs) of this chapter.

The criteria for payment of HCPCS code G0379 under either APC 0604 or APC 8002 include:

1. Both HCPCS codes G0378 (Hospital observation services, per hr) and G0379 (Direct admission of patient for hospital observation care) are reported with the same date of service.
2. No service with a status indicator of T or V or Critical Care (APC 0617) is provided on the same day of service as HCPCS code G0379.

If either of the above criteria is not met, HCPCS code G0379 will be assigned status indicator N and will be packaged into payment for other separately payable services provided in the same encounter.

Only a direct referral for observation services billed on a 13X bill type may be considered for a composite APC payment.

100-4, 4, 300.6

Common Working File (CWF) Edits

The CWF edit will allow 3 hours of therapy for MNT in the initial calendar year. The edit will allow more than 3 hours of therapy if there is a change in the beneficiary's medical condition, diagnosis, or treatment regimen and this change must be documented in the beneficiary's medical record. Two new G codes have been created for use when a beneficiary receives a second referral in a calendar year that allows the beneficiary to receive more than 3 hours of therapy. Another edit will allow 2 hours of follow up MNT with another referral in subsequent years.

Advance Beneficiary Notice (ABN)

The beneficiary is liable for services denied over the limited number of hours with referrals for MNT. An ABN should be issued in these situations. In absence of evidence of a valid ABN, the provider will be held liable.

An ABN should not be issued for Medicare-covered services such as those provided by hospital dietitians or nutrition professionals who are qualified to render the service in their state but who have not obtained Medicare provider numbers.

Duplicate Edits

Although beneficiaries are allowed to receive training and therapy during the same time period Diabetes Self-Management and Training (DSMT) and Medical Nutrition Therapy (MNT) services may not be provided on the same day to the same beneficiary. Effective April 1, 2010 CWF shall implement a new duplicate crossover edit to identify and prevent claims for DSMT/MNT services from being billed with the same dates of services for the same beneficiaries submitted from institutional providers and from a professional provider.

100-4, 4, 320

Outpatient Intravenous Insulin Treatment (OIVIT)

Effective for claims with dates of service on and after December 23, 2009, the Centers for Medicare and Medicaid Services (CMS) determines that the evidence is adequate to conclude that OIVIT does not improve health outcomes in Medicare beneficiaries. Therefore, CMS determines that OIVIT is not reasonable and necessary for any indication under section 1862(a)(1)(A) of the Social Security Act, and services comprising an OIVIT regimen are nationally non-covered.

See Pub. 100-03, *Medicare National Coverage Determinations Manual*, Section 40.7, Outpatient Intravenous Insulin Treatment (Effective December 23, 2009), for general information and coverage indications.

100-4, 4, 320.1

HCPCS Coding for OIVIT

HCPCS code G9147, effective with the April IOCE and MPFSDB updates, is to be used on claims with dates of service on and after December 23, 2009, billing for non-covered OIVIT and any services comprising an OIVIT regimen.

NOTE: HCPCS codes 99199 or 94681(with or without diabetes related conditions 250.00-250.93) are not to be used on claims billing for non-covered OIVIT and any services comprising an OIVIT regimen when furnished pursuant to an OIVIT regimen. Claims billing for HCPCS codes 99199 and 94681 for non-covered OIVIT are to be returned to provider/returned as unprocessable.

100-4, 4, 320.2

Outpatient Intravenous Insulin Treatment (OIVIT)

Effective for claims with dates of service on and after December 23, 2009, the Centers for Medicare and Medicaid Services (CMS) determines that the evidence does not support a conclusion that OIVIT improves health outcomes in Medicare beneficiaries. Therefore, CMS has determined that OIVIT is not reasonable and necessary for any indication under section 1862(a)(1)(A) of the Social Security Act. Services comprising an OIVIT regimen are nationally non-covered under Medicare when furnished pursuant to an OIVIT regimen.

See Pub. 100-03, Medicare National Coverage Determinations Manual, Section 40.7, Outpatient Intravenous Insulin Treatment (Effective December 23, 2009), for general information and coverage indications.

100-4, 5, 10.2

A. Financial Limitation Prior to the Balanced Budget Refinement Act (BBRA)

Section 4541(a)(2) of the Balanced Budget Act (BBA) (P.L. 105-33) of 1997, which added ¬ß1834(k)(5) to the Act, required payment under a prospective payment system for outpatient rehabilitation services (except those furnished by or under arrangements with a hospital). Outpatient rehabilitation services include the following services:

- Physical therapy (which includes outpatient speech-language pathology); and
- Occupational therapy.

Section 4541(c) of the BBA required application of a financial limitation to all outpatient rehabilitation services (except those furnished by or under arrangements with a hospital). In 1999, an annual per beneficiary limit of $1, 500 applied to all outpatient physical therapy services (including speech-language pathology services). A separate limit applied to all occupational therapy services. The limit is based on incurred expenses and includes applicable deductible and coinsurance. The BBA provided that the limits be indexed by the Medicare Economic Index (MEI) each year beginning in 2002.

The limitation is based on therapy services the Medicare beneficiary receives, not the type of practitioner who provides the service. Physical therapists, speech-language pathologists, occupational therapists as well as physicians and certain nonphysician practitioners could render a therapy service.

As a transitional measure, effective in 1999, providers/suppliers were instructed to keep track of the allowed incurred expenses. This process was put in place to assure providers/suppliers did not bill Medicare for patients who exceeded the annual limitations for physical therapy, and for occupational therapy services rendered by individual providers/suppliers. In 2003 and later, the limitation was applied through CMS systems.

B. Moratoria and Exceptions for Therapy Claims

Section 221 of the BBRA of 1999 placed a 2-year moratorium on the application of the financial limitation for claims for therapy services with dates of service January 1, 2000, through December 31, 2001.

Section 421 of the Medicare, Medicaid, and SCHIP Benefits Improvement and Protection Act (BIPA) of 2000, extended the moratorium on application of the financial limitation to claims for outpatient rehabilitation services with dates of service January 1, 2002, through December 31, 2002. Therefore, the moratorium was for a 3-year period and applied to outpatient rehabilitation claims with dates of service January 1, 2000, through December 31, 2002.

In 2003, there was not a moratorium on therapy caps. Implementation was delayed until September 1, 2003. Therapy caps were in effect for services rendered on September 1, 2003 through December 7, 2003.

Congress re-enacted a moratorium on financial limitations on outpatient therapy services on December 8, 2003 that extended through December 31, 2005. Caps were implemented again on January 1, 2006 and policies were modified to allow exceptions as directed by the Deficit Reduction Act of 2005 only for calendar year 2006. The Tax Relief and Health Care Act of 2006 extended the cap exceptions process through calendar year 2007. The Medicare, Medicaid, and SCHIP Extension Act of 2007 extended the cap exceptions process for services furnished through June 30, 2008.

Future exceptions. The cap exception for therapy services billed by outpatient hospitals was part of the original legislation and applies as long as caps are in effect. Exceptions to caps based on the medical necessity of the service are in effect only when Congress legislates the exceptions, as they did for 2007. References to the exceptions process in subsection C of this section apply only when the exceptions are in effect.

C. Application of Financial Limitations

Financial limitations on outpatient therapy services, as described above, began for therapy services rendered on or after on January 1, 2006. See C 1 to C 7 of this section when exceptions to therapy caps apply. The limits were $1740 in 2006 and $1780 in 2007. For 2008, the annual limit on the allowed amount for outpatient physical therapy and speech-language pathology combined is $1810; the limit for occupational therapy is $1810. Limits apply to outpatient Part B therapy services from all settings except outpatient hospital (place of service code 22 on carrier claims) and hospital emergency room (place of service code 23 on carrier claims). These excluded hospital services are reported on types of bill 12x or 13x on intermediary claims.

Contractors apply the financial limitations to the Medicare Physician Fee Schedule (MPFS) amount (or the amount charged if it is smaller) for therapy services for each beneficiary.

As with any Medicare payment, beneficiaries pay the coinsurance (20 percent) and any deductible that may apply. Medicare will pay the remaining 80 percent of the limit after the deductible is met. These amounts will change each calendar year. Medicare Contractors shall publish the financial limitation amount in educational articles. It is also available at 1-800-Medicare.

Medicare shall apply these financial limitations in order, according to the dates when the claims were received. When limitations apply, the Common Working File (CWF) tracks the limits. Shared System Maintainers are not responsible for tracking the dollar amounts of incurred expenses of rehabilitation services for each therapy limit.

In processing claims where Medicare is the secondary payer, the shared system takes the lowest secondary payment amount from MSPPAY and sends this amount on to CWF as the amount applied to therapy limits.

1. Exceptions to Therapy Caps - General
   The Tax Relief and Health Care Act of 2006 directed CMS to extend a process to allow for exceptions to the caps for services received in CY2007 in cases where continued therapy services are medically necessary. The following policies concerning exceptions to caps due to medical necessity apply only when the exceptions process is in effect. With the exception of the use of the KX modifier, the guidance in this section concerning medical necessity applies as well to services provided before caps are reached.

   Instructions for contractors to manage automatic process for exceptions will be found in the Program Integrity Manual, chapter 3, section 3.4.1.2. Provider and supplier information concerning exceptions is in this manual and in IOM Pub. 100-02, chapter 15, section 220.3. Exceptions shall be identified by a modifier on the claim and supported by documentation.

   Since the providers and suppliers will take an active role in obtaining an exception for a beneficiary, this manual section is written to address them as well as Medicare contractors.

   The beneficiary may qualify for use of the cap exceptions at any time during the episode when documented medically necessary services exceed caps. All covered and medically necessary services qualify for exceptions to caps.

   In 2006, the Exception Processes fell into two categories, Automatic Process Exceptions, and Manual Process Exceptions. Beginning January 1, 2007, there is no manual process for exceptions. All services that require exceptions to caps shall be processed using the automatic process. All requests for exception are in the form of a KX modifier added to claim lines. (See subsection C6 for use of the KX modifier.)

   Use of the automatic process for exceptions increases the responsibility of the provider/supplier for determining and documenting that services are appropriate.

   Also, use of the automatic process for exception does not exempt services from manual or other medical review processes as described in 100-08, Chapter 3, Section 3.4.1.1.1. Rather, atypical use of the automatic exception process may invite contractor scrutiny. Particular care should be taken to document improvement and avoid billing for services that do not meet the requirements for skilled services, or for services which are maintenance rather than rehabilitative treatment (See Pub. 100-02, chapter 15, sections 220.2, 220.3, and 230).

   The KX modifier, described in subsection C6, is added to claim lines to indicate that the clinician attests that services are medically necessary and justification is documented in the medical record.

2. Automatic Process Exceptions
   The term "automatic process exceptions" indicates that the claims processing for the exception is automatic, and not that the exception is automatic. An exception may be made when the patient's condition is justified by documentation indicating that the beneficiary

requires continued skilled therapy, i.e., therapy beyond the amount payable under the therapy cap, to achieve their prior functional status or maximum expected functional status within a reasonable amount of time.

No special documentation is submitted to the contractor for automatic process exceptions. The clinician is responsible for consulting guidance in the Medicare manuals and in the professional literature to determine if the beneficiary may qualify for the automatic process exception when documentation justifies medically necessary services above the caps. The clinician's opinion is not binding on the Medicare contractor who makes the final determination concerning whether the claim is payable.

Documentation justifying the services shall be submitted in response to any Additional Documentation Request (ADR) for claims that are selected for medical review. Follow the documentation requirements in Pub. 100-02, chapter 15, section 220.3. If medical records are requested for review, clinicians may include, at their discretion, a summary that specifically addresses the justification for therapy cap exception.

In making a decision about whether to utilize the automatic process exception, clinicians shall consider, for example, whether services are appropriate to--

- The patient's condition including the diagnosis, complexities and severity (A list of the excepted evaluation codes are in C.2.a. A list of the ICD-9 codes for conditions and complexities that might qualify a beneficiary for exception to caps is in 10.2 C3. The list is a guideline and neither assures that services on the list will be excepted nor limits provision of covered and medically necessary services for conditions not on the list);
- The services provided including their type, frequency and duration;
- The interaction of current active conditions and complexities that directly and significantly influence the treatment such that it causes services to exceed caps.

In addition, the following should be considered before using the automatic exception process:

a. Exceptions for Services

Evaluation. The CMS will except therapy evaluations from caps after the therapy caps are reached when evaluation is necessary, e.g., to determine if the current status of the beneficiary requires therapy services. For example, the following evaluation procedures may be appropriate:

92506, 92597, 92607, 92608, 92610, 92611, 92612, 92614, 92616, 96105, 97001, 97002, 97003, 97004.

These codes will continue to be reported as outpatient therapy procedures as described in the Claims Processing Manual, Chapter 5, Section 20(B) "Applicable Outpatient Rehabilitation HCPCS Codes." They are not diagnostic tests. Definition of evaluations and documentation is found in Pub 100-02, sections 220 and 230.

Other Services. There are a number of sources that suggest the amount of certain services that may be typical, either per service, per episode, per condition, or per discipline. For example, see the CSC- Utilization and Edit Report, 2006, Appendices at www.cms.hhs.gov/TherapyServices (Studies and Reports). Professional literature and guidelines from professional associations also provide a basis on which to estimate whether the type, frequency and intensity of services are appropriate to an individual. Clinicians and contractors should utilize available evidence related to the patient's condition to justify provision of medically necessary services to individual beneficiaries, especially when they exceed caps. Contractors shall not limit medically necessary services that are justified by scientific research applicable to the beneficiary. Neither contractors nor clinicians shall utilize professional literature and scientific reports to justify payment for continued services after an individual's goals have been met earlier than is typical. Conversely, professional literature and scientific reports shall not be used as justification to deny payment to patients whose needs are greater than is typical or when the patient's condition is not represented by the literature.

b. Exceptions for Conditions or Complexities Identified by ICD-9 codes.

Clinicians may utilize the automatic process for exception for any diagnosis for which they can justify services exceeding the cap. Based upon analysis of claims data, research and evidence based practice guidelines, CMS has identified conditions and complexities represented by ICD-9 codes that may be more likely than others to require therapy services that exceed therapy caps. This list appears in 10.2 C3. Clinicians may use the automatic process of exception for beneficiaries who do not have a condition or complexity on this list when they justify the provision of therapy services that exceed caps for that patient's condition.

NOT ALL patients who have a condition or complexity on the list are "automatically" excepted from therapy caps. See Pub. 100-02, chapter 15, section 230.3 for documenting the patient's condition and complexities. Contractors may scrutinize claims from providers whose services exceed caps more frequently than is typical.

Regardless of the condition, the patient must also meet other requirements for coverage. For example, the patient must require skilled treatment for a covered, medically necessary service; the services must be appropriate in type, frequency and duration for the patient's condition and service must be documented appropriately. Guidelines for utilization of therapy services may be found in Medicare manuals, Local Coverage Determinations of Medicare contractors, and professional guidelines issued by associations and states.

Bill the most relevant diagnosis. As always, when billing for therapy services, the ICD-9 code that best relates to the reason for the treatment shall be on the claim, unless there is a compelling reason. For example, when a patient with diabetes is being treated for gait training due to amputation, the preferred diagnosis is abnormality of gait (which characterizes the treatment). Where it is possible in accordance with State and local laws and the contractors Local Coverage Determinations, avoid using vague or general diagnoses. When a claim includes several types of services, or where the physician/NPP must supply the diagnosis, it may not be possible to use the most relevant therapy code in the primary position. In that case, the relevant code should, if possible, be on the claim in another position.

Codes representing the medical condition that caused the treatment are used when there is no code representing the treatment. Complicating conditions are preferably used in non-primary positions on the claim and are billed in the primary position only in the rare circumstance that there is no more relevant code.

The condition or complexity that caused treatment to exceed caps must be related to the therapy goals and must either be the condition that is being treated or a complexity that directly and significantly impacts the rate of recovery of the condition being treated such that it is appropriate to exceed the caps. Codes marked as complexities represented by ICD-9 codes on the list below are unlikely to require therapy services that would exceed the caps unless they occur in a patient who also has another condition (either listed or not listed). Therefore, documentation for an exception should indicate how the complexity (or combination of complexities) directly and significantly affects treatment for a therapy condition. For example, if the condition underlying the reason for therapy is V43.64, hip replacement, the treatment may have a goal to ambulate 60' with stand-by assistance and a KX modifier may be appropriate for gait training (assuming the severity of the patient is such that the services exceed the cap). Alternatively, it would not be appropriate to use the KX modifier for a patient who recovered from hip replacement last year and is being treated this year for a sprain of a severity which does not justify extensive therapy exceeding caps.

3. ICD-9 Codes That are Likely to Qualify for the Automatic Process Therapy Cap Exception Based Upon Clinical Condition or Complexity

When using this table, refer to the ICD-9 code book for coding instructions. Some contractors' Local Coverage Determinations do not allow the use of some of the codes on this list in the primary diagnosis position on a claim. If the contractor has determined that these codes do not characterize patients who require medically necessary services, providers/suppliers may not use these codes, but must utilize a billable diagnosis code allowed by their contractor to describe the patient's condition. Contractors shall not apply therapy caps to services based on the patient's condition, but only on the medical necessity of the service for the condition. If a service would be payable before the cap is reached and is still medically necessary after the cap is reached, that service is excepted. Providers/suppliers may use the automatic process for exception for medically necessary services when the patient has a billable condition that is not on the list below. The diagnosis on the list below may be put in a secondary position on the claim and/or in the medical records, as the contractor directs.

When two codes are listed in the left cell in a row, all the codes between them are also eligible for exception. If one code is in the cell, only that one code is likely to qualify for exception. The descriptions in the table are not always identical to those in the ICD-9 code book, but may be summaries. Contact your contractor for interpretation if you are not sure that a condition or complexity is applicable for automatic process exception.

It is very important to recognize that most of the conditions on this list would not ordinarily result in services exceeding the cap. Use the KX modifier only in cases where the condition of the individual patient is such that services are APPROPRIATELY provided in an episode that exceeds the cap. In most cases, the severity of the condition, comorbidities, or complexities will contribute to the necessity of services exceeding the cap, and these should be documented. Routine use of the KX modifier for all patients with these conditions will likely show up on data analysis as aberrant and invite inquiry. Be sure that documentation is sufficiently detailed to support the use of the modifier.

The following ICD-9 codes describe the conditions (etiology or underlying medical conditions) that may result in excepted conditions (marked X) and complexities (marked *) that MIGHT cause medically necessary therapy services to qualify for the automatic process exception for each discipline separately. When the field corresponding to the therapy discipline treating and the diagnosis code is marked with a dash (‚Äì) services by that discipline are not appropriate for that diagnosis and, therefore, services do not qualify for exception to caps.

These codes are grouped only to facilitate reference to them. The codes may be used only when the code is applicable to the condition being actively treated. For example, an exception should not be claimed for a diagnosis of hip replacement when the service provided is for an unrelated dysphagia.

ICD-9 Cluster	ICD-9 (Cluster) Description	PT	OT	SLP
V43.61-V43.69	Joint Replacement	X	X	--
V45.4	Arthrodesis Status	*	*	--
V45.81-V45.82 and V45.89	Other Postprocedural Status	*	*	--
V49-61-V49.67	Upper Limb Amputation Status	X	X	--
V49.71-V49.77	Lower Limb Amputation Status	X	X	--
V54.10-V54.29	Aftercare for Healing Traumatic or Pathologic Fracture	X	X	--
V58.71-V58.78	Aftercare Following Surgery to Specified Body Systems, Not Elsewhere Classified	*	*	*
244.0-244.9	Acquired Hypothyroidism	*	*	*
250.00-251.9	Diabetes Mellitus and Other Disorders of Pancreatic Internal Secretion	*	*	*
276.0-276.9	Disorders of Fluid, Electrolyte, and Acid-Base Balance	*	*	*
278.00-278.01	Obesity and Morbid Obesity	*	*	*
280.0-289.9	Diseases of the blood and blood-forming organs	*	*	*
290.0-290.43	Dementias	*	*	*
294.0-294.9	Persistent Mental Disorders due to Conditions Classified Elsewhere	*	*	*
295.00-299.91	Other Psychoses	*	*	*
300.00-300.9	Anxiety, Disassociative and Somatoform Disorders	*	*	*
310.0-310.9	Specific Nonpsychotic Mental Disorders due to Brain Damage	*	*	*
311	Depressive Disorder, Not Elsewhere Classified	*	*	*
315.00-315.9	Specific delays in Development	*	*	*
317	Mild Mental Retardation	*	*	*
320.0-326	Inflammatory Diseases of the Central Nervous System	*	*	*
330.0-337.9	Hereditary and Degenerative Diseases of the Central Nervous System	X	X	X
340-345.91 and 348.0-349.9	Other Disorders of the Central Nervous System	X	X	X
353.0-359.9	Disorders of the Peripheral Nervous system	X	X	--
365.00-365.9	Glaucoma	*	*	*
369.00-369.9	Blindness and Low Vision	*	*	*
386.00-386.9	Vertiginous Syndromes and Other Disorders of Vestibular System	*	*	*
389.00-389.9	Hearing Loss	*	*	*
401.0-405.99	Hypertensive Disease	*	*	*
410.00-414.9	Ischemic Heart Disease	*	*	*
415.0-417.9	Diseases of Pulmonary Circulation	*	*	*
420.0-429.9	Other Forms of Heart Disease	*	*	*

X Amutomatic (only ICD-9 needed on claim)
* Complexity (requires another ICD-9 on claim)
-- Does not serve as qualifying ICD-9 on claim

ICD-9 Cluster	ICD-9 (Cluster) Description	PT	OT	SLP
430-438.9	Cerebrovascular Disease	X	X	X
440.0-448.9	Diseases of Arteries, Arterioles, and Capillaries	*	*	*
451.0-453.9 and 456.0-459.9	Diseases of Veins and Lymphatics, and Other Diseases of Circulatory System	*	*	*
465.0-466.19	Acute Respiratory Infections	*	*	*
478.30-478.5	Paralysis, Polyps, or Other Diseases of Vocal Cords	*	*	*
480.0-486	Pneumonia	*	*	*
490-496	Chronic Obstructive Pulmonary Disease and Allied Conditions	*	*	*
507.0-507.8	Pneumonitis due to solids and liquids	*	*	*
510.0-519.9	Other Diseases of Respiratory System	*	*	*
560.0-560.9	Intestinal Obstruction Without Mention of Hernia	*	*	*
578.0-578.9	Gastrointestinal Hemorrhage	*	*	*
584.5-586	Renal Failure and Chronic Kidney Disease	*	*	*
590.00-599.9	Other Diseases of Urinary System	*	*	*
682.0-682.8	Other Cellulitis and Abscess	*	*	--
707.00-707.9	Chronic Ulcer of Skin	*	*	--
710.0-710.9	Diffuse Diseases of Connective Tissue	*	*	*
711.00-711.99	Arthropathy Associated with Infections	*	*	--
712.10-713.8	Crystal Arthropathies and Arthropathy Associated with Other Disorders Classified Elsewhere	*	*	--
714.0-714.9	Rheumatoid Arthritis and Other Inflammatory Polyarthropathies	*	*	--
715.00-715.98	Osteoarthrosis and Allied Disorders (Complexity except as listed below)	*	*	--
715.09	Osteoarthritis and allied disorders, multiple sites	X	X	--
715.11	Osteoarthritis, localized, primary, shoulder region	X	X	--
715.15	Osteoarthritis, localized, primary, pelvic region and thigh	X	X	--
715.16	Osteoarthritis, localized, primary, lower leg	X	X	--
715.91	Osteoarthritis, unspecified id gen. or local, shoulder	X	X	--
715.96	Osteoarthritis, unspecified if gen. or local, lower leg	X	X	--
716.00-716.99	Other and Unspecified Arthropathies	*	*	--
717.0-717.9	Internal Derangement of Knee	*	*	--
718.00-718.99	Other Derangement of Joint (Complexity except as listed below)	*	*	--
718.49	Contracture of Joint, Multiple Sites	X	X	--
719.00-719.99	Other and Unspecified Disorders of Joint (Complexity except as listed below)	*	*	--
719.7	Difficulty Walking	X	X	--
720.0-724.9	Dorsopathies	*	*	--
725-729.9	Rheumatism, Excluding Back (Complexity except as listed below)	*	*	--
726.10-726.19	Rotator Cuff Disorder and Allied Syndromes	X	X	--
727.61-727.62	Rupture of Tendon, Nontraumatic	X	X	--
730.00-739.9	Osteopathies, Chondropathies, and Acquired Musculoskeletal Deformities (Complexity except as listed below)	*	*	--
733.00	Osteoporosis	X	X	--

X Amutomatic (only ICD-9 needed on claim)
* Complexity (requires another ICD-9 on claim)
-- Does not serve as qualifying ICD-9 on claim

ICD-9 Cluster	ICD-9 (Cluster) Description	PT	OT	SLP
741.00-742.9 and 745.0-748.9 and 754.0-756.9	Congenital Anomalies	*	*	*
780.31-780.39	Convulsions	*	*	*
780.71-780.79	Malaise and Fatigue	*	*	*
780.93	Memory Loss	*	*	*
781.0-781.99	Symptoms Involving Nervous and Musculoskeletal System (Complexity except as listed below)	*	*	*
781.2	Abnormality of Gait	X	X	--
781.3	Lack of Coordination	X	X	--
783.0-783.9	Symptoms Concerning Nutrition, Metabolism, and Development	*	*	*
784.3-784.69	Aphasia, Voice and Other Speech Disturbance, Other Symbolic Dysfunction	*	*	X
785.4	Gangrene	*	*	--
786.00-786.9	Symptoms involving Respiratory System and Other Chest Symptoms	*	*	*
787.2	Dysphagia	*	*	X
800.00-828.1	Fractures (Complexity except as listed below)	*	*	--
806.00-806.9	Fracture of Vertebral Column With Spinal Cord Injury	X	X	--
810.11-810.13	Fracture of Clavicle	X	X	--
811.00-811.19	Fracture of Scapula	X	X	--
812.00-812.59	Fracture of Humerus	X	X	--
813.00-813.93	Fracture of Radius and Ulna	X	X	--
820.00-820.9	Fracture of Neck of Femue	X	X	--
821.00-821.39	Fracture of Other and Unspecified Parts of Femur	X	X	--
828.0-828.1	Multiple Fractures Involving Both Lower Limbs, Lower with Upper Limb, and Lower Limb(s) with Rib(s) and Sternum	X	X	--
830.0-839.9	Dislocations	X	X	--
840.0-848.8	Sprains and Strains of Joints and Adjacent Muscles	*	*	--
851.00-854.19	Intracranial Injury, excluding those with Skull Fracture	X	X	X
888.00-884.2	Open Wound of Upper Limb	*	*	--
885.0-887.7	Traumatic Amputation, Thumb(s), Finger(s), Arm and Hand (complete)(partial)	X	X	--
890.0-894.2	Open Wound Lower Limb	*	*	--
895.0-897.7	Traumatic Amputation, Toe(s), Foot/Feet, Leg(s) (complete) (partial)			
905.0-905.9	Late Effects of Musculoskeletal and Connective Tissue Injuries	*	*	*
907.0-907.9	Late Effect of Injuries to the Nervous System	*	*	*
941.00-949.5	Burns	*	*	*
952.00-952.9	Spinal Cord Injury Without Evidence of Spinal Bone Injury	X	X	X
953.0-953.8	Injury to Nerve Roots and Spinal Plexus	X	X*	
959.01	Head Injury, Unspecified	X	X	X

X Amutomatic (only ICD-9 needed on claim)
* Complexity (requires another ICD-9 on claim)
-- Does not serve as qualifying ICD-9 on claim

100-4, 5, 20

HCPCS Coding Requirement

A. Uniform Coding

Section 1834(k)(5) of the Act requires that all claims for outpatient rehabilitation therapy services and all comprehensive outpatient rehabilitation facility (CORF) services be reported using a uniform coding system. The current Healthcare Common Procedure Coding System/Current Procedural Terminology is used for the reporting of these services. The uniform coding requirement in the Act is specific to payment for all CORF services and outpatient rehabilitation therapy services - including physical therapy, occupational therapy, and speech-language pathology - that is provided and billed to carriers and fiscal intermediaries (FIs). The Medicare physician fee schedule (MPFS) is used to make payment for these therapy services at the nonfacility rate.

Effective for claims submitted on or after April 1, 1998, providers that had not previously reported HCPCS/CPT for outpatient rehabilitation and CORF services began using HCPCS to report these services. This requirement does not apply to outpatient rehabilitation services provided by:

- Critical access hospitals, which are paid on a cost basis, not MPFS;
- RHCs, and FQHCs for which therapy is included in the all-inclusive rate; or
- Providers that do not furnish therapy services.

The following "providers of services" must bill the FI for outpatient rehabilitation services using HCPCS codes:

- Hospitals (to outpatients and inpatients who are not in a covered Part A1 stay);
- Skilled nursing facilities (SNFs) (to residents not in a covered Part A1 stay and to nonresidents who receive outpatient rehabilitation services from the SNF);
- Home health agencies (HHAs) (to individuals who are not homebound or otherwise are not receiving services under a home health plan of care2 (POC);
- Comprehensive outpatient rehabilitation facilities (CORFs); and
- Providers of outpatient physical therapy and speech-language pathology services (OPTs), also known as rehabilitation agencies (previously termed outpatient physical therapy facilities in this instruction).

Note 1. The requirements for hospitals and SNFs apply to inpatient Part B and outpatient services only. Inpatient Part A services are bundled into the respective prospective payment system payment; no separate payment is made.

Note 2. For HHAs, HCPCS/CPT coding for outpatient rehabilitation services is required only when the HHA provides such service to individuals that are not homebound and, therefore, not under a home health plan of care.

The following practitioners must bill the carriers for outpatient rehabilitation therapy services using HCPCS/CPT codes:

- Physical therapists in private practice (PTPPs),
- Occupational therapists in private practice (OTPPs),
- Physicians, including MDs, DOs, podiatrists and optometrists, and
- Certain nonphysician practitioners (NPPs), acting within their State scope of practice, e.g., nurse practitioners and clinical nurse specialists.

Providers billing to intermediaries shall report:

- The date the therapy plan of care was either established or last reviewed (see Sec.220.1.3B) in Occurrence Code 17, 29, or 30.
- The first day of treatment in Occurrence Code 35, 44, or 45.

B. Applicable Outpatient Rehabilitation HCPCS Codes

The CMS identifies the following codes as therapy services, regardless of the presence of a financial limitation. Therapy services include only physical therapy, occupational therapy and speech-language pathology services. Therapist means only a physical therapist, occupational therapist or speech-language pathologist. Therapy modifiers are GP for physical therapy, GO for occupational therapy, and GN for speech-language pathology. Check the notes below the chart for details about each code.

When in effect, any financial limitation will also apply to services represented by the following codes, except as noted below

64550+	95834+	97032	97597+
90901+	95851+	97033	97598+ξ
92506■	95852+	97034	97602+****ξ
92507■	95992+****	97035	97605+ξ
92508	96105+	97036	97606+ξ
92526	96110+✓	97039*❋	97750
92597	96111+✓	97110	97755
92605***	96125	97112	97760**■
92606****	97001	97113	97761
92607	97002	97116	97762
92608	97003	97124	97799*
92609	97004	97139*❋	G0281
92610+	97010****	97140	G0283
92611+	97012	97150	G0329
92612+	97016	97530	0019T+***
92614+	97018	97532+	0029T+***
92616+	97022	97533	0183T+***E
95831+	97024	97535	
95832+	97026	97537	
95833+	97028	97542	

* The code is priced by the carrier. Contact the carrier for appropriate fee schedule amount.

❋ Effective January 1, 2006, these codes will no longer be valued under the Medicare physician fee schedule (MPFS) and will be priced by the carriers.

■ Effective January 1, 2006, the descriptors for these services have changed.

** CPT code 97760 should not be reported with CPT code 97116 for the same extremity.

*** Carrier priced codes.

**** Codes are bundled with any therapy codes. Regardless of whether they are billed alone or with another therapy code, separate payment will not be made for these codes.

✓ If billed by an outpatient hospital department, these are paid using the outpatient prospective payment system (OPPS).

U Underlined codes designate therapy services, regardless of who performs them, and always require therapy modifiers (GP, GO, GN).

ξ When billed by a hospital subject to OPPS for outpatient services, these codes (also indicated as "sometimes therapy" services) will be paid under the OPPS when the service is not performed by a qualified therapist and it is inappropriate to bill the service under a therapy plan of care. The requirements for other sometimes therapy codes, described below, apply.

\+ Codes sometimes represent therapy services. These codes and all codes on the above list always represent therapy services when performed by therapists.

NOTE: Listing of the following codes does not imply that services are covered or applicable to all provider settings.

92526	92597	92605****	92606****	92607
92608	92609	92610+	92611+	92612+
92614+	92616+	95831+	95832+	95833+
95834+	95851+	95852+	95992****	96105+
96110+				

100-4, 5, 20.4

Coding Guidance for Certain CPT Codes - All Claims

The following provides guidance about the use of codes 96105, 97026, 97150, 97545, 97546, and G0128.

CPT Codes 96105, 97545, and 97546.

Providers report code 96105, assessment of aphasia with interpretation and report in 1-hour units. This code represents formal evaluation of aphasia with an instrument such as the Boston Diagnostic Aphasia Examination. If this formal assessment is performed during treatment, it is typically performed only once during treatment and its medical necessity should be documented.

If the test is repeated during treatment, the medical necessity of the repeat administration of the test must also be documented. It is common practice for regular assessment of a patient's progress in therapy to be documented in the chart, and this may be done using test items taken from the formal examinations. This is considered to be part of the treatment and should not be billed as 96105 unless a full, formal assessment is completed.

Other timed physical medicine codes are 97545 and 97546. The interval for code 97545 is 2 hours and for code 97546, 1 hour. These are specialized codes to be used in the context of rehabilitating a worker to return to a job. The expectation is that the entire time period specified in the codes 97545 or 97546 would be the treatment period, since a shorter period of treatment could be coded with another code such as codes 97110, 97112, or 97537. (Codes 97545 and 97546 were developed for reporting services to persons in the worker's compensation program, thus we do not expect to see them reported for Medicare patients except under very unusual circumstances. Further, we would not expect to see code 97546 without also seeing code 97545 on the same claim. Code 97546, when used, is used in conjunction with 97545.) CPT Code 97026 Effective for services performed on or after October 24, 2006, the Centers for Medicare & Medicaid Services announce a NCD stating the use of infrared and/or near-infrared light and/or heat, including monochromatic infrared energy (MIRE), is non-covered for the treatment, including symptoms such as pain arising from these conditions, of diabetic and/or non-diabetic peripheral sensory neuropathy, wounds and/or ulcers of the skin and/or subcutaneous tissues in Medicare beneficiaries. Further coverage guidelines can be found in the National Coverage Determination Manual (Publication 100-03), section 270.6.

Contractors shall deny claims with CPT 97026 (infrared therapy incident to or as a PT/OT benefit) and HCPCS E0221 or A4639, if the claim contains any of the following ICD-9 codes: 250.60-250.63 354.4, 354.5, 354.9 355.1-355.4 355.6-355.9 356.0, 356.2-356.4, 356.8-356.9 357.0-357.7 674.10, 674.12, 674.14, 674.20, 674.22, 674.24 707.00-707.07, 707.09-707.15, 707.19 870.0-879.9 880.00-887.7 890.0-897.7 998.31-998.32 Contractors can use the following messages when denying the service: Medicare Summary Notice # 21.11 "This service was not covered by Medicare at the time you received it." Reason Claim Adjustment Code #50 "These are noncovered services because this is not deemed a medical necessity by the payer." Advanced Beneficiary Notice (ABN): Physicians, physical therapists, occupational therapists, outpatient rehabilitation facilities (ORFs), comprehensive outpatient rehabilitation facilities (CORFs), home health agencies (HHA), and hospital outpatient departments are liable if the service is performed, unless the beneficiary signs an ABN.

Similarly, DME suppliers and HHA are liable for the devices when they are supplied, unless the beneficiary signs an ABN.

100-4, 8, 60.4

Epoetin Alfa (EPO)

Coverage rules for Epoetin Alfa (EPO) are explained in the Medicare Benefit Policy Manual, Publication 100-02, chapter 11. For an explanation of Method I and Method II reimbursement for patients dialyzing at home, see §40.1.

Fiscal intermediaries (FIs) pay for EPO to end-stage renal disease (ESRD) facilities as a separately billable drug to the composite rate. No additional payment is made to administer EPO, whether in a facility or a home. Effective January 1, 2005, the cost of supplies to administer EPO may be billed to the FI. HCPCS A4657 and Revenue Code 270 should be used to capture the charges for syringes used in the administration of EPO.

If the beneficiary obtains EPO from a supplier for self-administration, the supplier bills the durable medical equipment regional carrier (DMERC) and the DMERC pays at the rate shown in §60.4.3

Program payment may not be made to a physician for EPO for self-administration. Where EPO is furnished by a physician payable as "incident to services" the carrier processes the claim.

EPO Payment Methodology

Type of Provider	Separately Billable	DMERC Payment	No payment
In-facility freestanding and hospital-based ESRD facility	X		
Self-administer Home Method I	X		
Self-administer Home Method II		X	
Incident to physician in facility or for self-administration *			X

Medicare pays for a drug if self-administered by a dialysis patient. When EPO is administered in a renal facility, the service is not an "incident to" service and not under the "incident to" provision.

Renal dialysis facilities are required to report hematocrit or hemoglobin levels for their Medicare patients receiving erythropoietin products. Hematocrit levels are reported in value code 49 and reflect the most recent reading taken before the start of the billing period. Hemoglobin readings before the start of the billing period are reported in value code 48. See §60.4.1.

Effective January 1, 2012, renal dialysis facilities are required to report hematocrit or hemoglobin levels on all ESRD claims irrespective of ESA administration. Reporting the value 99.99 is not permitted when billing for an ESA.

Effective for services provided on or after April 1, 2006, Medicare has implemented a national claims monitoring policy for EPO administered in Medicare renal dialysis facilities. This policy does not apply to claims for EPO for patients who receive their dialysis at home and self-administer their EPO.

While Medicare is not changing its coverage policy on erythropoietin use to maintain a target hematocrit level between 30% and 36%, we believe the variability in response to EPO warrants postponing requiring monitoring until the hematocrit reaches higher levels. For dates of services April 1, 2006, and later, the Centers for Medicare & Medicaid Services (CMS) will not initiate monitoring until the hematocrit level exceeds 39.0% or the hemoglobin level exceeds 13.0g/dL. This does not preclude the contractors from performing medical review at lower levels. The Food and Drug Administration (FDA) labeling for EPO notes that as the hematocrit approaches a reading of 36.0 (or hemoglobin 12.0g/dL), the dose of the drug should be reduced by 25%.

Effective for services provided on or after April 1, 2006, for claims reporting hematocrit or hemoglobin levels exceeding the monitoring threshold, the dose shall be reduced by 25% over the preceding month. Providers may report that a dose reduction did occur in response to the reported elevated hematocrit or hemoglobin level by adding a GS modifier on the claim. The definition of the GS modifier continues to be defined as: "Dosage of EPO or Darbepoetin Alfa has been reduced and maintained in response to hematocrit or hemoglobin level." Thus, for claims reporting a hematocrit level or hemoglobin level exceeding the monitoring threshold without the GS modifier, CMS will reduce the dosage reported on the claim by 25%. The excess dosage is considered to be not reasonable and necessary. Providers are reminded that the patient's medical records should reflect hematocrit/hemoglobin levels and any dosage reduction reported on the claim during the same time period for which the claim is submitted.

Effective for dates of service provided on and after January 1, 2008, requests for payments or claims for EPO for ESRD patients receiving dialysis in renal dialysis facilities reporting a hematocrit level exceeding 39.0% (or hemoglobin exceeding 13.0g/dL) shall also include modifier ED or EE. Claims reporting neither modifier or both modifiers will be returned to the provider for correction.

The definition of modifier ED is "The hematocrit level has exceeded 39.0% (or hemoglobin 1evel has exceeded 13.0g/dL) 3 or more consecutive billing cycles immediately prior to and including the current billing cycle." The definition of modifier EE is "The hematocrit level has exceeded 39.0% (or hemoglobin level has exceeded 13.0g/dL) less than 3 consecutive billing cycles immediately prior to and including the current billing cycle." The GS modifier continues to be defined as stated above.

Providers may continue to report the GS modifier when the reported hematocrit or hemoglobin levels exceed the monitoring threshold for less than 3 months and a dose reduction has occurred. When both modifiers GS and EE are included, no reduction in the reported dose will occur. Claims reporting a hematocrit or hemoglobin level exceeding the monitoring threshold and the ED modifier shall have an automatic 50% reduction in the reported dose applied, even if the claim also reports the GS modifier.

Below is a chart illustrating the resultant claim actions under all possible reporting scenarios:

Hct Exceeds 39.0% or Hgb Exceeds 13.0g/dL	ED Modifier? (Hct >39% or Hgb >13g/dL =3 cycles)	EE Modifier? (Hct >39% or Hgb >13g/dL <3 cycles)	GS Modifier? (Dosage reduced and maintained)	Claim Action
No	N/A	N/A	N/A	Do not reduce reported dose.
Yes	No	No	No	Return to provider for correction. Claim must report either ED or EE.
Yes	No	No	Yes	Return to provider for correction. Claim must report either ED or EE.
Yes	No	Yes	Yes	Do not reduce reported dose.
Yes	No	Yes	No	Reduce reported dose 25%.
Yes	Yes	No	Yes	Reduce reported dose 50%.
Yes	Yes	No	No	Reduce reported dose 50%.

In addition, for dates of service on and after January 1, 2008, CMS will implement a revised medically unbelievable edit (MUE). For dates of service on and after January 1, 2008, the MUE for claims for Epogen® is reduced to 400,000 units from 500,000. It is likely that claims reporting doses exceeding the new threshold reflect typographical errors and will be returned to providers for correction.

In some cases, physicians may believe there is medical justification to maintain a hematocrit above 39.0% or hemoglobin above 13.0g/dL. Beneficiaries, physicians, and/or renal facilities may submit additional medical documentation to justify this belief under the routine appeal process. You may reinstate any dosage reduction amounts under this first level appeal process when you believe the documentation supports a higher hematocrit/hemoglobin level.

Providers are reminded that, in accordance with FDA labeling, CMS expects that as the hematocrit approaches 36.0% (hemoglobin 12.0g/dL), a dosage reduction occurs. Providers are expected to maintain hematocrit levels between 30.0 to 36.0% (hemoglobin 10.0-12.0g/dL). Hematocrit levels that remain below 30.0% (hemoglobin levels below 10.0g/dL)) despite dosage increases, should have causative factors evaluated. The patient's medical record should reflect the clinical reason for dose changes and hematocrit levels outside the range of 30.0-36.0% (hemoglobin levels 10.0-12.0g/dL). Medicare contractors may review medical records to assure appropriate dose reductions are applied and maintained and hematological target ranges are maintained.

These hematocrit requirements apply only to EPO furnished as an ESRD benefit under §1881(b) of the Social Security Act. EPO furnished incident to a physician's service is not included in this policy. Carriers have discretion for local policy for EPO furnished as "incident to service."

100-4, 8, 60.7

Darbepoetin Alfa (Aranesp) for ESRD Patients

Coverage rules for Aranesp® are explained in the Medicare Benefit Policy Manual, Publication 100-02, chapter 11. For an explanation of Method I and Method II reimbursement for patients dialyzing at home see §40.1.

Fiscal intermediaries (FIs) pay for Aranesp® to end-stage renal disease (ESRD) facilities as a separately billable drug to the composite rate. No additional payment is made to administer Aranesp®, whether in a facility or a home. Effective January 1, 2005, the cost of supplies to administer Aranesp® may be billed to the FI. HCPCS A4657 and Revenue Code 270 should be used to capture the charges for syringes used in the administration of Aranesp®.

If the beneficiary obtains Aranesp® from a supplier for self-administration, the supplier bills the durable medical equipment regional carrier (DMERC), and the DMERC pays in accordance with MMA Drug Payment Limits Pricing File.

Program payment may not be made to a physician for self-administration of Aranesp®. When Aranesp® is furnished by a physician as "incident to services," the carrier processes the claim.

For ESRD patients on maintenance dialysis treated in a physician's office, code J0882, "injection, darbepoetin alfa, 1 mcg (for ESRD patients)," should continue to be used with the hematocrit included on the claim. (For ANSI 837 transactions, the hematocrit (HCT) value is reported in 2400 MEA03 with a qualifier of R2 in 2400 MEA02.) Claims without this information will be denied due to lack of documentation. Physicians who provide Aranesp® for ESRD patients on maintenance dialysis must bill using code J0882.

Darbepoetin Alfa Payment Methodology

Type of Provider	Separately Billable	DMERC Payment	No payment
In-facility freestanding and hospital-based ESRD facility	X		
Self-administer Home Method I	X		
Self-administer Home Method II		X	
Incident to physician in facility or for self-administration *			X

Medicare pays for a drug if self-administered by a dialysis patient. When Aranesp® is administered in a dialysis facility, the service is not an "incident to" service, and not under the "incident to" provision.

Renal dialysis facilities are required to report hematocrit or hemoglobin levels for their Medicare patients receiving erythropoietin products. Hematocrit levels are reported in value code 49 and reflect the most recent reading taken before the start of the billing period. Hemoglobin readings before the start of the billing period are reported in value code 48. See §60.4.1.

Effective January 1, 2012, renal dialysis facilities are required to report hematocrit or hemoglobin levels on all ESRD claims irrespective of ESA administration. Reporting the value 99.99 is not permitted when billing for an ESA.

Effective for services provided on or after April 1, 2006, Medicare has implemented a national claims monitoring policy for Aranesp® administered in Medicare renal dialysis facilities. This policy does not apply to claims for Aranesp® for patients who receive their dialysis at home and self-administer their Aranesp®.

While Medicare is not changing its coverage policy on erythropoietin use to maintain a target hematocrit level between 30% and 36%, we believe the variability in response to EPO warrants postponing requiring monitoring until the hematocrit reaches higher levels. For dates of services on and after April 1, 2006, the Centers for Medicare & Medicaid Services (CMS) will not initiate monitoring until the hematocrit level exceeds 39.0% or the hemoglobin level exceeds 13.0g/dL. This does not preclude the contractors from performing medical review at lower levels. The Food and Drug Administration (FDA) labeling for Aranesp® notes that as the hematocrit approaches a reading of 36.0% (or hemoglobin 12.0g/dL), the dose of the drug should be reduced by 25%.

Effective for dates of service provided on or after April 1, 2006, for claims reporting hematocrit or hemoglobin levels exceeding the monitoring threshold, the dose shall be reduced by 25% over the preceding month. Providers may report that a dose reduction did occur in response to the reported elevated hematocrit or hemoglobin level by adding a GS modifier on the claim. The definition of the GS modifier continues to be defined as: "Dosage of EPO or Darbepoetin Alfa has been reduced and maintained in response to hematocrit or hemoglobin level." Thus, for claims reporting a hematocrit level or hemoglobin level exceeding the monitoring threshold without the GS modifier, CMS shall reduce the dosage reported on the claim by 25%. The excess dosage is considered to be not reasonable and necessary. Providers are reminded that the patient's medical records should reflect hematocrit/hemoglobin levels and any dosage reduction reported on the claim during the same time period for which the claim is submitted.

Effective for dates of service provided on an after January 1, 2008, requests for payments or claims for Aranesp® for ESRD patients receiving dialysis in renal dialysis facilities reporting a hematocrit level exceeding 39.0% (or hemoglobin exceeding 13.0g/dL) shall also include modifier ED or EE. Claims reporting neither modifier or both modifiers will be returned to the provider for correction.

The definition of modifier ED is "The hematocrit level has exceeded 39.0% (or hemoglobin 1evel has exceeded 13.0g/dL) 3 or more consecutive billing cycles immediately prior to and including the current billing cycle." The definition of modifier EE is "The hematocrit level has exceeded 39.0% (or hemoglobin level has exceeded 13.0g/dL) less than 3 consecutive billing cycles immediately prior to and including the current billing cycle." The GS modifier continues to be defined as stated above.

Providers may continue to report the GS modifier when the reported hematocrit or hemoglobin levels exceed the monitoring threshold for less than 3 months and a dose reduction has occurred. When both modifiers GS and EE are included, no reduction in the reported dose will occur. Claims reporting a hematocrit or hemoglobin level exceeding the monitoring threshold and the ED modifier shall have an automatic 50% reduction in the reported dose applied, even if the claim also reports the GS modifier.

Below is a chart illustrating the resultant claim actions under all possible reporting scenarios.

Hct Exceeds 39.0% or Hgb Exceeds 13.0g/dL	ED Modifier? (Hct >39% or Hgb >13g/dL =3 cycles)	EE Modifier? (Hct >39% or Hgb >13g/dL <3 cycles)	GS Modifier? (Dosage reduced and maintained)	Claim Action
No	N/A	N/A	N/A	Do not reduce reported dose.
Yes	No	No	No	Return to provider for correction. Claim must report either ED or EE.
Yes	No	No	Yes	Return to provider for correction. Claim must report either ED or EE.
Yes	No	Yes	Yes	Do not reduce reported dose.
Yes	No	Yes	No	Reduce reported dose 25%.
Yes	Yes	No	Yes	Reduce reported dose 50%.
Yes	Yes	No	No	Reduce reported dose 50%.

These hematocrit requirements apply only to Aranesp® furnished as an ESRD benefit under §1881(b) of the Social Security Act. Aranesp® furnished incident to a physician's service is not included in this policy. Carriers have discretion for local policy for Aranesp® furnished as "incident to service."

100-4, 8, 60.4.1

Epoetin Alfa (EPO) Facility Billing Requirements

Revenue codes required for reporting EPO:

Revenue Codes Dates of Service	Bill Type 72x	Bill Type 12x	Bill type 13x	Bill type 85x
0634 - administrations under 10,000 units	1/1/04 - present	4/1/06 - present	1/1/04 - present	1/1/04 - present
0635 - administrations of 10,000 units or more	1/1/04 - present	4/1/06 - present	1/1/04 - present	1/1/04 - present
0636 - detailed drug coding	N/A	1/1/04 - 3/31/06	N/A	

N/A For additional hospital billing instructions related to bill types 12x, 13x and 85x see also sections 60.4.3.1 and 60.4.3.2 of this chapter.

The HCPCS code for EPO must be included:

HCPCS	HCPCS Description	Dates of Service
Q4055	Injection, Epoetin alfa, 1,000 units (for ESRD on Dialysis)	1/1/2004 through 12/31/2005
J0886	Injection, Epoetin alfa, 1,000 units (for ESRD on Dialysis)	1/1/2006 through 12/31/2006
Q4081	1 Injection, Epoetin alfa, 100	1/1/2007 to present

The number of units of EPO administered during the billing period is reported with value code 68. Medicare no longer requires value code 68 for claims with dates of service on or after January 1, 2008. Each administration of epoetin alfa (EPO) is reported on a separate line item with the units reported used as a multiplier by the dosage description in the HCPCS to arrive at the dosage per administration.

Append the GS modifier to report a line item that represents an administration of EPO at the reduced dosage following existing instructions in section 60.4 of this chapter. The hematocrit reading taken prior to the last administration of EPO during the billing period must also be reported on the UB-92/Form CMS-1450 with value code 49. Effective January 1, 2006 the definition of value code 49 used to report the hematocrit reading is changed to indicate the patient's most recent hematocrit reading taken before the start of the billing period.

The hemoglobin reading taken during the billing period must be reported on the UB- 92/Form CMS-1450 with value code 48. Effective January 1, 2006 the definition of value code 48 used for the hemoglobin reading is changed to indicate the patient's most recent hemoglobin reading taken before the start of the billing period.

To report a hemoglobin or hematocrit reading for a new patient on or after January 1, 2006, the provider should report the reading that prompted the treatment of epoetin alfa. The provider may use results documented on form CMS 2728 or the patient's medical records from a transferring facility.

The maximum number of administrations of EPO for a billing cycle is 13 times in 30 days and 14 times in 31 days.

100-4,8,60.6

Vaccines Furnished to ESRD Patients

The Medicare program covers hepatitis B, influenza virus and Pneumococcal pneumonia virus (PPV) vaccines and their administration when furnished to eligible beneficiaries in accordance with coverage rules. Payment may be made for both the vaccine and the administration. The costs associated with the syringe and supplies are included in the administration fee: HCPCS code A4657 should not be billed for these vaccines.

Vaccines and their administration are reported using separate codes. See Chapter 18 of this manual for the codes required for billing vaccines and the administration of the vaccine.

Payment for vaccine administration (PPV, Influenza Virus, and Hepatitis B Virus) to freestanding RDFs is based on the Medicare Physician Fee Schedule (MPFS) according to the rate in the MPFS associated with code 90782 for services provided prior to March 1, 2003 and code 90471 for services provided March 1, 2005 and later and on reasonable cost for provider-based RDFs.

Vaccines remain separately payable under the ESRD PPS.

100-4,8,60.7.3

Payment Amount for Darbepoetin Alfa (Aranesp)

For Method I patients, the FI pays the facility per one mcg of Aranesp administered, in accordance with the MMA Drug Payment Limits Pricing File rounded up to the next highest whole mcg. Effective January 1, 2005, Aranesp will be paid based on the ASP Pricing File. Effective January 1, 2005, the cost of supplies to administer Aranesp may be billed to the FI. HCPCS A4657 and Revenue Code 270 should be used to capture the charges for syringes used in the administration of Aranesp.

Physician payment is calculated through the drug payment methodology described in Chapter 17, of the Claims Processing Manual.

The coinsurance and deductible are based on the Medicare allowance payable, not on the provider,Äôs charges. The provider may not charge the beneficiary more than 20 percent of the Medicare Aranesp allowance. This rule applies to independent and hospital based renal facilities.

Payment for ESRD-related Aranesp is included in the ESRD PPS for claims with dates of service on or after January 1, 2011.

100-4, 8, 60.7.4

Darbepoetin Alfa (Aranesp) Furnished to Home Patients

Medicare covers Aranesp for dialysis patients who use Aranesp in the home, when requirements for a patient care plan and patient selection as described in the Medicare Benefit Policy Manual, Chapter 11, are met.

When Aranesp is prescribed for a home patient, it may be either administered in a facility, e.g., the one shown on the Form CMS-382 (ESRD Beneficiary Method Selection Form) or furnished by a facility or Method II supplier for self-administration to a home patient determined to be competent to administer this drug. For Aranesp furnished for self-administration to Method I and Method II home patients determined to be competent, the renal facility bills its FI and the Method II supplier bills its DMERC. No additional payment is made for training a prospective self-administering patient or retraining an existing home patient to self-administer Aranesp.

Method II home patients who self-administer may obtain Aranesp only from either their Method II supplier or a Medicare-certified ESRD facility. In this case, the DMERC makes payment at the same rate that applies to facilities.

Program payment may not be made for Aranesp furnished by a physician to a patient for self-administration.

The DMERCs pay for Aranesp for Method II ESRD beneficiaries only. DMERCs shall deny claims for Aranesp where the beneficiary is not a Method II home dialysis patient.

When denying line items for patients that are not Method II, use the following message on the remittance advice:

The ANSI message 7011: Claim not covered by this payer contractor. You must send the claim to the correct payer contractor. When denying line items for patients that are not Method II, use the following message on the Medicare Summary Notice (MSN):

English: 8.59- Durable Medical Equipment Regional Carriers pay for Epoetin Alfa and Darbepoetin Alfa only for Method II End Stage Renal Disease home dialysis patients.

Spanish: 8.59- Las Empresas Regionales de Equipo Médico Duradero pagan por los medicamentos Epoetina Alfa y Darbepoetina Alfa sÐŠlo a pacientes del Metodo II de dialisis con enfermedad renal en etapa final que estan confinados al hogar.

100-4, 9, 150

Initial Preventive Physical Examination (IPPE)

Effective for services furnished on or after January 1, 2005, Section 611 of the Medicare Prescription Drug Improvement and Modernization Act of 2003 (MMA) provides for coverage under Part B of one initial preventive physical examination (IPPE) for new beneficiaries only, subject to certain eligibility and other limitations. For RHCs the Part B deductible for IPPE is waived for services provided on or after January 1, 2009. FQHC services are always exempt from the Part B deductible. Coinsurance is applicable.

Payment for the professional services will be made under the all-inclusive rate. Encounters with more than one health professional and multiple encounters with the same health professionals that take place on the same day and at a single location generally constitute a single visit.

However, in rare circumstances an RHC/FQHC can receive a separate payment for an encounter in addition to the payment for the IPPE when they are performed on the same day.

RHCs and FQHCs must HCPCS code for IPPE for the following reasons:

- To avoid application of deductible (on RHC claims);
- To assure payment for this service in addition to another encounter on the same day if they are both separate, unrelated, and appropriate; and
- To update the CWF record to track this once in a lifetime benefit.

Beginning with dates of service on or after January 1, 2009 if an IPPE is provided in an RHC or FQHC, the professional portion of the service is billed to the FI or Part A MAC using TOBs 71X and 73X, respectively, and the appropriate site of service revenue code in the 052X revenue code series, and must include HCPCS G0402. Additional information on IPPE can be found in Chapter 18, section 80 of this manual. NOTE: The technical component of an EKG performed at a clinic/center is not a Medicare-covered RHC/FQHC service and is not billed by the independent RHC/FQHC. Rather, it is billed to Medicare carriers or Part B MACs on professional claims (Form CMS-1500 or 837P) under the practitioner's ID following instructions for submitting practitioner claims. Likewise, the technical component of the EKG performed at a provider-based clinic/center is not a Medicare-covered RHC/FQHC service and is not billed by the provider-based RHC\FQHC. Instead, it is billed on the applicable TOB and submitted to the FI or Part A MAC using the base provider's ID following instructions for submitting claims to the FI/Part A MAC from the base provider. For the professional component of the EKG, there is no separate payment and no separate billing of it. The IPPE is the only HCPCS for which the deductible is waived under this benefit. For more information on billing for a screening EKG see chapter 18 section 80 of this manual.

100-4, 9, 160

Ultrasound Screening for Abdominal Aortic Aneurysm (AAA)

Section 5112 of the Deficit Reduction Act of 2005 amended the Social Security Act to provide coverage under Part B of the Medicare program for a one-time ultrasound screening for abdominal aortic aneurysms (AAA). Payment for the professional services that meet all of the program requirements will be made under the all-inclusive rate. For RHCs the Part B deductible for screening AAA is waived for dates of service on or after January 1, 2007. FQHC services are always exempt from the Part B deductible. Coinsurance is applicable. Additional information on AAA can be found in Chapter 18, section 110 of this manual.

If the screening is provided in an RHC or FQHC, the professional portion of the service is billed to the FI or Part A MAC using TOBs 71X and 73X, respectively, and the appropriate site of service revenue code in the 052X revenue code series and must include HCPCS G0389.

If the AAA screening is provided in an independent RHC or freestanding FQHC, the technical component of the service can be billed by the practitioner to the carrier or Part B MAC under the practitioner's ID following instructions for submitting practitioner claims.

If the screening is provided in a provider-based RHC/FQHC, the technical component of the service can be billed by the base provider to the FI or Part A MAC under the base provider's ID, following instructions for submitting claims to the FI/Part A MAC from the base provider.

100-4, 9, 181

181 - Diabetes Self-Management Training (DSMT) Services Provided by RHCs and FQHCs

A - FQHCs Previously, DSMT type services rendered by qualified registered dietitians or nutrition professionals were considered incident to services under the FQHC benefit, if all relevant program requirements were met. Therefore, separate all-inclusive encounter rate payment could not be made for the provision of DSMT services. With passage of DRA, effective January 1, 2006, FQHCs are eligible for a separate payment under Part B for these services provided they meet all program requirements. See Pub. 100-04, chapter 18, section 120. Payment is made at the all-inclusive encounter rate to the FQHC. This payment can be in addition to payment for any other qualifying visit on the same date of service as the beneficiary received qualifying DSMT services.

For FQHCs to qualify for a separate visit payment for DSMT services, the services must be a one-on-one face-to-face encounter. Group sessions don't constitute a billable visit for any FQHC services. Rather, the cost of group sessions is included in the calculation of the all-inclusive FQHC visit rate. To receive separate payment for DSMT services, the DSMT services must be billed on TOB 73X with HCPCS code G0108 and the appropriate site of service revenue code in the 052X revenue code series. This payment can be in addition to payment for any other qualifying visit on the same date of service that the beneficiary received qualifying DSMT services as long as the claim for DSMT services contains the appropriate coding specified above. Additional information on DSMT can be found in Chapter 18, section 120 of this manual.

NOTE: DSMT is not a qualifying visit on the same day that MNT is provided.

Group services (G0109) do not meet the criteria for a separate qualifying encounter. All line items billed on TOBs 73x with HCPCS codes for DSMT services will be denied.

B - RHCs Separate payment to RHCs for these practitioners/services continues to be precluded as these services are not within the scope of Medicare-covered RHC benefits. Note that the provision of the services by registered dietitians or nutritional professionals, might be considered incident to services in the RHC setting, provided all applicable conditions are met. However, they do not constitute an RHC visit, in and of themselves. All line items billed on TOB 71x with HCPCS code G0108 or G0109 will be denied.

100-4, 9, 182

Medical Nutrition Therapy (MNT) Services

A - FQHCs

Previously, MNT type services were considered incident to services under the FQHC benefit, if all relevant program requirements were met. Therefore, separate all-inclusive encounter rate payment could not be made for the provision of MNT services. With passage of DRA, effective January 1, 2006, FQHCs are eligible for a separate payment under Part B for these services provided they meet all program requirements. Payment is made at the all-inclusive encounter rate to the FQHC. This payment can be in addition to payment for any other qualifying visit on the same date of service as the beneficiary received qualifying MNT services.

For FQHCs to qualify for a separate visit payment for MNT services, the services must be a one-on-one face-to-face encounter. Group sessions don't constitute a billable visit for any FQHC services. Rather, the cost of group sessions is included in the calculation of the all-inclusive FQHC visit rate. To receive payment for MNT services, the MNT services must be billed on TOB 73X with the appropriate individual MNT HCPCS code (codes 97802, 97803, or G0270) and with the appropriate site of service revenue code in the 052X revenue code series. This payment can be in addition to payment for any other qualifying visit on the same date of service as the beneficiary received qualifying MNT services as long as the claim for MNT services contain the appropriate coding specified above.

NOTE: MNT is not a qualifying visit on the same day that DSMT is provided.

Additional information on MNT can be found in Chapter 4, section 300 of this manual.

Group services (HCPCS 97804 or G0271) do not meet the criteria for a separate qualifying encounter. All line items billed on TOB 73x with HCPCS code 97804 or G0271 will be denied.

B - RHCs

Separate payment to RHCs for these practitioners/services continues to be precluded as these services are not within the scope of Medicare-covered RHC benefits. All line items billed on TOB 71x with HCPCS codes for MNT services will be denied.

100-4, 10, 90.1

Osteoporosis Injections as HHA Benefit

A - Billing Requirements

The administration of the drug is included in the charge for the skilled nursing visit billed under bill type 32X or 33X, as appropriate. The cost of the drug is billed under bill type 34X, using revenue code 0636. Drugs that have the ingredient calcitonin are billed using HCPCS code J0630. Drugs that have the ingredient teriparatide may be billed using HCPCS code J3110, if all existing guidelines for coverage under the home health benefit are met. All other osteoporosis drugs that are FDA approved and are awaiting an HCPCS code must use the miscellaneous code of J3490 until a specific HCPCS code is approved for use.

HCPCS code J0630 is defined as up to 400 units. Therefore, the provider must calculate units for the bill as follows:

Units Furnished During Billing Period	Units of Service Entry on Bill
100-400	1
401-800	2
801-1200	3
1201-1600	4
1601-2000	5
2001-2400	6

HCPCS code J3110 is defined as 10 mcg. Providers should report 1 unit for each 10 mcg dose provided during the billing period.

These codes are paid on a reasonable cost basis, using the provider's submitted charges to make initial payments, which are subject to annual cost settlement.

Coverage requirements for osteoporosis drugs are found in Pub. 100-02, Medicare Benefit Policy Manual, chapter 7, section 50.4.3. Coverage requirements for the home health benefit in general are found in Pub. 100-02, Medicare Benefit Policy Manual, chapter 7, section 30.

B - Denial Messages

If the claim for an osteoporosis drug is denied because it was not an injectable drug approved by the FDA, the Medicare contractor shall use the appropriate message below on the MSN:

MSN Message 6.2: "Drugs not specifically classified as effective by the Food and Drug Administration are not covered."

If the claim for an osteoporosis injection is denied because the patient did not meet the requirements for coverage, the Medicare contractor shall use:

MSN message 6.5, which reads, "Medicare cannot pay for this injection because one or more requirements for coverage were not met."

C - Edits

Medicare system edits require that the date of service on a 34X claim for covered osteoporosis drugs falls within the start and end dates of an existing home health PPS episode. Once the system ensures the service dates on the 34X claim fall within an HH PPS episode that is open for the beneficiary on CWF, CWF edits to assure that the provider number on the 34X claim matches the provider number on the episode file. This is to reflect that although the osteoporosis drug is paid separately from the HH PPS episode rate it is included in consolidated billing requirements (see Sec.10.1.25 regarding consolidated billing).

Claims are also edited to assure that the claim is an HH claim (type of bill 34X), the beneficiary is female and that the diagnosis code 733.01 (post-menopausal osteoporosis) is present.

100-4, 11, 10.1

Hospice Pre-Election Evaluation and Counseling Services

Effective January 1, 2005, Medicare allows payment to a hospice for specified hospice pre-election evaluation and counseling services when furnished by a physician who is either the medical director of or employee of the hospice.

Medicare covers a one- time only payment on behalf of a beneficiary who is terminally ill, (defined as having a prognosis of 6 months or less if the disease follows its normal course), has no previous hospice elections, and has not previously received hospice pre-election evaluation and counseling services.

HCPCS code G0337 "Hospice Pre-Election Evaluation and Counseling Services" is used to designate that these services have been provided by the medical director or a physician employed by the hospice. Hospice agencies bill their Medicare contractor with home health and hospice jurisdiction directly using HCPCS G0337 with Revenue Code 0657. No other revenue codes may appear on the claim.

Claims for "Hospice Pre-Election and Counseling Services", HCPCS code G0337, are not subject to the editing usually required on hospice claims to match the claim to an established hospice period. Further, contractors do not apply payments for hospice pre-election evaluation and counseling consultation services to the overall hospice cap amount.

Medicare must ensure that this counseling service occurs only one time per beneficiary by imposing safeguards to detect and prevent duplicate billing for similar services. If "new patient" physician services (HCPCS codes 99201-99205) are submitted by a Medicare contractor to CWF for payment authorization but HCPCS code G0337 (Hospice Pre-Election Evaluation and Counseling Services) has already been approved for a hospice claim for the same beneficiary, for the same date of service, by the same physician, the physician service will be rejected by CWF and the service shall be denied as a duplicate. Medicare contractors use the following messages in this case:

HCPCS code G0337 is only payable when billed on a hospice claim. Contractors shall not make payment for HCPCS code G0337 on professional claims. Contractors shall deny line items on professional claims for HCPCS code G0337 and use the following messages:

100-4, 11, 30.3

Data Required on the Institutional Claim to Medicare Contractor

See Pub. 100-02, Chapter 9, §§10 & 20.2 for coverage requirements for Hospice benefits. This section addresses only the submittal of claims. Before submitting claims, the hospice must submit a Notice of Election (NOE) to the Medicare contractor. See section 20, of this chapter for information on NOE transaction types.

The Social Security Act at §1862 (a)(22) requires that all claims for Medicare payment must be submitted in an electronic form specified by the Secretary of Health and Human Services, unless an exception described at §1862 (h) applies. The electronic form required for billing hospice services is the ANSI X12N 837 Institutional claim transaction. Since the data structure of the 837 transaction is difficult to express in narrative form and to provide assistance to small providers excepted from the electronic claim requirement, the instructions below are given relative to the data element names on the UB-04 (Form CMS-1450) hardcopy form. Each data element name is shown in bold type. Information regarding the form locator numbers that correspond to these data element names and a table to crosswalk UB-04 form locators to the 837 transaction is found in Chapter 25.

Because claim formats serve the needs of many payers, some data elements may not be needed by a particular payer. Detailed information is given only for items required for Medicare hospice claims. Items not listed need not be completed although hospices may complete them when billing multiple payers.

Provider Name, Address, and Telephone Number
The hospice enters this information for their agency.

Type of Bill
This three-digit alphanumeric code gives three specific pieces of information. The first digit identifies the type of facility. The second classifies the type of care. The third indicates the sequence of this bill in this particular benefit period. It is referred to as a "frequency" code.

Code Structure

1st Digit - Type of Facility
8 - Special facility (Hospice)

2nd Digit - Classification (Special Facility Only)
1 - Hospice (Nonhospital based)
2 - Hospice (Hospital based)

3rd Digit – Frequency	Definition
0 - Nonpayment/Zero Claims	Used when no payment from Medicare is anticipated.
I - Admit Through Discharge Claim	This code is used for a bill encompassing an entire course of hospice treatment for which the provider expects payment from the payer, i.e., no further bills will be submitted for this patient.
2 - Interim – First Claim	This code is used for the first of an expected series of payment bills for a hospice course of treatment.
3 - Interim - Continuing Claim	This code is used when a payment bill for a hospice course of treatment has already been submitted and further bills are expected to be submitted.
4 - Interim - Last Claim	This code is used for a payment bill that is the last of a series for a hospice course of treatment. The "Through" date of this bill is the discharge date, transfer date, or date of death.
5 - Late Charges	Use this code for late charges that need to be billed. Late charges can be submitted only for revenue codes not on the original bill.
	Effective April 1, 2012, hospice late charge claims are no longer accepted by Medicare. Providers should use type of bill frequency 7. See below.
7 - Replacement of Prior Claim	This code is used by the provider when it wants to correct (other than late charges) a previously submitted bill. This is the code used on the corrected or "new" bill.
	For additional information on replacement bills see Chapter 3.
8 - Void/Cancel of a Prior Claim	This code is used to cancel a previously processed claim. For additional information on void/cancel bills see Chapter 3.

Statement Covers Period (From-Through)
The hospice shows the beginning and ending dates of the period covered by this bill in numeric fields (MM-DD-YY). The hospice does not show days before the patient's entitlement began. Since the 12-month hospice "cap period" (see §80.2) ends each year on October 31, hospices must submit separate bills for October and November.

Patient Name/Identifier
The hospice enters the beneficiary's name exactly as it appears on the Medicare card.

Patient Address

Patient Birth date

Patient Sex
The hospice enters the appropriate address, date of birth and gender information describing the beneficiary.

Admission/Start of Care Date
The hospice enters the admission date, which must be the same date as the effective date of the hospice election or change of election. The date of admission may not precede the physician's certification by more than 2 calendar days.

The admission date stays the same on all continuing claims for the same hospice election.

Patient Discharge Status
This code indicates the patient's status as of the "Through" date of the billing period. The hospice enters the most appropriate National Uniform Billing Committee (NUBC) approved code.

Note that patient discharge status code 20 is not used on hospice claims. If the patient has died during the billing period, use codes 40, 41 or 42 as appropriate.

Medicare regulations at 42 CFR 418.26 define three reasons for discharge from hospice care:

1) The beneficiary moves out of the hospice's service area or transfers to another hospice,
2) The hospice determines that the beneficiary is no longer terminally ill or
3) The hospice determines the beneficiary meets their internal policy regarding discharge for cause.

Each of these discharge situations requires different coding on Medicare claims.

Reason 1: A beneficiary may move out of the hospice's service area either with, or without, a transfer to another hospice. In the case of a discharge when the beneficiary moves out of the hospice's service area without a transfer, the hospice uses the NUBC approved discharge status code that best describes the beneficiary's situation. The hospice does not report occurrence code 42 on their claim. This discharge claim will terminate the beneficiary's current hospice benefit period as of the "Through" date on the claim. The beneficiary may re-elect the hospice benefit at any time as long they remain eligible for the benefit.

In the case of a discharge when the beneficiary moves out of the hospice's service area and transfers to another hospice, the hospice uses discharge status code 50 or 51, depending on whether the beneficiary is transferring to home hospice or hospice in a medical facility. The hospice does not report occurrence code 42 on their claim. This discharge claim does not terminate the beneficiary's current hospice benefit period. The admitting hospice submits a transfer Notice of Election (type of bill 8xC) after the transfer has occurred and the beneficiary's hospice benefit is not affected.

Reason 2: In the case of a discharge when the hospice determines the beneficiary is no longer terminally ill, the hospice uses the NUBC approved discharge status code that best describes the beneficiary's situation. The hospice also reports occurrence code 42 on their claim and the date of their determination. This discharge claim will terminate the beneficiary's current hospice benefit period as of the occurrence code 42 date. This coding may also used if the beneficiary has chosen to revoke their hospice election. The beneficiary may re-elect the hospice benefit if they are certified as terminally ill and eligible for the benefit again in the future.

Reason 3: In the case of a discharge for cause, the hospice uses the NUBC approved discharge status code that best describes the beneficiary's situation. The hospice does not report occurrence code 42 on their claim. Instead, the hospice reports condition code H2 to indicate a discharge for cause. The effect of this discharge claim on the beneficiary's current hospice benefit period depends on the discharge status.

If the beneficiary is transferred to another hospice (discharge status codes 50 or 51) the claim does not terminate the beneficiary's current hospice benefit period. The admitting hospice submits a transfer Notice of Election (type of bill 8xC) after the transfer has occurred and the beneficiary's hospice benefit is not affected. If any other appropriate discharge status code is used, this discharge claim will terminate the beneficiary's current hospice benefit period as of the "Through" date on the claim. The beneficiary may re-elect the hospice benefit if they are certified as terminally ill and eligible for the benefit again in the future and are willing to be compliant with care.

Untimely Face-to-Face Encounters and Discharge
When a required face-to-face encounter occurs prior to, but no more than 30 calendar days prior to, the third benefit period recertification and every benefit period recertification thereafter, it is considered timely. A timely face-to-face encounter would be evident when examining the face-to-face attestation, which is part of the recertification, as that attestation includes the date of the encounter. If the required face-to-face encounter is not timely, the hospice would be unable to recertify the patient as being terminally ill, and the patient would cease to be eligible for the Medicare hospice benefit. In such instances, the hospice must discharge the patient from the Medicare hospice benefit because he or she is not considered terminally ill for Medicare purposes.

When a discharge from the Medicare hospice benefit occurs due to failure to perform a required face-to-face encounter timely, the claim should include the most appropriate patient discharge status code and occurrence code 42, as described in the Medicare Claims Processing Manual, Pub. 100-04, Chapter 11, Section 30.3. The hospice can re-admit the patient to the Medicare hospice benefit once the required encounter occurs, provided the patient continues to meet all of the eligibility requirements and the patient (or representative) files an election statement in accordance with CMS regulations. Where the only reason the patient ceases to be eligible for the Medicare hospice benefit is the hospice's failure to meet the face-to-face requirement, we would expect the hospice to continue to care for the patient at its own expense until the required encounter occurs, enabling the hospice to re-establish Medicare eligibility.

Occurrence span code 77 does not apply to the above described situations when the face-to-face encounter has not occurred timely.

While the face-to-face encounter itself must occur no more than 30 calendar days prior to the start of the third benefit period recertification and each subsequent recertification, its accompanying attestation must be completed before the claim is submitted.

Condition Codes

The hospice enters any appropriate NUBC approved code(s) identifying conditions related to this bill that may affect processing.

Codes listed below are only those most frequently applicable to hospice claims. For a complete list of codes, see the NUBC manual.

07	Treatment of Non-terminal Condition for Hospice	Code indicates the patient has elected hospice care but the provider is not treating the terminal condition, and is, therefore, requesting regular Medicare payment.
20	Beneficiary Requested Billing	Code indicates the provider realizes the services on this bill are at a noncovered level of care or otherwise excluded from coverage, but the beneficiary has requested a formal determination.
21	Billing for Denial Notice	Code indicates the provider realizes services are at a noncovered level of care or excluded, but requests a denial notice from Medicare in order to bill Medicaid or other insurers.
H2	Discharge by a Hospice Provider for Cause	Discharge by a Hospice Provider for Cause.~Note: Used by the provider to indicate the patient meets the hospice's documented policy addressing discharges for cause.

Occurrence Codes and Dates

The hospice enters any appropriate NUBC approved code(s) and associated date(s) defining specific event(s) relating to this billing period. Event codes are two numeric digits, and dates are six numeric digits (MM-DD-YY). If there are more occurrences than there are spaces on the form, use the occurrence span code fields to record additional occurrences and dates.

Codes listed below are only those most frequently applicable to hospice claims. For a complete list of codes, see the NUBC manual

Code	Title	Definition
23	Cancellation of Hospice Election Period (Medicare contractor USE ONLY)	Code indicates date on which a hospice period of election is cancelled by a Medicare contractor as opposed to revocation by the beneficiary.
24	Date Insurance Denied	Code indicates the date of receipt of a denial of coverage by a higher priority payer.
27	Date of Hospice Certification or Re-Certification	Code indicates the date of certification or re-certification of the hospice benefit period, beginning with the first 2 initial benefit periods of 90 days each and the subsequent 60-day benefit periods. Note regarding transfers from one hospice to another hospice: If a patient is in the first certification period when they transfer to another hospice, the receiving hospice would use the same certification date as the previous hospice until the next certification period. However, if they were in the next certification at the time of transfer, then they would enter that date in the Occurrence Code 27 and date.
42	Date of Termination of Hospice Benefit	Enter code to indicate the date on which beneficiary terminated his/her election to receive hospice benefits. This code can be used only when the beneficiary has revoked the benefit or has been decertified. It is not used in transfer situations.

Occurrence code 27 is reported on the claim for the billing period in which the certification or re-certification was obtained. When the re-certification is late and not obtained during the month it was due, the occurrence span code 77 should be reported with the through date of the span code equal to the through date of the claim.

Occurrence Span Code and Dates

The hospice enters any appropriate NUBC approved code(s) and associated beginning and ending date(s) defining a specific event relating to this billing period are shown. Event codes are two alphanumeric digits and dates are shown numerically as MM-DD-YY.

Codes listed below are only those most frequently applicable to hospice claims. For a complete list of codes, see the NUBC manual.

Code	Title	Definition
M2	Dates of Inpatient Respite Care	Code indicates From/Through dates of a period of inpatient respite care for hospice patients to differentiate separate respite periods of less than 5 days each. M2 is used when respite care is provided more than once during a benefit period.
77	Provider Liability – Utilization Charged	Code indicates From/Through dates for a period of non-covered hospice care for which the provider accepts payment liability (other than for medical necessity or custodial care).

Hospices must use occurrence span code 77 to identify days of care that are not covered by Medicare due to untimely physician recertification. This is particularly important when the non-covered days fall at the beginning of a billing period.

Value Codes and Amounts

The hospice enters any appropriate NUBC approved code(s) and the associated value amounts identifying numeric information related to this bill that may affect processing.

The most commonly used value codes on hospice claims are value codes 61 and G8, which are used to report the location of the site of hospice services. Otherwise, value codes are commonly used only to indicate Medicare is secondary to another payer. For detailed information on reporting Medicare secondary payer information, see the Medicare Secondary Payer Manual.

Code	Title	Definition
61	Place of Residence where Service is Furnished (Routine Home Care and Continuous Home Care)	MSA or Core-Based Statistical Area (CBSA) number (or rural State code) of the location where the hospice service is delivered. A residence can be an inpatient facility if an individual uses that facility as a place of residence. It is the level of care that is required and not the location where hospice services are provided that determines payment. In other words, if an individual resides in a freestanding hospice facility and requires routine home care, then claims are submitted for routine home care. Hospices must report value code 61 when billing revenue codes 0651 and 0652.
G8	Facility where Inpatient Hospice Service is Delivered (General Inpatient and Inpatient Respite Care).	MSA or Core Based Statistical Area (CBSA) number (or rural State code) of the facility where inpatient hospice services are delivered. Hospices must report value code G8 when billing revenue codes 0655 and 0656.

If hospice services are provided to the beneficiary in more than one CBSA area during the billing period, the hospice reports the CBSA that applies at the end of the billing period. For routine home care and continuous home care (e.g., the beneficiary's residence changes between locations in different CBSAs), report the CBSA of the beneficiary's residence at the end of the billing period. For general inpatient and inpatient respite care (e.g., the beneficiary is served in inpatient facilities in different CBSAs), report the CBSA of the latest facility that served the beneficiary. If the beneficiary receives both home and inpatient care during the billing period, the latest home CBSA is reported with value code 61 and the latest facility CBSA is reported with value code G8.

Revenue Codes

The hospice assigns a revenue code for each type of service provided and enters the appropriate four-digit numeric revenue code to explain each charge.

For claims with dates of service before July 1, 2008, hospices only reported the revenue codes in the table below. Effective on claims with dates of service on or after January 1, 2008, additional revenue codes will be reported describing the visits provided under each level of care. However, Medicare payment will continue to be reflected only on claim lines with the revenue codes in this table.

Hospice claims are required to report separate line items for the level of care each time the level of care changes. This includes revenue codes 0651, 0655 and 0656. For example, if a patient begins the month receiving routine home care followed by a period of general inpatient care and then later returns to routine home care all in the same month, in addition to the one line reporting the general inpatient care days, there should be two separate line items for routine home care. Each routine home care line reports a line item date of service to indicate the first date that level of care began for that consecutive period. This will ensure visits and calls reported on the claim will be associated with the level of care being billed.

Code	Description	Standard Abbreviation
0651*	Routine Home Care	RTN Home
0652*	Continuous Home Care	CTNS Home A minimum of 8 hours of primarily nursing care within a 24-hour period. The 8-hours of care do not need to be continuous within the 24-hour period, but a need for an aggregate of 8 hours of primarily nursing care is required. Nursing care must be provided by a registered nurse or a licensed practical nurse. If skilled intervention is required for less than 8 aggregate hours (or less than 32 units) within a 24 hour period, then the care rendered would be covered as a routine home care day. Services provided by a nurse practitioner as the attending physician are not included in the CHC computation nor is care that is not directly related to the crisis included in the computation. CHC billing should reflect direct patient care during a period of crisis and should not reflect time related to staff working hours, time taken for meal breaks, time used for educating staff, time used to report etc.
0655***	Inpatient Respite Care	IP Respite
0656***	General Inpatient Care	GNL IP
0657**	Physician Services	PHY SER (must be accompanied by a physician procedure code)

* Reporting of value code 61 is required with these revenue codes.

** Reporting of modifier GV is required with this revenue code when billing physician services performed by a nurse practitioner.

*** Reporting of value code G8 is required with these revenue codes.

NOTE: Hospices use revenue code 0657 to identify hospice charges for services furnished to patients by physician or nurse practitioner employees, or physicians or nurse practitioners receiving compensation from the hospice. Physician services performed by a nurse practitioner require the addition of the modifier GV in conjunction with revenue code 0657. Procedure codes are required in order for the Medicare contractor to determine the reimbursement rate for the physician services. Appropriate procedure codes are available from the Medicare contractor.

Effective on claims with dates of service on or after July 1, 2008, hospices must report the number of visits that were provided to the beneficiary in the course of delivering the hospice levels of care billed with the codes above. Charges for these codes will be reported on the appropriate level of care line. Total number of patient care visits is to be reported by the discipline (registered nurse, nurse practitioner, licensed nurse, home health aide (also known as a hospice aide), social worker, physician or nurse practitioner serving as the beneficiary's attending physician) for each week at each location of service. If visits are provided in multiple sites, a separate line for each site and for each discipline will be required. The total number of visits does not imply the total number of activities or interventions provided. If patient care visits in a particular discipline are not provided under a given level of care or service location, do not report a line for the corresponding revenue code.

To constitute a visit, the discipline, (as defined above) must have provided care to the beneficiary. Services provided by a social worker to the beneficiary's family also constitute a visit. For example, phone calls, documentation in the medical/clinical record, interdisciplinary group meetings, obtaining physician orders, rounds in a facility or any other activity that is not related to the provision of items or services to a beneficiary, do not count towards a visit to be placed on the claim. In addition, the visit must be reasonable and necessary for the palliation and management of the terminal illness and related conditions as described in the patient's plan of care.

Example 1: Week 1: A visit by the RN was made to the beneficiary's home on Monday and Wednesday where the nurse assessed the patient, verified effect of pain medications, provided patient teaching, obtained vital signs and documented in the medical record. A home health aide assisted the patient with a bath on Tuesday and Thursday. There were no social work or physician visits. Thus for that week there were 2 visits provided by the nurse and 2 by the home health aide. Since there were no visits by the social worker or by the physician, there would not be any line items for each of those disciplines.

Example 2: If a hospice patient is receiving routine home care while residing in a nursing home, the hospice would record visits for all of its physicians, nurses, social workers, and home health aides who visit the patient to provide care for the palliation and management of the terminal illness and related conditions, as described in the patient's plan of care. In this example the nursing home is acting as the patient's home. Only the patient care provided by the hospice staff constitutes a visit.

Hospices must enter the following visit revenue codes, when applicable as of July 1, 2008:

055x Skilled Nursing	Required detail: The earliest date of service this discipline was provided during the delivery of each level of care in each service location, service units which represent the number of visits provided in that location, and a charge amount.
056x Medical Social Services	Required detail: The earliest date of service this discipline was provided during the delivery of each level of care in each service location, service units which represent the number of visits provided in that location, and a charge amount.
057x Home Health Aide	Required detail: The earliest date of service this discipline was provided during the delivery of each level of care in each service location, service units which represent the number of visits provided in that location, and a charge amount.

For services provided on or after January 1, 2010, hospices report social worker phone calls and visits performed by hospice staff for other than General Inpatient (GIP) care in 15 minute increments using the following revenue codes and associated HCPCS:

Revenue Code	Required HCPCS	Required Detail
042x Physical Therapy	G0151	Required detail: Each visit is identified on a separate line item with the appropriate line item date of service and a charge amount. The units reported on the claim are the multiplier for the total time of the visit defined in the HCPCS description.
043x Occupational Therapy	G0152	Required detail: Each visit is identified on a separate line item with the appropriate line item date of service and a charge amount. The units reported on the claim are the multiplier for the total time of the visit defined in the HCPCS description.
044x Speech Therapy – Language Pathology	G0153	Required detail: Each visit is identified on a separate line item with the appropriate line item date of service and a charge amount. The units reported on the claim are the multiplier for the total time of the visit defined in the HCPCS description.
055x Skilled Nursing	G0154	Required detail: Each visit is identified on a separate line item with the appropriate line item date of service and a charge amount. The units reported on the claim are the multiplier for the total time of the visit defined in the HCPCS description.
056x Medical Social Services	G0155	Required detail: Each visit is identified on a separate line item with the appropriate line item date of service and a charge amount. The units reported on the claim are the multiplier for the total time of the visit defined in the HCPCS description.
0569 Other Medical Social Services	G0155	Required detail: Each social service phone call is identified on a separate line item with the appropriate line item date of service and a charge amount. The units reported on the claim are the multiplier for the total time of the call defined in the HCPCS description.

Revenue Code	Required HCPCS	Required Detail
057x Aide	G0156	Required detail: Each visit is identified on a separate line item with the appropriate line item date of service and a charge amount. The units reported on the claim are the multiplier the total time of the visit defined in the HCPCS description.

Visits by registered nurses, licensed vocational nurses and nurse practitioners (unless the nurse practitioner is acting as the beneficiary's attending physician) are reported under revenue code 055x.

All visits to provide care related to the palliation and management of the terminal illness or related conditions, whether provided by hospice employees or provided under arrangement, must be reported. The two exceptions are related to General Inpatient Care and Respite care. CMS is not requiring hospices to report visit data at this time for visits made by non-hospice staff providing General Inpatient Care or respite care in contract facilities. However, General Inpatient Care or respite care visits related to the palliation and management of the terminal illness or related conditions provided by hospice staff in contract facilities must be reported, and all General Inpatient Care and respite care visits related to the palliation and management of the terminal illness or related conditions provided in hospice-owned facilities must be reported.

Charges associated with the reported visits are covered under the hospice bundled payment and reflected in the payment for the level of care billed on the claim. No additional payment is made on the visit revenue lines. The visit charges will be identified on the provider remittance advice notice with remittance code 97 "Payment adjusted because the benefit for this service is included in the payment / allowance for another service/procedure that has already been adjudicated."

Effective January 1, 2010, Medicare will require hospices to report additional detail for visits on their claims. For all Routine Home Care (RHC), Continuous Home Care (CHC) and Respite care billing, Medicare hospice claims should report each visit performed by nurses, aides, and social workers who are employed by the hospice, and their associated time per visit in the number of 15 minute increments, on a separate line. The visits should be reported using revenue codes 055x (nursing services), 057x (aide services), or 056x (medical social services), with the time reported using the associated HCPCS G-code in the range G0154 to G0156. Hospices should report in the unit field on the line level the units as a multiplier of the visit time defined in the HCPCS description.

Additionally, providers should begin reporting each RHC, CHC, and Respite visit performed by physical therapists, occupational therapists, and speech-language therapists and their associated time per visit in the number of 15 minute increments on a separate line. Providers should use existing revenue codes 042x for physical therapy, 043x for occupational therapy, and 044x for speech language therapy, in addition to the appropriate HCPCS G-code for recording of visit length in 15 minute increments. HCPCS G-codes G0151 to G0153 will be used to describe the therapy discipline and visit time reported on a particular line item. Hospices should report in the unit field on the line level the units as a multiplier of the visit time defined in the HCPCS description. If a hospice patient is receiving Respite care in a contract facility, visit and time data by non-hospice staff should not be reported.

Social worker phone calls made to the patient or the patient's family should be reported using revenue code 0569, and HCPCS G-code G0155 for the length of the call, with each call being a separate line item. Hospices should report in the unit field on the line level the units as a multiplier of the visit time defined in the HCPCS description. Only phone calls that are necessary for the palliation and management of the terminal illness and related conditions as described in the patient's plan of care (such as counseling, or speaking with a patient's family or arranging for a placement) should be reported. Report only social worker phone calls related to providing and or coordinating care to the patient and family and documented as such in the clinical records.

When recording any visit or social worker phone call time, providers should sum the time for each visit or call, rounding to the nearest 15 minute increment. Providers should not include travel time or documentation time in the time recorded for any visit or call. Additionally, hospices may not include interdisciplinary group time in time and visit reporting.

HCPCS/Accommodation Rates/HIPPS Rate Codes

For services provided on or before December 31, 2006, HCPCS codes are required only to report procedures on service lines for attending physician services (revenue 657). Level of care revenue codes (651, 652, 655 or 656) do not require HCPCS coding.

For services provided on or after January 1, 2007, hospices must also report a HCPCS code along with each level of care revenue code (651, 652, 655 and 656) to identify the type of service location where that level of care was provided.

The following HCPCS codes will be used to report the type of service location for hospice services:non-hospice staff should not be reported.

HCPCS Code	Definition
Q5001	HOSPICE CARE PROVIDED IN PATIENT'S HOME/RESIDENCE
Q5002	HOSPICE CARE PROVIDED IN ASSISTED LIVING FACILITY
Q5003	HOSPICE CARE PROVIDED IN NURSING LONG TERM CARE FACILITY (LTC) OR NON-SKILLED NURSING FACILITY (NF)
Q5004	HOSPICE CARE PROVIDED IN SKILLED NURSING FACILITY (SNF)
Q5005	HOSPICE CARE PROVIDED IN INPATIENT HOSPITAL
Q5006	HOSPICE CARE PROVIDED IN INPATIENT HOSPICE FACILITY
Q5007	HOSPICE CARE PROVIDED IN LONG TERM CARE HOSPITAL (LTCH)
Q5008	HOSPICE CARE PROVIDED IN INPATIENT PSYCHIATRIC FACILITY
Q5009	HOSPICE CARE PROVIDED IN PLACE NOT OTHERWISE SPECIFIED (NOS)
Q5010	Hospice home care provided in a hospice facility

If care is rendered at multiple locations, each location is to be identified on the claim with a corresponding HCPCS code. For example, routine home care may be provided for a portion of the billing period in the patient's residence and another portion in an assisted living facility. In this case, report one revenue code 651 line with HCPCS code Q5001 and the number of days of routine home care provided in the residence and another revenue code 651 line with HCPCS code Q5002 and the number of days of routine home care provided in the assisted living facility.

Q5003 is to be used for hospice patients in an unskilled nursing facility (NF) or hospice patients in the NF portion of a dually certified nursing facility, who are receiving unskilled care from the facility staff.

Q5004 is to be used for hospice patients in a skilled nursing facility (SNF), or hospice patients in the SNF portion of a dually certified nursing facility, who are receiving skilled care from the facility staff.

NOTE: Q5003 should be used for hospice patients located in a NF; many of these patients may also have Medicaid. Q5004 should be used when the hospice patient is in a SNF, and receiving skilled care from the facility staff, such as would occur in a GIP stay. For Q5004 to be used, the facility would have to be certified as a SNF. Some facilities are dually certified as a SNF and a NF; the hospice will have to determine what level of care the facility staff is providing (skilled or unskilled) in deciding which type of bed the patient is in, and therefore which code to use. When a patient is in the NF portion of a dually certified nursing facility, and receiving only unskilled care from the facility staff, Q5003 should be reported. Note that GIP care that is provided in a nursing facility can only be given in a SNF, because GIP requires a skilled level of care.

These service location HCPCS codes are not required on revenue code lines describing the visits provided under each level of care (e.g. 055X, 056X, 057X).

Service Date

The HIPAA standard 837 Institutional claim format requires line item dates of service for all outpatient claims. Medicare classifies hospice claims as outpatient claims (see Chapter 1, §60.4). For services provided on or before December 31, 2006, CMS allows hospices to satisfy the line item date of service requirement by placing any valid date within the Statement Covers Period dates on line items on hospice claims.

For services provided on or after January 1, 2007, service date reporting requirements will vary between continuous home care lines (revenue code 652) and other revenue code lines.

Revenue code 652 – report a separately dated line item for each day that continuous home care is provided, reporting the number of hours, or parts of hours rounded to 15-minute increments, of continuous home care that was provided on that date.

Other payment revenue codes – report a separate line for each level of care provided at each service location type, as described in the instructions for HCPCS coding reported above. Hospices report the earliest date that each level of care was provided at each service location. Attending physician services should be individually dated, reporting the date that each HCPCS code billed was delivered.

Non-payment service revenue codes – report dates as described in the table above under Revenue Codes.

For services provided on or after January 1, 2010, hospices report social worker phone calls and visits performed by hospice staff for other than GIP care as separate line items for each with the appropriate line item date of service. GIP visit reporting has not changed with the January 2010 update. GIP visits will continue to be reported as the number of visits per week.

For service visits that begin in one calendar day and span into the next calendar day, report one visit using the date the visit ended as the service date.

Service Units
The hospice enters the number of units for each type of service. Units are measured in days for revenue codes 651, 655, and 656, in hours for revenue code 652, and in procedures for revenue code 657. For services provided on or after January 1, 2007, hours for revenue code 652 are reported in 15-minute increments. For services provided on or after January 1, 2008, units for visit discipline revenue codes are measured by the number of visits.

For services provided on or after January 1, 2010, hospices report social worker phone calls and visits performed by hospice staff for other than GIP care as a separate line item with the appropriate line item date of service and the units as an increment of 15 minutes. GIP visit reporting has not changed with the January 2010 update. The units for visits under GIP level of care continue to reflect the number of visits per week.

Report in the unit field on the line level the units as a multiplier of the visit time defined in the HCPCS description.

Total Charges
The hospice enters the total charge for the service described on each revenue code line. This information is being collected for purposes of research and will not affect the amount of reimbursement.

Payer Name
The hospice identifies the appropriate payer(s) for the claim.

National Provider Identifier – Billing Provider
The hospice enters its own National Provider Identifier (NPI).

Principal Diagnosis Code
The hospice enters diagnosis coding as required by ICD-9-CM Coding Guidelines. Hospices may not report V-codes as the primary diagnosis on hospice claims. The principal diagnosis code describes the terminal illness of the hospice patient and V-codes do not describe terminal conditions.

Other Diagnosis Codes
The hospice enters diagnosis coding as required by ICD-9-CM Coding Guidelines.

Attending Provider Name and Identifiers
For claims with dates of service before January 1, 2010, the hospice enters the National Provider Identifier (NPI) and name of the physician currently responsible for certifying the terminal illness, and signing the individual's plan of care for medical care and treatment.

For claims with dates of service on or after January 1, 2010 the hospice shall enter the NPI and and name of the attending physician designated by the patient as having the most significant role in the determination and delivery of the patient's medical care.

Other Provider Name and Identifiers
For claims with dates of service before January 1, 2010, if the attending physician is a nurse practitioner, the hospice enters the NPI and name of the nurse practitioner.

For claims with dates of service on or after January 1, 2010, the hospice enters the NPI and name of the hospice physician responsible for certifying that the patient is terminally ill, with a life expectancy of 6 months or less if the disease runs its normal course. Note: Both the attending physician and other physician fields should be completed unless the patient's designated attending physician is the same as the physician certifying the terminal illness. When the attending physician is also the physician certifying the terminal illness, only the attending physician is required to be reported.

100-4, 11, 40.1.3.1

Care Plan Oversight

Care plan oversight (CPO) exists where there is physician supervision of patients under care of hospices that require complex and multidisciplinary care modalities involving regular physician development and/or revision of care plans. Implicit in the concept of CPO is the expectation that the physician has coordinated an aspect of the patient's care with the hospice during the month for which CPO services were billed.

For a physician or NP employed by or under arrangement with a hospice agency, CPO functions are incorporated and are part of the hospice per diem payment and as such may not be separately billed.

For information on separately billable CPO services by the attending physician or nurse practitioner see Chapter 12, 180 of this manual.

100-4,12, 30.4

Cardiovascular System (Codes 92950-93799)

A. Echocardiography Contrast Agents
Effective October 1, 2000, physicians may separately bill for contrast agents used in echocardiography. Physicians should use HCPCS Code A9700 (Supply of Injectable Contrast Material for Use in Echocardiography, per study). The type of service code is 9. This code will be carrier-priced.

B. Electronic Analyses of Implantable Cardioverter-defibrillators and Pacemakers
The CPT codes 93731, 93734, 93741 and 93743 are used to report electronic analyses of single or dual chamber pacemakers and single or dual chamber implantable cardioverterdefibrillators. In the office, a physician uses a device called a programmer to obtain information about the status and performance of the device and to evaluate the patient's cardiac rhythm and response to the implanted device. Advances in information technology now enable physicians to evaluate patients with implanted cardiac devices without requiring the patient to be present in the physician's office. Using a manufacturer's specific monitor/transmitter, a patient can send complete device data and specific cardiac data to a distant receiving station or secure Internet server. The electronic analysis of cardiac device data that is remotely obtained provides immediate and long-term data on the device and clinical data on the patient's cardiac functioning equivalent to that obtained during an in-office evaluation. Physicians should report the electronic analysis of an implanted cardiac device using remotely obtained data as described above with CPT code 93731, 93734, 93741 or 93743, depending on the type of cardiac device implanted in the patient.

100-4, 12, 60

Payment for Pathology Services

B3-15020, AB-01-47 (CR1499)

A. General Payment Rule
Payment may be made under the fee schedule for the professional component of physician laboratory or physician pathology services furnished to hospital inpatients or outpatients by hospital physicians or by independent laboratories, if they qualify as the reassignee for the physician service.. Payment may be made under the fee schedule, as noted below, for the technical component (TC) of pathology services furnished by an independent laboratory to hospital inpatients or outpatients. Payment may be made under the fee schedule for the technical component of physician pathology services furnished by an independent laboratory, or a hospital if it is acting as an independent laboratory, to non-hospital patients. The Medicare physician fee schedule identifies those physician laboratory or physician pathology services that have a technical component service.

CMS published a final regulation in 1999 that would no longer allow independent laboratories to bill under the physician fee schedule for the TC of physician pathology services. The implementation of this regulation was delayed by Section 542 of the Benefits and Improvement and Protection Act of 2000 (BIPA). Section 542 allows the Medicare carrier to continue to pay for the TC of physician pathology services when an independent laboratory furnishes this service to an inpatient or outpatient of a covered hospital. This provision is applicable to TC services furnished in 2001, 2002, 2003, 2004, 2005 or 2006.

For this provision, a covered hospital is a hospital that had an arrangement with an independent laboratory that was in effect as of July 22, 1999, under which a laboratory furnished the TC of physician pathology services to fee-for-service Medicare beneficiaries who were hospital inpatients or outpatients, and submitted claims for payment for the TC to a carrier. The TC could have been submitted separately or combined with the professional component and reported as a combined service.

The term, fee-for-service Medicare beneficiary, means an individual who:

- Is entitled to benefits under Part A or enrolled under Part B of title XVIII or both; and
- Is not enrolled in any of the following: A Medicare + Choice plan under Part C of such title; a plan offered by an eligible organization under 1876 of the Social Security Act; a program of all-inclusive care for the elderly under 1894; or a social health maintenance organization demonstration project established under Section 4108 of the Omnibus Budget Reconciliation Act of 1987.

In implementing Section 542, the carriers should consider as independent laboratories those entities that it has previously recognized as independent laboratories. An independent laboratory that has acquired another independent laboratory that had an arrangement of July 22, 1999, with a covered hospital, can bill the TC of physician pathology services for that hospital's inpatients and outpatients under the physician fee schedule.

An independent laboratory that furnishes the TC of physician pathology services to inpatients or outpatients of a hospital that is not a covered hospital may not bill the carrier for the TC of physician pathology services during the time 542 is in effect.

If the arrangement between the independent laboratory and the covered hospital limited the provision of TC physician pathology services to certain situations or at particular times, then the independent laboratory can bill the carrier only for these limited services.

The carrier shall require independent laboratories that had an arrangement, on or prior to July 22, 1999 with a covered hospital, to bill for the technical component of physician pathology services to provide a copy of this agreement, or other documentation substantiating that an arrangement was in effect between the hospital and the independent laboratory as of this date. The independent laboratory must submit this documentation for each covered hospital that the independent laboratory services.

See Chapter 16 for additional instruction on laboratory services including clinical diagnostic laboratory services.

Physician laboratory and pathology services are limited to:

- Surgical pathology services;
- Specific cytopathology, hematology and blood banking services that have been identified to require performance by a physician and are listed below;
- Clinical consultation services that meet the requirements in subsection D below; and
- Clinical laboratory interpretation services that meet the requirements and which are specifically listed in subsection E below.

B. Surgical Pathology Services

Surgical pathology services include the gross and microscopic examination of organ tissue performed by a physician, except for autopsies, which are not covered by Medicare. Surgical pathology services paid under the physician fee schedule are reported under the following CPT codes:

88300, 88302, 88304, 88305, 88307, 88309, 88311, 88312, 88313, 88314, 88318, 88319, 88321, 88323, 88325, 88329, 88331, 88332, 88342, 88346, 88347, 88348, 88349, 88355, 88356, 88358, 88361, 88362, 88365, 88380.

Depending upon circumstances and the billing entity, the carriers may pay professional component, technical component or both.

C. Specific Hematology, Cytopathology and Blood Banking Services

Cytopathology services include the examination of cells from fluids, washings, brushings or smears, but generally excluding hematology. Examining cervical and vaginal smears are the most common service in cytopathology. Cervical and vaginal smears do not require interpretation by a physician unless the results are or appear to be abnormal. In such cases, a physician personally conducts a separate microscopic evaluation to determine the nature of an abnormality. This microscopic evaluation ordinarily does require performance by a physician. When medically necessary and when furnished by a physician, it is paid under the fee schedule.

These codes include 88104, 88106, 88107, 88108, 88112, 88125, 88141, 88160, 88161, 88162, 88172, 88173, 88180, 88182.

For services furnished prior to January 1, 1999, carriers pay separately under the physician fee schedule for the interpretation of an abnormal pap smear furnished to a hospital inpatient by a physician. They must pay under the clinical laboratory fee schedule for pap smears furnished in all other situations. This policy also applies to screening pap smears requiring a physician interpretation. For services furnished on or after January 1, 1999, carriers allow separate payment for a physician's interpretation of a pap smear to any patient (i.e., hospital or non-hospital) as long as: (1) the laboratory's screening personnel suspect an abnormality; and (2) the physician reviews and interprets the pap smear.

This policy also applies to screening pap smears requiring a physician interpretation and described in the National Coverage Determination Manual and Chapter 18. These services are reported under codes P3000 or P3001.

Physician hematology services include microscopic evaluation of bone marrow aspirations and biopsies. It also includes those limited number of peripheral blood smears which need to be referred to a physician to evaluate the nature of an apparent abnormality identified by the technologist. These codes include 85060, 38220, 85097, and 38221.

Carriers pay the professional component for the interpretation of an abnormal blood smear (code 85060) furnished to a hospital inpatient by a hospital physician or an independent laboratory.

For the other listed hematology codes, payment may be made for the professional component if the service is furnished to a patient by a hospital physician or independent laboratory. In addition, payment may be made for these services furnished to patients by an independent laboratory.

Codes 38220 and 85097 represent professional-only component services and have no technical component values.

Blood banking services of hematologists and pathologists are paid under the physician fee schedule when analyses are performed on donor and/or patient blood to determine compatible donor units for transfusion where cross matching is difficult or where contamination with transmissible disease of donor is suspected.

The blood banking codes are 86077, 86078, and 86079 and represent professional component only services. These codes do not have a technical component.

D. Clinical Consultation Services

- Clinical consultations are paid under the physician fee schedule only if they:
- Are requested by the patient's attending physician;
- Relate to a test result that lies outside the clinically significant normal or expected range in view of the condition of the patient;
- Result in a written narrative report included in the patient's medical record; and
- Require the exercise of medical judgment by the consultant physician.

Clinical consultations are professional component services only. There is no technical component. The clinical consultation codes are 80500 and 80502.

Routine conversations held between a laboratory director and an attending physician about test orders or results do not qualify as consultations unless all four requirements are met. Laboratory personnel, including the director, may from time to time contact attending physicians to report test results or to suggest additional testing or be contacted by attending physicians on similar matters. These contacts do not constitute clinical consultations. However, if in the course of such a contact, the attending physician requests a consultation from the pathologist, and if that consultation meets the other criteria and is properly documented, it is paid under the fee schedule.

EXAMPLE: A pathologist telephones a surgeon about a patient's suitability for surgery based on the results of clinical laboratory test results. During the course of their conversation, the surgeon ask the pathologist whether, based on test results, patient history and medical records, the patient is a candidate for surgery. The surgeon's request requires the pathologist to render a medical judgment and provide a consultation. The athologist follows up his/her oral advice with a written report and the surgeon notes in the patient's medical record that he/she requested a consultation. This consultation is paid under the fee schedule.

In any case, if the information could ordinarily be furnished by a nonphysician laboratory specialist, the service of the physician is not a consultation payable under the fee schedule.

See the Program Integrity Manual for guidelines for related data analysis to identify inappropriate patterns of billing for consultations.

E. Clinical Laboratory Interpretation Services

Only clinical laboratory interpretation services listed below and which meet the criteria in subsections D.1, D.3, and D.4 for clinical consultations and, as a result, are billable under the fee schedule. These services are reported under the clinical laboratory code with modifier 26. These services can be paid under the physician fee schedule if they are furnished to a patient by a hospital pathologist or an independent laboratory. Note that a hospital's standing order policy can be used as a substitute for the individual request by the patient's attending physician. Carriers are not allowed to revise CMS's list to accommodate local medical practice. The CMS periodically reviews this list and adds or deletes clinical laboratory codes as warranted.

Clinical Laboratory Interpretation Services

Code	Definition
83020	Hemoglobin; electrophoresis
83912	Nucleic acid probe, with electrophoresis, with examination and report
84165	Protein, total, serum; electrophoretic fractionation and quantitation
84181	Protein; Western Blot with interpretation and report, blood or other body fluid
84182	Protein; Western Blot, with interpretation and report, blood or other body fluid, immunological probe for band identification; each
85390	Fibrinolysin; screening
85576	Platelet; aggregation (in vitro), any agent
86255	Fluorescent antibody; screen
86256	Fluorescent antibody; titer
86320	Immunoelectrophoresis; serum, each specimen
86325	Immunoelectrophoresis; other fluids (e.g.urine) with concentration, each specimen
86327	Immunoelectrophoresis; crossed (2 dimensional assay)
86334	Immunofixation electrophoresis
87164	Dark field examination, any source (e.g. penile, vaginal, oral, skin); includes specimen collection
87207	Smear, primary source, with interpretation; special stain for inclusion bodies or intracellular parasites (e.g. malaria, kala azar, herpes)
88371	Protein analysis of tissue by Western Blot, with interpretation and report.
88372	Protein analysis of tissue by Western Blot, immunological probe for band identification, each
89060	Crystal identification by light microscopy with or without polarizing lens analysis, any body fluid (except urine)

100-4, 12, 80.1

Healthcare Common Procedure Coding System (HCPCS) Coding for the IPPE

The HCPCS codes listed below were developed for the IPPE benefit effective January 1, 2005, for individuals whose initial enrollment is on or after January 1, 2005.

G0344: Initial preventive physical examination; face-to-face visit, services limited to new beneficiary during the first 6 months of Medicare enrollment

Short Descriptor: Initial Preventive Exam

G0366: Electrocardiogram, routine ECG with 12 leads; performed as a component of the initial preventive examination with interpretation and report

Short Descriptor: EKG for initial prevent exam

G0367: tracing only, without interpretation and report, performed as a component of the initial preventive examination

Short Descriptor: EKG tracing for initial prev

G0368: interpretation and report only, performed as a component of the initial preventive examination

Short Descriptor: EKG interpret & report preve

The following new HCPCS codes were developed for the IPPE benefit effective January 1, 2009, and replaced codes G0344, G0366, G0367, and G0368 shown above beginning with dates of service on or after January 1, 2009:

G0402: Initial preventive physical examination; face-to-face visit, services limited to new beneficiary during the first 12 months of Medicare enrollment

Short Descriptor: Initial Preventive exam

G0403: Electrocardiogram, routine ECG with 12 leads; performed as a screening for the initial preventive physical examination with interpretation and report

Short Descriptor: EKG for initial prevent exam

G0404: Electrocardiogram, routine ECG with 12 leads; tracing only, without interpretation and report, performed as a screening for the initial preventive physical examination

Short Descriptor: EKG tracing for initial prev

G0405: Electrocardiogram, routine ECG with 12 leads; interpretation and report only, performed as a screening for the initial preventive physical examination

Short Descriptor: EKG interpret & report preve

100-4, 12, 100.1.1

Evaluation and Management (E/M) Services

A. General Documentation Instructions and Common Scenarios

Evaluation and Management (E/M) Services -- For a given encounter, the selection of the appropriate level of E/M service should be determined according to the code definitions in the American Medical Association's Current Procedural Terminology (CPT) and any applicable documentation guidelines.

For purposes of payment, E/M services billed by teaching physicians require that they personally document at least the following:

- That they performed the service or were physically present during the key or critical portions of the service when performed by the resident; and
- The participation of the teaching physician in the management of the patient.

When assigning codes to services billed by teaching physicians, reviewers will combine the documentation of both the resident and the teaching physician.

Documentation by the resident of the presence and participation of the teaching physician is not sufficient to establish the presence and participation of the teaching physician.

On medical review, the combined entries into the medical record by the teaching physician and the resident constitute the documentation for the service and together must support the medical necessity of the service.

Following are four common scenarios for teaching physicians providing E/M services:

Scenario 1:

The teaching physician personally performs all the required elements of an E/M service without a resident. In this scenario the resident may or may not have performed the E/M service independently.

In the absence of a note by a resident, the teaching physician must document as he/she would document an E/M service in a nonteaching setting.

Where a resident has written notes, the teaching physician's note may reference the resident's note. The teaching physician must document that he/she performed the critical or key portion(s) of the service, and that he/she was directly involved in the management of the patient. For payment, the composite of the teaching physician's entry and the resident's entry together must support the medical necessity of the billed service and the level of the service billed by the teaching physician.

Scenario 2:

The resident performs the elements required for an E/M service in the presence of, or jointly with, the teaching physician and the resident documents the service. In this case, the teaching physician must document that he/she was present during the performance of the critical or key portion(s) of the service and that he/she was directly involved in the

management of the patient. The teaching physician's note should reference the resident's note. For payment, the composite of the teaching physician's entry and the resident's entry together must support the medical necessity and the level of the service billed by the teaching physician.

Scenario 3:

The resident performs some or all of the required elements of the service in the absence of the teaching physician and documents his/her service. The teaching physician independently performs the critical or key portion(s) of the service with or without the resident present and, as appropriate, discusses the case with the resident. In this instance, the teaching physician must document that he/she personally saw the patient, personally performed critical or key portions of the service, and participated in the management of the patient. The teaching physician's note should reference the resident's note. For payment, the composite of the teaching physician's entry and the resident's entry together must support the medical necessity of the billed service and the level of the service billed by the teaching physician.

Scenario 4:

When a medical resident admits a patient to a hospital late at night and the teaching physician does not see the patient until later, including the next calendar day:

- The teaching physician must document that he/she personally saw the patient and participated in the management of the patient. The teaching physician may reference the resident's note in lieu of re-documenting the history of present illness, exam, medical decision-making, review of systems and/or past family/social history provided that the patient's condition has not changed, and the teaching physician agrees with the resident's note.
- The teaching physician's note must reflect changes in the patient's condition and clinical course that require that the resident's note be amended with further information to address the patient's condition and course at the time the patient is seen personally by the teaching physician.
- The teaching physician's bill must reflect the date of service he/she saw the patient and his/her personal work of obtaining a history, performing a physical, and participating in medical decision-making regardless of whether the combination of the teaching physician's and resident's documentation satisfies criteria for a higher level of service. For payment, the composite of the teaching physician's entry and the resident's entry together must support the medical necessity of the billed service and the level of the service billed by the teaching physician.

Following are examples of minimally acceptable documentation for each of these scenarios:

Scenario 1:

Admitting Note: "I performed a history and physical examination of the patient and discussed his management with the resident. I reviewed the resident's note and agree with the documented findings and plan of care."

Follow-up Visit: "Hospital Day #3. I saw and evaluated the patient. I agree with the findings and the plan of care as documented in the resident's note."

Follow-up Visit: "Hospital Day #5. I saw and examined the patient. I agree with the resident's note except the heart murmur is louder, so I will obtain an echo to evaluate."

(NOTE: In this scenario if there are no resident notes, the teaching physician must document as he/she would document an E/M service in a non-teaching setting.)

Scenario 2:

Initial or Follow-up Visit: "I was present with the resident during the history and exam. I discussed the case with the resident and agree with the findings and plan as documented in the resident's note."

Follow-up Visit: "I saw the patient with the resident and agree with the resident's findings and plan."

Scenarios 3 and 4:

Initial Visit: "I saw and evaluated the patient. I reviewed the resident's note and agree, except that picture is more consistent with pericarditis than myocardial ischemia. Will begin NSAIDs."

Initial or Follow-up Visit: "I saw and evaluated the patient. Discussed with resident and agree with resident's findings and plan as documented in the resident's note."

Follow-up Visit: "See resident's note for details. I saw and evaluated the patient and agree with the resident's finding and plans as written."

Follow-up Visit: "I saw and evaluated the patient. Agree with resident's note but lower extremities are weaker, now 3/5; MRI of L/S Spine today."

Following are examples of unacceptable documentation:

"Agree with above.", followed by legible countersignature or identity;

"Rounded, Reviewed, Agree.", followed by legible countersignature or identity;

"Discussed with resident. Agree.", followed by legible countersignature or identity;

"Seen and agree.", followed by legible countersignature or identity;

"Patient seen and evaluated.", followed by legible countersignature or identity; and

A legible countersignature or identity alone.

Such documentation is not acceptable, because the documentation does not make it possible to determine whether the teaching physician was present, evaluated the patient, and/or had any involvement with the plan of care.

B. E/M Service Documentation Provided By Students

Any contribution and participation of a student to the performance of a billable service (other than the review of systems and/or past family/social history which are not separately billable, but are taken as part of an E/M service) must be performed in the physical presence of a teaching physician or physical presence of a resident in a service meeting the requirements set forth in this section for teaching physician billing.

Students may document services in the medical record. However, the documentation of an E/M service by a student that may be referred to by the teaching physician is limited to documentation related to the review of systems and/or past family/social history. The teaching physician may not refer to a student's documentation of physical exam findings or medical decision making in his or her personal note. If the medical student documents E/M services, the teaching physician must verify and redocument the history of present illness as well as perform and redocument the physical exam and medical decision making activities of the service.

C. Exception for E/M Services Furnished in Certain Primary Care Centers

Teaching physicians providing E/M services with a GME program granted a primary care exception may bill Medicare for lower and mid-level E/M services provided by residents. For the E/M codes listed below, teaching physicians may submit claims for services furnished by residents in the absence of a teaching physician:

New Patient	Established Patient
99201	99211
99202	99212
99203	99213

Effective January 1, 2005, the following code is included under the primary care exception: HCPCS code G0402 (Initial preventive physical examination; face-to-face visit services limited to new beneficiary during the first 12 months of Medicare enrollment).

Effective January 1, 2011, the following codes are included under the primary care exception: HCPCS codes G0438 (Annual wellness visit, including personal preventive plan service, first visit) and G0439 (Annual wellness visit, including personal preventive plan service, subsequent visit).

If a service other than those listed above needs to be furnished, then the general teaching physician policy set forth in §100.1 applies. For this exception to apply, a center must attest in writing that all the following conditions are met for a particular residency program. Prior approval is not necessary, but centers exercising the primary care exception must maintain records demonstrating that they qualify for the exception.

The services must be furnished in a center located in the outpatient department of a hospital or another ambulatory care entity in which the time spent by residents in patient care activities is included in determining direct GME payments to a teaching hospital by the hospital's FI. This requirement is not met when the resident is assigned to a physician's office away from the center or makes home visits. In the case of a nonhospital entity, verify with the FI that the entity meets the requirements of a written agreement between the hospital and the entity set forth at 42 CFR 413.78(e)(3)(ii).

Under this exception, residents providing the billable patient care service without the physical presence of a teaching physician must have completed at least 6 months of a

GME approved residency program. Centers must maintain information under the provisions at 42 CFR 413.79(a)(6).

Teaching physicians submitting claims under this exception may not supervise more than four residents at any given time and must direct the care from such proximity as to constitute immediate availability. Teaching physicians may include residents with less than 6 months in a GME approved residency program in the mix of four residents under the teaching physician's supervision. However, the teaching physician must be physically present for the critical or key portions of services furnished by the residents with less than 6 months in a GME approved residency program. That is, the primary care exception does not apply in the case of residents with less than 6 months in a GME approved residency program.

Teaching physicians submitting claims under this exception must:

- Not have other responsibilities (including the supervision of other personnel) at the time the service was provided by the resident;
- Have the primary medical responsibility for patients cared for by the residents;
- Ensure that the care provided was reasonable and necessary;
- Review the care provided by the resident during or immediately after each visit. This must include a review of the patient's medical history, the resident's findings on physical examination, the patient's diagnosis, and treatment plan (i.e., record of tests and therapies); and
- Document the extent of his/her own participation in the review and direction of the services furnished to each patient.

Patients under this exception should consider the center to be their primary location for health care services. The residents must be expected to generally provide care to the same group of established patients during their residency training. The types of services furnished by residents under this exception include:

- Acute care for undifferentiated problems or chronic care for ongoing conditions including chronic mental illness;
- Coordination of care furnished by other physicians and providers; and,
- Comprehensive care not limited by organ system or diagnosis.

Residency programs most likely qualifying for this exception include family practice, general internal medicine, geriatric medicine, pediatrics, and obstetrics/gynecology.

Certain GME programs in psychiatry may qualify in special situations such as when the program furnishes comprehensive care for chronically mentally ill patients. These would be centers in which the range of services the residents are trained to furnish, and actually do furnish, include comprehensive medical care as well as psychiatric care. For example, antibiotics are being prescribed as well as psychotropic drugs.

100-4, 12, 180

Care Plan Oversight Services

The Medicare Benefit Policy Manual, Chapter 15, contains requirements for coverage for medical and other health services including those of physicians and non-physician practitioners.

Care plan oversight (CPO) is the physician supervision of a patient receiving complex and/or multidisciplinary care as part of Medicare-covered services provided by a participating home health agency or Medicare approved hospice.

CPO services require complex or multidisciplinary care modalities involving: Regular physician development and/or revision of care plans; Review of subsequent reports of patient status; Review of related laboratory and other studies; Communication with other health professionals not employed in the same practice who are involved in the patient's care; Integration of new information into the medical treatment plan; and/or Adjustment of medical therapy.

The CPO services require recurrent physician supervision of a patient involving 30 or more minutes of the physician's time per month. Services not countable toward the 30 minutes threshold that must be provided in order to bill for CPO include, but are not limited to: Time associated with discussions with the patient, his or her family or friends to adjust medication or treatment; Time spent by staff getting or filing charts; Travel time; and/or Physician's time spent telephoning prescriptions into the pharmacist unless the telephone conversation involves discussions of pharmaceutical therapies.

Implicit in the concept of CPO is the expectation that the physician has coordinated an aspect of the patient's care with the home health agency or hospice during the month for which CPO services were billed. The physician who bills for CPO must be the same physician who signs the plan of care.

Nurse practitioners, physician assistants, and clinical nurse specialists, practicing within the scope of State law, may bill for care plan oversight. These non-physician practitioners must have been providing ongoing care for the beneficiary through evaluation and management services. These non-physician practitioners may not bill for CPO if they have been involved only with the delivery of the Medicare-covered home health or hospice service.

A. Home Health CPO

Non-physician practitioners can perform CPO only if the physician signing the plan of care provides regular ongoing care under the same plan of care as does the NPP billing for CPO and either: The physician and NPP are part of the same group practice; or If the NPP is a nurse practitioner or clinical nurse specialist, the physician signing the plan of care also has a collaborative agreement with the NPP; or If the NPP is a physician assistant, the physician signing the plan of care is also the physician who provides general supervision of physician assistant services for the practice.

Billing may be made for care plan oversight services furnished by an NPP when: The NPP providing the care plan oversight has seen and examined the patient; The NPP providing care plan oversight is not functioning as a consultant whose participation is limited to a single medical condition rather than multidisciplinary coordination of care; and The NPP providing care plan oversight integrates his or her care with that of the physician who signed the plan of care.

NPPs may not certify the beneficiary for home health care.

B. Hospice CPO

The attending physician or nurse practitioner (who has been designated as the attending physician) may bill for hospice CPO when they are acting as an "attending physician".

An "attending physician" is one who has been identified by the individual, at the time he/she elects hospice coverage, as having the most significant role in the determination and delivery of their medical care. They are not employed nor paid by the hospice. The care plan oversight services are billed using Form CMS-1500 or electronic equivalent.

For additional information on hospice CPO, see Chapter 11, 40.1.3.1 of this manual.

100-4, 12, 180.1

Care Plan Oversight Billing Requirements

A. Codes for Which Separate Payment May Be Made

Effective January 1, 1995, separate payment may be made for CPO oversight services for 30 minutes or more if the requirements specified in the Medicare Benefits Policy Manual, Chapter 15 are met.

Providers billing for CPO must submit the claim with no other services billed on that claim and may bill only after the end of the month in which the CPO services were rendered. CPO services may not be billed across calendar months and should be submitted (and paid) only for one unit of service.

Physicians may bill and be paid separately for CPO services only if all the criteria in the Medicare Benefit Policy Manual, Chapter 15 are met.

B. Physician Certification and Recertification of Home Health Plans of Care

Effective 2001, two new HCPCS codes for the certification and recertification and development of plans of care for Medicare-covered home health services were created.

See the Medicare General Information, Eligibility, and Entitlement Manual, Pub. 100-01, Chapter 4, "Physician Certification and Recertification of Services," 10-60, and the Medicare Benefit Policy Manual, Pub. 100-02, Chapter 7, "Home Health Services", 30.

The home health agency certification code can be billed only when the patient has not received Medicare-covered home health services for at least 60 days. The home health agency recertification code is used after a patient has received services for at least 60 days (or one certification period) when the physician signs the certification after the initial certification period. The home health agency recertification code will be reported only once every 60 days, except in the rare situation when the patient starts a new episode before 60 days elapses and requires a new plan of care to start a new episode.

C. Provider Number of Home Health Agency (HHA) or Hospice

For claims for CPO submitted on or after January 1, 1997, physicians must enter on the Medicare claim form the 6-character Medicare provider number of the HHA or hospice providing Medicare-covered services to the beneficiary for the period during which CPO services was furnished and for which the physician signed the plan of care. Physicians are responsible for obtaining the HHA or hospice Medicare provider numbers.

Additionally, physicians should provide their UPIN to the HHA or hospice furnishing services to their patient.

NOTE: There is currently no place on the HIPAA standard ASC X12N 837 professional format to specifically include the HHA or hospice provider number required for a care plan oversight claim. For this reason, the requirement to include the HHA or hospice provider number on a care plan oversight claim is temporarily waived until a new version of this electronic standard format is adopted under HIPAA and includes a place to provide the HHA and hospice provider numbers for care plan oversight claims.

100-4, 12, 190.3

List of Medicare Telehealth Services

The use of a telecommunications system may substitute for an in-person encounter for professional consultations, office visits, office psychiatry services, and a limited number of other physician fee schedule (PFS) services. The various services and corresponding current procedure terminology (CPT) or Healthcare Common Procedure Coding System (HCPCS) codes are listed below.

- Consultations (CPT codes 99241 - 99275) - Effective October 1, 2001 – December 31, 2005;
- Consultations (CPT codes 99241 - 99255) - Effective January 1, 2006 – December 31, 2009;
- Initial inpatient telehealth consultations (HCPCS codes G0425 – G0427) - Effective January 1, 2010;
- Follow-up inpatient telehealth consultations (HCPCS codes G0406, G0407, and G0408) - Effective January 1, 2009;
- Office or other outpatient visits (CPT codes 99201 - 99215);
- Subsequent hospital care services, with the limitation of one telehealth visit every 3 days (CPT codes 99231, 99232, and 99233) – Effective January 1, 2011; Subsequent nursing facility care services, with the limitation of one telehealth visit every 30 days (CPT codes 99307, 99308, 99309, and 99310) – Effective January 1, 2011;
- Pharmacologic management (CPT code 90862);
- Individual psychotherapy (CPT codes 90804 - 90809); Psychiatric diagnostic interview examination (CPT code 90801) – Effective March 1, 2003;
- Neurobehavioral status exam (CPT code 96116) - Effective January 1, 2008;
- End Stage Renal Disease (ESRD) related services (HCPCS codes G0308, G0309, G0311, G0312, G0314, G0315, G0317, and G0318) – Effective January 1, 2005 – December 31, 2008;
- End Stage Renal Disease (ESRD) related services (CPT codes 90951, 90952, 90954, 90955, 90957, 90958, 90960, and 90961) – Effective January 1, 2009;
- Individual and group medical nutrition therapy (HCPCS codes G0270, 97802, 97803, and 97804) – Individual effective January 1, 2006; group effective January 1, 2011;
- Individual and group health and behavior assessment and intervention (CPT codes 96150 – 96154) – Individual effective January 1, 2010; group effective January 1, 2011.
- Individual and group kidney disease education (KDE) services (HCPCS codes G0420 and G0421) – Effective January 1, 2011; and
- Individual and group diabetes self-management training (DSMT) services, with a minimum of 1 hour of in-person instruction to be furnished in the initial year training period to ensure effective injection training (HCPCS codes G0108 and G0109) - Effective January 1, 2011.

NOTE: Beginning January 1, 2010, CMS eliminated the use of all consultation codes, except for inpatient telehealth consultation G-codes. CMS no longer recognizes office/outpatient or inpatient consultation CPT codes for payment of office/outpatient or inpatient visits. Instead, physicians and practitioners are instructed to bill a new or established patient office/outpatient visit CPT code or appropriate hospital or nursing facility care code, as appropriate to the particular patient, for all office/outpatient or inpatient visits.

100-4, 12, 190.3.1

Inpatient Telehealth Consultation Services versus Inpatient Evaluation and Management (E/M) Visits

A consultation service is an evaluation and management (E/M) service furnished to evaluate and possibly treat a patient's problem(s). It can involve an opinion, advice, recommendation, suggestion, direction, or counsel from a physician or qualified nonphysician practitioner (NPP) at the request of another physician or appropriate source.

Section 1834(m) of the Social Security Act includes "professional consultations" in the definition of telehealth services. Inpatient consultations furnished via telehealth can facilitate the provision of certain services and/or medical expertise that might not otherwise be available to a patient located at an originating site.

The use of a telecommunications system may substitute for an in-person encounter for initial and follow-up inpatient consultations.

Medicare contractors pay for reasonable and medically necessary inpatient telehealth consultation services furnished to beneficiaries in hospitals or SNFs when all of the following criteria for the use of a consultation code are met:

- An inpatient consultation service is distinguished from other inpatient evaluation and management (E/M) visits because it is provided by a physician or qualified nonphysician practitioner (NPP) whose opinion or advice regarding evaluation and/or management of a specific problem is requested by another physician or other appropriate source. The qualified NPP may perform consultation services within the scope of practice and licensure requirements for NPPs in the State in which he/she practices;
- A request for an inpatient telehealth consultation from an appropriate source and the need for an inpatient telehealth consultation (i.e., the reason for a consultation service) shall be documented by the consultant in the patient's medical record and included in the requesting physician or qualified NPP's plan of care in the patient's medical record; and
- After the inpatient telehealth consultation is provided, the consultant shall prepare a written report of his/her findings and recommendations, which shall be provided to the referring physician.

The intent of an inpatient telehealth consultation service is that a physician or qualified NPP or other appropriate source is asking another physician or qualified NPP for advice, opinion, a recommendation, suggestion, direction, or counsel, etc. in evaluating or treating a patient because that individual has expertise in a specific medical area beyond the requesting professional's knowledge.

Unlike inpatient telehealth consultations, the majority of subsequent inpatient hospital and nursing facility care services require in-person visits to facilitate the comprehensive, coordinated, and personal care that medically volatile, acutely ill patients require on an ongoing basis.

Subsequent hospital care services are limited to one telehealth visit every 3 days. Subsequent nursing facility care services are limited to one telehealth visit every 30 days.

100-4, 12, 190.3.2

Initial Inpatient Telehealth Consultations Defined

Initial inpatient telehealth consultations are furnished to beneficiaries in hospitals or SNFs via telehealth at the request of the physician of record, the attending physician, or another appropriate source. The physician or practitioner who furnishes the initial inpatient consultation via telehealth cannot be the physician of record or the attending physician, and the initial inpatient telehealth consultation would be distinct from the care provided by the physician of record or the attending physician. Counseling and coordination of care with other providers or agencies is included as well, consistent with the nature of the problem(s) and the patient's needs. Initial inpatient telehealth consultations are subject to the criteria for inpatient telehealth consultation services, as described in Sec.190.3.1.

Payment for initial inpatient telehealth consultations includes all consultation related services furnished before, during, and after communicating with the patient via telehealth. Pre-service activities would include, but would not be limited to, reviewing patient data (for example, diagnostic and imaging studies, interim labwork) and communicating with other professionals or family members. Intra-service activities must include the three key elements described below for each procedure code. Post-service activities would include, but would not be limited to, completing medical records or other documentation and communicating results of the consultation and further care plans to other health care professionals. No additional E/M service could be billed for work related to an initial inpatient telehealth consultation.

Initial inpatient telehealth consultations could be provided at various levels of complexity:

Practitioners taking a problem focused history, conducting a problem focused examination, and engaging in medical decision making that is straightforward, would bill HCPCS G0425. At this level of service, practitioners would typically spend 30 minutes communicating with the patient via telehealth.

Practitioners taking a detailed history, conducting a detailed examination, and engaging in medical decision making that is of moderate complexity, would bill HCPCS G0426. At this level of service, practitioners would typically spend 50 minutes communicating with the patient via telehealth.

Practitioners taking a comprehensive history, conducting a comprehensive examination, and engaging in medical decision making that is of high complexity, would bill HCPCS G0427. At this level of service, practitioners would typically spend 70 minutes or more communicating with the patient via telehealth. Although initial inpatient telehealth consultations are specific to telehealth, these services must be billed with either the "GT" or "GQ" modifier to identify the telehealth technology used to provide the service. (See Sec.190.6 et. al. for instructions on how to use these modifiers.)

100-4, 12, 190.3.3

Follow-Up Inpatient Telehealth Consultations Defined

Follow-up inpatient telehealth consultations are furnished to beneficiaries in hospitals or SNFs via telehealth to follow up on an initial consultation, or subsequent consultative visits requested by the attending physician. The initial inpatient consultation may have been provided in person or via telehealth.

Follow-up inpatient telehealth consultations include monitoring progress, recommending management modifications, or advising on a new plan of care in response to changes in the patient's status or no changes on the consulted health issue. Counseling and coordination of care with other providers or agencies is included as well, consistent with the nature of the problem(s) and the patient's needs.

The physician or practitioner who furnishes the inpatient follow-up consultation via telehealth cannot be the physician of record or the attending physician, and the follow-up inpatient consultation would be distinct from the follow-up care provided by the physician of record or the attending physician. If a physician consultant has initiated treatment at an initial consultation and participates thereafter in the patient's ongoing care management, such care would not be included in the definition of a follow-up inpatient consultation and is not appropriate for delivery via telehealth. Follow-up inpatient telehealth consultations are subject to the criteria for inpatient telehealth consultation services, as described in Sec.190.3.1

Payment for follow-up inpatient telehealth consultations includes all consultation related services furnished before, during, and after communicating with the patient via telehealth. Pre-service activities would include, but would not be limited to, reviewing patient data (for example, diagnostic and imaging studies, interim labwork) and communicating with other professionals or family members. Intra-service activities must include at least two of the three key elements described below for each procedure code. Post-service activities would include, but would not be limited to, completing medical records or other documentation and communicating results of the consultation and further care plans to other health care professionals. No additional evaluation and management service could be billed for work related to a follow-up inpatient telehealth consultation.

Follow-up inpatient telehealth consultations could be provided at various levels of complexity:

Practitioners taking a problem focused interval history, conducting a problem focused examination, and engaging in medical decision making that is straightforward or of low complexity, would bill a limited service, using HCPCS G0406, Follow-up inpatient telehealth consultation, limited. At this level of service, practitioners would typically spend 15 minutes communicating with the patient via telehealth.

Practitioners taking an expanded focused interval history, conducting an expanded problem focused examination, and engaging in medical decision making that is of moderate complexity, would bill an intermediate service using HCPCS G0407, Follow-up inpatient telehealth consultation, intermediate. At this level of service, practitioners would typically spend 25 minutes communicating with the patient via telehealth.

Practitioners taking a detailed interval history, conducting a detailed examination, and engaging in medical decision making that is of high complexity, would bill a complex service, using HCPCS G0408, Follow-up inpatient telehealth consultation, complex. At this level of service, practitioners would typically spend 35 minutes or more communicating with the patient via telehealth.

Although follow-up inpatient telehealth consultations are specific to telehealth, these services must be billed with either the "GT" or "GQ" modifier to identify the telehealth technology used to provide the service. (See Sec.190.6 et. al. for instructions on how to use these modifiers.)

100-4, 12, 190.7

Contractor Editing of Telehealth Claims

Medicare telehealth services (as listed in section 190.3) are billed with either the "GT" or "GQ" modifier. The contractor shall approve covered telehealth services if the physician or practitioner is licensed under State law to provide the service. Contractors must familiarize themselves with licensure provisions of States for which they process claims and disallow telehealth services furnished by physicians or practitioners who are not authorized to furnish the applicable telehealth service under State law. For example, if a nurse practitioner is not licensed to provide individual psychotherapy under State law, he or she would not be permitted to receive payment for individual psychotherapy under Medicare. The contractor shall install edits to ensure that only properly licensed physicians and practitioners are paid for covered telehealth services.

If a contractor receives claims for professional telehealth services coded with the "GQ" modifier (representing "via asynchronous telecommunications system"), it shall approve/pay for these services only if the physician or practitioner is affiliated with a Federal telemedicine demonstration conducted in Alaska or Hawaii. The contractor may require the physician or practitioner at the distant site to document his or her participation in a Federal telemedicine demonstration program conducted in Alaska or Hawaii prior to paying for telehealth services provided via asynchronous, store and forward technologies.

If a contractor denies telehealth services because the physician or practitioner may not bill for them, the contractor uses MSN message 21.18: "This item or service is not covered when performed or ordered by this practitioner." The contractor uses remittance advice message 52 when denying the claim based upon MSN message 21.18.

If a service is billed with one of the telehealth modifiers and the procedure code is not designated as a covered telehealth service, the contractor denies the service using MSN message 9.4: "This item or service was denied because information required to make payment was incorrect." The remittance advice message depends on what is incorrect, e.g., B18 if procedure code or modifier is incorrect, 125 for submission billing errors, 4-12 for difference inconsistencies. The contractor uses B18 as the explanation for the denial of the claim.

The only claims from institutional facilities that FIs shall pay for telehealth services at the distant site, except for MNT services, are for physician or practitioner services when the distant site is located in a CAH that has elected Method II, and the physician or practitioner has reassigned his/her benefits to the CAH. The CAH bills its regular FI for the professional services provided at the distant site via a telecommunications system, in any of the revenue codes 096x, 097x or 098x. All requirements for billing distant site telehealth services apply.

Claims from hospitals or CAHs for MNT services are submitted to the hospital's or CAH's regular FI. Payment is based on the non-facility amount on the Medicare Physician Fee Schedule for the particular HCPCS codes.

100-4, 12, 210.1

Application of Limitation

B3-2472 - 2472.5

A. Status of Patient

The limitation is applicable to expenses incurred in connection with the treatment of an individual who is not an inpatient of a hospital. Thus, the limitation applies to mental health services furnished to a person in a physician's office, in the patient's home, in a skilled nursing facility, as an outpatient, and so forth. The term "hospital" in this context means an institution, which is primarily engaged in providing to inpatients, by or under the supervision of physician(s): Diagnostic and therapeutic services for medical diagnosis, treatment and care of injured, disabled, or sick persons; Rehabilitation services for injured, disabled, or sick persons; or Psychiatric services for the diagnosis and treatment of mentally ill patients.

B. Disorders Subject to Limitation

The term "mental, psychoneurotic, and personality disorders" is defined as the specific psychiatric conditions described in the American Psychiatric Association's (APA) "Diagnostic and Statistical Manual of Mental Disorders, Third Edition - Revised (DSMIII- R)." When the treatment services rendered are both for a psychiatric condition as defined in the DSM-III-R and one or more nonpsychiatric conditions, separate the expenses for the psychiatric aspects of treatment from the expenses for the nonpsychiatric aspects of treatment. However, in any case in which the psychiatric treatment component is not readily distinguishable from the nonpsychiatric treatment component, all of the expenses are allocated to whichever component constitutes the primary diagnosis.

1. Diagnosis Clearly Meets Definition - If the primary diagnosis reported for a particular service is the same as or equivalent to a condition described in the APA's DSM-III-R, the expense for the service is subject to the limitation except as described in subsection D.
2. Diagnosis Does Not Clearly Meet Definition - When it is not clear whether the primary diagnosis reported meets the definition of mental, psychoneurotic, and personality disorders, it may be necessary to contact the practitioner to clarify the diagnosis. In deciding whether contact is necessary in a given case, give consideration to such factors as the type of services rendered, the diagnosis, and the individual's previous utilization history.

C. Services Subject to Limitation

Carriers apply the limitation to claims for professional services that represent mental health treatment furnished to individuals who are not hospital inpatients by physicians, clinical psychologists, clinical social workers, and other allied health professionals.

Items and supplies furnished by physicians or other mental health practitioners in connection with treatment are also subject to the limitation. (The limitation also applies to CORF claims processed by intermediaries.) Carriers apply the limitation only to treatment services. It does not apply to diagnostic services as described in subsection D. Testing services performed to evaluate a patient's progress during treatment are considered part of treatment and are subject to the limitation.

D. Services Not Subject to Limitation

1. Diagnosis of Alzheimer's Disease or Related Disorder - When the primary diagnosis reported for a particular service is Alzheimer's Disease (coded 331.0 in the "International Classification of Diseases, 9th Revision") or Alzheimer's or other disorders coded 290.XX in the APA's DSM-III-R, carriers look to the nature of the service that has been rendered in determining whether it is subject to the limitation. Typically, treatment provided to a patient with a diagnosis of Alzheimer's Disease or a related disorder represents medical management of the patient's condition (rather than psychiatric treatment) and is not subject to the limitation. However, when the primary treatment rendered to a patient with such a diagnosis is psychotherapy, it is subject to the limitation.
2. Brief Office Visits for Monitoring or Changing Drug Prescriptions - Brief office visits for the sole purpose of monitoring or changing drug prescriptions used in the treatment of mental, psychoneurotic and personality disorders are not subject to the limitation. These visits are reported using HCPCS code M0064 (brief office visit for the sole purpose of monitoring or changing drug prescriptions used in the treatment of mental, psychoneurotic, and personality disorders). Claims where the diagnosis reported is a mental, psychoneurotic, or personality disorder (other than a diagnosis specified in subsection A) are subject to the limitation except for the procedure identified by HCPCS code M0064.
3. Diagnostic Services - Carriers do not apply the limitation to tests and evaluations performed to establish or confirm the patient's diagnosis. Diagnostic services include psychiatric or psychological tests and interpretations, diagnostic consultations, and initial evaluations.

   An initial visit to a practitioner for professional services often combines diagnostic evaluation and the start of therapy. Such a visit is neither solely diagnostic nor solely therapeutic. Therefore, carriers deem the initial visit to be diagnostic so that the limitation does not apply. Separating diagnostic and therapeutic components of a visit is not administratively feasible, unless the practitioner already has separately identified them on the bill. Determining the entire visit to be therapeutic is not justifiable since some diagnostic work must be done before even a tentative diagnosis can be made and certainly before therapy can be instituted. Moreover, the patient should not be disadvantaged because therapeutic as well as diagnostic services were provided in the initial visit. In the rare cases where a practitioner's diagnostic services take more than one visit, carriers do not apply the limitation to the additional visits. However, it is expected such cases are few. Therefore, when a practitioner bills for more than one visit for professional diagnostic services, carriers request documentation to justify the reason for more than one diagnostic visit.
4. Partial Hospitalization Services Not Directly Provided by Physician - The limitation does not apply to partial hospitalization services that are not directly provided by a physician. These services are billed by hospitals and community mental health centers (CMHCs) to intermediaries.

E. Computation of Limitation

Carriers determine the Medicare allowed payment amount for services subject to the limitation.

They:

- Multiply this amount by 0.625;
- Subtract any unsatisfied deductible; and,
- Multiply the remainder by 0.8 to obtain the amount of Medicare payment.

The beneficiary is responsible for the difference between the amount paid by Medicare and the full allowed amount.

EXAMPLE A:

A beneficiary is referred to a Medicare participating psychiatrist who performs a diagnostic evaluation that costs $350. Those services are not subject to the limitation, and they satisfy the deductible. The psychiatrist then conducts 10 weekly therapy sessions for which he/she charges $125 each. The Medicare allowed amount is $90 each, for a total of $900.

Apply the limitation by multiplying 0.625 times $900, which equals $562.50.

Apply regular 20 percent coinsurance by multiplying 0.8 times $562.50, which equals $450 (the amount of Medicare payment).

The beneficiary is responsible for $450 (the difference between Medicare payment and the allowed amount).

EXAMPLE B:

A beneficiary was an inpatient of a psychiatric hospital and was discharged on January 1, 1992. During his/her inpatient stay he/she was diagnosed and therapy was begun under a treatment team that included a clinical psychologist. He/she received post-discharge therapy from the psychologist for 12 sessions, at which point the psychologist administered testing that showed the patient had recovered sufficiently to warrant termination of therapy. The allowed amount for the therapy sessions was $80 each, and the amount for the testing was $125, for a total of $1085. All services in 1992 were subject to the limitation, since the diagnosis had been completed in the hospital and the subsequent testing was a part of therapy.

Apply the limitation by multiplying 0.625 times $1085, which gives $678.13.

Since the deductible must be met for 1992, subtract $100 from $678.13, for a remainder of $578.13.

Determine Medicare payment by multiplying the remainder by 0.8, which equals $462.50.

The beneficiary is responsible for $622.50.

100-4, 13, 40

Magnetic Resonance Imaging (MRI) Procedures

Effective September 28, 2009

The Centers for Medicare & Medicaid Services (CMS) finds that the non-coverage of magnetic resonance imaging (MRI) for blood flow determination is no longer supported by the available evidence. CMS is removing the phrase "blood flow measurement" and local Medicare contractors will have the discretion to cover (or not cover).

Consult Publication (Pub.) 100-03, National Coverage Determinations (NCD) Manual, chapter 1, section 220.2, for specific coverage and non-coverage indications associated with MRI and MRA (Magnetic Resonance Angiography).

Prior to January 1, 2007

Carriers do not make additional payments for three or more MRI sequences. The relative value units (RVUs) reflect payment levels for two sequences.

The technical component (TC) RVUs for MRI procedures that specify "with contrast" include payment for paramagnetic contrast media. Carriers do not make separate payment under code A4647.

A diagnostic technique has been developed under which an MRI of the brain or spine is first performed without contrast material, then another MRI is performed with a standard (0.1mmol/kg) dose of contrast material and, based on the need to achieve a better image, a third MRI is performed with an additional double dosage (0.2mmol/kg) of contrast material. When the high-dose contrast technique is utilized, carriers:

- Do not pay separately for the contrast material used in the second MRI procedure;
- Pay for the contrast material given for the third MRI procedure through supply code Q9952, the replacement code for A4643, when billed with Current Procedural Terminology (CPT) codes 70553, 72156, 72157, and 72158;
- Do not pay for the third MRI procedure. For example, in the case of an MRI of the brain, if CPT code 70553 (without contrast material, followed by with contrast material(s) and further sequences) is billed, make no payment for CPT code 70551 (without contrast material(s)), the additional procedure given for the purpose of administering the double dosage, furnished during the same session. Medicare does not pay for the third procedure (as distinguished from the contrast material) because the CPT definition of code 70553 includes all further sequences; and
- Do not apply the payment criteria for low osmolar contrast media in §30.1.2 to billings for code Q9952, the replacement code for A4643.

Effective January 1, 2007

With the implementation for calendar year 2007 of a bottom-up methodology, which utilizes the direct inputs to determine the practice expense (PE) relative value units (RVUs), the cost of the contrast media is not included in the PE RVUs. Therefore, a separate payment for the contrast media used in various imaging procedures is paid. In addition to the CPT code representing the imaging procedure, separately bill the appropriate HCPCS "Q" code (Q9945 – Q9954; Q9958-Q9964) for the contrast medium utilized in performing the service.

Effective February 24, 2011

Medicare will allow for coverage of MRI for beneficiaries with implanted PMs or cardioverter defibrillators (ICDs) for use in an MRI environment in a Medicare-approved clinical study as described in section 220.C.1 of the NCD manual.

Effective July 7, 2011

Medicare will allow for coverage of MRI for beneficiaries with implanted pacemakers (PMs) when the PMs are used according to the Food and Drug Administration (FDA)-approved labeling for use in an MRI environment as described in section 220.2.C.1 of the NCD Manual.

100-4, 13, 40.1.2

HCPCS Coding Requirements

Providers must report HCPCS codes when submitting claims for MRA of the chest, abdomen, head, neck or peripheral vessels of lower extremities. The following HCPCS codes should be used to report these services:

MRA of head	70544, 70544-26, 70544-TC
MRA of head	70545, 70545-26, 70545-TC
MRA of head	70546, 70546-26, 70546-TC
MRA of neck	70547, 70547-26, 70547-TC
MRA of neck	70548, 70548-26, 70548-TC
MRA of neck	70549, 70549-26, 70549-TC
MRA of chest	71555, 71555-26, 71555-TC
MRA of pelvis	72198, 72198-26, 72198-TC
MRA of abdomen (dates of service on or after July 1, 2003) - see below.	74185, 74185-26, 74185-TC
MRA of peripheral vessels of lower extremities	73725, 73725-26, 73725-TC

Hospitals subject to OPPS should report the following C codes in place of the above HCPCS codes as follows:

- MRA of chest 71555: C8909 - C8911
- MRA of abdomen 74185: C8900 - C8902
- MRA of peripheral vessels of lower extremities 73725: C8912 - C8914

For claims with dates of service on or after July 1, 2003, coverage under this benefit has been expanded for the use of MRA for diagnosing pathology in the renal or aortoiliac arteries. The following HCPCS code should be used to report this expanded coverage of MRA:

- MRA, pelvis, with or without contrast material(s) 72198, 72198-26, 72198-TC

Hospitals subject to OPPS report the following C codes in place of HCPCS code 72198:

- MRA, pelvis, with or without contrast material(s) 72198: C8918 - C8920

Providers utilizing the UB-92 flat file, use record type 61, HCPCS code (Field No. 6) to report HCPCS/CPT code. Providers utilizing the hard copy UB-92, report the HCPCS/CPT code in FL 44 "HCPCS/Rates." Providers utilizing the Medicare A 837 Health Care Claim version 3051 implementations 3A.01 and 1A.C1, report the HCPCS/CPT in 2-395-SV202-02.

100-4, 13, 60

Positron Emission Tomography (PET) Scans - General Information

Positron emission tomography (PET) is a noninvasive imaging procedure that assesses perfusion and the level of metabolic activity in various organ systems of the human body. A positron camera (tomograph) is used to produce cross-sectional tomographic images which are obtained by detecting radioactivity from a radioactive tracer substance radiopharmaceutical) that emits a radioactive tracer substance (radiopharmaceutical FDG) such as 2 -[F-18] flouro-D-glucose FDG, that is administered intravenously to the patient.

The Medicare National Coverage Determinations (NCD) Manual, Chapter 1, Sec.220.6, contains additional coverage instructions to indicate the conditions under which a PET scan is performed.

A. Definitions

For all uses of PET, excluding Rubidium 82 for perfusion of the heart, myocardial viability and refractory seizures, the following definitions apply:

Diagnosis: PET is covered only in clinical situations in which the PET results may assist in avoiding an invasive diagnostic procedure, or in which the PET results may assist in determining the optimal anatomical location to perform an invasive diagnostic procedure. In general, for most solid tumors, a tissue diagnosis is made prior to the performance of PET scanning. PET scans following a tissue diagnosis are generally performed for the purpose of staging, rather than diagnosis. Therefore, the use of PET in the diagnosis of lymphoma, esophageal and colorectal cancers, as well as in melanoma, should be rare. PET is not covered for other diagnostic uses, and is not covered for screening (testing of patients without specific signs and symptoms of disease).

Staging: PET is covered in clinical situations in which (1) (a) the stage of the cancer remains in doubt after completion of a standard diagnostic workup, including conventional imaging (computed tomography, magnetic resonance imaging, or ultrasound) or, (b) the use of PET would also be considered reasonable and necessary if it could potentially replace one or more conventional imaging studies when it is expected that conventional study information is insufficient for the clinical management of the patient and, (2) clinical management of the patient would differ depending on the stage of the cancer identified.

NOTE: Effective for services on or after April 3, 2009, the terms "diagnosis" and "staging" will be replaced with "Initial Treatment Strategy." For further information on this new term, refer to Pub. 100-03, NCD Manual, section 220.6.17.

Restaging: PET will be covered for restaging: (1) after the completion of treatment for the purpose of detecting residual disease, (2) for detecting suspected recurrence, or metastasis, (3) to determine the extent of a known recurrence, or (4) if it could potentially replace one or more conventional imaging studies when it is expected that conventional study information is to determine the extent of a known recurrence, or if study information is insufficient for the clinical management of the patient. Restaging applies to testing after a course of treatment is completed and is covered subject to the conditions above.

Monitoring: Use of PET to monitor tumor response to treatment during the planned course of therapy (i.e., when a change in therapy is anticipated).

NOTE: Effective for services on or after April 3, 2009, the terms "restaging" and "monitoring" will be replaced with "Subsequent Treatment Strategy." For further information on this new term, refer to Pub. 100-03, NCD Manual, section 220.6.17.

B. Limitations

For staging and restaging: PET is covered in either/or both of the following circumstances:

The stage of the cancer remains in doubt after completion of a standard diagnostic workup, including conventional imaging (computed tomography, magnetic resonance imaging, or ultrasound); and/or

The clinical management of the patient would differ depending on the stage of the cancer identified. PET will be covered for restaging after the completion of treatment for the purpose of detecting residual disease, for detecting suspected recurrence, or to determine the extent of a known recurrence. Use of PET would also be considered reasonable and necessary if it could potentially replace one or more conventional imaging studies when it is expected that conventional study information is insufficient for the clinical management of the patient.

The PET is not covered for other diagnostic uses, and is not covered for screening (testing of patients without specific symptoms). Use of PET to monitor tumor response during the planned course of therapy (i.e. when no change in therapy is being contemplated) is not covered.

100-4, 13, 60.3

PET Scan Qualifying Conditions and HCPCS Code Chart

Below is a summary of all covered PET scan conditions, with effective dates.

NOTE: The G codes below except those a # can be used to bill for PET Scan services through January 27, 2005. Effective for dates of service on or after January 28, 2005, providers must bill for PET Scan services using the appropriate CPT codes. See section 60.3.1. The G codes with a # can continue to be used for billing after January 28, 2005 and these remain non-covered by Medicare. (NOTE: PET Scanners must be FDA-approved.)

Conditions	Coverage Effective Date	****HCPCS/CPT
*Myocardial perfusion imaging (following previous PET G0030-G0047) single study, rest or stress (exercise and/or pharmacologic)	3/14/95	G0030
*Myocardial perfusion imaging (following previous PET G0030-G0047) multiple studies, rest or stress (exercise and/or pharmacologic)	3/14/95	G0031
*Myocardial perfusion imaging (following rest SPECT, 78464); single study, rest or stress (exercise and/or pharmacologic)	3/14/95	G0032
*Myocardial perfusion imaging (following rest SPECT 78464); multiple studies, rest or stress (exercise and/or pharmacologic)	3/14/95	G0033
*Myocardial perfusion (following stress SPECT 78465); single study, rest or stress (exercise and/or pharmacologic)	3/14/95	G0034
*Myocardial Perfusion Imaging (following stress SPECT 78465); multiple studies, rest or stress (exercise and/or pharmacologic)	3/14/95	G0035
*Myocardial Perfusion Imaging (following coronary angiography 93510-93529); single study, rest or stress (exercise and/or pharmacologic)	3/14/95	G0036
*Myocardial Perfusion Imaging, (following coronary angiography), 93510-93529); multiple studies, rest or stress (exercise and/or pharmacologic)	3/14/95	G0037
*Myocardial Perfusion Imaging (following stress planar myocardial perfusion, 78460); single study, rest or stress (exercise and/or pharmacologic)	3/14/95	G0038
*Myocardial Perfusion Imaging (following stress planar myocardial perfusion, 78460); multiple studies, rest or stress (exercise and/or pharmacologic)	3/14/95	G0039
*Myocardial Perfusion Imaging (following stress echocardiogram 93350); single study, rest or stress (exercise and/or pharmacologic)	3/14/95	G0040
*Myocardial Perfusion Imaging (following stress echocardiogram, 93350); multiple studies, rest or stress (exercise and/or pharmacologic)	3/14/95	G0041
*Myocardial Perfusion Imaging (following stress nuclear ventriculogram 78481 or 78483); single study, rest or stress (exercise and/or pharmacologic)	3/14/95	G0042
*Myocardial Perfusion Imaging (following stress nuclear ventriculogram 78481 or 78483); multiple studies, rest or stress (exercise and/or pharmacologic)	3/14/95	G0043
*Myocardial Perfusion Imaging (following stress ECG, 93000); single study, rest or stress (exercise and/or pharmacologic)	3/14/95	G0044
*Myocardial perfusion (following stress ECG, 93000), multiple studies; rest or stress (exercise and/or pharmacologic)	3/14/95	G0045
*Myocardial perfusion (following stress ECG, 93015), single study; rest or stress (exercise and/or pharmacologic)	3/14/95	G0046
*Myocardial perfusion (following stress ECG, 93015); multiple studies, rest or stress (exercise and/or pharmacologic)	3/14/95	G0047
PET imaging regional or whole body; single pulmonary nodule	1/1/98	G0125
Lung cancer, non-small cell (PET imaging whole body) Diagnosis, Initial Staging, Restaging	7/1/01	G0210 G0211 G0212
Colorectal cancer (PET imaging whole body) Diagnosis, Initial Staging, Restaging	7/1/01	G0213 G0214 G0215
Melanoma (PET imaging whole body) Diagnosis, Initial Staging, Restaging	7/1/01	G0216 G0217 G0218
Melanoma for non-covered indications Lymphoma (PET imaging whole body)	7/1/01	#G0219
Diagnosis, Initial Staging, Restaging	7/1/01	G0220 G0221 G0222
Head and neck cancer; excluding thyroid and CNS cancers (PET imaging whole body or regional) Diagnosis, Initial Staging, Restaging	7/1/01	G0223 G0224 G0225

100-4, 13, 60.3.1

Appropriate CPT Codes Effective for PET Scans for Services Performed on or After January 28, 2005

NOTE: All PET scan services require the use of a radiopharmaceutical diagnostic imaging agent (tracer). The applicable tracer code should be billed when billing for a PET scan service. See section 60.3.2 below for applicable tracer codes.

CPT Code	Description
78459	Myocardial imaging, positron emission tomography (PET), metabolic evaluation
78491	Myocardial imaging, positron emission tomography (PET), perfusion, single study at rest or stress
78492	Myocardial imaging, positron emission tomography (PET), perfusion, multiple studies at rest and/or stress
78608	Brain imaging, positron emission tomography (PET); metabolic evaluation
78811	Tumor imaging, positron emission tomography (PET); limited area (eg, chest, head/neck)
78812	Tumor imaging, positron emission tomography (PET); skull base to mid-thigh
78813	Tumor imaging, positron emission tomography (PET); whole body

CPT Code	Description
78814	Tumor imaging, positron emission tomography (PET) with concurrently acquired computed tomography (CT) for attenuation correction and anatomical localization; limited area (eg, chest, head/neck)
78815	Tumor imaging, positron emission tomography (PET) with concurrently acquired computed tomography (CT) for attenuation correction and anatomical localization; skull base to mid-thigh
78816	Tumor imaging, positron emission tomography (PET) with concurrently acquired computed tomography (CT) for attenuation correction and anatomical localization; whole body

100-4, 13, 60.3.2

Tracer Codes Required for PET Scans

The following tracer codes are applicable only to CPT 78491 and 78492. They can not be reported with any other code.

Institutional providers billing the fiscal intermediary

HCPCS	Description
*A9555	Rubidium Rb-82, Diagnostic, Per study dose, Up To 60 Millicuries
* Q3000 (Deleted effective 12/31/05)	Supply of Radiopharmaceutical Diagnostic Imaging Agent, Rubidium Rb-82, per dose
A9526	Nitrogen N-13 Ammonia, Diagnostic, Per study dose, Up To 40 Millicuries

NOTE: For claims with dates of service prior to 1/01/06, providers report Q3000 for supply of radiopharmaceutical diagnostic imaging agent, Rubidium Rb-82. For claims with dates of service 1/01/06 and later, providers report A9555 for radiopharmaceutical diagnostic imaging agent, Rubidium Rb-82 in place of Q3000.

Physicians / practitioners billing the carrier:

*A4641	Supply of Radiopharmaceutical Diagnostic Imaging Agent, Not Otherwise Classified
A9526	Nitrogen N-13 Ammonia, Diagnostic, Per study dose, Up To 40 Millicuries
A9555	Rubidium Rb-82, Diagnostic, Per study dose, Up To 60 Millicuries

* NOTE: Effective January 1, 2008, tracer code A4641 is not applicable for PET Scans.

The following tracer codes are applicable only to CPT 78459, 78608, 78811-78816. They can not be reported with any other code:

Institutional providers billing the fiscal intermediary:

* A9552	Fluorodeoxyglucose F18, FDG, Diagnostic, Per study dose, Up to 45 Millicuries
*C1775 (Deleted effective 12/31/05)	Supply of Radiopharmaceutical Diagnostic Imaging Agent, Fluorodeoxyglucose F18, (2-Deoxy-2-18F Fluoro-D-Glucose), Per dose (4-40 Mci/Ml)
**A4641	Supply of Radiopharmaceutical Diagnostic Imaging Agent, Not Otherwise Classified
A9580	Sodium Fluoride F-18, Diagnostic, per study dose, up to 30 Millicuries

** NOTE: Effective January 1, 2008, tracer code A4641 is not applicable for PET Scans.
*** NOTE: Effective for claims with dates of service February 26, 2010 and later, tracer code A9580 is applicable for PET Scans.

NOTE: For claims with dates of service prior to 1/01/06, OPPS hospitals report C1775 for supply of radiopharmaceutical diagnostic imaging agent, Fluorodeoxyglucose F18. For claims with dates of service January 1, 2006 and later, providers report A9552 for radiopharmaceutical diagnostic imaging agent, Fluorodeoxyglucose F18 in place of C1775.

Physicians / practitioners billing the carrier:

A9552	Fluorodeoxyglucose F18, FDG, Diagnostic, Per study dose, Up to 45 Millicuries
*A4641	Supply of Radiopharmaceutical Diagnostic Imaging Agent, Not Otherwise Classified
A9580	Sodium Fluoride F-18, Diagnostic, per study dose, up to 30 Millicuries

* NOTE: Effective January 1, 2008, tracer code A4641 is not applicable for PET Scans.
*** NOTE: Effective for claims with dates of service February 26, 2010 and later, tracer code A9580 is applicable for PET Scans.

* NOTE: Effective January 1, 2008, tracer code A4641 is not applicable for PET Scans.
*** NOTE: Effective for claims with dates of service February 26, 2010 and later, tracer code A9580 is applicable for PET Scans.

Positron Emission Tomography Reference Table

CPT	Short Descriptor	Tracer/Code	or	Tracer/Code	Comment
78459	Myocardial imaging, positron emission tomography (PET), metabolic imaging	FDG A9552	--	--	N/A
78491	Myocardial imaging, positron emission tomography (PET), perfusion; single study at rest or stress	N-13 A9526	or	Rb-82 A9555	N/A
78492	Myocardial imaging, positron emission tomography (PET), perfusion; multiple studies at rest and/or stress	N-13 A9526	or	Rb-82 A9555	N/A
78608	Brain imaging, positron emission tomography (PET); metabolic evaluation	FDG A9552	--	--	Covered indications: Alzheimer's disease/dementias, intractable seizures Note: This code is also covered for dedicated PET brain tumor imaging.
78609	Brain imaging, positron emission tomography (PET); perfusion evaluation	--	--	--	Nationally noncovered
78811	Positron emission tomography (PET) imaging; limited area (e.g, chest, head/neck)	FDG A9552	or	NaF-18 A9580	NaF-18 PET is covered only to identify bone metastasis of cancer.

100-4, 13, 60.7.1

Darbepoetin Alfa (Aranesp) Facility Billing Requirements

Revenue code 0636 is used to report Aranesp.

The HCPCS code for aranesp must be included: HCPCS HCPCS Description Dates of Service Q4054 Injection, darbepoetin alfa, 1mcg (for ESRD on Dialysis) 1/1/2004 through 12/31/2005 J0882 Injection, darbepoetin alfa, 1mcg (for ESRD on Dialysis) 1/1/2006 to present The hematocrit reading taken prior to the last administration of Aranesp during the billing period must also be reported on the UB-92/Form CMS-1450 with value code 49. For claims with dates of service on or after April 1, 2006, a hemoglobin reading may be reported on Aranesp claims using value code 48.

Effective January 1, 2006 the definition of value code 48 and 49 used to report the hemoglobin and hematocrit readings are changed to indicate the patient's most recent reading taken before the start of the billing period.

To report a hematocrit or hemoglobin reading for a new patient on or after January 1, 2006, the provider should report the reading that prompted the treatment of darbepoetin alfa. The provider may use results documented on form CMS 2728 or the patient's medical records from a transferring facility.

The payment allowance for Aranesp is the only allowance for the drug and its administration when used for ESRD patients. Effective January 1, 2005, the cost of supplies to administer Aranesp may be billed to the FI. HCPCS A4657 and Revenue Code 270 should be used to capture the charges for syringes used in the administration of Aranesp. The maximum number of administrations of Aranesp for a billing cycle is 5 times in 30/ 31days.

100-4, 13, 60.13

Billing Requirements for PET Scans for Specific Indications of Cervical Cancer for Services Performed on or After January 28, 2005

Contractors shall accept claims for these services with the appropriate CPT code listed in section 60.3.1. Refer to Pub. 100-03, section 220.6.17, for complete coverage guidelines for this new PET oncology indication. The implementation date for these CPT codes will be April 18, 2005. Also see section 60.17, of this chapter for further claims processing instructions for cervical cancer indications.

100-4, 13, 60.14

Billing Requirements for PET Scans for Non-Covered Indications

For services performed on or after January 28, 2005, contractors shall accept claims with the following HCPCS code for non-covered PET indications:

- - G0235: PET imaging, any site not otherwise specified

Short Descriptor: PET not otherwise specified

Type of Service: 4

NOTE:This code is for a non-covered service.

100-4, 13, 60.15

Billing Requirements for CMS - Approved Clinical Trials and Coverage With Evidence Development Claims for PET Scans for Neurodegenerative Diseases, Previously Specified Cancer Indications, and All Other Cancer Indications Not Previously Specified - Carriers and FIs

Effective for services on or after January 28, 2005, contractors shall accept and pay for claims for PET scans for lung cancer, esophageal cancer, colorectal cancer, lymphoma, melanoma, head & neck cancer, breast cancer, thyroid cancer, soft tissue sarcoma, brain cancer, ovarian cancer, pancreatic cancer, small cell lung cancer, and testicular cancer, as well as for neurodegenerative diseases and all other cancer indications not previously mentioned in this chapter, if these scans were performed as part of a CMS-approved clinical trial. (See Pub. 100-03, NCD Manual, sections 220.6.13 and 220.6.17.)

Contractors shall also be aware that PET scans for all cancers not previously specified at Pub. 100-03, NCD Manual, section 220.6.17, remain nationally non-covered unless performed in conjunction with a CMS-approved clinical trial.

Carriers Only

Carriers shall pay claims for PET scans for beneficiaries participating in a CMS-approved clinical trial submitted with an appropriate CPT code from section 60.3.1, of this chapter and the -QR (Item or Service Provided in a Medicare Specified Study) modifier.

FIs Only

In order to pay claims for PET scans on behalf of beneficiaries participating in a CMS-approved clinical trial, FIs require providers to submit claims with ICD-9 code V70.7 in the second diagnosis position on the CMS-1450 (UB-04), or the electronic equivalent, with the appropriate principal diagnosis code and an appropriate CPT code from section 60.3.1. Effective for PET scan claims for dates of service on or after January 28, 2005, FIs shall accept claims with the -QR modifier on other than inpatient claims.

NOTE: Effective for services on or after January 1, 2008, -Q0 (investigational clinical service provided in a clinical research study that is in an approved clinical research study) replaces the -QR modifier.

100-4, 13, 60.16

Billing and Coverage Changes for PET Scans Effective for Services on or After April 3, 2009

A. Summary of Changes

Effective for services on or after April 3, 2009, Medicare will not cover the use of FDG PET imaging to determine initial treatment strategy in patients with adenocarcinoma of the prostate.

Medicare will also not cover FDG PET imaging for subsequent treatment strategy for tumor types other than breast, cervical, colorectal, esophagus, head and neck (non-CNS/thyroid), lymphoma, melanoma, myeloma, non-small cell lung, and ovarian, unless the FDG PET is provided under the coverage with evidence development (CED) paradigm (billed with modifier -Q0, see section 60.15 of this chapter).

Last, Medicare will cover FDG PET imaging for initial treatment strategy for myeloma.

For further information regarding the changes in coverage, refer to Pub.100-03, NCD Manual, section 220.6.17.

B. New Modifiers for PET Scans

Effective for claims with dates of service on or after April 3, 2009, the following modifiers have been created for use to inform for the initial treatment strategy of biopsy-proven or strongly suspected tumors or subsequent treatment strategy of cancerous tumors:

PI -Positron Emission Tomography (PET) or PET/Computed Tomography (CT) to inform the initial treatment strategy of tumors that are biopsy proven or strongly suspected of being cancerous based on other diagnostic testing.

Short descriptor: PET tumor init tx strat

PS - Positron Emission Tomography (PET) or PET/Computed Tomography (CT) to inform the subsequent treatment strategy of cancerous tumors when the beneficiary's treatment physician determines that the PET study is needed to inform subsequent anti-tumor strategy.

Short descriptor: PS - PET tumor subsq tx strategy

C. Billing Changes for A/B MACs, FIs and Carriers

Effective for claims with dates of service on or after April 3, 2009, contractors shall accept FDG PET claims billed to inform initial treatment strategy with the following CPT codes AND modifier -PI: 78608, 78811, 78812, 78813, 78814, 78815, 78816.

Effective for claims with dates of service on or after April 3, 2009, contractors shall accept FDG PET claims with modifier -PS for the subsequent treatment strategy for solid tumors using a CPT code above AND an ICD-9 cancer diagnosis code.

Contractors shall also accept FDG PET claims billed to inform initial treatment strategy or subsequent treatment strategy when performed under CED with one of the PET or PET/CT CPT codes above AND modifier -PI OR modifier -PS AND an ICD-9 cancer diagnosis code AND modifier -Q0 (Investigational clinical service provided in a clinical research study that is in an approved clinical research study).

NOTE: For institutional claims continue to use diagnosis code V70.7 and condition code 30 on the claim.

D. Medicare Summary Notices, Remittance Advice Remark Codes, and Claim Adjustment Reason Codes

Effective for dates of service on or after April 3, 2009, contractors shall return as unprocessable/return to provider claims that do not include the -PI modifier with one of the PET/PET/CT CPT codes listed in subsection C. above when billing for the initial treatment strategy for solid tumors in accordance with Pub.100-03, NCD Manual, section 220.6.17.

In addition, contractors shall return as unprocessable/return to provider claims that do not include the -PS modifier with one of the CPT codes listed in subsection C. above when billing for the subsequent treatment strategy for solid tumors in accordance with Pub.100-03, NCD Manual, section 220.6.17.

The following messages apply:

- Claim Adjustment Reason Code 4 - the procedure code is inconsistent with the modifier used or a required modifier is missing.
- Remittance Advice Remark Code MA-130 - Your claim contains incomplete and/or invalid information, and no appeal rights are afforded because the claim is unprocessable. Submit a new claim with the complete/correct information.
- Remittance Advice Remark Code M16 - Alert: See our Web site, mailings, or bulletins for more details concerning this policy/procedure/decision.

Also, effective for claims with dates of service on or after April 3, 2009, contractors shall return as unprocessable/return to provider FDG PET claims billed to inform initial treatment strategy or subsequent treatment strategy when performed under CED without one of the PET/PET/CT CPT codes listed in subsection C. above AND modifier -PI OR modifier -PS AND an ICD-9 cancer diagnosis code AND modifier -Q0.

The following messages apply to return as unprocessable claims:

- Claim Adjustment Reason Code 4 - the procedure code is inconsistent with the modifier used or a required modifier is missing.
- Remittance Advice Remark Code MA-130 - Your claim contains incomplete and/or invalid information, and no appeal rights are afforded because the claim is unprocessable. Submit a new claim with the complete/correct information.
- Remittance Advice Remark Code M16 - Alert: See our Web site, mailings, or bulletins for more details concerning this policy/procedure/decision.

Effective April 3, 2009, contractors shall deny claims with ICD-9 diagnosis code 185 for FDG PET imaging for the initial treatment strategy of patients with adenocarcinoma of the prostate.

Contractors shall also deny claims for FDG PET imaging for subsequent treatment strategy for tumor types other than breast, cervical, colorectal, esophagus, head and neck (non-CNS/thyroid), lymphoma, melanoma, myeloma, non-small cell lung, and ovarian, unless the FDG PET is provided under CED (submitted with the -Q0 modifier) and use the following messages:

- Medicare Summary Notice 15.4 - Medicare does not support the need for this service or item
- Claim Adjustment Reason Code 50 - These are non-covered services because this is not deemed a 'medical necessity' by the payer.
- Contractors shall use Group Code CO (Contractual Obligation)

If an ABN is provided with a GA modifier indicating there is a signed ABN on file, contractors shall use Group Code PR (Patient Responsibility) and the liability falls to the beneficiary.

If an ABN is provided with a GZ modifier indicating no ABN was provided, contractors shall use Group Code CO (Contractual Obligation) and the liability falls to the provider.

100-4, 13, 60.17

Billing and Coverage Changes for PET Scans for Cervical Cancer Effective for Services on or After November 10, 2009

A. Billing Changes for A/B MACs, FIs, and Carriers

Effective for claims with dates of service on or after November 10, 2009, contractors shall accept FDG PET oncologic claims billed to inform initial treatment strategy; specifically for staging in beneficiaries who have biopsy-proven cervical cancer when the beneficiary's treating physician determines the FDG PET study is needed to determine the location and/or extent of the tumor as specified in Pub 100-03, section 220.6.17.

EXCEPTION: CMS continues to non-cover FDG PET for initial diagnosis of cervical cancer related to initial treatment strategy.

NOTE: Effective for claims with dates of service on and after November 10, 2009, the -Q0 modifier is no longer necessary for FDG PET for cervical cancer.

B. Medicare Summary Notices, Remittance Advice Remark Codes, and Claim Adjustment Reason Codes

Additionally, contractors shall return as unprocessable /return to provider for FDG PET for cervical cancer for initial treatment strategy billed without the following: one of the PET/PET/ CT CPT codes listed in 60.16 C above AND modifier -PI AND an ICD-9 cervical cancer diagnosis code.

Use the following messages:

- Claim Adjustment Reason Code 4 - the procedure code is inconsistent with the modifier used or a required modifier is missing.
- Remittance Advice Remark Code MA-130 - Your claim contains incomplete and/or invalid information, and no appeal rights are afforded because the claim is unprocessable. Submit a new claim with the complete/correct information.
- Remittance Advice Remark Code M16 - Alert: See our Web site, mailings, or bulletins for more details concerning this policy/procedure/decision.

100-4, 13, 60.18

Billing and Coverage Changes for PET (NaF-18) Scans to Identify Bone Metastasis of Cancer Effective for Claims With Dates of Services on or After February 26, 2010

A. Billing Changes for A/B MACs, FIs, and Carriers

Effective for claims with dates of service on and after February 26, 2010, contractors shall pay for NaF-18 PET oncologic claims to inform of initial treatment strategy (PI) or subsequent treatment strategy (PS) for suspected or biopsy proven bone metastasis ONLY in the context of a clinical study and as specified in Pub. 100-03, section 220.6. All other claims for NaF-18 PET oncology claims remain non-covered.

B. Medicare Summary Notices, Remittance Advice Remark Codes, and Claim Adjustment Reason Codes

Effective for claims with dates of service on or after February 26, 2010, contractors shall return as unprocessable NaF-18 PET oncologic claims billed with modifier TC or globally (for FIs modifier TC or globally does not apply) and HCPCS A9580 to inform the initial treatment strategy or subsequent treatment strategy for bone metastasis that do not include ALL of the following:

- PI or –PS modifier AND
- PET or PET/CT CPT code (78811, 78812, 78813, 78814, 78815, 78816) AND
- ICD-9 cancer diagnosis code AND
- Q0 modifier – Investigational clinical service provided in a clinical research study, are present on the claim.

NOTE: For institutional claims, continue to include diagnosis code V70.7 and condition code 30 to denote a clinical study.

Use the following messages:

- Claim Adjustment Reason Code 4 – The procedure code is inconsistent with the modifier used or a required modifier is missing. Note: Refer to the 835 Healthcare Policy Identification Segment (loop 2110 Service Payment Information REF), if present.
- Remittance Advice Remark Code MA-130 - Your claim contains incomplete and/or invalid information, and no appeal rights are afforded because the claim is unprocessable. Submit a new claim with the complete/correct information.
- Remittance Advice Remark Code M16 - Alert: See our Web site, mailings, or bulletins for more details concerning this policy/procedure/decision.
- Claim Adjustment Reason Code 167 – This (these) diagnosis(es) is (are) not covered.

  Effective for claims with dates of service on or after February 26, 2010, contractors shall accept PET oncologic claims billed with modifier 26 and modifier KX to inform the initial treatment strategy or strategy or subsequent treatment strategy for bone metastasis that include the following:

  - PI or –PS modifier AND
  - PET or PET/CT CPT code (78811, 78812, 78813, 78814, 78815, 78816) AND
  - ICD-9 cancer diagnosis code AND
  - Q0 modifier – Investigational clinical service provided in a clinical research study, are present on the claim.

NOTE: If modifier KX is present on the professional component service, Contractors shall process the service as PET NaF-18 rather than PET with FDG.

Contractors shall also return as unprocessable NaF-18 PET oncologic professional component claims (i.e., claims billed with modifiers 26 and KX) to inform the initial treatment strategy or strategy or subsequent treatment strategy for bone metastasis billed with HCPCS A9580 and use the following message:

Claim Adjustment Reason Code 97 – The benefit for this service is included in the payment/allowance for another service/procedure that has already been adjudicated.

NOTE: Refer to the 835 Healthcare Policy identification Segment (loop 2110 Service Payment Information REF), if present.

100-4, 13, 140

Bone Mass Measurements (BMMs)

Sections H1861(s)(15)H and H(rr)(1)H of the Social Security Act (the Act) (as added by 4106 of the Balanced Budget Act (BBA) of 1997) standardize Medicare coverage of medically necessary bone mass measurements by providing for uniform coverage under Medicare Part B. This coverage is effective for claims with dates of service furnished on or after July 1, l998.

Effective for dates of service on and after January 1, 2007, the CY 2007 Physician Fee Schedule final rule expanded the number of beneficiaries qualifying for BMM by reducing the dosage requirement for glucocorticoid (steroid) therapy from 7.5 mg of prednisone per day to 5.0 mg. It also changed the definition of BMM by removing coverage for a single-photon absorptiometry as it is not considered reasonable and necessary under section 1862 (a)(1)(A) of the Act. Finally, it required that in the case of monitoring and confirmatory baseline BMMs, they be performed with a dual-energy xray absorptiometry (axial) test.

Conditions of Coverage for BMMs are located in Pub.100-02, Medicare Benefit Policy Manual, chapter 15.

100-4, 14, 40.3

Payment for Intraocular Lens (IOL)

Prior to January 1, 2008, payment for facility services furnished by an ASC for IOL insertion during or subsequent to cataract surgery includes an allowance for the lens. The procedures that include insertion of an IOL are: Payment Group 6: CPT-4 Codes 66985 and 66986 Payment Group 8: CPT-4 Codes 66982, 66983 and 66984 Physicians or suppliers are not paid for an IOL furnished to a beneficiary in an ASC after July 1, 1988. Separate claims for IOLs furnished to ASC patients beginning March 12, 1990 are denied. Also, effective March 12, 1990, procedures 66983 and 66984 are treated as single procedures for payment purposes.

Beginning January 1, 2008, the Medicare payment for the IOL is included in the Medicare ASC payment for the associated surgical procedure. Consequently, no separate payment for the IOL is made, except for a payment adjustment for NTIOLs established according to the process outlined in 42 CFR 416.185. ASCs should not report separate charges for conventional IOLs because their payment is included in the Medicare payment for the associated surgical procedure. The ASC payment system logic that excluded $150 for IOLs for purposes of the multiple surgery reduction in cases of cataract surgery prior to January 1, 2008 no longer applies, effective for dates of service on or after January 1, 2008.

Effective for dates of service on and after February 27, 2006, through February 26, 2011, Medicare pays an additional $50 for specified Category 3 NTIOLs that are provided in association with a covered ASC surgical procedure. The list of Category 3 NTIOLS is available at: http://www.cms.hhs.gov/ASCPayment/08_NTIOLs.asp#TopOfPage.

ASCs should use HCPCS code Q1003 to bill for a Category 3 NTIOL. HCPCS code Q1003, along with one of the approved surgical procedure codes (CPT codes 66982, 66983, 66984, 66985, 66986) are to be used on all NTIOL Category 3 claims associated with reduced spherical aberration from February 27, 2006, through February 26, 2011. The payment adjustment for the NTIOL is subject to beneficiary coinsurance but is not wage-adjusted.

Any subsequent IOL recognized by CMS as having the same characteristics as the first NTIOL recognized by CMS for a payment adjustment as a Category III NTIOL (those of reduced spherical aberration) will receive the same adjustment for the remainder of the 5-year period established by the first recognized IOL.

100-4, 14, 40.8

40.8 - Payment When a Device is Furnished With No Cost or With Full or Partial Credit Beginning January 1, 2008

Contractors pay ASCs a reduced amount for certain specified procedures when a specified device is furnished without cost or for which either a partial or full credit is received (e.g., device recall). For specified procedure codes that include payment for a device, ASCs are required to include modifier -FB on the procedure code when a specified device is furnished without cost or for which full credit is received. If the ASC receives a partial credit of 50 percent or more of the cost of a specified device, the ASC is required to include modifier -FC on the procedure code if the procedure is on the list of specified procedures to which the -FC reduction applies. A single procedure code should not be submitted with both modifiers -FB and -FC. The pricing determination related to modifiers -FB and -FC is made prior to the application of multiple procedure payment reductions. Contractors adjust beneficiary coinsurance to reflect the reduced payment amount. Tables listing the procedures and devices to which the payment adjustments apply, and the full and partial adjustment amounts, are available on the CMS Web site.

In order to report that the receipt of a partial credit of 50 percent or more of the cost of a device, ASCs have the option of either: 1) Submitting the claim for the procedure to their Medicare contractor after the procedure's performance but prior to manufacturer acknowledgement of credit for a specified device, and subsequently contacting the contractor regarding a claims adjustment once the credit determination is made; or 2) holding the claim for the procedure until a determination is made by the manufacturer on the partial credit and submitting the claim with modifier -FC appended to the implantation procedure HCPCS code if the partial credit is 50 percent or more of the cost of the device. If choosing the first billing option, to request a claims adjustment once the credit determination is made, ASCs should keep in mind that the initial Medicare payment for the procedure involving the device is conditional and subject to adjustment.

100-4, 14, 40.9

Payment and Coding for Presbyopia Correcting IOLs (P-C IOLs) and Astigmatism Correcting IOLs (A-C IOLs) (CMS payment policies and recognition of P-C IOLs and A-C IOLs are contained in Transmittal 636 (CR3927) and Transmittal 1228 (CR5527) respectively.

Effective for dates of service on and after January 1, 2008, when inserting an approved A-C IOL in an ASC concurrent with cataract extraction, HCPCS code V2787 (Astigmatism-correcting function of intraocular lens) should be billed to report the non-covered charges for the A-C IOL functionality of the inserted intraocular lens. Additionally, note that HCPCS code V2788 (Presbyopia-correcting function of intraocular lens) is no longer valid to report non-covered charges associated with the A-C IOL. However, this code continues to be valid to report non-covered charges for a P-C IOL. The payment for the conventional lens portion of the A-C IOL and P-C IOL continues to be bundled with the ASC procedure payment.

Effective for services on and after January 1, 2010, ASCs are to bill for insertion of a Category 3 new technology intraocular lens (NTIOL) that is also an approved A-C IOL or P-C IOL, concurrent with cataract extraction, using three separate codes. ASCs shall use HCPCS code V2787 or V2788, as appropriate, to report charges associated with the non-covered functionality of the A-C IOL or P-C IOL, the appropriate HCPCS code 66982 (Extracapsular cataract removal with insertion of intraocular lens prosthesis (one stage procedure), manual or mechanical technique (e.g., irrigation and aspiration or phacoemulsification), complex, requiring devices or techniques not generally used in routine cataract surgery (e.g., iris expansion device, suture support for intraocular lens, or primary posterior capsulorrhexis) or performed on patients in the amblyogenic developmental stage); 66983 (Intracapsular cataract extraction with insertion of intraocular lens prosthesis (1 stage procedure)); or 66984 (Extracapsular cataract removal with insertion of intraocular lens prosthesis (1 stage procedure), manual or mechanical technique (e.g., irrigation and aspiration or phacoemulsification)), to report the covered cataract extraction and insertion procedure; and Q1003 (New technology, intraocular lens, category 3 (reduced spherical aberration) as defined in Federal Register notice, Vol. 65, dated May 3, 2000) to report the covered NTIOL aspect of the lens on claims for insertion of an A-C IOL or P-C IOL that is also designated as an NTIOL. Listings of the CMS-approved Category 3 NTIOLs, A-C IOLs, and P-C IOLs are available on the CMS web site.

100-4, 14, 60.1

60.1 - Applicable Messages for NTIOLs

Contractors shall return as unprocessable any claims for NTIOLs containing Q1003 alone or with a code other than one of the procedure codes listed in 40.3. Use the following messages for these returned claims:

- Claim Adjustment Reason Code 16 - Claim/service lacks information which is needed for adjudication. Additional information is supplied using remittance advice remark codes whenever appropriate.
- RA Remark Code M67 - Missing/Incomplete/Invalid other procedure codes.
- RA Remark Code MA130 - Your claim contains incomplete and/or invalid information, and no appeal rights are afforded because the claim is unprocessable. Please submit a new claim with the complete/correct information.

Contractors shall deny payment for Q1003 if services are furnished in a facility other than a Medicare-approved ASC. Use the following messages when denying these claims:

- MSN 16.2 - This service cannot be paid when provided in this location/facility.
- Claims Adjustment Reason Code 58 - Payment adjusted because treatment was deemed by the payer to have been rendered in an inappropriate or invalid place of service.

Contractors shall deny payment for Q1003 if billed by an entity other than a Medicare-approved ASC. Use the following messages when denying these claims:

- MSN 33.1 - The ambulatory surgical center must bill for this service.
- Claim Adjustment Reason Code 170 - Payment is denied when performed/billed by this type of provider.

Contractors shall deny payment for Q1003 if submitted for payment past the discontinued date (after the 5-year period, or after February 26, 2011). Use the following messages when denying these claims:

- MSN 21.11 - This service was not covered by Medicare at the time you received it.
- Claim Adjustment Reason Code 27 - Expenses incurred after coverage terminated.

Carriers shall deny payment for Q1003 if services are furnished in a facility other than a Medicare-approved ASC. Use the following messages when denying these claims:

- MSN 16.2 - This service cannot be paid when provided in this location/facility.
- Claims Adjustment Reason Code 58 - Payment adjusted because treatment was deemed by the payer to have been rendered in an inappropriate or invalid place of service.

Carriers shall deny payment for Q1003 if billed by an entity other than a Medicare-approved ASC. Use the following messages when denying these claims:

- MSN 33.1 - The ambulatory surgical center must bill for this service.
- Claim Adjustment Reason Code 170 - Payment is denied when performed/billed by this type of provider.

Carriers shall deny payment for Q1003 if submitted for payment past the discontinued date (after the 5-year period, or after February 26, 2011). Use the following messages when denying these claims:

MSN 21.11 - This service was not covered by Medicare at the time you received it.

- Claim Adjustment Reason Code 27 - Expenses incurred after coverage terminated.

100-4, 15, 20.1.4

Components of the Ambulance Fee Schedule

The mileage rates provided in this section are the base rates that are adjusted by the yearly ambulance inflation factor (AIF). The payment amount under the fee schedule is determined as follows:

- For ground ambulance services, the fee schedule amount includes:
  1. A money amount that serves as a nationally uniform base rate, called a "conversion factor" (CF), for all ground ambulance services;
  2. A relative value unit (RVU) assigned to each type of ground ambulance service;
  3. A geographic adjustment factor (GAF) for each ambulance fee schedule locality area (geographic practice cost index (GPCI));
  4. A nationally uniform loaded mileage rate;
  5. An additional amount for certain mileage for a rural point-of-pickup; and

6. For specified temporary periods, certain additional payment amounts as described in section 20.1.4A, below.

- For air ambulance services, the fee schedule amount includes:
  1. A nationally uniform base rate for fixed wing and a nationally uniform base rate for rotary wing;
  2. A geographic adjustment factor (GAF) for each ambulance fee schedule locality area (GPCI);
  3. A nationally uniform loaded mileage rate for each type of air service; and
  4. A rural adjustment to the base rate and mileage for services furnished for a rural point-of-pickup.

A. Ground Ambulance Services

1. Conversion Factor
The conversion factor (CF) is a money amount used to develop a base rate for each category of ground ambulance service. The CF is updated annually by the ambulance inflation factor and for other reasons as necessary.

2. Relative Value Units
Relative value units (RVUs) set a numeric value for ambulance services relative to the value of a base level ambulance service. Since there are marked differences in resources necessary to furnish the various levels of ground ambulance services, different levels of payment are appropriate for the various levels of service. The different payment amounts are based on level of service. An RVU expresses the constant multiplier for a particular type of service (including, where appropriate, an emergency response). An RVU of 1.00 is assigned to the BLS of ground service, e.g., BLS has an RVU of 1; higher RVU values are assigned to the other types of ground ambulance services, which require more service than BLS.

The RVUs are as follows:

Service Level	RVU
BLS	1.00
BLS - Emergency	1.60
ALS1	1.20
ALS1- Emergency	1.90
ALS2	2.75
SCT	3.25
PI	1.75

3. Geographic Adjustment Factor (GAF)
The GAF is one of two factors intended to address regional differences in the cost of furnishing ambulance services. The GAF for the ambulance FS uses the non-facility practice expense (PE) of the geographic practice cost index (GPCI) of the Medicare physician fee schedule to adjust payment to account for regional differences. Thus, the geographic areas applicable to the ambulance FS are the same as those used for the physician fee schedule.

The location where the beneficiary was put into the ambulance (POP) establishes which GPCI applies. For multiple vehicle transports, each leg of the transport is separately evaluated for the applicable GPCI. Thus, for the second (or any subsequent) leg of a transport, the POP establishes the applicable GPCI for that portion of the ambulance transport.

For ground ambulance services, the applicable GPCI is multiplied by 70 percent of the base rate. Again, the base rate for each category of ground ambulance services is the CF multiplied by the applicable RVU. The GPCI is not applied to the ground mileage rate.

4. Mileage
In the context of all payment instructions, the term "mileage" refers to loaded mileage. The ambulance FS provides a separate payment amount for mileage. The mileage rate per statute mile applies for all types of ground ambulance services, except Paramedic Intercept, and is provided to all Medicare contractors electronically by CMS as part of the ambulance FS. Providers and suppliers must report all medically necessary mileage, including the mileage subject to a rural adjustment, in a single line item.

5. Adjustment for Certain Ground Mileage for Rural Points of Pickup (POP)
The payment rate is greater for certain mileage where the POP is in a rural area to account for the higher costs per ambulance trip that are typical of rural operations where fewer trips are made in any given period.

If the POP is a rural ZIP Code, the following calculations should be used to determine the rural adjustment portion of the payment allowance. For loaded miles 1-17, the rural adjustment for ground mileage is 1.5 times the rural mileage allowance.

For services furnished during the period July 1, 2004 through December 31, 2008, a 25 percent increase is applied to the appropriate ambulance FS mileage rate to each mile of a transport (both urban and rural POP) that exceeds 50 miles (i.e., mile 51 and greater).

The following chart summarizes the above information:

Service	Dates of Service	Bonus	Calculation
Loaded miles 1-17, Rural POP	Beginning 4/1/02	50%	FS Rural mileage * 1.5
Loaded miles 18-50, Rural POP	4/1/02 – 12/31/03	25%	FS Rural mileage * 1.25
All loaded miles (Urban or Rural POP) 51+	7/1/04 – 12/31/08	25%	FS Urban or Rural mileage * 1.25

The POP, as identified by ZIP Code, establishes whether a rural adjustment applies to a particular service. Each leg of a multi-leg transport is separately evaluated for a rural adjustment application. Thus, for the second (or any subsequent) leg of a transport, the ZIP Code of the POP establishes whether a rural adjustment applies to such second (or subsequent) transport.

For the purpose of all categories of ground ambulance services except paramedic intercept, a rural area is defined as a U.S. Postal Service (USPS) ZIP Code that is located, in whole or in part, outside of either a Metropolitan Statistical Area (MSA) or in New England, a New England County Metropolitan Area (NECMA), or is an area wholly within an MSA or NECMA that has been identified as rural under the "Goldsmith modification." (The Goldsmith modification establishes an operational definition of rural areas within large counties that contain one or more metropolitan areas. The Goldsmith areas are so isolated by distance or physical features that they are more rural than urban in character and lack easy geographic access to health services.)

For Paramedic Intercept, an area is a rural area if:

- It is designated as a rural area by any law or regulation of a State;
- It is located outside of an MSA or NECMA; or
- It is located in a rural census tract of an MSA as determined under the most recent Goldsmith modification.

See IOM Pub. 100-02, Medicare Benefit Policy Manual, chapter 10 – Ambulance Services, section 30.1.1 – Ground Ambulance Services for coverage requirements for the Paramedic Intercept benefit. Presently, only the State of New York meets these requirements.

Although a transport with a POP located in a rural area is subject to a rural adjustment for mileage, Medicare still pays the lesser of the billed charge or the applicable FS amount for mileage. Thus, when rural mileage is involved, the contractor compares the calculated FS rural mileage payment rate to the provider's/supplier's actual charge for mileage and pays the lesser amount.

The CMS furnishes the ambulance FS files to claims processing contractors electronically. A version of the Ambulance Fee Schedule is also posted to the CMS website (http://www.cms.hhs.gov/AmbulanceFeeSchedule/02_afspuf.asp) for public consumption. To clarify whether a particular ZIP Code is rural or urban, please refer to the most recent version of the Medicare supplied ZIP Code file.

6. Regional Ambulance FS Payment Rate Floor for Ground Ambulance Transports
For services furnished during the period July 1, 2004 through December 31, 2009, the base rate portion of the payment under the ambulance FS for ground ambulance transports is subject to a minimum amount. This minimum amount depends upon the area of the country in which the service is furnished. The country is divided into 9 census divisions and each of the census divisions has a regional FS that is constructed using the same methodology as the national FS. Where the regional FS is greater than the national FS, the base rates for ground ambulance transports are determined by a blend of the national rate and the regional rate in accordance with the following schedule:

Year	National FS Percentage	Regional FS Percentage
7/1/04 - 12/31/04	20%	80%
CY 2005	40%	60%
CY 2006	60%	40%
CY 2007 – CY 2009	80%	20%
CY 2010 and thereafter	100%	0%

Where the regional FS is not greater than the national FS, there is no blending and only the national FS applies. Note that this provision affects only the FS portion of the blended transition payment rate. This floor amount is calculated by CMS centrally and is incorporated into the FS amount that appears in the FS file maintained by CMS and downloaded by CMS contractors.

There is no calculation to be done by the Medicare B/MAC or A/MAC in order to implement this provision.

7. Adjustments for FS Payment Rate for Certain Rural Ground Ambulance Transports
For services furnished during the period July 1, 2004 through December 31, 2010, the base rate portion of the payment under the FS for ground ambulance transports furnished in certain rural areas is increased by a percentage amount determined by CMS . Section 3105 (c) and 10311 (c) of the Affordable Care Act amended section 1834 (1) (13) (A) of the Act to extend this rural bonus for an additional year through December 31, 2010. This increase applies if the POP is in a rural county (or Goldsmith area) that is comprised by the lowest quartile by population of all such rural areas arrayed by population density. CMS will determine this bonus amount and the designated POP rural ZIP Codes in which the bonus applies. Beginning on July 1, 2004, rural areas qualifying for the additional bonus amount will be identified with a "B" indicator on the national ZIP Code file. Contractors must apply the additional rural bonus amount as a multiplier to the base rate portion of the FS payment for all ground transports originating in the designated POP ZIP Codes.

Subsequently, section of 106 (c) of the MMEA again amended section 1843 (l) (13) (A) of the Act to extend the rural bonus an additional year, through December 31, 2011.

8. Adjustments for FS Payment Rates for Ground Ambulance Transports
The payment rates under the FS for ground ambulance transports (both the fee schedule base rates and the mileage amounts) are increased for services furnished during the period July 1, 2004 through December 31, 2006 as well as July 1, 2008 through December 31, 2010. For ground ambulance transport services furnished where the POP is urban, the rates are increased by 1 percent for claims with dates of service July 1, 2004 through December 31, 2006 in accordance with Section 414 of the Medicare Modernization Act (MMA) of 2004 and by 2 percent for claims with dates of service July 1, 2008 through December 31, 2010 in accordance with Section 146(a) of the Medicare Improvements for Patients and Providers Act of 2008 and Sections 3105(a) and 10311(a) of the Patient Protection and Affordable Care Act (ACA) of

2010. For ground ambulance transport services furnished where the POP is rural, the rates are increased by 2 percent for claims with dates of service July 1, 2004 through December 31, 2006 in accordance with Section 414 of the Medicare Modernization Act (MMA) of 2004 and by 3 percent for claims with dates of service July 1, 2008 through December 31, 2010 in accordance with Section 146(a) of the Medicare Improvements for Patients and Providers Act of 2008 and Sections 3105(a) and 10311(a) of the Patient Protection and Affordable Care Act (ACA) of 2010. Subsequently, section 106 (a) of the Medicare and Medicaid Extenders Act of 2010 (MMEA) again amended section 1834 (1) (12) (A) of the Act to extend the payment increases for an additional year, through December 31, 2011. These amounts are incorporated into the fee schedule amounts that appear in the Ambulance FS file maintained by CMS and downloaded by CMS contractors. There is no calculation to be done by the Medicare carrier or intermediary in order to implement this provision.

The following chart summarizes the Medicare Prescription Drug, Improvement, and Modernization Act (MMA) of 2003 payment changes for ground ambulance services that became effective on July 1, 2004 as well as the Medicare Improvement for Patients and Providers Act (MIPPA) of 2008 changes that became effective July 1, 2008 and were extended by the Patient Protection and Affordable Care Act of 2010 and the Medicare and Medicaid Extenders Act of 2010 (MMEA).

Summary Chart of Additional Payments for Ground Ambulance Services Provided by MMA, MIPPA and MMEA

Service	Effective Dates	Payment Increase*
All rural miles	7/1/04 - 12/31/06	2%
All rural miles	7/1/08 – 12/31/11	3%
Rural miles 51+	7/1/04 - 12/31/08	25% **
All urban miles	7/1/04 - 12/31/06	1%
All urban miles	7/1/08 – 12/31/11	2%
Urban miles 51+	7/1/04 - 12/31/08	25% **
All rural base rates	7/1/04 - 12/31/06	2%
All rural base rates	7/1/08 – 12/31/11	3%
Rural base rates (lowest quartile)	7/1/04 - 12/31/11	22.6 %**
All urban base rates	7/1/04 - 12/31/06	1%
All urban base rates	7/1/08 – 12/31/11	2%
All base rates (regional fee schedule blend)	7/1/04 - 12/31/09	Floor

NOTES: * All payments are percentage increases and all are cumulative.

**Contractor systems perform this calculation. All other increases are incorporated into the CMS Medicare Ambulance FS file.

B. Air Ambulance Services

1. Base Rates
   Each type of air ambulance service has a base rate. There is no conversion factor (CF) applicable to air ambulance services.
2. Geographic Adjustment Factor (GAF)
   The GAF, as described above for ground ambulance services, is also used for air ambulance services. However, for air ambulance services, the applicable GPCI is applied to 50 percent of each of the base rates (fixed and rotary wing).
3. Mileage
   The FS for air ambulance services provides a separate payment for mileage.
4. Adjustment for Services Furnished in Rural Areas
   The payment rates for air ambulance services where the POP is in a rural area are greater than in an urban area. For air ambulance services (fixed or rotary wing), the rural adjustment is an increase of 50 percent to the unadjusted FS amount, e.g., the applicable air service base rate multiplied by the GAF plus the mileage amount or, in other words, 1.5 times both the applicable air service base rate and the total mileage amount.

The basis for a rural adjustment for air ambulance services is determined in the same manner as for ground services. That is, whether the POP is within a rural ZIP Code as described above for ground services.

100-4, 15, 20.2

Payment for Mileage Charges

B3-5116.3, PM AB-00-131

Charges for mileage must be based on loaded mileage only, e.g., from the pickup of a patient to his/her arrival at destination. It is presumed that all unloaded mileage costs are taken into account when a supplier establishes his basic charge for ambulance services and his rate for loaded mileage. Suppliers should be notified that separate charges for unloaded mileage will be denied.

Instructions on billing mileage are found in Sec.30.

100-4, 15, 20.3

Air Ambulance

PHs AB-01-165, AB-02-036, and AB-02-131; B3-5116.5, B3-5205 partial

Refer to IOM Pub. 100-02, Medicare Benefit Policy Manual, chapter 10 - Ambulance Services, section 10.4 - Air Ambulance Services, for additional information on the coverage of air ambulance services. Under certain circumstances, transportation by airplane or helicopter may qualify as covered ambulance services. If the conditions of coverage are met, payment may be made for the air ambulance services.

Air ambulance services are paid at different rates according to two air ambulance categories:

- AIR ambulance service, conventional air services, transport, one way, fixed wing (FW) (HCPCS code A0430)
- AIR ambulance service, conventional air services, transport, one way, rotary wing (RW) (HCPCS code A0431)

Covered air ambulance mileage services are paid when the appropriate HCPCS code is reported on the claim:

HCPCS code A0435 identifies FIXED WING AIR MILEAGE

HCPCS code A0436 identifies ROTARY WING AIR MILEAGE

Air mileage must be reported in whole numbers of loaded statute miles flown. Contractors must ensure that the appropriate air transport code is used with the appropriate mileage code.

Air ambulance services may be paid only for ambulance services to a hospital. Other destinations e.g., skilled nursing facility, a physician's office, or a patient's home may not be paid air ambulance. The destination is identified by the use of an appropriate modifier as defined in Section 30(A) of this chapter.

Claims for air transports may account for all mileage from the point of pickup, including where applicable: ramp to taxiway, taxiway to runway, takeoff run, air miles, roll out upon landing, and taxiing after landing. Additional air mileage may be allowed by the contractor in situations where additional mileage is incurred, due to circumstances beyond the pilot's control. These circumstances include, but are not limited to, the following:

Military base and other restricted zones, air-defense zones, and similar FAA restrictions and prohibitions;

Hazardous weather; or

Variances in departure patterns and clearance routes required by an air traffic controller.

If the air transport meets the criteria for medical necessity, Medicare pays the actual miles flown for legitimate reasons as determined by the Medicare contractor, once the Medicare beneficiary is loaded onto the air ambulance.

IOM Pub. 100-08, Medicare Program Integrity Manual, chapter 6 - Intermediary MR Guidelines for Specific Services contains instructions for Medical Review of Air Ambulance Services.

100-4, 15, 30.1.2

Coding Instructions for Paper and Electronic Claim Forms

Except as otherwise noted, beginning with dates of service on or after January 1, 2001, the following coding instructions must be used.

In item 23 of the CMS-1500 Form, billers shall code the 5-digit ZIP Code of the point of pickup.

Electronic billers using ANSI X12N 837 should refer to the Implementation Guide to determine how to report the origin information (e.g., the ZIP Code of the point of pickup).

Since the ZIP Code is used for pricing, more than one ambulance service may be reported on the same paper claim for a beneficiary if all points of pickup have the same ZIP Code. Suppliers must prepare a separate paper claim for each trip if the points of pickup are located in different ZIP Codes.

Claims without a ZIP Code in item 23 on CMS-1500 Form item 23, or with multiple ZIP Codes in item 23, must be returned as unprocessable. Carriers use message N53 on the remittance advice in conjunction with reason code 16.

ZIP Codes must be edited for validity.

The format for a ZIP Code is five numerics. If a nine-digit ZIP Code is submitted, the last four digits are ignored. If the data submitted in the required field does not match that format, the claim is rejected.

Generally, each ambulance trip will require two lines of coding, e.g., one line for the service and one line for the mileage. Suppliers who do not bill mileage would have one line of code for the service.

Beginning with dates of service on or after January 1, 2011, if mileage is billed it must be reported as fractional units in Item 24G of the Form CMS-1500 paper claim or the corresponding loop and segment of the ANSI X12N 837P electronic claim for trips totaling up to 100 covered miles. When reporting fractional mileage, suppliers must round the total miles up to the nearest tenth of a mile and report the resulting number

with the appropriate HCPCS code for ambulance mileage. The decimal must be used in the appropriate place (e.g., 99.9).

For trips totaling 100 covered miles and greater, suppliers must report mileage rounded up to the next whole number mile without the use of a decimal (e.g., 998.5 miles should be reported as 999).

For trips totaling less than 1 mile, enter a "0" before the decimal (e.g., 0.9).

Fractional mileage reporting applies only to ambulance services billed on a Form CMS-1500 paper claim, ANSI X12N 837P, or 837I electronic claims. It does not apply to providers billing on the Form CMS-1450.

For mileage HCPCS billed on a Form CMS-1500 or ANSI X12N 837P only, contractors shall automatically default to "0.1" units when the total mileage units are missing in Item 24G.

100-4, 15, 30.2

Intermediary Guidelines

For SNF Part A, the cost of transportation to receive most services included in the RUG rate is included in the cost for the service. This includes transportation in an ambulance. Payment for the SNF claim is based on the RUGs, and recalibration for future years takes into account the cost of transportation to receive the ancillary services.

If the services are excluded from the SNF PPS rate, the ambulance service may be billed separately as can the excluded service.

Refer to section 10.5, of chapter 3, of the Medicare Claims Processing Manual, for additional information on hospital inpatient bundling of ambulance services.

In general, the intermediary processes claims for Part B ambulance services provided by an ambulance supplier under arrangements with hospitals or SNFs. These providers bill intermediaries using only Method 2.

The provider must furnish the following data in accordance with intermediary instructions. The intermediary will make arrangements for the method and media for submitting the data: A detailed statement of the condition necessitating the ambulance service; A statement indicating whether the patient was admitted as an inpatient. If yes the name and address of the facility must be shown; Name and address of certifying physician; Name and address of physician ordering service if other than certifying physician; Point of pickup (identify place and completed address); Destination (identify place and complete address); Number of loaded miles (the number of miles traveled when the beneficiary was in the ambulance); Cost per mile; Mileage charge; Minimum or base charge; and Charge for special items or services. Explain.

A. General

The reasonable cost per trip of ambulance services furnished by a provider of services may not exceed the prior year's reasonable cost per trip updated by the ambulance inflation factor. This determination is effective with services furnished during Federal Fiscal Year (FFY) 1998 (between October 1, 1997, and September 30, 1998).

Providers are to bill for Part B ambulance services using the billing method of base rate including supplies, with mileage billed separately as described below.

The following instructions provide billing procedures implementing the above provisions.

B. Applicable Bill Types

The appropriate type of bill (13X, 22X, 23X, 83X, and 85X) must be reported. For SNFs, ambulance cannot be reported on a 21X type of bill.

C. Value Code Reporting

For claims with dates of service on or after January 1, 2001, providers must report on every Part B ambulance claim value code A0 (zero) and the related ZIP code of the geographic location from which the beneficiary was placed on board the ambulance in FLs 39-41 "Value Codes." The value code is defined as "ZIP Code of the location from which the beneficiary is initially placed on board the ambulance." Providers report the number in dollar portion of the form location right justified to the left to the dollar/cents delimiter. Providers utilizing the UB-92 flat file use Record Type 41 fields 16-39. On the X-12 institutional claims transactions, providers show HI*BE:A0:::12345, 2300 Loop, HI segment.

More than one ambulance trip may be reported on the same claim if the ZIP code of all points of pickup are the same. However, since billing requirements do not allow for value codes (ZIP codes) to be line item specific and only one ZIP code may be reported per claim, providers must prepare a separate claim for a beneficiary for each trip if the points of pickup are located in different ZIP codes.

D. Revenue Code/HCPCS Code Reporting

Providers must report revenue code 054X and, for services provided before January 1, 2001, one of the following CMS HCPCS codes in FL 44 "HCPCS/Rates" for each ambulance trip provided during the billing period: A0030 (discontinued 12/31/2000); A0040 (discontinued 12/31/2000); A0050 (discontinued 12/31/2000); A0320 (discontinued 12/31/2000); A0322 (discontinued 12/31/2000); A0324 (discontinued 12/31/2000); A0326 (discontinued 12/31/2000); A0328, (discontinued 12/31/2000); or A0330 (discontinued 12/31/2000).

In addition, providers report one of A0380 or A0390 for mileage HCPCS codes. No other HCPCS codes are acceptable for reporting ambulance services and mileage.

Providers report one of the following revenue codes: 0540; 0542; 0543; 0545; 0546; or 0548.

Do not report revenue codes 0541, 0544, or 0547.

For claims with dates of service on or after January 1, 2001, providers must report revenue code 540 and one of the following HCPCS codes in FL 44 "HCPCS/Rates" for each ambulance trip provided during the billing period: A0426; A0427; A0428; A0429; A0430; A0431; A0432; A0433; or A0434.

Providers using an ALS vehicle to furnish a BLS level of service report HCPCS code, A0426 (ALS1) or A0427 (ALS1 emergency), and are paid accordingly.

In addition, all providers report one of the following mileage HCPCS codes: A0380; A0390; A0435; or A0436.

Since billing requirements do not allow for more than one HCPCS code to be reported for per revenue code line, providers must report revenue code 0540 (ambulance) on two separate and consecutive lines to accommodate both the Part B ambulance service and the mileage HCPCS codes for each ambulance trip provided during the billing period. Each loaded (e.g., a patient is onboard) 1-way ambulance trip must be reported with a unique pair of revenue code lines on the claim. Unloaded trips and mileage are NOT reported.

However, in the case where the beneficiary was pronounced dead after the ambulance is called but before the ambulance arrives at the scene: Payment may be made for a BLS service if a ground vehicle is dispatched or at the fixed wing or rotary wing base rate, as applicable, if an air ambulance is dispatched. Neither mileage nor a rural adjustment would be paid. The blended rate amount will otherwise apply. Providers report the A0428 (BLS) HCPCS code. Providers report modifier QL (Patient pronounced dead after ambulance called) in Form Locator (FL) 44 "HCPCS/Rates" instead of the origin and destination modifier. In addition to the QL modifier, providers report modifier QM or QN.

E. Modifier Reporting

Providers must report an origin and destination modifier for each ambulance trip provided in FL 44 "HCPCS/Rates." Origin and destination modifiers used for ambulance services are created by combining two alpha characters. Each alpha character, with the exception of x, represents an origin code or a destination code. The pair of alpha codes creates one modifier. The first position alpha code equals origin; the second position alpha code equals destination. Origin and destination codes and their descriptions are listed below: D - Diagnostic or therapeutic site other than "P" or "H" when these are used as origin codes; E - Residential, Domiciliary, Custodial Facility (other than an 1819 facility); H - Hospital; I - Site of transfer (e.g. airport or helicopter pad) between modes of ambulance transport; J - Nonhospital based dialysis facility; N - Skilled Nursing Facility (SNF) (1819 facility); P - Physician's office (Includes HMO nonhospital facility, clinic, etc.); R - Residence; S - Scene of accident or acute event; or X - (Destination Code Only) intermediate stop at physician's office enroute to the hospital. (Includes HMO nonhospital facility, clinic, etc.) In addition, providers must report one of the following modifiers with every HCPCS code to describe whether the service was provided under arrangement or directly: QM - Ambulance service provided under arrangement by a provider of services; or QN - Ambulance service furnished directly by a provider of services.

F. Line-Item Dates of Service Reporting

Providers are required to report line-item dates of service per revenue code line. This means that they must report two separate revenue code lines for every ambulance trip provided during the billing period along with the date of each trip. This includes situations in which more than one ambulance service is provided to the same beneficiary on the same day. Line-item dates of service are reported on the hard copy UB-92 in FL 45 "Service Date" (MMDDYY), and on RT 61, field 13, "Date of Service" (YYYYMMDD) on the UB-92 flat file.

G. Service Units Reporting

For line items reflecting HCPCS code A0030, A0040, A0050, A0320, A0322, A0324, A0326, A0328, or A0330 (services before January 1, 2001) or code A0426, A0427, A0428, A0429, A0430, A0431, A0432, A0433, or A0434 (services on and after January 1, 2001), providers are required to report in FL 46 "Service Units" each ambulance trip provided during the billing period. Therefore, the service units for each occurrence of these HCPCS codes are always equal to one. In addition, for line items reflecting HCPCS code A0380 or A0390, the number of loaded miles must be reported. (See examples below.) Therefore, the service units for each occurrence of these HCPCS codes are always equal to one.

In addition, for line items reflecting HCPCS code A0380, A0390, A0435, or A0436, the number of loaded miles must be reported.

H. Total Charges Reporting

For line items reflecting HCPCS code: A0030, A0040, A0050, A0320, A0322, A0324, A0326, A0328, or A0330 (services before January 1, 2001); OR HCPCS code A0426, A0427, A0428, A0429, A0430, A0431, A0432, A0433, or A0434 (on or after January 1, 2001); Providers are required to report in FL 47 "Total Charges" the actual charge for the ambulance service including all supplies used for the ambulance trip but excluding the charge for mileage.

For line items reflecting HCPCS code A0380, A0390, A0435, or A0436, report the actual charge for mileage.

NOTE: There are instances where the provider does not incur any cost for mileage, e.g., if the beneficiary is pronounced dead after the ambulance is called but before the ambulance arrives at the scene. In these situations, providers report the base rate ambulance trip and mileage as separate revenue code lines. Providers report the base rate ambulance trip in accordance with current billing requirements. For purposes of reporting mileage, they must report the appropriate HCPCS code, modifiers, and units as a separate line item. For the related charges, providers report $1.00 in FL48 for noncovered charges. Intermediaries should assign ANSI Group Code OA to the $1.00 noncovered mileage line, which in turn informs the beneficiaries and providers that they each have no liability.

Prior to submitting the claim to CWF, the intermediary will remove the entire revenue code line containing the mileage amount reported in FL 48 "Noncovered Charges" to avoid nonacceptance of the claim.

EXAMPLES:The following provides examples of how bills for Part B ambulance services should be completed based on the reporting requirements above. These examples reflect ambulance services furnished directly by providers. Ambulance services provided under arrangement between the provider and an ambulance company are reported in the same manner except providers report a QM modifier instead of a QN modifier. The following examples are for claims submitted with dates of service on or after January 1, 2001.

EXAMPLE 1: Claim containing only one ambulance trip:

For the UB-92 Flat File, providers report as follows:

Modifier Record Type	Revenue Code	HCPCS Modifier	Date of Service	Units	Total Charges
61	0540	A0428RHQN	082701	1 (trip)	100.00
61	0540	A0380RHQN	082701	4 (mileage)	8.00

For the hard copy UB-92 (Form CMS-1450), providers report as follows:

Modifier Record Type	Revenue Code	HCPCS Modifier	Date of Service	Units	Total Charges
FL 42, FL 44 FL 45, FL 46 FL 47	0540	A0428RHQN	082701	1 (trip)	100.00
	0540	A0380RHQN	082701	4 (mileage)	8.00

EXAMPLE 2: Claim containing multiple ambulance trips:
For the UB-92 Flat File, providers report as follows:

Modifier Record Type	Revenue Code	HCPCS Code	Modifiers #1	#2	Date of Service	Units	Total Charges
61	0540	A0429	RH	QN	082801	1 (trip)	100.00
61	0540	A0380	RH	QN	082801	2 (mileage)	4.00
61	0540	A0330	RH	QN	082901	1 (trip)	400.00
61	0540	A0390	RH	QN	082901	3 (mileage)	6.00
61	0540	A0426	RH	QN	083001	1 (trip)	500.00
61	0540	A0390	RH	QN	083001	5 (mileage)	10.00
61	0540	A0390	RH	QN	082901	3 (mileage)	6.00
61	0540	A0426	RH	QN	083001	1 (trip)	500.00

For the hard copy UB-92 (Form CMS-1450), providers report as follows:

Modifier	Revenue Code	HCPCS Code	#1	#2	Date of Service	Units	Total Charges
FL42, FL 44, FL 45, FL 46, FL 47	0540	A0429	RH	QN	082801	1 (trip)	100.00
	0540	A0380	RH	QN	082801	2 (mileage)	4.00

EXAMPLE 3:Claim containing more than one ambulance trip provided on the same day: For the UB-92 Flat File, providers report as follows:

Modifier Record Type	Revenue Code	HCPCS Code	#1	#2	Date of Service	Units	Total Charges
61	0540	A0429	RH	QN	090201	1 (trip)	100.00
61	0540	A0380	RH	QN	090201	2 (mileage)	4.00
61	0540	A0429	HR	QN	090201	1 (trip)	100.00
61	0540	A0380	HR	QN	090201	2 (mileage)	4.00

For the hard copy UB-92 (Form CMS-1450), providers report as follows:

Modifier	Revenue Code	HCPCS Code	#1	#2	Date of Service	Units	Total Charges
FL42, FL 44, FL 45, FL 46, FL 47	0540	A0429	RH	QN	090201	1 (trip)	100.00
	0540	A0380	RH	QN	090201	2 (mileage)	4.00
	0540	A0429	HR	QN	090201	1 (trip)	100.00
	0540	A0380	HR	QN	090201	2 (mileage)	4.00

I. Edits Intermediaries edit to assure proper reporting as follows:

For claims with dates of service before January 1, 2001, each pair of revenue codes 0540 must have one of the following ambulance trip HCPCS codes - A0030, A0040, A0050, A0320, A0322, A0324, A0326, A0328 or A0330; and one of the following mileage HCPCS codes - A0380 or A0390; For claims with dates of service on or after January 1, 2001, each pair of revenue codes 0540 must have one of the following ambulance HCPCS codes - A0426, A0427, A0428, A0429, A0430, A0431, A0432, A0433, or A0434; and one of the following mileage HCPCS codes - A0435, A0436 or for claims with dates of service before April 1, 2002, A0380, or A0390, or for claims with dates of service on or after April 1, 2002, A0425; For claims with dates of service on or after January 1, 2001, the presence of an origin and destination modifier and a QM or QN modifier for every line item containing revenue code 0540; The units field is completed for every line item containing revenue code 0540; For claims with dates of service on or after January 1, 2001, the units field is completed for every line item containing revenue code 0540; Service units for line items containing HCPCS codes A0030, A0040, A0050, A0320, A0322, A0324, A0326, A0328, A0330, A0426, A0427, A0428, A0429, A0430, A0431, A0432, A0433, or A0434 always equal "1" For claims with dates of service on or after July 1, 2001, each 1-way ambulance trip, line-item dates of service for the ambulance service, and corresponding mileage are equal.

100-4, 15, 30.2.1

A/MAC Bill Processing Guidelines Effective April 1, 2002, as a Result of Fee Schedule Implementation

For SNF Part A, the cost of medically necessary ambulance transportation to receive most services included in the RUG rate is included in the cost for the service. Payment for the SNF claim is based on the RUGs, which takes into account the cost of such transportation to receive the ancillary services.

Refer to IOM Pub. 100-04, Medicare Claims Processing Manual, chapter 6 – SNF Inpatient Part A Billing, Section 20.3.1 – Ambulance Services for additional information on SNF consolidated billing and ambulance transportation.

Refer to IOM Pub. 100-04, Medicare Claims Processing Manual, chapter 3 – Inpatient Hospital Billing, section 10.5 – Hospital Inpatient Bundling, for additional information on hospital inpatient bundling of ambulance services.

In general, the A/MAC processes claims for Part B ambulance services provided by an ambulance supplier under arrangements with hospitals or SNFs. These providers bill A/MACs using only Method 2.

The provider must furnish the following data in accordance with A/MAC instructions. The A/MAC will make arrangements for the method and media for submitting the data:

- A detailed statement of the condition necessitating the ambulance service;
- A statement indicating whether the patient was admitted as an inpatient. If yes the name and address of the facility must be shown;
- Name and address of certifying physician;
- Name and address of physician ordering service if other than certifying physician;
- Point of pickup (identify place and completed address);
- Destination (identify place and complete address);
- Number of loaded miles (the number of miles traveled when the beneficiary was in the ambulance);
- Cost per mile;
- Mileage charge;
- Minimum or base charge; and

Charge for special items or services. Explain.

A. Revenue Code Reporting

Providers report ambulance services under revenue code 540 in FL 42 "Revenue Code."

B. HCPCS Codes Reporting

Providers report the HCPCS codes established for the ambulance fee schedule. No other HCPCS codes are acceptable for the reporting of ambulance services and mileage. The HCPCS code must be used to reflect the type of service the beneficiary received, not the type of vehicle used.

Providers must report one of the following HCPCS codes in FL 44 "HCPCS/Rates" for each base rate ambulance trip provided during the billing period:

A0426;

A0427;

A0428;

A0429;

A0430;

A0431;

A0432;

A0433; or

A0434.

These are the same codes required effective for services January 1, 2001.

In addition, providers must report one of HCPCS mileage codes:

A0425;

A0435; or

A0436.

Since billing requirements do not allow for more than one HCPCS code to be reported per revenue code line, providers must report revenue code 540 (ambulance) on two separate and consecutive line items to accommodate both the ambulance service and the mileage HCPCS codes for each ambulance trip provided during the billing period. Each loaded (e.g., a patient is onboard) 1-way ambulance trip must be reported with a unique pair of revenue code lines on the claim. Unloaded trips and mileage are NOT reported.

For UB-04 hard copy claims submission prior to August 1, 2011, providers code one mile for trips less than a mile. Miles must be entered as whole numbers. If a trip has a fraction of a mile, round up to the nearest whole number.

Beginning with dates of service on or after January 1, 2011, for UB-04 hard copy claims submissions August 1, 2011 and after, mileage must be reported as fractional units. When reporting fractional mileage, providers must round the total miles up to the nearest tenth of a mile and the decimal must be used in the appropriate place (e.g., 99.9).

For trips totaling less than 1 mile, enter a "0" before the decimal (e.g., 0.9).

For electronic claims submissions prior to January 1, 2011, providers code one mile for trips less than a mile. Miles must be entered as whole numbers. If a trip has a fraction of a mile, round up to the nearest whole number.

Beginning with dates of service on or after January 1, 2011, for electronic claim submissions only, mileage must be reported as fractional units in the ANSI X12N 837I element SV205 for trips totaling up to 100 covered miles. When reporting fractional mileage, providers must round the total miles up to the nearest tenth of a mile and the decimal must be used in the appropriate place (e.g., 99.9).

For trips totaling 100 covered miles and greater, providers must report mileage rounded up to the nearest whole number mile (e.g., 999) and not use a decimal when reporting whole number miles over 100 miles.

For trips totaling less than 1 mile, enter a "0" before the decimal (e.g., 0.9).

C. Modifier Reporting

Providers must report an origin and destination modifier for each ambulance trip provided and either a QM (Ambulance service provided under arrangement by a provider of services) or QN (Ambulance service furnished directly by a provider of services) modifier in FL 44 "HCPCS/Rates".

D. Service Units Reporting

For line items reflecting HCPCS codes A0426, A0427, A0428, A0429, A0430, A0431, A0432, A0433, or A0434, providers are required to report in FL 46 "Service Units" for each ambulance trip provided. Therefore, the service units for each occurrence of these HCPCS codes are always equal to one. In addition, for line items reflecting HCPCS code A0425, A0435, or A0436, providers must also report the number of loaded miles.

E. Total Charges Reporting

For line items reflecting HCPCS codes A0426, A0427, A0428, A0429, A0430, A0431, A0432, A0433, or A0434, providers are required to report in FL 47, "Total Charges," the actual charge for the ambulance service including all supplies used for the ambulance trip but excluding the charge for mileage. For line items reflecting HCPCS codes A0425, A0435, or A0436, providers are to report the actual charge for mileage.

NOTE: There are instances where the provider does not incur any cost for mileage, e.g., if the beneficiary is pronounced dead after the ambulance is called but before the ambulance arrives at the scene. In these situations, providers report the base rate ambulance trip and mileage as separate revenue code lines. Providers report the base rate ambulance trip in accordance with current billing requirements. For purposes of reporting mileage, they must report the appropriate HCPCS code, modifiers, and units. For the related charges, providers report $1.00 in non-covered charges. A/MACs should assign ANSI Group Code OA to the $1.00 non-covered mileage line, which in turn informs the beneficiaries and providers that they each have no liability.

F. Edits (A/MAC Claims with Dates of Service On or After 4/1/02)

For claims with dates of service on or after April 1, 2002, A/MACs perform the following edits to assure proper reporting:

Edit to assure each pair of revenue codes 540 have one of the following ambulance HCPCS codes - A0426, A0427, A0428, A0429, A0430, A0431, A0432, A0433, or A0434; and one of the following mileage HCPCS codes - A0425, A0435, or A0436.

Edit to assure the presence of an origin, destination modifier, and a QM or QN modifier for every line item containing revenue code 540;

Edit to assure that the unit's field is completed for every line item containing revenue code 540;

Edit to assure that service units for line items containing HCPCS codes A0426, A0427, A0428, A0429, A0430, A0431, A0432, A0433, or A0434 always equal "1"; and

Edit to assure on every claim that revenue code 540, a value code of A0 (zero), and a corresponding ZIP Code are reported. If the ZIP Code is not a valid ZIP Code in accordance with the USPS assigned ZIP Codes, intermediaries verify the ZIP Code to determine if the ZIP Code is a coding error on the claim or a new ZIP Code from the USPS not on the CMS supplied ZIP Code File.

Beginning with dates of service on or after April 1, 2012, edit to assure that only non-emergency trips (i.e., HCPCS A0426, A0428) require an NPI in the Attending Physician field. Emergency trips do not require an NPI in the Attending Physician field (i.e., A0427, A0429, A0430, A0431, A0432, A0433, A0434)

G. CWF (A/MACs)

A/MACs report the procedure codes in the financial data section (field 65a-65j). They include revenue code, HCPCS code, units, and covered charges in the record. Where more than one HCPCS code procedure is applicable to a single revenue code, the provider reports each HCPCS code and related charge on a separate line, and the A/MAC reports this to CWF. Report the payment amount before adjustment for beneficiary liability in field 65g "Rate" and the actual charge in field 65h, "Covered Charges."

100-4, 15, 30.2.4

30.2.4 - Non-covered Charges on Institutional Ambulance Claims

Medicare law contains a restriction that miles beyond the closest available facility cannot be billed to Medicare. Non-covered miles beyond the closest facility are billed with HCPCS procedure code A0888 ("non-covered ambulance mileage per mile, e.g., for miles traveled beyond the closest appropriate facility"). These non-covered line items can be billed on claims also containing covered charges. Ambulance claims may use the -GY modifier on line items for such non-covered mileage, and liability for the service will be assigned correctly to the beneficiary.

The method of billing all miles for the same trip, with covered and non-covered portions, on the same claim is preferable in this scenario. However, billing the non-covered mileage using condition code 21 claims is also permitted, if desired, as long as all line items on the claims are non-covered and the beneficiary is liable. Additionally, unless requested by the beneficiary or required by specific Medicare policy, services excluded by statute do not have to be billed to Medicare.

When the scenario is point of pick up outside the United States, including U.S. territories but excepting some points in Canada and Mexico in some cases, mileage is also statutorily excluded from Medicare coverage. Such billings are more likely to be submitted on entirely non-covered claims using condition code 21. This scenario requires the use of a different message on the Medicare Summary Notice (MSN) sent to beneficiaries.

Another scenario in which billing non-covered mileage to Medicare may occur is when the beneficiary dies after the ambulance has been called but before the ambulance arrives. The -QL modifier should be used on the base rate line in this scenario, in place of origin and destination modifiers, and the line is submitted with covered charges. The -QL modifier should also be used on the accompanying mileage line, if submitted, with non-covered charges. Submitting this non-covered mileage line is optional for providers.

Non-covered charges may also apply is if there is a subsidy of mileage charges that are never charged to Medicare. Because there are no charges for Medicare to share in, the only billing option is to submit non-covered charges, if the provider bills Medicare at all (it is not required in such cases). These non-covered charges are unallowable, and should not be considered in settlement of cost reports. However, there is a difference in billing if such charges are subsidized, but otherwise would normally be charged to Medicare as the primary payer. In this latter case, CMS examination of existing rules relating to grants policy since October 1983, supported by Federal regulations (42CFR 405.423), generally requires providers to reduce their costs by the amount of grants and gifts restricted to pay for such costs. Thereafter, section 405.423 was deleted from the regulations.

Thus, providers were no longer required to reduce their costs for restricted grants and gifts, and charges tied to such grants/gifts/subsidies should be submitted as covered charges. This is in keeping with Congress's intent to encourage hospital philanthropy, allowing the provider receiving the subsidy to use it, and also requiring Medicare to share in the unreduced cost. Treatment of subsidized charges as non-covered Medicare charges serves to reduce Medicare payment on the Medicare cost report contrary to the 1983 change in policy.

Medicare requires the use of the -TQ modifier so that CMS can track the instances of the subsidy scenario for non-covered charges. The -TQ should be used whether the subsidizing entity is governmental or voluntary. The -TQ modifier is not required in the case of covered charges submitted when a subsidy has been made, but charges are still normally made to Medicare as the primary payer.

If providers believe they have been significantly or materially penalized in the past by the failure of their cost reports to consider covered charges occurring in the subsidy case, since Medicare had previous billing instructions that stated all charges in the case of a subsidy, not just charges when the entity providing the subsidy never charges another entity/primary payer, should be submitted as non-covered charges, they may contact their FI about reopening the reports in question for which the time period in 42 CFR 405.1885 has not expired. FIs have the discretion to determine if the amount in question warrants reopening. The CMS does not expect many such cases to occur.

Billing requirements for all these situations, including the use of modifiers, are presented in the chart below:

Mileage Scenario	*HCPCS*	*Modifiers**	*Liability*	*Billing*	*Remit. Requirements*	*MSN Message*
STATUTE: Miles beyond closest facility, OR **Pick up point outside of U.S.	A0888 on line item for the non-covered mileage	-QM or -QN, origin/destination modifier, and -GY unless condition code 21 claim used	Beneficiary	Bill mileage line item with A0888 -GY and other modifiers as needed to establish liability, line item will be denied; OR bill service on condition code 21 claim, no -GY required, claim will be denied	Group code PR, reason code 96	16.10 "Medicare does not pay for this item or service"; OR, "Medicare no paga por este artículo o servicio"
Beneficiary dies after ambulance is called	Most appropriate ambulance HCPCS mileage code (i.e., ground, air)	-QL unless condition code -21 claim	Provider	Bill mileage line item with -QL as non-covered, line item will be denied	Group Code CO, reason code 96	16.58 "The provider billed this charge as non-covered. You do not have to pay this amount."; OR, "El proveedor facuró este cargo como no cubierto. Usted no tiene que pagar ests cantidad."
Subsidy or government owned Ambulance, Medicare NEVER billed***	A0888 on line item for the non-covered mileage	-QM or -QN, origin/ destination modifier, and -TQ must be used for policy purposes	Provider	Bill mileage line item with A0888, and modifiers as non-covered, line item will be denied	Group Code CO, reason code 96	16.58 "The provider billed this charge as non-covered. You do not have to pay this amount."; OR, "El proveedor facuró este cargo como no cubierto. Usted no tiene que pagar ests cantidad."

* Current ambulance billing requirements state that either the -QM or -QN modifier must be used on services. The -QM is used when the "ambulance service is provided under arrangement by a provider of services," and the -QN when the "ambulance service is provided directly by a provider of services." Line items using either the -QM or -QN modifiers are not subject to the FISS edit associated with FISS reason code 31322 so that these lines items will process to completion. Origin/destination modifiers, also required by current instruction, combine two alpha characters: one for origin, one for destination, and are not non-covered by definition.

** This is the one scenario where the base rate is not paid in addition to mileage, and there are certain exceptions in Canada and Mexico where mileage is covered as described in existing ambulance instructions.

*** If Medicare would normally have been billed, submit mileage charges as covered charges despite subsidies.

Medicare systems may return claims to the provider if they do not comply with the requirements in the table.

100-4, 15, 40

Medical Conditions List and Instructions

The following list is intended as primarily an educational guideline. This list was most recently updated by CMS Transmittal 1185, Change Request 5542 issued February 23, 2007. It will help ambulance providers and suppliers to communicate the patient's condition to Medicare contractors, as reported by the dispatch center and as observed by the ambulance crew. Use of the medical conditions list does not guarantee payment of the claim or payment for a certain level of service. Ambulance providers and suppliers must retain adequate documentation of dispatch instructions, patient's condition, other on-scene information, and details of the transport (e.g., medications administered, changes in the patient's condition, and miles traveled), all of which may be subject to medical review by the Medicare contractor or other oversight authority. Medicare contractors will rely on medical record documentation to justify coverage, not simply the HCPCS code or the condition code by themselves. All current Medicare ambulance policies remain in place.

The CMS issued the Medical Conditions List as guidance via a manual revision as a result of interest expressed in the ambulance industry for this tool. While the International Classification of Diseases, 9th Revision, Clinical Modification (ICD-9-CM) codes are not precluded from use on ambulance claims, they are currently not required (per Health Insurance Portability and Accountability Act (HIPAA)) on most ambulance claims, and these codes generally do not trigger a payment or a denial of a claim. Some carriers and fiscal intermediaries have Local Coverage Determinations (LCD) in place that cite ICD-9-CM that can be added to the claim to assist in documenting that the services are reasonable and necessary, but this is not common. Since ICD-9-CM codes are not required and are not consistently used, not all carriers or fiscal intermediaries edit on this field, and it is not possible to edit on the narrative field. The ICD-9-CM codes are generally not part of the edit process, although the Medical Conditions List is available for those who do find it helpful in justifying that services are reasonable and necessary.

The Medical Conditions List is set up with an initial column of primary ICD-9-CM codes, followed by an alternative column of ICD-9-CM codes. The primary ICD-9-CM code column contains general ICD-9-CM codes that fit the transport conditions as described in the subsequent columns. Ambulance crew or billing staff with limited knowledge of ICD-9-CM coding would be expected to choose the one or one of the two ICD-9-CM codes listed in this column to describe the appropriate ambulance transport and then place the ICD-9-CM code in the space on the claim form designated for an ICD-9-CM code. The option to include other information in the narrative field always exists and can be used whenever an ambulance provider or supplier believes that the information may be useful for claims processing purposes. If an ambulance crew or billing staff member has more comprehensive clinical knowledge, then that person may select an ICD-9-CM code from the alternative ICD-9-CM code column. These ICD-9-CM codes are more specific and detailed. An ICD-9-CM code does not need to be selected from both the primary column and the alternative column. However, in several instances in the alternative ICD-9-CM code column, there is a selection of codes and the word "PLUS." In these instances, the ambulance provider or supplier would select an ICD-9-CM code from the first part of the alternative listing (before the word "PLUS") and at least one other ICD-9-CM code from the second part of the alternative listing (after the word "PLUS"). The ambulance claim form does provide space for the use of multiple ICD-9-CM codes. Please see the example below:

The ambulance arrives on the scene. A beneficiary is experiencing the specific abnormal vital sign of elevated blood pressure; however, the beneficiary does not normally suffer from hypertension (ICD-9-CM code 796.2 (from the alternative column on the Medical Conditions List)). In addition, the beneficiary is extremely dizzy (ICD-9-CM code 780.4 (fits the "PLUS any other code" requirement when using the alternative list for this condition (abnormal vital signs)). The ambulance crew can list these two ICD-9-CM codes on the claim form, or the general ICD-9-CM code for this condition (796.4 - Other Abnormal Clinical Findings) would work just as well. None of these ICD-9-CM codes will determine whether or not this claim will be paid; they will only assist the contractor in making a medical review determination provided all other Medicare ambulance coverage policies have been followed.

While the medical conditions/ICD-9-CM code list is intended to be comprehensive, there may be unusual circumstances that warrant the need for ambulance services using ICD-9-CM codes not on this list. During the medical review process contractors may accept other relevant information from the providers or suppliers that will build the appropriate case that justifies the need for ambulance transport for a patient condition not found on the list.

Because it is critical to accurately communicate the condition of the patient during the ambulance transport, most claims will contain only the ICD-9-CM code that most closely informs the Medicare contractor why the patient required the ambulance transport. This code is intended to correspond to the description of the patient's symptoms and condition once the ambulance personnel are at the patient's side. For example, if an Advanced Life Support (ALS) ambulance responds to a condition on the medical conditions list that warrants an ALS-level response and the patient's condition on-scene also corresponds to an ALS-level condition, the submitted claim need only include the code that most accurately reflects the on-scene condition of the patient as the reason for transport. (All claims are required to have HCPCS codes on them, and may have modifiers as well.) Similarly, if a Basic Life Support (BLS) ambulance responds to a condition on the medical conditions list that warrants a BLS-level response and the patient's condition on-scene also corresponds to a BLS-level condition, the submitted claim need only include the code that most accurately reflects the on-scene condition of the patient as the reason for transport.

When a request for service is received by ambulance dispatch personnel for a condition that necessitates the skilled assessment of an advanced life support paramedic based upon the medical conditions list, an ALS-level ambulance would be appropriately sent to the scene. If upon arrival of the ambulance the actual condition encountered by the crew corresponds to a BLS-level situation, this claim would require two separate condition codes from the medical condition list to be processed correctly. The first code would correspond to the "reason for transport" or the on-scene condition of the patient. Because in this example, this code corresponds to a BLS condition, a second code that corresponds to the dispatch information would be necessary for inclusion on the claim in order to support payment at the ALS level. In these cases, when MR is performed, the Medicare contractor will analyze all claim information (including both codes) and other supplemental medical documentation to support the level of service billed on the claim.

Contractors may have (or may develop) individual local policies that indicate that some codes are not appropriate for payment in some circumstances. These continue to remain in effect.

Information on appropriate use of transportation indicators:
When a claim is submitted for payment, an ICD-9-CM code from the medical conditions list that best describes the patient's condition and the medical necessity for the transport may be chosen. In addition to this code, one of the transportation indicators below may be included on the claim to indicate why it was necessary for the patient to be transported in a particular way or circumstance. The provider or supplier will place the transportation indicator in the "narrative" field on the claim.

- Air and Ground
- Transportation Indicator "C1": Transportation indicator "C1" indicates an interfacility transport (to a higher level of care) determined necessary by the originating facility based upon EMTALA regulations and guidelines. The patient's condition should also be reported on the claim with a code selected from either the emergency or non-emergency category on the list.
- Transportation Indicator "C2": Transportation indicator "C2" indicates a patient is being transported from one facility to another because a service or therapy required to treat the patient's condition is not available at the originating facility. The patient's condition should also be reported on the claim with a code selected from either the emergency or non-emergency category on the list. In addition, the information about what service the patient requires that was not available should be included in the narrative field of the claim.
- Transportation Indicator "C3": Transportation indicator "C3" may be included on claims as a secondary code where a response was made to a major incident or mechanism of injury. All such responses - regardless of the type of patient or patients found once on scene - are appropriately Advanced Level Service responses. A code that describes the patient's condition found on scene should also be included on the claim, but use of this modifier is intended to indicate that the highest level of service available response was medically justified. Some examples of these types of responses would include patient(s) trapped in machinery, explosions, a building fire with persons reported inside, major incidents involving aircraft, buses, subways, trains, watercraft and victims entrapped in vehicles.
- Transportation Indicator "C4": Transportation indicator "C4" indicates that an ambulance provided a medically necessary transport, but the number of miles on the claim form appear to be excessive. This should be used only if the facility is on divert status or a particular service is not available at the time of transport only. The provider or supplier must have documentation on file clearly showing why the beneficiary was not transported to the nearest facility and may include this information in the narrative field.
- Ground Only
- Transportation Indicator "C5": Transportation indicator "C5" has been added for situations where a patient with an ALS-level condition is encountered, treated and transported by a BLS-level ambulance with no ALS level involvement whatsoever. This situation would occur when ALS resources are not available to respond to the patient encounter for any number of reasons, but the ambulance service is informing you that although the patient transported had an ALS-level condition, the actual service rendered was through a BLS-level ambulance in a situation where an ALS-level ambulance was not available.

  For example, a BLS ambulance is dispatched at the emergency level to pick up a 76-yearold beneficiary who has undergone cataract surgery at the Eye Surgery Center. The patient is weak and dizzy with a history of high blood pressure, myocardial infarction, and insulin-dependent diabetes melitus. Therefore, the on-scene ICD-9-CM equivalent of the medical condition is 780.02 (unconscious, fainting, syncope, near syncope, weakness, or dizziness - ALS Emergency). In this case, the ICD-9-CM code 780.02 would be entered on the ambulance claim form as well as transportation indicator C5 to provide the further information that the BLS ambulance transported a patient with an ALS-level condition, but there was no intervention by an ALS service. This claim would be paid at the BLS level.

- Transportation Indicator "C6": Transportation indicator "C6" has been added for situations when an ALS-level ambulance would always be the appropriate resource chosen based upon medical dispatch protocols to respond to a request for service. If once on scene, the crew determines that the patient requiring transport has a BLS-level condition, this transportation indicator should be included on the claim to indicate why the ALS-level response was indicated based upon the information obtained in the operation's dispatch center. Claims including this transportation indicator should contain two primary codes. The first condition will indicate the BLS-level condition corresponding to the patient's condition found on-scene and during the transport. The second condition will indicate the ALS-level condition corresponding to the information at the time of dispatch that indicated the need for an ALS-level response based upon medically appropriate dispatch protocols.
- Transportation Indicator C7- Transportation indicator "C7" is for those circumstances where IV medications were required en route. C7 is appropriately used for patients requiring ALS level transport in a non-emergent situation primarily because the patient requires monitoring of ongoing medications administered intravenously. Does not apply to self-administered medications. Does not include administration of crystalloid intravenous fluids (i.e., Normal Saline, Lactate Ringers, 5% Dextrose in Water, etc.). The patient's condition should also be reported on the claim with a code selected from the list.
- Air Only
- All "transportation indicators" imply a clinical benefit to the time saved with transporting a patient by an air ambulance versus a ground or water ambulance.
- D1 Long Distance - patient's condition requires rapid transportation over a long distance.
- D2 Under rare and exceptional circumstances, traffic patterns preclude ground transport at the time the response is required.
- D3 Time to get to the closest appropriate hospital due to the patient's condition precludes transport by ground ambulance. Unstable patient with need to minimize out-of hospital time to maximize clinical benefits to the patient.
- D4 Pick up point not accessible by ground transportation.

Ambulance Fee Schedule - Medical Conditions List

(Rev. 1942; Issued: 04-02-10; Effective/Implementation Date: 05-03-10)

ICD 9 Primary Code	ICD9 Alternative Specific Code	Condition (General)	Condition (Specific)	Service Level	Comments and Examples (not all-inclusive)	HCPCS Crosswalk
Emergency Conditions - Non-Traumatic						
535.50	458.9, 780.2, 787.01, 787.02, 787.03, 789.01, 789.02, 789.03, 789.04, 789.05, 789.06, 789.07, 789.09, 789.60 through 789.69, or 789.40 through 789.49 PLUS any other code from 780 through 799 except 793, 794, and 795.	Severe abdominal pain	With other signs or symptoms	ALS	Nausea, vomiting, fainting, pulsatile mass, distention, rigid, tenderness on exam, guarding.	A0427/A0433
789.00	726.2, 789.01, 789.02, 789.03, 789.04, 789.05, 789.06, 789.07, or 789.09	Abdominal pain	Without other signs or symptoms	BLS		A0429
427.9	426.0, 426.3, 426.4, 426.6, 426.11, 426.13, 426.50, 426.53, 427.0, 427.1, 427.2, 427.31, 427.32, 427.41, 427.42, 427.5, 427.60, 427.61, 427.69, 427.81, 427.89, 785.0, 785.50, 785.51, 785.52, or 785.59.	Abnormal cardiac rhythm/Cardiac dysrythmia.	Potentially life-threatening	ALS	Bradycardia, junctional and ventricular blocks, non-sinus tachycardias, PVC's >6, bi- and trigeminy, ventricular tachycardia, ventricular fibrillation, atrial flutter, PEA, asystole, AICD/AED fired	A0427/A0433
780.8	782.5 or 782.6	Abnormal skin signs		ALS	Diaphorhesis, cyanosis, delayed cap refill, poor turgor, mottled.	A0427/A0433
796.4	458.9, 780.6, 785.9, 796.2, or 796.3 PLUS any other code from 780 through 799	Abnormal vital signs (includes abnormal pulse oximetry)	With or without symptoms.	ALS		A0427/A0433
995.0	995.1, 995.2, 995.3, 995.4, 995.60, 995.61, 995.62, 995.63, 995.64, 995.65, 995.66, 995.67, 995.68, 995.69, or 995.7	Allergic reaction	Potentially life-threatening	ALS	Other emergency conditions, rapid progression of symptoms, prior history of anaphylaxis, wheezing, difficulty swallowing.	A0427/A0433
692.9	692.0, 692.1, 692.2, 692.3, 692.4, 692.5, 692.6, 692.70, 692.71, 692.72, 692.73, 692.74, 692.75, 692.76, 692.77, 692.79, 692.81, 692.82, 692.83, 692.89, 692.9, 693.0, 693.1, 693.8, 693.9, 695.9, 698.9, 708.9, 782.1.	Allergic reaction	Other	BLS	Hives, itching, rash, slow onset, local swelling, redness, erythema.	A0429
790.21	790.22, 250.02, or 250.03.	Blood glucose	Abnormal <80 or >250, with symptoms.	ALS	Altered mental status, vomiting, signs of dehydration.	A0427/A0433
799.1	786.02, 786.03, 786.04, or 786.09.	Respiratory arrest		ALS	Apnea, hypoventilation requiring ventilatory assistance and airway management.	A0427/A0433
786.05		Difficulty breathing		ALS		A0427/A0433
427.5		Cardiac arrest – resuscitation in progress		ALS		A0427/A0433

ICD 9 Primary Code	ICD9 Alternative Specific Code	Condition (General)	Condition (Specific)	Service Level	Comments and Examples (not all-inclusive)	HCPCS Crosswalk
786.50	786.51, 786.52, or 786.59.	Chest pain (non-traumatic)		ALS	Dull, severe, crushing, substernal, epigastric, left sided chest pain associated with pain of the jaw, left arm, neck, back, and nausea, vomiting, palpitations, pallor, diaphoresis, decreased LOC.	A0427/A0433
784.99	933.0 or 933.1.	Chocking episode	Airway obstructed or partially obstructed	ALS		A0427/A0433
991.6		Cold exposure	Potentially life or limb threatening	ALS	Temperature < 95F, deep frost bite, other emergency conditions.	A0427/A0433
991.9	991.0, 991.1, 991.2, 991.3, or 991.4.	Cold exposure	With symptoms	BLS	Shivering, superficial frost bite, and other emergency conditions	A0429
780.97	780.02, 780.03, or 780.09.	Altered level of consciousness (nontraumatic)		ALS	Acute condition with Glascow Coma Scale < 15.	A0427/A0433
780.39	345.00, 345.01, 345.2, 345.3, 345.10, 345.11, 345.40, 345.41, 345.50, 345.51, 345.60, 345.61, 345.70 , 345.71, 345.80, 345.81, 345.90, 345.91, or 780.31.	Convulsions, seizures	Seizing, immediate post-seizure, postictal, or at risk of seizure and requires medical monitoring/observation.	ALS		A0427/A0433
379.90	368.11, 368.12, or 379.91	Eye symptoms, non-traumatic	Acute vision loss and/or severe pain	BLS		A0429
437.9	784.0 PLUS 781.0, 781.1, 781.2, 781.3, 781.4, or 781.8.	Non-traumatic headache	With neurologic distress conditions or sudden severe onset	ALS		A0427/A0433
785.1		Cardiac symptoms other than chest pain.	Palpitations, skipped beats	ALS		A0472/A0433
536.2	787.01, 787.02, 787.03, 780.79, 786.8, or 786.52.	Cardiac symptoms other than chest pain.	Atypical pain or other symptoms	ALS	Persistent nausea and vomiting, weakness, hiccups, pleuritic pain, feeling of impending doom, and other emergency conditions.	A0427/A0433
992.5	992.0, 992.1, 992.3, 992.4, or 992.5	Heat exposure	Potentially life-threatening	ALS	Hot and dry skin, Temp>105, neurologic distress, signs of heat stroke or heat exhaustion, orthostatic vitals, other emergency conditions.	A0427/A0433
992.2	992.6, 992.7, 992.8, or 992.9.	Heat exposure	With symptoms	BLS	Muscle cramps, profuse sweating, fatigue.	A0429
459.0	569.3, 578.0, 578.1, 578.9, 596.7, 596.8, 623.8, 626.9, 637.1, 634.1, 666.00, 666.02, 666.04, 666.10, 666.12, 666.14, 666.20, 666.22, 666.24, 674.30, 674.32, 674.34, 786.3, 784.7, or 998.11	Hemorrhage	Severe (quantity) and potentially life-threatening	ALS	Uncontrolled or significant signs of shock or other emergency conditions. Severe, active vaginal, rectal bleeding, hematemesis, hemoptysis, epistaxis, active post- surgical bleeding.	A0472/A0433
038.9	136.9, any other condition in the 001 through 139 code range which would require isolation.	Infectious diseases requiring isolation procedures / public health risk.		BLS		A0429
987.9	981, 982.0, 982.1, 982.2, 982.3, 982.4, 982.8, 983.0, 983.1, 983.2, 983.9, 984.0, 984.1, 984.8, 984.9, 985.0, 985.1, 985.2, 985.3, 985.4, 985.5, 985.6, 985.8, 985.9, 986, 987.0, 987.1, 987.2, 987.3, 987.4, 987.5, 987.6, 987.7, 987.8, 989.1, 989.2, 989.3, 989.4, 989.6, 989.7, 989.9, or 990.	Hazmat exposure		ALS	Toxic fume or liquid exposure via inhalation, absorption, oral, radiation, smoke inhalation.	A0472/A0433

ICD 9 Primary Code	ICD9 Alternative Specific Code	Condition (General)	Condition (Specific)	Service Level	Comments and Examples (not all-inclusive)	HCPCS Crosswalk
996.00	996.01, 996.02, 996.04, 996.09, 996.1, or 996.2.	Medical device failure	Life or limb threatening malfunction, failure, or complication.	ALS	Malfunction of ventilator, internal pacemaker, internal defibrillator, implanted drug delivery service.	A0427/A0433
996.30	996.31, 996.40, 996.41, 996.42, 996.43, 996.44, 996.45, 996.46, 996.47, 996.49, or 996.59.	Medical device failure	Health maintenance device failures that cannot be resolved on location.	BLS	Oxygen system supply malfunction, orthopedic device failure.	A0429
436	291.3, 293.82, 298.9, 344.9, 368.16, 369.9, 780.09, 780.4, 781.0, 781.2, 781.94, 781.99, 782.0, 784.3, 784.5, or	787.2.	Neurologic distress	Facial drooping; loss of vision; aphasia; difficulty swallowing; numbness, tingling extremity; stupor, delirium, confusion, hallucinations; paralysis, paresis (focal weakness); abnormal movements; vertigo; unsteady gait/ balance; slurred speech, unable to speak	ALS	A0427/A0433
780.96		Pain, severe not otherwise specified in this list.	Acute onset, unable to ambulate or sit due to intensity of pain.	ALS	Pain is the reason for the transport. Use severity scale (7-10 for severe pain) or patient receiving pharmalogic intervention.	A0427/A0433
724.5	724.2 or 785.9	Back pain – non-traumatic (T and/or LS).	Suspect cardiac or vascular etiology	ALS	Other emergency conditions, absence of or decreased leg pulses, pulsatile abdominal mass, severe tearing abdominal pain.	A0427/A0433
724.9	724.2, 724.5, 847.1, or 847.2.	Back pain – non-traumatic (T and/or LS).	Sudden onset of new neurologic symptoms.	ALS	Neurologic distress list.	A0427/A0433
977.9	Any code from 960 through 979.	Poisons, ingested, injected, inhaled, absorbed.	Adverse drug reaction, poison exposure by inhalation, injection, or absorption.	ALS		A0427/A0433
305.0	303.00, 303.01, 303.02, 303.03, or any code from 960 through 979.	Alcohol intoxication or drug overdose (suspected).	Unable to care for self and unable to ambulate. No airway compromise.	BLS		A0429
977.3		Severe alcohol intoxication.	Airway may or may not be at risk. Pharmacological intervention or cardiac monitoring may be needed. Decreased level of consciousness resulting or potentially resulting in airway compromise.	ALS		A0427/A0433
998.9	674.10, 674.12, 674.14, 674.20, 674.22, 674.24, 997.69, 998.31, 998.32, or 998.83.	Post-operative procedure complications.	Major wound dehiscence, evisceration, or requires special handling for transport.	BLS	Non-life threatening	A0429
650	Any code from 630 through 679.	Pregnancy complication/childbirth /labor		ALS		A0427/A0433
292.9	291.0, 291.3, 291.81, 292.0, 292.81, 292.82, 292.83, 292.84, or 292.89.	Psychiatric/Behavioral	Abnormal mental status; drug withdrawal.	ALS	Disoriented, DTs, withdrawal symptoms.	A0427/A0433
298.9	300.9	Psychiatric/Behavioral	Threat to self or others, acute episode or exacerbation of paranoia, or disruptive behavior.	BLS	Suicidal, homicidal, or violent.	A0429
036.9	780.6 PLUS either 784.0 or 723.5.	Sick person – fever	Fever with associated symptoms (headache, stiff neck, etc.). Neurological changes.	BLS	Suspected spinal meningitis.	A0429

ICD 9 Primary Code	ICD9 Alternative Specific Code	Condition (General)	Condition (Specific)	Service Level	Comments and Examples (not all-inclusive)	HCPCS Crosswalk
787.01	787.02, 787.03, or 787.91.	Severe dehydration	Nausea and vomiting, diarrhea, severe and incapacitating resulting in severe side effects of dehydration.	ALS		A0427/A0433
780.02	780.2 or 780.4	Unconscious, fainting, syncope, near syncope, weakness, or dizziness.	Transient unconscious episode or found unconscious. Acute episode or exacerbation.	ALS		A0427/A0433
Emergency Conditions - Trauma						
959.8	800.00 through 804.99, 807.4, 807.6, 808.8, 808.9, 812.00 through 812.59, 813.00 through 813.93, 813.93, 820.00 through 821.39, 823.00 through 823.92, 851.00 through 866.13, 870.0 through 879.9, 880.00 through 887.7, or 890.0 through 897.7.	Major trauma	As defined by ACS Field Triage Decision Scheme. Trauma with one of the following: Glascow <14; systolic BP<90; RR<10 or >29; all penetrating injuries to head, neck, torso, extremities proximal to elbow or knee; flail chest; combination of trauma and burns; pelvic fracture; 2 or more long bone fractures; open or depressed skull fracture; paralysis; severe mechanism of injury including: ejection, death of another passenger in same patient compartment, falls >20", 20" deformity in vehicle or 12" deformity of patient compartment, auto pedestrian/bike, pedestrian thrown/run over, motorcycle accident at speeds >20 mph and rider separated from vehicle.	ALS	See "Condition (Specific)" column	A0427/A0433
518.5		Other trauma	Need to monitor or maintain airway	ALS	Decreased LOC, bleeding into airway, trauma to head, face or neck.	A0427/A0433
958.2	870.0 through 879.9, 880.00 through 887.7, 890.0 through 897.7, or 900.00 through 904.9.	Other trauma	Major bleeding	ALS	Uncontrolled or significant bleeding.	A0427/A0433
829.0	805.00, 810.00 through 819.1, or 820.00 through 829.1.	Other trauma	Suspected fracture/dislocation requiring splinting/immobilization for transport.	BLS	Spinal, long bones, and joints including shoulder elbow, wrist, hip, knee and ankle, deformity of bone or joint.	A0429
880.00	880.00 through 887.7 or 890.0 through 897.7	Other trauma	Penetrating extremity injuries	BLS	Isolated bleeding stopped and good CSM.	A0429
886.0 or 895.0	886.1 or 895.1	Other trauma	Amputation – digits	BLS		A0429
887.4 or 897.4	887.0, 887.1, 887.2, 887.3, 887.6, 887.7, 897.0, 897.1, 897.2, 897.3, 897.5, 897.6, or 897.7.	Other trauma	Amputation – all other	ALS		A0427/A0433
869.0 or 869.1	511.8, 512.8, 860.2, 860.3, 860.4, 860.5, 873.8, 873.9, or 959.01.	Other trauma	Suspected internal, head, chest, or abdominal injuries.	ALS	Signs of closed head injury, open head injury, pneumothorax, hemothorax, abdominal bruising, positive abdominal signs on exam, internal bleeding criteria, evisceration.	A0427/A0433

ICD 9 Primary Code	ICD9 Alternative Specific Code	Condition (General)	Condition (Specific)	Service Level	Comments and Examples (not all-inclusive)	HCPCS Crosswalk
949.3	941.30 through 941.39, 942.30 through 942.39, 943.30 through 943.39, 944.30 through 944.38, 945.30 through 945.39, or 949.3.	Burns	Major – per American Burn Association (ABA)	ALS	Partial thickness burns > 10% total body surface area (TBSA); involvement of face, hands, feet, genitalia, perineum, or major joints; third degree burns; electrical; chemical; inhalation; burns with preexisting medical disorders; burns and trauma	A0472/A0433
949.2	941.20 through 941.29, 942.20 through 942.29, 943.20 through 943.29, 944.20 through 944.28, 945.20 through 945.29, or 949.2.	Burns	Minor – per ABA	BLS	Other burns than listed above.	A0429
989.5		Animal bites, stings, envenomation.	Potentially life or limb-threatening.	ALS	Symptoms of specific envenomation, significant face, neck, trunk, and extremity involvement; other emergency conditions.	A0427/A0433
879.8	Any code from 870.0 through 897.7.	Animal bites/sting/envonmation.	Other	BLS	Local pain and swelling or special handling considerations (not related to obesity) and patient monitoring required.	A0429
994.0		Lightning		ALS		A0427/A0433
994.8		Electrocution		ALS		A0427/A0433
994.1		Near drowning	Airway compromised during near drowning event	ALS		A0427/A0433
921.9	870.0 through 870.9, 871.0, 871.1, 871.2, 871.3, 871.4, 871.5, 871.6, 871.7, 871.9, or 921.0 through 921.9.	Eye injuries	Acute vision loss or blurring, severe pain or chemical exposure, penetrating, severe lid lacerations.	BLS		A0429
995.83	995.53 or V71.5 PLUS any code from 925.1 through 929.9, 930.0 through 939.9, 958.0 through 958.8, or 959.01 through 959.9.	Sexual assault	With major injuries	ALS	Reference codes 959.8, 958.2, 869.0/869.1	A0427/A0433
995.80	995.53 or V71.5 PLUS any code from 910.0 through 919.9, 920 through 924.9, or 959.01 through 959.9.	Sexual assault	With minor or no injuries	BLS		
Non-Emergency						
428.9		Cardiac/hemodynamic monitoring required en route.		ALS	Expectation monitoring is needed before and after transport.	A0426
518.81 or 518.89	V46.11 or V46.12.	Advanced airway management		ALS	Ventilator dependent, apnea monitor, possible intubation needed, deep suctioning.	A0426, A0434
293.0		Chemical restraint.		ALS		A0426
496	491.20, 491.21, 492.0 through 492.8, 493.20, 493.21, 493.22, 494.0, or 494.1.	Suctioning required en route, need for titrated O2 therapy or IV fluid management.		BLS	Per transfer instructions.	A0428
786.09		Airway control/positioning required en route.		BLS	Per transfer instructions.	A0428
492.8	491.20, 491.21, 492.0 through 492.8, 493.20, 493.21, 493.22, 494.0, or 494.1.	Third party assistance/attendant required to apply, administer, or regulate or adjust oxygen en route.		BLS	Does not apply to patient capable of self-administration of portable or home O2. Patient must require oxygen therapy and be so frail as to require assistance.	A0428

ICD 9 Primary Code	ICD9 Alternative Specific Code	Condition (General)	Condition (Specific)	Service Level	Comments and Examples (not all-inclusive)	HCPCS Crosswalk
298.9	Add 295.0 through 295.9 with 5th digits of 0, 1, 3, or 4, 296.00 or 299.90.	Patient safety: Danger to self or others – in restraints.		BLS	Refer to definition in 42 CFR Section 482.13(e).	A0428
293.1		Patient safety: Danger to self or others – monitoring.		BLS	Behavioral or cognitive risk such that patient requires monitoring for safety.	A0428
298.8	Add 295.0 through 295.9 with 5th digits of 0, 1, 3, or 4, 296.00 or 299.90	Patient safety: Danger to self or others – seclusion (flight risk).		BLS	Behavioral or cognitive risk such that patient requires attendant to assure patient does not try to exit the ambulance prematurely. Refer to 42 CFR Section 482.13(f) for definition.	A0428
781.3	Add 295.0 through 295.9 with 5th digits of 0, 1, 3, or 4, 296.00 or 299.90.	Patient safety: Risk of falling off wheelchair or stretcher while in motion (not related to obesity).		BLS	Patient's physical condition is such that patient risks injury during vehicle movement despite restraints. Indirect indicators include MDS criteria.	A0428
041.9		Special handling en route – isolation.		BLS	Includes patients with communicable diseases or hazardous material exposure who must be isolated from public or whose medical condition must be protected from public exposure; surgical drainage complications.	A0428
907.2		Special handling en route to reduce pain – orthopedic device.		BLS	Backboard, halotraction, use of pins and traction etc. Pain may be present.	A0428
719.45 or 719.49	718.40, 718.45, 718.49, or 907.2.	Special handling en route – positioning requires specialized handling.		BLS	Requires special handling to avoid further injury (such as with > grade 2 decubiti on buttocks). Generally does not apply to shorter transfers of < 1 hour. Positioning in wheelchair or standard car seat inappropriate due to contractures or recent extremity fractures – post-op hip as an example.	A0428

Transportation Indicators Air/Ground	Transportation Category	Transportation Indicator Description		Service Level	Comments and Examples (not all-inclusive)	HCPCS Crosswalk
Transportation Indicators						
C1	Inter-facility Transport	EMTALA-certified inter-facility transfer to a higher level of care.	Beneficiary requires higher level of care.	BLS, ALS, SCT, FW, RW	Excludes patient-requested EMTALA transfer.	A0428, A0429, A0426, A0427, A0433, A0434
C2	Inter-facility transport	Service not available at originating facility, and must meet one or more emergency or non-emergency conditions.		BLS, ALS, SCT, FW,RW		A0428, A0429, A0426, A0427, A0433, A0434
C3	Emergency Trauma Dispatch Condition Code	Major incident or mechanism of injury	Major Incident-This transportation indicator is to be used ONLY as a secondary code when the on-scene encounter is a BLS-level patient.	ALS	Trapped in machinery, close proximity to explosion, building fire with persons reported inside, major incident involving aircraft, bus, subway, metro, train and watercraft. Victim entrapped in vehicle.	A0427/A0433

Transportation Indicators Air/Ground	Transportation Category	Transportation Indicator Description		Service Level	Comments and Examples (not all-inclusive)	HCPCS Crosswalk
C4	Medically necessary transport but not to the nearest facility.	BLS or ALS response	Indicates to Carrier/Intermediary that an ambulance provided a medically necessary transport, but that the number of miles on the Medicare claim form may be excessive.	BLS/ALS	This should occur if the facility is on divert status or the particular service is not available at the time of transport only. In these instances the ambulance units should clearly document why the beneficiary was not transported to the nearest facility.	Based on transport level.
C5	BLS transport of ALS-level patient	ALS-level condition treated and transport by a BLS-level ambulance.	This transportation indicator is used for ALL situations where a BLS-level ambulance treats and transports a patient that presents an ALS-level condition. No ALS-level assessment or intervention occurs at all during the patient encounter.	BLS		A0429
C6	ALS-level response to BLS-level patient	ALS response required based upon appropriate dispatch protocols – BLS-level patient transport	Indicates to Carrier/Intermediary that an ALS-level ambulance responded appropriately based upon the information received at the time the call was received in dispatch and after a clinically appropriate ALS-assessment was performed on scene, it was determined that the condition of the patient was at a BLS level. These claims, properly documented, should be reimbursed at an ALS-1 level based upon coverage guidelines under the Medicare Ambulance Fee Schedule.	ALS		A0427
C7		IV meds required en route.	This transportation indicator is used for patients that require an ALS level transport in a non- emergent situation primarily because the patient requires monitoring of ongoing medications administered intravenously. Does not apply to self-administered medications. Does not include administration of crystalloid intravenous fluids (i.e., Normal Saline, Lactate Ringers, 5% Dextrose in Water, etc.). The patient's condition should also be reported on the claim with a code selected from the list	ALS	Does not apply to self-administered IV medications.	A0426

Air Ambulance Transportation Indicators	Transportation Indicator Description	Service Level	Comments and Examples (not all-inclusive)	HCPCS Crosswalk
Air Ambulance Transportation Indicators				
D1	Long Distance-patient's condition requires rapid transportation over a long distance	FW, RW	If the patient's condition warrants only.	A0430, A0431
D2	Under rare and exceptional circumstances, traffic patterns preclude ground transport at the time the response is required.	FW, RW	A0430, A0431	
D3	FW, RW	A0430, A0431		
D4	FW, RW	A0430, A0431		

Note: HCPCS Crosswalk to ALS1E (A0427) and ALS2 (A0433) would ultimately be determined by the number and type of ALS level services provided during transport. All medical condition codes can be cross walked to fixed wing and rotor wing HCPCS provided the air ambulance service has documented the medical necessity for air ambulance service versus ground or water ambulance. As a result, codes A0430 (Fixed Wing) and A0431 (Rotor Wing) can be included in Column 7 for each condition listed.

100-4, 16, 10

Background

B3-2070, B3-2070.1, B3-4110.3, B3-5114

Diagnostic X-ray, laboratory, and other diagnostic tests, including materials and the services of technicians, are covered under the Medicare program. Some clinical laboratory procedures or tests require Food and Drug Administration (FDA) approval before coverage is provided.

A diagnostic laboratory test is considered a laboratory service for billing purposes, regardless of whether it is performed in:

- A physician's office, by an independent laboratory;
- By a hospital laboratory for its outpatients or nonpatients;
- In a rural health clinic; or
- In an HMO or Health Care Prepayment Plan (HCPP) for a patient who is not a member.

When a hospital laboratory performs laboratory tests for nonhospital patients, the laboratory is functioning as an independent laboratory, and still bills the fiscal intermediary (FI). Also, when physicians and laboratories perform the same test, whether manually or with automated equipment, the services are deemed similar. Laboratory services furnished by an independent laboratory are covered under SMI if the laboratory is an approved Independent Clinical Laboratory. However, as is the case of all diagnostic services, in order to be covered these services must be related to a patient's illness or injury (or symptom or complaint) and ordered by a physician. A small number of laboratory tests can be covered as a preventive screening service.

See the Medicare Benefit Policy Manual, Chapter 15, for detailed coverage requirements.

See the Medicare Program Integrity Manual, Chapter 10, for laboratory/supplier enrollment guidelines.

See the Medicare State Operations Manual for laboratory/supplier certification requirements.

100-4, 16, 60.2

Travel Allowance

In addition to a specimen collection fee allowed under Sec.60.1, Medicare, under Part B, covers a specimen collection fee and travel allowance for a laboratory technician to draw a specimen from either a nursing home patient or homebound patient under Sec.1833(h)(3) of the Act and payment is made based on the clinical laboratory fee schedule. The travel allowance is intended to cover the estimated travel costs of collecting a specimen and to reflect the technician's salary and travel costs.

The additional allowance can be made only where a specimen collection fee is also payable, i.e., no travel allowance is made where the technician merely performs a messenger service to pick up a specimen drawn by a physician or nursing home personnel. The travel allowance may not be paid to a physician unless the trip to the home, or to the nursing home was solely for the purpose of drawing a specimen. Otherwise travel costs are considered to be associated with the other purposes of the trip. The travel allowance is not distributed by CMS. Instead, the carrier must calculate the travel allowance for each claim using the following rules for the particular Code. The following HCPCS codes are used for travel allowances:

- Per Mile Travel Allowance (P9603)
- The minimum "per mile travel allowance" is $1.035. The per mile travel allowance is to be used in situations where the average trip to patients' homes is longer than 20 miles round trip, and is to be pro-rated in situations where specimens are drawn or picked up from non-Medicare patients in the same trip. - one way, in connection with medically necessary laboratory specimen collection drawn from homebound or nursing home bound patient; prorated miles actually traveled (carrier allowance on per mile basis); or
- The per mile allowance was computed using the Federal mileage rate plus an additional 45 cents a mile to cover the technician's time and travel costs. Contractors have the option of establishing a higher per mile rate in excess of the minimum (1.035 cents a mile in CY 2008) if local conditions warrant it. The minimum mileage rate will be reviewed and updated in conjunction with the clinical lab fee schedule as needed. At no time will the laboratory be allowed to bill for more miles than are reasonable or for miles not actually traveled by the laboratory technician.

Example 1: In CY 2008, a laboratory technician travels 60 miles round trip from a lab in a city to a remote rural location, and back to the lab to draw a single Medicare patient's blood. The total reimbursement would be $62.10 (60 miles x 1.035 cents a mile), plus the specimen collection fee.

Example 2: In CY 2008, a laboratory technician travels 40 miles from the lab to a

Medicare patient's home to draw blood, and then travels an additional 10 miles to a non-Medicare patient's home and then travels 30 miles to return to the lab. The total miles traveled would be 80 miles. The claim submitted would be for one half of the miles traveled or $41.40 (40 x 1.035), plus the specimen collection fee.

Flat Rate (P9604)

The CMS will pay a minimum of $9.55 one way flat rate travel allowance. The flat rate travel allowance is to be used in areas where average trips are less than 20 miles round trip. The flat rate travel fee is to be pro-rated for more than one blood drawn at the same address, and for stops at the homes of Medicare and non-Medicare patients. The laboratory does the pro-ration when the claim is submitted based on the number of patients seen on that trip. The specimen collection fee will be paid for each patient encounter.

This rate is based on an assumption that a trip is an average of 15 minutes and up to 10 miles one way. It uses the Federal mileage rate and a laboratory technician's time of $17.66 an hour, including overhead. Contractors have the option of establishing a flat rate in excess of the minimum of $9.55, if local conditions warrant it. The minimum national flat rate will be reviewed and updated in conjunction with the clinical laboratory fee schedule, as necessitated by adjustments in the Federal travel allowance and salaries.

The claimant identifies round trip travel by use of the LR modifier

Example 3: A laboratory technician travels from the laboratory to a single Medicare patient's home and returns to the laboratory without making any other stops. The flat rate would be calculated as follows: 2 x $9.55 for a total trip reimbursement of $19.10, plus the specimen collection fee.

Example 4: A laboratory technician travels from the laboratory to the homes of five patients to draw blood, four of the patients are Medicare patients and one is not. An additional flat rate would be charged to cover the 5 stops and the return trip to the lab (6 x $9.55 = $57.30). Each of the claims submitted would be for $11.46 ($57.30 /5 = $11.46). Since one of the patients is non-Medicare, four claims would be submitted for $11.46 each, plus the specimen collection fee for each.

Example 5: A laboratory technician travels from a laboratory to a nursing home and draws blood from 5 patients and returns to the laboratory. Four of the patients are on Medicare and one is not. The $9.55 flat rate is multiplied by two to cover the return trip to the laboratory (2 x $9.55 = $19.10) and then divided by five (1/5 of $19.10 = $3.82).

Since one of the patients is non-Medicare, four claims would be submitted for $3.82 each, plus the specimen collection fee.

If a carrier determines that it results in equitable payment, the carrier may extend the former payment allowances for additional travel (such as to a distant rural nursing home) to all circumstances where travel is required. This might be appropriate, for example, if the carrier's former payment allowance was on a per mile basis. Otherwise, it should establish an appropriate allowance and inform the suppliers in its service area. If a carrier decides to establish a new allowance, one method is to consider developing a travel allowance consisting of:

- The current Federal mileage allowance for operating personal automobiles, plus a personnel allowance per mile to cover personnel costs based upon an estimate of average hourly wages and average driving speed.

Carriers must prorate travel allowance amounts claimed by suppliers by the number of patients (including Medicare and non-Medicare patients) from whom specimens were drawn on a given trip.

The carrier may determine that payment in addition to the routine travel allowance determined under this section is appropriate if:

- The patient from whom the specimen must be collected is in a nursing home or is homebound; and
- The clinical laboratory tests are needed on an emergency basis outside the general business hours of the laboratory making the collection.

Subsequent updated travel allowance amounts will be issued by CMS via Recurring Update Notification (RUN) on an annual basis.

100-4, 16, 70.8

Certificate of Waiver

Effective September 1, 1992, all laboratory testing sites (except as provided in 42 CFR 493.3(b)) must have either a CLIA certificate of waiver, certificate for provider-performed microscopy procedures, certificate of registration, certificate of compliance, or certificate of accreditation to legally perform clinical laboratory testing on specimens from individuals in the United States.

The Food and Drug Administration approves CLIA waived tests on a flow basis. The CMS identifies CLIA waived tests by providing an updated list of waived tests to the Medicare contractors on a quarterly basis via a Recurring Update Notification. To be recognized as a waived test, some CLIA waived tests have unique HCPCS procedure codes and some must have a QW modifier included with the HCPCS code.

For a list of specific HCPCS codes subject to CLIA see http://www.cms.hhs.gov/CLIA/downloads/waivetbl.pdf

100-4, 17, 80.4.1

Clotting Factor Furnishing Fee

Beginning January 1, 2005, a clotting factor furnishing fee is separately payable to entities that furnish clotting factor unless the costs associated with furnishing the clotting factor is paid through another payment system.

The clotting factor furnishing fee is updated each calendar year based on the percentage increase in the consumer price index (CPI) for medical care for the 12-month period ending with June of the previous year. The clotting factor furnishing fees applicable for dates of service in each calendar year (CY) are listed below:

CY 2005 - $0.140 per I.U.

CY 2006 - $0.146 per I.U.

CY 2007 - $0.152 per I.U.

CY 2008 - $0.158 per I.U.

CY 2009 - $0.164 per I.U.

CY 2010 - $0.170 per I.U.

CY 2011 - $0.176 per unit

Annual updates to the clotting factor furnishing fee are subsequently communicated by a Recurring Update Notification.

CMS includes this clotting factor furnishing fee in the nationally published payment limit for clotting factor billing codes. When the clotting factor is not included on the Average Sales Price (ASP) Medicare Part B Drug Pricing File or Not Otherwise Classified (NOC) Pricing File, the contractor must make payment for the clotting factor as well as make payment for the furnishing fee.

100-4, 17, 90.3

Hospital Outpatient Payment Under OPPS for New, Unclassified Drugs and Biologicals After FDA Approval But Before Assignment of a Product-Specific Drug or Biological HCPCS Code

Section 621(a) of the MMA amends Section 1833(t) of the Social Security Act by adding paragraph (15), Payment for New Drugs and Biologicals Until HCPCS Code Assigned. Under this provision, payment for an outpatient drug or biological that is furnished as part of covered outpatient department services for which a product-specific HCPCS code has not been assigned shall be paid an amount equal to 95 percent of average wholesale price (AWP). This provision applies only to payments under the hospital outpatient prospective payment system (OPPS).

Beginning January 1, 2004, hospital outpatient departments may bill for new drugs and biologicals that are approved by the FDA on or after January 1, 2004, for which a product-specific HCPCS code has not been assigned. Beginning on or after the date of FDA approval, hospitals may bill for the drug or biological using HCPCS code C9399, Unclassified drug or biological.

Hospitals report in the ANSI ASC X-12 837 I in specific locations, or in the "Remarks" section of the CMS 1450):

1. the National Drug Code (NDC),
2. the quantity of the drug that was administered, expressed in the unit of measure applicable to the drug or biological, and
3. the date the drug was furnished to the beneficiary. Contractors shall manually price the drug or biological at 95 percent of AWP. They shall pay hospitals 80 percent of the calculated price and shall bill beneficiaries 20 percent of the calculated price, after the deductible is met. Drugs and biologicals that are manually priced at 95 percent of AWP are not eligible for outlier payment.

HCPCS code C9399 is only to be reported for new drugs and biologicals that are approved by FDA on or after January 1, 2004, for which there is no HCPCS code that describes the drug.

100-4, 18, 10.2.1

Healthcare Common Procedure Coding System (HCPCS) and Diagnosis Codes

Vaccines and their administration are reported using separate codes. The following codes are for reporting the vaccines only.

90655 Influenza virus vaccine, split virus, preservative free, for children 6-35 months of age, for intramuscular use;

90656 Influenza virus vaccine, split virus, preservative free, for use in individuals 3 years and above, for intramuscular use;

90657 Influenza virus vaccine, split virus, for children 6-35 months of age, for intramuscular use;

90658 Influenza virus vaccine, split virus, for use in individuals 3 years of age and above, for intramuscular use;

90660 Influenza virus vaccine, live, for intranasal use;

90662 Influenza virus vaccine, split virus, preservative free, enhanced immunogenicity via increased antigen content, for intramuscular use

90669 Pneumococcal conjugate vaccine, polyvalent, for children under 5 years, for intramuscular use

90670 Pneumococcal conjugate vaccine, 13 valent, for intramuscular use

90732 Pneumococcal polysaccharide vaccine, 23-valent, adult or immunosuppressed patient dosage, for use in individuals 2 years or older, for subcutaneous or intramuscular use;

90740 Hepatitis B vaccine, dialysis or immunosuppressed patient dosage (3 dose schedule), for intramuscular use;

90743 Hepatitis B vaccine, adolescent (2 dose schedule), for intramuscular use;

90744 Hepatitis B vaccine, pediatric/adolescent dosage (3 dose schedule), for intramuscular use;

90746 Hepatitis B vaccine, adult dosage, for intramuscular use; and

90747 Hepatitis B vaccine, dialysis or immunosuppressed patient dosage (4 dose schedule), for intramuscular use.

The following codes are for reporting administration of the vaccines only. The administration of the vaccines is billed using:

G0008 Administration of influenza virus vaccine;

G0009 Administration of pneumococcal vaccine; and

*G0010 Administration of hepatitis B vaccine.

*90471 Immunization administration. (For OPPS hospitals billing for the hepatitis B vaccine administration)

*90472 Each additional vaccine. (For OPPS hospitals billing for the hepatitis B vaccine administration)

* NOTE: For claims with dates of service prior to January 1, 2006, OPPS and non-OPPS hospitals report G0010 for hepatitis B vaccine administration. For claims with dates of service January 1, 2006 and later, OPPS hospitals report 90471 or 90472 for hepatitis B vaccine administration as appropriate in place of G0010.

One of the following diagnosis codes must be reported as appropriate. If the sole purpose for the visit is to receive a vaccine or if a vaccine is the only service billed on a claim the applicable following diagnosis code may be used.

Diagnosis Code	Description
V03.82	Pneumococcus
V04.81**	Influenza
V06.6***	Pneumococcus and Influenza
V05.3	Hepatitis B

** Effective for influenza virus claims with dates of service October 1, 2003 and later.

*** Effective October 1, 2006, providers may report diagnosis code V06.6 on claims for pneumococcus and/or influenza virus vaccines when the purpose of the visit was to receive both vaccines.

If a diagnosis code for pneumococcus, hepatitis B, or influenza virus vaccination is not reported on a claim, contractors may not enter the diagnosis on the claim. Contractors must follow current resolution processes for claims with missing diagnosis codes.

If the diagnosis code and the narrative description are correct, but the HCPCS code is incorrect, the carrier or intermediary may correct the HCPCS code and pay the claim. For example, if the reported diagnosis code is V04.81 and the narrative description (if annotated on the claim) says "flu shot" but the HCPCS code is incorrect, contractors may change the HCPCS code and pay for the flu vaccine. Effective October 1, 2006, carriers/AB MACs should follow the instructions in Pub. 100-04, Chapter 1, Section 80.3.2.1.1 (Carrier Data Element Requirements) for claims submitted without a HCPCS code.

Claims for hepatitis B vaccinations must report the I.D. Number of the referring physician. In addition, if a doctor of medicine or osteopathy does not order the influenza virus vaccine, the intermediary claims require:

- UPIN code SLF000 to be reported on claims submitted prior to May 23, 2008, when Medicare began accepting NPIs, only
- The provider's own NPI to be reported in the NPI field for the attending physician on claims submitted on or after May 23, 2008, when NPI requirements were implemented.

100-4, 18, 10.2.2.1

FI Payment for Pneumococcal Pneumonia Virus, InfluenzaVirus, and Hepatitis B Virus Vaccines and Their Administration

Payment for Vaccines

Payment for all of these vaccines is on a reasonable cost basis for hospitals, home health agencies (HHAs), skilled nursing facilities (SNFs), critical access hospitals (CAHs), and hospital-based renal dialysis facilities (RDFs). Payment for comprehensive outpatient rehabilitation facilities (CORFs), Indian Health Service hospitals (IHS), IHS CAHs and independent RDFs is based on 95 percent of the average wholesale price (AWP). Section 10.2.4 of this chapter contains information on payment of these vaccines when provided by RDFs or hospices. See Sec.10.2.2.2 for payment to independent and provider- based Rural Health Centers and Federally Qualified Health Clinics.

Payment for these vaccines is as follows:

Facility	Type of Bill	Payment
Hospitals, other than Indian Health Service (IHS) Hospitals and Critical Access Hospitals (CAHs)	12x, 13x	Reasonable cost
IHS Hospitals	12x, 13x, 83x	95% of AWP
IHS CAHs	85x	95% of AWP
CAHs	85x	Reasonable cost
Method I and Method II		
Skilled Nursing Facilities	22x, 23x	Reasonable cost
Home Health Agencies	34x	Reasonable cost
Comprehensive Outpatient Rehabilitation Facilities	75x	95% of the AWP
Independent Renal Dialysis Facilities	72x	95% of the AWP
Hospital-based Renal Dialysis Facilities	72x	Reasonable cost

Payment for Vaccine Administration

Payment for the administration of Influenza Virus and PPV vaccines is as follows:

Facility	Type of Bill	Payment
Hospitals, other than IHS Hospitals and CAHs	12x, 13x	Outpatient Prospective Payment System (OPPS) for hospitals subject to OPPS Reasonable cost for hospitals not subject to OPPS
IHS Hospitals	12x, 13x, 83x	MPFS as indicated in guidelines below.
IHS CAHs	85x	MPFS as indicated in guidelines below.
CAHs	85x	Reasonable cost
Method I and II		
Skilled Nursing Facilities	22x, 23x	MPFS as indicated in the guidelines below
Home Health Agencies	34x	OPPS
Comprehensive Outpatient Rehabilitation Facilities	75x	MPFS as indicated in the guidelines below
Independent RDFs	72x	MPFS as indicated in the guidelines below
Hospital-based RDFs	72x	Reasonable cost

Guidelines for pricing PPV and Influenza vaccine administration under the MPFS.

Make reimbursement based on the rate in the MPFS associated with the CPT code 90782 or 90471 as follows:

HCPCS code	Effective prior to March 1, 2003	Effective on and after March 1, 2003
G0008	90782	90471
G0009	90782	90471

See Sec.10.2.2.2 for payment to independent and provider based Rural Health Centers and Federally Qualified Health Clinics.

Payment for the administration of Hepatitis B vaccine is as follows:

Facility	Type of Bill	Payment
Hospitals other than IHS hospitals and CAHs	12x, 13x	Outpatient Prospective Payment System (OPPS) for hospitals subject to OPPS Reasonable cost for hospitals not subject to OPPS
IHS Hospitals	12x, 13x, 83x	MPFS as indicated in the guidelines below
CAHs Method I and II	85x	Reasonable cost
IHS CAHs	85x	MPFS as indicated in guidelines below.
Skilled Nursing Facilities	22x, 23x	MPFS as indicated in the chart below
Home Health Agencies	34x	OPPS
Comprehensive Outpatient Rehabilitation Facilities	75x	MPFS as indicated in the guidelines below
Independent RDFs	72x	MPFS as indicated in the chart below
Hospital-based RDFs	72x	Reasonable cost

Guidelines for pricing Hepatitis B vaccine administration under the MPFS.

Make reimbursement based on the rate in the MPFS associated with the CPT code 90782 or 90471 as follows:

HCPCS code	Effective prior to March 1, 2003	Effective on and after March 1, 2003
G0010	90782	90471

See Sec.10.2.2.2 for payment to independent and provider based Rural Health Centers and Federally Qualified Health Clinics.

100-4, 18, 10.2.2.1

FI/AB MAC Payment for Pneumococcal Pneumonia Virus, Influenza Virus, and Hepatitis B Virus Vaccines and Their Administration

Payment for Vaccines

Payment for all of these vaccines is on a reasonable cost basis for hospitals, home health agencies (HHAs), skilled nursing facilities (SNFs), critical access hospitals (CAHs), and hospital-based renal dialysis facilities (RDFs). Payment for comprehensive outpatient rehabilitation facilities (CORFs), Indian Health Service hospitals (IHS), IHS CAHs and independent RDFs is based on 95 percent of the average wholesale price (AWP). Section 10.2.4 of this chapter contains information on payment of these vaccines when provided by RDFs or hospices. See Sec.10.2.2.2 for payment to independent and provider- based Rural Health Centers and Federally Qualified Health Clinics.

Payment for these vaccines is as follows:

Facility	Type of Bill	Payment
Hospitals, other than Indian Health Service (IHS) Hospitals and Critical Access Hospitals (CAHs)	12x, 13x	Reasonable cost
IHS Hospitals	12x, 13x, 83x	95% of AWP
IHS CAHs	85x	95% of AWP
CAHs Method I and Method II	85x	Reasonable cost
Skilled Nursing Facilities	22x, 23x	Reasonable cost
Home Health Agencies	34x	Reasonable cost
Comprehensive Outpatient Rehabilitation Facilities	75x	95% of the AWP
Independent Renal Dialysis Facilities	72x	95% of the AWP
Hospital-based Renal Dialysis	72x	Reasonable cost

Facilities

Payment for Vaccine Administration

Payment for the administration of influenza virus and pneumococcal vaccines is as follows:

Facility	Type of Bill	Payment
Hospitals, other than IHS Hospitals and CAHs	12x, 13x	Outpatient Prospective Payment System (OPPS) for hospitals subject to OPPS
Reasonable cost for hospitals not subject to OPPS IHS Hospitals	12x, 13x, 83x	MPFS as indicated in guidelines below.
IHS CAHs	85x	MPFS as indicated in guidelines below.
CAHs Method I and II	85x	Reasonable cost
Skilled Nursing Facilities	22x, 23x	MPFS as indicated in the guidelines below
Home Health Agencies	34x	OPPS
Comprehensive Outpatient Rehabilitation Facilities	75x	MPFS as indicated in the guidelines below
Independent RDFs	72x	MPFS as indicated in the guidelines below
Hospital-based RDFs	72x	Reasonable cost

Guidelines for pricing pneumococcal and influenza virus vaccine administration under the MPFS.

Make reimbursement based on the rate in the MPFS associated with the CPT code 90782 or 90471 as follows:

HCPCS code	Effective prior to March 1, 2003	Effective on and after March 1, 2003
G0008	90782	90471
G0009	90782	90471

See Sec.10.2.2.2 for payment to independent and provider based Rural Health Centers and Federally Qualified Health Clinics.

Payment for the administration of hepatitis B vaccine is as follows:

Facility	Type of Bill	Payment
Hospitals other than IHS hospitals and CAHs	12x, 13x	Outpatient Prospective Payment System (OPPS) for hospitals subject to OPPS
Reasonable cost for hospitals not subject to OPPS IHS Hospitals	12x, 13x, 83x	MPFS as indicated in the guidelines below
CAHs Method I and II	85x	Reasonable cost
IHS CAHs	85x	MPFS as indicated in guidelines below.
Skilled Nursing Facilities	22x, 23x	MPFS as indicated in the chart below
Home Health Agencies	34x	OPPS
Comprehensive Outpatient Rehabilitation Facilities	75x	MPFS as indicated in the guidelines below
Independent RDFs	72x	MPFS as indicated in the chart below
Hospital-based RDFs	72x	Reasonable cost

Guidelines for pricing hepatitis B vaccine administration under the MPFS.

Make reimbursement based on the rate in the MPFS associated with the CPT code 90782 or 90471 as follows:

HCPCS code	Effective prior to March 1, 2003	Effective on and after March 1, 2003
G0010	90782	90471

See Sec.10.2.2.2 for payment to independent and provider based Rural Health Centers and Federally Qualified Health Clinics.

100-4, 18, 10.2.5.2

Carrier/AB MAC Payment Requirements

Payment for pneumococcal, influenza virus, and hepatitis B vaccines follows the same standard rules that are applicable to any injectable drug or biological. (See chapter 17 for procedures for determining the payment rates for pneumococcal and influenza virus vaccines.) Effective for claims with dates of service on or after February 1, 2001, Sec.114, of the Benefits Improvement and Protection Act of 2000 mandated that all drugs and biologicals be paid based on mandatory assignment. Therefore, all providers of influenza virus and pneumococcal vaccines must accept assignment for the vaccine.

Prior to March 1, 2003, the administration of pneumococcal, influenza virus, and hepatitis B vaccines, (HCPCS codes G0008, G0009, and G0010), though not reimbursed directly through the MPFS, were reimbursed at the same rate as HCPCS code 90782 on the MPFS for the year that corresponded to the date of service of the claim.

Prior to March 1, 2003, HCPCS codes G0008, G0009, and G0010 are reimbursed at the same rate as HCPCS code 90471. Assignment for the administration is not mandatory, but is applicable should the provider be enrolled as a provider type "Mass Immunization Roster Biller," submits roster bills, or participates in the centralized billing program.

Carriers/AB MACs may not apply the limiting charge provision for pneumococcal, influenza virus vaccine, or hepatitis B vaccine and their administration in accordance with Secs.1833(a)(1) and 1833(a)(10)(A) of the Social Security Act (the Act.) The administration of the influenza virus vaccine is covered in the influenza virus vaccine benefit under Sec.1861(s)(10)(A) of the Act, rather than under the physicians' services benefit. Therefore, it is not eligible for the 10 percent Health Professional Shortage Area (HPSA) incentive payment or the 5 percent Physician Scarcity Area (PSA) incentive payment.

No Legal Obligation to Pay Nongovernmental entities that provide immunizations free of charge to all patients, regardless of their ability to pay, must provide the immunizations free of charge to Medicare beneficiaries and may not bill Medicare. (See Pub. 100-02, Medicare Benefit Policy Manual, chapter 16.) Thus, for example, Medicare may not pay for influenza virus vaccinations administered to Medicare beneficiaries if a physician provides free vaccinations to all non-Medicare patients or where an employer offers free vaccinations to its employees. Physicians also may not charge Medicare beneficiaries more for a vaccine than they would charge non-Medicare patients. (See Sec.1128(b)(6)(A) of the Act.)

When an employer offers free vaccinations to its employees, it must also offer the free vaccination to an employee who is also a Medicare beneficiary. It does not have to offer free vaccinations to its non-Medicare employees.

Nongovernmental entities that do not charge patients who are unable to pay or reduce their charges for patients of limited means, yet expect to be paid if the patient has health insurance coverage for the services provided, may bill Medicare and expect payment.

Governmental entities (such as PHCs) may bill Medicare for pneumococcal, hepatitis B, and influenza virus vaccines administered to Medicare beneficiaries when services are rendered free of charge to non-Medicare beneficiaries.

100-4, 18, 10.3.1.1

Centralized Billing for Influenza Virus and Pneumococcal Vaccines to Medicare Carriers/AB MACs

The CMS currently authorizes a limited number of providers to centrally bill for influenza virus and pneumococcal immunization claims. Centralized billing is an optional program available to providers who qualify to enroll with Medicare as the

provider type "Mass Immunization Roster Biller," as well as to other individuals and entities that qualify to enroll as regular Medicare providers. Centralized billers must roster bill, must accept assignment, and must bill electronically.

To qualify for centralized billing, a mass immunizer must be operating in at least three payment localities for which there are three different contractors processing claims. Individuals and entities providing the vaccine and administration must be properly licensed in the State in which the immunizations are given and the contractor must verify this through the enrollment process.

Centralized billers must send all claims for influenza virus and pneumococcal immunizations to a single contractor for payment, regardless of the jurisdiction in which the vaccination was administered. (This does not include claims for the Railroad Retirement Board, United Mine Workers or Indian Health Services. These claims must continue to go to the appropriate processing entity.) Payment is made based on the payment locality where the service was provided. This process is only available for claims for the influenza virus and pneumococcal vaccines and their administration. The general coverage and coding rules still apply to these claims.

This section applies only to those individuals and entities that provide mass immunization services for influenza virus and pneumococcal vaccinations and that have been authorized by CMS to centrally bill. All other providers, including those individuals and entities that provide mass immunization services that are not authorized to centrally bill, must continue to bill for these claims to their regular carrier/AB MAC per the instructions in Sec.10.3.1 of this chapter.

The claims processing instructions in this section apply only to the designated processing contractor. However, all carriers/AB MACs must follow the instructions in Sec.10.3.1.1.J, below, "Provider Education Instructions for All Carriers/AB MACs." A. Processing Contractor

Trailblazers Health Enterprises is designated as the sole contractor for the payment of influenza virus and pneumococcal claims for centralized billers from October 1, 2000, through the length of the contract. The CMS central office will notify centralized billers of the appropriate contractor to bill when they receive their notification of acceptance into the centralized billing program.

B. Request for Approval

Approval to participate in the CMS centralized billing program is a two part approval process. Individuals and corporations who wish to enroll as a CMS mass immunizer centralized biller must send their request in writing. CMS will complete Part 1 of the approval process by reviewing preliminary demographic information included in the request for participation letter. Completion of Part 1 is not approval to set up vaccination clinics, vaccinate beneficiaries, and bill Medicare for reimbursement. All new participants must complete Part 2 of the approval process (Form CMS-855 Application) before they may set up vaccination clinics, vaccinate Medicare beneficiaries, and bill Medicare for reimbursement. If an individual or entity's request is approved for centralized billing, the approval is limited to 12 months from September to August 31 of the next year. It is the responsibility of the centralized biller to reapply for approval each year. The designated contractor shall provide in writing to CMS and approved centralized billers notification of completion and approval of Part 2 of the approval process. The designated contractor may not process claims for any centralized biller who has not completed Parts 1 and 2 of the approval process. If claims are submitted by a provider who has not received approval of Parts 1 and 2 of the approval process to participate as a centralized biller, the contractor must return the claims to the provider to submit to the local carrier/AB MAC for payment.

C. Notification of Provider Participation to the Processing Contractor

Before September 1 of every year, CMS will provide the designated contractor with the names of the entities that are authorized to participate in centralized billing for the 12 month period beginning September 1 and ending August 31 of the next year.

D. Enrollment

Though centralized billers may already have a Medicare provider number, for purposes of centralized billing, they must also obtain a provider number from the processing contractor for centralized billing through completion of the Form CMS-855 (Provider Enrollment Application). Providers/suppliers are encouraged to apply to enroll as a centralized biller early as possible. Applicants who have not completed the entire enrollment process and received approval from CMS and the designated contractor to participate as a Medicare mass immunizer centralized biller will not be allowed to submit claims to Medicare for reimbursement.

Whether an entity enrolls as a provider type "Mass Immunization Roster Biller" or some other type of provider, all normal enrollment processes and procedures must be followed. Authorization from CMS to participate in centralized billing is dependent upon the entity's ability to qualify as some type of Medicare provider. In addition, as under normal enrollment procedures, the contractor must verify that the entity is fully qualified and certified per State requirements in each State in which they plan to operate.

The contractor will activate the provider number for the 12-month period from September 1 through August 31 of the following year. If the provider is authorized to participate in the centralized billing program the next year, the contractor will extend the activation of the provider number for another year. The entity need not re-enroll with the contractor every year. However, should there be changes in the States in which the entity plans to operate, the contractor will need to verify that the entity meets all State certification and licensure requirements in those new States.

E. Electronic Submission of Claims on Roster Bills

Centralized billers must agree to submit their claims on roster bills in an Electronic Media Claims standard format using the appropriate version of American National Standards Institute (ANSI) format. Contractors should refer to the appropriate ANSI Implementation Guide to determine the correct location for this information on electronic claims. The processing contractor must provide instructions on acceptable roster billing formats to the approved centralized billers. Paper claims will not be accepted.

F. Required Information on Roster Bills for Centralized Billing

In addition to the roster billing instructions found in Sec.10.3.1 of this chapter, centralized billers must complete on the electronic format the area that corresponds to Item 32 and 33 on Form CMS 1500 (08-05). The contractor must use the ZIP Code in Item 32 to determine the payment locality for the claim. Item 33 must be completed to report the provider of service/supplier's billing name, address, ZIP Code, and telephone number. In addition, the NPI of the billing provider or group must be appropriately reported.

For electronic claims, the name, address, and ZIP Code of the facility are reported in:

- The HIPAA compliant ANSI X12N 837: Claim level loop 2310D NM101=FA. When implemented, the facility (e.g., hospitals) NPI will be captured in the loop 2310D NM109 (NM108=XX) if one is available. Prior to NPI, enter the tax information in loop 2310D NM109 (NM108=24 or 34) and enter the Medicare legacy facility identifier in loop 2310D REF02 (REF01=1C). Report the address, city, state, and ZIP Code in loop 2310D N301 and N401, N402, and N403. Facility data is not required to be reported at the line level for centralized billing.

G. Payment Rates and Mandatory Assignment

The payment rates for the administration of the vaccinations are based on the Medicare Physician Fee Schedule (MPFS) for the appropriate year. Payment made through the MPFS is based on geographic locality. Therefore, payments vary based on the geographic locality where the service was performed.

The HCPCS codes G0008 and G0009 for the administration of the vaccines are not paid on the MPFS. However, prior to March 1, 2003, they must be paid at the same rate as HCPCS code 90782, which is on the MPFS. The designated contractor must pay per the correct MPFS file for each calendar year based on the date of service of the claim. Beginning March 1, 2003, HCPCS codes G0008, G0009, and G0010 are to be reimbursed at the same rate as HCPCS code 90471.

In order to pay claims correctly for centralized billers, the designated contractor must have the correct name and address, including ZIP Code, of the entity where the service was provided.

The following remittance advice and Medicare Summary Notice (MSN) messages apply:

- Claim adjustment reason code 16, "Claim/service lacks information which is needed for adjudication. At least one Remark Code must be provided (may be comprised of either the Remittance Advice Remark Code or NCPDP Reject Reason Code.)" and Remittance advice remark code MA114, "Missing/incomplete/invalid information on where the services were furnished." and MSN 9.4 - "This item or service was denied because information required to make payment was incorrect." The payment rates for the vaccines must be determined by the standard method used by Medicare for reimbursement of drugs and biologicals. (See chapter 17 for procedures for determining the payment rates for vaccines.) Effective for claims with dates of service on or after February 1, 2001, Sec.114, of the Benefits Improvement and Protection Act of 2000 mandated that all drugs and biologicals be paid based on mandatory assignment. Therefore, all providers of influenza virus and pneumococcal vaccines must accept assignment for the vaccine. In addition, as a requirement for both centralized billing and roster billing, providers must agree to accept assignment for the administration of the vaccines as well. This means that they must agree to accept the amount that Medicare pays for the vaccine and the administration. Also, since there is no coinsurance or deductible for the influenza virus and pneumococcal benefit, accepting assignment means that Medicare beneficiaries cannot be charged for the vaccination.

H. Common Working File Information

To identify these claims and to enable central office data collection on the project, special processing number 39 has been assigned. The number should be entered on the HUBC claim record to CWF in the field titled Demonstration Number.

I. Provider Education Instructions for the Processing Contractor

The processing contractor must fully educate the centralized billers on the processes for centralized billing as well as for roster billing. General information on influenza virus and pneumococcal coverage and billing instructions is available on the CMS Web site for providers.

J. Provider Education Instructions for All Carriers/AB MACs

By April 1 of every year, all carriers/AB MACs must publish in their bulletins and put on their Web sites the following notification to providers. Questions from interested providers should be forwarded to the central office address below. Carriers/AB MACs must enter the name of the assigned processing contractor where noted before sending.

NOTIFICATION TO PROVIDERS

Centralized billing is a process in which a provider, who provides mass immunization services for influenza virus and pneumococcal pneumonia virus (PPV) immunizations, can send all claims to a single contractor for payment regardless of the geographic locality in which the vaccination was administered. (This does not include claims for the Railroad Retirement Board, United Mine Workers or Indian Health Services. These claims must continue to go to the appropriate processing entity.) This process is only available for claims for the influenza virus and pneumococcal vaccines and their administration. The administration of the vaccinations is reimbursed at the assigned rate based on the Medicare physician fee schedule for the appropriate locality. The vaccines are reimbursed at the assigned rate using the Medicare standard method for reimbursement of drugs and biologicals.

Individuals and entities interested in centralized billing must contact CMS central office, in writing, at the following address by June 1 of the year they wish to begin centrally billing.

Center for Medicare & Medicaid Services Division of Practitioner Claims Processing Provider Billing and Education Group 7500 Security Boulevard Mail Stop C4-10-07 Baltimore, Maryland 21244 By agreeing to participate in the centralized billing program, providers agree to abide by the following criteria.

CRITERIA FOR CENTRALIZED BILLING

To qualify for centralized billing, an individual or entity providing mass immunization services for influenza virus and pneumococcal vaccinations must provide these services in at least three payment localities for which there are at least three different contractors processing claims.

Individuals and entities providing the vaccine and administration must be properly licensed in the State in which the immunizations are given.

Centralized billers must agree to accept assignment (i.e., they must agree to accept the amount that Medicare pays for the vaccine and the administration).

NOTE: The practice of requiring a beneficiary to pay for the vaccination upfront and to file their own claim for reimbursement is inappropriate. All Medicare providers are required to file claims on behalf of the beneficiary per Sec.1848(g)(4)(A) of the Social Security Act and centralized billers may not collect any payment.

The contractor assigned to process the claims for centralized billing is chosen at the discretion of CMS based on such considerations as workload, user-friendly software developed by the contractor for billing claims, and overall performance. The assigned contractor for this year is [Fill in name of contractor.]

The payment rates for the administration of the vaccinations are based on the Medicare physician fee schedule (MPFS) for the appropriate year. Payment made through the MPFS is based on geographic locality. Therefore, payments received may vary based on the geographic locality where the service was performed. Payment is made at the assigned rate.

The payment rates for the vaccines are determined by the standard method used by Medicare for reimbursement of drugs and biologicals. Payment is made at the assigned rate.

Centralized billers must submit their claims on roster bills in an approved Electronic Media Claims standard format. Paper claims will not be accepted.

Centralized billers must obtain certain information for each beneficiary including name, health insurance number, date of birth, sex, and signature. [Fill in name of contractor] must be contacted prior to the season for exact requirements. The responsibility lies with the centralized biller to submit correct beneficiary Medicare information (including the beneficiary's Medicare Health Insurance Claim Number) as the contractor will not be able to process incomplete or incorrect claims.

Centralized billers must obtain an address for each beneficiary so that a Medicare Summary Notice (MSN) can be sent to the beneficiary by the contractor. Beneficiaries are sometimes confused when they receive an MSN from a contractor other than the contractor that normally processes their claims which results in unnecessary beneficiary inquiries to the Medicare contractor. Therefore, centralized billers must provide every beneficiary receiving an influenza virus or pneumococcal vaccination with the name of the processing contractor. This notification must be in writing, in the form of a brochure or handout, and must be provided to each beneficiary at the time he or she receives the vaccination.

Centralized billers must retain roster bills with beneficiary signatures at their permanent location for a time period consistent with Medicare regulations. [Fill in name of contractor] can provide this information.

Though centralized billers may already have a Medicare provider number, for purposes of centralized billing, they must also obtain a provider number from [Fill in name of contractor]. This can be done by completing the Form CMS-855 (Provider Enrollment Application), which can be obtained from [Fill in name of contractor].

If an individual or entity's request for centralized billing is approved, the approval is limited to the 12 month period from September 1 through August 31 of the following year. It is the responsibility of the centralized biller to reapply to CMS CO for approval each year by June 1. Claims will not be processed for any centralized biller without permission from CMS.

Each year the centralized biller must contact [Fill in name of contractor] to verify understanding of the coverage policy for the administration of the pneumococcal vaccine, and for a copy of the warning language that is required on the roster bill.

The centralized biller is responsible for providing the beneficiary with a record of the pneumococcal vaccination.

The information in items 1 through 8 below must be included with the individual or entity's annual request to participate in centralized billing:

1. Estimates for the number of beneficiaries who will receive influenza virus vaccinations;
2. Estimates for the number of beneficiaries who will receive pneumococcal vaccinations;
3. The approximate dates for when the vaccinations will be given;
4. A list of the States in which influenza virus and pneumococcal clinics will be held;
5. The type of services generally provided by the corporation (e.g., ambulance, home health, or visiting nurse);
6. Whether the nurses who will administer the influenza virus and pneumococcal vaccinations are employees of the corporation or will be hired by the corporation specifically for the purpose of administering influenza virus and pneumococcal vaccinations;
7. Names and addresses of all entities operating under the corporation's application;
8. Contact information for designated contact person for centralized billing program.

100-4, 18, 10.4.1

In order to prevent duplicate payment by the same FI/AB MAC, CWF edits by line item on the FI/AB MAC number, the beneficiary Health Insurance Claim (HIC) number, and the date of service, the influenza virus procedure codes 90654, 90655, 90656, 90657, 90658, 90660, or 90662 and the pneumococcal procedure codes 90669, 90670, or 90732, and the administration codes G0008 or G0009.

If CWF receives a claim with either HCPCS codes 90654, 90655, 90656, 90657, 90658, 90660, or 90662 and it already has on record a claim with the same HIC number, same FI/AB MAC number, same date of service, and any one of those HCPCS codes, the second claim submitted to CWF rejects.

If CWF receives a claim with HCPCS codes 90669, 90670, or 90732 and it already has on record a claim with the same HIC number, same FI/AB MAC number, same date of service, and the same HCPCS code, the second claim submitted to CWF rejects when all four items match.

If CWF receives a claim with HCPCS administration codes G0008 or G0009 and it already has on record a claim with the same HIC number, same FI/AB MAC number, same date of service, and same procedure code, CWF rejects the second claim submitted when all four items match.

CWF returns to the FI/AB MAC a reject code "7262" for this edit. FIs/AB MACs must deny the second claim and use the same messages they currently use for the denial of duplicate claims.

100-4, 18, 10.4.2

CWF Edits on Carrier/AB MAC Claims

In order to prevent duplicate payment by the same carrier/AB MAC, CWF will edit by line item on the carrier/AB MAC number, the HIC number, the date of service, the influenza virus procedure codes 90654, 90655, 90656, 90657, 90658, 90660, or 90662; the pneumococcal procedure codes 90669, 90670, or 90732; and the administration code G0008 or G0009.

If CWF receives a claim with either HCPCS codes 90654, 90655, 90656, 90657, 90658, 90660, or 90662 and it already has on record a claim with the same HIC number, same carrier/AB MAC number, same date of service, and any one of those HCPCS codes, the second claim submitted to CWF will reject.

If CWF receives a claim with HCPCS codes 90669, 90670, or 90732 and it already has on record a claim with the same HIC number, same carrier/AB MAC number, same date of service, and the same HCPCS code, the second claim submitted to CWF will reject when all four items match.

If CWF receives a claim with HCPCS administration codes G0008 or G0009 and it already has on record a claim with the same HIC number, same carrier/AB MAC number, same date of service, and same procedure code, CWF will reject the second claim submitted.

CWF will return to the carrier/AB MAC a specific reject code for this edit. Carriers/AB MACs must deny the second claim and use the same messages they currently use for the denial of duplicate claims.

In order to prevent duplicate payment by the centralized billing contractor and local carrier/AB MAC, CWF will edit by line item for carrier number, same HIC number, same date of service, the influenza virus procedure codes 90654, 90655, 90656, 90657, 90658, 90660, or 90662; the pneumococcal procedure codes 90669, 90670, or 90732; and the administration code G0008 or G0009.

If CWF receives a claim with either HCPCS codes 90654, 90655, 90656, 90657, 90658, 90660, or 90662 and it already has on record a claim with a different carrier/AB MAC number, but same HIC number, same date of service, and any one of those same HCPCS codes, the second claim submitted to CWF will reject.

If CWF receives a claim with HCPCS codes 90669, 90670, or 90732 and it already has on record a claim with the same HIC number, different carrier/AB MAC number, same date of service, and the same HCPCS code, the second claim submitted to CWF will reject.

If CWF receives a claim with HCPCS administration codes G0008 or G0009 and it already has on record a claim with a different carrier/AB MAC number, but the same HIC number, same date of service, and same procedure code, CWF will reject the second claim submitted.

CWF will return a specific reject code for this edit. Carriers/AB MACs must deny the second claim. For the second edit, the reject code should automatically trigger the following Medicare Summary Notice (MSN) and Remittance Advice (RA) messages.

MSN: 7.2 – "This is a duplicate of a claim processed by another contractor. You should receive a Medicare Summary Notice from them."

Claim adjustment reason code 18 – duplicate claim or service

100-4, 18, 10.4.3

When CWF receives a claim from the carrier/AB MAC, it will review Part B outpatient claims history to verify that a duplicate claim has not already been posted.

CWF will edit on the beneficiary HIC number; the date of service; the influenza virus procedure codes 90654, 90655, 90656, 90657, 90658, 90660, or 90662; the pneumococcal procedure codes 90669, 90670, or 90732; and the administration code G0008 or G0009.

CWF will return a specific reject code for this edit. Contractors must deny the second claim and use the same messages they currently use for the denial of duplicate claims.

100-4, 18, 20.4

Billing Requirements - FI/A/B MAC Claims

Contractors use the weekly-updated MQSA file to verify that the billing facility is certified by the FDA to perform mammography services, and has the appropriate certification to perform the type of mammogram billed (film and/or digital). (See Sec.20.1.) FIs/A/B MACs use the provider number submitted on the claim to identify the facility and use the MQSA data file to verify the facility's certification(s). FIs/A/B MACs complete the following activities in processing mammography claims:

If the provider number on the claim does not correspond with a certified mammography facility on the MQSA file, then intermediaries/A/B MACs deny the claim.

When a film mammography HCPCS code is on a claim, the claim is checked for a "1" film indicator.

If a film mammography HCPCS code comes in on a claim and the facility is certified for film mammography, the claim is paid if all other relevant Medicare criteria are met.

If a film mammography HCPCS code is on a claim and the facility is certified for digital mammography only, the claim is denied.

When a digital mammography HCPCS code is on a claim, the claim is checked for "2" digital indicator.

If a digital mammography HCPCS code is on a claim and the facility is certified for digital mammography, the claim is paid if all other relevant Medicare criteria are met.

If a digital mammography HCPCS code is on a claim and the facility is certified for film mammography only, the claim is denied.

NOTE: The Common Working File (CWF) no longer receives the mammography file for editing purposes.

Except as provided in the following sections for RHCs and FQHCs, the following procedures apply to billing for screening mammographies: The technical component portion of the screening mammography is billed on Form CMS-1450 under bill type 12X, 13X, 14X**, 22X, 23X or 85X using revenue code 0403 and HCPCS code 77057* (76092*).

The technical component portion of the diagnostic mammography is billed on Form CMS-1450 under bill type 12X, 13X, 14X**, 22X, 23X or 85X using revenue code 0401 and HCPCS code 77055* (76090*), 77056* (76091*), G0204 and G0206.

Separate bills are required for claims for screening mammographies with dates of service prior to January 1, 2002. Providers include on the bill only charges for the screening mammography. Separate bills are not required for claims for screening mammographies with dates of service on or after January 1, 2002.

See separate instructions below for rural health clinics (RHCs) and federally qualified health centers (FQHCs).

* For claims with dates of service prior to January 1, 2007, providers report CPT codes 76090, 76091, and 76092. For claims with dates of service January 1, 2007 and later, providers report CPT codes 77055, 77056, and 77057 respectively.

** For claims with dates of service April 1, 2005 and later, hospitals bill for all mammography services under the 13X type of bill or for dates of service April 1, 2007 and later, 12X or 13X as appropriate. The 14X type of bill is no longer applicable. Appropriate bill types for providers other than hospitals are 22X, 23X, and 85X.

In cases where screening mammography services are self-referred and as a result an attending physician NPI is not available, the provider shall duplicate their facility NPI in the attending physician identifier field on the claim.

100-4, 18, 60.1

Payment

Payment (contractor) is under the MPFS except as follows:

- Fecal occult blood tests (82270* (G0107*) and G0328) are paid under the clinical diagnostic lab fee schedule except reasonable cost is paid to all non-OPPS hospitals, including CAHs, but not IHS hospitals billing on TOB 83x. IHS hospitals billing on TOB 83x are paid the ASC payment amount. Other IHS hospitals (billing on TOB 13x) are paid the OMB approved AIR, or the facility specific per visit amount as applicable. Deductible and coinsurance do not apply for these tests. See section A below for payment to Maryland waiver on TOB 13X. Payment from all hospitals for non-patient laboratory specimens on TOB 14X will be based on the clinical diagnostic fee schedule, including CAHs and Maryland waiver hospitals

Flexible sigmoidoscopy (code G0104) is paid under OPPS for hospital outpatient departments and on a reasonable cost basis for CAHs; or current payment methodologies for hospitals not subject to OPPS.

Colonoscopies (G0105 and G0121) and barium enemas (G0106 and G0120) are paid under OPPS for hospital outpatient departments and on a reasonable costs basis for CAHs or current payment methodologies for hospitals not subject to OPPS. Also colonoscopies may be done in an Ambulatory Surgical Center (ASC) and when done in an ASC the ASC rate applies. The ASC rate is the same for diagnostic and screening colonoscopies. The ASC rate is paid to IHS hospitals when the service is billed on TOB 83x.

Prior to January 1, 2007, deductible and coinsurance apply to HCPCS codes G0104, G0105, G0106, G0120, and G0121. Beginning with services provided on or after January 1, 2007, Section 5113 of the Deficit Reduction Act of 2005 waives the requirement of the annual Part B deductible for these screening services. Coinsurance still applies. Coinsurance and deductible applies to the diagnostic colorectal service codes listed below.

The following screening codes must be paid at rates consistent with the diagnostic codes indicated.

Screening Code	Diagnostic Code
G0104	45330
G0105 and G0121	45378
G0106 and G0120	74280

A. Special Payment Instructions for TOB 13X Maryland Waiver Hospitals

For hospitals in Maryland under the jurisdiction of the Health Services Cost Review Commission, screening colorectal services HCPCS codes G0104, G0105, G0106, 82270* (G0107*), G0120, G0121 and G0328 are paid according to the terms of the waiver, that is 94% of submitted charges minus any unmet existing deductible, co-insurance and non-covered charges. Maryland Hospitals bill TOB 13X for outpatient colorectal cancer screenings.

B. Special Payment Instructions for Non-Patient Laboratory Specimen (TOB 14X) for all hospitals

Payment for colorectal cancer screenings (82270* (G0107*) and G0328) to a hospital for a non-patient laboratory specimen (TOB 14X), is the lesser of the actual charge, the fee schedule amount, or the National Limitation Amount (NLA), (including CAHs and Maryland Waiver hospitals). Part B deductible and coinsurance do not apply.

*NOTE: For claims with dates of service prior to January 1, 2007, physicians, suppliers, and providers report HCPCS code G0107. Effective January 1, 2007, code G0107 is discontinued and replaced with CPT code 82270.

100-4, 18, 60.2

HCPCS Codes, Frequency Requirements, and Age Requirements (If Applicable)

Effective for services furnished on or after January 1, 1998, the following codes are used for colorectal cancer screening services:

- 82270* (G0107*) - Colorectal cancer screening; fecal-occult blood tests, 1-3 simultaneous determinations;
- G0104 - Colorectal cancer screening; flexible sigmoidoscopy;
- G0105 - Colorectal cancer screening; colonoscopy on individual at high risk;
- G0106 - Colorectal cancer screening; barium enema; as an alternative to G0104, screening sigmoidoscopy;
- G0120 - Colorectal cancer screening; barium enema; as an alternative to G0105, screening colonoscopy.

Effective for services furnished on or after July 1, 2001, the following codes are used for colorectal cancer screening services:

- G0121 - Colorectal cancer screening; colonoscopy on individual not meeting criteria for high risk. Note that the description for this code has been revised to remove the term "noncovered."
- G0122 - Colorectal cancer screening; barium enema (noncovered).

Effective for services furnished on or after January 1, 2004, the following code is used for colorectal cancer screening services as an alternative to 82270* (G0107*):

- G0328 - Colorectal cancer screening; immunoassay, fecal-occult blood test, 1-3 simultaneous determinations

*NOTE: For claims with dates of service prior to January 1, 2007, physicians, suppliers, and providers report HCPCS code G0107. Effective January 1, 2007, code G0107 is discontinued and replaced with CPT code 82270.

- G0104 - Colorectal Cancer Screening; Flexible Sigmoidoscopy

Screening flexible sigmoidoscopies (code G0104) may be paid for beneficiaries who have attained age 50, when performed by a doctor of medicine or osteopathy at the frequencies noted below.

For claims with dates of service on or after January 1, 2002, contractors pay for screening flexible sigmoidoscopies (code G0104) for beneficiaries who have attained age 50 when these services were performed by a doctor of medicine or osteopathy, or by a physician assistant, nurse practitioner, or clinical nurse specialist (as defined in Sec.1861(aa)(5) of the Act and in the Code of Federal Regulations at42 CFR 410.74, 410.75, and410.76) at the frequencies noted above. For claims with dates of service prior to January 1, 2002, contractors pay for these services under the conditions noted only when a doctor of medicine or osteopathy performs them.

For services furnished from January 1, 1998, through June 30, 2001, inclusive:

- Once every 48 months (i.e., at least 47 months have passed following the month in which the last covered screening flexible sigmoidoscopy was done).
- For services furnished on or after July 1, 2001:
- Once every 48 months as calculated above unless the beneficiary does not meet the criteria for high risk of developing colorectal cancer (refer to Sec.60.3 of this chapter) and he/she has had a screening colonoscopy (code G0121) within the preceding 10 years. If such a beneficiary has had a screening colonoscopy within the preceding 10 years, then he or she can have covered a screening flexible sigmoidoscopy only after at least 119 months have passed following the month that he/she received the screening colonoscopy (code G0121).

NOTE:If during the course of a screening flexible sigmoidoscopy a lesion or growth is detected which results in a biopsy or removal of the growth; the appropriate diagnostic procedure classified as a flexible sigmoidoscopy with biopsy or removal should be billed and paid rather than code G0104.

G0105 - Colorectal Cancer Screening; Colonoscopy on Individual at High Risk

Screening colonoscopies (code G0105) may be paid when performed by a doctor of medicine or osteopathy at a frequency of once every 24 months for beneficiaries at high risk for developing colorectal cancer (i.e., at least 23 months have passed following the month in which the last covered G0105 screening colonoscopy was performed). Refer to Sec.60.3of this chapter for the criteria to use in determining whether or not an individual is at high risk for developing colorectal cancer.

NOTE:If during the course of the screening colonoscopy, a lesion or growth is detected which results in a biopsy or removal of the growth, the appropriate diagnostic procedure classified as a colonoscopy with biopsy or removal should be billed and paid rather than code G0105.

A. Colonoscopy Cannot be Completed Because of Extenuating Circumstances

1 FIs

When a covered colonoscopy is attempted but cannot be completed because of extenuating circumstances, Medicare will pay for the interrupted colonoscopy as long as the coverage conditions are met for the incomplete procedure. However, the frequency standards associated with screening colonoscopies will not be applied by CWF. When a covered colonoscopy is next attempted and completed, Medicare will pay for that colonoscopy according to its payment methodology for this procedure as long as coverage conditions are met, and the frequency standards will be applied by CWF. This policy is applied to both screening and diagnostic colonoscopies.

When submitting a facility claim for the interrupted colonoscopy, providers are to suffix the colonoscopy HCPCS codes with a modifier of "-73" or" -74" as appropriate to indicate that the procedure was interrupted. Payment for covered incomplete screening colonoscopies shall be consistent with payment methodologies currently in place for complete screening colonoscopies, including those contained in42 CFR 419.44(b). In situations where a critical access hospital (CAH) has elected payment Method II for CAH patients, payment shall be consistent with payment methodologies currently in place as outlined in Chapter 3. As such, instruct CAHs that elect Method II payment to use modifier "-53" to identify an incomplete screening colonoscopy (physician professional service(s) billed in revenue code 096X, 097X, and/or 098X). Such CAHs will also bill the technical or facility component of the interrupted colonoscopy in revenue code 075X (or other appropriate revenue code) using the "-73" or "-74" modifier as appropriate.Note that Medicare would expect the provider to maintain adequate information in the patient's medical record in case it is needed by the contractor to document the incomplete procedure.

2. Carriers

When a covered colonoscopy is attempted but cannot be completed because of extenuating circumstances (see Chapter 12), Medicare will pay for the interrupted colonoscopy at a rate consistent with that of a flexible sigmoidoscopy as long as coverage conditions are met for the incomplete procedure. When a covered colonoscopy is next attempted and completed, Medicare will pay for that colonoscopy according to its payment methodology for this procedure as long as coverage conditions are met. This policy is applied to both screening and diagnostic colonoscopies.

When submitting a claim for the interrupted colonoscopy, professional providers are to suffix the colonoscopy code with a modifier of "-53" to indicate that the procedure was interrupted. When submitting a claim for the facility fee associated with this procedure, Ambulatory Surgical Centers (ASCs) are to suffix the colonoscopy code with "-73" or "-74" as appropriate. Payment for covered screening colonoscopies, including that for the associated ASC facility fee when applicable, shall be consistent with payment for diagnostic colonoscopies, whether the procedure is complete or incomplete.Note that Medicare would expect the provider to maintain adequate information in the patient's medical record in case it is needed by the contractor to document the incomplete procedure.

- G0106 - Colorectal Cancer Screening; Barium Enema; as an Alternative to G0104, Screening Sigmoidoscopy

Screening barium enema examinations may be paid as an alternative to a screening sigmoidoscopy (code G0104). The same frequency parameters for screening sigmoidoscopies (see those codes above) apply. In the case of an individual aged 50 or over, payment may be made for a screening barium enema examination (code G0106) performed after at least 47 months have passed following the month in which the last screening barium enema or screening flexible sigmoidoscopy was performed. For example, the beneficiary received a screening barium enema examination as an alternative to a screening flexible sigmoidoscopy in January 1999. Start counts beginning February 1999. The beneficiary is eligible for another screening barium enema in January 2003. The screening barium enema must be ordered in writing after a determination that the test is the appropriate screening test. Generally, it is expected that this will be a screening double contrast enema unless the individual is unable to withstand such an exam. This means that in the case of a particular individual, the attending physician must determine that the estimated screening potential for the barium enema is equal to or greater than the screening potential that has been estimated for a screening flexible sigmoidoscopy for the same individual. The screening single contrast barium enema also requires a written order from the beneficiary's attending physician in the same manner as described above for the screening double contrast barium enema examination.

- 82270* (G0107*) - Colorectal Cancer Screening; Fecal-Occult Blood Test, 1-3 Simultaneous Determinations

Effective for services furnished on or after January 1, 1998, screening FOBT (code 82270* (G0107*) may be paid for beneficiaries who have attained age 50, and at a frequency of once every 12 months (i.e., at least 11 months have passed following the month in which the last covered screening FOBT was performed). This screening FOBT means a guaiac-based test for peroxidase activity, in which the beneficiary completes it by taking samples from two different sites of three consecutive stools. This screening requires a written order from the beneficiary's attending physician. (The term "attending physician" is defined to mean a doctor of medicine or osteopathy (as defined in Sec.1861(r)(1)of the Act) who is fully knowledgeable about the beneficiary's medical condition, and who would be responsible for using the results of any examination performed in the overall management of the beneficiary's specific medical problem.)

Effective for services furnished on or after January 1, 2004, payment may be made for a immunoassay-based FOBT (G0328, described below) as an alternative to the guaiacbased FOBT, 82270* (G0107*). Medicare will pay for only one covered FOBT per year, either 82270* (G0107*) or G0328, but not both.

*NOTE: For claims with dates of service prior to January 1, 2007, physicians, suppliers, and providers report HCPCS code G0107. Effective January 1, 2007, code G0107 is discontinued and replaced with CPT code 82270.

- G0328 - Colorectal Cancer Screening; Immunoassay, Fecal-Occult Blood Test, 1-3 Simultaneous Determinations

Effective for services furnished on or after January 1, 2004, screening FOBT, (code G0328) may be paid as an alternative to 82270* (G0107*) for beneficiaries who have attained age 50. Medicare will pay for a covered FOBT (either 82270* (G0107*) or G0328, but not both) at a frequency of once every 12 months (i.e., at least 11 months have passed following the month in which the last covered screening FOBT was performed). Screening FOBT, immunoassay, includes the use of a spatula to collect the appropriate number of samples or the use of a special brush for the collection of samples, as determined by the individual manufacturer's instructions. This screening requires a written order from the beneficiary's attending physician. (The term "attending physician" is defined to mean a doctor of medicine or osteopathy (as defined in Sec.1861(r)(1) of the Act) who is fully knowledgeable about the beneficiary's medical condition, and who would be responsible for using the results of any examination performed in the overall management of the beneficiary's specific medical problem.)

- G0120 - Colorectal Cancer Screening; Barium Enema; as an Alternative to or G0105, Screening Colonoscopy

Screening barium enema examinations may be paid as an alternative to a screening colonoscopy (code G0105) examination. The same frequency parameters for screening colonoscopies (see those codes above) apply. In the case of an individual who is at high risk for colorectal cancer, payment may be made for a screening barium enema examination (code G0120) performed after at least 23 months have passed following the month in which the last screening barium enema or the last screening colonoscopy was performed. For example, a beneficiary at high risk for developing colorectal cancer received a screening barium enema examination (code G0120) as an alternative to a screening colonoscopy (code G0105) in January 2000. Start counts beginning February 2000. The beneficiary is eligible for another screening barium enema examination (code G0120) in January 2002. The screening barium enema must be ordered in writing after a determination that the test is the appropriate screening test. Generally, it is expected that this will be a screening double contrast enema unless the individual is unable to withstand such an exam. This means that in the case of a particular individual, the attending physician must determine that the estimated screening potential for the barium enema is equal to or greater than the screening potential that has been estimated for a screening colonoscopy, for the same individual. The screening single contrast barium enema also requires a written order from the beneficiary's attending physician in the same manner as described above for the screening double contrast barium enema examination.

- G0121 - Colorectal Screening; Colonoscopy on Individual Not Meeting Criteria for High Risk - Applicable On and After July 1, 2001

Effective for services furnished on or after July 1, 2001, screening colonoscopies (code G0121) performed on individuals not meeting the criteria for being at high risk for developing colorectal cancer (refer to Sec.60.3 of this chapter) may be paid under the following conditions:

- At a frequency of once every 10 years (i.e., at least 119 months have passed following the month in which the last covered G0121 screening colonoscopy was performed.)

If the individual would otherwise qualify to have covered a G0121 screening colonoscopy based on the above but has had a covered screening flexible sigmoidoscopy (code G0104), then he or she may have covered a G0121 screening colonoscopy only after at least 47 months have passed following the month in which the last covered G0104 flexible sigmoidoscopy was performed.

NOTE:If during the course of the screening colonoscopy, a lesion or growth is detected which results in a biopsy or removal of the growth, the appropriate diagnostic procedure classified as a colonoscopy with biopsy or removal should be billed and paid rather than code G0121.

- G0122 - Colorectal Cancer Screening; Barium Enema

The code is not covered by Medicare.

100-4, 18, 60.6

Billing Requirements for Claims Submitted to FIs

(Follow the general bill review instructions in Chapter 25. Hospitals use the ANSI X12N 837I to bill the FI or on the hardcopy Form CMS-1450. Hospitals bill revenue codes and HCPCS codes as follows:

Screening Test/Procedure	Revenue Code	HCPCS Code	TOB
Fecal Occult blood test	030X	82270*** (G0107***), G0328	12X, 13X, 14X**, 22X, 23X, 83X, 85X
Barium enema	032X	G0106, G0120, G0122	12X, 13X, 22X, 23X, 85X****
Flexible Sigmoidoscopy	*	G0104	12X, 13X, 22X, 23X, 83X, 85X****
Colonoscopy-high risk	*	G0105, G0121	12X, 13X, 22X, 23X, 83X, 85X****

* The appropriate revenue code when reporting any other surgical procedure.

** 14X is only applicable for non-patient laboratory specimens.

*** For claims with dates of service prior to January 1, 2007, physicians, suppliers, and providers report HCPCS code G0107. Effective January 1, 2007, code G0107, is discontinued and replaced with CPT code 82270.

**** CAHs that elect Method II bill revenue code 096X, 097X, and/or 098X for professional services and 075X (or other appropriate revenue code) for the technical or facility component.

Special Billing Instructions for Hospital Inpatients

When these tests/procedures are provided to inpatients of a hospital or when Part A benefits have been exhausted, they are covered under this benefit. However, the provider bills on bill type 12X using the discharge date of the hospital stay to avoid editing in the Common Working File (CWF) as a result of the hospital bundling rules.

100-4, 18, 80

Initial Preventive Physical Examination (IPPE)

(NOTE: For billing and payment requirements for the Annual Wellness Visit, see chapter 18, section 140, of this manual.)

Background: Effective for services furnished on or after January 1, 2005, Section 611 of the Medicare Prescription Drug Improvement and Modernization Act of 2003 (MMA) provides for coverage under Part B of one initial preventive physical examination (IPPE) for new beneficiaries only, subject to certain eligibility and other limitations. CMS amended §§411.15 (a)(1) and 411.15 (k)(11) of the Code of Federal Regulations (CFR) to permit payment for an IPPE as described at 42 CFR §410.16, added by 69 FR 66236, 66420 (November 15, 2004) not later than 6 months after the date the individual's first coverage period begins under Medicare Part B.

Under the MMA of 2003, the IPPE may be performed by a doctor of medicine or osteopathy as defined in section 1861 (r)(1) of the Social Security Act (the Act) or by a qualified mid-level nonphysician practitioner (NPP) (nurse practitioner, physician assistant or clinical nurse specialist), not later than 6 months after the date the individual's first coverage begins under Medicare Part B. (See section 80.3 for a list of bill types of facilities that can bill fiscal intermediaries (FIs) for this service.) This examination will include: (1) review of the individual's medical and social history with attention to modifiable risk factors for disease detection, (2) review of the individual's potential (risk factors) for depression or other mood disorders, (3) review of the individual's functional ability and level of safety; (4) a physical examination to include measurement of the individual's height, weight, blood pressure, a visual acuity screen, and other factors as deemed appropriate by the examining physician or qualified nonphysician practitioner (NPP), (5) performance and interpretation of an electrocardiogram (EKG); (6) education, counseling, and referral, as deemed appropriate, based on the results of the review and evaluation services described in the previous 5 elements, and (7) education, counseling, and referral including a brief written plan (e.g., a checklist or alternative) provided to the individual for obtaining the appropriate screening and other preventive services, which are separately covered under Medicare Part B benefits. The EKG performed as a component of the IPPE will be billed separately. Medicare will pay for only one IPPE per beneficiary per lifetime. The Common Working File (CWF) will edit for this benefit.

As required by statute under the MMA of 2003, the total IPPE service includes an EKG, but the EKG is billed with its own unique HCPCS code(s). The IPPE does not include other preventive services that are currently separately covered and paid under Section 1861 of the Act under Medicare Part B screening benefits. (That is, pneumococcal, influenza and hepatitis B vaccines and their administration, screening mammography, screening pap smear and screening pelvic examinations, prostate cancer screening tests, colorectal cancer screening tests, diabetes outpatient self-management training services, bone mass measurements, glaucoma screening, medical nutrition therapy for individuals with diabetes or renal disease, cardiovascular screening blood tests, and diabetes screening tests.)

Section 5112 of the Deficit Reduction Act of 2005 allows for one ultrasound screening for Abdominal Aortic Aneurysm (AAA) as a result of a referral from an IPPE effective January 1, 2007. For AAA physician/practitioner billing, correct coding, and payment policy information, refer to section 110 of this chapter.

Effective January 1, 2009, Section 101(b) of the Medicare Improvement for Patients and Providers Act (MIPPA) of 2008 updates the IPPE benefit described under the MMA of 2003. The MIPPA allows the IPPE to be performed not later than 12 months after the date the individual's first coverage period begins under Medicare Part B, requires the addition of the measurement of an individual's body mass index to the IPPE, adds end-of-life planning (upon an individual's consent) to the IPPE, and removes the screening EKG as a mandatory service of the IPPE. The screening EKG is optional effective January 1, 2009, and is permitted as a once-in-a-lifetime screening service as a result of a referral from an IPPE.

The MIPPA of 2008 allows for possible future payment for additional preventive services not otherwise described in Title XVIII of the Act that identify medical conditions or risk factors for eligible individuals if the Secretary determines through the national coverage determination (NCD) process (as defined in section 1869(f)(1)(B) of the Act) that they are: (1) reasonable and necessary for the prevention or early detection of illness or disability, (2) recommended with a grade of A or B by the United States Preventive Services Task Force, and, (3) appropriate for individuals entitled to benefits under Part A or enrolled under Part B, or both. MIPPA requires that there be education, counseling, and referral for additional preventive services, as appropriate, under the IPPE, if the Secretary determines in the future that such services are covered.

For the physician/practitioner billing correct coding and payment policy, refer to chapter 12, section 30.6.1.1, of this manual.

100-4, 18, 80.1

The HCPCS codes listed below were developed for the IPPE benefit effective January 1, 2005, for individuals whose initial enrollment is on or after January 1, 2005.

G0344: Initial preventive physical examination; face-to-face visit, services limited to new beneficiary during the first 6 months of Medicare enrollment

Short Descriptor: Initial Preventive Exam

G0366: Electrocardiogram, routine ECG with 12 leads; performed as a component of the initial preventive examination with interpretation and report

Short Descriptor: EKG for initial prevent exam

G0367: tracing only, without interpretation and report, performed as a component of the initial preventive examination

Short Descriptor: EKG tracing for initial prev

G0368: interpretation and report only, performed as a component of the initial preventive examination

Short Descriptor: EKG interpret & report preve

The following new HCPCS codes were developed for the IPPE benefit effective January 1, 2009, and replaced codes G0344, G0366, G0367, and G0368 shown above beginning with dates of service on or after January 1, 2009:

G0402: Initial preventive physical examination; face-to-face visit, services limited to new beneficiary during the first 12 months of Medicare enrollment

Short Descriptor: Initial Preventive exam

G0403: Electrocardiogram, routine ECG with 12 leads; performed as a screening for the initial preventive physical examination with interpretation and report

Short Descriptor: EKG for initial prevent exam

G0404: Electrocardiogram, routine ECG with 12 leads; tracing only, without interpretation and report, performed as a screening for the initial preventive physical examination

Short Descriptor: EKG tracing for initial prev

G0405: Electrocardiogram, routine ECG with 12 leads; interpretation and report only, performed as a screening for the initial preventive physical examination

Short Descriptor: EKG interpret & report preve

100-4, 18, 80.2

A/B Medicare Administrative Contractor (MAC) and Contractor Billing Requirements

Effective for dates of service on and after January 1, 2005, through December 31, 2008, contractors shall recognize the HCPCS codes G0344, G0366, G0367, and G0368 shown above in §80.1 for an IPPE. The type of service (TOS) for each of these codes is as follows:

G0344: TOS = 1

G0366: TOS = 5

G0367: TOS = 5

G0368: TOS = 5

Contractors shall pay physicians or qualified nonphysician practitioners for only one IPPE performed not later than 6 months after the date the individual's first coverage begins under Medicare Part B, but only if that coverage period begins on or after January 1, 2005.

Effective for dates of service on and after January 1, 2009, contractors shall recognize the HCPCS codes G0402, G0403, G0404, and G0405 shown above in §80.1 for an IPPE. The TOS for each of these codes is as follows:

G0402: TOS = 1

G0403: TOS = 5

G0404: TOS = 5

G0405: TOS = 5

Under the MIPPA of 2008, contractors shall pay physicians or qualified nonphysician practitioners for only one IPPE performed not later than 12 months after the date the individual's first coverage begins under Medicare Part B only if that coverage period begins on or after January 1, 2009.

Contractors shall allow payment for a medically necessary Evaluation and Management (E/M) service at the same visit as the IPPE when it is clinically appropriate. Physicians and qualified nonphysician practitioners shall use CPT codes 99201-99215 to report an E/M with CPT modifier 25 to indicate that the E/M is a significant, separately identifiable service from the IPPE code reported (G0344 or G0402, whichever applies based on the date the IPPE is performed). Refer to chapter 12, § 30.6.1.1, of this manual for the physician/practitioner billing correct coding and payment policy regarding E/M services.

If the EKG performed as a component of the IPPE is not performed by the primary physician or qualified NPP during the IPPE visit, another physician or entity may perform and/or interpret the EKG. The referring physician or qualified NPP needs to make sure that the performing physician or entity bills the appropriate G code for the screening EKG, and not a CPT code in the 93000 series. Both the IPPE and the EKG should be billed in order for the beneficiary to receive the complete IPPE service. Effective for dates of service on and after January 1, 2009, the screening EKG is optional and is no longer a mandated service of an IPPE if performed as a result of a referral from an IPPE.

Should the same physician or NPP need to perform an additional medically necessary EKG in the 93000 series on the same day as the IPPE, report the appropriate EKG CPT code(s) with modifier 59, indicating that the EKG is a distinct procedural service.

Physicians or qualified nonphysician practitioners shall bill the contractor the appropriate HCPCS codes for IPPE on the Form CMS-1500 claim or an approved electronic format. The HCPCS codes for an IPPE and screening EKG are paid under the Medicare Physician Fee Schedule (MPFS). The appropriate deductible and coinsurance applies to codes G0344, G0366, G0367, G0368, G0403, G0404, and G0405. The deductible is waived for code G0402 but the coinsurance still applies.

100-4, 18, 80.3.3

Outpatient Prospective Payment System (OPPS) Hospital Billing

Hospitals subject to OPPS (TOBs 12X and 13X) must use modifier -25 when billing the IPPE G0344 along with the technical component of the EKG, G0367, on the same claim. The same is true when billing IPPE code G0402 along with the technical component of the screening EKG, code G0404. This is due to an OPPS Outpatient Code Editor (OCE) which contains an edit that requires a modifier -25 on any evaluation and management (E/M) HCPCS code if there is also a status "S" or "T" HCPCS procedure code on the claim.

100-4, 18, 80.4

Coinsurance and Deductible

The Medicare deductible and coinsurance apply for the IPPE provided before January 1, 2009.

The Medicare deductible is waived effective for the IPPE provided on or after January 1, 2009. Coinsurance continues to apply for the IPPE provided on or after January 1, 2009.

As a result of the Affordable Care Act, effective for the IPPE provided on or after January 1, 2011, the Medicare deductible and coinsurance (for HCPCS code G0402 only) are waived.

100-4, 18, 120.1

Coding and Payment of DSMT Services

The following HCPCS codes are used to report DSMT: G0108 - Diabetes outpatient self-management training services, individual, per 30 minutes.

G0109 - Diabetes outpatient self-management training services, group session (2 or more), per 30 minutes.

The type of service for these codes is 1.

Type of Facility	Payment Method	Type of Bill
Physician (billed to the carrier)	MPFS	NA
Hospitals subject to OPPS	MPFS	12X, 13X

Type of Facility	Payment Method	Type of Bill
Method I and Method II Critical Access Hospitals (CAHs) (technical services)	101% of reasonable cost	12X and 85X
Indian Health Service (IHS) providers billing hospital outpatient Part B	OMB-approved outpatient per visit all inclusive rate (AIR)	13X
IHS providers billing inpatient Part B	All-inclusive inpatient ancillary per diem rate	12X
IHS CAHs billing outpatient Part B	101% of the all-inclusive facility specific per visit rate	85X
IHS CAHs billing inpatient Part B	101% of the all-inclusive facility specific per diem rate	12X
FQHCs*	All-inclusive encounter rate with other qualified services. Separate visit payment available with HCPCS.	73X
Skilled Nursing Facilities **	MPFS non-facility rate	22X, 23X
Maryland Hospitals under jurisdiction of the Health Services Cost Review Commission (HSCRC)	94% of provider submitted charges in accordance with the terms of the Maryland Waiver	12X, 13X
Home Health Agencies (can be billed only if the service is provided outside of the treatment plan)	MPFS non-facility rate	34X

* Effective January 1, 2006, payment for DSMT provided in an FQHC that meets all of the requirements as above, may be made in addition to one other visit the beneficiary had during the same day, if this qualifying visit is billed on TOB 73X, with HCPCS G0108 or G0109, and revenue codes 0520, 0521, 0522, 0524, 0525, 0527, 0528, or 0900.

** The SNF consolidated billing provision allows separate part B payment for training services for beneficiaries that are in skilled Part A SNF stays, however, the SNF must submit these services on a 22 bill type. Training services provided by other provider types must be reimbursed by X the SNF.

NOTE: An ESRD facility is a reasonable site for this service, however, because it is required to provide dietician and nutritional services as part of the care covered in the composite rate, ESRD facilities are not allowed to bill for it separately and do not receive separate reimbursement. Likewise, an RHC is a reasonable site for this service, however it must be provided in an RHC with other qualifying services and paid at the all-inclusive encounter rate.

Deductible and co-insurance apply.

100-4, 18, 130

Healthcare Common Procedure Coding System (HCPCS) for HIV Screening Tests

Healthcare Common Procedure Coding System (HCPCS) for HIV Screening Tests

Effective for claims with dates of service on and after December 8, 2009, implemented with the April 5, 2010, IOCE, the following HCPCS codes are to be billed for HIV screening:

G0432 Infectious agent antibody detection by enzyme immunoassay (EIA) technique, HIV-1 and/or HIV-2, screening,

G0433 Infectious agent antibody detection by enzyme-linked immunosorbent assay (ELISA) technique, HIV-1 and/or HIV-2, screening, and,

G0435 Infectious agent antibody detection by rapid antibody test, HIV-1 and/or HIV-2, screening

100-4, 18, 130.1

Billing Requirements

Effective for dates of service December 8, 2009, and later, contractors shall recognize the above HCPCS codes for HIV screening.

Medicare contractors shall pay for voluntary HIV screening as follows in accordance with Pub. 100-03, Medicare National Coverage Determinations Manual, sections 190.14 and 210.7:

A maximum of once annually for beneficiaries at increased risk for HIV infection (11 full months must elapse following the month the previous test was performed in order for the subsequent test to be covered), and,

A maximum of three times per term of pregnancy for pregnant Medicare beneficiaries beginning with the date of the first test when ordered by the woman's clinician. Claims that are submitted for HIV screening shall be submitted in the following manner:

For beneficiaries reporting increased risk factors, claims shall contain HCPCS code G0432, G0433, or G0435 with diagnosis code V73.89 (Special screening for other specified viral disease) as primary, and V69.8 (Other problems related to lifestyle), as secondary.

For beneficiaries not reporting increased risk factors, claims shall contain HCPCS code G0432, G0433, or G0435 with diagnosis code V73.89 only.

For pregnant Medicare beneficiaries, claims shall contain HCPCS code G0432, G0433, or G0435 with diagnosis code V73.89 as primary, and one of the following ICD-9 diagnosis codes: V22.0 (Supervision of normal first pregnancy), V22.1 (Supervision of other normal pregnancy), or V23.9 (Supervision of unspecified high-risk pregnancy), as secondary.

100-4, 18, 130.4

Diagnosis Code Reporting

A claim that is submitted for HIV screening shall be submitted with one or more of the following diagnosis codes in the header and pointed to the line item:

a. For claims where increased risk factors are reported: V73.89 as primary and V69.8 as secondary.

b. For claims where increased risk factors are NOT reported: V73.89 as primary only.

c. For claims for pregnant Medicare beneficiaries, the following diagnosis codes shall be submitted in addition to V73.89 to allow for more frequent screening than once per 12-month period:

V22.0 – Supervision of normal first pregnancy, or,

V22.1 – Supervision of other normal pregnancy, or,

V23.9 - Supervision of unspecified high-risk pregnancy).

100-4, 18, 140

Annual Wellness Visit (AWV)

Pursuant to section 4103 of the Affordable Care Act of 2010, the Centers for Medicare & Medicaid Services (CMS) amended section 411.15(a)(1) and 411.15(k)(15) of 42 CFR (list of examples of routine physical examinations excluded from coverage) effective for services furnished on or after January 1, 2011. This expanded coverage is subject to certain eligibility and other limitations that allow payment for an annual wellness visit (AWV), including personalized prevention plan services (PPPS), for an individual who is no longer within 12 months after the effective date of his or her first Medicare Part B coverage period, and has not received either an initial preventive physical examination (IPPE) or an AWV within the past 12 months.

The AWV will include the establishment of, or update to, the individual's medical/family history, measurement of his/her height, weight, body-mass index (BMI) or waist circumference, and blood pressure (BP), with the goal of health promotion and disease detection and encouraging patients to obtain the screening and preventive services that may already be covered and paid for under Medicare Part B. CMS amended 42 CFR §§411.15(a)(1) and 411.15(k)(15) to allow payment on or after January 1, 2011, for an AWV (as established at 42 CFR 410.15) when performed by qualified health professionals.

Coverage is available for an AWV that meets the following requirements:

1. It is performed by a health professional;

2. It is furnished to an eligible beneficiary who is no longer within 12 months after the effective date of his/her first Medicare Part B coverage period, and he/she has not received either an IPPE or an AWV providing PPPS within the past 12 months.

See Pub. 100-02,Medicare Benefit Policy Manual, chapter 15, section 280.5, for detailed policy regarding the AWV, including definitions of: (1) detection of cognitive impairment, (2) eligible beneficiary, (3) establishment of, or an update to, an individual's medical/family history, (4&5) first and subsequent AWVs providing PPPS, (6) health professional, and, (7) review of an individual's functional ability/level of safety.

100-4, 18, 140.1

Healthcare Common Procedure Coding System (HCPCS) Coding for the AWV

HCPCS codes listed below were developed for the AWV benefit effective January 1, 2011, for individuals whose initial enrollment is on or after January 1, 2011.

G0438 - Annual wellness visit; includes a personalized prevention plan of service (PPPS); first visit

G0439 – Annual wellness visit; includes a personalized prevention plan of service (PPPS); subsequent visit

100-4, 18, 140.5

Coinsurance and Deductible

Sections 4103 and 4104 of the Affordable Care Act provide for a waiver of Medicare coinsurance/copayment and Part B deductible requirements for the AWV effective for services furnished on or after January 1, 2011.

100-4, 18, 150

Counseling to Prevent Tobacco Use

Effective for claims with dates of service on and after August 25, 2010, the Centers for Medicare & Medicaid Services (CMS) will cover counseling to prevent tobacco use services for outpatient and hospitalized Medicare beneficiaries:

1. Who use tobacco, regardless of whether they have signs or symptoms of tobacco-related disease;
2. Who are competent and alert at the time that counseling is provided; and,
3. Whose counseling is furnished by a qualified physician or other Medicare-recognized practitioner. These individuals who do not have signs or symptoms of tobacco-related disease will be covered under Medicare Part B when the above conditions of coverage are met, subject to certain frequency and other limitations.

Conditions of Medicare Part A and Medicare Part B coverage for counseling to prevent tobacco use are located in the Medicare National Coverage Determinations (NCD) Manual, Publication 100-3, chapter 1, section 210.4.1.

100-4,18,150.1

Healthcare Common Procedure Coding System (HCPCS) and Diagnosis Coding

The CMS has created two new G codes for billing for tobacco cessation counseling services to prevent tobacco use for those individuals who use tobacco but do not have signs or symptoms of tobacco-related disease. These are in addition to the two CPT codes 99406 and 99407 that currently are used for smoking and tobacco-use cessation counseling for symptomatic individuals.

The following HCPCS codes should be reported when billing for counseling to prevent tobacco use effective January 1, 2011:

- G0436 - Smoking and tobacco cessation counseling visit for the asymptomatic patient; intermediate, greater than 3 minutes, up to 10 minutes

  Short descriptor: Tobacco-use counsel 3-10 min

- G0437 - Smoking and tobacco cessation counseling visit for the asymptomatic patient; intensive, greater than 10 minutes

  Short descriptor: Tobacco-use counsel >10min

NOTE: The above G codes will not be active in contractors' systems until January 1, 2011. Therefore, contractors shall advise non-outpatient perspective payment system (OPPS) providers to use unlisted code 99199 to bill for counseling to prevent tobacco use and tobacco-related disease services during the interim period of August 25, 2010, through December 31, 2010.

On January 3, 2011, contractor's systems will accept the new G codes for services performed on or after August 25, 2010.

Two new C codes have been created for facilities paid under OPPS when billing for counseling to prevent tobacco use and tobacco-related disease services during the interim period of August 25, 2010, through December 31, 2010:

- C9801 - Smoking and tobacco cessation counseling visit for the asymptomatic patient, intermediate, greater than 3 minutes, up to 10 minutes

  Short descriptor: Tobacco-use counsel 3-10 min

- C9802 - Smoking and tobacco cessation counseling visit for the asymptomatic patient, intensive, greater than 10 minutes

  Short descriptor: Tobacco-use counsel >10min

Claims for smoking and tobacco use cessation counseling services G0436 and G0437 shall be submitted with diagnosis code V15.82, history of tobacco use, or 305.1, non-dependent tobacco use disorder.

Contractors shall allow payment for a medically necessary E/M service on the same day as the smoking and tobacco-use cessation counseling service when it is clinically appropriate. Physicians and qualified non-physician practitioners shall use an appropriate HCPCS code to report an E/M service with modifier -25 to indicate that the E/M service is a separately identifiable service from G0436 or G0437.

100-4,18,150.2

Carrier Billing Requirements

Carriers shall pay for counseling to prevent tobacco use services billed with code G0436 or G0437 for dates of service on or after January 1, 2011. Carriers shall pay for counseling services billed with code 99199 for dates of service performed on or after August 25, 2010 through December 31, 2010. The type of service (TOS) for each of the new codes is 1.

Carriers pay for counseling services billed based on the Medicare Physician Fee Schedule (MPFS). Deductible and coinsurance apply for services performed on August 25, 2010, through December 31, 2010. For claims with dates of service on and after January 1, 2011, coinsurance and deductible do not apply on G0436 and G0437.

Physicians or qualified non-physician practitioners shall bill the carrier for counseling to prevent tobacco use services on Form CMS-1500 or an approved electronic format.

NOTE: The above G codes will not be active in contractors' systems until January 1, 2011. Therefore, contractors shall advise providers to use unlisted code 99199 to bill for counseling to prevent tobacco use services during the interim period of August 25, 2010, through December 31, 2010.

100-4,18,150.2.1

Fiscal Intermediary (FI) Billing Requirements

The FIs shall pay for counseling to prevent tobacco use services with codes G0436 and G0437 for dates of service on or after January 1, 2011. FIs shall pay for counseling services billed with code 99199 for dates of service performed on or after August 25, 2010, through December 31, 2010. For facilities paid under OPPS, FIs shall pay for counseling services billed with codes C9801 and C9802 for dates of service performed on or after August 25, 2010, through December 31, 2010.

Claims for counseling to prevent tobacco use services should be submitted on Form CMS-1450 or its electronic equivalent.

The applicable bill types are 12X, 13X, 22X, 23X, 34X, 71X, 77X, and 85X.

Payment for outpatient services is as follows:

- Type of Facility
- Method of Payment
- Rural Health Centers (RHCs) TOB 71X/Federally Qualified Health Centers (FQHCs)TOB 77X
- All-inclusive rate (AIR) for the encounter
- Hospitals TOBs 12X and 13X
- OPPS for hospitals subject to OPPS
- MPFS for hospitals not subject to OPPS
- Indian Health Services (IHS) Hospitals TOB 13X
- AIR for the encounter
- Skilled Nursing Facilities (SNFs) TOBs 22X and 23X
- Medicare Physician Fee Schedule (MPFS)
- Home Health Agencies (HHAs) TOB 34X
- MPFS
- Critical Access Hospitals (CAHs) TOB 85X
- Method I: Technical services are paid at 101% of reasonable cost. Method II: technical services are paid at 101% of reasonable cost, and Professional services are paid at 115% of the MPFS Data Base
- IHS CAHs TOB 85X
- Based on specific rate
- Maryland Hospitals

Payment is based according to the Health Services Cost Review Commission (HSCRC). That is 94% of submitted charges subject to any unmet deductible, coinsurance, and non-covered charges policies.

100-4,18,150.4

Common Working File (CWF)

The Common Working File (CWF) shall edit for the frequency of service limitations of counseling to prevent tobacco use sessions and smoking and tobacco-use cessation counseling services (G0436, G0437, 99406, 99407) rendered to a beneficiary for a combined total of 8 sessions within a 12-month period. The beneficiary may receive another 8 sessions during a second or subsequent year after 11 full months have passed since the first Medicare covered counseling session was performed. To start the count for the second or subsequent 12-month period, begin with the month after the month in which the first Medicare covered counseling session was performed and count until 11 full months have elapsed.

By entering the beneficiary's health insurance claim number (HICN), providers have the capability to view the number of sessions a beneficiary has received for this service via inquiry through CWF.

100-4, 20, 100.2.2

Evidence of Medical Necessity for Parenteral and Enteral Nutrition (PEN) Therapy

The PEN coverage is determined by information provided by the treating physician and the PEN supplier. A completed certification of medical necessity (CMN) must accompany and support initial claims for PEN to establish whether coverage criteria are met and to ensure that the PEN therapy provided is consistent with the attending or ordering physician's prescription.

Contractors ensure that the CMN contains pertinent information from the treating physician. Uniform specific medical data facilitate the review and promote consistency in coverage determinations and timelier claims processing.The medical and prescription information on a PEN CMN can be most appropriatelycompleted by the treating physician or from information in the patient's records by an employee of the physician for the physician's review and signature.

Although PEN suppliers sometimes may assist in providing the PEN services, they cannot complete the CMN since they do not have the same access to patient information needed to properly enter medical or prescription information. Contractors use appropriate professional relations issuances, training sessions, and meetings to ensure that all persons and PEN suppliers are aware of this limitation of their role. When properly completed, the PEN CMN includes the elements of a prescription as well as other data needed to determine whether Medicare coverage is possible. This practice will facilitate prompt delivery of PEN services and timely submittal of the related claim.

100-4, 20, 160.1

Billing for Total Parenteral Nutrition and Enteral NutritionFurnished to Part B Inpatients

A3-3660.6, SNF-544, SNF-559, SNF-260.4, SNF-261, HHA-403, HO-438, HO-229

Inpatient Part A hospital or SNF care includes total parenteral nutrition (TPN) systems and enteral nutrition (EN).

For inpatients for whom Part A benefits are not payable (e.g., benefits are exhausted or the beneficiary is entitled to Part B only), total parenteral nutrition (TPN) systems and enteral nutrition (EN) delivery systems are covered by Medicare as prosthetic devices when the coverage criteria are met. When these criteria are met, the medical equipment and medical supplies (together with nutrients) being used comprise covered prosthetic devices for coverage purposes rather than durable medical equipment. However, reimbursement rules relating to DME continue to apply to such items.

When a facility supplies TPN or EN systems that meet the criteria for coverage as a prosthetic device to an inpatient whose care is not covered under Part A, the facility must bill one of the DMERCs. Additionally, HHAs, SNFs, and hospitals that provide PEN supplies, equipment and nutrients as a prosthetic device under Part B must use the CMS-1500 or the related NSF or ANSI ASC X12N 837 format to bill the appropriate DMERC. The DMERC is determined according to the residence of the beneficiary. Refer to Sec.10 for jurisdiction descriptions.

FIs return claims containing PEN charges for Part B services where the bill type is 12x,

13x, 22x, 23x, 32x, 33x, or 34x with instructions to the provider to bill the DMERC.

100-4, 23, 60.3

(Rev.2340, Issued: 11-04-11, Effective, 01-01-12, Implementation: 01-03-12)

The DME MACs and local carriers must gap-fill the DMEPOS fee schedule for items for which charge data were unavailable during the fee schedule data base year using the fee schedule amounts for comparable equipment, using properly calculated fee schedule amounts from a neighboring carrier, or using supplier price lists with prices in effect during the fee schedule data base year. Data base "year" refers to the time period mandated by the statute and/or regulations from which Medicare allowed charge data is to be extracted in order to compute the fee schedule amounts for the various DMEPOS payment categories. For example, the fee schedule base year for inexpensive or routinely purchased durable medical equipment is the 12 month period ending June 30, 1987. Mail order catalogs are particularly suitable sources of price information for items such as urological and ostomy supplies which require constant replacement. DME MACs will gap-fill based on current instructions released each year for implementing and updating the new year's payment amounts.

If the only available price information is from a period other than the base period, apply the deflation factors that are included in the current year implementation instructions against current pricing in order to approximate the base year price for gap-filling purposes.

The deflation factors for gap-filling purposes are:

Year*	OX	CR	PO	SD	PE
1987	0.965	0.971	0.974	n/a	n/a
1988	0.928	0.934	0.936	n/a	n/a
1989	0.882	0.888	0.890	n/a	n/a
1990	0.843	0.848	0.851	n/a	n/a
1991	0.805	0.810	0.813	n/a	n/a
1992	0.781	0.786	0.788	n/a	n/a
1993	0.758	0.763	0.765	0.971	n/a
1994	0.740	0.745	0.747	0.947	n/a
1995	0.718	0.723	0.725	0.919	n/a
1996	0.699	0.703	0.705	0.895	0.973
1997	0.683	0.687	0.689	0.875	0.951
1998	0.672	0.676	0.678	0.860	0.936
1999	0.659	0.663	0.665	0.844	0.918
2000	0.635	0.639	0.641	0.813	0.885
2001	0.615	0.619	0.621	0.788	0.857
2002	0.609	0.613	0.614	0.779	0.848
2003	0.596	0.600	0.602	0.763	0.830
2004	0.577	0.581	0.582	0.739	0.804
2005	0.563	0.567	0.568	0.721	0.784
2006	0.540	0.543	0.545	0.691	0.752
2007	0.525	0.529	0.530	0.673	0.732
2008	0.500	0.504	0.505	0.641	0.697
2009	0.508	0.511	0.512	0.650	0.707
2010	0.502	0.506	0.507	0.643	0.700
2011	0.485	0.488	0.490	0.621	0.676

* Year price in effect

Payment Category Key:

OX	Oxygen & oxygen equipment (DME)
CR	Capped rental (DME)
IN	Inexpensive/routinely purchased (DME)
FS	Frequently serviced (DME)
SU	DME supplies
PO	Prosthetics & orthotics
SD	Surgical dressings
OS	Ostomy, tracheostomy, and urological supplies
PE	Parental and enteral nutrition

After deflation, the result must be increased by 1.7 percent and by the cumulative covered item update to complete the gap-filling (e.g., an additional .6 percent for a 2002 DME fee).

Note that when gap-filling for capped rental items, it is necessary to first gap-fill the purchase price then compute the base period fee schedule at 10 percent of the base period purchase price.

For used equipment, establish fee schedule amounts at 75 percent of the fee schedule amount for new equipment.

When gap-filling, for those carrier areas where a sales tax was imposed in the base period, add the applicable sales tax, e.g., five percent, to the gap-filled amount where the gap-filled amount does not take into account the sales tax, e.g., where the gap-filled amount is computed from pre-tax price lists or from another carrier area without a sales tax. Likewise, if the gap-filled amount is calculated from another carrier's fees where a sales tax is imposed, adjust the gap-filled amount to reflect the applicable local sales tax circumstances.

DME MACs and local carriers send their gap-fill information to CMS. After receiving the gap-filled base fees each year, CMS develops national fee schedule floors and ceilings and new fee schedule amounts for these codes and releases them as part of the July update file each year and during the quarterly updates.

Attachment A 2012 Fees for Codes K0739, L4205, L7520

STATE	K0739	L4205	L7520	STATE	K0739	L4205	L7520
AK	$26.47	$30.16	$35.48	SC	$14.05	20.94	28.43
AL	14.05	20.94	28.43	SD	15.70	20.92	38.00
AR	14.05	20.94	28.43	TN	14.05	20.94	28.43
AZ	17.37	20.92	34.98	TX	14.05	20.94	28.43
CA	21.56	34.38	40.07	UT	14.09	20.92	44.27
CO	14.05	20.94	28.43	VA	14.05	20.92	28.43
CT	23.47	21.41	28.43	VI	14.05	20.94	28.43
DC	14.05	20.92	28.43	VT	15.08	20.92	28.43
DE	25.88	20.92	28.43	WA	22.39	30.69	36.45
FL	14.05	20.94	28.43	WI	14.05	20.92	28.43
GA	14.05	20.94	28.43	WV	14.05	20.92	28.43
HI	17.37	30.16	35.48	WY	19.59	27.91	39.64
IA	14.05	20.92	34.03				
ID	14.05	20.92	28.43				
IL	14.05	20.92	28.43				
IN	14.05	20.92	28.43				
KS	14.05	20.92	35.48				
KY	14.05	26.81	36.35				
LA	14.05	20.94	28.43				
MA	23.47	20.92	28.43				
MD	14.05	20.92	28.43				
ME	23.47	20.92	28.43				
MI	14.05	20.92	28.43				
MN	14.05	20.92	28.43				
MO	14.05	20.92	28.43				
MS	14.05	20.94	28.43				
MT	14.05	20.92	35.48				
NC	14.05	20.94	28.43				
ND	17.51	30.10	35.48				
NE	14.05	20.92	39.64				
NH	15.08	20.92	28.43				
NJ	18.96	20.92	28.43				
NM	14.05	20.94	28.43				
NV	22.39	20.92	38.75				
NY	25.88	20.94	28.43				
OH	14.05	20.92	28.43				
OK	14.05	20.94	28.43				
OR	14.05	20.92	40.88				
PA	15.08	21.54	28.43				
PR	14.05	20.94	28.43				
RI	16.75	21.56	28.43				

Attachment B

HCPCS Codes Selected for the Round One of the DMEPOS Competitive Bidding Program in 2008

PRODUCT CATEGORY 1

Oxygen Supplies and Equipment

E1390 OXYGEN CONCENTRATOR, SINGLE DELIVERY PORT, CAPABLE OF DELIVERING 85 PERCENT OR GREATER OXYGEN CONCENTRATION AT THE PRESCRIBED FLOW RATE

E1391 OXYGEN CONCENTRATOR, DUAL DELIVERY PORT, CAPABLE OF DELIVERING 85 PERCENT OR GREATER OXYGEN CONCENTRATION AT THE PRESCRIBED FLOW RATE, EACH

E0424 STATIONARY COMPRESSED GASEOUS OXYGEN SYSTEM, RENTAL; INCLUDES CONTAINER, CONTENTS, REGULATOR, FLOWMETER, HUMIDIFIER, NEBULIZER, CANNULA OR MASK, AND TUBING

E0439 STATIONARY LIQUID OXYGEN SYSTEM, RENTAL; INCLUDES CONTAINER, CONTENTS, REGULATOR, FLOWMETER, HUMIDIFIER, NEBULIZER, CANNULA OR MASK, & TUBING

E0431 PORTABLE GASEOUS OXYGEN SYSTEM, RENTAL; INCLUDES PORTABLE CONTAINER, REGULATOR, FLOWMETER, HUMIDIFIER, CANNULA OR MASK, AND TUBING

E0434 PORTABLE LIQUID OXYGEN SYSTEM, RENTAL; INCLUDES PORTABLE CONTAINER, SUPPLY RESERVOIR, HUMIDIFIER, FLOWMETER, REFILL ADAPTOR, CONTENTS GAUGE, CANNULA OR MASK, AND TUBING

A4608 TRANSTRACHEAL OXYGEN CATHETER, EACH

A4615 CANNULA, NASAL

A4616 TUBING (OXYGEN), PER FOOT

A4617 MOUTH PIECE

A4620 VARIABLE CONCENTRATION MASK

E0560 HUMIDIFIER, DURABLE FOR SUPPLEMENTAL HUMIDIFICATION DURING IPPB TREATMENT OR OXYGEN DELIVERY

E0580 NEBULIZER, DURABLE, GLASS OR AUTOCLAVABLE PLASTIC, BOTTLE TYPE, FOR USE WITH REGULATOR OR FLOWMETER

E1353 REGULATOR

E1355 STAND/RACK

PRODUCT CATEGORY 2

Standard Power Wheelchairs, Scooters, and Related Accessories

E0950 WHEELCHAIR ACCESSORY, TRAY, EACH

E0951 HEEL LOOP/HOLDER, ANY TYPE, WITH OR WITHOUT ANKLE STRAP,

PRODUCT CATEGORY 1

Oxygen Supplies and Equipment

E1390 OXYGEN CONCENTRATOR, SINGLE DELIVERY PORT, CAPABLE OF DELIVERING 85 PERCENT OR GREATER OXYGEN CONCENTRATION AT THE PRESCRIBED FLOW RATE

E1391 OXYGEN CONCENTRATOR, DUAL DELIVERY PORT, CAPABLE OF DELIVERING 85 PERCENT OR GREATER OXYGEN CONCENTRATION AT THE PRESCRIBED FLOW RATE, EACH

E0424 STATIONARY COMPRESSED GASEOUS OXYGEN SYSTEM, RENTAL; INCLUDES CONTAINER, CONTENTS, REGULATOR, FLOWMETER, HUMIDIFIER, NEBULIZER, CANNULA OR MASK, AND TUBING

E0439 STATIONARY LIQUID OXYGEN SYSTEM, RENTAL; INCLUDES CONTAINER, CONTENTS, REGULATOR, FLOWMETER, HUMIDIFIER, NEBULIZER, CANNULA OR MASK, & TUBING

E0431 PORTABLE GASEOUS OXYGEN SYSTEM, RENTAL; INCLUDES PORTABLE CONTAINER, REGULATOR, FLOWMETER, HUMIDIFIER, CANNULA OR MASK, AND TUBING

E0434 PORTABLE LIQUID OXYGEN SYSTEM, RENTAL; INCLUDES PORTABLE CONTAINER, SUPPLY RESERVOIR, HUMIDIFIER, FLOWMETER, REFILL ADAPTOR, CONTENTS GAUGE, CANNULA OR MASK, AND TUBING

A4608 TRANSTRACHEAL OXYGEN CATHETER, EACH

A4615 CANNULA, NASAL

A4616 TUBING (OXYGEN), PER FOOT

A4617 MOUTH PIECE

A4620 VARIABLE CONCENTRATION MASK

E0560 HUMIDIFIER, DURABLE FOR SUPPLEMENTAL HUMIDIFICATION DURING IPPB TREATMENT OR OXYGEN DELIVERY

E0580 NEBULIZER, DURABLE, GLASS OR AUTOCLAVABLE PLASTIC, BOTTLE TYPE, FOR USE WITH REGULATOR OR FLOWMETER

E1353 REGULATOR

E1355 STAND/RACK

PRODUCT CATEGORY 2

Standard Power Wheelchairs, Scooters, and Related Accessories

E0950 WHEELCHAIR ACCESSORY, TRAY, EACH

E0951 HEEL LOOP/HOLDER, ANY TYPE, WITH OR WITHOUT ANKLE STRAP, EACH

E0952 TOE LOOP/HOLDER, ANY TYPE, EACH

E0955 WHEELCHAIR ACCESSORY, HEADREST, CUSHIONED, ANY TYPE, INCLUDING FIXED MOUNTING HARDWARE, EACH

E0956 WHEELCHAIR ACCESSORY, LATERAL TRUNK OR HIP SUPPORT, ANY TYPE, INCLUDING FIXED MOUNTING HARDWARE, EACH

E0957 WHEELCHAIR ACCESSORY, MEDIAL THIGH SUPPORT, ANY TYPE, INCLUDING FIXED MOUNTING HARDWARE, EACH

E0960 WHEELCHAIR ACCESSORY, SHOULDER HARNESS/STRAPS OR CHEST STRAP, INCLUDING ANY TYPE MOUNTING HARDWARE

E0973 WHEELCHAIR ACCESSORY, ADJUSTABLE HEIGHT, DETACHABLE ARMREST, COMPLETE ASSEMBLY, EACH

E0978 WHEELCHAIR ACCESSORY, POSITIONING BELT/SAFETY BELT/PELVIC STRAP, EACH

E0981 WHEELCHAIR ACCESSORY, SEAT UPHOLSTERY, REPLACEMENT ONLY, EACH

E0982 WHEELCHAIR ACCESSORY, BACK UPHOLSTERY, REPLACEMENT ONLY, EACH

E0990 WHEELCHAIR ACCESSORY, ELEVATING LEG REST, COMPLETE ASSEMBLY, EACH

E0995 WHEELCHAIR ACCESSORY, CALF REST/PAD, EACH

E1016 SHOCK ABSORBER FOR POWER WHEELCHAIR, EACH

E1020 RESIDUAL LIMB SUPPORT SYSTEM FOR WHEELCHAIR

E1028 WHEELCHAIR ACCESSORY, MANUAL SWINGAWAY, RETRACTABLE OR REMOVABLE MOUNTING HARDWARE FOR JOYSTICK, OTHER CONTROL INTERFACE OR POSITIONING ACCESSORY

E2208 WHEELCHAIR ACCESSORY, CYLINDER TANK CARRIER, EACH

E2209 ACCESSORY, ARM TROUGH, WITH OR WITHOUT HAND SUPPORT, EACH

E2210 WHEELCHAIR ACCESSORY, BEARINGS, ANY TYPE, REPLACEMENT ONLY, EACH

E2361 POWER WHEELCHAIR ACCESSORY, 22NF SEALED LEAD ACID BATTERY, EACH, (E.G. GEL CELL, ABSORBED GLASSMAT)

E2363 POWER WHEELCHAIR ACCESSORY, GROUP 24 SEALED LEAD ACID BATTERY, EACH (E.G. GEL CELL, ABSORBED GLASSMAT)

E2365 POWER WHEELCHAIR ACCESSORY, U-1 SEALED LEAD ACID BATTERY, EACH (E.G. GEL CELL, ABSORBED GLASSMAT)

E2366 POWER WHEELCHAIR ACCESSORY, BATTERY CHARGER, SINGLE MODE, FOR USE WITH ONLY ONE BATTERY TYPE, SEALED OR NON-SEALED, EACH

E2367 POWER WHEELCHAIR ACCESSORY, BATTERY CHARGER, DUAL MODE, FOR USE WITH EITHER BATTERY TYPE, SEALED OR NON-SEALED, EACH

E2368 POWER WHEELCHAIR COMPONENT, MOTOR, REPLACEMENT ONLY

E2369 POWER WHEELCHAIR COMPONENT, GEAR BOX, REPLACEMENT ONLY

E2370 POWER WHEELCHAIR COMPONENT, MOTOR AND GEAR BOX COMBINATION, REPLACEMENT ONLY

E2371 POWER WHEELCHAIR ACCESSORY, GROUP 27 SEALED LEAD ACID BATTERY, (E.G. GEL CELL, ABSORBED GLASSMAT), EACH

E2381 POWER WHEELCHAIR ACCESSORY, PNEUMATIC DRIVE WHEEL TIRE, ANY SIZE, REPLACEMENT ONLY, EACH

E2382 POWER WHEELCHAIR ACCESSORY, TUBE FOR PNEUMATIC DRIVE WHEEL TIRE, ANY SIZE, REPLACEMENT ONLY, EACH

E2383 POWER WHEELCHAIR ACCESSORY, INSERT FOR PNEUMATIC DRIVE WHEEL TIRE (REMOVABLE), ANY TYPE, ANY SIZE, REPLACEMENT ONLY, EACH

E2384 POWER WHEELCHAIR ACCESSORY, PNEUMATIC CASTER TIRE, ANY SIZE, REPLACEMENT ONLY, EACH

E2385 POWER WHEELCHAIR ACCESSORY, TUBE FOR PNEUMATIC CASTER TIRE, ANY SIZE, REPLACEMENT ONLY, EACH

E2386 POWER WHEELCHAIR ACCESSORY, FOAM FILLED DRIVE WHEEL TIRE, ANY SIZE, REPLACEMENT ONLY, EACH

E2387 POWER WHEELCHAIR ACCESSORY, FOAM FILLED CASTER TIRE, ANY SIZE, REPLACEMENT ONLY, EACH

E2388 POWER WHEELCHAIR ACCESSORY, FOAM DRIVE WHEEL TIRE, ANY SIZE, REPLACEMENT ONLY, EACH

E2389 POWER WHEELCHAIR ACCESSORY, FOAM CASTER TIRE, ANY SIZE, REPLACEMENT ONLY, EACH

E2390 POWER WHEELCHAIR ACCESSORY, SOLID (RUBBER/PLASTIC) DRIVE WHEEL TIRE, ANY SIZE, REPLACEMENT ONLY, EACH

E2391 POWER WHEELCHAIR ACCESSORY, SOLID (RUBBER/PLASTIC) CASTER TIRE (REMOVABLE), ANY SIZE, REPLACEMENT ONLY, EACH

E2392 POWER WHEELCHAIR ACCESSORY, SOLID (RUBBER/PLASTIC) CASTER TIRE WITH INTEGRATED WHEEL, ANY SIZE, REPLACEMENT ONLY, EACH

E2394 POWER WHEELCHAIR ACCESSORY, DRIVE WHEEL EXCLUDES TIRE, ANY SIZE, REPLACEMENT ONLY, EACH

E2395 POWER WHEELCHAIR ACCESSORY, CASTER WHEEL EXCLUDES TIRE, ANY SIZE, REPLACEMENT ONLY, EACH

E2396 POWER WHEELCHAIR ACCESSORY, CASTER FORK, ANY SIZE, REPLACEMENT ONLY, EACH

E2601 GENERAL USE WHEELCHAIR SEAT CUSHION, WIDTH LESS THAN 22 INCHES, ANY DEPTH

E2602 GENERAL USE WHEELCHAIR SEAT CUSHION, WIDTH 22 INCHES OR GREATER, ANY DEPTH

E2603 SKIN PROTECTION WHEELCHAIR SEAT CUSHION, WIDTH LESS THAN 22 INCHES, ANY DEPTH

E2604 SKIN PROTECTION WHEELCHAIR SEAT CUSHION, WIDTH 22 INCHES OR GREATER, ANY DEPTH

E2605 POSITIONING WHEELCHAIR SEAT CUSHION, WIDTH LESS THAN 22 INCHES, ANY DEPTH

E2606 POSITIONING WHEELCHAIR SEAT CUSHION, WIDTH 22 INCHES OR GREATER, ANY DEPTH

E2607 SKIN PROTECTION AND POSITIONING WHEELCHAIR SEAT CUSHION, WIDTH LESS THAN 22 INCHES, ANY DEPTH

E2608 SKIN PROTECTION AND POSITIONING WHEELCHAIR SEAT CUSHION, WIDTH 22 INCHES OR GREATER, ANY DEPTH

E2611 GENERAL USE WHEELCHAIR BACK CUSHION, WIDTH LESS THAN 22 INCHES, ANY HEIGHT, INCLUDING ANY TYPE MOUNTING HARDWARE

E2612 GENERAL USE WHEELCHAIR BACK CUSHION, WIDTH 22 INCHES OR GREATER, ANY HEIGHT, INCLUDING ANY TYPE MOUNTING HARDWARE

E2613 POSITIONING WHEELCHAIR BACK CUSHION, POSTERIOR, WIDTH LESS THAN 22 INCHES, ANY HEIGHT, INCLUDING ANY TYPE MOUNTING HARDWARE

E2614 POSITIONING WHEELCHAIR BACK CUSHION, POSTERIOR, WIDTH 22 INCHES OR GREATER, ANY HEIGHT, INCLUDING ANY TYPE MOUNTING HARDWARE

E2615 POSITIONING WHEELCHAIR BACK CUSHION, POSTERIOR-LATERAL, WIDTH LESS THAN 22 INCHES, ANY HEIGHT, INCLUDING ANY TYPE MOUNTING HARDWARE

E2616 POSITIONING WHEELCHAIR BACK CUSHION, POSTERIOR-LATERAL, WIDTH 22 INCHES OR GREATER, ANY HEIGHT, INCLUDING ANY TYPE MOUNTING HARDWARE

E2619 REPLACEMENT COVER FOR WHEELCHAIR SEAT CUSHION OR BACK CUSHION, EACH

E2620 POSITIONING WHEELCHAIR BACK CUSHION, PLANAR BACK WITH LATERAL SUPPORTS, WIDTH LESS THAN 22 INCHES, ANY HEIGHT, INCLUDING ANY TYPE MOUNTING HARDWARE

E2621 POSITIONING WHEELCHAIR BACK CUSHION, PLANAR BACK WITH LATERAL SUPPORTS, WIDTH 22 INCHES OR GREATER, ANY HEIGHT, INCLUDING ANY TYPE MOUNTING HARDWARE

K0015 DETACHABLE, NON-ADJUSTABLE HEIGHT ARMREST, EACH

K0017	DETACHABLE, ADJUSTABLE HEIGHT ARMREST, BASE, EACH
K0018	DETACHABLE, ADJUSTABLE HEIGHT ARMREST, UPPER PORTION, EACH
K0019	ARM PAD, EACH
K0020	FIXED, ADJUSTABLE HEIGHT ARMREST, PAIR
K0037	HIGH MOUNT FLIP-UP FOOTREST, EACH
K0038	LEG STRAP, EACH
K0039	LEG STRAP, H STYLE, EACH
K0040	ADJUSTABLE ANGLE FOOTPLATE, EACH
K0041	LARGE SIZE FOOTPLATE, EACH
K0042	STANDARD SIZE FOOTPLATE, EACH
K0043	FOOTREST, LOWER EXTENSION TUBE, EACH
K0044	FOOTREST, UPPER HANGER BRACKET, EACH
K0045	FOOTREST, COMPLETE ASSEMBLY
K0046	ELEVATING LEGREST, LOWER EXTENSION TUBE, EACH
K0047	ELEVATING LEGREST, UPPER HANGER BRACKET, EACH
K0050	RATCHET ASSEMBLY
K0051	CAM RELEASE ASSEMBLY, FOOTREST OR LEGREST, EACH
K0052	SWINGAWAY, DETACHABLE FOOTRESTS, EACH
K0053	ELEVATING FOOTRESTS, ARTICULATING (TELESCOPING), EACH
K0098	DRIVE BELT FOR POWER WHEELCHAIR
K0195	ELEVATING LEG RESTS, PAIR (FOR USE WITH CAPPED RENTAL WHEELCHAIR BASE)
K0733	POWER WHEELCHAIR ACCESSORY, 12 TO 24 AMP HOUR SEALED LEAD ACID BATTERY, EACH (E.G., GEL CELL, ABSORBED GLASSMAT)
K0734	SKIN PROTECTION WHEELCHAIR SEAT CUSHION, ADJUSTABLE, WIDTH LESS THAN 22 INCHES, ANY DEPTH
K0735	SKIN PROTECTION WHEELCHAIR SEAT CUSHION, ADJUSTABLE, WIDTH 22 INCHES OR GREATER, ANY DEPTH
K0736	SKIN PROTECTION AND POSITIONING WHEELCHAIR SEAT CUSHION, ADJUSTABLE, WIDTH LESS THAN 22 INCHES, ANY DEPTH
K0737	SKIN PROTECTION AND POSITIONING WHEELCHAIR SEAT CUSHION, ADJUSTABLE, WIDTH 22 INCHES OR GREATER, ANY DEPTH
K0800	POWER OPERATED VEHICLE, GROUP 1 STANDARD
K0801	POWER OPERATED VEHICLE, GROUP 1 HEAVY DUTY
K0802	POWER OPERATED VEHICLE, GROUP 1 VERY HEAVY DUTY
K0806	POWER OPERATED VEHICLE, GROUP 2 STANDARD
K0807	POWER OPERATED VEHICLE, GROUP 2 HEAVY DUTY
K0808	POWER OPERATED VEHICLE, GROUP 2 VERY HEAVY DUTY
K0813	POWER WHEELCHAIR, GROUP 1 STANDARD, PORTABLE, SLING/SOLID SEAT AND BACK
K0814	POWER WHEELCHAIR, GROUP 1 STANDARD, PORTABLE, CAPTAINS CHAIR
K0815	POWER WHEELCHAIR, GROUP 1 STANDARD, SLING/SOLID SEAT AND BACK
K0816	POWER WHEELCHAIR, GROUP 1 STANDARD, CAPTAINS CHAIR
K0820	POWER WHEELCHAIR, GROUP 2 STANDARD, PORTABLE, SLING/SOLID SEAT/BACK
K0821	POWER WHEELCHAIR, GROUP 2 STANDARD, PORTABLE, CAPTAINS CHAIR
K0822	POWER WHEELCHAIR, GROUP 2 STANDARD, SLING/SOLID SEAT/BACK
K0823	POWER WHEELCHAIR, GROUP 2 STANDARD, CAPTAINS CHAIR
K0824	POWER WHEELCHAIR, GROUP 2 HEAVY DUTY, SLING/SOLID SEAT/BACK
K0825	POWER WHEELCHAIR, GROUP 2 HEAVY DUTY, CAPTAINS CHAIR
K0826	POWER WHEELCHAIR, GROUP 2 VERY HEAVY DUTY, SLING/SOLID SEAT/BACK
K0827	POWER WHEELCHAIR, GROUP 2 VERY HEAVY DUTY, CAPTAINS CHAIR
K0828	POWER WHEELCHAIR, GROUP 2 EXTRA HEAVY DUTY, SLING/SOLID SEAT/BACK
K0829	POWER WHEELCHAIR, GROUP 2 EXTRA HEAVY DUTY, CAPTAINS CHAIR

PRODUCT CATEGORY 3

Complex Rehabilitative Power Wheelchairs and Related Accessories

E0950	WHEELCHAIR ACCESSORY, TRAY, EACH
E0951	HEEL LOOP/HOLDER, ANY TYPE, WITH OR WITHOUT ANKLE STRAP, EACH
E0952	TOE LOOP/HOLDER, ANY TYPE, EACH
E0955	WHEELCHAIR ACCESSORY, HEADREST, CUSHIONED, ANY TYPE, INCLUDING FIXED MOUNTING HARDWARE, EACH
E0956	WHEELCHAIR ACCESSORY, LATERAL TRUNK OR HIP SUPPORT, ANY TYPE, INCLUDING FIXED MOUNTING HARDWARE, EACH
E0957	WHEELCHAIR ACCESSORY, MEDIAL THIGH SUPPORT, ANY TYPE, INCLUDING FIXED MOUNTING HARDWARE, EACH
E0960	WHEELCHAIR ACCESSORY, SHOULDER HARNESS/STRAPS OR CHEST STRAP, INCLUDING ANY TYPE MOUNTING HARDWARE
E0973	WHEELCHAIR ACCESSORY, ADJUSTABLE HEIGHT, DETACHABLE ARMREST, COMPLETE ASSEMBLY, EACH
E0978	WHEELCHAIR ACCESSORY, POSITIONING BELT/SAFETY BELT/PELVIC STRAP, EACH
E0981	WHEELCHAIR ACCESSORY, SEAT UPHOLSTERY, REPLACEMENT ONLY, EACH
E0982	WHEELCHAIR ACCESSORY, BACK UPHOLSTERY, REPLACEMENT ONLY, EACH
E0990	WHEELCHAIR ACCESSORY, ELEVATING LEG REST, COMPLETE ASSEMBLY, EACH
E0995	WHEELCHAIR ACCESSORY, CALF REST/PAD, EACH
E1002	WHEELCHAIR ACCESSORY, POWER SEATING SYSTEM, TILT ONLY
E1003	WHEELCHAIR ACCESSORY, POWER SEATING SYSTEM, RECLINE ONLY, WITHOUT SHEAR REDUCTION
E1004	WHEELCHAIR ACCESSORY, POWER SEATING SYSTEM, RECLINE ONLY, WITH MECHANICAL SHEAR REDUCTION
E1005	WHEELCHAIR ACCESSORY, POWER SEATNG SYSTEM, RECLINE ONLY, WITH POWER SHEAR REDUCTION
E1006	WHEELCHAIR ACCESSORY, POWER SEATING SYSTEM, COMBINATION TILT AND RECLINE, WITHOUT SHEAR REDUCTION
E1007	WHEELCHAIR ACCESSORY, POWER SEATING SYSTEM, COMBINATION TILT AND RECLINE, WITH MECHANICAL SHEAR REDUCTION
E1008	WHEELCHAIR ACCESSORY, POWER SEATING SYSTEM, COMBINATION TILT AND RECLINE, WITH POWER SHEAR REDUCTION
E1010	WHEELCHAIR ACCESSORY, ADDITION TO POWER SEATING SYSTEM, POWER LEG ELEVATION SYSTEM, INCLUDING LEG REST, PAIR
E1016	SHOCK ABSORBER FOR POWER WHEELCHAIR, EACH
E1020	RESIDUAL LIMB SUPPORT SYSTEM FOR WHEELCHAIR
E1028	WHEELCHAIR ACCESSORY, MANUAL SWINGAWAY, RETRACTABLE OR REMOVABLE MOUNTING HARDWARE FOR JOYSTICK, OTHER CONTROL INTERFACE OR POSITIONING ACCESSORY
E1029	WHEELCHAIR ACCESSORY, VENTILATOR TRAY, FIXED
E1030	WHEELCHAIR ACCESSORY, VENTILATOR TRAY, GIMBALED
E2208	WHEELCHAIR ACCESSORY, CYLINDER TANK CARRIER, EACH
E2209	ACCESSORY, ARM TROUGH, WITH OR WITHOUT HAND SUPPORT, EACH
E2210	WHEELCHAIR ACCESSORY, BEARINGS, ANY TYPE, REPLACEMENT ONLY, EACH
E2310	POWER WHEELCHAIR ACCESSORY, ELECTRONIC CONNECTION BETWEEN WHEELCHAIR CONTROLLER AND ONE POWER SEATING SYSTEM MOTOR, INCLUDING ALL RELATED ELECTRONICS, INDICATOR FEATURE, MECHANICAL FUNCTION SELECTION SWITCH, AND FIXED MOUNTING HARDWARE
E2311	POWER WHEELCHAIR ACCESSORY, ELECTRONIC CONNECTION BETWEEN WHEELCHAIR CONTROLLER AND TWO OR MORE POWER SEATING SYSTEM MOTORS, INCLUDING ALL RELATED ELECTRONICS, INDICATOR FEATURE, MECHANICAL FUNCTION SELECTION SWITCH, AND FIXED MOUNTING HARDWARE

E2321 POWER WHEELCHAIR ACCESSORY, HAND CONTROL INTERFACE, REMOTE JOYSTICK, NONPROPORTIONAL, INCLUDING ALL RELATED ELECTRONICS, MECHANICAL STOP SWITCH, AND FIXED MOUNTING HARDWARE

E2322 POWER WHEELCHAIR ACCESSORY, HAND CONTROL INTERFACE, MULTIPLE MECHANICAL SWITCHES, NONPROPORTIONAL, INCLUDING ALL RELATED ELECTRONICS, MECHANICAL STOP SWITCH, AND FIXED MOUNTING HARDWARE

E2323 POWER WHEELCHAIR ACCESSORY, SPECIALTY JOYSTICK HANDLE FOR HAND CONTROL INTERFACE, PREFABRICATED

E2324 POWER WHEELCHAIR ACCESSORY, CHIN CUP FOR CHIN CONTROL INTERFACE

E2325 POWER WHEELCHAIR ACCESSORY, SIP AND PUFF INTERFACE, NONPROPORTIONAL, INCLUDING ALL RELATED ELECTRONICS, MECHANICAL STOP SWITCH, AND MANUAL SWINGAWAY MOUNTING HARDWARE

E2326 POWER WHEELCHAIR ACCESSORY, BREATH TUBE KIT FOR SIP AND PUFF INTERFACE

E2327 POWER WHEELCHAIR ACCESSORY, HEAD CONTROL INTERFACE, MECHANICAL, PROPORTIONAL, INCLUDING ALL RELATED ELECTRONICS, MECHANICAL DIRECTION CHANGE SWITCH, AND FIXED MOUNTING HARDWARE

E2328 POWER WHEELCHAIR ACCESSORY, HEAD CONTROL OR EXTREMITY CONTROL INTERFACE, ELECTRONIC, PROPORTIONAL, INCLUDING ALL RELATED ELECTRONICS AND FIXED MOUNTING HARDWARE

E2329 POWER WHEELCHAIR ACCESSORY, HEAD CONTROL INTERFACE, CONTACT SWITCH MECHANISM, NONPROPORTIONAL, INCLUDING ALL RELATED ELECTRONICS, MECHANICAL STOP SWITCH, MECHANICAL DIRECTION CHANGE SWITCH, HEAD ARRAY, AND FIXED MOUNTING HARDWARE

E2330 POWER WHEELCHAIR ACCESSORY, HEAD CONTROL INTERFACE, PROXIMITY SWITCH MECHANISM, NONPROPORTIONAL, INCLUDING ALL RELATED ELECTRONICS, MECHANICAL STOP SWITCH, MECHANICAL DIRECTION CHANGE SWITCH, HEAD ARRAY, AND FIXED MOUNTING HARDWARE

E2351 POWER WHEELCHAIR ACCESSORY, ELECTRONIC INTERFACE TO OPERATE SPEECH GENERATING DEVICE USING POWER WHEELCHAIR CONTROL INTERFACE

E2361 POWER WHEELCHAIR ACCESSORY, 22NF SEALED LEAD ACID BATTERY, EACH, (E.G. GEL CELL, ABSORBED GLASSMAT)

E2363 POWER WHEELCHAIR ACCESSORY, GROUP 24 SEALED LEAD ACID BATTERY, EACH (E.G. GEL CELL, ABSORBED GLASSMAT)

E2365 POWER WHEELCHAIR ACCESSORY, U-1 SEALED LEAD ACID BATTERY, EACH (E.G. GEL CELL, ABSORBED GLASSMAT)

E2366 POWER WHEELCHAIR ACCESSORY, BATTERY CHARGER, SINGLE MODE, FOR USE WITH ONLY ONE BATTERY TYPE, SEALED OR NON-SEALED, EACH

E2367 POWER WHEELCHAIR ACCESSORY, BATTERY CHARGER, DUAL MODE, FOR USE WITH EITHER BATTERY TYPE, SEALED OR NON-SEALED, EACH

E2368 POWER WHEELCHAIR COMPONENT, MOTOR, REPLACEMENT ONLY

E2369 POWER WHEELCHAIR COMPONENT, GEAR BOX, REPLACEMENT ONLY

E2370 POWER WHEELCHAIR COMPONENT, MOTOR AND GEAR BOX COMBINATION, REPLACEMENT ONLY

E2371 POWER WHEELCHAIR ACCESSORY, GROUP 27 SEALED LEAD ACID BATTERY, (E.G. GEL CELL, ABSORBED GLASSMAT), EACH

E2373 KC POWER WHEELCHAIR ACCESSORY, HAND OR CHIN CONTROL INTERFACE, COMPACT REMOTE JOYSTICK, PROPORTIONAL, INCLUDING FIXED MOUNTING HARDWARE

E2374 POWER WHEELCHAIR ACCESSORY, HAND OR CHIN CONTROL INTERFACE, STANDARD REMOTE JOYSTICK (NOT INCLUDING CONTROLLER), PROPORTIONAL, INCLUDING ALL RELATED ELECTRONICS AND FIXED MOUNTING HARDWARE, REPLACEMENT ONLY

E2375 POWER WHEELCHAIR ACCESSORY, NON-EXPANDABLE CONTROLLER, INCLUDING ALL RELATED ELECTRONICS AND MOUNTING HARDWARE, REPLACEMENT ONLY

E2376 POWER WHEELCHAIR ACCESSORY, EXPANDABLE CONTROLLER, INCLUDING ALL RELATED ELECTRONICS AND MOUNTING HARDWARE, REPLACEMENT ONLY

E2377 POWER WHEELCHAIR ACCESSORY, EXPANDABLE CONTROLLER, INCLUDING ALL RELATED ELECTRONICS AND MOUNTING HARDWARE, UPGRADE PROVIDED AT INITIAL ISSUE

E2381 POWER WHEELCHAIR ACCESSORY, PNEUMATIC DRIVE WHEEL TIRE, ANY SIZE, REPLACEMENT ONLY, EACH

E2382 POWER WHEELCHAIR ACCESSORY, TUBE FOR PNEUMATIC DRIVE WHEEL TIRE, ANY SIZE, REPLACEMENT ONLY, EACH

E2383 POWER WHEELCHAIR ACCESSORY, INSERT FOR PNEUMATIC DRIVE WHEEL TIRE (REMOVABLE), ANY TYPE, ANY SIZE, REPLACEMENT ONLY, EACH

E2384 POWER WHEELCHAIR ACCESSORY, PNEUMATIC CASTER TIRE, ANY SIZE, REPLACEMENT ONLY, EACH

E2385 POWER WHEELCHAIR ACCESSORY, TUBE FOR PNEUMATIC CASTER TIRE, ANY SIZE, REPLACEMENT ONLY, EACH

E2386 POWER WHEELCHAIR ACCESSORY, FOAM FILLED DRIVE WHEEL TIRE, ANY SIZE, REPLACEMENT ONLY, EACH

E2387 POWER WHEELCHAIR ACCESSORY, FOAM FILLED CASTER TIRE, ANY SIZE, REPLACEMENT ONLY, EACH

E2388 POWER WHEELCHAIR ACCESSORY, FOAM DRIVE WHEEL TIRE, ANY SIZE, REPLACEMENT ONLY, EACH

E2389 POWER WHEELCHAIR ACCESSORY, FOAM CASTER TIRE, ANY SIZE, REPLACEMENT ONLY, EACH

E2390 POWER WHEELCHAIR ACCESSORY, SOLID (RUBBER/PLASTIC) DRIVE WHEEL TIRE, ANY SIZE, REPLACEMENT ONLY, EACH

E2391 POWER WHEELCHAIR ACCESSORY, SOLID (RUBBER/PLASTIC) CASTER TIRE (REMOVABLE), ANY SIZE, REPLACEMENT ONLY, EACH

E2392 POWER WHEELCHAIR ACCESSORY, SOLID (RUBBER/PLASTIC) CASTER TIRE WITH INTEGRATED WHEEL, ANY SIZE, REPLACEMENT ONLY, EACH

E2394 POWER WHEELCHAIR ACCESSORY, DRIVE WHEEL EXCLUDES TIRE, ANY SIZE, REPLACEMENT ONLY, EACH

E2395 POWER WHEELCHAIR ACCESSORY, CASTER WHEEL EXCLUDES TIRE, ANY SIZE, REPLACEMENT ONLY, EACH

E2396 POWER WHEELCHAIR ACCESSORY, CASTER FORK, ANY SIZE, REPLACEMENT ONLY, EACH

E2601 GENERAL USE WHEELCHAIR SEAT CUSHION, WIDTH LESS THAN 22 INCHES, ANY DEPTH

E2602 GENERAL USE WHEELCHAIR SEAT CUSHION, WIDTH 22 INCHES OR GREATER, ANY DEPTH

E2603 SKIN PROTECTION WHEELCHAIR SEAT CUSHION, WIDTH LESS THAN 22 INCHES, ANY DEPTH

E2604 SKIN PROTECTION WHEELCHAIR SEAT CUSHION, WIDTH 22 INCHES OR GREATER, ANY DEPTH

E2605 POSITIONING WHEELCHAIR SEAT CUSHION, WIDTH LESS THAN 22 INCHES, ANY DEPTH

E2606 POSITIONING WHEELCHAIR SEAT CUSHION, WIDTH 22 INCHES OR GREATER, ANY DEPTH

E2607 SKIN PROTECTION AND POSITIONING WHEELCHAIR SEAT CUSHION, WIDTH LESS THAN 22 INCHES, ANY DEPTH

E2608 SKIN PROTECTION AND POSITIONING WHEELCHAIR SEAT CUSHION, WIDTH 22 INCHES OR GREATER, ANY DEPTH

E2611 GENERAL USE WHEELCHAIR BACK CUSHION, WIDTH LESS THAN 22 INCHES, ANY HEIGHT, INCLUDING ANY TYPE MOUNTING HARDWARE

E2612 GENERAL USE WHEELCHAIR BACK CUSHION, WIDTH 22 INCHES OR GREATER, ANY HEIGHT, INCLUDING ANY TYPE MOUNTING HARDWARE

E2613 POSITIONING WHEELCHAIR BACK CUSHION, POSTERIOR, WIDTH LESS THAN 22 INCHES, ANY HEIGHT, INCLUDING ANY TYPE MOUNTING HARDWARE

E2614 POSITIONING WHEELCHAIR BACK CUSHION, POSTERIOR, WIDTH 22 INCHES OR GREATER, ANY HEIGHT, INCLUDING ANY TYPE MOUNTING HARDWARE

E2615 POSITIONING WHEELCHAIR BACK CUSHION, POSTERIOR-LATERAL, WIDTH LESS THAN 22 INCHES, ANY HEIGHT, INCLUDING ANY TYPE MOUNTING HARDWARE

E2616 POSITIONING WHEELCHAIR BACK CUSHION, POSTERIOR-LATERAL, WIDTH 22 INCHES OR GREATER, ANY HEIGHT, INCLUDING ANY TYPE MOUNTING HARDWARE

E2619 REPLACEMENT COVER FOR WHEELCHAIR SEAT CUSHION OR BACK CUSHION, EACH

E2620 POSITIONING WHEELCHAIR BACK CUSHION, PLANAR BACK WITH LATERAL SUPPORTS, WIDTH LESS THAN 22 INCHES, ANY HEIGHT, INCLUDING ANY TYPE MOUNTING HARDWARE

E2621 POSITIONING WHEELCHAIR BACK CUSHION, PLANAR BACK WITH LATERAL SUPPORTS, WIDTH 22 INCHES OR GREATER, ANY HEIGHT, INCLUDING ANY TYPE MOUNTING HARDWARE

K0015 DETACHABLE, NON-ADJUSTABLE HEIGHT ARMREST, EACH

K0017 DETACHABLE, ADJUSTABLE HEIGHT ARMREST, BASE, EACH

K0018 DETACHABLE, ADJUSTABLE HEIGHT ARMREST, UPPER PORTION, EACH

K0019 ARM PAD, EACH

K0020 FIXED, ADJUSTABLE HEIGHT ARMREST, PAIR

K0037 HIGH MOUNT FLIP-UP FOOTREST, EACH

K0038 LEG STRAP, EACH

K0039 LEG STRAP, H STYLE, EACH

K0040 ADJUSTABLE ANGLE FOOTPLATE, EACH

K0041 LARGE SIZE FOOTPLATE, EACH

K0042 STANDARD SIZE FOOTPLATE, EACH

K0043 FOOTREST, LOWER EXTENSION TUBE, EACH

K0044 FOOTREST, UPPER HANGER BRACKET, EACH

K0045 FOOTREST, COMPLETE ASSEMBLY

K0046 ELEVATING LEGREST, LOWER EXTENSION TUBE, EACH

K0047 ELEVATING LEGREST, UPPER HANGER BRACKET, EACH

K0050 RATCHET ASSEMBLY

K0051 CAM RELEASE ASSEMBLY, FOOTREST OR LEGREST, EACH

K0052 SWINGAWAY, DETACHABLE FOOTRESTS, EACH

K0053 ELEVATING FOOTRESTS, ARTICULATING (TELESCOPING), EACH

K0098 DRIVE BELT FOR POWER WHEELCHAIR

K0195 ELEVATING LEG RESTS, PAIR (FOR USE WITH CAPPED RENTAL WHEELCHAIR BASE)

K0733 POWER WHEELCHAIR ACCESSORY, 12 TO 24 AMP HOUR SEALED LEAD ACID BATTERY, EACH (E.G., GEL CELL, ABSORBED GLASSMAT)

K0734 SKIN PROTECTION WHEELCHAIR SEAT CUSHION, ADJUSTABLE, WIDTH LESS THAN 22 INCHES, ANY DEPTH

K0735 SKIN PROTECTION WHEELCHAIR SEAT CUSHION, ADJUSTABLE, WIDTH 22 INCHES OR GREATER, ANY DEPTH

K0736 SKIN PROTECTION AND POSITIONING WHEELCHAIR SEAT CUSHION, ADJUSTABLE, WIDTH LESS THAN 22 INCHES, ANY DEPTH

K0737 SKIN PROTECTION AND POSITIONING WHEELCHAIR SEAT CUSHION, ADJUSTABLE, WIDTH 22 INCHES OR GREATER, ANY DEPTH

K0835 POWER WHEELCHAIR, GROUP 2 STANDARD, SINGLE POWER OPTION, SLING/SOLID SEAT/BACK, PATIENT WEIGHT CAPACITY UP TO AND INCLUDING 300 POUNDS

K0836 POWER WHEELCHAIR, GROUP 2 STANDARD, SINGLE POWER OPTION, CAPTAINS CHAIR, PATIENT WEIGHT CAPACITY UP TO AND INCLUDING 300 POUNDS

K0837 POWER WHEELCHAIR, GROUP 2 HEAVY DUTY, SINGLE POWER OPTION, SLING/SOLID SEAT/BACK, PATIENT WEIGHT CAPACITY 301 TO 450 POUNDS

K0838 POWER WHEELCHAIR, GROUP 2 HEAVY DUTY, SINGLE POWER OPTION, CAPTAINS CHAIR, PATIENT WEIGHT CAPACITY 301 TO 450 POUNDS

K0839 POWER WHEELCHAIR, GROUP 2 VERY HEAVY DUTY, SINGLE POWER OPTION SLING/SOLID SEAT/BACK, PATIENT WEIGHT CAPACITY 451 TO 600 POUNDS

K0840 POWER WHEELCHAIR, GROUP 2 EXTRA HEAVY DUTY, SINGLE POWER OPTION, SLING/SOLID SEAT/BACK, PATIENT WEIGHT CAPACITY 601 POUNDS OR MORE

K0841 POWER WHEELCHAIR, GROUP 2 STANDARD, MULTIPLE POWER OPTION, SLING/SOLID SEAT/BACK, PATIENT WEIGHT CAPACITY UP TO AND INCLUDING 300 POUNDS

K0842 POWER WHEELCHAIR, GROUP 2 STANDARD, MULTIPLE POWER OPTION, CAPTAINS CHAIR, PATIENT WEIGHT CAPACITY UP TO AND INCLUDING 300 POUNDS

K0843 POWER WHEELCHAIR, GROUP 2 HEAVY DUTY, MULTIPLE POWER OPTION, SLING/SOLID SEAT/BACK, PATIENT WEIGHT CAPACITY 301 TO 450 POUNDS

K0848 POWER WHEELCHAIR, GROUP 3 STANDARD, SLING/SOLID SEAT/BACK, PATIENT WEIGHT CAPACITY UP TO AND INCLUDING 300 POUNDS

K0849 POWER WHEELCHAIR, GROUP 3 STANDARD, CAPTAINS CHAIR, PATIENT WEIGHT CAPACITY UP TO AND INCLUDING 300 POUNDS

K0850 POWER WHEELCHAIR, GROUP 3 HEAVY DUTY, SLING/SOLID SEAT/BACK, PATIENT WEIGHT CAPACITY 301 TO 450 POUNDS

K0851 POWER WHEELCHAIR, GROUP 3 HEAVY DUTY, CAPTAINS CHAIR, PATIENT WEIGHT CAPACITY 301 TO 450 POUNDS

K0852 POWER WHEELCHAIR, GROUP 3 VERY HEAVY DUTY, SLING/SOLID SEAT/BACK, PATIENT WEIGHT CAPACITY 451 TO 600 POUNDS

K0853 POWER WHEELCHAIR, GROUP 3 VERY HEAVY DUTY, CAPTAINS CHAIR, PATIENT WEIGHT CAPACITY 451 TO 600 POUNDS

K0854 POWER WHEELCHAIR, GROUP 3 EXTRA HEAVY DUTY, SLING/SOLID SEAT/BACK, PATIENT WEIGHT CAPACITY 601 POUNDS OR MORE

K0855 POWER WHEELCHAIR, GROUP 3 EXTRA HEAVY DUTY, CAPTAINS CHAIR, PATIENT WEIGHT CAPACITY 601 POUNDS OR MORE

K0856 POWER WHEELCHAIR, GROUP 3 STANDARD, SINGLE POWER OPTION, SLING/SOLID SEAT/BACK, PATIENT WEIGHT CAPACITY UP TO AND INCLUDING 300 POUNDS

K0857 POWER WHEELCHAIR, GROUP 3 STANDARD, SINGLE POWER OPTION, CAPTAINS CHAIR, PATIENT WEIGHT CAPACITY UP TO AND INCLUDING 300 POUNDS

K0858 POWER WHEELCHAIR, GROUP 3 HEAVY DUTY, SINGLE POWER OPTION, SLING/SOLID SEAT/BACK, PATIENT WEIGHT 301 TO 450 POUNDS

K0859 POWER WHEELCHAIR, GROUP 3 HEAVY DUTY, SINGLE POWER OPTION, CAPTAINS CHAIR, PATIENT WEIGHT CAPACITY 301 TO 450 POUNDS

K0860 POWER WHEELCHAIR, GROUP 3 VERY HEAVY DUTY, SINGLE POWER OPTION, SLING/SOLID SEAT/BACK, PATIENT WEIGHT CAPACITY 451 TO 600 POUNDS

K0861 POWER WHEELCHAIR, GROUP 3 STANDARD, MULTIPLE POWER OPTION, SLING/SOLID SEAT/BACK, PATIENT WEIGHT CAPACITY UP TO AND INCLUDING 300 POUNDS

K0862 POWER WHEELCHAIR, GROUP 3 HEAVY DUTY, MULTIPLE POWER OPTION, SLING/SOLID SEAT/BACK, PATIENT WEIGHT CAPACITY 301 TO 450 POUNDS

K0863 POWER WHEELCHAIR, GROUP 3 VERY HEAVY DUTY, MULTIPLE POWER OPTION, SLING/SOLID SEAT/BACK, PATIENT WEIGHT CAPACITY 451 TO 600 POUNDS

K0864 POWER WHEELCHAIR, GROUP 3 EXTRA HEAVY DUTY, MULTIPLE POWER OPTION, SLING/SOLID SEAT/BACK, PATIENT WEIGHT CAPACITY 601 POUNDS OR MORE

PRODUCT CATEGORY 4

Mail-Order Diabetic Supplies

A4233 KL REPLACEMENT BATTERY, ALKALINE (OTHER THAN J CELL), FOR USE WITH MEDICALLY NECESSARY HOME BLOOD GLUCOSE MONITOR OWNED BY PATIENT, EACH

A4234 KL REPLACEMENT BATTERY, ALKALINE, J CELL, FOR USE WITH MEDICALLY NECESSARY HOME BLOOD GLUCOSE MONITOR OWNED BY PATIENT, EACH

A4235 KL REPLACEMENT BATTERY, LITHIUM, FOR USE WITH MEDICALLY NECESSARY HOME BLOOD GLUCOSE MONITOR OWNED BY PATIENT, EACH

A4236 KL REPLACEMENT BATTERY, SILVER OXIDE, FOR USE WITH MEDICALLY NECESSARY HOME BLOOD GLUCOSE MONITOR OWNED BY PATIENT, EACH

A4253 KL BLOOD GLUCOSE TEST OR REAGENT STRIPS FOR HOME BLOOD GLUCOSE MONITOR, PER 50 STRIPS

A4256 KL NORMAL, LOW AND HIGH CALIBRATOR SOLUTION / CHIPS

A4258 KL SPRING-POWERED DEVICE FOR LANCET, EACH

A4259 KL LANCETS, PER BOX OF 100

PRODUCT CATEGORY 5

Enteral Nutrients, Equipment, and Supplies

B4034 ENTERAL FEEDING SUPPLY KIT; SYRINGE FED, PER DAY

B4035 ENTERAL FEEDING SUPPLY KIT; PUMP FED, PER DAY

B4036 ENTERAL FEEDING SUPPLY KIT; GRAVITY FED, PER DAY

B4081 NASOGASTRIC TUBING WITH STYLET

B4082 NASOGASTRIC TUBING WITHOUT STYLET

B4083 STOMACH TUBE - LEVINE TYPE

B4087 GASTROSTOMY / JEJUNOSTOMY TUBE, ANY MATERIAL, ANY TYPE, (STANDARD), EACH

B4088 GASTROSTOMY / JEJUNOSTOMY TUBE, ANY MATERIAL, ANY TYPE, (LOW PROFILE), EACH

B4149 ENTERAL FORMULA, MANUFACTURED BLENDERIZED NATURAL FOODS WITH INTACT NUTRIENTS, INCLUDES PROTEINS, FATS, CARBOHYDRATES, VITAMINS AND MINERALS, MAY INCLUDE FIBER, ADMINISTERED THROUGH AN ENTERAL FEEDING TUBE, 100 CALORIES = 1 UNIT

B4150 ENTERAL FORMULA, NUTRITIONALLY COMPLETE WITH INTACT NUTRIENTS, INCLUDES PROTEINS, FATS, CARBOHYDRATES, VITAMINS AND MINERALS, MAY INCLUDE FIBER, ADMINISTERED THROUGH AN ENTERAL FEEDING TUBE, 100 CALORIES = 1 UNIT

B4152 ENTERAL FORMULA, NUTRITIONALLY COMPLETE, CALORICALLY DENSE (EQUAL TO OR GREATER THAN 1.5 KCAL/ML) WITH INTACT NUTRIENTS, INCLUDES PROTEINS, FATS, CARBOHYDRATES, VITAMINS AND MINERALS, MAY INCLUDE FIBER, ADMINISTERED THROUGH AN ENTERAL FEEDING TUBE, 100 CALORIES = 1 UNIT

B4153 ENTERAL FORMULA, NUTRITIONALLY COMPLETE, HYDROLYZED PROTEINS (AMINO ACIDS AND PEPTIDE CHAIN), INCLUDES FATS, CARBOHYDRATES, VITAMINS AND MINERALS, MAY INCLUDE FIBER, ADMINISTERED THROUGH AN ENTERAL FEEDING TUBE, 100 CALORIES = 1 UNIT

B4154 ENTERAL FORMULA, NUTRITIONALLY COMPLETE, FOR SPECIAL METABOLIC NEEDS, EXCLUDES INHERITED DISEASE OF METABOLISM, INCLUDES ALTERED COMPOSITION OF PROTEINS, FATS, CARBOHYDRATES, VITAMINS AND/OR MINERALS, MAY INCLUDE FIBER, ADMINISTERED THROUGH AN ENTERAL FEEDING TUBE, 100 CALORIES = 1 UNIT

B4155 ENTERAL FORMULA, NUTRITIONALLY INCOMPLETE/MODULAR NUTRIENTS, INCLUDES SPECIFIC NUTRIENTS, CARBOHYDRATES (E.G. GLUCOSE POLYMERS), PROTEINS/AMINO ACIDS (E.G. GLUTAMINE, ARGININE), FAT (E.G. MEDIUM CHAIN TRIGLYCERIDES) OR COMBINATON, ADMINISTERED THROUGH AN ENTERAL FEEDING TUBE, 100 CALORIES = 1 UNIT NOTE: (SEE J7060, J7070, J7042 FOR SOLUTION CODES FOR OTHER THAN PARENTERAL NUTRITION THERAPY USE)

B9000 ENTERAL NUTRITION INFUSION PUMP - WITHOUT ALARM

B9002 ENTERAL NUTRITION INFUSION PUMP - WITH ALARM

E0776 IV POLE

PRODUCT CATEGORY 6

Continuous Positive Airway Pressure Devices, Respiratory Assist Devices, and Related Supplies and Accessories

A4604 TUBING WITH INTEGRATED HEATING ELEMENT FOR USE WITH POSITIVE AIRWAY PRESSURE DEVICE

A7030 FULL FACE MASK USED WITH POSITIVE AIRWAY PRESSURE DEVICE, EACH

A7031 FACE MASK INTERFACE, REPLACEMENT FOR FULL FACE MASK, EACH

A7032 CUSHION FOR USE ON NASAL MASK INTERFACE, REPLACEMENT ONLY, EACH

A7033 PILLOW FOR USE ON NASAL CANNULA TYPE INTERFACE, REPLACEMENT ONLY, PAIR

A7034 NASAL INTERFACE (MASK OR CANNULA TYPE) USED WITH POSITIVE AIRWAY PRESSURE DEVICE, WITH OR WITHOUT HEAD STRAP

A7035 HEADGEAR USED WITH POSITIVE AIRWAY PRESSURE DEVICE

A7036 CHINSTRAP USED WITH POSITIVE AIRWAY PRESSURE DEVICE

A7037 TUBING USED WITH POSITIVE AIRWAY PRESSURE DEVICE

A7038 FILTER, DISPOSABLE, USED WITH POSITIVE AIRWAY PRESSURE DEVICE

A7039 FILTER, NON DISPOSABLE, USED WITH POSITIVE AIRWAY PRESSURE DEVICE

A7044 ORAL INTERFACE USED WITH POSITIVE AIRWAY PRESSURE DEVICE, EACH

A7045 EXHALATION PORT WITH OR WITHOUT SWIVEL USED WITH ACCESSORIES FOR POSITIVE AIRWAY DEVICES, REPLACEMENT ONLY

A7046 WATER CHAMBER FOR HUMIDIFIER, USED WITH POSITIVE AIRWAY PRESSURE DEVICE, REPLACEMENT, EACH

E0470 RESPIRATORY ASSIST DEVICE, BI-LEVEL PRESSURE CAPABILITY, WITHOUT BACKUP RATE FEATURE, USED WITH NONINVASIVE INTERFACE, E.G., NASAL OR FACIAL MASK (INTERMITTENT ASSIST DEVICE WITH CONTINUOUS POSITIVE AIRWAY PRESSURE DEVICE)

E0471 RESPIRATORY ASSIST DEVICE, BI-LEVEL PRESSURE CAPABILITY, WITH BACK-UP RATE FEATURE, USED WITH NONINVASIVE INTERFACE, E.G., NASAL OR FACIAL MASK (INTERMITTENT ASSIST DEVICE WITH CONTINUOUS POSITIVE AIRWAY PRESSURE DEVICE)

E0472 RESPIRATORY ASSIST DEVICE, BI-LEVEL PRESSURE CAPABILITY, WITH BACKUP RATE FEATURE, USED WITH INVASIVE INTERFACE, E.G., TRACHEOSTOMY TUBE (INTERMITTENT ASSIST DEVICE WITH CONTINUOUS POSITIVE AIRWAY PRESSURE DEVICE)

E0561 HUMIDIFIER, NON-HEATED, USED WITH POSITIVE AIRWAY PRESSURE DEVICE

E0562 HUMIDIFIER, HEATED, USED WITH POSITIVE AIRWAY PRESSURE DEVICE

E0601 CONTINUOUS AIRWAY PRESSURE (CPAP) DEVICE

PRODUCT CATEGORY 7

Hospital Beds and Related Supplies

E0250 HOSPITAL BED, FIXED HEIGHT, WITH ANY TYPE SIDE RAILS, WITH MATTRESS

E0251 HOSPITAL BED, FIXED HEIGHT, WITH ANY TYPE SIDE RAILS, WITHOUT MATTRESS

E0255 HOSPITAL BED, VARIABLE HEIGHT, HI-LO, WITH ANY TYPE SIDE RAILS, WITH MATTRESS

E0256 HOSPITAL BED, VARIABLE HEIGHT, HI-LO, WITH ANY TYPE SIDE RAILS, WITHOUT MATTRESS

E0260 HOSPITAL BED, SEMI-ELECTRIC (HEAD AND FOOT ADJUSTMENT), WITH ANY TYPE SIDE RAILS, WITH MATTRESS

E0261 HOSPITAL BED, SEMI-ELECTRIC (HEAD AND FOOT ADJUSTMENT), WITH ANY TYPE SIDE RAILS, WITHOUT MATTRESS

E0265 HOSPITAL BED, TOTAL ELECTRIC (HEAD, FOOT AND HEIGHT ADJUSTMENTS), WITH ANY TYPE SIDE RAILS, WITH MATTRESS

E0266 HOSPITAL BED, TOTAL ELECTRIC (HEAD, FOOT AND HEIGHT ADJUSTMENTS), WITH ANY TYPE SIDE RAILS, WITHOUT MATTRESS

E0271 MATTRESS, INNERSPRING

E0272 MATTRESS, FOAM RUBBER

E0280 BED CRADLE, ANY TYPE

E0290 HOSPITAL BED, FIXED HEIGHT, WITHOUT SIDE RAILS, WITH MATTRESS

E0291 HOSPITAL BED, FIXED HEIGHT, WITHOUT SIDE RAILS, WITHOUT MATTRESS

E0292 HOSPITAL BED, VARIABLE HEIGHT, HI-LO, WITHOUT SIDE RAILS, WITH MATTRESS

E0293 HOSPITAL BED, VARIABLE HEIGHT, HI-LO, WITHOUT SIDE RAILS, WITHOUT MATTRESS

E0294 HOSPITAL BED, SEMI-ELECTRIC (HEAD AND FOOT ADJUSTMENT), WITHOUT SIDE RAILS, WITH MATTRESS

E0295 HOSPITAL BED, SEMI-ELECTRIC (HEAD AND FOOT ADJUSTMENT), WITHOUT SIDE RAILS, WITHOUT MATTRESS

E0296 HOSPITAL BED, TOTAL ELECTRIC (HEAD, FOOT AND HEIGHT ADJUSTMENTS). WITHOUT SIDE RAILS, WITH MATTRESS

E0297 HOSPITAL BED, TOTAL ELECTRIC (HEAD, FOOT AND HEIGHT ADJUSTMENTS), WITHOUT SIDE RAILS, WITHOUT MATTRESS

E0300 PEDIATRIC CRIB, HOSPITAL GRADE, FULLY ENCLOSED

E0301 HOSPITAL BED, HEAVY DUTY, EXTRA WIDE, WITH WEIGHT CAPACITY GREATER THAN 350 POUNDS, BUT LESS THAN OR EQUAL TO 600 POUNDS, WITH ANY TYPE SIDE RAILS, WITHOUT MATTRESS

E0302 HOSPITAL BED, EXTRA HEAVY DUTY, EXTRA WIDE, WITH WEIGHT CAPACITY GREATER THAN 600 POUNDS, WITH ANY TYPE SIDE RAILS, WITHOUT MATTRESS

E0303 HOSPITAL BED, HEAVY DUTY, EXTRA WIDE, WITH WEIGHT CAPACITY GREATER THAN 350 POUNDS, BUT LESS THAN OR EQUAL TO 600 POUNDS, WITH ANY TYPE SIDE RAILS, WITH MATTRESS

E0304 HOSPITAL BED, EXTRA HEAVY DUTY, EXTRA WIDE, WITH WEIGHT CAPACITY GREATER THAN 600 POUNDS, WITH ANY TYPE SIDE RAILS, WITH MATTRESS

E0305 BED SIDE RAILS, HALF LENGTH

E0310 BED SIDE RAILS, FULL LENGTH

E0316 SAFETY ENCLOSURE FRAME/CANOPY FOR USE WITH HOSPITAL BED, ANY TYPE

E0910 TRAPEZE BARS, A/K/A PATIENT HELPER, ATTACHED TO BED, WITH GRAB BAR

E0911 TRAPEZE BAR, HEAVY DUTY, FOR PATIENT WEIGHT CAPACITY GREATER THAN 250 POUNDS, ATTACHED TO BED, WITH GRAB BAR

E0912 TRAPEZE BAR, HEAVY DUTY, FOR PATIENT WEIGHT CAPACITY GREATER THAN 250 POUNDS, FREE STANDING, COMPLETE WITH GRAB BAR

E0940 TRAPEZE BAR, FREE STANDING, COMPLETE WITH GRAB BAR

PRODUCT CATEGORY 8

Negative Pressure Wound Therapy Pumps and Related Supplies and Accessories

A6550 WOUND CARE SET, FOR NEGATIVE PRESSURE WOUND THERAPY ELECTRICAL PUMP, INCLUDES ALL SUPPLIES AND ACCESSORIES

A7000 CANISTER, DISPOSABLE, USED WITH SUCTION PUMP, EACH

E2402 NEGATIVE PRESSURE WOUND THERAPY ELECTRICAL PUMP, STATIONARY OR PORTABLE

PRODUCT CATEGORY 9

Walkers and Related Accessories

A4636 REPLACEMENT, HANDGRIP, CANE, CRUTCH, OR WALKER, EACH

A4637 REPLACEMENT, TIP, CANE, CRUTCH, WALKER, EACH.

E0130 WALKER, RIGID (PICKUP), ADJUSTABLE OR FIXED HEIGHT

E0135 WALKER, FOLDING (PICKUP), ADJUSTABLE OR FIXED HEIGHT

E0140 WALKER, WITH TRUNK SUPPORT, ADJUSTABLE OR FIXED HEIGHT, ANY TYPE

E0141 WALKER, RIGID, WHEELED, ADJUSTABLE OR FIXED HEIGHT

E0143 WALKER, FOLDING, WHEELED, ADJUSTABLE OR FIXED HEIGHT

E0144 WALKER, ENCLOSED, FOUR SIDED FRAMED, RIGID OR FOLDING, WHEELED WITH POSTERIOR SEAT

E0147 WALKER, HEAVY DUTY, MULTIPLE BRAKING SYSTEM, VARIABLE WHEEL RESISTANCE

E0148 WALKER, HEAVY DUTY, WITHOUT WHEELS, RIGID OR FOLDING, ANY TYPE, EACH

E0149 WALKER, HEAVY DUTY, WHEELED, RIGID OR FOLDING, ANY TYPE

E0154 PLATFORM ATTACHMENT, WALKER, EACH

E0155 WHEEL ATTACHMENT, RIGID PICK-UP WALKER, PER PAIR

E0156 SEAT ATTACHMENT, WALKER

E0157 CRUTCH ATTACHMENT, WALKER, EACH

E0158 LEG EXTENSIONS FOR WALKER, PER SET OF FOUR (4)

E0159 BRAKE ATTACHMENT FOR WHEELED WALKER, REPLACEMENT, EACH

PRODUCT CATEGORY 10

Support Surfaces

E0193 POWERED AIR FLOTATION BED (LOW AIR LOSS THERAPY)

E0277 POWERED PRESSURE-REDUCING AIR MATTRESS

E0371 NONPOWERED ADVANCED PRESSURE REDUCING OVERLAY FOR MATTRESS, STANDARD MATTRESS LENGTH AND WIDTH

E0372 POWERED AIR OVERLAY FOR MATTRESS, STANDARD MATTRESS LENGTH AND WIDTH

E0373 NONPOWERED ADVANCED PRESSURE REDUCING MATTRESS

100-4, 32, 11.1

Electrical Stimulation

A. Coding Applicable to Carriers & Fiscal Intermediaries (FIs)

Effective April 1, 2003, a National Coverage Decision was made to allow for Medicare coverage of Electrical Stimulation for the treatment of certain types of wounds. The type of wounds covered are chronic Stage III or Stage IV pressure ulcers, arterial ulcers, diabetic ulcers and venous stasis ulcers. All other uses of electrical stimulation for the treatment of wounds are not covered by Medicare. Electrical stimulation will not be covered as an initial treatment modality.

The use of electrical stimulation will only be covered after appropriate standard wound care has been tried for at least 30 days and there are no measurable signs of healing. If electrical stimulation is being used, wounds must be evaluated periodically by the treating physician but no less than every 30 days by a physician. Continued treatment with electrical stimulation is not covered if measurable signs of healing have not been demonstrated within any 30-day period of treatment. Additionally, electrical stimulation must be discontinued when the wound demonstrates a 100% epithelialzed wound bed.

Coverage policy can be found in Pub. 100-03, Medicare National Coverage Determinations Manual, Chapter 1, Section 270.1 (http://www.cms.hhs.gov/manuals/103_cov_determ/ncd103index.asp)

The applicable Healthcare Common Procedure Coding System (HCPCS) code for Electrical Stimulation and the covered effective date is as follows:

HCPCS	Definition	Effective Date
G0281	Electrical Stimulation, (unattended), to one or more areas for chronic Stage III and Stage IV pressure ulcers, arterial ulcers, diabetic ulcers and venous stasis ulcers not demonstrating measurable signs of healing after 30 days of conventional care as part of a therapy plan of care.	04/01/2003

Medicare will not cover the device used for the electrical stimulation for the treatment of wounds. However, Medicare will cover the service. Unsupervised home use of electrical stimulation will not be covered.

B. FI Billing Instructions

The applicable types of bills acceptable when billing for electrical stimulation services are 12X, 13X, 22X, 23X, 71X, 73X, 74X, 75X, and 85X. Chapter 25 of this manual provides general billing instructions that must be followed for bills submitted to FIs. FIs pay for electrical stimulation services under the Medicare Physician Fee Schedule for a hospital, Comprehensive Outpatient Rehabilitation Facility (CORF), Outpatient Rehabilitation Facility (ORF), Outpatient Physical Therapy (OPT) and Skilled Nursing Facility (SNF).

Payment methodology for independent Rural Health Clinic (RHC), provider-based RHCs, free-standing Federally Qualified Health Center (FQHC) and provider based FQHCs is made under the all-inclusive rate for the visit furnished to the RHC/FQHC patient to obtain the therapy service. Only one payment will be made for the visit furnished to the

RHC/FQHC patient to obtain the therapy service. As of April 1, 2005, RHCs/FQHCs are no longer required to report HCPCS codes when billing for these therapy services.

Payment Methodology for a Critical Access Hospital (CAH) is on a reasonable cost basis unless the CAH has elected the Optional Method and then the FI pays115% of the MPFS amount for the professional component of the HCPCS code in addition to the technical component.

In addition, the following revenues code must be used in conjunction with the HCPCS code identified:

Revenue Code	Description
420	Physical Therapy
430	Occupational Therapy
520	Federal Qualified Health Center *
521	Rural Health Center *
977, 978	Critical Access Hospital- method II CAH professional services only

* NOTE: As of April 1, 2005, RHCs/FQHCs are no longer required to report HCPCS codes when billing for these therapy services.

C. Carrier Claims

Carriers pay for Electrical Stimulation services billed with HCPCS codes G0281 based on the MPFS. Claims for Electrical Stimulation services must be billed on Form CMS-1500 or the electronic equivalent following instructions in chapter 12 of this manual (http://www.cms.hhs.gov/manuals/104_claims/clm104c12.pdf).

D. Coinsurance and Deductible

The Medicare contractor shall apply coinsurance and deductible to payments for these therapy services except for services billed to the FI by FQHCs. For FQHCs, only co-insurance applies.

100-4, 32, 11.2

Electromagnetic Therapy

A. HCPCS Coding Applicable to Carriers & Fiscal Intermediaries (FIs)

Effective July 1, 2004, a National Coverage Decision was made to allow for Medicare coverage of electromagnetic therapy for the treatment of certain types of wounds. The type of wounds covered are chronic Stage III or Stage IV pressure ulcers, arterial ulcers, diabetic ulcers and venous stasis ulcers. All other uses of electromagnetic therapy for the treatment of wounds are not covered by Medicare. Electromagnetic therapy will not be covered as an initial treatment modality.

The use of electromagnetic therapy will only be covered after appropriate standard wound care has been tried for at least 30 days and there are no measurable signs of healing. If electromagnetic therapy is being used, wounds must be evaluated periodically by the treating physician but no less than every 30 days by a physician. Continued treatment with electromagnetic therapy is not covered if measurable signs of healing have not been demonstrated within any 30-day period of treatment. Additionally, electromagnetic therapy must be discontinued when the wound demonstrates a 100% epithelialzed wound bed.

Coverage policy can be found in Pub. 100-03, Medicare National Coverage Determinations Manual, Chapter 1, Section 270.1. (www.cms.hhs.gov/manuals/103_cov_determ/ncd103index.asp)

The applicable Healthcare Common Procedure Coding System (HCPCS) code for Electrical Stimulation and the covered effective date is as follows:

HCPCS	Definition	Effective Date
G0329	ElectromagneticTherapy, to one or more areas for chronic Stage III and Stage IV pressure ulcers, arterial ulcers, diabetic ulcers and venous stasis ulcers not demonstrating measurable signs of healing after 30 days of conventional care as part of a therapy plan of care.	07/01/2004

Medicare will not cover the device used for the electromagnetic therapy for the treatment of wounds. However, Medicare will cover the service. Unsupervised home use of electromagnetic therapy will not be covered.

B. FI Billing Instructions

The applicable types of bills acceptable when billing for electromagnetic therapy services are 12X, 13X, 22X, 23X, 71X, 73X, 74X, 75X, and 85X. Chapter 25 of this manual provides general billing instructions that must be followed for bills submitted to FIs. FIs pay for electromagnetic therapy services under the Medicare Physician Fee Schedule for a hospital, CORF, ORF, and SNF.

Payment methodology for independent (RHC), provider-based RHCs, free-standing FQHC and provider based FQHCs is made under the all-inclusive rate for the visit furnished to the RHC/FQHC patient to obtain the therapy service. Only one payment will be made for the visit furnished to the RHC/FQHC patient to obtain the therapy service. As of April 1, 2005, RHCs/FQHCs are no longer required to report HCPCS codes when billing for the therapy service.

Payment Methodology for a CAH is payment on a reasonable cost basis unless the CAH has elected the Optional Method and then the FI pays pay 115% of the MPFS amount for the professional component of the HCPCS code in addition to the technical component.

In addition, the following revenues code must be used in conjunction with the HCPCS code identified:

Revenue Code	Description
420	Physical Therapy
430	Occupational Therapy
520	Federal Qualified Health Center *
521	Rural Health Center *
977, 978	Critical Access Hospital- method II CAH professional services only

* NOTE: As of April 1, 2005, RHCs/FQHCs are no longer required to report HCPCS codes when billing for the therapy service.

C. Carrier Claims

Carriers pay for Electromagnetic Therapy services billed with HCPCS codes G0329 based on the MPFS. Claims for electromagnetic therapy services must be billed on Form CMS-1500 or the electronic equivalent following instructions in chapter 12 of this manual (www.cms.hhs.gov/manuals/104_claims/clm104index.asp).

Payment information for HCPCS code G0329 will be added to the July 2004 update of the Medicare Physician Fee Schedule Database (MPFSD).

D. Coinsurance and Deductible

The Medicare contractor shall apply coinsurance and deductible to payments for electromagnetic therapy services except for services billed to the FI by FQHCs. For FQHCs only co-insurance applies.

100-4, 32, 30.1

Billing Requirements for HBO Therapy for the Treatment of Diabetic Wounds of the Lower Extremities

Hyperbaric Oxygen Therapy is a modality in which the entire body is exposed to oxygen under increased atmospheric pressure. Effective April 1, 2003, a National Coverage Decision expanded the use of HBO therapy to include coverage for the treatment of diabetic wounds of the lower extremities. For specific coverage criteria for HBO Therapy, refer to the National Coverage Determinations Manual, chapter 1, section 20.29.

NOTE: Topical application of oxygen does not meet the definition of HBO therapy as stated above. Also, its clinical efficacy has not been established. Therefore, no Medicare reimbursement may be made for the topical application of oxygen.

I. Billing Requirements for Intermediaries

Claims for HBO therapy should be submitted on Form CMS-1450 or its electronic equivalent.

a. Applicable Bill Types

The applicable hospital bill types are 11X, 13X and 85X.

b. Procedural Coding

- 99183 - Physician attendance and supervision of hyperbaric oxygen therapy, per session.
- C1300 - Hyperbaric oxygen under pressure, full body chamber, per 30-minute interval.

NOTE: Code C1300 is not available for use other than in a hospital outpatient department. In skilled nursing facilities (SNFs), HBO therapy is part of the SNF PPS payment for beneficiaries in covered Part A stays.

For hospital inpatients and critical access hospitals (CAHs) not electing Method I, HBO therapy is reported under revenue code 940 without any HCPCS code. For inpatient services, show ICD-9-CM procedure code 93.59.

For CAHs electing Method I, HBO therapy is reported under revenue code 940 along with HCPCS code 99183.

c. Payment Requirements for Intermediaries

Payment is as follows:

- Intermediary payment is allowed for HBO therapy for diabetic wounds of the lower extremities when performed as a physician service in a hospital outpatient setting and for inpatients. Payment is allowed for claims with valid diagnostic ICD-9 codes as shown above with dates of service on or after April 1, 2003. Those claims with invalid codes should be denied as not medically necessary.
- For hospitals, payment will be based upon the Ambulatory Payment Classification (APC) or the inpatient Diagnosis Related Group (DRG). Deductible and coinsurance apply.

Payment to Critical Access Hospitals (electing Method I) is made under cost reimbursement. For Critical Access Hospitals electing Method II, the technical component is paid under cost reimbursement and the professional component is paid under the Physician Fee Schedule.

NOTE: Information regarding the form locator numbers that correspond to these data element names and a table to crosswalk UB-04 form locators to the 837 transaction is found in Chapter 25.

II. Carrier Billing Requirements
Claims for this service should be submitted on Form CMS-1500 or its electronic equivalent.

The following HCPCS code applies:

- 99183 - Physician attendance and supervision of hyperbaric oxygen therapy, per session.

a. Payment Requirements for Carriers

Payment and pricing information will occur through updates to the Medicare Physician Fee Schedule Database (MPFSDB). Pay for this service on the basis of the MPFSDB. Deductible and coinsurance apply. Claims from physicians or other practitioners where assignment was not taken, are subject to the Medicare limiting charge.

III. Medicare Summary Notices (MSNs)
Use the following MSN Messages where appropriate:

In situations where the claim is being denied on the basis that the condition does not meet our coverage requirements, use one of the following MSN Messages:

"Medicare does not pay for this item or service for this condition." (MSN Message 16.48)

The Spanish version of the MSN message should read:

"Medicare no paga por este articulo o servicio para esta afeccion."

In situations where, based on the above utilization policy, medical review of the claim results in a determination that the service is not medically necessary, use the following MSN message:

"The information provided does not support the need for this service or item." (MSN Message 15.4)

The Spanish version of the MSN message should read:

"La informacion proporcionada no confirma la necesidad para este servicio o articulo."

IV. Remittance Advice Notices
Use appropriate existing remittance advice and reason codes at the line level to express the specific reason if you deny payment for HBO therapy for the treatment of diabetic wounds of lower extremities.

100-4, 32, 40.1

Coverage Requirements

Effective January 1, 2002, sacral nerve stimulation is covered for the treatment of urinary urge incontinence, urgency-frequency syndrome and urinary retention. Sacral nerve stimulation involves both a temporary test stimulation to determine if an implantable stimulator would be effective and a permanent implantation in appropriate candidates. Both the test and the permanent implantation are covered.

The following limitations for coverage apply to all indications:

- Patient must be refractory to conventional therapy (documented behavioral, pharmacologic and/or surgical corrective therapy) and be an appropriate surgical candidate such that implantation with anesthesia can occur.
- Patients with stress incontinence, urinary obstruction, and specific neurologic diseases (e.g., diabetes with peripheral nerve involvement) that are associated with secondary manifestations of the above three indications are excluded.
- Patient must have had a successful test stimulation in order to support subsequent implantation. Before a patient is eligible for permanent implantation, he/she must demonstrate a 50% or greater improvement through test stimulation. Improvement is measured through voiding diaries.
- Patient must be able to demonstrate adequate ability to record voiding diary data such that clinical results of the implant procedure can be properly evaluated.

100-4, 32, 50

Deep Brain Stimulation for Essential Tremor and Parkinson's Disease

Deep brain stimulation (DBS) refers to high-frequency electrical stimulation of anatomic regions deep within the brain utilizing neurosurgically implanted electrodes. These DBS electrodes are stereotactically placed within targeted nuclei on one (unilateral) or both (bilateral) sides of the brain. There are currently three targets for DBS -- the thalamic ventralis intermedius nucleus (VIM), subthalamic nucleus (STN) and globus pallidus interna (GPi).

Essential tremor (ET) is a progressive, disabling tremor most often affecting the hands. ET may also affect the head, voice and legs. The precise pathogenesis of ET is unknown. While it may start at any age, ET usually peaks within the second and sixth decades. Beta-adrenergic blockers and anticonvulsant medications are usually the first line treatments for reducing the severity of tremor. Many patients, however, do not adequately respond or cannot tolerate these medications. In these medically refractory ET patients, thalamic VIM DBS may be helpful for symptomatic relief of tremor.

Parkinson's disease (PD) is an age-related progressive neurodegenerative disorder involving the loss of dopaminergic cells in the substantia nigra of the midbrain. The disease is characterized by tremor, rigidity, bradykinesia and progressive postural instability. Dopaminergic medication is typically used as a first line treatment for reducing the primary symptoms of PD. However, after prolonged use, medication can become less effective and can produce significant adverse events such as dyskinesias and other motor function complications. For patients who become unresponsive to medical treatments and/or have intolerable side effects from medications, DBS for symptom relief may be considere

100-4, 32, 60.4.1

Allowable Covered Diagnosis Codes

For services furnished on or after July 1, 2002, the applicable ICD-9-CM diagnosis code for this benefit is V43.3, organ or tissue replaced by other means; heart valve.

For services furnished on or after March 19, 2008, the applicable ICD-9-CM diagnosis codes for this benefit are:

V43.3 (organ or tissue replaced by other means; heart valve),

289.81 (primary hypercoagulable state),

451.0-451.9 (includes 451.11, 451.19, 451.2, 451.80-451.84, 451.89) (phlebitis & thrombophlebitis),

453.0-453.3 (other venous embolism & thrombosis),

453.40-453.49 (includes 453.40-453.42, 453.8-453.9) (venous embolism and thrombosis of the deep vessels of the lower extremity, and other specified veins/unspecified sites)

415.11-415.12, 415.19 (pulmonary embolism & infarction) or,

427.31 (atrial fibrillation (established) (paroxysmal)).

100-4, 32, 60.5.2

Applicable Diagnosis Codes for Carriers

For services furnished on or after July 1, 2002, the applicable ICD-9-CM diagnosis code for this benefit is V43.3, organ or tissue replaced by other means; heart valve.

For services furnished on or after March 19, 2008, the applicable ICD-9-CM diagnosis codes for this benefit are:

- V43.3 (organ or tissue replaced by other means; heart valve),
- 289.81 (primary hypercoagulable state),
- 451.0-451.9 (includes 451.11, 451.19, 451.2, 451.80-451.84, 451.89) (phlebitis & thrombophlebitis),
- 453.0-453.3 (other venous embolism & thrombosis),
- 453.40-453.49 (includes 453.40-453.42, 453.8-453.9) (venous embolism and thrombosis of the deep vessels of the lower extremity, and other specified veins/unspecified sites)
- 415.11-415.12, 415.19 (pulmonary embolism & infarction) or,
- 427.31 (atrial fibrillation (established) (paroxysmal)).

100-4, 32, 80

Billing of the Diagnosis and Treatment of Peripheral Neuropathy with Loss of Protective Sensation in People with Diabetes

Coverage Requirements - Peripheral neuropathy is the most common factor leading to amputation in people with diabetes. In diabetes, peripheral neuropathy is an anatomically diffuse process primarily affecting sensory and autonomic fibers; however, distal motor findings may be present in advanced cases. Long nerves are affected first, with symptoms typically beginning insidiously in the toes and then advancing proximally. This leads to loss of protective sensation (LOPS), whereby a person is unable to feel minor trauma from mechanical, thermal, or chemical sources. When foot lesions are present, the reduction in autonomic nerve functions may also inhibit wound healing.

Peripheral neuropathy with LOPS, secondary to diabetes, is a localized illness of the feet and falls within the regulation's exception to the general exclusionary rule (see 42 C.F.R. Sec.411.15(l)(l)(i)). Foot exams for people with diabetic peripheral neuropathy with LOPS are reasonable and necessary to allow for early intervention in serious complications that typically afflict diabetics with the disease.

Effective for services furnished on or after July 1, 2002, Medicare covers, as a physician service, an evaluation (examination and treatment) of the feet no more often than every 6 months for individuals with a documented diagnosis of diabetic sensory neuropathy and LOPS, as long as the beneficiary has not seen a foot care specialist for some other reason in the interim. LOPS shall be diagnosed through sensory testing with the 5.07 monofilament using established guidelines, such as those developed by the National Institute of Diabetes and Digestive and Kidney Diseases guidelines. Five sites should be tested on the plantar surface of each foot, according to the National Institute of Diabetes and Digestive and Kidney Diseases guidelines. The areas must be tested randomly since the loss of protective sensation may be patchy in distribution, and the patient may get clues if the test is done rhythmically. Heavily callused areas should be avoided. As suggested by the American Podiatric Medicine Association, an absence of sensation at two or more sites out of 5 tested on either foot when tested with the 5.07 Semmes-Weinstein monofilament must be present and documented to diagnose peripheral neuropathy with loss of protective sensation.

100-4, 32, 80.2

Applicable HCPCS Codes

G0245 - Initial physician evaluation and management of a diabetic patient with diabetic sensory neuropathy resulting in a loss of protective sensation (LOPS) which must include:

1. The diagnosis of LOPS;
2. A patient history;
3. A physical examination that consists of at least the following elements:
   - (a) visual inspection of the forefoot, hindfoot, and toe web spaces,
   - (b) evaluation of a protective sensation,
   - (c) evaluation of foot structure and biomechanics,
   - (d) evaluation of vascular status and skin integrity,
   - (e) evaluation and recommendation of footwear, and
4. Patient education.

G0246 - Follow-up physician evaluation and management of a diabetic patient with diabetic sensory neuropathy resulting in a loss of protective sensation (LOPS) to include at least the following:

1. a patient history;
2. a physical examination that includes:
   - (a) visual inspection of the forefoot, hindfoot, and toe web spaces,
   - (b) evaluation of protective sensation,
   - (c) evaluation of foot structure and biomechanics,
   - (d) evaluation of vascular status and skin integrity,
   - (e) evaluation and recommendation of footwear, and
3. patient education.

G0247 - Routine foot care by a physician of a diabetic patient with diabetic sensory neuropathy resulting in a LOPS to include if present, at least the following:

- (1) local care of superficial (i.e., superficial to muscle and fascia) wounds;
- (2) debridement of corns and calluses; and
- (3) trimming and debridement of nails.

NOTE: Code G0247 must be billed on the same date of service with either G0245 or G0246 in order to be considered for payment.

The short descriptors for the above HCPCS codes are as follows:

G0245 - INITIAL FOOT EXAM PTLOPS

G0246 - FOLLOWUP EVAL OF FOOT PT LOP

G0247 - ROUTINE FOOTCARE PT W LOPS

100-4, 32, 80.8

CWF Utilization Edits

Edit 1 - Should CWF receive a claim from an FI for G0245 or G0246 and a second claim from a contractor for either G0245 or G0246 (or vice versa) and they are different dates of service and less than 6 months apart, the second claim will reject. CWF will edit to allow G0245 or G0246 to be paid no more than every 6 months for a particular beneficiary, regardless of who furnished the service. If G0245 has been paid, regardless of whether it was posted as a facility or professional claim, it must be 6 months before G0245 can be paid again or G0246 can be paid. If G0246 has been paid, regardless of whether it was posted as a facility or professional claim, it must be 6 months before G0246 can be paid again or G0245 can be paid. CWF will not impose limits on how many times each code can be paid for a beneficiary as long as there has been 6 months between each service.

The CWF will return a specific reject code for this edit to the contractors and FIs that will be identified in the CWF documentation. Based on the CWF reject code, the contractors and FIs must deny the claims and return the following messages:

> MSN 18.4 -- This service is being denied because it has not been __ months since your last examination of this kind (NOTE: Insert 6 as the appropriate number of months.)
>
> RA claim adjustment reason code 96 - Non-covered charges, along with remark code M86 - Service denied because payment already made for same/similar procedure within set time frame.

Edit 2

The CWF will edit to allow G0247 to pay only if either G0245 or G0246 has been submitted and accepted as payable on the same date of service. CWF will return a specific reject code for this edit to the contractors and FIs that will be identified in the CWF documentation. Based on this reject code, contractors and FIs will deny the claims and return the following messages:

> MSN 21.21 - This service was denied because Medicare only covers this service under certain circumstances.
>
> RA claim adjustment reason code 107 - The related or qualifying claim/service was not identified on this claim.

Edit 3

Once a beneficiary's condition has progressed to the point where routine foot care becomes a covered service, payment will no longer be made for LOPS evaluation and management services. Those services would be considered to be included in the regular exams and treatments afforded to the beneficiary on a routine basis. The physician or provider must then just bill the routine foot care codes, per Pub 100-02, Chapter 15, Sec.290.

The CWF will edit to reject LOPS codes G0245, G0246, and/or G0247 when on the beneficiary's record it shows that one of the following routine foot care codes were billed and paid within the prior 6 months: 11055, 11056, 11057, 11719, 11720, and/or 11721.

The CWF will return a specific reject code for this edit to the contractors and FIs that will be identified in the CWF documentation. Based on the CWF reject code, the contractors and FIs must deny the claims and return the following messages:

> MSN 21.21 - This service was denied because Medicare only covers this service under certain circumstances.
>
> The RA claim adjustment reason code 96 - Non-covered charges, along with remark code M86 - Service denied because payment already made for same/similar procedure within set time frame.

100-4, 32, 100

Billing Requirements for Expanded Coverage of Cochlear Implantation

Effective for dates of services on and after April 4, 2005, the Centers for Medicare & Medicaid Services (CMS) has expanded the coverage for cochlear implantation to cover moderate-to-profound hearing loss in individuals with hearing test scores equal to or less than 40% correct in the best aided listening condition on tape-recorded tests of open-set sentence recognition and who demonstrate limited benefit from amplification. (See Publication 100-03, chapter 1, section 50.3, for specific coverage criteria).

In addition CMS is covering cochlear implantation for individuals with open-set sentence recognition test scores of greater than 40% to less than or equal to 60% correct but only when the provider is participating in, and patients are enrolled in, either:

- A Food and Drug Administration (FDA)-approved category B investigational device exemption (IDE) clinical trial; or
- A trial under the CMS clinical trial policy (see Pub. 100-03, section 310.1); or
- A prospective, controlled comparative trial approved by CMS as consistent with the evidentiary requirements for national coverage analyses and meeting specific quality standards.

100-4, 32, 110.5

DMERC Billing Instructions

Effective for dates of service on or after April 27, 2005, DMERCs shall allow payment for ultrasonic osteogenic stimulators with the following HCPCS codes:

- E0760 for low intensity ultrasound (include modifier "KF"), or;
- E1399 for other ultrasound stimulation (include modifier "KF")

100-4, 32, 120.1

Payment for Services and Supplies

For an IOL inserted following removal of a cataract in a hospital, on either an outpatient or inpatient basis, that is paid under the hospital Outpatient Prospective Payment System (OPPS) or the Inpatient Prospective Payment System (IPPS), respectively; or in a Medicare-approved ambulatory surgical center (ASC) that is paid under the ASC fee schedule:

Medicare does not make separate payment to the hospital or ASC for an IOL inserted subsequent to extraction of a cataract. Payment for the IOL is packaged into the payment for the surgical cataract extraction/lens replacement procedure.

Any person or ASC, who presents or causes to be presented a bill or request for payment for an IOL inserted during or subsequent to cataract surgery for which payment is made under the ASC fee schedule, is subject to a civil money penalty.

For a P-C IOL or A-C IOL inserted subsequent to removal of a cataract in a hospital, on either an outpatient or inpatient basis, that is paid under the OPPS or the IPPS, respectively; or in a Medicare-approved ASC that is paid under the ASC fee schedule:

The facility shall bill for the removal of a cataract with insertion of a conventional IOL, regardless of whether a conventional, P-C IOL, or A-C IOL is inserted. When a beneficiary receives a P-C or A-C IOL following removal of a cataract, hospitals and ASCs shall report the same CPT code that is used to report removal of a cataract with insertion of a conventional IOL. Physicians, hospitals and ASCs may also report an additional HCPCS code, V2788, to indicate any additional charges that accrue when a P-C IOL or A-C IOL is inserted in lieu of a conventional IOL until Janaury 1, 2008. Effective for A-C IOL insertion services on or after January 1, 2008, physicians, hospitals and ASCs should use V2787 to report any additional charges that accrue. On or after January 1, 2008, physicians, hospitals, and ASCs should continue to report HCPCS code V2788 to indicate any additional charges that accrue for insertion of a P-C IOL. See Section 120.2 for coding guidelines.

There is no Medicare benefit category that allows payment of facility charges for services and supplies required to insert and adjust a P-C or A-C IOL following removal of a cataract that exceed the facility charges for services and supplies required for the insertion and adjustment of a conventional IOL.

There is no Medicare benefit category that allows payment of facility charges for subsequent treatments, services and supplies required to examine and monitor the beneficiary who receives a P-C or A-C IOL following removal of a cataract that exceeds the facility charges for subsequent treatments, services and supplies required to examine and monitor a beneficiary after cataract surgery followed by insertion of a conventional IOL.

A - For a P-C IOL or A-C IOL inserted in a physician's office

A physician shall bill for a conventional IOL, regardless of a whether a conventional, P-C IOL, or A-C IOL is inserted (see section 120.2, General Billing Requirements)

There is no Medicare benefit category that allows payment of physician charges for services and supplies required to insert and adjust a P-C or A-C IOL following removal of a cataract that exceed the physician charges for services and supplies for the insertion and adjustment of a conventional IOL.

There is no Medicare benefit category that allows payment of physician charges for subsequent treatments, service and supplies required to examine and monitor a beneficiary following removal of a cataract with insertion of a P-C or A-C IOL that exceed physician charges for services and supplies to examine and monitor a beneficiary following removal of a cataract with insertion of a conventional IOL.

B - For a P-C IOL or A-C IOL inserted in a hospital

A physician may not bill Medicare for a P-C or A-C IOL inserted during a cataract procedure performed in a hospital setting because the payment for the lens is included in the payment made to the facility for the surgical procedure.

There is no Medicare benefit category that allows payment of physician charges for services and supplies required to insert and adjust a P-C or A-C IOL following removal of a cataract that exceed the physician charges for services and supplies required for the insertion of a conventional IOL.

C - For a P-C IOL or A-C IOL inserted in an Ambulatory Surgical Center

Refer to Chapter 14, Section 40.3 for complete guidance on payment for P-C IOL or A-C IOL in Ambulatory Surgical Centers.

100-4, 32, 120.2

Coding and General Billing Requirements

Physicians and hospitals must report one of the following Current Procedural Terminology (CPT) codes on the claim:

- 66982 - Extracapsular cataract removal with insertion of intraocular lens prosthesis (one stage procedure), manual or mechanical technique (e.g., irrigation and aspiration or phacoemulsification), complex requiring devices or techniques not generally used in routine cataract surgery (e.g., iris expansion device, suture support for intraocular lens, or primary posterior capsulorrhexis) or performed on patients in the amblyogenic development stage.
- 66983 - Intracapsular cataract with insertion of intraocular lens prosthesis (one stage procedure)
- 66984 - Extracapsular cataract removal with insertion of intraocular lens prosthesis (one stage procedure), manual or mechanical technique (e.g., irrigation and aspiration or phacoemulsification)
- 66985 - Insertion of intraocular lens prosthesis (secondary implant), not associated with concurrent cataract extraction
- 66986 - Exchange of intraocular lens

In addition, physicians inserting a P-C IOL or A-C IOL in an office setting may bill code V2632 (posterior chamber intraocular lens) for the IOL. Medicare will make payment for the lens based on reasonable cost for a conventional IOL. Place of Service (POS) = 11.

Effective for dates of service on and after January 1, 2006, physician, hospitals and ASCs may also bill the non-covered charges related to the P-C function of the IOL using HCPCS code V2788. Effective for dates of service on and after January 22, 2007 through January 1, 2008, non-covered charges related to A-C function of the IOL can be billed using HCPCS code V2788. The type of service indicator for the non-covered billed charges is Q. (The type of service is applied by the Medicare carrier and not the provider). Effective for A-C IOL insertion services on or after January 1, 2008, physicians, hospitals and ASCs should use V2787 rather than V2788 to report any additional charges that accrue.

When denying the non-payable charges submitted with V2787 or V2788, contractors shall use an appropriate Medical Summary Notice (MSN) such as 16.10 (Medicare does not pay for this item or service) and an appropriate claim adjustment reason code such as 96 (non-covered charges) for claims submitted with the non-payable charges.

Hospitals and physicians may use the proper CPT code(s) to bill Medicare for evaluation and management services usually associated with services following cataract extraction surgery, if appropriate.

A - Applicable Bill Types

The hospital applicable bill types are 12X, 13X, 83X and 85X.

B - Other Special Requirements for Hospitals

Hospitals shall continue to pay CAHs method 2 claims under current payment methodologies for conditional IOLs.

100-4, 32, 130

External Counterpulsation (ECP) Therapy

Commonly referred to as enhanced external counterpulsation, is a non-invasive outpatient treatment for coronary artery disease refractory medical and/or surgical therapy. Effective for dates of service July 1, 1999, and after, Medicare will cover ECP when its use is in patients with stable angina (Class III or Class IV, Canadian Cardiovascular Society Classification or equivalent classification) who, in the opinion of a cardiologist or cardiothoracic surgeon, are not readily amenable to surgical intervention, such as PTCA or cardiac bypass, because:

- Their condition is inoperable, or at high risk of operative complications or post-operative failure;
- Their coronary anatomy is not readily amenable to such procedures; or
- They have co-morbid states that create excessive risk.

(Refer to Publication 100-03, section 20.20 for further coverage criteria.)

100-4, 32, 130.1

Billing and Payment Requirements

Effective for dates of service on or after January 1, 2000, use HCPCS code G0166 (External counterpulsation, per session) to report ECP services. The codes for external cardiac assist (92971), ECG rhythm strip and report (93040 or 93041), pulse oximetry (94760 or 94761) and plethysmography (93922 or 93923) or other monitoring tests for examining the effects of this treatment are not clinically necessary with this service and should not be paid on the same day, unless they occur in a clinical setting not connected with the delivery of the ECP. Daily evaluation and management service, e.g., 99201-99205, 99211-99215, 99217-99220, 99241-99245, cannot be billed with the ECP treatments. Any evaluation and management service must be justified with adequate documentation of the medical necessity of the visit. Deductible and coinsurance apply.

100-4, 32, 140.2.2.1

Correct Place of Service (POS) Code for CR and ICR Services on Professional Claims

Effective for claims with dates of service on and after January 1, 2010, place of service (POS) code 11 shall be used for CR and ICR services provided in a physician's office and POS 22 shall be used for services provided in a hospital outpatient setting. All other POS codes shall be denied. Contractors shall adjust their prepayment procedure edits as appropriate.

The following messages shall be used when contractors deny CR and ICR claims for POS:

Claim Adjustment Reason Code (CARC) 58 - Treatment was deemed by the payer to have been rendered in an inappropriate or invalid place of service.

NOTE: Refer to the 832 Healthcare Policy Identification Segment (loop 2110 Service payment Information REF), if present.

Remittance Advice Remark Code (RARC) N428 - Service/procedure not covered when performed in this place of service.

Medicare Summary Notice (MSN) 21.25 - This service was denied because Medicare only covers this service in certain settings.

Group Code PR (Patient Responsibility) - Where a claim is received with the GA modifier indicating that a signed ABN is on file.

Group Code CO (Contractor Responsibility) - Where a claim is received with the GZ modifier indicating that no signed ABN is on file.

100-4, 32, 140.3.1

Coding Requirements for Intensive Cardiac Rehabilitation Services Furnished On or After January 1, 2010

The following are the applicable HCPCS codes for intensive cardiac rehabilitation services:

G0422 (Intensive cardiac rehabilitation; with or without continuous ECG monitoring, with exercise, per hour, per session)

G0423 (Intensive cardiac rehabilitation; with or without continuous ECG monitoring, without exercise, per hour, per session)

Effective for dates of service on or after January 1, 2010, hospitals and practitioners may report a maximum of 6 1-hour sessions per day. In order to report one session of cardiac rehabilitation services in a day, the duration of treatment must be at least 31 minutes. Additional sessions of intensive cardiac rehabilitation services beyond the first session may only be reported in the same day if the duration of treatment is 31 minutes or greater beyond the hour increment. In other words, in order to report 6 sessions of intensive cardiac rehabilitation services on a given date of service, the first five sessions would account for 60 minutes each and the sixth session would account for at least 31 minutes. If several shorter periods of intensive cardiac rehabilitation services are furnished on a given day, the minutes of service during those periods must be added together for reporting in 1-hour session increments.

Example: If the patient receives 20 minutes of intensive cardiac rehabilitation services in the day, no intensive cardiac rehabilitation session may be reported because less than 31 minutes of services were furnished.

Example: If a patient receives 20 minutes of intensive cardiac rehabilitation services in the morning and 35 minutes of intensive cardiac rehabilitation services in the afternoon of a single day, the hospital or practitioner would report 1 session of intensive cardiac rehabilitation services under 1 unit of the appropriate HCPCS G-code for the total duration of 55 minutes of intensive cardiac rehabilitation services on that day.

Example: If the patient receives 70 minutes of intensive cardiac rehabilitation services in the morning and 25 minutes of intensive cardiac rehabilitation services in the afternoon of a single day, the hospital or practitioner would report two sessions of intensive cardiac rehabilitation services under the appropriate HCPCS G-code(s) because the total duration of intensive cardiac rehabilitation services on that day of 95 minutes exceeds 90 minutes.

Example: If the patient receives 70 minutes of intensive cardiac rehabilitation services in the morning and 85 minutes of intensive cardiac rehabilitation services in the afternoon of a single day, the hospital or practitioner would report three sessions of intensive cardiac rehabilitation services under the appropriate HCPCS G-code(s) because the total duration of intensive cardiac rehabilitation services on that day is 155 minutes, which exceeds 150 minutes and is less than 211 minutes.

100-4, 32, 140.4

Pulmonary Rehabilitation Program Services Furnished On or After January 1, 2010

As specified in 42 CFR 410.47, Medicare covers pulmonary rehabilitation items and services for patients with moderate to very severe COPD (defined as GOLD classification II, III and IV), when referred by the physician treating the chronic respiratory disease.

Pulmonary rehabilitation programs must include the following components:

- Physician-prescribed exercise. Some aerobic exercise must be included in each pulmonary rehabilitation session;
- Education or training closely and clearly related to the individual's care and treatment which is tailored to the individual's needs, including information on respiratory problem management and, if appropriate, brief smoking cessation counseling;
- Psychosocial assessment;
- Outcomes assessment; and,
- An individualized treatment plan detailing how components are utilized for each patient.

Pulmonary rehabilitation items and services must be furnished in a physician's office or a hospital outpatient setting. All settings must have a physician immediately available and accessible for medical consultations and emergencies at all time items and services are being furnished under the program. This provision is satisfied if the physician meets the requirements for direct supervision of physician office services as specified at 42 CFR 410.26 and for hospital outpatient therapeutic services as specified at 42 CFR 410.27.

As specified at 42 CFR 410.47(f), pulmonary rehabilitation program sessions are limited to a maximum of 2 1-hour sessions per day for up to 36 sessions, with the option for an additional 36 sessions if medically necessary. Contractors shall accept the inclusion of the KX modifier on the claim lines as an attestation by the provider of the service that documentation is on file verifying that further treatment beyond the 36 sessions is medically necessary up to a total of 72 sessions for that beneficiary.

100-4, 32, 140.4.1

Coding Requirements for Pulmonary Rehabilitation Services Furnished On or After January 1, 2010

The following is the applicable HCPCS code for pulmonary rehabilitation services:

G0424 (Pulmonary rehabilitation, including exercise (includes monitoring), per hour, per session)

Effective for dates of service on or after January 1, 2010, hospitals and practitioners may report a maximum of 2 1-hour sessions per day. In order to report one session of pulmonary rehabilitation services in a day, the duration of treatment must be at least 31 minutes. Two sessions of pulmonary rehabilitation services may only be reported in the same day if the duration of treatment is at least 91 minutes. In other words, the first session would account for 60 minutes and the second session would account for at least 31 minutes, if two sessions are reported. If several shorter periods of pulmonary rehabilitation services are furnished on a given day, the minutes of service during those periods must be added together for reporting in 1-hour session increments.

Example: If the patient receives 20 minutes of pulmonary rehabilitation services in the day, no pulmonary rehabilitation session may be reported because less than 31 minutes of services were furnished.

Example: If a patient receives 20 minutes of pulmonary rehabilitation services in the morning and 35 minutes of pulmonary rehabilitation services in the afternoon of a single day, the hospital or practitioner would report 1 session of pulmonary rehabilitation services under 1 unit of the HCPCS G-code for the total duration of 55 minutes of pulmonary rehabilitation services on that day.

Example: If the patient receives 70 minutes of pulmonary rehabilitation services in the morning and 25 minutes of pulmonary rehabilitation services in the afternoon of a single day, the hospital or practitioner would report two sessions of pulmonary rehabilitation services under the HCPCS G-code because the total duration of pulmonary rehabilitation services on that day of 95 minutes exceeds 90 minutes.

Example: If the patient receives 70 minutes of pulmonary rehabilitation services in the morning and 85 minutes of pulmonary rehabilitation services in the afternoon of a single day, the hospital or practitioner would report two sessions of pulmonary rehabilitation services under the HCPCS G-code for the total duration of pulmonary rehabilitation services of 155 minutes. A maximum of two sessions per day may be reported, regardless of the total duration of pulmonary rehabilitation services.

100-4, 32, 250.1

Coverage Requirements

Effective August 3, 2009, pharmacogenomic testing to predict warfarin responsiveness is covered only when provided to Medicare beneficiaries who are candidates for anticoagulation therapy with warfarin; i.e., have not been previously tested for CYP2C9 or VKORC1 alleles; and have received fewer than five days of warfarin in the anticoagulation regimen for which the testing is ordered; and only then in the context of a prospective, randomized, controlled clinical study when that study meets certain criteria as outlined in Pub 100-03, section 90.1, of the NCD Manual.

NOTE: A new temporary HCPCS Level II code effective August 3, 2009, G9143, warfarin responsiveness testing by genetic technique using any method, any number of specimen(s), was developed to enable implementation of CED for this purpose.

100-4, 32, 250.2

Billing Requirements

Institutional clinical trial claims for pharmacogenomic testing for warfarin response are identified through the presence of all of the following elements:

Value Code D4 and 8-digit clinical trial number (when present on the claim) - Refer to Transmittal 310, Change Request 5790, dated January 18, 2008;

ICD-9 diagnosis code V70.7 - Refer to Transmittal 310, Change Request 5790, dated January 18, 2008;

Condition Code 30 - Refer to Transmittal 310, Change Request 5790, dated January 18, 2008;

HCPCS modifier Q0: outpatient claims only - Refer to Transmittal 1418, Change Request 5805, dated January 18, 2008; and,

HCPCS code G9143 (mandatory with the April 2010 Integrated Outpatient Code Editor (IOCE) and the January 2011 Clinical Laboratory Fee Schedule (CLFS) updates. Prior to these times, any trials should bill FIs for this test as they currently do absent these instructions, and the FIs should process and pay those claims accordingly.)

Practitioner clinical trial claims for pharmacogenomic testing for warfarin response are identified through the presence of all of the following elements:

ICD-9 diagnosis code V70.7;

8-digit clinical trial number(when present on the claim);

HCPCS modifier Q0; and HCPCS code G9143 (to be carrier priced for claims with dates of service on and after August 3, 2009, that are processed prior to the January 2011 CLFS update.)

100-4, 32, 260.1

Policy

The Centers for Medicare & Medicaid Services (CMS) received a request for national coverage of treatments for facial lipodystrophy syndrome (LDS) for human immunodeficiency virus (HIV)-infected Medicare beneficiaries. Facial LDS is often characterized by a loss of fat that results in a facial abnormality such as severely sunken cheeks. This fat loss can arise as a complication of HIV and/or highly active antiretroviral therapy. Due to their appearance and stigma of the condition, patients with facial LDS may become depressed, socially isolated, and in some cases may stop their HIV treatments in an attempt to halt or reverse this complication.

Effective for claims with dates of service on and after March 23, 2010, dermal injections for facial LDS are only reasonable and necessary using dermal fillers approved by the Food and Drug Administration for this purpose, and then only in HIV-infected beneficiaries who manifest depression secondary to the physical stigmata of HIV treatment.

100-4, 32, 260.2.1

Hospital Billing Instructions

For hospital outpatient claims, hospitals must bill covered dermal injections for treatment of facial LDS by having all of the required elements on the claim:

A line with HCPCS codes Q2026 or Q2027 with a Line Item Date of service (LIDOS) on or after March 23, 2010,

A line with HCPCS code G0429 with a LIDOS on or after March 23, 2010,

ICD-9-CM diagnosis codes 042 (HIV) and 272.6 (Lipodystrophy)

Note to Outpatient Prospective Payment System (OPPS) hospitals or Ambulatory Surgical Centers (ASCs): For line item dates of service on or after march 23, 2010, and until HCPCS codes Q2026 and Q2027 are billable, facial LDS claims shall contain a temporary HCPCS code C9800, instead of HCPCS G0429 and HCPCS Q2026/Q2027, as shown above.

For hospital inpatient claims, hospitals must bill covered dermal injections for treatment of facial LDS by having all of the required elements on the claim:

Discharge date on or after March 23, 2010, ICD-9-CM procedure code 86.99 (other operations on skin and subcutaneous tissue, i.e., injection of filler material),

ICD-9-CM diagnosis codes 042 (HIV) and 272.6 (Lipodystrophy).

Note on all hospital claims: An ICD-9-CM diagnosis code for a comorbidity of depression may also be required for coverage on an outpatient and/or inpatient basis as determined by the individual Medicare contractor's policy.

100-4, 32, 260.2.2

Practitioner Billing Instructions

Practitioners must bill covered claims for dermal injections for treatment of facial LDS by having all of the required elements on the claim:

Performed in a non-facility setting:

A line with HCPCS codes Q2026 or Q2027 with a LIDOS on or after March 23, 2010,

A line with HCPCS code G0429 with a LIDOS on or after March 23, 2010,

ICD-9-CM diagnosis codes 042 (HIV) and 272.6 (Lipodystrophy).

NOTE: An ICD-9-CM diagnosis code for a comorbidity of depression may also be required for coverage based on the individual Medicare contractor's policy.

Performed in a facility setting:

A line with HCPCS code G0429 with a LIDOS on or after March 23, 2010,

ICD-9-CM diagnosis codes 042 (HIV) and 272.6 (Lipodystrophy).

NOTE: An ICD-9-CM diagnosis code for a comorbidity of depression may also be required for coverage based on the individual Medicare contractor's policy.

100-4, 32, 280.1

Autologous Cellular Immunotherapy Treatment of Prostate Cancer

Effective for services furnished on or after June 30, 2011, a National Coverage Determination (NCD) provides coverage of sipuleucel-T (PROVENGE®) for patients with asymptomatic or minimally symptomatic metastatic, castrate-resistant (hormone refractory) prostate cancer. Conditions of Medicare Part A and Medicare Part B coverage for sipuleucel-T are located in the Medicare NCD Manual, Publication 100-3, section 110.22.

100-4, 32, 280.2

Healthcare Common Procedure Coding System (HCPCS) Codes and Diagnosis Coding

Effective for claims with dates of service on June 30, 2011, Medicare providers shall report one of the following HCPCS codes for PROVENGE®:

- C9273 - Sipuleucel-T, minimum of 50 million autologous CD54+ cells activated with PAP-GM-CSF, including leukapheresis and all other preparatory procedures, per infusion, or
- J3490 – Unclassified Drugs, or
- J3590 – Unclassified Biologics.

NOTE: Contractors shall continue to process claims for HCPCS code C9273, J3490, and J3590, with dates of service June 30, 2011, as they do currently.

Effective for claims with dates of service on and after July 1, 2011, Medicare providers shall report the following HCPCS code:

- Q2043 – Sipuleucel-T, minimum of 50 million autologous CD54+ cells activated with PAP-GM-CSF, including leukapheresis and all other preparatory procedures, per infusion; short descriptor, Sipuleucel-T auto CD54+.

ICD-9 Diagnosis Coding

For claims with dates of service on and after July 1, 2011, for PROVENGE®, the on-label indication of asymptomatic or minimally symptomatic metastatic, castrate-resistant (hormone refractory) prostate cancer, must be billed using ICD-9 code 185 (malignant neoplasm of prostate) and at least one of the following ICD-9 codes:

ICD-9 code	Description
196.1	Secondary and unspecified malignant neoplasm of intrathoracic lymph nodes
196.2	Secondary and unspecified malignant neoplasm of intra-abdominal lymph nodes
196.5	Secondary and unspecified malignant neoplasm of lymph nodes of inguinal region and lower limb
196.6	Secondary and unspecified malignant neoplasm of intrapelvic lymph nodes

ICD-9 code	Description
196.8	Secondary and unspecified malignant neoplasm of lymph nodes of multiple sites
196.9	Secondary and unspecified malignant neoplasm of lymph node site unspecified - The spread of cancer to and establishment in the lymph nodes.
197.0	Secondary malignant neoplasm of lung – Cancer that has spread from the original (primary) tumor to the lung. The spread of cancer to the lung. This may be from a primary lung cancer, or from a cancer at a distant site.
197.7	Malignant neoplasm of liver secondary - Cancer that has spread from the original (primary) tumor to the liver. A malignant neoplasm that has spread to the liver from another (primary) anatomic site. Such malignant neoplasms may be carcinomas (e.g., breast, colon), lymphomas, melanomas, or sarcomas.
198.0	Secondary malignant neoplasm of kidney - The spread of the cancer to the kidney. This may be from a primary kidney cancer involving the opposite kidney, or from a cancer at a distant site.
198.1	Secondary malignant neoplasm of other urinary organs
198.5	Secondary malignant neoplasm of bone and bone marrow – Cancer that has spread from the original (primary) tumor to the bone. The spread of a malignant neoplasm from a primary site to the skeletal system. The majority of metastatic neoplasms to the bone are carcinomas.
198.7	Secondary malignant neoplasm of adrenal gland
198.82	Secondary malignant neoplasm of genital organs

Coding for Off-Label PROVENGE® Services

The use of PROVENGE® off-label for the treatment of prostate cancer is left to the discretion of the Medicare Administrative Contractors. Claims with dates of service on and after July 1, 2011, for PROVENGE® paid off-label for the treatment of prostate cancer must be billed using either ICD-9 code 233.4 (carcinoma in situ of prostate), or ICD-9 code 185 (malignant neoplasm of prostate) in addition to HCPCS Q2043. Effective with the implementation date for ICD-10 codes, off-label PROVENGE® services must be billed with either ICD-10 code D075(carcinoma in situ of prostate), or C61 (malignant neoplasm of prostate) in addition to HCPCS Q2043.

ICD-10 Diagnosis Coding

Contractors shall note the appropriate ICD-10 code(s) that are listed below for future implementation. Contractors shall track the ICD-10 codes and ensure that the updated edit is turned on as part of the ICD-10 implementation effective October 1, 2013.

ICD-10	Description
C61	Malignant neoplasm of prostate (for on-label or off-label indications)
D075	Carcinoma in situ of prostate (for off-label indications only)
C77.1	Secondary and unspecified malignant neoplasm of intrathoracic lymph nodes
C77.2	Secondary and unspecified malignant neoplasm of intra-abdominal lymph nodes
C77.4	Secondary and unspecified malignant neoplasm of inguinal and lower limb lymph nodes
C77.5	Secondary and unspecified malignant neoplasm of intrapelvic lymph nodes
C77.8	Secondary and unspecified malignant neoplasm of lymph nodes of multiple regions
C77.9	Secondary and unspecified malignant neoplasm of lymph node, unspecified
C78.00	Secondary malignant neoplasm of unspecified lung
C78.01	Secondary malignant neoplasm of right lung
C78.02	Secondary malignant neoplasm of left lung
C78.7	Secondary malignant neoplasm of liver
C79.00	Secondary malignant neoplasm of unspecified kidney and renal pelvis
C79.01	Secondary malignant neoplasm of right kidney and renal pelvis
C79.02	Secondary malignant neoplasm of left kidney and renal pelvis
C79.10	Secondary malignant neoplasm of unspecified urinary organs
C79.11	Secondary malignant neoplasm of bladder
C79.19	Secondary malignant neoplasm of other urinary organs
C79.51	Secondary malignant neoplasm of bone
C79.52	Secondary malignant neoplasm of bone marrow
C79.70	Secondary malignant neoplasm of unspecified adrenal gland
C79.71	Secondary malignant neoplasm of right adrenal gland
C79.72	Secondary malignant neoplasm of left adrenal gland
C79.82	Secondary malignant neoplasm of genital organs

100-4, 36, 50.14

Purchased Accessories & Supplies for Use With Grandfathered Equipment

Purchased Accessories & Supplies for Use With Grandfathered Equipment

Purchased Accessories & Supplies for Use With Grandfathered Equipment

Non-contract grandfathered suppliers must use the KY modifier on claims for CBA-residing beneficiaries with dates of service on or after January 1, 2011, for purchased, covered accessories or supplies furnished for use with rented grandfathered equipment. The following HCPCS codes are the codes for which use of the KY modifier is authorized:

Continuous Positive Airway Pressure Devices, Respiratory Assistive Devices, and Related Supplies and Accessories – A4604, A7030, A7031, A7032, A7033, A7034, A7035, A7036, A7037, A7038, A7039, A7044, A7045, A7046, E0561, and E0562

Hospital Beds and Related Accessories – E0271, E0272, E0280, and E0310

Walkers and Related Accessories – E0154, E0156, E0157 and E0158 Grandfathered suppliers that submit claims for the payment of the aforementioned purchased accessories and supplies for use with grandfathered equipment should submit the applicable single payment amount for the accessory or supply as their submitted charge on the claim. Non-contract grandfathered suppliers should be aware that purchase claims submitted for these codes without the KY modifier will be denied. In addition, claims submitted with the KY modifier for HCPCS codes other than those listed above will be denied.

After the rental payment cap for the grandfathered equipment is reached, the beneficiary must obtain replacement supplies and accessories from a contract supplier. The supplier of the grandfathered equipment is no longer permitted to furnish the supplies and accessories once the rental payment cap is reached.

100-4, 36, 50, 15

Hospitals Providing Walkers and Related Accessories to Their Patients on the Date of Discharge

Hospitals may furnish walkers and related accessories to their own patients for use in the home during an admission or on the date of discharge and receive payment at the applicable single payment amount, regardless of whether the hospital is a contract supplier or not. Separate payment is not made for walkers furnished by a hospital for use in the hospital, as payment for these items is included in the Part A payment for inpatient hospital services.

To be paid for walkers as a non-contract supplier, the hospital must use the modifier J4 in combination with the following HCPCS codes: A4636; A4637; E0130; E0135; E0140; E0141; E0143; E0144; E0147; E0148; E0149; E0154; E0155; E0156; E0157; E0158; and E0159. Under this exception, hospitals are advised to submit the claim for the hospital stay before or on the same day that they submit the claim for the walker to ensure timely and accurate claims processing.

Hospitals that are located outside a CBA that furnish walkers and/or related accessories to travelling beneficiaries who live in a CBA must affix the J4 modifier to claims submitted for these items.

The J4 modifier should not be used by contract suppliers.

100-8, 10, 2.2.8

Cardiac Rehabilitation (CR) and Intensive Cardiac Rehabilitation (ICR)

A. General Background Information

Effective January 1, 2010, Medicare Part B covers Cardiac Rehabilitation (CR) and Intensive Cardiac Rehabilitation (ICR) program services for beneficiaries who have experienced one or more of the following:

- An acute myocardial infarction within the preceding 12 months;
- A coronary artery bypass surgery;
- Current stable angina pectoris;
- Heart valve repair or replacement;
- Percutaneous transluminal coronary angioplasty or coronary stenting;

- A heart or heart-lung transplant; or,
- Other cardiac conditions as specified through a national coverage determination (NCD) (CR only).

ICR programs must be approved by CMS through the national coverage determination (NCD) process and must meet certain criteria for approval. Individual sites wishing to provide ICR services via an approved ICR program must enroll with their local contractor or MAC as an ICR program supplier.

B. ICR Enrollment

In order to enroll as an ICR site, a supplier must complete a Form CMS-855B, with the supplier type of "Other" selected. Contractors shall verify that the ICR program is approved by CMS through the NCD process. A list of approved ICR programs will be identified through the NCD listings, the CMS Web site and the Federal Register. Contractors shall use one of these options to verify that the ICR program has met CMS approval.

ICR suppliers shall be enrolled using specialty code 31. ICR suppliers must separately enroll each of their practice locations. Therefore, each enrolling ICR supplier can only have one practice location on its CMS-855B enrollment application and shall receive its own PTAN.

Contractors shall only accept and process reassignments (855R's) to ICR suppliers for physicians defined in 1861(r)(1) of the Act.

C. Additional Information

For more information on ICR suppliers, refer to:

42 CFR Sec.410.49;

Pub. 100-04, Medicare Claims Processing Manual, chapter 32, sections 140.2.2 - 140.2.2.6; and

Pub. 100-02, Medicare Benefit Policy Manual. chapter 15, section 232.

APPENDIX 5 — NEW, CHANGED, DELETED, AND REINSTATED HCPCS CODES FOR 2012

NEW CODES

A5056 Ostomy pouch, drainable, with extended wear barrier attached, with filter, (1 piece), each

A5057 Ostomy pouch, drainable, with extended wear barrier attached, with built in convexity, with filter, (1 piece), each

A9272 Mechanical wound suction, disposable, includes dressing, all accessories and components, each

A9584 Iodine I-123 ioflupane, diagnostic, per study dose, up to 5 millicuries

A9585 Injection, gadobutrol, 0.1 ml

C1830 Powered bone marrow biopsy needle

C1840 Lens, intraocular (telescopic)

C1886 Catheter, extravascular tissue ablation, any modality (insertable)

C9285 Lidocaine 70 mg/tetracaine 70 mg, per patch

C9286 Injection, belatacept, 1 mg

C9287 Injection, brentuximab vedotin, 1 mg

C9366 EpiFix, per sq cm

C9732 Insertion of ocular telescope prosthetic including removal of crystalline lens

E0988 Manual wheelchair accessory, lever-activated, wheel drive, pair

E2358 Power wheelchair accessory, group 34 nonsealed lead acid battery, each

E2359 Power wheelchair accessory, group 34 sealed lead acid battery, each (e.g., gel cell, absorbed glass mat)

E2626 Wheelchair accessory, shoulder elbow, mobile arm support attached to wheelchair, balanced, adjustable

E2627 Wheelchair accessory, shoulder elbow, mobile arm support attached to wheelchair, balanced, adjustable Rancho type

E2628 Wheelchair accessory, shoulder elbow, mobile arm support attached to wheelchair, balanced, reclining

E2629 Wheelchair accessory, shoulder elbow, mobile arm support attached to wheelchair, balanced, friction arm support (friction dampening to proximal and distal joints)

E2630 Wheelchair accessory, shoulder elbow, mobile arm support, monosuspension arm and hand support, overhead elbow forearm hand sling support, yoke type suspension support

E2631 Wheelchair accessory, addition to mobile arm support, elevating proximal arm

E2632 Wheelchair accessory, addition to mobile arm support, offset or lateral rocker arm with elastic balance control

E2633 Wheelchair accessory, addition to mobile arm support, supinator

G0442 Annual alcohol misuse screening, 15 minutes

G0443 Brief face-to-face behavioral counseling for alcohol misuse, 15 minutes

G0444 Annual depression screening, 15 minutes

G0445 High intensity behavioral counseling to prevent sexually transmitted infection; face-to-face, individual, includes: education, skills training and guidance on how to change sexual behavior; performed semi-annually, 30 minutes

G0446 Intensive behavioral therapy to reduce cardiovascular disease risk, individual, face-to-face, bi-annual, 15 minutes

G0447 Face-to-face behavioral counseling for obesity, 15 minutes

G0448 Insertion or replacement of a permanent pacing cardioverter-defibrillator system with transvenous lead(s), single or dual chamber with insertion of pacing electrode, cardiac venous system, for left ventricular pacing

G0449 Annual face-to-face obesity screening, 15 minutes

G0450 Screening for sexually transmitted infections, includes laboratory tests for chlamydia, gonorrhea, syphilis and hepatitis B

G0451 Development testing, with interpretation and report, per standardized instrument form

G0908 Most recent hemoglobin (HgB) level > 12.0 g/dl

G0909 Hemoglobin level measurement not documented, reason not otherwise specified

G0910 Most recent hemoglobin level <= 12.0 g/dl

G0911 Assessed level of activity and symptoms

G0912 Level of activity and symptoms not assessed

G0913 Improvement in visual function achieved within 90 days following cataract surgery

G0914 Patient care survey was not completed by patient

G0915 Improvement in visual function not achieved within 90 days following cataract surgery

G0916 Satisfaction with care achieved within 90 days following cataract surgery

G0917 Patient satisfaction survey was not completed by patient

G0918 Satisfaction with care not achieved within 90 days following cataract surgery

G0919 Influenza immunization ordered or recommended (to be given at alternate location or alternate provider); vaccine not available at time of visit

G0920 Type, anatomic location, and activity all documented

G0921 Documentation of patient reason(s) for not being able to assess

G0922 No documentation of disease type, anatomic location, and activity, reason not otherwise specified

G8694 Left ventriucular ejection fraction (LVEF) < 40%

G8695 Left ventricular ejection fraction (LVEF) >= 40% or documentation as mildly depressed left ventricular systolic function or normal

G8696 Antithrombotic therapy prescribed at discharge

G8697 Antithrombotic therapy not prescribed for documented reasons

G8698 Antithrombotic therapy was not prescribed at discharge, reason not otherwise specified

G8699 Rehabilitation services (occupational, physical or speech) ordered at or prior to discharge

G8700 Rehabilitation services (occupational, physical or speech) not indicated at or prior to discharge

G8701 Rehabilitation services were not ordered, reason not otherwise specified

G8702 Documentation that prophylactic antibiotics were given within 4 hours prior to surgical incision or intraoperatively

G8703 Documentation that prophylactic antibiotics were neither given within 4 hours prior to surgical incision nor intraoperatively

G8704 12-lead electrocardiogram (ECG) performed

G8705 Documentation of medical reason(s) for not performing a 12-lead electrocardiogram (ECG)

G8706 Documentation of patient reason(s) for not performing a 12-lead electrocardiogram (ECG)

G8707 12-lead electrocardiogram (ECG) not performed, reason not otherwise specified

G8708 Patient not prescribed or dispensed antibiotic

G8709 Patient prescribed or dispensed antibiotic for documented medical reason(s)

G8710 Patient prescribed or dispensed antibiotic

G8711 Prescribed or dispensed antibiotic

G8712 Antibiotic not prescribed or dispensed

NEW CODES (continued)

G8713 SpKt/V greater than or equal to 1.2 (single-pool clearance of urea [Kt] / volume V])

G8714 Hemodialysis treatment performed exactly 3 times per week

G8715 Hemodialysis treatment performed less than 3 times per week or greater than 3 times per week

G8716 Documentation of reason(s) for patient not having greater than or equal to 1.2 (single-pool clearance of urea [Kt] / volume [V])

G8717 SpKt/V less than 1.2 (single-pool clearance of urea [Kt] / volume V]), reason not specified

G8718 Total Kt/V greater than or equal to 1.7 per week (total clearance of urea [Kt] / volume V])

G8720 Total Kt/V less than 1.7 per week (total clearance of urea [Kt] / volume V]), reason not specified

G8721 PT category (primary tumor), pN category (regional lymph nodes), and histologic grade were documented in pathology report

G8722 Medical reason(s) documented for not including pT category, pN category and histologic grade in the pathology report

G8723 Specimen site is other than anatomic location of primary tumor

G8724 PT category, pN category and histologic grade were not documented in the pathology report, reason not otherwise specified

G8725 Fasting lipid profile performed (triglycerides, LDL-C, HDL-C and total cholesterol)

G8726 Clinician has documented reason for not performing fasting lipid profile

G8727 Patient receiving hemodialysis, peritoneal dialysis or kidney transplantation

G8728 Fasting lipid profile not performed, reason not otherwise specified

G8730 Pain assessment documented as positive utilizing a standardized tool and a follow-up plan is documented

G8731 Pain assessment documented as negative, no follow-up plan is required

G8732 No documentation of pain assessment

G8733 Documentation of a positive elder maltreatment screen and documented follow-up plan

G8734 Elder maltreatment screen documented as negative, no follow-up required

G8735 Elder maltreatment screen documented as positive, follow-up plan not documented, reason not specified

G8736 Most current LDL-C < 100 mg/dL

G8737 Most current LDL-C >= 100 mg/dL

G8738 Left ventricular ejection fraction (LVEF) < 40% or documentation of severely or moderately depressed left ventricular systolic function

G8739 Left ventricular ejection fraction (LVEF) >= 40% or documentation as normal or mildly depressed left ventricular systolic function

G8740 Left ventricular ejection fraction (LVEF) not performed or assessed, reason not specified

G8741 Patient not treated for spoken language comprehension disorder

G8742 Patient not treated for attention disorder

G8743 Patient not treated for memory disorder

G8744 Patient not treated for motor speech disorder

G8745 Patient not treated for reading disorder

G8746 Patient not treated for spoken language expression disorder

G8747 Patient not treated for writing disorder

G8748 Patient not treated for swallowing disorder

G8749 Absence of signs of melanoma (cough, dyspnea, tenderness, localized neurologic signs such as weakness, jaundice or any other sign suggesting systemic spread) or absence of symptoms of melanoma (pain, paresthesia, or any other symptom suggesting the possibility of systemic spread of melanoma)

G8750 Presence of signs of melanoma (cough, dyspnea, tenderness, localized neurologic signs such as weakness, jaundice or any other sign suggesting systemic spread) or presence of symptoms of melanoma (pain, paresthesia, or any other symptom suggesting the possibility of systemic spread of melanoma)

G8751 Smoking status and exposure to secondhand smoke in the home not assessed, reason not specified

G8752 Most recent systolic blood pressure < 140 mm Hg

G8753 Most recent systolic blood pressure >= 140 mm Hg

G8754 Most recent diastolic blood pressure < 90 mm Hg

G8755 Most recent diastolic blood pressure >= 90 mm Hg

G8756 No documentation of blood pressure measurement, reason not otherwise specified

G8757 All quality actions for the applicable measures in the chronic obstructive pulmonary disease measures group have been performed for this patient

G8758 All quality actions for the applicable measures in the inflammatory bowel disease measures group have been performed for this patient

G8759 All quality actions for the applicable measures in the obstructive sleep apnea measures group have been performed for this patient

G8760 All quality actions for the applicable measures in the epilepsy measures group have been performed for this patient

G8761 All quality actions for the applicable measures in the dementia measures group have been performed for this patient

G8762 All quality actions for the applicable measures in the Parkinson's disease measures group have been performed for this patient

G8763 All quality actions for the applicable measures in the hypertension measures group have been performed for this patient

G8764 All quality actions for the applicable measures in the cardiovascular prevention measures group have been performed for this patient

G8765 All quality actions for the applicable measures in the cataract measures group have been performed for this patient

G8767 Lipid panel results documented and reviewed (must include total cholesterol, HDL-C, triglycerides and calculated LDL-C)

G8768 Documentation of medical reason(s) for not performing lipid profile (e.g., patients who have a terminal illness or for whom treatment of hypertension with standard treatment goals is not clinically appropriate)

G8769 Lipid profile not performed, reason not otherwise specified

G8770 Urine protein test result documented and reviewed

G8771 Documentation of diagnosis of chronic kidney disease

G8772 Documentation of medical reason(s) for not performing urine protein test (e.g., patients who have a terminal illness or for whom treatment of hypertension with standard treatment goals is not cllinically appropriate)

G8773 Urine protein test was not performed, reason not otherwise specified

G8774 Serum creatinine test result documented and reviewed

G8775 Documentation of medical reason(s) for not performing serum creatinine test (e.g., patients who have a terminal illness or for whom treatment of hypertension with standard treatment goals is not clinically appropriate)

G8776 Serum creatinine test not performed, reason not otherwise specified

G8777 Diabetes screening test performed

G8778 Documentation of medical reason(s) for not performing diabetes screening test (e.g., patients who have a terminal illness or for whom treatment of hypertension with standard treatment goals is not clinically appropriate, or patients with a diagnosis of diabetes)

G8779 Diabetes screening test not performed, reason not otherwise specified

G8780 Counseling for diet and physical activity performed

NEW CODES (continued)

G8781 Documentation of medical reason(s) for patient not receiving counseling for diet and physical activity (e.g., patients who have a terminal illness or for whom treatment of hypertension with standard treatment goals is not clinically appropriate)

G8782 Counseling for diet and physical activity not performed, reason not otherwise specified

G8783 Blood pressure screening performed as recommended by the defined screening interval

G8784 Blood pressure not assessed, patient not eligible

G8785 Blood pressure screening not performed as recommended by screening interval, reason not otherwise specified

G8786 Severity of angina assessed according to level of activity

G8787 Angina assessed as present

G8788 Angina assessed as absent

G8789 Severity of angina not assessed according to level of activity

G8790 Most recent office visit systolic blood pressure < 130 mm hg

G8791 Most recent office visit systolic blood pressure, 130-139 mm hg

G8792 Most recent office visit systolic blood pressure >= 140 mm Hg

G8793 Most recent office visit diastolic blood pressure, < 80 mm hg

G8794 Most recent office visit diastolic blood pressure, 80-89 mm hg

G8795 Most recent office visit diastolic blood pressure >= 90 mm Hg

G8796 Blood pressure measurement not documented, reason not otherwise specified

G8797 Specimen site other than anatomic location of esophagus

G8798 Specimen site other than anatomic location of prostate

G8799 Anticoagulation ordered

G8800 Anticoagulation not ordered for reasons documented by clinician

G8801 Anticoagulation was not ordered, reason not specified

G8802 Pregnancy test (urine or serum) ordered

G8803 Pregnancy test (urine or serum) not ordered for reasons documented by clinician

G8805 Pregnancy test (urine or serum) was not ordered, reason not specified

G8806 Performance of transabdominal or transvaginal ultrasound

G8807 Transabdominal or transvaginal ultrasound not performed for reasons documented by clinician

G8808 Performance of transabdominal or transvaginal ultrasound not ordered, reason not specified

G8809 Rh immune globulin (RhoGam) ordered

G8810 R immune globulin (RhoGam) not ordered for reasons documented by clinician

G8811 Documentation Rh immune globulin (RhoGam) was not ordered, reason not specified

G8812 Patient is not eligible for follow-up CTA, duplex, or MRA

G8813 Follow-up CTA, duplex, or MRA of the abdomen and pelvis performed

G8814 Follow-up CTA, duplex, or MRA of the abdomen and pelvis not performed

G8815 Statin therapy not prescribed for documented reasons

G8816 Statin medication prescribed at discharge

G8817 Statin therapy not prescribed at discharge, reason not specified

G8818 Patient discharge to home no later than postoperative day #7

G8819 Aneurysm minor diameter <= 5.5 cm

G8820 Aneurysm minor diameter 5.6-6.0 cm

G8821 Abdominal aortic aneurysm is not infrarenal

G8822 Male patients with aneurysms minor diameter > 6 cm

G8823 Female patients with aneurysm minor diameter > 6 cm

G8824 Female patients with aneurysm minor diameter 5.6-6.0 cm

G8825 Patient not discharged to home by postoperative day #7

G8826 Patient discharged to home no later than postoperative day #2 following EVAR

G8827 Aneurysm minor diameter <= 5.5 cm for women

G8828 Aneurysm minor diameter <= 5.5 cm for men

G8829 Aneurysm minor diameter 5.6-6.0 cm for men

G8830 Aneurysm minor diameter > 6 cm for men

G8831 Aneurysm minor diameter > 6 cm for women

G8832 Aneurysm minor diameter 5.6-6.0 cm for women

G8833 Patient not discharged to home by postoperative day #2 following EVAR

G8834 Patient discharged to home no later than postoperative day #2 following CEA

G8835 Asymptomatic patient with no history of any transient ischemic attack or stroke in any carotid or vertebrobasilar territory

G8836 Symptomatic patient with ipsilateral stroke or TIA within 120 days prior to CEA

G8837 Other symptomatic patient with ipsilateral carotid territory TIA or stroke > 120 days prior to CEA, or contralateral carotid territory TIA or stroke or vertebrobasilar TIA or stroke

G8838 Patient not discharged to home by postoperative day #2

G8839 Sleep apnea symptoms assessed, including presence or absence of snoring and daytime sleepiness

G8840 Documentation of reason(s) for not performing an assessment of sleep symptoms (e.g., patient didn't have initial daytime sleepiness, patient visits between initial testing and initiation of therapy)

G8841 Sleep apnea symptoms not assessed, reason not otherwise specified

G8842 Apnea hypopnea index (AHI) or respiratory disturbance index (RDI) measured at the time of initial diagnosis

G8843 Documentation of reason(s) for not measuring an apnea hypopnea index (AHI) or a respiratory disturbance index (RDI) at the time of initial diagnosis

G8844 Apnea hypopna index (AHI) or respiratory disturbance index (RDI) not measured at the time of initial diagnosis, reason not specified

G8845 Positive airway pressure therapy prescribed

G8846 Moderate or severe obstructive sleep apnea (apnea hypopnea index (AHI) or respiratory disturbance index (RDI) of 15 or greater)

G8847 Positive airway pressure therapy not prescribed

G8848 Mild obstructive sleep apnea (apnea hypopnea index (AHI) or respiratory disturbance index (RDI) of less than 15)

G8849 Documentation of reason(s) for not prescribing positive airway pressure therapy

G8850 Positive airway pressure therapy not prescribed, reason not otherwise specified

G8851 Objective measurement of adherence to positive airway pressure therapy, documented

G8852 Positive airway pressure therapy prescribed

G8853 Positive airway pressure therapy not prescribed

G8854 Documentation of reason(s) for not objectively measuring adherence to positive airway pressure therapy

G8855 Objective measurement of adherence to positive airway pressure therapy not performed, reason not otherwise specified

G8856 Referral to a physician for an otologic evaluation performed

G8857 Patient is not eligible for the referral for otologic evaluation measure (e.g., patients who are already under the care of a physician for acute or chronic dizziness)

G8858 Referral to a physician for an otologic evaluation not performed, reason not specified

NEW CODES (continued)

Code	Description
G8859	Patient receiving corticosteroids greater than or equal to 10 mg/day for 60 or greater consecutive days
G8860	Patients who have received dose of corticosteroids greater than or equal to 10 mg/day for 60 or greater consecutive days
G8861	Central dual-energy x-ray absorptiometry (DXA) ordered or documented, review of systems and medication history or pharmacologic therapy (other than minerals/vitamins) for osteoporosis prescribed
G8862	Patients not receiving corticosteroids greater than or equal to 10 mg/day for 60 or greater consecutive days
G8863	Patients not assessed for risk of bone loss, reason not otherwise specified
G8864	Pneumococcal vaccine administered or previously received
G8865	Documentation of medical reason(s) for not administering or previously receiving pneumococcal vaccine (e.g., patient allergic reaction, potential adverse drug reaction)
G8866	Documentation of patient reason(s) for not administering or previously receiving pneumococcal vaccine (e.g., patient refusal)
G8867	Pneumococcal vaccine not administered or previously received, reason not otherwise specified
G8868	Patients receiving a first course of anti-TNF therapy
G8869	Patient has documented immunity to hepatitis B and is receiving a first course of anti-TNF therapy
G8870	Hepatitis B vaccine injection administered or previously received and is receiving a first course of anti-TNF therapy
G8871	Patient not receiving a first course of anti-TNF therapy
G8872	Excised tissue evaluated by imaging intraoperatively to confirm successful inclusion of targeted lesion
G8873	Patients with needle localization specimens which are not amenable to intraoperative imaging such as MRI needle wire localization, or targets which are tentatively identified on mammogram or ultrasound which do not contain a biopsy marker but which can be verified on intraoperative inspection or pathology
G8874	Excised tissue not evaluated by imaging intraoperatively to confirm successful inclusion of targeted lesion
G8875	Clinician diagnosed breast cancer preoperatively by a minimally invasive biopsy method
G8876	Documentation of reason(s) for not performing minimally invasive biopsy to diagnose breast cancer preoperatively
G8877	Clinician did not attempt to achieve the diagnosis of breast cancer preoperatively by a minimally invasive biopsy method, reason not otherwise specified
G8878	Sentinel lymph node biopsy procedure performed
G8879	Clinically node negative (T1N0M0 or T2N0M0) invasive breast cancer
G8880	Documentation of reason(s) sentinel lymph node biopsy not performed
G8881	Stage of breast cancer is greater than T1N0M0 or T2N0M0
G8882	Sentinel lymph node biopsy procedure not performed
G8883	Biopsy results reviewed, communicated, tracked and documented
G8884	Clinician documented reason that patient's biopsy results were not reviewed
G8885	Biopsy results not reviewed, communicated, tracked or documented
G8886	Most recent blood pressure under control
G8887	Documentation of medical reason(s) for most recent blood pressure not being under control (e.g., patients with comorbid conditions that cause an increase in blood pressure or require treatment with medications that cause an increase in blood pressure, or patients who had a terminal illness or for whom treatment of hypertension with standard treatment goals is not clinically appropriate)
G8888	Most recent blood pressure not under control, results documented and reviewed
G8889	No documentation of blood pressure measurement, reason not otherwise specified
G8890	Most recent LDL-C under control, results documented and reviewed
G8891	Documentation of medical reason(s) for most recent LDL-C not under control (e.g., patients who had a terminal illness or for whom treatment of hypertension with standard treatment goals is not clinically appropriate)
G8892	Documentation of medical reason(s) for not performing LDL-C test (e.g., patients who had a terminal illness or for whom treatment of hypertension with standard treatment goals is not clinically appropriate)
G8893	Most recent LDL-C not under control, results documented and reviewed
G8894	LDL-C not performed, reason not specified
G8895	Oral aspirin or other anticoagulant/antiplatelet therapy prescribed
G8896	Documentation of medical reason(s) for not prescribing oral aspirin or other anticoagulant/antiplatelet therapy (e.g., under age 30, patient documented to be low risk, patient with terminal illness or treatment of hypertension with standard treatment goals is not clinically appropriate)
G8897	Oral aspirin or other anticoagulant/antiplatelet therapy was not prescribed, reason not otherwise specified
G8898	I intend to report the chronic obstructive pulmonary disease measures group
G8899	I intend to report the inflammatory bowel disease measures group
G8900	I intend to report the obstructive sleep apnea measures group
G8901	I intend to report the epilepsy measures group
G8902	I intend to report the dementia measures group
G8903	I intend to report the Parkinson's disease measures group
G8904	I intend to report the hypertension measures group
G8905	I intend to report the cardiovascular prevention measures group
G8906	I intend to report the cataract measures group
G9156	Evaluation for wheelchair requiring face-to-face visit with physician
J0131	Injection, acetaminophen, 10 mg
J0221	Injection, alglucosidase alfa, (Lumizyme), 10 mg
J0257	Injection, alpha 1 proteinase inhibitor (human), (GLASSIA), 10 mg
J0490	Injection, belimumab, 10 mg
J0588	Injection, incobotulinumtoxinA, 1 unit
J0712	Injection, ceftaroline fosamil, 10 mg
J0840	Injection, crotalidae polyvalent immune fab (ovine), up to 1 g
J0897	Injection, denosumab, 1 mg
J1557	Injection, immune globulin, (Gammaplex), intravenous, nonlyophilized (e.g., liquid), 500 mg
J1725	Injection, hydroxyprogesterone caproate, 1 mg
J2265	Injection, minocycline HCl, 1 mg
J2507	Injection, pegloticase, 1 mg
J7131	Hypertonic saline solution, 1 ml
J7180	Injection, factor XIII (antihemophilic factor, human), 1 IU
J7183	Injection, von Willebrand factor complex (human), Wilate, 1 IU vWF:RCo
J7326	Hyaluronan or derivative, Gel-One, for intra-articular injection, per dose
J7665	Mannitol, administered through an inhaler, 5 mg
J8561	Everolimus, oral, 0.25 mg
J9043	Injection, cabazitaxel, 1 mg
J9179	Injection, eribulin mesylate, 0.1 mg
J9228	Injection, ipilimumab, 1 mg

NEW CODES (continued)

K0741 Portable gaseous oxygen system, rental, includes portable container, regulator, flowmeter, humidifier, cannula or mask, and tubing, for cluster headaches

K0742 Portable oxygen contents, gaseous, 1 month's supply = 1 unit, for cluster headaches, for initial months supply or to replace used contents

K0743 Suction pump, home model, portable, for use on wounds

K0744 Absorptive wound dressing for use with suction pump, home model, portable, pad size 16 sq in or less

K0745 Absorptive wound dressing for use with suction pump, home model, portable, pad size more than 16 sq in but less than or equal to 48 sq in

K0746 Absorptive wound dressing for use with suction pump, home model, portable, pad size greater than 48 sq in

L5312 Knee disarticulation (or through knee), molded socket, single axis knee, pylon, SACH foot, endoskeletal system

L6715 Terminal device, multiple articulating digit, includes motor(s), initial issue or replacement

L6880 Electric hand, switch or myolelectric controlled, independently articulating digits, any grasp pattern or combination of grasp patterns, includes motor(s)

Q0162 Ondansetron 1 mg, oral, FDA approved prescription antiemetic, for use as a complete therapeutic substitute for an IV antiemetic at the time of chemotherapy treatment, not to exceed a 48 hour dosage regimen

Q2043 Sipuleucel-T, minimum of 50 million autologous cd54+ cells activated with PAP-GM-CSF, including leukapheresis and all other preparatory procedures, per infusion

Q4122 DermACELL, per sq cm

Q4123 AlloSkin RT, per sq cm

Q4124 OASIS ultra tri-layer wound matrix, per sq cm

Q4125 Arthroflex, per sq cm

Q4126 MemoDerm, per sq cm

Q4127 Talymed, per sq cm

Q4128 FlexHD or AllopatchHD, per sq cm

Q4129 Unite biomatrix, per sq cm

Q4130 Strattice TM, per sq cm

S0119 Ondansetron, oral, 4 mg (for circumstances falling under the Medicare statute, use HCPCS Q code)

S3722 Dose optimization by area under the curve (AUC) analysis, for infusional 5-fluorouracil

S8130 Interferential current stimulator, 2 channel

S8131 Interferential current stimulator, 4 channel

CHANGED CODES

C8931 Magnetic resonance angiography with contrast, spinal canal and contents

E0637 Combination sit-to-stand frame/table system, any size including pediatric, with seat lift feature, with or without wheels

E0638 Standing frame/table system, one position (e.g., upright, supine or prone stander), any size including pediatric, with or without wheels

E0641 Standing frame/table system, multi-position (e.g., 3-way stander), any size including pediatric, with or without wheels

E0642 Standing frame/table system, mobile (dynamic stander), any size including pediatric

E0691 Ultraviolet light therapy system, includes bulbs/lamps, timer and eye protection; treatment area 2 sq ft or less

G0159 Services performed by a qualified physical therapist, in the home health setting, in the establishment or delivery of a safe and effective physical therapy maintenance program, each 15 minutes

G0160 Services performed by a qualified occupational therapist, in the home health setting, in the establishment or delivery of a safe and effective occupational therapy maintenance program, each 15 minutes

G0161 Services performed by a qualified speech-language pathologist, in the home health setting, in the establishment or delivery of a safe and effective speech-language pathology maintenance program, each 15 minutes

G0164 Skilled services of a licensed nurse (LPN or RN), in the training and/or education of a patient or family member, in the home health or hospice setting, each 15 minutes

G0406 Follow-up inpatient consultation, limited, physicians typically spend 15 minutes communicating with the patient via telehealth

G0407 Follow-up inpatient consultation, intermediate, physicians typically spend 25 minutes communicating with the patient via telehealth

G0408 Follow-up inpatient consultation, complex, physicians typically spend 35 minutes communicating with the patient via telehealth

G0425 Telehealth consultation, emergency department or initial inpatient, typically 30 minutes communicating with the patient via telehealth

G0426 Telehealth consultation, emergency department or initial inpatient, typically 50 minutes communicating with the patient via telehealth

G0427 Telehealth consultation, emergency department or initial inpatient, typically 70 minutes or more communicating with the patient via telehealth

G0435 Infectious agent antigen detection by rapid antibody test of oral mucosa transudate, HIV-1 or HIV-2, screening

G0437 Smoking and tobacco cessation counseling visit for the asymptomatic patient; intermediate, greater than 10 minutes

G8431 Positive screen for clinical depression using an age appropriate standardized tool and a follow-up plan documented

G8432 No documentation of clinical depression screening using an age appropriate standardized tool

G8433 Screening for clinical depression using an age appropriate standardized tool not documented, patient not eligible/appropriate

G8482 Influenza immunization administered or previously received

G8509 Documentation of positive pain assessment; no documentation of a follow-up plan, reason not specified

G8510 Negative screen for clinical depression using an age appropriate standardized tool, follow-up not required

G8511 Positive screen for clinical depression using an age appropriate standardized tool documented, follow up plan not documented, reason not specified

G8539 Documentation of a current functional outcome assessment using a standardized tool and documentation of a care plan based on identified deficiencies

G8542 Documentation of a current functional outcome assessment using a standardized tool; no functional deficiencies identified, care plan not required

G8553 Prescription(s) generated and transmitted via a qualified ERX system or a certified EHR system

G8573 Stroke following isolated CABG surgery

G8574 No stroke following isolated CABG surgery

G8575 Developed postoperative renal failure or required dialysis

G8576 No postoperative renal failure/dialysis not required

G8577 Reexploration required due to mediastinal bleeding with or without tamponade, graft occlusion, valve dysfunction or other cardiac reason

G8578 Reexploration not required due to mediastinal bleeding with or without tamponade, graft occlusion, valve dysfunction or other cardiac reason

G8580 Antiplatelet medication contraindicated

G8583 Beta blocker contraindicated

G8586 Antilipid treatment contraindicated

CHANGED CODES (continued)

G8605 Patient treated for spoken language comprehension but not scored on the spoken language comprehension functional communication measure either at admission or at discharge

G8608 Patient treated for attention but not scored on the attention functional communication measure either at admission or at discharge

G8611 Patient treated for memory but not scored on the memory functional communication measure either at admission or at discharge

G8614 Patient treated for motor speech but not scored on the motor speech comprehension functional communication measure either at admission or at discharge

G8617 Patient treated for reading but not scored on the reading functional communication measure either at admission or at discharge

G8620 Patient treated for spoken language expression but not scored on the spoken language expression functional communication measure either at admission or at discharge

G8623 Patient treated for writing but not scored on the writing functional communication measure either at admission or at discharge

G8626 Patient treated for swallowing but not scored on the swallowing functional communication measure at admission or at discharge

J0129 Injection, abatacept, 10 mg (code may be used for Medicare when drug administered under the direct supervision of a physician, not for use when drug is self-administered)

J0220 Injection, alglucosidase alfa, 10 mg, not otherwise specified

J0256 Injection, alpha 1-proteinase inhibitor (human), not otherwise specified, 10 mg

J1561 Injection, immune globulin, (Gamunex/Gamunex-C/Gammaked), nonlyophilized (e.g., liquid), 500 mg

L0470 TLSO, triplanar control, rigid posterior frame and flexible soft anterior apron with straps, closures and padding extends from sacrococcygeal junction to scapula, lateral strength provided by pelvic, thoracic, and lateral frame pieces, rotational strength provided by subclavicular extensions, restricts gross trunk motion in sagittal, coronal, and transverse planes, provides intracavitary pressure to reduce load on the intervertebral disks, includes fitting and shaping the frame, prefabricated, includes fitting and adjustment

L6000 Partial hand, thumb remaining

L6010 Partial hand, little and/or ring finger remaining

L6020 Partial hand, no finger remaining

L7368 Lithium ion battery charger, replacement only

Q4113 GRAFTJACKET XPRESS, injectable, 1cc

S9900 Services by a Journal-listed Christian Science practitioner for the purpose of healing, per diem

DELETED CODES

C9270	C9272	C9273	C9274	C9276	C9277	C9278
C9280	C9281	C9282	C9283	C9284	C9365	C9406
C9729	C9730	C9731	E0571	G0440	G0441	G8440
G8441	G8508	G8534	G8537	G8538	G8636	G8637
G8638	G8639	G8640	G8641	G8675	G8676	G8677
G8678	G8679	G8680	G8681	G8684	G8686	G8687
G8688	G8689	G8690	G8691	G8692	G8693	G9041
G9042	G9043	G9044	J7130	J7184	L1500	L1510
L1520	L3964	L3965	L3966	L3968	L3969	L3970
L3972	L3974	L4380	L5311	L7266	L7272	L7274
L7500	Q0179	Q1003	Q2040	Q2041	Q2042	Q2044
S0181	S0625	S2270	S2344	S3628	S3905	S9075

REINSTATED CODES

*There are no reinstated codes for 2012

APPENDIX 6 — PLACE OF SERVICE AND TYPE OF SERVICE

Place-of-Service Codes for Professional Claims

Listed below are place of service codes and descriptions. These codes should be used on professional claims to specify the entity where service(s) were rendered. Check with individual payers (e.g., Medicare, Medicaid, other private insurance) for reimbursement policies regarding these codes. To comment on a code(s) or description(s), please send your request to posinfo@cms.gov.

Code	Place of Service	Description
01	Pharmacy	A facility or location where drugs and other medically related items and services are sold, dispensed, or otherwise provided directly to patients.
02	Unassigned	N/A
03	School	A facility whose primary purpose is education.
04	Homeless shelter	A facility or location whose primary purpose is to provide temporary housing to homeless individuals (e.g., emergency shelters, individual or family shelters).
05	Indian Health Service freestanding facility	A facility or location, owned and operated by the Indian Health Service, which provides diagnostic, therapeutic (surgical and non-surgical), and rehabilitation services to American Indians and Alaska natives who do not require hospitalization.
06	Indian Health Service provider-based facility	A facility or location, owned and operated by the Indian Health Service, which provides diagnostic, therapeutic (surgical and nonsurgical), and rehabilitation services rendered by, or under the supervision of, physicians to American Indians and Alaska natives admitted as inpatients or outpatients.
07	Tribal 638 freestanding facility	A facility or location owned and operated by a federally recognized American Indian or Alaska native tribe or tribal organization under a 638 agreement, which provides diagnostic, therapeutic (surgical and nonsurgical), and rehabilitation services to tribal members who do not require hospitalization.
08	Tribal 638 Provider-based Facility	A facility or location owned and operated by a federally recognized American Indian or Alaska native tribe or tribal organization under a 638 agreement, which provides diagnostic, therapeutic (surgical and nonsurgical), and rehabilitation services to tribal members admitted as inpatients or outpatients.
09	Prison/correctional facility	A prison, jail, reformatory, work farm, detention center, or any other similar facility maintained by either federal, state or local authorities for the purpose of confinement or rehabilitation of adult or juvenile criminal offenders.
10	Unassigned	N/A
11	Office	Location, other than a hospital, skilled nursing facility (SNF), military treatment facility, community health center, State or local public health clinic, or intermediate care facility (ICF), where the health professional routinely provides health examinations, diagnosis, and treatment of illness or injury on an ambulatory basis.
12	Home	Location, other than a hospital or other facility, where the patient receives care in a private residence.
13	Assisted living facility	Congregate residential facility with self-contained living units providing assessment of each resident's needs and on-site support 24 hours a day, 7 days a week, with the capacity to deliver or arrange for services including some health care and other services.
14	Group home	A residence, with shared living areas, where clients receive supervision and other services such as social and/or behavioral services, custodial service, and minimal services (e.g., medication administration).
15	Mobile unit	A facility/unit that moves from place-to-place equipped to provide preventive, screening, diagnostic, and/or treatment services.
16	Temporary lodging	A short-term accommodation such as a hotel, campground, hostel, cruise ship or resort where the patient receives care, and which is not identified by any other POS code.
17	Walk-in retail health clinic	A walk-in health clinic, other than an office, urgent care facility, pharmacy, or independent clinic and not described by any other place of service code, that is located within a retail operation and provides preventive and primary care services on an ambulatory basis.
18-19	Unassigned	N/A
20	Urgent care facility	Location, distinct from a hospital emergency room, an office, or a clinic, whose purpose is to diagnose and treat illness or injury for unscheduled, ambulatory patients seeking immediate medical attention.
21	Inpatient hospital	A facility, other than psychiatric, which primarily provides diagnostic, therapeutic (both surgical and nonsurgical), and rehabilitation services by, or under, the supervision of physicians to patients admitted for a variety of medical conditions.
22	Outpatient hospital	A portion of a hospital which provides diagnostic, therapeutic (both surgical and nonsurgical), and rehabilitation services to sick or injured persons who do not require hospitalization or institutionalization.
23	Emergency room—hospital	A portion of a hospital where emergency diagnosis and treatment of illness or injury is provided.
24	Ambulatory surgical center	A freestanding facility, other than a physician's office, where surgical and diagnostic services are provided on an ambulatory basis.
25	Birthing center	A facility, other than a hospital's maternity facilities or a physician's office, which provides a setting for labor, delivery, and immediate post-partum care as well as immediate care of new born infants.
26	Military treatment facility	A medical facility operated by one or more of the uniformed services. Military treatment facility (MTF) also refers to certain former U.S. Public Health Service (USPHS) facilities now designated as uniformed service treatment facilities (USTF).
27-30	Unassigned	N/A
31	Skilled nursing facility	A facility which primarily provides inpatient skilled nursing care and related services to patients who require medical, nursing, or rehabilitative services but does not provide the level of care or treatment available in a hospital.
32	Nursing facility	A facility which primarily provides to residents skilled nursing care and related services for the rehabilitation of injured, disabled, or sick persons, or, on a regular basis, health-related care services above the level of custodial care to other than mentally retarded individuals.
33	Custodial care facility	A facility which provides room, board, and other personal assistance services, generally on a long-term basis, and which does not include a medical component.

34	Hospice	A facility, other than a patient's home, in which palliative and supportive care for terminally ill patients and their families are provided.
35-40	Unassigned	N/A
41	Ambulance—land	A land vehicle specifically designed, equipped and staffed for lifesaving and transporting the sick or injured.
42	Ambulance—air or water	An air or water vehicle specifically designed, equipped and staffed for lifesaving and transporting the sick or injured.
43-48	Unassigned	N/A
49	Independent clinic	A location, not part of a hospital and not described by any other place-of-service code, that is organized and operated to provide preventive, diagnostic, therapeutic, rehabilitative, or palliative services to outpatients only.
50	Federally qualified health center	A facility located in a medically underserved area that provides Medicare beneficiaries preventive primary medical care under the general direction of a physician.
51	Inpatient psychiatric facility	A facility that provides inpatient psychiatric services for the diagnosis and treatment of mental illness on a 24-hour basis, by or under the supervision of a physician.
52	Psychiatric facility-partial hospitalization	A facility for the diagnosis and treatment of mental illness that provides a planned therapeutic program for patients who do not require full time hospitalization, but who need broader programs than are possible from outpatient visits to a hospital-based or hospital-affiliated facility.
53	Community mental health center	A facility that provides the following services: outpatient services, including specialized outpatient services for children, the elderly, individuals who are chronically ill, and residents of the CMHC's mental health services area who have been discharged from inpatient treatment at a mental health facility; 24 hour a day emergency care services; day treatment, other partial hospitalization services, or psychosocial rehabilitation services; screening for patients being considered for admission to state mental health facilities to determine the appropriateness of such admission; and consultation and education services.
54	Intermediate care facility/mentally retarded	A facility which primarily provides health-related care and services above the level of custodial care to mentally retarded individuals but does not provide the level of care or treatment available in a hospital or SNF.
55	Residential substance abuse treatment facility	A facility which provides treatment for substance (alcohol and drug) abuse to live-in residents who do not require acute medical care. Services include individual and group therapy and counseling, family counseling, laboratory tests, drugs and supplies, psychological testing, and room and board.
56	Psychiatric residential treatment center	A facility or distinct part of a facility for psychiatric care which provides a total 24-hour therapeutically planned and professionally staffed group living and learning environment.
57	Non-residential substance abuse treatment facility	A location which provides treatment for substance (alcohol and drug) abuse on an ambulatory basis. Services include individual and group therapy and counseling, family counseling, laboratory tests, drugs and supplies, and psychological testing.
58-59	Unassigned	N/A
60	Mass immunization center	A location where providers administer pneumococcal pneumonia and influenza virus vaccinations and submit these services as electronic media claims, paper claims, or using the roster billing method. This generally takes place in a mass immunization setting, such as, a public health center, pharmacy, or mall but may include a physician office setting.
61	Comprehensive inpatient rehabilitation facility	A facility that provides comprehensive rehabilitation services under the supervision of a physician to inpatients with physical disabilities. Services include physical therapy, occupational therapy, speech pathology, social or psychological services, and orthotics and prosthetics services.
62	Comprehensive outpatient rehabilitation facility	A facility that provides comprehensive rehabilitation services under the supervision of a physician to outpatients with physical disabilities. Services include physical therapy, occupational therapy, and speech pathology services.
63-64	Unassigned	N/A
65	End-stage renal disease treatment facility	A facility other than a hospital, which provides dialysis treatment, maintenance, and/or training to patients or caregivers on an ambulatory or home-care basis.
66-70	Unassigned	N/A
71	State or local public health clinic	A facility maintained by either state or local health departments that provides ambulatory primary medical care under the general direction of a physician.
72	Rural health clinic	A certified facility which is located in a rural medically underserved area that provides ambulatory primary medical care under the general direction of a physician.
73-80	Unassigned	N/A
81	Independent laboratory	A laboratory certified to perform diagnostic and/or clinical tests independent of an institution or a physician's office.
82-98	Unassigned	N/A
99	Other place of service	Other place of service not identified above.

Type of Service

Common Working File Type of Service (TOS) Indicators

For submitting a claim to the Common Working File (CWF), use the following table to assign the proper TOS. Some procedures may have more than one applicable TOS. CWF will produce alerts on codes with incorrect TOS designations.

The only exceptions to this table are:

- Surgical services billed for dates of service through December 31, 2007, containing the ASC facility service modifier SG must be reported as TOS F. Effective for services on or after January 1, 2008, the SG modifier is no longer applicable for Medicare services. ASC providers should discontinue applying the SG modifier on ASC facility claims. The indicator F does not appear in the TOS table because its use depends upon claims submitted with POS 24 (ASC facility) from an ASC (specialty 49). This became effective for dates of service January 1, 2008, or after.
- Surgical services billed with an assistant-at-surgery modifier (80-82, AS,) must be reported with TOS 8. The 8 indicator does not appear on the TOS table because its use is dependent upon the use of the appropriate modifier. (See Pub. 100-4 *Medicare Claims Processing Manual*, chapter 12, "Physician/Practitioner Billing," for instructions on when assistant-at-surgery is allowable.)
- Psychiatric treatment services that are subject to the outpatient mental health treatment limitation should be reported with TOS T.
- TOS H appears in the list of descriptors. However, it does not appear in the table. In CWF, "H" is used only as an indicator for hospice. The carrier should not submit TOS H to CWF at this time.
- For outpatient services, when a transfusion medicine code appears on a claim that also contains a blood product, the service is paid under reasonable charge at 80 percent; coinsurance and deductible apply. When

transfusion medicine codes are paid under the clinical laboratory fee schedule they are paid at 100 percent; coinsurance and deductible do not apply.

Note: For injection codes with more than one possible TOS designation, use the following guidelines when assigning the TOS:

When the choice is L or 1:

- Use TOS L when the drug is used related to ESRD; or
- Use TOS 1 when the drug is not related to ESRD and is administered in the office.

When the choice is G or 1:

- Use TOS G when the drug is an immunosuppressive drug; or
- Use TOS 1 when the drug is used for other than immunosuppression.

When the choice is P or 1:

- Use TOS P if the drug is administered through durable medical equipment (DME); or
- Use TOS 1 if the drug is administered in the office.

The place of service or diagnosis may be considered when determining the appropriate TOS. The descriptors for each of the TOS codes listed in the following table are:

0	Whole blood
1	Medical care
2	Surgery
3	Consultation
4	Diagnostic radiology
5	Diagnostic laboratory
6	Therapeutic radiology
7	Anesthesia
8	Assistant at surgery
9	Other medical items or services
A	Used DME
B	High risk screening mammography
C	Low risk screening mammography
D	Ambulance
E	Enteral/parenteral nutrients/supplies
F	Ambulatory surgical center (facility usage for surgical services)
G	Immunosuppressive drugs
H	Hospice
J	Diabetic shoes
K	Hearing items and services
L	ESRD supplies
M	Monthly capitation payment for dialysis
N	Kidney donor
P	Lump sum purchase of DME, prosthetics, orthotics
Q	Vision items or services
R	Rental of DME
S	Surgical dressings or other medical supplies
T	Outpatient mental health treatment limitation
U	Occupational therapy
V	Pneumococcal/flu vaccine
W	Physical therapy

Berenson-Eggers Type of Service (BETOS) Codes

The BETOS coding system was developed primarily for analyzing the growth in Medicare expenditures. The coding system covers all HCPCS codes; assigns a HCPCS code to only one BETOS code; consists of readily understood clinical categories (as opposed to statistical or financial categories); consists of categories that permit objective assignment; is stable over time; and is relatively immune to minor changes in technology or practice patterns.

BETOS Codes and Descriptions:

1. Evaluation and Management

1. M1A Office visits—new
2. M1B Office visits—established
3. M2A Hospital visit—initial
4. M2B Hospital visit—subsequent
5. M2C Hospital visit—critical care
6. M3 Emergency room visit
7. M4A Home visit
8. M4B Nursing home visit
9. M5A Specialist—pathology
10. M5B Specialist—psychiatry
11. M5C Specialist—ophthalmology
12. M5D Specialist—other
13. M6 Consultations

2. Procedures

1. P0 Anesthesia
2. P1A Major procedure—breast
3. P1B Major procedure—colectomy
4. P1C Major procedure—cholecystectomy
5. P1D Major procedure—TURP
6. P1E Major procedure—hysterectomy
7. P1F Major procedure—explor/decompr/excis disc
8. P1G Major procedure—other
9. P2A Major procedure, cardiovascular—CABG
10. P2B Major procedure, cardiovascular—aneurysm repair
11. P2C Major procedure, cardiovascular—thromboendarterectomy
12. P2D Major procedure, cardiovascular—coronary angioplasty (PTCA)
13. P2E Major procedure, cardiovascular—pacemaker insertion
14. P2F Major procedure, cardiovascular—other
15. P3A Major procedure, orthopedic—hip fracture repair
16. P3B Major procedure, orthopedic—hip replacement
17. P3C Major procedure, orthopedic—knee replacement
18. P3D Major procedure, orthopedic—other
19. P4A Eye procedure—corneal transplant
20. P4B Eye procedure—cataract removal/lens insertion
21. P4C Eye procedure—retinal detachment
22. P4D Eye procedure—treatment of retinal lesions
23. P4E Eye procedure—other
24. P5A Ambulatory procedures—skin
25. P5B Ambulatory procedures—musculoskeletal
26. P5C Ambulatory procedures—groin hernia repair
27. P5D Ambulatory procedures—lithotripsy
28. P5E Ambulatory procedures—other
29. P6A Minor procedures—skin
30. P6B Minor procedures—musculoskeletal

31. P6C Minor procedures—other (Medicare fee schedule)
32. P6D Minor procedures—other (non-Medicare fee schedule)
33. P7A Oncology—radiation therapy
34. P7B Oncology—other
35. P8A Endoscopy—arthroscopy
36. P8B Endoscopy—upper gastrointestinal
37. P8C Endoscopy—sigmoidoscopy
38. P8D Endoscopy—colonoscopy
39. P8E Endoscopy—cystoscopy
40. P8F Endoscopy—bronchoscopy
41. P8G Endoscopy—laparoscopic cholecystectomy
42. P8H Endoscopy—laryngoscopy
43. P8I Endoscopy—other
44. P9A Dialysis services (Medicare fee schedule)
45. P9B Dialysis services (non-Medicare fee schedule)

3. **Imaging**

1. I1A Standard imaging—chest
2. I1B Standard imaging—musculoskeletal
3. I1C Standard imaging—breast
4. I1D Standard imaging—contrast gastrointestinal
5. I1E Standard imaging—nuclear medicine
6. I1F Standard imaging—other
7. I2A Advanced imaging—CAT/CT/CTA; brain/head/neck
8. I2B Advanced imaging—CAT/CT/CTA; other
9. I2C Advanced imaging—MRI/MRA; brain/head/neck
10. I2D Advanced imaging—MRI/MRA; other
11. I3A Echography/ultrasoundography—eye
12. I3B Echography/ultrasoundography—abdomen/pelvis
13. I3C Echography/ultrasoundography—heart
14. I3D Echography/ultrasoundography—carotid arteries
15. I3E Echography/ultrasoundography—prostate, transrectal
16. I3F Echography/ultrasoundography—other
17. I4A Imaging/procedure—heart, including cardiac catheterization
18. I4B Imaging/procedure—other

4. Tests

1. T1A Lab tests—routine venipuncture (non-Medicare fee schedule)
2. T1B Lab tests—automated general profiles
3. T1C Lab tests—urinalysis
4. T1D Lab tests—blood counts
5. T1E Lab tests—glucose
6. T1F Lab tests—bacterial cultures
7. T1G Lab tests—other (Medicare fee schedule)
8. T1H Lab tests—other (non-Medicare fee schedule)
9. T2A Other tests—electrocardiograms
10. T2B Other tests—cardiovascular stress tests
11. T2C Other tests—EKG monitoring
12. T2D Other tests—other

5. **Durable Medical Equipment**

1. D1A Medical/surgical supplies
2. D1B Hospital beds
3. D1C Oxygen and supplies
4. D1D Wheelchairs
5. D1E Other DME
6. D1F Prosthetic/orthotic devices
7. D1G Drugs administered through DME

6. **Other**

1. O1A Ambulance
2. O1B Chiropractic
3. O1C Enteral and parenteral
4. O1D Chemotherapy
5. O1E Other drugs
6. O1F Hearing and speech services
7. O1G Immunizations/vaccinations

7. **Exceptions/Unclassified**

1. Y1 Other—Medicare fee schedule
2. Y2 Other—Non-Medicare fee schedule
3. Z1 Local codes
4. Z2 Undefined codes